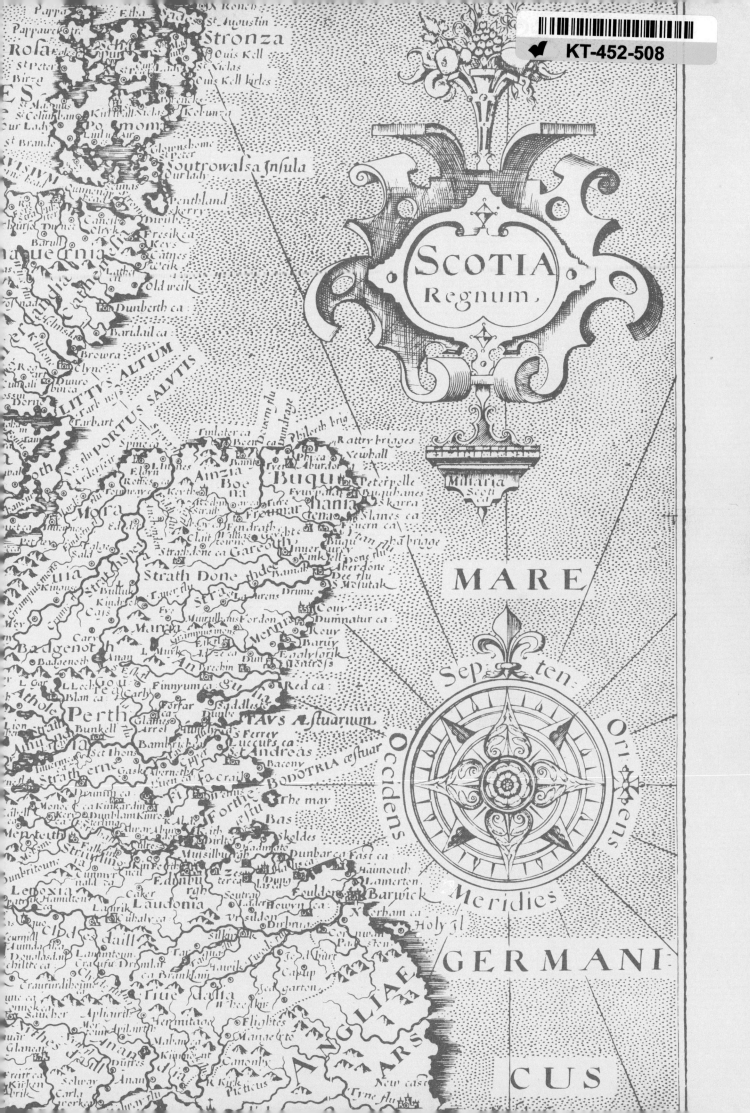

AA TOURING GUIDE TO SCOTLAND

From the treeless brae
All green and grey,
To the wooded ravine I wind my way,
Dashing, and foaming, and leaping with glee,
The child of the mountain wild and free.
Under the crag where the stone-crop grows,
Fringing with gold my shelvy bed,
Where over my head
Its fruitage red,
The rock-rooted rowan tree blushfully shows . . .

from the Song of The Highland River by Professor John Stuart Blackie

2

Contents

Produced by the Publications Division of the
Automobile Association

Editor Russell Beach
Art Editor Michael Preedy MSIA

Assistant editor Michael Cady
Assistant designer Robert Johnson

Feature writers:
W F Inglis, Ross Finlay

Day Drives compiled by the Publications
Research Unit of the Automobile Association

Gazetteer revised by Linda O'Donnell

Artists:
Anderson Dykes Organization, Bernard Baker,
Don Cordery, Fleet Design, Outline Art Services

Picture researchers: Diana Phillips, Angela Murphy

Tartans supplied by The Scotch House,
Knightsbridge, London

Extract from *The Song of the Highland River*
from *Contemporary Scottish Verse*, published
by Walter Scott Ltd *c*1893

Day Drives, Town Plans, Leisure Maps,
and Special Feature Maps by
the Cartographic Services Unit of the
Automobile Association

Touring Atlas © Copyright by Geographia Ltd

Maps in this book are based upon the
Ordnance Survey maps, with the sanction of the
Controller of Her Majesty's Stationery Office
Crown Copyright Reserved

Phototypeset by Petty and Sons Ltd, Leeds

Colour Separations by Mullis Morgan Ltd, London

Printed and bound by Purnell and Sons Ltd,
Paulton, Bristol

Published in England by The Automobile Association,
Fanum House, Basingstoke, Hampshire RG21 2EA

Pride in Adversity

For centuries the Scottish people have known adversity. Whether from the Highlands or Lowlands they have been torn by martial strife, persecuted by grasping landowners, and crushed by bitter climatic conditions. Yet they have nurtured famous men, cradled the arts, and fostered an unbending pride in their stern homeland.

Pride and poverty – that sums up the story of Scotland and explains the character of her people. Pride in the natural beauty provided by stern Nature; poverty caused by the strictures of the same hard mistress. Generations of Scots have been poor while their English neighbours have been richer. Adversity has bred virtues however, for though Scotland has not been able to afford great possessions and dreams of grandeur, she has produced men like David Hume, Adam Smith, Robert Burns, Walter Scott, William Dunbar, and the Adam family.

It has been estimated that some 20 million Scots live abroad, all boasting of their lovely homeland but refusing to live there. For centuries poor Scotland, sustained by her oatmeal and haggis, has said goodbye to her most venturesome people – soldiering in the Low Countries and in France, trading and peddling in the Baltic and in Poland, penetrating the Russias and seeking new worlds in America, Canada, New Zealand, and Australia. For a long time the noblest prospect for the Scot, in Dr Johnson's words, was the high road that leads to England. Now the wheel is turning. English and Americans – and more important the Scots themselves – see a noble prospect in Scotland. For long the image of Scotland has been one of mountains and meanness, of aggressive, rather drunken little men wearing tartan tammies and yelling football slogans. Every year Hampden Park in Glasgow or London's Wembley Stadium sees Scotland and England meet on the football field; depending on the result it is Bannockburn or Flodden all over again. This spirit of aggression is a reminder to the English that Scotland is still a different country – despite the absence of border-control and customs points.

The visitor who thinks he can 'do' Scotland in a day or two is in for a surprise. It is two-thirds the size of England and, besides its famed Highland mountains and glens, has rolling pastoral acres, picturesque fishing ports, and handsome towns and villages as well as a splendid capital. Its fishing and golf can be ludicrously cheap, and enthusiasts of these sports look upon the country with a kind of reverence. But it also has wide facilities for sailing, water ski-ing, pony-trekking, and other less strenuous pursuits. The weather can be excellent; it can also be maddeningly overcast, wet, and in places ferociously windy.

Most visitors or would-be visitors go wrong in their conception of Scotland and the Scots by equating the whole country with the Highlands. The Lowlands – only so called because they are marginally less high than the Highlands – cover half the country, house almost all the people, and are rich in the variety of their life. The population of the Highlands is not much more than a quarter of a million. Only in recent years has the discovery of North Sea oil and the activity of the Highlands and Islands Development Board in promoting all kinds of small industries arrested depopulation.

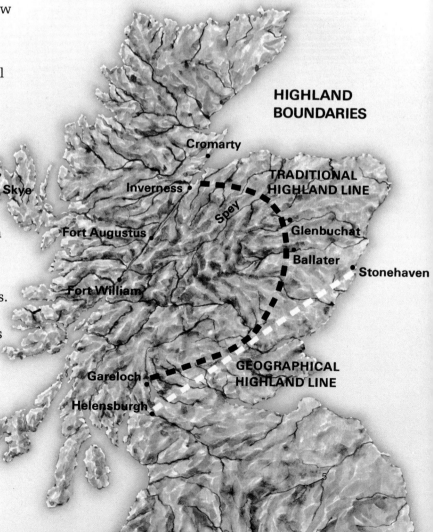

HIGHLAND BOUNDARIES

Cromarty

TRADITIONAL HIGHLAND LINE

Skye
Inverness
Spey
Glenbuchat

Fort Augustus
Ballater
Stonehaven

Fort William

GEOGRAPHICAL HIGHLAND LINE

Gareloch

Helensburgh

Distribution of Clans and Families from *c*1600

After the 1745 Rising a large part of the clan system became outlawed and dispersed, and many of the smaller clans emigrated *en bloc* or were forced to change their names. Further depopulation resulted from the Highland Clearances. By the time that Sir Walter Scott's romantic but highly dubious versions of Scottish history – which 19th-c England accepted as fact –

became popular, the system had become totally confused. Clan boundaries had moved, splinter clans had formed, and the Highlands had been extensively infiltrated by Lowland family names. This map illustrates the approximate distribution of clans and families just prior to the Rising.

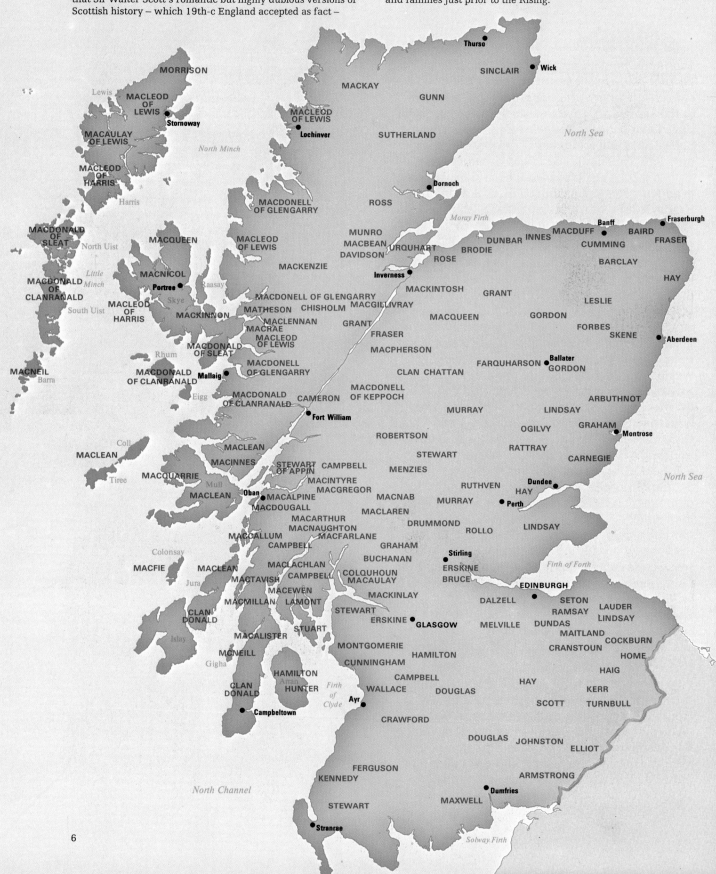

The Enigmatic Tartan

The reason that tartans were proscribed by the English after the 1745 Rising was because they were associated with the Jacobite cause – not because they served any military purpose. Popular belief that they served as badges of clan loyalty during battles can be discounted because the clansmen set aside their colourful plaids before a conflict and fought half naked. The whole tartan myth is a modern one, perpetrated by the romantic if inaccurate works of Sir Walter Scott. Scott's writings inflamed 19th-c England with a love for all things north of the border and a need to identify with the poet's Highland heroes. This need was amply catered for by haberdashers who were used to following the fickle dictates of fashion, and very soon anybody who had a tenuous claim to Scottish ancestry could have their very own tartan designed and made up to order. Even kings were not immune – George IV is recorded to have attended a function in full Highland dress. Of the bewildering array of tartans in existence today some are genuinely old, others are the products of wishful thinking on the part of people from every corner of the globe, and still more are town or area tartans unconnected with any particular clan or family. In spite of this they are all colourful and ingenious designs, as the selection illustrated below confirms.

Chisholm
(Highland clan)

Chattan
(Highland clan)

Kennedy
(Lowland family)

Stewart dress tartan
(Highland clan)

MacDonald ancient hunting tartan
(Highland clan)

Macnab
(Highland clan)

MacGregor
(Highland clan)

Red Comyn
(Highland clan – branch of Cumming)

Sinclair
(Highland clan)

Home
(Lowland family)

Maclean of Duart
(Highland clan)

Carnegie
(Lowland family)

Crawford
(Lowland family)

Huntly
(District tartan)

MacFarlane black and white
(Highland clan)

Fraser
(Highland clan)

Galloway
(District tartan)

MacLeod of Lewis
(Highland clan)

Lennox
(District tartan)

Stirling
(Town tartan)

7

Above the Highland line

Broadly speaking the Highland Line divides two contrasting ways of life. The southern limit of the Highlands where they meet the Central Lowlands is the tremendous escarpment of the Highland Plateau, traversing the country north-eastwards from Helensburgh to Stonehaven. But this geological fault differs from the more truly high-land boundary defined by the traditional line. This follows the escarpment from the Gareloch to the River Isla in old Angus, north and then westwards to cross the Dee at Ballater, the Don about Glenbuchat, and the Spey at the confluence of the Avon – reaching just west of the Highland capital of Inverness. To the south and east the people of the Lowlands could prosper in agriculture, industry, and commerce, while nature left the north and west little but hunting, herding, and war. The hard primary rocks of the Highlands give only a shallow soil, which the heavy rain brought by the prevailing westerly winds from the Atlantic has kept wet and sour for thousands of years. The steep slopes left by the glaciers of the Ice Age make agriculture even more difficult, and the chief aim of Highland economy became the breeding of cattle, sheep, and goats. They set out to achieve this by collective farming, in which the productive units were 'townships'. To these farm-communities the grain crops that they managed to grow were vitally important. 'The High-landers' wrote Thomas Morer in 1689, 'are not without considerable quantities of corn, yet have not enough to satisfie their numbers, and therefore yearly come down with their cattle, of which they have greater plenty, and so traffick with the Low-landers'. The picture emerges of a croft too small to support a family and with insufficient opportunity of outside labour to make up the deficiency. That, of course, was before the mixed blessing of oil arrived, bringing more jobs and new social problems.

The Highlands cover a sixth of Britain, so there are vast, empty, and spectacular unscathed regions to be enjoyed. There are old folk in the islands and west Highlands who have rarely, if ever, seen a train, but to whom planes are more common than puffins. To be rushed to hospital is to be rushed by air. Scottish Gaelic is confined to these areas and is spoken by 70,000 people. Its status is not strong, though it is well taught in some schools and is served by radio programmes, writers, and publishers. But many Gaelic-speakers are apathetic, and this differs sharply from the Welsh situation; Welsh Gaelic is spoken by 600,000 people. Before the Reformation, boys of position in the Highlands received some education at religious houses, but most of the smaller chieftains and their men were illiterate up to the end of the 16thc. They signed documents with hands 'led on the pen'. Gaelic culture depended largely on song and spoken verse.

Two sets of people populated the Highlands – the Picts and Scots, with a bit of interference from the Vikings. Some historians believe that the pre-Celtic invaders, who became ancestors of the Picts, mingled with an older non-Celtic race speaking a non-Celtic language which was used concurrently with Celtic. Pictish personal names are not all clearly Celtic, and Pictish inscriptions are written in a language which was not Celtic. The pre-Celts probably called themselves *Priteni* (the people of the designs or tattoos), but there is no reason to believe they adopted the Latin name *Picti* (the Painted Men) which the Romans gave to tribes threatening them from the north. These people may still at that time have tattooed their bodies, and it is as Picts they are known to history. The first home of the Scots was Ireland, and those who settled in Scotland – eventually giving their name to that country – were Gaelic-speaking Irish Celts. The sea passage from Ireland to Scotland at its shortest is less than 12m, between Antrim and the Mull of Kintyre, though this crossing where the North Channel and the Atlantic meet is liable to be more dangerous than the longer passage from Ireland to Islay, farther west. A settlement may have been made during the Roman period, and there is contemporary evidence that there were Scots not far from the Clyde area during St Patrick's mission to Ireland between 432 and 464. Immigration from Ireland set up a kingdom of the Scots in Argyll *c*498.

Bloody Glencoe

So Pict and Scot were the ancestors of a predominantly Celtic Highlands, and the fastnesses of remote glen and island created the clan system which lasted for a thousand years and survives today in sentiment if not in fact. The clan was a large family bound by ties of blood. The Highland chief was more powerful than the Lowland baron, for his rule over his clan was absolute. The clansmen looked on him as a father rather than as a feudal superior, and he regarded them as children to whom he was bound to give protection and support. Clan loyalties caused feuds between chieftains to be fierce, protracted, and bloodthirsty. Glencoe in Gaelic means 'the Glen of Weeping', and in 1692 was the scene of one of the last and the most notorious of Highland massacres – symbolizing the traditional hatred between the clans MacDonald and Campbell. Many Highlanders disapproved of the Glorious Revolution which robbed James II of his throne, and clan chiefs were required to take an oath of allegiance to William III by the end of 1691. At the time of the massacre the bleak glen belonged to the MacIans, a branch of the MacDonalds. Their chief was an old man who had toiled through deep snow to Inveraray, but was six days late in making his pledge. The villain of the piece, Master of Stair Sir John Dalrymple, was determined to make an example of old MacIan and used the king's authority to order the massacre. Captain Campbell of Glenlyon, commanding a Government regiment, was given the job. Campbell's niece was the wife of MacIan's second son, and when the soldiers arrived in the glen they were received with Highland hospitality and billeted in the cottages. For twelve days the hospitality continued, until 05.00 hrs on 13 February when the indiscriminate killing of men, women, and children began. Yet the massacre was botched. Of a clan numbering more than 140 whom Stair had ordered to be 'extirpated' only 38 died. The passes were to have been closed to troops, but many of the intended victims escaped in spite of the freezing weather. The Highlands had seen many more bloodthirsty massacres than this one – for example, the massacre of the entire population of Eigg – but when the news reached the outside world the broadening humanity of the age was outraged.

The outlaw and the prince

The mountain and loch country around the Trossachs and the shores of Loch Lomond was where a Scottish Robin Hood made his forays to rob the rich in the late 17th and early 18thc. He was Rob Roy MacGregor, a powerful red-haired Highlander born to a freebooter in 1671 at a time when few people from the central plain ventured north. His story is an insight into life on the Highland-Lowland frontier in more rugged times. The MacGregor country lies around the Braes of Balquhidder, which rise near Loch Voil and Loch Doine, and the MacGregors were long associated with 'blood, slaughter, theft, and robbery'. Feuds were pursued relentlessly, as shown by the one between the MacGregors and the Colquhouns, whose laird lived at a Loch Lomond-side hamlet of Luss. One night two MacGregors who were refused shelter by a Colquhoun took a lamb and killed it for supper. They offered payment to the owner, but the Laird of Luss had them condemned to death and executed. The sequel was the bloody battle of Glen Fruin, where a 300-strong band of MacGregors routed the 700-strong force led by Sir Humphrey Colquhoun. Feeling against the victorious clan was such that in 1603 the Privy Council 'expressly abolished' the name MacGregor. Another edict put a death sentence on any of the clan formerly called MacGregor who assembled in numbers larger than four. Bitterly the MacGregors bided their time, and this was the atmosphere in which Rob Roy grew up. At 20 he was leading a raid in the parish of Kippen and he made many raids on the softer south and west before he was captured. He escaped and passed the years as a fugitive until pardoned in 1727. Even enemies admitted he was courteous, but a chronicler said: 'Few who lived within his reach could promise to themselves security, whether for their persons or effects, without subjecting themselves to pay him a heavy and shameful tax.' His daring brought him much money, popularity, and many cattle.

The clans gathered when Bonnie Prince Charlie landed off the west coast of Scotland. It was at Glenfinnan, on the Road to the Isles, that the prince raised the royal standard of the Stuarts, proclaiming his father James as king and himself as regent. The story of his triumphal progress to Edinburgh and south as far as Derby, then his retreat and defeat at Culloden, is well known. Culloden was the deathbed of the clan system as well as Stuart hopes, but the prince's five months as a fugitive in the Hebrides and West Highlands added more romance to his story. Flora MacDonald was only one of many who gave him shelter and active help, despite the £30,000 on his head.

After Culloden
In the 18thc the Highlands had 20 per cent of Scotland's population; now it is less than five per cent. The job of breaking up the clan system was done thoroughly – 'Butcher' Cumberland, victor of Culloden, had terrorized the Highlands; tartan was proscribed; an Act was passed taking away the chief's old heritable jurisdiction. The chief became just another landowner, and the presence of a multitude of half-starved peasants on his land became an embarrassment. Once he had counted his wealth in men, but now he counted it in money and became an absentee living in Edinburgh or London and sending his sons to public school. Sometimes he sold his land to a

Lowland or English (and later still American) proprietor. Soon it was found that sheep farming was more profitable, and the Highland Clearances drove the clansmen to Glasgow or America, into crofts or small farms on the sea coast, or into the new Highland Regiments. By the mid 19thc the Balmoral era was gathering pace and millions of acres were devoted to red deer.

Time has painted a rosier picture of life in the Highlands than the facts justify, a picture perhaps more in keeping with the magnificent and heroic scenery. The romantic Highlands, with their tartans, souvenirs, and legendary figures, were more or less invented by prolific poet and novelist Sir Walter Scott after the old clan system broke up. Before the summer of 1810 the world outside considered the landscape of the Highlands desolate and the people barbarous. Then Scott's poem *The Lady of the Lake* opened people's eyes to the grandeur of the Trossachs ('the bristly country') and the poetry of the Highland legends. Within days of the poem's publication post-chaises were carrying sightseers to Loch Katrine. A shrewd Highlander called James Stuart made a small fortune out of showing tourists the Trossachs, Ben Venue, and Ellen's Isle; a hotel was built; the Scottish tourist industry was born. The Waverley novels did wonders for the kilt. George IV paid his momentous visit to Scotland in 1822, the first reigning monarch to do so for two centuries, and showed himself at Holyroodhouse in a kilt of Royal Stewart tartan. Scott took charge of the ceremonial, clad in Campbell trews, and Scotland entered a tartan age which still continues to obscure the difference between Highlander and Lowlander.

State within a state
Today the Highlands are in a sense a vast nationalized industry, even discounting the state interest in oil. Two great empires flourish – the Forestry Commission and the North of Scotland Hydro-Electric Board. The Forestry Commission builds its own roads and houses and is almost a state within a state. The Hydro-Electric Board's achievement is immense. In 1948, when it began operations in earnest, only five per cent of the farms and crofts had electricity; now virtually all are covered. Hydro-electric schemes have shown a consistently high standard of architectural and engineering design. Upper Shira dam near Inveraray is a good example. It is more than 700 yards long and is built chiefly of mass concrete, forming part of a system feeding the Clachan hydro-electric power station in the Glen Shira scheme. Another dam built to give English people the use of Highland water-power is the one which has become a great tourist attraction at Pitlochry. Near it is a fish ladder to help migrating salmon surmount the dam, for the board's powers include a

'Butcher' Cumberland's victory at Culloden saw the end of the traditional clan system and the start of Highland depopulation.

9

PRIDE IN ADVERSITY

The Scott monument in Edinburgh is a fit memorial to one of Scotland's most famous and well-known national heroes.

provision that it 'shall have regard to the desirability of avoiding as far as possible injury to fisheries and to the stock of fish in any waters.' A great deal of money has been spent on fish ladders and fish lifts, and on traps and hatcheries to strip the salmon of their eggs and rear the young. Ben Cruachan, part of the Awe scheme, shows how the board has tried to build the dams without spoiling the scenery. Cruachan has its power station in a man-made underground cavern which is another tourist attraction.

The confused Lowlands

Today many Lowland Scots wear the kilt proudly and claim the best Highland traditions as their own. They talk of 'Caledonia stern and wild', but would not dream of living through a Highland winter. In Rob Roy's time there was more difference between a burgess of Perth and a MacGregor of Balquidder than there was between the Perth burgess and the burgess of an English or even a French town. The Lowlander, in his broad blue Scots bonnet, developed a culture, traditions, and for a brief time even a language of his own, untrammelled by the existence of an alien Scotland on the other side of the Highland Line. The two have become confused, even in the mind of the average Scot, partly because of the chain reaction set up by Walter Scott and partly because of a generation of kilted comedians like Harry Lauder. But the chief reason is that the Unions, first of the crowns and then of parliaments, anglicized the Lowlands and destroyed the Lallans (Lowlands) tongue. At the same time the Lowlander, ever suspicious of England's size, wealth, and attitudes, was driven closer to the Highlands in his determination to remain Scottish and different. Scots from Ireland were one of the ingredients in the mixing bowl that created the Lowlander, and in modern times many more Irish have settled – particularly in the Glasgow area. Another ingredient was the Romanized ancient Briton – men like St Ninian – and the third was the Angles who, with the Saxons, invaded Britain's eastern seaboard in the dark ages. In the 7thc Edinburgh was 'Edwin's borough' – Edwin being King of Northumbria at that time.

Lowlands is a name of convenience and does not describe countryside which forms some kind of northern Fenland. Much of the terrain on the Lowlands side of the Highland line rises over 2,000ft. There are low lands, too, like the stretch of the Lothians beside the Firth of Forth, the green plain from the Carse of Stirling west to the foothills of Ben Lomond, and the Wigtown peninsula. For 16 of its 100m the Tweed, perhaps most romantic of all Scottish rivers, marks the boundary between Scotland and England before it winds its way into the heart of the Border Country. The hills of the Lowlands lie in a great loose chain across the country from the Lammermuirs in the east to the Merrick far to the south-west in old Galloway. It seems an error that the Borders and the south-west should have been overlooked for so long. Thousands of square miles of some of the most unspoilt countryside in Europe are wedged comfortably between the central belt of Scotland and England's industrial north. Yet this stretch of the country has suffered from depopulation faster than the Highlands and Islands. They are perhaps too dependent on traditional industries like knitwear and tweeds, and are ignored by visitors driving north to Edinburgh and the Highlands. This neglect is all the more surprising because each gateway into Scotland from the south offers immediate reward. The 1,371ft summit at Carter Bar on the A68 provides a panorama of the Border country: the Merse of Berwickshire lies below the long line of the Cheviot Hills and the Eildons raise their triple heads in the distance. The A697 crosses the Tweed Bridge into the historic little town of Coldstream. Beyond Berwick-upon-Tweed the A1 leads on to the golf courses and seaside resorts of Lothian. A turn west along the A75 at Gretna Green leads to the lochs, ancient castles, tropical gardens, sandy beaches, forests, and the glens of Dumfries and Galloway.

Most of Scotland's people are the Lowlanders who live in the central belt formed by the Forth-Clyde isthmus, and most of those live in the area in and around Glasgow. Whether the folk of Edinburgh accept it or not the likeliest typical Lowlander is a Glaswegian, whose voice has a harsh, metallic edge contrasting vividly with the genteel throatiness of middle-class Edinburgh and the soft tones of the Highlander. For more than a century Glasgow called itself the Second City of the Empire and in the closing decade of the Victorian era it was one of the largest cities in Europe. That cannot be said now, but with neighbouring towns the population is about $2\frac{1}{2}$ million – almost half Scotland's total. Approximately a million of these people live within Glasgow's boundaries, and the city is still bigger than Edinburgh, Aberdeen, and Dundee put together. Despite its industrial setting Glasgow has a large number of overseas visitors each year. It is the gateway to the Burns country and to the Western Highlands, and many people living in the city will say that the Highlands begin just beyond their back gardens. There are more Gaelic-speaking people in Glasgow than in any other city in the world.

City on the Clyde
The predominant feature of the region, both economically and geographically, is the River Clyde, traditionally a shipbuilding centre and home port of the Scots chief engineers who are known in ports all over the world. The Glaswegian male is a football fanatic – in the vernacular, 'he's fitba daft'. The city has three of the largest stadia in Britain – Hampden Park and the grounds of the great rival clubs Celtic and Rangers. The pressure on housing brought by the Industrial Revolution gave Glasgow some of the worst slums in Britain and a reputation it is fighting hard to live down. Modern redevelopment is on a scale hard to match elsewhere in Europe. Victorian tenements are being demolished and modern accommodation put up for a large number of the people. No city so apparently prosperous in the 19thc was left a worse housing mess to clear up. Its area never increased as rapidly as the population, and many districts were dense mixtures of houses, factories, and schools. Docks and quays built here on the Clyde brought shipping far upstream and concentrated all bridges in the heart of the city. As traffic grew so did congestion. Many of the older houses came to the end of their useful lives at the same time as the old, traditional, industries passed their peak of employment potential. As the reshaped city struggles to emerge the Glaswegian goes on singing its praises defiantly.

A Lowlander's praise is not likely to be couched in flowery language, and the Glaswegian might think he is being fulsome enough if he utters a simple 'No' bad'. For Edinburgh, the capital, Glasgow people have another short phrase. 'East windy, West endy,' they say. Edinburgh does have a more or less permanent east wind and a vaguely pseudo atmosphere of upper class. Because it is a beautiful city and a festival centre which attracts visitors by the million, there is a tendency to think of it as a professional city populated by bank clerks and musicians,

lawyers and architects, with never a workman's overall to be seen. Edinburgh does, in fact, have a lot of industry. Tourists who have never wandered through the Old Town's back streets and closes have seen only one side of the picture. Reality is not Princes Street, which is built on one side of the road only; nor is it the gardens sweeping down to the valley and up again to the castle; nor is it the great banks and insurance offices. It is the city's massive printing industry, the beer being brewed, the fishing and deep water harbours, the electronics complexes, the biscuit factories, and the bakeries. The difference between Edinburgh's industry and that of Glasgow and most other Scottish cities is that it is spread out. Less than 25 per cent of the working population are professionals in the academic sense of the word.

Truly brewed and blended
Food and drink are often the clue to a man's character and attitude to life. Scotch whisky was undoubtedly a drink to accompany an outdoor life, and never intended for soft southern stomachs. Scotch has an unfair reputation as a tipple for hardened drinkers – though it is true that a really serious drinker in Scotland will alternate his whisky with beer until he can hardly taste the difference. But there is justification given the right circumstances. The climate is more bracing, and to have taken malt whisky while walking in the Cairngorms or fishing in clear waters is exhilarating. Until the 1830's Scotch whisky was little seen outside the Highlands, where it was distilled in small, frequently illicit distilleries sought out by excise officers. Until then the only Scotch was malt whisky made – as it is today – from malted barley and distilled in copper pot-stills. The malted barley, peat smoke, water, and the shape of the still all help to give a pronounced bouquet and flavour. In the 1860's several pioneers of the embryo whisky industry, with eyes on the drawing-rooms and drinking establishments of London, lightened the single malts with grain whiskies to create the famous blends. Each has its own formula and may contain up to

Turning the barley in a Scottish whisky distillery.

11

40 different malt and grain whiskies. For years whisky has been Scotland's biggest single export, and the United States has taken almost half of the export total. To be sold in Britain whisky must be at least three years old and the youngest in a blend is usually a few years older. Blends account for about 85 per cent of sales, with only 15 per cent for single malts. Single malts may be eight, ten, twelve, or even fifteen years old, but all favourably compare with best cognac. There is no 'best' single malt. It is a matter of taste.

A taste for the malt

The 17thc in Scotland saw whisky begin to take the place of ale as the general drink. 'A man of the Hebrides,' said Dr Johnson, 'as soon as he appears in the morning, swallows a glass of whisky; yet they are not a drunken race.' But another observer declared that the aquavitae houses, which were very numerous, were 'the bane and ruin' of the Highlands. There farmers consumed their substance and vagrants drank the profits of their robberies while planning new thieving. For years illicit distilling was rife, but in 1823 an Act was passed to sanction distilling on payment of a duty of 2s 3d per gallon of proof spirit and a licence of £10 for all stills with a capacity of 40 gallons and over. George IV, when he visited Scotland in 1822, would drink nothing but malt whisky once he had tasted it. He asked for Glenlivet and caused a panic because it was unobtainable. The situation was saved by Miss Elizabeth Grant of Rothiemurchus, who sent supplies to the king from her own bin 'long in wood, mild as milk, and the true contraband gout in it'. For this timely service Miss Grant's father was rewarded with an Indian judgeship. Before George IV's time whisky had been the drink of the peasants. When lairds and prosperous merchants gathered round the glowing embers of a fire to converse, their tipple was claret imported from France, Scotland's partner in the Auld Alliance.

Home grown, home made

Scottish food and eating habits are much maligned, and the Scottish people are branded as a race filling their stomachs with haggis and porridge like the Irish do with potatoes. In fact Scotland has done a great deal for the world's diet – think of Aberdeen-Angus beef for a start – and haggis, which the English also ate in earlier centuries as a way to make use of the offal, is produced nowadays chiefly for tourists and Burns suppers. Dr Johnson's dictionary defines oats as 'a grain which in England is generally given to horses, but in Scotland supports the people . . .' Oats will grow in cold, wet climates and poorer soil than any other cereal. As a food it offers a good balance of protein, carbohydrate, and fats. On a cold morning there is nothing more sustaining than a bowl of steaming, creamy porridge, either taken neat in Scottish fashion, or laced with golden syrup. Oatmeal can also form the basis of a wide variety of cakes and biscuits, but its major rôle is played at breakfast time – and not only in Britain. The Emperor of Japan insisted on porridge when he visited London during 1971.

For a long time soup was associated with charity, and even Mrs Beeton wrote of its 'benevolent uses'. The less affluent people of Britain have never forgiven soup enough to make it regularly in the way the great continental soup-makers do. But the hard-headed Scots housewife is an exception; she recognizes the food value of a good soup, and does not mind the work that goes into making it. Scotch broth and leek soup are household regulars. Cock-a-leekie, properly made with a whole boiling fowl, is too costly for every day – as is partan (crab) bree. There are many others, like Cullenskink, a fish soup originating on the Moray Firth, and powsowdie, a sheep's head broth. Scotland's smoked salmon is the best in the world, and a grilled salmon steak should be a must for every visitor. Scampi-fishing has developed, particularly on the west coast, into a major industry. Methods of curing the herring and haddock came from the Vikings and local invention. Favourites are Finnan haddie and Arbroath smokies, fresh-caught haddock cleaned then smoked over an oak-wood fire. Among a host of meat-course dishes are potted hough (a kind of brawn made with beef shin and veal knuckles), potted head (pig's head brawn), mutton with rowan jelly, venison pasty, and Forfar bridies (meat and onions in shortcake pastry). High tea, the usual Scottish evening meal, is not a meal for slimmers. The main course is often fish and is followed by large quantities of scones and baps, cakes and biscuits – such things as girdle scones (made with buttermilk), Abernathy biscuits, shortbread, Dundee cake (with currants, almonds and glace cherries), pancakes, crumpets, gingerbread, and black bun.

Game and the gun

Game in season, like venison and grouse, is traditionally Scottish, though most of the venison is now exported to Germany because it is too strong for the majority of British palates. Between 12 August and 10 December the purple moors are inhabited by sportsmen, usually operating in costly syndicates, shooting a russet gallinaceous game bird with feathered feet. This is the grouse season, a time when the soft-spoken Highland gillie can draw silent amusement from the antics of the Sassenachs. The gillie, whose forefathers were perhaps attendants to a chief, also guides the hands of those who go deerstalking and salmon fishing on the great estates.

Influence of the kirk

John Knox, rabble-rousing
leader of the Reformation, may be
long dead; the 'meenisters' no longer
have the power to sit people on the penitent's
stool; the Scotsman of today is not theologically-
minded as he once was; children are no longer brought
up on the Shorter Catechism and the Bible is a less familiar
book. But the influence of the kirk is still strong in Scottish
life. More than three million people owe it an allegiance,
real or nominal, and Scotland remains stoutly
Presbyterian. The Kirk or Church of Scotland is the
national church established by the state. Its constitution
represents ecclesiastical government by a hierarchy of
courts as opposed to an episcopal hierarchy of people. At
the foot of the pyramid is the parochial kirk-session,
consisting of the parish minister and a number of lay
elders elected by the congregation. Then come the
presbyteries. The General Assembly of the Church of
Scotland is one of the most impressive bodies in
Christendom, consisting of both clerical and lay
commissioners from each of the presbyteries. Among its
lay membership are representatives of all walks of
Scottish life. Sunday observance is still strong, and parts
of the Highlands and Islands have no public transport on
that day. Licensing laws are strict, and in some areas
public houses have been vetoed by local poll. Most pubs
have only six-day licences. A wit has remarked that the
country which produces the best drink in the world has
made it difficult to sample. The God of John Knox was the
unforgiving Old Testament God, hellfire was preached
from the pulpits, and pleasure of all kinds was frowned
on. After Cromwell's Puritans had gone the English could
enjoy Charles II's Restoration, but to many Scots the
Covenant remained sacrosanct and much blood was spilt
in its defence.

Kirk and climate combined to make the Scot dour. This in
turn has earned him a reputation for meanness and led to
remarks such as 'like Aberdeen on a flag day'. Scots
humour is rarely of the uproarious kind – unless much
whisky has been taken – but usually concerns either death
or money. These are two typical examples:

*An elderly Scot died and the widow permitted one
of his old cronies to have a last look at him on his
death-bed. The visitor returned from the bedroom and
said to the widow: 'He looks very happy.' 'Ay,' agreed
the widow, 'Willie was always gey slow in the uptak' –
he probably doesna' ken whaur he is yet.'*

*The chemist was furious with Angus for knocking
him up in the early hours of the morning. 'Three
pennyworth of sodium bicarbonate at this time of
night,' he fumed. 'A glass of hot water would have
served just as well.' 'Weel, fancy that!' said Angus.
'I thank ye for your advice and I'll no' be bothering
ye after all. Goodnicht.'*

A law to themselves

Visitors to the Edinburgh Festival may go to Parliament
House behind the High Kirk of St Giles. This was the seat
of Scottish government until the Union of 1707. Now its
polished floor is trodden, while the courts are sitting, by
advocates in wig and gown who show by their numbers
that the law is one thing Scotland cannot export.
Parliament House, with fine hammer-beam roof and
Raeburn portraits in its Great Hall, is now the supreme
Law Courts of Scotland – and Scots are proud that they
have their own law. It is something to boast about, for
Scottish Law – based on an amalgam of ancient Roman
Law and sturdy common sense – is enlightened and simple.

Parliament House in Edinburgh was the seat of Scottish
government until the Union of crowns in 1707.

When there is a significant 'reform' in English law it is
often something the Scots have been doing for centuries.
'Are we for ever to be behind Scotland?' Lord Denning,
Master of the Rolls and senior English Appeal Court judge,
has asked. In England the Legal Aid and Advice Act
introduced State legal aid in 1949. A system of free legal
aid for the poor has existed in Scotland since 1424, and in
1587 it was enacted that all those accused of crimes
should be legally represented. In 1926 England at last
passed an Act allowing for 'legitimation by subsequent
marriage'. That has been the law in Scotland, stemming
from a Roman Law principle, since time immemorial.
In 1938 England passed an Act preventing a man cutting
his wife or family out of his will. In Scotland, through
another ancient Roman principle, a man's family is
entitled to a fixed proportion of part of his assets as of
right. The Scots were first with majority verdicts for
juries, non-publicity for magistrates' court hearings in
major crimes, no more last-minute 'alibi' defences, and
'diminished responsibility' as a partial defence in murder
cases. It is a jealously-guarded privilege that Scottish
banks like the Royal Bank of Scotland and the Bank of
Scotland issue their own bank notes. The notes seem to
have the sole purpose of annoying the English, for they
are an accounting fiction; they must almost all be backed
by deposits at the Bank of England.

Mediterranean gardens

One can spend days in downpour in the west of Scotland,
only to learn infuriatingly that friends who went there a
month later enjoyed the scenery amid golden sunshine.
The Scots are touchy about their weather, and in its
defence they point to their gardens. If it rains after a few

dry days they say things like, 'The garden was badly needing that rain'. They are keen gardeners, and that provokes the question: Why are the gardens of Scotland so luxuriant? The answer is the Gulf Stream. It is important to remember that Scotland and England are divided climatically into east and west, not north and south. When the Gulf Stream, which originates in the Caribbean, crosses the Atlantic it washes the shores of Cornwall, western Ireland, and the west coast of Scotland. Ireland imposes a barrier between the Gulf Stream and much of the west coast of England and Wales, but the west coast of Scotland has many gardens which are almost sub-tropical. A famous one is the Logan Botanical Garden in old Wigtownshire. Close by is the great Scottish garden of Lochinch, which was laid out in the 18thc. Trees are a great beauty here and an impressive surprise is a magnificent avenue of Araucaria imbricata – the common Monkey Puzzle. In Wester Ross the contrast between the wild interior and the Mediterranean-type coast is striking. At Poolewe, where Loch Maree flows into the sea, is a great sub-tropical garden of over 2,000 acres. Until 1862 the headland where the Inverewe Gardens now flourish was a barren and rocky place. Then Osgood MacKenzie, laird, sportsman, and gardener, put in shelter-belts of trees, dragged huge quantities of rich soil up to the headland in baskets, and planted endless varieties of shrubs, trees, and flowers. The garden has the largest magnolia tree in existence, a 50ft hydrangea, exotics from all over the world, miles of rhododendrons, and is one of the finest in Britain.

The practical kilt

The kilt is a useful garment and the modern version is built on lavish lines. Anything up to 8yds of material, thickly pleated at the back and sides but with pleats stitched together only at the waistband, can be used in a single garment. Below the waistband pleats swing free. As a walking-dress it is both warm and airy, leaves the legs free, stands rain for hours before it soaks, and hangs well

Scottish piper in full dress.

above the mud and grass which wet other garments. It is warm enough for a cold day, cool enough for a warm one, and it is a fine dress to look at. It was not always used in its present form. In the days of the clans it was the breacan-feile, the belted plaid, a sort of tartan blanket about 2yds wide by 5yds or 6yds long. One end of this was wrapped round the body like a modern kilt, and the rest thrown over the shoulder and pinned in place. The plaid could be used as a blanket at night. In battle the Highlanders sometimes laid aside their plaids to allow freer actions, and fought near naked or in their shirts if they had any. Highlanders delighted in bright colours, and those who could afford it wore plaids that were striped in hues generally in both warp and weft, but sometimes in one direction only. They called such cloth *breacan* ('variegated'). Our word 'tartan' comes from French *tiretaine*, which referred to a kind of cloth.

Mythology of the tartan

Neither existing examples of pre-1745 tartans, nor Highland portraits painted before 1745, justify a belief that Highland chiefs had come to use tartan as a sort of military uniform by which one clan could be distinguished from another. Tartan would have been of little service for such a purpose when the belted plaid was laid aside before an engagement, though this objection would not have applied to the trews (tight trousers and a hose in one piece), nor to the kilt or philabeg ('little wrap'). The latter was the lower half of the belted plaid cut off at the waist, but may not have come into general use until about 1730. Such a uniformity within a clan – in view of the cost and labour of producing a plaid – would in any case have been difficult to attain. This destroys a plausible theory on the origin of clan tartans. The truth seems to be that the kilt was proscribed after 1745 because it had been worn as a badge of Jacobite sympathies. When Walter Scott introduced his romanticized stories of the Highlands the haberdashers listened and devised clan tartans out of a confusion of colours. The kilt became the middle-class Scotsman's suit and glamour wear. Now every Scottish clan has a tartan or tartans of its own, each one different in some respect from all the others. If one's name is on the clan list one is said to be 'entitled' to wear a certain tartan, but there is no law, written or unwritten, about it.

Piper, piper . . .

Scots do not claim to have invented the bagpipes, but they do claim to have developed the music into an art. A set consists of a sheepskin bag (devout pipers anoint the bag with whisky to keep it in heart), from which five wooden pipes project. One of these is a mouthpiece, and another is the chanter on which notes can be fingered. The remaining three play fixed notes in harmony as the air is squeezed out through them from the bag, which is held under the elbow of the piper. The volume of sound is constant and cannot be varied. Broadly speaking there are two kinds of music – the march, strathspey, and reel composed for dancing or for armies on the move, and the great pibroch, symphony music of the pipes. The first is catchy music with a lilt, excellent for lifting men up and over the last long mile or rocking a ballroom to its foundations. The second has to 'grow on the ear'. Most of the pibrochs are constructed in five movements, beginning with a simple statement of the melody (the urlar), then working up through three successively more complicated variations of the original theme, and finally dropping back to the urlar. There are scores of pibrochs and thousands of marches, strathspeys, and reels. They are still being composed, but the making of bagpipes is a highly-skilled trade and there are fewer than ten firms now doing it.

Visitors who arrive in a Border town and find horses cantering through streets gay with flags and bunting will have arrived at the time of the annual Common Riding Festivals (usually June), when the citizens celebrate their ancient origins by riding round their local boundaries or marches. The festivals have names like the Braw Lads Gathering at Galashiels, or the Guid Nychburris (Good Neighbours) Festival at Dumfries. Often the celebrations go on for several days. In most of these celebrations the central figures are a Cornet or standard-bearer, and his Lass, chosen by popular vote among the young men and girls of the town. They have to be skilled on a horse, for the Marches are always ridden on horseback, usually at an early-morning hour with a large crowd of spectators up with the lark to follow on. The custom goes back to the days when the common lands of a town were closely inspected each year to prevent encroachment.

Heroes and villains

History is one of the most compelling of magnets for visitors to Scotland from all over the world. They flock to Sir Walter Scott's home Abbotsford House near Galashiels; to Falkland Palace in Fife; Stirling and Edinburgh Castles, and other places associated with Mary Queen of Scots; to Bannockburn and Culloden where the country's two most famous battles were fought; and to the places where the memory of the national bard, Robert Burns, is enshrined. The cult of Burns is almost a religion, illustrated by the story of the Scot who burst out after a recitation from his work: 'Whaur's your Wullie Shakespeare noo?' Ayr, biggest of the popular Firth of Clyde resorts, is the start of the Burns country. It was just on its fringe at Alloway that Robert Burns, poet of the common man, was born in 1759. Burns Cottage, the 'auld clay biggin' – its thatched roof recently renewed by an English thatcher – had been built a few years before by Robert's father William Burns on $7\frac{1}{2}$ acres of land he had rented to start a market garden. This cottage today is one of the most-visited houses in Scotland – about 130,000 people go every year to see it and the adjoining museum, which houses a major collection of Burns relics. Close by is the Brig o' Doon, which is believed to date from the 13thc and figures in *Tam o' Shanter*.

A large number of towns and villages in south west Scotland boast of their associations with the bard. Dumfries, where he lived the last six years of his life, is one. Another is the immaculate white-painted village of Gatehouse-of-Fleet, where the Murray Arms Hotel carries the genteel advertisement: 'Patronized by Robert Burns'. At the bright little port of Kirkcudbright, much loved by artists, the *Selkirk Grace* was written:

Some hae meat and canna eat,
And some wad eat that want it:
But we hae meat and we can eat
And sae the Lord be thankit.

Robert the Bruce and Robert Burns are the heroes of the average Scot. Bonnie Prince Charlie and Mary Queen of Scots are loved for the tragedy in their stories – and the fact that the English can be identified as their enemies. But Walter Scott is hardly read now, and the wonder is that so many generations managed to plough through his prose. So the Scots are a people full of native genius and with many great men. But few are national heroes, for many had to leave Scotland before finding fame in the wider world.

One of doubtful fame was John Law, a shrewd 17th-c financier who won £100,000 by gambling at the tables all over Europe, established the Bank of France, and then

Scott and Burns, both literary giants and beloved of every true-blooded Scot.

died in poverty in Venice when his bank collapsed without enough money to back the notes it had issued. William Paterson founded the Bank of England, but his Darien Scheme which was to give Scotland prosperity brought disaster instead. Andrew Carnegie, millionaire industrialist and philanthropist, was born at Dunfermline in 1835 to a poor weaver who emigrated to Allegheny in Pennsylvania. At 14 Carnegie became a telegram boy, then joined the Pennsylvania Railroad. He laid the foundation of his fortune by introducing sleeping cars on the railway and investing in oil lands, but his great work began with the development of the Pittsburgh iron and steel industries. In 1901 he retired to live at Skibo 'castle', in one-time Sutherland, in the style of a great Scots laird. The rest of his life (until 1919) was devoted to giving away money to save his soul.

Glasgow and its university produced many great men. James Watt (1736 to 1819), Greenock-born designer of the first economical steam engine, developed in the academic environment as one of the first and greatest applied scientists. Adam Smith (1723 to 1790), a Fifer who held the chairs of logic and moral philosophy, wrote the most influential of all books on political economy. David Livingstone (1813 to 1873) studied medicine, applied science, and divinity before he went to Africa. William Thomson, Lord Kelvin (1824 to 1907), professor of natural philosophy for 50 years, declined the Cavendish chair at Cambridge three times. His genius was applying his theoretical knowledge of heat, light, sound, and electricity to practical problems. Kelvin was given the freedom of the city after the laying of the Atlantic cable in 1866. Other products of the university were James Boswell, John

Buchan, and A J Cronin. Natives of the city included Sir John Moore, hero of Corunna; Colin MacLiver – Lord Clyde – who crushed the Indian Mutiny; and Sir Thomas Lipton, who built a butter-and-ham empire and played a big part in turning the British into a nation of tea drinkers.

Many workshops and factories open their doors to visitors and are glad to demonstrate how their products are made. These places may be one- or two-man enterprises producing craft work – Scottish glass, jewellery, pottery, and woodcarving, for example – souvenirs of a visit to Scotland. They may be the mills making tweeds and knitwear or they may be distilleries producing malt whisky. Many of the places welcome visitors without prior notice, others need to be contacted in advance. The list of possibilities includes atomic energy establishments (*eg* Dounreay and Caithness), bagpipe and kilt makers (Glasgow), and golf-club manufacturers (North Berwick).

Of sport and kings

Golf is so much a Scottish national game that it seems right to put it first when talking about sport. Scotland, where it all began, offers the golfer some of the world's most historic and most challenging courses. Yet the game was so much frowned upon by King James II that he banned it in 1457. He wanted his subjects to take up archery instead. James III and James IV also tried to produce archers instead of golfers, but after a treaty with England in 1502 James IV decided to take up the game. He bought clubs and balls from a bow-maker in Perth, and two years later an item in the royal accounts shows two guineas paid out for the king's game of golf with the Earl of Bothwell. In 1567 Mary Queen of Scots caused some resentment when she went off to play golf just after her husband Lord Darnley had been assassinated. In 1552 St Andrews had a course; Leith near Edinburgh got one in 1593; and links were set up 200m north at Dornoch in 1616. James I and James VI took the game to England. Today 350 courses in Scotland welcome visitors. Most are seaside links with sandy soil and springy turf, but there are also many fine inland courses amid magnificent scenery. St Andrews, on the Fife coast, is a town dedicated to golf. Its Old Course is claimed to be the most famous – and beloved – in the world, and most of the world's great names in the game have played there. In Scotland golf is an artisan's sport as well as that of the professional classes, and a round on the Old Course is still comparatively cheap. North from Fife across the Tay estuary is Carnoustie, a seaside town which has staged several British Open Championships. Over the sea in Skye there is good golf at Portree and Sconser, but for first-class golf in an out-of-the-way place few courses match Machrie on the island of Islay. Gleneagles, 37m from Edinburgh, has two of the finest inland courses to be found anywhere. Henry Cotton called it 'a golfer's paradise'. Gullane in Lothian has four courses, of which the best known is Muirfield – home of the Honourable Company of Edinburgh Golfers and venue for the Ryder Cup in 1973. On the Firth of Clyde the names of Gailes, Barassie, Troon, Prestwick, and Turnbarry ring for the enthusiast. The Old Course at Troon, where the British Open Championship was played in 1974, is a tough test even for leading professionals.

The 'glorious twelfth' of August marks the start of the grouse season, when the moors are busy with gentlemen and dogs.

16

Cairngorm ski slopes

Ski-ing is possible in many more Scottish mountains than will ever be developed for the sport, and is regularly practised in many more areas than can be considered holiday propositions by skiers living far south of the border'. Glenshee and Cairngorm offer good facilities in terms of accommodation, ski schools, equipment hire, and apres-ski interests. The official season at Cairngorm is from mid-December to May, and at Glenshee extends to April. The best time is between early March and late April. Scottish mountain weather is unpredictable. Poor visibility, suddenly-descending chill mist, and bitter, damp, cold frequently grip the slopes. But when conditions are at their best they are excellent. In spring, although the mountains are not high (Cairngorm is 4,084ft) it is possible to ski in warm sunshine over perfect powder, when the Alpine snows are rotting fast. Scotland should not be compared with the resorts of the Alps however; the climate is Arctic, not Alpine. Aviemore village has been transformed into the main accommodation centre for Cairngorm ski-ing, with hotels, chalets, artificial ski-slope, swimming pool, skating rink, restaurants, cinema, and pin-bowling. It is now truly a 'resort'. The ski slopes are reached by a fast access road which ends at car parks 2,000ft up the mountain and just below the chairlift station. There is a tow near the car park on ground suitable for beginners, but the main tows are reached from the mid-station of the two-stage double chairlift. Close by there is a trainer tow, and just above the wide bowl of Coire Cas offers ski-ing that is easy but interesting and varied. The steeper, fast runs of the White Lady give good sport for advanced skiers and are reached either by continuing to the top station of the chairlift or by tow from the middle station. A third coire, Coire na Ciste (narrow, steep, excellent run), is also reached from the top. Hotels throughout the Spey Valley cater for the winter-sporters, and many of them arrange evening entertainment. Some also have their own ski school or resident instructor, equipment-hire service, and provide transport to the slopes. A profusion of ski schools on Speyside employ the services of both home-grown and imported instructors.

Glenshee does not hold its snow so long as Cairngorm, and there has been no development comparable with the Aviemore centre. The apres-ski scene is split around the hotels serving the area, a few in Glenshee itself and several in the nearby town of Blairgowrie. The slopes are only fifteen to twenty-minutes drive from the nearest Glenshee hotels. The single-seater chairlift rises to the top of the 3,059ft Cairnwell, and the Tiger Run down this steep and often icy face of the mountain can be avoided by traversing screes to Butchart's Corrie, a pleasant wide bowl with tows and fine terrain for beginners and intermediate skiers. The Cairnwell gets little sunshine, but when the shadows start the sun can be chased to the facing slopes by way of the Sunny Slope tow.

An angler's paradise

The scope for salmon and trout fishing in hundreds of rivers and lochs is well-known, but what is not always appreciated is how cheap fishing can be in Scotland. Permits for trout fishing are never expensive. Salmon may be a different matter, but while some beats on exclusive waters are admittedly costly, the opportunity often exists elsewhere at not too great a cost. Many hotels have salmon

Strathspey Hotel at Aviemore has the appearance of an alpine winter-sports centre transplanted straight from Europe.

St Andrew's Old Course has been played on since the 16thc and is a mecca for golfers all over the world.

fishing available to residents. Often the recommended best times to fish are spring, early summer, and in the autumn; fishing apart, it is during these off-peak periods that Scotland is at its most enjoyable. The governing body for national and international competitions for sea angling is the Scottish Federation of Sea Anglers, which sponsors open boat and shore championships and publishes a special brochure listing the main festivals and competitions. The federation is in membership with the European Federation of Sea Anglers and runs European championships in Scotland each year. The main season is from May to October. New British records are made regularly in Scottish waters, and the federation keeps note of these and Scottish record fish of all species. A skate of 226lb 8oz heads the list, and the record halibut weighed in at 162lb 12oz. These fish were taken in northern waters around the Shetland and Orkney Isles, but in Luce Bay there are tope and sharks, and the British haddock and cod records are being closely pressed in the Firth of Clyde and other marks.

Only in recent years have the extensive coarse-fishing opportunities that exist in Scotland for pike, perch, roach, grayling, and other species been realized. In Scotland the right to fish for coarse fish and brown trout belongs to those owning land adjoining water. So someone owning land adjoining a river may fish for those species in that part of the river opposite his land. On the other hand, someone having land adjoining a loch may pursue coarse fish and brown trout anywhere in that loch. Permission to fish must therefore be obtained from the riparian owner, or if the fishings are leased to a club or association then permission must be obtained from the lessees. Visitors

may find their interest in coarse fish regarded with some amusement, but permission to fish will generally be readily forthcoming, and in some cases payment will not be requested. Where a charge is made it is usually to cover any game fish which may inhabit that particular water. A point which causes some confusion, particularly with visiting English anglers, concerns river-board licences. Scotland has no direct equivalent to the English river board, and district fisheries boards are concerned only with the preservation of salmon fisheries, having no powers applicable to coarse fisheries. There is, therefore, no such thing as a Scottish river-board licence for coarse fish. Nor is there a statutory close season for coarse fish.

The moorland chase
Scotland has vast areas of hunting ground for those inclined to stalking or shooting, and the quarry varies from the majestic red deer stag to the common wood pigeon. Whether the visitor is out on the 'Glorious 12th' (of August), or content with some rough shooting during the fresh, frosty days of winter, there is ample sport. The season for stalking red deer stags begins on 1 July, but stalking seldom starts before early September, when the antlers are clear of velvet and the stags have reached prime condition. The season is short and ends on 20 October. A shootable stag is not necessarily the one with the finest antlers. To shoot only the best heads would mean deterioration of the stock. Weather conditions, the lie of the ground, and the presence of other animals to alarm the quarry are all problems to be overcome if the stalk is to succeed. Two methods are employed in shooting the red grouse – walking up and driving. Walking up is carried out by a line of six to eight guns, interspersed by gillies

Nobody really knows how Highland games first started, but most agree that their colour and music contribute a great deal to the Scottish way of life.

and beaters who carry the shot game. The birds are flushed by the approach of the line and are shot as they go away, usually forward. Later in the season they become wary and wild; if a substantial bag is to be obtained driving must be resorted to. This is perhaps the most difficult form of game shooting. A party of eight guns is placed in a line of butts sited on the flank of a sloping moor. A wide semi-circle of beaters and flankers walk in across a large area of moor, driving the birds forward over the butts.

During a day's shooting four or five such drives will take place. Skill is required both in driving the birds and in shooting. Only with long experience is the correct use of the wind and ground acquired. Against the wind birds in coveys of six to twelve, and sometimes in packs of 60 to 100, travel at a speed fast enough for most sportsmen. Down wind, at a speed of 60mph, few experts can claim any degree of consistency in killing 'two in front'. On moors where there are large numbers of birds and bags of 100 brace are expected, each shooter uses two guns, the second one being re-loaded by a 'loader'. Partly by tradition, but also because they are slow to re-load, automatic shotguns are not generally used in Scotland. Both blackgame and capercailzie are members of the grouse family and regarded as a welcome addition to a day's bag. However, since neither are regarded as special delicacies on the table, they are seldom made the object of a shoot. A number of estates have begun to offer excellent pheasant shooting during November and December.

Games and open spaces

Highland games or gatherings are held mainly in August and September in majestic settings amid a swirl of tartan and the skirl of bagpipes. Their origin is obscure, but the first Braemar Games are said to have been organized by King Malcolm Canmore in the 11thc, because he was dissatisfied with the speed of his messengers and wanted to find the best for his service. Dances at the games include the Highland fling, the seann truibhas, and the ghillie calum or sword dance. Many experts consider these are best danced by men. The seann truibhas is a Gaelic expression for old trews or old trousers, and the dance originated after the battle of Culloden when the kilt was banned. The Highlander had to wear trousers, and the actions of the seann truibhas show the dancer's distaste for them. The Highland fling expresses a zest for life and is danced on one spot. Athletic events include putting the stone (a 16lb or 22lb stone) and throwing hammers of the same weights. Tossing the caber is the most spectacular contest. A tall pine log has to be tossed, end over end, to land pointing away from the thrower. The skill is to balance it properly before tossing. The largest of the cabers at the Braemar Gathering is over 19ft long and weighs 120lb, and rarely is it tossed successfully. Other events include foot races and tug of war, but for many visitors the highlight comes near the end when the pipe bands take part in a grand parade.

Walking is a popular pastime because so often the best things in Scotland are guarded by distance. The forest parks of Argyll, Glenmore, Galloway, and the Borders and the Queen Elizabeth forest park (between the Trossachs and Loch Lomond) all have fine forest trails. Hill walking is to be found all over the Scottish mountains because by Alpine standards they are not high. Only seven exceed

19

4,000ft, and most lie within a few miles of a public road. Most can be climbed easily in a single day by anyone with a car who drives to the nearest point on a road. Unlike the Alps, where there are many mountain huts, most climbers and hill walkers in Scotland can either camp in the glens or stay in hotels, guest houses, or youth hostels. But the Scottish mountains can be dangerous. Sudden weather changes can turn a simple walk up an easy hillside into a serious undertaking requiring a high degree of mountain skill in route finding, and the Arctic weather of the mountains makes proper clothing and equipment essential.

Holidays on horseback can mean anything from riding lessons in a city school or country estate to rough riding over open country. It may be a Highland pony or one of the other native ponies of Britain; it may be a hunter or a hack; but the rider will care for it, groom it, and feed it, whether riding from a hotel, guest house, or youth hostel. Pony-trekking began on Speyside at Newtonmore. In its simplest form it offers a means of exploring wild country in the company of other adventure-loving people. The ponies used are sturdy and sure-footed. They know their job and many of them can carry heavy people for long distances. The pace is steady for the ground is often rough, and the treks lead across moors and mountains, along forest paths, through burns and rivers, and up and down steep glens. Trail riding is offered for experienced riders at two centres in the Borders. Horses are used and the pace is faster, including spells of trotting and cantering. Potted details of many Scottish leisure activity centres can be found at the end of the main gazetteer in this guide.

Pony-trekking is a delightful way of exploring the wild Scottish countryside.

A History in Stone

Stone is an inescapable part of Scottish heritage;
the culture which has grown from living rock and stern
landscapes is as tough and beautiful as the
mountains which formed it.

Though Scotland is a comparatively poor country – more than 60 per cent moor and mountain – she has no need to apologize for her architecture. Man-made scenery can almost rival the mountains and glens, and her highly-individual heritage in stone is both a monument to the past and an adornment to the present. The prehistoric peoples, Picts and those who came before them, have left vivid evidence of their existence. Castles and keeps are grim reminders of the blood spilled by harsh men living a harsh life. Noble Renaissance palaces succeeded the castles, cathedrals and humble kirks starkly demonstrate the watershed of the Reformation, and simple stones pay tribute to the heroes of lost causes. In the 16th and 17thc came the tower houses of the north-east, castellated vertical mansions that created a unique native style surviving into Victorian times as 'Scottish baronial'. At the same time came the more humble homes of merchants and craftsmen in the old burghs – 'little houses' which have been given a new lease of life by the National Trust for Scotland. Scotland enjoyed a golden age in literature and the arts in the 18thc. With it came classic style in architecture, the Adam family, the new town of Edinburgh, the handsome burgh of Haddington, and glorious Culzean Castle. All these buildings, whether simple or splendid, owe their existence to the land of Scotland – the actual bedrock from which the country is formed. This foundation has been racked, contorted, and smoothed through geological time, resulting in the stern grandeur of today's panoramas. Places detailed in this feature are tied to their old, pre-reorganization county names to allow easier location.

Ice the sculptor

Landscapes of wild, stern beauty were torn out of the original Scottish plateau by the glaciers of the Ice Age. As the glaciers withdrew, rivers of moving ice and running water scoured out the valleys and gouged the narrow lochs and sea lochs, leaving peaks and mountain plateaus between them. The glaciers bit deep into the glens making the Highland slopes steeper. Some of the sea lochs, like Loch Fyne, are deeper than the sea outside. A geological slip running diagonally across Scotland, from Stonehaven in the north-east to the Mull of Kintyre far in the south-west, divides Highlands and Lowlands. This is the Highland Boundary Fault, which passes through the Queen Elizabeth forest park around Aberfoyle and the Trossachs, then continues through Loch Lomond with the isles of Inchmurrin, Creinch, Torrinch, and Inchcailloch looking like great stepping stones. North and west from Stirling

David Marshall Lodge, a beautifully-sited Forestry Commission visitor centre situated almost at the top of the Highland Boundary Fault.

Castle is the great wall of the Grampian mountains. Beyond these are the Cairngorms and the Monadliaths, beyond which rise the north-west Highlands and the Cuillins of Skye. To the south and east is the central plain, where the cities of Glasgow, Edinburgh and Dundee sit on the banks of the Clyde, Forth, and Tay, and the hills are the gentle Campsies, Pentlands, Ochils and Sidlaws. Set almost on top of the fault is the David Marshall Lodge, a Forestry Commission visitor centre offering a panorama in all directions. It lies off the Duke's Pass (A821), a wild road winding from Aberfoyle over the hills to the Trossachs.

High or low land?

It is impossible to draw a clear line between Highlands and Lowlands. Many areas in the north are not 'Highland' at all, among them the city of Aberdeen, the area around the Moray Firth, and Caithness in the farthest north-east. And the term 'Lowlands' includes the Southern Highlands – the hills, mountains and glens of the wild Galloway and Carrick country around the 2,770ft Merrick. But the Highland barrier seen from Stirling is real enough, for most of Scotland's mountains and glens lie beyond the north-west frontier of the Highland Boundary Fault, and the rocks are among the most ancient in the British Isles. Running parallel to this fault is another geological phenomenon, the Great Glen – a gigantic rift valley which carves its way from Inverness in the north-east to Fort William and the Irish Sea in the south-west. In the glen are Loch Ness, Loch Oich, and Loch Lochy, connected by the Caledonian Canal which was built by Thomas Telford in the 19thc. Between the two great faults lie the Grampians, the result of volcanic activity while ancient sandstone was being laid down. The rich, fruit-growing soils of the Carse (or vale) of Gowrie are also products of the sandstone.

Granites appear chiefly as mountain masses extending east from the Cairngorms to Lochnagar (which is a mountain). Aberdeen is both built on and of granite. The straths (or valleys) of the Spey and Dee are floored with drifts of granite scree. Precipitous corries and glens, high tundras, semi-permanent snow fields, and remote lochs . . . all are features of the Cairngorms, the highest and largest mountain mass in Britain, including four giants over 4,000ft that follow Ben Nevis as the country's second,

The Great Glen is a gigantic rift valley which carves its way north east from Inverness to the Irish Sea.

third, fourth, and fifth peaks. These mountains lie between Strathspey and Royal Deeside, and summits like 4,300ft Ben Macdui dominate the neighbouring hills because the granite they are made of has resisted erosion. Less granite and more of the harder rocks appear in the west Highlands, where the heaviest granite concentration is Ben Nevis and its neighbours. The harder materials are the metamorphic grits of Ben Ledi and Ben Lomond, the gabbro of the hills of Rhum, and the red basalt and black gabbro of the Cuillins of Skye. The islands of the Hebrides have some dramatic geological features, like Fingal's Cave and the Gribun cliffs on the Isle of Mull. The region north of Inverness has a belt of old red sandstone which follows the east coast up to Caithness. Moving from east to west, the crystalline rocks of the central area give place to rocks of the most ancient geological period on the coastal belt, and the massive sandstone Torridon mountains of Wester Ross thrust their white quartzite peaks to the sky.

Stone forms both of Scotland's landscapes – natural and man made. A random few of the well-conserved beauty spots carved out of the living rock by the Ice Age include Glencoe, scene of a notorious clan massacre, where Bidean nam Bian and Buachaille Etive Mor offer testing rock and ice climbs; Ben Lawers, at 3,984ft old Perthshire's highest mountain and called by some 'the real beginning of the Highlands', noted for its variety of Alpine flowers; Grey Mare's Tail, a 200ft waterfall in Dumfries-shire, just one example of the spectacular scenery to be found in the Southern Highlands. Corrieshalloch Gorge is a 1m,

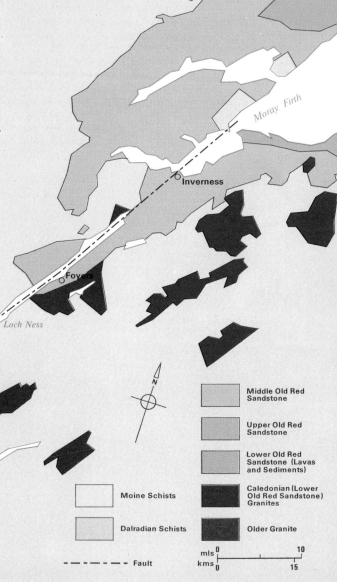

Middle Old Red Sandstone	
Upper Old Red Sandstone	
Lower Old Red Sandstone (Lavas and Sediments)	
Moine Schists	Caledonian (Lower Old Red Sandstone) Granites
Dalradian Schists	Older Granite

mls 0 — 10
kms 0 — 15
– – – – Fault

200-ft deep gorge near the road to Ullapool at Braemore, spanned by a suspension bridge which affords views of the 150ft Falls of Measach. Lairig Ghru, the bare wilderness of a glen in the heart of the Cairngorms, can be explored only on foot. Suilven rises to 2,399ft from the old county of Sutherland and is known as 'the Pillar'. Its dangerous cliff faces are remnants of ancient sandstone.

Stone speaks volumes

Thousands of years of pre-history are recorded in Scottish stone. Archaeologists have found a rich harvest in the work of stone, bronze, and iron-age peoples, and later the Picts, the Roman invaders, and the Vikings. In Orkney, Shetland, and the Hebrides particularly there are bronze and iron-age sites of stone circles, burial cairns, earth houses, and circular stone towers or brochs. For example, Jarlshof near Sumburgh is the site of three village settlements – bronze-age, iron-age, and Viking. The northerly and north-westerly parts were probably the first to be inhabited. Peoples from northern Europe and the Baltic came to the north and east, and from Ireland to the west. Also to the west came people from the Mediterranean, given the name megalithic (or big stone) because of the huge stones used in their burial chambers.

Orkney has an average of three recorded places of antiquarian interest to every square mile and claims to be the richest archaeological area in Britain. Here one can see history in unbroken sequence from stone-age times. Skara Brae (c2500–2000BC) is a village settlement of a stone-age pastoral community, where one-roomed houses with their stone furniture, hearths, and drains were preserved by drift sand. This was a place designed to be lived in, and the life of its occupants is revealed by such things as beds, cupboards, covered passages from one house to another, and a paved open court. Here the stone-age becomes real. Maeshowe dates from 2000BC and is the most magnificent chambered tomb in Western Europe. A spacious central chamber and three mural cells, majestically fashioned with gigantic stones, are covered by a huge mound 24ft high and 110ft in diameter. Ring of Brodgar and the Standing Stones of Stenness show how the bronze-age people left their mark in upright stone circles. Both are near Stromness, and the Ring of Brodgar – the earlier of the two – is still a magnificent sight. Midhowe Broch and the Broch of Gurness (100BC to 200AD) demonstrate the flowering of the iron-age in the North of Scotland, and no comparable structures are to be found elsewhere in Europe. In Orkney the grass-covered

remains of over a hundred brochs may be seen, but only two have been fully excavated. Within the great thickness of the massive defensive walls are narrow passages, stairways, and galleries. The brochs of Northern Scotland all seem to follow the same master plan and were probably used as defensive homesteads.

A well-preserved broch can also be seen on Mousa, just off the east coast of Shetland's Mainland. Near Lerwick is Clickhimin Broch, occupied in the late bronze age and fortified in the iron age. Dun Carloway Broch in Lewis is one of the best-preserved iron-age brochs in the Western Isles and still stands at 30ft high. Edin's Hall Broch lies 13m west of Eyemouth in Berwickshire and is among the ten iron-age brochs known in Lowland Scotland. The site was occupied well into Roman times. The Glenelg Brochs can be seen $1\frac{1}{2}$m south of Glenelg in the old county of Inverness-shire, and are known as Dun Telve and Dun Troddan. Both are iron-age towers with well-preserved broch features and walls which still rise to 30ft in places. The Callanish Standing Stones on the Isle of Lewis are in a cruciform setting unique in Scotland, and consist of 50 stones – some as much as 16ft high. Loanhead Stone Circle near Daviot in old Aberdeenshire is the best-known of a group of recumbent circles in east Scotland. A circle of bronze-age upright stones is almost complete at East Aquhorthies, $2\frac{1}{2}$m west of Inverurie, also in old Aberdeenshire. The circle at Auchagallon, 4m north of Blackwaterfoot on the Isle of Arran, is a bronze-age burial cairn surrounded by 15 standing stones. At Port William in one-time Wigtownshire is the Wren's Egg, originally a double ring of stones but now surviving as three stones, including the central monolith.

Pictish magic

By the 7thc all the north and east of Scotland from the Firth of Forth to Shetland was inhabited by the Picts. These people left symbol-stones all over the area, either incised or carved in relief. But the meaning of the various devices is unknown. Symbol stones are also found in the Hebrides and a few in the Lowlands. Old Aberdeenshire was probably the centre of dispersion of the incised stones. Relief stones predominate farther south. Pictish symbol stones can be seen at Insch (the Picardy Stone) and Inverurie (Brandsbutt Stone). The Aberlemno Sculptured Stones found 5m north-east of Forfar include an upright cross-slab with Pictish symbols and figure sculpture on the reverse. The Dunfallandy Stone found $1\frac{1}{2}$m south-east of

A hut from the prehistoric village of Skara Brae.

Abandoned shortly after it was built, the Antonine Wall developed from a line of military posts established across the Forth-Clyde isthmus by Julius Agricola.

Pitlochry is an 8th-c Pictish cross-slab with a cross, beasts, and angels on one side and with a horseman, seated figures, and Pictish symbols on the other. Sueno's Stone lies 1m north-east of Forres in one-time Morayshire, and is one of the most remarkable early sculptured monuments in Scotland. It stands 20ft high and is decorated with elaborate carving. It was probably of 9th- or 10th-c origin, but remains something of a riddle.

Temples and walls

Near Bathgate in old West Lothian is Cairnapple Hill, a remarkable series of ceremonial and burial monuments spanning at least 500 years (c2000–1500BC). Originally a stone-age sanctuary, this was remodelled in the early bronze-age as an open-air temple in the form of a stone circle enclosed by a ditch. Later it was despoiled and covered by a bronze-age cairn, which was itself considerably enlarged over several centuries. Bronze-age and earlier burial cairns are among the prehistoric relics to be seen in the area of Kilmartin. Others are Clava Cairns, situated 6m east of Inverness on the south bank of the Nairn facing Culloden battlefield. This group of burial cairns includes three concentric rings of great stones, of which the principal features are now exposed. The Caterthuns lie 5m north-west of Brechin and are iron-age hill forts. The Brown Caterthun has four concentric ramparts and ditches; the White Caterthun is a well-preserved hill fort with massive stone rampart, defensive ditch, and outer earthworks.

The iron-age peoples lived in earth houses until the first centuries AD, and good examples of these are to be found in the north-east and Orkney. Culsh Earth House at Tarland in one-time Aberdeenshire is well preserved, with roofing slabs intact over a large chamber and entrance. Some 7m east of Dundee near Monifieth are Ardestie and Carlugie, two examples of large earth-houses attached to surface dwellings used during the first centuries AD. At Tealing, 5m north of Dundee, another iron-age house consists of a passage, a long curved gallery, and a small inner chamber. Grain Earth-House at Kirkwall has an entrance stair, passage, and underground chamber.

North of Hadrian's Wall there is little to mark Roman times – no town, no temple, no forum, no theatre. *Caledonia*, as the Romans called it, passed straight from the iron age to the dark ages. AD80–83 Julius Agricola, Governor of Roman Britain, established a line of posts across the Forth-Clyde isthmus and a temporary legionary fortress at *Inchtuthill* (Perth) on the River Tay. Some 60 years later Governor Lollins Urbicus transformed the line of posts into the Antonine Wall, but it was never more than temporary and was abandoned after 40 years. The wall stretched 36m from Old Kilpatrick to Bo'ness in the one-time county of West Lothian. It was 14ft wide and 10ft or 12ft high – clay and sods on a stone foundation. In front was a wide, dry, V-section ditch. The wall is best seen at Rough Castle near Bonnybridge, where a one-acre fort had a headquarters building, barracks, and a bathhouse. A unique feature to be seen here is the series of defensive pits outside the Antonine ditch. Also near Bonnybridge is Seabegs Wood, a good length of rampart and ditch. Of other forts the best known are Birrens, Dumfriesshire, Newstead, Roxburghshire – on the trunk road from Corbridge to the Wall, and Ardoch in Perthshire. Cardean (Angus) was the most northerly fort, beyond which a line of marching camps reached across Aberdeenshire as far as the River Spey. Birrens was a seven-acre fort for less than 1,000 men with headquarters, commandant's house, barracks, granaries, and six surrounding ditches and ramparts. Nearby Birrenswark Hill features an iron-age fort with two Roman siege encampments below, one with emplacements for siege engines.

Power to the church

Christianity came to Scotland early and brought centuries of fine church building with it. One thinks immediately of the four magnificent Border abbeys founded by David I in the 12thc, of Iona and of the great cathedrals of Glasgow, Kirkwall, Elgin, and Dunkeld. But, Iona apart, there is no single monument that captures Scottish religious minds like the English York Minster and Canterbury, Salisbury and Durham Cathedrals. King David's abbeys and Elgin Cathedral – the beautiful 'Lantern of the North' – are in ruins. In a poor country only the church, the king, and the most powerful barons could afford to build great stone edifices. When the

Reformation robbed the church of its riches neglect set in. Congregational worship needed only a single-chamber building and the subdivisions of nave, chancel, apse, transepts, and chapel interfered with this. Smaller parish churches were easily adapted, but in larger churches often only part of the building was maintained and the remainder used for other purposes or allowed to decay. The responsibility for maintaining the church fabric and providing the stipend fell on local landholders, who were usually reluctant or unable to do so.

Missions and missionaries

Christianity was brought by two missions. The first, led by St Ninian in 397 after the Roman Empire had become Christian, established itself in Galloway and carried the faith into the remote fastnesses of Southern Pictland. The oldest Christian site in Scotland is at Whithorn in the one-time county of Wigtownshire, where the foundations of the saint's *Candida Casa* or White House church lie beneath a later medieval structure. There is little trace of this mission, apart from some inscribed crosses and cave shrines on the coasts of Wigtownshire and Fife. The Kirkmadrine Stones, near Sandhead in the Rhinns of Galloway, are three of the earliest Christian monuments in Britain and show the Chi-Rho symbol (which was used by early Christians in various forms) and inscriptions dating from the 5th or early 6thc. St Ninian's Cave, 4m south west of Whithorn, is said to have been his retreat.

It was with the second mission, nearly 200 years after Ninian's, that the real history of the Scottish Church began. Columba, a noisy cleric, crossed from Ireland *c*563, at a time when the Scots from Ireland were invading in great numbers, and established a monastery on Iona off the tip of Mull. Many of the remains found there are Columban. Two round towers of the Irish type can still be seen at Brechin in Angus and Abernethy in Perthshire. These are evidence of the spread of the Irish Celtic Church into Pictland from the 9thc, and indicate the site of a monastic community. They were used as places of refuge – hence the elevated entrance – and also served as belfries. Eassie Sculptured Stone can be seen 3m south-west of Glamis and is a fine, elaborately sculptured example of an early-Christian monument. The Kildalton Crosses are two of the first Celtic crosses in Scotland.

While early Christianity was spreading, Norse immigrant farming communities were settling in the northern islands. Many Norse churches remain, but the finest is St Magnus' Cathedral at Kirkwall, which was begun in the 12thc and ranks with Glasgow Cathedral in its Gothic completeness. St Magnus', the greatest monument left by the Norsemen, took more than 300 years to build. and is still in use after major repairs made in 1903. Roman Christianity returned to Scotland with the marriage of Malcolm III (Canmore) to the saintly English princess Margaret in the 11thc. It soon absorbed the old Celtic Church, just as it had done in Northumbria in the 7thc. Margaret's son David I was also Earl of Huntingdon, and by the early 12thc Norman influences were replacing the austere Celtic churches and towers with Romanesque buildings. The first monastic house was Benedictine Dunfermline Abbey, which owes its beginnings to Queen Margaret. The foundations of her modest church remain beneath th late-Norman nave. King Robert the Bruce is buried in the choir and his grave is marked by a modern brass.

Four great abbeys

Over the next two centuries master masons were brought in from England and France. The Romanesque style is

The Kildalton crosses are two fascinating Celtic monuments which were sculpted in the dawn of Scottish Christianity.

recognized by its simple massive forms. The walls were of great thickness, built of dressed stone and filled with rubble, and the windows were small and widely spaced. Arches over doors, windows, and arcades were semi-circular. Narrow spaces were sometimes vaulted in stone, but wood was more common for roofing. Sculptured decoration was simple but vigorous. Building often extended over a long period, so different styles can be seen. Holyrood Abbey in Edinburgh is now a picturesque ruin but was founded by David I in 1128. The four great Border abbeys were also founded by David. Melrose is notable for its fine traceried stonework. It suffered the attacks usual for all the Border abbeys during English invasions, but the nave and choir dating from a rebuilding of 1385 include some of the best and most elaborate work of the period. Kelso was the largest and perhaps the finest, Jedburgh has noble and extensive remains, and Dryburgh has cloister buildings which are more complete than in most Scottish monasteries. Sir Walter Scott and Earl Haig are buried there. Other 12th-c foundations include Arbroath Abbey, where important remains of the cloisters survive and the abbot's house has been restored as a museum. Dundrennan Abbey, ruins of a Cistercian house which preserve much late-Norman work, is situated 7m east of Kirkcudbright.

The gothic revolution

In the 13thc came the gothic style, which was already dominating architecture in Northern Europe. It continued to do so until the end of the 15thc, and for rather longer in Scotland. The gothic pointed arch had been used in buildings together with the round arch during the period of transition – for example at Jedburgh Abbey – but it gradually replaced the round arch entirely. This added to the height and grace of gothic churches. Walls were less massive. Vaulting over narrow areas was generally of the rib and panel kind, though roofs continued to be built of timber. Sculptured decoration was more refined, with pronounced mouldings. Glasgow Cathedral is the only unmutilated survivor of the great gothic churches of South Scotland. Parts date from late 12thc, though several periods are represented in its architecture. The crypt

displays fan vaulting over the tomb of
St Mungo and is the cathedral's chief glory. The
exterior shows the vertical tendency characteristic
of gothic architecture. Two towers at the western
end were removed in the 19thc. Elgin Cathedral,
once the most beautiful of Scottish cathedrals,
was founded 750 years ago. In spite of the
ravages of fire and time it is still a noble
monument to its 13th- and 15th-c builders. In 1567 the
Privy Council ordered the roof of the cathedral to be
stripped of its lead to pay troops, and the building steadily
deteriorated until the great, 196ft central tower collapsed
in 1711. The cathedral had been built and rebuilt several
times over. In 1390, after it had been laid waste
by the Earl of Buchan (the notorious Wolf of
Badenoch), a bishop wrote to King Robert III
seeking money to restore it and recalling how it
had been 'the ornament of the district, the glory of
the kingdom, and the praise and admiration of foreigners'.

Architectural wealth

In the 14th and 15thc ecclesiastical architecture received
a renewed impetus from the establishment of collegiate
and new-burgh churches. Castellated and domestic
architecture began to appear in church building in the
form of crenellated parapets, round towers with conical
roofs, crow-stepped gables, and stepped buttresses.
Carved enrichments, including heraldry, were more
common. St Giles Church in Edinburgh was elevated to
collegiate status, with merchant burgesses and craftsmen
founding chaplainries and altars within the church.
Additions and alterations were made to cathedrals and
abbeys such as Elgin, Dunkeld, Dryburgh, Melrose, and
Paisley in the 15thc. Dunkeld Cathedral, for example, was
founded in the 9thc but in the 15thc it was given its great
north-west tower and nave. Prior to the Reformation in
the early 16thc Romanesque, gothic, and castellated
features continued to be combined to form a picturesque
national style. Decorated gothic was preferred to the
more subtle English perpendicular gothic. King's College
Chapel in Aberdeen is typical. The crown steeple is also to
be found at St Giles' in Edinburgh and the Tolbooth in
Glasgow. St Machar's, also in Aberdeen, is the only
cathedral built of granite. The west front is a heroic
design with two spire-capped towers. St Mary's Abbey
stands on the island of Iona where Columba founded his
settlement, and the surviving structure dates mainly from
the late 15th and early 16thc, when it became a cathedral
church. It stayed conservatively with the older and simpler
forms. The Chapel Royal of Stirling Castle is a royal
foundation built in 1594 and shows early classic
Renaissance architecture not seen widely until the 18thc,
but was a foretaste of things to come. Churches built in
the 17thc were generally small and appropriate to the
simple needs of Reformed worship. Plans were of three
types – rectangular, which was most common; 'T'-plan,
which was peculiarly Scottish, and rare cruciform.

Lyne Church in old Peebles-shire was built to the
rectangular plan. The exterior rubble walls were originally
harled, leaving the window dressings exposed. The church
contains the original pulpit and canopied pews, and has a
belfry which was rebuilt in the 19thc. Towers on churches
were less common than a belfry, usually over the west
gable. Two Edinburgh churches of the time have unusual
features. Canongate is a unique example in Britain of a
church which recalls the pre-Reformation Latin Cross,
and the south front is a fine example of Netherlandish
Renaissance. Greyfriars Church has an exceptionally large
aisle and arcades. Here the National Covenant was signed

Fan vaulting above St Mungo's tomb in Glasgow Cathedral.

and later 1,200 Covenanters were imprisoned for five
months. Outside is a fountain with the figure of 'Greyfriars
Bobby', a Skye terrier who watched over his master's
grave in the churchyard for fourteen years and was
eventually buried in the same grave.

Halls of worship . . .

Post-Reformation churches are more likely to have
interesting fittings than medieval churches ruined by John
Knox's 'rascal multitude'. The old kirk at Ayr was built
from funds provided by Oliver Cromwell and has separate
'lofts' for 'sailors, traders and merchants'. At Burntisland
in Fife the kirk has a sailor's loft and an outside stair. Town
churches showed a marked change to the classical in the
18thc. Steeples rose from the roofs and classical porticoes
appeared. Internal arrangements were changing too.
Galleries along both long walls and across one end, with
the pulpit near the centre of the opposite end, introduced
the 'hall-church'. This was derived from the designs of
Christopher Coren and James Gibbs. Gibbs, who was born
in Aberdeen and trained in Rome by the Baroque architect
Carlo Fontana, came home to make a name for himself in
London – where he designed St Martin-in-the-Fields –
and disseminate Wren's ideas. Sadly his only notable
Scottish work is the West Church of St Nicholas in
Aberdeen, which was completed in 1755. Also dating from
the mid 18thc is St Andrew's parish church in Glasgow,
which Allan Dreghorn based on St Martin-in-the-Fields.
St Andrew's episcopal church, also in Glasgow, dates from
the same period.

Hall churches with galleries continued to be popular in
the 19thc. They were either in the Georgian-gothic or the
neo-classical styles. In the larger burghs the neo-classical
designs often included a temple-like portico to distinguish
the entrance at one end, and a tower of classical
proportions rose from the roof to add dignity. Episcopal
and Roman Catholic churches differed from the Church
of Scotland in their internal arrangements, but were built
in the current architectural styles. Generally they favoured

gothic. Alexander Thomson, nicknamed 'Greek' Thomson, showed his bent in his Glasgow churches of the 1850's and 60's – the Free Church at Queen's Park, and the Presbyterian Church in St Vincent Street. The second of these had to deal with an awkward sloping site. James Gillespie Graham's St Andrew's RC Cathedral in Glasgow was an early attempt at a genuine gothic revival. In the 1870's Sir George Gilbert Scott, architect of Glasgow University and Britain's most prominent gothicist, built St Mary's Episcopal Cathedral in Edinburgh, a huge church with three tall spires. There are several gothic-revival churches in both Glasgow and Edinburgh – and also the cathedral at Inverness. The Fife burghs have many distinguished old kirks and a worthy 20th-c successor at the new town of Glenrothes – St Columba's, the new parish kirk by Anthonay Wheeler – a fine piece of ecclesiastical architecture with a detached campanile. But the materials are brick, steel, and wood – not Scottish stone.

. . . And castle homes

'An Englishman's home is his castle', the saying goes. For a long time – and in some cases even today – a Scotsman's castle was his home. The Scottish baronial of Victorian times and the vertical style of tower houses, popular for several centuries, owe their origins to the castles and pele towers of earlier times. Most of the 'castles' in ruins and classed as ancient monuments are really historic houses, and many of them are still lived in. Balmoral Castle, the Queen's Scottish home, and Inveraray Castle, ancestral home of the Dukes of Argyll, are just two of the better-known examples.

Norman influence brought the motte-and-bailey castle to Scotland, and a fine example is Duffus Castle, situated north-west of Elgin in one-time Morayshire. The massive ruins stand in an eight-acre area still surrounded by a water-filled moat. In the 14thc a great stone tower was built on the Norman motte. The motte-and-bailey castle consisted of a motte, or moated artificial mound. On it was a wooden tower, the keep, surrounded by a stout stockade. Attached to the motte was a bailey, or lower court, surrounded by a stockaded bank and ditch, and containing the buildings of the lord's household. Ancient burghs were enclosed in this way, with 'ports' for entry – a term surviving in many towns. Another motte-and-bailey site later became one of the largest castles in Scotland, the 14th- to 17th-c ruin of Castle Urquhart on the banks of Loch Ness, near Drumnadrochit, a spot favoured by seekers of the Loch Ness monster. From the palisaded motte was developed the shell keep, a thick stone wall round the top of the earthwork. An example in one-time Aberdeenshire is the Pele of Lumphanan, where masonry

foundations can be seen on the summit of a motte. Rothesay Castle on Bute was also a shell keep, but it was extensively added to later. Early stone castles consisted of a single high wall – stone and lime with a rubble core – enclosing a courtyard area. Castles of enclosure rose to a considerable height, finishing in a crenellated wall-walk. They were usually built on a natural place of strength, a rocky outcrop or on an island in a loch. Much photographed and well known because of its proximity to the A87 at Dornie on the way to Kyle of Lochalsh and Skye is Eilean Donan Castle, situated on an islet in Loch Duich and now connected to the mainland by causeway. It dates from 1220 and has been restored as a war memorial to the Clan Macrae. Loch Doon Castle, south of Dalmellington in old Ayrshire, was built in the early 14thc to fit an island in Loch Doon. Its massive walls vary from 7ft to 9ft thick and are 26ft high. When the waters of the loch were raised for a hydro-electric scheme the castle was dismantled and put up again on the shores.

Another famous island stronghold is Loch Leven Castle, where Mary Queen of Scots was held prisoner for a year between 1567 and 1568 before she made a dramatic escape. This has an early enclosure wall, though the rectangular tower is probably 15th or 16thc. The absence of wall chambers and scarcity of stairs show its early date. Threave Castle is a grim fortress of the Black Douglases which stands on an island in the Kirkcudbrightshire Dee. Once it was four storeys high with enclosure wall. The castle fell to James II of Scotland and his great cannon Mons Meg (now in Edinburgh Castle) in 1455. The success of cannon meant that castles became status symbols rather than strongholds – but that is anticipating. Back in the 13thc developments in methods of warfare – the use of assault towers and battering rams – brought improvements in the castle design. Round corner towers were used on enclosure towers, rising from ground to wall head. Later one of these towers was built large enough to be a refuge if the enclosure had been breached in time of siege. This was called the 'keep' tower or 'donjon'.

Impregnable stone

Inverlochy Castle near Fort William shows the new round corner towers built on a square building. Dunstaffnage Castle lies 4m north of Oban and is a well-preserved example of a 13th-c castle with enclosure wall and round towers. Rothesay Castle on Bute, one of the most important medieval castles in Scotland, was given higher walls with four round towers enclosing a circular courtyard unique in

Melrose Abbey shows the evolution of architectural styles up to the late 15thc.

27

Scotland. It is difficult to classify many castles by period because they were constantly being developed, added to, and rebuilt. Edinburgh Castle is an outstanding example. King Edwin of Northumbria had a fortress on the rock in the 7thc, and the oldest of the present cluster of buildings is Queen Margaret's Chapel built in the 11thc. It stands on the highest point of the rock. James IV built the Palace block and the Great Hall in the early 16thc, and this was restored between 1888 and 1889. Craigmillar Castle lies 3m away and has a massive 14th-c keep, a 15th-c embattled enclosure wall, and inside it are the remains of stately ranges of apartments dating from the 16th and 17thc. Mary Queen of Scots was in residence here when the plot to murder Darnley was devised.

Grim guardians

An example of the 13th-c change from timber to stone is Bothwell Castle, 7½m south-east of Glasgow on the River Clyde. It was once the largest and finest stone castle in Scotland, and the ruins include the great donjon plus a high enclosure wall to the prison tower built in the early 15thc when it was reconstructed. Another 13th-c stronghold is Hermitage Castle. Situated 16m south of Hawick, this grim building comprises four towers and connecting walk and is outwardly almost perfect even now. The interior contains remains of the original tower. Stirling Castle was at the heart of Scotland's constant strife from the time it was built at least 900 years ago. As early as the 12thc the castle was the residence of the King of Scotland, Alexander I. Much of the present building dates from early and mid-Stuart times, but these parts were built long after the turbulent time when Wallace recaptured it from the English in 1297, Edward I retook it in 1304, then Bruce won it back at nearby Bannockburn in 1314. The old towers built by James III remain, as do the 15th-c hall, the Renaissance palace of James V, the Parliament Hall, and the Chapel Royal of 1594. St Andrew's Castle stands on a promontory thrust out into the North Sea and isolated by a deep wide ditch. The oldest parts of the ruin date from the 13thc, but much of the work is later than the near destruction of 1547. Notable features are the bottle-dungeon, and the mine and counter-mine tunnelled in the rock during a siege in 1546. One of the most impressive fortresses, and the home of some grim stories, is Dunnottar Castle at Stonehaven, set 160ft above the sea on a near-impregnable peninsula that is almost an island. It was a stronghold of the Earls Marischal from the 14thc and was the last to fall to Cromwell.

The hall house or fortified manor appears in Scotland in small numbers at the end of the 13th and beginning of the 14thc. Well-preserved remains can be seen at Hailes Castle, 5m east of Haddington, and Morton Castle, 15m north of Dumfries. These hall houses were more vulnerable than the tower-house, which first appeared in the 14thc. Continuing danger to life and property were responsible for the noble and laird adopting the tower-house as a residence. It was a modest structure which provided the necessary security, a tall, vertical, castle-like building with one room on each floor. More of these were built in Scotland from the 14th to the 17thc than all other types of fortified buildings. Drum Castle, 10m west of Aberdeen, is one of the early ones. The massive granite tower can still be seen joined to a mansion of 1619. The oldest part of Aberdour Castle, overlooking the harbour at Aberdour, is the 14thc tower house. Another 14th-c keep forms part of Crichton Castle, 15m south-east of Edinburgh. As the century progressed the tower house was changed for greater comfort. Additional wall chambers, cupboards and bigger window embrasures with stone seats became typical. A short wing provided more accommodation and greater privacy. The addition of the wing made the plan L-shaped rather than rectangular. Craigmillar and Dunnottar Castles, already mentioned, were L-shaped tower houses. Another was Neidpath Castle, situated 1m west of Peebles and a stronghold of the Frasers set above the Tweed. Yet another was Huntly Castle in old Aberdeenshire, which displays elaborate heraldic adornments on the tower.

The comforts of home

During the 15thc came variations to the tower house. It is symptomatic of the concern for greater comfort that Borthwick Castle had many chimneys, and it is still inhabited. Even more significant and part of the same change is the fact that this was the century when palaces began to appear, and royal castles were transformed into palaces. The palace buildings in Edinburgh and Stirling Castles have already been mentioned. Mary Queen of Scots was born at Linlithgow Palace in West Lothian while her father James V lay dying at Falkland Palace. Linlithgow was started in 1425 but not completed until 1539, so it spans several architectural styles. The Great Hall was late gothic. A fine quadrangle inside the building contains a richly-carved, 16th-c fountain. Buildings to be seen now at Falkland Palace – perhaps loveliest of the old Scottish

Grim Hermitage Castle dates from the 13thc and symbolizes the unrest that gripped Scotland for centuries.

Stirling Castle has been the seat of Scottish kings and the centre of constant strife since its building some 900 years ago.

royal palaces – date from 1530 to 1540, but an ornamental string-course discovered around the remains of the great circular well-house tower shows that the Castle of Falkland was already built by the 13thc. The south range has been described as 'the finest work of its period in Scotland', and includes the French Renaissance façade of James V's time and the Chapel Royal with original entrance screen. The east range is now roofless but still shows changes made by the same king; that on the north was destroyed by Cromwell's soldiers. The gatehouse – with flanking towers surmounted by pointed roofs – survives, as does the Cross House where the King's bedchamber has been beautifully restored. One of the most famous 16th-c tower-houses on the L-plan is Crathes Castle in one-time Aberdeenshire, which was begun in 1553. Among its glories are its painted ceilings – found more often in Scotland and the Continent than in England – which were always done after beam and boards were in position. Conservation work by the National Trust for Scotland has made Crathes a must on any visitor's list. Its outstanding characteristic on first sight is the emphasis on slender height. The castle also has an 18th-c wing.

Tower house to mansion
In the late 17thc the tower house began to develop into the mansion. To the L-plan were added T and Z-shaped houses and others of irregular plan. Elcho Castle, which stands on the banks of the Tay east of Perth, shows this development in its tower-like wings. Traquair House in old Peeblesshire is said to be the oldest continuously-inhabited house in Scotland and has a 14th-c tower, but was developed as a mansion in the 15th and 16thc. Its service wings, screen wall, and gateway were built by James Smith from 1695 to 1705. Another tower-house altered in the 15thc to a castellated mansion providing greater accommodation is Huntingtower Castle. Edzell Castle in one-time Angus is one of Scotland's finest. It was built in the early 16thc and extended in the 17thc. The tower is preserved, walls are decorated with bas-reliefs of the virtues, the sciences, and the planets, and square holes in the fabric represent the Lindsay arms. Renaissance

motifs were applied decoratively to traditional forms by William Wallace, principal master mason to the Crown from 1617 to 1631. But the Renaissance movement was more than ornamental additions. Wallace was concerned with an overall conception of symmetrical planning and dignified façades. He did more than anyone to clear away gothic tradition and make way for the Italianate classicism of William Bruce at the end of the century. Winton House near Haddington, a building dating from 1627 by Wallace, is architecturally a Scottish Renaissance gem. It has carved pediments, strapwork motifs, and other classical enrichments. Glamis Castle near Forfar in the one-time county of Angus, although built earlier, owes its turrets and other ornaments to this period.

Dignity in symmetry
The transition to the Renaissance style is shown by George Heriot's Hospital in Edinburgh, and Drumlanrig Castle in old Dumfries-shire – a ducal mansion. In both a square encloses a courtyard, but they differ from earlier courtyard buildings in that they were designed that way in the first place instead of being adaptations. George Heriot's Hospital was begun by William Wallace in 1627 and completed by William Ayton c1650. The building, rising above a balustraded terrace, has four square towers at the corners and four stair towers in the courtyard angles. It has many towers and turrets with cupolas, tall chimneys, and pedimented windows. In the centre of the main front is a tower carrying a domed and lanterned octagon. The Scottish tower-house influence remains, but there are many French, Flemish, and English ideas. Drumlanrig Castle, built between 1679 and 1689 by the first Duke of Queensberry, is like Heriot's in the symmetrical layout and orderly arrangement of windows and doors. The addition of decorative details of a classical origin is seen in the entrance to Drumlanrig, and this was one of the first houses to have corridors incorporated as an essential part of the plan. Elevations of buildings were lengthened by adding a range with a classical front to the tower house and constructing another at the other end to balance it. Two

Traquair House is a good example of the late 17th-c development of practical tower houses into more decorative mansions.

buildings illustrate the point well. Fyvie Castle, overlooking the River Ythan 24m west of Peterhead is one of the stateliest castellated mansions in Scotland. The four turreted towers are named after their builders – Gordon, Meldrum, Preston, and Seton. It is also noted for its imposing but graceful staircase. The Palace of Holyroodhouse in Edinburgh originated as a guest-house for the Abbey of Holyrood, and became a royal palace at the beginning of the 16thc. The palace as seen today is mainly the work of William Bruce. Its extension and remodelling was his first design in the neo-classical style. Bruce became Sir William and a politician as well as an architect, and built the impressive sandstone Kinross House for himself at the end of the 17thc. He was never able to finish the interior as he had planned, but externally it displays giant pilasters and some elaborate carving – probably from the hands of Dutch craftsmen. Fine stables, garden pavilions, and the grand Fish Gate – adorned with cupids, cornucopias, and fish – survive from Bruce's days.

'Georgian' is a term used for all British architecture of the 18th and 19thc until about the 1830's. William Adam (1689 to 1748) was one of its main exponents in Scotland at the start of the period. His admiration for the work of contemporaries like James Gibbs and Sir John Vanbrugh led him to study the classical style closely, and his three famous sons – John, Robert, and James – carried the 'Adam' style of design and decoration all over Britain. Typical architecture of the time had symmetry in plans and elevations, the main floor at entrance level, larger windows, and flat, lead-covered roofs. Renaissance motifs or new interpretations from antique originals were incorporated. Careful attention was given to external appearance and Hopetoun House in old West Lothian was one of the grandest in Scotland, set in spaciously-landscaped grounds near the Forth bridges. It was begun to Sir William Bruce's design, enlarged by William Adam between 1721 and 1746, and completed by his sons in the second half of the century. The exterior is splendidly adorned with balustrades and urns, steps, colonnades, and pavilions. Early wainscoting with carving in the Grinling-Gibbons manner survives in the Bruce building. The Yellow and Red Drawing Rooms have Adam rococo decoration and beautiful damask wall coverings. It was the home of the Earls of Hopetoun, later Marquesses of Linlithgow. Also designed by William Adam were Duff House in Banff, which combines rich classical treatment in the lower, main storeys, with a 'baronial' skyline and projecting corners; Haddo House near Methlick in old Aberdeenshire, home of the Gordons of Haddo, Earls of Aberdeen; Pollok House in Glasgow, which has later additions by Rowland Anderson. Mellerstain House, near Kelso, was begun by William Adam and completed by son Robert.

Gothic romance revisited

The fashionable study of Greek and Roman architecture was extended by mid-century to medieval art, and this brought the application of gothic forms to buildings with elevations and to plans of regular symmetrical design. This 'Romantic Medieval' style has an outstanding example in Culzean Castle, superbly placed above the sea in the old Ayrshire area and one of the most visited houses in Scotland. It was built around an ancient tower by Robert Adam and shows castellated features characteristic of his designs, though some changes have since been made, particularly in 1879. The romantic exterior's towers and turrets form a marked contrast to the interior, where nothing of the gothic intrudes. In the Round Drawing Room most of the fittings are from Adam's design. His grand oval staircase includes Corinthian and Ionic columns, and various rooms have his typical ceilings and chimney-pieces. The 565-acre grounds include a walled garden established in 1783, aviary, swan pond, camellia house, and a home farm (also by Adam). Inveraray Castle in Argyll is the ancestral home of the chiefs of the Clan Campbell – the Dukes of Argyll – and was one of the earliest Georgian houses in Scotland to show the new fashion for gothic dress. All the Adam family were involved with its transformation, which coincided with the creation of a model township to replace the untidy village of Inveraray.

Classical and medieval styles continued into the first part of the 19thc, though the original Greek and Roman

The whole Adam family worked together to design Inveraray Castle, a building which amply illustrates the Georgian fashion for 'gothicization'.

models were now more closely re-created, and the revival of medieval architecture received a fresh impetus from writers like Sir Walter Scott, with his romantic novels. Victorian architects shook off the formal rules partly because of the varied building needs of the new industrial society. The best Victorian architecture was an expression of the architect's pride and self-confidence in his own interpretations. Then in mid-century the Prince Consort found an Aberdeen architect, William Smith, to put his ideas for a new Balmoral into effect, transforming a house built by the architect's father. A fashion for castellated and contrived neo-baronial Scottish mansions took hold. The main part of Dunrobin Castle, a ducal pile by the sea in old Sutherland, is mid-Victorian; also from this period are Carbisdale Castle, Sutherland; Ingliston House, Midlothian; Beaufort Castle at Beauly. Even the prosperous commercial and professional middle classes took to living in 'baronial' villas.

Black-house people
Leaving the rich man behind in his castle, Scotland has abundant evidence of how and where ordinary folk lived for centuries past. Surviving 'black houses' in the Highlands and Hebrides tell much of the lives of humble crofters for more than 1,000 years, and in towns and villages like Culross the National Trust for Scotland has conserved much vernacular architecture by restoring what it calls the 'little houses'. Before the 16thc there were humbler kinds of stone houses than the warlike tower houses already described, but not many. Most were of timber, wattle, and turf – quickly burned and almost as quickly rebuilt. The Scots peasant farmer or crofter lived in a miserable hovel, often without windows and with a hole in the roof as chimney to the central stone hearth. It was usually shared with livestock. Its low thick walls were built of unmortared stone with a core of turf or earth. Loose thatch covered the roof and was held in place by ropes of heather or straw weighted by stones. Life for the poorest was little better than in the iron age. Black houses were

still being built in the 19thc, and remains can be found in outlying parts of the country. At Kingussie, Inverness-shire, is *Am Fasgadh*, an interesting Highland folk museum which exhibits relics of old crafts, farm implements and a black house. The islands also have black house folk museums.

Rise of the burgh
In the Lowlands the rise of 'burghs' can be followed from the 12thc. These were settlements of the merchants whose overseas trade was the country's chief source of wealth by the 14thc – hence the number of old burghs on the Fife coast. Or they might be found around a castle like Edinburgh or Stirling. Until the 16thc only king, baron, and church built in stone, and houses in the burghs were timber constructions – despite the obvious risks. The physical presence of these burghs at their newest has mostly disappeared, apart from remnants of old kirks and castles and the layout of market, ports (gates), and wynds. Such evidence can be found, for example, at Ayr and Stirling. The earliest stone buildings seem to have incorporated timber for overhanging galleries and extensions, supported on wooden posts or brackets. Plans varied according to site, and in congested burghs buildings might have three or four floors plus an attic. At the tiny royal burgh of Culross there are houses surviving almost as they were in the 16th and 17thc, when it was a thriving community trading over the North Sea to Scandinavia, Germany, and the Netherlands. A Mercat cross forms the hub of the burgh, and old buildings include Snuff Cottage, Tanner's House, The Study, The Ark (possibly a home for old sailors), and so on. The burgh's new look is the result of 40 years' work by the National Trust for Scotland, and there is more to be done when funds permit. Other schemes to preserve the 'Little Houses' are going on at Dunkeld in old Perthshire; on the Fife coast at Crail, Pittenweem, and Dysart; and in Inverness. These houses may be no more than 'but-and-ben' (room and kitchen). They seldom had more than six rooms, were rectangular or built to L or U plans, and the walls were of free-stone,

whinstone, or granite. Roofs were originally of thatch, later of stone, tile, or pantile, and later still of slate. Panelled doors appeared in the 17thc and no authentic window from the 16thc has survived. From the late 17thc until the recent past windows were wood-framed. Peat was the fuel of the Highlands, but these houses were coal-fired and included a chimney stack in each end-gable.

Flowering domesticity

A typical Scottish touch was a central gable topped by a third chimney stack, a feature common in tenement blocks with their greater number of chimneys. The tenement is the typical larger domestic building of this tradition, and it attained great dignity. Until the early 17thc stairs continued to be the early spiral or turnpike stone-built kind, combining strength with economy of space. Later staircases rose in flights within a rectangle to the landings, and were known as 'scale and plot' stairs. Distinctive features in Scottish domestic architecture include the forestairs leading up to the door; marriage lintels over the doors, carved with the initials of the owner, builder, and his wife, often combined with a date; crow-stepped gables, the square stones set one above the other like a small flight of steps up the gable end of a house; Dutch gables, a curved shape of gable-end which became popular in Scotland from the end of the 17thc; the close, courtyard, or passage often giving access to a number of dwellings; the skew-butt, a projecting bottom stone of a set of crow-steps or the stone at the foot of the sloping coping stones (skews) on a gable, often decorated with carved motifs such as dates, initials, grotesque masks, or flower heads; and the yett (a gate), usually of iron bars. Harling is the Scottish form of roughcast, and the ingredients are a mixture of lime and grit with an aggregate of fine gravel or stone chippings. Because lime is used the harled finish is usually white, but the other ingredients can colour the mixture or it can be colour washed.

Out of the Reformation the lairds had acquired new wealth from church lands, and trade grew with the Union of the Crowns in 1603. The burghs of the 17thc included many houses which were built with their fronts at least of stone, though the poorest people were still living in primitive constructions like the black houses. The cottage Robert Burns was born in at Alloway near Ayr in 1759' was built and thatched by his father. A burgh's function as a trade centre was marked by the Tolbooth or Town House, and early examples are to be found on the quay at Stonehaven in old Kincardineshire, in Edinburgh's Canongate, and at Culross. It served as courtroom, council chamber, and prison for debtors. The tolbooth usually had a tower, perhaps with crow-stepped gables or spire, and those built in later centuries were a matter of civic pride. Sanquhar in one-time Dumfries-shire, and Haddington in old East Lothian have town houses designed by William Adam. There are also good examples at Aberdeen and Dunbar. A feature in the High Street of every burgh was the Mercat cross, a symbol of municipal authority. Many survive in their original places, like the one at Preston-pans. Aberdeen has two fine examples of 16th-c houses. Provost Ross's House has dormer windows, projecting tower, and arcading; Provost Skene's House has turrets and painted ceilings. Near the Border is Jedburgh, where Queen Mary's House displays turrets and corbie gables. Historically important burghs like St Andrews and Stirling are good places to look for domestic vernacular architecture. Argyll's Lodging in Stirling was the town residence of a nobleman and reached its present form – enclosing an irregular quadrangle – by a number of 17th-c additions. It has a heavily rusticated Renaissance street gate. Old Hamilton House in Prestonpans was built by an Edinburgh burgess and is similar but smaller, showing burgh architecture at its best. Unusual for the 17thc was the use of the ground floor for living accommodation instead of storage. In Edinburgh's Royal Mile are Huntly House, which was built in 1570 and was once the town house of the Marquis of Huntly; Lady Stair's House, built in 1622; and White Horse Close, a restored group of 17th-c houses. The progress made by the 18thc is seen in Carlyle's House at Ecclefechan, where Thomas Carlyle was born. It was built by his father and uncle – both master-masons.

Well-built little houses like these at Culross were home to ordinary working people during the 16th and 17thc.

As the 18thc progressed the Industrial Revolution gathered momentum and industrial architecture began to appear. Many people moved to the new industrial areas, and medieval towns like Glasgow and Edinburgh had to build beyond their old boundaries. Fashionable suburbs were built for the well-to-do and new towns were laid out. New roads were built and old ones improved. In the Highlands, after the '15 Rebellion General Wade embarked on a road-building campaign such as had not been seen since Roman times. He saw that while the Lowlands could easily be invaded from the Highlands, the absence of roads and bridges made counter-invasion difficult for an army. He set his soldiers to work, and in eleven years 250 miles of road and 42 bridges were built. The Wade bridges are to be seen all over the Highlands, but few are as elaborate as the five-arch bridge over the Tay at Aberfeldy.

New towns, old styles

New architectural developments in street planning and building came with the expansion of old towns in the second half of the 18thc. The New Town of Edinburgh was the most impressive of these developments. Old Edinburgh had grown through the centuries by piling up its tenements ever higher and more closely, first along the ridge of the Royal Mile and then in the Cowgate valley to the south. Up until the closing years of the century the prosperous merchants had been content to live in flats, but then merchants, doctors, and lawyers forsook the Old Town for the New Town. A competition promoted by the town council was won by James Craig (1740 to 1795), who devised a symmetrical layout with George Street as a main axis terminating in a square at each end – St Andrew's and St George's. Parallel on the north and south sides are two similarly broad streets – Princes Street and Queen Street. Behind the houses facing the main streets and running parallel to them were to be narrow lanes leading to the tradesmen's houses and mews. One of these was Rose Street, which became a haunt of poets, artists, and drinking men. Craig's orderly plan was adopted and

added to in the early 19thc, and houses of the first new-town developments were gable-roofed terraces of varying heights which were joined to one another. Robert Adam designed one of the first unified street frontages for Charlotte Square (Craig's St George's Square) in 1791. The design is typically Adam and shows classical motifs from Roman architecture. Charlotte Square has been called 'the first architectural triumph of the New Edinburgh . . . something as good as the best that London or Paris could show'. Today it is still impressive, and No. 5 is the headquarters of the National Trust for Scotland. Other Edinburgh buildings of this period included the university, which was founded in 1582 but whose present old college buildings were erected between 1789 and 1834. The original design by Robert Adam was modified by William Henry Playfair, but the pillared portico on South Bridge is considered one of Adam's most impressive works. Register House is Scotland's Public Record Office and was built mainly between 1774 and 1789 from designs by Robert Adam. It was finished between 1822 and 1827 by Robert Reid.

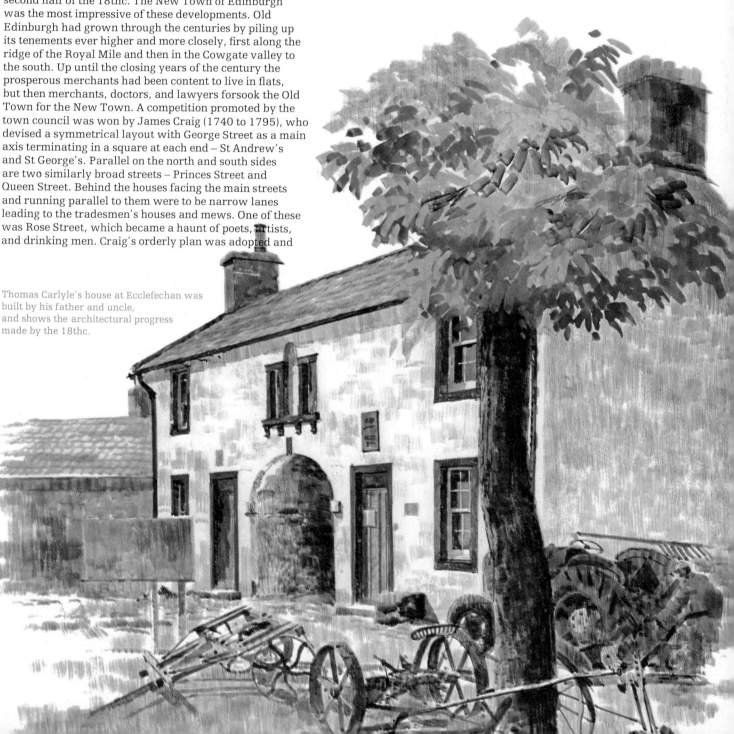

Thomas Carlyle's house at Ecclefechan was built by his father and uncle, and shows the architectural progress made by the 18thc.

33

New village planning in the 18th and early 19thc followed the Edinburgh principles of a grid-like layout incorporating a broad central main street. These can be seen in Fochabers, Grantown-on-Spey, Inverary, and Newcastleton. Inveraray is an important example of town planning on a small scale. The original street plan was by John Adam and Robert Mylne, and Mylne also designed the church. Like in other planned towns and villages of this time the church was situated at a focal point. New Lanark, late 18th- to 19th-c cotton mills and village, was the scene of Robert Owen's social experiment for a self-contained industrial community. It can be regarded as a model village of the Industrial Revolution, for it became a world-famous example of social and economic reform. Its mellow sandstone buildings are situated in a narrow gorge of the Clyde about 1½m from the ancient burgh of Lanark.

Classicism and civic pride

Classicism asserted itself in regular frontages and larger windows where architects were called in for civic building. Glasgow, Aberdeen, and Dundee all joined Edinburgh at this time in acquiring fine buildings by well-known architects. Neo-Greek was an international style, and the chief architects practising it in Scotland in the first half of the 19thc were Playfair and Hamilton in Edinburgh, 'Greek' Thomson in Glasgow, and Archibald Simpson in Aberdeen. It is not without reason that Edinburgh is called 'the Athens of the North'. William Henry Playfair was born in London, trained in Glasgow, and did his best work in Edinburgh. The Royal Scottish Academy (in Doric) and the National Gallery of Scotland

(in Ionic) were his work, as was the eastern extension to the New Town, which produced the Royal Circus and the Calton, Royal, and Regent Terraces. Neo-Greek works include Thomas Hamilton's Royal High School, his Burns Monument, and his Royal College of Physicians.

Glasgow, which has more good buildings than it is given credit for, had fine neo-classical works in David Hamilton's Graeco-Roman Royal Exchange (now Stirling's Library), the Royal Bank of Scotland by Archibald Elliott, and the Kelvinside terraces of Decimus Burton. But the outstanding name in the city's Greek revival was Alexander Thomson – nicknamed 'Greek' though he had never been to Greece. (Nor had Playfair or Thomas Hamilton.) Thomson's churches have already been mentioned, but in the 1870's he was producing monumental terraces like 21 to 39 Hyndland Road and Great Western Terrace which were to have an important influence on the city's street architecture, and symmetrically embellished public buildings like the Egyptian Halls in Union Street. Charles Wilson gave some Glasgow buildings an Italian Renaissance style, like the Bank of Scotland in St Vincent Place. A similar influence affects William Young's City Chambers, where round arches and spacious marble halls abound. A highly-individual example of the historical revival was Abbotsford House near Melrose, built for Sir Walter Scott by a then little-known architect and antiquarian, Edward Blore. It

Robert Adam designed Edinburgh's Charlotte Square as one of the first unified street frontages in 1791.

was a mansion of many turrets and gables in Romantic style, and Scott's reputation launched Blore on a career that included the restoration of Glasgow Cathedral and work at Hampton Court, Windsor, and Buckingham Palace.

Victorian architecture (1840 to 1900) produced a broad contrast in historical styles, with classical public buildings, banks, and commercial houses, gothic churches, and the freely adopted use of many styles for private houses. The best work showed both academic achievement and artistic originality. Before the end of the century 'art nouveau' was challenging historical revivalism. Among the leaders of this movement was Charles Rennie Mackintosh from Glasgow, now acknowledged as a pioneer of 20th-c architecture. At the turn of the century Mackintosh and the art-nouveau circle in Glasgow made a considerable impression on the Continent, though their influence in Scotland was limited to Glasgow and its environs. His School of Art, built on bold, straightforward lines, was the first large building to depart from period styles and was a portent of things to come. But the 20thc also added to the traditional building materials. Iron, steel, plate glass, and brick had been taking over from stone and timber as the 19thc progressed. Now came reinforced concrete, new alloys like aluminium and stainless steel, and new synthetic substances.

The great despoiler

The expansion of industry and the railways gradually broke down the good town planning of the late 18th and early 19thc. Honey- and rose-coloured tenements, soon to turn black, engulfed the hills and green fields around Glasgow. The great demand for housing was met by speculative builders who willy-nilly threw up imposing villas for the well-to-do and great tenement blocks for the artisans. Now 20th-c architects and planners have begun to collaborate and design for whole communities – as they did before the Industrial Revolution. Buildings have become plainer and more massive, but stone still sometimes finds a place. Structures with a framework of steel girders encased in concrete often have walls faced with dressed stone.

The Glasgow School of Art shows a departure from period styles, and is one of the few Scottish examples of art-nouveau influence.

Byways of masonry

The uses of stone are not confined to buildings. A country with a long and turbulent history is certain, for example, to have many monuments, and a country with many rivers rushing from its mountainsides is sure to have built bridges along its roads of progress.

Architect-engineers were pioneers in the field of structural engineering who also created works of artistic merit. They built bridges, viaducts, railway stations, and harbour installations. Among these was Thomas Telford (1757 to 1834), a Dumfries-shire shepherd's son and stone-mason's apprentice who won fame farther afield, but built many roads and bridges in his native Scotland. His Spey Bridge at Craigellachie has stone turrets as a concession to the taste of the time, but of greater significance is the use of pre-fabricated cast iron in its construction. Most of his Scottish bridges were stone built, like Dean Bridge in Edinburgh and others at Melrose and Dunkeld. Early stone bridges dating from the 15thc were narrow and spanned the river with a series of elliptical or semi-circular arches, carried on heavy piers incorporating pointed cut-waters. Wall recesses were built at intervals along the parapet to allow pedestrians to stand aside while traffic passed by. Devorgilla Bridge in old Dumfries was built at this time and still spans the Nith although it is now used as a footbridge. Six arches remain from the original nine. Stirling Old Bridge was the only dry crossing over the River Forth at this strategic spot for nearly 400 years. It has four graceful semi-circular arches strengthened by triangular abutments on the piers, but is no longer in use.

Aberdeen's Brig o' Dee was built in the early 16thc by Bishop Gavin Dunbar and has seven arches spanning 400ft. It is a solid structure enlivened by heraldic carvings and until recent times was the gateway to 'the granite city'. Most of Aberdeen's granite came from its own quarry at Rubishaw. The bridge is as old as the medieval university town, though the soaring Marischal College was rebuilt in 1844. Tweed Bridge at Coldstream was built in 1776 and still carries the A697 across its 300ft length from England into Scotland, at a spot where many rival armies crossed in both directions. Later eloping English couples came here to take advantage of the Scottish

Stone is often seen at its best in bridge building – as in the old Devorgilla Bridge which spans the Nith at Dumfries.

marriage laws. Design improvements from the beginning of the 18thc included wider carriageways and longer spans. The increasing use of wheeled transport and new road building helped to open up the country. Most of the Wade bridges were of simple design – one or more semi-circular arches spanning the river and carrying a road wide enough to take a carriage. Most hump-backed bridges date from this time. Where a bridge was on the approach to an estate the owner sometimes used an architect – hence distinguished 18th-c work like Shira Bridge near Inveraray, and Kilravock Bridge (the White Bridge) near Cawdor in the one-time county of Nairnshire.

To famous men

West of Fort William along the Road to the Isles is the Glenfinnan Monument, which commemorates the raising of Bonnie Prince Charlie's standard in the '45 rebellion. Glenfinnan was the rallying point for the clans. The monument, erected in 1815 by Macdonald of Glenaladale, is an imposing round tower surmounted by the carved figure of a Highlander. Wigtown has the Martyrs' Monument, a cairn and pillar by Wigtown Bay where two women aged 18 and 63 were tied to stakes and drowned for their religious beliefs. North-east of Stirling is the Wallace Monument, commemorating William Wallace who defeated the English at the Battle of Stirling Bridge in 1297. The monument was built in 1870 and has a statue of Wallace on the side of the tower. Princes Street in Edinburgh is the site of the Scott Monument, which was completed in 1844. A statue of Sir Walter Scott and his dog Maida stands under a 200ft spire, with 64 statuettes of Scott characters. The spire springs from a huge gothic-arched canopy containing the Scott statue. This gothic shrine, by G Meikle Kemp, is a vivid contrast to the massive neo-Greek buildings that were at that time finding favour in 'the Athens of the North'. At Culloden, where the '45 Rising ended in defeat, are the Graves of the Clans, the Well of the Dead, the Memorial Cairn, the

Cumberland Stone, and the Old Leanach farmhouse – now restored as a museum. Covenanters' graves can be seen in various parts of the country. Robert Paterson was a stonemason who lived at Balmaclellan near New Galloway and spent much of his life travelling around Scotland repairing the graves of the Covenanters. Sir Walter Scott met him, and his occupation inspired *Old Mortality.*

Fancies and friends

Perhaps the most famous of Scotland's follies – those eye-catching monuments to the builder's foolish fancy – is McCaig's Tower, surmounting a hill above Oban. The tower resembles Rome's Colosseum except that it is a circle instead of being oval. It was built in the 1890's by John Stuart McCaig, a prosperous local banker who lectured the young men of Oban on Greek and Roman art, and is claimed to be the earliest example of work for relief of the unemployed. Edinburgh's Calton Hill Monument is

Famous Bell Rock Lighthouse is one of 23 such structures designed and built by Robert Stevenson, grandfather of the poet Robert Louis Stevenson.

an acropolis that was never finished – twelve columns with steps up to the base. It is part of Edinburgh's early 19th-c tribute to great men, and on a precipice stands the Nelson Monument. At Alves in old Morayshire is York Tower, a folly built by Alexander Forteath in 1827 amid heathery hills. History is not helpful, but this is said to mark the spot where Macbeth met the three witches. Travellers on the B970 on the east side of the Spey pass the gaunt, eerie shell of Ruthven Barracks, built from 1716 to 1718 to keep the Highlands in check and extended by General Wade in 1734. But they failed when Bonnie Prince Charlie landed. After the disaster of Culloden the Highlanders assembled at Ruthven hoping he might take the field again. When they realized the cause was lost they set fire to the barracks to prevent them falling into English hands.

Robert Stevenson (1772 to 1850), grandfather of poet Robert Louis, built 23 Scottish lighthouses, among which was the Bell Rock Lighthouse on Inchcape Rock off Arbroath. He supervised the building of a lighthouse on the island of Little Cumbrae when he was 19. His sons

followed in his footsteps; Alan built the Skerryvore Lighthouse near Tiree and Thomas built one on top of an old tower at Kinnaird's Head, Fraserburgh.

The old county of East Lothian is particularly rich in dovecots, which were introduced into Britain by the Normans. They have survived because they are sturdy and attractive stone buildings – and a tradition says ill-luck will befall anyone demolishing a dovecot. They were built to provide fresh meat in the centuries before cattle and sheep could be kept through the winter. Young pigeons called 'squabs' in England and 'peesers' in Scotland were considered particularly delicious. In 1697 an Act restricted the privilege of building dovecots to lairds who owned land in the vicinity. As the lairds' households got larger, so did the dovecots, and the largest in the old county of East Lothian has 2,000 nesting boxes.

Four distinctive types can be seen. The earliest are round-domed structures with a circular hole in the roof to admit the birds, and a string course of projecting stones to keep out rats. A dovecot at Northfield has walls $3\frac{1}{2}$ft thick with 600 stone nests 9in high by 6in wide and 12in deep. These 'beehive' dovecots can be seen at Dirleton Castle and East Linton. At the end of the 16thc a square type appeared with a slated sloping roof and entry holes half way down the roof. Preston Tower has a good example, with walls $2\frac{1}{2}$ft thick and 985 nests 12in high by 9in wide and 15in deep. Sometimes these are found in pairs – as at Tantallon Castle, where there were 1,200 nests and an earlier vaulted stone roof. Other pairs survive at The Abbey, North Berwick and Johnstounburn. Decorative or drum types of dovecots appeared next. These were built with an eye to their effect in the landscape, and a notable example is at Lady Kitty's Garden in Haddington. Here the lower storey was used as a shed and the upper part battlemented. The fourth type is incorporated in a tower, such as at Aberlady Church, or in farm buildings. The nests for these were usually made of wood.

Stone of destiny

Finally the most important Scottish stone of all – the Stone of Destiny. Scone, near Perth, became the centre of Scottish monarchy in the 10thc not long after Kenneth, son of Alpin, had united the Picts and Scots. Here the Stone of Destiny, a block of red sandstone 26in by 16in by $10\frac{1}{2}$in, was part of the coronation ceremony. The Scots had brought the stone (legend says it was once Jacob's pillow) with them during their invasions from Ireland, and for centuries it had been at Dunstaffnage Castle in old Argyll. For the ceremony the stone was carried from the Abbey of Scone to a moot hill close by. The central act was the setting of the king upon the stone. Scottish kings continued to be crowned at Scone down to James VI (later James I of England) in 1567 – though Edward I of England had removed the stone in 1296 and carried it off to Westminster Abbey. Now there is a castellated 19th-c mansion called Scone Palace here.

Dunure Castle, in the one-time county of Ayrshire, boasts an ancient dovecot which may have been constructed from the remains of an even older broch.

Islands of Enchantment

The Scottish islands form a world within a world, an unexplored Eldorado offering scenic and historic riches unsurpassed elsewhere in the whole of Great Britain. They are also the last strongholds of ancient culture, rare wildlife, and a simplicity of outlook which evades most of modern civilization.

Situated on the north-west fringe of Europe, Orkney and Shetland and the Outer and Inner Hebrides are remote, romantic little other-worlds where strangers are still a source of wonder and the 20thc only a small part of everyday life. This atmosphere of timelessness combines with the sternly-beautiful surroundings and the ever-present sea to make them a splendid choice for escape holidays. They are numbered in hundreds and the majority are uninhabited, but they were once home to prehistoric man. He has left abundant clues to prove it, and they are still home to countless wild birds. Their long white or golden beaches amaze resort-conditioned visitors, but population is sparse, so accommodation is limited and early booking for the summer months essential.

For a long time the turbulent sea was the only link with the Scottish mainland, and the quirk of geography brought the aeroplane to the islands almost before the motor car. In the past few years speedy improvement has come to car ferries, and more frequent services use more roll-on/roll-off vessels to more places. Many islanders are still deeply religious, and generally speaking services do not operate on Sundays. As with accommodation, reservations should be made for car ferries or car-ferrying steamers in the summer. Driving manners are good on the islands' single-track roads, and there is no rushing to beat the other fellow to the passing-bay. Sheep abound on the roads so speeding is always unwise; a driver is expected to hurry only if he is late for a ferry or a doctor on an urgent case. The islands are full of surprises. They are places for gentle touring and the discovery of solitude – unless the visitor chooses to go to Skye in high summer, and so long as he avoids the enclaves of oil development.

The Ice Age came to the great plateau that contained what is now Scotland and carved out mountains and glens before a sudden subsidence plunged much of the northern and western seaboards under the sea, leaving only the mountain tops to survive as islands. Orkney and Shetland, similar in structure to neighbouring Norway and the North of Scotland, are situated on a ridge which separates the basins of the Atlantic and North Sea. The Hebrides include more than 700 islands which stretch in a great 250m archipelago from the Butt of Lewis in the north to Islay in the south. Visitors should not expect endless sunshine and must be prepared for rain and wind-lashed seas. But they are also likely to have placid hours of clear sunny skies in settings that are unforgettable – especially in May, June, and September. During July and August the temperature climbs into the 60's Fahrenheit, but both months have an average of 20 days with some rain. The more northerly islands are so near the Arctic Circle that they hardly get dark at all in June. This is the land of the 'Simmer Dim' where it is possible to play golf until nearly midnight.

KEY TO MAPS

HEIGHTS			
feet SL 400 1200			
metres SL 122 366			

Sandy beaches	Bird watching	Gardens	Nature reserve
A road	Car ferry	Golf course	Notable building
B road	Castle	Harbour	Other places of interest
Minor road	Craft centre	Industrial workings	Pony trekking
Footpath	Croft museum	Information centre	Ruined building

Airport	Deer	Lighthouse	Sailing
Archæological site	Ecclesiastical building	Monument/cairn	Sand yachting
Bird sanctuary	Freshwater fishing	Mountain climbing	Sea angling
			Seal colony
			Standing stones
			Surfing
			Town/village
			Wild ponies

Roads to the Western Isles

The Outer Hebrides form a sparkling crescent 40 to 50m from the mainland, and are made up of Lewis and Harris, North and South Uist with Benbecula between them, Eriskay and Barra, plus a multitude of satellites. These are known as the Western Isles, a name sometimes wrongly applied to the Inner Hebridean group also. Adding to the confusion the outer isles are also collectively known as 'the Long Island'. Roll-on/roll-off ferries from Ullapool and Oban on the mainland, and Uig in Skye, carry cars and passengers to Stornoway (Lewis), Tarbert (Harris), Lochmaddy (North Uist), Lochboisdale (South Uist), and Castlebay (Barra). There are also a number of inter-island services. Details of ferry services can be obtained from Caledonian MacBrayne Ltd, The Pier, Gourock, Renfrewshire. The Western Isles are the home of the Macleods, Macdonalds, Mackenzies, Morrisons and Macneils, and the last strongholds of the Gaelic language in Scotland. The people use their own language more than English, though almost all are bi-lingual, and the islands are rich in Gaelic culture, folklore, poetry, and song. There is little that could be called urban apart from Stornoway, and even there the streets signs are bi-lingual. All along the Atlantic coasts are long beaches and quiet bays, from the silver-white sands of Barra and the Uists to the clean golden arcs around Lewis and Harris. These beaches are unspoiled, yet to be discovered by the holiday masses, and safe for children. The beaches of Northton in Harris, Sollas in North Uist, and the Cockle Strand in Barra are ideal for sand-yachting.

For anglers there are brown trout in the thousands of lochs and lochans; the thrills of grassing salmon; and exciting sea angling for giant skate, halibut, cod, ling, pollack and conger. Active sea angling centres include Stornoway (Lewis), Tarbert (Harris) and Castlebay (Barra). Stornoway has become something of a mecca for sea anglers, having played host to several major festivals in recent years. Visitors can apply for temporary membership to its sea angling club, and for the energetic the islands offer boating, sailing, skin-diving, water ski-ing, golf, tennis, climbing in Harris and Barra, and walking over the moors in Lewis and the Uists. Photographers will find landscapes, seascapes, quiet lochs, roaring waves, crofters at work, sea birds in flight, busy harbours, movement in peat cutting, and the fisherman contemplating the fish he is about to catch.

Ancient landscapes

Those with a sense of history will discover the Standing Stones at Callanish, the Broch at Carloway, the Black House at Arnol, the Folk Museum at Shawbost, old houses at Kinlochresort, the Ui Chapel by the Braighe Sands – all in Lewis; St Clement's Church at Rodel in Harris; Trinity Temple in North Uist; Flora Macdonald's birthplace at Milton in South Uist; Kismul Castle at Castlebay in Barra, the restored stronghold of the ancient Macneils of Barra. These islands have been inhabited since the end of the stone age and the beginning of the bronze age, and evidence of megalithic builders is prolific. These early people were superseded by the Celts from Ireland, who were responsible for raising other prehistoric fortifications – duns and brochs. The Hebrides became part of the Kingdom of Norway at the end of the 9thc and towards the end of the Norwegian domination the Lordship of the Isles was created. The islands were ruled by a minor king, answerable to Norway, but in 1266 the Battle of Largs was fought and the islands were returned to Scotland. Various components were governed by individual chieftains and their clans under the rule of the Lord of the Isles.

Standing Stones at Callanish – an enduring heritage from megalithic builders.

Two of the rare bird species to be seen in the Western Isles – the Arctic skua (in flight) and red-necked phalarope.

The pleasures of bird-watching attract both professional and amateur ornithologists, who come to see birds such as the skua and red-necked phalarope breeding at the southern limit of their range; birds more plentiful in these islands than elsewhere, like the golden eagle, red-throated diver, and corncrake; and birds peculiar to the area, such as the Hebridean sub-species of song-thrush, wren, twite, and dunnock. In spring and autumn immense numbers of migrants are to be seen in passage, using the Long Island as one of the fly-aways while travelling to or from Greenland and Iceland. These migrants favour the Butt of Lewis or any of the western promontories. There is a RSPB reserve at Balranald in North Uist, a nature reserve and bird sanctuary at Loch Druidibog in South Uist, plus bird life in the grounds of Lewis Castle.

Board and travel

Castlebay and Stornoway have tennis courts, and Stornoway has an eighteen-hole golf course with a licensed clubhouse. There is a nine-hole course at Askernish in South Uist and concerts, *ceilidhs*, and dances are frequent in town and village halls. The *ceilidhs* (pronounced *Kay-ly*) are gatherings for impromptu singing and story-telling in Gaelic. All the islands except Barra hold Highland and agricultural shows in summer, and accommodation improves each year. Stornoway has seven licensed hotels; there are three and a number of guest houses in rural Lewis; Harris has two licensed hotels; North Uist three; South Uist and Benbecula two; Barra three. Guest houses, private residences, and croft houses cater for visitors on a full board, half board, and bed and breakfast basis. There are also vacant holiday houses, cottages, and caravans available. Early closing days vary – Stornoway, Wednesday; Tarbert, Thursday; Lochmaddy, Thursday; Lochboisdale, Tuesday; Daliburgh, Wednesday; Castlebay, Thursday.

The ferry company Caledonian MacBrayne Ltd operates a summer and winter service with the summer service usually starting at the beginning of May and ending at the end of September. Visitors planning travel through the islands over the April to May and September to October periods should study the timetables closely. Self-drive cars can be hired from Stornoway, Lochmaddy, Balivanich, Lochboisdale, and Castlebay. British Airways Scotland operates a daily service (except Sunday) from Glasgow to Barra and from Glasgow and Inverness to Stornoway and Benbecula. The Stornoway airport serves Lewis and Harris, while the Benbecula airport serves North and South Uist. It is possible to motor right through Lewis and Harris without touching water, and a continuous road links North Uist, Benbecula, and South Uist. The distance between Stornoway (Lewis) and Tarbert (Harris) is 38m, and between Lochmaddy (North Uist) and Lochboisdale (South Uist) 45m. Single petrol pumps are dotted all over the islands, with garages, filling, and service stations mainly in Stornoway, Tarbert, Northton, Lochmaddy, Balivanich, Homore, Lochboisdale, and Castlebay. Further details about the Western Isles are available from Western Isles Tourist Organisation, Administration and Information Centre, (Dept I/H 971), South Beach Quay, Stornoway, Isle of Lewis. Seasonal information offices operate from May to September at Pier Road, Tarbert; Lochmaddy Pier, North Uist; Lochboisdale, South Uist; Castlebay, Barra. Each island is sufficiently different to merit a tour of its own. The following pages provide island-by-island information which may help the holidaymaker to make the most of his visit.

Rural Lewis

The Isles of Lewis and Harris are not in fact separate, but a distinct geographical boundary exists where the wild Lewis moorland reaches the rugged mountains of Harris. The two areas were cut off from one another by the natural barrier of 2,622ft Clisham for centuries, and even their dialects of Gaelic differ. Lewis is the largest and most northerly island in the group. It is sometimes called Eilean an Fhraoich (the Island of Heather), and its rural aspect is of moorland, peat bog, loch, and vigorous crofting communities. Stornoway is the only town in the Western Isles, and comes as a surprise to anyone who has reached it by motoring up from Harris. It is no sleepy backwater however, but a bustling seaport sheltered in all weather and accessible at all states of the tide. The harbour has a mile of quayside with more than 20ft of water at low tide, and can usually offer something of interest. Local trawlers land prawns and whitefish to be processed in the town; foreign ships put in for bunkers; the local lifeboat has one of the biggest patrol areas in Britain; cargo boats discharge among sailing dinghies; even large liners call. The town is a shopping centre with an enclave of Pakistani shops whose owners are more at ease with Gaelic than most English immigrants, but it also has the familiar names of nationwide multiple stores. One modern shop, James Mackenzie and Sons, is run exclusively as a charity for the town's aged and infirm.

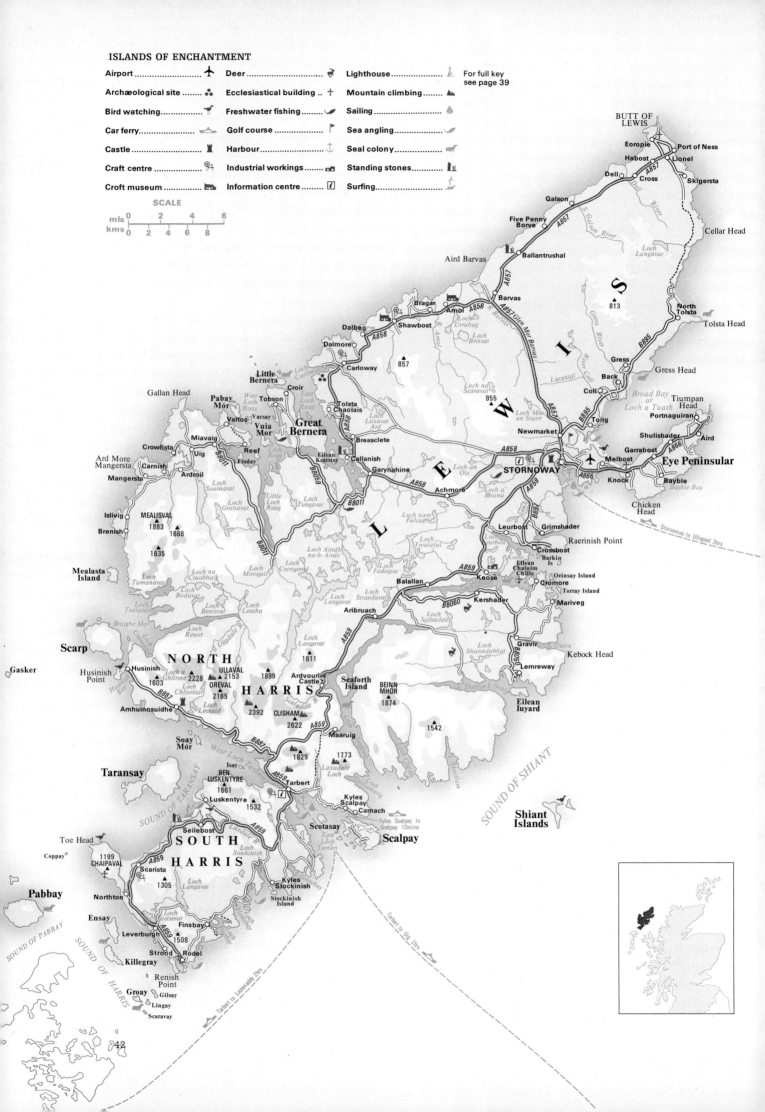

ISLANDS OF ENCHANTMENT

Airport .... ✈	Deer .... 🦌	Lighthouse .... ⚓
Archæological site .... ⁂	Ecclesiastical building .. †	Mountain climbing .... ▲
Bird watching............... 🐦	Freshwater fishing .... ⌐	Sailing .... ⛵
Car ferry .... ⛴	Golf course .... ⚑	Sea angling .... ⌐
Castle .... ♜	Harbour .... ⚓	Seal colony .... 🦭
Craft centre .... ⊕	Industrial workings .... ▣	Standing stones............ ⵢ
Croft museum .... ⌂	Information centre .... ⓘ	Surfing........................ 🏄

For full key
see page 39

SCALE

mls 0 ___ 2 ___ 4 ___ 6
kms 0 __ 2 __ 4 __ 6 __ 8

BUTT OF LEWIS

Eoropie
Port of Ness
Habost · Lionel
Dell · Cross
Skigersta

Galson

Five Penny Borve

S Galson River

Cellar Head

Aird Barvas
Ballantrushal

Loch Langavat

Barvas
813
North Tolsta
Bragar
Arnol · Loch Urrahag
Shawbost
Dalbeg
Dalmore
Carloway
857

Loch na Scaravat
955

Loch Mor an Stair

Tolsta Head

Gress
Gress Head

Back
Coll
Tong

Broad Bay or Loch a Tuath
Tiumpan Head
Portnaguiran

Little Bernera
Croir
Pabay Mór
Tobson
Valtos · Vacsay
Vuia Mor
Great Bernera
Tolsta Chaolais
East Loch Roag
West Loch Roag
Miavaig
Crowlista
Reef · Floday
Uig
Carnish
Ardroil

Breasclete
Eilean Kearstay
Callanish
Garynahine

Newmarket
Stornoway

Shulishader
Garrabost
Melbost
Eye Peninsular
Knock · Bayble
Bayble Bay

Ard More Mangersta
Mangersta
Islivig
Brenish

Achmore
Loch an Ois
Loch a' Bhuna

Chicken Head

Stornaway to Ullapool 3hrs

MEALISVAL
1883 · 1688
1635

Loch Suainaval
Loch Grunavat
Little Loch Roag
Loch Tungavat

Loch nam Falcag
Loch Trealaval

Loch Ainidh na-h-Airde
Loch Coirigerod
Loch Fadagoa

Leurbost
Crossbost
Grimshader

Raerinish Point

Barkin Is
Eilean Chalum Chille
Orinsay Island
Cromore
Torray Island
Mariveg

Mealasta Island

Loch Tamanavay
Loch Bodavat
Loch Tealavay
Loch Benisval
Loch Leatha
Loch Morsgail
Loch Cleshuig

Balallan
Keose
Kershader

Scarp
Gasker

Husinish Point
Husinish
Loch a Ghlinne
ULLAVAL 2153
2228
OREVAL
2165

NORTH HARRIS

Aribruach

Loch Langavat
1611

Loch Sgaileit

Loch Shanndabhat

Gravir
Lemreway

Kebock Head

Eilean Iuyard

1603
Amhuinnsuidhe
B887
Loch Chliostair
2392
CLISHAM
2622
Loch Leosaid

Ardvourlie Castle
Seaforth Island
BEINN MHOR
1874

1542

Soay Mór
West Loch Tarbert
Maaruig
1829
1773
Laxadale Loch

Sound of Shiant

Taransay
Isay
BEN LUSKENTYRE
1661
Tarbert
Luskentyre
1532

Scaladale R

A859

Kyles Scalpay
Carnach
Scalpay

Shiant Islands

Kyles Scalpay to Scalpay 10mins

Sound of Taransay

Seilebost
SOUTH HARRIS
Scotasay
East Loch Tarbert

Toe Head
Coppay
1199
CHAIPAVAL
Scarista
1305

Scarista
Loch Langavat
Loch Stockinish

Kyles Stockinish
Stockinish Island

Pabbay
Northton
Ensay
Leverburgh
1508
Strond · Rodel
Killegray

Finsbay

Sound of Pabbay
Sound of Harris

Renish Point
Groay · Gilsay
Lingay
Scaravay

Tarbert to Uig 2hrs
Tarbert to Lochmaddy 2hrs

42

Near-record catches from the sea around the Scottish islands are common, and are likely to include most species – including sharks.

Provision vans go out to many parts of the island, and Britain's first travelling bank operates from Stornoway, through Lewis and Harris, transacting most classes of business.

Islanders at work

Manufacturing interests include kippers, scampi, and hand-knitted garments, but the most important facet of the local economy is the Harris-tweed industry. This manufactures about five million yards of tweed a year, giving work to around 800 self-employed weavers, who contract to work for various mills, and 800 millworkers. The popularity of Harris tweed – the *clo mor*, or big cloth – is a success story based on the quality of the product and the determined patronage of a few women. Originally the tweed was woven exclusively for the islanders own use, but at the turn of the century the wife of a big Harris landowner realized the potential of the cloth. In 1909 the Harris Tweed Association was formed to protect the industry and its customers from imitators. Genuine Harris tweed carries the orb trade mark, which means that the tweed has been made from virgin Scottish wool, then spun-dyed and finished in the Outer Hebrides and hand-woven by islanders at their own homes in Lewis, Harris, the Uists, and Barra. Raw Scottish wool is shipped to Stornoway in bales and then taken to the mills, where it is spun. The yarn is taken to the crofters all over the islands, and later the lengths of tweed are collected from the weavers. No matter what the weather the cloth can be seen lying at the roadside for collection, a sure sign of its durability. Harris tweed has more than 5,000 designs and is made in a variety of weights to suit all types of weather. Stornoway has many shops selling tweeds, locally-made blankets, knitwear, and other craft works. The economic pulse of the islands can be measured by the clack of the weavers' looms, and a visitor can usually find a weaver willing to demonstrate his skill.

The name Lewis is derived from *leogach*, meaning marshy, and the island is locally known as the 'Lews'. Lewis Castle, built in 1840 on a site overlooking the bay at Stornoway, was the home of the first Lord Leverhulme, who bought the island after the first world war with the grand design of turning it into a fishing and fish-canning centre. When he left, frustrated by the government and land grabbers, he gave the castle to the town. It now serves as a technical college where navigation, textiles, and building skills are taught. Splendidly-wooded Lady Lever Park surrounds the castle and is a blaze of colour during summer and autumn. East of Stornoway the A866 leads through the village of Sandwick and past Melbost, where wildfowl and waders can be seen on the sands. The airport here is also a NATO base. The road penetrates the Minch on the rugged 12m Eye Peninsula, eventually reaching Tiumpan Head lighthouse. The peninsula has two safe sandy beaches at Braighe (3½m from Stornoway) and Bayble (7m). At its western end is the roofless Chapel of Ui and the burial ground of the Macleod chiefs of Lewis, while to the north of the peninsula lie the beaches of Broad Bay. The B895 out of Stornoway follows this coast through small crofting villages and continues as far as Tolsta Head. Apart from its fine beaches this coast also has interesting caves; the Seal Cave at Gress Head can be reached by hired boat, and seals can also be sighted around Tolsta Head.

Starting a tour

By taking a 48m circular tour from Stornoway and adding two major diversions the visitor can cover much of rural Lewis. The route runs north west through the parish of Laxdale on the A857, and crosses the island over 10m of bleak, boggy moorland. At first the moorland is dotted with huts erected by Stornoway families at the places where they go to cut peats in early summer. This is hard work, and it takes about a fortnight to cut a year's supply. Peat is decomposed vegetable matter which has

Dun Carloway Broch is a superb example of iron-age building which has survived the rigours of centuries.

become partly carbonized while being deposited over 7,000 years to an average depth of 5ft. It is a vital source of fuel universally used throughout the islands. The road divides when it reaches Barvas crossroads near the island's Atlantic seaboard, and remains the A857 where it turns right to the island's northern tip – the Butt of Lewis. This is where the first of the suggested major diversions begins. Many of Lewis's 20,000 inhabitants live in the string of crofting and weaving villages placed at regular intervals along the Atlantic coast, from Loch Roag in the south to the Butt of Lewis. This coast is more rugged than the rest of the Long Island's Atlantic side, and is made up of a succession of little sandy bays contained by high cliffs.

A crofter holds his small parcel of land on a yearly tenancy from his landlord. The landlord cannot dispossess him as long as the land is cultivated, the buildings kept in repair, and the rent is paid; the crofter's right descends from father to son or can be willed to others. It is hard to extract a living from a croft, even with the various government subsidies available, and the crofting population is diminishing throughout the islands. Some 4m north of Barvas at Ballanthrushal is the Thrushell Stone, a 20ft-high prehistoric monolith. A lighthouse at the Butt of Lewis stands on cliffs more than 100ft high and faces the open Atlantic. St Molnag's Church, built *c*12thc

to commemorate a disciple of St Columba, is episcopalian and still in use after restoration. The keys can be obtained from Macleod's Store at the village of Eropie. Back at Barvas crossroads the tour continues along a road which turns south along the Atlantic coast and becomes the A858.

Stones and seaweed
Arnol, also called 'Little Holland' because of its many stone dykes, preserves a traditional black house as a museum. These black houses, or *tigh dubh*, are traditionally Hebridean and have thatched roofs, tiny doors and windows as a protection against winter winds, a central peat fire, and byre and house under the same roof. At the village of Bragar is an arch made of a giant whale bone, with the harpoon which killed the mammal hanging from its centre. A little farther on at Shawbost is another museum and a renovated Norse mill. Also in the village is a Harris-tweed spinning and finishing mill. A few miles on is the village of Doune Carloway, which derives its name from the dun or broch which stands here on a prominent and easily defended hill. Dun Carloway Broch is a well-preserved, 30ft-high remnant of the iron age. The road passes picturesque Tolsta Chaolais and continues to a gigantic, 3,000-year old megalithic temple which rivals Stonehenge – the Callanish Standing Stones. These are arranged in a cruciform setting, unique in Scotland. At Garynahine the A858 continues back to

Thanks to the efforts of preservation movements the endearing Atlantic grey seal can still be seen around the islands' coasts.

44

Lewis Castle, once the home of would-be island industrialist Lord Leverhulme.

Stornoway and completes the circular journey, but the B8011 here allows the second major diversion. It leads out to Uig, winds around the many branches of Loch Roag, and passes the Grimersta River – claimed by some to be the best salmon river in Western Europe.

The B8059 branches off this road and leads to the island of Great Bernera via a bridge over Loch Roag. The inhabitants got the bridge built in 1953 by threatening to blow up the cliffs to create a causeway. Great Bernera is one of the main lobster fishing areas and has many fine angling lochs. Places of interest in the Uig area include the Isle of Berisay – retreat of an outlawed Macleod – and the Selaro, a vast chasm in the moor connected underground with the sea. Good beaches abound in this area: Dalmore and Dalberg, near Carloway, have white sand and green Atlantic rollers; Uig has sandy beaches at Valtos, Reef, Cliff, Ardoil, Carnish, and Mangersta; Bernera has Bosta Sands. The A859 road from Stornoway to Harris runs south-west through the Parish of Lochs, which takes its name from the large number of lochs it contains, then winds past the end of the road to Keose – a village with a seaweed factory where alginate is made. Seaweed is making a useful contribution to the economy of the islands, with the extraction of alginates leading to exports of over £1 million. The weed is processed in factories at Lochmaddy and Lochboisdale as well as Keose, and is dried and ground into powder before being shipped across the Minch to be used in food manufacture on the mainland. More than 40 crofter-cutters working in Lewis and Harris supplement their earnings by selling seaweed.

Prince's refuge
At Balallan, the longest village in Lewis, the A859 reaches the head of Loch Erisort where the B8060 creates a tempting diversion along its shores and into the scenic district of Park. Park Deer Forest has herds of small red deer, and seals can be seen near the entrance of Loch Erisort. Just off the village of Cromore is St Columba's Isle, where the ruins of an ancient church and an old graveyard are of interest. After Balallan the A859 runs by the side of Loch Seaforth near where Bonnie Prince Charlie, a fugitive after the Battle of Culloden, landed at dead of night. He sent to Stornoway in the hope of raising a ship which would aid his escape, but his attempt was frustrated by two Lewis ministers, father and son – ancestors of the historian Lord Macaulay. Half way down

the loch and just before Ardvourlie the road crosses into Harris.

The Harris moonscape
Harris's boundary with Lewis runs between Loch Resort and Loch Seaforth, and the landscape here is typical Highland scenery of bare hills and dramatic peaks. Much of Harris, like its neighbour, is accessible only on foot or by boat. White-painted Tarbert is the island's biggest village and stands on an isthmus between West Loch Tarbert and East Loch Tarbert. The isthmus also divides North and South Harris, making South Harris almost an island, and the village is where car ferries dock from Uig in Skye and Lochmaddy in North Uist. It is a thriving, lively community nestling under a mountain at the head of the sheltered anchorage of East Loch Tarbert, attracting sailing enthusiasts and anglers. Boats can be hired for fishing, sight-seeing cruises, and visits to nearby islands. The shops deal particularly in Harris tweeds. The population has been steadily declining for years, and the people left today get most of their income from crops and stock. They try to augment their earnings by weaving Harris tweed or producing warm knitwear, plus more modern craft items – utilizing shells, wood, and sealskin. The island passed out of the hands of the hereditary chieftain in 1779 and was held in two large estates until again united by Lord Leverhulme. He planned a large fishing industry centred in Obbe, which was renamed Leverburgh. He died in 1925 and large parts of Harris passed to absentee landlords.

Areas of the lands 'cleared' to make way for sheep 100 years earlier were broken up into crofts, allowing some of the people to return and use the fertile ground of the west coast. This is the pattern today, with the crofts providing a place to live and contributing a modest amount to family incomes. North Harris presents good opportunities for climbers, and has eight summits exceeding 2,000ft. Clisham is the highest at 2,622ft and has no major climbs, but its neighbour – 1,805ft Tomnaval – has the fine precipice of Sgurr Scaladale. North of Tarbert 1,544ft Gillavel Glas and 1,829ft Sgaoth Ard have possibilities, and east are 1,731ft Toddun and 2,392ft Uisgnavel More provide magnificent views and some short faces. The 2,227ft Tirga More and 2,165ft Oreval are worth investigation, while 2,153ft Ullavel

Famous and highly durable Harris tweed
is the product of thriving cottage industry.

offers the towering headland of Strone Ulladale – a
climbing face of 800ft with severe overlaps. This is of
most interest to serious climbers and is considered one of
the best outcrops in the British Isles. South Harris has
1,506ft Roneval and 1,654ft Ben Luskentyre, but only the
latter offers any challenge – although the steep glen of
Beesdale is worth a visit.

Island mountains

A tour of Harris can start by the shores of Loch Seaforth,
where the A859 crosses the border from Lewis. To the
west lie Clisham and its treeless attendant peaks, and the
scenery becomes increasingly wild as a diversion on the
B887 is taken between the hills and the shores of West
Loch Tarbert. Isolated villages find a precarious foothold
on the few patches of level and fertile ground here, and
the hills are inhabited by wild deer. Nearly all this area is
owned by the proprietors of the North Harris Estate and
includes Amhuinnguidhe Castle (12m from Tarbert), which
was built during the last century by the Earl of Dunmore.
The castle stands just beside the main road and is only a
stone's throw from where a salmon river runs into the sea.
In late June and early July huge shoals of salmon and sea
trout can be seen leaping the falls and running from pool to
pool on their way up river. Close by is the hydro-electric
scheme at Loch Chliostair, where the small arch dam is
the first of its kind to be built in the Western Isles. Small
stations like this serve scattered crofts and villages
huddled by shore and lochside, bringing them light and the
power for small industries and tourist developments. The
B887 ends at the village of Husinish, where a glorious
stretch of golden sand sweeps the sea in a gentle curve. On
the far side a fine cliff harbours nesting seabirds and
overlooks the island of Scarp. Birds in the hilly country
are scarce but include breeding pairs of golden eagles.

Husinish is the crossing point for Scarp. Within the last
decade this island supported a population of nearly 50 and
had its own school, but all the inhabitants have now left.
Scarp was the site of an ill-fated experiment to project
mail to the mainland by rocket on 28 July, 1934. A special
stamp was produced, but the rocket exploded on impact
and most of the mail was damaged. The experiment was
not repeated. A minor road from Tarbert runs along the

northern shore of East Loch Tarbert and gives access to
pleasant hill walks, one of which leads beside the Laxdale
Lochs and to the village of Maaruig. The road ends at the
village of Kyles Scalpay, overlooking the Isle of Scalpay.
Unlike Scarp this island is thriving and derives most of its
living from herring and lobster fishing. A pier was
completed here in 1971, and it is the home port of three
coasters and two smaller trading vessels. Access to the
island is by vehicular ferry across the narrow sound.
Bonnie Prince Charlie is said to have landed on Scalpay in
1746. Glass Island lighthouse stands like a sentinel over
the Minch at the south-east end and affords views which
take in Skye, Lewis and Harris, North and South Uist, and
parts of the mainland. East of Scalpay and some 10m out
to sea are the Shiant Islands, where the massive sheer
cliffs are a wonderful spot for bird-watching. Hiring a
boat for the Shiants is not easy, but it is sometimes
possible when weather permits. A 48m circular round trip
around South Harris can be taken from Tarbert.

South of Tarbert is a rough, winding minor road which
follows the east coast and connects villages where the
people spend much time on the old local crafts – spinning,
weaving, boat-building, and inshore fishing – before
meeting the A859 at Rodel. The east coast is known as the
Bays of Harris and includes good walking country, either
by the sea or on heather-clad slopes studded with lochs.
Sea angling can be pursued in many parts of the Bays, and
the sea lochs yield herring, mackerel, lythe, saith, and
pollack. Local boat owners will help to arrange trips.
Rodel is the site of one of the finest examples of
ecclesiastical architecture in the Hebrides, the early 16th-c
St Clement's Church. This was probably built by one of the
Macleods of Dunvegan because it was their traditional
burial place. The key may be obtained from Rodel Hotel.
The standard bearers of the Macleods were buried in a
tomb comprising a stone coffin with an iron grating about
a foot below the cover, on which the body was laid. Each
time the tomb was opened the remains of the previous
incumbent were shaken down through the bars into the
coffin, and his successor was laid to rest on the grating.
There is a sheltered little harbour here, and Rodel has
excellent salmon and sea trout fishing.

Short-lived bustle

The road from Rodel runs through a narrow glen and
descends into Leverburgh, which Lord Leverhulme
turned to in 1923 after his failure to make Lewis a major
fishing centre. He built piers, jetties, roads, houses, and
huge kippering sheds, but although the initial landings in
1924 were enormous and many people had been
employed, the project was abandoned in 1925 when he
died. Installations which cost about £250,000 were sold
to a demolition company for £5,000. Several 'manager's'
houses remain, and are among the best built on the
island. The only public building, Hulme Hall, was
originally intended for recreation and now serves as a
school. Another legacy of the short-lived bustle is the
cross-country road from this village to Finsbay, and a road
leading from Leverburgh along the coast to Strond and
Borrisdale. These villages afford lovely views across the
Sound of Harris, and a footpath which connects this road
to Rodel forms the basis of an interesting 5m walk. In
summer a regular ferry and mail service links Leverburgh
with Berneray, the only inhabited island in the sound, and
Newton Ferry in North Uist. Boats can be hired at
Leverburgh or Strond to explore islands in the sound.
Berneray has a small population of lobster fishermen and
sheep farmers, and can be visited by arrangement with
D A MacAskil, who runs the ferry service. Peeping above

the Atlantic horizon about 45m to the west are the tops of St Kilda, a small group of islands which are part of Harris but which have not been inhabited on a permanent basis since the last 30 residents were evacuated in 1930. The islands were given to the National Trust for Scotland in 1957, who leased them to the Nature Conservancy. Occupancy is shared with the military authorities, who have a radar station to track rockets fired from their range in Benbecula. Among the spectacular rock scenery here are massive sea-cliffs which support the world's largest gannetry, enormous quantities of fulmars, and numerous puffins. The St Kilda wren, the St Kilda mouse, and the wild Soay sheep are three unique species. Usually it is only possible to visit as a member of the working parties which undertake conservation work on Hirta.

On the way from Leverburgh back to Tarbert the A859 follows the west coast and passes Northton, a village linked by a low-lying isthmus to the heathery slopes of Chaipaval and the promontory of Toe Head. An important prehistoric site discovered at the head in 1964 has yielded neolithic pottery and bone tools. The steep cliffs at the far end of the promontory provide nesting sites for sea-birds, which include a colony of fulmars, and a little chapel standing exposed to the Atlantic is assumed to have been built about the same time as St Clement's at Rodel. The view from the 1,200ft peak of Chaipaval encompasses the Cuillins of Skye and the islands and stacks of St Kilda. Between Chaipaval and Northton is a broad stretch of machair land (sand and grass), which is still cultivated with oats and potatoes in the ancient strip system. Marshy ground bordering the extensive saltings, and an expanse of sand in Northton's sheltered estuary, form the habitat of lapwings and dunlins, plus wild flowers which include many orchids.

Machair lands
The road from Northton follows the coast by a beach of golden shell sand and through the straggling village of Scarista. Beyond Borve Lodge, where Lord Leverhulme lived, it hugs a rocky shore pounded in winter by wild Atlantic seas which send clouds of spray up the slopes of Cleitt Nisabost. In summer Nisabost is safe for bathing and surfing, and it has a fine beach. Above is a headland with a huge standing stone put up by inhabitants of the earth-houses and cairns which are from time to time revealed among the sand dunes. A large sheltered bay on the other side of the headland has a mile of white sand. In the autumn the sea is alive with duck. From here the road

winds through the village of Seilebost, where the sand dunes provide a home for the hundreds of rabbits; past saltings which make a pink carpet in May and June when the sea thrift is in bloom; and past the artificial salmon loch of Fincastle. A turn-off along the foreshore leads to Luskentyre, a beauty spot set beneath Ben Luskentyre. The village faces south over the Sound of Taransay and has long stretches of golden sand backed by large areas of machair, which are thick with flowers in July and August. The crofting land is rich and fertile, and trees have survived in small numbers round the meadow of one farm. Traigh Luskentyre is a refuge for waders, wildfowl, and numerous migrant birds, while the pools left by the ebbing tide provide good sea-trout fishing. A fine stretch of recently-built road covers the 7m back to Tarbert, crossing the Laxdale River and climbing the southern slopes of Ben Luskentyre to meet a road from the Bays.

North Uist, Benbecula, South Uist
The A865 links Lochmaddy in the north with Lochboisdale 45m away in the south, and acts as an artery which virtually makes the three islands into one. Little roads link it to villages, and it is never more than a few miles from the Atlantic to the west and the Little Minch to the east. Benbecula, 'the Mountain of the Fords', lies in the middle and is joined to North Uist by a causeway, as well as to South Uist by a bridge across the tidal sands of the old fords which gave the island its name. Some of the most beautiful and least-frequented beaches in Britain await the visitor to this part of the Hebrides. The western shores are low-lying and sandy, and by contrast the eastern coast is rocky and broken by long sea lochs – a playground for seals. It is fairly easy to get a boat for a day's sailing among the coves and islets, and the inland moors are so dotted with lochans (small lochs) that in North Uist particularly there seems to be more water than earth. This water abounds with trout. Every July sees the Uist Games, where pipers from far and wide play tunes which reflect old stories and island characters.

Numerous islands lie off the coast of North Uist, but the sea ebbs twice daily and many of them can be reached by walking across the sand. The attraction of the island lies in its miles of silver-white beach, lush vegetation, historic

Picturesque St Clement's Church at Rodel dates from the early 16thc and is a traditional clan burial place.

47

ISLANDS OF ENCHANTMENT

Berneray
Boreray
Borve
Lingay
Torogay
Sursay
Tahay
Hermetray

SOUND OF HARRIS

Lochmaddy to Tarbert 2hrs

Haskeir Island
Haskeir Eagach

Griminish Point
Vallay
Oronsay
Newton
Rubha an Duine
Weaver's Point

Scolpaig
Natural Arches
A865
Grenetote
Sollas
A865
B893
Lochmaddy to Uig 2hrs

Kettle Spout
Tigharry
Pigeon Caves
Hougharry
Kilmuir Churchyard
Bayhead
Paible

Loch nan Geireann
756 ▲ MARRIVAL
Loch Scadavay
Loch Skealtar
Lochmaddy

NORTH UIST

NORTH LEE ▲ 821
SOUTH 898 LEE

Heisker or Monach Islands

Kirkibost Island

Baleshare

Clachan
B894
Locheport

A867

Loch Obisary
▲ 1139 EAVAL

Carinish

Beul an Toim

Floddaymore

Bailivanish
Grimsay
Ronay

Culla Bay

B892
A865
409 ▲ RUEVAL

BENBECULA

Liniclett
Loch Heouravay

Wiay

Creagorry
Eochar
B891
Loch a Chips

Ardivachar Point

Carnan
Steisay

West Geirinish

B890
Loch Skiport
Ornish Island

Loch Druidibeg
Howmore
1988 ▲ HECLA
Rubha Rossel

Rubha Ardvule

Loch Ollay
1723 ▲
2033 ▲ BEINN MHOR
Rubha Bolum

SOUTH UIST

Loch Kildonan

Milton
822 ▲
Loch Snigisclett
Askernish
Loch Stulaval
1227 ▲ STULAVAL
Stuley

Daliburgh
TRIUIREBHEINN
1168 ▲
Lochboisdale
Loch Boisdale
Lochboisdale to Oban 5hrs

Orosay
Calvay
Kilbride
Pollacher Inn
Ludac
Rubha na h-Ordaig

Lingay
Eriskay

Fiaray
Fuday
Stack Islands

Scurrival Point
SOUND OF BARRA

Eoligarry
Sound of Fuday
Gighay

Greian Head
Cliad Caves
Sound of Hellisay
Hellisay
Flodday
Fuiay

A888
Borve
HEAVAL ▲ 1260
BARRA

1092 ▲
Castlebay
Castlebay to Lochboisdale 90mins

Vatersay
Muldoanich
Vatersay Bay

Flodday
Sound of Sandray
Castlebay to Oban 5hrs

Lingay
678 ▲
Sandray

Pabbay
Sound of Pabbay

Sound of Mingulay
735 ▲
Mingulay 48

Sound of Berneray
Barra Head
Berneray

SCALE
mls 0 2 4 6
kms 0 2 4 6 8

Airport .... ✈
Archæological site .... ⛯
Bird sanctuary .... ◈
Bird watching .... 🐦
Car ferry .... ⛴
Castle .... ♜
Craft centre .... ⚒
Croft museum .... 🏚
Freshwater fishing .... 🎣
Golf course .... ⚑
Harbour .... ⚓
Industrial workings .... ⛏
Information centre .... ⓘ
Lighthouse .... 🗼
Monument/cairn .... ⚲
Mountain climbing .... ⛰
Notable building .... 🏛
Other places of interest ■
Sand yachting .... ⛵
Sea angling .... 🐟
Seal colony .... 🦭

For full key see page 39

and prehistoric treasures, sailing and fishing facilities, and crafts. To the east of Benbecula is a maze of tiny islands and sea lochs where the fugitive Bonnie Prince Charlie landed after Culloden, and where Flora MacDonald smuggled him 'over the sea to Skye' from Rosinish. West beyond the crofting lands and fresh water lochs, the Atlantic rollers break impressively over vast empty beaches. South Uist's east coast features rugged 2,000ft-plus peaks with the anchorages of Lochs Carnan, Skipport, Eynort, and Boisdale cutting into their sides fiord-fashion. In the centre of the island are peat bogs and fresh water lochs, and in the west flower-spangled machair contrasts with more white sandy beaches. These islands are a happy hunting ground for ornithologists. The Monach Isles lie off the Atlantic coast and attract seabirds in crowded colonies; Wiay in Benbecula has a bird sanctuary; Loch Bee in South Uist is the place to see mute swans, wildfowl, and waders; Loch Druidibeg is the habitat of graylag geese. The Monach Isles, Balranald, and Loch Druidibeg are all national nature reserves.

A tour route round the islands follows the length of the A865 and includes a series of short diversions. The road starts at Lochmaddy – North Uist's business centre and principal port – where car ferries from Uig and Tarbert dock at a modern pier. The village has been a fishing port since the 17thc and derives its name from three basalt rocks shaped like crouching dogs at the entrance of the harbour. These rocks are called 'The Maddies' from the Gaelic *madadh*, meaning a dog. South are the two hills of North Lee and South Lee, both a little under 1,000ft and worth the climb for the views. About 1m north is Sponish, where an alginate factory processes seaweed. From here the A865 sweeps in a coastal circle round the north of the island, and after a few miles a short diversion on the B893 leads out to Newton at the north-east corner. Boats can sometimes be hired from here for visits to the islands of Pabbay (seals), Boreray, and Berneray. Local beaches are carved by deep channels, and walkers should take care not to be trapped by the incoming tide. A small, shallow loch is crossed by a causeway which leads to the remains of Dun an Sticer, an iron-age fortress occupied by Hugh Macdonald. Hugh was a lineal descendant of Macdonald of Sleat who vainly attempted to lay claim to North Uist. He took refuge in the fort to defend himself from the real heir *c*1601, but was later betrayed,

captured, and imprisoned in Skye. Tradition says he was fed on salt beef until he died of thirst. Grenitote village boasts Coilegan an Udal, an archaeological site which is still being excavated. This area was the scene of evictions which formed part of the Highland Clearances, when people were forcibly removed from their crofts.

Rocks fantastic

From Newton the coast becomes increasingly rocky as the road heads towards Scolpaig, which lies in the north-west corner of the island. Dun Scolpaig, a miniature castle-type building put up by a former chamberlain to the MacDonald Estates, stands on an islet in Loch Scolpaig. This part of the island is nearest point to St Kilda, which is plainly visible. A mile north of the village are cliffs which have been carved into a series of natural arches. On the shore side of the road from Scolpaig stands Kilphedar Cross, a Latin monument unearthed from an old cemetery. Out to sea are Hasgeir and Hasgeir Eagach, island breeding grounds of the grey seal. Hasgeir Eagach was the scene of Lewis Spence's book *Island of Disaster.* Near the village of Tigharry are a natural rock arch, a blow-hole commonly called the Kettle Spout, and the bird-infested Pigeon Caves. Kilmuir Churchyard lies near the next village, Hougharry, and is the resting place of the Uist nobility and site of some interesting gravestones. Some 8m away across the Sound of Monach are the Monach Isles, a reserve for geese and grey seals. Lobster fishermen from Grimsay in North Uist stay on the island during summer weekdays, and permission to visit the reserve should be obtained from North Uist Estates Ltd, Lochmaddy. The Nature Conservancy must also be informed. There is water on the main island, but the lobstermen have the monopoly of the only inhabitable house. From October until the spring the islands are visited only occasionally by lobstermen, but it is usually possible to charter a fishing boat for the day.

Benbecula is linked to North Uist by causeway, and to South Uist by a bridge which spans an ancient tidal ford.

49

South from Hougharry is Balranald, where another reserve cares for rare marshland birds; farther south and close to the shore are the islands of Kirkibost and Baleshare, both with extensive dunes. Baleshare is connected to North Uist by a causeway, but walkers should beware of the tides. At Clachan the A867 runs east to Lochmaddy, and the B894 runs along the shore of Loch Eport to the fishing village of Locheport. This village is noted for its modern and old techniques of making Harris tweed. This road continues for 3m beyond the village, and provides a starting point for solitary walks towards 1,139ft Eaval, North Uist's highest hill. At the southern end of North Uist on the A865 is Carinish, where Trinity Temple was founded in 1203 on the site of an earlier church. The Battle of Carinish was fought near here between the MacLeods of Harris and the MacDonalds of Uist in 1601, and a ditch on the battlefield is still known by the name *Feithe Na Fala* – Ditch of Blood. The road then crosses North Ford Causeway, which was built to link the islands of North Uist, Grimsay, and Benbecula and opened in 1960. A lobster-fishing industry with a storage factory thrives at Grimsay. The A865 runs south over the shoulder of 500ft Rueval, Benbecula's only hill, but it is worth turning west on the B892.

Clan Ranald country

Bailivanich, the first place reached on this road, once housed a monastery but now has a huge Royal Artillery rocket range, a large influx of army personnel and their families, an airport, and a garage which provides car hire. Beaches around this coast are divided by outcrops of rock, and Culla Bay is a beautiful crescent of sand where bathing is safe. Farther south are the ruins of 14th-c Borve

Boats and castles encapsulate the mood of the islands. Illustrated is Kismul, the 15th-c stronghold and seat of the MacNeils of Barra.

Castle, which was once a stronghold of Clan Ranald of Benbecula; and Creagorry, a village which offers good fishing in freshwater lochs and is convenient for the west coast or the more rugged eastern coves on the Peter's Port Road. At the south end of the bridge from Benbecula is the village of Eochar, where the South Uist Black-House Museum displays mementoes of Bonnie Prince Charlie. Miles of white sand to the west of the A865 make South Uist an attractive island for family holidays, but in the Loch Bee area red flags mean that missiles are being fired from a rocket range and the beaches are closed. A few miles south is the Loch Druidibeg reserve and a viewing tower, and the hill of Rueval is surmounted by a statue of the Madonna and Child which was erected in 1957 by the Roman Catholic community to commemorate Marian Year. Visible traces of island history include the graves of the ancient chiefs of Clan Ranald at Howmore, west of Loch Druidibeg, and farther south are the gaunt ruins of Ormaclete Castle. This took seven years to build, and had been lived in for only seven when venison being roasted for a celebration caught fire and burnt the castle down in 1715. A monument known as the Flora Macdonald Cairn marks the brave lady's birthplace at Milton.

Lochboisdale is a busy little port surrounded by hills in the south. The car ferry from here connects with Oban on the mainland and Barra, and the port is a good shopping and fishing centre. At the south end of the island is Pollacher Inn. The road along the shore leads to a jetty where ferries cross to Eriskay and Barra at times which are dependant on the tides. In South Uist the brown trout season starts in April, and sea trout can be sought after in mid-July. Sea trout and salmon centres in the Benbecula and South Uist Estates include Lochs Roag, Fada, Castle, and Schoolhouse; in the Howmore district Lochs Kildonan and Mill; and at Lochboisdale, Loch Bharp. The chief brown trout lochs are Grogarry, Skilligarry, West Ollay, Lower Barrish, and Upper Kildonan. The South Uist Angling Society has eighteen lochs, all near roads, most of which contain brown trout.

Eriskay and Barra

Colonies of grey seals are commonly seen by passengers crossing the sound from Uist to the small green island of Eriskay, where Bonnie Prince Charlie first set foot on Scottish soil. Pink sea-bindweed that grows by the shore at Prince's Bay is said to have sprung from seeds that he dropped. Modern fishing boats with local crews operate from the island, and sturdy Eriskay ponies are still used for carrying peats from the hills and seaweed fertilizer from the shore. SS 'Politician', carrying 243,000 bottles of whisky, was wrecked here in 1941 – inspiring Compton Mackenzie's novel *Whisky Galore*. The A888 road running round Barra is only 14m long, and the island's population of 1,200 is served by Castlebay's car-ferry port and an airport. Cars can be hired, although the more energetic can walk round this lovely island in an afternoon. Picturesque Castlebay is a sheltered anchorage beautifully set amid hills in the south part of Barra. Kismul Castle, perched on a rock in the middle of the bay, is the 15th-c seat of the MacNeils of Barra and was uninhabited for over 200 years until restored by the late Robert Lister MacNeil, an American architect and 45th chief of the clan. It is usually open to the public on summer Saturday afternoons. Associated with the castle is the herald who used to mount the Great Tower and proclaim: 'Hear, ye people and listen, ye nations. The great MacNeil of Barra having finished his meal, the princes of the earth may dine'. It is also recorded that a MacNeil of Barra refused Noah's offer of hospitality because he had a boat of his own.

Two traditional aspects of island life – peat cutting and an original black house.

Fishing has always been the main industry here and has recently revived. A number of small firms set up in recent years include a shell grit factory which makes harl for roughcasting houses, and a firm which began making perfume in a croft house and has now moved into a small factory. Another factory assembles thermostat components for a company manufacturing switches for electric radiators, blankets, and kettles. All these industries have brought new life to the traditional fishing and crofting communities. Barra is believed to have been named after St Findbarr of Cork (c550 to 623), who is said to have converted the inhabitants of the island to Christianity. A church dedicated to him once stood in the north of the island at Eoligarry. Good walks include routes from Garrygall to Brevig, Bentangval to Tangusdale, Glen Dorcha to Northbay, and Cliat to Vaslane Sands – past the Cliat caves and Ardmaor, where seals and a variety of birds fascinate the visitor. Hills include 1,092ft Bentangval and 1,260ft Heaval, both of which offer spectacular views. Boats can be hired for sea and loch angling, a ferry runs to the neighbouring island of Vatersay, and trips to Eriskay and Mingulay can be arranged. In the north the great sweep of beach known as the Cockle Strand serves as Barra's airfield, though it is covered by the sea twice daily, and is one of the world's most exciting landings. The island is so hilly that there was no other place for the daily plane to come down.

The Inner Hebrides

The tempo of life is as leisurely in these islands, which hug the mainland coast from Skye in the north to Islay in the south, as it is in the more remote Outer Hebrides. They are away-from-it-all places now being made more accessible by 'marine motorways' – a new name being given to steadily-improving roll on/roll off car ferry services. With Skye are the small isles – Scalpay, Raasay, Rhum, Eigg, Muck, and Canna; with Mull are Iona, Coll, Tiree, Staffa, and the Treshnish Isles. Yet each island has a flavour of its own. Think of the Cuillins of Skye, the red deer of Rhum, the treasure ship sunk in Mull's Tobermory Bay, the monks of Iona, and Fingal's Cave on Staffa. In the south are Colonsay, Jura, Islay, and Gigha, all of which can be linked with the Firth of Clyde for transport reasons.

Skye and the small isles

Skye is a grotesquely shaped island which is the largest of the Inner Hebrides. It measures about 50m long and is at no point more than 5m from the sea – yet its jagged coastline is about 2,000m long. There is neither railway nor airport, and the visitor must travel 'over the sea to Skye'. The attraction of Skye is the Cuillin range, majestic peaks of blue, red, and black rock with hills and valleys of purple heather in summer and swirling mist and 'small' rain which is said to 'wet an Englishman to the skin' at other times of the year. But the lure of the island is not just for climbers. Many come with cameras and many just to stare. Others come for hill-walking or scrambling, fishing, swimming, bird-watching, golf, pony trekking, or for the solitude which is to be found in the lesser known areas. Between April and July the weather is at its best. Caledonian MacBraynes operate car ferry services from Kyle of Lochalsh to Kyleakin – over a few hundred yards of water – and Mallaig to Armadale, near the south-west corner of the island. There is also a passenger steamer service from Mallaig by way of Kyle of Lochalsh and Raasay to Portree, the island's chief town, and a car ferry service from Glenelg to Kylerhea; a projected service may be instituted from Portree to Raasay in 1975. There is always a bonus in Highland scenery on the roads of the isles.

Each of the Small Isles is served by a Caledonian MacBrayne's steamer from Kyle of Lochalsh and Mallaig, with the exception of Muck in winter, and other day trips are easy to arrange in summer. But facilities for overnight stays are limited. The road to Dunvegan and the castle of the Clan MacLeod's chiefs carries banners saying 'This is the Faery Isle', for legends tell of mythical warrior queens, legendary heroes, goblins haunting the glens, and fearsome water horses in the lochs. Nearer the truth are tales of cruel and bloody clan feuds, particularly between the MacLeods and the MacDonalds. Above all else Skye is associated with Bonnie Prince Charlie's perilous escape from government troops. About 8,000 people live on this island, most of whom still speak Gaelic and live by crofting, salmon fishing between May and August, local crafts, and whisky distilling. Peaty, purple moorland and green valleys are set against the rounded Red Hills and the Black Cuillins. The two northerly peninsulas of Trotternish and Vaternish feature grassy plateau land which descends to the sea in a series of sliced off escarpments. Trees, rare elsewhere on the island, grow in the southerly peninsula of Sleat, also known as 'the garden of Skye'.

Croftlands cover 450,000 acres of the island, and about 96 per cent of this area comprises rough hill grazing. The number of croft units is around 1,650, and the nature of the land dictates stock rearing. Skye has about 5,000 head of breeding cows and some 85,000 breeding ewes. This is an island of volcanic rock, red basalt and black gabbro thrown up 70 million years ago and later carved by Ice Age glaciers. For experienced mountaineers the Cuillins offer an almost continuous 18m chain of naked rock peaks, linked by narrow ridges which rarely fall below 3,000ft. The black gabbro provides good foot and hand holds, but this range can bring danger to the inexperienced. The weather can change rapidly, with sudden mists clamping down or high winds suddenly shrieking out of nowhere. Even experienced climbers must take care, for in these conditions there is no quick way to safety from the complicated ridges. One path which is safe for any novice with enough energy in clear weather is up 3,143ft

The majestic Cuillin peaks offer a rich wilderness of rock and a wealth of rare wildlife.

Bruach na Frithe. More difficult is Sgurr nan Gillean, 'the peak of the young men', which has tiring steps near the top. An ascent from Sligachan takes about four hours, and the descent three; the other Cuillins' climbing centre is Glen Brittle. Some peaks have moderate slopes which can be scaled by rough walking or scrambling and afford fine mountain scenery. The going is usually tough, and the prospective walker or climber should be prepared to get wet. However, he should not clutter himself with waterproof gear, but should wear boots, strong trousers, and gloves to minimize abrasions from the rough gabbro; take a water flask and biscuits in case of delays; find an experienced companion; not bother with a compass because the rock is magnetic; try one or two of the western corries to become acquainted with the area and adjusted to the exercise before long trips.

Crofts and castles

The visitor crossing to Kyleakin will be rewarded with views of one of Skye's many castles or keeps – Castle Maoil. This stands on a grassy promontory overlooking the narrows and once belonged to the MacKinnons. The oldest parts of the building date from the 10thc, and it is much photographed by tourists who are just setting foot on the island. From Kyleakin the A850 leads round the island's east coast to Broadford, then continues to Portree with the reddish granite screes of the Red Hills on the left and the Inner Sound of the Minch and the islands of Scalpay and Raasay on the right. Behind Broadford is 2,400ft Beinn na Caillich, where tradition says a Norwegian princess was buried so that she would be in the wake of the winds from Norway. An ever-growing cairn which is constantly added to by climbers marks the grave A diversion on the A881 from Broadford leads across to Elgol on the west coast, then makes a 30m return trip which affords rewarding panoramas of the Cuillins. A side road off the A881 at Kilbride leads down to Loch Slapin and a marble quarry, while the A881 continues through the crofting village of Torrin. Among the hills here are the ruins of Mackinnon's House, where Samuel Johnson and James Boswell stayed on their visit in 1773.

Elgol is a scattered crofting village on the eastern shore of Loch Scavaig. A boat takes visitors across the loch to a landing place at the southern edge of the Cuillins, from where a short walk leads to Loch Coruisk. This spectacular lake was carved out of the mountains by glaciers, measures 200ft deep, and looks like an amphitheatre surrounded by peaks. From Broadford the A850 runs through the hamlet of Sconser, which has a nine-hole golf course, and runs along the shores of Loch Sligachan. A diversion west along the A863 and B8009 at Sligachan leads to a minor road at Carbost, which runs to Talisker, the home of a famous whisky. The distillery can be visited by appointment, and Talisker Bay has a fine beach. A minor road near Carbost leads towards Glen Brittle, and a journey through the glen affords superb views of the Cuillins before the road meets Loch Brittle and the Glen Brittle Forest on the west coast. This is good country for hill walking. After returning to Sligachan by the same route the tour takes the A850 to continue through Glen Varragill and descend into Portree, a compact hillside town of 2,000 people. Comprising clusters of white houses around the harbour on Portree Loch, this is Skye's biggest town and the name means 'The King's Harbour'. It is also the island's chief holiday centre. The Skye provincial Gaelic mod is held in June, Skye Week on the last full week in May, the agricultural show at the end of July, and the Highland Games in August. Steamers from

the harbour make trips round the island and to the 15m-long isle of Raasay, where Prince Charlie was a fugitive and where Dr Johnson stayed at Raasay House.

The visitor can discover breathtaking views on a 46m circular tour of Trotternish, Skye's most northerly peninsula. Seven miles out along the A855 is The Storr, a 2,360ft height which is shaped like a crown and offers a stiff two-hour climb; to its east is the Old Man of Storr, an isolated, 150ft pinnacle of rock. Between The Storr and Staffin the road crosses the River Lealt, where the salmon fishing is part of the workaday life. Some 6m beyond the river is sandy Staffin Bay, with its trim crofts, and after Staffin is the Quirang – so broken up with massive rock faces that it looks like a range in miniature rather than a single mountain. Round the top of the peninsula the road reaches first Duntulm Castle, ancient seat of the MacDonalds of the Isles, then Kilmuir where there is a monument to Flora MacDonald (1722 to 1790) in an old graveyard. Her shroud was a sheet from the bed in which Bonnie Prince Charlie slept. The prince travelled to Skye disguised as 'Betty Burke', Flora's Irish spinning maid, while on the run after Culloden. They said good-bye in Portree as he followed the escape route that was to put him on a boat to France, and Flora spent some time in the Tower of London before returning to Skye to marry.

Mystic Dunvegan

Uig is the terminus for some of the car-ferries to the Outer Hebrides. Its name is of Norse origin and means 'the bay' – a broad curve which is sheltered by bluff basalt cliffs to the north and south and has a wide pebble beach. As it returns towards Portree the A856 road meets the A850 at Borve. Turn right here on to the A850 Dunvegan road; before reaching Dunvegan itself the road divides, with the B886 heading north into the Vaternish peninsula before dwindling to a minor road and continuing to Trumpan Church. This was where the Macleods massacred the Macdonalds of Uist after waving their Fairy Flag, a torn, delicate piece of silk weaving which can still be seen in Dunvegan Castle. The latter is one of the oldest inhabited castles in the country, and has been the ancestral home of the MacLeods since the 13thc. Across Loch Dunvegan and to the north is Boreraig, where the MacCrimmons – hereditary pipers of the MacLeod chiefs – had a piping school for 300 years. The castle is battlemented, has walls 10ft thick, and was originally accessible only by boat, but

Mystic Dunvegan Castle, keeper of the magical Fairy Flag of the Macdonalds of Uist.

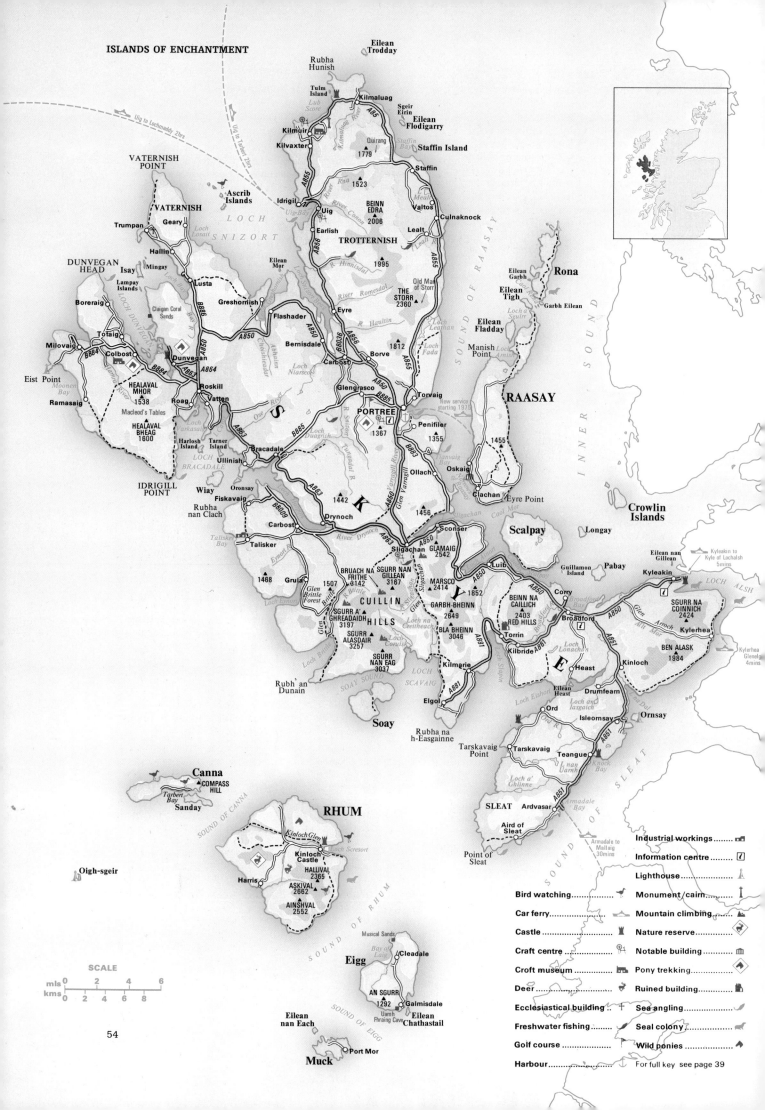

ISLANDS OF ENCHANTMENT

TROTTERNISH

Rubha Hunish
Eilean Trodday
Tulm Island
Kilmaluag
Kilmuir
Kilvaxter
Quiraing 1779
Staffin
Beinn Edra 2006
Valtos
Culnaknock
Lealt
The Storr 2360
Old Man of Storr

Sgeir Eirin
Eilean Flodigarry
Staffin Island

Uig to Lochmaddy 2hrs
Uig to Tarbert 2hrs

VATERNISH POINT
VATERNISH
Geary
Trumpan
Hallin
Mingay
Ascrib Islands

DUNVEGAN HEAD
Isay
Lampay Islands
Boreraig
Totaig
Milovaig
Colbost
Eist Point
Ramasaig
HEALAVAL MHOR 1538
Macleod's Tables
HEALAVAL BHEAG 1600
Roag
Harlosh Island
Tarner Island
Ullinish
Bracadale

Lusta
Greshornish
Flashader
Bernisdale
Borve 1812
Carbost
Glengrasco
Portree 1367

LOCH SNIZORT
Idrigil
Uig
Earlish
Eyre
1995
Eilean Mor

THE STORR 2360

Rona
Eilean Garbh
Eilean Tigh
Garbh Eilean
Eilean Fladday
Manish Point
1455

RAASAY

Torvaig
New service starting 1975
Penifiler 1355
Ollach
Oskaig
Clachan
Eyre Point

Crowlin Islands
Longay

IDRIGILL POINT
Wiay
Oronsay
Fiskavaig
Rubha nan Clach
Carbost
Talisker
1468
Grula
1507
Drynoch
1442
K
1456

Scalpay
Pabay
Guillamon Island
Eilean nan Gillean
Kyleakin to Kyle of Lochalsh 5mins

SGURR NAN GILLEAN 3167
BRUACH NA FRITHE 3142
CUILLIN HILLS
SGURR A' GHREADAIDH 3197
SGURR ALASDAIR 3257
SGURR NAN EAG 3037
Rubh' an Dunain

Sconser
Sligachan
GLAMAIG 2542
MARSCO 2414
GARBH-BHEINN 2649
1852
BLA BHEINN 3046
Torrin
Kilbride
Kilmarie
Elgol
Rubha na h-Easgainne

Luib
BEINN NA CAILLICH 2403 RED HILLS
Corry
Broadford
Heast
E
Ord
Isleornsay

Kyleakin
SGURR NA COINNICH 2424
Kylerhea
BEN ALASK 1984
Kinloch
Drumfearn
Eilean Heast
Ornsay

Kylerhea Glenelg 4mins

Soay
Loch Scavaig

Tarskavaig Point
Tarskavaig
Teangue
SLEAT
Ardvasar
Aird of Sleat
Point of Sleat

Armadale Bay
Armadale to Mallaig 30mins

Oigh-sgeir

CANNA
COMPASS HILL
Tarbert Bay
Sanday

RHUM
Kinloch Glen
Kinloch Castle
Harris
HALLIVAL 2365
ASKIVAL 2662
AINSHVAL 2552
Loch Scresort

EIGG
Musical Sands
Bay of Laig
Cleadale
AN SGURR 1292
Galmisdale
Uamh Fhraing Cave
Eilean Chathastail
Eilean nan Each

MUCK
Port Mor

54

SCALE
mls 0 2 4 6
kms 0 2 4 6 8

Industrial workings ....
Information centre ....
Lighthouse ....
Monument/cairn ....
Bird watching ....
Mountain climbing ....
Car ferry ....
Nature reserve ....
Castle ....
Notable building ....
Craft centre ....
Pony trekking ....
Croft museum ....
Deer ....
Ruined building ....
Ecclesiastical building ....
Sea angling ....
Freshwater fishing ....
Seal colony ....
Golf course ....
Wild ponies ....
Harbour ....
For full key see page 39

Thousands of years of erosion have produced these weird pinnacles on Ben Storr – formations as mysterious as the primeval rock from which they have been carved.

the moat is now bridged and the castle opens from mid April to mid October on weekday afternoons. Among the relics preserved here is a half-gallon drinking horn which Rory More, the 13th clan chief, is said to have been able to quaff at a draught. Colbost, a few miles away on the B884, boasts a folk museum which is open daily during summer. Ponies can be hired for trekking from local stables.

As the visitor heads south from Dunvegan on the A863 he crosses the Duirinish peninsula, with the twin, flat-topped hills of basalt known as MacLeod's Tables on the right. The road then follows the shores of Loch Bracadale, one of the finest fiords on the west coast, with the black basalt wall of Talisker Head away to the south. A return to Portree can be made by turning left at Bracadale and taking the B885 or continuing on the A863 to Sligachan. The second road leads to Drynoch Bridge, which spans a burn flowing into Loch Harport and is said to be the highest masonry bridge in Scotland. In order to explore Sleat – the south, or 'boot' of Skye – it is necessary to return from Portree or Sligachan on the A850 to Broadford and take the A851 Armadale road. Sleat is an area of cliffs and rocky beaches, with a lush coastal strip of woodland, farmland, and wild flowers along its east coast. About 3m beyond Isleornsay, a whitewashed fishing village with a lighthouse, are the ruins of Castle Camus or Knock – a 15th-c building which was once a stronghold of the MacDonalds. A few miles farther on is Armadale Bay, terminal for the car ferry from Mallaig. A minor road just north of Armadale allows access to the western shore of Sleat. The rocky offshore pinnacle near Tarskavaig Point carries the ruins of Dun Scaich Castle and is separated from the mainland by a 20ft-wide chasm, spanned at one time by a drawbridge. It is possible that this is the oldest castle in Skye and is sited near a lovely bay and a stretch of fine sand. North of Tarskavaig is Ord, situated on a prominent rocky headland which affords views across Loch Eishort and Loch Slapin, with the Cuillins in the distance. Ord is a good place for a final view of Skye's splendours before leaving the island by the Armadale ferry.

Around the small isles

A boat trip from Mallaig to and around the Small Isles is rather like taking a day-long marine nature trail. Rhum has three peaks over 2,500ft and is the most rugged of the four islands, though all are hilly. There are few harbours and the coasts are exposed to Atlantic winds, so travellers to Eigg, Muck, and Rhum on the Caledonian MacBraynes steamer transfer to and from the ship by ferry boat. Canna is exceptional in having a good harbour and a sheltered anchorage. Privately-run cruises round the isles are usually available between June and September.

Singing sands

The nearest island to Mallaig, Eigg measures some 5m long by 3m wide and has two outstanding features: 1,291ft Sgurr of Eigg is a castle-like mass of smooth naked rock and one of the most impressive inland cliffs in Britain; the white Camas Musical Sands are so named because of the sound they make when walked upon. The 'singing' is caused by friction between rounded grains of quartz. South-east of the sands is the scattered crofting community of Cleadale, linked by a narrow road to the island's landing place at Galmisdale. Uamh Fhraing, a cave near Galmisdale, was the scene of a 16th-c massacre after the entire population of Eigg – about 200 – hid in the cave to escape from a party of raiding MacLeods. The MacLeods suffocated the cave's occupants by making a huge bonfire at the entrance. A mini-bus service provides transport on the island, but Eigg has no hotels. Accommodation can sometimes be arranged in crofters' houses, and visitors should contact The Factor, Eigg Estates Ltd.

Muck is the smallest of the four islands and acquired its name from the Gaelic word for 'swine'. It is 2m long, lies south-west of Eigg, and has several sandy beaches. The extremely sparse population are mainly crofters and fishermen, and there are no cars, no public transport, and no accommodation facilities for the visitor. Mountainous Rhum is a haven for dozens of Atlantic grey seals, tiny ponies which run wild on the hillsides, and some 1,500 red deer. The Nature Conservancy took over Rhum's 42 square miles as a reserve in 1957, and employs the entire population of 10 families. This island is Britain's main area for studying red deer and is noted for geological and botanical research. The only way to stay is to be a self-sufficient camper – and then only by permission from the Nature Conservancy. Loch Scresort is overlooked by the large and ornate red sandstone Kinloch Castle, built in the early 1900's as the whim of an English textile magnate, and provides a sheltered anchorage. The shores of the loch are a mixture of muddy sand and seaweed-covered mussel beds which attract many birds, and the upper slopes of

2,365ft Hallival are riddled with burrows made by nesting shearwaters. Nature Conservancy work leaves little of the island open to day visitors, but two interesting nature trails start near Loch Scresort's pier. The first runs for 1½m along the loch's southern shores to Port na Caranean, a ruined fishing village founded in 1827 and finally deserted 16 years later; the other follows Kinloch Glen inland for about 2m.

A boat rounding the north side of Canna, which lies beyond Rhum, sails under 1,000ft cliffs populated by guillemots, puffins, fulmars, and razorbills. It is unusual not to see two or three golden eagles here. Passengers can land on the east side of the island at a harbour sheltered by the small island of Sanday. Canna is a green, fertile island with rocky outcrops and a coast serrated by caves, stacks, and cliffs up to 400ft high. Small areas of sand can be found at Tarbert Bay, on the opposite side of the island from the bay, and at the harbour. Compass Hill rises 458ft from the eastern end of the island and is composed of rocks which are said to be so magnetic that they affect ships' compasses. Bed-and-breakfast accommodation is available in the cottages of the Gaelic-speaking crofters, and visitors are made welcome.

Mull and Iona, Coll and Tiree

Mull, an island of mountains, moors, lochs, forested glens and towering cliffs, is the third largest in the Hebrides but less well known than Skye. For that reason it is more tranquil. Roads follow the old cattle trails, and even the new road through Glen More to Iona follows an old meandering trail rather than a straight route blasted through the rocks. Campers can find ample space for a caravan or tent, though they should do the farmer or landowner the courtesy of asking permission first. The island's 300m coastline is carved by sea lochs, sandy bays, shingle coves, and cliff caves, while the sea to the west is studded with islands. Among these are the holy island of Iona, with a religious heritage founded by St Columba 1,400 years ago; Staffa, where Mendelssohn saw Fingal's Cave 150 years ago; and the crofting islands of Coll and Tiree, washed by the salt spray of Atlantic storms. Tobermory is Mull's only burgh and is the centre for most activities, particularly shopping and local crafts. Furnished cottage accommodation is available, and shops in Tobermory send provision vans round the island at regular intervals. Each village has its general store, and in some of the larger villages these stores also have travelling shops which supply remote districts. Shops throughout the island advertise the *ceilidhs* and dances frequently held in Aros Hall, Main Street, Tobermory.

Roll-on/roll-off car ferries from Oban cross the Firth of Lorn into the Sound of Mull and offload at Craignure, where the south-east point of the island overlooks Loch Linnhe at the southern end of the Great Glen. A car ferry from Oban to Coll and Tiree calls at Tobermory but is not of the roll-on/roll-off type, and a launch runs regularly from Kilchoan on the Ardnamurchan peninsula to Tobermory. The A848 and A849 roads follow the east

coast of the island, affording views across the narrow Sound of Mull to Morvern and Loch Aline, and link Craignure with Salen and Tobermory. A regular summer air service links Glasgow, Oban, and Mull and cars are available for hire at Salen and Tobermory. Mull and Iona Week is in early September. Other special events held here include angling competitions at Craignure, a golf tournament at Tobermory, music and drama at Iona Abbey, and a piping competition south of Craignure at Torosay Castle. Few places contain more complex geological formations than Mull, and the island's westerly seaboard in particular exposes cliffs and drastically-landslipped areas which tell most of the earth's story. The layers vary from the most ancient rock known to science – over 2,600 million years old – through periods of igneous accretions, lava outbursts, sedimentary deposition, and the comparatively recent Ice Ages.

Ocean treasure

The island is noted for its fossil remains, notably the MacCulloch Tree lodged in basalt columns at Armeanach, and the Ardtun Leaf Beds at Bunessan. The latter have yielded many superbly-preserved fossilized leaves and twigs. Mull's huge variety of rock includes Ross of Mull granite, which was used for the Albert Memorial in London. Diligent searchers may find sapphires on the north shore of Loch Scridain – not very valuable but fun to find. Stories of a Spanish galleon sunk in Tobermory Bay, with treasure said to be worth 30-million ducats, are partly borne out by records which prove that a treasure ship did come to Tobermory. The galleon was named 'Florida' and she was commanded by Don Fureiga. The storm which split up the ships of the Spanish Armada in 1588 forced her to take shelter in the bay, and it seems that both ship and crew were well received. Trouble arose when it became evident the Spaniards were going to leave without paying the Clan Macleans for goods taken aboard, and Maclean of Duart sent Donald Glas Maclean of Morvern to obtain payment. The Spanish commander imprisoned Donald, who somehow managed to set fire to the powder magazine and blew the bow off the ship. Although sunk by the Macleans the galleon became the property of the Dukes of Argyll and there have been many attempts to recover the treasure over the years. Relics were brought to the surface from time to time, and in 1968 the late duke engaged the services of an expert to make a complete survey of the sea bed in Tobermory Bay.

Fingal's Cave on Staffa, the inspiration for great music and cloudy myth.

Much of the history of Mull and the Hebrides revolved round grim Duart Castle, home of the Clan Maclean chiefs since the 13thc.

There is now no doubt in the minds of experts who have uncovered other sunken ships of the Armada that the 'Florida' lies 80yds off the town-side corner of the pier. It is thought the only way to get at the remains might be to build a steel caisson round the sunken vessel and pump the enclosure dry – an enormously expensive operation. There are those, however, who maintain that no Maclean living in the 16thc would have lost such a treasure.

Cathedral cavern

Mull can be divided into three parts for touring – north, central, and south. These routes are from Salen up to the northern coastline between Ardmore Point and Treshnish Point; a central circle from Salen to Craignure, through Glen More to the head of Loch Scridain, then back by the shore of Loch na Keal; and to Ross of Mull in the extreme south via the Glen More route again, but this time along the shore of Loch Scridain to Fionnphort for the ferry to Iona. The northern tour starts from Salen, crosses the narrow neck of the island on the B8035, and on reaching Loch na Keal at Gruline turns right on the B8073 to Killichronan. An estate here combines sheep and cattle farming, forestry, building, and the sale of building materials with the provision of game, fishing, and deer stalking for visitors. The road begins to turn from the loch just after it passes the small uninhabited island of Eorsa, and climbs a hill on the Ard Dearg headland. Below the headland lie the islands of Ulva and Inch Kenneth. Ulva is privately owned and cannot be visited, but it evokes thoughts of *Lord Ullin's Daughter* – the poem written by Thomas Campbell about the chief of Ulva's Isle and his bride:

A Chieftain to the Highlands bound
Cries 'Boatman do not tarry!
And I'll give thee a silver pound
To row us o'er the ferry!'

Beyond Ulva lie Staffa and the Treshnish Isles, which can be visited by passenger launch from Ulva Ferry, Tobermory, and Oban on the mainland. Visitors can cruise around Staffa, which is privately owned, and see Fingal's Cave which so inspired the composer Mendelssohn during his Scottish tour of 1829. The cave, one of the world's most famous pieces of natural architecture, cuts 200ft into the basalt cliff and features many awesome rock columns. Puffins and other sea birds, grey seals, basking sharks, and porpoises can be seen in the area. The Treshnish Isles were once fortified, and ruins of the old strongholds can still be seen. Lunga, the main island of the group, is home to a mass of sea birds from May to July, and the island of Dutchman's Cap is so called because of the silhouette shape of its terraced lavas.

North on the B8073 and just beyond Lagganulva is a mountain stream which falls sheer into the sea from a height of 60ft, known as Eas Fors. Achleck offers a choice of roads, one over the hills to Dervaig and one to Dervaig by way of the B8073 and Calgary Bay – said to have given its name to the Canadian Calgary when people from Mull emigrated there. This unspoiled bay has a beautiful silver sand beach and calm sea for bathing. Outside Calgary a croft road leads left to a salmon fishing station at Caliach Point. Another road to the left leads to Croig, where there are remains of an old stone pier and small harbour where drovers from other islands brought their cattle on their way to mainland markets. Croig has three sandy bays to the right of the harbour, each facing a different direction at the entrance to Loch a'Chumhainn. At least one of them will be sheltered no matter from which direction the wind blows. The B8073 then twists over the bridge at Penmore Mill and runs to West Ardhu, a craft centre on Loch a'Chumhainn. The village of Dervaig, popular with artists and a good walking centre, is perhaps best known as the home of Mull Little Theatre. This is a converted byre which seats 35 people and is claimed to be the smallest professional theatre in the world. It is open from late May to the end of September. The Dervaig/Tobermory road twists and turns past the man-made Loch Torr, along the shores of three Mishnish Lochs – which run into each other – then drops right down into Tobermory by way of the Main Street and the Esplanade. The town's name is derived from the Gaelic *Tobar Mhoire*, meaning the 'Well of St Mary', and was founded in its present form in 1788.

Calve Island sits strategically in the Sound of Mull, making Tobermory Bay a safe anchorage which attracts yachtsmen from all over the world. The main regatta staged by the Western Isles Yacht Club of Tobermory is in early August, and visitors are welcome to enter the events. The club also holds dinghy races during the summer, and again visitors are welcome. The Clyde Cruising Club Race, a major event in Scottish yachting, finishes at Tobermory on the first Monday of the Glasgow Fair Holiday. The town has a nine-hole golf course and an old church where hand weaving can be seen and tweed products are sold. Walks from Tobermory include one along a path into the Aros forest park, and another along the shore to the lighthouse at Rubha nan Gall on the small headland at Bloody Bay. This bay was the scene of a sea battle when the Macleans of Duart, Lochbuie, and Ardgour supported John, 4th Lord of the Isles, against his rebel son Angus in 1439. On the way back to Salen down the Sound of Mull a road passes the ruins of the 12th-c Aros Castle, a stronghold of the MacDonalds when they were Lords of the Isles. The forest on the right opens up and the road to the right continues to Loch Frisa – the largest

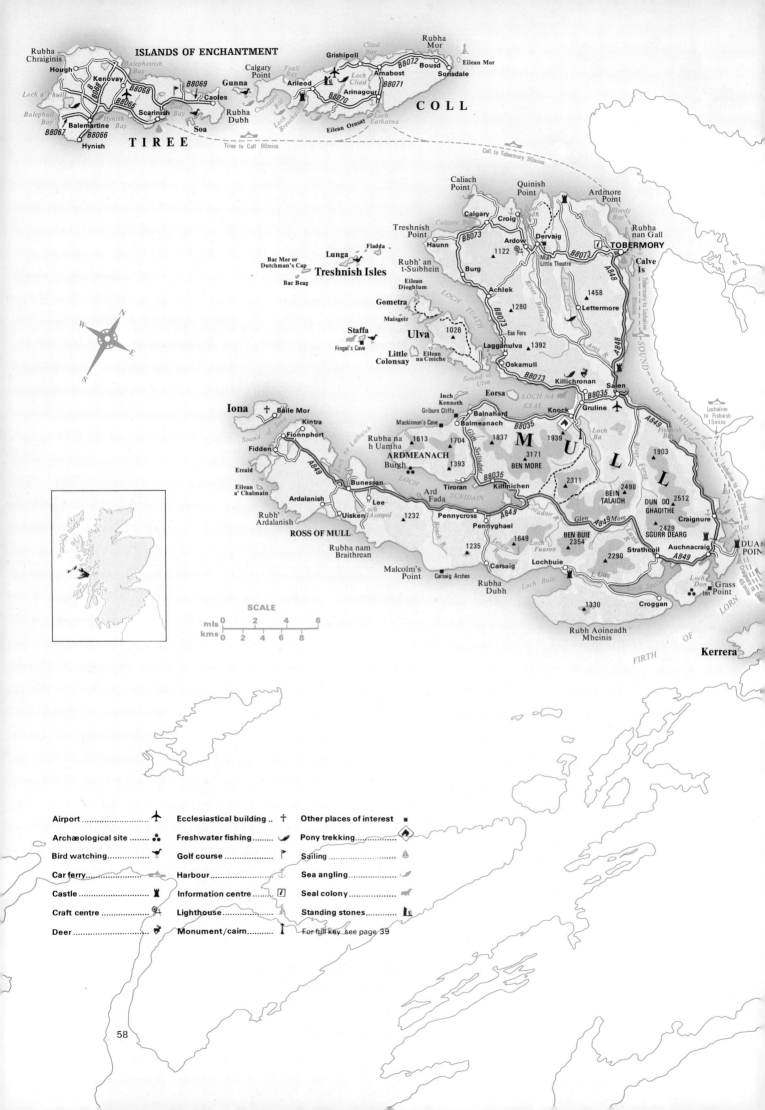

ISLANDS OF ENCHANTMENT

TIREE

Rubha Chraiginis
Hough
Kenovay
Caoles
Balephetrish Bay
B8069
Gunna
B8068
B8065
Scarinish
Gott Bay
Rubha Dubh
Soa
Balemartine
B8067
B8066
Hynish
Loch a' Phuill
Balephuil Bay
Hynish Bay

Calgary Point
Feall Bay
Arileod
Crossapol Bay
Loch Breachacha
Eilean Ornsay

COLL

Grishipoll
Arnabost
B8072
Bousd
Sorisdale
Rubha Mor
Eilean Mor
Arinagour
B8071
B8070
Cliad Bay
Loch Cliad
Loch Eatharna

Tiree to Coll 60mins
Coll to Tobermory 90mins

MULL

Caliach Point
Quinish Point
Ardmore Point
Bloody Bay
Calgary
Croig
Ardow
Dervaig
Rubha nan Gall
TOBERMORY
Calve Is
Calgary Bay
Treshnish Point
Haunn
B8073
1122
Burg
Achlek
1280
1458
Lettermore
B8073
A848
Mull Little Theatre
River Bellart
Treshnish Isles
Lunga
Fladda
Bac Mor or Dutchman's Cap
Bac Beag
Rubh' an t-Suibhein
Eilean Dioghlum
Gometra
Maisgeir
Staffa
Fingal's Cave
Ulva
1026
Little Colonsay
Eilean na Creiche
Lagganulva
1392
Eas Fors
Oskamull
B8073
Killichronan
Salen
B8035
Sound of Ulva
LOCH TUATH
Aros R.
SOUND OF MULL
Lochaline to Fishnish 15mins
Iona
Baile Mor
Kintra
Fionnphort
Fidden
Erraid
Eilean a' Chalmain
Rubh' Ardalanish
Ardalanish
Bunessan
Uisken
Lee
Loch Assopol
1232
ROSS OF MULL
Rubha nam Braithrean
Malcolm's Point
A849
Loch na Lathaich
Sound of Iona
Inch Kenneth
Griburn Cliffs
Mackinnon's Cave
Eorsa
Balnahard
Balmeanach
ARDMEANACH
Burgh
Rubha na h Uamha
1613
1704
1393
1837
1939
Knock
Gruline
LOCH NA KEAL
3171
BEN MORE
M U L L
1903
Loch Ba
River Forsa
B8035
Tiroran
Kilfinichen
Ard Fada
LOCH SCRIDAIN
2311
2498
BEIN TALAIDH
2512
DUN DO GHAOITHE
A849
Craignure
Pennycross
Pennyghael
A849
Glen More
Leidle R.
2429
SGURR DEARG
2290
Auchnacraig
A849
DUA POIN
1235
Beach R.
1649
Loch Fuaron
BEN BUIE
2354
Strathcoil
Grass Point
1330
Carsaig
Carsaig Arches
Rubha Dubh
Lochbuie
L. Uisg
Croggan
Loch Buie
Loch Spelve
Loch Don
Rubh Aoineadh Mheinis
FIRTH OF LORN
Kerrera

SCALE

mls 0 · · · 2 · · · 4 · · · 6
kms 0 · · 2 · · 4 · · 6 · · 8

Airport	✈	Ecclesiastical building	†
Archæological site	♣	Freshwater fishing	
Bird watching		Golf course	⚑
Car ferry		Harbour	
Castle	♜	Information centre	ⓘ
Craft centre		Lighthouse	
Deer		Monument/cairn	

Other places of interest	◆
Pony trekking	
Sailing	
Sea angling	
Seal colony	
Standing stones	

For full key see page 39

freshwater loch on the island. During the summer season many *ceilidhs*, dances, and barbecues are held at Salen.

A tour of central Mull is a circuit of massive, 3,169ft Ben More. This mountain owes its birth to eruptions of a volcanic range which ended at a point where the present cliffs of Burg fall to the sea at the mouth of Loch Scridain. From Salen the tour route takes the A849 to Craignure, and then continues past Torosay Castle on the left to a well-marked turning point. This leads to a headland and Duart Castle, home of the Clan Maclean chiefs since the 13thc. From then until the middle of the 18thc much of the history of Mull and the Hebrides revolved around this huge fortress. In 1691 the castle was put 'to fire and sword' by the Duke of Argyll, then after the 18th-c Jacobite troubles and occupation by the 'Red Coats' it was left uninhabited. It fell into disrepair to the point of ruin, but in 1912 was restored by Sir Fitzroy Maclean of Duart – chief of Clan Maclean and grandfather of the present chief, Lord Maclean of Duart, Morven, and Brolas. Duart Castle is open to the public from May to September and should certainly be on the itinerary of any visitor to the island. It contains relics of Scotland's history, and a comprehensive record of scouting from its inception in 1907 to the present day. Lord Maclean is Chief Scout of the Commonwealth.

Pilgrim's path

At the entrance to Loch Don from the Firth of Lorne is Grasspoint, start of the pilgrim's way to Iona. Summer launches bring visitors over from Oban for a short visit and refreshment at Grasspoint's 250-year-old inn, now a tearoom and showplace for local crafts and paintings. A prehistoric burial ground has been discovered close by. At Strathcoil another branch road off the A849 leads to Croggan on the far shore of Loch Spelve, and to the beautiful countryside around Loch Buie. For over 500 years the chiefs of the MacLaines of Loch Buie lived here at Moy Castle, which is now in ruins. Lochbuie village, dominated by Ben Buie, is a beauty spot well worth seeing. As the main road continues through Glen More, mountains rise to the right and three freshwater lochs lie to the left. The mountains include Sgurr Dearg and Beinn Talaidh; legends of 'Little Folk'; and a grimly majestic glen which brings the road to the head of Loch Scridain on the west side of the island. To continue on the A849 would be to anticipate the third suggested tour, described later. Instead this route takes a right turn on the B8035 along the northern shore of Loch Scridain, the largest of Mull's sea lochs, to Kilfinichen.

Beyond this village is a turning off to Tiroran, where the land along the lochside is privately owned. The road can be used but soon becomes a track which ends in a walk to the high headland of Burg – 2,000 acres of which were bequeathed to the National Trust in 1932. Here by Loch Scridain is the MacCulloch Fossil Tree, possibly 50-million years old, which can be reached at low water. As it passes through Glen Seilisdeir the B8035 climbs, with the terraced rocks of Ardmeanach towering around newly-planted forests to the west. Tide permitting it is possible to walk from Bolmeanach to MacKinnon's Cave, just over 1m to the south. The cave is said to penetrate the headland of Burg and emerges at Tiroran, but as yet no one has proved this. Later the road skirts Gribun Cliffs, which rise sheer from its side to about 1,000ft then passes through Knock and continues to Gruline. Here a footpath to the right leads up the side of Loch Ba. Also near here is the entrance to MacQuarrie's Tomb, a monument to Major General Lachlan MacQuarrie, first Governor-General of New South Wales and sometimes called 'father of

Australia'. The major founded Salen in 1808. Stay on the B8035 for the return to Salen.

The Road to Iona

Ross of Mull and Iona can be approached from Salen either via the B8035 through Gruline or the A849 through Glen More. These roads meet at the head of Loch Scridain, and the A849 continues through Ross of Mull to Fionphort. Close to the southern shore of Loch Scridain is Pennyghael, and just beyond this is a left turn for the notable rock formations of Carsaig Arches, which can be reached by a 3m trip along the shore at low tide. Beyond Pennyghael, past the towering cliffs of Burg on the far side of the loch, is Bunessan, a village overlooking a sheltered sea loch used by fishing boats and private craft. To the left a narrow road leads to Port Uisken, a safe sandy beach with several small islets that can be reached on foot at low tide. The western part of the Ross of Mull is a geologist's treasure house, but left and right turns on the way to Fionnphort lead to sands at Fidden and Kintra.

Iona has neither cars nor motor roads and is reached from Fionnphort across the mile-wide Sound of Iona by passenger ferry. It was to this low-lying, gentle isle in the year 563 that St Columba came from Ireland with twelve followers and started his mission. By the 7thc Iona was a European centre of Christian teaching and a place of pilgrimage. In the late 19thc the buildings were in ruins. Now, chiefly because of the dedicated work of the Iona community, the cathedral and associated buildings have been restored. Services of every Christian denomination are held within the cathedral precincts. St Oran's Chapel is said to be on the site of St Columba's original church, and in St Oran's cemetery are the graves of 60 kings of Scotland, Norway, and Ireland. Farther along this Street of the Dead is St Mary's Abbey, which dates from the 13thc. St Columba's Tomb is situated in the grounds, and St John's Cross, considered one of the best surviving examples of Celtic stone carving. The essence of Iona's tranquillity is found in the farmlands above the shore of the island's west coast. South east of

Detail from St Columba's Cathedral on the holy island of Iona.

Iona is the tiny island of Erraid, which Robert Louis Stevenson used in *Kidnapped*. As David Balfour discovered after days of living on shellfish, the sound separating it from Mull can be crossed at low tide 'dry shod or at most by wading'. A return journey from the head of Loch Scridain can be made via the route alternative to that used on the outward journey. This would have the effect of combining this tour with the circuit of Ben More.

Coll and Tiree lie off the western coast of Mull and are served by car-carrying steamers from Oban, plus a Glasgow to Tiree air service. The sea trip from Oban takes about four hours. Both are treeless crofting islands – Coll rocky with low hills and Tiree flat and fertile. Tiree measures 12m by 3m and has a population of about 850, most of whom are Gaelic speaking. It has long been a granary island but has recently turned to tulip growing. Scarinish, the central village, has a snug harbour and is flanked by two long, lonely, and impressive sandy beaches at Hynish Bay and Gott Bay. The eastern end of the island has a nine-hole golf course, and dozens of rocky islets can be reached at low tide. Sea birds abound – terns, razorbills, red-throated divers, and Arctic skuas. Other little townships include Balemartine, which is the largest and has the only licensed store, hotel accommodation, and a bus service. Boating and fishing are popular holiday pastimes. Between Tiree and Coll is the tiny isle of Gunna, the haunt of barnacle geese, and 10m to the west is the Skerryvore Lighthouse, which was built in 1843 and has a beam which can be seen for 18m.

Coll has fewer than 150 inhabitants and only 25m of road. Facilities for visitors are limited to one hotel, bed-and-breakfast houses, and camping areas, but its moors delight ramblers and walkers and there are many safe, sandy beaches. Permits for fishing the little lochs are easily obtained, and locals will readily take visitors sea fishing. Rock fishing is worth a try for cod, mackerel, and conger. Most of the people live near Arinagour, a village with a sheltered anchorage on the western shore of Loch Eatharna. There are several prehistoric stone forts and standing stones on Coll. Ruined 12th-c Breachacha Castle overlooks the sea from the west coast and was originally the stronghold of the Macleans, who ruled Coll for many years. A new castle, built in 1750 for the 13th chieftain Hector Maclean, was where Johnson and Boswell spent most of their time when stranded on Coll for ten days during their Highland tour. Giant dunes, more than 100ft high in places, separate the long sandy beaches of Feall Bay and Crossapol Bay – but neither Johnson nor Boswell were energetic men.

Isles of the South West

In the south-west corner of the Highlands, at a southerly latitude which surprises those who do not know the Highlands, the long peninsular finger of the Mull of Kintyre points across the water at Northern Ireland. To the west of this are the most southerly islands of the Hebrides – Islay, Jura, Colonsay, Oronsay, and Gigha. To the east are the popular islands of the Firth of Clyde, holiday places known to Glaswegians as 'Doon the water'. These are Arran, Bute, the Cumbraes, and Ailsa Craig. Each has its own fascination – the verdant peace of Islay, the gardens of Colonsay and Gigha, and the hill climbing, sea-angling, and sailing in and around Arran. May and June are the sunniest months, and although July and August are warmer they can also be wetter. Car ferry services to Arran, Bute, and the larger of the two Cumbraes are frequent in summer and easily accessible; but to reach the southern Hebrides by car the visitor must drive down the A83 to the western shore of Loch Fyne, past Inveraray Castle, and round Loch Gilp to the isthmus that so narrowly prevents Kintyre from being an island. Car ferries serve Islay from West Tarbert, a fishing village at the head of West Loch Tarbert, and from Kennacraig farther down the loch. There are also links with the other islands, and a Glasgow to Campbeltown air service to Islay.

Islay

In the same way that the whisky from the island's distilleries at Laphroaig, Lagavulin and Ardbeg should be savoured, so should this green and pleasant isle itself. Some 25m long, 20m wide, and with nearly 200m of road, it is home to a bewildering variety of birds and features pretty coastal villages with a fair choice of hotels. Camping and caravanning are permitted at selected sites, details of which are available from the tourist information office at Bowmore. The island supports a growing population of around 4,000, while its neighbours have only a total of 500 to 600 inhabitants among them, a hotel each, and a few bed-and-breakfast places. The chief reasons for this comparative affluence are the distilleries and dairy farms. Though much of the island is green and arable about a quarter of the land is peat, an important ingredient in preparing the malt for the distinctive Islay whiskies. Woodlands, moors, cliffs, sand-dunes, marshes, rivers, and lochs provide an astonishing variety of scenery and a great variety of birds.

Some 97 different species were recorded on two winter days – a total unlikely at the same season elsewhere in Britain except perhaps in East Anglia. Islay is the principal wintering resort – possibly in the world – of the barnacle goose, and a recent count showed over 10,000 of this species as well as greylags and greenland whitefronts. Pink-footed and Brent geese are rarities. Duck are numerous, particularly on Loch Indaal where great rafts of scaup float out on the middle, flocks of wigeon nibble the grass at the sea's edge, eiders rest in the rocks, and shelduck stalk about on the machair. Scaup, merganser, and golden-eye come right inside the pier at Bowmore. In winter the island has woodcock and in few places can the great northern diver be seen in greater numbers; some stay for summer, but not for nesting. Bird sanctuaries and observation points exist at Loch Gruinart, the head of Loch Indaal, and on the Mull of Oa. Other facilities for visitors include yachting and boating at Port Ellen, Bowmore, Port Charlotte, Port Askaig, and Portnahaven; eighteen-hole golf at Machrie; pony-trekking at Port Ellen; shooting, fishing, and sea angling. Laggan Bay is one of Scotland's best surfing beaches, but swimming around Islay can be dangerous and local advice should be sought to find safe places. Port Charlotte is noted for its cheese and Bridgend has a tweed mill. Islay has a history going back to neolithic times, and boasts several exquisitely carved crosses – particularly at Kildalton.

18th-c Bowmore Church was made round so that the devil could find no corners to hide in.

The roads on Islay are excellent, especially the straight stretch from Port Ellen to Bowmore. Port Ellen is a neat, attractive village with a harbour flanked by the sands of Kilnaughton Bay and is the island's principal port. This bay is safe for bathing, and west of the town a narrow road leads over the Oa Peninsula to Mull of Oa, where the cliffs are crowned with a memorial to American soldiers and sailors drowned when two ships were torpedoed off Islay in the first world war. East of Port Ellen a road runs to Ardbeg through the whisky distilling villages of Laphroaig, Lagavulin, and Ardbeg itself. Beyond the latter an unclassified road through wooded country provides the only convenient access to the south-east coast. A 9th-c cross at Kildalton Church is considered to be one of the finest in existence. The road peters out to the north of Claggain Bay, from where lonely walks lead north to McArthur's Head and north-west to the 1,609ft peak of Beinn Bheigeir. North from Port Ellen towards Bowmore are two roads which run almost parallel. The A846 low road passes the airport and provides access to tracks and footpaths which lead to Laggan Bay and 6m of sandy beach. Bowmore, the island's main centre, was founded in 1693 and has an 18th-c, white-walled, circular parish church – made round so that the devil could find no corners to hide in.

Beyond Bowmore the main road follows the shore of Loch Indaal into Bridgend, where it forks left. The A847 branch leads along the western shore of Loch Indaal and through the Rhinns of Islay villages of Bruichladdich, Port Charlotte, Portnahaven, and Port Wemyss. A narrow road west of Port Charlotte leads to sandy Kilchiaran Bay, and paths along the cliffs north of this beach pass Machir Bay to join a road to Saligo Bay, where the beach is flanked by rocks, cliffs, and natural arches. Kilchoman stands on Machir Bay and has many prehistoric and early-Christian monuments. Portnahaven and Port Wemyss are sheltered from the full force of the Atlantic by two small islands. The shore near the twin villages is rocky, but there is a secluded sandy beach 3½m north at Lossit Bay. Near Blackrock on the A847 an ithsmus between Lochs Indaal and Gruinart is spanned by the B8017, which provides access to other roads leading to small freshwater lochs and hamlets in the island's north-west corner. Back at Bridgend, the A846 crosses the island to Port Askaig, which is surrounded by steep, wooded slopes and has a pier for car ferries from the mainland and Feolin on the Isle of Jura.

Jura

Perhaps the least known of the Inner Hebrides, this island is ruggedly beautiful and largely uninhabited. Its farming community of some 250 people live on the eastern shore. The A846, continuing from Islay over the Feolin Ferry and skirting the southern and eastern shores, is the island's only main road and runs for 28m. Jura is 28m long by 8m wide and has only one village – Craighouse. There is only one hotel, although some families welcome visitors. The city dweller who finds accommodation here and is willing to explore on foot or by boat will find ample reward. Beaches of silver and white at Tarbert and Corran contrast with miles of tall cliffs and a shingle-strewn foreshore teeming with sea birds. Jura has around 5,000 red deer, and stalking and trout fishing can be arranged at the hotel. Sea angling for mackerel, saithe, and lythe is good, whether from a boat or from the rocks.

The island is dominated by the Paps of Jura, three peaks between 2,400ft and 2,600ft high which offer good climbing and afford fine views. West of Tarbert Bay – which is 5m north of Craighouse – a track leads to the lonely shores of Loch Tarbert, a long sea loch which bites far into the island from the west and almost cuts it in two. There are many sandy coves and towards the open sea the explorer will find some of the largest and most interesting caves in Scotland. North of Loch Tarbert is a roadless wilderness of moorland, peat bogs, and small lochs, and a coastline to please the long-distance walker. A walker should never set off into these remote areas without telling someone. The west-coast area bordering Loch Tarbert features good examples of raised beaches; those at Shian Bay are more than 100ft above sea-level and several-hundred yards inland. A better-known feature is the great and fearsome whirlpool of Corryevreckan, situated between the small island of Scarba and the north tip of Jura. The Strait of Corryevreckan is roughly 1m in breadth, and the 10-knot currents which race in and around the whirlpool are considered by mariners to be unparalleled about the coasts of Britain. The Royal Navy has officially classed it as un-navigable.

Colonsay

Some 10m west of Jura is Colonsay, an attractive, craggy little island owned by Lord Strathcona. The island has a hotel, several houses to let, and bed-and-breakfast cottages. Besides farming its Gaelic-speaking people go in

The stately red deer – still king of the wild island places.

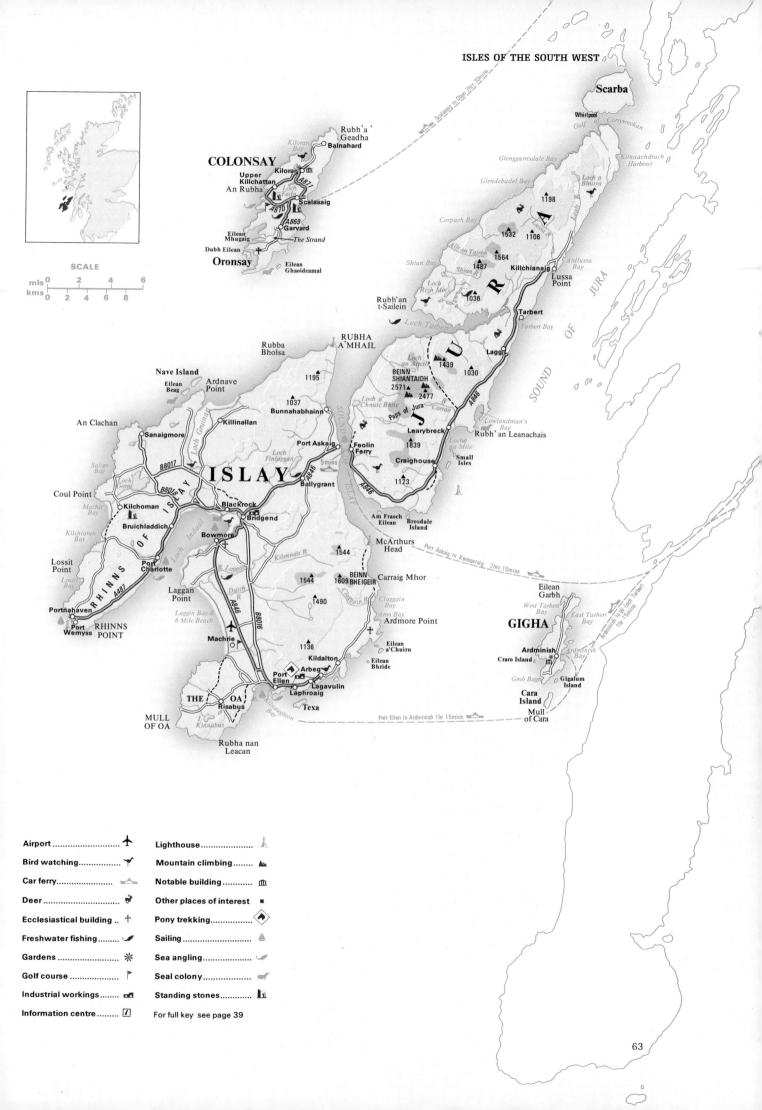

Scarba
Whirlpool
Gulf *Corryvreckan*

Scalasaig to Oban 2hrs 30mins

COLONSAY
Rubh'a'
Geadha
Kiloran Bay
Balnahard
Kiloran
Upper
Killchattan
An Rubha
Loch Fada
Scalasaig
A871
A870
A869
Garvard
Eilean
Mhugaig
The Strand
Dubh Eilean
Oronsay
Eilean
Ghaoideamal

Glenggarrisdale Bay
Kilnuachdrach Harbour
Glendebadel Bay
Loch a Bhurra
1198
Corpach Bay
Allt an Tairbh
1532
1106
1564
1487
Killchianaig
Shian Bay
Loch Righ Mor
Shian R
Ardlussa
Lussa
Point
1036
Leall R

Rubh'an
t-Sailein
Loch Tarbert
Tarbert
Tarbert Bay
Loch an Airicl
1439
Laggi
1030
BEINN
SHIANTAIDH
2571
2477
Loch a'
Chnuic Bhric
Paps of Jura
Corran
1839
Learybreck
Lowlandman's Bay
Rubh'an Leanachais
Craighouse
Loch na Mile
1123
Small
Isles

Rubba
Bholsa
RUBHA A'MHAIL
1195
Nave Island
Ardnave
Point
Eilean
Beag
1037
Bunnahabhainn
Loch Gruinart
Killinallan
Port Askaig
An Clachan
Sanaigmore
Loch Finlaggan
Feolin
Ferry
5mins
B8017
ISLAY
A846
Ballygrant
Sound of Islay
Am Fraoch
Eilean
Brosdale
Island
Coul Point
Saligo Bay
Machir Bay
Kilchoman
Blackrock
Bridgend
A846
Bruichladdich
Loch Gorm
Bowmore
Kilchiaran Bay
Port
Charlotte
Loch Indaal
Kilennan R
R Laggan
1544
McArthurs
Head
Port Askaig to Kennacraig 2hrs 10mins
Lossit
Point
RHINNS OF ISLAY
A847
1544
BEINN
1609 BHEIGEIR
Carraig Mhor
Eilean
Garbh
West Tarbert Bay
Lossit Bay
Duich R
A846
1490
Claggain R
Claggain Bay
Portnahaven
Port
Wemyss
**RHINNS
POINT**
*Laggin Bay &
6 Mile Beach*
Laggan
Point
B8016
Machrie
1136
Aros Bay
Ardmore Point
Eilean
a'Chuirn
GIGHA
Ardminish
Craro Island
Kildalton
Arbeg
Eilean
Bhride
Gigalum
Island
THE OA
Risabus
Port
Ellen
Lagavulin
Laphroaig
Texa
Cara
Island
Mull
of Cara
MULL
OF OA
L Kinnabus
Kintnaughton Bay
Port Ellen to Ardminish 1hr 15mins
Rubha nan
Leacan
Grob Bagh

SCALE

mls 0 — 2 — 4 — 6
kms 0 — 2 — 4 — 6 — 8

Airport ✈	**Lighthouse**
Bird watching	**Mountain climbing** ▲
Car ferry	**Notable building**
Deer	**Other places of interest** ▪
Ecclesiastical building †	**Pony trekking** ◆
Freshwater fishing	**Sailing** ⚓
Gardens ✳	**Sea angling**
Golf course ⚑	**Seal colony**
Industrial workings	**Standing stones**
Information centre	For full key see page 39

for sea fishing, poultry, and bee keeping. The little port of Scalasaig lies half-way up the eastern shore and is the main village. A car ferry operates from Oban and a boat from Port Askaig. The road system is surprisingly good, and from Scalasaig the A870 runs west to the golf course before turning north-east to Upper Kilchattan, the thickly-forested Vale of Kiloran, and Lord Strathcona's home of Colonsay House. Just 1m out of Scalasaig the A869 forks south off this road to The Strand, a sandy channel between Colonsay and the smaller island of Oronsay, which can be reached on foot at low tide. Oronsay is known for the ruins of a 14th-c priory and seal sightings. By tradition this was a place where St Columba paused on his journey to Iona, and he is said to have consecrated the island as a sanctuary.

Perhaps the best-known of Colonsay's attractions are the exotic tropical Gardens of Kiloran, which are open to the public from April to September, dawn till dusk, and display magnificent rhododendrons, azaleas, embrithriums, magnolias, bamboo, and palm trees growing in the open. The west coast of the island has many raised beaches, and there are standing stones about 1m south-west of Scalasaig and at the westernmost tip of Loch Fada, near the hamlet of Lower Kilchattan. The coast south of Kiloran Bay is impressive, and is where Atlantic waves surge over the rocks below towering cliffs populated by seabirds. This is an island for the game angler, ornithologist, archaeologist, walker, botanist, geologist, photographer, and sea angler. Seekers after local crafts will find locally-made rugs and woven goods at Kiloran.

Gigha

This little island lies 3m west of the Kintyre peninsula and is more fertile than its rocky, barren appearance suggests. The climate is warm and moist enough to support dairy

farms, and a valuable collection of plants can be seen in the gardens of Achamore House, including rhododendrons, azaleas, hydrangeas, lilies, and roses; Australasian and Chilean shrubs and trees; agapanthus, irises, camellias, cherries, and sorbus. The island measures 8m long by less than 2m wide and can be reached from Tayinloan on Kintyre by passenger ferry, or by car ferry from West Loch Tarbert. There is no tourist accommodation. Its name is Norse and means 'God's island', and it formed part of the Norse empire until the 13thc.

Arran

It may seem trite to call Arran 'Scotland in miniature', but there seems no better way to describe this lovely Firth of Clyde island. The 56m road which rings its coast encloses eleven peaks over 2,000ft, the highest being 2,866ft Goat Fell. Magnificent scenery apart, Arran has ten villages and no towns, a population of 3,500, seven golf courses, safe bathing, water ski-ing, sailing, fishing, and pony-trekking. Most of the villages are set on the coast road, but two other roads suitable for cars also cross the island. These are the String Road from Brodick to Blackwaterfoot and Machrie, and the Ross Road from Lamlash to Sliddery. Frequent car ferries which cross from Ardrossan on the mainland coast arrive at Brodick, where the red-sandstone mass of the castle – former home of the Dukes of Hamilton – commands the bay. Car ferries also operate from Claonaig on Kintyre to Lochranza in the north of Arran. The compactness of the Arran Hills is one of their chief delights. Granite ridges have been thrust through slate and sandstone to form a chain of knobbly peaks cut by three distinctive glens. They appear difficult to climb but in fact prove easy by their line of least resistance, and strong hill walkers can traverse all of them in one long day. Such energetic people are rewarded with views of the peaks of Ireland, the Lake District, and the mountains of Scotland's western seaboard on a clear day. Cir Mhor is a sharp peak with a mighty cascade of boiler-plate slabs. The well-textured granite has been shaped into fantastic flying buttresses and overhanging chimneys, and this is

Castle ruins on the shore of Arran's beautiful Lochranza.

The magnificent golden eagle is one of the many birds of prey to be seen hunting over wild Arran glens.

the nearest thing Scotland has to the Chamonix Aiguilles of Mount Blanc. The best climbing is to be had on the Rosa Pinnacle, but there is no difficulty in climbing to the peak by easy ways from the adjacent summits.

The only other potentially-difficult summit on Arran is the Witch's Step, an intimidating pinnacle best avoided by all but the most experienced rock climbers. Goat Fell affords pleasant and easily-accessible hill walking and has a clearly-defined path to the summit. Views from the gentler slopes of the western hills make Mull and Jura seem a stone's throw away, and there are many easy walks over the softer country in the south-west of Arran. Visitors to the 'tops' will often see the broad-winged golden eagle soaring over the glens, with its great head out-thrust as it searches the corries for prey. Another bird of the Arran hills is the short-eared owl, which hunts in daylight and has the most buoyant flight of all predators. Peregrine falcons, merlins, hen harriers, buzzards, sparrow hawks, and kestrels may also be met with on or around these granite heights. Among Arran's many geological features are 'The Rents' – spectacular crevasses on the Scriodan near Lochranza. The finest walks available are in the glens, and for these stout shoes or boots are necessary to combat the soggy ground. Little of the island's surface is enclosed and most of the roads are unfenced. Forestry Commission roads over the southern uplands make the going easy, but agility is needed for the moors. From Lochranza the northern segment affords lovely seascapes, and the three glens of Rosa, Shurig, and Cloy converge on Brodick. Glen Sannox in the north is wild, Glen Iorsa the island's largest, and Glen Ashdale in the south has a 200ft waterfall.

Lamlash's Spring Festival, which attracts sea anglers from all over the country, is one of many competitive events held during the season. Cod and haddock are usually plentiful, and for those who prefer to hunt for big or specimen fish there are tope, plaice, whiting, skate, ray, dogfish, conger, and wrasse. Shore fishers have miles of easily-accessible beach where good sport may be enjoyed in peace and safety, and the larger holiday villages organize fishing trips or offer boats for hire. The island has six freshwater lochs and extensive river fishing. Many visitors have found semi-precious stones – including cairngorms – on and around Goat Fell, and pebbles of cornelian, chalcedony, agate, jasper, and amethyst on the beaches at King's Cross and Corriegills. A workshop at Whiting Bay has specimens of these local stones and the equipment to cut and polish them. Arran craftsmen also work with pottery, wood, leather, and wool.

To tour Arran the visitor must obviously take the circular A841 coast road, which either actually runs through the villages or provides access to feeder roads. Brodick is the chief port and the obvious starting place. Besides catering for the ordinary tourist it is also a centre for ridge walking and rock climbing. The pier is on the south side, and to the north are wooded hills which descend to a beach overlooked by Brodick Castle and Goat Fell. The castle is a mixture of ancient and comparatively modern styles, with a 16th-c centre block and a north wing which may date from the 14thc. The original structure was seized by Edward I and later garrisoned by Cromwell, whose soldiers were massacred by the islanders, and the 600 acre grounds have a formal walled garden which was established in 1710 by the Duchess Anne, daughter of the first Duke of Hamilton. A woodland garden here includes rhododendrons and plants from the Himalayas, Burma, and China, and both the castle and gardens are open from Easter to September. A few miles to the north is Corrie, a picturesque village of closely-packed white-washed cottages at the foot of the mountains. The shore here mostly comprises low-lying rock with a sandy patch in the harbour. Ferry Rock is so called because in the early days of this century passengers to Corrie were ferried to this spot from the steamers. Corrie is a favourite place for mountaineers because of the proximity of the peaks to the north and south of Glen Sannox, and Sannox village offers two boarding houses, furnished cottages, a nine-hole golf course, and a shore of unbroken sand. A new forestry road over the North Sannox burn to the Fallen Rocks provides a pleasant walk.

Lochranza, the most northerly village, has a sheltered anchorage for yachts and a bay dominated by a ruined 17th-c castle. A car ferry operates from here to Kintyre on the mainland. Earlier structures existed on the same site, and Robert the Bruce is said to have landed here in 1306 after coming from Rathlin Island off Northern Ireland to fight for Scottish independence. Lochranza has a golf course, tennis courts, and sea and river fishing. Farther down the west coast the village of Pirnmill stretches along the shore near the foot of Beinn Bharrain and includes an old mill which once made 'pirns' – wooden bobbins – but has since been converted to flats. The coast road continues through Imachar, Dougrie, and Auchagallon, with Kilbrannan Sound on the right. Just south of Auchagallon is wide Machrie Bay, a quiet and sandy place with a golf course and pleasant walks by the south

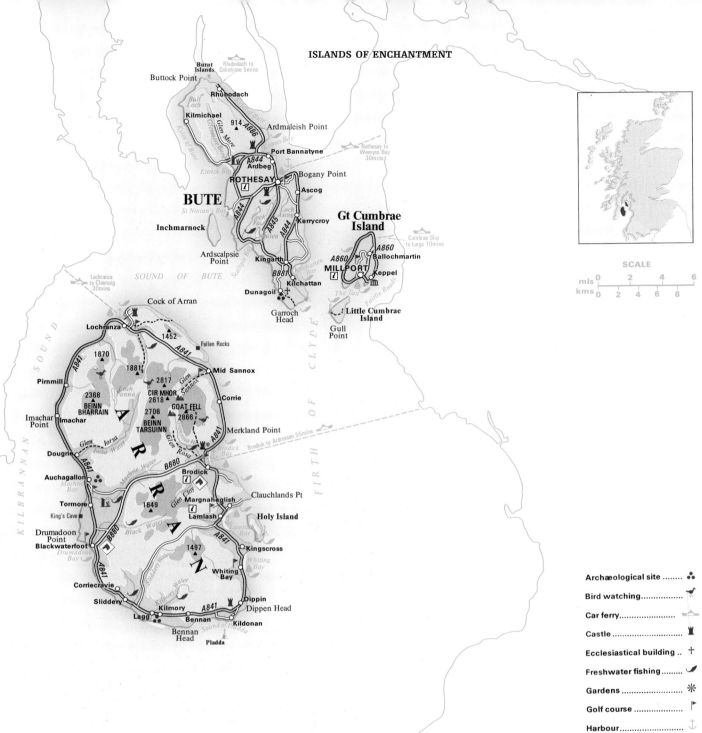

SCALE

mls 0 2 4 6
kms 0 2 4 6 8

Archæological site ....
Bird watching................
Car ferry......................
Castle ....
Ecclesiastical building ..
Freshwater fishing........
Gardens ....
Golf course ....
Harbour.........................
Information centre .,......
Lighthouse....................
Mountain climbing........
Notable building............
Other places of interest
Pony trekking.................
Sailing ....
Sea angling...................
Standing stones............

For full key see page 39

Rothesay Castle is an imposing structure which dates from the time of the Vikings.

shore to the King's Cave – so called because it has associations with Bruce's advance party. After Machrie Moor, which has a stone circle, the road south passes the village of Tormore and a nearby collection of standing stones. Blackwaterfoot, a centre for pony trekking and one of the best bathing areas, offers good fishing, tennis courts, and a golf course.

Kilmory covers the south of Arran and includes Corriecravie, Sliddery, Lagg, and Bennan – all villages on the A841. This pastoral district includes wide stretches of moorland and is rich in megalithic structures. Arran cheese is made at Torrylin Creamery, Lagg has a Continental air, palm trees, and a tea garden, and Laggburn offers good fishing. Carn Ban is a chambered cairn of the new-stone age sited at Kilmory, and Kildonan occupies a headland at the island's south-east corner, looking down on the island and lighthouse of Pladda. The shore at the foot of the cliffs is sand with stretches of rock, and a ruined castle dominates the landscape. Up the east coast lies Whiting Bay, a modern village near Glen Ashdale, and on the northern part of the bay is King's Cross, where Bruce and a fleet of 30 vessels set sail for the mainland in 1307. Whiting Bay is a tourist centre with facilities for most sports and entertainments. Farther up the east coast and south of Brodick is Lamlash, the administrative centre of the island, a good tourist centre, and the headquarters of the Arran Yacht Club. The 2m-long Holy Isle is so placed in the bay that it forms a narrow channel at either end for ships to pass, and a sheltered anchorage at Lamlash. A private ferry operates to Holy Isle, which has a 1,000ft central peak and is almost sheer on the seaward side.

Bute

The centre of this little 15m by 5m island is Rothesay, a bustling place and one of Scotland's leading resorts. Bute is softer and more fertile than Arran and is separated from the Cowal peninsula by the narrow Kyles of Bute, which many claim to be one of the loveliest sailing areas in Scotland. From Armaleish Point to the Burnt Islands the East Kyle is about 4m long, and the Cowal Hills fall steeply to the sea on the right. The Gaelic word *kyle* means 'the narrow water', and these straits are only about 400yds wide. Just beyond the Rhubodach ferry are the Burnt Islands, a handful of islets which create an almost complete barrier, and cause the passage to narrow until it is measured in feet. The old pleasure steamer 'Queen Mary II' gets through on her frequent summer cruises, then swings hard to port and steams down the western arm of the Kyles to Tighnabruaich. Car ferry services operate between Wemyss Bay on the mainland and Rothesay, and between Colintraive on the mainland and Rhubodach. A host of passenger steamers serve trains from Glasgow,

and the island has a good internal transport system. Steamer tours are a traditional speciality of the Firth of Clyde.

Rothesay is a fine yachting centre which also offers most of the popular indoor and outdoor entertainments. Its castle was an important medieval stronghold, and the title 'Duke of Rothesay' was originally conferred on the heir to the Scottish throne. It is now held by the Prince of Wales. Sited in the centre of the town, the castle dates from the time of the Vikings and has walls which were heightened in the late 13thc and enclose a circular courtyard unique in Scotland. An esplanade from the town's pier stretches along the two arms of the bay, reaching Craigmore in the east and Ardbeg in the west. The A844 circles the dairy-farming southern part of the island, and beyond the fishing village of Port Bannatyne the A886 leaves it and heads along the north-east coast. The latter starts from Kames Bay, with its 14thc castle, and follows the eastern arm of the Kyles of Bute as far as Rhubodach – where the ferry from Colintraive docks. To the west of the A886 is the hilly northern part of the island, which is without roads but does have nature trails and several good walks. From Rhubodach it is possible to have a full day's walk round the top of the island to Glenmore and return over the moors by Bull Loch. Another walk from Rhubodach runs over the hills of the western arm of the Kyles of Bute and down to Ettrick Bay on the west coast.

From Ettrick Bay the A844 and a few diversions offer a tour of the south end of the island, finishing back in Rothesay. This bay lies 5m across the island from Rothesay and boasts 2m of safe sands. A few miles south is St Ninian's Bay, which is deeply inset, sandy, and sheltered from the westerly winds by the island of Inchmarnock. About $\frac{1}{2}$m east of Ettrick Bay is a stone circle, just one of several prehistoric sites on the island, and a few miles south of St Ninian's are the red sands of Scalpsie Bay. At Kingarth there is a minor road which leads on to Dunagoil Bay and the southernmost point at Garroch Head. High above the sea at Dunagoil are remains of a pre-Roman vitrified fort, the ruins of St Blane's Chapel of *c*1700, and the foundations of a monastery founded by St Blane in the 16thc. Also leading south from Kingarth is the B881 to the beaches and picturesque countryside of Kilchattan Bay. Here the route turns to the east shores of the island. Nearer Rothesay it meets Kerrycroy – a model village designed in the English style with half timbered houses and a village green – and Ascog Bay. In the south the island offers good walks, particularly round wooded Loch Fad. This can be reached via the A845, which runs across the island from Rothesay to Scalpsie Bay. One walk ends at the gatehouse of a cottage built by Edmund Kean the actor in 1827, and farther south a shore walk from Kilchattan Pier leads between rocks to a lighthouse guarding the entrance to the upper firth. From here the walker can continue to Glencallum Bay, round Garroch Head, and back to Dunagoil. As in the north these hills and moors are without roads or tracks.

The Cumbraes and Ailsa Craig

Great Cumbrae is easily reached by car ferries and steamers which operate from Largs, and has been a holiday island since the 18thc. It is best known for the resort of Millport, and can offer good sandy beaches, safe bathing, boating, and a golf course. Little Cumbrae, which is rocky, barren, and uninhabited, lies with Great Cumbrae between the mainland coast and the south-east shores of Bute. A 12m road running right round the island allows access to beaches, cliffs, and rocky foreshores. The Scottish Marine Biological Station at Keppel has a museum and aquarium which are open to the public. A narrow hilly road leads inland.

Far out in the firth and some 10m offshore from Girvan is a volcanic pyramid of rock called Ailsa Craig. This is also known as 'Paddy's Milestone', because it lies halfway on the sea route from Belfast to Ardrossan. It measures 1,114ft high by 2m round, and features a gannetry plus numerous puffin and guillemot colonies. Granite from here is used for making curling stones, and the island can be visited from Girvan.

Puffins are among the many different species of sea bird that congregate on isolated Ailsa Craig.

Orkney and Shetland

These two groups of storm-lashed isles are essentially different from the rest of Scotland – and not only because they lie so far to the north. The Norse influence is apparent in St Magnus's 12th-c cathedral, which is still in use at Kirkwall, and both Orkney and Shetland only became part of Scotland some 500 years ago – not long in the language of history. Each group has its own Mainland island, and there are still Orcadians and Shetlanders who look on Scotland as a foreign country. Here amid majestic landscapes and seascapes which provide a home for seabirds rather than men, the thinly-spread population has followed the ancient crafts of fishing, farming, and spinning. They remained remote from industrial turmoil until a few years ago, when the East Shetlands Basin of the North Sea was established as a major oil-producing area. For the people of Shetland and Orkney oil meant change and disruption, as they came under pressure from both oil companies and government. But all was not lost. The Shetland planning authority insisted on concentrating oil development in one area of about 2,760 acres round a sea loch called Sullom Voe. In summer there is a brief half-light between sunset and sunrise – the Simmer Dim. May and June are usually the sunniest months, and the average temperature is in the high 50's Fahrenheit.

British Airways operate services from Aberdeen, Edinburgh, Glasgow, Inverness, and Wick to Grimsetter in Orkney and Sumburgh in Shetland. Loganair Ltd operate inter-island services, and sea services are in the hands of the North of Scotland Orkney and Shetland Shipping Company. This firm runs vehicle-carrying steamer services from Aberdeen to Lerwick, similar services by way of Kirkwall, and a roll-on/roll-off ferry between Scrabster on the mainland and Stromness in Orkney. Kirkwall and Lerwick both have tourist information centres, and cars and boats can be hired on the major

islands. Regular bus services link Kirkwall and Stromness with other centres in Orkney, and Lerwick is similarly connected with centres in Shetland. The major islands in each group can be reached by ferry services and mailboats.

Orkney

This group of 70-odd islands lies 20m across the Pentland Firth from Caithness and can be divided into three – the North Isles, the South Isles, and between them the largest island – Mainland. But most spectacular is Hoy, with its 1,000ft cliffs at St John's Head and the impressive stack known as the Old Man of Hoy, a pillar of rock rearing 450ft out of the sea. Cliffs are perhaps the most exciting aspect of Orkney, and are mostly vertical – as at St John's Head – due to the horizontal bedding of the rocks. Caves have been formed by the pounding of waves, and where these have collapsed a headland and stack has been left. Some of these are insignificant, but others vie with the Old Man. Scandinavians visit the ancient Norwegian province of Orkney in increasing numbers each year, for a permanent record in stone displays aspects of the way of life of their Viking ancestors better than in their native

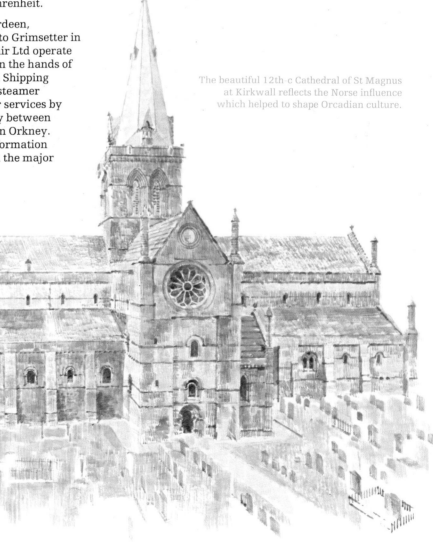

The beautiful 12th-c Cathedral of St Magnus at Kirkwall reflects the Norse influence which helped to shape Orcadian culture.

ISLANDS OF ENCHANTMENT

SCALE

mls 0   2   4   6

kms 0   2   4   6   8

MULL HEAD

Seal Skerry

North Ronaldsay

Dennis Head

Bow Head

Papa Westray

Hollandstoun

Linklet Bay

NOUP HEAD

Holland

Holm of Papa

Rack Wick

Pierowall

NORTH RONALDSAY FIRTH

B9067

Tafts Ness

Westray

THE NORTH SOUND

OTTERS WICK

Midbea

Bay of Tuquoy

B9066

Sanday

START POINT

Berst Ness

B9068

Rapness

B9069

Skea Skerries

Holm of Faray

Roadside

B9070

Bay of Lopness

Faray

Kettletoft

Bay of Newark

SANDAY SOUND

Sacquoy Head

Rusk Holm

Calf of Eday

Braeswick

Tres Ness

Quoy Ness

SOUND OF FARAY

Rousay

Wasbister

Saviskaill Bay

Eday

Kirkwall to Lerwick 8hrs

Papa Stronsay

Muckle Water

B9064

B9063

Linga Holm

Whitehall

Grice Ness

Brough Head

Eynhallow

821

Egilsay

FALL OF WARNESS

B9062

Odness

Birsay

B9064

Brinyan

EDAY SOUND

Stronsay

Aith

Marwick Head

Georth

Aiker Ness

Muckle Green Holm

B9061

B9061

Burgh Head

Kitchener Memorial

Loch of Swannay

Wyre

STRONSAY

Bay of Holland

Twatt

Loch of Boardhouse

B9051

A966

Gairsay

GAIRSAY SOUND

Sweyn Holm

FIRTH

Lamb Head

Tor Ness

B9056

A967

Loch of Sabiston

735

STRONSAY

AUSKERRY SOUND

Sandwick

B9057

Dounby

Ness of Ork

Veantrow Bay

B9058

Edmonstone

Rothiesholm Head

Auskerry

Bay of Skaill

Harray

Loch of Harray

Isbister

Shapinsay

Yesnaby

B9055

A986

Finstown

Balfour

B9059

Helliar Holm

Hacksness

WIDE FIRTH

THE STRING

A967

A986

A965

Rerwick Head

Mull Head

ORKNEY
(West Mainland)

A965

KIRKWALL

Ingansay Bay

Tankerness

DEER SOUND

STROMNESS

Scapa

B9050

Skaill

Graemsay

WARD HILL 881

A964

St Andrews

Deerness

The Gloup

HOY SOUND

Linksness

A960

A961

Gritley

Point of Ayre

St John's Head

1420

Howth

(East Mainland)

Foubister

B9052

Stromness to Scrabster 2hrs 30mins

1577 WARD HILL

B9047

SCAPA FLOW

St Marys

BRING DEEPS

Corn Holm

Old Man of Hoy

Rackwick

Dwarfie Stone

Cava

BARRIER 1

Copinsay

RORA HEAD

1309

Rysa Little

Lamb Holm

BARRIER 2

Kirkwall to Aberdeen 11hrs

HOY

Calf of Flotta

Glims Holm

BARRIER 3

Sneuk Head

Fara

Hunda

Burray

Lyness

Flotta

Water Sound

Burray Ness

HOLM SOUND

B9047

Bow

Rose Ness

Wateringhouse

FLOTTA SOUND

BARRIER 4

Swartha

B9043

St Margarets Hope

Meisetter

Longhope

Widewall Bay

Grim Ness

Tor Ness

Cantick Head

OF HOXA

Herston

Brims Ness

South Walls

B9042

South Ronaldsay

Swona

B9041

Windwick Bay

Halcro Head

Burwick

Brough Ness

B9041

A961

PENTLAND

Island of Stroma

Muckle Skerry

FIRTH

Mell Head

Pentland Skerries

Key

Airport	✈		
Archæological site			
Bird watching			
Car ferry		Harbour	⚓
Castle	♜	Industrial workings		Other places of interest	◼
Craft centre		Sailing	⛵
Ecclesiastical building	✝	Information centre		Sea angling	
Gardens	✳	Lighthouse		Standing stones	
		Notable building	🏛	For full key see page 39

lands. *The Orkneyinga Saga* chronicle of the Norse earls of Orkney records prominent people, places, and events from *c*900 to 1200; not only have the structural remains of many Viking habitations survived, but it is known who lived in the island and the important events that occurred here. East Mainland and West Mainland are joined by a narrow isthmus which holds the city and royal burgh of Kirkwall. To the north lies a harbour and anchorage, and to the south is the great expanse of Scapa Flow. Kirkwall got its name from two old Norse words, *Kirku Vagr*, meaning 'the Church on the Bay'. The church then was St Olaf's, but today it is the 12th-c cathedral of St Magnus.

In the Norse era of the Middle Ages this beautiful cathedral, built by Earl Rognvald and dedicated to the memory of his uncle Earl Magnus, was second only to Nidaros in magnificence and importance. For eight centuries it has dominated Kirkwall and shaped the lives of Orcadians. Caskets containing the relics of St Magnus and St Rognvald are sealed within two pillars flanking the position where the high altar stood. On West Mainland is the fishing town of Stromness, which also has links with history. It was *Hamnavoe* to the Norsemen, and much later was a thriving seaport which received ships from the Hudson's Bay Company before they set out across the

Atlantic to Canada. These two towns are the only communities of any size in the islands. Air services ply to the North Isles of Westray, Stronsay, Eday, Sanday, North Ronaldsay, Papa Westray, and to the island of Hoy in the South Isles. Sea services operate to the same northern isles, as well as to Rousay, Egilsay, Wyre, and Shapinsay. A round-of-the-isles trip is available to visitors. The South Isles can be visited from Stromness and/or Scapa, and these trips take in Hoy, Flotta, and Graemsay.

A tour of Orkney must almost certainly begin at Kirkwall. The top of the 125ft tower of the St Magnus Cathedral affords views of two other antiquities – the Bishop's Palace and the Earl's Palace. The Bishop's Palace was built about the same time as the cathedral, and although subsequently much altered it still retains a 16th-c round tower added by Bishop Reid. The Earl's Palace was built in 1607 by Earl Patrick Stewart, who was executed before he could fulfil his plan and link it with the other palace. The building is roofless but still magnificent. Opposite the cathedral the gardens and museum of Tankerness House show how a 16th-c Orkney merchant-laird lived, and Scandinavian influences can still be seen in the many gable-ended houses and narrow twisting streets.

Stromness is of ancient origin and was known to the Norsemen as *Hamnavoe*. Now a fishing village, it was once the last stopping place for ships of the Hudson's Bay Company before they started out across the Atlantic for Canada.

As the visitor leaves Kirkwall on the A965 for West Mainland he immediately appreciates the wide range of colour which the islands offer, and has his first sight of prehistoric cairns and earth houses. At Finstown, which has many lovely private gardens, the route turns right on to the A966. A feature of Aikerness is the Broch of Gurness, a well-preserved iron-age broch which still stands 10ft high and is surrounded by other buildings plus a rock cut ditch, is sited here. Continuing along the northerly coastal road of Mainland, the visitor comes to the Loch of Swannay and thence to the parish of Birsay, a peaceful hamlet containing the impressive Earl's Palace which was built by Earl Robert Stewart at the end of the 16thc. The palace is being renovated. From Birsay it is possible to walk over a narrow causeway to the tidal island of the Brough of Birsay, an unsurpassed reminder of the Viking age. Remains of 12th-c Earl Thorfinn's Hall, the cathedral church he built and in which St Magnus was buried, a bishop's palace, and the nucleus of an old Norse town can be seen here. The Brough of Birsay affords views of Marwick Head, where the Orkney people erected a Kitchener Memorial after he was killed during the first world war. To the south on the A967 is the old Click Mill, which was built c1800 and is the last Orkney horizontal water-mill. Beyond Twatt the A986 passes through the parish of Harray and turns right to rejoin the A965 Kirkwall to Stromness route. Tormiston Mill, now a restaurant, is sited on this road and preserves mill equipment still in working order. Opposite the mill is the Maeshowe Chambered Cairn, some 4,000 years old and possibly the finest megalithic tomb in Western Europe.

From here the B9055 leads to the Bay of Skaill. On the narrow neck of land separating the Loch of Stenness from the Loch of Harray are the Standing Stones of Stenness, which probably date from c1800 BC and are the remains of a once great circle. A short distance away is an impressive bronze-age structure known as the Ring of Brodgar, meaning 'The Circle of the Sun'. Of the 27 stones that remain standing the tallest is 15ft. After this the road approaches the parish of Sandwick and the most remarkable of the United Kingdom's archaeological treasures – the prehistoric village settlement of Skara Brae. Some of the houses here date from 2500–2000 BC, have been well preserved by drift sand, and still contain their stone furniture, hearths, and drains. South of Skara Brae and accessible via a minor road off the B9056 is Yesnaby, where the fascinating geographical feature of Yesnaby Castle is shaped like an old red-sandstone tower standing on two legs. Stromness is a town of the sea where the houses project gable-ended into the water and are complemented by their own private jetties. It retains much of its history and has a library, Orkney's first indoor swimming pool, and an eighteen-hole golf course. Stromness is the major port for the South Isles, and is often the first port of call to visitors who travel across on the ferry from Scrabster. The tour returns to Kirkwall via the A964, skirting Scapa Flow on the way.

Yesnaby Castle is a naturally-formed stack of old-red sandstone shaped like a tower and perilously supported on two legs.

The East Mainland is not as rich in archaeological treasures as the west, but has much to offer in the tranquil beauty of nature. The A960 from Kirkwall runs past the airport before minor left turns lead to uncrowded bays and lonely beaches at Tankerness and St Andrews. The B9050 road leads across to the extreme easterly parish on Mainland, Deerness, where there is beautiful rock scenery and numerous sandy bays. Some 60yds back from the edge of the cliff at Sandside is a vast chasm which encloses a natural arch in the rock face. This strange geographical feature is known as The Gloup. The village of Skaill has a Viking site dating from the 11thc and provides boat trips under The Gloup. On the south side of the East Mainland peninsula the A961 runs along the Churchill Barriers to reach South Ronaldsay over the islands of Lamb Holm, Glims Holm, and Burray, with Scapa Flow to the right. These barriers join the eastern half of the South Isles to Mainland and are four causeways which were built in the second world war to seal up the approaches to Scapa Flow. They are now used as roadways. As the visitor travels back to Kirkwall on the A961 from the road's southern extremity at Burwick he covers the entire 4m length of South Ronaldsay. This island has lovely spots which include Windwick Bay, hidden by 260ft Hesta Head; Widewall Bay, popular for boating and fishing; and the picturesque village of Herston. At the head of another fine bay and overlooking Burray is St Margaret's Hope, the island's chief village.

Barrier 4 allows access to the fertile island of Burray, once owned by the notorious Earl Patrick Stewart and now the home of a major boat-building yard. Barrier 3 leads to Glims Holm and Barrier 2 to Lamb Holm. Lamb Holm features an Italianate Chapel which was built inside a Nissen hut by Italian prisoners of war. The ironwork was formed from scrap metal, and the hand painting gives a three-dimensional marble effect. Barrier 1 leads back to Mainland and Kirkwall. The other South Isles are not so conveniently joined to Mainland, but regular shipping services and motorboat charters are available from Stromness. These islands include Graemsay, Hoy, and Flotta – all worth visiting for their cliff scenery. Hoy is the second largest of the Orkney Islands and is the 'high island'. The highest point is 1,577ft Ward Hill, and the Cuilags rise to 1,420ft in the north. The point where the Cuilags meet the Atlantic is called St John's Head and displays a dramatic perpendicular cliff. Some 2m farther south is 'Orkney's oldest inhabitant', the Old Man of Hoy rock stack. The Dwarfie Stone is a rock-cut tomb dating from 1900 BC, and although similar tombs have been found in the Mediterranean this one is unique in the British Isles. Hoy has a rich variety of flowers and trees. Alpine varieties which grow at about 2,000ft in Scotland can be seen after a modest climb of 500ft on the Hoy hills. Great black-backed gulls nest on the island's moorland in huge numbers, and puffins can be seen at St John's Head.

One of the most impressive of the prehistoric monuments in the Orkneys is the Ring of Brodgar, a well-preserved bronze-age temple.

One of the most curious features of the Orkneys is the chapel on Lamb Holm – based on a Nissen hut and built from scrap by Italian prisoners of war.

Air and sea services link the visitor with the outermost North Isles. North Ronaldsay, low lying and fertile, is the most northerly and much favoured by migratory birds. Prehistoric remains here include the iron-age Broch of Burrian, where an ox-bone incised with Pictish symbols was found, and a high stone dyke round the island keeps the sheep outside to feed on seaweed. A 184ft lighthouse is also of interest here. Sanday lies 2½m to the south and offers marvellous beaches, good fishing areas, and Quoyness – a cairn dating from 2,000 BC. Westray is west of Sanday. It is an island of hills, lochs, cliffs, and sandy beaches and was once a Viking base; tiny Papa Westray lies north-east of Westray and includes the 12th-c church and graveyard of St Boniface. Colonies of Arctic skua, great skua, kittiwake, and guillemot populate these and the islands of Eday, which is almost cut in two by Fersness Bay and Eday Sound, and Stronsay, only 8m long but so oddly shaped that it has almost 50m of coast. The shores of rugged Stronsay are mainly rocky, with 100ft cliffs above Odin Bay, but there are also long sandy beaches. Whitehall is a pleasant fishing village and harbour strung out along a bay which is sheltered by the island of Papa Stronsay. Shapinsay island is so close to Kirkwall that it is almost suburbia, and it has a number of small archaeological sites. Also here and unique in Orkney is baronial-style Balfour Castle, which was built in 1847 by Col David Balfour.

It is possible to visit Rousay, Egilsay, and Wyre by taking a boat from Tingwell Jetty on Mainland. Rousay's rich prehistoric remains include the huge, twelve-chambered Midhowe Cairn and nearby Midhowe Broch. About 110ft above sea level lies Egilsay, a flat arrow-shaped island dominated by the 45ft, cylindrical tower of 12th-c St Magnus' Church. Wyre takes its name from *vigr*, meaning spearhead, and is a similar shape to Egilsay. Its main features are Cobbie Row's Castle, perhaps the earliest stone castle in Scotland, and the Norse Wyre Chapel.

Orkney has many local crafts and industries. Stromness has lobster ponds, salmon are smoked in Kirkwall, and both places have an Orkney chairmaker. Kirkwall also has two silversmiths, a tweed mill, and the Highland Park Distillery, and there is a craft centre at Tormiston Mill on Mainland, and Westray has crab processing. Look out for Orkney fudge from Stromness, sheepskin rugs, Orkney straw-backed chairs, home knitting, sealskin articles, and wrought iron.

Shetland

The Shetland Isles are closer to Norway than to England, and Lerwick the capital is 100m north of John o'Groats. There are at least 100 islands in the group, but fewer than 20 of them inhabited, although some are quite large. Mainland is the most important and measures 50m long and 20m across at its widest point. Shetland is similar in structure to Norway and the North of Scotland, with coastlines deeply indented with sea lochs which are really ice-scoured valleys. These penetrate for miles and the sea is dominant everywhere. Being the main port Lerwick is a crossroads for the northern seas, and 5,000 of the group's 20,000 people live here. Fishing goes on despite the oil, and other exports include fine knitwear and small, sturdy ponies from the island of Fetlar. The near-Arctic position gives many hours of daylight in summer, and an opportunity to see the spectacular Aurora Borealis. Equally spectacular is the January festival of *Up Helly Aa*, when a Viking ship is escorted through the narrow streets of Lerwick and then burnt amid great celebrations.

Norse influence is found in many place names, and many Norse festivals have been absorbed into the local way of life. Most important of these were the feasts of *Beltane* (Spring), Midsummer feast (June), Hallomas (end of Harvest), and Yule (Christmas). In years past Yule was the most lengthy of all the feasts, lasting three weeks and ending with a mighty binge, but with the coming of Christianity the Yule festival became Christmas and the 24th night after Christmas was called *Up Helly Aa* – 'the up-ending' of the holy days. The pagan Norsemen were compelled by torture to adopt Christianity, so they looked forward to *Up Helly Aa* as the end of the enforced holy period and the beginning of celebrations. These islands have been inhabited for 4,000 years – perhaps longer – and the remains of houses, tombs, and temples built by late stone-age people who came here between 2000 and 1500 BC are widespread. Few areas of Britain are richer in archaeological interest. More than 1,000 antiquities have been recorded in the islands, only a few of which have so far been excavated. Those that have been uncovered include some of Northern Europe's most important sites. All around are some of the richest

cont page 76

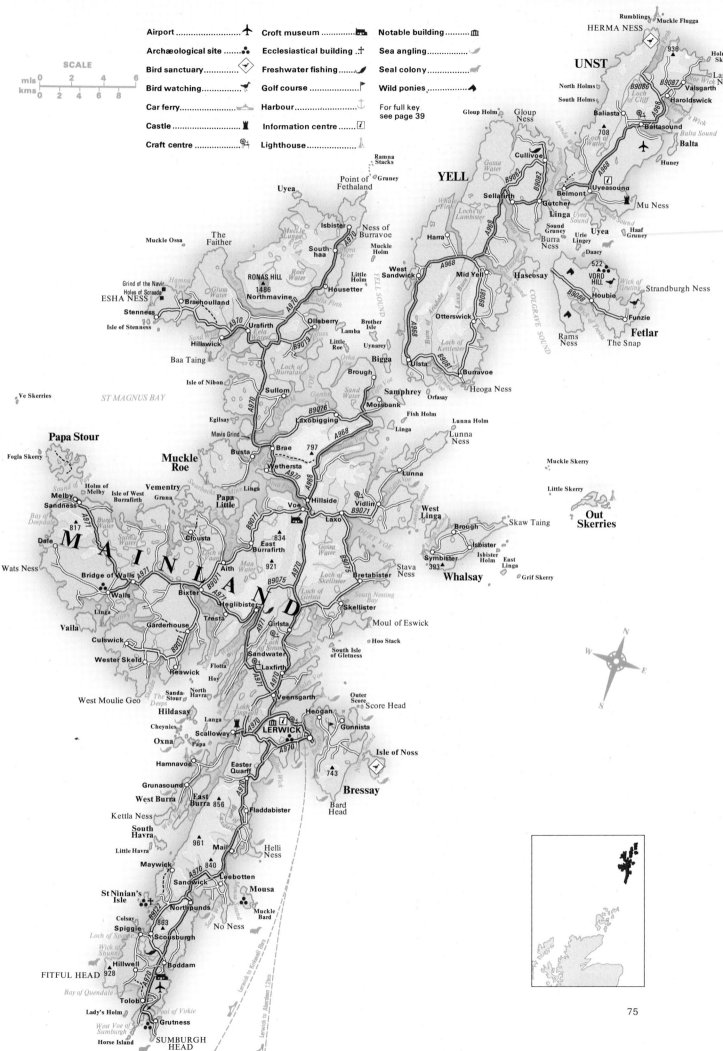

Key

✈	Airport
⚫⚫⚫	Archæological site
◇	Bird sanctuary
🐦	Bird watching
🚢	Car ferry
♜	Castle
📷	Craft centre
🏠	Croft museum
✝	Ecclesiastical building
🎣	Freshwater fishing
⛳	Golf course
⚓	Harbour
ⓘ	Information centre
🗼	Lighthouse
🏛	Notable building
🐟	Sea angling
🦭	Seal colony
🐴	Wild ponies

For full key
see page 39

SCALE

mls 0   2   4   6
kms 0   2   4   6   8

UNST

Rumblings   Muckle Flugga
HERMA NESS
936
Holm of Skaw
North Holms
South Holms
Lamba Ness
Valsgarth
Haroldswick
Baliasta
Balta
Baltasound
Huney
Balta Sound
Uyeasound
Mu Ness
Linga
Sound Gruney
Burra Ness
Urie Lingey
Uyea
Haaf Gruney
Daaey
VORD HILL
522
Strandburgh Ness
Houbie
Funzie
Fetlar
Rams Ness
The Snap

Point of Fethaland
Ramna Stacks
Gruney
Uyea

YELL

Gloup Holm
Gloup Ness
Cullivoe
Gossa Water
Sellafirth
Gutcher
Harra
Mid Yell
West Sandwick
Hascosay
Otterswick
Loch of Kettlester
Ulsta
Burravoe
Heoga Ness

Isbister
Ness of Burravoe
South-haa
Muckle Holm
Housetter
Little Holm
Ollaberry
Lamba
Brother Isle
Little Roe
Uynarey
Bigga
Brough
Samphrey
Mossbank
Orfasay
Fish Holm
Linga
Lunna Holm
Lunna Ness

Uyea
The Faither
Muckle Ossa
RONAS HILL
1486
Northmavine
ESHA NESS
Grind of the Navir
Holes of Scraada
Braehoulland
Stenness
Isle of Stenness
Hillswick
Baa Taing
Urafirth
B9019
Isle of Nibon
Sullom
Egilsay
Mavis Grind
Busta
Brae
797
Wethersta
B9076
Laxobigging
Sand Water
A968
Lunna
Lunna Voe
West Linga
Brough
Skaw Taing
Isbister
Symbister
393
Isbister Holm
East Linga
Bretabister
Grif Skerry
Whalsay
Stava Ness

Muckle Skerry
Little Skerry
Out Skerries

Ve Skerries
ST MAGNUS BAY

Papa Stour
Fogla Skerry
Holm of Melby
Melby
Sandness
Vementry
Gruna
Isle of West Burrafirth
Papa Little
Voe
Hillside
Laxo
Vidlin
B9071
Dale
817
MAINLAND
Bridge of Walls
Walls
Bixter
Aith
East Burrafirth
834
921
B9075
Loch of Skellister
Bretabister
Skellister
Heglibister
Tresta
Girlsta
Moul of Eswick
Garderhouse
Culswick
Wester Skeld
Reawick
Sandwater
Laxfirth
Hoo Stack
South Isle of Gletness
Wats Ness
Linga
Vaila
West Moulie Geo
Hildasay
Sanda Stour
North Havra
Flotta
Hoy
Veensgarth
Heogan
Outer Score
Score Head
Langa
Cheynies
Scalloway
Papa
LERWICK
Gunnista
Oxna
Hamnavoe
Grunasound
Easter Quarff
Isle of Noss
West Burra
East Burra
856
Bressay
Fladdabister
743
Bard Head
Kettla Ness
South Havra
Little Havra
961
Mail
Helli Ness
Maywick
840
Leebotten
Sandwick
Mousa
St Ninian's Isle
Nortpunds
Muckle Bard
Colsay
863
No Ness
Spiggie
Scousburgh
Loch of Spiggie
Wick of Shunni
Hillwell
Boddam
FITFUL HEAD
928
Bay of Quendale
Tolob
Lady's Holm
Grutness
West Voe of Sumburgh
Horse Island
SUMBURGH HEAD
SUMBURGH ROOST

Lerwick to Aberdeen 12hrs
Lerwick to Kirkwall 8hrs

75

fishing grounds in the Northern Hemisphere, and the sea angler can reap a rich harvest around the islands' coasts. He can always find some sheltered fishing spot around the tiny islets or in the narrow voes, whatever the wind direction. Sea angling for fun is a recent development, but 40 people who took part in a recent competition landed 2,000lb of fish in only five hours. Between the halibut and the haddock lies a wide selection of game fish for the rock as well as boat angler. Species caught regularly include ling, whiting, cod, herring, mackerel, turbot, flatfish, skate, eels, dog-fish, hake, coalfish, and tope.

Few places offer the bird-watcher more. The coastline provides ideal nesting sites for seabirds, and the lochs and moorland behind the cliffs are favourite breeding-grounds of other species. Noss is one of the places on the bird-watcher's 'must' list, a little island which rises to a peak of 600ft beyond Bressay and which forms the eastern shore of Lerwick Harbour. Thousands of birds nest on Noss, and the cliff ledges are crammed with puffins, razorbills, guillemots, kittiwakes, shags, gannets, and fulmars. The visitor here can watch the great skua swoop within inches of anyone daring to come too close to its nest, or the Arctic skua feign injury when it thinks that its eggs or chicks are threatened. The nature reserve of Hermaness is situated on the north-west coast of Unst and is known for its skua sightings. Several Arctic tern and puffin colonies exist around the shores of Mainland, common and herring gulls and oystercatchers breed here, and throughout the year rare or unusual species can occur practically anywhere. King eiders are seen offshore from time to time and ospreys appear most years, sometimes staying in one area for several days.

The visitor arriving by air would land at the airport on Sumburgh Head, which is the most southerly point of Mainland and the starting point of the A970. This road runs the length of the island, so the island is a good place from which to start a Shetland tour. Almost immediately the traveller finds a justifiably famous prehistorical site, Jarlshof, where six distinct levels of occupation lie one over the other and outline the Shetland story from neolithic to historic times. On the site are fragmentary remains of one of the earliest houses; a village which lived through the late bronze age into the early iron age; a late iron-age complex of well-preserved and spacious circular houses

clustering round the stump of a broch tower built about 2,000 years ago; an extensive Viking settlement; a medieval farmstead; and a 17th-c laird's house. About 4m north a traditional croft house of the last century has been restored and now contains a croft museum. A water-mill close by has also been restored. A left turn onto the B9122 at Boddam leads to Spiggie, where there is a loch, a sandy beach, and two small bays. Beyond here and just off the west shore is St Ninian's Isle, which is linked to Mainland by a narrow isthmus and features the ruins of an ancient chapel. The foundations of this revealed a medieval apse, altar, and nave on excavation, and near by are a bronze-age burial ground and the remains of a pre-Norse church.

After rejoining the A970 the tour continues across moorland into Sandwick, one of Shetland's most populous rural districts. Over a half-mile channel to the east lies the uninhabited isle of Mousa, site of the most complete iron-age broch in existence. This is still over 40ft high all round and can be reached by boat from Leebotten or Sandwick. Ahead and also out to sea is the island of Bressay, which lies across the mouth of Lerwick's bay and helps to create a fine natural harbour. A feature of Lerwick is Fort Charlotte, a roughly pentagonal building which was begun in 1665 to protect the Sound of Bressay against the Dutch – a job it failed to do because the Dutch burned it in 1673. It was repaired in 1781. The Town Hall is in the Scottish baronial style and displays stained-glass windows. The view from its tower is panoramic, but access to the top is by a steep wooden ladder. The 18th-c part of the town nestles round the harbour, where many of the houses are built Norwegian-style on the sea wall. Norse influence is apparent everywhere – for example in the absence of a street pattern, which creates problems for visitors because many of the streets tend to look the same. For a long time the town relied on its fishing economy, and visitors can see the fish markets and live-lobster ponds at a crab and lobster processing factory. Lerwick is also the centre of the Shetland wool industry, and the island's cottage knitting industry is still strong. The wool, the finest of which comes from the neck of the sheep, is used to produce fine-spun garments which are exported the world over. It is said that the measure of a good Shetland garment is to be able to draw it through a wedding ring.

Lerwick's development into one of the main Shetland communities is largely due to its fine natural harbour, sheltered by the island of Bressay.

About half-a-dozen car hire firms are based in the town, but although getting around Mainland island is no problem, it is not possible to take a car to any of the other major islands. A daily bus service links with a ferry which crosses to them all. Even remote Unst and the North Isles can be reached by inter-island steamer. Vehicle ferries soon to come into operation will allow motorists to 'drive' all over Shetland. Some 6m from Lerwick and on the west coast is Scalloway, the ancient capital and now a fishing village. It overlooks a sheltered harbour and is huddled round Scalloway Castle, which was built by Earl Patrick Stewart in 1600. Inland between Scalloway and Lerwick is Clickhimin Broch, an ancient structure which was first occupied in the bronze age and later fortified during the iron age.

Sheer Foula Cliffs are $\frac{1}{4}$m high and can be visited by boat from Scalloway. Foula lies 24m to the west and is dominated by the 1,373ft Sneug. West of the Sneug is the Kame, a cliff 1,220ft high, and about 50 people still live on this remote, fortress-like isle. A mailboat crosses once a week, weather permitting. Scalloway lies at the southern extremity of Tingwall, so called because the site of the old Norse parliament or *ting* was sited at the north end of Tine wall loch. As the tour runs north through Tingwall on the B9074 it crosses the A971, which runs north-west from Lerwick to Walls and Sandness. Walls lies to the south of Shetland's lake district, a wilderness of lochs and burns, and the road ends at Melby, a scattered settlement overlooking the island of Papa Stour, (big isle of the priests). This island's many rock formations include a sea-tunnel almost $\frac{1}{2}$m long and caves which can be explored by boat. After crossing the A971 the B9074

runs north to join the A970 from Lerwick to pass Strand Loch, Girlsta, and Sandwater. A diversion along the east coast on the B9075 is longer but more interesting. The traveller rejoins the A970 near Voe, a prosperous looking village with a Norwegian atmosphere, and beyond here the road crosses the isthmus of Mavis Grind. The parish of Northmavine is so nearly severed from the rest of Mainland that it is said to be possible to throw a stone from the North Sea to the Atlantic.

A diversion to the west leads to Urafirth and Hillswick. The Drongs of Hillswick are spectacular rocks rising like giant's teeth from the sea, and about 7m beyond is Esha Ness, where a lighthouse perches on the edge of a precipice. A walk from here leads to the Grind of Navir, where the Atlantic has found a weakness in the cliff wall and torn a huge, boulder-strewn gateway. Also here are the strange Holes of Scraada. Continue past 1,486ft Ronas Hill towards Isbister. Across the racing tides of Yell Sound lie the North Isles of Yell, Fetlar, and Unst, while to the east lie Whalsay and the Skerries.

Fetlar is where the rare snowy owl breeds, and is so fertile that it has been called the 'garden of Shetland'. Several

burial cairns on 522ft Vord Hill are probably Pictish, and there are remains of Funzie Girt – a stone wall that once divided the island – to the west of the hill. Whalsay is dappled with lochs and dominated by the Ward of Clett, a 393ft hill which affords fine views north-eastwards towards Skerries and Yell. The latter is the second largest of the Shetland Isles and features beautiful cliff scenery. Unst, apart from the rocky islet of Muckle Flugga, is the northernmost point of the British Isles and features the ruins of 16th-c Muness Castle. The northern part of the island has fine cliff scenery. Boats can be hired at the village of Baltasound, and there is a bird sanctuary on the headland of Hermaness. South of Shetland and halfway to

Orkney is Fair Isle – 3m long and only half as wide – which is famous for knitting patterns still wrought by the island women. This island of green fields, bare moors, and sandstone cliffs is owned by the National Trust for Scotland. Its bird observatory is one of the most important in Britain for the study of migrants, has a hostel attached, and has recorded more than 300 species. Fair Isle has a population of about 50 and is accessible by a boat which sails to the island from Grutness near Sumburgh Head twice a week.

The bird observatory on Fair Isle has recorded over 300 species, and is one of the most important centres for the study of migrants in Britain.

Here Be Monsters . . .

The first person to survive a face-to-face encounter with Scotland's most famous monster was a man called Lugne Mocumin. This hero's name has an unfamiliar ring to it, because the incident happened more than 1,400 years ago in the time of St Columba. In the second book of Adamnan's biography of the saint, which was written in the following century, the story is told in some detail. Knowing he was on rather delicate ground, Adamnan went to some pains to assure his readers that he was reporting a historical fact and not just a piece of folklore. During a mission in the country of the Picts, the saint and his followers encountered what Adamnan's Latin called an *aquatilis bestia* in the River Ness, which flows out of Loch Ness into the Moray Firth. They were about to cross the river at a point near present-day Inverness when they noticed a Pictish burial party. It was for a man who had been savaged by a water monster, despite the best efforts of his friends to rescue him with boathooks. Columba, who still wanted to get across, told one of his companions to swim over and bring back a boat which was lying on the far bank. It was then that Lugne Mocumin stepped briefly into recorded history by stripping to his underclothes and diving into the Ness. Halfway across the monster caught sight of him, 'rushed up with a great roar and open mouth' and was within a few feet of sinking its jaws into him when Columba loudly rebuked it, whereupon it scuttled away. Mocumin's attacker may

have been nothing more than a shark in from the open water, and the incident did happen in the River Ness rather than on the loch itself; but the beast from which he escaped may have been an ancestor of the present Loch Ness monster – or, rather, of the breeding species that produces it. Certainly there are many enthusiasts who take Adamnan's 7th-c account as the first recorded sighting of a creature which has defied capture, and even identification, right up to the present day.

Sceptics often say that modern sightings of the Loch Ness monster began to be reported only when the A82 road from Fort Augustus to Inverness was blasted out of the north-west shore in the 1930's, thus opening up the district to floods of gullible tourists. But the people who lived by the loch had spoken about a mysterious creature long before that, and it was in the 1870's that newspapers began to take an interest. A Mr Mackenzie of Abriachan was one of the first to report seeing what he thought at first was a log or an upturned boat suddenly move off at speed across the loch. That 'upturned boat' shape was to be mentioned dozens of times in the years to come. Other reports of strange things in the loch were made by the crew of one of the boats which regularly sailed down from Inverness, along the Caledonian Canal of which Loch Ness is the biggest single part. A workman washing his feet by the shore had the shock of his life, he said,

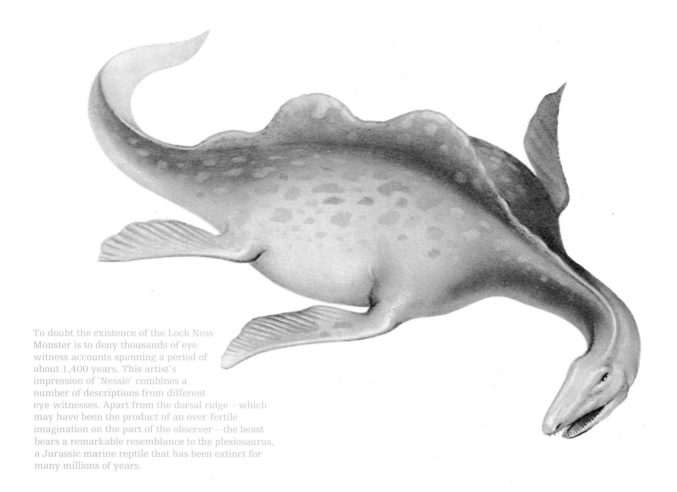

To doubt the existence of the Loch Ness Monster is to deny thousands of eye-witness accounts spanning a period of about 1,400 years. This artist's impression of 'Nessie' combines a number of descriptions from different eye-witnesses. Apart from the dorsal ridge – which may have been the product of an over-fertile imagination on the part of the observer – the beast bears a remarkable resemblance to the plesiosaurus, a Jurassic marine reptile that has been extinct for many millions of years.

when a great head reared out of the water beside him. Two boys fishing out from Urquhart Castle were so frightened by something like a serpent in the loch that they rushed home and were forbidden to mention it again. Even the head keeper on one of the local estates was so shattered by the sight of an enormous animal surfacing alongside his boat that he needed a brandy in the Drumnadrochit Hotel to regain his composure.

A more significant incident involved some divers who were sent down to search for the body of a visitor who had drowned in the loch. The first diver came up almost at once, saying that it was far too dangerous because of the massive eels which interfered with his air line; so did the second, who was a Royal Navy man from Invergordon; and so did the third, who was imported from London and knew nothing of the previous misadventures. All said that the eels were giants of their kind. It was in 1933, after the new road opened, that the sightings began to increase in number. One very respected local man who claimed to have seen a 30ft creature with a small tapering head and a long thin neck was Alex Campbell of Fort Augustus, who was a correspondent for the *Inverness Courier* and also the water bailiff on one of the lochside estates. Tourists began to write to the newspapers too, although a local police constable who went to check one story about a great red beast with fearsome horns rampaging about the edge of the loch met only a calm red Highland cow. The pilot of an aeroplane reported seeing something like a giant alligator. National newspapers sent special correspondents to Loch Ness, and they usually returned to their city offices making rude remarks about ignorant countryfolk. The monster was mentioned in the House of

Commons, and its protection was discussed at the annual general meeting of the Ness Fishery Board. A circus offered £20,000 to anyone who would capture it alive, and the Chief Constable of Inverness-shire was prodded into issuing an order that it should not be molested.

It was in November 1933 that the first of many photographs was offered in evidence. Hugh Gray, who lived by the lochside, produced a picture of some unidentified object creating a disturbance in the water. Kodak certified that the film had not been faked. One scientist said it obviously showed a whale, another that there was no reason to believe it showed a living creature at all. Soon afterwards, an expedition headed by somebody who called himself a big-game hunter was financed by the *Daily Mail*. In a remarkably short time he found tracks which, he said, reminded him of hippopotamus spoor he had seen in Africa. Plaster casts of the footprints were sent to the Natural History Department of the British Museum, who reported back that this must be a very strange creature indeed, because all its tracks appeared to be made by the stuffed and mounted right hind hoof of the same juvenile hippo. Films were made and have mysteriously disappeared, or have survived only as vague single frames. Sir Edward Mountain, an insurance tycoon, financed a more serious expedition which produced no definite evidence. Monster parties dedicated and frivolous came and went. Theories were battered back and forth between scientists and amateur naturalists. Some said the monster was a seal, others that it was simply the occasional appearance on the surface of logs of wood shot up from the bottom by the gases from their own decomposition. One learned

Some schools of thought consider it possible that giant, ancient reptiles like the plesiosaurus may have been able to survive devastating climatic changes by seeking the shelter of very deep water. Whether such creatures could survive the Ice Age and keep their numbers up sufficiently to become the monsters of Scottish legend is a matter of opinion – but it is still a serious and exciting possibility. Creatures which the scientific world has thought extinct have been found – very much alive – in recent years, so a surviving, if greatly evolved, plesiosaur is not entirely beyond the bounds of reason.

gentleman decided that a photograph he examined was of the dorsal fin of a whale which had sneaked through the series of canal locks at Inverness at the same time as a coaster. Gradually, as hoax followed honest report, and possibly genuine picture followed obvious fake, national interest in the monster died away. But even though the armchair pundits had finished with Loch Ness for a while, few of the people who lived round its shores treated the monster stories as a joke. Several of the monks at the Benedictine abbey of Fort Augustus were eye-witnesses, and local boatmen, estate workers, foresters, and gamekeepers were less likely than excited visitors to be fooled by rafts of rotting vegetation or the wake of out-of-sight motor boats. During the second world war there were obviously fewer sightings, as the former tourists were far away on grimmer business; but one was reported by a member of the Royal Observer Corps on duty looking out for German bombers. Nessie also played her part in the Axis war effort, when the Italian air force, with few other successes to crow about, reported gleefully that one of its heroic pilots had not only located the monster but had actually managed to sink it.

In peacetime again the hunt continued. Between 1949 and 1957 Mrs Constance Whyte compiled an imposing list of sightings made by local people. In 1960 Tim Dinsdale, an aeronautical engineer, shot 50ft of telephoto film which showed something swimming towards the far shore. It was played over on *Panorama*, and some years later the Joint Air Reconnaissance Centre of the Ministry of Defence, Britain's most experienced photo-interpretation organization, analysed the film carefully. After a mass of technical detail, its report concluded that what was shown

on the film was probably an animate object with a body not less than 6ft wide and 5ft high in cross-section. In 1962 and 1963 came the first two short expeditions organized by the Loch Ness Phenomena Investigation Bureau, whose founders included Mrs Whyte, the naturalist Peter Scott, and Richard Fitter, nature correspondent of the *Observer*. Science began to move in. Several expeditions tried out underwater microphones and sonar, following a strange record on the echo-sounding chart of the trawler 'Rival', which seemed to show something 50ft long passing through the loch 500ft below the boat. Cambridge University came into the act with an expedition which kept watch from four boats for a total of 480 hours. The result was a total of sixteen reported 'sightings', eight of which were reckoned to be wave formations, six birds, one an otter, and one a leaping salmon. But even they would not go as far as to say that they had disproved the monster theory.

Despite a continuing series of what seemed like hoaxes – including one photograph, treated for a while with reverence, which looks like a bad picture of a polythene bag and was eventually suspected to be nothing more than that – Loch Ness attracted more and more businesslike searchers. In 1968 Birmingham University came along with a sonar probe. After several days it recorded a large object rising from the bottom of the loch and moving at 9 knots. It never surfaced, but was tracked underwater for thirteen minutes. Next year more mysterious objects were tracked by sonar from a specially chartered boat. In 1969 baited hooks were let down from a trawler, which also trailed its nets far down in the loch; but nothing came up. A one-man submarine was brought from America, and its pilot complained that nobody had told him the peaty water brought down by the mountain burns restricts visibility in places to no more than 12in. Infra-red cameras were used as a way round this problem. A Vickers research submarine went to Loch Ness for trials, discovered that the bed of the loch was much deeper than earlier soundings had suggested, and picked up another sonar trace in 520ft of water near Urquhart Castle.

Interested parties who either believe in some unknown monster inhabiting the loch, or believe that there is some perfectly ordinary explanation, have said that what has appeared on photographs – apart from the obvious hoaxes – must be a seal, a seal flipper, a sea-cow, a mat of vegetable matter, a tree trunk, the wake of a boat, an upturned boat, a boat the right way up, a dinosaur, a plesiosaurus, a giant newt, a giant worm, a giant eel, a dragon, a line of otters or swimming deer, a slug, a mollusc, or a dozen other things. Certainly, Loch Ness itself is a strange enough place. It is 24m long, reaches 970ft in its deepest recorded area, and contains an estimated 263,000,000,000 cubic feet of water – three times as much as Loch Lomond – for the most part impenetrable to the human eye. When monks, gamekeepers, fishermen, and schoolteachers who have lived for years round the shores – and would have nothing to gain from a hoax – say they believe there is an unexplained 'something' in the loch, casual visitors can ill afford to scoff. And most of Scotland would like there to be a monster of Loch Ness.

Although it has captured most of the headlines, Loch Ness is not the only inland Scottish water to have its monster stories. Years ago, there were recognized Gaelic names for creatures in three Highland lochs: *An Niseag* lived in Loch Ness, *An Seileag* in Loch Shiel and *A'Mhorag* in Loch Morar; and these were only the most often discussed. Loch Shiel has not played much part in recent investigations,

but attention has been directed to lovely Loch Morar, east of the road from Arisaig to Fort William. This is another unusual place, an 11m loch edged by mountains, with a scatter of islands and the deepest bed of any inland water in western Europe; and yet the seaward end is only 400yds from the Atlantic shore. Being in the West Highlands, the district has had tales of the supernatural for centuries. The Grey Dog of Meoble, for instance, was supposed to appear red-eyed and slavering to travellers in the woods between Arisaig and Morar. An unearthly monster surfacing in the loch was believed to signal a death in one of the local families. More solid and less supernatural occurrences began to be mentioned about a century ago. There were tales of what sounded like the humped creature sometimes described in Loch Ness – like a sail-less boat towing other boats across the loch. In 1931 an experienced angler reported losing his fishing line and the end of his rod to the heaviest creature he had ever hooked. In 1948 something unknown displayed itself to a boat-load of tourists. Then in 1969 came the adventure that brought Loch Morar into the headlines.

Two Mallaig men were coming back one evening from a boat trip to the head of the loch. Suddenly a heavy creature of some kind bumped against the boat and seemed likely to upset it. One of the men tried to fend it off with an oar, and the other fired a shot to frighten it. Newspapers all over the western world got hold of the story and sensationalized it; but the sober evidence was that the men claimed to have seen a creature 25ft to 30ft long, with rough, dirty-brown skin and three separate humps or undulations. It had a snakelike head and stayed in their sight for five minutes. In 1970 the Loch Morar Survey was founded. It gathered reports of 33 sightings from 1887 onwards. Experiments were made with hydrophones, and camera points were set up; but nothing positive came to light. Another organization which had already made a sonar survey had ambitions to use tranquilizer darts in an underwater pursuit; whatever may be in the loch, few people would relish a confrontation with it 1,000ft below the surface. Not much more has been heard of the scheme. There are monster stories from other Highland lochs, and many of them do not need to

Loch Ness is not the only Scottish water to hold a monster. Two men returning from the head of Loch Morar in 1969 encountered a 25ft to 30ft 'something' which very nearly upset their boat. Their description of the beast tallies with various Loch Ness sightings, even down to the undulating dorsal ridge.

be treated too seriously, even by believers in Nessie and Morag. North west of Poolewe in Wester Ross, on the road to a beautifully situated place called Mellon Udrigle on the shore of Gruinard Bay, is a stretch of water still called Loch na Beiste. In the 1840's the estate was the property of a wealthy English shipowner called Bankes. One Sunday Sandy Macleod, a Free Church elder on his way home with two friends from a service at Aultbea, was astonished to see a beast in the loch. It was as big as a good-sized boat with the keel turned up. Another day a second elder saw much the same thing. His tenants appealed to Mr Bankes to do something about it.

He owned a yacht called the 'Iris', crewed by James and Allan Mackenzie. The two seamen and other helpers were instructed to man a large pump which was set up on the outflow from the loch, to drain off all the water. It was by no means a casual job, because channels were cut and pipes were laid to take the water away without causing any damage. The work continued intermittently, as was the way of the west, for something like two years. Unfortunately the capacity of the pump was not much greater than the inflow of water to the loch from the various burns and seepages which fed it. After two years, the level of Loch na Beiste had gone down by no more

than 6in. Mr Bankes lost his temper, realizing that it would be doomsday at that rate before the little loch was drained. He sent the 'Iris' to Broadford in Skye to pick up fourteen barrels of lime, which would be poured into the monster's lair. The 'Iris's' dinghy was launched on the loch, and the estate factor was instructed to climb aboard. Like a sensible man he would have nothing to do with it. The two Mackenzies were given the job, and began by rowing over the whole surface of the loch, which is about 600yds long and a third of that wide. They plumbed the water with an oar, finding it in few places more than a fathom deep, except at one part which they reckoned at $2\frac{1}{2}$ fathoms. All fourteen barrels of lime were emptied into that hole. It did not improve the fishing, but there was no sign whatever of a monster. Mr Bankes was not happy, especially as he had been made to look a fool in an account of the two-year hunt which appeared in *Punch*. To revenge himself on his tenants he slapped an extra charge of £1 on their year's rents, thus helping to recover part of the cost of an embarrassing episode. The beast of Loch na Beiste was never heard of again.

Monster fever also gripped appropriately-named Loch na Beiste in the 19thc, when a Free Church elder saw a large, ill-defined shape in the water. Attempts to drain the loch were unsuccessful, so Mr Bankes the owner attempted to flush the beast out by pouring large quantities of lime into the deepest part. This story has picturesque rather than believable qualities, as the depth of the loch averaged little more than a fathom.

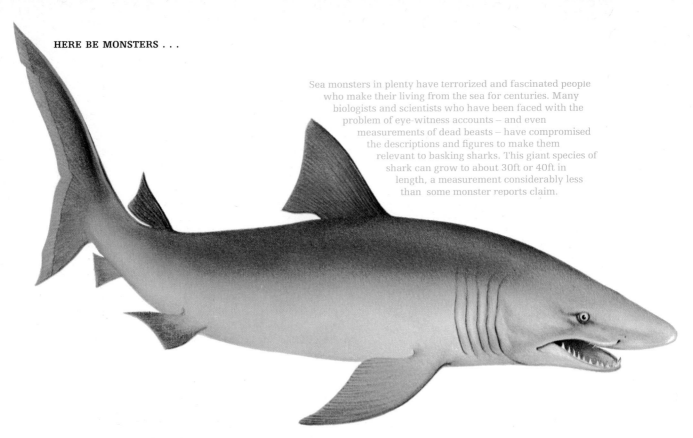

A similar escapade enlivened the district of Sleat in Skye during the year 1840. Loch nan Dubhrachan was said to be infested by a fearsome beast which tried to drag unwary night-time travellers into the water. The laird agreed to try to flush it out. A holiday was declared, the children were let out of school, and dozens of local families came to see the loch being dragged by a long net fixed to a pair of boats. All went well until the net snagged on something underwater, at which point the bystanders took to their heels. The dragging was completed, and all that ever came out of the loch was a pair of pike. In the last century, when tales of sea-serpents came from all over the world, the north and west coasts of Scotland were not missed out. An early report came from the Reverend Donald Maclean of the island of Eigg, who wrote about his experience to the Wernerian Natural History Society of Edinburgh. In June 1808 he was forced to beach a rowing boat on the coast of Coll when attacked by a creature that surfaced near him. After being almost stranded in shallow water as it made for the boat, it swam off to sea, but not before Mr Maclean had noted its broad head, 'of a form somewhat oval'. The neck was thinner, but the body widened again before tapering towards the tail. He could see no fins, and reported that it seemed to 'move progressively by undulation up and down'. Its length he estimated at 70ft to 80ft. In his letter, he added that at about the same time the monster was seen off the island of Canna. The crews of thirteen fishing boats were so terrified that they fled in a body to the nearest shore.

Three months later it may have reappeared. At least, in September 1808 came the strange occurrence of the Stronsay monster. John Peace, who lived at Rothiesholm on the Orkney island of Stronsay, was fishing from his boat when he noticed what he took at first to be a dead whale on some sunken rocks. Six weeks later, in a statement he made before two Justices of the Peace in Kirkwall, he said that when he reached it he found it to be different from a whale, particularly in having six fins or arms which ended in toes and had rows of long bristles on them. He pulled off some of the bristles and kept them for souvenirs. Ten days afterwards a gale drove the remains ashore, and when he measured the body with

a fathom-line he reckoned it to be nearly 55ft long. Similar statements about the length were made by two other farmers and a carpenter. The neck alone, they said, was 15ft long, and they all agreed that the creature, even in its decomposing state, had six bristled fins or legs or arms. A local artist made a picture from a sketch which George Sherar, one of the eye-witnesses, had drawn in chalk on a table. Some bones which Sherar had rescued were sent to an eminent anatomist in London, who was at that time preparing a weighty tome on the basking shark. He regarded the carpenter's measurement of 55ft as 'at least doubtful', cavalierly reduced it to 30ft to fit in with his own theories, and entered the Stronsay monster in his new book as a fine example of a basking shark. Baulking at his patronizing tone, Scots-based scientists reacted fiercely. One went so far as to claim that 'the existence of the seasnake, a monster 55ft long, is placed beyond doubt. However, some of the vertebrae were preserved at the Royal Scottish Museum in Edinburgh, and 120 years after the event the Keeper of the Natural History Department agreed that, national pride apart, the Stronsay monster really must have been a basking shark; even he reduced the length to 40ft, so part of the mystery remains.

Perhaps the most detailed of all encounters with what might have been a sea-serpent happened in August 1872. The Reverend John Macrae, a keen amateur naturalist, was minister of Glenelg, a parish on the Sound of Sleat facing Skye. He was one of a party of six who sailed from Glenelg village the few miles south into Loch Hourn, another part of his vast and scattered charge. One of his companions was the Reverend David Twopeny of Stockbury in Kent, and after their strange experience the two men wrote an article that was published in the *Zoologist* magazine. It was a calm day, and they had to start rowing: 'As we got the cutter along with the oars we perceived a dark mass about 200yds astern of us, to the north. While we were looking at it with our glasses (we had three on board) another similar black lump rose to the left of the first, leaving an interval between; then another and another followed, all in regular order. We did not doubt its being one living creature: it moved slowly across our wake, and disappeared. Presently the first mass, which was evidently the head, reappeared and was followed by the rising of the other black lumps, as before.' The ministers – and Mr Macrae knew the waters of the sound well – estimated its length at 45ft. It seemed to notice them: 'Presently, as we were watching the creature, it began to approach us rapidly, causing a great agitation in the sea. Nearly the whole of its body, if not all of it, had now disappeared, and the head advanced at a great rate in the midst of a shower of fine spray, which was evidently raised in some way by the quick movement of the animal . . . When within about 100yds of us it sank and moved away in the direction of Skye, just under the surface of the water, for we could trace its course by the waves it raised on the still sea for a mile or more.'

When they came back from Loch Hourn the next day the party were becalmed again, and saw the creature making at high speed up the loch, where a fishing boat crew later reported seeing it. The ministers were rowing round the coast some time later, past Sandaig (which years afterwards was to be the 'Camusfearna' of Gavin Maxwell's otter books) when they were overtaken again: 'It went with great rapidity, its black head only being visible through the clear sea, followed by a long trail of agitated water. As it shot along the noise of its rush through the water could be distinctly heard on board. There were no organs of motion to be seen, nor was there any shower of spray as on the day before, but merely such a commotion in the sea as its quick passage might be expected to make. Its progress was equable and smooth, like that of a log towed rapidly.'

That same evening the ferrymen on both sides of Kylerhea, where there was a crossing to Skye, saw and heard the creature rush through the narrow strait. They wondered

By no stretch of the imagination can the basking shark be equated with the traditional sea serpent. This gigantic animal is reported to move by means of undulations through its entire eel-like body, which occasionally breaks the surface of the water as a series of humps. Illustrated is an impression of the Stronsay monster, sighted by the Rev John Macrae in 1872.

if it might be a school of porpoises, which still disport themselves in the Sound of Sleat, but for the unusual speed. Whatever it was, it seems to have stayed in the district. Ten days later Alexander Hamilton, a Dornie boatbuilder, saw it in Loch Duich, heard the noise as it rushed through the water, and was 'much alarmed'. In a separate article, Mr Twopeny said that the two ministers had been offered all kinds of explanations for what they had seen, from porpoises and lumps of seaweed to empty herring barrels, logs of wood, waves of the sea, and inflated pigskins: 'But as all these theories present to our minds much greater difficulties than the existence of the animal itself, we feel obliged to decline them.' This was not the last time a strange creature was seen in these waters. In September 1893 Dr Farquhar Matheson, an ear, nose, and throat specialist on holiday from London, was sailing across Loch Alsh from Dornie to the farm of Ardintoul on the south shore. His boat was sailing well in a gusty wind when something suddenly rose up out of the water in front of it, 200yds away and coming closer:

'It began to draw its neck down, and I saw clearly that it was a large sea-monster – of the saurian type, I should think. It was brown in colour, shining, and with a sort of ruffle at the junction of the head and neck. I can think of nothing with which to compare it so well as the head and neck of the giraffe, only the neck was much longer, and the head was not set upon the neck like that of a giraffe; that is, it was not so much at right angles to it as a continuation of it in the same line. The creature made off at great speed towards Kyle of Lochalsh: I saw no body – only a ripple of water where the line of the body should be. I should judge, however, that there must have been a large base of body to support such a neck . . . It was something of the nature of a giant lizard, I should think. An eel could not lift up its body like that, nor could a snake.'

One of the last accounts of a sea monster off the Scottish coast came in August 1919 from Mr J Mackintosh Bell, a lawyer who lived in Moffat. He was taking a month's holiday working on an Orkney fishing boat which belonged to some friends of his. As they sailed from the island of Hoy to lift some lobster creels laid between Brims Ness and Tor Ness, something appeared in the water close by: 'A long neck as thick as an elephant's foreleg, all rough-looking like an elephant's hide, was sticking up. On top of this was the head, which was much smaller in proportion, but of the same colour. The head was like that of a dog, coming sharp to the nose. The eye was black and small, and the whiskers were black. The neck, I should say, stuck about 5ft to 6ft, possibly more, out of the water.' In years to come Mr Bell's Monster was to be dismissed as some unusual species of long-necked seal, just as the Stronsay monster was considered a basking shark. But what about

The sea serpent seen off the Orkneys by a lawyer in 1919 was said to have had a neck the thickness of an elephant's leg. There is a ring of truth about his description, in that the neck ruffles might form a gill arrangement performing a similar function to that of an ordinary eel.

the sea-serpent of the Sound of Sleat and the incident in Loch Alsh? Many people involved in monster hunts have been guilty of hoaxes, but it would be a brave man who would say that a Highland parish minister, a vicar of the Church of England, a successful surgeon, or a lawyer would lay themselves open to the chance of ridicule which could ruin their professional careers and standing.

Scotland has not much to offer in the way of land-based monsters. One of these, however, managed to weave itself into the story of a noble family, and is recalled in a faded carving above the door of a Norman parish church. The place was Linton, south east of Kelso and a few miles on the Scottish side of the border with England. About 800 years ago, the story goes, the district round the village and as far away as the town of Jedburgh was terrorized by a great 'worm' or dragon which lived in a place still pointed out as the worm's den. William de Somerville, laird of nearby Larriston whose family had come from

France with William the Conqueror, decided to destroy it. He knew that the beast always attacked with its great mouth wide open, and planned to deal with it accordingly. On the day he rode out to tackle it he carried a lance tipped with peat, which was soaked in pitch. When the dragon appeared Somerville's servant lit the peat and ran for his life. As the monster reared up at him, Somerville plunged the blazing peat down its throat, and it expired in the flames. In its final agonies the Worm of Linton coiled its tail round a hillock, and there are people who will point out the ridges it squeezed out of the hill. Somerville was rewarded by being made the royal falconer and was granted the barony of Linton as an extra reward. Well, there was a historical character called William de Somerville, who was a witness to a document dated 1124 and to various later papers. He was indeed the overlord of Linton, and one of his successors was later created Lord Somerville. The story of the original Somerville of Linton and his fight with the dragon is still told; but the *Scots Peerage*, a definitive work, deals brusquely with the old tale and declares that it was produced to match the carved stone above the church door which shows a knight battling with a hazy monster, and not the other way round.

Scotland also has a few land-based monsters, or dragons. This creature is said to have terrorized the people of Linton some 800 years ago before being despatched in true George-and-the-Dragon style by William de Somerville. The size of this 'worm' prompts the question as to where it could hide!

All was quiet at Fyvie Castle until rebuilding work earlier this century revealed a skeleton. Soon after the bones were removed a Green Lady appeared, and stayed until the remains were reburied.

Monsters, sea-serpents, and dragons are tangible things, even in the imagination. Throughout the centuries, Scotland has had more than its fair share of less substantial creatures: apparitions, ghosts, and eerie presences. One of the most famous is the haunting of Duncan Campbell of Inverawe, laird of an estate to the east of Oban. Campbell's home was Inverawe House, which is still occupied as a private residence today. One stormy night in 1740 a frantic stranger begged to be let in because he had killed a man whose friends were in hot pursuit. According to the laws of Highland hospitality Duncan Campbell had to shelter the man, only to learn later the same night that the victim had been one of his own family. The murdered man's ghost appeared before Inverawe that night and the next demanding vengeance. The fugitive slipped away, but the apparition came back on the third night. It pointed at Campbell and cried farewell, 'till we meet at Ticonderoga'.

Campbell told his household the strange tale next morning, making note of the odd and unfamiliar name. For years after that it slipped his memory. In 1744 he joined the Black Watch, rose to the rank of major, and in 1756 sailed with his regiment to North America to join the fight against the French. In July 1758 the British forces prepared to attack the French garrison at Fort Carillon. A friend of Campbell's suddenly learned from a scout that the Indian name of the place was none other than Ticonderoga. The secret was kept from Campbell, but not for long. On the night before the final assault he saw again the spectre which had not appeared to him for eighteen years. He guessed at once that this was the place where he was to die. And so he did, although he was at first wounded only in the arm. It was a small thing, but infection set in and the arm had to be amputated. Campbell waited for the inevitable, and death came to him nine days later. The room where the ghost appeared at Inverawe House is still known as the Ticonderoga Room.

Many of Scotland's great houses have their unearthly tenants. At Glamis Castle guests have reported nightly visions of murder and assault. The castle is said to be haunted by the ghost of Jane Douglas, who was burned at the stake in the time of James V. Earlier this century a skeleton was uncovered during some rebuilding work at Fyvie Castle. The bones were removed. Soon a Green Lady began to appear, and her restless spirit was laid to rest only when the old skeleton was reburied. A similar apparition has appeared at Crathes Castle, the 16th-c showpiece near Banchory now in the care of the NTS. She appears sometimes with a baby, and the story is that she is the ghost of a daughter of one of the early lairds who disgraced her family by having a child by some low-born local man. Again, skeletons matching the story have been found during rebuilding work. At another NTS property in the north-east, Leith Hall near Kennethmont, guests have reported hearing groans and violent argument.

A well-known West Highland story is that of the 17th-c piper of Duntrune. During one of the civil wars a force of Macdonalds under their chief Coll Ciotach planned to attack the Campbell stronghold of Duntrune, which stands near the western end of the Crinan Canal. Coll sent his piper as a spy to find out the castle's defences. Seeing that the place was too heavily guarded, the piper began to play a tune well known as a warning. The sound carried to the waiting Macdonalds; but the Campbells heard it too. Seizing the piper, they slashed off his fingers and put him to death. Just before the first world war a fingerless skeleton was disinterred; and even in the 1970's an uneasy presence has been sensed at Duntrune.

At the grim ruined keep of Hermitage Castle in a lonely Border valley, there were tales for generations of the ghost of the evil Lord Soulis, a black magician said to have captured the young children of some of his tenants for his grisly rituals. The outraged parents stormed the castle, bound Lord Soulis in chains and a jacket of lead, and boiled him alive. Craigcrook Castle in the north west of Edinburgh was built in the 1540's. It has been restored and turned into offices for architects and engineers; despite this prosaic modern use, the building is affected by some kind of poltergeist which enjoys throwing lighter items of office equipment around. Outside Glasgow, at Bedlay Castle near Chryston on the Stirling road, the owner has been running an antiques business since 1969. Reports of a Bedlay ghost first appeared 80 years before that, and today there are still unexpected footsteps and a strange something that has been felt brushing against a woman's hair. There is even a modern council house in Irvine said to be haunted by the spirit of an old woman in white. There are outdoor hauntings too. In the great sweep of wild, deserted coastline between Kinlochbervie and Cape Wrath is Sandwood Bay, with a lonely ruined cottage. Not many people find their way to Sandwood, but several of those who have walked by the bay have been surprised by the figure of a man in old-fashioned sailor's clothes. He was once greatly annoyed by a visitor who picked up some driftwood, and did not dissolve until she had put it down.

The eeriest place in all of outdoor Scotland, however, is the mountain top of Ben MacDhui, more than 4,000ft up in the Cairngorm plateau. It is the second-highest mountain in Britain, not far from the ski-ing grounds of Glenmore and the busy holiday centres of the Spey Valley. The story of *Am Fear Liath Mor*, the Big Grey Man, is no vague yarn from out of the Celtic twilight. It was originally mentioned in the 18thc; but the first firm account of a meeting with

some hostile presence on the mountain came from Norman Collie, professor of organic chemistry at London University. It was only in 1925 that Collie told in detail of an experience on Ben MacDhui 34 years before. Coming down from the summit in misty conditions, he began to hear a crunching noise that sounded like someone else's footsteps. But there were no other climbers to be seen near by. As the descent continued and the sound kept pace with him, he realized that, although the footsteps were always close behind, whatever was making them took steps three or four times as long as his own. A terror took hold of him, and he ended up by running as hard as he could down the bouldery slope until he was safe in the valley some 5m away. Other climbers have written of sensing some unseen companion on Ben MacDhui. Unexplained footsteps have been reported many more times, and several accounts have been published of weird psychic experiences on the mountain. Some climbers have felt themselves being pulled by a near-fatal attraction towards the edge of a precipice. Similar happenings have been reported from the Lairig Ghru, the right of way from Aviemore to Deeside which runs between Ben MacDhui and Braeriach. Even the formation of the Glenmore forest park and the Cairngorms national nature reserve has not quelled the feeling that some unearthly force has its home on Ben MacDhui's wild, sub-Arctic slopes.

Mountains all over the world have their supernatural guardians and elemental spirits, and the Scottish peaks are no exception. The *Am Fear Liath Mor* of Ben MacDhui is a formless grey presence that dogs the footsteps of anyone caught in the grey mist of the Cairngorm plateau. It was first mentioned in the 18thc and has been well documented by various climbers and walkers since then.

In a country with a violent history it is not surprising that ghostly battles have been seen. From Loch Ashie, south of Inverness, there have been several reports of a phantom army sweeping across the high moorland and the road. Beside the A9 between Dunkeld and Blair Atholl, visitors claim to have seen spectral soldiers fleeing from the rout of Killiecrankie. Even Iona, the sacred isle of St Columba, has been the scene of ghostly fights.

With so much coastline and so many islands, Scotland is a prime place for mermaids. Often they were referred to as the seal-folk, and even in this century there have been tales of fishermen in lonely places frightened nearly out of their wits when they wandered into a darkened inlet among the cliffs and saw a dim figure watching them from a rock. A favourite story from the island of Unst in Shetland and elsewhere is of a man walking by a beach in moonlight who sees the seal-folk in human form, dancing on the shore with their sealskins thrown on the sand. He is suddenly discovered, but in the general rush of the seal-folk to dive beneath the waves he manages to escape with one of the skins. Later he goes back to the shore to discover a beautiful girl – there are few ugly mermaids – weeping for the skin without which she can never return to her real home. They marry and have children, but she is often unhappy, spending hours by the shore looking helplessly to sea. One day her son or daughter finds the long-hidden skin; she slips it on, and her human husband is just too late to stop her from rushing to the beach and swimming off to join her seal husband, who is conveniently close by. In the 1880's a man called Roderick Mackenzie, who lived near Gairloch in Wester

Ross, used to tell a fine tale of how he once surprised a sleeping mermaid. He grasped her by the hair, and she cried that if he would only let her go she would grant him one special wish. He said he wished that nobody would ever be drowned from one of his boats; but as Roderick Mackenzie was by trade the boatbuilder of Port Henderson, he may simply have found it useful to be able to give his customers a better than usual guarantee.

Inland lochs and running water used to be considered the territory of all manner of strange creatures. Loch Achtriochtan in Glencoe was believed to be the home of a water-bull, St Mary's Loch in the Borders the home of a prolific water-cow. A small loch beside the road from Corgarff to Tomintoul was thought to be the home of some water-spirit who kept dragging travellers to their doom. An expedition was formed to drain the loch and so reveal the bodies. The men had just arrived with their picks and spades to hack out a channel that would act as a drain when there was a great bellow, and a little man with a red cap bounded outraged from the water. As the men ran off in terror he hurled all the picks and spades into the loch, gave a roar that echoed round the hills, and went back to the peace from which he has never again been disturbed. Fords were always considered especially dangerous places. Three centuries ago, according to one tale, a ford on the River Conon in Easter Ross near an old graveyard and a now-ruined church, was the home of a kelpie. Sometimes, determined people throwing stones at it could make a kelpie keep out of innocent travellers' way; but the kelpie of the River Conon claimed at least one victim. Local people cutting corn in a field near the ford heard an eerie voice calling. They looked around

Always beautiful and usually sad, the maidens of the seal people live in legends from the Duchy of Cornwall to Wales and the Scottish coast. Their form varies; this Shetland mermaid could only take to the sea with the aid of her seal skin.

and saw the kelpie standing in the river at a place that was called the false ford. Although the water looked shallow there it was really a deep pool, and the genuine ford was some distance away. A rider was seen urging his horse to the false ford. The locals, realizing his danger, ran over to stop him and show him the correct way; but he was too impatient to pay any attention, and they finally dragged him off his horse and locked him in the church out of harm's way. The kelpie stayed for an hour, and then disappeared. When his rescuers went to release the man from the church they found – with all the inevitability of the best horror stories – that in trying to climb out of a window he had fallen head-first into a trough of water and drowned on dry land.

Occasionally water-spirits could be put to work. Graham of Morphie, laird of a property north of Montrose, once managed to put shafts and a harness on a water-horse from the Pontage Pool on the River North Esk that ran close to his estate. He harnessed it to a cart, with which he carried load after load of stones to build a castle, now to be seen in ruins. Once the work was finished the water-horse was released. Exhausted by its labours, it put a rhyming curse on the Grahams of Morphie, that they would never flourish as long as he lived in the North Esk. In time, of course, the last of the family died without an heir and the estate passed into other hands. Sir Walter Scott recalled the story of another water-spirit at the old house of Gorrenberry, in the same lonely Border valley as Hermitage Castle. This one was a bogle called Shellycoat, from his suit of shells which rattled whenever he appeared. His habit was to groan 'Lost! Lost!' when some late-night travellers came by, and as they searched for him, lead them higher and higher into the hills until he had them miles off their intended route, when he would laugh and disappear to his watery home.

Kelpies and bogles are masters of black mischief. The Shellycoat bogle is said to have derived great amusement from luring travellers miles out of their way and leaving them bemused and stranded in the hills.

More friendly creatures were the brownies or glaistigs, which in different parts of the country acted like unpaid servants in castles and farmhouses. The lucky household which sheltered one of these hard-working creatures would find its bread baked, the cows milked, the fires set, pots and pans cleaned. But they were very sensitive to slights real or imagined. One which used to help about a farm near Moffat took offence at something and moved to the nearby mansion of Leithen Hall, where it worked happily for 300 years while the original farm sank into bankruptcy and decay. There was a brownie at Castle Lachlan by the shore of Loch Fyne; another on the island of Cara off Kintyre; still more at Cullachy House near Fort Augustus, the Doune of Rothiemurchus near Aviemore, and Dunollie Castle near Oban. Island House on Tiree, built in 1748, is the home of the estate factor. In years gone by stories were told of a hard-working glaistig which served the household and could even be heard scolding the human servants when their work was carelessly done. In 1972 the current occupier of the house wrote a magazine article explaining that there was still

91

an unseen friendly presence there. Even yet there are sounds as of furniture being dragged across the floor, of low uncanny music, and lights have been seen from outside the house showing in unlit rooms.

When the Norsemen came to settle and control the Scottish islands they brought stories of their homeland trolls with them. In Orkney and Shetland the ugly dwarfs became known as trows. Some lived on land, and when their children sickened crept into houses and exchanged them for human babies. They delighted in making things difficult for young couples about to be married, but in some households acted much as the brownies did in the rest of Scotland. The sea trows were stupid creatures who did nothing more than steal fish from lines rather than find food for themselves. The last of the Orkney trows, according to one old story, tried to escape from the advance of civilization by walking a tightrope to the safe, secluded island of Hoy; but the rope broke and they were all drowned. Trows are now nothing more than memories.

Trows or trolls came with the Norsemen and could either be helpful or irritating and stupid. Tradition has it that the last trows died when a tightrope which they were walking to the secluded island of Hoy broke, plunging them all into the sea.

Dunvegan Castle in Skye, ancestral home of the chiefs of Clan Macleod, is perhaps Scotland's only tangible link with fairyland. The fairy flag of Dunvegan came into the family's hands at some mysterious time in the long-dead past, but its tattered remains are still kept safe in the castle. Several versions are told of how it came to be in the Macleods' possession; but all are agreed that when unfurled the flag can conjure out of the air a great army of armed men. A terrible penalty would be exacted from the island of Skye if the flag were to be unfurled for some unworthy reason, and its magic properties will be seen on only three occasions, two of which are long since past. In many parts of Scotland there are places called Elfhill or Elfhillock, where fairies are supposed to have lived or suddenly appeared. A much more solid reminder is a gravestone in the old churchyard at the Kirkton of Aberfoyle, beside one of the entrance roads to Loch Ard Forest. It is to the Reverend Robert Kirk, parish minister at the end of the 17thc; but there are severe doubts about whether his body is buried there, or indeed anywhere on earth. Mr Kirk was a noted Gaelic scholar, and as well as ministering at Aberfoyle from 1685 to 1692 he produced a fine Gaelic translation of the Bible. It is for another literary work, however, that he is best remembered.

Known as *The Secret Commonwealth*, it was an examination of 'the Nature and Actions of the Subterranean (and, for the most part) Invisible People, heretofore going under the names of Elves, Faunes, Fairies, and the lyke, among the Low-Country Scots . . . and now, to occasion further Inquiry, collected and compared, by a Circumspect Inquirer residing among the Scottish-Irish in Scotland'.

Fairies, wrote Mr Kirk, are 'of intelligent studious Spirits, and light changeable Bodies (lyke those called Astral) somewhat of the Nature of a condensed Cloud, and best seen in Twilight. These Bodies be so plyable through the Subtilty of the Spirits that agitate them, that they can make them appear or disappear att Pleasure.' 'Mortals,' he said, 'have a chance to see fairies four times every year. They are condemned till doomsday to change their lodgings at every quarter: Their chamaelion-lyke Bodies swim in the Air near the Earth with Bag and Bagadge; and at such revolution of Time, Seers, or Men of the Second Sight (Faemales being seldome so qualified) have very terrifying Encounters with them even on High Ways.' Perhaps Mr Kirk got too close, during his detailed researches, to the truth about fairies. When still in middle age, and with his wife expecting a child, he died. What happened then has been recounted in the district for generations, and even into this century has been the subject of several books and pamphlets. His funeral took place in the old churchyard in 1692; soon afterwards, he appeared as a ghost to a local man who was well known

to himself and to Graham of Duchray, laird of a large estate nearby. The man was to explain to Duchray that Mr Kirk was not in fact dead, but had simply been spirited away to fairyland. There was only one chance to bring him back. When his child was baptized, he would appear in the church. Duchray was to attend the service, and take a knife with him. At the moment when his old friend materialized he was to hurl the knife over the apparition's head, and Mr Kirk would be restored to the human world. The message was passed on. In due course the baptismal service was held, and Graham of Duchray was waiting in the church. Mr Kirk materialized before the congregation – and Graham somehow failed to play his part. With a last reproachful look Robert Kirk faded from view and disappeared for ever. When he published *The Secret Commonwealth* in 1691 Scotland was still a superstitious place, and witches were still being burned for communing with supernatural forces. It was a curious paradox that a man who made a serious examination of the subject should himself become the central character in such a strange, other-worldly tale.

As well as fairies, Scotland was believed to have been inhabited hundreds of years ago by a race of giants. They were the Feinn, who came, like their original stories, from Ireland. Legendary tales of these giants were told all over Scotland, and can be traced today from curious names on maps of the Highlands. Kylerhea, where the sea-serpent sighted by the ministers Twopeny and Macrae left

Fairies are said to have helped and hindered individuals or entire clans in Scotland throughout history, and many placenames are derived from the belief that these ethereal people existed.

the Sound of Sleat for the waters of the north, is one of these places. It is said to have taken its name from Reidh, a giant who vaulted across the narrow strait from Skye to Glenelg. At the beginning of the last century there was what might have been a confirmation of at least some of these old legends. Not far from Glenelg is a place which used to be called in Gaelic the 'Field of the Big Men'. About 150 years ago some gentlemen decided to dig open a great mound that stood there, and was traditionally the burial ground of the giants. Precisely what happened then is lost in the usual bewildering confusion of accounts. It seems fairly certain that skeletons of more than usual size were discovered. One account said that a skull was found which was big enough for one of the excavators to place over his own head, something which must have taken a cool nerve. Another version was that a doctor examined two of the skeletons and said they were the remains of people who must have been 8½ft and 11ft tall. A third story claimed that the bones were seen to be far bigger than average, when a sudden thunderstorm convinced the local men present that the giants' graves were not meant to be disturbed, and the whole excavation was filled in again.

Scottish maps are helpful in tracking down the sites of other more traditional tales. Still near Glenelg, in a valley overlooked by Forestry Commission plantations, is Loch Iain Mhic Aonghais, or John MacInnes's Loch. He was an unfortunate crofter who captured a water-horse. All went well until he tried to ride it – which is, as anybody in the west would have told him, an unwise thing to attempt. It bounded into the loch, and neither it nor John MacInnes was ever seen again. A few miles to the north, beside the A890 which runs from Lochcarron to Achnasheen, Loch Sgamhain is sandwiched between the road and the enterprising railway to Kyle of Lochalsh. It was once the scene of another incident when somebody tried to ride a water-horse. That time the man did not disappear without trace, because a few days later his lungs floated to the surface, giving the loch for evermore its Gaelic name – which in English is 'Loch of the Lungs'.

So the roads of Scotland lead through a land of monsters and dragons, giants and fairies, ghosts, phantom armies, mermaids, sea-serpents, bogles, kelpies, brownies, water-horses, snatches of ancient folk-tales, and faint stirrings of an ancient dread. Loch monsters are things to be examined by scientific means. Haunted houses and castles offer no apparitions to casual passers-by. Sea-serpents know their place. But what, in a lonely twilight, of the beings that wander at will, free of natural or supernatural boundaries? Like the deadly and mysterious *Cu-Saeng*, which flits silently over the roughest moors and the wildest hills, and will never be described because no man who has ever glimpsed it has survived to tell the tale.

Near Glenelg is a place which was traditionally held to be the burial ground of giants. About 150 years ago a group of people decided to excavate the mound, and a somewhat confused account speaks of skulls big enough to fit over a human head. It appears that this was proved by a practical – if somewhat gruesome – demonstration.

Day Drives

Key to Day Drives

DAY DRIVE SYMBOLS

AA Viewpoint

Abbey

Airport

Battle Site   1189

Boating Centre

Bridge

Castle

Church

Crags

Drive Route   A40

Heights in Feet   ▲ 2323

Hillfort

Houses Open to the Public

Industrial Building

Inn

Lighthouse

Marshland

Motorway   M3 6

Motorway Service Station   S

Other Roads   B5913

Places off Main Route   Helham

Places of Interest   Museum ■

Places on Route   Gralen

Racecourse

Rivers and Lakes   R Ure

Sandy Beaches

Station

Tower

TV or Radio Mast

Waterfall

Windmill

Woodland

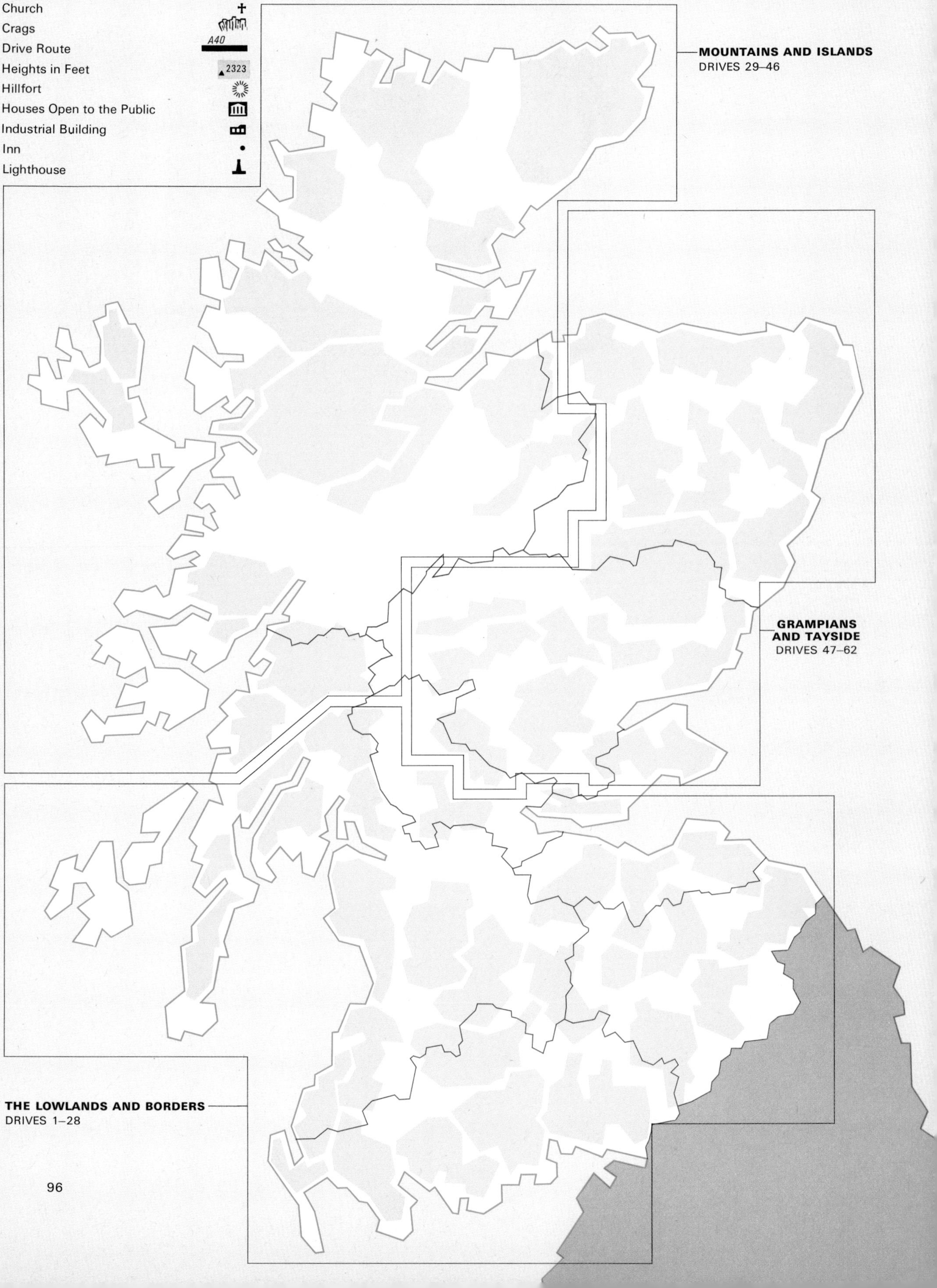

MOUNTAINS AND ISLANDS
DRIVES 29–46

**GRAMPIANS
AND TAYSIDE**
DRIVES 47–62

THE LOWLANDS AND BORDERS
DRIVES 1–28

96

Discovering a Nation

Scotland is a country of bewildering variety and constant surprises. The world's most famous monster rises from the depths of a mysterious loch, where the stern reality of Victorian engineering placed the first-ever hydroelectric scheme. A building in the heart of an industrial city is modelled on the Doge's Palace in Venice. The most closely guarded secret in a nation of hard-headed, practical folk is the location of the lonely eyries of the golden eagle. In a hundred lifetimes Scotland would never reveal itself fully, even to the most persistent traveller. But its wild mountains, rich arable land tilled by generations of patient farmers, lochside scenery of heart-aching beauty, forests, ancient estates, and castles drowsing in the memory of some far-off clash of weapons are an ideal background to motoring in a certain style. Not the frantic hustle of trunk roads and time schedules, but a kind of exploring in which the destination is less than the journey itself; a gentler pace which would appeal to Robert Louis Stevenson, who wrote that 'to travel hopefully is better than to arrive' and that 'I travel not to go somewhere, but to go.' Stevenson knew the country well. His movements can be traced along the roads of Scotland; at the old hamlet of Swanston on the edge of Edinburgh where he was born; at Bridge of Allan, where the cave in which he spun his boyish dreams still looks out over the rushing Allan Water; at Moulin near Pitlochry, where a cottage still retains his memory.

Other famous writers can be pursued, both in their own lives and in the works of their lively imaginations. Robert Burns' birthplace in 'auld clay biggin' at Alloway now stands at the side of a prosaic B-class road. Not far away is Kirkoswald, where as a schoolboy studying trigonometry he fell in love for the first of all too many times. Through the jocular debating days at the Bachelors' Club of Tarbolton, his life can be traced to the hard times on the farm of Ellisland in Nithsdale – 'the very riddlings of Creation,' he called it – where his landlord was, by one of those curious interweavings of history, the first man to launch a steamboat, on a private loch only minutes from the farm. Then came the later days in the revenue service at Dumfries, and the last, sad, unavailing attempts to save his health and his life at the bathing resort of Brow, itself now little more than a memory on the Solway shore.

Burns wove his poetic fancies round real places and real people. The splendid, rollicking ballad of *Tam o'Shanter* was based on Ayrshire characters. There is a real farm of Shanter, in the hills behind the Carrick coast. The man of the house did often ride home less than sober from the market-days in Ayr. He did have a drinking crony called Souter Johnnie – John Davidson, the shoemaker of

Kirkoswald, whose cottage is still there in the village street. Alloway Kirk, where Tam disturbed the warlocks' revels, survives in ruins, and the Auld Brig, where he escaped the chase only by leaving his mare's tail clutched firmly in a witch's grasp, still spans the Doon.

On the other side of southern Scotland, every village, castle, and lonely glen seemed to attract the attention of Sir Walter Scott. His great mansion of Abbotsford is much as he left it, after ploughing more of his hard-won fortune than he could afford into creating his heart's desire out of a pig's-ear of a rundown farm called Cartley Hole. He left his stamp throughout the Borders, recalling in poem, ballad and novel the vicious, blood-soaked days when Scot and Englishman alike stole cattle, tore down churches, swept out of nowhere to terrorise quaking villages, and created the Debateable Land that could only be held by brute force of arms.

Despite its gory history, beauty is never far away in the Border country. Scott's View from Bemersyde is of the triple-peaked Eildon Hills above Melrose, haunted yet by tales of wizardry and intrigue. The old monks of Kelso planted orchards and gardens, mellowed a wild landscape, and are still remembered in places like Gattonside, founded to feed an ancient abbey. Sir Walter himself is buried in a graceful aisle of the ruined Dryburgh Abbey, a soothing place where the Tweed murmurs quietly by. One of his eeriest characters was the Black Dwarf, based on the real-life David Ritchie, whose low-built cottage still stands in the peaceful Manor Valley near Peebles.
Scott made his mark on the Highlands too. Callander, Aberfoyle, the Trossachs, and Balquhidder came into the adventures that flowed from his magic pen. Few people may read him now, but the first floods of visitors came from a vast readership captivated by his tales of Highland chieftains, sturdy outlaws, and the thrills of the chase.

Other men of imagination can be followed round the map of Scotland. Mendelssohn wrote his *Hebrides* overture after seeing the waves lash against Fingal's Cave on Staffa. Wordsworth enthused poetically about a Highland girl at Inversnaid, yearned for the leafy dens of the Yarrow Water near Selkirk, gave the Duke of Queensberry a drubbing in verse for despoiling the woodlands round Neidpath Castle on the Tweed. And Bram Stoker composed the fearful story of *Dracula* while strolling along Cruden Bay. As in Scott's time, the mountains of Scotland are perhaps its greatest attraction. Motorists can drive into the great gorge of Glen Nevis, towered over by Britain's loftiest peak. North of Glasgow every horizon is ringed with hills: Ben Lomond, the Arrochar Alps, range after range of summits on the Highland

Line. The most striking mountains are perhaps those of Wester Ross, some weathered from Torridon sandstone, seven hundred and fifty million years old, and among the most ancient rocks on Earth. Hairpinned roads twist and soar among the peaks, across the Pass of the Cattle to lonely Applecross, by Mam Ratagan to Glenelg on the Sound of Sleat, over the Pass of the Wind and plummeting down into the rocky amphitheatre that encircles the scattered township of Diabaig.

In Wester Ross is the superb mountain estate of Kintail, where within living memory visitors were almost hounded from the hills; it is now owned by the National Trust for Scotland and is open to all. Balmacara estate and the glorious peaks of Torridon are also in the Trust's care. Beinn Eighe with its majestic ridge is controlled by the Nature Conservancy, and mountain trails have been laid out to display the landscape and the wildlife. Farther north there are still vast estates preserved strictly for deerstalkers and wealthy anglers. There are seemingly limitless tracts of wild country through which occasional roads stumble their narrow way, dominated by the strange, harsh landscapes and there only, it appears, with grudging permission. There are island mountains too, brought within motoring reach by the network of car ferries: Skye and the magical Cuilins, Mull and its soaring cliffs, Lewis and Harris and the Uists which are worlds apart, even if crofters gathering peat rub shoulders with modern rocket bases. Nearer the industrial heartland are the almost Hebridean island of Arran, set down with its spiky peaks in the middle of the Firth of Clyde, and gentler neighbours like Bute, the patrician landscape of its interior contrasting vividly with the bustle of the holiday resort of Rothesay.
The Grampians, in the geographical heart of Scotland, have a variety of their own. In the Cairngorm plateau there are sub-arctic conditions at 4,000ft, home of the ptarmigan, the mountain hare, and Britain's only herd of reindeer. This fierce landscape, sometimes swept by deadly storms, is the province of the climber and skier; but a road has been built to 2,500ft, and chairlifts can whisk visitors to the highest restaurant in Britain.

Round the foothills of the Grampians is motorist country again. Roads of all kinds pick their way through the ancestral lands of Mackintosh and Campbell, Drummond, Stewart and Fraser, Shaw, Farquharson, Ogilvy, Menzies, Murray, Gordon, Robertson, Grant, and Forbes. There's away-from-it-all motoring in the Angus glens of Isla, Prosen, Clova, and Esk. In the long valley of the Spey there are splendid pinewood walks, nesting ospreys to be observed, famous distilleries to be visited, even a wildlife park at Kincraig where wolves are on the prowl. The royal family's estates at

97

Balmoral have public roads round the edges, and the railway line from Ballater – which Queen Victoria vetoed because it would invade her privacy – is a famous walk. All this is a country of fine mansions and castles, many of them still in their prime despite long years of clan battles and pointless feuds, the desires of Highland noblemen to advance their power to the south and the even greater determination of the southerners to hold them at bay. A castle was built at Blair Atholl in 1296, and the Duke of Atholl's great house is on the same site today. Turreted Braemar Castle dates from 1628. It was the home of the Earl of Mar who convened a hunting party in 1715 as a decoy for the start of the first great Jacobite rebellion. Craigievar near Alford, only two years older, is a fairytale in stone created for a rich Baltic merchant called William Forbes, whose family have lived in it ever since. Crathes Castle at Banchory is Jacobean by design, Leith Hall at Kennethmont is Jacobite by political persuasion.

These are all open to the public, like many other superb buildings. Hopetoun House near South Queensferry was begun by one of Scotland's first great architects, Sir William Bruce, and extended by his worthy successors, the Adams. Mellerstain, in the Borders, was by William and Robert Adam, and remains a masterpiece of Georgian design. Scone Palace near Perth stands near the ancient capital of the Picts, where the kings of Scotland were crowned on the Stone of Destiny until it was stolen to the south in 1296. On the Firth of Clyde, Culzean was created for a Kennedy Earl and now stands surrounded by a countryside park. Haunted Glamis was borrowed by Shakespeare for *Macbeth*. Falkland in Fife was a hunting palace of the Scottish kings, and from little coastal villages there can still be traced the Cadgers' Roads along which carts were hurried with fresh fish for the royal banquets. Cullen House has art treasures, tapestries and an underground passage to the parish church. Inveraray and Eilean Donan, Brodick and Doune and Traquair – in these changing days, almost all the great houses of Scotland now welcome visitors.

Even in what looks like inhospitable country, Scottish gardeners have triumphed. At Inverewe in Wester Ross, careful planting and the softening effect of the Gulf Stream helped to create a tropical garden, begun in 1862 on a rocky penninsula farther north than Moscow. At Crarae and Cairndow on Lochfyneside, at Kilchrenan in the lonely country near Loch Awe, the mountains and lochsides of Argyll are speckled with private gardens open to passers-by. In Argyll too are the great showpieces of Scottish forestry and botany. The Holy Loch may be best known to protesters as a nuclear submarine base; but climbing the mountainside above is Kilmun Arboretum, plot after plot of eucalyptus, larch, pine and hemlock – species both native and from half a world away. Grander still are the nearby Younger

Botanic Gardens, where a giant avenue of soft-barked sequoias leads into displays of magnolias and rhododendrons, deodars and monkey-puzzles, azaleas and lantern trees, riotous flowering shrubs from six continents. One former owner planted six and a half million trees, and added as an afterthought the Golden Gates from the Great Exhibition in London.

Galloway too has its gardens. One is in an Earl's estate at Lochinch near Stranraer, another massed in sub-tropical profusion at Logan, a third prepared in professional splendour at Threave near Castle Douglas, where the National Trust for Scotland runs its School of Practical Gardening. Some of the graduates from Threave go on to look after the Trust's own properties, from lochside woodlands at Balmacara to intricate formal designs at Pitmedden.

Galloway is too wild to have always been a land of gardeners. Along its coast live the memories of harder, ruthless men – the Solway smugglers. Villages, farms, and lonely houses have their brandy holes where cargoes of contraband were hidden from prying eyes. Night after night the boats would sidle into Solway creeks, oars muffled at the end of another profitable journey from the tax-free haven of the Isle of Man. Desperate stories were told of the lintowers, men who led strings of pack-horses through the Galloway hills to the waiting markets of the Lowland cities; and of characters like Captain Yawkins, who outwitted the revenue men again and again in his Black Prince. Eventually the government stamped out the secret trade, and by that time more regimented industry had begun to flourish in Scotland, sometimes in foul, cramped factories in the cities and sometimes in unexpected rural situations. Mills were established where water supplies were assured – at Deanston on the River Teith, at Stanley by the Tay, at Alva where the local laird was clever enough to run water pipes down one of the dizzy gorges of the Ochil Hills. Many survive today.

Canals were cut at Crinan and the Great Glen. Only those two are working now, but travellers still come across an unexpected aqueduct, bridge, or cutting that reveals the presence of the old Union Canal from Falkirk to Edinburgh, or the Forth and Clyde from Grangemouth to Bowling. There were short-lived ventures like the Aberdeenshire Canal to Inverurie, and the Glasgow-Johnstone, remembered now in little more than the name of the station at Paisley Canal. There are occasional traces of others which faded quickly from the reference books, as canal mania overtook the usually sober calculations of Scottish businessmen, and many a fortune dwindled in a flurry of reckless speculation.

In the end, though, it is the countryside itself which cries out to be explored. More and more of it is being opened up to motorists who like to park their cars and walk out into the open air. There are nature trails and forest walks from the inland cliffs of Knocken near Ullapool to Kilsture Forest on the edge of the Solway

Firth. At Caladh Castle near Tighnabruaich there are precipitous walks overlooking the unforgettable Kyles of Bute. At Inverliever on Loch Awe, where the state forest pre-dates the founding of the Forestry Commission, there are red and roe deer, badgers and sparrowhawks, waterfalls and the remains of long-lost crofts. Perhaps the finest of all views of Loch Lomond is over the spread of islands from a walk above Balmaha.

There are splendid nature trails at the Birks of Aberfeldy, where beside one of the steep pathways is the seat on which Robert Burns rested and composed a famous song. The Hermitage trail near Dunkeld leads to the aristocratic fancy of a summer-house built in 1758 above the raging Falls of Braan. At Yellowcraig near North Berwick, where sea-buckthorn lines the coast for miles, seabirds wheel by from the great gannetry on the Bass Rock.

Travellers in the Scottish countryside are always stalking history. To admire the mountain scenery of Glen Shiel, on the main road to Kyle of Lochalsh, means looking over the only battlefield of the rarely-remembered Jacobite rebellion of 1719; the defeated contingent of Spanish soldiers were the last foreign troops to fight on Scottish soil. Bonnie Prince Charlie's later, more romantic attempt to put a Stuart king back on the British throne can be traced along many a Highland road. At Loch nan Uamh on the road to Mallaig he first set foot on the mainland of Scotland. At nearby Glenfinnan a monument marks the spot where his standard was unfurled. Prestonpans on the Firth of Forth is where the Jacobites first defeated a government army, and devoted time afterwards to making up derisive songs about the beaten general, Johnny Cope. The retreat from Derby, back into the Highlands, is marked by sadder tales, and the bloodied field of Culloden is a woeful place even today. Ruined Ruthven Barracks near Kingussie is where the Jacobite army disbanded for ever, and the Young Chevalier began a hunted summer through the land of those who loved him most.

Motoring in Scotland is not a dull, predictable business. It can mean exploring the recesses of Glen Trool, where Robert the Bruce was a guerrilla leader long before he became king. It can mean picking a way through the old wynds and archways of St Andrews to find the home of golf. It can mean identifying Alpine flowers in the mountain reserve of Ben Lawers. It can mean wandering through half-silent villages, where the most pleasureable activity is tracing the tiny movements of local history from faded inscriptions in ivied churchyards. It can mean – in a different world – discovering that the replica of the Doge's Palace is a carpet factory on Glasgow Green. The following one-day drives have been selected to help the adventurous motorist discover Scotland – the true Scotland that only the individual can find.

The Lowlands and Borders

Rolling hills and wooded valleys, networks of green-hedged lanes through long-settled acres of farmland, independent little towns and long coastlines of fishing villages and holiday resorts allow the south of Scotland to offer motoring of many kinds. Wandering roads exert themselves in the keen upland air of the Lammermuir Hills, the Moorfoots, the Lowthers and the old Ettrick Forest, once a hunting preserve of the Scottish kings. In the valleys the very names are an evocation of long-ago tales which come alive again in their own surroundings: Tweeddale and Lauderdale, Annandale, Nithsdale, Teviotdale, and Eskdale.

There are sleepy hamlets like Abbey St Bathans in its quiet fold of the Lammermuirs, busy fishing villages like Eyemouth on the rocky North Sea coast, upland settlements like Carsphairn where the memory of the old Covenanters seems never far away. Industry in some places has left its scars. In others it has simply faded, leaving only an added interest behind. Gatehouse of Fleet was once a minor boom town of the south-west; now it is a paradise for the antiquarian. In the

Glenkens the great Galloway power scheme created a chain of lochs where none had been before, and left the valley of the Dee perhaps a better place. One glance at a map shows, by the concentration of little country roads, where the well-worked farmlands are. In the Lothian plains, in the Merse that stretches inland from Berwick, in Nithsdale and Annandale, in the dairy country by Stranraer, in the hinterland of Ayr – motorists must always be ready to give way to tractors, hay-balers, or occasional parties of ambling cows.

In the north are the great flat carselands over which the Forth writhes and meanders to Stirling, where long years ago the ocean rested its giant, aqueous belly. When the water receded it left behind a thickness of peat. A shrewd-thinking laird had it whittled away and floated through channels to the Firth of Forth, revealing some of Scotland's richest arable ground. The Border burghs keep their independent views; even the casual vistor can hardly help being caught up in the summer festivals and the riding of the marches.

There are orchardlands round Lanark, cheery holiday towns on the Clyde coast, unlikely places like Dirleton, where beside the village green the bowling club is within the grounds of a 13th-c castle. The Romans built their northernmost wall to keep the troublesome Picts beyond the Forth and Clyde, and parts of it can be seen today. New Abbey, south of Dumfries, is where the word sweetheart was invented seven centuries ago, by the sorrowing widow who built the memorial abbey called Dulce Cor. Near Lochmaben are the little settlements of Greenhill, Hightae, Smallholm and Heck, the Royal Four Towns with ancient privileges granted by no less a person than Robert the Bruce. Lochmaben's Castle Loch contains a rare fish called the vendace, discovered nowhere else in the world; William Paterson, educated at the local school, was the founder of the Bank of England; a few years later Dr Thomas Mounsey retired to an estate in the same district, happy in the knowledge that he was the man who introduced rhubarb to Britain from Russia.

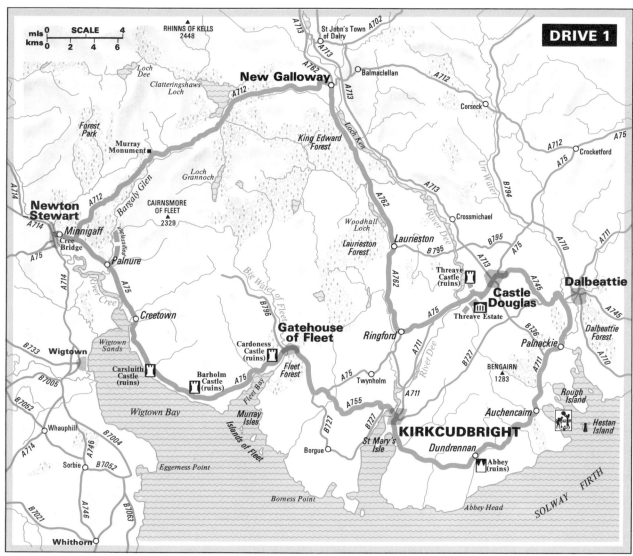

See text for Drive 1 overleaf

Among the Galloway Hills

From Kirkcudbright

Drive 1   88 miles

The small market town of *Kirkcudbright*, with its gaunt ruined castle, stands on the E bank of the River Dee. From here the route runs along the coast before turning to climb into the Galloway Hills.

The route leaves the town by Bridge Street, crosses the River Dee and follows the A755 *Gatehouse of Fleet* road for a relaxing drive across agricultural country. In 4½m turn left on to the A75, signposted *Stranraer*, to follow a winding road skirting Fleet Forest to Gatehouse of Fleet. This tiny Galloway town on the Water of Fleet is popular with anglers, and it also has associations with the poet Robert Burns and the novelist Sir Walter Scott.

Continuing on the A75 the drive passes the remains of late 15th-c Cardoness Castle, perched to the right of the road on a rocky outcrop overlooking Fleet Bay. Beyond Cardoness, the high Galloway hills come close to the shore forcing the road to follow one of the most scenic coastal routes in all of Scotland. There are widesweeping views across Wigtown Bay to the Marchers Peninsula and also to the nearer Murray Isles just off the coast. Two ruined castles, Barholm – not open – and Carsluith, can be seen from the road nearer *Creetown*. A clock tower here commemorates Queen Victoria's Diamond Jubilee. To the N of the town rises the 2,329ft mass of Cairnsmore of Fleet.

From *Palnure* a detour to the right on an unclassified and dead-end road leads beside the clear waters of Palnure Burn to the attractive Bargaly Glen and part of the *Glen Trool Forest Park*. The drive reaches the market town of *Newton Stewart* through the village of *Minnigaff* and across the Cree Bridge.

Return along the A75 through Minnigaff and after 1m turn left on to the A712 *New Galloway* road. This road winds through the attractive woodland of a forest park and affords splendid views of the high Galloway Hills to the N and S. Later the drive passes the lonely Murray Monument, commemorating a shepherd boy who became a professor of oriental language. Near by is the Grey Mare's Tail, a fine waterfall. In 4½m the road dips to the water's edge for a pleasant ride alongside the shore of *Clatteringshaws Loch*. This was created as part of the Galloway hydro-electric power scheme. In 6m turn right on to the A762 to enter New Galloway, a tiny Royal Burgh and angling centre. Follow the Kirkcudbright road to the shores of Loch Ken, with the Cairn Edward Forest stretching to the W. Later the drive skirts the shore of Woodhall Loch before reaching the hamlet of *Laurieston*. To the W lies the conifered Laurieston Forest, as the road leads through attractive hill country to *Ringford* where the drive turns left on to the A75 *Dumfries* road. In 4m, shortly after crossing the River Dee, a track leads left to reach lonely 14th-c Threave Castle. It stands on an islet in the River and can be reached

by rowing boat. Continue with the A75 towards *Castle Douglas*. Before entering the town an unclassified right turn leads to Threave Estate and its 19th-c mansion. The extensive grounds are particularly attractive during the daffodil and rhododendron seasons.

The pleasant market town of Castle Douglas is set at the N end of Carlingwark Loch and is the commercial centre of the Stewartry of Kirkcudbright. The shores of the loch are used as a civic park, offering boating, fishing and other sports. The drive takes the A745 Dumfries then *Dalbeattie* road, dipping and climbing through rolling countryside for 5m before slipping down past granite quarries and joining the A711 *Auchencairn* road. The small town of Dalbeattie lies across the Urr Water to the left. The drive turns S to pass through *Palnackie* to the attractive village of Auchencairn, lying close to a sand and pebble beach a little way inland from the *Solway Firth*. Follow the A711 to *Dundrennan*, a village that is partly built of stone from the nearby 12th-c ruined abbey.

Occasional glimpses of the sea are afforded from the next section of road, before the drive drops to the shore of Manxman's Lake and returns to Kirkcudbright.

The Marchers Country

From Newton Stewart

Drive 2   78 miles

Newton Stewart, an attractive little weaving town spread along the W bank of the River Cree, is linked by the Cree Bridge to the old village of *Minnigaff*. The area offers fine fishing facilities.

The drive follows the *Stranraer* road and then the A714 *Wigtown* road, to leave the town along Queen Street for a short relaxing ride to Wigtown. This ancient settlement stands on its bay below the estuary of the Cree and near the mouth of the River Bladnoch.

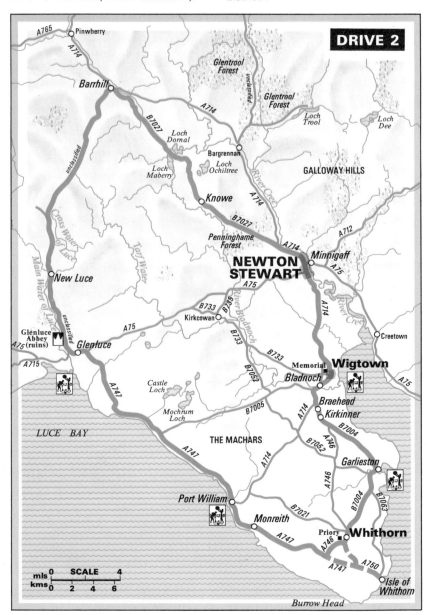

Drive 2 continued

Leave the town on the *Whithorn* road and pass through the village of *Bladnoch*. Cross the river bridge and in 1m keep forward on to the A746 for Braehead and *Kirkinner*. Drive beyond the village for 1m and branch left on to the B7004, signposted *Garlieston*. After 4m the drive reaches the edge of Garlieston, a small coastal port on Garlieston Bay. Turn right here with Whithorn signposts and in ¼m turn left with the B7004 to historic Whithorn, set amid the bleak Marchers countryside. The local shrine of St Ninian was once a popular object of pilgrimage, and James II and Mary Queen of Scots both journeyed to this holy place. From the S end of the main street a detour can be made by turning left on to the A750 to visit *Isle of Whithorn*, a small port perched on rocky shores and sheltered by headlands. From here the drive returns along the A750 for 2m. It then goes forward on to the A747 *Port William* road, continuing across windswept and often treeless countryside before reaching the coast and

Luce Bay at *Monreith*. The main tour from Whithorn continues on the A746 Port William road, and after 1½m turns right on to the A747 to rejoin the coast at Monreith. Port William, a few miles along the coast, is a little port with one of the few sandy beaches in the area. The drive continues beside the coastline along a quiet road which gives beautiful, panoramic views across Luce Bay. Sharks are not uncommon in these waters. The road finally turns inland over the bleak Marchers countryside to *Glenluce*. Turn left on to the A75 and enter the village, which clings to a steep valley slope. After ½m turn right on to an unclassified road signposted *Barrhill*, passing ruined Glenluce Abbey as the drive nears *New Luce* where the Main Water of Luce meets Cross Water of Luce. The drive climbs towards Barrhill across lonely and bleak moorland on a narrow, hilly road. In 4m turn right across a river bridge before the road winds down to Barrhill. Turn right on to the A714, and at end of village right again on to B7027, signposted Newton Stewart via Knowe. This pleasant road passes

through countryside interspersed with typically Scottish lochs and rivers, with the added grandeur of the high Galloway hills to the E. After 6m the drive enters the old county of Wigtownshire, then after the hamlet of Knowe passes through the leafy Penningham Forest. Later it turns right on to the A714 to re-enter Newton Stewart.

Cradle of a Poet

From Ayr

Drive 3   101 miles

This drive leaves *Ayr* on the A719 *Maidens* road, and climbs beyond Butlin's holiday camp to over 300ft with panoramic sea views across the Firth of Clyde to the *Isle of Arran*. The small fishing village of *Dunure* lies to the right below the main road, with the remains of a cliff-top castle overlooking the sea. After 2m the drive reaches the so-called *Electric Brae*, where because of the configuration of the land a car will start to roll backwards although appearing to face downhill. In another 2m the drive turns right with the A719, following an attractive wooded valley to the entrance to *Culzean Castle*. Set on the top of craggy cliffs, the castle was designed in the 18thc by Robert Adam and is set in 500-acre grounds which are graced by exotic trees and wildfowl. The ceilings and staircase of the house are especially noteworthy. Follow the A719 beyond Maidens, a small fishing village and resort, to reach *Turnberry* – one of the most famous golfing resorts in the world. Overlooking the sea are the ruins of Turnberry Castle, the childhood home of Robert the Bruce. The lonely island peak of the 1,110ft Ailsa Craig lies 12m off the coast.

Once in the village turn left on to the A77 Ayr road to *Kirkoswald*, a village rich in Burns' associations. Beyond the village the drive passes impressive Crossraguel Abbey. At *Maybole*, one of the larger towns of the area the drive takes the B7023 Crosshill road. At Crosshill turn right in the village with the B7023 *Dailly* road, and in 1m join the B741. The road follows the Valley of the Water of Girvan for 2¾m before turning left on to an unclassified road signposted *Barr*. This narrow and sometimes gated road winds through lonely moorland for 5m before crossing the River Stinchar and turning right to follow the river to Barr. This secluded village is a popular angling resort and nestles beneath the Changue Forest. At the T-junction turn right then left on to the B734, signposted *Barrhill*, and in 6m turn left again on to the A714 *Newton Stewart* road to *Pinwherry*. Turn right to cross the Duisk River, passing a ruined castle on the left. The drive continues along the attractive Duisk Valley to Barrhill, then crosses more exposed moorland with fine views of the Carrick Hills to the E. At the hamlet of *Bargrennan* turn left with *Straiton* signposts on to an unclassified road, and enter the 110,000 acreage of *Glen Trool Forest Park*. Some of the most picturesque forest scenery in Scotland is to be found within this park. Beyond *Glentrool* village a detour may

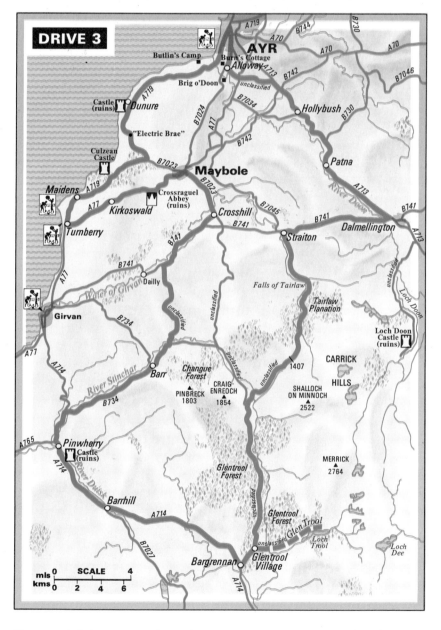

DRIVE 3

Drive 3 continued

be made by turning right to visit Glen Trool.
The scenery around here is very beautiful,
with pine-clad hills rising to over 2,300ft
from the shores of Loch Trool. At the N
end a monument commemorates the victory
by Bruce over an English force in 1307.

The main drive continues through the
forest park for 8m before branching right.
In this less forested area the 2,764ft
Merrick and 2,522ft Shalloch on Minnoch
are among the most prominent hills rising to
the right. The 1,854ft Craigenreoch is to the
left. The road now climbs to its 1,407ft
summit, then winds down through the
Tairlow Plantation of Carrick Forest into the
Girvan Valley. Several waterfalls are passed
before the drive reaches Straiton, a village
picturesquely situated beside the Water of
Girvan. Straiton church houses a pre-
Reformation aisle.

The drive turns right from Straiton on to the
B741 *Dalmellington* road, and in 6m turns
left on to the A713 Ayr road. The iron-
working town of Dalmellington lies 1m to
the right. Several mining settlements for
both iron and coal are passed as the tour
runs through the Doon Valley to reach
Patna. After 3½m pass through the hamlet of
Hollybush, then in 2½m turn left on to an
unclassified road signposted *Alloway*. In
1¾m turn right then left to cross the A77 for
Alloway. Robert Burns, the Scottish national
poet, was born here in 1759. His cottage
birthplace has been preserved, and a
museum with various relics of the poet
stands in the grounds.

The drive turns right on to the B7024
and continues N, passing a golf course
before returning to Ayr.

Across the Lowther Heights

From Thornhill

Drive 4   93 miles

Leave *Thornhill*, a small Nithsdale town amid
pleasant rolling hillsides, on the A76
Kilmarnock road and follow the valley of the
River Nith to *Carronbridge*. Turn right here
on to the A702, signposted *Edinburgh*, then
continue along the wooded Carron Valley
into the high Lowther Hills through the
strikingly-attractive Dalveen Pass, which
winds through steep, bare hills to over
1,100ft. To the E of the pass rises
2,268ft Ballencleuch Law, and to the W
are 2,403ft Green Lowther and 2,378ft
Lowther Hill. The run down to the Clyde
Valley is gentler, and beyond *Elvanfoot* the
drive turns left on to the A74 past the small
resort of *Crawford*, lying off the road to the
right.

Some 3m beyond Crawford the drive turns
left on to the B797, signposted *Leadhills*.
The road dips back S and climbs steadily
towards Leadhills, which at 1,350ft above
sea level is the second highest village in
Scotland. Lead, gold, and silver have all
been mined in the area. The road climbs to
the 1,531ft summit through the Lowther

Hills, with 1,808ft Wanlock Dod
prominent to the right and 2,403ft Green
Lowther and 2,378ft Lowther Hill to the left.

Wanlockhead, another old mining settlement
at an altitude of 1,380ft is the loftiest
village in Scotland. The drive drops down to
Nithsdale by the fine Mennock Pass,
following Mennock Water through a
beautifully-wooded valley. Later turn right on
to the A76 for Mennock, and 2m farther
pass the ruined Sanquhar Castle to
Sanquhar. The A76 continues through the
mining town of *Kirkconnel* to *New
Cumnock*, where the drive turns left on to
the B741 *Dalmellington* road. At
Dalmellington, which is another old mining
town, turn left on to the A713 *Dumfries*
road. For a detour to *Loch Doon* reservoir
turn right after 1½m on to an unclassified
road. The picturesque Ness Glen is to the
right of the loch approach; the loch is
surrounded by high hills which include
2,668ft Corserine in the Rhinns of Kells
range to the SE. Part of the W side of
the loch is within the *Glen Trool Forest
Park*. Loch Doon Castle dates from the
14thc and was removed from its former
island home to a new site beside the loch
before a hydro-electric scheme was
introduced.

Continue on the main route with the A713
to *Carsphairn*, with its open views to the
nearby mountains, and beyond the village
turn left on to the B729, signposted
Moniaive. After skirting the artificial
Kendoon Loch, the drive turns left with the
B729 and crosses bleak moorland to reach
Moniaive, a pleasant village lying on both
sides of the Dalwhat Water. A cross dating

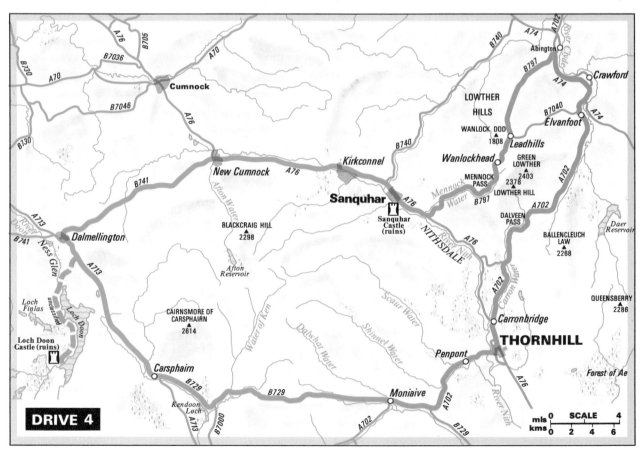

Drive 4 continued

from 1638 is an interesting feature of the village.

Enter the village and join the A702 Thornhill road, later passing through the Shinnel Valley to *Penpont* before crossing the River Nith to re-enter Thornhill.

Lowland Seascapes

From Gourock

Drive 5   97 miles

Gourock is one of the most picturesquely situated resorts in Scotland, and overlooks pleasant scenery across the *Firth of Clyde* to the *Cowal Peninsula*. Set on steep hills, it is an important Clyde ferry port with services to *Dunoon* and *Kilcreggan*. The drive leaves the town on the A78 *Largs* road, and after 3m passes the *Cloch Lighthouse*. The seascapes now extend across to the beautiful Cowal coast, S of Dunoon, and the *Isle of Bute*.

Beyond the greystone village of *Inverkip*, where there is a marina, the road returns to the tree-lined coast at *Wemyss Bay*, a popular resort and ferry port for the Islands of Bute and *Rothesay*. The drive continues alongside the waters of the Firth of Clyde to another resort, *Skelmorlie*, where the views encompass the S tip of Cowal. As the drive continues along the coast, the dark shape of the island of *Great Cumbrae* is prominent only 1m offshore at Largs. This major Firth of Clyde resort is also a ferry port with services to Great Cumbrae.

Leaving the town along the A78 *Irvine* road, the drive passes Bowen Craig where a monument commemorates the defeat of the Norsemen in 1263, resulting in their loss of the Hebrides and the Isle of Man. The smaller island 4m out to sea beyond the resort and port of *Fairlie* is the deserted *Little Cumbrae*. The road turns inland for the next 4m, and to the right on the coast is the nuclear power station at *Hunterston*. This overlooks a wide beach of sand and shingle popular with sea birds. The dark mass of the *Isle of Arran* is increasingly prominent to the SW with 2,866ft Goat Fell, rising steeply from the shore. The road dips towards the sea again beyond Seamill, with its parent settlement of *West Kilbride* lying 1m inland on the slopes of Law Hill, and continues along the coast on the A78 Irvine road. The drive then skirts the resorts and ports of *Ardrossan* and *Saltcoats*. The A78 continues through *Stevenston* to Irvine, a port and manufacturing town which has associations with Burns. There is a sandy beach to the S of the resort. Before entering the town turn right on to the ring road, signposted *Ayr*. In 4m turn right on to the B746 towards Irvine Bay for Barassie, one of the well-known golfing resorts along this coast. On reaching the sea-front turn left and after 1m pass under a railway bridge and turn right into *Troon*, with its docks and popular beaches. Offshore lies the bird sanctuary of Lady Isle. Leave by the B749 Ayr road, and in 1¼m cross the railway bridge and turn right. In 1½m turn right on to the A79 for

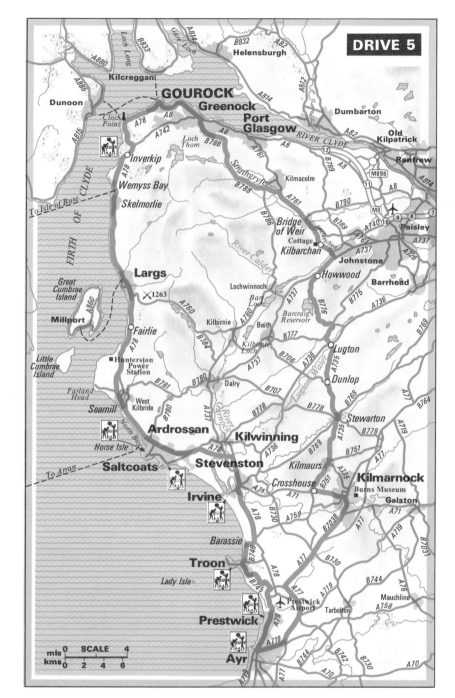

DRIVE 5

Prestwick, where giant jetliners start their flight across the Atlantic from the large international airport. For golfing enthusiasts there is another fine course, before the drive enters Ayr. Leave Ayr by following By-pass, then *Kilmarnock* signposts to join the A77 Ayr by-pass. Skirt Prestwick Airport, then enter a roundabout and turn right with the A77 for a pleasant drive across undulating countryside. In 3¾m branch left on to the B7038 to reach the important manufacturing town of Kilmarnock. To avoid the town centre turn left on to the Ring Road, then follow Irvine signposts to leave by the A71. After 2m, at Crosshouse, turn right on to the B751, signposted *Kilmaurs*. At Kilmaurs turn right then left on to the A735 for the wool town of *Stewarton*.

At the crossroads turn left with the A735, signposted *Paisley*, and continue through

the cheese town of *Dunlop* to Lugton. Turn left here on to the A736, then right on the B777, signposted *Beith*. In ¾m turn right again on to the B775, signposted Paisley. After another 1m turn left on the B776, signposted *Howwood*. This cross-country route winds over high ground and passes Barcraig Reservoir before descending into the Black Cart Valley at Howwood. Turn right here on to the A737 Paisley road, and on reaching the outskirts of *Johnstone* turn left on to the B787, signposted *Kilbarchan*. In ½m meet a T-junction and turn left on to an unclassified road for Kilbarchen, where an 18th-c weaver's cottage is preserved. The drive continues to *Bridge of Weir*, a pleasant residential and golfing town. Join the A761 across the railway bridge to continue through the town. In 2¼m turn left

Drive 5 continued

on to the B788, signposted *Greenock*. This scenic road crosses high ground, affording magnificent views over *Port Glasgow* and across the Clyde to the Dunbartonshire Hills. On the run down into Greenock the drive passes under a railway viaduct and turns left, then at the T-junction turns right. At the next roundabout take the second exit, and on reaching the A8 turn left on to the Gourock road to pass the famous shipbuilding yards spread along the banks of the Clyde estuary. The drive continues along the A8 for the return to Gourock.

Forests of Dalbeattie and Ae

From Dumfries

Drive 6   89 miles

Leave *Dumfries* on the A75 *Stranraer* road and cross the Buccleuch Street bridge into adjoining Maxwelltown. In ¼m turn left on to the A710, signposted *New Abbey*, to follow the Nith Valley downstream. Beyond here is the prominent moorland of Islesteps. New Abbey, a small town beautifully set amid woodland, is dominated by 1,868ft Criffell to the S. Near by is the aptly named Sweetheart Abbey.

The drive continues on the A710 beneath the steep slopes of Criffell, overlooking the *Solway Firth* to the left. The little village of *Kirkbean* has connections with John Paul Jones, 'father' of the United States Navy. Continue for 1¼m beyond the hamlet of Mainsriddle, then branch left with A710 and pass through woodlands beside Sandyhills Bay. In 3m a short detour can be made by turning left on to an unclassified road for *Rockcliffe*, a quite resort overlooking Rough Firth. The Mote of Mark W of the village is the site of a prehistoric vitrified fort; Rough Island is a bird sanctuary with waders, shelduck, and mergansers. The main

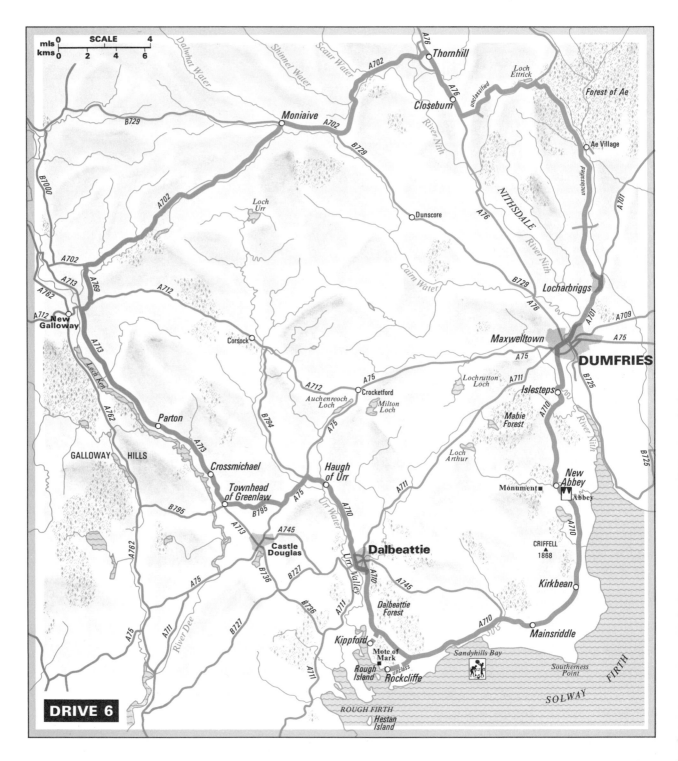

Drive 6 continued

drive continues along the *Dalbeattie* road to pass between the wooded hills of Dalbeattie Forest. In 2m another detour can be taken on an unclassified left turn for beautifully situated *Kippford*, a yachting centre on Rough Firth. The main drive follows the Urr Valley and skirts the small market town of Dalbeattie. Accompany the river on the Haugh of Urr road to remain on the A710, and pass through attractive scenery to Haugh of Urr. A mile beyond the village turn left on to the A75 Stranraer road. After 2m turn right on to the B795, signposted *Lauriston*, to Townhead of Greenlaw. Turn right here with Ayr signposts to follow the A713 along the picturesque shores of the wide River Dee.

The area around *Crossmichael* has been changed by hydro-electric schemes, and the artificially widened River Dee merges with Loch Ken in the N. Beyond Parton there are excellent views W across Loch Ken to the High Galloway Hills. The drive continues alongside Loch Ken, and after 6m turns right on to the A712 Corsock and *Crocketford* road. In ½m turn left on to the unsignposted A769. This is a 1½m link road to the A702, where the drive turns right on to the *Moniaive* road to climb across bleak moorland before reaching Moniaive. Turn right on to the *Thornhill* road, and later pass through the Shinnel Valley to Penpont before crossing the River Nith to enter Thornhill. Turn right in Thornhill on to the A76, signposted Dumfries, for the drive through Lower Nithsdale to *Closeburn*. The massive Closeburn Tower preserves an iron yett (gate).

Drive beyond the village for 1m and turn left on to an unclassified road signposted Loch Ettrick and *Ae*, then in ¾m turn left towards the Forest of Ae. Just beyond Loch Ettrick turn right to pass through dark forest land to Ae, a Forestry Commission village. Before the village branch right to continue on an unclassified road through open countryside. In 3½m go over the crossroads, and after another 2½m turn right on to the A701 into Locharbriggs for the return to Dumfries.

Tail of the Grey Mare

From Moffat

Drive 7   100 miles

This drive starts at *Moffat*, a small inland resort pleasantly situated in the Lowland hills, and leads through rolling countryside and river valleys.

Follow the A708 *Selkirk* road out of the town for the attractive drive through the

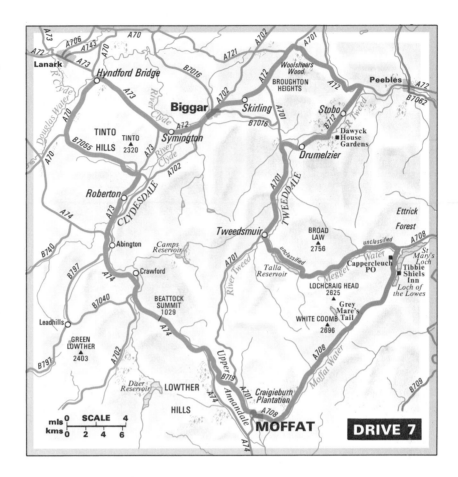

steep valley of Moffat Water. After the Craigieburn Plantation the valley becomes increasingly narrow, with hills rising to over 2,100ft on both sides. Near the head of the valley the road reaches the notable 200ft waterfall known as the Grey Mare's Tail. After a short climb to over 1,100ft, the drive runs down to the shore of Loch of the Lowes and later to St Mary's Loch. These two lochs are attractively situated amongst the green hills of the almost treeless *Ettrick* Forest. Standing on the narrow spit of land dividing the two lochs is *Tibbie Shiel's Inn*, an attractive place popular with anglers.

Continue beyond Cappercleuch post office for 1½m, then turn left on to an unclassified road signposted *Tweedsmuir*. Drive into the valley of the Cross Megget Water. This thinly populated valley is bounded by 2,000ft-plus hills, with 2,625ft Lochcraig Head prominent to the left and 2,765ft Broad Law rising to the right. The road climbs to a height of 1,483ft, then follows a steep descent which affords grandstand views as it drops to Talla Reservoir, which serves *Edinburgh*.

At the hamlet of Tweedsmuir the drive crosses the River Tweed, and turns right on to the A701 Edinburgh road to drop through Tweeddale. After 7m turn right on to the B712 *Peebles* road and pass through the attractive village of *Drumelzier*, situated near the Tweed. The Dawyck House Gardens, with their collection of trees and shrubs, is passed before *Stobo*. Continue through the village, and after 3m turn left on to the A72 *Glasgow* road. Drive through the winding valley of the Lyne Water among

bare hillsides. After 4½m Woolshears Wood stands out on the N slopes of 1,800ft Broughton Heights to the left. Stay with the A72 through the small and pleasant village of *Skirling*, then beyond the village join the A702 to reach *Biggar*, a small market town in the broad vale of the Biggar Water. A feature of the town is its spacious main street.

Leave by following Glasgow signposts, and in 1m turn right on to the A72. After ¾m the drive crosses the River Clyde and continues to *Symington*. To the W rises the prominent conical peak of 2,320ft Tinto. In ¾m turn right on to the A73 for the gentle run down through farming country to *Hyndford Bridge*, beside the Clyde. Here the drive goes forward on to the A70 *Ayr* road, keeping to the hillside above the valley of Douglas Water. After 4¼m turn left on to the B7055, signposted *Wiston*, and climb to cross the wild Tinto Hills at a height of 1,125ft. After 4m bear right and in 1½m turn right on to the A73 to enter Clydesdale. Continue through the hamlet of *Roberton* and in 3m join the A74 Carlisle road. The valley now closes in and skirts the villages of *Abington* and *Crawford*. Throughout the length of the valley the road runs alongside the Glasgow to Carlisle railway line, and 5m beyond Crawford the summit of the railway is passed at a height of 1,029ft.

A long and winding descent through the bleak Lowther Hills lasts for 3¾m before the drive turns left on to the B719 Moffat road. This crosses into upper Annandale, where the tour turns right on to the A701 for the final descent to Moffat.

The Border Vales and Marshes

From Lockerbie

Drive 8   110 miles

Lockerbie, now by-passed by the busy A74, is a market town with an annual August sheep fair. The drive leaves the town to join the A74 *Glasgow* road for the drive through Annandale. After 12m leave the dual carriageway and turn left to follow the A701 *Dumfries* road. The high hills beyond the Forest of *Ae*, with Queensberry prominent at 2,286ft, rise to the W. Kinnel Water is bridged at the hamlet of *St Ann's* before the route continues through rolling country to Locharbriggs and lower Nithsdale, and thence to Dumfries.

Meet a roundabout and follow the *Stranraer* road, then turn left with Carlisle signposts to travel alongside the River Nith. At end of the road turn left then right, signposted *Glencaple*, to continue on the B725. Later the drive reaches the widening River Nith, and follows it to Glencaple. Beyond the village the road is bounded by marshes and the shallow waters of the *Solway Firth*, with 1,868ft Criffell prominent across the water to the right. After 3m the ruins of *Caerlaverock* Castle lie ¼m off the road to the right. Although mainly of 14th- and 15th-c origins, this building is best known for its Renaissance wing of 1638. At Bankend turn right, signposted *Ruthwell*, to cross flat and often marshy countryside. After 4¾m turn right on to the B724. After ½m an unclassified road

to the left leads to Ruthwell Church. Inside the parish church is the famous Ruthwell Cross, an 18in-high preaching cross which probably dates from the 18thc. Continue with the B724 through *Cummertrees* and in 3m join the A75 to enter the Solway Firth market town of *Annan*. In the gardens of Moat House is the Burgh Museum of exhibits connected with local history and Thomas Carlyle. After crossing the River Annan turn left at the traffic signals on to the B722 Eaglesfield road. In 2m turn left on to an unclassified road signposted *Ecclefechan*. After 2½m cross the River Mein and turn right to Ecclefechan, where the birthplace of Thomas Carlyle houses personal relics. A right turn in the village leads to the A74 Carlisle road. After 8m branch left, signposted *Gretna Green*, to reach *Springfield*.

Continue along the Longtown road into England across Solway Moss, site of the 1542 battle in which the Scots were defeated by the English. After ¾m turn left on to the A6071. Before reaching Longtown turn left on to the A7, signposted *Galashiels*, and follow the River Esk back into Scotland and the village of *Canonbie*. The hills close in on wooded Eskdale N from here, making an attractive run to *Langholm*. This pleasant town is popular with anglers and is noted for its woollens. The 1,163ft Whita Hill rises to the E and is crowned by a monument commemorating General Malcolm, a one-time governor of Bombay. Leave the town on the B709 Eskdalemuir road and continue through the

pleasantly relaxing river and valley scenery of Eskdale to the hamlet of Bentpath. After 2m the tour crosses the River Esk and climbs over bleak moorland into Castle O'er Forest, before winding down to the valley and reaching the hamlet of *Eskdalemuir*, a well-known weather station. Turn left here on to the B723, signposted Lockerbie. Continue through the conifered Castle O'er Forest, and beyond Boreland follow the valley of the Dryfe Water for the return to Lockerbie.

To the Rhinns of Galloway

From Stranraer

Drive 9   74 miles

Stranraer, a resort at the head of Loch Ryan, is an important port from which mail steamers operate to Larne in Northern Ireland.

The drive leaves the town along the seafront on the A718 *Kirkcolm* road and in 2½m, at the roundabout, turns right to run alongside the edge of Loch Ryan to Kirkcolm. The road then veers inland to join the B738 Ervie road. After another 2m turn sharp left,

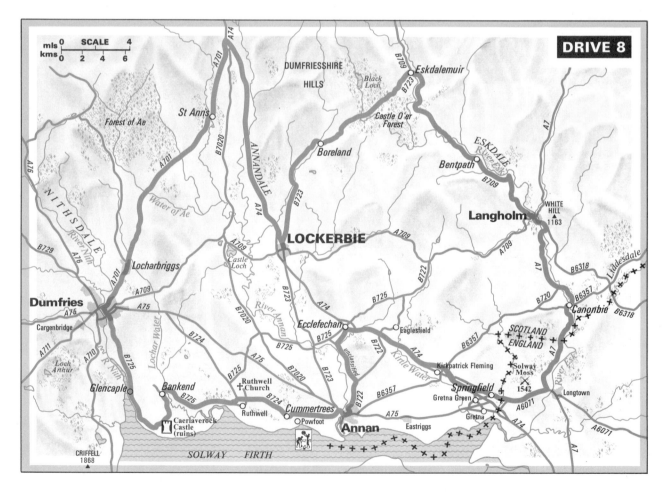

Drive 9 continued

signposted *Leswalt*, and pass the Marian
Tower on the left. After 1m go forward on
to the B798 and in 2¾m, at the edge of
Leswalt, go over the crossroads on to the
B7043, signposted *Lochnaw*. For a short
while the drive runs through the Aldouran
Glen, then after 2¼m turns left to rejoin the
B738, signposted *Portpatrick*. After 2¾m
there are occasional sea views over the
craggy headland to the right as the route
continues on the A764.

In another 1½m a detour can be made by
turning right on to a narrow unclassified
road to visit the Killantringan Lighthouse,
with its fine views of the wild, gale-swept
coast. At the junction with the A77 turn
right to reach Portpatrick. This small, exposed
resort was once the main Scottish port for
Irish traffic, but it declined because the
harbour was often closed by severe gales.
The sheltered port of Stranraer gradually
took over Portpatrick's rôle. The Ulster
coast is 20m to the W and can be seen on a
clear day.

Return along the A77 and on the climb out
of the town turn sharp right on to an
unclassified and unsignposted road. The
drive continues to climb, and after ½m the
road affords occasional views of the coast,
including ruined 16th-c Dunskey Castle.
Continue with the narrow road and in 1½m
turn left, signposted B7042. In 1m meet
crossroads and turn right on to the
unsignposted B7042, then in 1m turn right
again, signposted *Sandhead*. The road dips
and climbs for 3m and meets a T-junction
at which the route turns right. After ¾m turn
right again, signposted A716, to skirt the
coastal village of Sandhead. In ½m go
forward with the A716 and follow the coast,
with views across *Luce Bay* to the hamlet
of *Ardwell*.

After 1¼m branch right on to the B7065,
signposted *Port Logan*; after ½m a road leads
to Logan Gardens, which contain many rare
and exotic plants and trees. The village of
Port Logan nestles on the S shore of
Port Logan Bay. It is famous for its tidal fish
pond where cod and bass come to be fed
when a bell is rung. By the near-side of the
village turn left with the B7065, signposted
Drummore, to follow a winding road across
the Rhinns of Galloway peninsular. In
3¼m keep right to enter *Kirkmaiden*. Keep
forward, following the signposts for the Mull
of Galloway, and after ¾m the drive reaches
the junction with the B7041. From this point
an 8m diversion can be made by keeping
forward with the B7041 to visit the *Mull of
Galloway* at the extremity of the Rhinns of
Galloway peninsular. This is the farthest
S point on the mainland of Scotland.
The lighthouse here stands on remote,
windswept cliffs 210ft high. On a clear day
it is possible to see the coast of Ireland and
the Isle of Man. The final 3m is along a
narrow unclassified road with passing bays.
Return along the same roads for 4m to the
junction with the B7065.

The main drive turns left on to the B7041,
signposted Drummore. In ¾m at the
T-junction turn left, then right into the small
fishing village of Drummore. Turn left here

on to the A716 Stranraer road, which runs
along Luce Bay with attractive coastal
scenery before turning inland. The road
then turns back to the coast at the hamlet of
Ardwell. In 2½m go forward with an
unclassified road to skirt the coastal village
of Sandhead once more, and rejoin the A716.
In ½m join the A715 *Newton Stewart* and
Dumfries road, skirting sand dunes on the
right which in places rise to over 50ft in height.

In 3¾m the road turns right and passes
through the dark banks of a coniferous
plantation. In 1m turn right again with the
A715. After 1¼m turn right on to the A75,
and after 2m pass beneath a railway viaduct
and turn left on to an unclassified road
signposted *New Luce*. The drive follows a

quiet road alongside the Water of Luce,
passing the beautiful 12th-c remains of
Glenluce Abbey as it nears New Luce. The
latter village is where the Main Water of
Luce joins Cross Water of Luce. Turn left
over the river towards Stranraer; climbing
over the hills, and in 5½m turn right on to
the A75. After ½m the entrance for
Lochinch and *Castle Kennedy* Gardens lies
to the right. The ivy-clad castle is now in
ruins, but to the N Lochinch Castle
stands in magnificent gardens which are
graced by fine azaleas and rhododendrons.
Both of these castles lie in attractive wooded
settings on a strip of land separating the
White Loch from the Black Loch. The return
to Stranraer is through flat countryside.

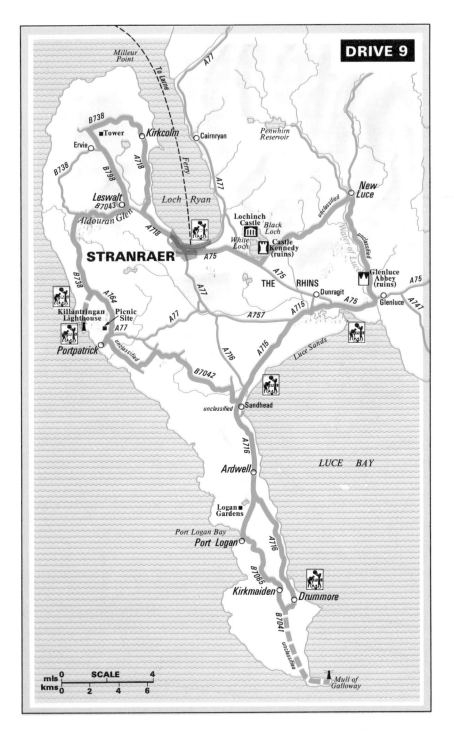

A Short Tour to Moscow

From Glasgow

Drive 10   75 miles

Leave *Glasgow* on the A77 *Ayr* and *Kilmarnock* road, passing through suburbs for 7m to *Newton Mearns* before climbing on to wild moorland. Turn left after 7½m on to the A719, signposted *Galston*. An undulating road continues through the hamlets of Waterside and *Moscow*. After another 2½m turn right on to the A71 to enter Galston, in the valley of the River Irvine. Enter the town and turn right, then leave by the A719 Ayr road. In another 2½m turn left on to the A76, signposted *Dumfries*, heading towards *Mauchline* with its many

Robert Burns' associations. The Burns Memorial tower contains a small museum and can be seen before the drive enters Mauchline. Near the castle is the house where Burns and Jean Armour were married. In the town turn left on to the B743 *Sorn* road. The route then climbs to 600ft before passing through pleasant woods and dropping down into the valley of the River Ayr at Sorn. This village boasts a 17th-c church with lofts which are reached by external stairs. Continue along the B743 *Muirkirk* road with landscapes which become increasingly barren, with hills rising to over 1,400ft to the left. The bog known as Airds Moss extends beyond the River Ayr to the right. After 7m turn left on to the A70 to reach the small iron- and coal-mining

town of Muirkirk. Here the drive turns left on to the A723 *Strathaven* road, later crossing high moorland close to Glengaval Reservoir before reaching the weaving town of Strathaven. Follow Hamilton signposts to leave by the A723, and later enjoy wide views over *Hamilton* and across to Glasgow before descending into the Clydesdale industrial town of Hamilton. An unusual octagonal parish church dating from 1732 stands behind the Celtic Netherton Cross.

Leave by the A74 Glasgow and *Uddingston* road, passing along Cadzow Street and Bothwell Road. To the right is Low Parks, with a racecourse and an impressive 19th-c mausoleum built by the Duke of Hamilton. A crossing of the River Clyde is made near the site of the 1679 Battle of *Bothwell* Bridge. The bridge was originally built *c*1400, but was modernized in 1826. The entrance to Bothwell Castle is near a road from Uddingston Cross, by traffic signals. The castle ruins date from the 13th and 15th c and occupy a pleasant position beside the wooded Clyde. Douglas Tower took 36 years to construct and was modelled on a French design. The return to Glasgow is along the A74 through mainly industrial and suburban areas.

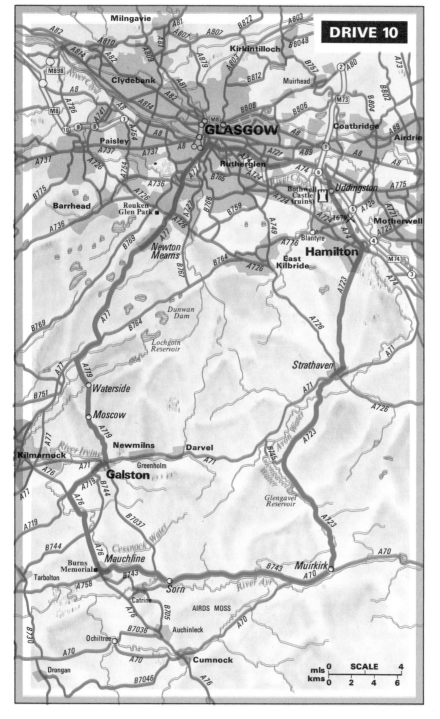

Coal, Iron, and The Clyde

From Lanark

Drive 11   84 miles

The starting point of this drive is *Lanark*, a Clydesdale market town built on rising ground on the E side of the valley.

Leave the town by following the A73 *Glasgow* road and turn left on to the A72, signposted *Hamilton*. Immediately descend to cross the Clyde and enter the village of *Kirkfieldbank* on the far bank. The Clyde is spanned by two bridges here, one of which dates from the 17thc. Beyond Hazelbank the A72 stays very close to the Clyde before reaching *Crossford*, a settlement built on the spur between Rivers Nethan and Clyde. Continue with the A72 to the small Clydeside village of Dalserf. Pass through the village, and after 1m branch left on to the A71, signposted *Kilmarnock*. Make a gradual climb out of the valley then in 2½m pass beneath the M74 and continue to Stonehouse, high above the Avon Water. Beyond *Strathaven* the drive turns left on to the A723 *Muirkirk* road to cross bleak moorland. Glenagavel Reservoir is passed before the tour reaches the small mining town of Muirkirk. Turn right here on to the A70, signposted *Cumnock*, and continue through desolate countryside beside the Bellow Water. Much of the area to the right comprises the marsh and bog lands of Airds Moss. Coal mining activities and the iron

works at *Lugar* become increasingly prominent towards Cumnock, a coalfield's centre.

Leave Cumnock on the A76 *Dumfries* road and cross bleak country to *New Cumnock*, another mining community. As the drive continues along the A76 it passes between hills which become higher and more impressive, with 2,298ft Blackcraig to the right and 1,559ft Corseacon Hill to the left. Drive through *Kirkconnel*, and after 3m turn left on to the B740, signposted *Crawfordjohn*. Follow the winding valley of the Crawick Water then after 10½m turn sharp left on to an unclassified road towards *Douglas*. Settlement in this area is sparse and the countryside is almost treeless. In 4½m bear right with an unclassified road, and on reaching a junction with the A70 turn right to reach Douglas. Continue down the valley of the Douglas Water, and in 2m turn left on to the A74, then right with *Edinburgh* signposts to rejoin the A70. Continue to *Hyndford Bridge*, then turn left on to the A73 and cross the River Clyde before passing the local racecourse and re-entering Lanark.

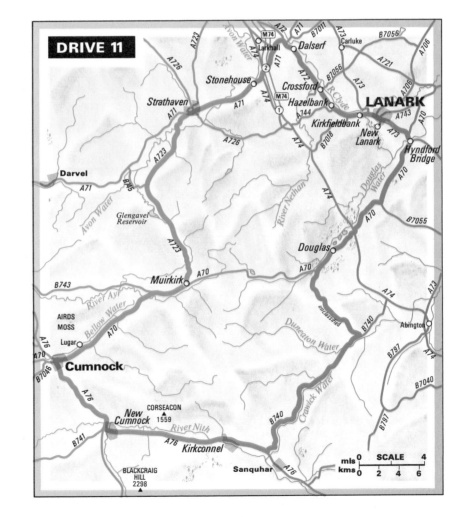

Placenames in *italic* type are worth stopping at; each is listed and described in the main gazetteer section of the book

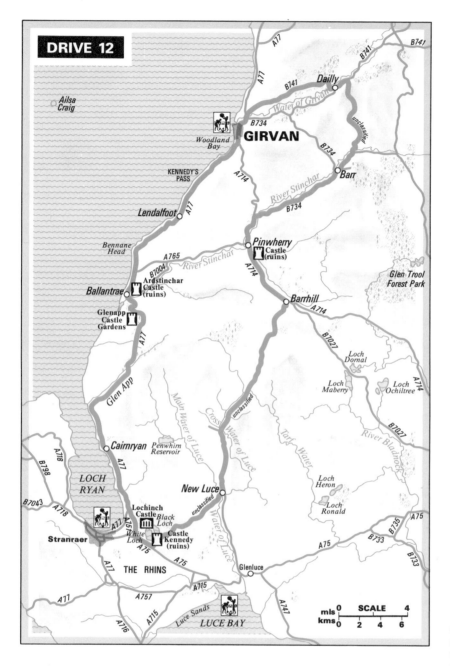

DRIVE 12

Edinburgh is Scotland's second largest city and the historic and cultural capital of the country, impressively situated between the Firth of Forth and the 2,000ft high *Pentland Hills.* The drive climbs from here on to bleak moorland, a stark contrast to the rolling green scenery around the city. Leave Edinburgh on the A702 Carlisle road, passing the 1,600ft summits of the N

Where Moors Meet the Sea

From Girvan

Drive 12   76 miles

This drive begins at *Girvan*, a popular resort in an attractive position on the Firth of Clyde, at the foot of a pleasant Galloway landscape.

Leave the town by the A77 *Ayr* road. After crossing the Water of Girvan turn right on to the B741 with *Dailly* signposts and enter a valley softened by extensive woodlands. Re-cross the river before entering Dailly, with its 18th-c church. Continue with the B741 and beyond the town turn left, signposted *Straiton*. After ¾m turn right on to an unclassified road signposted *Barr*. This narrow and sometimes gated road leads through lonely moorland for 5m before crossing the River Stinchar and turning right to follow the river to Barr, a popular

angling resort nestling beneath the Changue Forest.

Meet a T-junction and turn right, then turn left on to the B734 with *Barrhill* signposts. Continue for 6m and turn left again on to the A714 *Newton Stewart* road. Drive to *Pinwherry* and turn right to cross the Duisk River, passing a ruined castle on the left. The road now passes through the attractive Duisk Valley to Barrhill. With the prospect of wild scenery ahead, turn right on to an unclassified road with *New Luce* signposts and cross bleak, often boggy moorland on a narrowing highway. After 9m cross a river bridge and turn right, then continue to New Luce. Turn right with *Stranraer* signposts, and in 5½m turn right again on to the A75. To the right, after ½m, is the entrance for Lochinch and *Castle Kennedy* Gardens.

Continue with the A75 and in ½m turn right on to the A751, signposted Ayr. After 1¾m

turn right on to the A77 and drive along the shore of Loch Ryan. Fine backward views take in Stranraer and the Rhinns district of old Wigtownshire. *Cairnryan* is an attractive lochside village with many whitewashed houses. To the N of the village the road is hemmed in by steep, 600ft slopes on the right. After a short distance the drive turns inland with the A77, and passes through wooded Glen App before crossing open moorland and heading downhill to Glenapp Castle. The latter stands in fine gardens. Cross the River Stinchar into the small holiday resort of *Ballantrae*; near the Stinchar Bridge are the ruins of Ardstinchar Castle, an ancient Kennedy stronghold. The island of *Ailsa Craig* rises from the sea to the N. Superb coastal scenery accompanies the drive along the A77, which later rounds Bennane Head to *Lendalfoot*. High moors sweep down to the coast and make the drive N from Ballantrae one of the most spectacular in Britain. Beyond Lendalfoot the drive crosses rocky and beautiful Kennedy's Pass before entering a coastal plain and rounding Woodland Bay on the return to Girvan.

Drive 13 continued

Pentland Hills which overshadow much of the route between Edinburgh and *Lanark*. Beyond *Fairmilehead* the road negotiates the wooded, undulating foothills, reaching a height of 950ft below the main summits of 1,890ft Carnethy, and 1,899ft Scald. Left are the bleak, extensive moorlands of Auchencorth Moss, lying in the shadows of the Moorfoot Hills where the summits of 2,042ft Dundreich and 2,004ft Jeffries Corse dominate the range. After a while pass through the pleasant village of *Carlops* before crossing open country to *West Linton*, situated on the Lyne Water and once famous for its stonemasons. It was these craftsmen who carved Lady Gifford's Well.

Continue through *Dolphinton*, and after 2m pass the 1,689ft Black Mount on the right before turning right on to the A721, signposted *Glasgow*. Continue through Elsrickle and *Newbigging* to *Carnwath*, where a market cross dates from 1516 and indicates several mileages. Only the aisle of the local 15th-c church survives. Join the A70 with *Ayr* signposts, and in 2¾m turn left to pass through *Carstairs*. In 1¼m go forward to the A743 for Lanark, a market town set on rising ground E of the attractive wooded Clyde Valley. Leave the town by following Glasgow then *Linlithgow* signposts along the A706, and in 2m cross the wooded Mouse Water Valley.

After the drive crosses the A721 it continues through a rising landscape which becomes increasingly desolate. Forth is a town built at an altitude of 940ft above sea level, and is surrounded by moorland. In 2¼m bear right on to the A704, signposted Edinburgh, and pass Woodmuir Plantation. This is the start of a long descent, with good forward views, before the drive turns right on to the A71 to enter *West Calder*. Distinctive tips or 'bings' betray the numerous oil-shale workings of the area. Towards *Mid Calder* the route passes through pleasant stretches of woodland, and the town itself is attractively sited between the Almond and Linhouse Water.

Continue on the A71 through *East Calder*, then in 3m reach Wilkieston and turn left on to the B7030, signposted Ratho. Pass through Ratho, crossing the Union Canal, and climb to meet the A8. Turn left, then in ½m meet a roundabout and take the second exit on to an unclassified road to enter *Newbridge*. The interesting crow-stepped and gabled inn dates from 1683. Meet the main road and turn left on to the A89, then cross the River Almond and turn right on to the B800. Follow the river to *Kirkliston*, where the church has associations with Scott's *Bride of Lammermoor*. Parts of the church date from the 12thc – notably the west tower.

At the crossroads go forward. In ½m enter a roundabout and take the second exit on to the A8000. In ½m at a point near the private

grounds of 15th-c Dundas Castle there are views of the two *Forth Bridges*. From here the drive continues down to South Queensferry. Cross the A90 and turn right on to the B907 to enter the town. Formerly a ferry port, *Queensferry* adopted its name after Queen Margaret crossed the estuary from here. Dominating the town are two bridges; the massive, 19th-c cantilever railway bridge is 1½m long and 361ft high, and the 20th-c road bridge is one of the largest suspension bridges in Europe. The latter is 1½m long and has a 3,300ft centre span.

Leave by the B924 and pass under the railway bridge. An unclassified road on the right leads to *Dalmeny*, a village boasting one of the finest Norman churches in Scotland.

Drive to the church and turn left to rejoin the B924. In 2m join the A90 for a short scenic drive with views S of the Pentland Hills. In 2m reach the Barnton Hotel and turn left into unclassified Whithouse Road for *Cramond*. Cramond church is signposted and stands on the site of a Roman fort, close to the estuary. The village was described in Stevenson's *St Ives*. Leave by Cramond Road North and in 1m pass the entrance to the late 16th-c mansion of *Lauriston Castle*. In 1¼m go forward to traffic signals and turn left on to the A90, following City Centre signposts for the return to Edinburgh.

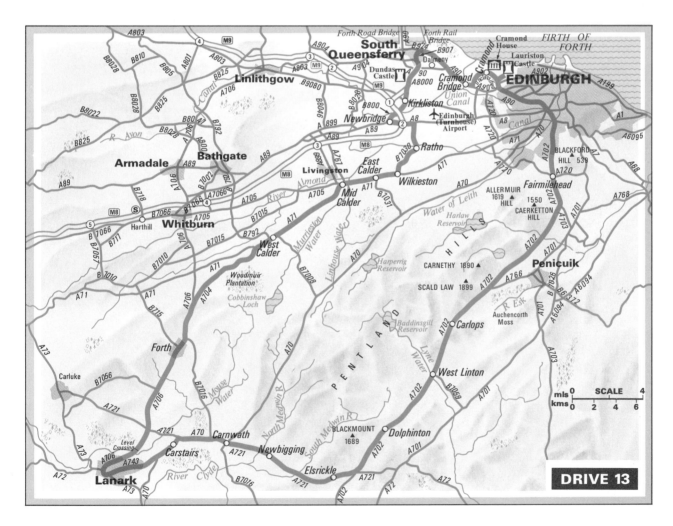

Over the Southern Uplands

From Hawick

Drive 14   85 miles

The Teviotdale community of *Hawick* is the largest and most important of the Border towns. As well as being well-known for its textiles and woollens, it is associated with Wordsworth and Anne, Duchess of Monmouth.

Leave by the B6399 *Newcastleton* road and follow a narrow, winding valley which is also occupied by Slitrig Water and the former Waverley railway line from *Edinburgh* to Carlisle. The road turns away from the valley for a short distance after the woodland at Stobs, and takes in impressive views of 1,300ft hills. *Shankend* viaduct stands out on the right as the drive rejoins the valley, after which the road climbs to its 1,182ft summit and affords views of 1,662ft Wyndburgh Hill and 1,412ft Kiln Knowe to the left. These peaks form a

watershed from which the headstreams of Slitrig Water flow NE to the North Sea, and those of Liddel Water drop SW to the *Solway Firth.*

In 1½m the descent past 1,544ft Leap Hill crosses the former railway close to its 1,006ft summit. From here the road drops rapidly down Whitrope Burn, passing 1,966ft Greatmoor Hill to the right and affording pleasant forward views. Arnton Fell rises to 1,464ft on the left as the drive approaches Hermitage. In ½m cross the river bridge; 14th-c *Hermitage Castle*, associated with Mary Queen of Scots, lies 1m farther on the right. In 3½m meet a junction with the B6357 and turn right. Turn left to visit the Border Forest Park and museum by following the B6357 to Saughtree, adding another 28m to the drive. Turn right to Kielder on a signposted but unclassified road. The museum lies 2m beyond the village. The weaving village of Newcastleton nestles in the delightful Liddesdale Valley, associated with Scott's *Guy Mannering.*

Follow *Canonbie* signposts through more wooded, undulating country and at the edge of Canonbie turn right on to the A7, signposted *Galashiels.* Continue along the attractively wooded Esk Valley. After 2m the 16th-c Hollows Tower pele can be seen on the right.

Langholm is a woollen-manufacturing town which is also a popular angling resort. It has associations with a 16th-c Border outlaw known as Johnny Armstrong, and the poet Hugh McDiarmid. East of the town is Whita Hill, a fine 1,163ft viewpoint surmounted by a monument. The direct return to Hawick is along Ewes Water and Teviotdale with the A7, thus saving 24m, but the drive takes a left turn on to the B709, signposted Eskdalemuir, to continue through the Esk Valley between rounded, 1,100ft hills. Pass through Bentpath and after 2m go forward on an unclassified road with Lockerbie signposts, keeping S of the river. In 2½m bear right with Eskdalemuir signposts, and after a short distance cross the Black Esk

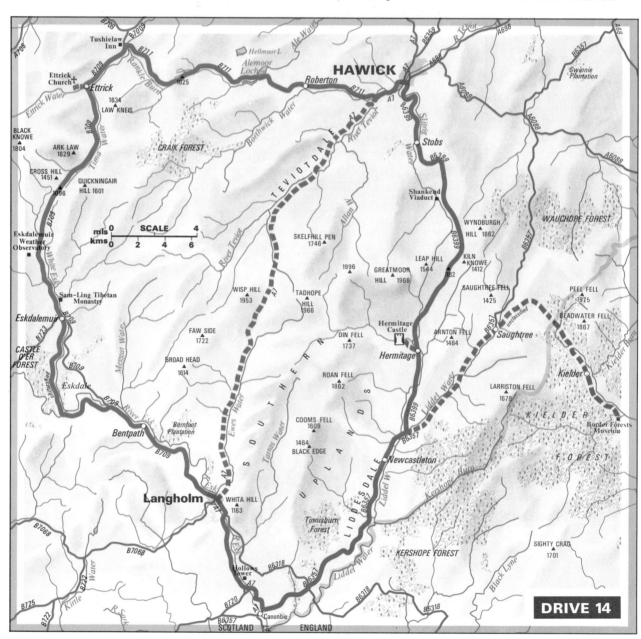

Drive 14 continued

River to enter Castle O'er Forest. The White Esk River lies to the right.

In 5m keep forward on the B709, signposted *Ettrick*, passing the hamlet of *Eskdalemuir*. In 1½m on the right is the curious Sam-Ling Tibetan Monastery, and 1¾m farther on the left, the famous Eskdalemuir weather observatory. From this point the road climbs steadily to a summit of 1,096ft, with 1,601ft Quickningair Hill to the right. Several heights of over 1,700ft lie to the left, but the most prominent are 1,451ft Cross Hill and 1,629ft Ark Law. As the road turns away from the hills it runs alongside Tima Water, on the descent to Ettrick. After 1m Ettrick Church lies to the left. It is here that James Hogg — Ettrick shepherd, poet, ballad writer, and friend of Scott — is buried. His birthplace is near by and marked by a monument.

Continue on the B709 along Ettrick Water. At *Tushielaw Inn* turn right on to the B711, signposted Hawick, and climb alongside Rankle Burn. The drive now continues through open country and descends to cross tree-shrouded Alemoor Loch. A short climb to 1,085ft leads to a long descent through *Roberton* and Borthwick Water; continue to the A7 and take a left turn signposted Galashiels. Return to Hawick alongside the Teviot.

The Rolling Cheviots

From Kelso

Drive 15   76 miles

Kelso, an attractive Border town where the Rivers Teviot and Tweed join, was once the home and school place of Sir Walter Scott. The 250-mile Pennine Way, a rugged walk down the backbone of England, starts at Kirk Yetholm 7m to the SE and just inside the Scottish border. Leave by the A699 *St Boswells* and *Selkirk* road, cross the River Tweed and turn right to cross the River Teviot. In ½m the site of the former town of *Roxburgh* — with the remains of its castle — is passed. It was during the siege of Roxburgh that James II was killed by a bursting cannon in 1460. The present hamlet of *Roxburgh* lies 2½m to the SW of the original site. Continue for 9m and turn right on to the A68, then turn right again on to the B6404 and enter St Boswells. Keep forward and in 1m cross the River Tweed. In ¼m turn left on to the B6356, signposted Dryburgh, for pleasant riverside scenery. In 1¼m go forward for the ruins of the beautiful 12th-c Dryburgh Abbey, which stand in a lovely riverside setting. Sir Walter Scott and Field Marshal Earl Haig are buried here.

Return along the B6356, and after ½m turn left to pass the massive Wallace statue. On the left after ½m is Bemersyde House (not open), the hereditary home of the Haig family. In ¼m turn left, and in ½m pass famous *Scott's View* where an AA viewpoint looks out over the conical peaks of

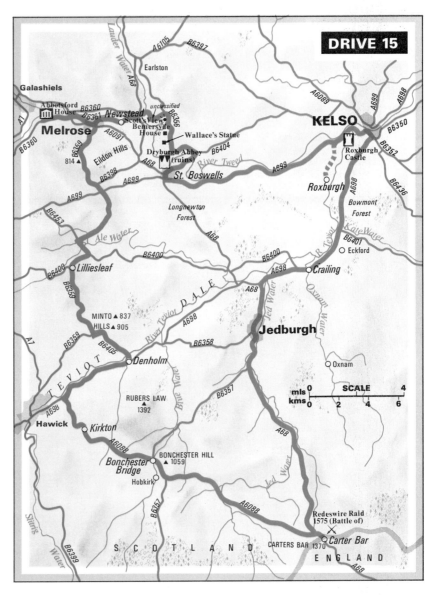

the Eildon Hills, much loved by Scott. In ½m go forward on an unclassified road signposted *Melrose*, for the wooded descent to cross Leader Water. At crossroads turn left on to the A68 to cross the Tweed, then immediately turn right on to the B6361. Continue through *Newstead* to the pleasant old town of Melrose, famous for the finest of all ruined Border abbeys. This was founded in 1136 and described by Scott in *The Lay of the Last minstrel*. Follow signposts for *Galashiels* on the A6091, and after 1¼m turn left on to the B6360, signposted Selkirk. In 1¼m on the right stands *Abbotsford House*, the famous 19th-c home of Sir Walter Scott. A car park is provided on the left.

Return to Melrose, and at the roundabout turn right on to the B6359, signposted *Lilliesleaf* and *Hawick*. Climb to a summit of 814ft for forward views over the rolling Cheviot hills. In 1¾m go forward over the crossroads. After 3m turn left over a river bridge, continue to Lilliesleaf, and turn left to follow the signposts for *Denholm*. In 3½m turn left on to the B6405, passing the twin peaks of the Minto Hills, and 1½m farther cross the River Teviot into Denholm. John Leyden,

a poet and friend of Scott, was born here.

Turn right on to the A698, signposted Hawick, and after 3½m turn left on to the A6088, signposted *Bonchester Bridge* and Newcastle. The route now climbs on to open moorland, affording rewarding views of high, rounded hills. To the S Wyndburgh Hill and Fanna Hill rise above the W expanses of Wauchope Forest. The long descent to Bonchester Bridge on Rule Water is followed by a long climb to moorland past the ancient hill fort on Bonchester Hill. A final climb is made prior to joining the A68 for *Carter Bar* situated at 1,370ft on the England-Scotland border. Extensive views to the NW take in the 18m distant Eildon Hills. Near by is the site of the last border battle, the Redeswire Raid of 1575.

Turn away from the border and return on the A68, signposted *Jedburgh*, winding down to the wooded valley of Jed Water. Jedburgh is one of the most attractive Border towns and preserves many crow-stepped and gabled houses. Continue on the A68 with *Edinburgh* signposts, then in 2m turn right on to the A698 for the return to Kelso along the Teviot Valley.

Where Merlin Sleeps

From Peebles

Drive 16   70 miles

Attractively situated in the Vale of Tweed, *Peebles* is an inland resort which is popular as an angling centre and well-known for its tweed mills.

Leave by the A72 *Glasgow* road and drive along the winding Tweed Valley. In 1m pass *Neidpath Castle*, a building with 11ft-thick walls and built in a situation which affords commanding views. After a further 1m an unclassified road to the left leads up the Manor Valley for 8m and ends below the 2,682ft slopes of Dollar Law. Sir Walter

Scott described this valley as 'the sweetest vale of all the south'. Pass the entrance to this road, and after 2m turn left on to the B712, signposted *Moffat*. At *Stobo* the Norman church retains its 'jougs', an iron collar used for punishment. After 2m the road crosses the River Tweed, then passes the Dawyck House Gardens which are noted for fine collections of trees and shrubs. Several species new to Scotland were introduced here in the 17th and 18thc. Behind the woods rise the 2,348ft Scrape, and 1,886ft Breach Law. The area of *Drumelzier* is said to contain the burial place of Merlin, the Arthurian wizard. After 1½m turn left on to the A701, signposted *Moffat*. On the left for several miles are a series of 1,500ft spurs leading to a string of summits

which rise to over 2,000ft. To the right are 1,600ft ridges running parallel with the road.

At the hamlet of *Tweedsmuir* the unclassified road signposted Talla road leads past Talla Reservoir to *St Mary's Loch*, a 3m curve of water popular with fishermen. This route can be taken to avoid Moffat, saving 20m on the detour. A climb to the edge of Talla Reservoir reveals four peaks over 2,250ft at its E end; the road begins a steep climb between these at first, but becomes gentler before the 1,483ft summit is reached near to the Megget Stone on the old Peebles-Roxburgh border. To the N stands the 2,756ft peak of Broad Law, and Molls Cleuch Dod rises to 2,572ft in the S — just two of the seven summits which top 2,500ft in the area. A long run down alongside Megget Water leads to Cappercleuch on St Mary's Loch, where the main drive is rejoined.

From Tweedsmuir the main route continues up the Tweed Valley. At the 1,334ft summit there is a tablet to a mail-coach crew killed in a snowstorm in 1831. Near by are the sources of the rivers Tweed, Clyde, and Annan. In 1¼m on the descent is the deep precipitous hollow at the head of Annandale known as the Devil's Beef-tub. The 2,651ft Hart Fell rises to the left across Annandale on the long descent to the market town of Moffat. Moffat's Colvin fountain is surmounted by a ram and indicates the importance of local sheep-farming.

Bear left on to the A708, signposted *Selkirk*, and follow Moffat Water. Beyond Craigieburn Plantation the valley becomes deeper and U-shaped, dominated by a 2,000ft ridge on the right. After 3m the valley narrows, and the spectacular Grey Mare's Tail Waterfall can be seen dropping 200ft on the left. Beyond its 1,108ft summit the road descends through bare countryside to Loch of the Lowes, which has a monument to James Hogg the Ettrick Shepherd. Opposite stands *Tibbie Shiel's Inn*. Named after the landlady, it was visited by Scott and became a centre for literary gatherings. Today it is popular with anglers. St Mary's Loch lies beyond the inn and was the 'lone St Mary's silent lake' of Scott's *Marmion*. Continue on the A708, skirting the loch and winding down alongside Yarrow Water to the Gordon Arms Hotel, where Scott and Hogg met for the last time. Hogg died in 1835 at Eldinhope, 1m to the SW. Turn left on to the B709, signposted *Innerleithen*, and climb to the 1,170ft summit. From here a long descent leads to *Traquair*. Go forward to reach Traquair House, one of the oldest and most interesting mansions in Scotland. Return to Traquair and turn right on to the B7062 for Peebles, following the Tweed Valley and skirting Cardrona Forest.

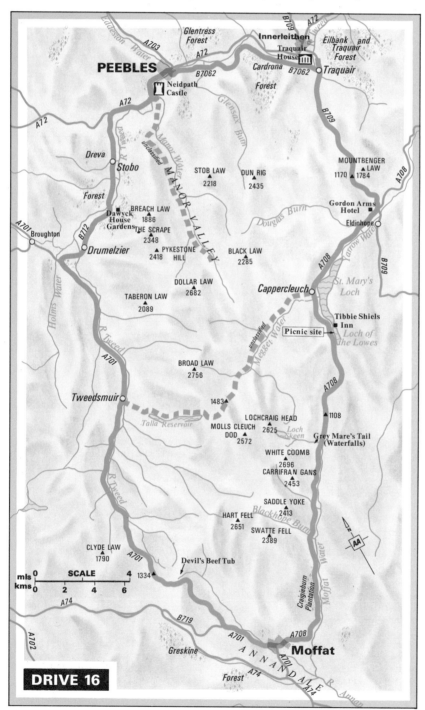

DRIVE 16

Through the Vale of Tweed

From Berwick-upon-Tweed

Drive 17   88 miles

At Berwick-upon-Tweed the river is spanned by the impressive Royal Border Railway Bridge of 1850. The town hall is of 18th-c origin, and remains of both the 12th-c castle and the medieval town walls survive.

Leave by the A1 *Edinburgh* road for attractive coastal scenery on the approach to the small fishing village of *Burnmouth*. Turn right here on to the A1107, signposted *Eyemouth*. Drive into this small fishing port and continue with *Coldingham* and *Dunbar* signposts along the A1107. Views of the coast take in rugged cliffs, alive with the noise of gulls. Coldingham church includes abbey ruins which are associated with Scott's *Marmion*. Turn right on to the B6438, signposted *St Abbs*, and drive to the quaint little fishing village of St Abbs. To the N are the 300ft cliffs of St Abbs Head, and the sandy Coldingham Bay curves to the S. Bathing is dangerous here on the ebb tide.

Return to Coldingham and turn right on to the A1107, signposted Dunbar. A long climb winds through hilly country to a moorland summit of 750ft before the drive turns downhill to face fine coastal scenery. Meet a T-junction with the A1; Pease Bridge spans Heriot Water to the right, and at 124ft was once known as the world's highest bridge. The drive turns left with the A1 and Berwick signposts. Continue to *Grantshouse* and turn right on to the A6112, signposted *Duns*. Climb through hilly country before the descent to the Whiteadder Valley at *Preston*. In 1½m approach the market town of Duns, passing 714ft Duns Law and the original site of the town on the way. Duns Burgh

Chambers contain a Jim Clark Room which houses trophies won by the famous racing driver. He lived near here before he was killed. Turn right on to the A6105 with *Greenlaw* signposts, and motor through open country before descending to Greenlaw, a one-time county town. Turn right then left for *Gordon*. Standing W of the village, off the A6105 *Earlston* road, is Greenknowe Castle. At the crossroads in Gordon and turn left on to the A6089, signposted *Kelso*. In 2¼m turn right on an unclassified road signposted *Mellerstain*. This road skirts the Mellerstain House estate, which includes a fine mansion by Adam. In 1½m turn left on to the unsignposted B6397, and continue to *Smailholm*. Smailholm Tower stands to the SW.

In 4m skirt the park of 18th-c *Floors Castle* before turning right on to the A6089 for Kelso, once the home of Sir Walter Scott. In the town follow *Coldstream* signposts on the A698 to run alongside the River Tweed.

Coldstream, which is well-known for the Guards Regiment raised here in 1659, has a museum housed in the old regimental headquarters. Leave by the A6112 Duns road and in 1¾m meet crossroads and turn right on to the B6437, signposted Norham. In 3¾m meet more crossroads and turn right on to the B6470. After 1½m the road crosses the River Tweed into England, and in ½m enters Norham. Turn left on the unclassified road to Berwick and pass the 12th-c keep of Norham Castle. Continue, and in 2½m turn left with Horncliffe signposts. At the edge of Horncliffe go

forward and follow signposts indicating the Chain Bridge and Berwick, then in ½m turn left. This road crosses the River Tweed and re-enters Scotland by the 19th-c Union Suspension Bridge – the first of its kind. In 1¼m turn right on to the A699 for the return to Berwick.

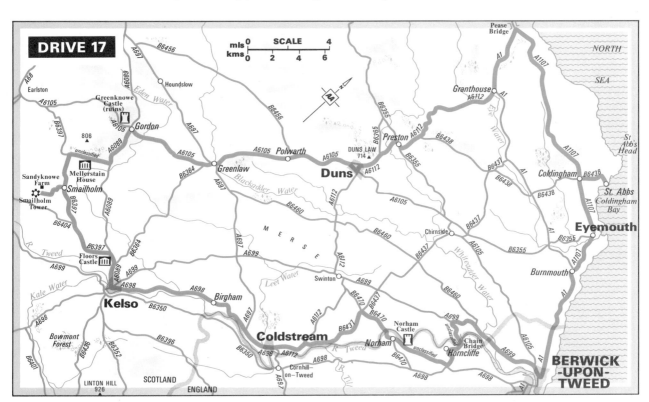

Among the Lammermuir Hills

From Dunbar

Drive 18 75 miles

Dunbar is a quiet town which was once the scene of historic and violent conflict, and interesting features of the community include a 17th-c town house and a ruined 14th-c castle. On a gentler note, a branch of the Myreton Motor Museum is also situated here.

Leave by the A1087 Berwick road and in 1¼m turn left on to the A1 to head S along the coast. In ½m on the right is the site of the Battle of Dunbar in 1650. Pass through *Cockburnspath* and after ½m turn right on to an unclassified road signposted *Abbey St Bathans*. As the road climbs to the 909ft summit of Ecclaw Hill there are wide views in several directions. Continue for 3½m over high ground, following signposts for *Preston* and *Duns*, before the road dips down again. Continue uphill and turn right on to the A6112. After Preston village turn right on to the B6355, signposted *Gifford* and *Cranshaws*. The valley of the Whiteadder Water lies to the left beyond the ford. After 2m the road skirts the Whiteadder Reservoir below the 1,500ft mass of Spartleton Edge. A long climb brings the road to a moorland summit of 1,346ft. A steep descent affords wide-sweeping views over East Lothian to the Firth of Forth. At Gifford turn right on to the B6369 for a short run through pleasant, wooded country, then turn right on to the A6137 for *Haddington*. Situated on the River Tyne, Haddington is known for its grain market.

Follow *Edinburgh* signposts on the A6093 for the B6471, and in 1m turn left on to the A1. In 2¼m pass Gladsmuir, then in ½m meet crossroads and turn right on to the B6363, signposted *Longniddry*. After 2m turn right on to the A198 with North Berwick signposts to pass Longniddry. In 1m meet a T-junction and turn right by the wooded shores of the Forth. Fine views across the dunes of Gosford Bay can be enjoyed before the drive turns inland to *Aberlady*, which is situated on a wide inlet overlooking a nature reserve. One mile beyond the village is 16th-c Luffness House, containing the Myreton Motor Museum; farther on is the well-known golfing centre of *Gullane*. The attractive village of *Dirleton* is dominated by an impressive 13th- to 16th-c castle with an enclosed bowling green.

The coast is rejoined at the fishing and golfing resort of North Berwick. Continue on the A198, signposted Berwick-upon-Tweed, and in 2½m reach 14th-c *Tantallon Castle* – associated with Scott's *Marmion*. This striking fortress is set on a rocky headland overlooking the sea. Offshore is the 350ft mass of Bass Rock. Boat trips to the island run from North Berwick. *Whitekirk's* 15th-c cruciform church has a barrel-vaulted chancel and porch. Continue to *Tyninghame* and turn right on to the B1407 to pass along the Tyne Valley to *East Linton*. In 1½m Preston Mill stands beside the river. This is the oldest working grain-mill in Scotland. At East Linton turn

left, and in ¼m left again with Dunbar signposts. Cross the river and its shallow gorge. For a short detour to 13th- and 15th-c Hailes Castle, turn right on to an unclassified road immediately beyond the bridge and pass under the railway bridge. Cross the main road and turn right.

The main drive continues forward after ¼m to join the A1, passing Phantassie House – birth-place of John Rennie in 1761 – on the left. Rennie was a famous engineer and bridge-builder. In 3m meet a roundabout and take the first exit on the A1087 for the return to Dunbar.

Road to the Moorfoot Hills

From Edinburgh

Drive 19 90 miles

From *Edinburgh* city centre follow *Galashiel's* signposts, passing Salisbury Crags and Arthur's Seat. In 2m go forward on to the A701, signposted *Penicuik* and *Peebles*, for *Kames*. In 2½m turn left on to the B7003, signposted *Roslin*, and in ¾m at the edge of the village turn right with Rosewell signposts.

To visit the remains of Roslin Chapel go forward. The chapel was founded in 1446,

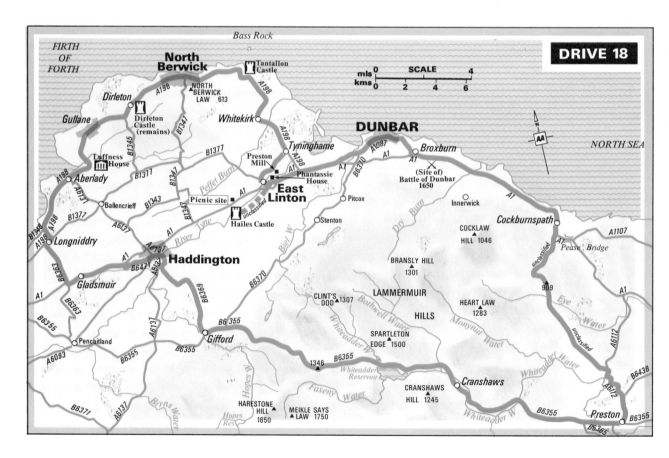

Drive 19 continued

and is well-known for the Prentice pillar, richly carved in a continental style. The former Old Rosslyn Inn on College Hill, and the attractively situated 14th- to 17th-c castle are worth visiting. Roslin is the site of a famous battle fought between the English and the Scots in 1302, the English suffering a severe reverse. Descend to cross the wooded valley of the North Esk River and continue to Rosewell.

Meet a T-junction and turn right on to the A6094. In 2¼m turn left on to an unclassified road and cross Cauldhall Moor, with views of the Moorfoot Hills ahead. In 1¾m meet crossroads and turn left on to the B6372. After another 1¼m turn right on to an unclassified road signposted Peebles. In 1¼m a road to the left winds to the shores of Gladhouse Reservoir. After 3m descend and turn left on to the A703. At *Eddleston* turn right with signposts indicating *Lyne* via Eldons, on to an unclassified road which gradually climbs to 900ft. Continue downhill and in 1¼m bear left. In ½m turn left on to the A72, with Peebles signposts, driving alongside the Lyne Water and River Tweed. In 2½m on the right stands Neidpath Castle, formerly known as the Castle of Peebles. After 1m the road enters Peebles and continues on the A72, signposted Galashiels, to the woollen-manufacturing town of *Innerleithen*. For *Traquair* House turn right on to the B709.

Turn left on to the B709 with *Heriot* signposts, and continue alongside Leithen Water to follow the river for 4m. As the main river is left behind the road climbs to 1,250ft over a narrow pass, then descends to the Dewar Burn. In 2m go forward on to the B7007 for the gradual climb to a 1,324ft summit at the back of the Moorfoot scarp. On a clear day the views are extensive, taking in the *Pentland Hills*, the 1,900ft summits of Scald Law and Carnethy, Arthur's Seat in Edinburgh, and the waters of the Firth of Forth. In 3¼m turn right on to the A7, signposted Galashiels, and 1¼m farther turn left on to the B6367, signposted *Pathhead*. In 3¼m reach *Crichton* and turn left, then right. For the ruins of Crichton Castle turn left into the village, then go forward and bear left. At Pathhead, turn right then left following *Haddington* signposts. In 2m turn right on to the A6093, and 3m farther pass through *Pencaitland* on the River Tyne. Meet crossroads and turn left on to the B6355, signposted *Tranent*, then take the next turning right on to the B6363 and follow *Longniddry* signposts through to the golfing resort of Longniddry. Turn right on to the A198, drive into the town, and follow signposts for *North Berwick*. In 1m meet a T-junction and turn left on to the B1348, signposted *Cockenzie*. Continue alongside the Firth of Forth.

Entering the fishing villages of Cockenzie and *Port Seton*, where an unclassified road on the left leads to the Adam mansion of Seton Castle and the collegiate church of *Seton*. After another 2m reach the site of the battle in which Prince Charles Edward – Bonnie Prince Charlie – defeated General Cope in 1745, on the approach to

Prestonpans. The town's name originated from salt-pans established here by the monks of *Newbattle Abbey*. At the end of the town is Preston Grange historical site, preserving Scotland's last working beam-engine at what is thought to be Britain's oldest coal-mine.

In 1½m enter a roundabout and take the third exit on to the A1. Return to Edinburgh through *Musselburgh*, a community on the wooded banks of the River Esk.

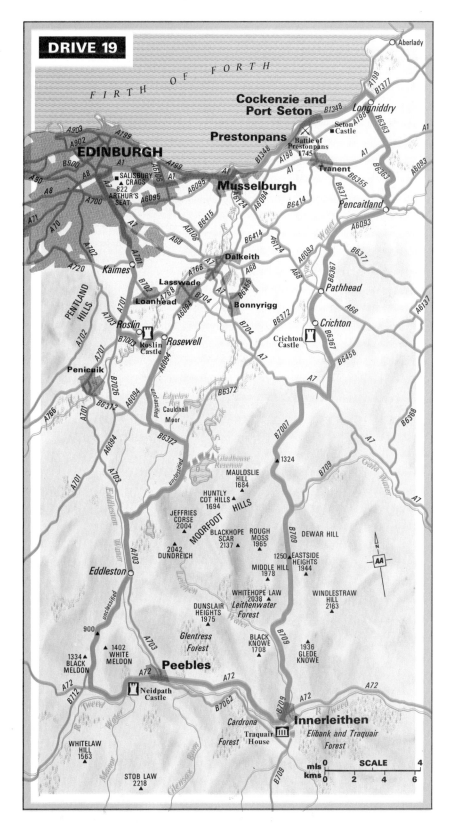

Scott's Country

From Galashiels

Drive 20   83 miles

Galashiels is a large Border town where tweeds and woollens are manufactured. A technical college here specializes in local industry.

Leave by the A6091, signposted *Jedburgh* (A68). In 1½m at Langlee there is a tablet recording Sir Walter Scott's last journey from Italy to his home at *Abbotsford*, shortly before his death. In 1½m go forward on to the B6360, signposted Gattonside. For Abbotsford turn right across the bridge, then right again on to the B6360. The main route runs alongside the River Tweed, with views of the Eildon Hills to the right. In 3m meet crossroads and turn left on to the A68, signposted *Edinburgh*, to follow the valley of the Leader Water. Beyond *Earlston* there are distant views of Lammermuir Hill as the valley broadens.

The historic royal burgh of *Lauder* is an angling centre and the venue for the Common or Border Riding ceremony. From here the route continues along the broad valley for several miles before starting a long, gradual climb through increasingly bare country to a moorland summit of 1,192ft. In 2m the famous 1,130ft *Soutra Hill* viewpoint overlooks the Eildon Hills, the 822ft peak of Arthur's Seat at Edinburgh, and the Ochil Hills beyond the Forth estuary. This route across the hills was first used by the Romans, and centuries later by the kings Edward I and II and James IV. In 3¾m turn left on to the B6458, signposted Tynehead, descending from Soutra Hill and passing the flat expanse of Fala Moor. In 2½m at Tynehead go forward on to the B6367, with views of the 1,700ft Moorfoot Hills scarp. In 1¼m turn left on to the A7, signposted Galashiels. In 1½m the track-bed of the former railway from Edinburgh to Carlisle is crossed, close to the 870ft road summit of the climb from Edinburgh. After 3m the road and the former railway track share the Gala Water's winding, partly-wooded valley almost to Galashiels. At *Stow* there is a fine, mid 17th-c pack-horse bridge. After 4m turn right on to the B710, signposted *Clovenfords*, where Scott once lodged as county sheriff. Meet crossroads here and turn right on to the A72, signposted *Peebles*. The road now descends to the Tweed Valley, where the drive turns right. Across the river is *Ashiesteel House*, where Scott lived from 1804 to 1812 and wrote *Marmion*, *Lady of the Lake*, and *The Lay of the Last Minstrel*. The drive then passes the extensive Elibank and Traquair Forest, opposite the 19th-c textile village of *Walkerburn*.

At *Innerleithen*, a woollen-manufacturing town with mineral springs on the Leithen Water, turn left with *Yarrow* signposts on to the B709 and cross the River Tweed. In ½m on the right stands Traquair House, one of Scotland's oldest and finest houses. The pleasant, relaxing drive continues forward through *Traquair* and joins Paddock Burn at the start of a long climb to the 1,170ft summit. Mountbenger Law rises to 1,784ft on the left as the drive descends to the Gordon Arms Hotel. Meet crossroads and turn left on to the A708 with *Selkirk* signposts, following the valley of Yarrow Water – praised by Scott, Wordsworth, and many others for its beauty.

In 9m on the left stands Foulshiels, where the explorer Mungo Park was born in 1771. On the opposite bank of the river are the ruins of 15th-c Newark Castle, retreat of Anne, Duchess of Monmouth, for whom Scott wrote *The Lay of the Last Minstrel*. On the left after 2m are the gardens of Philiphaugh, a fine mansion associated with a nearby battle in 1645.

In 1m bear right, then turn right into the tweed mill town of Selkirk. The town hall carries a 110ft spire and still sounds a nightly curfew. Return to Galashiels along the A7, through the Ettrick and Tweed Valleys.

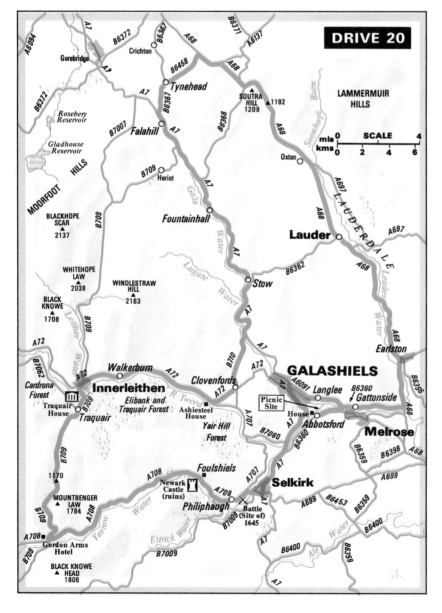

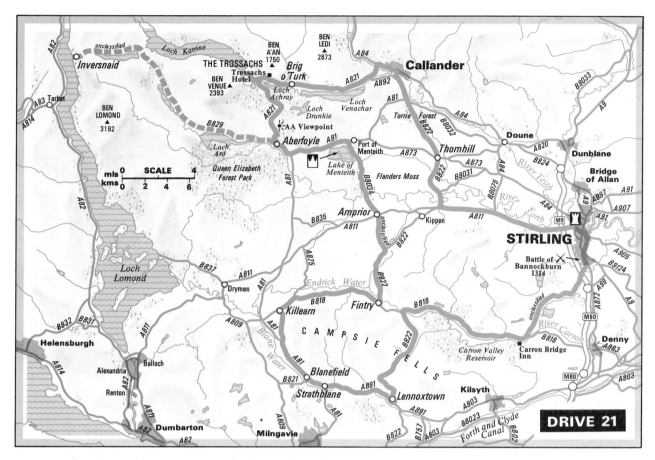

Gateway to the Highlands

From Stirling

Drive 21   86 miles

Strategically set beside the River Forth, *Stirling* is known as the Gateway to the Highlands. From here tourists head N or to *Loch Lomond* and the *Trossachs*. The town is dominated by its imposing castle, standing proudly on a sheer 250ft crag. The present structure dates from the 15thc, but earlier castles were built on the site to command routes across the surrounding plain. Near here were the battles of Stirling Bridge in 1297 and Bannockburn in 1314, both severe reverses for the English. Scenes from the BBC series *Colditz* were filmed at the castle, and it is still used as a barracks. Crowning Abbey Craig, 1m NE at *Causewayhead*, is the Wallace monument – a good viewpoint.

Follow *Erskine* signposts to leave by the A811, continuing W along the level Forth Valley. In 8¾m turn right on to the B822, signposted *Thornhill*, and after ½m cross the River Forth. At Thornhill join the A873, then keep forward with the B822 towards *Callander*. The road passes the edge of Torrie Forest before joining the A81 to reach Callander, the starting point for a Trossachs tour. Follow the A84 *Crianlarich* road, then in 1¼m turn left on to the A821 towards the Trossachs. Cross the River Leny, then turn alongside the shores of Loch Vennachar with the 2,873ft peak of Ben Ledi to the right. After Brig o'Turk there is relaxing scenery through the Queen Elizabeth Forest Park beside Loch Auchray.

After ¼m beyond the Trossachs Hotel, a diversion can be made by going forward to the pier at the E end of Loch Katrine. Pleasure steamer trips are very popular here during the summer. The loch, which inspired Sir Walter Scott's poem *The Lady of the Lake*, is set in the heart of the Trossachs area, a delightful combination of mountains, woodland, and water. The rugged 2,393ft peak of Ben Venue stands out to the S.

The main drive continues along the *Aberfoyle* road, winding through the Queen Elizabeth Forest, and after 2½m offers views of Loch Drunkie to the left. In another 2½m pass the David Marshall Lodge viewpoint, a delightful place to relax before the short winding descent to the small resort of Aberfoyle. From here a detour may be taken along the B829 for *Inversnaid*, picturesquely set at the end of Loch Lomond. This scenic road runs alongside Loch Ard and Loch Chon. The final 4m is on an unclassified road passing Loch Arklet. The return is along the same roads; 28m is added to the drive if the full detour is made.

The main drive continues with the A821 Stirling road, and after 1m branches left on to the A81, signposted Callander. To the right after 2½m is the Lake of Menteith, where the 13th-c island ruins of Inchmahome Priory are occasionally open to the public. In 1m turn right on to the B8034, towards Arnprior. The passenger ferry for Inchmahome Priory is shortly to the right by Menteith Church.

At Arnprior turn right on the A811, then left on to an unclassified road signposted *Fintry*. After 2m the drive crosses the moors below the Fintry Hills and turns right on to the B822 to Fintry. This village is pleasantly set in the valley of the Endrick Water, between the Fintry Hills and Campsie Fells, which form the Lennox Hills. Turn right on to the B818 Killearn road, then in 5½m join the A875 *Glasgow* road and pass through *Killearn*. After 2m turn left on to the A81, following Strath Blane to Blanefield and the edge of *Strathblane*. Turn left here on to the A891. At *Lennoxtown* turn left with Fintry signposts on to the B822, which climbs out of the valley and passes the head of Campsie Glen. The road reaches a height of over 1,000ft as it crosses the moors of Campsie Fells. After the run down into the valley of Endrick Water, turn right on to the B818, signposted *Denny*. The road later runs alongside the Carron Valley Reservoir, backed by attractive pine forests. Beyond the dam, after 1¾m, turn left at *Carronbridge* Inn on to an unclassified road signposted Stirling. In 1¾m the road passes the small Loch Coulter Reservoir on the right. After another 2¼m meet a T-junction and turn left. The drive later crosses the M9 motorway, and in ¾m turns right then left to join the A80. Immediately to the left is the *Bannockburn* Battleground where an open-air rotunda and equestrian statue of Robert the Bruce commemorates the battle of 1314. The A80 and A9 are taken for the short return into Stirling.

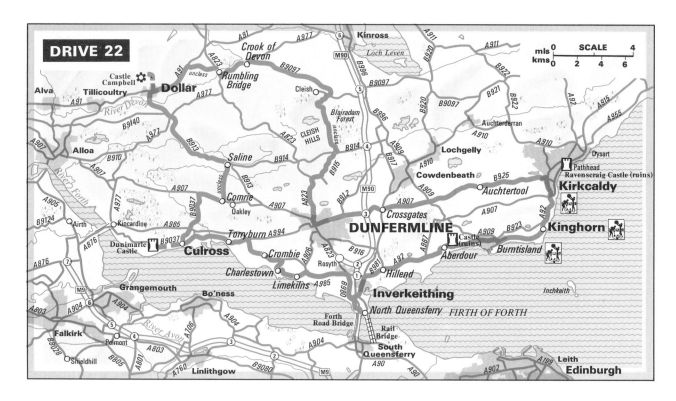

Around South Fife

From Dunfermline

Drive 22   70 miles

Dunfermline, once the capital of Scotland, is well-known for its industries, including the manufacture of linen.

Follow *Crieff* signposts to leave by the A823, and in 2½m turn right on to the B915, signposted *Kelty*. After ¼m turn left, then in another 1½m take the second turning left on to the unclassified *Cleish* road, which crosses the moorland Cleish Hills and skirts Blairadam Forest. After 3¾m meet a T-road and turn right, then turn left on to the B9097, signposted *Crook of Devon*. The road passes through pleasant agricultural country before turning left on to the A977 to Crook of Devon. In 1m turn right on to the A823, signposted Crieff, and cross the River Devon by *Rumbling Bridge*, a local beauty spot. After ¼m turn left on to an unclassified road signposted *Dollar*, then in 1½m left again on to the A91. Dollar is a mainly residential town sitting at the foot of the Ochil Hills in the valley of the River Devon. A diversion can be made 1m N of the town to Castle Campbell, a 15th-c tower in a picturesque setting above Dollar Glen. The splendid views from this vantage point are worth the slight diversion.

The main drive turns left towards *Kincardine* to leave by the B913. In 2m, at the junction with the A977, turn right then immediately left following signposts for Dunfermline. Continue to *Saline*. Turn right here on to the unclassified *Oakley* road, and in 2m right again on to the A907. Pass over the level crossing into *Comrie*. After 1¼m turn left on to the B9037 towards *Culross*, a charming little place which still retains much of its old character. Later the route crosses the A985 on to an unclassified road

for Culross. There are attractive views across the River Forth before the road turns downhill past the remains of a Cistercian abbey which was founded in 1217. On the B9037, 1m W, is Dunimarle Castle with its impressive collection of art treasures.

The drive turns left on to the B9037 and continues along the Forth to *Torryburn*. In 1m enter a roundabout and take the fourth exit on to the A985 for Crombie. After ¾m turn right on to an unclassified road for the small coalport of *Charlestown*, and run alongside the river to *Limekilns*. The road veers inland before turning right to rejoin the A985. At the edge of *Rosyth* keep forward at a roundabout, then at the next roundabout take the fourth exit on to the B980, signposted *North Queensferry*. In 1¼m meet a roundabout and take the third exit to join the B981 for North Queensferry. The main features here are the two impressive bridges across the Firth of Forth. The cantilever rail bridge, completed in 1890, is one of the finest examples of engineering in the world. The new road bridge, opened in 1964, is one of Europe's largest suspension bridges and has a centre span of 3,300ft. The two bridges provide a marked contrast — the rail bridge big and powerful, the other slim and elegant.

Return along the B981. In 1¼m enter a roundabout and take the second exit for *Inverkeithing*. At the end of town turn right on to the A92, signposted *Kirkcaldy*, for *Hillend* and *Aberdour*, a small Firth of Forth resort which has a Norman church and a ruined 14th-c castle. Continue with the *Burntisland* road and in 3m at a

roundabout take the third exit to Burntisland, another Firth of Forth resort and coaling port. Turn left along the coast with the A92 Kirkcaldy road. Offshore lies the fortified island of Inchkeith. After *Kinghorn* the drive reaches the outskirts of Kirkcaldy, an industrial town and coalport. To the NE of the town, at Pathead, a diversion along the A92 coast road leads to the gaunt, impressive ruin of Ravenscraig Castle.

The main drive avoids the town by turning right then immediately left on to the A907, passing Raith Rovers' football ground. After ½m take the first exit at a roundabout on to the B925, signposted Dunfermline. This road passes through undulating countryside to *Auchertool*. In 2¼m meet a roundabout and join the A907, then at *Crossgates* turn right then immediately left. The M90 motorway is crossed before the drive returns to Dunfermline.

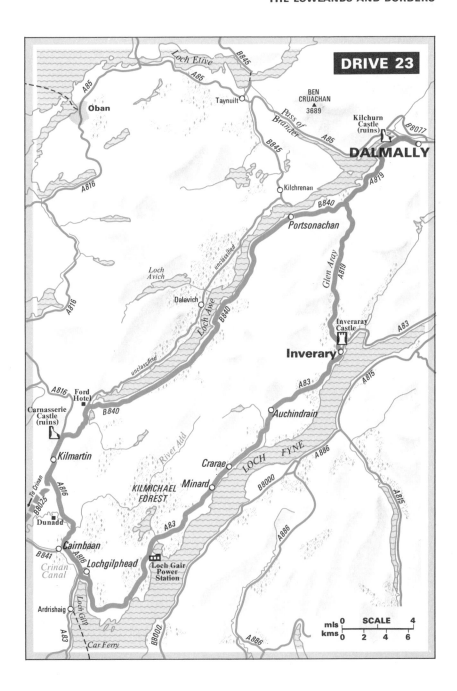

DRIVE 23

Loch Landscapes

From Dalmally

Drive 23   78 miles

Leave the small Loch Orchy town of *Dalmally* on the A85 *Oban* road, looking for an early turn left on to the A819. The ruins of *Kilchurn Castle* can be seen on the right and there are fine views across Loch Awe to 3,689ft Ben Cruachan. Turn right on to the B840. This leads along a narrow undulating road alongside the shores of Loch Awe for about 20m. Beyond the end of the loch, opposite the Ford Hotel, turn left and in 2¾m, at the A816, turn left again. Near by are the ruins of 16th-c Carnasserie Castle. At *Kilmartin* there is an ancient carved cross in the churchyard. Prehistoric remains have been found in the area.

Once S of Kilmartin a diversion of 35m can be made on the B8025, to *Crinan* on Crinan Loch at the W end of the Crinan Canal. As the route continues on the B8025 it passes through *Knapdale* Forest to *Tayvallich* on the arm of Loch Sween, ending at *Keills* on

the Sound of Jura. The main route continues on the A816, and after 3½m the prehistoric hill fort of Dunadd Fort lies to the right. The structure incorporates walled enclosures. This was once the capital of the ancient Scots kingdom of Dalriada. From near *Cairnbaan* the Crinan Canal runs on the right of the road to *Lochgilphead*, at the head of Loch Gilp, an attractive small inlet of Loch Fyne.

Take the A83 *Inveraray* road beside the shores of Loch Fyne, passing Loch Gair power station on the right. Points of interest at *Minard* include the gardens of Crarae Lodge and Crarae Forest Garden. At *Auchindrain* there is a recently-founded museum of Farming Life. Inveraray is without doubt one of the most picturesque small towns in Scotland. Beautifully set beside Loch Fyne, it is famous for an 18th-c castle set in a fine wooded park.

To leave this historic scene take the A819 and pass through richly-wooded Glen Aray to open moorland. There are good views of Ben Cruachan, Cruachan Dam, and Loch Awe as the drive runs down to *Cladich* for the return to Dalmally.

Placenames in *italic* type are worth stopping at; each is listed and described in the main gazetteer section of the book   121

A Short Tour of Knapdale

From Lochgilphead

Drive 24   46½ miles

Leave *Lochgilphead* on the A83 for a pleasant drive along the shores of Loch Gilp to the little town of *Ardrishaig* at the E end of the Crinan Canal. The road continues S for 2½m, sandwiched between Loch Fyne and pleasantly-wooded slopes. Turn right on to the B8024 and climb inland to bleak, open country. Pass Loch Errol before running down to Loch Caolisport, a sea-loch. As the route runs beside the shore there are wide-sweeping views across the loch. The Point of Knap may be seen, and across the Sound of Jura the prominent Paps of Jura are outlined against the sky. At Kilberry there is a collection of sculptured stones dating from medieval times. The castle, which was rebuilt in 1844, is not open to the public. Beyond Kilberry bear left to take an undulating, wooded road to the shore of West Loch Tarbert — the sea-loch that divides Knapdale from Kintyre. On the left of the road is the coniferous Achaglachach Forest. After passing through a short wooded glen the route goes forward on to the A83 for the return to Lochgilphead, again flanked on one side by wooded slopes and on the other by the loch. The final views across the loch take in the *Cowal* Peninsula.

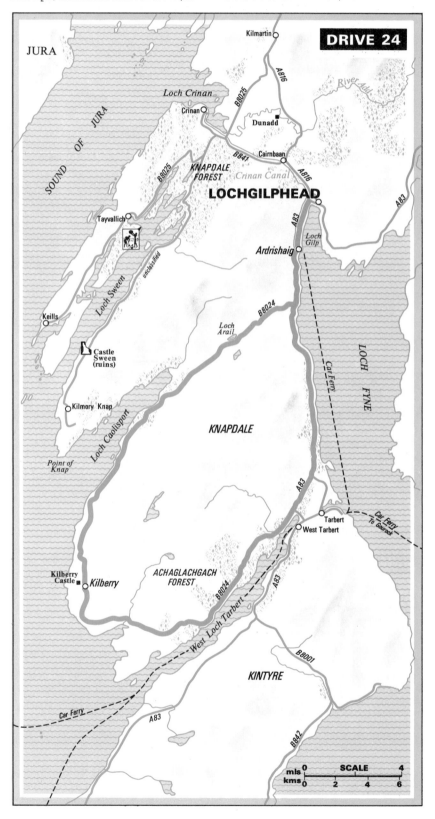

The Kintyre Peninsula

From Tarbert

Drive 25   73¼ miles

The fishing port of *Tarbert* lies on East Loch Tarbert, an inlet of Loch Fyne but separated from West Loch Tarbert by a narrow isthmus linking the *Kintyre* Peninsula and Knapdale. The route starts its run on the A83 *Campbeltown* road, passing West Loch Tarbert. At Kennacraig there is a car-ferry service to the beautiful islands of *Islay, Jura,* and *Gigha*. From the W coast of Kintyre these islands stand out prominently to the right. A passenger ferry operates between *Tayinloan* and Gigha. There is attractive scenery as the drive continues along the coast between agricultural land and the rocky shore, with occasional glimpses of sandy beaches.

Northern Ireland can be seen in the distance before the drive turns inland and heads for Campbeltown. This is the main commercial centre for Kintyre, a fishing port and popular holiday resort.

From Campbeltown the A83 leads W to the B843, which continues for 5½m to *Machrihanish*, a golfing resort with fine sands. From the junction of the A83 and the B843 the B842 leads to *Southend*, which also has a golf course and fine sands. A narrow, hilly road leads from Southend to the *Mull of Kintyre*, where the distant coast of Northern Ireland can be seen across the water.

The route leaves Campbeltown by the B842 and passes through *Saddell*, with its ruined castle and the 12th-c abbey. Saddell lies in the South Kintyre Forest, an area which merges with Carradale Forest farther N. As the road enters hilly country, open stretches reveal fine views clear to the hills of Arran, and in particular to the 2,345ft peak of Beinn Bharrain. Skirt the shore of Kilbrannan Sound and pass near

Carradale, a popular resort with fine sands. In 13m the drive reaches Claonaig, which is the terminal for the Arran car-ferry service during the summer. The route turns left on to the B8001 to Kennacraig, but straight on is *Skipness*, a village with a ruined 13th-c castle. The main route first makes a short climb, then dips to give views to Knapdale and West Loch Tarbert. At Kennacraig turn right on to the A83 for the return to Tarbert.

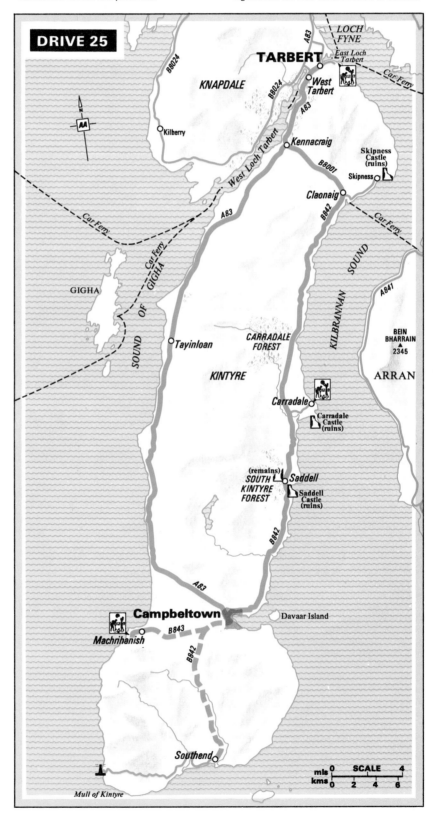

123

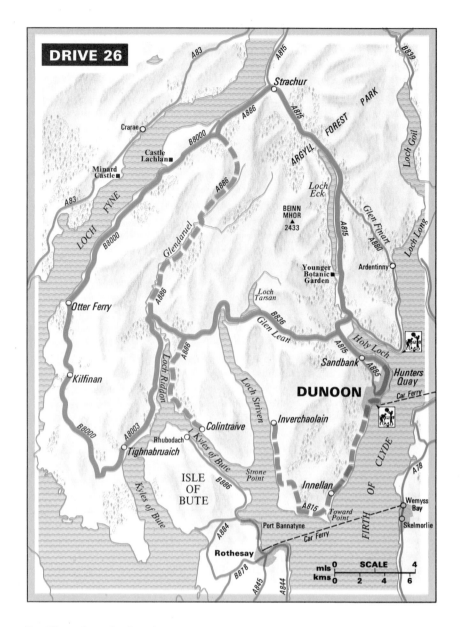

Sea-Views from the Cowal

From Dunoon

Drive 26   69 miles

Dunoon is a popular *Firth of Clyde* resort linked by car-ferry to *Gourock* on the old Renfrewshire coast. It is an ideal point from which to sample Scotland's fine scenery. Take the A815 through *Kirn* to *Hunters Quay* where another car-ferry service operates to Gourock, and follow the S shore of Holy Loch. The road turns right at the yacht-building centre of *Sandbank* to run alongside Holy Loch. In 2½m turn left to pass the Younger Botanic Garden at *Benmore* Estate, which is incorporated in the *Argyll Forest Park*. The drive continues pleasantly along the shores of Lock Eck, with 2,433ft Beinn Mhor rising above the loch to the left of the road. Continue through a thickly-forested valley to Strachur on the shore of Loch Fyne and turn left on to the A886. After 3m turn right on to the B8000. A short cut, saving 19m, can be taken by continuing on the A886 through *Glendaruel*.

There are attractive views across Loch Fyne as the narrow and hilly B8000 leads past Castle Lachlan, *Otter Ferry*, and *Kilfinan*. The dark outlines of the island of *Arran* and 2,866ft Goat Fell stand out as the road runs down into *Tighnabruaich*, a small resort on the *Kyles of Bute* – the narrow strait that separates the *Island of Bute* from the mainland.

Take the A8003 *Strachur* road along the slopes above Loch Riddon. On this stretch of road there are several places set aside as viewpoints, as well as picnic areas, forestry walks, and a wildlife enclosure. Excellent views of Arran, Bute, and *Cowal* can be enjoyed from these marked points. Beyond the head of the loch turn right on to the A886 and in 1½m left on to the B836. Continue on the A886 for the 5¼m to *Colintraive* and the car ferry to *Rhubodach* on the Isle of Bute.

The B836 winds uphill to open moorland then falls steeply, passing first the head of Loch Striven and then on the left Loch Tarsan reservoir. Descend through thickly-forested Glen Lean to Holy Loch. Turn right on to the A815 Dunoon road for *Sandbank*, then take the A885 to Dunoon.

A short excursion of 28m can be made by taking the A815 – a no-through road – S from Dunoon along the *Firth of Clyde* shore through *Innellan* to Toward Point. As the road rounds the headland it affords splendid views across to the Isle of Bute and the Kyles of Bute before an unclassified road takes the drive alongside Loch Striven. Finish the tour N of the remote settlement of *Inverchaolain*.

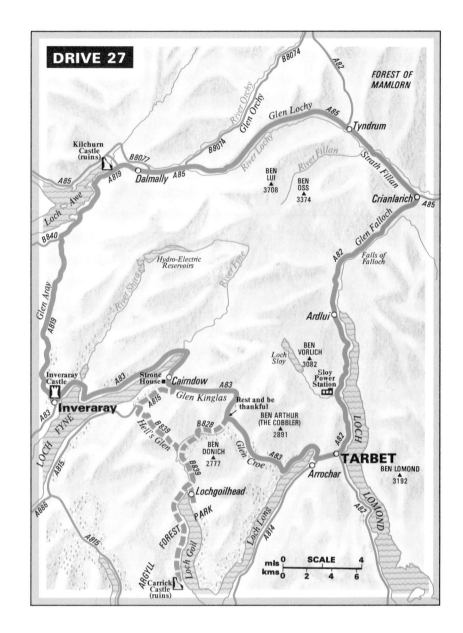

DRIVE 27

Banks of Loch Lomond

From Tarbet

Drive 27   71 miles

This drive starts from *Tarbet*, a little town overlooking *Loch Lomond* with the 3,192ft peak of Ben Lomond dominating the scenery. Leave on the A82 *Crianlarich* road with the loch on the right, passing Sloy power station. This is part of the Loch Sloy hydro-electric scheme. After *Ardlui* the attractive wooded Glen Falloch and the Falls of Falloch can be seen on the right on the way to Crianlarich. This is an important Highland centre, with the twin peaks of 3,843ft Ben More, and 3,821ft Stobinian rising to the SE. As the route follows the *Fort William* road along Strath Fillan, it is dominated by mountains that rise above the glen on both sides. To the left are 3,374ft Ben Oss and 3,708ft Ben Lui, while to the right is the Forest of Mamlorn group. At *Tyndrum* join the A85 *Oban* road to continue below Ben Lui through Glen Lochy to *Dalmally*. Beyond the town join the A819 *Inveraray* road, and run past ruined

Kilchurn castle to the right. For a while the drive follows the shore of Loch Awe and offers splendid views across to the 3,689ft peak of Ben Cruachan. The road regretfully leaves the loch side for a stretch of open country before making a climb through Glen Aray. On the run down to picturesque Inveraray the drive passes to the right of Inveraray Castle, seat of the Duke of Argyll. From Inveraray take the A83 *Glasgow* road, which at first follows the shore of Loch Shira. Carry on to the shores of Loch Fyne and round the head of the loch for *Cairndow*. The gardens of Strone House are open to the public during the summer. The route then takes a long easy ascent through Glen Kinglas to the pass's 380ft summit, *Rest and be Thankful*, at the head of wild Glen Croe.

An alternative route can be taken from a point E of Cairndow to the Rest and be Thankful summit. Follow the A815 for 2m then turn left on to the B839 through Hell's Glen. Join the B828 and continue through *Glenmore Forest Park* below 2,777ft Ben Donich, to the summit. If at the junction with the B828 the B839 is followed, the drive

leads to Loch Goil at *Lochgoilhead* and then 5m on to the ruins of Carrick Castle. The main route continues through *Glen Croe* and the N edge of the extensive *Argyll Forest Park*, with 2,981ft Ben Arthur – or the Cobbler – rising to the left. The drive finally runs down to Loch Long and round the head of the loch for Arrochar and Tarbet.

Placenames in *italic* type are worth stopping at; each is listed and described in the main gazetteer section of the book   125

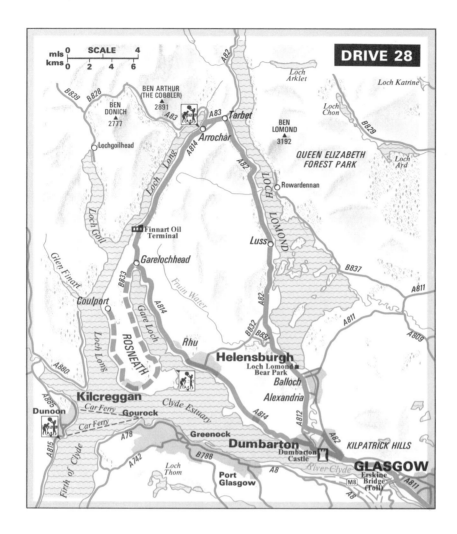

The Loch Country

From Glasgow

Drive 28   78½ miles

Glasgow is the largest city and seaport in Scotland, with extensive docks and ship-building yards sprawled along the banks of the Clyde.

Leave Glasgow by the A82 Great Western Road. As the route continues to Alexandria, the Kilpatrick Hills can be seen to the right and the Clyde on the left. At *Balloch* the drive reaches *Loch Lomond*, the largest loch in Britain. The S end is now a nature reserve. Steamer excursions are run from Balloch Pier during the summer, and the recently-opened Loch Lomond Bear Park can be reached from a point close to Balloch Pier. As the road follows the loch to *Tarbet*, there are pretty views of many wooded islets and the hills beyond the E shore, including 3,192ft Ben Lomond.

At Tarbet turn left on to the A83, crossing the narrow neck of land that separates Loch Lomond from Loch Long, for Arrochar. Among the mountains that can be seen in this area is the 2,891ft peak of Ben Arthur, also known as the Cobbler. Turn sharp left at *Arrochar* to join the A814 along the shores of Loch Long. Pass the *Finnart* oil terminal, and cross another neck of land to reach Gare Loch at *Garelochhead.* For a detour of 29m take the B833, a no-through

road from Garelochhead, to run along the shores of Gare Loch. Around the *Rosneath* Peninsula the B833 passes through *Kilcreggan*, which overlooks the Clyde Estuary. The road ends at *Coulport* on Loch Long, with a view across the loch to the densely-wooded slopes of Glen Finart on the *Cowal Peninsula.*

The main drive continues, with Gare Loch on the right, through *Rhu* where the gardens of Glenaran are open to visitors during the spring and summer. On reaching *Helensburgh*, a residential town and popular tourist centre, the drive carries on to the industrial town of *Dumbarton*. The town's former importance as the ancient capital of Strathclyde is emphasized by the castle, perched high on a rock overlooking the entrance to the River Clyde. As the drive leaves the town it passes several of Dumbarton's world-famous whisky distilleries, then rejoins the A82 for the return to Glasgow.

126

Mountains and Islands

Majestic mountains, sea lochs, and offshore islands are the appeal of the Atlantic edge of Scotland. Deep indentations of the sea make the west coast a fjord country similar to Norway's, though smaller in scale. Loch Sunart, Loch Nevis, Loch Hourn, Loch Duich, Loch Carron, Loch Torridon and Loch Broom bite into the mountains to provide breathtaking scenery of peaks soaring unhindered from the sea.

This is a country of dead-end motoring. There are through roads where needed, but Ardnamurchan, Morar, Glenelg, Torridon, and Gairloch can only be explored fully by drivers who persevere to the end of a road, appreciating that the outlook is always different on the return drive. That is the only way to discover places like Mellon Udrigle, a tiny hamlet by a sandy beach on the shore of Gruinard Bay, with a superb view over the Summer Isles to the peaks of Coigach; Killilan in the deer forest country of Kintail; lonely Polloch by Loch Shiel, at the end of an adventurous drive over the hills from Strontian; remote Kinlochhourn at the head of a nearly land-locked loch, reached by a wild road through almost theatrical mountains.

Through much of the area, in valley after valley and on hillside after hillside, stand the shattered remains of settlements abandoned within the last 200 years. Their people were driven out to make way for sheep-walks and deer-forests, or could no longer in years of famine wheedle a living from the unhelpful soil. That is a summary of the history of old Sutherland; why the interior is an empty wilderness and villages are crowded round the coast, on land that was useless for grazing or stalking.

The area that used to be Caithness is a different kind of country — lowlands beyond the Highlands, once settled by Vikings who left their outlandish names behind after the longships sailed away. There are places called Scarfskerry and Staxigoe, Broubster and Shebster, Freswick, Sarclet, Huna, and Keiss. Off the north coast, from Dunnet Head and John o'Groats, there are spectacular views to Orkney. From Scrabster the Orkney mail boat sails over the often intimidating Pentland Firth, still sometimes known by the more poetic name of the Northern Gate.

Orkney, despite its appearance on the map, is a land of prosperous farms, not a scattering of wild islands. Farther north still, Shetland is the land of the summer dim, romantic midnights in June when the sky is never fully dark. Shetlanders are Shetlanders first and Scotsmen second, no surprise in people who live closer to the Arctic ice floes than to Edinburgh and Glasgow.

In the last few years the Western Isles have come into the motorists' net, thanks to the web of car ferries that link Mallaig with South Uist and Skye; Skye with Harris and North Uist; Ullapool with Stornoway across the Minch. Inter-island ferries and causeways have brought within reach this Atlantic land of crofters and fishermen, trout lochs and weavers of traditional tweed.

Away from coasts and islands there are beautiful valleys like Glen Affric and Strathconon, lonely roads through Strathnaver and Strathmore, inland resorts like Strathpeffer. But the most lasting memory is likely to be a west Highland sunset, with island mountains silhouetted against great fiery cathedrals in the sky.

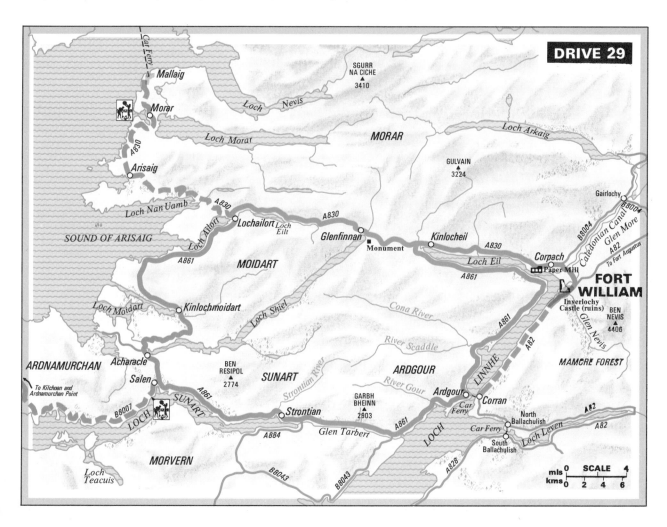

See text for Drive 29 overleaf

Road to the Isles

From Fort William

Drive 29   103¾ miles

Fort William is a well-known touring centre at the SW end of the Great Glen – Glen More – and at the head of the Loch Linnhe. *Ben Nevis*, at 4,406ft, the highest mountain in Britain, rises behind the town. For general interest, the town's West Highland Museum is worth visiting.

Take the A82 N out of the town, passing 15th-c Inverlochy Castle, a ruined stronghold between the main road and the River Lochy. Beyond the castle turn left to join the A830 *Mallaig* road, the famous 'Road to the Isles'. Although once notoriously difficult this has now been greatly improved.

After crossing the River Lochy and the Caledonian Canal, the drive follows the N shore of Loch Eil and passes a recently-built paper mill at *Corpach*. At *Glenfinnan*, with its superb view down the 18m long Loch Shiel, stands the Prince Charles Edward Monument. This was erected in 1815 to commemorate the raising of the Bonnie Prince's standard in 1745. The National Trust of Scotland has an information centre here, and a passenger ferry service runs along Loch Shiel to Archaracle. The road continues along Loch

Eilt to *Lochailort*. From here a diversion of 39m can be made to Mallaig. Leave Lochailort by the A830, driving alongside Loch Ailort and Loch Nan Uamh. It was here, in July 1745, that Prince Charles Edward landed from France at the start of the second Jacobite rebellion. Here also, after the collapse of the rising a year later, he boarded another boat for the beginning of his long exile.

Across the Sound of Arisaig the islands of *Rum* and *Eigg* may be seen, and at *Arisaig* there are lovely views over the sea. *Morar*, famous for its white sands, stands on the narrow neck of land that separates 180-fathom *Loch Morar* from the sea. Mallaig, on the Sound of Sleat, is a fishing port and a car-ferry terminal for services to the *Isle of Skye*.

From Lochailort the main drive takes the A861 along the E shore of the loch and the Sound of Arisaig before turning S towards Loch Moidart and Acharacle. This ferry terminal stands at the S end of Loch Shiel and dominated by the 2,774ft peak of Ben Resipol. From *Salen*, which is attractively situated on the N shore of Loch Sunart, a diversion of 43m can be taken to

Kilchoan and *Ardnamurchan Point*. Take the B8007, a narrow winding road W alongside the loch and then drive inland through the Ardnamurchan Peninsula to Kilchoan. Ardnamurchan Point and the lighthouse are 6m farther W – the farthest W point of the Scottish mainland – and offer magnificent marine views.

The main route from Salen continues along Loch Sunart and offers superb views across the loch to the Morven Hills. Ben Resipol can be seen rising in the background to the left of the road before the drive reaches *Strontian*. It was near here that the mineral strontianite was found. From it comes Strontium 90, which is present in nuclear fallout. After Strontian the drive joins Glen Tarbert and continues to Loch Linnhe. Among the mountains that can be seen on the E shore is the 4,406ft peak of Ben Nevis. Continue along the W shore of Loch Linnhe, passing the ferry point at *Ardgour Hotel* before following the shore of Loch Eil round the head of the loch. Turn right on to the A830 for *Kinlocheil* and Fort William. Alternatively the ferry may be taken from Ardgour to *Corran*, and Fort William reached by the A82, cutting the journey by 25¼m.

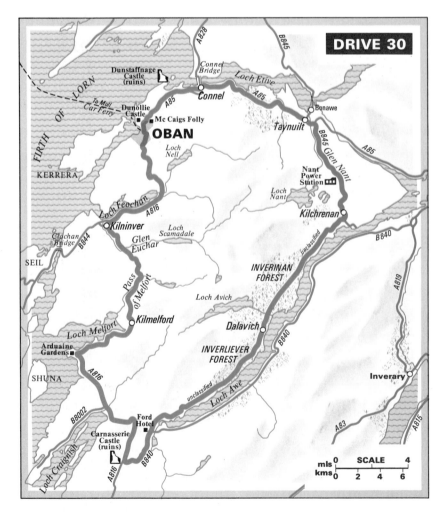

To the Falls of Lora

From Oban

Drive 30   65 miles

Take the A816 *Campbeltown* road from Oban. After a short inland stretch along the S shore of Loch Feochan pass *Kilninver*. The slate-quarrying island of Seil, linked to the mainland by *Clachan Bridge*, can be reached on the B844 through Kilninver. A second island, Luing, is accessible from Seil on the Cuan ferry. Continuing S on the A816, another short detour can be made along Glen Euchar – left of the road – to Loch Scamadale, which is attractively set among hills. Pass wooded Glen Gallain for the run down to *Kilmelford*. From here follow the shores of Loch Melfort towards the sea, passing Arduaine Gardens. The latter are open to visitors during the summer.

After passing the head of Loch Craignish the drive turns inland. Near the ruins of the 16th-c Carnasserie Castle turn left on to the B840, and from the Ford Hotel follow an unclassified road bounded by the waters of Loch Awe on the right. As the road runs through Inverliever Forest it passes marked viewpoints, nature trails, and walks before reaching Dalavich on the shore of Loch Awe. There are fine views of the loch to the right and of 3,689ft peak of Ben Cruachan ahead.

Just before *Kilchrenan* the drive joins the B845 to make a pretty run through Glen Nant, passing Nant power station on the left. At the main road turn left on to the A85 for *Taynuilt*. Near by are the 18th-c

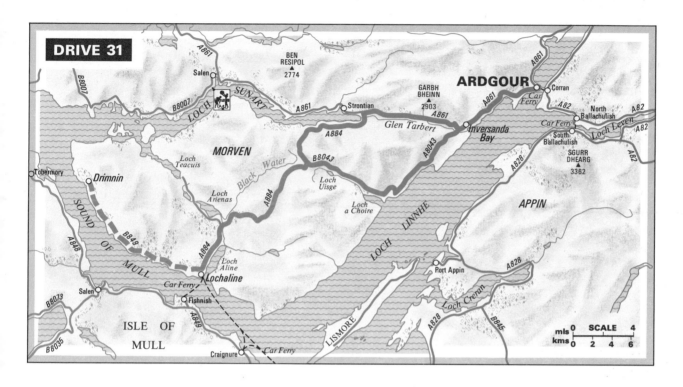

The Morven District

From Ardgour

Drive 31   61 miles

From the Ardgour Hotel in *Ardgour* take the A861 *Strontian* road to *Inversanda Bay* and turn left on to the B8043. This narrow road leads inland before rejoining the shores of Loch Linnhe, which afford superb views across the water to the flat island of Lismore and the Appin Hills. After turning inland alongside Loch a Choire, first 2,136ft Beinn Na Cille, and then 2,511ft Fuar Bheinn may be seen to the right. Continue past the lonely shores of Loch Uisage before turning left on to the A884. The road crosses wild country to an area of forest land at the head of Loch Aline. *Lochaline*, a small port at the seaward end of the loch on the *Sound of Mull*, is linked by car ferry with Fishnish on the *Island of Mull* and with *Oban*. The tour may be extended by 22m by following the B849 alongside the Sound of Mull, a drive offering magnificent mountain views across the sound to 1,903ft Beinn Chreagach Mhor, 2,087ft Beinn Mheadon, and 2,512ft Dun da Ghaoithe, on the Island of Mull.

Return N from Lochaline along the A884, leaving the outward route at the junction with the A8043 and climbing a lonely col before the run down to the S shore of Loch Sunart. At the head of the loch turn right on to the A861. Return to Loch Linnhe and Ardgour through Glen Tarbert, where rugged hills rise to either side and include the 2,903ft rock peak of Garbh Bheinn.

Drive 30 continued

Bonawe iron-smelting furnaces, which are of interest to the industrial archaeologist. Follow the shores of Loch Etive before passing under the cantilever bridge at *Connel*. A series of whirlpools known as the Falls of Lora can be seen under the bridge. On the return to Oban the drive passes mainly 15th-c *Dunstaffnage Castle*, which stands to the right of the road and guards the entrance to Loch Etive.

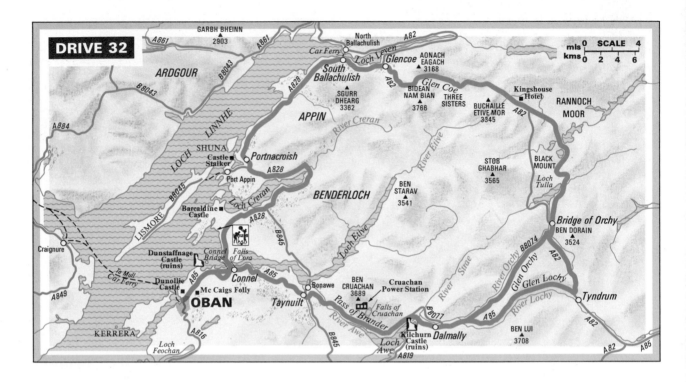

In the Glen of Weeping

From Oban

Drive 32   102 miles

Oban is both a popular resort and the port for goods and car-carrying services to the islands of *Mull, Coll, Tiree, Barra* and *South Uist.* The smaller islands of *Iona* and *Staffa* can also be reached from here.

The drive begins by heading N on the A85 from Oban, passing on the left after 3m *Dunstaffnage Castle* – mainly 15thc – which guards the entrance to Loch Etive. Later, on the approach to *Connel*, the Falls of Lora can be seen below *Connel Bridge.* Follow Loch Etive to *Taynuilt.* Beyond here the twin peaks of 3,698ft Ben Cruachan, one of the highest mountains in Argyll, rise to the left of the road. The scenery is very rugged as the drive then enters the wild Pass of Brander, with the *Falls of Cruachan* and the Cruachan Reservoir on the left. Cruachan power station is built underground and is open to the public in the summer. A minibus service is provided for visitors. Continue alongside *Loch Awe*, which is also used in the production of hydro-electricity, to the ruins of *Kilchurn Castle*, strategically set on a spit projecting into the loch.

A short cut through Glen Orchy on the B8074 saves 5½m between *Dalmally* and *Bridge of Orchy.* One of the many features here are the numerous waterfalls which can be seen alongside the road. The main drive continues through Glen Lochy to *Tyndrum*, with 3,708ft Ben Lui rising to the right.

Leave Tyndrum on the A82 *Fort William* road, with the 3,524ft conical peak of Ben Doran visible to the right before reaching Bridge of Orchy. Beyond the village the road passes Loch Tulla then climbs on to the bleak bog and lochan waste of Rannoch Moor. This stretch of road was built in the 1930's to replace the narrow, exposed road

over the Black Mount. The Kingshouse Hotel, on the right, faces Buchaille Etive Mor. At 3,345ft this is one of Scotland's most famous rock peaks, and is a well-known winter-sports district. As the road runs down through wild and impressive Glen Coe it is overshadowed by the rugged peaks of 3,766ft Bidean nam Bian, the highest mountain in Argyll, and its outliers the Three Sisters. On the right can be seen the great 3,000ft ridge of Aonach Eagach.

From *Glencoe* the drive follows the A828 *Ballachulish* road. It was from the Signal Rock in the vicinity of this village that the signal for the hideous massacre of the Macdonalds of Glencoe by the Campbells of Glen Lyon came during the winter of 1692. More than 40 died in the attack and others fled into the hills to die of hunger and exposure. To the right is Loch Leven, backed by the peaks of the Mamore Forest.

The road continues through Ballachulish, where there is a monument to James of the Glen, wrongly hanged in 1752 after a notorious trial known as the Appin murder case. The identity of the real culprit was never discovered but the story is graphically portrayed by R L Stevenson in *Kidnapped.* Along the Appin shore of Loch Linnhe there are splendid views of the Ardgour Hills across the loch. Castle Stalker can be seen on an island site at *Portnacroish* before the drive meets the edge of Loch Creran. As the road continues, *Barcaldine Castle* can be seen to the right. The fine cantilevered Connel Bridge is crossed before the drive turns left along the A85 for Oban.

Seals and Small Bays

From Helmsdale

Drive 33   125 miles

This drive starts from the small fishing village of *Helmsdale* and leaves along the A9 *Wick* road. After climbing on to open moorland with good views of the sea, the road descends steeply to *Berriedale*, with its small harbour and 12th-c ruined castle. The cliff scenery here is rugged.

Lonely moorland 3m N bears a memorial marking the spot where the Duke of Kent was killed in an air crash in 1942. There are more views along this rocky coast as the drive passes *Dunbeath* Castle, on the right, before descending through the village. An interesting feature to be seen on the approach to Latheronwheel is an arch made from the bones of a whale, standing to the right of the road. More small fishing villages are skirted as the drive continues N, with extensive views along the coast. The fishing port of Wick is an important centre for

DRIVE 33

Drive 33 continued

coastguard operations in the N of Scotland, and the glassworks are open to the public. To the N of the town the road passes the airport, then continues to *Reiss*. Here turn right with the main road for *Keiss*, skirting Sinclair's Bay – the longest stretch of sand on the old Caithness Coast – on the right. The A9 comes to an end at *John o'Groats*, but the splendid views reach across to the Island of *Stroma*. Return for ½m before turning right on to the A836. An unclassified road to the left leads to the spectacular cliff scenery around Duncansby Head. Small bays on the Pentland Firth can be reached to the right off the A836. The sleek shapes of seals are a common sight here. On the right just before *Mey* village is the Castle of Mey, which is owned by the Queen Mother. The gardens are open at times during the summer. At *Dunnet* the

B855 leads N to Dunnet Head, the farthest N point on the Scottish mainland. There are beautiful views from here across to the *Orkney Islands*.

The road skirts the fine sands of Dunnet Bay before passing through *Castletown* to reach *Thurso*, a resort and fishing port and the farthest N town on the British mainland. Continue with the *Tongue* road, passing the road to the *Scrabster* ferry terminal for Stromness in Orkney. *Dounreay* is the site of Scotland's first nuclear power station, and an exhibition is open to the public. Pass through *Reay*, where there are good sands at Sandside Bay, and where the original village was buried by shifting sand dunes in the early 18thc. In 3m turn left on to the A897 *Helmsdale* road to enter the lonely Strath Halladale, which is popular with anglers. The route then passes through the hamlet of *Forsinard*, then crosses bleak moorland with the peaks of

1,903ft Ben Criam Beg and 1,936ft Ben Criam More to the right before passing the small Loch an Ruathair.

After skirting *Kinbrace* the drive follows the River Helmsdale through Strath Kildonan for the return to Helmsdale.

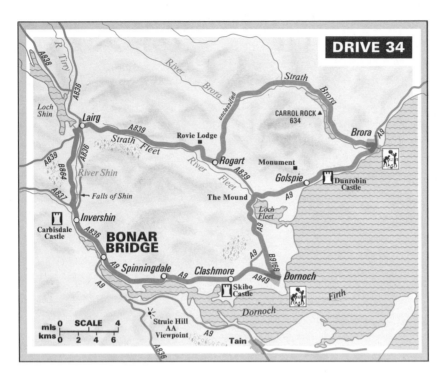

An Angler's Paradise

From Lairg

Drive 35   138 miles

The numerous lochs and fast-flowing rivers make this tour a fisherman's paradise.

From *Lairg* follow the A836 *Tongue* road, skirting the shore of Loch Shin before climbing through Strath Tirry then crossing the Crask Pass Descend through pleasant Strath Vagastie with 3,154ft Ben Kilbreck rising to the right, then pass through the small angling resort of *Altnaharra* and turn right on to the B873, signposted *Syre*. The road now follows a narrow winding route beside Loch Naver, and gradually falls to join the B871 through Strath Naver, famous for its salmon. Meet the main road and turn left on to the A836 for attractive rock scenery. Descend through Coldbackie, beside Tongue Bay, keeping right on to the A838 for Tongue. Follow the *Durness* road and cross the Kyle of Tongue via a causeway built in 1971. Magnificent sandy

Across the Mound

From Bonar Bridge

Drive 34   68 miles

This drive leaves *Bonar Bridge* on the A9 *Wick* road and follows the N side of Dornoch Firth. Pass through *Spinningdale*, then beyond Clashmore turn right on to the A949 for *Dornoch*, a popular resort with golf and a good bathing beach. The majestic cathedral here dates from the 13thc, but has been much restored. A single lofty tower remains from the Bishop's Palace, which was destroyed in 1570. Return along the A949, then at the war memorial turn right on to the B9168 to rejoin the A9 Wick road. The route now crosses the head of Loch Fleet via the Mound, an embankment built by Thomas Telford in 1815.

As the drive approaches *Golspie*, a statue by Chantrey to the first Duke of Sutherland can be seen high on a hill to the left. Beyond the village on the right stands *Dunrobin* Castle, the magnificent seat of the Duke of Sutherland. Part of the castle dates from the 13thc.

Continue along the coast to *Brora*, where a small 16th-c coal-mine is said to be the only one in the N of Scotland. Turn left on to an unclassified road signposted Gordonrush, and follow Strath Brora inland to pass Loch Brora where the Carroll Rock looms high above the water. The road gradually climbs beside the river to cross higher ground before the descent into Strath Fleet and *Rogart*. Turn right on to the A839 and in 1½m on the right pass the gardens of Rovie Lodge, which are open during the summer. Another gradual climb is made before a descent to *Lairg*, a small town at the S end of Loch Shin popular with anglers. Leave by the A839 *Lochinver* road, turning right across the River Shin, then in ½m branch left on to the

B864 with *Inveran* signposts. In 4m a footpath to the left leads to the Falls of Shin, where leaping salmon are a popular attraction. Continue to the main road and turn left on to the A837, joining the A836. This road runs through *Invershin*, on the Kyle of Sutherland opposite Carbisdale Castle, before leading back to Bonar Bridge.

Drive 35 continued

beaches abound in the vicinity, and can be reached by turning right on to an unclassified road beyond the causeway. After a further stretch of desolate country the main route runs down to the head of Loch Hope. The 3,042ft peak of Ben Hope dominates the S end of the loch. Continue round steep-sided Loch Eriboll, with its small sand and shingle beaches, to Smoo Cave and Durness. An

unclassified road leads to Balnakeil, a craft village established in 1964, then the tour turns S. After 2m an unclassified road on the right leads to the Kyle of Durness ferry, which is for passengers only. This links with a minibus service to *Cape Wrath*, Scotland's most NW point. More mountain scenery is passed on the journey to *Rhiconich*, which stands at the head of Loch Inchard with the high ridges of 2,980ft Foinaven and 2,580ft Arkle prominent to the left.

The area is dotted with numerous small lochans. At *Laxford Bridge* take a left turn to pass beneath 2,634ft Ben Stack, overlooking the waters of Loch Stack. Foinaven is again prominent to the left. On the return to Lairg the drive passes a string of lochs, first Loch More followed by Loch Merkland and the small Loch a'Ghriama. A last long stretch runs beside Loch Shin before the drive ends at Lairg.

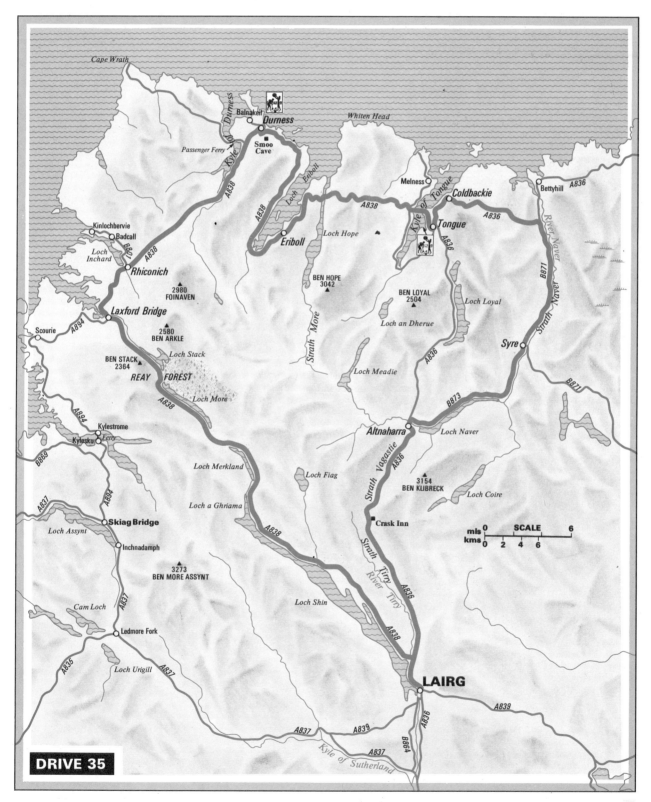

DRIVE 35

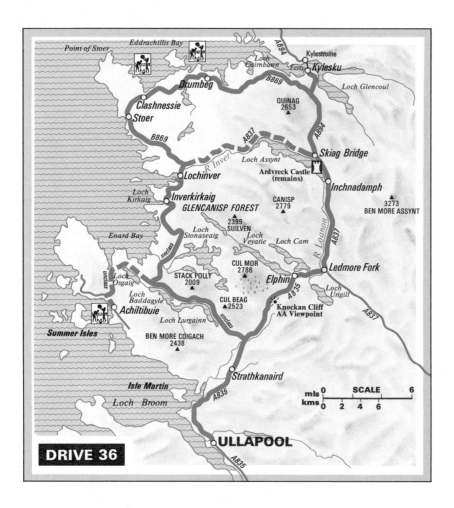

DRIVE 36

Among the Mountains

From Ullapool

Drive 36   87 miles

From *Ullapool* follow the A835 N to skirt Loch Broom. The route immediately gives splendid views of the mountains, including the impressive 2,438ft ridge of Ben More Coigach, the 2,009ft pinnacled peak of Stack Polly, and 2,786ft Cul Mor. Drive through Strathcanaird to the viewpoint at Knockan Cliff, which is also the starting point for a nature trail. As the road runs through the hamlet of *Elphin* the 2,399ft double-peak of Suilven stands out on the left. Continue through Ledmore Fork; after the drive turns left on to the A837 the 2,779ft peak of Canisp is prominent to the left. The mountains to the right include 3,273ft Ben More Assynt.

Beyond *Inchnadamph* the road skirts the shore of Loch Assynt, passing the ruins of Ardvreck Castle on the way to Skiag Bridge. Turn right on to the A894 and start a long climb to skirt the many-peaked ridge of 2,653ft Quinag on the left. After the summit the road leads down to *Kylesku*, which is linked by ferry to *Kylestrome* on the far side of Loch Cairn-Dawn. Return for 2m, then turn right on to the B869. As the route switchbacks along this narrow, winding road it allows spectacular coastal and mountain views. Continue through the remote hamlets of *Drumbeg*, Clashnessie, and *Stoer* before turning right on to the

A837 for *Lochinver*, sited at the end of the sea-loch of the same name. Go forward through the town and cross the bridge, then turn left with the unclassified road to *Inverkirkaig*, at the end of Loch Kirkaig. The route enters the Inverpolly nature reserve then follows an extremely winding and narrow road which gives marvellous views of the wild and rugged coast. Meet a T-junction and turn left to skirt Loch Baddagyle. The road to the right leads to the remote village of *Achiltibuie*, set beside Badentarbat Bay in a position overlooking the Summer Isles. On the main route the 2,009ft peak of Stack Polly is now very prominent to the left of the road, and at the far end of Loch Lurgainn the 2,533ft peak of Cul Bezg stands out. Continue to the main road. Turn right at the A835 and pass through Strathcanaird on the return to Ullapool.

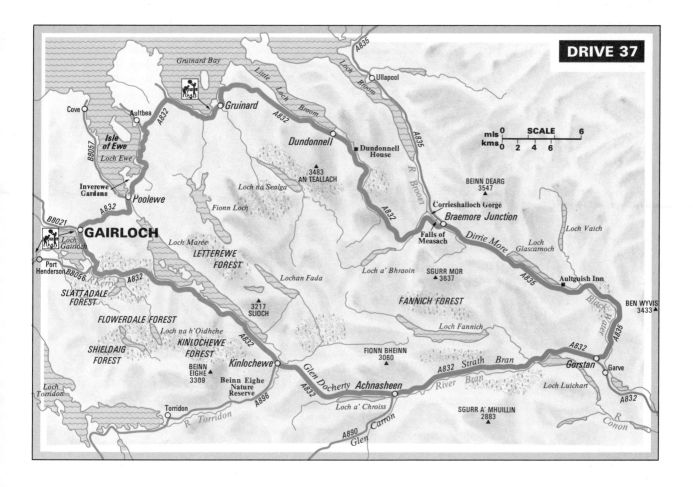

DRIVE 37

Peaks and Forests

From Gairloch

Drive 37   107 miles

This tour starts at *Gairloch*, a small village picturesquely set on Loch Gairloch. Leave by the A832 *Achnasheen* road and follow the River Kerry inland to pass Gairloch Dam. The road runs through Slattadale Forest before reaching the shore of Loch Maree, with its many small tree-covered islands. On the far side of the loch are the mountain peaks of Letterewe Forest with 3,217ft Slioch prominent towards the S.

Approaching *Kinlochewe* the drive skirts the Beinn Eighe national nature reserve, where nature trails start at the trail car park. The road continues forward and climbs Glen Docherty to skirt Loch a'Chroisg on the way to the small village of Achnasheen. To the right the 2,883ft peak of Sgurr a'Mhuilinn is prominent. The tour then follows the *Inverness* road through Strath Bran, skirting the end of Loch Luichart to Gorstan, where a sharp left turn is made on to the A835 *Ullapool* road. Ben Wyvis rises to 3,433ft on the right. This pleasant run follows the Glascarnoch River to the Glascarnoch Reservoir, then the road runs across bleak Dirrie More with the high peaks of Beinn Dearg to the right. Continue to *Braemore Junction* and turn left on to the A832 Gairloch road, passing on the right a footpath to the Corrieshalloch Gorge. A fragile bridge spans the narrow, 200ft-deep chasm, which drops 150ft in 1m of foaming water. Below the bridge lie the spectacular falls of Measach. From here the road runs down beside Dundonnel river to *Dundonnel* beneath the slopes of 3,483ft An Teallach.

The tour now skirts the shore of little Loch Broom before rounding the headland and slipping down to the fine sands of *Gruinard Bay*. Splendid coastal views are offered before the route skirts *Aultbea*, a small village on the shore of Loch Ewe. The sheltered harbour is used by naval craft.

As it approaches *Poolewe* the road passes the remarkable Inverewe Garden, which contains rare and sub-tropical plants. At Poolewe the tour turns S and affords further attractive views to the left down the length of Loch Maree. High ground is crossed on the return to Gairloch.

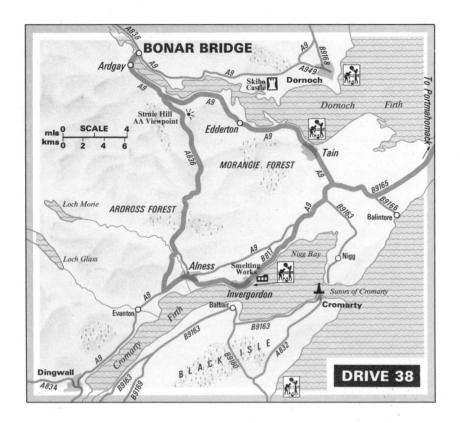

The Kyle of Sutherland

From Bonar Bridge

Drive 38   50 miles

Starting at *Bonar Bridge*, this drive follows the A9 *Inverness* road and crosses the Kyle of Sutherland. After passing through *Ardgay* the road skirts the Dornoch Firth for 3m before turning right on to the A836, signposted '*Dingwall*-Direct Route', to start the climb of *Struie Hill*. Just before the summit is an AA viewpoint which affords spectacular views over the surrounding mountains and coastline. After crossing high open moorland a descent is made towards the Cromarty Firth through Ardross Forest. Beautiful views of the *Black Isle* are offered by this section of the drive. At the main road turn left on to the A9 for *Alness*, then at the end of the town turn right on to the B817 for *Invergordon* — a former naval base and scene of a naval mutiny in 1931. The fine harbour is still used as a re-fuelling base for ships.

Continue alongside the Firth, where a large aluminium smelting plant and its long ore-unloading pier dominates the shore. The route now skirts the fine sands of Nigg Bay, then turns right to rejoin the A9 and passes through pleasant farming country to *Tain*. The shores of Nigg Bay are now the site of heavy industrial plants which produce equipment for the North Sea oil field. An interesting detour can be made to the Tarbat Peninsula and the small resort of *Portmahomack* by turning right on to the B9165, 3½m after rejoining the A9. Tain features a 17th-c tollbooth and an old collegiate church, and offers a fine sandy

beach. The drive continues along the S shore of Dornoch Firth, passing through *Edderton* on the return to Bonar Bridge.

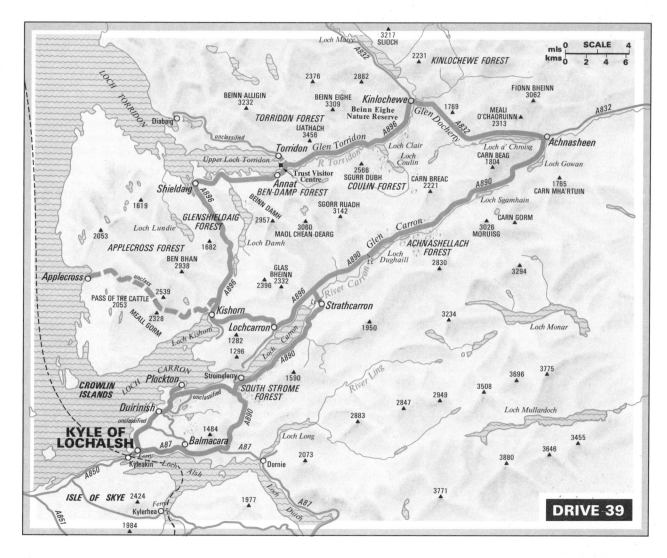

DRIVE 39

Mountains of the North West

From Kyle of Lochlash

Drive 39   105 miles

This drive encompasses some of the finest mountain scenery in the NW highlands, and starts at *Kyle of Lochalsh* – situated at the W end of *Loch Alsh*. Sometimes known as the gateway to *Skye*, the town operates a frequent ferry service to the island and steamer connections to the *Outer Hebrides*. There is also a thriving fishing industry.

Leave by the unclassified *Plockton* road and follow the winding coastline towards the wild Applecross Mountains, keeping left for Duirinish. Turn left and cross the river bridge for Plockton, a fishing village beautifully situated on a small inlet of Loch Carron. Return for 1½m and turn left, signposted *Strome* ferry, and follow a winding road which affords beautiful views from high above Loch Carron.

On reaching the main road turn left on to the A890 and continue through South Strome Forest, passing the Loch Carron viewpoint before descending to the loch shores for *Strathcarron*. Cross the railway and at the T-junction turn left on to the A896 for the pleasant loch-side village of *Lochcarron*. At the end of the village turn right on to the

Shieldaig road, which provides fine views as it climbs.

The descent to Loch Kishorn affords views across to the remarkable red-sandstone peaks of Applecross Forest. From the end of the loch a road to the left winds across the mountains over the 2,054ft-high Pass of the Cattle. There are severe hairpin bends on the run to the isolated fishing village of *Applecross*. The views from this road are superb, but drivers are warned that care should be exercised on the crossing of the pass. The main route continues through wild mountain scenery to Shieldaig, on Loch Shieldaig, an inlet of Loch Torridon.

Continue with the *Kinlochewe* road and skirt the S shore of Upper Loch Torridon. Magnificent views of the Torridon Mountains include the 3,232ft peak of Beinn Alligin. As the road slips down to the loch side it passes through the hamlet of Annat, past the road to *Torridon* village and the entrance to the Trust visitor centre. The latter features a deer museum and an audio-visual information unit on wild life. The road enters the wild Glen Torridon, with the great 3,456ft red sandstone peak of Liathach towering above to the left. A few miles farther the quartzite peaks of Beinn Eighe, all over 3,000ft high, rise into view on the left. Part of its slopes form a 10,000-

acre national nature reserve which protects flourishing birch and pine woods, plus varied wildlife which includes deer and eagles.

The 3,217ft ridge of Slioch can be seen on the approach to Kinlochewe, where a right turn is made on to the A832 to climb through Glen Docherty and pass Loch a'Chroisg to the edge of *Achnasheen*. The drive here turns right on to the A890 Lochcarron road, crossing open moorland and passing Lochs Gowan and Sgamhain before slipping down through *Achnashellach* Forest. The clear waters of the River Carron are followed before the drive turns left on to the Kyle of Lochalsh road for Strathcarron.

The tour now reverses an earlier part of the drive and climbs from Loch Carron through South Strome Forest. It continues along the main road crossing *Auchtertyre Hill*. The latter affords fine mountain views that include the Five Sisters of Kintail, above *Loch Duich* to the left. At the foot of the descent turn right on to the A87 for a fine run beside Loch Alsh. Pass through *Balmacara* and return to Kyle of Lochalsh.

Placenames in *italic* type are worth stopping at; each is listed and described in the main gazetteer section of the book

Capital of the Highlands

From Inverness

Drive 40   119 miles

Inverness is an important road and rail centre known as the Capital of the Highlands. Leave the town on the A9 *Dingwall* road, skirting the S shore of Beauly Firth. In 11m the drive crosses the River Beauly and turns left with the A831 towards *Cannich*, following the thickly-wooded river banks. This is the gateway to a beautiful part of Scotland; the road passes through *Struy* to continue with Strath Glass to Cannich. Glen Cannich and Glen Affric are two of the most attractive and richly-wooded glens in NW Scotland. Roads continue into each glen for 10m but are not through-ways for motor traffic. Loch Mullardoch in Glen Cannich and Loch Benevean in Glen Affric have both been dammed as hydro-electricity reservoirs, and there is a power station at Fasnakyle in Glen Affric. The

highest mountain peaks NW of the Great Glen are to be found in this area, including 3,775ft Sgurr na Lapaich, N of Loch Mullardoch, plus 3,880ft Carn Eige and 3,862ft Mam Sodhail to the S.

The drive continues with the *Drumnadrochit* road, climbing away from Strath Glass to enter Glen Urquhart. Pass Loch Meiklie and follow the River Enrick between pine-clad slopes, through *Milton* to Drumnadrochit.

Turn right on to the A82 and pass the ruins of Urquhart Castle before entering the Great Glen. Continue along the shore of *Loch Ness*. On the left at *Invermoriston* is the memorial to John Cobb, who died trying to break the water speed record. Turn right on to the A887 *Kyle of Lochalsh* road to enter attractively-wooded Glen Morriston, and climb slowly beside the river past the *Torgyle* power station before reaching more open country. Meet the *Fort William* road and turn left on to the A87. Climb on to the bare mountains beside Loch Loyne. This road

gives spectacular views of the surrounding peaks before descending beside Loch Garry, where a single track road to the right leads 22m W to *Loch Quoich* and *Kinloch Hourn*, passing through some of W Scotland's wildest and loveliest scenery. The main route passes the Falls of Garry and continues to *Invergarry* where it turns left on to the A82, skirting the N end of Loch Oich. Cross the Caledonian Canal for a short run to *Fort Augustus*, a former fort associated with General Wade. The Benedictine Abbey here was built in 1876. Leave by the A862 *Errogie* road and follow the former military road to Inverness, climbing steeply through Glen Doe to enjoy magnificent scenery N along Loch Ness.

The road then passes Loch Tarff and crosses lonely open moorland to *Whitebridge*. In 1m the route turns left on to the B852, signposted *Foyers*. This is followed by a descent through wooded hillsides to the E shore of Loch Ness at Foyers, well known

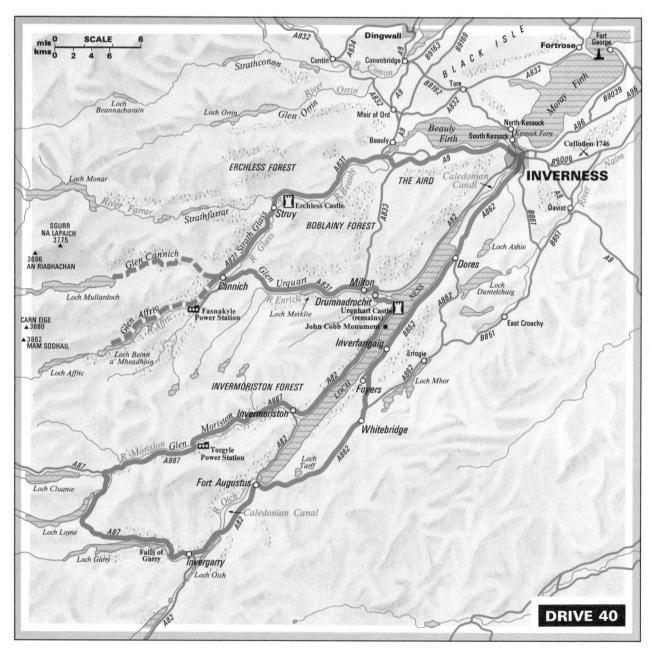

Drive 40 continued

for its two waterfalls. There is a hydro-
electric power station and an aluminium
smelting works here – the latter was the
first to be built in Britain (1894). Continue
beside this beautiful loch, with its fine views
of the mountains to the W, and drive through
the hamlet of *Inverfarigaig*. A Forestry
Commission exhibition can be visited here,
and there are forest walks near *Dores*. Join
the A862 to follow Strath Dores and the
River Ness for the return to Inverness.

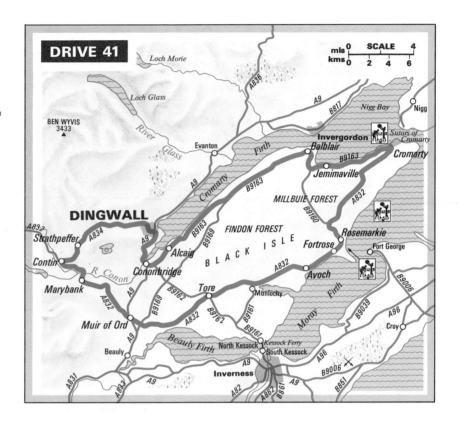

Into the Black Isle

From Dingwall

Drive 41   59 miles

This tour starts from *Dingwall*, a busy town
with a harbour built by Thomas Telford in
the early 19thc. Follow the A9 *Inverness*
road to *Conon Bridge*, where an old Toll
House stands on the river bridge. At the end
of the village turn left on to the B9162,
signposted *Cromarty*. Turn left again at
crossroads with Alcaig signposts and
continue along the B9163. The drive now
enters the *Black Isle* and follows the shore
of Cromarty Firth, passing through Alcaig
and turning left. After a while skirt
Balblair, then go through Jemimaville and
follow the coastline closely to Cromarty.
This is a small seaport at the entrance to the
Firth, which at this point is guarded by two
headlands known as The Sutors. Across the
water on the shores of Nigg Bay are
heavy industrial sites where equipment for
the North Sea oil field is manufactured.

Leave the town by the A832 *Fortrose* road,
and pass through Millbuie Forest before
running down to *Rosemarkie*, a small resort
on Rosemarkie Bay. Drive through Fortrose;
a road to the left leads to the remains of a
cathedral which was founded in the 12thc
by David I of Scotland. The next section runs
alongside the Moray Firth and passes
through the fishing village of *Avoch* before
turning inland. Reach Tore and turn left to
leave the Black Isle for *Muir of Ord*. Follow
the *Ullapool* road and beyond *Marybank*
cross the River Conon for *Contin*. Turn right
on to the A834 for *Strathpeffer*, the well-
known spa and resort. A few miles to the left
rises 3,433ft Ben Wyvis, a notable landmark
for many miles around. Continue with A834
for the return to Dingwall.

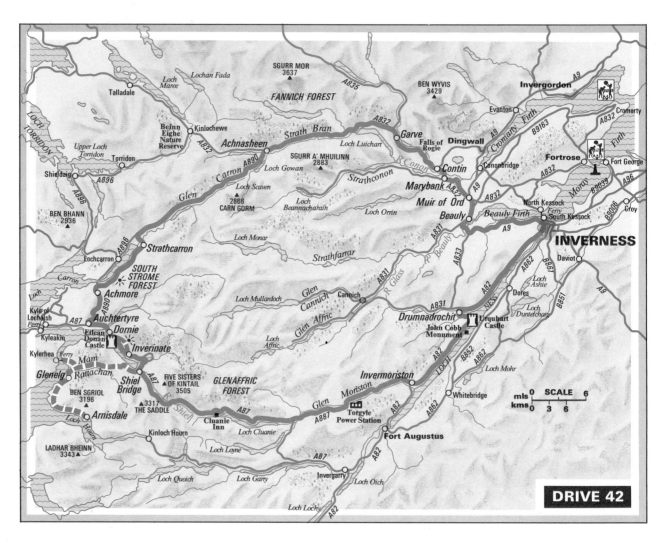

DRIVE 42

Shores of Loch Ness

From Inverness

Drive 42   150 miles

From *Inverness* follow the A9 Dingwall road
and skirt the S shore of the Beauly Firth for
Beauly, with its ruined 13th-c priory.
Continue to *Muir of Ord*, then turn left on to
the A832 *Ullapool* road and drive to
Marybank. Cross the River Conon to *Contin*.

On the right after 2m a footpath leads to
Rogie Falls. Continue past Loch Garve and
pass through the village of *Garve*. Keep
forward with the *Gairloch* road, skirting Loch
Luichart before the gradual ascent of Strath
Bran. On the left of *Achnasheen* is the
2,883ft peak of Sgurr a'Mhuilinn. Turn left
on to the A890 *Kyle of Lochalsh* road for the
run through open moorland, passing Lochs
Gowan and Scaven before slipping down
through *Achnashellach* Forest. The road
follows the River Carron before turning left
for *Strathcarron*. The drive now continues up
the shore of *Loch Carron* before climbing
through South Strome Forest, passing the
Loch Carron viewpoint on the way. Through
Achmore the road begins the long climb of
Auchtertyre Hill. Wide views of the *Wester
Ross* Mountains, including on the left the
Five Sisters of Kintail above *Loch Duich*,
are afforded by the summit. At the foot of
the descent turn left on to the A87 Inverness

road for *Dornie*. Just beyond the village the
former main road, now unclassified, can be
taken to the left for the fine Carr Brae
viewpoint on Keppoch Hill. On the main
route the picturesque Eilean Donan Castle
is passed on the right as the drive continues
on the A87 beside Loch Duich through
Inverinate to *Shiel Bridge*. An unclassified
road to the right crosses the spectacular
Mam Rattachan Pass to *Glenelg* and
Arnisdale, 18m away.

Continue through *Glen Shiel*, with the slopes
of the Five Sisters of Kintail rising sheer on
the left. A gradual climb is made to Loch
Cluanie, which is now part of a hydro-
electric scheme. The drive continues with
the A887 through Glen Morriston, passing
the *Torgyle* hydro-electric power station
before entering an attractively-wooded
stretch beside the River Morriston to
Invermoriston. The route now runs into the
Great Glen and a left turn on to the A82 is
made to follow the shore of *Loch Ness*.
After 9m the memorial to John Cobb, the
racing motorist who lost his life when his
speedboat capsized on the loch in 1952,
can be seen on the right. The ruins of
Urquhart Castle are also to the right of the

road, and can be seen before the village of
Drumnadrochit. The next section follows the
loch and the Caledonian Canal, then leads
back to Inverness.

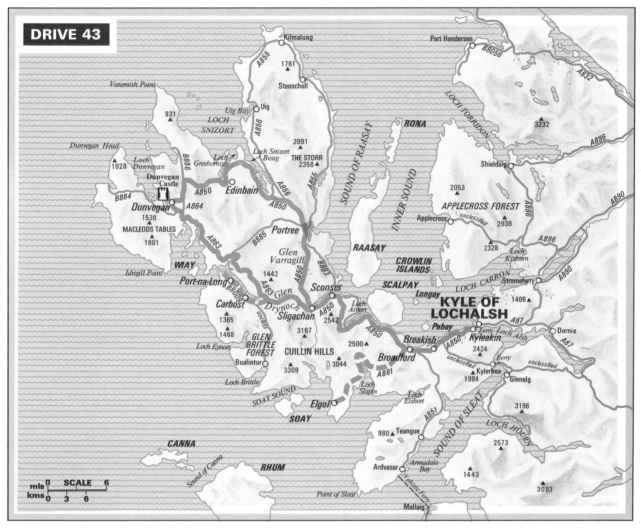

DRIVE 43

Exploring Skye

From Kyle of Lochalsh

Drive 43   104 miles

From *Kyle of Lochalsh* on the mainland, take the Skye ferry to *Kyleakin* and follow the A850 through Breakish to *Broadford*. The Broadford group of Red Hills rises to the left beyond the town, with the island of Scalpay lying offshore. From Broadford a detour can be made on the A881 to *Elgol* and *Loch Scavaig*. Motor boat trips run from here to the wild and beautiful *Loch Coruisk*, which is surrounded by the wild peaks of the *Cuillins* amid some of the finest scenery in Britain. The main route follows the *Portree* road to skirt Loch Ainort, with its views of the 3,044ft Bla Bheinn Cuillin peak to the left. On the left of the climb from the loch is the area known as Lord Macdonald's Forest. The Red Hills of Marsco and Glamaig, and the island of Raasay can be seen on the descent.

After the road passes through *Sconser*, on the shores of Loch Sligachan, it reaches the hamlet and famous climbing centre of *Sligachan*. The peak of 3,167ft Sgurrnan Gillean is prominent to the left. The tour now turns N and follows Glen Varragill before winding down to Portree Loch and the town of Portree, the chief centre of the island. A steamer operates from here.

Follow the *Dunvegan* road and in 4m keep left to follow the shores of Loch Snizort Beag and Loch Greshornish to *Edinbane*. In the distance to the right the Outer Hebrides can be seen before the drive passes through Dunvegan to reach the castle. This ancestral home of the Macleods stands to the N of the town. The peninsula W of the town is dominated by Macleod's Tables, two flat-topped peaks of solid basalt.

Return to Dunvegan and turn right on to the A863 Sligachan road for fine forward views of the Cuillins. Continue along high ground above Loch Harport before winding down to Glen Drynoch. From here a detour on the B8009 can be taken to *Carbost*, with its famous Talisker distillery, and the tiny weaving village of *Port-na-Long*. The main route continues to Sligachan, with views of the Morsco and Glamaig peaks. Turn right and follow the outward route in reverse for further magnificent scenery across to the mainland mountains of *Applecross*, *Torridon*, and *Kintail*. Return to the car ferry at Kyleakin.

Placenames in *italic* type are worth stopping at; each is listed and described in the main gazetteer section of the book

The Trotternish of Skye

From Portree

Drive 44   48 miles

Leave *Portree* by the A850 *Uig* and *Dunvegan* road, then in 4m join the A856. This passes through the village of Kensaleyre on the shore of Loch Eyre, an inlet of Loch Snizort Beag. From Uig, a village of crofts scattered over a hillside above the harbour, a car-ferry service operates to the *Outer Hebrides*. On the outskirts of the town turn right on to the A855 *Staffin* road and climb Idrigil Hill for beautiful views over Uig Bay, then follow the coast road through *Kilmuir*. Beyond the village Flora Macdonald's burial place is marked by a Celtic cross near the Skye Cottage Museum. Far out to sea the hills of the Outer Hebrides stand darkly against the sky. Pass the ruins of *Duntulm* Castle, the ancient residence of Clan Macdonald, to skirt *Flodigarry*, the early home of Flora

Macdonald. There are splendid views over the sea to the mainland *Applecross* and *Torridon* Hills. The weird collection of rocks and pinnacles forming the *Quiraing* are on the right and can be visited on foot. Pass through Staffin, with its basalt cliffs, to reach Loch Mealt; the well-known Kilt Rock is near by.

After the drive has passed Lealt Falls, the long Trotternish Ridge and precipices of the *Storr* come into view. The curious, detached, 160ft-high pinnacle that can be seen is known as the Old Man of Storr. The drive passes Loch Leathan and Loch Fada, both now harnessed to a local hydro-electric scheme, on the return to Portree.

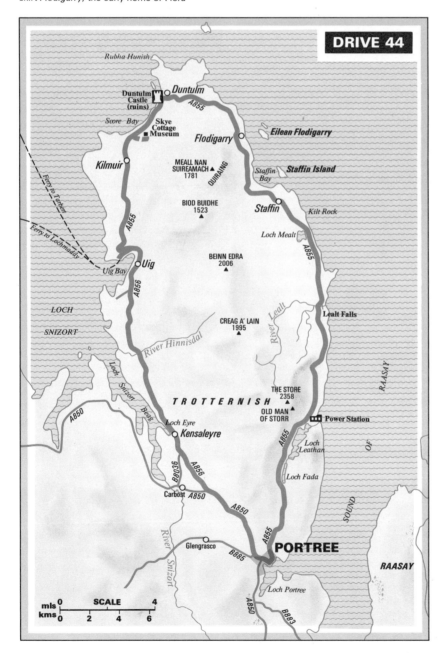

142

Ladder Hills and Balmoral

From Ballater

Drive 45   96 miles

The drive starts from *Ballater*, a popular
Deeside resort set at a height of nearly 700ft
amid beautifully wooded hills. Leave by the
A93 *Aberdeen* road and drive along the Dee
Valley to the Cambus o'May Hotel, where
the river flows through an attractive
woodland setting. After 1m turn left on to
the A97, signposted *Huntly*. Two small
lochs – Kinord and Davan, are passed before
the road turns left again after 3½m, still with
the A97. Beyond Logie Coldstone the road
climbs through moorland with the 2,862ft
peak of Morven to the W, and eventually
achieves a summit of over 1,200ft before
running down to Deskry Water and later the
River Don. The drive turns right here, still
with the A97, and runs parallel with the
river to *Glenkindie*. On the left after 2½m
are the ruins of *Kildrummy* Castle, a
13th-c fortress with an imposing gatehouse.
At the foot of this medieval castle is the
Kildrummy Castle Garden Trust – an
attractive alpine garden laid out by
Japanese designers in 1904.

Beyond the hamlet of Mossat turn left and
continue to *Lumsden*, attractively set in a
valley between the Correen Hills on the
right and the 2,368ft Buck of Cabrach to the
left. In 2m turn left on to the B9022 and
pass ruined Auchindoir church, with its
richly carved 12th- and 13th-c doorway.
Beyond the church the road climbs across
bleak moorland to a height of 1,400ft. After
4¾m turn left on to the A941 *Dufftown*
road. Make a gradual descent into the upper
valley of the Deveron, following the river
for a short distance before continuing
through moorland landscapes to Dufftown.
This small town operates numerous
distilleries in the area, including the
Glenfiddich plant which is open regularly
to the public. Just N of the town is ruined
Balvenie Castle, a large and well-
preserved structure with a notable iron
'yett', or grillegate.

The drive leaves by the B9009 *Tomintoul*
road, then follows Dullan Water through
Glen Rinnes with 2,755ft Ben Rinnes rising
to the right. Later the road passes Glenlivet
Forest to enter *Glenlivet*, where the drive
keeps left on to the unsignposted B9008.
This road climbs out of the glen after 1½m
to reach the Pole Inn at Knockandhu. The
route now crosses moors at over 1,200ft,
and after 4¼m turns left on to the A939 with
Cock Bridge and *Braemar* signposts. Ahead
lies *Tomintoul*, the loftiest village in the
Highlands. The A939 at first follows
Conglass Water, then the landscape
becomes more bleak and desolate as the
drive crosses the Ladder Hills and climbs to
a 2,050ft road summit. This is known as the
Lecht road, and was built for military
purposes in 1754. Deep snow often makes
it impassable during the winter, and although
much improved in recent years the road still
includes steep gradients before the River
Don is crossed at Cock Bridge. The ruins of
Corgarff Castle, associated with Jacobite
uprisings of the 18thc, can be seen near by.

In 2½m turn right with the A939, signposted
Braemar, and cross the Don. From here the
road runs over further open moorland, and
after 6m crosses a fine old bridge over the
River Gairn. Branch right with the B976
(A939). After 5m the drive reaches Royal
Deeside at the junction with the A93. Turn
left here on to the *Aberdeen* road. Shortly
to the right and across the Dee is *Balmoral
Castle*, the Highland residence of HM the
Queen. Grounds only are open to the public
on weekdays from May to July. To the left
is granite-built, 19th-c *Crathie* Church,
which is attended by the Royal Family when
in residence at Balmoral. Continue with the
A93 alongside the Dee, passing through
attractive woodland on the return to Ballater.

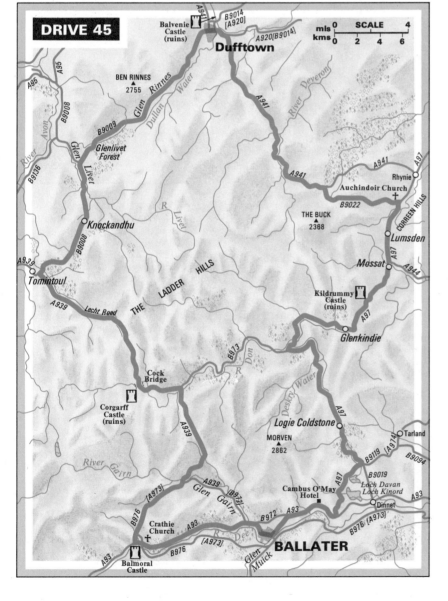

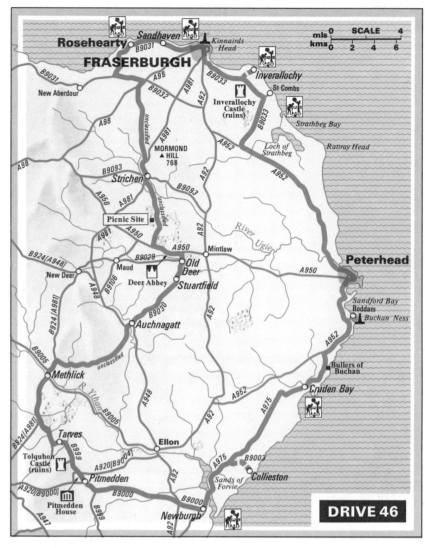

Village in the Sands

From Fraserburgh

Drive 46   84 miles

The resort and herring port of *Fraserburgh* sits on the W side of the sandy Fraserburgh Bay, and is sheltered to the W by Kinnairds Head. Near the lighthouse on Kinnairds Head is the Wine Tower, which is built above a 100ft-long cave called Scaleh's Holte.

Leave by the A98 *Inverness* road, and after $\frac{3}{4}$m turn right on to the B9031, following *Rosehearty* signposts. Continue alongside the coast for *Sandhaven* and Rosehearty, small fishing ports with sands for pleasant bathing. Continue on the B9031 with *New Aberdour* signposts, and in $2\frac{1}{2}$m turn left on to the B9032, signposted Rathen. After $1\frac{1}{2}$m meet crossroads and turn left on to the A98 Inverness road, then in $\frac{1}{4}$m turn left on to an unclassified road signposted *Strichen*.

Pass through undulating countryside for $4\frac{1}{4}$m before turning right on to the A981 for Strichen, sited in the valley of the North Ugie Water. At the end of the village turn right, following the signposts for New Deer, and pass under a bridge before branching left on to an unclassified road signposted *Old Deer*. On the climb out of the valley there are rearward views of a white horse which was carved on the slopes of Mormond Hill in 1700. After $2\frac{1}{2}$m the drive passes a picnic site in White Cow Wood – part of the Forest of Deer. In $1\frac{1}{2}$m turn left on to the A950. To the right after $1\frac{1}{4}$m are the remains of the 13th-c Cistercian Deer Abbey. In $\frac{1}{2}$m turn right on to the B9030 with Auchnagatt signposts, then cross the South Ugie Water to enter Old Deer.

Continue with the B9030 through Stuartfield, and at end of village keep right. At Auchnagatt turn right on to the A948 and cross the railway bridge, then turn left on to an unclassified, unsignposted road. In 2m keep forward with the *Methlick* road to follow a cross-country route for $3\frac{1}{2}$m, then turn left on to the B922 (A981). The clear waters of the River Ythan are crossed before the drive enters Methlick. Turn right with the B922 (A981), and in $2\frac{3}{4}$m turn left on to the B999 with *Tarves* signposts. After $1\frac{3}{4}$m turn left for Tarves. Continue with the B999 and after $1\frac{1}{2}$m pass the road to Tolquhou Castle, which lies 1m to the right.

This ruined 16th-c mansion includes an interesting 15th-c tower. After 1m another detour can be made by turning right on to the A920 (B9004) to *Pitmedden House*, where the 17th-c Great Garden is open daily. The main drive keeps forward with the B999 *Aberdeen* road to Pitmedden. Drive through the village, and after $\frac{1}{2}$m turn left on to the B9000 towards *Newburgh*. In 5m turn right on to the A92, then left to remain on the B9000 for Newburgh. This town stands on the estuary of the River Ythan and is noted for mussel pearls. Due to the action of coastal deposition, its sandy coastline is gradually moving seawards. Turn left on to the A975 with *Cruden Bay* signposts. Beyond the town the drive crosses the River Ythan; seaward are the Sands of Forvie, which rise to heights of over 180ft in places and hide the buried village of Forvie. To the N of these sands a diversion may be taken along the B9003 to Collieston, a neat fishing village situated in a cove and especially noted for speldings (small haddock).

The main road strikes inland before rejoining the coast at Cruden Bay, a resort which is set back from the sea and offers golfing facilities and good sands. Continue with the *Peterhead* road. After $1\frac{3}{4}$m the Bullers of Buchan can be seen off the road to the right – a spectacular natural amphitheatre measuring 200ft deep and 50ft wide, which becomes a cauldron of foaming sea water during storms. The A975 again heads inland before turning right on to the A952. This road joins the coast and runs close to the cliff-tops. Off to the right lies the pink-granite fishing village of *Boddam*. To the E of this village is Buchan Ness and its lighthouse, the farthest E point in Scotland. The drive passes Sandford Bay and Peterhead prison before arriving at the largest of the Buchan towns, Peterhead, another important herring port set between Peterhead Bay and the point where the River Ugie empties into the sea.

Leave by the A952 with Fraserburgh signposts, then cross the River Ugie. The countryside is predominantly flat as the drive runs through *St Fergus* to *Crimond*. Continue through the village and after $1\frac{1}{2}$m turn right on to the B9033 towards *St Combs*. This road heads towards the coast and after $3\frac{1}{4}$m turns left with Fraserburgh signposts. Ahead lies the small fishing village of St Combs. The remains of Inverallochy Castle are on the left before the drive passes the turning on to the B9107 for *Inverallochy*, a coastal village set in a golfing area. The return to Fraserburgh is along the B9033 and A92, often behind sand dunes which are high enough to seriously restrict views of Fraserburgh Bay.

Grampians and Tayside

Many travellers are content to know the mountainous heart of Scotland from the great river valleys, deeply etched by retreating glaciers. Queen Victoria and Prince Albert assured the popularity of Royal Deeside when they bought the estate of Balmoral in 1852. Speyside and Strathspey include holiday centres busy both in summer and in winter, taking advantage of splendid pinewood scenery and Cairngorm snows alike. As the Tay spills out of its loch at Kenmore, it sets off on a long journey past ancient clan castles, mansions built by wealthy families attracted north in Queen Victoria's wake, steeply-wooded hillsides around historic Dunkeld, and a gentler landscape towards the Fair City of Perth.

Other Grampian rivers are more elusive. The Findhorn is worth pursuing for its strange eroded valley of the Streens and the tortured rock scenery of Randolph's Leap upstream from Forres. The Deveron rises in the heather moors of the Cabrach and reaches the sea at Banff, a town which holds on determinedly to the fading grace of its Georgian houses and remembers even farther back to when it was a proud member of the Hanseatic League. Don and Ythan, North and South Esk, Earn and Almond are all, in their various ways, rivers the motorist can follow to escape the busy tourist routes.

The roads can offer exhilarating driving. The Devil's Elbow may have been engineered away, but the Lecht Road to Tomintoul, the highest village in the Highlands, still swoops and dips adventurously over the Ladder Hills. One of the best is Cairn o'Mount, which follows an ancient route across the rounded heather hills and famous sporting estates from Fettercairn in the rich and long-settled Howe of the Mearns to Banchory on Deeside.

Ideal hill motoring can also be found in less elevated country. In the Braes of the Carse, between Perth and Dundee, little roads linking Kinfauns and Kilspindie, Kinnaird and Abernyte give superb views over the Carse of Gowrie and the far shore of the widening Tay.

The coastal districts are full of change. There are forests and farms in the Moray lowlands. Eastwards are the cliffs where fishing ports were built to haul in the harvest of the North Sea, with names as no-nonsense as the people who live in them: Macduff and Buckie, Findochty and Portknockie. The granite cliffs of Buchan, teeming with seabirds, swing south to meet long miles of sandy beaches on the way to Aberdeen. Still clearly the Granite City and with a university founded in 1494, Aberdeen has a new reputation as, half-smothered in flowers, it captures prize after prize in the competition for Britain in Bloom. Inland again, the mountain country which includes many of Britain's state forests is balanced by districts like Strathmore, where arable farms, stock farms, and fruit farms make use of every lush and productive acre. Upland valleys call on local resources of barley, peat, and clear tumbling water to float the world on Scottish whisky.

Pontius Pilate, many people firmly believe, was born at Fortingall when his father served there with a Roman legion. Captain Scott planned his last great Antarctic journey in Glen Prosen. Beatrix Potter invented Peter Rabbit in a garden by the Tay. In this often reticent country, it is the traveller who stops to look around who learns the secrets behind the scenery.

Glen Shee and Glamis Castle

From Kirriemuir

Drive 47   71 miles

The drive starts from *Kirriemuir*, a small market town noted for jute manufacture. The novelist Sir James Barrie was born here in 1860, and his birthplace is open to the public. Follow the signposts for *Clova* to leave by the B955, heading towards the S slopes of the Grampians to *Dykehead*. From here a 19½m diversion can be made by keeping forward with the B955 to visit picturesque Glen Clova. Beyond Dykehead a left fork after 3m allows the traveller to see most of the glen from a circular route. The approach to Clova is accompanied by increasingly rugged scenery and steep-sided valleys, as the road pushes into the heart of the Braes of Angus Hills. The return is along the E side of the glen back to Dykehead.

The main tour from Dykehead turns left on to an unclassified road – or right if the detour has been taken – to follow signposts for Prosen. In 1m the road enters the attractive Glen Prosen and follows Prosen Water along the E side of the valley. After 4½m turn left and cross the river bridge, then left again with Kirriemuir signposts to follow the W bank of the Prosen Water. In 5¼m meet crossroads and turn right, signposted Glenisla. In 1m meet a T-junction and turn right again along an unsignposted road. The drive then follows a narrow road along the S slopes of the Grampians, and in 4m passes modern Balintore Castle on the right. This is not open to the public. After a short descent keep left, then in 2½m meet crossroads and turn right on to the B951, signposted Glenisla. Accompany Melgam Water for a short distance before following the River Isla through attractive Glen Isla, which penetrates deep into the Grampians. After 5½m the drive keeps left and leaves the glen. In 2½m cross Shee Water and at the junction with the A93 turn left on to the *Perth* road. Continue down Glen Shee and in 7¾m turn sharp left on to an unclassified road signposted Drimmie. In

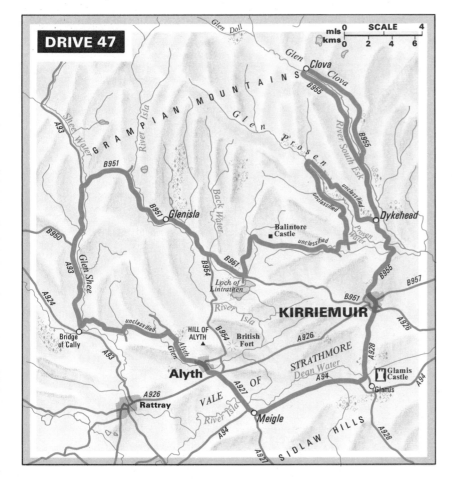

Drive 47 continued

¼m cross the river bridge, then branch right and climb above the valley of the River Ericht. After 2m turn left and cross open countryside, then in 3m meet a T-junction and turn right. Continue to *Alyth*, a small linen-manufacturing town on the N edge of Strathmore.

Leave by the A927 *Dundee* road, and at the end of the town turn left. In ½m enter a roundabout and take the third exit, then after 2½m turn left on to the A94 to *Meigle*. A museum here houses a collection of ancient stones. Continue with the A94 *Aberdeen* road across the fertile Vale of Strathmore, and in 6m turn left on to an unclassified road. This leads to the outskirts of *Glamis*, famous for the predominantly 17th-c castle which was the birthplace of Princess Margaret. The village also boasts Kirkwynd Cottages, now housing the Angus folk collection. The drive follows the A928 N for the return to Kirriemuir.

On the Angus Coast

From Dundee

Drive 48   82 miles

The Firth of Tay is spanned by a new road bridge and a 2m 19th-c rail bridge at the university city of *Dundee*. There are beautiful grandstand views across the Firth from Dundee Law, a large hill within the city. Commercially the city is known for the manufacture of preserves, and for its jute processing concerns.

The drive starts by following *Aberdeen* signposts to leave by the A92, passing through agricultural country to Muirdrum. After 2m along the A930 the well-known golfing and sea resort of *Carnoustie* lies to the right. Continue with the A92 and in 5m turn right under the railway bridge to *Arbroath*, a port, industrial town, and resort. The red-sandstone cliffs to the NE are known for their caves. The drive continues on the A92 Aberdeen road, and just N of the town passes a left turning for *St Vigeans*. A notable collection of sculptured stones dating from early-Christian and medieval periods is housed in a cottage here.

After *Inverkeilor* the road crosses Lunan Water and later affords views of the Montrose Basin before crossing the River South Esk to enter the resort and fishing port of *Montrose*. Beyond the town the drive keeps forward with the A937, signposted *Laurencekirk*. In 4½m turn right under a railway bridge, then cross the River North Esk to *Marykirk*. Turn left here on to the B974, following the signposts for *Fettercairn*. At the junction with the A94 turn right then left, still with the B974 and in 3¼m turn right to reach Fettercairn. This attractive village lies in the fertile agricultural area known as the Howe of the Mearns. A commemorative arch recalls the visit of Queen Victoria in 1861.

Leave by the B966 *Edzell* road; after 3½m a diversion can be made by turning right on to an unclassified road to visit Glen Esk. Superb glen scenery can be enjoyed as the road accompanies the River North Esk into the E Grampian mountains. After 9½m the drive passes the Retreat, a former shooting lodge which now houses a museum of local country life and handicrafts. The road ends at *Lochlee* church. Away to the N is the 3,077ft peak of Mount Keen. The entire detour adds 31m to the tour.

The main drive continues with the B966 and crosses the River North Esk before reaching the pleasant small town of Edzell. Edzell Castle lies 2m W and features a fine walled garden dating from 1604. On leaving the town the road passes through an arch which was erected in 1887 in memory of the 13th Earl of Dalhousie. In 3½m turn right on to the A94 *Perth* road and continue to the small city of *Brechin*. the much-restored cathedral has one of the only two round towers on the Scottish mainland, dating from the 10th or 11thc. Follow the Arbroath signposts to leave by the A933 and cross the River South Esk.

The drive skirts the private *Kinnaird* deer park and Montreathmont Moor Forest before turning right after 7m on to the A932, signposted *Forfar*. On the right after ¾m are the grounds of *Guthrie* Castle. The gardens here are occasionally open to the public. The drive continues to Forfar, the main market town for the NE extremity of the fertile Vale of Strathmore. This is known locally as the How of Angus. Leave by the A929 Dundee road and pass through agricultural countryside before crossing the low Sidlaw Hills on the return to Dundee.

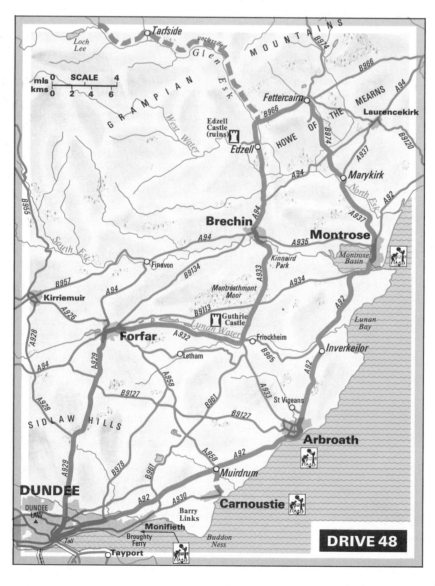

Golfing Country

From St Andrews

Drive 49   109 miles

St Andrews is a university town and resort which is famous for the Royal and Ancient Golf Club, acknowledged as the leading authority on golf. The harbour is guarded by steep cliffs, but wide sands lie NW.

The drive follows Tay Bridge signposts to leave by the A91. At Guardbridge cross the River Eden and turn right on to the A919 to reach *Leuchars*. The village is perhaps best known for its RAF base, but it also has one of the finest small Norman churches in Scotland. In 1¼m, at St Michael's Hotel, turn right on to the B945 to *Tayport*. There are fine views across the Firth of Tay to *Dundee* as the B946 winds W and passes beneath the new Tay road bridge into *Newport-on-Tay*. At *Wormit* there are views of the 2m long Tay railway bridge, which was completed in 1888.

The B946 continues inland and after ¾m the route branches left on to an unclassified road signposted St Andrews. At the roundabout in 1m take the second exit, then in another 1½m turn right on to the A92 and return to St Michael's Hotel. At the crossroads turn right towards *Cupar* and continue through Balbullo. After 2m join the A91 to enter *Dairsie*. Turn left here on to an unclassified road towards *Pitscottie*. In 1m the River Eden is crossed by a 16th-c bridge, and as the drive turns right there are views of ruined Dairsie Castle on the N bank. Picturesquely-wooded Dura Glen – noted for its fossils – is then followed to Pitscottie. Turn left then immediately right on to the B939, towards *Kirkcaldy*, for the attractive village of *Ceres*. After 1½m turn right at Craigrothie on to the A916, which passes

the entrance to the Hill of Tarvit mansion. Built in 1696 and enlarged in 1906, this house contains fine collections of tapestries and furniture. The A916 later winds down into the attractive valley of the River Eden, and joins the A92 for the run into Cupar. This is the main town of the fertile agricultural area known as the *Howe of Fife*. The town has a fine 15th-c church, plus an ancient and unusual Mercat cross.

Follow *Kincardine* signposts to leave by the A91, and at end of the town turn right on to the A913, towards *Perth*. After 1¾m turn right on to an unclassified road, following the signposts for Luthrie, and in 1m pass the ruins of an old castle on the left. At the junction with the A914 turn left and in ½m turn right on to another unclassified road for the hamlet of Luthrie. In 1m bear left.

After a while the drive affords fine views across the Firth of Tay before turning left and following the river to *Newburgh*. As the route enters this small town it passes the remains of *Lindores* Abbey before turning right on to the A913 Perth road. Newburgh itself is noted for the manufacture of linoleum and as the site of the Magdrum Cross, which is more than 1,000 years old.

Continue on the A913 to *Abernethy*, where there is an early 12th-c round tower – one of only two on the Scottish mainland. Beyond Aberargie turn left on to the A90, following the signposts for the Forth Road Bridge, and pass through wooded Glen Farg. Beyond the village of *Glenfarg* keep forward after 2½m on to the B996, signposted *Glenrothes*. At the T-road turn right on to the A91, then turn left on to the B919. In 1¾m reach Balgedie and join the A911 to pass through *Kinnesswood*, with the Lomond Hills to the left. At *Scotlandwell* there is a picnic site. Turn left here and continue to the small industrial town of *Leslie*. Drive along the

main street and pass the church. In 300yds, opposite the Clansman public house, turn left at a concealed and unsignposted entrance on to an unclassified road to *Falkland*. Turn right to enter the town and keep left through the attractive square, passing the interesting 16th-c Palace – former residence of the Stuart Kings and Queens. At the T-road turn right on to the A912 and in ¼m turn left on to the B936, signposted Freuchie.

Continue through Newton of Falkland, then Freuchie, and at the end of the latter village go over crossroads on to an unclassified and unsignposted road. At the junction with the A92 turn right then immediately left on to the Kennoway road for a relaxing drive through rolling country. In 4¼m turn left to enter Kennoway. At the main road turn right and immediately left towards *Leven*. After 2m the drive reaches the outskirts of Leven, a resort and port on Largo Bay. Turn left on to the A915 St Andrews road and continue past Lundin Links to Upper *Largo*. Keep forward on the A921 with *Crail* signposts, and in 2¼m turn right on to the A917 for *Elie*. Both this resort and *Earlsferry* are situated on a sheltered crescent-shaped bay, and are noted for their fine golf courses. Leave by the A917 *Anstruther* road in order to follow the next stage of the drive along the East Neuk coastline. The road passes the fishing villages of *St Monance* and *Pittenweem* to Anstruther, where the Scottish Fisheries museum is situated. The Isle of May national nature reserve lies offshore.

The route continues on the A917 to Crail. This is the farthest E of the East Neuk fishing villages, and retains an early 16th-c tolbooth. The return to St Andrews is made along the A918, with the drive passing through *Kingsbarns* and mainly agricultural country.

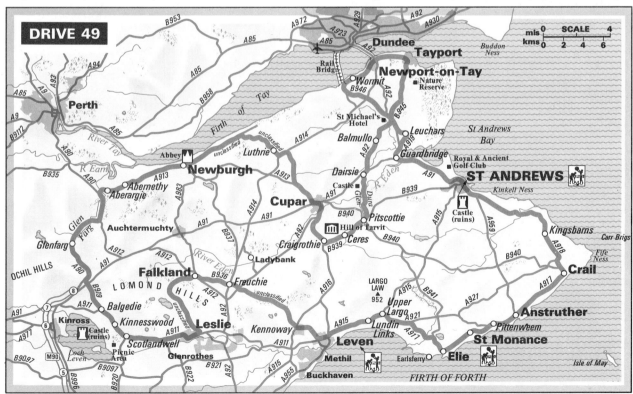

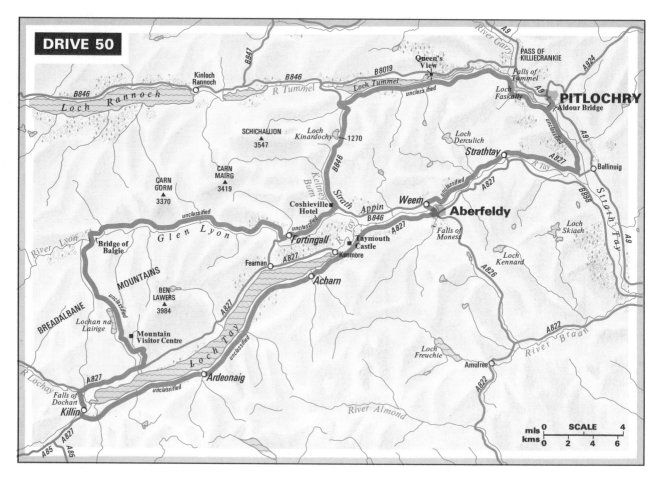

DRIVE 50

Through Glen Lyon

From Pitlochry

Drive 50   84 miles

Pitlochry is a popular resort beside the Tummel, in an attractive setting of lochs, rivers, mountains, and woods. A modern Festival Theatre set in the hills presents plays and concerts in the summer. The artificial Loch Faskally was created when the hydro-electric power station was built, and includes an extensive fish ladder with an observation chamber. A fish ladder is a device to help springing salmon negotiate difficult ascents.

Leave by the A9 *Perth* road and in $\frac{1}{2}$m turn right on to an unclassified road signposted *Logierait*, then cross the new Aldour Bridge. On the far side turn right with Foss signposts on to a narrow road which runs beside Loch Faskally to pass the Clunie Memorial Arch. The drive continues through magnificent scenery as the road follows the S bank of the River Tummel and Loch Tummel. After 12m turn left on to the B846 towards *Aberfeldy* and climb out of the valley to a summit of over 1,270ft. This section follows the line of a military road built by General Wade in the 18thc. The tour turns down into the valley of the Keltney Burn and continues to the Coshieville Hotel. Turn right here on to an unclassified road for *Fortingall.* Pass through the village and after $\frac{1}{2}$m turn right, following Glen Lyon signposts. Continue beside the River Lyon into Glen Lyon, one of the longest and most picturesque glens in Scotland. After 11m

turn left towards Loch Tay and cross the Bridge of Balgie. This narrow moorland road climbs to a height of 1,805ft as it crosses the Breadalbane Mountains. The descent affords views of Lochan na Lairige, and 3,984ft Ben Lawers rises to the left. This mountain is considered of great botanical interest. The drive passes the Ben Lawers mountain visitor centre, then after 2m turns right to join the A827 along the N side of Loch Tay.

Killin is a pleasant village resort at the W extremity of the loch. Drive to the end and cross the River Dochart, then keep right. Take the next turning left on to an unclassified road signposted Ardeonaig. This scenic road returns along the S side of Loch Tay, passing through the hamlets of Ardeonaig and later Acharn. In 1$\frac{1}{2}$m turn right on to the A827, signposted Aberfeldy. To the left is the small resort of *Kenmore*, sited at the E end of Loch Tay.

The A827 continues along the valley of the River Tay, with views of modern Taymouth Castle to the left. This is not open to the public. Aberfeldy is a market town and holiday centre. The River Tay is spanned here by a stone bridge built in 1733 by General Wade.

Turn left on to the B846 towards *Kinloch Rannoch*, and cross Wade's bridge for Weem. Turn right on to an unclassified

road signposted Strathtay. The route now follows the N bank of the river to Strathtay, and beyond the hamlet joins the A827 Ballinluig road. In 4m turn left on to an unclassified road towards Dunfallandy. This narrow road follows the W bank of the River Tummel before turning right, after another 4m, to recross the Aldour bridge. On the far side of the Tummel turn left on to the A9 for the return to Pitlochry.

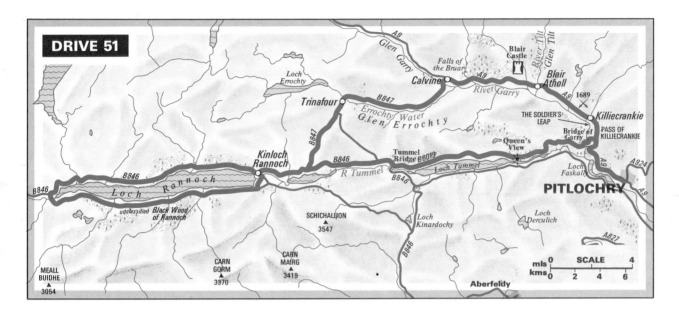

Loch Tummel and the Black Wood

From Pitlochry

Drive 51   67 miles

From *Pitlochry* take the A9 *Inverness* road along the wooded shores of Loch Faskally and follow the River Garry through the Pass of *Killiecrankie*. A spot where two rocks almost bridge the gorge is known as Soldier's Leap. A fugitive escaped death here by a daring leap to freedom while being pursued by Highlanders during the Battle of Killiecrankie. To the N of the village is the site of the battle fought in 1689, when the Highlanders defeated a royalist force. Further along Glen Garry is *Blair Atholl*, pleasantly situated in attractive Highland scenery. To the right of the village is Blair Castle, home of the Dukes of Atholl. Although dating back to 1269 the structure was greatly altered during the 18th and 19thc. Before the village of Calvine are the Falls of Bruar, which lie off the main road to the right. At Calvine turn left on to the B847 towards *Kinloch Rannoch*, and continue through Glen Errochty to *Trinafour*, pleasantly set amongst lonely moorland. The road then leaves the glen and later runs down into the Tummel Valley before turning right on to the B846 for the small fishing resort of Kinloch Rannoch. A circuit of Loch Rannoch, which now forms part of the Tummel-Garry hydro-electric scheme, is made by following the B846 with *Rannoch Station* signposts along the N shore of the loch.

There are splendid views of the mountains on the S side from this route, including 3,419ft Cairn Mairg, 3,370ft Cairn Gorm, and 3,054ft Meall Buidhe. After 10¾m, at the far end of the loch, turn left on to an unclassified road and follow the S Loch Rannoch road. Part of this stretch is through the picturesque Black Wood of Rannoch, where the native Caledonian pine still grows. The drive turns left after 11½m and returns to Kinloch Rannoch. Rejoin the B846 *Aberfeldy* road, and in 2½m go forward towards *Tummel Bridge*. There are views to the right of the 3,547ft conical peak of

Schichallion as the road follows the River Tummel to Tummel Bridge – built by General Wade in 1730.

By the nearside of the bridge keep left on to the B8019 along the N side of Loch Tummel. This road provides some impressive views of the mountains, which sweep grandly down to the S side of the loch. After 6½m the drive passes the Queen's View, a notable AA viewpoint named after Queen Victoria. In the car park is the Tummel Forest information centre. In 3¾m cross the *Bridge of Garry* and turn right on to the A9 for the return to Pitlochry.

Placenames in *italic* type are worth stopping at; each is listed and described in the main gazetteer section of the book

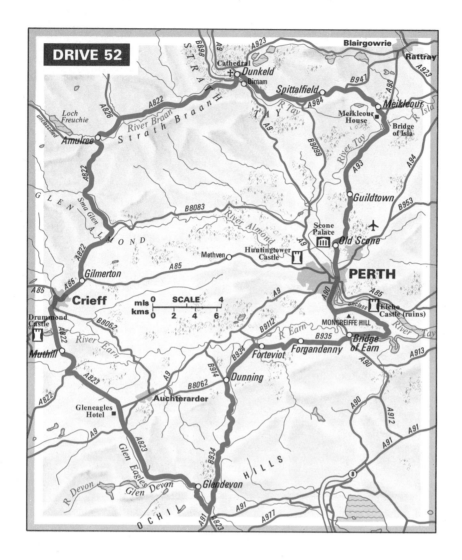

Through the Ochil Hills

From Perth

Drive 52   88 miles

The city of *Perth* is built on the banks of the River Tay and lies between the Sidlaw and the Ochil Hills. Some 2m W on the *Crieff* road is historic 15th- to 16th-c *Huntingtower Castle* – formerly Ruthven Castle – which is open to the public. Follow *Braemar* signposts across the Tay to leave by the A93. On the left after 1m are the grounds of Scone Palace. The present building replaced the original Abbey of Scone, which was destroyed in the 16thc. The Motehill of Scone was the residing place for the Stone of Scone until it was removed to Westminster Abbey by Edward I in the 13thc. The house, grounds, and pinetum are open to the public during the summer.

Continue through *Old Scone* and Guildtown, then follow the pleasant valley of the River Tay. Later the drive crosses the Bridge of Isla and reaches the grounds of Meikleour House, which is bordered by a magnificent 85ft-high beech hedge, planted in 1746. At the far end of the hedge turn left on to an unclassified road for *Meikleour*. Join the A984 *Dunkeld* road and continue through Spittalfield before entering the attractive and well-wooded

Strath Tay to reach Dunkeld. Leave by the Crieff road, crossing the Tay by Telford's fine 19th-c bridge into Little Dunkeld. Turn right on to the A822, then turn left and climb. Enter Glen Almond and follow one of General Wade's military roads through the lonely Sma' Glen. At *Gilmerton* turn right on to the A85 for Crieff, a pleasant hillside town overlooking Strath Earn. The Mercat cross here is dated 1688 and the ancient market cross is possibly of 10th-c origin.

Leave by the A822 *Stirling* road. On the right after 2m are the grounds of Drummond Castle, which are occasionally open to the public during the summer. Continue through Muthill and in 1¾m turn left on to the A823, signposted *Dunfermline*. After 4m the drive passes the entrance to *Gleneagles Hotel*, with its world-famous golf course. There is more fine scenery ahead; the route crosses the A9 and takes the A823 to pass through Glen Eagles into the heart of the Ochil Hills, entering Glen Devon to reach the village of *Glendevon*. After 2m turn left on to the B934 towards *Dunning*. This road re-crosses the Ochil Hills through well-wooded countryside to Dunning in Strath Earn. The church here retains a notable 13th-c tower. In the village turn right with the B934 then keep left, following the signposts for Perth. In 1¾m turn right with *Bridge of Earn*

signposts on to the B935, and immediately keep left. Continue through *Forteviot* and Forgandenny to Bridge of Earn. Turn left here on to the A90 Perth road, then after crossing the River Earn turn right towards Rhynd on to an unclassified road. This follows the foot of wooded Moncreiffe Hill.

In 2¼m meet a T-junction and turn left. After 1m a track to the right leads to Elcho Castle, a 16th-c stronghold beside the River Tay. There are good views of the Tay and the city of Perth as the unclassified road continues to a junction with the A90, where the drive turns right for the return to Perth.

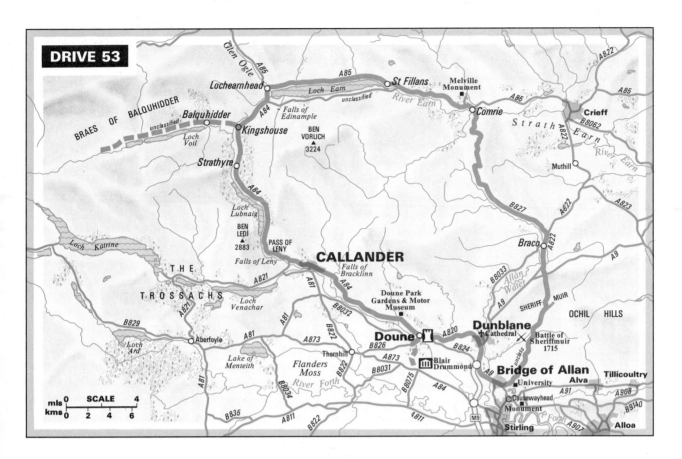

Strath Earn and Strathyre

From Callander

Drive 53   62 miles

The drive starts from *Callander*, a well-known resort and tourist centre attractively set at the confluence of the Rivers Teith and Leny. It is a good starting point for touring the Trossachs. Overlooking the town to the NW is Ben Ledi, which rises to 2,883ft. Scenes from the BBC series *Dr Finlay's Casebook* were filmed in Callander. Leave by the A84 *Stirling* road along the valley of the River Teith, and after 6m pass a turning for Doune Park gardens and motor museum. After 1m the drive turns left on to the A820 with *Dunblane* signposts to enter *Doune*, a small town once known for the manufacture of pistols. A detour can be made from Doune by remaining on the A84 to visit Blair Drummond safari park and the Victorian Blair Drummond House and gardens.

The main drive continues with the A820 to Dunblane, a small cathedral city in the S extremity of Strath Allan. Turn right on to the Stirling road and after 1m, at the roundabout, take the first exit for *Bridge of Allan*, a spa resort beneath the Ochil Hills. Ahead there are good views of the Wallace Monument. At the far end of town turn left on to an unclassified road towards Sheriffmuir, then bear right on the climb to pass the grounds of Stirling University. Use this unclassified road to cross the Ochil Hills, then after 4m keep forward with the *Blackford* road to cross Sheriff Muir, a battleground in 1715. In another 1½m turn left towards Greenloaning. At the junction

with the A9 turn left then right, towards *Braco*, then in ¼m right again on to the A822 for Braco.

After ¾m turn left with *Comrie* signposts on to the B827. The road runs through moorland scenery to this small but attractive resort in Strath Earn. To the N Dunmore Hill is crowned by the Melville monument. As this point is on the Highland geological fault, earth tremors are sometimes experienced in the area.

Leave by the A85 *Crianlarich* road and follow the River Earn to *St Fillans*. Beyond this village the drive takes the N bank of Loch Earn, with fine views across to the 3,224ft peak of Ben Vorlich. At the W end of the loch is *Lochearnhead*, another small resort and centre for water ski-ing and sailing. Turn left on to the A84 Stirling road and continue to Kingshouse. From here a minor road to the right leads to *Balquhidder* and Loch Voil, and although not a through-road it offers pleasing scenery along the lochside beneath the Braes of Balquhidder. Rob Roy is buried in the churchyard of the roofless Balquhidder Kirk.

The A84 continues through *Strathyre* to the small village of the same name, then follows the wooded E shore of Loch Lubnaig – a narrow winding stretch of water enclosed by steep hillsides. The attractive Pass of Leny, including the Falls, is passed before the drive returns to Callander.

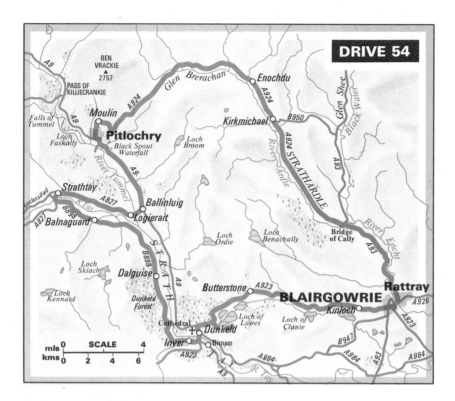

Skirting Dunkeld Forest

From Blairgowrie

Drive 54   59 miles

The drive starts from *Blairgowrie*, an angling resort and touring base on the River Ericht and the centre of a strawberry and raspberry-growing region. Follow the signposts for *Braemar* and cross the River Ericht into the neighbouring town of Rattray. Turn left to leave by the A93. The road follows the winding valley of the Ericht before re-crossing the river at *Bridge of Cally*. Turn left here on to the A924 towards *Pitlochry*, and follow Strath Ardle to *Kirkmichael*. The road continues to Enochdu and later climbs across the moors to over 1,200ft. The 2,757ft peak of Ben Vrachie is prominent to the right before the road runs down into the Tummel Valley for *Moulin* and Pitlochry.

Leave by the A9 *Perth* road and follow the River Tummel to Ballinluig. Turn right here on to the A827 towards *Aberfeldy*, and go over the level crossing and River Tummel to enter Strath Tay. The route continues through *Logierait* and follows the N bank of the Tay to the hamlet of Strathtay. In ¼m cross the river bridge and turn left on to the B898 towards *Dunkeld*. The road runs along the S side of Strath Tay, passing through Balnaguard to Dalguise. The drive then passes the edge of Dunkeld Forest to Inver, where there is a Forestry Commission information centre and picnic site. Cross the River Braan and in ½m join the A822, then turn left on to the A9. Telford's fine bridge of 1809 is used to re-cross the Tay and enter the tiny cathedral town of Dunkeld.

Continue with the A9 *Inverness* road, and in ½m turn right on to the A923, signposted Blairgowrie. After 1m a minor road to the right leads to the Loch of the Lowes, where there is a Scottish Wild Life Trust bird sanctuary. The drive continues with the A923 passing Loch Craiglush and Loch Butterstone before the hamlet of *Butterstone*. Later there are views of Loch Clunie as the road follows the valley of the Lunan Burn, before passing through Kinloch and returning to Blairgowrie.

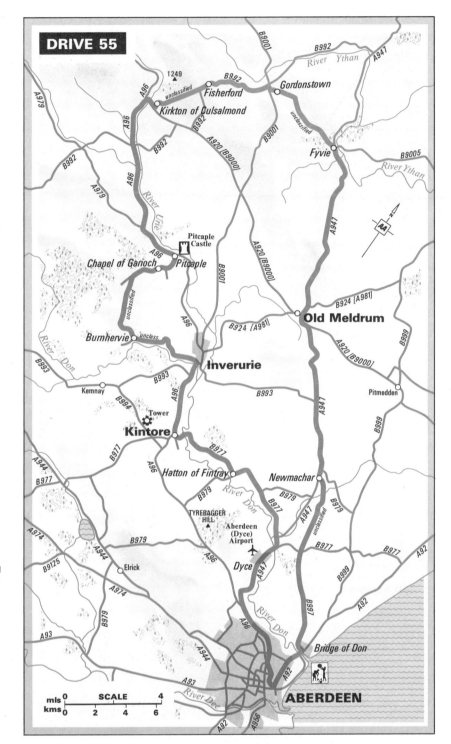

DRIVE 55

The Formartime District

From Aberdeen

Drive 55   68 miles

Leave *Aberdeen* by the A92 King Street, and follow the signposts for *Fraserburgh* to cross the Bridge of Don. On the far side of river turn left on to the B997, signposted Parkhill. Pass through agricultural country, then after 4½m go over crossroads on to an unclassified road towards Newmachar. At the main road turn right on to the A947 and continue through more agricultural country to *Old Meldrum*.

The drive remains on the A947, signposted *Turriff*, passing through undulating country for 8m to reach *Fyvie* beside the River Ythan. Turn left here on to an unclassified road signposted *Rothie Norman*, and immediately turn right then bear left. In 1½m turn right towards Gordonstown, and continue across rolling countryside to the hamlet of Gordonstown. In ½m turn right at a T-junction on to the unsignposted B9001. Meet crossroads and turn left on to the B992, signposted Fisherford. After 3m meet crossroads beyond the hamlet of Fisherton and go forward on to an unclassified road signposted *Culsamond*. The conical Hill of Tillymorgan rises to 1,249ft on the right before the drive reaches Kirkton of Culsamond. Follow the road down, and at the crossroads turn right on to the A920 (B9000), signposted Colepy. Meet a T-junction and turn left on to the A96

Aberdeen road. Continue along the valley of the River Urie to *Pitcaple*. Pitcaple Castle lies to the E of the village and is occasionally open to visitors during the summer.

The main drive turns sharp right on to an unclassified road signposted *Chapel of Garioch*. In 1¼m turn right, then at Chapel of Garioch post office bear left. In 1m go left again towards Bernhervie. Continue across the lower slopes of Bennachie, with 1,698ft Mither Tap rising to the right, and enter the valley of the River Don at Bernhervie. Turn left here towards *Inverurie*, and in 1¼m keep right. There are good views of the Don before the drive

reaches the outskirts of Inverurie. Avoid the town centre by turning right on to the A96 Aberdeen road and crossing the Don. At *Kintore*, where there is a tollbooth dated 1740, turn left on to the A977 with Hatton of Fintray signposts. In ¼m turn left and go over the level crossing, then re-cross the Don and follow the river to *Fintray*.

Turn left towards *Dyce*; views of the Don can be enjoyed before the tour reaches the A947 Aberdeen road, which leads into Dyce. The local airport lies to the right and is backed by the wooded Tyrebagger Hill. At Bucksburn the route joins the A96 for a suburban trek to Aberdeen.

Placenames in italic type are worth stopping at; each is listed and described in the main gazetteer section of the book   153

A Tour of Deeside

From Braemar

Drive 56   115 miles

Braemar is an attractive winter and summer resort 1,100ft up in the Highlands, well-known for the annual Royal Highland Gathering held in September. The village is set among heather-clad hills, dominated to the W by the Cairngorm massif of 4,241ft Cairn Toul, and to the SE by the 3,786ft peak of Lochnagar. Braemar Castle, dating from 1628 and rebuilt in 1748, stands N of the village near the River Dee.

An interesting 6m excursion to the W may be made beyond the hamlet of *Inverey* to the Lin of Dee, where the Dee flows through a rocky cleft. Here the road crosses the river and doubles back along the N bank, passing by Mar Lodge and its modern ski-ing developments.

The main drive leaves by the A93 *Perth* road and passes through Glen Clunie, gradually rising to 2,199ft at the *Cairnwall Pass* – Britain's highest main road summit. Extensive ski-ing developments have taken place here, and a chair lift operates throughout the year up to the 3,059ft peak of Cairnwell. To the left is 3,502ft Glas Maol.

The road runs down the Devil's Elbow, once well-known for its severe gradients and hairpin bends, but now re-aligned with an easier maximum gradient of 1 in 8. The drive continues down the valley to *Spittal of Glenshee*, another all-the-year-round resort, then crosses Shee Water and continues

alongside it before passing the new plantations of Strathardle Forest. After the forest turn sharp left on to the B951 with *Kirriemuir* and Glenisla signposts. Re-cross Shee Water and in ¼m keep right. After 2m keep right again to follow the course of the River Isla through attractive Glen Isla. Carry on along the Kirriemuir road, then after 6m the drive leaves the valley and after 3m passes the Loch of Lintrathen to enter the fertile Vale of Strathmore. Drive through Kirkton of Kingoldrum, then after 3m turn left on to the A926. Turn right to enter the small market town of Kirriemuir, which is noted for jute manufacture. The town makes a good centre for exploration of the beautiful Braes of Angus, including Glen Clova and Glen Prosen, which penetrate deep into the E Grampian mountains to the N.

Follow *Brechin* signposts to leave by the B957, and after 5½m cross the River South Esk to reach *Tannadice*. Pass through the village and after 1½m turn left on to the A94 *Aberdeen* road to the small city of Brechin. Continue on the A94 towards Aberdeen, and in 2m turn left on to the B966 for *Edzell*. The attractive small town is approached through an arch which was erected during 1887 in memory of the 13th Earl of Dalhousie. Edzell Castle lies 2m W and features a fine walled garden dating from 1604. Continue with the B966 through the Howe of the Mearns, a fertile agricultural area, to *Fettercairn*. This village is entered through an arch which commemorates the visit of Queen Victoria in 1861.

Follow the B947 *Strachan* and *Banchory* road to cross the Grampians over the Cairn O'Mounth, which affords a fine view from its

1,488ft summit. The run down towards Deeside passes through wooded Glen Dye and later crosses the Bridge of Dye, which dates from 1680. In 2m at AA box 753, turn left on to an unclassified road towards *Aboyne*. Two fords are then crossed, and after 2¼m the drive turns left on to the B976. In 5½m keep forward with the B976 (A973) with Aboyne signposts to reach Deeside. After 3¼m, across the River Dee, lies the small resort of Aboyne. As the road continues forward towards *Ballater* it runs along S Deeside, passing through attractive pine forests beside the river. At the edge of Ballater keep forward towards Balmoral, and in ½m bear right across the River Muick towards Braemar. On the right after 5½m is Abergeldie Castle, home of Edward VII while Prince of Wales. After another 2m the drive passes the entrance to *Balmoral Castle*, the Highland home of HM the Queen. The grounds only are open to the public on weekdays from May to July.

The River Dee is crossed to reach the junction with the A93, and a short distance to the right is granite-built *Crathie* church of 1895. The Royal Family attend services here when in residence at Balmoral. The main drive turns left to follow the Braemar road along the N side of the Dee, passing through more pine forests with fine views of the E Cairngorm mountains. Later the Dee is re-crossed, and after 2m the entrance to Braemar Castle is passed on the right before the return to Braemar.

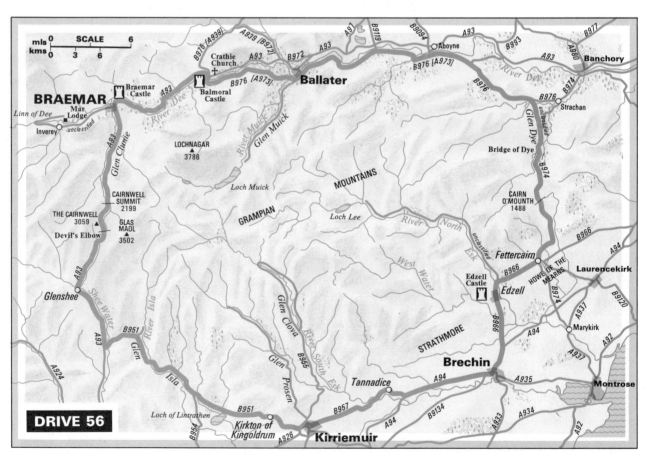

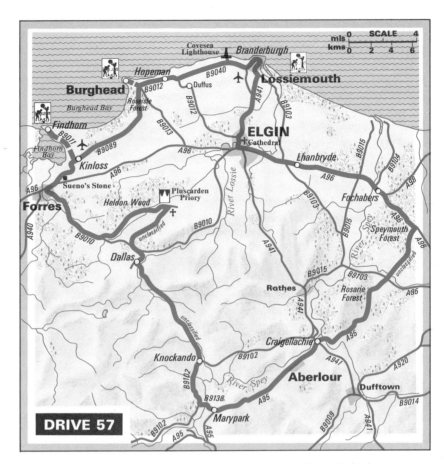

DRIVE 57

Bays of the Moray Firth

From Elgin

Drive 57   77 miles

The city of *Elgin* is neatly set on the banks of the River Lossie, 5m inland from the Moray Firth. The drive leaves by the A941 towards *Lossiemouth*, and crosses low-lying land to reach Lossiemouth, a resort on the W extremity of Spey Bay. The town is

linked with Branderburgh, which serves as the port for Elgin. From the seafront follow the B9040 towards *Hopeman* and *Burghead*. The road runs parallel with the coast passing Lossiemouth Airfield on the left and the *Covesea* Lighthouse to the right. Sand dunes rise to heights of over 200ft on the way to Hopeman. Just beyond Cummingstown the drive reaches the junction with the B9089. From here a diversion can be made by turning right to visit Burghead, a fishing village overlooking Burghead Bay.

The main drive keeps left on to the unsignposted B9089, then turns right with *Forres* signposts and passes through the Roseisle Forest to *Kinloss*, with its large RAF base. To the NE of the village on Findhorn Bay lies the fishing village and resort of *Findhorn*, which can be reached by the B9011. The drive continues with the B9011 Forres road. After 2m, before the junction with the A96, stands the Sueno's stone, a carved pillar of unknown origin. The route turns right here on to the A96 towards *Inverness* to enter Forres, the centre of rich agricultural country. Overlooking the town is Clunny Hill, capped by the notable viewpoint of Nelson Monument.

In the town turn left on to the B9010, signposted *Dallas*, and at the roundabout take the second exit. After 4½m branch left on to an unclassified road towards Elgin and Pluscarden. A pleasant road, well-wooded in places, is taken along the N side of the Blackburn valley, and after 4m the drive passes a left turn to *Pluscarden Priory*. This interesting 13th-c monastery has recently been restored and re-occupied by

Benedictine monks, and guided tours are available at certain times. In ¼m, at Pluscarden church, turn right and return along the S side of the valley. After 3¼m take an unsignposted left turn to rejoin the B9010; and in 1m turn right on to an unclassified road signposted *Knockando*. Drive into Dallas, which is pleasantly sited in the valley of the River Lossie. At the end of the village turn left and cross the River Lossie. The scenery becomes increasingly wild and desolate over the moors on the long run down to Knockando. At the post office turn right on to the B9102 *Grantown* road and enter Strath Spey. After 3m turn left on to the B9138, following the signposts to Marypark, then cross the River Spey. At Marypark post office turn left on to the A95 Elgin road. The 2,755ft peak of Ben Rinnes rises to the right before the drive reaches the Speyside villages of *Aberlour* and *Craigellachie*. The latter is picturesquely set at an important crossroads. A bridge which takes the A941 over the Spey was originally designed by Telford, but has been superseded by a new structure.

The drive continues with the A95 *Keith* road and passes through the scattered Craigellachie and Rosarie Forests. After 6½m meet crossroads and keep forward on to an unclassified road signposted Rumbach. After ¾m keep forward, and in 2¾m turn left on to the A96 for a pleasant run through the Speymouth Forest to *Fochabers*. Beyond the town the drive re-crosses the River Spey, and then passes through *Lhanbryde* before returning to Elgin.

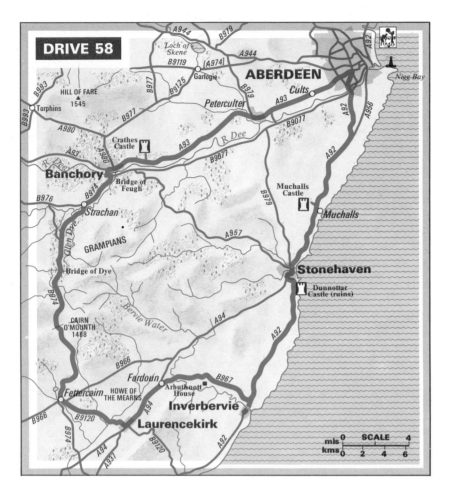

Over the Howe of Mearns

From Aberdeen

Drive 58   80 miles

The drive leaves *Aberdeen* by the A93, following the signposts to *Braemar* and running parallel to the River Dee. Pass through Cults to *Peterculter*, then on the right after 7¼m stands *Crathes Castle*, dating from the late 16thc. It is in the baronial style and includes fine woodwork, painted ceilings, and noted walled gardens. *Banchory* is a pleasant Deeside resort near the confluence of the Dee and Water of Feugh. In the town turn left on to the B974 (A943) *Stonehaven* road to cross the Dee, then in ¼m keep forward with the B974, signposted *Fettercairn*. At *Strachan* turn left and cross the Water of Feugh, then keep right.

The drive continues through wooded Glen Dye and after 4½m crosses the 17th-c Bridge of Dye. There are some fine views as the road climbs up into the Grampians, reaching its summit at the *Cairn O'Mounth* viewpoint. From here the road leads down into the fertile area known as Howe of the Mearns to reach Fettercairn. In the village square is the old Kincardine town cross, dated 1670 and notched to show a Scottish measurement known as an ell. Turn left on to the B966 with *Laurencekirk* signposts, then in ½m join the B9120 to reach Laurencekirk. Turn left on to the A94 Aberdeen road to Fordoun. Turn right here on to the B967 *Inverbervie* road, and at the

next crossroads turn left to follow the valley of the Bervie Water. After 3m *Arbuthnott House*, a 16th- to 18th-c mansion which is occasionally open during the summer, lies to the right. On reaching the junction with the A92 turn left towards *Aberdeen*. A short detour may be made by turning right to visit the flax-spinning town of Inverbervie. This attractive place is set on rising ground around Bervie Bay. To the S is fine coastal scenery, but this is not easily accessible by car.

The main drive continues with the A92 through undulating countryside, and after 6m runs parallel with the coast to Stonehaven. Before the descent into the town is *Dunnottar Castle*, a ruined fortress situated on a rocky headland overlooking the North Sea. Stonehaven is a fishing port and charming resort noted for its setting amid magnificent cliff scenery. The drive continues with the Aberdeen road, and hugs the cliff tops for much of the route before skirting *Muchalls*. Off the road to the left lies 17th-c Muchalls Castle — open occasionally during the summer. The A92 veers inland for the return to Aberdeen, and later offers fine views of the city before entering the suburbs and re-crossing the River Dee.

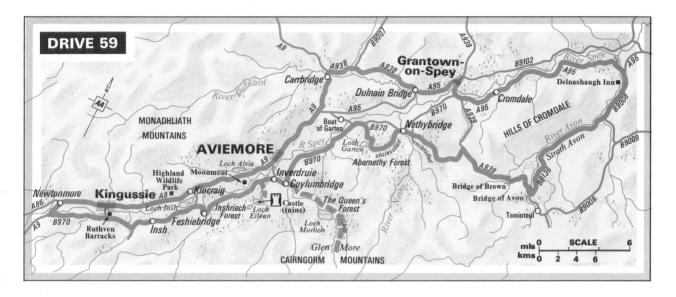

The Scottish Alps

From Aviemore

Drive 59   101 miles

Aviemore, in a picturesque setting beside the River Spey, has been greatly affected by rapid developments to promote winter sports. These activities have made the town an all-the-year-round resort.

Follow the A9 *Perth* road. After 2½m a monument to the Duke of Gordon stands out on the hillside to the left. The drive then skirts the shores of Loch Alvie; beyond the village of *Kincraig* is the Highland Wildlife Park, where many species of wild animals can be seen. *Kingussie*, the most populated township in upper Strath Spey, has a Highland folk museum. Newtonmore is a smaller resort, with the Clan Trust museum containing treasures of the Clan Macpherson. After crossing the Spey on the A9 the drive turns left on to the B970 towards *Insh*, to follow the S side of Strath Spey. In 3¾m keep forward with signposts for *Rothiemurchas*, and pass the remains of 18th-c Ruthven Barracks. These were later added to by General Wade, the famous Highland road maker. After 1¾m cross the River Tromie and turn left. The route continues through the hamlet of Insh, then in 2½m keeps forward with the Rothiemurchas road and later crosses the River Feshie at *Feshiebridge*. Beyond this hamlet the drive enters attractive Inshriach Forest. After 4½m a short diversion can be made by turning right on to an unclassified road to visit the shores of Loch an Eilein, where the ruined island-castle was once a stronghold of the notorious Wolf of Badenoch.

The B970 continues to Inverdruie, where the drive turns right on to the A951 for *Coylumbridge*, a small village on the River Druiel. The unclassified road ahead leads into the Cairngorm Mountains, passing through the Queen's Forest to the shores of Loch Morlich. This new ski road climbs to nearly 2,250ft. The ski-tows and chair lifts are open throughout the year and the views from the car park are extensive. This whole area is now part of the Glen More

forest park, and reindeer have inhabited the mountain slopes since their introduction in 1952. The Cairngorms themselves form a vast national nature reserve covering some 60,000 acres. This diversion would add some 15m to the tour.

From Coylumbridge the main drive turns left to rejoin the B970 with *Nethy Bridge* signposts, and continues along Strath Spey. In 6¾m turn right on to an unclassified road towards Loch Garten, and enter the *Abernethy* Forest. The route passes Loch Garten, where the famous osprey nest is now closely screened since the return of the birds to the area. Pass the loch and after ½m keep forward on to the Nethy Bridge road. In 2½m turn right to rejoin the B970 for Nethy Bridge, a small resort on the River Nethy. After crossing the river turn right on to an unclassified road towards *Tomintoul*, and in ½m go over the crossroads. The drive continues across bleak moorland and after 4½m turns right on to the A939 towards Tomintoul. The Hills of Cromdale rise away to the left, and the dark outline of the Cairngorms are prominent to the right. The road climbs to a height of over 1,420ft before slipping down to the *Bridge of Brown*. A further climb and fall takes the drive across the *Bridge of Avon*, where it turns left on to the B9136, signposted *Craigellachie*. Follow the prettily wooded Strath Avon, then in 8½m cross the River Livet and turn left to join the B9008, which continues alongside the river. After 4m turn left on to the A95 Grantown road and re-cross the Avon to enter Strath Spey. The road keeps to the S side of the Spey, with the Hills of Cromdale to the left. After a while pass through the hamlet of *Cromdale* before reaching *Grantown-on-Spey*. This resort is almost totally surrounded by woodlands, which together with the nearby River Spey and mountains give it an attractive position.

Leave by the Perth road, staying on the A95, and at *Dulnain Bridge* keep forward on to the

A938 towards *Carrbridge*. Follow the valley of the River Dulnain to Carrbridge. This small village is developing fast as a winter-sports centre, and is one of Scotland's leading resorts. Take the A9 Perth road for the return to Aviemore.

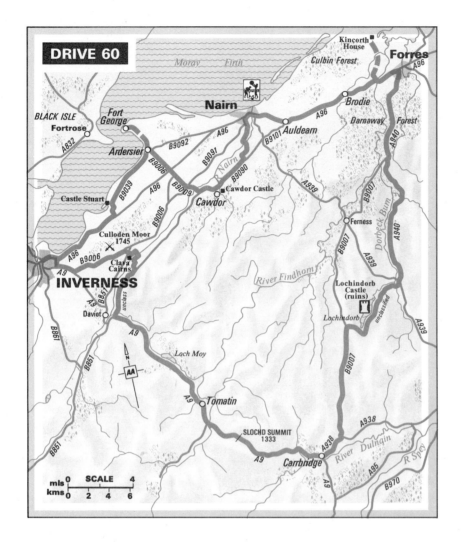

DRIVE 60

Around Culloden Moor

From Inverness

Drive 60   89 miles

From *Inverness* the drive follows the A9
Perth road to climb out of the town, and
after 2½m turns left on to the B9006
towards *Croy*. Ahead is *Culloden Moor*,
the site of the great battle in 1745 in which
Bonnie Prince Charlie was defeated by
George II's troops, led by the Duke of
Cumberland. A cairn marks the site of the
battle. Old Leanach Farmhouse survived the
battle and is now a National Trust information
centre. The Cumberland Stone from which
the Duke viewed the battle is also visible.

Pass the information centre and after ¼m
turn right on to an unclassified road
signposted Clava Cairns. Go over the next
crossroads, then cross the River Nairn and
turn right to pass the Clava Cairns, three
concentric rings of great stones dating from
neolithic or early bronze-age times. In 1m
turn right towards *Daviot*, to follow a narrow
road alongside the railway line, and after
3¼m turn left on to the unsignposted A9.
The A9 continues across moorland and
passes Loch Moy before entering the valley
of the River Findhorn to reach *Tomatin*.
After crossing the river, the road climbs
from the valley to 1,333ft Slochd Summit,
before running down to *Carrbridge*.

From here the A938 *Grantown* road is
followed for a short stretch along the
Dulnain Valley, then after 1¾m the drive
turns left on to the B9007 towards *Forres*.
The scenery here is bleak as the road crosses
treeless moors for 6¾m before turning right
on to a narrow unclassified road which runs
down to the shores of Lochindorb. The
ruined castle which stands on an island was
once a stronghold of the Wolf of
Badenoch, whose infamous conduct is
associated with the sacking of *Elgin*
Cathedral. The drive continues across
bleak Dava Moor to the junction with the
A939. Turn left here towards Forres, then
turn right on to the A940 to follow the
Dorback Valley. Later the route runs through
the picturesque Darnaway Forest before
reaching Forres. Leave Forres by the A96
Inverness road, and in 1¼m cross the River
Findhorn. Beyond the bridge a side road to
the right, signposted Kintessach, leads to
Kincorth House. This is noted for its
beautiful gardens. The A96 continues
through *Brodie* to *Auldearn*, where the
circular, 17th-c Boath Dovecot
stands on the spot where Montrose raised
the Scottish standard prior to the battle in
1645. The prosperous town of Nairn is
situated on the Moray Firth, and is well
known for its golf courses. Leave by the
B9090, following the signposts for *Cawdor*,
and in 1¾m cross the River Nairn. After 1m
turn right to reach the edge of Cawdor. The

village church has an unusual tower and a
Norman doorway. Cawdor Castle is one of
the most picturesque and finest medieval
structures in Scotland, but is not open to the
public. Traditionally it was the scene of
Duncan's murder in *Macbeth*. Continue with
the B9090 and in 1¼m turn right towards
Inverness. Re-cross the River Nairn.

After ½m go over crossroads towards
Ardersier, and in 1m keep forward with the
B9006 then cross the A96. The route of
General Wade's military road is followed
across flat countryside to the fishing village
of Ardersier, on the shores of Inverness Firth
– Inner Moray Firth. The coastal views here
stretch across the water to the *Black Isle*
and distant mountains beyond Inverness.
A detour can be made by continuing with
the B9006 to Fort George, dating from the
18thc and now housing a military museum.
From Ardersier the main drive turns left on
to the unsignposted B9039, following the
coastline of the Moray Firth. After 4¼m
Castle Stewart stands on the right. It dates
from 1625 and has been restored. This fine
example of the Scottish baronial style is,
however, not open to the public. On
reaching the A96 turn right for the return to
Inverness.

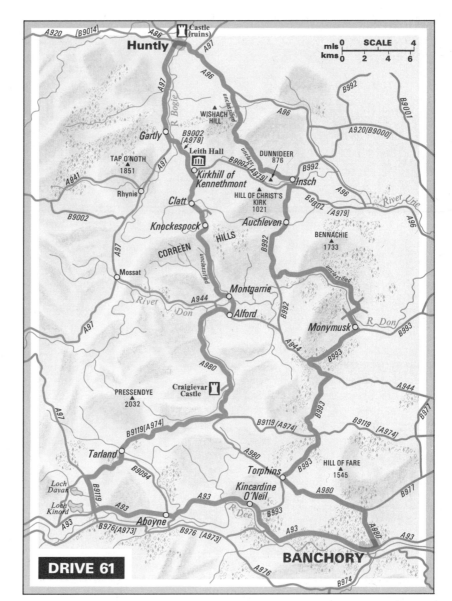

DRIVE 61

Castles and the Dee

From Banchory

Drive 61   100 miles

Banchory is a pleasant Deeside resort near the confluence of the River Dee and Water of Feugh. Leave by the A93 *Aberdeen* road and in ½m turn left on to the A980 towards *Torphins*. After 2¼m the drive turns left and skirts the 1,545ft Hill of Fare, site of a battle in 1562. At Torphins turn right on to the B993, with *Inverurie* signposts, to run through pleasantly wooded country. At the junction with the B9119 (A974) the drive turns left, then immediately right (no signpost), but still continues with the B993. In 4m turn left on to the A944 *Alford* road, and 1½m farther turn right to rejoin the B993 towards Inverurie. After 3¼m turn left on to an unclassified road for the village of *Monymusk* in the valley of the River Don. Turn right 1m beyond the village, following the signposts for *Chapel of Garioch*. Cross the River Don and in ¼m turn left. In ¼m turn left again, signposted *Keig* via Lords Throat, and continue through a very attractive, well-wooded stretch alongside the Don. This pleasant section lasts for 6m before the route turns right on to the B992, towards *Insch*. The drive then crosses open country to Auchleven. In 2¼m turn right on to the B9002 (A979), then go over the level crossing and immediately turn left on to the B992 to enter Insch — a small town and a centre for the surrounding agricultural-based community.

Pass the telephone box and turn left into unsignposted Western Road. The drive then passes the conical hill of Dunnideer — which is crowned by a vitrified fort — and a ruined 16th-c castle before climbing round the E slopes of wooded Wishach Hill. This landmark rises to 1,375ft and is part of Huntly Forest. Meet the junction with the A96 and turn left, then continue to the

market town of *Huntly* — prettily set near the confluence of the River Bogie and River Deveron. The town makes a pleasant summer resort and is noted for its good fishing facilities. Situated N of the town are the imposing ruins of a castle, formerly known as the Palace of Strathbogie and dating from 1602.

Follow the signposts for *Rhynie* to leave by the A97, and follow Strathbogie to Gartly. Later the drive turns left on to the B9002 (A979), signposted Insch. After 1½m the drive passes the entrance to *Leith* Hall, a NTS property built during the 17thc and noted for its rock garden. In ½m, before Kirkhill of Kennethmont, turn right on to an unclassified road which leads to Clatt. Keep forward here on the Knockespock road and in ½m keep right. Beyond the hamlet of Knockespock the drive climbs to splendid views as the road crosses the Corren Hills at a height of 1,281ft. This road is followed across the moors for 4m before turning left to Montgarrie. Turn right here, then cross the River Don and continue to Alford — a small market town attractively situated in the centre of the fertile Howe of Alford.

Turn right on to the A944 and in 1m keep forward to join the A980, signposted Banchory. After 5¼m the drive passes the entrance of *Craigievar Castle* on the right, perhaps the loveliest of Scottish castles. Built early in the 17thc in the baronial style, it commands a fine position between the valleys of the Dee and Don. It is noted for the splendid Renaissance hall ceiling. Continue with the A980 and in 2¼m turn right on to the B9119 (A974) towards *Tarland*. Later the road slips gently down into the small fertile area known as Cromar, of which Tarland is the centre.

Continue with the B9119 (A974) for 3m and turn left with *Dinnet* signposts to reach Deeside again. At the junction with the A93 turn left towards Aberdeen, and follow the Dee Valley to *Aboyne*, a small resort noted for its Highland gathering every September. The A93 veers inland for a short distance before rejoining the Dee near *Kincardine O'Neil*. The road often accompanies the river through picturesque woodlands on the return to Banchory.

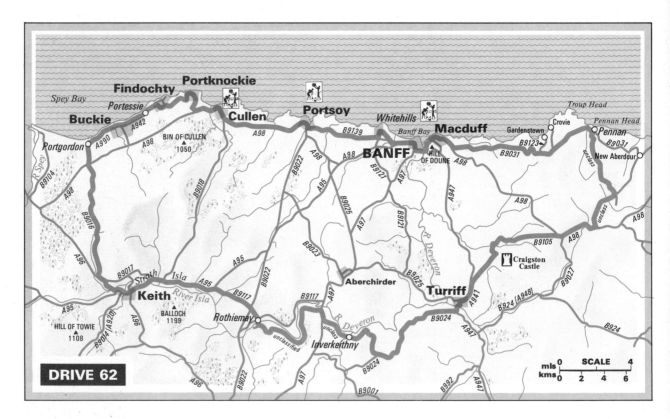

DRIVE 62

Sea and Serpentine

From Banff

Drive 62 89 miles

Banff is an ancient seaport and resort on the mouth of the River Deveron. The drive leaves by the A98 *Inverness* road, and after 1½m turns right on to the B9038 which leads to the small fishing village of *Whitehills*. Turn left here on to an unsignposted road, and in ½m meet crossroads. Turn right on to the B9139, signposted *Portsoy*. After 4m turn right on to the A98 to Portsoy itself, which is set on a rocky coastline. The economy here relies mainly on fishing and the marketing of serpentine, which is known as Portsoy marble. Continue along the A98 through agricultural country, parallel to the coast with 1,050ft Bin of Cullen prominent to the W. *Cullen* is a fishing port and resort with sandy beaches. The rocks called the Three Kings of Cullen are on the foreshore, and to the S of the town is partly 16th-c Cullen House.

Remain on the A98 Inverness road for 1¼m, then turn right on to the A942 for *Portknockie*. From here the drive follows Inverness Coast Road signposts, passing the small fishing villages of *Findochty* and *Portessie* to reach *Buckie*. Set on Spey Bay, this is the largest coastal town between *Fraserburgh* and Inverness. Beyond the harbour turn right with the A990, still following the Inverness coast road, and continue to *Portgordon*. The drive leaves the coast by turning left with the A990 and after 1¼m, at the junction with the A98, turns right and immediately left on to the B9016 *Keith* road.

An undulating, cross-country road takes the drive for 6½m to the junction with the A96, where the route turns left on to the

Aberdeen road and continues to Keith. This town is the centre for the agricultural area of Strath Isla, and one of the two bridges over the River Isla was built in 1609. Leave on the A95, with Banff signposts, and follow Strath Isla. After 5m turn right on to the B9117, following *Rothiemay* signposts. In 2½m turn right then immediately left, and after ¾m follow the B9118 to Rothiemay. For some pleasant pastoral scenery go forward on to an unclassified road and cross the River Deveron, then turn left. A narrow road runs through attractive, well-wooded country following the valley of the River Deveron.

On the main route continue for 5¾m and turn right on to the A97 *Huntly* road. In ½m turn left on to an unclassified road signposted Inverkeithny. After 1½m keep left for the run down to Inverkeithny, a hamlet at the confluence of the Burn of Forgue and the Deveron. The drive again climbs high above the river before leaving the valley and crossing open country to the junction with the B9024. Turn left here on to the *Turriff* road, and in 6m left again on to the B947 towards Banff. Continue to the market town of Turriff. Stay on the Banff road, and in 2m turn right on to the B9103 towards *Fraserburgh*. After 2½m Craigston Castle, which dates from the 17thc and is open by appointment only, lies to the right. The drive continues through the Buchan countryside and in 3½m turns right on to the A98. In another 2½m turn left on to an unclassified road with *New Aberdour* signposts. After 2¼m turn left again, towards Pennan. The road affords bleak moorland scenery before

winding down to reach the coast at the junction with the B9031. Go over the crossroads for the steep run down into *Pennan*, an attractive fishing village nestling amongst high and precipitous cliffs.

Return to the B9031 and turn right towards Banff. As the road dips and climbs it offers occasional coastal views. Diversions off the main road lead to the attractive fishing villages of *Crovie* and *Gardenstowns*. After 8¾m turn right on to the A98 towards Inverness, to reach the herring fishing port of *Macduff*. Overlooking the town is the Hill of Doune, a good viewpoint which retains the name given to Macduff until 1783. The A98 leads across the River Deveron for the return to Banff.

Gazetteer

Key to Town Plans and Gazetteer

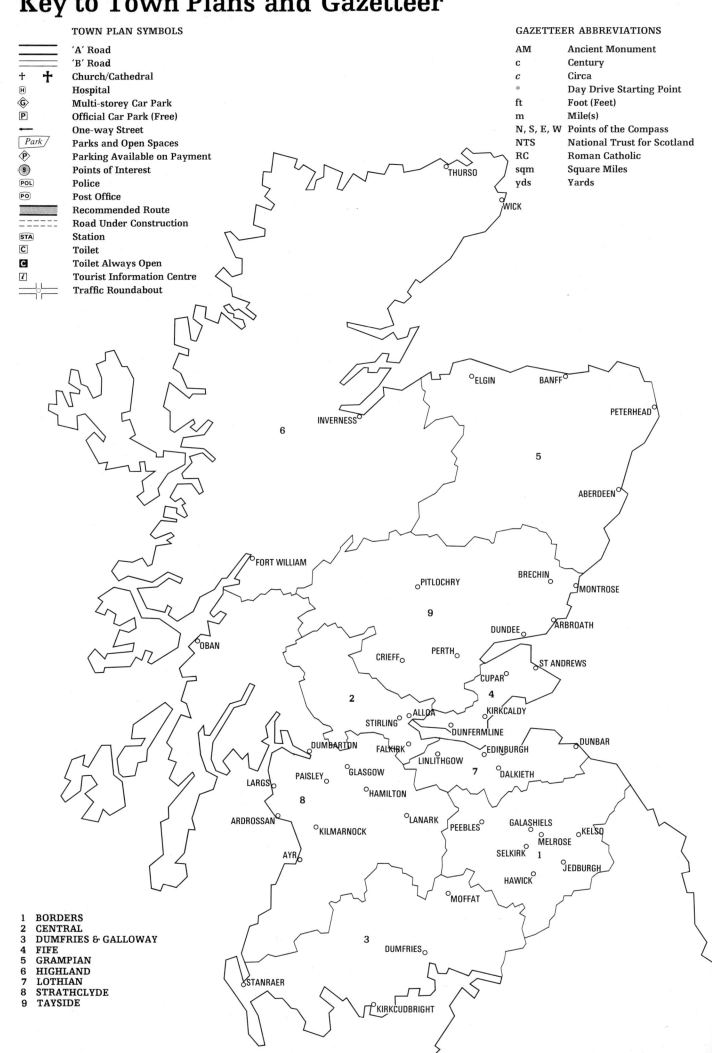

TOWN PLAN SYMBOLS

═══	'A' Road
───	'B' Road
† ✝	Church/Cathedral
Ⓗ	Hospital
Ⓖ	Multi-storey Car Park
Ⓟ	Official Car Park (Free)
←	One-way Street
Park	Parks and Open Spaces
Ⓟ	Parking Available on Payment
⑨	Points of Interest
POL	Police
PO	Post Office
▓▓	Recommended Route
- - -	Road Under Construction
STA	Station
Ⓒ	Toilet
🅒	Toilet Always Open
ⓘ	Tourist Information Centre
┼	Traffic Roundabout

GAZETTEER ABBREVIATIONS

AM	Ancient Monument
c	Century
c	Circa
*	Day Drive Starting Point
ft	Foot (Feet)
m	Mile(s)
N, S, E, W	Points of the Compass
NTS	National Trust for Scotland
RC	Roman Catholic
sqm	Square Miles
yds	Yards

1 BORDERS
2 CENTRAL
3 DUMFRIES & GALLOWAY
4 FIFE
5 GRAMPIAN
6 HIGHLAND
7 LOTHIAN
8 STRATHCLYDE
9 TAYSIDE

ABBEY ST BATHANS, Borders   *31 NT76*

This village is situated on the Whiteadder Water amongst the Lammermuir Hills. The parish church contains the tomb of a prioress and portrays her pet dog; the tomb was taken from the former 12th-c abbey church. Near by lies the Holy Well of St Bathans, within the grounds of the manor house. To the S, on the slopes of Cockburn Law, stands Edins Hall (AM) – an ancient tower or broch which is a rare example of its type outside the N Highlands. The long ridge of Monynut Edge rises NW of the village.

ABBOTSFORD HOUSE, Borders   *26 NT53*

Originally known as Cartleyhole, Abbotsford House was Sir Walter Scott's last and most famous home, which he himself designed and where he died in 1832. The house was built between 1817 and 1824 and contains a collection of Scottish relics, some interesting portraits, and a bust of Scott by Chantrey. Scott's study has been preserved as he left it; his library contains some 20,000 rare books. There is also a comprehensive collection of historic weapons. The Border country around Abbotsford was a major inspiration for Scott's historical novels, and he particularly loved the view from Bemersyde Hill across the Tweed towards the Eildon Hills, to the SE of Abbotsford.

ABERCHIRDER, Grampian   *35 NJ65*

A small Royal Burgh, Aberchirder was founded in 1764. Kinnairdy Castle, a Crichton stronghold, lies 2m SW where the River Deveron is joined by Auchintoul Burn.

ABERCORN, Lothian   *46 NT07*

Abercorn is a tiny hamlet on the shores of the Forth, notable for Hopetoun House – seat of the Hope family, Earls of Hopetoun and later Marquesses of Linlithgow. It is considered one of Scotland's most splendid mansions. The central section was built by Sir William Bruce of Kinross between 1696 and 1703, and the wings were added by the famous architectural family of William Adam and his sons during the next 50 years. Works by Rubens, Rembrandt, and Titian hang in the Yellow Drawing Room, and the elegant furniture in the State Room was made by Thomas Chippendale, the famous 18th-c cabinet-maker. The mansion lies amid parkland with formal gardens in the style of Versailles surrounding the house.

Bishop Trumuini established an Anglican bishopric in Abercorn in the 7thc and the present church, restored in 1597 and 1838, has some Celtic cross-shafts, a pre-Reformation pulpit and the curious Binns Aisle. The retiring rooms and elaborate laird's pew were designed by Sir William Bruce, the builder of Hopetoun House. Ancient carved stones have been preserved in the churchyard. The Royal Scots Greys were raised near Abercorn in 1681 by General Tam Dalyell, who defeated the Covenanters at Rullion Green in 1666.

On the opposite shores of the Forth is the naval base of Rosyth. Midhope Tower, dating from the 16thc stands ½m SW; 3m WSW lies the 15th-c mansion of The Binns (NTS), begun in 1478 and added to later. Its 17th-c plaster ceilings survive.

*ABERDEEN, Grampian   *35 NJ90*
Plan overleaf

The Royal Burgh of Aberdeen is the third largest city in Scotland and an important university and cathedral centre. It is also the largest fishing port in Scotland. Apart from the university it houses a number of research institutes, and being one of the biggest seaside resorts in Scotland is also a major touring centre. It lies on the estuaries of the Rivers Dee and Don, and is built almost entirely of local granite. Year after year it is judged the most floral city in Britain, its parks and gardens being outstanding. Its major industries include fishing, engineering, shipbuilding, paper making, granite, and chemicals. It is also a major market centre, the leading commercial centre in N Scotland, and now of outstanding importance as the North Sea oil capital.

The city charters were granted in *c*1179, but the castle has long since disappeared. Edward I was in Aberdeen in 1296 and Robert the Bruce campaigned here against the Comyns, rival contenders for the Scottish throne. Bruce was also a refugee here after the Battle of Methven in 1306. Edward III burned Aberdeen in 1337; the city was rebuilt and divided into Old Aberdeen – containing the cathedral precincts – and Aberdeen. It was made a Burgh of Barony in 1498. Montrose occupied it three times in the 17thc, and in 1891 Aberdeen and Old Aberdeen were united.

The broad central thoroughfare, Union Street, is a fine example of the use of local granite. Just off it lies the church of St Nicholas, which is divided by a 12th- and 13th-c transept into the East and West Churches. The East Church was rebuilt in the 19thc, but the West Church dates from 1763. It is the work of James Gibbs and represents the finest piece of Scottish ecclesiastical architecture of the time. Drum's Aisle, a part of the transept, contains a fine medieval brass. Original woodwork has been preserved in the 15th-c crypt below the apse. Other treasures include a stone effigy of Sir Alexander Irvine, Captain Governor of Aberdeen from 1439 to 1442, and his wife. A 48-bell carillon is rung daily in summer.

In Huntly Street, W of Union Bridge, is St Mary's RC cathedral. A statue of the 5th Duke of Gordon, Sir Walter Scott's *Cock o' the North*, stands in Golden Square. The 16th-c Provost Ross's House (NTS) in Shiprow is one of the city's oldest buildings and has been restored. It was probably built by the master-mason Andrew Jamesone in 1593, and is a fine example of early Scottish domestic architecture with dormer windows, a projecting tower, and arcading.

Aberdeen Art Gallery and Museum in Schoolhill has some good English and French paintings, Epstein bronzes, and a Henry Moore sculpture. Near by stand Robert Gordon's Colleges, founded in 1739. The house of Sir George Skene, Provost of Aberdeen from 1676 to 1685, stands in Guestrow. Its remarkable painted ceilings have been preserved, and it now contains a museum of local history and rural life. The Duke of Cumberland stayed here in 1746 before marching to Culloden, where he defeated Bonnie Prince Charlie. The municipal buildings in Castle Street incorporate the tower and spire of the 14th-c Tolbooth, which was the scene of public executions until 1857. The Tolbooth still preserves the 'Aberdeen Maiden', said to have been the model for the French guillotine. Also in Castle Street stands the old Mercat cross, built for the sum of £100 from the guild wine funds. It dates from 1686 but has been moved from its original site.

The modern St Andrew's Episcopal Cathedral stands in King Street. Farther W in front of Aberdeen Grammar School is a statue of Lord Byron, a pupil there from 1794 to 1798. Aberdeen University combines two medieval colleges – Marischal (1593) in Broad Street and King's (1494) in High Street. Old Aberdeen. Marischal College, founded in 1593 by George Keith the Earl Marischal, was rebuilt in 1844. With its soaring perpendicular façade it is considered one of the finest granite buildings in the world. The college was originally housed in the buildings of the former Greyfriars monastery.

The Music Hall is a complex which comprises two contiguous buildings. The frontage, six massive Ionic columns supporting a classical pediment, was designed by Archibald Simpson and built in 1820. A 19th-c Town House contains a fine collection of portraits, and the fine Union Bridge is one of the widest single-span granite arches in Britain. Wonderful views over Aberdeen can be enjoyed from the top of the 233ft Mitchell

Abbotsford House, Sir Walter Scott's last and best-loved home.

tower of the college. The museum of Marischal College houses a collection of Egyptian weapons, head-dresses, Chinese bronzes and jades, together with local exhibits. King's College still has its 16th-c chapel, and its fine crown tower was rebuilt after a storm in 1633. The chapel contains some beautiful woodwork, particularly the screen with its wide rood-loft and the carved, canopied stalls. The Senator's Room and the library with its fine old manuscripts, are also of interest. Also in Old Aberdeen is the Cathedral of St Machar (AM), founded in 1136. This is a partly castellated 15th-c granite building with two 14th-c sandstone pillars. The old choir has gone.

Of particular note is the painted wooden nave ceiling, dated 1540. The cathedral houses some fine monuments to Bishops

Scougal and Dunbar, the Nun's Library, modern stained glass, and a beautiful series of early 16th-c heraldic wooden nave bosses.

Beyond the cathedral in a lovely wooded setting stands the picturesque Auld Brig o' Don, or Bridge of Balgownie. Its single span dates from the early 14thc. Near by in Seaton Park stands a Norman motte and a 17th-c fortified tower house. Fishing plays a major part in Aberdeen's prosperity; the public can watch fish being auctioned at the lively fish market at 07.00 hrs. Some 2m SSW of central Aberdeen lies the seven-arched Brig o' Dee, which formerly carried the main road to Deeside. It was built by Bishop Gavin Dunbar in c1520 and is carved with coats of arms. Near by stands the Ruthriston packhorse bridge of 1693 and

1694, with similar decoration. In Queen's Road, 2m W of the city centre, is the Gordon Highlanders' Regimental Museum.

ABERDOUR, Fife *47 NT18*

A little resort on the Firth of Forth, Aberdour has a sandy beach and is popular with yachtsmen. St Fillons Church is Norman and 16thc with later restoration, and has a leper window blocked by the Pilgrim's Stone. Ruined Aberdour Castle (AM), overlooking the harbour, was built between the 14thc and 17thc. Later additions were the work of the 8th Earl of Morton. Remarkable wall paintings have survived, and a lovely circular dovecot stands near by. To the SW at Dalgety lies the ruined 12th-c church of St Bridget (AM), the resting place of the

1	Art Gallery and Museum
2	Bridge of Dee
3	East and West Churches of St Nicholas
4	Fish Market
5	Gordon's College
6	Gordon Highlanders' Regimental Museum
7	Grammar School and Byron Statue
8	King's College
9	Marischal College
10	Mercat Cross
11	Municipal Buildings and Tolbooth
12	Music Hall
13	Provost Ross's House
14	Provost Skene's House
15	St Andrew's Episcopal Cathedral
16	St Machar's Cathedral
17	St Mary's Cathedral (RC)
18	Seaton Park
19	Town House
20	Union Bridge

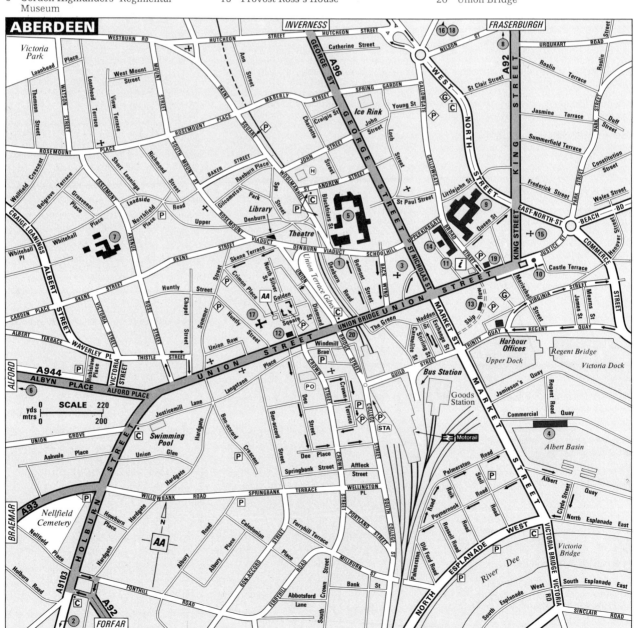

early Bishops of Dunkeld. In Dalgety Bay to the W stands Donibristle House. The surviving buildings date from c1720, and the fine wrought-iron entrance gates are still in good condition. An old ballad commemorates the murder of the Earl of Moray by the Earl of Huntly near Donibristle in 1592. Braefoot Point overlooks Inchcolm Island and is situated E of Dalgety Bay.

ABERFELDY, Tayside 30 NN84
This market town and touring centre lies on the River Tay, which is spanned by a five-arched stone bridge built by General George Wade to carry a military road in 1733. The cost of this bridge is recorded as £4,095 5s 10d. A monument erected N of the bridge in 1887 marks the enrolment of the Black Watch, a Highland Regiment, into the British Army in 1740. The regiment, which had been raised in the area fifteen years earlier, received its name because of its tartan uniform. Burns' poem *The Birks of Aberfeldy* probably refers to Abergeldie and not Aberfeldy.

Some distance N beyond Lochs Glassie and Derculich rises the fine viewpoint of 2,559ft Farragon Hill. Along the footpath from Bank Street are the three falls of Moness (1m S), on the Moness Burn. The Amulree road runs S through Glen Cochill and climbs high over lonely moorland, with the 2,258ft peak of Meall Dearg to the S.

ABERFOYLE, Central 30 NN50
Situated to the E of Loch Ard, this village is known as the Gateway to the Trossachs. It has grown rapidly since the Duke's Road was built by the Duke of Montrose in the 19thc, to give easier access N towards the Trossachs. This road affords fine views of Loch Drunkie and Loch Vennachar, backed by 2,875ft Ben Ledi. The former clachan of Aberfoyle, associated with Scott's *Rob Roy* lies 1m E. A plough coulter hanging from a tree opposite recalls a scene from the book. Two mortsafes in the churchyard record the horrible exploits of the early 19th-c bodysnatchers, Burke and Hare, who were eventually brought to justice at Edinburgh.

Loch Ard Forest extends E and W of Aberfoyle, and forms part of the Forestry Commission's Queen Elizabeth forest park. The grassy Menteith Hills and Lake of Menteith lie E of the village. A road W of Aberfoyle runs through the Pass of Aberfoyle to beautiful Loch Ard. Near the W end of the loch are the two waterfalls on the Ledard Burn described in Scott's *Waverley*. Near by stands 16th-c Duchray Castle.

ABERLADY, Lothian 47 NT47
This Firth-of-Forth village has a sandy beach and safe bathing. Its church has a 15th-c tower and an old mounting stone, or loupin-on-stane, outside. Late 16th-c Liffness House has modern additions and ornate chimneys, plus a lovely 16th-c circular dovecot. Also in the village is a monument to Lady Elibank, made by Canova in 1763. Aberlady Bay is reached by a footbridge from the car park, and is a nature reserve. Myreton Motor Museum is the largest of its kind in Scotland.

ABERLEMNO, Tayside 31 NO55
In the churchyard stands a splendid upright cross-slab with Pictish symbols (AM), probably of 8th-c origin, and at

Flemington Farm are three Celtic stones (AM) with reliefs of fights. To the E lies the wooded expanse of Montreathmont Moor. A vitrified fort tops the Hill of Finhaven, a good viewpoint W of the village.

ABERLOUR, Grampian 35 NJ24
The full name of this Spey-Valley village is Charlestown of Aberlour, named after its 19th-c founder Charles Grant. There are 19th-c distilleries near by, and fine views can be had from the high ground around the village. Ben Rinnes rises to 2,755ft 6m SSW, and to the N the Linn of Ruthie cascade flows from the mountains in Aberlour Burn.

ABERNETHY, Tayside 30 NO11
Once a Pictish capital, Abernethy is well-known for its Irish-type round church tower (AM). This 74ft-high tower is probably of early 12th-c origin and one of only two on the Scottish mainland. Tradition has it that Malcolm Canmore did homage to William the Conqueror here. To the N the River Earn flows into the Firth of Tay, and the Ochil Hills rise to the S. About 4m S lies 15th- and 16th-c Balvaird Castle. At the Roman port of Carpow, 1m NE, Roman baths have been excavated; a double-passageway gate was discovered in 1969.

ABERUTHVEN, Tayside 30 NN91
To the N of the Ochil Hills in Strath Earn lies Aberuthven. A mausoleum to the Dukes of Montrose stands beside the ruined church of St Kattan. About 4m NNE, beyond Dalreoch Bridge and across the River Earn, is 19th-c Gask House. This mansion has a collection of Prince Charles Edward relics, and in its grounds is a fragment of the 17th-c house where the prince spent several hours on his way to Edinburgh in 1745. To the N of Gask House is a 5m stretch of Roman road which has been excavated many times, notably by Pennant in 1770. Further excavations were conducted in 1890.

ABINGTON, Strathclyde 25 NS92
Prince Louis Napoleon stayed at a former coaching inn in this Clydesdale village before going on to the tournament at Eglinton Castle, near Kilwinning, in 1839. A memorial to Matthew McKendrick, a local 19th-c postmaster and fisherman, stands on the A73 overlooking the River Clyde. Gold has been found SW in the valley of Glengonnar Water.

ABOYNE, Grampian 35 NO59
Bordered to the S by the Forest of Birse and backed by the 2,435ft Hill of Cat, Aboyne is a popular Deeside resort where the Highland Gathering is held during September. Aboyne Castle, a Gordon stronghold with a history dating back to the 13thc, lies to the N. This was rebuilt in the 17thc as a tower house, and part of the W wing survives from this date. A mansion house was built on the site in 1801, then this was also transformed in the 1880's by Sir Cunliffe Brookes. The grounds feature the Formaston Stone, which dates from between AD800 and 1000 and bears a mirror symbol. Other markings include part of an elaborately decorated Celtic cross and an inscription in the ancient Ogham script. The house and grounds are not open to the public.

A track known as Fungle Road runs S from the village and penetrates deep into the Forest of Birse. To the SW of the village the long wooded valley of Glen Tanner stretches into the hills of Glen

Tanner Forest and continues up to 3,077ft Mount Keen.

A track known as the Fir Mounth Road leads from the church in the glen and crosses the hills E of the Hill of Cat to reach Glen Esk, near Tarpside. The Mounth Road diverges higher up Glen Tanner and, after crossing a shoulder of Mount Keen reaches Glen Mark near Lochlee.

ABRIACHAN, Highland 34 NH53
Abriachan lies on the W side of Loch Ness, and is reached via a steep and winding road. A narrow road runs NW into the hills, passing tiny Loch Laide, and finally descends into Glen Convinth and Beauly.

ACHARACLE, Highland 32 NM66
Situated on the W tip of Loch Shiel, this little anglers' resort is the departure point for summer cruises along the loch. Prince Charles Edward roamed the hills and surrounding countryside in these parts. Offshore lies the picturesque 14th-c Castle Tioram of the MacDonalds of Clanranald, which was burnt in 1715. The castle can be reached from the mainland except at high spring tides. A road runs N from Acharacle alongside the Shiel River, past Shiel Bridge, to its outlet in Loch Moidart. Near by, in a richly-wooded setting, is Dorlin; opposite this is the large island of Eilean Shona. To the E of Acharacle rises imposing, 2,774ft Ben Resipol, with wonderful views from the summit. A by-road from Acharacle leads W across Kentra Moss to Ardtoe, where fish farming has recently been established. Fine views of the islands of Eigg and Rum are afforded from this part of Ardnamurchan.

ACHFARY, Highland 36 NC23
This village lies between Loch Stack and Loch More, two of a chain of lochs which accompany the road from Lairg to Loch Laxford, on the wild coast of old Sutherland. Near by the strange shape of Ben Stack rises to 2,364ft; N are the lonely hills of the great Reay Forest.

ACHILTIBUIE, Highland 36 NC00
A beautiful and remote Wester Ross hamlet, Achiltibuie lies on the sandy shores of Baden Bay. Offshore lie the lovely Summer Islands; the largest of these is Tanera More, and Horse Island lies to the SE. These islands once supported a community of inshore fishermen, but the herring shoals diminished and the last islanders left in 1946. The Rhu More peninsula extends N to Rhu Coigach, overlooking Enard Bay and the Minch. Ben More Coigach rises to 2,438ft SE of Achiltibuie, and affords splendid views of the Coigach district – particularly along Loch Broom. The lonely peaks of 2,009ft Stack Polly, 2,399ft Suilven, and 2,779ft Carisp dominate the country to the NE.

ACHILTY INN, Highland 33 NH45
This old coaching inn is set in the woods along the Blackwater River. To the W is the little Loch Achilty, beyond which are the Conon Falls. Access to the latter is by paths leading to the SE tip of Loch Luichart.

ACHMORE, Highland 33 NG83
Achmore lies along the picturesque road from Strome to the shores of Loch Alsh.
cont

The fine viewpoint of Auchtertyre Hill is near by.

ACHNACARRY, Highland   *33 NN18*

The Dark Mile of trees, near which Bonnie Prince Charlie hid in 1746, lies to the N of Achnacarry Estate. Commandos were trained at Achnacarry House, which has been the seat of the Camerons since the mid 17thc, during the last war. The house was reconstructed in 1952.

ACHNASHEEN, Highland   *35 NH15*

Dominated to the N by the 3,060ft peak of Fionn Bhein, Achnasheen lies between Strath Bran and Glen Carron. Beyond Fionn Bhein lies lonely Loch Fannick, with the Fannick peaks in the background. The area is now used in the production of hydro electricity. Sgurr Vuillin rises to 2,845ft in the SE, and overlooks lonely Glen Conon and Loch Beannachan. Running S from the village, the road to Kyle of Lochalsh crosses the Drum Alban watershed W of Loch Gowan, to the SE of which 3,033ft Moruisg can be seen rising from Glencarron Forest. Magnificent distant views of Loch Maree can be enjoyed from

the head of Glen Docherty, which is reached by a climb from Loch a'Chroisg or Rosque, on the road W of Achnasheen to Loch Maree.

ACHNASHELLACH, Highland   *33 NH04*

The 2,968ft peaks of Fuar Tholl and 3,142ft Sgurr Ruadh dominate the NW side of this village, rising from Glen Carron and Achnashellach Forest by Loch Doule. Moruisg tops 3,033ft and stands E in the Glencarron Forest. A beautiful private road runs NE over Coulin Pass, by Lochs Coulin and Clair, to Glen Torridon and Kinlochewe. The public road runs through Achnasheen.

AE, Dumfries and Galloway   *25 NY08*

The Forestry Commission founded this village in 1947, and there are walks with viewpoints through the surrounding forests. Ae Bridge spans the Water of Ae 2½m SE; the river flows E to join the Annan near Lochmaben. The Ae rises on 2,285ft Queensberry Hill to the N, near the Lanark border.

AIRD CASTLE, Strathclyde   *24 NR83*

This ruined castle lies off the B879, 17m

N of Campbeltown. Its dungeons can still be seen, and an old ruined fort lies near by.

AIRTH, Central   *46 NS88*

Situated at the S end of the Kincardine roadbridge over the Forth, Airth has an interesting history. A Royal Dockyard existed here in the 15thc, and an old Mercat cross dated 1697 stands near by. It has two sundials and displays the Elphinstone arms and motto 'Doe well let them say'. Airth Castle, now a hotel, is of 14th-c origin and although modernized incorporates Wallace's tower. Dunmore Tower and Park lies to the N and was built in 1820. Its grounds contain the curious Pineapple garden-conceit.

ALEXANDRIA, Strathclyde   *44 NS38*

Lying on the River Leven, which flows from the S end of Loch Lomond into the Clyde, Alexandria is triplet to the neighbouring manufacturing towns of Renton and Bonhill. Scottish Argyll cars were once made here (see inset below), and Tobias Smollett the novelist was born at the old house of Dalquharn in 1721. He has a memorial in Renton.

BIRTH OF THE ARGYLL

In the pioneering days of the motor industry, one of the best Scottish cars was the Argyll. Although the company which built them has been extinct for almost 50 years, their memory is kept alive by a spectacular factory still standing by the side of the main road in Alexandria.

Argylls were originally built in Glasgow, the first of them being designed in 1899 by Alex Govan. Demand increased, and within six years the Glasgow factory, with a production limit of 25 cars per week, had no chance of keeping up. A new £500,000 company was formed, and £220,000 of this was promptly spent in building the Alexandria factory, which opened in 1906 and was in many ways undeniably extravagant.

Preserved facade of the imposing Argyll offices.

Facing the main road was the imposing office block, designed like some vast town hall. Sandstone was brought from Dumfries, granite from Aberdeen, even marble from Italy. The best possible machinery was installed, and the machine shop, chassis shop, assembly shop, coachbuilding shop, painting, varnishing, and upholstery departments were among the most advanced of their time.

The Argyll company were enlightened employers. Hygiene was one of their great concerns, and 500 wash basins with hot and cold running water were installed. Workers had clothes lockers, there were restaurants, sports clubs (the factory once produced 35 separate teams for a five-a-side football competition), a male voice choir, and an orchestra under the general direction of Signor Veneri, the convenor of entertainments.

Alex Govan had designed the factory to produce 2,500 cars per year. It never had a chance to build up to that figure, but in 1906 and 1907 – the company's heyday – Argyll managed to complete 800 vehicles per year, a rate beaten at that time only by Ford in Detroit. Tragically

Govan died of food poisoning in 1907, and Argyll did not survive the loss for long. In the following year the company went into liquidation.

Production never stopped, however, and in 1909 the company was re-formed. The Alexandria works flourished again, and the Argyll won acclaim as the first car in the world to go into production with four-wheel brakes. Development costs, a protracted lawsuit about sleeve-valve engine patents, and the management's wasteful introduction of more and more new models overstretched the finances once again. In 1914 the second company was liquidated, and the Alexandria works and machinery put on the market.

After the war a third company produced Argyll cars back in the original Glasgow factory; but it too went out of business in the depression. The Alexandria works survived. In 1936, to reduce local unemployment, they became a Royal Navy torpedo factory. This closed down in the 1960's. An electronics firm took over, but soon moved away again. Now the factory is used by several smaller firms, but it is still largely intact and the grand office block remains from the outside as it was in 1906 – one of the great might-have-beens of Scottish industry.

ALFORD, Grampian   35 NJ51

The village lies S of the River Don, where it flows through the fertile Howe of Alford. The Correen Hills rise to the NW, with Bennachie to the NE. In 1645 the Marquis of Montrose defeated General Baillie here during the civil war, and battle relics have been unearthed from time to time. The battle was fought near the church 2m W of the village, and near by stands ruined Asloun Castle. The Bridge of Alford, NE of the church, is where the Huntly Road crosses the Don. Balfluig Castle dates from 1556 and lies 1m SE of Alford.

ALLOA, Central   46 NS89

Alloa lies just N of the River Forth and is backed by the long spread of the Ochil Hills. Double tides are a feature of the Forth here. Alloa is noted for the spinning of worsted yarns, its breweries, and its glassworks. Alloa Tower has associations with Mary Queen of Scots. A house dating from 1695 still stands in Kirkgate, and its magnificent contemporary sundial was built by Thomas Beauchop – master-mason of Kinross House and Mid Steeple of Dumfries. The Church of St Mungo retains an old tower, and some 19th-c breweries and maltings can be seen. Also of interest is the new Lornshill Academy.

ALLOWAY, Strathclyde   24 NS31

Robert Burns, Scotland's national poet, was born here on 25 January 1759, a date celebrated by Scotsmen all over the world as Burns' Night. The thatched cottage where he was born has been preserved, and a Burns Museum adjoins the cottage. The famous Auld Brig mentioned in Burns' poem *Tam o' Shanter* still spans the Doon – a simple arched bridge, perhaps of 13th-c date, flanked by beautiful gardens. Haunted Kirk Alloway, also mentioned in the poem, stands roofless not far away. The poet's father is buried in the graveyard. Above the bridge stands the 19th-c Burns Monument, containing among other items bibles belonging to Burns and his Highland Mary. Brown Carrick Hill is a fine viewpoint to the SW.

ALNESS, Highland   34 NH66

North-Sea oil developments have greatly enlarged this Cromarty-Firth village, which lies on the Alness River where it flows into the firth after its journey down Strath Rusdale. A curious monument said to be a copy of the Indian gate of Negapatam can be found on Fyrish Hill to the W. It was set up by Sir Hector Munro of Novar in the 18thc, who helped to capture an Indian town of the same name.

ALTGUISH INN, Highland   36 NH37

This lonely old coaching inn lies on the moorland road between Garve and Ullapool. Glascarnoch River, alongside the road, flows SE into Loch Garve after being joined by other streams. On the A835 near by lies Loch Glascarnoch, a reservoir belonging to the Fannich hydro-electric scheme. To the E rises 3,426ft Ben Wyvis and W are the lovely Fannicks, the highest of which is 3,637ft Sgurr Mor. Loch Droma is situated 5m WNW in a desolate spot known as Dirrie More.

ALTNACEALGACH, Highland   36 NC21

Altnacealgach is said to have been claimed by Ross and Cromarty men who walked the ground with Ross soil on their boots. On the shores of Loch Borralan stands a lonely inn. The mountain scenery is magnificent, with 2,399ft Breabag rising in the N. A line of hills stretches from Breabag to 3,273ft Ben More Assynt, and stone-age remains have been found in Breabag's caves. To the W rise 2,523ft Cul Beag, 2,786ft Cul Mor, and the sharp cone of 2,399ft Suilver in the distance. Near tiny Loch Awe, on the road to Inchnadamph, are several bronze-age burial cairns. Cam Loch and Loch Veyatie lie 4m NW in the heart of the weird and isolated mountains of old Sutherland.

ALTNAHARRA, Highland   37 NC53

Situated in Strath Naver on the W tip of Loch Naver, this angling resort is dominated to the S by the schist peak of 3,154ft Ben Klibreck. On the far side of

this peak lies lonely Loch Choire. Several prehistoric remains exist around Loch Naver. Near Klibreck Farm at the SW end of the loch are hut circles and a Celtic cross, and further along the lochside is the Pictish broch known as Dun Creagach. On the road through Strath Naver on the opposite side of the loch is another broch. A lovely but narrow road runs NW from Altnaharra, passing Loch na Meadie and reaching Strath More near its junction with Glen Golly.

Some 10m NW of Altnaharra stands perhaps the best known of the mainland brochs, Dun Dornadilla. Allt-na-Caillich waterfall can be found a little to the N of Dun Dornadilla, E of the Strath More road. To the N rises the splendid viewpoint of 3,040ft Ben Hope, overlooking narrow Loch Hope.

ALVA, Central   46 NS89

Records of wool-working in this area go back to 1550, and Alva is still a weaving town. Ben Cleuch rises to 2,363ft in the NE, and wonderful views can be enjoyed from here. The River Devon flows S of Alva, and Craighall waterfall drops at the head of Alva Glen. Silver was mined in Silver Glen from 1712, until the ore was exhausted. Alva Church has two communion cups made from local silver. The Ochil Hills dominate the area.

ALVES, Highland   34 NJ16

Situated in the fertile Laigh of Moray are the village of Alves and its neighbouring hamlet, Crook of Alves. To the NE stands modern York Tower on the summit of the Knock – Macbeth's traditional rendezvous with the Weird Sisters. Beyond Alves Wood to the SW stand the ruins of Asliesk Castle.

ALYTH, Tayside   30 NO24

This small linen-manufacturing town lies just N of the Blairgowrie-Kirriemuir road in Strath More. Alyth is overlooked by the Hill of Alyth, and to the E stands an old British fort on Barry Hill. Alyth's Auld Brig is of 16th-c origin. Bamff House, built chiefly during the 16thc,

1   Alloa Tower
2   17th-c House

3   Lornshill Academy

4   St Mungo's Church

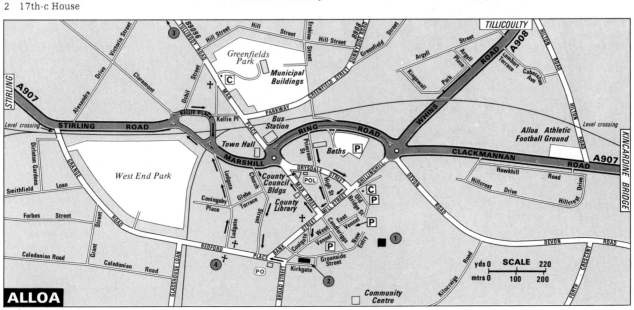

stands 4m N. Restored Airlie Castle, the ancient seat of the Ogilvies, lies 4m E of Alyth beyond the River Isla. Little remains of the Bonnie Hoose o' Airlie, which was plundered in 1640. Near by is a rare Pict's house with a crudely sculptured roof.

AMISFIELD, Dumfries and Galloway 25 NY08

Amisfield is also known as Amisfield Town, and has been associated with the Charteris family since the 12thc. The ancestral seat of the Charteris family, Amisfield Tower, stands 1m NW. One of the best preserved and most beautiful of Scottish towers, this was built largely in the second half of the 16thc. Heraldic panels bear the date 1600, and an oak door with carvings is now exhibited at the National Museum of Antiquities in Edinburgh. About 3m SW beyond the village of Kirkmahoe is Carnsalloch House. This dates from 1759 and has an old walled garden.

AMULREE, Tayside 30 NN93

A good centre for exploring Glen Quaich, Loch Freuchie, and Glens Cochill and Almond, Amulree is situated at the W corner of Strath Bran. The clans met in Amulree in 1715 and were armed for the Jacobite rebellion. The road to Aberfeldy, through Glen Cochill, runs partly along one of General Wade's old roads. The Wade road runs S from Amulree through the lovely Sma' Glen. Beyond beautiful Glen Almond Ben Chonzie rises to 3,048ft in the SW. A road running NW from the village climbs through Glen Quaich then descends a steep gradient to Kenmore on Loch Tay.

ANCRUM, Borders 26 NT62

Lying on Ale Water, which flows S to join the Teviot at Ancrum Bridge, this village is steeped in history. On the banks of the Ale are several old caves, probably used in ancient Border warfare. The remains of the cross on the village green are 13thc, and Chesters House dates from 1790. Ancrum House stands in a beautiful wooded setting. To the N of the village is Ancrum Moor, or Lilliards Edge, where one of the last major Border conflicts took place in 1545. A Roman road can be traced through Ancrum Moor. Some 2m NE of the village is the well-known Border-country landmark of Waterloo Monument, erected in 1815 on Peniel Heugh by the Marquis of Lothian and his tenants.

ANNAN, Dumfries and Galloway 26 NY16

This busy town lies on the tidal River Annan on the Solway Firth and is noted for its shrimps. Views take in Bowness in Cumbria and the Lake-District peak of Skiddaw. Robert Stevenson built the local bridge in 1826, and Thomas Carlisle attended the old grammar school – which he later described as Hinterschlag Gymnasium in his *Sartor Resartus*. The town hall contains the inscribed Brus Stone, which many think is associated with Robert the Bruce. A nuclear power station has been built on the outskirts of the town at Chapelcross. The scenery N along Annandale becomes increasingly hilly and beautiful, particularly beyond Moffat. The 16th-c Stapleton Tower stands 3m NE of Annan.

Just S of the town are the remains of the Solway Viaduct, opened in 1869 to carry iron-ore across the Solway Firth from Cumberland. Badly damaged by a storm in 1881, the viaduct was repaired but closed again in 1921 because of a decline in the demand for iron-ore.

ANSTRUTHER, Fife 31 NO50

On either side of the harbour stand the Royal Burghs of Anstruther Easter and Anstruther Wester, each boasting pretty churches with unbuttressed 16th-c towers. The village is well-known for its herring catch, and there is sand at the Hynd although the foreshore is rocky. Anstruther Easter has a 16th-c manse, and St Ayles House was used by monks from Balmerino Abbey. The house now contains an interesting fisheries museum. The ancient Dreel Inn carries a plaque recording an incident connected with James V of Scotland. Cellardyke, another Royal Burgh, is situated on the NE side of Anstruther Easter. A little inland is Kilrenny, where the church has a similar tower to those in Anstruther.

The little Island of May was one of the first Scottish lighthouse sites. Today it incorporates a major national nature reserve, with a bird-watching station and a record of over 200 species of birds.

ANTONINE WALL

Also known as Graham's or Grime's Dyke, this Roman Wall (AM) was set up between a line of nineteen forts built by Agricola in AD 78. Starting from the W, the forts were at Old Kilpatrick; Duntocher; Castlehill; New Kilpatrick; Balmuildy; Cadder; Kirkintilloch; Auchendary; Barhill; Croyhill; Westerwood; Castlecary; Seabegs; Rough Castle; Falkirk; Mumrills; Inveravan; Kinneil, and Bridgeness. The wall itself was built between AD 138 and 143, and consisted of.a turf rampart with a ditch to the N and a military road to the S. It stretched 36m from the Forth estuary, 1m E of Bo'ness, across the narrow waist of Scotland to reach the Clyde near Bowling.

The wall was built as a protection against raids from the northern tribes but was abandoned before the end of the 2ndc. Unlike Hadrian's Wall, in Northumberland, little is left of the fortifications. The best preserved fort is Rough Castle, to the W of Falkirk; good portions of the wall survive near Falkirk, in the private grounds of Callendar House, and near Bearsden.

One of the largest Roman forts in Britain lies at Ardoch, near Braco, while others are described under Lockerbie and Newstead. Traces of Roman occupation exist at Ythan Wells in Aberdeen, the farthest N Roman penetration in Britain. The earliest of the Roman roads in Scotland is Agricola's Dere Street, shown on some maps as a branch of Watling Street. This crosses the Cheviots near Carter Bar, and S of the Border to the E lies the large camp of Chew Green near the head-waters of the River Coquet. The road ran N across Kale Water, and traces can still be seen near Oxnam.

ANWORTH, Dumfries and Galloway 25 NX55

A medieval bell hangs in the 17th-c ruined church, which also shows the remarkable 8ft-high inscribed tomb of a 17th-c Gordon. Samuel Rutherford, a one-time minister here, is commemorated by an obelisk on a nearby hill.

APPIN, Strathclyde 29 NM94

Robert Louis Stevenson described the countryside around Appin in his novel *Kidnapped*. The beautiful stretch between Loch Creran and the confluence of Lochs Leven and Linnhe is generally known as Appin, though it is really part of the land of Lorne. The village was the scene of the murder of Colin Campbell, the Red Fox, in 1752. Later James Stewart (James of the Glen) was brought to trial at Inverary and hanged at Ballachulish, though many vowed that the trial was unfair. Ben Vair, with its two peaks topping 3,000ft, stretches in a semi-circle from Glen Dwon to Ballachulish and provides fine mountain walking with wonderful views.

APPLECROSS, Highland 32 NG74

Access to this quiet little W Highland village is by road through the famous Pass of the Cattle, or Bealach nam Bo. This spectacular pass zigzags from sea level to 2,054ft in 6m, and the road is one of the highest in Scotland. Gradients reach a maximum of 1 in 4, and the road climbs through the grey landscape of the Applecross Mountains. It is often blocked with snow in winter. Applecross Bay looks across the water to the Island of Raasay, with Skye beyond. A monastery was founded here in AD 673 by St Maelrulsha or Maree, one of the Irish missionaries who brought Christianity to Scotland. The saint was buried in a little church N of the village, where a carved stone marks his grave.

Passenger ferries from the Kyle of Lochalsh call at Toscaig, 4m S, at the head of the inlet of Loch Toscaig. Beyond the loch lie the three small Crowlin Islands. Although Applecross is on a dead-end road, a new road under construction at time of printing will run N along the coast to the mouth of Outer Loch Torridon and Kenmore.

ARBIRLOT, Tayside 31 NO64

Arbirlot village stands on Elliot Water, with Kelly Castle a little to the SE. This fine tower was extended by Sir William Irvine of Drum in 1614, and well restored in the 19thc. It is still inhabited.

ARBROATH, Tayside 31 NO64

A resort and fishing port, Arbroath is also a Royal Burgh and industrial town. Its name is a contraction of Aberbrothock. This is the home of the famous smokies – haddock flavoured and browned by smoke from an oak fire. The aroma of the smoking process can be savoured in the streets. The resort has sands and safe bathing, plus indoor and open-air swimming pools. The red-sandstone cliffs and caves to the NE are irresistible for explorers, particularly Dickmont's Den, Mason's, and the Forbidden Cave. Perched on top is a curious rock formation known as the Pint Stoup. Brothock Water flows through the town into the North Sea. Scott wrote about Arbroath in his novel *The Antiquary*, where he called it 'Fairport'.

Only ruins remain of Arbroath Abbey (AM) where Scotland's Declaration of Independence was signed by Robert the Bruce in 1320. The Lords of Scotland, in a letter to the Pope, asserted Scotland's independence and acknowledged Robert the Bruce as their King. A transcript of the declaration is in the town library. The abbey was built and dedicated to St Thomas à Becket in the 13thc. The south transept gable and the west front are the most complete portions left, and in the south transept is a circular window known as the O of Arbroath. This window was lit in ancient times as a beacon for mariners. King William the Lion, founder of the abbey in 1176, is buried before the high altar. This is where the Stone of Scone was discovered in 1951 after it had been removed from beneath the Coronation Chair in Westminster Abbey. The Abbot's House has a 12th-c vaulted kitchen and now serves as a Folk Museum.

The beautiful old mansion of Hospitalfield lies to the W of Arbroath. Now restored, the mansion is mentioned in Scott's *The Antiquary* as 'Monkbarn', and nowadays serves as an art college. Arbroath has several 19th-c mills and the Court House (Trades Hall) was built in 1814. The famous Bell Rock or Inchcape Rock lies some 11m out to sea to the SE, and an old Scottish ballad tells how the Bell Rock was named. Inchcape Rock lighthouse, erected between 1808 and 1811, is the outstanding achievement of Robert Stevenson, a kinsman of Robert Louis Stevenson.

ARBUTHNOTT, Grampian   35 NO87
The *Arbuthnott Missal* was written in 1491 in the church of this remote Bervie Water village. The church was collegiate and parts of the building are of 13th- and 15th-c date. Arbuthnott Aisle is heavily buttressed with a vaulted ceiling. The mansion of Arbuthnott House dates back to the 16thc and displays beautiful 17th-c plaster ceilings.

ARDCHATTAN, Strathclyde   29 NM93
The local church is reached by a by-road running NE from Connel road bridge across Loch Etive. Some 3m E of the church lie the remains of Ardchattan

Priory (AM), a 13th-c foundation with some interesting carved stones, an 11th-c cross slab, and a carved coffin cover. The priory has associations with Bruce's parliament of 1308, and the murder of the 'Red Fox' in 1752 – which Robert Louis Stevenson portrays in his novel *Kidnapped*. The road E forks, one branch continuing to the Bonawe granite quarries and the other turning N and climbing through Glen Salach to reach the shore of Loch Creran, on the road to the lovely Appin country.

ARDCLACH CHURCH, Highland 34 NH94
Near this church is Ardclach Bell Tower (AM). A detached belfry built in 1655, it stands high above the River Findhorn and used to summon worshippers to church – or warn the neighbourhood in case of alarm.

ARDELVE, Highland   33 NG82
A village in a beautiful setting at the junction of Loch Alsh and Duich, Ardelve is surrounded by the NW Highland mountains. The summer ferry crosses Loch Duich from the W side of the road bridge at Dornie, a little to the SE, to Totaig. There are fine views along the loch to the Five Sisters of Kintail. NE from Ardelve a by-road follows the shores of Loch Long and passes Killilan. The valley here is dominated by 2,466ft Ben Killilan and 2,188ft Sguman Coinntich, and leads into Glen Elchaig. Those enjoying long walks can take the path from the head of the glen and carry on E to reach Cannich, one of Scotland's loveliest wooded glens. The Falls of Glomach can be reached by a climb from the W end of the tiny Loch na Leitreach in Glen Elchaig. An old heather-thatched croft stands beside Loch Alsh, and was used in

the filming of Robert Louis Stevenson's *Master of Ballantrae*.

ARDENTINNY, Strathclyde   44 NS18
A good road from Dunoon follows the W side of Loch Long N and ends at Ardentinny. Across the loch is the village of Coulport on the Rosneath peninsula. From Ardentinny a hilly road runs NW along Glen Finart to the shores of Loch Eck, with 2,433ft Beinn Mhor to the W. This little road connects with the A815 running N to Strachur, near the shores of Loch Fyne.

ARDERSIER, Highland   34 NH75
Known also as Campbelltown, Ardersier is situated on the Inner Moray Firth and until recently was a fishing village. It is now a major centre for the construction of production platforms and other offshore ironmongery for the North-Sea oil industry.

ARDGAY, Highland   37 NH59
Ardgay lies on the Inner Dornoch Firth, with Strath Carron and its river to the W. The White Stone of Kincardine, marking the annual winter market, stands in the market square but was originally built into an inn wall for safety. Roads run along both banks of the River Carron as far as the edge of Amat Forest. Lonely hills rise farther to the W, with the vast Diebidale and Freevater Forests beyond.

*ARDGOUR, Highland   33 NN06
The name Ardgour is generally applied to the whole district between Loch Linnhe and Loch Shiel, but the village lies where the Corran Narrows almost divide Loch Linnhe into two. A car ferry crosses the Narrows for Fort William and the S. Corran Lighthouse guards the Narrows with 2,397ft Sgurr na h'Eanchainne, soaring beyond. Garbh Bheinn rises to

1   Arbroath Abbey and Abbot's House
2   Court House (Trades Hall)

3   Hospitalfield

4   Town Library

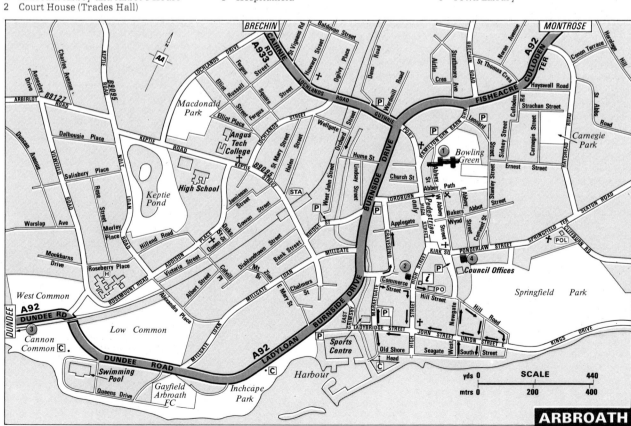

ARBROATH

2,903ft in the W, and is a mecca for rock climbers. About 3m SW of the village, on Loch Linnhe, is the entrance to Glen Gour (no road). Sgurr Dhomhail stands at 2,915ft at the head of the glen, and is Ardgour's highest peak. Some 4m NW of Ardgour, also on Loch Linnhe, is Inverscaddle Bay. Glen Scaddle and Cona Glen (no roads) converge at this point. Wonderful views across Loch Linnhe into Lochaber and away towards Ben Nevis can be enjoyed from here.

ARDLUI, Strathclyde   29 NN31
A beautiful mountain village at the N tip of Loch Lomond, Ardlui is dominated by 3,092ft Ben Vorlich to the SW. Near by is a curious pulpit which was hewn out from the rock-face many years ago. The road through Ardlui continues N through the lovely Glen Fallock towards Crianlarich, with the peaks of 3,374ft Beinn Oss, to the W and 3,428ft Cruach Ardran to the E.

ARDMAIR BAY, Highland   36 NH19
The pebbly foreshore of this bay looks out over Loch Kanaird – a branch of Loch Broom – towards the Coigach Mountains.

ARDNADAM, Strathclyde   44 NS18
Ardnadam lies on the S shore of Holy Loch and is a favourite spot with yachtsmen.

ARDNAMURCHAN POINT, Highland 32 NM46
This name is Gaelic for 'point of the great ocean', and the point is the farthest W part of the British mainland – 23m farther W than Land's End. It is served by the lonely Ardnamurchan Point lighthouse, built by Alan Stevenson in 1848. A rough road from the B8007 leads almost to the point, where the islands of Muck, Eigg and Rum can be seen to the N with Coll and Tiree stretching out to the W and Mull to the S. Sanna Bay, NE of the point, has pure white sand and is overlooked by Sanna Point. The whole peninsula is bordered to the N and S by the sea lochs of Sunart and Moidart, and

is known as Ardnamurchan. The B8007 runs along the S side of the peninsula, affording attractive views of the coast and inland areas.

ARDRISHAIG, Strathclyde   28 NR88
Ardrishaig village lies on Loch Gilip, a shingle inlet of Loch Fyne. Crinan Canal runs 9m from Crinan to Ardrishaig, linking the Sound of Jura with Loch Fyne. The road S from the village forks within 2½m, with the W branch leading through the Knapdale Hills towards Loch Killisport. The main road continues S along the shores of Loch Fyne to Tarbert.

ARDROSSAN, Strathclyde   29 NS24
This holiday resort offers sands and bathing, and is also the point of departure for car ferries to the Isle of Arran. Its harbour was built in 1806 and scattered remains still exist of a 12th-c castle of the Montgomerys. On the old Customs House are the Royal Arms, and the town has a modern RC Church – St Peter-in-Chains – of striking Swedish design. Ardrossan stands between the North and South Bay. Beyond the South Bay lies the popular resort of Saltcoats, and off North Bay is the bird sanctuary of Horse Island. Magnificent views from the town across the Firth of Clyde take in the granite peaks of Arran, 15m away.

ARDWELL, Dumfries and Galloway 24 NX14
Situated on the Rhinns of Galloway peninsula, Ardwell lies on the W shore of Luce Bay. Ardwell House, now restored, was built in the late 17thc and stands in fine gardens.

ARISAIG, Highland   32 NM68
This village lies amid rocks and sand in the green landscape of South Morar. It has a ruined 16th-c chapel with some old sculptured tombstones, and the tower to the RC church can be seen for miles around. In the church is a memorial clock to Alexander Macdonald, or Alisdair MacMhaigstir Alasdair, the Gaelic poet. Near Arisaig House, with its

beautiful gardens, lies the cave in which Bonnie Prince Charlie hid before escaping to France in 1746. From the romantic Road to the Isles it is possible to look across Loch nan Cilltean to the islands of Eigg and Rum, and N towards the distant Cuillins S of Skye. The Sound of Arisaig and little inlet of Loch nan Uamh – with its associations with Bonnie Prince Charlie – lie S. The hills of Moidart and 2,876ft Fros Beinn can be seen across the sound.

ARMADALE, Isle of Skye, Highland 32 NG60
Armadale is sited on the fertile peninsula of Sleat – the garden of Skye. A steamer service from Mallaig on the mainland carries visitors to Skye, disembarking at Armadale. Dr Johnson and Boswell stayed at a local house – now reconstructed and known as Armadale Castle – built in 1815 by Lord Macdonald of Sleat in neo-gothic style. A road running SW from Armadale passes Ardvasar and ends by the Aird of Sleat. From here the walker can continue to the Point of Sleat – the farthest S tip of Skye. Some 2m NE of Armadale a little by-road off the coast road climbs NW over a water-shed, giving wonderful views of the Cuillins before descending to Tarskavaig Bay on Loch Eishort, facing Strathaird.

ARMADALE, Highland   37 NC76
Lying on the stormy N coast of Scotland just off the Bettyhill to Thurso road, Armadale is a crofting and fishing township noted for its sheep. It has a rocky shoreline and sandy bays. Remote Kirtomy Bay lies 4m NW, and N of this is Kirtomy Point where boats pass under the rocks via a curious tunnel.

ARNISDALE, Highland   32 NG81
Beautiful mountain scenery is a feature of this tiny and remote village, built on the rocky shores of Outer Loch Hourn. The steep, twin-peaked Ben Sgriol soars to 3,196ft behind the village, and across

1   Castle Remains
2   Customs House

3   St Peter In Chains Church (RC)
4   North Ayrshire Museum

5   Maritime Museum

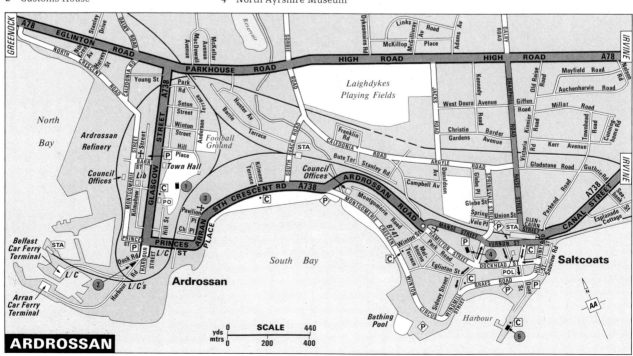

the loch is 3,343ft Ladhar Bheinn. The narrow, winding road from Glenelg to Arnisdale affords fine views of the islands of Skye and Rum before entering Eileanreach Forest. Situated W of the village, in the loch, are the Rassaidh Islands. A little path leads SE from Arnisdale and the clachan of Corran – where the Arnisdale River flows into Loch Hourn from Glens Arnisdale and Dubh – under the slopes of Druim Fada. It affords views of the wonderful fiord-like scenery of Inner Loch Hourn, facing Barrisdale Bay on the S side of the loch.

ARNPRIOR, Central   45 NS69
Arnprior Garden is a fine Georgian mansion in a wooded setting.

ARRAN, ISLE OF, Strathclyde   24
Mountains, low hills, streams, glens and lochs earn the Island of Arran its description of Scotland in miniature. Arran is 20m long, 10m wide and some 14m from the mainland coast, and can be reached from the mainland by steamer from Ardrossan and Fairlie. The finest scenery is in the N, where lofty granite ridges are shadowed by Goat Fell (NTS), the summit of which affords one of the best panoramic views in Scotland. Goat Fell is first recorded as having been climbed in 1628. The surrounding wild areas of Glen Sannox to the N and Glen Rosa to the S are popular with walkers, and there are many attractive sandy and rocky bays on the island.

A good 56m road encircles the island and another crosses it from Brodick on the E coast, the chief port and holiday village, to the little resorts of Machrie and Blackwaterfoot on the W. Near Blackwaterfoot are bronze-age cairns and the King's Caves, which sheltered Robert the Bruce in the early 14thc. Picturesque Lochranza on 'the loch of safe anchorage' is where Bruce landed from Ireland in 1306.

Three large bays lie in the shelter of the undulating E coast. Brodick Bay is dominated by a 15th-c castle which was once the home of the Dukes of Hamilton (NTS). Lamlash Bay, protected by the craggy Holy Island on which is St Molais's cave, the cell of a hermit in the 6th-c days of St Columba, is a haven for yachts. Whiting Bay is another popular holiday centre. In the S of Arran the landscape is more pastoral. Popular Arran cheese is made at Torrylin. The shore is sandy and the countryside is rich in c4,000-year-old standing stones.

ARROCHAR, Strathclyde   29 NN20
Situated in the heart of Macfarlane country, Arrochar stands at the N end of Loch Long and has a steamer pier on the sandy shore of the loch. The W shores of Loch Lomond are only 2m away. Wordsworth, his sister, and Coleridge were visitors here in 1803. Ardgartan lies 2m SW in the vast Argyll forest park. The park, mainly devloped by the Forestry Commission, covers 37,000 acres and includes many beautiful mountains. Camping sites are situated at Arrochar and Ardgartan. The 2,580ft Brock rises to the W of Ardgartan.

Some of Argyll's finest mountains rise to the NW of the village, particularly 2,891ft Ben Arthur, or the Cobbler (after its Gaelic name 'An Gobaileach'), and 3,036ft Ben Narnain – both popular with rock climbers. Another wonderful Cowal viewpoint is 3,318ft Ben Ime. The road from Arrochar to Ardgartan then runs W through Glen Croe, past Rest and be Thankful, before climbing down to Loch Fyne. To the SW of Glen Croe is the Ardgoil Estate of Argyll forest park, with the 2,774ft peak of Ben Donich predominant.

ASCOG, Isle of Bute, Strathclyde   44 NS16
Ascog lies on the E shore of the island, with Loch Ascog to the W.

ASHIESTIEL, Borders   26 NT43
Scott, during his time as Sheriff of Selkirk (1804 to 1812) lived at Ashiestiel or Ashiesteel House, which lies on the S bank of the Tweed. Mungo Park the explorer visited Scott here. It was during his time as sheriff that Scott penned *The Lay of the Last Minstrel*, *The Lady of the Lake*, and *Marmion*.

ASSYNT, Highland   36
This is the district around Loch Assynt, with Quinag mountain forming a long ridge between Loch Assynt and Kylesku. On a spit of land in the loch stands the ruins of 16th-c Ardvreck Castle.

ATHELSTANEFORD, Lothian   31 NT57
The Saxon King Athelstan is said to have been defeated in a battle against the Picts and Scots here in the 10thc. This conflict is said to have resulted in St Andrew's Cross being taken up as the Scottish flag. The event is commemorated by a plaque in the churchyard, where a flag perpetually flies. The church, though originally built c1100, has been rebuilt. Behind it stands a remarkable old stone-built dovecot with a crow-stepped gable. John Home, the writer of *Douglas*, was once a minister at this church. *Douglas* was produced at Covent Garden in 1775.

ATHOLL, Tayside   34
Atholl is a district of N Tayside in the Grampians, bounded to the W by the main road from Perth to Inverness. It includes the forests of Atholl and Gaick. At Blair Atholl, on the River Garry, stands Blair Castle, the ancient seat of the Dukes of Atholl who were heads of the Clan Murray. Glen Tilt runs from the N of Blair Atholl to the Grampian border, hemmed in by lofty hills.

AUCHENCAIRN, Dumfries and Galloway   25 NX75
This attractive village stands on Auchencairn Bay on the Solway Firth, with the little Hestan Island lying a short distance off-shore. The island has a lighthouse and was called 'Isle Rathan' in S R Crockett's *Raiders*. Near the school lies an ancient circular burial cairn, with Balcary House, originally built by smugglers, to the SE. Beyond Balcary House is Balcary Point.

AUCHENCROW, Borders   31 NT86
Gruesome stories of the treatment meted out to witches here in the 18thc abound; the village itself lies beneath Horseley Hill.

AUCHINCRUIVE, Strathclyde   24 NS32
West of Scotland Agriculture College uses Auchincruive House and its extensive grounds. The house is attractively set among the woods and sandstone cliffs of the River Ayr, and was presented to the nation in 1930. Burns and Wallace both came to Auchincruive, and Wallace is reputed to have hidden from pursuit in nearby Leglen Wood.

AUCHINDOWN CASTLE, Grampian   35 NJ34
The remains of this castle (AM) are surrounded by prehistoric earthworks overlooking the Fiddich River. Thought to have been founded in the 11thc, the castle was built partly by Thomas Cochrane, who was a favourite of James III.

AUCHINDRAIN, Strathclyde   29 NN00
A fascinating local museum of farming life comprises a cluster of 18th- and 19th-c houses, with farm buildings preserved amid their fields.

AUCHINEDEN, Central   45 NS48
Queen Victoria saw Loch Lomond for the first time from here in 1869, and the 1,171ft point from which she looked is now called Queen's View. It is an AA viewpoint.

AUCHINLECK, Strathclyde   25 NS52
The father of James Boswell built Auchinleck House, also known as Place Affleck, which lies 3m W near the banks of the Lugar. Designed partly by the brothers Adam, the house dates from c1780. Nearer the river lie the remains of an old castle. The local church is the last resting place of James Boswell, who died in 1795.

AUCHMITHIE, Tayside   31 NO64
Scott writes about Auchmithie in his book *The Antiquary*, in which he refers to the village as 'Musselcrag'. The community is perched high up on a sandstone cliff with a sandy beach below. Cliffs continue NE towards impressive Red Head and Lang Craig, overlooking Lunan Bay. Some way S lies a pretty stretch of foreshore with fascinating caves known by such names as Dickmont's Den, Mason's, and the Forbidden Cave. Pint Stoup's curious rock stack perches overhead.

AUCHTERARDER, Tayside   30 NN91
In 1716 the old town of Auchterarder, to the N of the Ochil Hills, was burnt by the Earl of Mar. It is now a Royal Burgh boasting a 1m-long main street. Just N of the town are remains of 11th-c Auchterarder. A modern castle lies S near Ruthven Water. Strathallan Castle can be seen 2½m NW near Machary Water.

AUCHTERDERRAN, Fife   47 NT29
An 18th-c church with a doorway of 1676 stands in this village, which lies on the winding River Ore. Bowhill Colliery operates near by. At Dogton Farm, 2½m NE, is the inscribed Dogton Stone (AM) which is believed to be of Celtic origin.

AUCHTERLESS, Grampian   35 NJ74
Towie-Barclay Farm incorporates Tolly Castle and lies 2m NE of this village. The castle, once a Barclay stronghold, was built during the 16thc and earlier and has a fine 14th-c hall. Prehistoric traces near Auchterless include stone circles and earthen hut remains.

AUCHTERMUCHTY, Fife   30 NO21
Lying on the fertile Howe of Fife and looking NW to the Ochill Hills, Auchtermuchty was once a Royal Burgh. On the Perth road 1⅓m NW of the village is the Thirlestone – a stone block once used for a beam which held wool-scales. A Tolbooth dating from 1728 is also preserved, and several weavers' thatched houses – unusual in Scotland – are of interest. Myres Castle is of 16th-c and later date.

AUCHTERTOOL, Fife *47 NT29*
Knockdavie Castle stands in ruins 2½m S across the A907.

AUCHTERTYRE, Highland *32 NG82*
From Auchtertyre Hill, NE on the hilly road leading towards Strome, there is a wonderful view towards the Five Sisters of Kintail and 3,505ft Scour Ouran at the head of Loch Duich. A small hydro-electric scheme operates in Glen Udalain beneath Scour Ouran.

AULDEARN, Highland *34 NH95*
Montrose raised the Royal Standard here in 1645 before he defeated the Covenanters. A circular 17th-c Boath Doocot (NTS) marks the spot. The ruined parish church lies ½m E, and various cairns and cists can be seen in the neighbourhood. The wooded Hardmuir, reputed scene of Macbeth's and Banquo's encounter with the witches, lies 3m E off the Forres road. Ruined Inshoch Tower stands 2m NE.

AULDGIRTH, Dumfries and Galloway *25 NX98*
A late 18th-c bridge which Carlyle's father helped to build spans the River Nith. Below the bridge the river rushes through a beautiful gorge. Near the river, 2m SE, is Ellisland Farm where Burns composed *Tam o' Shanter* and other works. Tiny Dalswinton Castle Loch lies beyond the river and is where Patrick Millar experimented with a steam-driven vessel in 1788; Burns was a passenger. Isle Tower, built in 1587 and still well preserved, lies 3m SE on the W bank of the river. The ruined 16th-c tower of Lag can be seen 2m W.

AULTBEA, Highland *36 NG88*
This crofting village stands on Loch Ewe and faces the Isle of Ewe. Loch Ewe is a sea loch which was of considerable naval importance in both world wars. The peninsula of Rudha Mor extends N and ends at Greenstone Point. The road from Aultbea runs NE, passing the curiously-named clachans of First Coast and Second Coast.

AULTNAHARRIE, Highland *36 NH19*
A passenger ferry across Loch Broom connects Aultnaharrie with Ullapool. Ben Goleach rises to 2,052ft in the W, and affords fine views over Loch Broom and Little Loch Broom. Near the village are two ruined brochs. Walkers can take the S track from the village and climb over the hills. The views of the great Teallach mountains are breathtaking.

AULTNAMAIN INN, Highland *37 NH68*
The inn was once a resting place for drovers going S, and it stands on the fine moorland road linking Evanton and Bonar Bridge. A fine view over Dornoch Firth can be enjoyed on the ascent from Struie Hill, 3m N (AA viewpoint). To the SW rises 2,270ft Beinn Tharsuinn. A tree 3m N was planted in July 1937 to commemorate the march of the London Scottish through the Scottish Highlands.

*AVIEMORE, Highland *34 NH81*
A once unremarkable Speyside village between the Monadhliath and Cairngorm Mountains, Aviemore was transformed in the 1960's by the building of a multi-million pound all-year-round holiday complex. The Aviemore Centre is a massive concrete plaza with shops, restaurants, luxury hotels, chalets, a theatre and concert hall, ice-rinks for

skating and curling, a swimming pool, a dry ski-slope, a go-kart track, bars, and many other facilities. The village lies at the heart of Britain's main winter-sports area, and the centre's bold modern design in local granite and wood harmonizes with its setting near the foot of the historic rock of Craigellachie. This rock was the rallying place of the Clan Grant, whose war cry was Stand Fast – Craigellachie. A 600-acre national nature reserve is also situated in the area.

The great Glen More Forest is reached by way of Coylumbridge on the road to Nethybridge, which keeps to the E of the Spey. Queen's Forest of Glen More has been developed as the Forestry Commission's 12,500-acre Glen More forest park. At Glen More Lodge, situated on the E end of beautiful Loch Morlich, the Scottish Council for Physical Education runs courses for young people and youth leaders in climbing, sailing, canoeing, fly fishing, ski-ing, and gem hunting for local semi-precious stones. The loch is backed by 4,084ft Cairn Gorm and 3,983ft Cairn Lochan. The district is popular with skiers. There is a camping ground near by.

A path climbs over Ryvoan Pass, with picturesque Green Loch, and leads eventually to Nethybridge through the Forest of Abernethy. The once-vast Rothiemurchus Forest lies S of the River Luineag between Aviemore and Glen More Forest, and the cleft of the well-known Lairig Ghru Pass can be seen to the SE. A long-distance walker's path leads through the pass towards the upper reaches of the River Dee in Glen Dee. Sluggan Pass can be reached from Loch Morlich and is an alternative track towards Abernethy Forest. Strathspey Railway Association plan to re-open the Aviemore to Boat of Garten line for steam locomotives.

AVOCH, Highland *34 NH75*
This fishing village lies in the Black Isle on the sandy shores of the Inner Moray Firth. The harbour works were built in the early 19thc by Telford. Traces of the old Avoch Castle lie S on Ormond Hill.

*AYR, Strathclyde *24 NS32*
In the heart of Burns Country, the town of Ayr is an attractive resort with excellent beaches and a fishing harbour on Ayr Bay. It is also a Royal Burgh and industrial area. Prestwick, with its airport, and Troon are well-known golfing centres to the N of Ayr. The old thatched Tam o' Shanter Inn was bought for the town in 1943, and houses a Burns museum.

Of the Twa Brigs, the Auld Brig o' Ayr is probably 13thc. Burns wrote of it as a poor narrow footpath of a street, where two wheel-barrows tremble when they meet'. The Auld Brig was renovated in 1910 and carries pedestrians only. The other bridge of the Twa Brigs is a modern replacement of a structure which was first erected in 1788. Burns was baptized in the Auld Kirk of Ayr, which dates from 1655 and replaced the 12th-c Church of St John. The kirk, with its Cromwellian associations, was renovated in 1952 and contains three lofts known as the Merchants', Sailors', and Traders' Lofts.

Ayr's oldest building is Loudoun Hall, a 16th-c structure of great architectural importance. The hall originally belonged to James Tait, Burgess of Ayr, and passed into the hands of the Campbells who

extended it. Some 200 years ago the hall entered a decline which continued until restoration began in 1938. St John's Tower affords panoramic views across to the island of Arran, and is the tower of old Greyfriars Church of St John. Bruce's parliament met here in 1315. A slender spire tops the 19th-c Town Buildings, and the Academy is a 13th-c foundation. Wallace's tower was erected in 1832 and is surmounted by a statue of Wallace; a statue of Burns stands near the station. John Macadam the road designer was born in Ayr in 1756. The racecourse lies E of Ayr. Ruined Greenan Castle stands on the coast 2½m S of the town near a cape known as the Heads of Ayr.

AYTON, Borders *31 NT96*
Ayton is situated on the N bank of Eye Water, where a single-arched bridge spans the water's wooded reaches. A modern castle stands near by, and a modern church has replaced an old ruined one. The church lodge was once a toll-house.

BADDAGYLE, Highland *36 NC01*
This village lies at the W end of Loch Baddagyle in the Aird of Coigach. The road W of the village passes Loch Owskeich and continues to Achiltibuie, dominated by 2,438ft Ben More Coigach. The beautiful N road climbs high over moorland on its tortuous way to Inverkirkaig and Lochinver. Breathtaking views of the distant mountains abound. Across the River Polly 2½m N of Baddagyle is curious Loch Sionascaig. It is situated in Inverpolly Forest, which is part of a 27,000-acre national nature reserve. To the SE of Loch Baddagyle is the curious Loch Lurgain and its circle of mountains. The 50m Inverpolly Motor Trail begins at Knockan AA viewpoint and provides good coverage of the area.

BADENOCH, Highland *34 NN58*
A mountainous district in the Grampian Mountains, Badenoch extends roughly from Loch Laggan to the Cairngorms. Kingussie is a good central point for exploration. Badenoch was once Comyn-family country but, after their annihilation, passed into the hands of the Earls of Moray. At Kingussie the ruins of Ruthven Barracks (AM) stand on the site of a stronghold once held by the notorious Wolf of Badenoch. The Barracks were built in 1716, enlarged by General Wade in 1734, and destroyed by the Highlanders after the '45 Rising.

BALBEGGIE, Tayside *30 NO12*
Dunsinane Hill, NE of the village, is topped by an ancient fort which many believe to have been Macbeth's castle.

BALERNO, Lothian *47 NT16*
Malleny House (NTS) was built in the early 17thc. Its features include a fine old dovecot and beautiful rose shrubberies.

BALFRON, Central *45 NS58*
Balfron village lies near Endrick Water, with the Campsie and the Fintry Hills stretching away to the S and E.

BALINTORE, Highland *37 NH87*
Once known as Abbotshaven, Balintore is a fishing village on the Moray Firth. A little to the N is Hilton of Cadboll, where a sculptured 7th-c stone was found. This is now in the Edinburgh Museum of National Antiquities.

Entries marked * are the starting point of drives included in the Day Drive section of the book (pages 95 to 160).

BALLACHULISH, Highland 29 NN05

The busy Ballachulish Ferry crosses Loch Leven to North Ballachulish, 1m to the W. The ferry, due to be replaced by a road bridge in the autumn of 1975, provides motorists with an alternative to the long route round Loch Leven for Fort William. Behind the straggling village rise the two 3,000ft peaks of Ben Vair and N beyond the loch are the mountains of Mamore Forest. Roofing slates are quarried near by.

Near the ferry is a monument to James of the Glen, who was hanged for allegedly shooting Colin Roy Campbell of Glenure in 1752. Campbell was also known as the Red Fox, and the crime was never proved. The white stone at the top of the monument is visible from the ferry mid-stream. Robert Louis Stevenson graphically portrays the story in his novel *Kidnapped*. Wonderful sunsets can sometimes be seen across Loch Linnhe towards the Ardgour Hills, which are dominated by 2,903ft Garbh Bheinn. Another magnificent view ranges E along Loch Leven to the conical Pap of Glencoe at the entrance to the famous pass of Glencoe. The road from Ballachulish runs SW towards Oban through Appin country, along the shores of Outer Loch Linnhe. The delightful scenery includes the massif of Ben Vair with its peaks of 3,362ft Sgurr Dhearg, and 3,284ft Sgurr Dhonuill – both fine viewpoints.

BALLANTRAE, Strathclyde 24 NX08

Robert Louis Stevenson took the name of this little holiday resort for his novel *The Master of Ballantrae*. The town, with its sand and shingle beach, lies in the Carrick district of Ballantrae Bay N of the estuary of the River Stinchar. The view out to sea is dominated by the impressive rock island of Ailsa Crag. This was Kennedy country, and many of their castles are still in evidence.

Near the bridge over the Stinchar is ruined Ardstinchar Castle, once held by the Bargany Kennedys and visited by Robert Louis Stevenson in 1876. Farther up the valley are the other Kennedy castles of Knockdolian and Kirkhill.

cont

1 Academy
2 Auld Brig
3 Auld Kirk
4 Burns' Statue
5 Greenan Castle
6 Loudon Hall
7 Racecourse
8 St John's Tower
9 Tam O'Shanter Inn
10 Town Buildings
11 Wallace's Tower

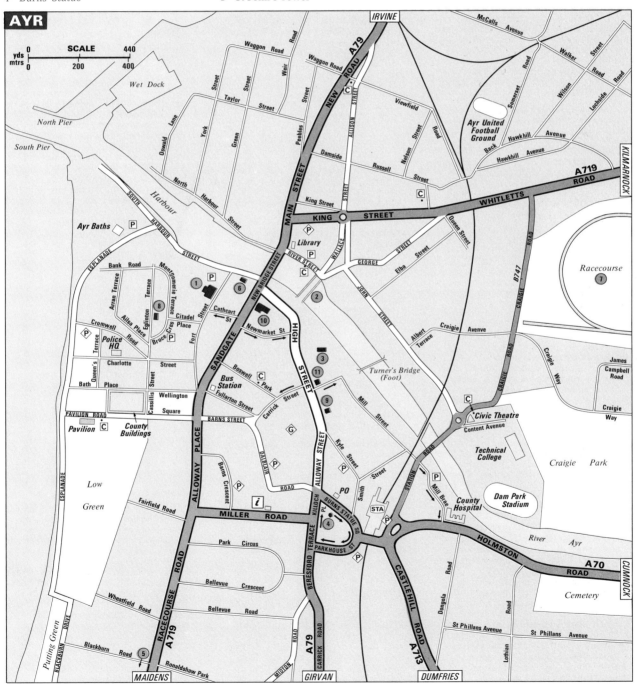

Beautifully wooded Glen App lies S of the town on the road to Stranraer. Also here is a little mid 19th-c church which was restored during this century in memory of the Hon Elsie Mackay, lost when flying the Atlantic in 1928. Glenapp Castle houses a collection of paintings and furniture, and stands in extensive gardens. Kennedy's Pass is the highlight of a beautiful coastal drive from Ballantrae to Girvan and lies 7m N of Ballantrae.

*BALLATER, Grampian   35 NO39
A busy holiday resort on Royal Deeside, Ballater is surrounded by beautiful wooded hills which are dominated by Lochnagar rising majestically to 3,786ft in the SW. The pretty pass of Ballater is threaded by the old Deeside road and runs beneath Craig-an-Darroch. Ruined Kirk of St Nathalan of Tullich, with its sculptured Celtic stones, stands near the road. Queen Victoria was particularly fond of the long valley of Glen Muick, which lies SW of Ballater and is shadowed by 3,268ft Broad Cairn. Those who enjoy long walks can trek along Glen Muick to the White Mounth plateau and Lochnagar, then continue down the long Capel Mounth track to Braedownie at the head of Glen Clova.

Birkhall, in Glen Muick, is a royal home which was built in 1715. It was bought by Edward VII while he was Prince of Wales, and is now used by the Queen Mother. Although a road runs 9m down the glen, Loch Muick is only accessible on foot. The Forest of Glen Tanner lies E of Glen Muick and includes 3,077ft Mount Keen. A narrow road N of Ballater links the Dee Valley with the upper valley of the Don, and crosses the hills by Gairnshiel Bridge. The higher portions of this road very often become snow-bound in winter. Bridge of Tullich affords fine views of Lochnagar and lies 1½m NE of the town.

BALLINGRY, Fife   47 NT19
This village lies below Benarty Hill. A bell inscribed 'Malcome of Lochore, 1658' is preserved in the church, and coal is mined near by.

BALLOCH, Strathclyde   44 NS38
Although the town actually stands on the River Leven, which flows S from Loch Lomond to the Clyde, it has a steamer pier on the Lomond shore. The beautiful journey along the loch should not be missed. Balloch also has a yachting marina, and Cameron House boasts Britain's first Bear Park plus a collection of fine furniture and a model aircraft exhibition. To the N of Balloch, on the E shores of Loch Lomond, stands 19th-c Balloch Castle. Just S of this is an older ruined structure known as Boturich Castle.

BALMACARA, Highland   32 NG82
The 8,000-acre Balmacara Estate includes Kyle of Lochalsh and Plockton, and about 6,400 acres are now owned by the National Trust for Scotland. Balmacara House is now a field-study centre. Beinn na Caillich rises to 2,396ft on Skye and faces Balmacara across Loch Alsh. There are also fine views over the loch towards Kylerhea, also on Skye. A 19th-c monument facing Loch Alsh commemorates Colonel Donald Murchison. Murchison was factor to the Earl of Seaforth during the '45 Rising, and sent the rents to the earl for seven years

while the latter was in exile. The earl is said to have ignored him on his return.

BALMACLELLAN, Dumfries and Galloway   25 NX67
A monument to Robert Paterson, Scott's *Old Mortality*, stands in the churchyard of this delightful village. Paterson's wife kept a school here for 20 years while he repaired Covenanter's tombstones all over Scotland. Interesting tombstones include an inscribed Covenanter's stone, and another showing weapons used in the Crimean War. Celtic relics which have been unearthed near by are now on display in Edinburgh.

BALMAHA, Central   44 NS49
This hamlet lies on the E bank of Loch Lomond, opposite a picturesque group of wooded islands. The road along the loch side runs NW through the Pass of Balmaha towards Rowardennan.

BALMERINO ABBEY, Fife   31 NO32
This ruined Cistercian abbey (NTS) was founded in 1226 and stands in a lovely setting on the S shore of the Firth of Tay. It was built by monks from Melrose, burnt by English troops in 1547, and suppressed during the Reformation. The beautiful Chapter House dates from the 15thc. Nearby Naughton House has a fine old dovecot. Each house of a modern group facing the firth bears an inscription from the last words which Lt-Col David Scrymgeour-Wedderburn of the Scots Guards addressed to his troops prior to the Anzio battle of the second world war. The houses were built by Mr Henry J Scrymgeour-Wedderburn, in memory of his brother the colonel who died of wounds at Anzio in 1944.

BALMORAL CASTLE, Grampian   35 NO29
First mentioned in 1484, Balmoral Castle was then known as Bouchmorale, which is Gaelic for 'majestic dwelling'. It lies on a curve of the river in Royal Deeside, in the district of Mar. Craig Gowan is surmounted by a cairn and faces the castle. The Prince Consort purchased the estate in 1852 for £31,000, and had it rebuilt in the Scottish baronial style before it was used as a royal residence in 1855. Queen Victoria later added Ballochbuie Forest to the property, which has been used by the Royal Family ever since. Crathie Church is a granite building standing to the E, which was built in 1895 and is the Royal Family's place of worship when in residence at Balmoral.

Glen Gelder is S of the castle, and leads to Balmoral Forest and the White Mounth group. This was the route taken by Queen Victoria and Prince Albert when they climbed Lochnagar on ponies in 1848. The countryside around Balmoral is old Clan Farquharson country, and 1m W of Balmoral is a mound known as Carn na Cuimhne, associated with the clan. To the NW of Balmoral, beyond Invercauld Forest, rises 3,843ft Ben Avon – one of the Cairngorm's highest peaks.

BALQUHIDDER, Central   30 NN52
Best known as the burial place of Robert Campbell or MacGregor (Rob Roy), Balquhidder is beautifully situated at the E end of Loch Voil. Rob Roy was a famous freebooter and was immortalized in Scott's novel of the same name. He died at Inverlochlaraig in 1734. The churchyard of the ruined kirk also

contains the tombs of Rob Roy's wife Mary, and two of his sons – Coll and Robin Oig. Near the family grave the walls of a 13th-c or earlier pre-Reformation church can be traced. Another church, dated 1631 and now in ruins, was built partly on top of the earlier church. The present church was built in 1855. St Angus' Stone in the north wall may be 8thc, and the font may be of 13th-c or earlier origin. The bell of the old church is dated 1684 and lies on top of a session chest said to have belonged to Black Duncan Campbell of Glenorchy, who died in 1631. The offering ladles are over 200-years-old and still in use.

The surrounding countryside is the traditional home of the Clan Laurin (the McLarens), and the churchyard of the ruined kirk contains a stone which commemorates members of the clan murdered in 1588 by incendiaries from Glen Dochart. Three members of the clan were outlawed in 1533 for the murder of Sir John MacLaurin, vicar of Balquhidder. This is also MacGregor country, and 3m E near Loch Earn and Glen Kendrum is Edinchip, the present seat of the MacGregors.

In 1589 the Clan MacGregor met at old Balquhidder Church and swore over the severed head of their enemy John Drummond, the King's Forester, that they would never give away the murderers, who were members of the clan. The Braes of Balquhidder, steep-sided valleys which are praised in a popular Scottish ballad by the 18th-c poet Robert Tannahill, are situated N of Loch Voil. Rough roads and paths lead through the braes to Loch Doine, beyond which is a path to Inverlochlaraig. This lonely place is overlooked by 3,821ft Stobinian and 3,099ft Beinn Tulachan.

BANAVIE, Highland   33 NN17
Standing on the road from Corpach to Gairlochy, Banavie provides splendid views of Britain's highest mountain, Ben Nevis (4,406ft). On the W bank of the River Lochy 2m NE is Tor Castle, near which lies a ruined tower of the Clan Chattan. The entrance to Glen Loy, through which Prince Charles Edward marched in 1745, lies 4m NE on the W side of the road. A chain of eight locks on the Caledonian Canal, built here by Telford in the 19thc, is popularly known as Neptune's Staircase (see inset opposite).

*BANCHORY, Grampian   35 NO69
Lavender grows in abundance in this attractive Royal Deeside village, and is locally distilled into Dee Lavender Water. On the Brig o' Feugh, a narrow 18th-c bridge over a rugged gorge E of the village, an observation platform has been built from which visitors can watch springing salmon leaping the rapids.

Away to the N rises the Hill of Fare, on the slopes of which a battle was fought in 1562. Durris House, built in the 17thc and added to later, stands 8m E. The road from Banchory leads SE towards Stonehaven and affords fine views. To the S of this road and 4m from Banchory lies 16th-c Tilquhillie Castle, now a farmhouse. From Banchory a road runs S to follow the Water of Feugh through Glen Dye towards the Cairn o' Mounth Pass.

*BANFF, Grampian   35 NJ66
Plan on page 176
This ancient seaport is a Royal Burgh, and a holiday resort with good sands. It

Entries marked * are the starting point of drives included in the Day Drive section of the book (pages 95 to 160).

is situated at the mouth of the River Deveron, and Macduff lies on the opposite shore. Traces of a castle can be seen in Banff, and the later castle was built in 1750. Duff House (AM), built by William Adam c1735, is the town's showpiece and was donated to the town by the Duke of Fife. The house stands in beautiful grounds which can now be enjoyed by everyone as a public park. The shaft of an old cross stands at Planestones, and the 18th-c Town House has an earlier tower.

Other old buildings include a few 17th-c houses and the remains of an old church. The Biggar Fountain stands on the site of a former gallows where James Macpherson, a Highland freebooter, played the fiddle as he was led to his execution in 1701. Off the Huntly road 3m S is Kirktown of Alvah. The village of Whitehills is sheltered by Knock Head and lies 2½m WNW of Banff on a rocky piece of coast.

BANKFOOT, Tayside   29 NO03

This Strathmore village lies on the Garry Burn, with Cornleith Moss and the Muir of Thorn lying to the NE.

BANNOCKBURN, Stirling   46 NS89

The Battle of Bannockburn which established Robert the Bruce on his throne was fought on 23 June, 1314, for the possession of Stirling Castle. Bruce won against odds of nearly three to one. Edward II's army was hemmed between two bogs and Bruce's infantry inflicted heavy casualties upon the packed ranks of English knights. Part of the 58-acre battlefield just W of Bannockburn is owned by the National Trust for Scotland, and an open-air rotunda encircles the Borestone – in which the shaft of Bruce's standard is said to have been set.

An equestrian statue of Bruce by C d'O Pilkington Jackson was unveiled by the Queen in 1964, on the 650th anniversary of the battle. An auditorium and information centre were added in 1967, and there is a special permanent exhibition on the 'Forging of a Nation'. Scott's *Lord of the Isles* describes the conflict between Bruce and De Bohun. The area is also the site of the battle of Sauchieburn, where James III was defeated in 1488 and fatally stabbed. Prince Charles Edward made Bannockburn House, to the S, his

headquarters in January 1746. The house has some beautiful carvings. The Royal George Hill is of early 19th-c origin.

BARCALDINE CASTLE, Strathclyde 29 NM94

This 16th-c home of the Campbells of Barcaldine stands on a piece of land jutting out from the Benderloch district, with the waters of Loch Creran, the Lynn of Lorne, and Ardmucknish Bay on three sides. Built in 1579 in the Scottish baronial style, the castle was restored by the 10th Laird in 1896. A by-road off the main Oban to Ballachulish road leads to the castle, terminating on the shores of Loch Creran opposite the island of Eriska.

BARGRENNAN, Dumfries and Galloway 24 NX37

From Bargrennan Church, near the River Cree, a road runs NE to Loch Trool in beautiful Glen Trool, with the extensive Glen Trool forest park all around. At the SW tip of the Loch stands the Martyr's Stone, dated 1685. Beyond the loch rise the 2,764ft Merrick, highest peak in the Lowlands, and the Rhinns of Kells with the dominating Corserine farther E. Some

NEPTUNE'S STAIRCASE

The idea of a canal through the Great Glen of Scotland was first treated seriously in 1773. James Watt was commissioned to report on its feasibility, but his favourable report was shelved and only in 1803 was an Act of Parliament passed, authorizing the construction of a Caledonian Canal to the design of the great civil engineer Thomas Telford.

The southern end of the canal is at Corpach on Loch Eil. The scenery here is superb, with the sea loch to the south and the great bulk of Ben Nevis to the south-east. Telford needed to raise the canal level substantially not far from Corpach, and settled on a chain of 8 locks at Banavie, which the workmen christened Neptune's Staircase. It remains the most important feat of canal engineering in Scotland.

Excavations at Banavie started in 1805. There were eight connected locks, each 180ft long and 40ft wide, which raised the level 64ft. In the beginning work at

Corpach and Banavie proceeded slowly. James Hogg the Border poet visited the site and was amazed at the leisurely rate of progress by the Highland labourers, unused to strict work schedules – 'I could not help viewing it as a hopeless job . . . I felt the same sort of quandary as I used to do formerly, when thinking of eternity.'

A brewery was built at Corpach to wean the workmen from 'the pernicious habit of drinking whisky'. The first three locks of Neptune's Staircase were finished in 1809, three more the next year, and the project was unwisely declared perfect in 1811.

After many delays the canal was finally opened in 1822. A celebration cruise was arranged from Inverness to Fort William and back, with many of the local gentry on board. At a dinner in Fort William's masonic hall, toasts in whisky were offered with staggering rapidity. The representative of the *Inverness Courier* lost count after 32 and confessed that

'we cannot pretend to detail all the proceedings of the evening.'

In service the canal never prospered as originally hoped, and Neptune's Staircase soon received a very bad name. Not only was it a traffic bottleneck needing up to four hours for a single ship's passage, but John Simpson the original contractor had let Telford down. George May, the resident canal engineer, reported in 1837 that the masonry throughout the Staircase could not be characterized 'by any other term than that of execrable'.

May had seen the walls of the second lock from the top bulge ominously. Similar complaints were made throughout the years, but it was not until 1920 that the canal was closed for two months and the stonework of Neptune's Staircase completely rebuilt. The effects of John Simpson's treachery are long forgotten. Neptune's Staircase remains a monument to Scotland's most famous civil engineer, in one of the most dramatic situations in Britain's network of canals.

Telford's impressive flight of locks at Banavie lifts the Caledonian Canal 64ft.

10½m N of Bargrennan on the narrow and winding moorland road to Maybole, is the lonely Nick o' the Balloch Pass, with Shalloch on Minnock and Loch Macaterick to the E. Before the pass is reached the road affords views to Loch Maon to the W and Kirriereoch Hill away to the E, facing Mullwharchar. To the W of Bargrennan are the three small lochs of Ochiltree, Dornal, and Maberry.

BARNTON (EDINBURGH), Lothian 47 NT17
Lauriston Castle stands a little to the NE of Barnton near Davidson's Mains. Although attached to a modern house, the castle still retains 16th-c work by Sir Archibald Napier, father of the inventor of logarithms. It was once the home of John Law, who sponsored the disastrous Mississippi Scheme of 1720, and now belongs to Edinburgh Corporation.

BARR, Strathclyde 24 NX29
This little angling resort lies in the Carrick district, in the valley of the Upper Stinchar River with Polmadie Hill to the SE. The Nick o' Balloch Pass affords fine views towards Shalloch on Minnoch and the 2,764ft Merrick, and lies 6m ESE. To the S and E of Barr are the Changue and Carrick Forests, part of the huge Glen Trool forest park.

BARRHEAD, Strathclyde 45 NS45
The textile town of Barrhead lies on Levern Water, with extensive moorland dotted with reservoirs to the S. Remains of old textile mills can be seen; the three-storeyed Cross Arthurlic Mill was built in the 18thc and is particularly well preserved. John Davidson the poet was born in Barrhead in 1857.

BARRHILL, Strathclyde 24 NX28
Moorland country rises to the E and W of this Duisk Valley village. A narrow road which runs S towards New Luce crosses lonely hilly moorland which is threaded by the Cross Water of Luce. Views of the surrounding area are afforded.

BATHGATE, Lothian 46 NS96
The industrial town of Bathgate has iron and steel foundries, and a large factory which produces commercial vehicles. Silver used to be mined near by. Sir James Simpson, who pioneered the use of chloroform in midwifery, was born at Bathgate in 1811. To the N are the Bathgate Hills and the prominent peak of the Knock.

BEARSDEN, Strathclyde 45 NS57
Known also as New Kilpatrick, Bearsden is situated near some of the best-preserved portions of the great Antonine Wall.

BEATTOCK, Dumfries and Galloway 25 NT00
Situated in hilly country on the Evan Water in Upper Annandale, Beattock lies near four prehistoric forts. These are all sited above the station, and the one on Beattock Hill is the best preserved. Auchen Castle, built in the 13thc and now a hotel, stands 1m NWN of the village. Farther N along the Evan valley are the ruined towers of Blacklaw, Mellingshaw, and Raecleuch. Some 10m NW of Beattock near Elvanfoot is the 1,029ft Beattock Summit, the highest point on the main road between Carlisle and Glasgow. The 15th-c Johnstone Tower, once a Johnstone seat, stands in a wooded setting 4m S of Beattock.

BEAULY, Highland 34 NH54
This name is a corruption of the French beaulieu, meaning beautiful place. The village lies on the salmon river of Beauly at a point where it begins to widen into the Beauly Firth. Remains of a Valliscaulian priory (AM), founded by Sir John Bisset of Lovat in 1230, can be seen here, and alongside are monuments and graves of the Chisholms, Frasers, and Mackenzies of Kintail. Abbot Reid erected the façade after 1530. In the market place a monument commemorates the raising of the Lovat Scouts.

BEITH, Strathclyde 44 NS35
This town manufactures gloves and furniture, and has an 18th-c mill. To the NE is Cuff Hill, crowned by a long barrow and overlooking the Threepwood Reservoir.

BELLSHILL, Strathclyde 45 NS76
Situated to the NE of the Clyde valley, Bellshill has iron, steel, and engineering works. It forms part of the Bothwell industrial centre.

BEMERSYDE, Borders 26 NT53
Bemersyde House is the traditional home of the Haigs and was presented to the nation in 1921 by Field-Marshal Earl Haig. The field marshal is buried in Dryburgh Abbey to the S. The house includes an ancient restored tower which was burnt during a raid in 1545. Thomas the Rhymer once made the prophecy – 'Tide, 'tide what'er betide, Haig shall be Haig of Bemersyde'. Sir Walter Scott frequently visited the house and loved the views of the winding Tweed, backed by the triple-peaked Eildon Hills to the W, afforded by Bemersyde Hill. This is an AA viewpoint.

BENBECULA, Western Isles 39 NF75
See Hebrides, Outer.

BENDERLOCH, Strathclyde 29 NM93
A vitrified fort tops a low twin-peaked hill, erroneously called Beregonium, near Benderloch on the shores of Ardmucknish Bay. Benderloch is the name generally given to the area between Loch Etive and Loch Creran, dominated by 3,059ft Beinn Sguliaird. Strictly speaking it is a part of the much larger district of Lorne. A by-road from Benderloch runs NW to 16th-c Baracaldine Castle.

BENMORE ESTATE, Strathclyde 44 NS18
Forming part of the huge Argyll forest park, Benmore Estate includes magnificent mountain and loch scenery – particularly around Lochs Eck and Long. Benmore House is now a centre for outdoor pursuits and belongs to Edinburgh Corporation. To the N lie the forests of Glenbranter and Glenfinart. Picturesque Puck's Glen and Glen Masson, both near Holy Loch, are notable beauty spots. The highest peak in the district is 2,433ft Beinn Mhor.

BEN NEVIS, Highland 33 NN17
Britain's highest mountain, 4,406ft Ben Nevis, dominates Fort William and the district of Lochaber from the SW end of the Great Glen or Glen More. Glen Nevis

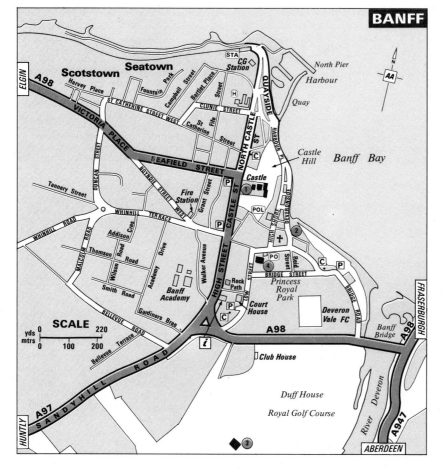

1 Castle Remains
2 Church Remains
3 Duff House
4 Town House, Biggar Fountain, and Old Cross

lies round the mountain's S and W flanks and is one of the loveliest Scottish glens, with the wooded gorge of the River Nevis at its farthest end. A narrow switchback road follows the glen and passes near Glen Nevis House, the headquarters of Lochiel when besieging Fort William in 1746. Remains of a vitrified fort can be seen on the hill of Dun Dearduil, to the W of the road. Polldubh waterfall is a little farther along the road, which at this point turns E and deteriorates. At the end of the road the slopes of Ben Nevis rise 4,000ft above, and the Allt Coire Eaghainn waterfalls drop from a hidden corrie. The path is now only suitable for walkers. At the end of the glen is the Steall waterfall in its wild setting below An Gearanach, among the peaks of the Mamores.

A long, lonely track leads towards Loch Treig from here. The magnificent N flanks of Ben Nevis can be seen from the remote Mhuilinn Glen, which leads to Coire Leis. There are also good views from the upper slopes of 4,012ft Carn Mor Dearg, which is linked to the Ben by a spectacular, narrow arête overlooking upper Glen Nevis. Snow often fills these great corries all the year round, and only very experienced climbers should tackle the precipitous cliffs on the Ben's N flanks. The Ben can be climbed starting from Achintree Farm, 2½m from Fort William on the E bank of the River Nevis. The 5m-long path is well defined but rough and stony. Walkers should take extreme care – accidents occur on the Ben every year. Halfway up the mountain is the little Lochan Meall-an-t-Suidhe, near which a descent over moorland can be made to view the N precipices from Mhuilinn Glen.

At the summit, an exposed wilderness of massive boulders, are the ruins of an observatory which was erected in 1883. A hostel which was closed in 1915 also stood here. A car climbed the track in 1911, and again in 1961, though the track has narrowed since the turn of the century. There is a mountain indicator at the summit, and on clear days the whole country from the Cairngorms to the Hebrides can be seen, as well as the far-distant Irish coast on occasions. Across Glen Nevis to the S is almost the entire Mamore group of mountains, with the white quartzite peak of 3,061ft Sgurr a' Mhaim dominating the lesser heights. Aonach Beag rises to 4,060ft, and together with 3,999ft Aonach Mor forms a 3m ridge at the upper reaches of the glen to the E. A 15m pipeline for the Lochaber power scheme has been driven through the Ben from Loch Treig near Tulloch to the outskirts of Fort William. The seldom-visited Grey Corries (3,858ft) lie E of the Aonach peaks.

BERRIEDALE, Highland *37 ND12*
This village lies at the mouth of Berriedale Water and preserves traces of 14th-c Berriedale Castle. The post office and old smithy are curiously decorated with antlers from local red deer. Berriedale Water is joined near its mouth by Langwell Water, which rises on a distant slope of Morven. Nearer to the village lies the long ridge of Scaraben, overlooking the bare expanse of Langwell Forest. Neill Gunn has written about the wild and rocky coast to the N in his novels, and the road S threads its steep and winding way past a number of deep ravines before reaching the Ord of Caithness.

BETTYHILL, Highland *37 NC76*
Situated at the mouth of the River Naver, this village was once known as Bettyhill of Farr and was founded by Elizabeth, Marchioness of Stafford for crofters evicted during the Highland clearances. The clearances were to make room for sheep and deer. Nowadays it is a touring and fishing resort with a sandy though exposed beach. Invernaver national nature reserve lies W and has a wide range of wildlife and plants, including rare Alpine plants. There is a bird sanctuary at Torrisdale Bay. Beyond the bay to the NW are the islands of Eilean Co'omb and Roan. Prehistoric remains are to be found in abundance in Strath Naver, 3 of the village, including tumuli, hut circles, and cairns. Some 4m S, on a by-road to the E of the River Naver, are several horned burial cairns.

BIGGAR, Strathclyde *25 NT03*
Biggar is largely one long street along the valley of the Biggar Water, a tributary of the Tweed which has been known to empty its waters into the Clyde (W) in times of flood. Only a tower remains of Boghall Castle, the home of Mary Fleming, one of the Four Marys who were ladies-in-waiting to Mary Queen of Scots; the others were Mary Seton, Mary Beaton, and Mary Livingstone. Mary Fleming is remembered every July in the crowning of the Fleming Queen. Near the end of the wide main street is Cadger's Brig, which has been restored. Also restored is the cruciform church of 1545. Gladstone's ancestors lie in the churchyard, and in the Gladstone Court Museum a street of 19th-c shops has been re-created. The Victorian prime minister himself came from the district. Dr John Brown, the author of *Rab and his Friends*, was born in the nearby manse in 1810. Culter House shows a 1m-long avenue of trees and was built in the 17thc. Coulter Motte Hill (AM) can be seen 1¼m SW.

BIRGHAM, Borders *27 NT73*
The Treaty of Birgham was signed in 1290 and established the details of Scotland's independence. Birgham is a Tweed-side village on the edge of the fertile plain of the Merse.

BIRKHILL, Dumfries and Galloway *26 NT11*
Surrounded by green lowland hills, Birkhill is overshadowed by 2,695ft White Coomb and stands at the summit of Birkhill Pass. A little to the S is Dob's Linn, a one-time refuge for the persecuted Covenanters. The spectacular 200ft-high Grey Mare's Tail waterfall (NTS) lies 1m SW and is where the Tail Burn joins Moffat Water. Loch Skene, in its lonely setting under Lochcraig Head, lies to the W of Birkhill.

BIRNAM, Tayside *30 NO04*
Known as the Mouth of the Highlands, Birnam Pass was used by both Montrose and Prince Charles Edward. The village lies in a delightful wooded setting between Birnam Hill and the River Tay. Duncan's Castle is a hill fort on Birnam Hill, associated with Shakespeare's 'King Duncan'. The Birnam Oaks (actually an oak and a sycamore), stand on the S bank of the Tay behind Birnam Hotel and are thought to be survivors of Shakespeare's 'Great Birnam Wood'. Murthly Castle, with Caputh Bridge beyond, lies 4m SE on a bend of the Tay.

BIRNIE, Grampian *34 NJ25*
A Celtic bell known as the Ronnel Bell is preserved in the little 12th-c kirk at Birnie. The kirk also houses a Norman font and chancel windows, and there is an 18th-c sundial and a Druid stone in the kirkyard.

BIRSAY, Orkney Isles *40 HY22*
See Orkney Isles.

BISHOPBRIGGS, Strathclyde *45 NS67*
Situated on the N outskirts of Glasgow near the Forth and Clyde canal, Bishopbriggs lies on the line of the Roman Antonine Wall.

BISHOPTON, Strathclyde *44 NS47*
This town lies off the Glasgow to Gourock road. Bishopton House was once a home of the Brisbanes, and the Maxwells lived 1½m S at the restored 16th-c Dargavel House. A gable carrying their arms is dated 1584. The modern mansion of Formakin was built by Sir Robert Lorimer and can be seen 2m SW. To the NW are views of Dumbarton Castle, backed by the distant 3,192ft peak of Ben Lomond.

BLACKBURN, Grampian *35 NJ81*
Kirkhill Forest lies on Tyrebagger Hill to the E of Blackburn.

BLACKFORD, Tayside *30 NN80*
Blackford lies on the Allan Water, 1m NW of the remains of Ogilvie Castle and the nearby Ochil Hills. Carsebreck Curling Pond lies 4m WNW and was once the venue for an annual match between N and S Scotland.

BLACK ISLE, Highland *34*
This fertile peninsula is bordered by the Firth of Cromarty and the Beauly and Inner Moray Firths. It is so named because it is seldom whitened by snow. The Millbuie, or Ardneanach, is a wooded ridge along the backbone of the Black Isle, and was originally granted to Darnley by Mary Queen of Scots. Castle Craig, a former home of the Bishops of Ross, faces Cromarty Firth beyond the B9163. It can be seen from the A9 on the farther shores of the firth.

BLACK MOUNT, Strathclyde *29*
This is an apt name for the bleak and hilly moors between Loch Tulla and Rannoch Moor. The main Glencoe road follows Black Mount's E border, with the old road to Glencoe further W. The fine peaks of 3,565ft Stob Ghabhar, 3,602ft Clachlet, and 3,636ft Meall a Bhuiridh, rise to the W of Black Mount.

BLACKNESS, Central *46 NT07*
Blackness was once the third port of Scotland. Blackness Castle (AM), built during the 15thc but with later additions, is often called Ship Castle because of its shape – one oblong tower and one circular stair tower. It was one of the most important fortresses in Scotland, and one of the four castles which by the Articles of Union were to be left fortified. The castle was used in the 17thc as a prison for Covenanters – Scottish Presbyterians who pledged themselves to maintain their chosen form of church government and worship. It served as a powder magazine in the 1870's, and recently has been used as a youth hostel.

The Binns (NTS), a mansion built in 1478, was once linked to Blackness Castle by an underground passage. In the 17thc it was the home of General Thomas Tam Dalyell, an ardent Royalist who was captured by Cromwell's army at the Battle of Worcester. He later escaped from the Tower of London and found his way to Russia, where he reorganized the Czar's army. He was recalled to command Charles II's forces in Scotland at the Restoration. According to legend, Dalyell consorted with the Devil, and traditionally was responsible for raising the Scots Greys in 1681. The mansion has been occupied continuously by the Dalyell family for over 350 years, and is still a family home.

BLACKSHIELS, Lothian 47 NT46

Lying on the edge of the Lammermuir Hills, Blackshiels and Fala are surrounded by sheep farming country. Some 2½m SW is Cakemuir Castle, standing by the Cakemuir Burn. It is said that Mary Queen of Scots changed out of her page's clothing here after escaping from Borthwick Castle in 1567. Cakemuir Castle was built between the 15th and 18thc, and the chamber which Mary was supposed to have used is on the first floor.

BLACKWATERFOOT, Isle of Arran, Strathclyde 24 NR82

Kintyre Peninsula can be seen from the fine cliffs near this little Drumadoon Bay village. The road from Brodick links with the coast road here, which follows the W shores of Arran. On the beach N of the village is King's Cave, where Robert the Bruce is said to have sheltered. Shiskine Church, where an ancient carved tombstone can be seen, lies 2m NE of the village.

BLADNOCH, Dumfries and Galloway 24 NX45

This little village lies on the Bladnoch Water, which is spanned here by a bridge. The river flows E past an old quay to enter Wigtown Bay N of the Baldoon Sands. Ruined Baldoon Castle stands about 1m SE of the village, and Scott mentions it in his *Bride of Lammermoor*. The castle was once the home of David Dunbar, who Scott made the bridegroom in his novel.

BLAIRADAM, Tayside 46 NT19

William Adam, father of the four distinguished 18th-c architects, was born here. His most eminent son was Robert (1728–1792), who became well-known for the interior decoration of his buildings. Blairadam was once known as Maryburgh, and the countryside around is described by Scott in his novel *The Abbot*. Scott was a visitor to Blairadam House.

Two nearby bridges have historic connections. The one over the Drumnagoil Burn is dated 1696, and the other, to the NE where the village of Paranwell once stood, displays two tablets which recall an abortive attempt on the lives of Mary Queen of Scots and Darnley in 1564. The Cleish Hills rise to the W, and Benarty Hill rises NE.

BLAIR ATHOLL, Tayside 34 NN86

A village in the midst of magnificent Highland scenery on the River Garry, Blair Atholl stands at the meeting point of several glens. Its position once made it strategically important as the key to the Central Highlands, and the Duke of Atholl built his castle here in 1269. The imposing pile of Blair Castle stands in a fine sweep of parkland, and has been

altered over the years. It was renovated in the mid 18thc, and restored in 1868 by David Bryce, an architect noted for his revival of the Scottish baronial style.

The oldest part of the castle is the 13th-c Cumming's Tower. Features of the castle include a lovely tapestry room, Jacobite relics, and fine collections of furniture and armour. It is still the seat of the Duke of Atholl, head of the Clan Murray. The duke is the only British subject permitted to maintain a private army – the Atholl Highlanders. James V, Mary Queen of Scots, and Montrose were all associated with Blair Castle, and at one time it was a Cromwellian garrison. When the castle was in Hanoverian hands during the 18thc, General Lord George Murray laid siege to it on behalf of Bonnie Prince Charlie. It was thus the last castle in Britain to have withstood a siege. The 16th-c parish church of Kilmaveonaig was rebuilt in 1794, and in St Bride's churchyard at Old Blair lies the grave of Claverhouse of Dundee, slain in 1689 at the Battle of Killiecrankie.

Glen Tilt lies to the N of the village, and the Falls of Fender can be found at its start – near the Old Bridge of Tilt. The glen runs N into the mountains of the Forest of Atholl, with 3,671ft Ben-y-Gloe to the E, and is hemmed in by steep hills for over 6m. Further N the Tarf Water joins the River Tilt in lonely hill country, with the deer forests of Glen Ey and Mar beyond.

*BLAIRGOWRIE, Tayside 30 NO14

The 19th-c Brig o' Blair spans the River Ericht to link the town to Rattray, on the edge of Strathmore. Blairgowrie is an angling resort and the centre of a prosperous strawberry and raspberry growing area. Part of the Lornty spinning mill of 1755 can still be seen, and white Newton Castle is of partly 17th-c date. The river rushes through a 200ft-deep gorge 2m N of the town. Craighall Rattray, a 17th-c mansion rebuilt in 1832 and still occupied by the Rattray family for whom it was originally built, stands above the gorge. This mansion may be the original of Scott's Tully-Veolan in his novel *Waverley*.

The road from Blairgowrie continues through Bridge of Cally and climbs along Glen Shee to the lofty Cairnwell Pass and Braemar. Off the Dunkeld road W of Blairgowrie are Lochs Ardblair and Marlee. Ardblair Castle is a 16th-c building which stands near its loch. Ruined Glasclune Castle, once home of the Blairs, lies 2m NW of the town. A battle was fought here in 1392.

BLAIRLOGIE, Central 46 NS89

Scotland's first conserved village, Blairlogie was a goat-milk spa in the 18thc. It lies under the Ochil Hills, with the fine viewpoint of 1,375ft Dumyat rising in the background. The Blair is of 16th-c date with later additions, and Powis House, built c1750, displays Adam features. Sir William Alexander, the founder of Nova Scotia, once worshipped in the former old church.

BLAIRS, Grampian 35 NJ80

A fine portrait of Mary Queen of Scots hangs in Blairs House. The painting was found concealed at Douai after the French Revolution, and is one of the very few portraits of Mary painted from life. Blairs House is now a college.

BLANTYRE, Strathclyde 45 NS65

Dr Livingstone was born in a local tenement in 1813. His birthplace in Shuttle Row was built in 1780 and has been restored as a national memorial and museum. The explorer's statue stands on the tower of the Livingstone Memorial Church. Some 2m N, at a point where the Clyde flows through woodland, there are traces of ancient Blantyre Priory. To the W, near Rotten Calder Water, is 16th-c and later Crossbasket Castle.

BLYTH BRIDGE, Borders 30 NT14

Blyth Bridge is a village on the Tarth Water, set amid the Lowland hills. The lovely old local mill is now a restaurant.

BOAT OF GARTEN, Highland 34 NH91

This curiously-named River Spey village is so-called because a ferry used to operate before the bridge was built in 1898. The Royal Society for the Protection of Birds maintains an observation point 2m E on Loch Garten, from which visitors can watch the rare ospreys in their nesting area. The last ospreys were killed off in Britain in 1910, but a pair returned to Loch Garten in 1958. Abernethy Forest is criss-crossed by many paths and tracks, and surrounds little Loch Garten. A track from the Nethybridge to Aviemore road runs S over the Sluggan Pass SE of the village, passing close to the foot of 2,237ft Craiggowrie and continuing into the Cairngorms. The Strathspey Railway Association intend to re-open the Aviemore to Boat of Garten line for the operation of steam locomotives.

BODDAM, Grampian 35 NK14

Buchan Ness boasts a lighthouse and is the farthest E point in Scotland, providing shelter for this little pink-granite fishing village which lies just off the Peterhead road. A ruined 14th-c castle lies to the S of the road, near the site of a new £100m North of Scotland Hydro-Electric Board power station. Peterhead granite quarries are situated SW of the village.

BOLTON, Lothian 31 NT57

The graves of Burns' mother, sister, and brother lie in the local churchyard. Visitors can see the Gifford Water well where Burns' mother drew water. The well, restored in 1932, is inscribed 'Drink of the pure crystals and not only be ye succoured but also refreshed in mind. Agnes Broun, 1732–1820'.

Lennoxlove mansion, formerly called Lethington Tower after William Maitland, stands 2m N. Maitland was the 'Mr Secretary Lethington to Mary Queen of Scots'. The 15th-c tower forms the centre of later additions. Features of the mansion include a great hall and two sundials dated 1644 and 1679 respectively. Above the entrance door, which still preserves its iron yett, is an inscription dated 1626. Pilmuir House is a delightfully gabled mansion 2m SW of Bolton. It was built by the Cairns family in 1624 and still has an original dovecot.

*BONAR BRIDGE, Highland 37 NH69

After 99 lives had been lost in the Meikle Ferry disaster of 1809, Telford built a bridge across the channel connecting the Inner Dornoch Firth with the Kyle of Sutherland. The present bridge replaces the one by Telford. The area around Bonar Bridge is dotted with hut circles

Entries marked * are the starting point of drives included in the Day Drive section of the book (pages 95 to 160).

and stone-age burial cairns, and a vitrified fort stands on Duncreich 4m SE. Loch Migdale lies in a wooded setting to the E of Bonar Bridge, and the picturesque glens of Strath Carron and Strath Oykell can be found to the W and NW of the bridge respectively. A road runs through Strath Oykell to Oykell Bridge and the mountains of the W coast.

IRONMASTERS OF BONAWE

Although ironworks are now thought of as part of the Lowland scene, it was to the Highlands that ironmasters looked in the days when charcoal furnaces were the most up-to-date method of extracting iron from its ore. The attraction was the great stretches of woodland which could be cut down to produce charcoal, although from time to time regulations were drawn up to reduce the amount of felling that was permitted. One of the earliest Highland iron furnaces was on the shore of Loch Maree, where Sir John Hay began operations in 1607. In the following century an iron company from Furness in Lancashire took a timber lease at Invergarry, but this was a foolish and reckless adventure' that did not survive for long.

In 1752 there was a much more businesslike approach when Richard Ford and Company, again from Furness, negotiated an agreement with Sir Duncan Campbell of Lochnell to lease ground and timber rights at Bonawe, on the south shore of Loch Etive. The woods around Bonawe abounded with oak, ash, birch, hazel, and alder.

At the time there was no iron being produced anywhere in Scotland, but the Lorn Furnace was to remain very much an English-controlled concern. The company rented no less than 34sqm of land, adding timber rights from the Earl of Breadalbane's vast estates when Campbell of Lochnell's woods seemed too small. They built their furnace near Taynuilt, employed hundreds of local people at low wages during their busiest seasons, rented · farms, set up a church, an inn, a school, and a quay on the shore of the loch.

BONAWE, Strathclyde 29 NN03

The River Awe enters Loch Etive near here, dividing it into the lower and upper lochs. Ben Starav rises to 3,541ft in the NE, near the head of the upper loch. Inverawe House, a 16th-c haunted building, stands on the E bank of the River Awe. Beyond the N side of the loch are the Bonawe granite quarries. These can

Ford's plan was to import raw iron ore direct to the quayside from Ulverston in Lancashire. Pig iron was produced in the Lorn Furnace and carried back to Ulverston in the same ships. It may seem a cumbersome way of doing business, but lower costs at Bonawe and the high quality of the product made it worthwhile.

Ford himself died in 1757, and control of the undertaking passed to the Newland Company, again of Furness, which was run by George Knott. Once he took over Knott visited Bonawe several times, and when he was back south sent a stream of complaining letters to McFarlin, the Lorn Furnace manager. One letter dated March 6, 1781 showed Knott's exasperation with the way his Scottish business was being conducted:

'I thought I had a right to know what was going on at the Furnace, but I imagine I am to be kept in total ignorance of everything . . . You have carried it to such a length as to become a disgrace to your employers by your retailing whisky out of bottles . . . I have also had a distinct intimation of the Quay being noted at Oban for the principal smuggling harbour. I therefore desire that it may be entirely put a stop to . . . I find by the Bank Account there is a most enormous sum of money expended about what or on what Account I know not, nor can I conceive . . . Put a stop, if possible, to that confounded drinking in general, and by your shewing the example it may be more easily done, for I believe there is not such another drunken hole in the Kingdom.'

This direct speaking had little effect, and McFarlin was soon replaced. Knott's reference to smuggling was no

exaggeration, because the excisemen once seized 34 casks of brandy hidden in a shed on the quay. George Knott died in 1784, thoroughly disgruntled by the Lorn Furnace, apart from the profits it made thanks to the low wages paid to local labourers while skilled men brought up from Furness were paid at Lancashire rates. He was little more enthusiastic about the Highland landowners with whom he had to deal: 'I doubt if a single honest man could be discovered among the landed proprietors of the district.'

The original lease expired in 1863, but another lasting for 21 years was arranged with Alexander Kelly of Bonawe, who had bought over this part of the Lochnell estate. The old furnace still made money, but its usefulness and profitability dwindled during this period of lease, and it was finally closed down.

In more than a century no major changes or additions were ever made to the original furnace or the buildings round about. The only deviation from the production of pig iron came in times of war, when shot was cast. To the end it remained an old-style furnace, separated by geography from the great strides made during Victorian times by Lowland ironmasters.

For a century or more the buildings crumbled away. Now they are in the hands of the Department of the Environment and have been painstakingly restored to something like their former glory. The furnace itself, built as usual into the side of a hill so that it could be fed from the top, still has the original lintels dated 1753. The site includes a casting house, a filling house, and storage sheds, with all the masonry and roofing carefully rebuilt. In an unlikely situation, surrounded by mountains and fronted by a sea loch, Bonawe is a worthy memorial to the charcoal-burners and furnacemen of Lorn.

These 18th-c workmen's cottages form the oldest tenement in one-time Argyll, and are connected to the Bonawe Ironworks.

BONCHESTER BRIDGE, Borders
26 NT51
Rule Water flows N under the bridge and beneath Bonchester Hill to join the Teviot. The late-Georgian Greenriver House stands near by. Roads run NE to Jedburgh and NW to Hawick from Bonchester Bridge, and the road S forks; the fine Liddesdale road runs SW from the fork into the hills reaching an altitude of 1,250ft at Note o' the Gate, below the Cheviot summits of Peel Fell and Carter Fell. This is Wauchope Forest country, which combines with Newcastleton Forest to form part of the Border forest park.

BO'NESS, Central *46 NS98*
Borrowstounness, to give the town its full name, was Scotland's third port in the 19thc but lost trade as Grangemouth, a few miles along the Firth of Forth, was developed. Bo'ness is now an industrial town and has associations with James Watt, who experimented with his steam engine at nearby Kinneil House (AM) in 1764. The estate is now a public park. Henry Bell launched an early steamship called the 'Comet' on the Clyde in 1812, and is similarly associated with the town.

The E end of the Antonine Wall was E of Bo'ness, and a distance slab unearthed in 1868 is now in the National Museum of Antiquities at Edinburgh. A copy of the stone has been set in a framework of Roman stones and erected near Bridgeness Tower, at the E end of the town. Wall paintings illustrating the story of the Good Samaritan have been discovered in a room of 16th-c Kinneil House. Bo'ness car hill-climb takes place in the grounds of Kinneil House. Carriden House, part of which is dated 1602 stands 1½m E of Bo'ness.

BONHILL, Strathclyde *44 NS37*
This town lies on the River Leven, between the Clyde estuary and the S tip of Loch Lomond. Bonhill House was the birthplace of 18th-c surgeon, novelist, and satirist, Tobias Smollett.

BONNYBRIDGE, Stirling *46 NS88*
Part of the Antonine Wall once stood here, and a well-preserved Roman fort can be seen to the E at Rough Castle. Bonnybridge is now an industrial town on the Forth and Clyde Canal.

BORDER COUNTRY, The
From the Cheviot Hills the moorlands and pastures of the Border Country stretch deep into the old counties of Roxburghshire, Selkirkshire, and Berwickshire. Peebles-shire and parts of Dumfries-shire complete the one-time Border counties. The Rivers Teviot, Yarrow and Jed flow through the valleys to join the Tweed. These rivers abound with purposeful salmon and bright, darting trout, and the hills provide pasture for sheep whose wool is made into the famous Border tweed. Roxburgh, Peebles, and Selkirk display true Border scenery – rounded green hills with delightful glens and dales.

The bare bones of a turbulent past occasionally break through the skin of this peaceful land; the gutted abbeys of Melrose, Jedburgh, Kelso, and Dryburgh (all AM) exist as gaunt reminders of the havoc wreaked by marauding English raiders from the 13th to 17thc. The English were not the only despoilers. For centuries the Border Bandits, known as reivers or mosstroopers, fought out their private feuds, murdered, and plundered until the Borders were pacified by James II in the 15thc, when he over-ruled the powerful Border Earls. The violence, the stories of medieval wizards, and the romance of the countryside inspired the writing of Sir Walter Scott, who lived at Abbotsford mansion in the very heart of the Border Country.

James Hogg, son of a Selkirkshire farmer who was dubbed 'The Ettrick Shepherd', followed the tradition of the Border ballad writers in his 18th-c poems of romance and local patriotism. Each year the towns remember the stormy past with the Common Ridings – when horse-men and women gallop over rough moors and hillsides.

BORGIE BRIDGE, Highland *37 NC65*
The River Borgie flows N from the bridge into Torrisdale Bay, and a by-road follows the river towards the coast before turning NW for the crofting town of Skerray.

BORGUE, Dumfries and Galloway
25 NX64
Robert Louis Stevenson used the setting of this village in his novel *The Master of Ballantrae*. Borgue lies to the W of Kirkcudbright Bay, and is noted for its summer flowers.

BORTHWICK, Lothian *47 NT35*
Borthwick Castle dates from 1430 and was the home of Mary Queen of Scots and Bothwell after their marriage in 1566. The massive restored castle displays two towers and a machicolated parapet. The barrel-vaulted great hall still has its splendid hooded fireplace. Mary escaped from the castle disguised as a man and rejoined Bothwell on his way to Dunbar. Borthwick Castle surrendered to Cromwell in 1650, and is now used as a centre for executive training courses. The church was burnt in 1775, but its 15th-c aisle was spared and later incorporated into the rebuilding. It contains well-preserved effigies of the first Lord and Lady Borthwick.

BOTHWELL, Strathclyde *45 NS75*
The Battle of Bothwell Brig was fought near here in 1679, resulting in the defeat of the Covenanters and a five-month sentence of imprisonment in Greyfriars churchyard at Edinburgh for 1,200 of their number. A monument commemorates the defeat. Bothwell Castle (AM) belongs to the Douglas family and was one of the largest and finest stone castles in Scotland. It was built during the 13th and 15thc and stands to the NW of the town in a lovely setting.

The castle has had a turbulent past, and though now ruined is still a most impressive sight. Its great Douglas Tower resembles its prototype at Coucy, in France, and was probably built by French craftsmen over a period of 36 years. The great hall was also one of the finest in the country. The bridge at Bothwell spans the Clyde and was erected *c*1400. It underwent major repair work in 1826. Bothwell's collegiate church has a wonderful pointed barrel vault and houses fine 18th-c monuments to the Douglas family. The earliest parts of the church date from 1398. Joanna Baillie the poetess was born in the town in 1762, and Scott wrote *Young Lochinvar* here.

BOWDEN, Borders *26 NT53*
A church was founded here in the 12thc, and the present restored church is mainly of 17th-c origin. An interesting laird's loft can be seen in the latter. Bowden received permission to hold a market in 1571, the first non-burghal licence to be permitted in Scotland. Its 16th-c market cross is now a war memorial. The triple-peaked Eildon Hills can be seen to the N, and the distant Cheviots are visible from high ground near the village.

BOWLAND, Borders *31 NT43*
Bowland stands on Gala Water. A road running S passes between Knowle Hill and Torwoodlee Woods, the latter with their old Castle of Torwoodlee. Near the castle is a Georgian house dating from 1793. Foundations of an ancient broch known as The Rings are to be found on Crosslee Hill within the boundaries of a British camp.

BOWLING, Strathclyde *45 NS47*
The Forth and Clyde Canal, built by Smeaton in 1790, enters the Clyde at Bowling. The great Antonine Wall across the waist of Scotland had its W end here. Symington tried out the first practical steamboat, 'The Charlotte Dundas', here in 1802, and in 1812 Bell launched the famous 'Comet' – the first Clyde passenger steamer. At Dunglass Point to the W of the village stands a ruined castle overlooking the Clyde, and near the point is Henry Bell's obelisk. The Kilpatrick Hills, dotted with reservoirs, lie to the N.

BOWMORE, Isle of Islay, Strathclyde
28 NR35
The Islay parliament met at this large fishing village between 1718 and 1843. The community is sited on Loch Indaal. The tower of the curious circular parish church of Kilmarrow includes a panel inscribed with the information that the church was built in 1767 by Daniel Campbell 'Lord of this Island'. It is said that the church was made round so that the Devil could find no corners to hide in. The high-road, running NE but later turning S, takes the inland route to Port Ellen; the low-road runs S from Bowmore and keeps near the shores of Laggan Bay.

BOW OF FIFE, Fife *31 NO31*
To the N of this curiously-named village is Fernie Castle. The earliest portions of the house, now used as a hotel, date from the 16thc.

BRACADALE, Isle of Skye, Highland
32 NG33
The scattered crofting village of Bracadale lies on Loch Beag, an inlet of Loch Harport. The rough hill road to Skye's capital, Portree, leads to the E and a better road runs S to Sligachan. Dunvegan Castle lies to the N beyond the shores of Loch Bracadale, a beautiful fjord with views W to the islands of Wiay, Harlosh, and Tarner. Beyond the islands is the Duirinish peninsula, topped by the twin peaks of Macleod's Tables. To the W of the village lie the ruins of two brochs – Dun Mor and Dun Beag. Dun Beag is Skye's best preserved broch and was visited by Dr Johnson and James Boswell on their tour of W Scotland in 1773.

BRACO, Tayside *30 NN81*
Ardoch Roman Camp lies in the grounds of Ardoch House to the E of the old bridge over the Knaik Water. The fort and its defences are some of the largest in

Copy of a Roman distance stone which marked the E terminal point of the Antonine Roman Wall at Bo'ness.

Britain, and are particularly well-preserved. Coins from the time of Hadrian have been excavated here. The Roman Great Camp lies NW of Ardoch Camp, adjacent to a smaller camp. A possible 40,000 troops could have been accommodated at any one time within the confines of these two camps. Braco Castle was built in the 16thc and later extended.

BRAEDOWNIE, Tayside 35 NO27
Beautifully situated in the Braes of Angus Mountains, Braedownie lies at the head of long Glen Clova. The road ends here. Two valleys with walking tracks run NW into the hills. The farthest E leads onto the lofty White Mounth plateau, with Lochnagar to the N. Capel Mounth is a track which branches off near the beginning to lead to Loch Muick in Glen Muick, with access to Ballater. The old drove road known as Jock's Road threads the valley of White Water, the farthest W of the two, and climbs high above White Water. Overlooking the road are 3,268ft Broad Cairn and 3,143ft Tolmount. The hills of 3,105ft Driesh and 2,815ft Craig Mellon overshadow the glen to the S and N. Craig Rennet crags overlook the head of the glen. A picnic site and car park have been established where the tracks to Jock's Road and Capel Mounth divide.

*BRAEMAR, Grampian 34 NO19
First popularized by Queen Victoria, Braemar is a Royal Deeside summer and winter resort made up of Castleton of Braemar and Auchindryne. These two districts face each other from opposite sides of Clunie Water, which flows into the Dee N of the village. Braemar is set among heather-carpeted hills, dominated to the W by the massive 4,241ft peak of Cairn Toul, and to the SE by 3,786ft Lochnagar. The annual Royal Highland Gathering in September is often attended by the Queen. In 1715 the 6th Earl of Mar raised the Jacobite standard on a mound where the Invercauld Arms now stands.

Braemar Castle, on a bluff overlooking the Dee, was built by the 2nd Earl of Mar in 1628; it was attacked and burnt in 1689 by the Farquharsons, and after the 1715 Jacobite Rising was garrisoned by English troops to keep the Highlanders in check. It was rebuilt c1748 with a round tower, a barrel-vaulted ceiling, a massive iron gateway, and a spiral stairway.

Robert Louis Stevenson wrote part of *Treasure Island* in a cottage at the S end of Castleton Terrace in Braemar. The foundations of Kindrochet Castle, a hunting lodge of Robert II, lie near Clunie Water. It is known that the castle was built in 1390 and became derelict by 1600. Below Invercauld Bridge and 3m E is the Old Bridge of Dee, built in 1753. Garbh-Allt Falls, in the Royal Forest of Ballochbuie, can sometimes be reached from the lodge near the Old Bridge. Invercauld House stands N of the river and is of partly 15th-c origin. Wonderful views of Lochnagar are afforded by Invercauld Bridge itself. Morrone Hill rises SW of Braemar and offers splendid views NW to the Cairngorms.

The main road S from the resort climbs through Glen Clunie and over the Cairnwell Pass. The old descent over the famous Devil's Elbow to reach Spittal of Glenshee was often snowbound in winter, but an easier road has recently been constructed. A steep, narrow road links the Dee valley with the upper valley of the Don, and leaves Deeside near Balmoral Castle, climbing N into the hills past Gairnshiel Bridge in Glen Gairn. The highest sections of this road are sometimes impassable in winter. Before Gairnshiel Bridge a by-road turns W, following the River Gairn; this becomes a private road beyond Daldownie, and leads to Loch Builg.

BRAEMORE JUNCTION, Highland 36 NH27
This is where the Dundonnell and Ullapool roads converge on their way E to Inverness. Deep Corrieshalloch Gorge (NTS) lies near the Dundonnell road and a fragile bridge spanning the gorge allows views of the magnificent Falls of Measach. The road down to Ullapool, on Loch Broom, follows the beautiful Strathmore valley with 3,547ft Beinn Dearg and 3,200ft Cona Mheall rising to the E. Little Loch Choire Ghranda, in its wild and precipitous setting, lies under the shadow of Cona Mheall.

The lonely vertical cliffs of 3,041ft Seana Bhraigh rise to the NE between the Inverlael and Freevater Forests. To the S of Braemore Junction are the remote Fannick Mountains, with 3,637ft Sgurr Mor overlooking Loch Fannich. The road SE to Inverness crosses bleak moorland known as the Dirrie More, on which lies little Loch Droma. The Dundonnell Road was built during the area's terrible famine of 1851, and is sometimes called Destitution Road. It runs through lonely Dundonnell Forest and affords fine views across the forest to the wild Teallach Mountains, nearly 3,500ft in height.

BRAIDWOOD, Strathclyde 30 NS84
Limestone is quarried at Braidwood, and a mansion known as The Lee stands in a park 2m SSE. This house is associated with the well-known Lee Penny amulet, which inspired Scott's novel *The Talisman*.

BREADALBANE, Central 30
This district includes Ben Laurens and the Tay Valley, including Loch Tay, plus the Earn and Forth river basins. The Grampian mountains cover much of the area, and the panoramic view from the 3,984ft summit of Ben Lawers (NTS) takes in the ranges of the Breadalbane Hills, including the lofty Forest of Mamlorn range. Glen Lyon, one of Scotland's longest and finest glens, lies in Breadalbane with Loch Rannoch to the N.

BRECHIN, Tayside 34 NO56
Plan overleaf
Brechin is a town which stands on the South Esk River and faces the valley of Strathmore. The hills in the background gradually rise to the E Grampians. The streets of the old town are lined with many buildings of local red sandstone, and rise steeply from the river. A good view of the old town can be enjoyed from the river bridge on the Arbroath road. The cathedral, now the parish church, was built c1150 but partly demolished in 1807. Restoration began in 1900, but some of the original building is still preserved. The spired tower dates from c1360.

Next to the cathedral is Brechin's most treasured possession – an 87ft-high round tower (AM) built in the 10th or 11thc. The only other remaining round tower such as this on the Scottish mainland is at Abernethy. Both structures are similar to those found in Ireland, and were built as watchtowers which doubled as places of refuge for the minister and church treasures. A fragment of the 13th-c Maison Dieu Chapel (AM) is also preserved in the town.

A large deer park 5m SE surrounds Kinnaird Castle, a 19th-c building with parts dating from 1405. A little farther SE is Farnell Castle, built during the late 16thc. Montreathmont Forest lies a few miles S of the town, and 5m W is 15th- and 18th-c Careston Castle. Two prehistoric hill forts (AM), known as Black Caterthun and White Caterthun, stand 6m NW of Brechin on a ridge overlooking the Howe of Mearns.

BRIDGEND, Isle of Islay, Strathclyde 28 NR36
Lying in a wooded setting at the head of the sea loch Indaal, Bridgend is the junction of roads running E, S, and W of the island. Islay House stands near by, and a sandy beach can be enjoyed 2½m W at Blackrock. A road leads N over

Entries marked * are the starting point of drives included in the Day Drive section of the book (pages 95 to 160).

181

Gruinart Flats from here and continues to the head of Loch Gruinart. A clan battle took place here in 1598. A little road running N from the head of the loch borders its W shores as far as Ardnave. Beyond here are Ardnave Point and Nave Island, on a rocky stretch of coastline.

BRIDGE OF ALLAN, Central 45 NS79

Popular as a spa for over 150 years, Bridge of Allan still has its pump room and baths. Robert Louis Stevenson was among those who took the waters at the Airthrey mineral spring, ½m SE. Now also a touring centre, the town lies on Allan Water which joins the Forth S of the town. Stirling University has a fine campus and is set here in the Airthrey estate. The Ochil Hills rise to the NE of the town, with the fine viewpoint of Dumyat prominent. Chopin was a guest 2m NW at Keir in 1848, and the house stands in fine gardens.

BRIDGE OF AVON, Grampian 34 NJ13

This is where the Tomintoul to Grantown-on-Spey road crosses the River Avon before continuing through hill country by way of Bridge of Brown and Strath Spey. At Bridge of Avon a road follows the River Avon N, with the Cromdale Hills to the W.

BRIDGE OF BALGIE, Tayside 30 NN54

Bridge of Balgie is situated on the Glen Lyon road, at the point where it is joined by the steep (1 in 6) mountain road which eventually leads to Killin. The mountain road leading S climbs high over a shoulder of 3,984ft Ben Lawers, with tiny Lochan na Lairige on the right. Beyond the Lochan to the SE are the peaks of the Tarmachan group. Hydro-electricity is produced hereabouts. Beautiful Glen Lyon is one of Scotland's longest glens, and its road running W from Bridge of Balgie into bleak hill country passes picturesque Meggernie Castle. This is sited by the River Lyon and dates partly from c1582. Lochs Giorra and Dhamh, in the hills to the W, have been joined to form one huge reservoir.

The road ends at Loch Lyon, which has also been extended and near which a large dam has been constructed. Ben Achallader rises to 3,404ft and dominates the head of the glen to the NW; 3,530ft Ben Heasgarnich can be seen to the S.

BRIDGE OF BROWN, Grampian 34 NJ12

This moorland bridge carries the Tomintoul to Grantown-on-Spey road. To the S lies little Glen Brown, with its stream. The road climbs high to the N before descending into wooded Strath Spey, with the Cromdale Hills rising gently to the N. The lofty Cairngorms with 3,843ft Ben Avon can be seen SW from the road.

BRIDGE OF CALLY, Tayside 30 NO15

The River Ardle meets the Black Water from Glenshee near this point, to become the River Ericht. Heading N the road from the village climbs 2,000ft to the popular Glenshee ski slopes. On the way is the once-notorious Devil's Elbow; its hazardous double bends have now been replaced by a new section of road. The moorland area of Clunie Forest, with the Forest of Alyth to the E, lies W of Bridge of Cally.

BRIDGE OF CRAIG, Tayside 31 NO25

Bridge of Craig spans the River Isla, and a little to the E are the fine waterfalls of Reekie Linn. Still farther E is the waterfall known as Slug of Auchrannie. Lintrathen Loch, Dundee's water supply, lies to the N.

BRIDGE OF EARN, Tayside 30 NO11

Part of the original medieval bridge is still preserved here. The fine old mansion of Balmanno was well-restored by Sir Robert Lorimer and lies 2½m SE. The once well-known Pitkeathly Wells are 1m W.

BRIDGE OF ESS, Grampian 35 NO59

This bridge spans the Water of Tanner at the entrance to wooded Glen Tanner. A by-road running W from the Bridge of Ess follows the river for a short way then turns N; the river valley can be followed on foot. Glentanar House stands in Glentanar Forest at this point, and a path

1   Cathedral and Round Tower
2   Farnell Castle
3   Kinnaird Castle
4   Maison Dieu Chapel

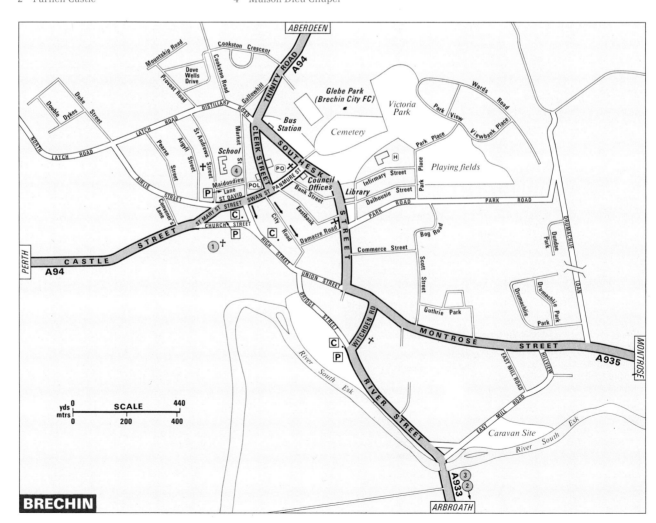

BRECHIN

leading S from the nearby church crosses the hills E of the Hill of Cat to reach Glen Esk, near Tarpside. This track is known as the Fir Mounth Road. The Mounth Road is another hill path, which diverges S near the head of Glen Tanner and, after crossing a shoulder of Mount Keen, reaches Glen Mark near Lochlee. Glentanner Churchyard, 2m NW of the bridge on the S bank of the Dee, is where Byron's Highland Mary is buried. She died in Aberdeen in 1887.

BRIDGE OF FEUGH, Grampian
35 NO79
Though dated 1799 this bridge is probably older, and its tollhouse is of 18th-c origin. The Bridge of Feugh spans the rocky Water of Feugh near its junction with the Dee, on the outskirts of Banchory.

BRIDGE OF FORSS, Highland   37 ND06
Close to the bridge is an old mill surrounded by trees, near the rapids of the Forss Water which flows N to Crosskirk Bay. Brims Ness is E of the bay and shelters the ruined 16th-c Brims Castle, now part of a farm. The tiny chapel of St Mary, possibly 12thc, lies to the NW.

BRIDGE OF GARRY, Tayside   34 NN96
River Garry flows under the bridge and joins the River Tummel a short distance to the S. A path leads to the junction of the two rivers. The new Loch Faskally was created by the construction of the Pitlochry dam across the River Tummel. Salmon can swim to the upper reaches of the river by way of a special ladder, and visitors can watch the fish from the Pitlochry hydro-electric station. The falls can be reached by road from Pitlochry over the new Aldour Bridge, thence along a new road by the W side of Loch Faskally. The Linn of Tummel (NTS) can be reached by footpath from the Bridge of Garry. A road W from the bridge leads to Loch Tummel, with the famous Queen's View (AA viewpoint) at its E end.

BRIDGE OF ORCHY, Strathclyde
29 NN23
Bridge of Orchy stands at the entrance to Glen Orchy, where the new Glencoe road leaves the line of the old one. The more recent road was built in 1935 and skirts the E side of Loch Tulla, where old pine trees stand as reminders of the once extensive Caledonian Forest. It avoids Black Mount by crossing Rannoch Moor, passing near Loch Bà. The old road climbs high over Black Mount. The steep, furrowed slopes of 3,524ft Ben Dorain dominate the countryside near the bridge, and 3,404ft Ben Achallader rises farther N on the E side of Loch Tulla. Ruined Achallader Castle stands in the shadow of the mountain on a rough by-road in Glen Tulla, which nurtures the ancient pines of Crannach. Glen Orchy runs SW from the bridge. A narrow road follows the river through the glen to join the main road to Oban.

BRIDGE OF WEIR, Strathclyde
44 NS36
Situated on Gryfe Water, Bridge of Weir is a residential district with golfing facilities. Tanning is carried out here, and the well-known Quarrier's Orphan Homes lie to the NW.

BROADFORD, Isle of Skye, Highland
32 NG62
Roads from the ferry ports of Armadale, Kylerhea, and Kyleakin meet at Broadford, making it a convenient touring centre for Skye. In Broadford Bay is the little island of Pabay, noted for its fossils. Granite screes of the Red Hills overlook the village. On top of 2,403ft Beinn na Caillich is the largest cairn on any hill in Scotland. Tradition has it that a 13th-c Norwegian princess who wished to have the winds of Norway blow over her grave lies beneath the cairn.

The Red Hills can be easily climbed from Corry, and the effort is amply repaid by beautiful views of S Skye and the hills of Wester Ross. Another wing of Skye can be explored by following the road from Broadford SW to Elgol. At the highest point above Broadford is An Sidhean, or the Fairy Hill, from which fine views of Strath Swordddale and the Red Hills can be enjoyed. From here the ruins of Mackinnon's house in Coire Chatachain can be reached on foot. Dr Johnson and James Boswell were entertained here in 1773.

Farther down the lochside the creeper-covered ruins of the old Church of Strath stand in a disused churchyard. This was where St Maolrubha set up his cell in the 7thc. The road to Elgol encircles the sea loch Slapin, which is dominated by two of the finest hills on Skye – 3,042ft Blaven and Clach Glas. Past Kilmaree a rocky path leads to the lovely beach and machair of Camasunary. The road descends through Elgol to the shore of the magnificent Loch Scavaig, where a jetty provides an embarkation point for launches leaving for the beautiful Loch Coruisk – the corrie of waters. Loch Coruisk impressed Scott and can be reached on foot from Camasunary, over a bridge, then along a path winding round attractive headlands. The coast road NW from Broadford to Sligachan offers fine views across the islands of Scalpay and Raasay.

BROADMEADOWS, Borders   26 NT43
Broadmeadows is a beautiful village near Yarrow Water, which flows through the Vale of Yarrow. Newark Castle stands 1m SE and was first mentioned in 1423. Newark, or New Wark, was so called to distinguish it from the older Auldwark Castle which once stood near by. It is a ruined tower house which had five storeys and was a royal hunting seat for the Forest of Ettrick. Royal Arms of James I are displayed by the W gable. A hundred prisoners from the Battle of Philiphaugh were shot in the courtyard by Leslie in 1645. The castle was the retreat of the widowed Anne, Duchess of Buccleuch, who was visited here by Scott and Wordsworth. It was to Anne that Scott addressed the lay of his minstrel in *Lay of the Last Minstrel.*

On the opposite side of Yarrow Water, in a lovely wooded reach, lies Foulshiels. A little ruined cottage still stands where Mungo Park the explorer was born in 1771. About 1m W of Broadmeadows is Hangingshaw, where the Hangingshaw Burn joins Yarrow Water. Remains of a castle belonging to the outlaw Murray can be seen near by. Minch Road is an old drover's track which runs NE from Broadmeadows towards Traquair.

BRODICK, Isle of Arran, Strathclyde
24 NS03
Brodick's correct name is Invercloy, and the village lies on sandy Brodick Bay. Steamers from Ardrossan on the mainland call at the pier. Brodick Castle (NTS) is the ancestral mansion of the Duke of Hamilton, and its mixture of ancient and comparatively modern styles is not displeasing. The centre block was built in the 16thc but the N wing may be of 14th-c origin. The W end and tower were built in 1844. The original castle was seized by Edward I, and later garrisoned by Cromwell, whose soldiers were massacred by the islanders. Brodick Castle's 600-acre grounds include a formal walled garden laid out in 1710.

The peak of 2,866ft Goat Fell (NTS), Arran's highest point, dominates Brodick Bay. Glen Rosa, the SW ridge of 2,618ft Cir Mhor, the Rosa pinnacle, and the nearby a'Chir ridge offer some of Scotland's finest rock climbing and ridge walking country. There are easier routes to the summits for the less strenuous. Caisteal Abhail (Peak of the Castles) rises to 2,817ft; this, Beinn Tarsuinn, and Beinn Nuis all offer wonderful opportunities to climbers. The String Road SW of Brodick crosses the island, passing through Glen Shurig and reaching the W coast at Blackwaterfoot. Fine views can be enjoyed from high ground on the way.

A road branches W from the String Road after Glaister and passes within sight of the Standing Stones of Tormore, where the remains of some ten circles survive S of Machrie Water. The Glen Rosa valley N of Brodick offers wonderful scenery, and walkers can reach Glen Sannox and Sannox after climbing a col at the head of Glen Rosa. Although the road S from Brodick to Lamlash runs inland, a path with beautiful views follows round the low Clauchland Hills and borders the coast.

BRODIE, Grampian   34 NH95
Imposing Brodie Castle, seat of the ancient family of Brodie, stands just N of the Muckle Water. The latter flows E to Findhorn Bay.

BRORA, Highland   37 NC90
A thriving golf and fishing resort on a river of the same name, Brora is surrounded by magnificent mountain and moorland scenery. The rocky coastline is indented by attractive sandy bays. There are many Pictish remains in the area, and 4m NE is the Kintradwell broch, a drystone tower which was used as a fortification by the Picts between 200BC and AD50. The River Brora flows from Loch Brora, over which hangs the 700ft-high Carrol Rock. Near the head of the loch stands the Pictish Cole Castle. Brora Bridge was the old county of Sutherland's only bridge prior to Telford's 18th-c road making, and a coal mine opened in 1598 and recently closed was the only one in the N of Scotland. Uppat House dates from the 18thc and lies 3m SW of Brora.

BROUGHTON, Borders   26 NT13
Biggar Water and the Broughton Burn unite here to flow into the Tweed SE of the village. Beside the ruined old church in the cemetery is a restored vault which is thought to be the remains of a cell founded in the 7thc by St Llolan, a Pictish saint. John Buchan (Lord Tweedsmuir) spent many holidays in Broughton, and Murray of Broughton once lived in the former house of Broughton Place. This has now been rebuilt. Murray of Broughton was secretary to Prince Charles Edward in 1745, and was later captured. He turned King's Evidence and eventually died in England.

Claypotts Castle, perhaps the best 16th-c tower-house extant.

BROUGHTY FERRY, Tayside   31 NO43
A popular holiday resort and a residential suburb of Dundee, Broughty Ferry was built around the cottages of an old fishing village. Broughty Castle (AM), a 15th-c tower on a rocky headland, was restored in 1860 and now houses a whaling museum. Claypotts Castle (AM) is one of the most complete examples of an old tower house extant. Once the home of James Graham of Claverhouse, it bears the dates 1569 and 1588 and was forfeited to the Douglases in 1689. Claypott's angle towers display crow-stepped gables, and there is a gunport in the kitchen. Part of the castle now houses a museum.

BROW, Dumfries and Galloway 25 NY06
Brow was once a small watering place and is situated on an inlet of the Solway Firth. The Brow Well stands on the B725, 1m SW of Ruthwell Church. It was visited by Burns a week before his death in 1796.

BROXBURN, Lothian   31 NT67
The Battle of Dunbar was fought in 1650 to the SE of Broxburn, just off the present A1 road. Cromwell defeated Leslie and the Covenanters, and later in 1950 a stone was erected to commemorate the battle. White Sands picnic area lies on the coast to the E, near Barn's Ness lighthouse. A restored kiln stands nearby.

BROXBURN, Lothian   46 NT07
Once a shale-mining village, this town lies SE of the curious Solar Stone at Kirkhill Farm. This was erected in the 18thc by the 11th Earl of Buchan, founder of the Society of Antiquaries in Scotland.

BUCCLEUCH, Borders   26 NT31
The Dukes of Buccleuch took their name from the tower which once stood near Buccleuch Farm.

BUCHAN, Grampian   35
This district of the new Grampian county is almost completely flat and rather bleak. Mormond Hill, with its carved white horse and stags, is a prominent feature of the landscape. The fishing ports of Fraserburgh and Peterhead lie on a stretch of coastline

which is changing under the influence of the North-Sea oil industry. Buchan Ness lies S of Peterhead and is the farthest E point in Scotland. Its lighthouse was erected in 1827. The River Deveron forms the W boundary of Buchan for a few miles, and the River Ythan flows along the S boundary. Magnificent Fyvie Castle stands on the River Ythan, 24m W of Peterhead.

The Bullers of Buchan, a vast 200ft-deep chasm in the cliffs, was pronounced by Dr Johnson to be a 'rock perpendicularly tubulated' in 'which no man can see with indifference' when he visited the Bullers by boat in 1773. The Bullers lie 1m NE of Cruden Bay. Parts of this coastal area are also being developed for the production of North-Sea oil and gas.

BUCHLYVIE, Central   45 NS59
Hand-weaving is a craft still practised in the area. Some 2m W is 18th-c Auchentroig House, which is associated with Rob Roy.

BUCKHAVEN, Fife   47 NT39
Quaint Buckhaven, once a ferry port and fishing centre, has the old-world corners and stepped streets common to many Fife villages. Its church was brought in sections from St Andrews by local fishermen and re-erected.

BUCKIE, Grampian   35 NJ46
Situated in Spey Bay, Buckie is an important fishing town with a good harbour. A number of fishing villages, including lovely Findochty and Portnockie, nestle in the cliffs on the coast to the E.

BUNESSAN, Isle of Mull, Strathclyde 28 NM32
This village lies on the Ross of Mull peninsula, well known for its granite quarries. The latter are no longer worked. Some 5m E along the road is Fionnphort, where a passenger ferry connects with Iona. Tiny Erroid Island lies in the Sound of Iona, S of Fionnphort. Robert Louis Stevenson writes about the island in *Kidnapped*, and Dr Johnston visited it in 1773. The sea loch of Na Lathaich lies N of Bunessan, with Loch Assapol to the SE.

BURGHEAD, Grampian   34 NJ16
Ptolemy's *Alata Castra* may have been here, and a rampart known as Broch

Bailies can be seen near by. The fishing village boasts a harbour and lighthouse, and stands on the E horn of Burghead Bay. Burghead's local landmark is its 550ft BBC radio transmitter post, set up in 1936. Burghead still carries out its old custom of Burning the Clavie on Old Yule Night, 11 January. A tar-filled barrel is set alight and rolled down Dorrie Hill in order to ward off evil spirits. Burghead Well (AM) is of interest.

BURNHAVEN, Grampian   35 NK14
Burnhaven village was built during the last century and lies adjacent to Peterhead Prison, between the bays of Peterhead and Sandford. To the S across Sandford Bay is Buchan Ness, Scotland's farthest E point of land.

BURNHOUSES, Borders   31 NT75
Cockburn Law rises to the N of this hamlet, with Whiteadder Water wandering to the E.

BURNMOUTH, Borders   31 NT96
Situated 3m N of the Border, this delightful fishing village lies at the foot of sandstone cliffs with Ross Point to the S. Beyond Ross Bay to the N is a rocky stretch of coast which leads to Nestends, facing Hare Point across the Eye estuary. Two Border treaties were signed at Burnmouth, one in 1384 and the other in 1497.

BURNS COUNTRY, THE
The great poet Robert Burns drew much of his inspiration from the Ayrshire – now Dumfries and Galloway – landscape. Its towns and villages – Alloway, Kirkoswald, Ayr, Mauchline, Tarbolton – have been immortalized in his verses. He was born at Alloway in 1759. His birthplace has been preserved, and a museum now adjoins the house. This is the start of the Burns Heritage Trail which may be followed to trace the places linked with him. Ayr has another Burns museum at the thatched Tam O'Shanter Inn in the High Street, and Burns' House in Mauchline was where he took a room for Jean Armour in 1788. The latter can be visited, as can Gavin Hamilton's House where he married Jean. Auld Nanse Tinnock's, where a Burns exhibition has been set up, stands near by.

Mossgiel Farm was rebuilt in 1859 and lies near Mauchline; it was here that Burns wrote much of his first volume of poems between 1784 and 1788. Prior to this, from 1777 onwards, the Burns family lived at Lochlea Farm 2m SE of Mossgiel. Burns moved to Dumfries in 1791 and worked there for five years until his death in 1796. The house where the family lived in Mill Vennel (now renamed as Burns Street) can be visited. Burns and members of his family are buried at St Michael's churchyard in Dumfries. Near Auldgirth is Ellisland, the farm which he built with his own hands and where he wrote *Tam O'Shanter* and other poems.

BURNTISLAND, Fife   47 NT28
Burntisland is a Royal Burgh and port which was once occupied by Cromwell and is noted for its parish church of St Columba. This was built in 1592, probably to a Dutch design, and is square with an octagonal tower which was added in 1749. It was at a meeting in this church in 1601 that the General Assembly proposed the Authorized Version of the Bible, which was published

ten years later. An outside staircase gives access to the Sailors' Loft. Inside is a magistrate's pew of 1606, plus special seats marked for the various town guilds. Somerville Street displays several 17th-c houses. Burntisland offers a sandy beach and safe bathing, and is overlooked by the 632ft Binn. Granton stands 5m across the Firth of Forth. Rossend Castle stands on the N shore of the Firth of Forth and was built in the 12thc. The building was extended in the 14th and 16thc, and it was here that Chastelard – a young French admirer of Mary Queen of Scots was arrested and executed. Cromwell captured the castle without too much damage in 1651. This building is not open to the public.

BUTE, ISLE OF, Strathclyde 29 NS06
The 15m-long island of Bute nestles at the foot of the hilly Cowal peninsula, from which it is separated by a beautiful stretch of water known as the Kyles of Bute. Cattle used to be made to swim from Colintraive on the mainland to Rhubodach on Bute; now a car ferry makes the crossing. To the S is the Sound of Bute, in which lies the tiny island of Inch Marnock. The sound divides the Isle of Bute from the larger island of Arran.

The N of the island is hilly, the S flatter and more fertile. Rothesay, the principal town, is one of Scotland's most popular resorts and can be reached by steamer from several Clyde ports. It has sandy bays for bathing, and the remains of a 13th-c castle (AM) are surrounded by a deep moat. The castle was destroyed by Cromwell in the 17thc. Remains of St Mary's Chapel (AM) are of interest.

BUTTERSTONE, Tayside 34 NO04
The three small lochs of Butterstone, Lowes, and Craignish lie to the SW, and N the exposed moors of the Forest of Clunie include the lonely lochs Ordie and Benachally. The Loch of the Lowes is now a Scottish Wildlife Trust nature reserve. Ospreys have nested here since 1972 and may be seen from a hide.

CABRACH, Grampian 35 NJ32
Cabrach village lies on the fine road to Dufftown. This highway continues NW over the hills, crossing the Deveron valley and the Glacks of Balloch Pass (1,197ft-high). To the SE is the 2,368ft Buck of Cabrach, with the lonely source of the River Deveron lying in the hills W of the mountain.

CADDONFOOT, Borders 26 NT43
Caddon Water flows into the Tweed W of this village, which lies in the wooded Tweed valley between Craig Hill to the S and a group that includes Meigle to the NE.

CAERLAVEROCK, Dumfries and Galloway 25 NY06
Robert Paterson (1715–1801), the *Old Mortality* immortalized by Scott, lies buried in a churchyard which is situated 1m NW of Bankend off a by-road near Lochar Water. Caerlaverock is thought to be the Ellangowan of Scott's *Guy Mannering*. The 6,200-acre Caerlaverock Estate is now a nature reserve, with saltmarsh and a sandy foreshore between the River Nith and Lochar Water – a winter haunt of wildfowl.

Caerlaverock Castle (AM), a Maxwell stronghold, lies off the B725 3m S of Caerlaverock. The castle was first mentioned in 1220, but dates mainly from the 15thc. Its stormy history includes an attack by Edward I in 1300,

and a thirteen-week siege in 1638. After this the castle capitulated to the Covenanters. It has a triangular enclosure with round towers, and the heavy machicolation is of 15th-c date. Over the gateway between two splendid towers is the Maxwell crest and motto. The interior was reconstructed, starting in 1638, as a Renaissance mansion.

CAIRNBAAN, Strathclyde 28 NR89
This village lies midway along the Crinan Canal. About 200yds N of the hotel are two prehistoric cup-and-ring marked rocks (AM). The ruined hill-fort of Dunadd (AM), once the capital of Dalriada, Kingdom of the Scots, lies 1m SE. Numerous bronze age stone circles can be seen in the vicinity.

CAIRNDOW, Strathclyde 29 NN11
Situated at the W end of Glen Kinglas on the shores of upper Loch Fyne, Cairndow is overlooked by 2,658ft Binnein an Fhidhleir. To the N the River Fyne flows through Glen Fyne into the loch. Impressive Eagle's Falls are 1,278ft high and can be seen to the E of Glen Fyne. Ardkinglas House, a mansion built by Sir Robert Lorimer, lies 1m SW.

CAIRNGORMS RANGE
The granite tops of the Cairngorms thrust their massive peaks toward the sky in a rugged, jagged line between the valleys of the Spey and Dee. Nine summits in the range top 4,000ft, with at least a dozen more at over 3,000ft. The mountains face across the Dee Valley towards the well-known mountain of Lochnagar, King of the Mounth group. Four of the best-defined high peaks in the Cairngorms are: 4,296ft Ben Macdhui, Scotland's second highest mountain and one with a view-indicator on the summit; 4,248ft Braeriach, rising from the 2m-long Garbh Choire cliffs – the source of the River Dee – and overlooking the pass of Lairig Ghru; 4,241ft Cairn Toul, prominent in the W from Braemar; and 4,084ft Cairn Gorm, the gently-rounded shape of which has given its name to the entire range.

Cairn Gorm has the most accessible summit. The road from Aviemore ends at a car park, from which the Cairngorm chairlift takes visitors to within 150yds of the summit. At these heights the weather can become sub-arctic within minutes, even in summer, so warm clothes, food, a compass, and a map are essential to anyone planning a walk in the mountains. Near Cairn Gorm is 3,983ft Cairn Lochan, on the edge of wild Coire-an-t-Sneachda, overlooked by the spectacular Fiacaill Ridge. Cairn Gorm and 3,883ft Beinn Mheadoin both overlook gloomy Loch Avon, with the Shelter Stone at the W end of the loch. Ben Macdui, Braeriach, and Cairn Toul can be climbed by the energetic. Their summits offer good views of Loch Avon to the NE, and glimpses of Caithness and the distant Atlantic. The climbing routes pass gigantic boulders, drifts of snow, and spectacular waterfalls. Tiny Loch Etchachan, frozen solid for over half the year, lies to the SW of Loch Avon.

Wild Loch Einich lies deep below the great cliffs of 3,658ft Sgoran Dubh on the W fringe of the range, overlooked by the bare plateau known as the Great Moss, or Am Moine Mhor, sheltering the tiny Lochan nan Cnapan. Among the lesser peaks are 3,843ft Ben Avon in the extreme E, overlooking the great Slochd

Mor rift and the waters of the Upper Avon; 3,924ft and 3,860ft Bheinn a'Bhuird, rising above Glen Quoich; 3,788ft Derry Cairngorm between Glen Derry and Glen Lui Beg; and 3,797ft Beinn Bhrotain to the W of Glen Dee. One of the finest panoramas of the range can be enjoyed from the summit of 2,702ft Geal Charn Mor, to the NW of Lynwilg.

The two main passes through the Cairngorms are Lairig Ghru and the lesser-known Lairig an Laoigh, both ancient rights of way which were formerly used by cattle drovers. The 20m walk through Lairig Ghru takes nine hours in fine weather and will test the most experienced walker, but it presents some of Europe's loneliest and most striking scenery as a reward. More than 600 acres of this rugged country make up the Cairngorm national nature reserve – the largest in Britain. Golden eagles, capercaillize, ptarmigan, deer, and wildcats all live here. Access to most of the area is unrestricted, though local lairds impose some restrictions on walkers and climbers in the grouse-shooting and deer-stalking seasons.

Aviemore is a good centre for visiting the 12,500-acres Glen More forest park in the foothills of the Cairngorms. The park offers unparalleled mountain walks and the best ski-ing in Britain. There are easy, intermediate, and difficult runs on Coire na Ciste, Coire Cas, and White Lady, plus several good nursery slopes. Snow lies from November to late May; summer ski-ing is possible around the summit of Cairn Gorm.

Aviemore, Carrbridge, and Grantown-on-Spey are the main Cairngorm ski resorts. The forest park includes Loch Morlich – one of Scotland's most beautiful inland lochs, lying to the NE of Rothiemurchus Forest where there are scanty survivors of the once-vast Caledonian Forest which covered the highlands. Reindeer have been re-introduced from Lapland and roam the mountain slopes around Loch Morlich. The old name for the Cairngorms was the Monadruadh or Red Mountains, as opposed to the much lower Monadhliath or Grey Mountains which rise to the W of the Spey valley. Peat-coloured, transparent quartz crystals found in the granite Cairngorms are themselves known as Cairngorms and often set in jewellery.

CAIRN O' MOUNTH, Grampian 35 NO68
A well-known pass through the E Grampians from Banchory to Fettercairn, Cairn o' Mounth is likely to be blocked by snow in winter. Gradients on the ascent from Fettercairn reach 1 in $5\frac{1}{2}$, and on the descent 1 in $6\frac{1}{2}$. The 1,475ft summit of the pass is 5m N of Fettercairn and affords fine views. Mount Battock rises to 2,555ft in the W, with Clachnaben to the N. The view E takes in the fertile Howe of the Mearns and the distant Kincardine coast. Edward I, Montrose, and Glaverhouse are all associated with the pass, and Macbeth used it when he fled N to Lumphanan across the Dee. Some 4m N of the summit, in the heart of the lovely, wooded Glen Dye, is a little bridge dated 1680 over Dye Water.

CAIRN RYAN, Dumfries and Galloway 24 NX06
Once known as Macherie, this town of whitewashed cottages lies on the shore

of Loch Ryan and was an important war-time port. Troopships called here and parts of Mulberry Harbour, the floating dock used in the D-Day invasion of Normandy in 1944, were assembled here. The Wig, a bay on the opposite shore of the loch, was a flying-boat base. In Cairn Ryan stands Lochryan, an 18th-c house standing in beautiful gardens. To the N on Leight Moor is the so-called Taxing Stone, supposedly marking the tomb of an ancient Scottish king murdered in 741. Beyond Leight Moor the lovely Glen App guides the Water of App into Loch Ryan at Finnart Bay.

CAIRNWELL PASS, Grampian, Tayside 34 NO17

The 2,199ft summit of Cairnwell Pass makes it the highest main road in Britain; it forms part of the original military road linking Coupar Angus with Braemar, built in the mid-18thc by General Caulfeild, one of roadbuilder Wade's successors. The Devil's Elbow section was once notorious for its hairpin bends, but has recently been bypassed by an easier road. The 3,059ft Cairnwell lies W and 3,502ft Glas Maol to the E, dominating the pass. Below the summit, S towards Blairgowrie, is the well-known Devil's Elbow at 1,950ft. There are ski-ing facilities in the area, with a chairlift up the Cairnwell from the W side of the road, and a draglift on the E side of the road which connects with Meall Odhar tow up to 3,019ft. The N descent from the summit of the pass leads through Glen Clunie to Braemar.

The long, 3,318ft Monega Pass is the highest right-of-way in Scotland and crosses the E shoulder of Glas Maol. This allows walkers access to the head of Glen Isla and Kirkton of Glenisla. To the NE lies an unbroken chain of mountains, including Glas Maol and 3,484ft Cairn na Glasha, and Lochnagar in the White Mounth range.

CALDERCRUIX, Strathclyde 46 NS86

Hillend Reservoir lies to the E of Caldercruix.

CALEDONIAN CANAL

This canal is a magnificent piece of 19th-c engineering which was begun in 1803 by Thomas Telford and opened 44 years later in 1847. It was a wonder of its time, and provided sailing boats which passed between the Irish and North Seas with a fast and safe alternative passage to the stormy N route round Cape Wrath. However, the 60½m waterway, with its 22m of canal, became obsolete with the coming of large steamships. Its main craft today are fishing boats and pleasure steamers. The canal cost 1¼ million pounds to build and virtually splits Scotland in two, running along the Great Glen of Alban and linking Lochs Linnhe, Lochy, Oich, and Ness with the Moray Firth. The 29 locks are still solid and smooth in operation; eight locks at Corpach are called Neptune's Staircase (see page 175).

CALGARY, Isle of Mull, Strathclyde 28 NM35

Lying on Calgary Bay at the NW end of Mull, Calgary offers fine sands for bathing. Calgary in Canada is said to have been founded by emigrants from this village, and the poet Campbell once lived to the N near lonely Callach Point. Some of his works were composed there. The scattered Treshnish Islands

can be seen to the SW, with the islands of Coll and Tiree farther away to the W.

*CALLANDER, Central 30 NN60

A resort and touring centre where the Rivers Teith and Leny meet, Callander makes a good starting point for tours of the Trossachs and Loch Katrine. Callander is the 'Tannochbrae' of television's Dr Finlay's Casebook. From 2,875ft Ben Ledi, which overlooks the town from the NW, the view on a clear day extends 2m N to Ben Lawers, and 40m SE to the Forth Bridge.

Scott was a frequent visitor to Callander, and the Roman Camp Hotel has associations with J M Barrie. A sundial dated 1753 can be seen in South Church Street. A road NW from Callander leads through the beautiful Pass of Leny, where the River Leny rushes through a narrow gorge. St Bride's Chapel, partly restored in memory of Scott, stands beyond the pass on the way to Loch Lubnaig. Another road runs 6m W from Callander along the N bank of Loch Vennachar to Brig o' Turk, a lovely village which has long attracted artists. An early 19th-c bridge over Finglas (or Turk) Water carries the main road on towards Loch Katrine, which inspired Scott's Lady of the Lake. Ellen's Isle on Loch Katrine is named after Ellen Douglas, the lady in Scott's poem.

From the Middle Ages to the early 18thc the MacGregors used the island to hide cattle they had stolen in raids on the Lowlands. There is no road round Loch Katrine, but a steamer trip along its 9m-length or a short walk from the pier to the Pass of Achray gives some idea of the rugged splendour of the Trossachs. To the NE of Callander are the Falls of Bracklinn – on Keltie Water – from which a path continues through the hills to lonely Glen Artney and Comrie.

CAMASNACROISE, Highland 29 NM85

Camasnacroise village lies on an inlet of Loch Linnhe, with the tiny Loch a' Choire a little to the W and 2,800ft Creach Bheinn rising to the N at the head of Glenalmadale. Fine views from the village take in the island of Lismore and the Appin coast as far as the distant Lochaber Mountains. A road leading NE into the hills forks after about 6m, with the N branch leading to the shores of Loch Sunart and the SW branch continuing through Gleann Geal towards Morven country and the shores of the Sound of Mull at Lochaline.

CAMBUSLANG, Strathclyde 45 NS66

Extensive iron and steel works operate in this town, but SW lies the wooded public park and viewpoint of Cathkin Braes. Gilbertfield, a 17th-c house, stands off the Hamilton Road to the SE.

CAMBUS O'MAY, Grampian 35 NO49

The wooded River Dee flows near Cambus o'May, and the small lochs of Kinord and Davan lie to the NE. Loch Davan is an ancient crannog or lake-dwelling. Across the Dee to the S is Ballaterach, the farmhouse where Lord Byron spent part of his youth. Culblean Hill stands to the N of the hamlet and is the site where the Battle of Culblean was fought in 1335. A commemorative stone was erected here in 1956 by the Deeside Field Club. Culblean Hill displays a curious rock chamber known as The Vat. Morven, the highest mountain in the district, rises to 2,862ft beyond the hill.

CAMELON, Central 46 NS88

A Roman town once stood here, and the famous Antonine Wall ran to the S of the settlement. Overlooking the River Carron to the N is the site of a double Roman camp. Camelon is now an area of industrial development.

CAMPBELTOWN, Strathclyde 24 NR72

Chief centre in the long peninsula of Kintyre, Campbeltown lies on Campbeltown Loch and has a rocky beach used for sea angling. Herring, whitefish, and lobsters are landed at the harbour. The town is a Royal Burgh and was once known as Kilkerran. Its facilities include a steamer pier. Offshore lies the island and lighthouse of Davaar, which can be reached across a bank of shingle or by boat. In a cave on the island, illuminated only by a shaft of light from a hole in the rock, is a Crucifixion scene painted by Archibald Mackinnon in 1887 and retouched by a local artist in 1956. At the Old Quay Head of the town stands Campbeltown Cross, a richly-carved Celtic cross dating from c1500.

About 1m SE is the ruined castle of Kilkerran. St Kieran's Cave, 2m SE of town near Achinhoan Head and E of the coast road, may be the earliest Christian chapel in Scotland. It is situated 25ft above high-water mark. Machrihanish Airport, linking with Glasgow (Abbotsinch Airport) and Islay, lies to the W of the town. The village of Machrihanish, with its famous golf course, lies farther W on the W coast of the peninsula.

CAMPSIE, Strathclyde 45 NS67

Campsie village stands at the foot of Campsie Glen, surrounded by the Campsie Fells. Crow Road, connecting Lennoxtown with Fintry, runs through the glen and affords fine views along the way. Earl's Seat lies NW of the village and is also a good point from which to view the fells.

CAMUSNAGAUL, Highland 33 NN07

At the head of Loch Linnhe, on its W shore and near the junction with Loch Eil, Camusnagaul stands on a narrow, winding road linking Kinlocheil with Ardgow. The view across the loch to Fort William takes in the 4,406ft bulk of Ben Nevis. A fine hilly ridge lying to the W of Camusnagaul includes 2,527ft Stob Choire a' Chearcail, overlooking the junction of Cona Glen with Glen Scaddle.

CANISBAY, Highland 37 ND37

Scotland's farthest N mainland church overlooks Gills Bay here. It is of mainly 18th-c origin and preserves the gravestone of Jan Groot in the S wall. An old mill lies near by. Jan Groot came to this part of Scotland from Holland with his two brothers in the reign of James IV. The Groots increased until there were eight families of the same name, and a question of precedency arose. To satisfy them all Jan Groot built an octagonal house, with a door to each side, and an octagonal table inside. The house gave the name John o' Groats to the lonely outpost a little to the E; it no longer stands but its site is marked by a mound and flagstaff.

CANNICH, Highland 33 NH33

Situated in a beautiful wooded setting, Cannich lies at the SW end of Strath Glass near the union of the Rivers Cannich and Glass. The two exceptionally

Entries marked * are the starting point of drives included in the Day Drive section of the book (pages 95 to 160).

lovely glens of Affric and Cannich run W of the village. A hydro-electric scheme operates in the Cannich area, its power station being sited at Fasnakyle. The road through Glen Affric passes near Fasnakyle. Prince Charles Edward wandered in the woods round here when he was a fugitive in 1746.

The road runs through Chisholm's Pass, and after passing the Dog Fall emerges by the shores of Loch Benevean amid birch and pine trees. The loch has been dammed at its E end, raising the level of the water and producing little islets. The road continues along the N shores of the loch, with views S towards the extensive Guisachan Forest. Scenery becomes more and more magnificent as Loch Affric is approached. Sgurr na Lapaich rises to 3,401ft above the loch, with 3,862ft Mam Sodhail and 2,877ft Carn Eige beyond. Though the road ends here, lonely tracks continue W beyond the loch, passing under the slopes of 3,771ft Sgurr nan Ceathreamhnan and heading towards Croe Bridge near Loch Duich. The road through Glen Cannich leaves Cannich and passes NW under the slopes of 2,119ft Beinn Acharain before entering densely-wooded hill country. Following the River Cannich all the way, the road then skirts tiny Loch Carrie and reaches Loch Mullardoch, the E end of which is restricted by a main dam for the Cannich hydro-electricity scheme.

The waters of the loch pass along a tunnel aqueduct to Loch Benevean. To the NW of Loch Mullardock are the bare summits of 3,773ft Sgurr na Lapaich and 3,370ft An Riabhachan. Long tracks lead W from the loch, passing Loch Lungard and eventually reaching Glen Elchaig and Loch Long. Telford built a road to the E which links Cannich with Drumnadrochit on Loch Ness.

CANONBIE, Dumfries and Galloway 26 NY37

Standing on the River Esk 3m N of the Border, Canonbie has an interesting old coaching inn and was the site of the Priory of Canonbie – destroyed by the English in 1542. The river is joined a little to the S by Liddell Water. This flows along the long valley of Liddesdale, associated with Dandie Dinmont in Scott's *Guy Mannering*, and forms the Border boundary for some 5m. The Esk flows towards the Solway Firth and used to form the Border boundary farther W. A tract of land between the Rivers Sark and Esk became known as the Debateable Land, an area of lawlessness where ground was held by force of arms.

In 1552 the Scots Dyke was constructed to form the new boundary and end the troubles. Remains of this earth and stone wall can be seen on the English side. A Roman Camp 2m N of Canonbie is situated N of Gilnockie station. Beyond Gilnockie Bridge, 2m NNW on the main Langholm road, is Hollows or Holehouse Tower. This was once the home of the 16th-c Border reiver, or freebooter, Johnny Armstrong. Hollows Tower is of 16th-c date and its walls are 6ft thick. Johnny Armstrong had another home near Gilnockie Bridge, but this no longer stands.

CAPE WRATH, Highland 36 NC27

Extreme NW point of the Scottish mainland, Cape Wrath is named after the Viking word *hvraf* – a turning point.

Inscribed 18th-c sundial in Callander's South Church Street.

This was where the Vikings turned S on their way to the Hebrides, which they held from the 9th to 13thc. The land stretching out to the isolated cape is lonely and barren, with few signs of human life and few roads. A pedestrian ferry crosses the Kyle of Durness 10m SE of the cape. There is no way to reach the cape by car, but in summer a minibus service runs several times a day across lonely moorland known as The Parph between the ferry and the lighthouse at the cape.

The road passes within 2m of the cliffs at Cleit Dhubb, which rise 850ft out of the sea and are the highest on the mainland of Britain. Scrishven rises to 1,216ft behind, and 1,498ft Fashven stands farther S. The lighthouse was built in 1828 and faces across The Minch towards Lewis in the Outer Hebrides. The islands of North Rona and Sula Sgeir lie 50m out into the Atlantic and both form national nature reserves. They foster two rare species – the Atlantic grey seal and Leach's fork-tailed petrel.

CAPUTH, Tayside 30 NO03

A bridge spans the River Tay at Caputh. The Roman Camp of Inchtuthil is 3m E in the private grounds of Delvine House. A 7-ton hoard of Roman nails has been unearthed here, the largest nail being 16in long. Across the river to the W is 16th-c and later Murthly Castle, with huge specimens of Sitka Spruce and Douglas Firs in the parkland.

CARBERRY HILL, Lothian 47 NT36

Mary Queen of Scots surrendered to the Lords of the Congregation after Bothwell had fled, as a result of the battle fought here in 1567. Mary was taken away to Loch Leven Castle. To the W is Carberry Tower, rebuilt in 1830, but still with its old tower. It is now used as a Church of Scotland youth leadership training and conference centre.

CARBOST, Isle of Skye, Highland 32 NG33

The Talisker Whisky Distillery is situated here on the W shores of Loch Harport. The little road S leads through Glen Eynort, to a loch of the same name, through landscape which is being slowly changed by afforestation. Another little road runs W over the hills to Talisker Bay, and the road to Carbost

from Sligachan runs N along the W shores of Loch Harport, almost to Ardtreck Point. Harris-Tweed weavers work near by at Port na Long.

CARDROSS, Strathclyde 44 NS37

Robert the Bruce died in 1329 at the castle which once stood 3m E of the village. Cardross parish church, where the grandfather of the historian Macaulay once ministered, was destroyed in the second world war. Facing the Clyde is Ardoch House, an 18th-c mansion which was once the home of author and explorer R B Cunninghame-Graham. Kilmahew lies N of Cardross and features a ruined castle and a 15th-c chapel which was restored in 1955. The latter is now St Peter's College for RC priests.

CARFIN, Strathclyde 45 NS75

The population of this village is almost entirely of Irish extraction. The Garfin Grotto was dedicated to Our Lady of Lourdes in 1922, and is visited by thousands of pilgrims every year. Two fragments of rock from Lourdes have been set in a marble block from Iona above the pool of holy water. Several shrines stand in lovely gardens by the Grotto.

CARFRAEMILL, Borders 31 NT55

Situated in Lauderdale, Carfraemill is bordered by the Lammermuir Hills to the NE. The Leader Water flows S on its way to join the Tweed, and the Edinburgh road climbs steadily NW to Soutra Hill, on the line of an ancient pilgrims' way. Soutra Hill affords fine views from the Eildon Hills in the S to the Ochils beyond the Forth estuary, taking in Arthur's Seat which overlooks the city of Edinburgh.

CARLOPS, Borders 47 NT15

A Pentland-Hills village on the North Esk River, Carlops is a well-known inland resort overshadowed by a curious rocky outcrop. The village has associations with Allan Ramsay, author of the pastoral play *The Gentle Shepherd*. Following the river is a path which leads into the hills past North Esk Reservoir to the Bore Stone. From here the East Cairn Hill, with its fine views, can be climbed.

CARLUKE, Strathclyde 46 NS85

Fertile Clyde Valley lies beneath this town, and the area has been used for fruit growing as far back as the 12thc. Moorland lies to the E. The tower of the former 18th-c church still stands, and 2m SW is Waygateshaw, built in the 16th and 17thc. Some 2m NW, near Milton Lockhart farm, a plaque marks the site of Miltonhead, birthplace of Major General William Roy. Roy died in 1790 and is considered the father of the Ordnance Survey. The Ordnance Survey of Great Britain grew from a military map drawn by the general between 1747 and 1755.

CARNACH, Highland   *29 NN05*
Carnach is where the road from Glen Coe divides, with the E fork continuing right the way round Loch Leven to North Ballachulish. The W fork leads to Ballachulish, where a ferry connects with North Ballachulish, considerably shortening the journey to Fort William. Across the entrance to Glen Coe the conical 2,430ft Pap of Glencoe can be seen. This is an outlier of the long high ridge of Aonach Eagach, and faces 3,766ft Bidean nam Bian across the deep rift of Glen Coe.

CARNOUSTIE, Tayside   *31 NO53*
The local championship golf course is considered by professionals to be one of the world's leading courses. Carnoustie has another well-known course – the Burnside – plus fine beaches offering good bathing and lovely coastal walks. The Barry Links extend S to Buddon Ness, a military training area, and comprise deep sand dunes which are the result of red sandstone being eroded by the weather and sea over the ages.

CARNWATH, Strathclyde   *30 NS94*
Only the aisle remains of Carnwath's *c*1424 church, and the shaft of the 16th-c market cross gives various road distances. One of these includes the mileage to Ayr, misspelt Air. An old drove road called Lang Whang leads NE across the lower slopes of the Pentland Hills towards Edinburgh. Traces of the Somerville stronghold of Cowthally Castle exist 2m NW of Carnwath. This originally comprised three separate towers, and James IV, V, and VI were all entertained within the castle walls.

CARRADALE, Strathclyde   *24 NR83*
A small Kintyre resort with a fishing harbour and sheltered bay, Carradale

stands opposite the Isle of Arran. The ruins of Aird Castle lie near the pier, and a vitrified oval fort, with its bricks and stones fused into a glassy substance by fire, stands at Carradale Point. The latter is a narrow peninsula which is sometimes isolated from the island at high water. Beinn an Tuirc rises to a height of 1,491ft inland and is the highest point on Kintyre.

CARRBRIDGE, Highland   *34 NH92*
A modern bridge standing beside the arch of a bridge dating from 1715 spans the River Dulnain at this pleasant Highland resort and winter-sports centre. The older structure was built by the Earl of Seafield for the use of funeral parties to Duthil. The Landmark visitor centre has an exciting audio-visual exhibition which covers topics including 10,000 years of Highland history. A narrow moorland road 1½m NE turns N from the Grantown-on-Spey road, and in 7m a little road branches E to the Lochindorb in the centre of the wild and lonely Dava Moor.

Lochindorb has a romantic island castle, now in ruins, which was one of the strongholds of the Wolf of Badenoch, who terrorized the Lowlands of Moray in the 14thc. About 2½m W of Carrbridge is Wade's 1728 Sluggan Bridge, which carries one of his military roads over the river. Remains of Inverlaidnan House, where Prince Charles Edward spent the night on the way to Culloden in 1746, stand about 1m W of Sluggan Bridge.

CARRICK, Strathclyde   *24 NX29*
Lying to the S of the River Doon, Carrick was once part of the district of Galloway, which was administered by hereditary stewards up until 1747. The best scenery is to be found in the SE where the foothills of the Galloway Highlands extend over the border. Carrick's best-known hills are 2,562ft Kirrereoch, and 2,520ft Shalloch on Minnoch, both lying in the N part of the vast Glen Trool forest park. Two narrow and hilly moorland roads lead N from Rowantree; the E road leads over the hills past Shalloch on Minnoch towards Straiton in the valley of the Water of Girvan, and the W road climbs over the Nick o' the Balloch Pass. A lovely stretch of coastline lies between Ballantrae and Girvan, including picturesque Kennedy's Pass.

Built in 1715, the arch of the old Dulnain bridge still stands beside the new structure at Carrbridge.

CARRINGTON, Lothian   *47 NT36*
A little cruciform church at Carrington carries an ogee-capped tower and dates from 1710.

CARRONBRIDGE, Dumfries and Galloway   *25 NX89*
This Nithsdale village lies a little NE of the point where Carron Water joins the River Nith. A road runs NE towards the lovely Dalveen Pass, which reaches a summit of 1,140ft and is shadowed by 1,998ft Comb Head, an outlier of the Lowther Hills. Morton Castle stands in a glen overlooking Morton Loch 2½m NE. Probably of 15th-c origin, the castle was occupied by Randolf, 1st Earl of Moray, as Regent for David II. It afterwards passed to the Douglases and is now a well-preserved ruin. Traces of Tibbers Castle can be seen W of the village, across the Nith.

CARSAIG, Isle of Mull, Strathclyde   *28 NM52*
Situated on the wild S shores of the island, Carsaig has beautiful rock scenery with cliffs which rise to nearly 1,000ft along the coast. To the SE lie the remarkable Carsaig Arches, natural tunnels in the basalt rock. The Nun's Cave, with carvings supposed to be the original designs of a Cross on Iona, lies to the E. The seaward end of Loch Buie, dominated at its head by 2,354ft Ben Buie, lies to the E of Carsaig Bay. The only road in the area leads N from Carsaig Bay and along Glen Leidle countryside that was used as a setting for the filming of *I Know Where I'm Going*.

CARSE OF GOWRIE, Tayside   *31 NO22*
This strip of fertile, level country lies between the Sidlaw Hills and the Firth of Tay. It is especially noted for its strawberries.

CARSETHORN, Dumfries and Galloway   *25 NX95*
Several 18th- and 19th-c fishermen's houses still stand near the little harbour on Carse Bay.

CARSPHAIRN, Dumfries and Galloway   *25 NX59*
This small Galloway village lies on the Water of Deugh between 2,612ft Cairnsmore of Carsphairn to the NE, and 2,688ft Corserine and 2,650ft Carlins Cairn to the SW. Knockgray Park, where a cairn indicates the place where the last wild deer in the Lowlands is said to have been slain, is situated E of the village. A prehistoric chambered cairn known as Cairn Avel lies S, and 3m SE in the Glenkens district is the man-made Kendoon Loch. Situated by the Moniave road, this forms part of the Galloway power scheme. The gorge known as Tinkler's Loup has been flooded.

Beyond this the High Bridge of Ken spans the Water of Ken, with the large Carsfad Dam further S. A track leading W from Carsphairn past the Woodhead lead mines gives access to Loch Doon – also part of the Galloway power scheme. The loch's former island castle (AM) has been carefully re-positioned on the W shore.

Farther W lies Carrick Forest, part of the vast Glen Trool forest park, with the lonely lochs Recar and Macaterick lying deep in the Galloway Hills. The remains of Lagwine Tower, home of the Macadams, lie NW of the village. The tower was burnt down before the famous road builder John Loudon Macadam was born.

CARSTAIRS, Strathclyde *30 NS94*
A rare 15th-c crucifixion stone is preserved in the parish church. Mouse Water winds N of the village on its way to join the Clyde, and to the E is the White Loch which is famous for curling matches. The Roman fort of Castledykes, stands S of the village, with the broad Clyde valley farther to the S.

CARTER BAR,
Northumberland, Borders *26 NT60*
Situated at 1,371ft in the Cheviot Hills of the Scottish/English border, Carter Bar is a favourite stopping place for people wishing to compare the two countries. Scotland seems the more inviting, with lush green pastures, red ploughed fields, and trim plantations stretching N, and the triple peaked Eildon Hills rising in the distance to the NW. About ½m NE is the spot where the Scottish Jeddarts beat the Redesdale men in the last great Border battle – the Redeswire Raid of 1575. The large Roman camp and earthworks of Chew Green lie to the E, just across the English border near the source of the River Coquet. The earliest Roman road into Scotland, the Dere Street of Agricola, crossed the Border near the camp and descended towards Oxnam. Traces of it can still be seen. Catcleugh Reservoir is 4m SE of Carter Bar across the Border, and measures over 1m in length and more than 78ft in depth.

CASTLEBAY, Western Isles *39 NL69*
See Hebrides, Outer.

CASTLECARY, Strathclyde *45 NS77*
One of Agricola's Roman forts, part of the great Antonine Wall (AM) was sited here. Castlecary takes its name from a square tower that was built here and almost destroyed in 1715. Traces dating from the 15th and 16thc survive.

CASTLE DOUGLAS,
Dumfries and Galloway *25 NX76*
This market town and one-time commercial capital was founded in the 18thc around the village and loch of Carlingwark. On the shores of the loch traces of prehistoric crannogs – artificial island dwellings – have been found. A civic park has been created on the lochside. The town has associations with novelist S L Crockett.

Bengarin rises to 1,250ft in the S and 1½m SW is Threave House (NTS) a Scottish baronial mansion which opens its gardens to visitors. A school for gardeners and a wildfowl refuge have also been created. Some 2m W of the town on an islet in the River Dee is ruined, mainly 14th-c Threave Castle (AM), once a stronghold of the Black Douglases. This black-haired branch of the family was so-called to distinguish it from the Red Douglases. Mons Meg, the famous cannon now in Edinburgh Castle, was probably forged by a local blacksmith called McKim. It was used by James II to overcome Threave and the rebellious Douglases in 1455.

A gallows knob over the doorway of the castle was the means by which the Douglases dispatched their enemies. In 1640 the castle was captured by the Covenanters, who wrecked the interior. A road leads NW from Castle Douglas to New Galloway, and thence along the shores of Loch Ken, artificially enlarged for the Galloway power scheme.

CASTLE KENNEDY,
Dumfries and Galloway *25 NX16*
Lochinch Castle was built in 1867 and stands between the Black and White Lochs to the N of this village. The seat of the Earl of Stair, the castle stands in magnificent landscaped grounds which include a fine pinetum. The ivy-clad ruin of Castle Kennedy stands in Lochinch Gardens to the E. This Kennedy stronghold was built by the 5th Earl of Cassillis in 1607 and burnt in 1715.

CASTLE SEMPLE, Strathclyde *44 NS35*
Near Castle Semple Loch are the remains of a collegiate church (AM) with a three-sided apse and a monument to John, 1st Lord Semple. He founded the church and was killed at Flodden Field in 1513.

CASTLETOWN, Highland *37 ND16*
Dunnet Bay lies to the N of the village, which had a thriving flagstone industry founded in 1837. Fences made from flagstones can be seen locally. A brooch was found in a burial cist here in 1786, and can now be seen in the National Museum of Antiquities in Edinburgh.

CATRINE, Strathclyde *25 NS52*
Situated on the River Ayr, Catrine includes an old mill which was once noted for its huge waterwheel. Burns dined with Professor Dugald Stewart at Catrine House, W of the village, before visiting Edinburgh in 1786. Scotland's largest concrete arch can be seen in the shape of Howford Bridge, which carries the A76 across the River Ayr W of Catrine. Ballochmyle House, a little to the NW of the village, is the setting for two of Burns' well-known songs.

CAUSEWAYEND, Lothian *46 NT06*
This curiously named village lies to the E of the Harper Rig Reservoir. Cauld Stane Slap, an old drove road, which passes near 1,839ft East Cairn Hill on its way to West Linton, runs near the shore of the reservoir. Near the S tip of the reservoir are the remains of Cairns Castle, once the home of the Warden of the Slap. Cobbinshaw Reservoir can be seen 6m SW of the village.

CAUSEWAY HEAD, Central *46 NS89*
Powis House dates from c1746 and stands to the E of this village.

CAWDOR, Highland *34 NH85*
Shakespeare's Macbeth was Thane of Cawdor, and Cawdor Castle is traditionally the scene of Duncan's murder. The castle retains a central tower dating from 1454, a drawbridge with its gateway and iron yett, and some 16th-c building which has been altered at a later date. It is considered one of Scotland's finest and most picturesque medieval buildings.

The church at Cawdor carries an unusual tower and includes a Norman doorway. The countryside around Dulsie Bridge in the valley of the Findhorn, 8m SE of Cawdor, is particularly lovely and can be reached by a road on the line of a former military highway. Cawdor Wood is watered by Hermitage Burn, S of the village, and two roads run SW from Cawdor on both sides of the River Nairn towards Daviot.

The N bank road passes Culloden. Kilravock Castle stands 3m W of Cawdor across the Nairn, and dates from 1460. Prince Charles Edward was entertained here in 1746.

CERES, Fife *31 NO31*
Ceres is a lovely old village with a green surrounded by old cottages. The medieval hump-backed Bishop's Bridge is of interest, and the church above the village contains medieval tombs of the Earls of Crawford. A wall in the village carries a carving of the last Provost of Ceres, who received this office in 1578.

On the last Saturday in June every year the village holds Highland Games to commemorate the safe return of Ceres villagers from Robert the Bruce's victory over Edward II at Bannockburn in 1314. An obelisk in the Bow Butts recalls Ceres' association with Bannockburn. Above the doorway of a 17th-c weigh-house in the village is a carving of a bale being weighed on iron scales, with an inscription which reads 'God bless the just'. Near by hang jougs, medieval instruments of punishment. The 18th-c St John's Lodge has been restored, and ruined 17th-c Craighall Castle stands 1m SE of the village.

CHAPEL OF GARIOCH, Grampian
35 NJ72
Ruined Balquhain Tower dates from 1530 and was where Mary Queen of Scots is said to have spent a night. This lies 1m SE of the village, and 17th-c Pittodrie House stands 1m W. The famous Maiden Stone (AM) can be seen a little to the NW near Drumdurno Farm. The stone is a 10ft-high early-Christian monument which carries a Celtic-cross design, and Pictish symbols including a comb and a mirror.

CHARLESTOWN, Fife *46 NT08*
A small Forth-estuary coal port, Charlestown lies a little to the W of Limekilns, which is associated with Robert Louis Stevenson's *Kidnapped*. The fine mansion of Broomhall stands near by.

CHEVIOT HILLS, THE
For much of its length the Cheviot range forms the border with England, and the grassy slopes provide pasture for hardy Cheviot and black-faced sheep. The Northumberland national park and Border forest park, both in England, include part of the range. The highest point of the hills is the 2,676ft Cheviot, situated in England. Carter Bar is a favourite Border stopping place for people wishing to view the Cheviots – particularly 1,964ft Peel Fell and 1,815ft Carter Fell to the SW. The Roman Dere Street of Agricola traversed the Cheviots to the E of the main A68 road. Away to the SW of Peel Fell the road from Riccarton cuts through the hills to reach the lonely North Tyne valley, across the old Northumberland border.

CHIRNSIDE, Borders *31 NT85*
Views S of the village, beyond the junction of the Whiteadder and Blackadder Waters, are considered notable. Chirnside's parish church features a Norman S doorway with tympanum, and the churchyard contains the grave and memorial to Jim Clark, the racing driver killed in Germany in 1968. Traces of Edington Castle and a fine old crow-step gabled dovecot lie to the E of the village.

CLACHAN BRIDGE, Strathclyde
28 NM71
Often described as the only bridge to span the Atlantic – though there are others – Clachan Bridge crosses the

189

narrow Seil Sound, which is an arm of the Atlantic Ocean. It is a lovely old bridge which was designed by Telford in 1792, and connects the island of Seil with the mainland. Seil and the little island of Easdale were once noted for slates.

Cuan Sound is crossed by a ferry and separates Seil from Luing, another slate-quarrying island, with the little port of Cullipool on its NW coast. Luing Sound separates Luing from Lunga, hilly Scarba, and the smaller Garvellach group; among the latter is Eileach an Naoimh, with its ruined chapel associated with St Brandan and St Columba. Scarba rises to 1,500ft and forms an island sanctuary for herds of deer. To the S is a treacherous tide-race in the Gulf of Corryvreckan, a maelstrom which can be heard from a great distance and is classed by the Royal Navy as unnavigable. Ardmaddy Castle stands on the mainland 3m S of Clachan Bridge and overlooks Ardmaddy Bay, near Seil Sound.

CLACHNAHARRY, Highland   34 NH64
The Caledonian Canal enters Beauly Firth at this point after passing through six locks. A good vitrified fort stands on Craig Phadraig a little to the S.

CLACKMANNAN, Central   46 NS99
This town stands on the Black Devon River, which flows S into the Forth Estuary at Clackmannan Pow. An old tolbooth in Clackmannan is near the ancient Stone of Manau and the stepped town cross. Clackmannan Tower (AM) stands 79ft-high on a hill to the W of the town. Robert the Bruce may have built the stronghold, which before the partial collapse of its 14th-c tower was one of the most complete tower-houses in Scotland. It retains some 14th- and 15th-c work, plus 17th-c additions, and is finely machicolated.

CLADICH, Strathclyde   29 NN02
The road from Dalmally forks here. The W branch continues along the E side of Loch Awe, and the S branch leads to Glen Aray and Inverary, climbing over the hills with fine views of 3,689ft Ben Cruachan to the N across the loch.

CLAGGAIN BAY, Isle of Islay, Strathclyde   28 NR45
Fine views of the island of Jura and the Kintyre peninsula can be enjoyed from this rocky and sandy bay. The road from Port Ellen ends at the bay, which is dominated to the NW by 1,609ft Beinn Bheigeir, the highest point on Islay.

CLARENCEFIELD, Dumfries and Galloway   25 NY06
To the W stands 15th-c Comlongan Castle, with its 10ft to 13ft-thick walls and a well-preserved iron yett, or gate.

CLARKSTON, Strathclyde   45 NS55
About 2m N of Clarkston, on the White Cart River, lie the remains of Cathcart Castle. This was demolished in the 15thc and later replaced by Cathcart House, which stands near by. Mary Queen of Scots is supposed to have watched the Battle of Langside from a window of the castle in 1568. This has since been known as Queen Mary's Window. As a result of this battle Mary fled to Dundrennan prior to leaving Scotland for good.

CLASHMORE, Highland   37 NH78
Skibo Castle lies 1m SW of Clashmore village. The structure was built for

Andrew Carnegie and replaced a former episcopal residence. A standing stone traditionally believed to commemorate the killing of the Danish chief Ospis lies 2m W by the A9 main road.

CLASHNESSIE, Highland   36 NC03
The sandy beach at Clashnessie invites bathers and sea anglers.

CLATTERING BRIDGE, Grampian   35 NO67
This oddly-named bridge lies at the foot of a moorland road which runs from the Dee valley at Banchory to Fettercairn, via the 1,488ft Cairn o' Mounth. Slack Burn flows through a deep gorge a little to the N, overlooked by Finella Hill. The latter is encircled by the little road leading to Fordoun by way of Drumtochty Castle, now a school.

CLATTERINGSHAWS DAM
Dumfries and Galloway   25 NX57
This dam restricts the Black Water of Dee and has created a reservoir for the Galloway power scheme. Robert the Bruce was active hereabouts, and a boulder (NTS) on Moss Raploch marks the site of one of his early skirmishes.

The area lies in Cairn Edward Forest, part of the great Glen Trool forest park. Meikle Millyea is a 2,446ft height in the beautiful Rinns of Kells range, and can be seen rising N of the dam with lonely Loch Dungeon beyond. The prominent Murray Monument lies 4½m SW above the A712 and commemorates Dr Alexander Murray, a shepherd's son who rose to become Professor of Oriental Languages at Edinburgh University in the 18thc.

An impressive waterfall, a wild goat park, and the Talnotry forest trail are near by. Farther to the SW, beyond remote Loch Grennoch, rises 2,331ft Cairnsmore of Fleet in the Galloway Hills. This is associated with John Buchan's novel *The Thirty-Nine Steps*. Loch Dee lies W of the dam near the bogland Silverflowe nature reserve.

CLEISH, Tayside   46 NT09
A rare burial boundary stone is set into the local churchyard wall, and Cleish Castle is a 16th-c house which has been restored. Aldie Castle, built during the 16th and 17thc but since renovated, lies 4m W.

CLOSEBURN, Dumfries and Galloway   25 NX89
The massive 14th-c Closeburn Tower retains an iron yett (gate) to its first-floor entrance doorway. The tower was once visited by Burns. In a ravine 2½m N is Crichope Linn, described in Scott's *Old Mortality*. Lonely moorland and hill country rises to the E, with the fine viewpoint of Queensberry Hill beyond.

CLOVA, Tayside   35 NO37
Situated in the lovely Glen Clova, one of the fine Braes of Angus glens, this hamlet is also known as Milton of Clova. The River South Esk tumbles down among the rare plants and ferns that grow locally on the rocky hills. Traces of a castle can be seen to the NW, and a track leads 1½m N from Clova to Loch Brandy, set at 2,098ft among mountains and overlooked by a sharp ridge known as the Snub of Clova. The road through Clova runs NW to the head of the glen in the heart of the wild E Grampians, or Benchinnan Mountains. The same road

running S forks near Clova church, with the two branches running either side of the river before joining up again 6m farther on the way to Dykehead.

CLOVENFORDS, Borders   26 NT43
This little hamlet lies on the Caddon Water, which flows S to join the Tweed. The Tweed Vineries, planted by the Duke of Buccleuch's head gardener in 1868, grow near by. Scott, when Sheriff of Selkirk, lodged in an inn here before moving to Ashiestiel; his statue stands in front of the inn. Dorothy and William Wordsworth were visitors to the little village in 1803. An inscribed tablet in memory of John Leyden, the poet and orientalist who was a schoolmaster here in 1792, can also be seen.

CLUANIE, Highland   33 NH01
Here, amid lonely, grassy hills at the W end of Loch Cluanie, the road to Kyle of Lochalsh and Skye begins the beautiful descent of Glen Shiel. Lochs Cluanie and Loyne are reservoirs, and the old road S from Cluanie to Tomdoun is now unusable where it once crossed Loch Loyne. Hydro-electricity developments have raised the level of the loch. Tomdoun can now be reached by following the road S at the E end of Loch Cluanie, crossing the low hills which lead to Loch Garry, and by following the road W along Loch Garry's N shore. Good hill-walking country lies around Cluanie, and to the N is 3,673ft A'Chralaig. This, the highest point in the area, affords fine views of the remote peak of 3,771ft Sgurr nan Ceathreamhnan to the NW.

CLUNIE, Tayside   30 NO14
Clunie village lies on the W side of the little Loch of Clunie, which boasts a ruined island castle that is supposed to have been the early home of the Admirable Crichton, born in 1560. Loch of Marlee lies 2½m E on the Blairgowrie road.

CLYDEBANK, Strathclyde   45 NS56
Ship building is surprisingly not an old Clyde trade. During the 16thc Glasgow's only boat-builder had to be bribed to remain in the district. It was not until the 19thc that steam and steel provided the incentive to dredge and widen the Clyde sufficiently to launch big ships. Clydebank's most famous shipyard is John Brown's – birthplace of the 'Lusitania', the 'Queen Mary', the 'Queen Elizabeth', and 'QE2'. The town was severely bombed during the last war. To the SE is Yoker, where a car ferry gives access to Renfrew and the S.

COATBRIDGE, Strathclyde   45 NS76
This large industrial town is noted for its ironworks and was the birthplace of Lord Reith, first head of the BBC. A fountain stands on the site of the old Monkland to Kirkintilloch railway, a 19th-c experimental venture which tried to use umbrellas and windpower for traction. Sturdy Clydesdale horses were used for rough travel against the wind. Bedlay House lies 4m NW and was built during the 16th and 17thc.

COCK BRIDGE, Grampian   35 NJ20
The famous Lecht road starts here on its journey N across the NE Grampians, locally known as the Ladder Hills. The road is part of a military road constructed by the 33rd Regiment under Lord Charles Hay in 1754. An old carved stone on the Well of the Lecht 4m NNW commemorates

this. The first part of the route runs alongside Conglass Water on the descent to Tomintoul. Some 2½m N of Cock Bridge the road reaches its highest point at 2,090ft, with hills on either side rising to over 2,600ft. One of the loftiest sections of road in Britain, this stretch is likely to become snow-bound in winter.

To the S of Cock Bridge the road ascends over the 1 in 5 Hill of Allargue, and 2½m E of the bridge another road turns S for Gairnshiel Bridge and climbs into the hills, reaching over 1,800ft in the steep and narrow Glas Choille section. This is also sometimes blocked by snow. Long Glen Avon stretches to the W of Cock Bridge, shadowed by 3,843ft Ben Avon which rises from the E edge of the mighty Cairngorm range.

COCKBURNSPATH, Borders 31 NT77
A village lying near the rocky North-Sea coast, Cockburnspath is also on the edge of the Lammermuir Hills. A deep wooded valley to the SE contains sections of the A1 road and the Edinburgh to London railway line. The village's partly 14th-c church carries a curious round tower, and an early 17th-c Mercat cross is crowned with a thistle.

Just outside the village, at the Coldingham road junction, stands ruined Cockburnspath Tower. Near sandy Pease Bay 2m E of the village is the ruined Norman Church of St Helen, and 6½m E the fragments of the cliff-top Fast Castle stand near a little farm road running E from the A1.

The castle was built in 1521 as a fortress for the Homes family, and rumour has it that Spanish Armada treasure is buried near by. Scott wrote of the fortress in his *Bride of Lammermoor*. Pease Bridge, built c1780, straddles the Coldingham road 2m SE of Cockburnspath. Measuring 300ft long and 124ft high, the bridge was thought to be the highest in the world when it was first erected.

COCKENZIE, Lothian 47 NT47
Fisherman's Walks is the name of a picturesque custom which is still carried out in this little Firth of Forth fishing village. A large coal-fired power station was recently erected near by.

COCKPEN, Lothian 47 NT36
The Marquis of Dalhousie – Viceroy of India at the time of the great mutiny – is buried in little Cockpen church. Dalhousie Castle dates from the 12thc and stands near the W bank of the South Esk River. Little remains of the original structure, except parts of the 11ft-thick walls and the drawbridge grooves in the old entrance. Henry IV, Edward I, and Queen Victoria were all visitors to the castle. Today it serves as a hotel, and is the scene of mock medieval banquets throughout the year.

COLDINGHAM, Borders 31 NT96
Situated a little inland from sandy Coldingham Bay, Coldingham's buildings date mainly from the 18thc. Coldingham's priory is now the parish church, but was originally founded in 1098 by Edgar, King of Scots. It is one of the oldest Scottish churches where public worship is still observed. The priory retains some 12th- and 13th-c work, even though it was burnt, plundered, and later partly blown up by Cromwell in 1648. A female skeleton found embedded upright in the S transept was mentioned by Scott in

Marmion. Excavation works still continue on this fascinating site. The underwater rocks near Coldingham are popular with sub-aqua clubs.

COLDSTREAM, Borders 27 NT83
For centuries the warring Scots and English forded the Tweed here between Cornhill in England and Coldstream in Scotland. Each year a procession visits Flodden, 3m E across the Border, where the Scots were defeated in 1513 by the Earl of Surrey's men. According to various estimates between 9,000 and 16,000 English and Scottish soldiers were killed in the Battle of Flodden Field – one of the bloodiest battles on English soil. James IV lost his life during the fighting.

The need to cross by the ford at Coldstream was ended in 1766 when John Smeaton completed the five-arched bridge, and up to 1856 marriages were frequently conducted at the former toll-house on the Scottish side. A plaque placed on the bridge in 1926 records that Burns first visited England by this route on 7 May 1787, and a tall fluted column erected in 1832 commemorates Charles Marjoribanks, a former Berwick MP. General Monk raised the Coldstream Guards for Cromwell's New Model Army in 1659 at a house which stood near the market. This has since been demolished, but the site is marked by a plaque. The Hirsel, a mansion standing in lovely grounds which include a small loch, lies 2m NW and is the home of Sir Alec Douglas Home.

COLINSBURGH, Fife 31 NO40
Founded in 1705 by Colin, 3rd Earl of Balcarres, Colinsburgh is renowned for its cattle shows. Balcarres House lies a little to the NW and dates from 1595. This mansion is a seat of the Lindsays. A folly tower stands on nearby Balcarres Crag.

COLINTON (Edinburgh), Lothian 47 NT26
Situated on the Water of Leith, Colinton includes an imposing modern church which preserves an old mortsafe in its churchyard. Robert Louis Stevenson was a frequent visitor to the Manse here in his youth, and Colinton house includes both Merchiston School and the Redford Barracks. To the NE stands the old 16th-c castle of Merchiston, where John

Napier the inventor of logarithms was born in 1550.

The castle stands in grounds which now belong to the Napier College of Science and Technology. The college can be seen in Colinton Road, leading towards Edinburgh city centre. Bonaly Tower was once the home of a well-known judge, Lord Cockburn, and lies 1m S in the foothills of the Pentland Hills. Near by is Dreghorn Castle, where the 18th-c writer of the ballad *William and Margaret* lived. Beyond Juniper Green, to the W of Colinton, is 17th-c Baberton House. This was built between 1622 and 1623, and at one time was the residence of Charles X of France.

COLINTRAIVE, Strathclyde 29 NS07
A small Cowal resort with a shingle beach, Colintraive lies on a beautiful stretch of water known as the Kyles of Bute. Years ago cattle used to be made to swim from the village to Rhubodach on the Isle of Bute, but this strait is now crossed by a car ferry. The ferry docks at Rhubodach for the drive down to Rothesay, the popular resort in the Isle of Bute. To the SE of Colintraive, beyond Strone Point, is the sea loch Striven; the smaller inlet of Loch Riddon is to the NW of the village.

COLLIESTON, Grampian 35 NK02
This lovely little fishing village is noted for its speldings or small haddock and lies in a cove. Near by are smugglers' caves in the cliffs. In 1588 a Spanish Armada ship sank in St Catherine's Dub, a deep creek to the N of the village. Traces of Old Slains Castle, which was demolished in 1594, can be seen 2m SE. To the SW near the Ythan estuary are the Sands of Forvie, a nature reserve beneath which lies a buried village.

COLMONELL, Strathclyde 24 NX18
Colmonell is set in the lovely valley of the River Stinchar. A Covenanter's memorial can be seen in the old churchyard. Ruined Kirkhill, built in 1589 but with later additions, was once a Kennedy stronghold. Craigneil Castle is a ruined 13th-c structure which lies across the stream, with 17th-c Knockdolian Tower further to the W beneath Knockdolian Hill.

A picturesque group at Clackmannan – Tolbooth, Town Cross, and the ancient stone of Manau.

COLONSAY, ISLE OF, Strathclyde
28 NR39
One of Inner Hebridean islands, Colonsay lies N of tiny Oronsay and is linked by steamer to Tarbert on the Kintyre Peninsula, by way of the Isle of Islay. Colonsay and Oronsay are separated by a narrow strait which is dry for three hours at low tide. Colonsay has a pier at Scalasaig and good pasture land. Inland near Kiloran is Colonsay House, standing in sub-tropical gardens. Out to sea on a reef to the NW is the lonely Dubh Heartach lighthouse, built by David and Thomas Stevenson.

COLVEND, Dumfries and Galloway
25 NX85
To the N of Colvend lies the little White Loch, with the tiny lochs Clonyard and Barean beyond. Some 1½m SW along a by-road is Rockcliffe, situated on Rough Firth.

COMRIE, Tayside *30 NN72*
This resort stands on the River Earn at the meeting points of Glen Artney to the SW and Glen Lednock to the NW. St Fillans lies to the W on the edge of Loch Earn. During Hogmanay a midnight torch procession, featuring quaintly-dressed mummers, is staged at Comrie. The two glens face each other across the Highland Boundary Fault, a 20,000ft-deep earth fracture which divides the Highlands and Lowlands and along which minor tremors have occurred. Most of these are very mild, but a more severe tremor in 1839 cracked the walls of houses. The tiny Earthquake House, built in 1869 to record earthquakes is situated at Drumearn. Comrie is a popular centre for hikers, and a particularly pleasant short walk can be taken via a path up Glen Lednock to the Devil's Cauldron, where the River Lednock rushes down a narrow channel and through a hole in the rock.

Loch Tay can be reached from the head of Glen Lednock. Glen Artney was used by Scott as the setting for parts of *The Lady of the Lake* and *Legend of Montrose*, and a long-distance path through the glen eventually leads to Callander after following Keltie Water for 3m. Comrie Church dates from 1805 and carries a steeple which was the work of John Stewart. Good views can be enjoyed from the top of Dunmore Hill, crowned by the 19th-c Melville Monument which was set up in memory of Viscount Melville who died in 1811. Aberuchill Castle is mostly of 17th-c origin and stands 2m WSW of Comrie.

CONNEL, or CONNEL FERRY, Strathclyde *29 NM93*
The road bridge spanning the mouth of Loch Etive, with the Falls of Lora – a sea cataract – on the E side is the largest cantilever bridge in Europe after the great Forth Bridge. Connel Ferry lies on the S side of the bridge and the road N leads to Benderloch and the beautiful Appin countryside past Loch Creran.

CONON BRIDGE, Highland *34 NH55*
An attractive village at the E end of the wooded Strath Conon, Conon Bridge stands on the River Conon which flows into the Firth of Cromarty NE of the village. A hydro-electric scheme operates in the valley, and a former toll-house stands on the river bridge at the village. A new bridge now carries the main road. A road runs NE of Conon

Bridge along the E shores of the Firth of Cromarty, with the Black Isle district to the E. The road reaches Udale and Cromarty Bays and ends at Cromarty. Conon House lies 2m S of the village near the river, and a huge beech tree with a girth of 25ft stands in the extensive grounds.

CONTIN, Highland *33 NH45*
Two roads from Dingwall meet at Contin, a village where the River Blackwater forms two channels. Contin church stands on an island between the channels.

CORGARFF, Grampian *35 NJ20*
Corgarff Castle (AM) is a 16th-c tower house which was enclosed within a star-shaped loophole wall in 1748. The old tower was besieged in 1571 and was involved in the Jacobite risings of 1715 and 1745. Later it became a garrison and was used as a military depot against smugglers until c1830.

CORNHILL, Grampian *35 NJ55*
Park House dates from the 16thc and stands in fine gardens at Cornhill.

CORPACH, Highland *34 NN07*
Near Corpach, on the shores of Loch Linnhe, are several large new paper mills. The eight Telford locks on the Caledonian Canal known as Neptune's Staircase are also of interest (see inset page 175). Kilmallie Church lies a little to the W next to an obelisk dedicated to Colonel John Cameron, who fell at the battle of Quatre Bras during the Waterloo campaign of 1815. The inscription on the monument is thought to have been penned by Sir Walter Scott. The modern Road to the Isles leads W from Corpach, affording picturesque views as it runs along the shores of Loch Eil to Glenfinnan.

CORRAN (Nether Lochaber), Highland
33 NN06
A car ferry is situated just off the main Ballachulish to Fort William road on the E side of the Corran Narrows. The narrows almost divide Loch Linnhe into two and the ferry gives access to the beautiful Ardgour district. Nether Lochaber is the name given to a district stretching from Loch Leven to Fort William – Cameron country. Brae Lochaber lies beyond Ben Nevis in the direction of Glen Spean.

CORRIE, Isle of Arran, Strathclyde
29 NS04
Corrie is a beautiful coastal village lying at the foot of 2,866ft Great Fell, Arran's highest point. White posts on the hillside and N as far as Sannox Bay indicate the measured mile for large ships on speed trials. A path leads off from the A841 N of Corrie to the picturesque Fallen Rocks.

CORRIEYAIRACK PASS, Highland
33 NN49
General Wade built a road through this pass to link Kingussie with Fort Augustus in 1735. Although little of it can be seen today, it ranks as one of Wade's greatest achievements. Neil Munro describes its construction in *New Road*. Prince Charles Edward crossed from W to E in 1745, and up until 1899 sheep were regularly driven through the pass. Although the road has deteriorated and vehicles are now unable to use the pass, it is still open to hikers.

The E side is paralleled by the River Spey, and the summit is reached after thirteen zigzag bends. The pass is 2,507ft high at this point, with the Corrieyairack itself rising to 2,922ft in the N. Wonderful views extend from the Moray Firth to the distant Cuillins of Skye. The descent on the NW side continues through Glen Tarff.

CORSTORPHINE (Edinburgh), Lothian
47 NT27
The extensive grounds of the Scottish National Zoological Park are situated on Corstorphine Hill, along with the viewpoint of Rest and Be Thankful. The latter is linked with Robert Louis Stevenson's *Kidnapped*. Clermiston Tower tops Corstorphine Hill and commemorates the centenary of Sir Walter Scott. The 15th-c Corstorphine church became collegiate in 1429 and is noted for the Forrest memorials, separate gabled roofs, and coats of arms on the exterior. To the E of the hill lies Craigcrook Castle, the earliest part of which dates from the early 17thc. Some 2m E is the rugby-football ground of Murrayfield, venue for Scotland's international matches. Roseburn House was begun in 1562 and stands near the ground. Cromwell is thought to have stayed at the house during 1659.

CORTACHY, Tayside *31 NO35*
The Earl of Airlie, head of the Clan Ogilvie, owns Cortachy Castle; this was restored in 1872. Cortachy church preserves a 15th-c window. Cat Law rises to a height of 2,196ft NW of the village.

COSHIEVILLE, Tayside *30 NN74*
The road from Aberfeldy divides at Coshieville, with one branch continuing W to Fortingall and beautiful Glen Lyon. The N road passes by the W end of Loch Tummel and traverses the N shore of Loch Rannoch. Garth Castle, dating from the 14thc and restored, lies 2m N. A walker's track leaves the B846 farther N before White Bridge and runs W up the slopes of 3,547ft Schiehallion.

COULPORT, Strathclyde *44 NS28*
Situated on the E shore of Loch Long opposite Ardentinny, Coulport is the end of a road which runs round the Rosneath peninsula.

COUPAR ANGUS, Tayside *30 NO23*
Fruit is grown in abundance in the valley of Strathmore, around the village which lies S of the winding Tay. Remains of a Cistercian abbey founded by Malcolm IV in 1164 stand in a corner of the churchyard. The abbey was destroyed in 1559. Outlines of an extensive Roman camp can be seen 2m S, and the Sidlaw Hills rise farther S with 1,235ft King's Seat and 1,012ft Dunsinane Hill predominant. Stormont Loch lies NW of Coupar Angus off the Blairgowrie road.

COVE, Grampian *35 NJ90*
This little village lies on a fascinating stretch of coast off the Aberdeen to Stonehaven road. The rocky shores of Nigg Bay can be found 2½m NNE, sheltered by Girdle Ness and its lighthouse. A road follows the shore as far as the ness and continues towards Aberdeen Bay.

COVESEA, Grampian *34 NJ17*
Covesea Skerries lighthouse of 1844 is a notable example of Alan Stevenson's work.

COWAL PENINSULA, Strathclyde

The hill country of the Cowal forms a
peninsula between Loch Fyne and the
Clyde estuary. Loch Striven and Loch
Goil, both beautiful sea lochs, indent the
peninsula. To the E of Loch Goil is Loch
Long, with Arrochar at its head. Arrochar
is surrounded by lofty hills, mostly part
of the Argyll forest park, and the Island
of Bute lies to the S of Cowal. The stretch
of water which divides the island from
the mainland is called the Kyles of Bute.
Colintraive is a mainland community
connected with Rhubodach on Bute by
car ferry.

COWDENBEATH, Fife 47 NT19

Fife's principal coal-mining town,
Cowdenbeath is bordered by the E by
Loch Gelly and to the W by Loch Fitty,
backed by the low Roscobie Hills.

COWIE, Grampian 35 NO88

This little fishing village is situated on a
rocky bay and has a ruined chapel.

COYLTON, Strathclyde 24 NS41

The winding Water of Coyle flows to the E
of this town. Martnaham Loch lies
2½m SW, and coal used to be mined in
the area.

COYLUMBRIDGE, Highland 34 NH91

A tempting stopping place on the way
from Aviemore to the Cairngorm
chairlifts, Coylumbridge has a hotel and
sports complex of its own. The resort
also lies on the long track to the Lairig
Ghru Pass through the Cairngorms. A
road runs N from Coylumbridge past the
lovely Loch Pityoulish, and later passes
Kincardine Church on the way to the
Forest of Abernethy and Nethybridge.
A road E leads into Glen More forest
park, and a little to the W at Inverdruie
is a by-road which leads to the beautiful
Loch an Eilean. On an island in the loch
are the sinister ruins of the castle of the
Comyns, once a fortress of the Wolf of
Badenoch.

CRAIGELLACHIE, Grampian 35 NJ24

Beautifully situated in wooded Strath

Spey, Craigellachie lies near the point
where the River Fiddich joins the Spey.
The village is sometimes known as
Lower Craigellachie to avoid confusion
with the well-known Craigellachie (Rock
of Alarm) at Aviemore. Thomas Telford,
constructed the single-arched iron bridge
which spans the Spey here (see inset
below). This is now by-passed by a new
bridge. Many distilleries can be found in
the area. Ben Aigan rises to 1,544ft 2½m
NE and affords beautiful views of the
Spey valley. The old mansion of Kininvie
stands 3½m ESE of Craigellachie, above
Glen Fiddich.

CRAIGENDORAN, Strathclyde 44 NS38

Lying on the SE outskirts of Helensburgh,
Craigendoran has a railway station and
steamer pier.

CRAIGIEVAR CASTLE, Grampian
35 NJ50

Considered one of the loveliest Scottish
castles, Craigievar (NTS) is an
extravagance of turrets, gables, and

TELFORD'S IRON ARCH

Thomas Telford is remembered in
countless civil engineering works all over
Scotland. One of the most attractive is
the bridge over the River Spey at
Craigellachie, which he designed as part
of his work for the Commissioners for
Highland Roads and Bridges. Begun in
1812, it was the second bridge over the
lower Spey, the first being some miles
downstream at Fochabers.

This was a very difficult situation for a
bridge to be built. The river itself flowed
swiftly round a bend. On the right bank
were low-lying meadows, and on the left
an almost vertical cliff soaring up to the
pine-covered hill which was Craigellachie
itself. Telford's design called for a 100-yd
approach road to be blasted out of the
cliff on the northern side, 70ft above the
water. The 150-ft main span was a
splendid piece of work, cast in iron at
Plas Kynaston in Wales, in the foundry
of William Hazeldine, whom Telford
called 'the arch conjuror, Merlin
Hazeldine'. There is no truth whatever
in the story still told locally that
Hazeldine delivered to Craigellachie the
component parts for a bridge intended to
be built somewhere hundreds of miles
away.

Each entrance to the bridge was guarded
by a pair of entirely ornamental stone
towers, looking like rooks in a chess set,
a concept which fits in remarkably well
with the rugged surroundings. Three
stone arches were included in the design
to bring the lower approach road level
with the bridge, a feature which Telford
considered would be useful in times of
flood.

The total price of the bridge and its
approach roads, including rock-blasting
on the north side, was no more than
£8,200, which was considered very
satisfactory. Extra expenses incurred
after the opening in 1815 included £130
for painting the metal structure and
more than £100 to provide parapets and
railings along the exposed roadway
halfway up the cliff.

Craigellachie bridge faced its stiffest test
during the terrible Lammas floods of
3 and 4 August 1829. Despite spilling
over the fields on its right bank, the Spey
rose 15½ft higher than usual as it tore
round the Craigellachie bend. Telford's
three stone arches saved the day,
although they were themselves destroyed.

By that time his successor with the
Commission was Joseph Mitchell, who
had been on a visit to Orkney and
Shetland and read about the floods on
11 August in Thurso. His first thought
was for the beautiful Craigellachie
bridge: 'As the mail coach started for the
South in half an hour, I took my place,
and proceeded, without halting, to
Craigellachie, some 200 miles distant to
see if I could save the iron arch.' His
assistants on the spot had the situation
well under control, and the main bridge
works survived.

Craigellachie bridge continued to take
modern traffic over the Spey. By 1964
the heavier loads were imposing a great
strain on it, and the old county councils
of Banff, Moray, and Nairn financed a
restoration which included replacing
some of the original metalwork, although
its appearance is just as Telford left it.
More recently it was bypassed for vehicle
traffic by a new bridge a little way
downstream. Happily, Telford's most
graceful design remains.

The iron arch of Telford's Spey bridge is
integrated with the surrounding scenery
by harmonious stone towers.

conical roofs which was constructed between 1610 and 1626. Completed by William Forbes, the castle has no later additions and stands high above Leochel Burn, affording views across the Don Valley. Inside is a hall with a superb Renaissance ceiling. A well-known inscription in the castle reads 'Doe not vaiken sleeping dogs'.

CRAIGMILLAR CASTLE (Edinburgh), Lothian 47 NT27

The ruins of this 14th-c fortress (AM) on the edge of the city have their share of dark legend. James II's youngest son, the Earl of Mar, is said to have been bled to death here in 1477. The castle was burnt by Hertford in 1544, and Mary Queen of Scots is believed to have plotted her husband's death with Bothwell here. She certainly visited the castle after Rizzio's death in 1566, but historians have since argued whether she had any direct hand in Darnley's murder. Fine views can be enjoyed from the massive 14th-c keep, which stands within its early 15th-c embattled curtain wall, and remains of the stately 16th- and 17th-c apartments still exist. On the nearby road to Dalkeith are some old houses known as Little France, where Mary's French attendants once lived. A tree planted by the queen grows near by.

CRAIGNURE, Isle of Mull, Strathclyde 28 NM73

Facing the flat island of Lismore, Craignure lies at the meeting place of Loch Linnhe and the Sound of Mull and boasts a steamer pier. Views of the mountains of Appin on the mainland and the distant peak of Ben Nevis can be enjoyed. At Duart Point 3½m SE lies the ruined stronghold of the Lord of the Isles – Duart Castle. The castle's 13th-c keep dominates the Sound of Mull, and the building is the ancestral home of the chief of the Clan Maclean. A royal charter of 1390 confirmed the lands to the Macleans, and the castle was extended in 1633. The Duke of Argyll took the castle from the Macleans, who supported the Stuarts, in 1691 and left it in ruins. During the 1745 Rising Sir Hector Maclean of Duart was imprisoned in the Tower of London and his estates forfeited. It was not until 1911 that Sir Fitzroy Maclean restored the castle. The 26th chief of the clan died in 1937 at the age of 101. Torosay Castle, 2m S of Craignure, was built in 1860 and features a walk lined with French statues.

A road runs S from Craignure by the head of Loch Don and later traverses the shores of the almost land-locked Loch Spelve. The mountain and cliff scenery here is very fine, dominated by 2,289ft Creach Bheinn. At the N end of Loch Spelve a road runs W along lonely Glen More, with wild hills dominated by 2,354ft Ben Buie, and continues to the shores of Loch Scridain. A range of 2,500ft-high hills borders the road NW from Craignure, which passes the shores of Scallastle Bay on the way to Salen.

CRAIL, Fife 31 NO60

A most picturesque fishing town huddled on the East Neuk's rocky coast, Crail is East Neuk's oldest Royal Burgh. The crow-stepped and red-tiled houses clustering round the harbour were once the haunt of smugglers, but now attract no-one more sinister than artists. The

early 16th-c Tolbooth or toll-house displays a gilded-copper salmon on its weather vane and a coat-of-arms dated 1602. Prisoners were formerly taken through the now blocked-up doorway under the window at the side of the Tolbooth. The building itself was added to in the 18th and early 19thc. A unicorn decorates the Mercat cross, and the mainly 13th-c collegiate church preserves its plain, short-spiked tower and some 17th-c woodwork. It houses an 8th-c carved cross, and in the chancel is a picture of a sailor taking a bearing with a sextant.

Many carved memorials can be seen in the churchyard. An old dovecot stands near the shore and in the Victoria Gardens is the Sauchope Stone, an ancient inscribed standing stone. The tower of Balcomie Castle stands on the coast 2m NE, and Mary of Guise, mother of Mary Queen of Scots, was entertained here in 1538. Beyond the castle is Fife Ness, facing the North Carr lighthouse which marks the perilous Carr Rocks. Lonely Bell Rock lighthouse can be seen to the NE from Crail in fine weather. Out to sea to the SE of Crail is the Isle of May, with its powerful lighthouse and bird observatory. The caves of Caiplie lie 2m SW of the town; the largest of these is some 40ft long.

CRAILING, Borders 26 NT62

Crailing House is a fine Regency mansion of 1803.

CRAMOND (Edinburgh), Lothian 47 NT17

A small village only 5m from Edinburgh's Princess Street, Cramond lies on the lovely Almond estuary and is a favourite resort for dinghy sailing. James V was attacked by thieves in the 16thc on a predecessor of Old Cramond Bridge (1619), and was rescued by a miller named James Howison. Howison afterwards received all the land around Braehead. A proviso on the gift of land was that the miller's descendants should always have a ewer of water and a basin ready to present to his sovereign. This condition was fulfilled at the last Coronation, when a member of the family presented Elizabeth II with a silver ewer and a bowl of rose water. Cramond Church stands on the site of Caer Almond Roman Fort, built by Antoninus Pius in AD 142.

Recent excavations have produced coins, glass, and other objects which can be seen in Huntly House Museum in Edinburgh. A corner of the fort forms part of a garden in the village. Robert Louis Stevenson stayed at Cramond and described the village in his novel St Ives. He once cut his initials on a table in the Cramond Inn. Cramond House dates from the 17th and 18thc. Many of Cramond's 18th-c houses have been restored, and a fine promenade leads along the shore to Granton. There is a pleasant path along the wooded banks of the Almond to an old mill. Cramond Island lies 1m out into the Firth of Forth, with the tiny bird sanctuary of Inchmickery Island beyond.

CRANSHAWS, Borders 31 NT66

This tiny village lies in a lonely, isolated setting on the Whiteadder Water, amid the Lammermuir Hills. Cranshaws Tower was once a Douglas stronghold and is still inhabited. Near by are the remains of an old church which once bore the arms of James VI. The arms have now

been transferred to the inner N door of the present church. A narrow, hilly road runs NW from Cranshaws, up over the Hungry Snout with Spartleton Edge away to the E, and on to Gifford. Beyond Whiteadder Reservoir a little road runs N below Clints Dod, with its fine views, to the village of Garvald.

CRARAE, Strathclyde 29 NR99

Crarae Forest and Lodge gardens have been planted in a glen near Loch Fyne.

CRASK, Highland 36 NC52

The low-road pass of the Crask runs a little to the N and affords views across to 3,154ft Ben Klibreck in the E, and 3,273ft Ben More Assynt in the W. Remote Loch Choire lies beneath Ben Klibreck to the E of the village. The Crask itself is a watershed.

CRASK OF AIGAS, Highland 33 NH44

Eilean Aigas house stands in lovely gardens between two arms of the beautiful Beauly River. The house, a refuge for Lord Lovat in 1697, was once a home of Sir Robert Peel and is associated with the Sobiéski Stuarts – two brothers who claimed to be the descendants of Prince Charles Edward. To the NE is the low Druim Pass with its thickly-wooded cliffs.

CRATHES CASTLE, Grampian 35 NO79

This fine castle (NTS) stands to the N of the River Dee 3m E of Banchory, and has belonged to the Burnetts of Leys since 1323. Its double square tower dates from 1553, and the rest of the structure – rich in turrets and gables – was completed between 1596 and 1600. The wonder of Crathes is its magnificent painted ceilings of 1599, in the Chamber of the Nine Worthies, the Chamber of the Nine Muses, and the Green Lady's Room. The Queen Anne and Victorian wings were destroyed by fire in 1966 but have been rebuilt and house an information centre. The bejewelled Horn of Leys dates from 1324 and was possibly connected with Robert the Bruce; this is preserved in the castle. Crathes also displays some fine woodwork, and stands in 575-acre grounds which include one of the best collections of trees and shrubs in Britain. Other features are beautiful walled gardens, and massive yew hedges which enclose a series of small gardens and were planted in 1702.

CRATHIE, Grampian 35 NO29

The Royal Family attend Crathie Church when in residence at Balmoral. Queen Victoria laid the church's foundation stone in 1895 and John Brown, her personal attendant for many years, lies buried in the graveyard of the ruined Old Church. Abergeldie Castle lies 1m E on the S side of the Dee. Built in c1550 and now showing 19th-c additions, the castle was garrisoned by Mackay in 1689. It has been leased as a royal residence since 1848, and was the Highland home of Edward VII when Prince of Wales.

CRAWFORD, Strathclyde 25 NS92

Camps Water flows from the Camps Reservoir in the hills to the E and enters the Clyde at Crawford. Surrounded by green Lowland hills, Crawford is a good centre for walking and boasts a late 19th-c stone pillar which was once a tombstone of the Cranston family. These were the former owners of the Crawford Hotel and ran the last mail coach in the area. The pillar was to have been set up in the churchyard, but owing to a family quarrel this was never carried out. Traces of Tower Lindsay, once visited by James IV, can also be seen.

CRAWFORDJOHN, Strathclyde
25 NS82
The road from Clydesdale follows Crawick Water before reaching Crawfordjohn, at the foot of 1,400ft Mountherrick Hill.

CREAGAN, Strathclyde *29 NM94*
A beautiful road from Benderloch to Appin winds round the head of Loch Creran, which provides a picturesque setting for Creagan. Glens Creran and Ure stretch beyond the road, overshadowed by 3,139ft Beinn Fhionnlaidh.

CREETOWN, Dumfries and Galloway
25 NX45
This sheltered and peaceful village is the Porton Ferry of Scott's novel *Guy Mannering*. Known as Ferrytown until 1785, the village supplied granite for Liverpool's docks. Queen Victoria's Diamond Jubilee is commemorated by the clock tower, and the village has an interesting rock and gem museum. When Queen Victoria asked Thomas Carlyle what was the finest road in the kingdom, he replied 'The coast road from Creetown to Gatehouse of Fleet'. This road is one of Scotland's loveliest and runs through good walking country for 18m, with magnificent seascapes to one side and lush hedgerows and trees to the other.

Some 4m S along the road from Creetown stands Carsluith Castle, a roofless 16th-c tower house built on an L-plan. To the W of Ravenshall Point is a cave used as a hiding place by Dick Hatteraick, the smuggler captain in Scott's *Guy Mannering*. Near by is Barholm Castle, once a refuge for John Knox, who led the Protestant Reformation in Scotland. Up the valley of the Kirkdale Burn from

Barholm are the 4,000-year-old standing stones and chambered tombs of Cairnholy. Prominent Cairnsmore of Fleet rises to 2,331ft 5m N of Creetown and was featured in John Buchan's spy novel *The Thirty-Nine Steps.*

CREICH, Highland *37 NH68*
Near the local church is the 7ft-high St Demhan's Cross. To the SE on the Dornoch Firth stands a vitrified fort known as Dun Creich, with several chambered cairns near by.

CRIANLARICH, Central *29 NN32*
Fine mountain scenery surrounds Crianlarich, which has become a centre for climbing and walking. Set in Breadalbane country, the village lies at the meeting point of Strath Fillan, Glen Dochart, and Glen Falloch. Loch Dochart and its glen lies to the E of Crianlarich, and traces of an old castle where Iver Campbell of Strachur was besieged in 1597 can be seen on a little wooded island in the loch. Beyond Loch Dochart is Loch Lubhair, backed by the well-known twin peaks of 3,843ft Ben More and 3,821ft Stobinian, with 3,428ft Cruach Ardran a little to the W. A picturesque road runs SW of the village by way of Glen Falloch to Ardlui at the head of Loch Lomond. Beinn Oss rises to 3,374ft to the W of Crianlarich, and 3m NW in Strath Fillan are fragments of St Fillan's Chapel, lying E of Fillan Water. The chapel dates from 1314 and was dedicated by Bruce as a thank-offering for the victory at Bannockburn. St Fillan's bell is now preserved in the National Museum of Antiquities at Edinburgh.

CRICHTON, Lothian *47 NT36*
Above the steep, wooded banks of Tyne Water stands a little collegiate church which dates from 1449. This is notable for its tower and barrel vaulting, and displays a quaint bellcote. To the S stands Crichton Castle (AM), more elaborate in style than many in Scotland.

The keep is of 14th-c origin, but the remaining castle ruins are mostly of 15th- to 17th-c date. An unusual Italianate N wing was erected by the Earl of Bothwell in the 16thc. Massie More is the name given to the dungeons. Mary Queen of Scots visited Crichton Castle in 1562 and the structure was also associated with Scott's *Marmion.*

CRIEFF, Tayside *30 NN82*
Crieff is a pleasant little hillside town overlooking beautiful Strath Earn. The River Earn is joined to the N of Crieff by Turret Water, flowing from lovely Loch Turret. The latter includes picturesque waterfalls. The loch lies in remote Glen Turret beneath 3,048ft Ben Chonzie. At the entrance to Crieff's Town Hall is the octagonal Drummond Cross, dated 1688, and near the 17th-c Tolbooth are iron stocks which were used until 1816. A 10th-c cross slab of red sandstone, sculptured with interlaced Celtic knots, has been re-used as the old Market Cross. Crieff was burnt in 1716 and 1745, and Prince Charles Edward held a council of war in the Drummond Arms Hotel in 1746. To the N of the town is the Knock of Crieff, topped by a view indicator and overlooking the mansion of Ochtertyre. A small loch in the area was visited by Burns in 1787.

Ruined Innerpeffray Castle is dated 1610 and lies 4m SE. Near by in an 18th-c building is the Innerpeffray Library, one of Scotland's oldest collections of books, founded in 1691 by David Drummond. Its valuable contents include a pocket Bible which was carried by the Marquis of Montrose during his last battle at Carbisdale in 1648. One of the eight remaining 17th-c Treacle Bibles is preserved here – so-called because of its reading of '. . . is there no balm in Gilead?' as '. . . is there no treacle in Gilead?'. The adjoining burial chapel of the Drummonds (AM), with its curious tombs, was once a collegiate church and dates from 1508.

Drummond Castle was built by the 1st Lord Drummond in 1491 and stands 3½m SSW of Crieff. It survived bombardment by Cromwell, but was partly demolished in 1745. Only the square tower of the original building still exists, now housing an armoury. Other features of the castle include a multiple sundial of 1630 and fine gardens. Tomachastle Hill, crowned by a monument to Sir David Baird, the hero of Seringapatam, stands 3m W.

CRINAN, Strathclyde *28 NR79*
A yachtsman's haven on the sound of Jura, Crinan is overlooked by early 11th-c Duntrune Castle, one of Scotland's oldest inhabited castles. The 9m-long Crinan Canal dates from 1793 to 1801 and flows into the Sound of Jura here. It is now used by pleasure craft but was originally constructed so that ships could reach the Atlantic from Loch Fyne

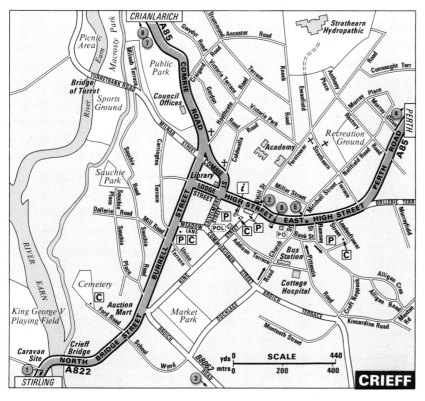

1 Drummond Castle
2 Drummond Arms Hotel
3 Innerpeffray Castle, Library, and Chapel
4 Knock of Crieff
5 Market Cross
6 Ochtertyre
7 Sir David Baird Monument
8 Town Hall with Drummond Cross, Iron Stocks and 17th-c Tolbooth

without having to make the long and often stormy circuit of the Kintyre peninsula to the S. Queen Victoria was taken by barge along the canal in 1847. Some 3m SE of Crinan is the Moss of Crinan, or Moine Mhor. Well-wooded Loch Sween lies to the S in the Knapdale district. Roads run along its E and W shores, terminating at the Sound of Jura with fine views across to the island of Jura.

CROCKETFORD, Dumfries and Galloway 25 NX87
A religious sect called the Buchanites founded this village, which lies between the little lochs Auchenreoch and Milton. On the hills to the NW are memorials to four martyred Covenanters who were shot in 1685.

CROE BRIDGE, Highland 33 NG92
Situated near the head of picturesque Loch Duich on the lovely road leading to Kyle of Lochalsh, Croe Bridge is a good starting point for hill walks. The wonderful Falls of Glomach (NTS) lie 7m NE, and can be reached by a path from Croe Bridge which climbs over steep, 2,000ft Bealach na Sroine. One of the highest falls in Britain at 370ft, the Falls of Glomach tumble down above wild Glen Elchaig. The falls can also be reached by a road running NE from Ardelve, along the shores of Loch Long to Killilan.

A small road runs along Glen Elchaig from Killilan to tiny Loch na Leitreach, and from the W end of the loch the falls can be reached after an arduous 1½-hour climb. Another path runs by the River Croe, heading SE from Croe Bridge through Glen Lichd and under the slopes of 3,383ft Ben Attow. It comes to the head-waters of the River Affric, then runs along the long Glen Affric. The little church and manse of Kintail lie W of Croe Bridge, on the way to Inverinate.

CROFTER COUNTIES
These were the Highland and Island counties of Caithness, Ross and Cromarty, Sutherland, Inverness, Argyll, Orkney, and Shetland. Most have been changed or eliminated under the county-reorganization scheme. Although they make up half the total area of Scotland – 9,000,000 acres in all – the crofter counties have a population density of only 20 per sqm.

Crossford's Craignethan Castle, possibly the 'Tillietudlem Castle' of Scott's *Old Mortality*.

CROMARTY, Highland 34 NH76
Birthplace of geologist Hugh Miller in 1802, Cromarty is a small Black-Isle seaport of Easter Ross which guards the narrows of Cromarty Firth. Much of the area around the town has been developed for North-Sea oil production. South Sutor headland juts out to the E of the town, with the North Sutor across the narrows; the two headlands together are known as the Sutors of Cromarty. A passenger ferry crosses the narrows to Dunskeath. Hugh Miller's cottage (NTS) dates from c1650 and houses a geological collection. This can be visited, and his statue stands on a hill above the town. Among the 17th- and 18th-c houses in the town is Albion House in Church Street. To the SE of the town is 18th-c Cromarty House, which stands on the site of the former castle. Cromarty's parish church has an interesting interior.

CROMDALE, Highland 34 NJ02
To the N of this village is the River Spey. The Haughs of Moray, where the Jacobites fought and lost a battle in 1690, lie 2m E of Cromdale. Carn Eachie rises to 2,136ft SE of the village and is the highest of the Cromdale Hills.

CROOK INN, Borders 26 NT12
Crook Inn was once a famous posting house on the Edinburgh to Dumfries road, and is surrounded by hill country. A former Jacobite landlord, who was captured at Culloden in 1746, saved his life by escaping down the steep slopes of the Devil's Beef Tub when on his way to be tried at Carlisle. The Beef Tub is situated near Moffat. Walkers can follow the Hearthstane Burn to the flat summit of 2,754ft Broad Law, which rises to the E of lonely Talla Reservoir with 2,680ft Dollar Law to the NE.

CROOK OF DEVON, Tayside 30 NO00
A sharp bend or crook in the River Devon gives this picturesque spot its name. It is thought that the flow of the river was once to the E, along the course of the present Gairney Water. Tullibole Castle is an old tower of 1608 which lies 1m ENE. Cleish Hills, with Dumglow rising to 1,241ft, can be seen to the SE.

CROSSFORD, Strathclyde 30 NS84
Orchards flourish around Crossford, the point where the River Nethan flows into the Clyde. About 1m NE in a ravine

along the Fiddler's Burn is 16th-c Hallbar Tower. Craignethan Castle (AM) lies 1m WSW and overlooks the Nethan. This large, well-preserved ruin was the main stronghold of the Hamiltons, supporters of Queen Mary, and was repeatedly attacked by Protestants who partly destroyed the castle in 1579. The oldest part of the building is a large, 16th-c tower-house of an unusual and ornate design. Recent excavations have revealed what may be the earliest example of a caponier – a covered passageway across a defensive ditch – in Britain. Craignethan Castle may be the 'Tillietudlem Castle' in Scott's *Old Mortality*.

CROSSGATES, Fife 46 NT18
A little to the SE of this town are the low wooded Cullalo Hills, which rise gently over the Burntisland Reservoir.

CROSSMICHAEL, Dumfries and Galloway 25 NX76
The waters of the River Dee widen here to form a reservoir which was formed by means of the Glenlochar barrage. Loch Ken is now a N continuation of the reservoir. In the local kirkyard is the tomb of William Graham, a Covenanter martyr of 1682. Tiny Loch Roan lies on high ground 2m NE of Crossmichael.

CROSSRAGUEL ABBEY, Strathclyde 24 NS20
This Cluniac monastery (AM) was originally founded in the 12thc by the Earl of Carrick during the reign of Alexander II. It was inhabited by Benedictine monks from 1244 until the end of the 16thc. The ruins display mostly 15th-c work and are of high architectural distinction. Of special interest are the gate-house, a dovecot with 240 nesting boxes, and the Abbot's Tower. Baltersan Tower was a Kennedy stronghold and stands a little to the NE. Wide views can be enjoyed from the 16th-c tower.

CROVIE, Grampian 35 NJ86
Sheltered by Crovie Head, this secluded little fishing village lies beneath the lofty red cliffs in Gamrie Bay. Troup Head juts into the sea to the NE.

CROY, Highland 34 NH74
Little Flemington Loch lies to the N of Croy, with 17th-c Kilravock Castle standing to the E by the River Nairn. Prince Charles Edward was entertained here in 1746. Dalcross Castle was built in 1621 and later modernized, and can be seen 2m SW of Croy.

CRUDEN BAY, Grampian 35 NK03
Features of this well-known resort include fine sands and a championship golf course. Bishop's Bridge spans Cruden Water and dates from 1697. A little to the E is ruined Slains Castle. The old castle of Slain once stood 4m away near Collieston, and was given to the Earl of Errol by Robert the Bruce in the early 14thc. It was demolished by James VI in 1594 when the 9th Earl conspired against him. The Earl returned from exile some years later and built a new Slains Castle. The 17th-c castle was rebuilt three times, and the round towers were added in 1836. Dr Johnson and James Boswell were guests at the castle in 1773.

On a headland near the church is the fishing village of Port Errol, where the Forties-Field oil pipeline comes ashore.

An immense rock ampitheatre carved out by the sea and known as the Bullers of Buchan lies 2m NE of Cruden Bay. Particularly impressive in rough weather, the chasm is 200ft deep and 50ft wide. Dr Johnson visited it by boat in 1773 and said it was a sight 'which no man can see with indifference'. Dun Bay, or Yellow Rock, lies to the SE of the Bullers and is associated with Scott's *The Antiquary*.

CRUGGLETON, Dumfries and Galloway 25 NX44
A little Norman church at Cruggleton displays a chancel arch, doors and windows dating from the 12thc. It was restored in the 19thc by the Marquess of Bute. Remains of Cruggleton Castle lie near the shore, and farther to the N beyond Sliddery Point is Cruggleton (or Rigg) Bay. The site of the castle is thought to have been first fortified by the Norsemen.

CUILLIN HILLS, THE, Isle of Skye, Highland 32
Also known as the Coolins or Cuchullins – maybe after an Ossianic hero – the main ridges of this magnificent range extend over the SW of the island and are known as the Black Cuillins. They overlook spectacular Loch Coruisk which was described by Scott in *Lord of the Isles.* The Black Cuillins form a 6m semi-circle of black gabbro mountains, with 3,309ft Sgurr Alasdair soaring above the rest. Although this is the highest peak, the finest is perhaps the jagged, pinnacled, 3,167ft Sgurr Gillean. The less-impressive Red Cuillins face the main ridge across Glen Sligachan, and comprise rounded, pink-granite mountains. The chief peaks are 2,537ft Glamaig and the lovely 2,414ft Marsco.

Sligachan is a famous climbing centre on the E coast of the island, and though the main Cuillin ridge is suitable for experienced climbers only, it is possible to reach the peak of 3,143ft Bruach na Frithe from the village without serious difficulty. Views of the rugged summit ridge and wild corries from the top of Bruach na Frithe are breathtaking, and quite unrivalled anywhere else in Scotland except from the main summits themselves. Mist is a constant danger to the climber. The River Sligachan flows through the U-shaped glacial valley of Glen Sligachan and forms a boundary of the Black and Red Cuillins.

At least fifteen of the Black Cuillins are Munros – *ie* peaks over 3,000ft in height. The gabbro rock has a rough surface and is one of the safest to climb. Blaven, a magnificent 3,042ft outlier of the Black Cuillins, is noted for the rocky traverse of Clach Glas and overlooks both Loch na Creitheach and Loch Slapin. The Cuillins are of great interest to geologists; from the mainland their serrated outline can be seen from the tops of the loftier peaks, and from points on the coast from Kyle of Lochalsh to Gairloch.

Boat trips on Loch Scavaig afford wonderful close views of the range with 2,934ft Gars Bheinn, the farthest S of the Cuillins, overlooking the loch. John Mackenzie was a famous 19th-c Scottish guide who made numerous ascents of the Cuillins. One peak is named after him.

CULBIN SANDS, Grampian 34 NH96
In 1694 a disastrous sandstorm overwhelmed this formerly fertile district.

The Barony of Culbin had previously been affected by sandstorms, and in the final storm the mansion of Culbin, home of the Kinnairds, was completely buried. The 3,600-acre wastes of Culbin Sands have now been afforested with Scots and Corsican pines.

CULLEN, Grampian 35 NJ56
Once known as Invercullen, this resort and fishing town offers sands and good bathing. Three rocks on the shore are known as the Three Kings of Cullen, and the headlands of Scar Nose and Logie Head project out to the W and E respectively. Features of the town itself include a Mercat cross and Cullen House. The latter affords fine views out to sea and stands where the old town was before it was demolished in 1822. It is a 16th-c fortified mansion which was greatly extended in 1861. The interior includes a 17th-c painting of the *Siege of Troy*, plus fine portraits by Van Dyck, Kneller, and Ramsay.

Near the house is cruciform St Mary's Church, which was founded by Bruce and became collegiate in 1543. The present building is of 16th-c origin and is largely original. In the chancel are the sacrament house, a large Ogilvie monument, and a fine laird's pew of the Seafield family of Clan Grant. The latter displays 17th-c woodwork. Many fine table tombs can be seen in the churchyard. Picturesque Findlater Castle lies in ruins 2m E on the coast.

CULLICUDDEN, Highland 34 NH66
Remains of 16th-c Castle Craig, once residence of the Bishops of Ross, lie 2m W on the shores of Cromarty Firth.

CULLODEN, Highland 34 NH74
The site (NTS) of the great Battle of Culloden, fought on 16 April 1746, is marked by a huge memorial cairn on Drummossie Muir (Culloden Moor). It was here that Bonnie Prince Charlie's hopes of restoring the Stuart monarchy were dashed after the slaughter of a quarter of his Highland army of 5,000 by the Duke of Cumberland's men, who outnumbered the clansmen two to one. The main cause for such bloodshed was the opening English cannonade, followed by the tactics of the redcoats when the clansmen charged. Each English soldier bayonetted the exposed side of the Highlander to his right, instead of attacking to the front. During the 40-minute battle 1,200 Scotsmen and 310 Englishmen died.

Old Leanach farmhouse around which the battle raged still stands, and was inhabited until 1912. A path from the farmhouse leads through the Field of the English where 76 of the Duke of Cumberland's men are thought to be buried. Simple headstones erected in 1881 distinguish the graves of the clans, alongside the main road. The victorious Duke of Cumberland, George II's son, surveyed the scene from a huge stone now known as the Cumberland Stone.

Across the River Nairn 1m to the SE are the Stones of Clava (AM) – an extensive group of bronze-age standing stones and cairns dated 1800 to 1500BC. Culloden House of late 18th-c date and stands 2m NW of the battle ground. It replaced a mansion where the prince spent some hours before the battle.

CULNAKNOCK, Isle of Skye, Highland 32 NG56
Situated on the E coast of the Trotternish peninsula, Culnaknock lies a little to the S of the Lealt Fall. A good view of the Kilt Rock can be enjoyed 3m N, where the road approaches the very edge of the cliffs. The top rock is composed of columnar basalt and the lower portion displays horizontal beds, giving the viewer an impression of pleats in a kilt. To the S of Culnaknock, a splendid panorama of sea and islands is afforded by the ridge before Rigg. Across the Sound of Raasay is the rocky island of South Rona, now uninhabited; the larger island of Raasay lies farther S.

CULROSS, Fife 46 NS98
One of the best examples of a 16th- to 17th-c small town in Scotland, Culross stands in Torry Bay and was once famous for its girdles or baking plates. The NTS has splendidly restored the old houses, with their crow-stepped gables and red pantiled roofs.

Culross is associated with both St Serf and St Kentigern, and the 13th-c church preserves its choir and central tower – the latter is built over the rood-screen and pulpitum. However, the nave of the church is ruined. Interesting 17th-c alabaster effigies of the Bruce family can be seen inside. Near the church is Abbey House, built in the 17th and 19thc from the stones of the monastic building it replaced.

Famous little Culross Palace (AM) features old painted ceilings and a terraced garden, and was built between 1597 and 1611 by Sir George Bruce of Carnock. Carnock developed the town's sea-going trade in salt and coal. James VI was a visitor to Culross Palace and the salt pans. Other lovely old buildings include the Study – with its panelled Culross Room, the Ark, the Nunnery, Parley Hill House, and the Manse. The delightful Tolbooth faces the estuary and dates from 1626, and the snuffmaker's house of 1693 carries the inscription 'Who would have thocht it, noses would have bocht it'.

The hospital was founded in 1637 and the modern Mercat cross, on its original steps, is approached by a paved road called the Crown o' the Causey. The crown of this was for the use of the upper classes only. Only the choir remains of the 13th-c abbey (AM) which was sited on a hillside N of the town. Dunimarle Castle stands to the W.

CULSALMOND, Grampian 35 NJ63
Kirkton of Culsalmond is the full name of this village. To the S lies Williamston House with its fine gardens. Glen Foudland is traversed by the main Aberdeen to Huntly road, and stretches NW with the Hill of Foudland rising to 1,529ft above it.

CULTER, Grampian 35 NJ80
More generally known as Peterculter, the village of Culter is situated on the River Dee. Leuchar Burn flows into the Dee at this point and once supplied water for paperworks dating from 1751. Above the burn is a statue of Rob Roy, the famous freebooter. Normandykes earthworks lie to the SW of the village. Modern Maryculter church is sited across the Dee in Kincardine, with the wild ravine of Corbie Linn near by.

CULTER, Strathclyde *25 NT03*

This village lies on Culter Water near the point where it joins the Clyde. Culter House is a white-harled 17th-c building with a 1m-long avenue of trees. Tinto Hill rises to 2,335ft in the W, with 2,454ft Culter Fell to the SE.

CULZEAN CASTLE, Strathclyde *24 NS21*

One of Robert Adam's finest creations, this splendid castle (NTS) dates mainly from 1777 but was built around an ancient tower of the Kennedy family. The castle overlooks the Firth of Clyde, and its 565 acres of ground include a walled garden established in 1783, an aviary, swan pond, camellia house, and home farm. Interesting Kennedy relics are preserved at Culzean, which also includes a magnificent staircase, fine plaster ceilings, and the notable Round Drawing Room. President Eisenhower was given the top flat in 1946 as his Scottish residence.

The splendid grounds became Scotland's first countryside park (NTS) in 1970, and in 1973 the farm buildings – also designed by Adam – were opened as a reception and interpretation centre.

CUMBERNAULD, Strathclyde *45 NS77*

Cumbernauld Development Corporation was established in 1956 to plan a new town for Glasgow's overspill population, and Cumbernauld New Town has become a model for town planners all over the world. Shops, offices, hotels, and entertainments are centralized into a multi-storey complex. Late 18th-c locks and a bridge can be seen on the Forth and Clyde Canal. To the SE are Fannyside Muir and a small loch – once part of the former Caledonian Forest.

CUMMERTREES, Dumfries and Galloway *26 NY16*

The notorious spring tides of the Firth can be observed from this village. The local church is thought to have been founded by Robert the Bruce. The district round Cummertrees was described by Scott in *Redgauntlet*.

CUMNOCK, Strathclyde *25 NS51*

An industrial and market town, Cumnock lies on Lugar Water and is the centre of a mining area. Snuff boxes were once made here, and the town's restored Mercat cross was erected in 1703. Outside the town hall is a bust of James Keir Hardie, one of the founders of the Labour Party, who lived in the town while secretary of the Miners' Federation.

Airds Moss is a barren expanse of moorland where government troops defeated the Covenanters in 1680, and which lies 2m N. Between Cumnock and Lugar 2m NE is a 150ft-high viaduct over a deep river gorge. Great ironworks were built at Lugar in 1845. Dumfries House, a fine unspoilt Adam mansion, stands 2m W of Cumnock in grounds which include ruined Terrenzean Castle.

CUPAR, Fife *31 NO31*

Cupar is the market centre for the agricultural produce of the fertile Howe of Fife, and a Royal Burgh with a charter dating back to 1363. Its Mercat cross is topped by a unicorn and was brought back to the town from Wemysshall Hill in 1897. A treaty was signed on the hill in 1559 between the Queen Regent and the Lords of the Congregation, with the result that invading French troops left Fife.

The parish church has a tower of 1415 which carries a spire dated two

centuries later. A 17th-c gravestone, carved with two heads and a hand, records the murder of martyrs of the period. Sir David Lyndsay gave the first performance of his nine-hour play *Ane Satyre of the Three Estaits* here in 1535. This attack on the Church of Scotland has had several successful 20th-c revivals at the Edinburgh Festival.

Scotstarvit Tower (AM), known to have been in existence in 1579, stands on the Hill of Tarvit Estate (NTS) 2m S. The estate's mansion overlooks the Howe of Fife and was restored in 1906 by Sir Robert Lorimer. It houses several art treasures. Off the Newburgh road 3m NW of Cupar is an obelisk to the 4th Earl of Hopetoun. This surmounts Mount Hill, with ruined 16th-c Collairnie Castle farther to the W.

CURRIE, Lothian *47 NT16*

Paper milling was once an important local industry both here and at neighbouring Balerno. The Water of Leith flows through the village, with the long range of the Pentland Hills to the S. An ancient bridge crosses the river near the little 18th-c church, and halfway to Balerno is the ruined Lennox Tower. Lang Whang is the curious name given to an old drove road that ran across the lower slopes of the Pentlands to Carnwath. Beyond Threipmuir Reservoir, some 2½m S of Balerno, is the old hunting seat of Bavelaw Castle. This is of 17th-c origin and displays modern additions.

DAILLY (Old & New), Strathclyde *24 NS20 and 24 NX29*

Old and New Dailly villages stand 3m apart in the wooded valley of the Water of Girvan. New Dailly church is 18thc and contains former lairds' lofts. To the

1 Collairnie Castle
2 Hill of Tarvit Mansion
3 Hopetoun Monument
4 Mercat Cross
5 Parish Church
6 Scotstarvit Tower

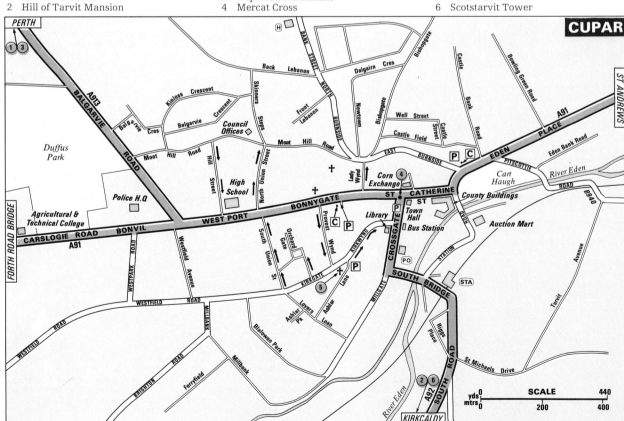

N of the village is ruined, 17th-c Dalquharran Castle. In the vicinity stands the newer castle of 1790, which was designed by Robert Adam.

Brunston Castle was built during the 16thc and stands to the W of New Dailly. To the NE of Old Dailly the 17th-c house of Bargany stands near the river in beautiful gardens. Penwhapple Glen is S of Old Dailly and is guarded by Penkill Castle, which dates from the 16th and 17thc. Penkill is one of the oldest inhabited houses in the one-time county of Ayrshire. Dante Gabriel Rossetti composed poetry here in 1869.

DAIRSIE, Fife   31 NO41

Situated 3m E of Cupar, Dairsie lies on the main Cupar to St Andrews Road. Ruined Dairsie Castle stands on a hill near by. The little church dates from 1621. To the S of the village on the Pitscottie road, the River Eden is spanned by a bridge dating from 1522. Farther S the road runs through the charming wooded Dura Den, an area where fossilized fish have been found.

DALBEATTIE, Dumfries and Galloway   25 NX86

Granite quarries brought Dalbeattie great prosperity, and the shiny, grey local stone was used for building all over the world. Granite chips from the quarries at nearby Craignair are still used today for road surfacing. Lying in the wooded vale of Urr Water, Dalbeattie itself is built of the local stone. The 80ft-high Mote of Urr, is a well-preserved Saxon or early-Norman circular mound within a fortified enclosure lying 2½m N. It is considered one of the finest examples in Britain.

The tower of Buittle Place stands 1½m NW and was built in the 16thc from stones taken from the old castle of Buittle, or Botel. John Baliol, a vassal king of Scotland known to his subjects as Toom Tabard (Empty Coat), was born in the castle in 1249. St Constantine was a missionary in the area round Dalbeattie, and several local churches are dedicated to him.

DALGETY BAY, Fife   47 NT18

A new town of private housing has been developed here, and 1m N stands an ancient church which was dedicated to St Bridget in 1244.

DALHALVAIG, Highland   37 NC85

Remains of several hut circles and brochs are to be found around this Strath-Halladale hamlet.

DALILEA, Highland   32 NM76

This angling resort lies in the historic Moidart district and can be reached by the road from Acharacle. The Gaelic Jacobite Bard Alexander Macdonald lived here, and in 1745 Prince Charles Edward and his Clanranald followers sailed up Loch Shiel from here in three boats to Glenaladale. They continued along the lonely, roadless glen into hills farther up the loch, where they received hospitality. Fine views of the Sunart district can be enjoyed from prominent, 2,774ft Ben Resipol, taking in the loch to the SE.

DALKEITH, Lothian   47 NT36

Electronics and diary printing are two of the many new industries which this ancient milling and market town has adopted. The North and South Esk rivers unite beyond the park of Dalkeith House, which dates from the 12thc.

The palace was remodelled by Vanbrugh in c1700 for Anne, Duchess of Buccleuch, widow of the rebel Duke of Monmouth. Monmouth was beheaded in London in 1685. James IV, James VI, and Prince Charles Edward all visited the palace, and Queen Victoria stayed here in 1842. The Duchess of Buccleuch was associated with Scott's Lay of the Last Minstrel, and she lived for some years at Newark Castle near Broadmeadows. She was buried in the now roofless eastern apse of St Nicholas Church, which was restored in 1852. To the S of the town is interesting Newbattle Abbey.

DALLAS, Grampian   34 NJ15

Circular Dallas Lodge was built in 1680 and stands in fine gardens.

*DALMALLY, Strathclyde   29 NN12

River Orchy flows through Dalmally in Strath Orchy on its way to Loch Awe, which lies W of the village. During its journey it passes near Kilchurn Castle, which affords views of 3,689ft Ben Cruachan across the loch. To the N of the village beyond Glen Strae is 3,242ft Ben Euniach. Ben Lui is one of old Argyll's highest peaks, and its 3,708ft-bulk dominates Glens Orchy and Lochy 6m E of the village. This mountain stands in a national nature reserve.

Glen Orchy is traversed by a narrow road which branches off the Tyndrum road. A prominent monument to the famous bard Duncan Ban MacIntyre, described as the Burns of the Highlands, crowns a piece of high ground off the old Inveraray road 2m SW of Dalmally.

DALMELLINGTON, Strathclyde   25 NS40

The River Doon flows into Bogton Loch to the W of this small town, near the Calcairnie Linn waterfall. The town itself is involved in the iron-working industry, and the source of the river is in the long and narrow Loch Doon, farther to the S. This loch lies in the shadow of the Rhinns of Kells, which are dominated by 2,668ft Corserine and 2,650ft Carlins Cairn. Picturesque Ness Glen lies at the N end of the loch. Good views of the area are afforded by 1,521ft Benbeoch, a hill to the N of Dalmellington.

DALMENY, Lothian   46 NT17

Probably Scotland's finest example of a Norman church stands here. Of special interest are the richly-carved south doorway, and the finely-arched chancel and semi-circular vaulted apse. Curious mythological beasts can be made out in the carvings. The church dates from the 12thc and has been restored; the recent tower replaces one which collapsed in the 15thc. Modern Dalmeny House stands in its own park E of the village, and 1m N is restored Barnbougle Castle. The latter overlooks Drum Sands on the Firth of Forth, and an oil terminal now stands near by.

DALNACARDOCH, Tayside   34 NN77

This is the point where a road built by General Wade in 1730 joins the main

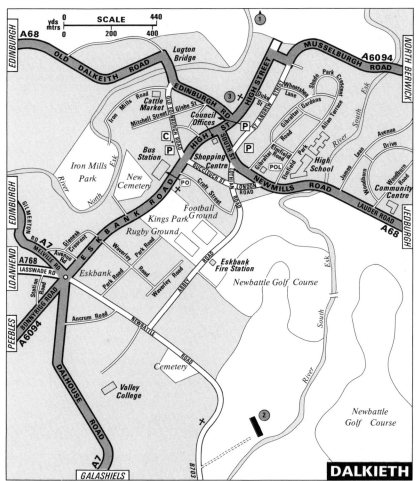

1   Dalkeith House
2   Newbattle Abbey
3   St Nicholas' Church

DALKIETH

road through Glen Garry towards Inverness. Part of the main road itself runs along the same course as another Wade road. General Wade had a hut at Dalnacardoch, which later became an inn where Prince Charles Edward spent a night in 1745.

To the N of the road junction is the vast hill and moorland area known as the Forest of Atholl. The Wade Stone, an 8ft-high pillar erected in 1729 to mark the completion of part of the Wade road, stands 2m NW of Dalnacardoch in lonely hill country. It is said that General Wade, a man of great stature, placed a coin on the top of the stone and found it still in position a year later.

DALNASPIDAL, Tayside   34 NN67
At this lonely spot in the Grampian moorlands the main road and railway from Perth to Inverness leave Glen Garry to pass through the bleak and lofty Pass of Drumochter. To the E the desolate, 3,000ft-high hills of the Forest of Atholl stretch N to the great Gaick Forest. Loch Garry lies a little to the S and is joined by a tunnel to Loch Ericht as part of a hydro-electric scheme. Ben Alder rises to 3,757ft and dominates Loch Ericht from the W, while 3,306ft Beinn Udlaman guards the E shores of the loch. Two prominent hills – the Sow of Atholl and the Boar of Badenoch – stand to the NW of Dalnaspidal.

DALRY, Dumfries and Galloway 25 NX68
Properly named St John's Town of Dalry, this little village lies in the Glenkens district and provides a good centre from which to tour the Galloway Highlands. Ancient St John's Stone stands in the village street and recalls the dedication name of John the Baptist, originally given to the church by the Knights Templars. A Covenanter's stone can be seen in the churchyard, which is encircled by the Water of Ken.

James IV was a visitor to the village in 1507 and 1508. Across the river valley to the W is the Glenlee power station of the Galloway power scheme, supplied from Clatteringshaws Loch. Earlston Linn can be found 2½m NNW along the road to Carsphairn, where the Water of Ken is joined by the Polharrow Burn. The tower of Earlston stands a little to the E and dates from 1655. Near by is the later Earlston Lodge. Dalry affords distant NW views to the Rhinns of Kells, particularly 2,668ft Corserine and 2,650ft Carlins Cairn.

DALRY, Strathclyde   29 NS24
Dalry is a one-time iron-working town in the Ayrshire coal field, situated on the River Garnock. Blair House stands 1½m SE and is a fine mansion which incorporates a 14th-c keep and two 17th-c doorways. Dusk Water flows through the grounds of the house, and a stalactite cave can be seen in the glen.

DALVOURN, Highland   34 NH63
Culloden battlefield lies to the NE of this Strath Nairn village, and the road N to Inverness crosses Drummossie Muir. Dunlichity church lies 3m SW of Dalvourn off a by-road, and a watchtower near the entrance of the church was used during the 19thc as a lookout for body snatchers. The church itself was built in 1758, and part of the walls of an earlier building were incorporated in the structure. It is said

that cuts on two of the stones here were made by clansmen sharpening their weapons before Culloden in 1746.

DALWHINNIE, Highland   34 NN68
This village name is a corruption of the Gaelic 'dell of the meeting'. Highland chiefs and lowland barons often met to parley or fight to the death on this desolate ground. Dalwhinnie lies on the Perth to Inverness road and the River Truim at the head of Glen Truim. General Wade's road to Inverness, and his now derelict road to Fort Augustus over the Corrieyairack Pass, fork just N of the village. Sir John Hope failed to intercept Prince Charles Edward at the fork in 1745, and a year later the prince was a fugitive in the same area. One of his hiding-places was Cluny's Cage, situated below the slopes of 3,757ft Ben Alder and described by R L Stevenson in *Kidnapped*. The Inverness road is N of the village and descends gradually through Glen Truim, past the Falls of Truim into gentler country.

Wild Gaick Forest extends to the E of the village and lonely, 15m-long Loch Ericht stretches away to the SW on the fringe of Badenoch. The loch is used in a hydro-electric scheme and at its W extremity are Ben Alder and 3,306ft Beinn Udlaman facing each other across the water.

DARNICK, Borders   26 NT53
Fine old Darnick Tower, beloved by Scott, stands in a lovely setting near the Tweed a little W of Melrose. It was originally built in 1425 but was burnt by the English under Hertford; rebuilding by Andrew Heiton began in 1569, and the old iron entrance gate can still be seen. A Border battle took place between the tower and the river at aptly-named Skirmish Hill in 1526, and was described by Scott in *The Monastery*.

To the SE of Darnick rise the triple-peaked Eildon Hills, and the lovely wooded Rhymer's Glen lies to the S of the hamlet. Little Cauldshiels Loch is to the W of the Glen. Off the Galashiels road, 2m NW of Darrick, is the entrance to the lonely valley of the Allan Water. The Border pele towers of Glendearg, Colmslie, and Langshaw lie in the hills farther N. Scott mentions Glendearg tower in *The Monastery*.

DARVEL, Strathclyde   25 NS53
Sir Alexander Fleming, the discoverer of penicillin, was born in this lace-making town in 1881. New Year's Day processions were once held round the prehistoric Dragon Stone in Burn Road.

DAVA, Highland   34 NJ03
Lofty Dava Moor lies between the valleys of the Spey and the Findhorn, and allows wide views N towards Moray Firth and S to the distant Cairngorms. The Knock of Braemoray rises a little to the N, with lonely hills and moorland culminating in Cairn Kitty.

DAVIOT, Highland   34 NH73
With the high ground of the Glen of Moy to the SE and Drummossie Moor to the NW, Daviot lies in a dip of Strath Nairn. Wade's old military road follows a parallel course with the main Daviot to Inverness road, but keeps about 1m W along the W side of wooded Dunmore Hill. The church's unusual steeple is a well-known landmark. Roads run along both banks of the Nairn NE of Daviot, and head towards Cawdor. The N bank road passes through Culloden on the way.

DEESIDE, Grampian   34
The Dee is a salmon river in a long and beautiful valley which stretches from the estuary at Aberdeen, across the Mar division of the old county, and briefly into old Kincardineshire near Banchory and Crathes Castle. From this point Royal Deeside becomes increasingly lovely, with dense woodlands on either bank. Near Aboyne are SW views of the lofty Forest of Birse hills, with the 2,433ft Hill of Cat and 2,555ft Mount Battock predominant.

The area between the Highland resorts of Ballater and Braemar is perhaps the best known part of Deeside. It includes the Royal castle of Balmoral, and little Crathie Church where the Royal Family worship when in residence at Balmoral. Queen Victoria popularized the district when she first visited it in 1848, and she and Prince Albert made many excursions into the surrounding mountains – including a pony ascent of the great Lochnagar peak.

This peak dominates the Royal Forest of Ballochbuie from its position at the N end of the lofty White Mount plateau. Grouse and deer are shot in season on many of the heather-clad Deeside moors. Between Aboyne and Balmoral good roads on both banks of the river offer fine views of this beautiful part of the Highlands, much of which is given over to deer.

Braemar is a summer and winter resort which is famed for its annual Highland Gathering – held on the first Saturday in September. Surrounded as it is by forested and heather-clad hills, Braemar illustrates the full character of Deeside. Fine views of the magnificent Cairngorms range, the largest 4,000ft-plus area in Scotland, can be enjoyed from the area. The highest peak is 4,296ft Ben Macdhui which can be seen to the NW from high ground around Braemar. The Dee's upper reaches W of Braemar are much wilder and faster flowing. Lord Byron nearly lost his life in the Linn of Dee, a rockly cleft beyond Inverey. Situated in the wild and lonely pass of Lairig Ghru are the Pools of Dee, beyond 3,303ft Devil's Point and 4,241ft Cairn Toul, far up Glen Dee in the fastnesses of the Cairngorms.

The Dee actually rises at the Wells of Dee, high up near the summit of 4,248ft Braeriach. Narrow hill roads running N from points near Balmoral and Ballater link Deeside with the upper valley of the Don near Cock Bridge, and converge at Gairnshiel Bridge to continue over the steep and narrow Glas Choille section. The latter is often snowbound in winter.

DELNASHAUGH INN, Grampian 34 NJ13
The lovely old Bridge of Avon spans the River Avon in a beautiful setting on the Grantown-on-Spey road, N of Delnashaugh Inn. Beyond the picturesque grounds of Ballindalloch Castle the Avon joins the River Spey. Ballindalloch Castle bears the arms of the Macpherson-Grants and was begun in the 16thc. It is now linked to a modern building. The Hill of Delnapot rises N of the meeting of the two rivers. A road follows the Avon S of Delnashaugh Inn to the river's junction with Livet Water, by Downan. The famous Glenlivet whisky distillery is near by.

DENHOLM, Borders   26 NT51
Both John Leyden, the 18th-c poet and friend of Scott, and editor of the *Oxford*

English Dictionary Sir James Murray, were born in this little village on the River Teviot. An obelisk was set up to Leyden's memory in 1861, and a tablet on a thatched cottage records his birth. Denholm has a village green, and Westgate Hall dates from the 17thc. Text House is of a strange design and was erected by Dr Haddon, a local eccentric. The ruins of oddly-named Fatlips Castle, built in the 16thc for the Lockharts, stand 2m NE on the summit of steep Minto Crags. Dark Ruberslaw rises to 1,392ft S of Denholm, and was once a Covenanters' retreat. Alexander Peden often preached from a rock now known as Peden's Pulpit, near the summit of Ruberslaw.

DENNY, Central　46 NS88
Together with Dunipace, Denny is a small manufacturing town on the River Carron to the E of the Kilsyth Hills. To the N is the small Georgian house of Quarter. A narrow and hilly moorland road runs W from Denny towards Fintry, following the Carron and later the Endrick Water between the Campsie Fells and the Fintry Hills.

DERVAIG, Isle of Mull, Strathclyde 28 NM45
A little theatre has been established for some years at Dervaig, which lies in a lovely setting at the head of narrow Loch Cuan in Glen Bellart. Hairpin bends characterize the narrow road which runs E to Tobermory past the Mishnish Lochs. A road leading SE from Dervaig to Salen passes near Loch Frisa and through Glen Aros.

DESKFORD, Grampian　35 NJ56
Properly named Kirktown of Deskford, this village lies on the Burn of Deskford. The ruined church (AM) has a richly-carved sacrament house which was donated by Alexander Ogilvy of Deskford in 1551. Inscribed in both Latin and English, this structure is considered a fine example of its kind. To the NW of the village is the 1,050ft Bin of Cullen.

*DINGWALL, Highland　34 NH55
Created a Royal Burgh in 1226, Dingwall is the one-time county town of old Ross and Cromarty and lies near the mouth of the River Conon. Dingwall's harbour was the work of Telford, and traces of the old castle can still be seen. The town arms – a starfish – adorn the Tolbooth of 1730, and in front of this is the shaft of a former Mercat cross. An iron yett, or gate, from the old town gaol stands beside the shaft. Near the church is a statue erected in 1714 to the 1st Earl of Cromarty, and a tower commemorating the birth of General Sir Hector Macdonald stands on a hill S of the town. Tulloch Castle lies N of Dingwall and was a Davidson seat for many years. The countryside to the NW is dominated for miles around by 3,426ft Ben Wyvis.

DINNET, Grampian　35 NO49
Prehistoric remains are to be found on Dinnet Moor, which can be reached from the road N from Dinnet to Huntly. Glen Tanner and Glen Tanar Forest lie to the S, beyond the Dinnet Bridge over the River Dee.

DIRLETON, Lothian　31 NT58
A village with an early 17th-c church and houses round a green, Dirleton lies halfway between the golfing resorts of Gullane and North Berwick. The beautiful sandstone ruins of Dirleton Castle (AM) rise from sheer rock near the village green. Built by the Norman de Vaux family in 1225, the castle displays 15th- to 17th-c additions and has had an eventful history. Wallace's Scottish supporters held out against a siege by Edward I's army in 1298, but the castle was subsequently captured for the king by the Bishop of Durham. In the 17thc it resisted Cromwell's troops before falling to Lambert, who dismantled it in 1650.

The group of 13th-c towers forms the earliest example of a clustered donjon extant. The ruins contain a flower garden, and a 17th-c bowling green which is surrounded by yew trees and is still in use. A 16th-c dovecot stands near the castle, and to the W is Archerfield House, which replaced the castle as a residence. Little Fidra Island and its lighthouse lie off the coast to the N.

DOLLAR, Central　46 NS99
The fine Dollar Academy was erected in 1818 by WH Playfair, and is one of the town's proud possessions. Dollar lies at the foot of the Ochil Hills near the River Devon; 1m N between the Burn of Sorrow, flowing through the steep Windy Pass, and the Burn of Care stands ruined Castle Campbell (AM) in Dollar Glen (NTS). This romantic wooded glen, with its paths and bridges, makes a wonderful setting for the castle. Views S over the winding Devon towards the Firth of Forth and the distant Pentland Hills can be enjoyed from here.

The castle was once known as Castle Gloume or Gloom, and includes a fine 14th-c square tower joined to a 16th-c wing. Also of interest are the courtyard, great hall, and the great barrel roof on the third floor. John Knox preached here in 1556. In 1645 Montrose ravaged the countryside but failed to take the castle, which was burnt by Cromwell's troops some ten years later. Off the Milnathort road 2m NE of Dollar are remains of Cowden House; 2m NW are the Ochils, with King's Seat rising to 2,111ft. Ben Cleuch stands behind King's Seat, and at 2,363ft is the highest point in the range. It affords splendid views.

DOLPHINTON, Strathclyde　30 NT14
Outside the door of the little ancient church is a Covenanter's grave. A c2,000-year-old sandstone cist was uncovered in 1920 on Kippit Hills, NE of the village.

DORES, Highland　34 NH53
Situated in Stath Dores at the point where it meets Loch Ness, Dores is bordered to the E by Loch Ashie, with the larger Loch Duntelchaig farther S. Both lochs lie at an altitude of more than 700ft. Aldourie Castle stands 2m N, where Loch Ness begins to narrow. First built in 1626 by MacIntoch, the castle has had alterations up to 1903 and has been the seat of the Frasers since 1750. The earliest structure now visible is of 18th-c origin. A choice of routes can be taken S from Dores to Fort Augustus. The W road follows the shores of Loch Ness, and the E one climbs over moorland by way of Errogie.

DORNIE, Highland　33 NG82
Dornie lies in a beautiful mountain and loch setting and is where Loch Duich meets Loch Long. A road bridge which spans Loch Long here replaces a ferry which once linked the little crofting village with Ardelve on Loch Alsh. Just to the NE on Loch Long is the clachan of Bundalloch, where byres of several old crofters' cottages known as black houses are still to be found. At the meeting point of Lochs Duich, Alsh, and Long – between Dornie and Totaig – is the picturesque offshore castle of Eilean Donan, built in 1220 by Alexander II.

Once completely surrounded by water, the castle is now linked by a causeway to the A87 on the mainland. Early in its history it passed into the hands of the Mackenzies of Kintail, who became Earls of Seaforth. In 1719 it was bombarded by the English frigate 'Worcester' in order to dislodge a party of Spanish Jacobite troops. The Macrae family held Eilean Donan as hereditary constables for the Mackenzies, and rebuilt the structure in 1932 at a cost of £230,000. It now houses a war memorial and museum of the Clan Macrae. On the way to Shiel Bridge, 2m SE of Dornie, the old road climbs above Loch Duich to a height of more

Entrance gate and lodge of 16th-c Ballindalloch Castle at Delnashaugh Inn.

than 500ft at Carr Brae. Also known as Keppoch, this point affords fine views towards the Five Sisters of Kintail, which are dominated by 3,505ft Scour Ouran. A new road follows the coast.

DORNOCH, Highland   37 NH78
An old woman accused of turning her daughter into a pony, which was then shod by the Devil, was burnt in Dornoch in 1722. She has the doubtful distinction of having been the last woman to be judicially executed in Scotland for witchcraft. The execution site is marked by a rough stone. Dornoch was the county town of old Sutherland, and is a Royal Burgh. The town is popular with golf enthusiasts and holiday makers.

Little Dornoch Cathedral was founded in 1224 by Gilbert, Archdeacon of Moray and Bishop of Caithness. It has been a place of worship ever since. Bishop Gilbert was killed by the Danes at the Battle of Embo near the town in 1248. A landmark for miles around, the cathedral was largely destroyed by fire in 1570 but restored in 1835, 1837, and 1924 after much neglect. As many as sixteen Earls of Sutherland are buried in here, and a fine statue of the Duke of Sutherland by Chantrey can be seen at the west end. An effigy of Sir Richard of Moray stands in the nave. Bishop's Castle was ruined in 1570, and only the tower remains. This has been incorporated into a hotel.

DORNOCK, Dumfries and Galloway   26 NY26
Remains of a stone circle and two ancient towers can be found in the vicinity of Dornock.

DOUGLAS, Strathclyde   25 NS83
Douglas Castle was rebuilt by Adam in 1759 and demolished as a result of colliery undermining in the 1940's. All that remains are the chapel and the porch. The castle was the model for Scott's *Castle Dangerous*, and an earlier castle on the same site was the Douglases' stronghold; many of the family are buried in partly 12th-c St Bride's Church (AM). The tombs include those of 'the good Sir James of Douglas', who was killed by the Moors in Spain in 1330 while taking the heart of Robert the Bruce to the Holy Land, and of Archibald Bell-the-Cat, 5th Earl of Angus who died in 1514. He was given the nickname after killing Robert Cochrane, low-born favourite of James III, in 1482.

The restored chancel of St Bride's stands in the churchyard and contains some 13th- and 15th-c French stained glass. Mary Queen of Scots is thought to have given the clock dated 1565, which is set in the tower of 1618 near the chancel. Douglas has two old inns – the Sun dating from 1621, and Crosskeys. A house in Main Street has an inscribed panel of 1695 recalling an atrocity perpetrated on James Gavin, a Covenanter. A monument commemorates the raising of the Cameronian Regiment in 1689.

DOUGLAS HALL, Dumfries and Galloway   25 NX85
This small resort on Sandyhills Bay overlooks the Solway Firth, with 1,866ft Criffel rising to the NE. Two natural rock archways can be seen on the coast near by.

DOUNE, Central   30 NN70
James Spittal, wealthy tailor to James IV, built the picturesque bridge over the Teith in 1535 after being refused passage by the ferryman because he had no money on him. Doune was once noted for its fine pistols and boasts an old Mercat cross. Doune Castle is one of Scotland's best-preserved medieval castles.

Built in the early 15thc by the Regent Albany, the castle overlooks the swift flowing Rivers of Teith and Ardoch. The Regent Albany was executed in 1424, and Castle Doune passed into the hands of the Stuarts of Doune, Earls of Moray, in the 16thc. The 2nd Earl of Moray, hero of the ballad *The Bonnie Earl of Moray*, lived here until his murder in 1592. In 1745 the castle was held for Prince Charles Edward, and the hero of Scott's *Waverley* was confined within. Home, the author of *Douglas*, escaped from the castle using a rope of bedclothes. Castle Doune's ruins include two fine towers flanking the hall.

Doune Park Gardens, 60 acres in all, lie $1\frac{1}{2}$m NW of the village with the Doune Motor Museum near by. The entrance to the African Safari Park at Blair Drummond is 2m SE of Doune.

DOUNREAY, Highland   37 NC96
Vast tracts of one-time Caithness have remained almost uninhabited since the early 19th-c Highland clearances, and in 1954 a spot on the N coast was chosen for the site of Dounreay's atomic reactor. This was Scotland's first experimental nuclear power station. The United Kingdom Atomic Energy Authority has an exhibition here.

DOWNAN, Grampian   34 NJ13
The Livet Water joins the River Avon at Dowan, near the road junction close to the famous whisky distillery at Glenlivet. Tomintoul can be reached along several routes, the W one following Strath Avon backed by the Cromdale Hills, and the E road crossing the Braes of Glenlivet.

DREGHORN, Strathclyde   24 NS33
Birthplace of inventor of the pneumatic tyre – John Dunlop – in 1845, Dreghorn stands on the Annick Water. The River Irvine joins Annick Water to the W of the town and eventually empties into Irvine Bay. An early 19th-c corn mill can be seen in Dreghorn.

DREM, Lothian   31 NT57
Some $2\frac{1}{2}$m E of Drem a monument at East Fortune marks the start of the first Atlantic double crossing by air. This was effected by the British airship R34 in July 1919 (see inset on page 247). A museum of flight is being established here.

DRIMNIN, Highland   28 NM55
Situated on the Sound of Mull, Drimnin has a pier for steamers and affords views across the Sound to the island of Mull. The village is situated on a narrow, hilly road in the Morven district, NW of Lochaline. Loch Teacuis, an inlet of Loch Sunart, lies beyond the hills to the NE with the islands of Carna and Oronsay off-shore.

DRUMBEG, Highland   36 NC13
Many small lochs litter the crofting district around Drumbeg, which lies on the beautiful but narrow coast road from Lochinver to Kylesku. Loch Nedd, a sandy inlet of Eddrachillis Bay, lies to the E. The bay itself is studded with

islands and affords noted seascapes. The isolated Torridon-sandstone peaks of old Sutherland rise to the E and S, from 2,653ft Quinag down to the $1\frac{1}{2}$m-long summit ridge of Suilven, which tops 2,399ft at its highest point. To the NW of Drumbeg is Oldany Island, which lies in Eddrachillis Bay.

DRUMELZIER, Borders   26 NT13
The burial place of Merlin the Arthurian wizard is supposed to be close to the confluence of Drumelzier Burn and the River Tweed. Drumelzier Church preserves the ancient burial vault of the Tweedies, and to the E lies the ruined Tinnis or Thanes Castle, reached via a sheep track and backed by 2,414ft Pykestone Hill. Tinnis Castle was built at the beginning of the 16thc and was the seat of the Clan Tweedie. Fragments of 16th-c Drumelzier Castle, which once stood near the Tweed, can be seen 1m SW of the village.

DRUMGASK, Highland   34 NN69
Roads from Dalwhinnie and Newtonmore meet here in the lonely valley of the Upper Spey, on their way through Strath Mashie to Loch Laggan. The lonely Monadhliath Mountains, with Carn Dearg rising to 3,093ft, extend NE. Some 2m NE beyond Laggan church and the bridge lies Cluny Castle, ancient home of the Macphersons. Cluny Macpherson was a fellow fugitive of Prince Charles Edward, with whom he hid in a cave in 1746.

A little to the SE of the castle on the S bank of the Spey near the Glen Truim Estate, is a stone which is said to mark the geographical centre of Scotland. The old Wade road to Fort Augustus over the Corrieyairack Pass diverges $\frac{1}{2}$m W of Drumgask, and 6m W beyond Loch Crunachan along the track is Wade's Garva Bridge. Also known as St George's Bridge, this structure spans the River Spey and dates from 1732.

DRUMLANRIG CASTLE, Dumfries and Galloway   25 NX89
The first Duke of Queensberry, for whom the castle was built between 1676 and 1689, was so horrified by its expense that he only spent one night in it. Designed by Sir William Bruce, the magnificent building displays much fine old woodwork and stands amid woodland in Nithsdale, a little to the W of River Nith. Prince Charles Edward occupied the castle in 1745. It is now the seat of the Dukes of Buccleuch. A feature of its fine park is ruined Tibber's Castle, destroyed by Bruce in 1311.

DRUMLITHIE, Grampian   35 NO78
A slender weavers' bell tower of 1777, the bell of which was rung to regulate weavers' working hours, can be seen here. The village lies off the Brechin to Stonehaven road NE of the fertile Howe of the Mearns. Delightful little Fiddes Castle stands $3\frac{1}{2}$m E of Drumlithie, and to the W are the fine old mansion and gardens of Glenbervie House.

DRUMMORE, Dumfries and Galloway   24 NX13
Situated in Kirkmaiden, the farthest S parish in Scotland, Drummore is a small fishing port standing in the Rhinns of Galloway facing Luce Bay. The church dates from 1639 and has an unusual gravestone in the shape of a lighthouse. An older church once stood 3m S near Mull Farm. Fragments of St Medan's

Chapel, the oldest in Galloway, lie at the foot of cliffs 4m S of Drummore.

DRUMMUIR, Grampian   35 NJ34
Drummuir Castle stands in a park near the village, with the 1,219ft Knockan to the N and 1,366ft Carran Hill to the S. Drummuir itself lies in a beautifully-wooded section of Strath Isla, with tree-shrouded Loch Park lying to the SW on the road to Dufftown.

DRUMNADROCHIT, Highland   34 NH53
A centre for angling, pony trekking, and hill-walking, Drumnadrochit stands on the River Enrick which traverses the green and fertile Glen Urquhart before entering Loch Ness 2m E of the village. The clachan of Lewiston lies 1m S of Drumnadrochit, and from here a footpath leads to the beautiful Divach Falls. Urquhart Castle (AM), one of Scotland's largest castles, stands 1½m SE on Strone Point. This promontory overlooks Loch Ness, and the castle was probably built by the Lord of the Isles in the 13thc. It was owned by the Chiefs of Grant in the 16thc and most of the ruins date from this later period. In 1692 the castle was blown up by the Grants to prevent it from becoming a Jacobite stronghold.

Many sightings of the Loch Ness monster have been reported from the area around Urquhart Castle. To the S of the village is the extensive Balmacaan Forest. Telford's road W from Drumnadrochit runs through Glen Urquhart and past little Loch Meiklie. It allows access to the magnificent scenery of Glens Affric and Cannick. A little road turns N off the road through the glen 1m W of the village, and climbs over moors into Glen Convinth.

DRUMOAK, Grampian   35 NO79
To the NE stands Drum Castle, a massive late 13th-c granite tower adjoining a mansion of 1619. In 1323 the tower, which has walls 12 to 15ft thick, was conferred by Robert the Bruce on Sir William de Irvine. Relics and portraits of the Irvine family are preserved in the mansion.

DRUMOCHTER PASS,
Highland and Tayside   34 NN67
Wade built the original road through this pass, which was used by Bonnie Prince Charlie in 1734. Parts of the old road – with its derelict bridges – can be seen on the hills at the side of the present road, redesigned by Telford in 1829. The pass carries the main Inverness road and railway through the Grampians and reaches its 1,506ft summit near the old county boundary of Inverness-shire and Perthshire. To the W rise the oddly named hills Sow of Atholl and Boar of Badenoch, with the 3,000ft summits of the vast Forest of Atholl to the E. Drumochter Forest lies on both sides of the N end of the pass, bordered to the E by 3,004ft Chaoruinn, and to the W by 3,306ft Beinn Udlaman. Ski-ing is sometimes possible in this area. Away to the NE stretches Gaick Forest.

DRYBURGH ABBEY, Borders   26 NT53
Sir Walter Scott, members of his family, his biographer J G Lockhart, and the British Army's first world war Commander-in-Chief Field Marshal Earl Haig, are all buried in St Mary's Aisle. The beautiful ruins of the abbey lie in a loop of the Tweed, and it (AM) was originally founded during the 12thc

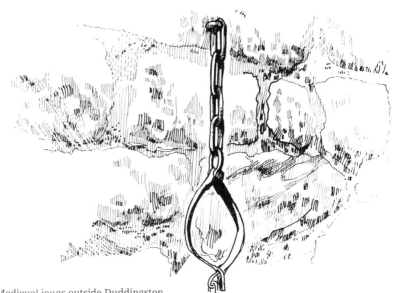

Medieval jougs outside Duddingston Church.

in the reign of David I. Repeatedly attacked by English invaders, it was badly damaged in 1322, 1385, and 1544. Meagre survivals of the church itself include the W front, with its 13th-c portal and parts of the nave, the transepts, and the chapterhouse. The cloister buildings survived in a more complete state than any other Scottish monastery except Iona and Incholm, particularly the refectory with its rose window, and the calefactory, retaining a large fireplace.

Lord Glenconner presented the abbey remains to the nation in 1918. One of Scott's favourite views, now known as Scott's View, is afforded by Bemersyde Hill 2m N of the abbey and takes in the Eildon Hills across the Tweed. The lofty Wallace statue stands on the slopes of the hill. Bemersyde House, ancient home of the Haigs, stands near by.

DRYMEN, Central   45 NS48
Lovely Loch Lomond can be seen from the gardens of the Buchanan Arms Inn. Drymen Bridge spans Endrick Water and dates from 1765. It was widened in 1929. Buchanan Castle was the 19th-c seat of the Duke of Montrose, head of the Clan Graham, and once stood by the river W of the village.

DRYNOCH
Isle of Skye, Highland   32 NG43
The village of Drynoch lies at the head of the sea-loch Harport, and Drynoch Bridge spans a burn flowing into the loch. The bridge was once the highest masonry bridge in Scotland.

DUDDINGSTON (Edinburgh), Lothian
47 NT27
Remains of prehistoric and Roman earthworks have been found in this pretty village, which lies in the shadow of Queen's Drive and the famous 822ft Arthur's Seat. Prince Charles Edward's Highlanders camped here. The Norman church displays a great deal of 17th-c alteration, but the S doorway and chancel arch are original. Outside the church hang medieval jougs – iron collars for punishing wrongdoers – last used c1850. Near by is an ancient louping-an-stane or mounting block.

Sheep's Heid Inn is the oldest licensed premises in Scotland. Duddingston's several interesting old houses include

Duddingston House, built by Sir William Chambers in 1768, the delightful 19th-c Peffermill House, and 17th-c Prestonfield House which is now a hotel. The latter was designed by Sir William Bruce in 1687, and visited by Dr Johnson and Boswell as guests of the Dick family in 1773. Little Duddingston Loch is now a bird sanctuary.

DUFFTOWN, Grampian   35 NJ33
Famous for its distilleries, Dufftown lies near the junction of the River Fiddich and Dullan Water. The latter flows to the SW along the attractive Glen Rinnes, under the slopes of 2,755ft Ben Rinnes. Dufftown was laid out by James Duff, 4th Earl of Fife, in 1817.

The picturesque 15th-c ruins of Balvenie Castle (AM) lie 1m N near the station. This moated stronghold, with its two-leaved iron yett or grille gate, originally belonged to the Comyns. It passed first into the hands of the Douglases, and then the Atholl family, and was visited by Edward I in 1304. Mary Queen of Scots came here in 1562. In 1746 the castle was occupied by the Duke of Cumberland during the Jacobite Rising. Near the castle is the famous Glenfiddich Distillery, which may be visited by the public.

The road to Keith runs NE from Dufftown through wooded Strath Isla, past tiny Loch Park and via Drummuir. A good road SE from Dufftown runs over the 1,197ft Glacks of Balloch Pass to Rhynie. The pass runs from the River Fiddich, flowing through lonely Glen Fiddich backed by 2,478ft Cooks Cairn to the River Deveron, which flows NE into the Strathbogie district of old Aberdeenshire. Just S of Dufftown the 12th-c Church of Mortlach – now modernized – stands in a lovely spot near Dullan Water. In the churchyard is the Battle Stone, reputed to commemorate a defeat of the Danes in 1010.

DUFFUS, Grampian   34 NJ16
Gordonstoun School, where the Duke of Edinburgh and the Prince of Wales were once pupils, stands to the NE of Duffus. It was founded in 1934 and is housed in a 17th- and 18th-c mansion. St Peter's Kirk (AM), in Duffus, is ruined but displays a fine 16th-c vaulted porch. The church was founded by a member of the Freskyns, ancestors of the Murrays and

several other Scottish families. Facing the church is the shaft of the old parish cross (AM), probably dating from the 14thc. The massive ruins of Duffus Castle (AM), a fine motte and bailey structure, stand on a mound 1½m SE of the village. A water-filled moat still surrounds the building, which was once seat of the de Moravia family. The Murrays are now represented by the Dukedoms of Atholl and Sutherland. The Norman motte is crowned by a fine 14th-c tower. Hopeman and Burghead are fishing villages which lie a little to the NW of Duffus.

DULL, Tayside 30 NN84
Prehistoric cairns, standing stones, and remains of stone circles can be found in the countryside surrounding the Strath-Appin hamlet of Dull. Part of one of the three ancient crosses of the abbey still stands near the old church. A college was founded at Dull in memory of Adamnan (or Eonan), the biographer of St Columba. He is said to have been buried near here. Ruined Comrie Castle lies a little to the W.

DULNAIN BRIDGE, Highland 34 NH92
Roads from Aviemore and Carrbridge converge here, near the point where the River Dulnain flows into the Spey. The old tower of Muckerach dates from 1598 and lies 1m W.

DULSIE BRIDGE, Highland 34 NH94
This single-arched 18th-c bridge spans the River Findhorn at what is considered its most picturesque reach. The great Moray floods of 1892 came near to damaging the bridge when the Findhorn rose 40ft above normal. To the N the grounds of Glenferness House contain the Princess Stone, a sculptured tablet lying near a cairn supposed to mark the grave of a Celtic princess. The River Findhorn follows the lonely Streens valley of Strath Dearn upstream, and is overlooked by hills rising to over 2,000ft. An old military road runs NW from Dulsie Bridge towards Cawdor and the Moray Firth.

DUMBARTON, Strathclyde 44 NS37
Known as Dunbreaton – Gaelic for 'Fort of the Britons' – from the 5thc to 1018, Dumbarton was the centre of the independent Kingdom of Strathclyde. It is now a Royal Burgh situated at the confluence of rivers Leven and Clyde, and operates a number of industries. St Patrick is said to have been born here and later taken to Ireland by a party of marauding raiders.

A royal castle stood on Dumbarton Rock, a majestic 240ft-high rock commanding the river, until the Middle Ages. Little survives of medieval Dumbarton Castle (AM), but 17th- and 18th-c fortifications can still be seen. A 12th-c gateway and a dungeon survive, plus a sundial which was given to the town by Mary Queen of Scots during her brief stay at the castle in 1548. The queen was aged five when sent from here to France, and in 1571 the castle was captured from her followers under cover of night. It is now used as a barracks.

An ancient arch known as College Bow was originally in St Mary's collegiate church, but has been re-erected in Church Street. Glencairn House dates from 1623. Castlehill comprises two wooded mounds, and near by is the Cunningham-Graham Memorial (NTS). *Dumbarton's Drums* is the regimental march of the Royal Scots, the oldest British regiment.

*DUMFRIES, Dumfries and Galloway 25 NX97
Dumfries is a Royal Burgh on the River Nith, situated opposite its sister town of Maxwelltown. The two towns were amalgamated in 1929.

1 Castle	3 Cunninghame – Graham Memorial
2 College Bow	4 Glencairn House

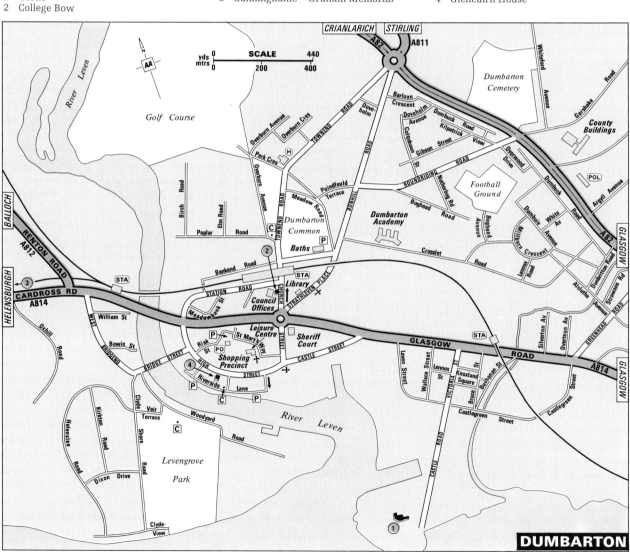

The Nith is spanned by five bridges, the oldest of which is a stone-built, six-arched structure. The Old Bridge, now used by pedestrians only, was built by Lady Devorgilla who also founded New Abbey (5m S) and endowed Balliol College in Oxford. The town has had a stormy history ever since Robert the Bruce stabbed the Red Comyn in the former Greyfriars monastery church in 1306. This action may well have altered the course of Scottish history. A plaque on a building in Castle Street records the supposed murder site. Dumfries was badly treated by Prince Charles Edward in 1745.

In 1791 Robert Burns came to live in the town and wrote some of his most famous songs here, including *Auld Lang Syne* and *Ye Banks and Braes o' Bonnie Doon.* At first he rented a three-roomed flat in the Wee Vennel, now Bank Street, but in 1793 he moved to a better house in Mill Vennel, now Burns Street. He died at the latter in 1796. His wife Jean Armour stayed in the house until her death in 1834, and the building is now a Burns museum containing his manuscripts and personal relics. The Hole in the Wa' Tavern and Globe Inn also contain Burns relics, and a fine statue of the poet stands in front of modern Greyfriars Church.

Burns was buried in the churchyard of the local Church of St Michael, together with his wife and several of his children.

St Michael's Church was built between 1744 to 1754 and later restored. A tablet recording the gratitude of Norwegians who took refuge in Scotland during the second world war is mounted on its interior south wall. A pew once used by Burns is marked by a plaque.

Picturesque Mid Steeple was built in 1707 as municipal buildings, a courthouse and a prison. Its south face carries a carved Scots ell measure of 37in. A table

1	Academy	5	Globe Inn	9	Old Bridge
2	Burns's House	6	Greyfriars Church	10	St Michael's Church
3	Burns's Mausoleum	7	Hole in the Wa'	11	Town Museum
4	Burns's Statue	8	Mid Steeple		

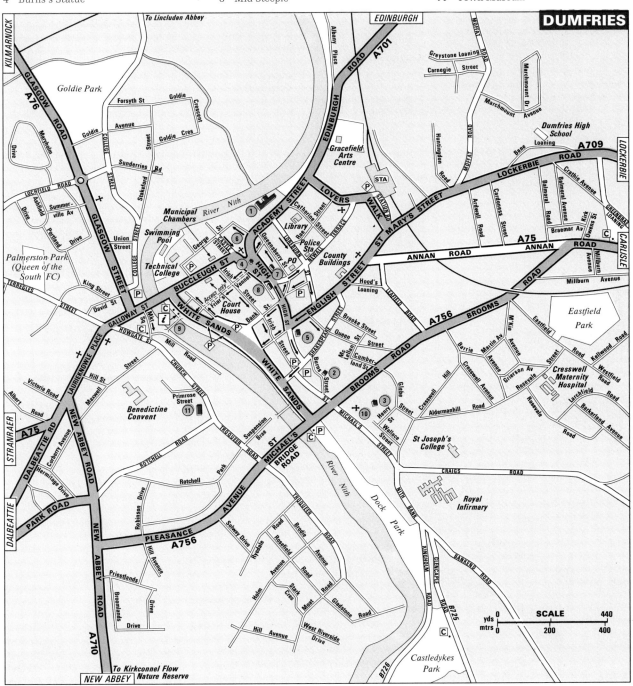

of distances on the building includes the mileage to Huntingdon in England, which was the 18th-c destination for Scottish cattle drovers pushing their animals S for the markets of London.

The Earldom of Huntingdon was held by three successive early Kings of Scotland, and Sir James Barrie was once a pupil at the Academy in Dumfries. The Guid Nychburris Festival takes place in the town annually, usually in early summer. Across the Nith in Maxwelltown is the interesting Town Museum, with an observatory and camera obscura. Kirkconnel Flow national nature reserve lies 4m S of Dumfries. The mansion of Terregles was rebuilt in 1789 and stands 2m NW of the town. This was once thought to have been the last resting place of Mary Queen of Scots before her final journey to England, but Dundrennan is now thought to have been her last Scottish stopping place.

The 18th-c Terregles Church includes a restored choir dating from 1583. Other features include several interesting tombs and stalls, plus a fine medieval painting on wood.

DUNAN, Isle of Skye, Highland   32 NG52
Situated at the mouth of Loch Ainart, Dunan faces the island of Scalpay across Loch na Cairidh. The tiny islands of Longay and the Crowlins lie beyond Scalpay. The road from Broadford to Sligachan is backed by the Red Cuillins in Lord Macdonald's Forest. Magnificent, 3,042ft Blaven rises SW of roadless Strath Mor, and can be seen from the road.

*DUNBAR, Lothian   31 NT67
Mary Queen of Scots stayed here with Bothwell for a few days before surrendering to the rebellious nobles in 1567. Dunbar is an old fishing port and Royal Burgh situated on the edge of rich farming country which is noted for its red soil. It is this which produces the famous Dunbar Red potato. The town's Myreton Motor Museum is of interest.

The charming town house dates from c1620 and carries a six-sided tower. The old market cross stands close by. The

parish church, which was rebuilt in 1821, houses a large, ornate marble monument to George Home, 1st Earl of Dunbar and Lord High Treasurer of Scotland, who died in 1610. The church's 108ft-high tower is visible from the sea.

The ruins of Dunbar Castle perch high on a rock above the harbour and also form a local landmark. In 1339 the castle was besieged, and its final destruction came after the downfall of Mary Queen of Scots in 1568. White Sands lie 2m E and offer safe bathing. Barns Ness, on the E edge of White Sands, includes limestone cliffs whicn are rich in fossils. St Abb's Head is a distant headland on the coast-line stretching SE from Dunbar. Just SE of the town, off the A1 close to Broxburn, is the site of the Battle of Dunbar which was fought in 1650. The result was a victory for Cromwell over the Covenanters under General Leslie. A stone erected in 1950 marks the battle site. The Lammermuir Hills rise to the S of the town, and there is safe bathing 1m W of Dunbar at Belhaven Beach. Out to sea to the NW is lovely Bass Rock, near North Berwick.

DUNBEATH, Highland   37 ND12
A broch known as Dun Beath stands in the angle formed by the Dunbeath River and the Burn of Houstry, and probably gave its name to the fishing village which lies SE. Built on a lofty promontory 1m S and just off the road to Berriedale, Dunbeath Castle still retains its 15th-c keep. Montrose captured the castle in 1650, and the building was enlarged during the 19thc. A coast road running SW from Dunbeath offers fine views of the lofty Caithness plateau, delicately sculpted by its rivers. Near Barriedale Water on moorland W of the village, a granite cross marks the place where the Duke of Kent was killed in a flying accident in 1942.

DUNBLANE, Central   30 NN70
This ancient town of narrow streets sits on the Allan Water at the SW tip of Strath Allan. Convenient for touring the Ochil Hills to the E and the one-time Perthshire Highlands to the W and N, Dunblane is also noted for its mainly 13th-c cathedral (AM).

The building's Norman tower is probably of 11th-c date. John Ruskin considered the W front, with its central doorway and lancet windows, to be a masterpiece of Scottish church architecture. The nave roof collapsed after the Reformation and remained in ruins until restoration began in 1892 to 1895. In the south aisle of the nave are the six wonderfully-carved, 15th-c Ochiltree stalls. These were installed in memory of Bishop Ochiltree, who died in 1447.

Restoration of the choir took place in 1914, and the north aisle includes an ancient and curiously-carved stone. Three blue slabs set in the pavement of the choir commemorate the three Drummond sisters associated with James IV – all poisoned in 1501. Traces of the Bishop's Palace can also be seen, and a little museum is housed in the 17th-c Dean's House. Leighton Library is housed in a building of 1687 near the churchyard gate. An indecisive battle took place between the Pretender's forces under the Earl of Mar, and the Royal troops led by the Duke of Argyll, on moorland 2½m E of Dunblane in 1715. The Gathering Stone of the clans commemorates this battle.

*DUNDEE, Tayside   31 NO33
Now extensively rebuilt, Dundee lies on the Firth of Tay and operates considerable light industry to supplement its old staple industries of jute production and jam making. The jute industry originated as a by-product of the whaling industry, which supplied oil for the city's lamps during the 18thc. In the early 19thc it was found that raw jute imported from India could be mixed with whale oil and woven into a useful coarse material with many applications from carpets to sacks. Mrs Keiller started making the renowned Dundee marmalade in 1797, and the fertile Carse of Gowrie to the NE produces the fruit used in the city's jam industry.

Dundee has been a Royal Burgh since 1190 and is Scotland's fourth largest city. Its eventful past bears the scars of several battles for Scottish independence. The English seized Dundee in the 14th and 16thc. In 1645 Montrose stormed the

1   Castle
2   Monument to Battle of Dunbar

3   Myreton Motor Museum
4   Parish Church and Home Monument

5   Town House and Market Cross

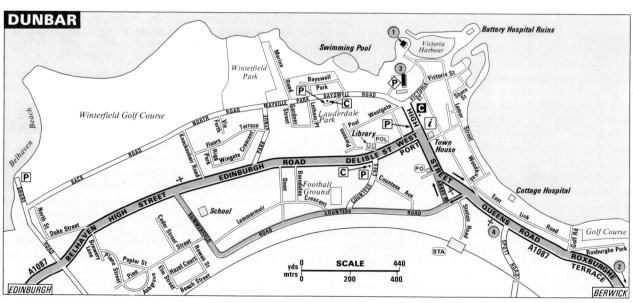

Entries marked * are the starting point of drives included in the Day Drive section of the book (pages 95 to 160).

city, and General Monk captured it in 1651. Dundee also has associations with the Old and the Young Pretenders, in 1715 and 1745 respectively. Early buildings which survive include the splendid 156ft, 15th-c Old Steeple, or St Mary's Tower – a survivor from one of the four City Churches, which were repeatedly sacked and almost destroyed by fire in 1841. The Old Steeple only surrendered to General Monk in 1651, after burning straw had been piled at its base.

Cowgate Port is the only surviving gate of the old town walls, and George Wishart is said to have preached here in 1544 during an outbreak of the plague. Restored Dunhope Castle was the 15th-c home of the Scrymgeours, hereditary constables of Dundee, and later the residence of Graham of Claverhouse – Scott's Bonnie Dundee. The castle is now a meeting place for clubs and societies. In Caird Park are the ruins of 16th-c Mains of Fintry Castle, ancient seat of the Grahams. Many quaint gravestones are to be found in the old Howff cemetery, and a plaque on the wall of St Paul's Episcopal Cathedral in the High Street records the site of the former

Dundee Castle, destroyed c1314.

Dundee University was founded in 1881 and affiliated to St Andrew's University in 1897. It is now independent. The city boasts many fine schools and colleges, including the well-known Duncan of Jordanstowne College of Art. William Wallace was educated at the grammar school, and Hector Boece the historian, was born in the city c1465. Hector Boece first used the name Grampians to describe the famous mountains after finding and misreading the name *Mons Grampius*, which Tacitus gave as the scene of Agricola's victory over the Picts cAD84.

Camperdown House lies to the NW of the city and was built by the son of Lord Duncan, victor of the Battle of Camperdown, in 1797. The mansion now houses a fascinating golf museum displaying exhibits which cover the history of the game over three centuries. An astrolabe of 1555 – an instrument used in navigation – is preserved in the Albert Institute, which houses the city museum and art gallery. In Balgay Park is the Mills Observatory, and Caird Hall is an outstanding example of Dundee's 20th-c building (1914 to 1923).

The city's dockland covers more than 35 acres and includes shipyards which built Shackleton's 'Terra Nova' and Scott's 'Discovery', both polar exploration vessels. HMS 'Unicorn', the oldest floating wooden warship extant, dates from the early 19thc and is preserved in Victoria Dock. The Barrack Street Shipping and Industrial Museum illustrates the history of Dundee's commercial and maritime life. The original ill-fated railway bridge over the Tay blew down in a gale in 1879 with great loss of life (see inset overleaf). Its 2m-long successor, also called Tay Bridge, was built between 1883 and 1888 and carries the railway line from Edinburgh to Aberdeen. A road bridge opened in 1965 is one of the longest in Europe. Dundee Law is an extinct volcano which forms the city's highest point; it stands at 571ft, and carries the war memorial.

DUNDONALD, Strathclyde 24 NS33

Dundonald Castle (AM) stands in ruins high on an isolated hill W of the town. It was built by Robert II, the first Stuart King, who died there in 1390. Robert III died here in 1406. Dr Johnson visited the castle in 1773 and was entertained by

1	Albert Institute	6	Cowgate Port
2	Balgay Park	7	Dunhope Castle
3	Barrack Street Museum	8	Dundee Law
4	Caird Hall	9	HMS 'Unicorn'
5	Camperdown House	10	Mains of Fintry Castle

11	St Mary's Tower
12	St Paul's Cathedral
13	Tay Railway Bridge
14	University

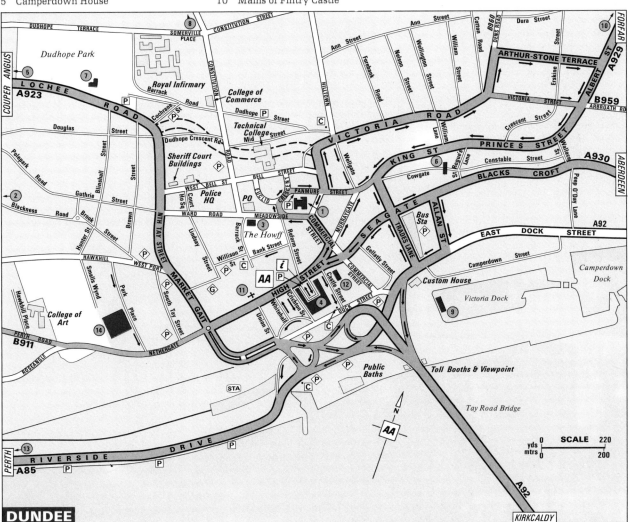

DUNDEE

the Countess of Eglinton at 17th-c Auchans House, NW of the castle. Dundonald has a church dating from 1803.

DUNDONNELL, Highland   *36 NH18*

Dundonnell is a climbing centre near the head of Little Loch Broom, in the green valley of Strath Beg beneath the towering peaks of 3,484ft An Teallach. The mountain's name means the forge – from the smoke-like mists which wreath its peaks.

In the heart of the Teallach range at a height of some 2,000ft is tiny loch Toll an Lochain, set in spectacular rocky country overlooked by a fascinating ridge of white quartzite slabs facing the great cliffs of 3,474ft Sgurr Fiona. This loch, one of the most remarkable sights in the Highlands, can be reached from a point on the Braemore Junction road about 2m SE of Dundonnell. A mile farther down the road near Corryhaillie is a picturesque gorge and waterfall.

The road climbs to over 1,100ft at Fain Hill along a stretch called Destitution Road, built during the potato famine of 1851. Strath Beg lies E of the village and is the site of Dundonnell Lodge. A track from here runs N to Aultnaharrie on Loch Broom. Aultnaharrie faces Ullapool, to which it is linked by passenger ferry. Ben Goleach rises to 2,052ft above Little Loch Broom beyond the track. Dundonnell House dates from the 18thc and stands 3m SE of the village in Oriental gardens. A fine waterfall can be seen 2½m WNW at Ardessie.

DUNDRENNAN, Dumfries and Galloway   *25 NX74*

The small village of Dundrennan stands on Abbey Burn and is partly built of stones from the ruined abbey (AM). Founded in 1142, this Cistercian abbey was annexed to the Chapel Royal at Stirling. Parts of the 13th-c chapter house and transepts of the church remain, together with some incised slabs and the Cellarer's Monument of 1480. A 13th-c monument to a former abbot is well-preserved, and the effigy on which he stands may have been his murderer. After being defeated at the Battle of Langside, Mary Queen of Scots probably spent her last night on Scottish soil in Dundrennan Abbey.

Port Mary lies 2m S; here stands the rock from which Mary stepped on to the boat which took her to Workington in England. She travelled S to seek help from Elizabeth, who imprisoned her instead. Abbey Burnfoot is sheltered by Abbey Head 4m SE of Dundrennan, near the point where Abbey Burn enters the Solway Firth.

DUNECHT, Grampian   *30 NJ70*

Off the Echt road and to the S of this village, Dunecht House stands in a fine park and gardens and was once famed for its observatory. Mainly 16th-c Corsindae House stands 5m W, with Castle Fraser 2½m NW. The castle is a magnificent example of the Scottish baronial style and dates from 1454 to 1618.

THE DISASTROUS TAY BRIDGE

In July 1871 a foundation stone was laid on the south side of the Tay estuary near Wormit, to mark the beginning of work on the Tay Bridge that was to take the North British Railway across to Dundee, and do away with the need for an inconvenient ferry. The designer of the bridge was Thomas Bouch, who had been pressing for it to be built for the past 22 years.

His bridge extended for 3,450yds, the longest in Britain, with 85 arches and a long curve three-quarters of the way across the often stormy waters, to meet up with the north-side rail link at Dundee. A feature of the design was the series of High Girders in the centre section; here the latticed metal girders were built above the track rather than below, to provide an agreed clearance for the masts of ships making their way up and down river. The best engineering firms had declined to tender, and the company which took it on was over-optimistic in estimating a cost of £217,000 and a completion date only three years away.

One person at least had grave doubts about the wisdom of building the bridge at all. Patrick Mather, an 80-year-old local man, wrote a series of letters to the *Dundee Advertiser* in 1869 and 1870 prophesying that the bridge would collapse, with a great cost in human lives. He was ridiculed in the speeches and commemorative book which marked the official opening on 31 May 1878.

Scheduled services began the next day. Trains were supposed to be limited to 25mph on the bridge, but several were timed through the High Girders at 42mph. Passengers began to notice an uncomfortable vibration, especially in windy weather, and some regular travellers went back to the ferries. However, the directors of the North British managed to persuade Queen Victoria to travel over the bridge in the royal train, and Bouch was knighted for his services.

In the late afternoon of Saturday 27 December 1879, a great storm sprang up. It increased in violence overnight, and mainland reports suggest that it reached its peak at 07.20hrs on the Sunday morning. At exactly that time the 05.20 train from Burntisland to Dundee was making its way across the bridge. In the murk and howling gale, neither the driver nor the signalling staff noticed in time that the High Girders and 1,000yds of bridge had been completely swept away. The engine, all five coaches, and the guard's van plunged headlong over the edge, dropping like stones into the raging water far below. All 75 people on board were killed.

A Board of Trade inquiry put the blame squarely on Sir Thomas Bouch, finding him wholly or partly to blame for faults in design, construction and maintenance. He damned himself by his admission that in the design he had made no special allowance for the effects of wind. Crowds shouted for his blood; but he retired to his home at Moffat, went quietly mad, and died four months later.

A new and far more substantial bridge was built, which still gives excellent service today. But alongside it can be seen the stumps of the far too close-set pairs of columns that took Bouch's bridge across the Tay, a grim monument to an enterprise whose designer and builders were not equal to their task.

About 75 people died because the designers and builders of the old Tay Bridge were not equal to their task.

*DUNFERMLINE, Fife   46 NT08

Scotland's capital for six centuries, Dunfermline is the burial place of Robert the Bruce and many other kings. James I was born here in 1394, Charles I in 1600, and Charles' sister Elizabeth. Nowadays the Royal Burgh manufactures linen. Andrew Carnegie was born in a small cottage, now a museum, in 1835. He emigrated to America and became an industrial millionaire and a great philanthropist. The first of nearly 3,000 Carnegie libraries was established here in 1881, and Carnegie presented Pittencrieff Glen – with its beautiful park – to the town in 1903. A fine 17th-c mansion house in the park has a costume gallery and is the venue for numerous temporary exhibitions.

The great Benedictine abbey (AM) was founded by Queen Margaret, wife of Malcolm Canmore in the 11thc. The foundations of her modest church lie beneath the present nave, a splendid piece of late-Norman work reminiscent of Durham Cathedral. At the east end of the nave are the remains of St Margaret's shrine, dating from the 13thc. Robert the Bruce was buried in the choir in 1329 and his grave is marked by a modern brass plate. The abbey's original steeple and SW tower fell in 1753 and 1807 respectively, and the choir was rebuilt between 1817 and 1822. Of special note are the massive 16th-c buttresses against the N and S sides of the nave. The W front, with its fine door and twin towers, has been rebuilt; around the four sides of the battlemented, 100ft-high square tower are carved the words 'King Robert the Bruce'.

Of the monastic buildings, only the ruins of the refectory and pend remain. The monastic guesthouse was later reconstructed as Dunfermline Palace (AM), but of this only a 200ft-long buttressed wall and the remains of Malcolm's Tower on a mound survive. Pends Archway links the palace with the abbey. Scott made use of the inscription on the door lintel of the 16th-c Abbot's House in his *Fair Maid of Perth*. Dunfermline Museum is of interest.

Hill House lies S of the town and dates from the 16th and 17thc. Some 2½m SW of the town is Pitfirraine Castle, which preserves a 15th-c tower and now serves as a golf club house.

DUNGLASS, Lothian   31 NT77

The grounds of modern Dunglass House include the partly-restored cruciform collegiate church (AM). Founded in 1450, the church displays a richly-embellished interior which boasts fine sedilia.

1   Abbey
2   Abbot's House
3   Carnegie's Birthplace and Memorial
4   Carnegie Library
5   Dunfermline Museum
6   Dunfermline Palace
7   Hill House
8   Pittencrieff Park and Museum
9   Pitfirraine Castle

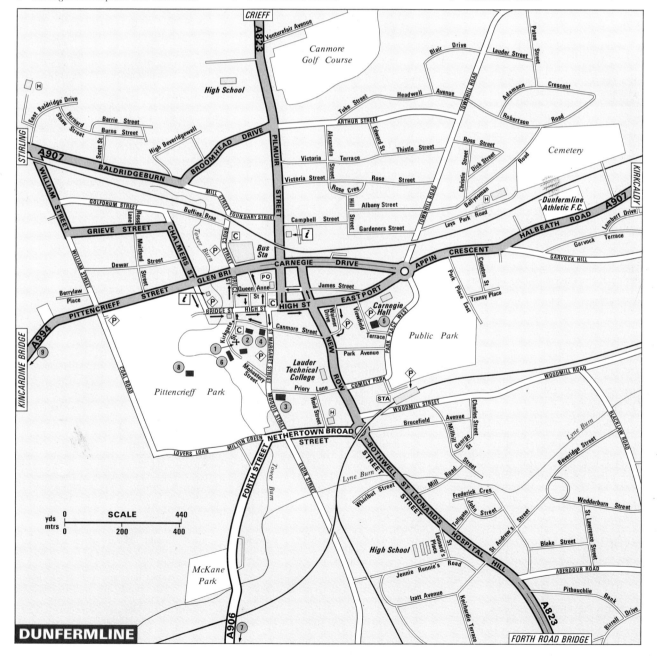

Entries marked * are the starting point of drives included in the Day Drive section of the book (pages 95 to 160).

Gateway to the grounds of Dunkeld House.

DUNINO, Fife   31 NO51
Near the church a very ancient carved stone is topped by a sundial of 1698. A beautiful small glen can be seen near by.

DUNKELD, Tayside   30 NO04
A delightful small cathedral town in the wooded Tay valley, Dunkeld boasts a fine bridge which was erected by Telford in 1809. Across the bridge is Little Dunkeld, burial place of Neil Gow. Neil was a violinist, composer, and player of reels and Strathspeys, who was born 1m W at Inver in 1727. Dunkeld's beautiful ruined cathedral (AM) is set among lawns and was founded in the 9thc. Only the 14th-c choir remains complete and restored, and this now serves as the parish church. A tomb in the choir is thought to be that of the notorious Wolf of Badenoch, despoiler of Elgin Cathedral.

The building was desecrated in 1560 and further damaged during the Battle of Dunkeld in 1689, when the Highlanders were defeated. Fine window tracery can be seen in the ruined nave, which was begun in 1406. The massive 15th-c tower contains some wall paintings, and the 15th-c chapter house is now the tomb-chapel of the Atholls.

Dunkeld Little Houses date from the rebuilding of the town after the battle of Dunkeld in 1689, and have been well restored by the NTS. The wall of a house in the small peaceful square bears an upright ell – the Scottish equivalent of a yard – which dates from 1706. Remains of a prehistoric fort exist to the W in the grounds of Dunkeld House. About 1m SW of Dunkeld is Ossian's Hall, a restored 18th-c folly with splendid views of the River Bran. Close by is Hermitage Bridge (NTS) below the Falls of Bran, and beyond the falls is Rumbling Bridge. This bridge is situated in Craigvinean Forest, at a point where the river enters a picturesque gorge. Fine views of Dunkeld and the cathedral can be enjoyed from Craig Vinean, a hill NW of Inver, and the wooded hill of Craigiebarns. The latter rises to 1,106ft above the river NW of Dunkeld.

DUNLOP, Strathclyde   29 NS44
Dunlop cheeses are produced in this district. Laigh Kirk dates from 1835 and contains the Dunlop aisle of 1641, plus numerous examples of stained glass. Viscount Clandeboyes erected the adjacent mausoleum and church hall.

DUNNET, Highland   37 ND27
Dunnet Head has a lighthouse and is the farthest N point on the Scottish mainland. Views from here extend to the Orkneys. Dunnet village overlooks Dunnet Bay S of St John's Loch, and its little early-Presbyterian church may be of 14th-c date. A feature of the church is its saddleback tower, and an early cartographer called Timothy Pont was minister here from 1601 to 1608. His revised surveys were incorporated in Blaeu's Atlas, which was published in Amsterdam in 1654. Across the waters of stormy Pentland Firth is the Old Man of Hoy, an impressive isolated rock stack rising almost sheer to 450ft.

DUNNING, Tayside   30 NO01
Dunning overlooks Strath Earn and lies N of the Ochil Hills. St Serf's Church has been rebuilt but preserves a fine 13th-c tower. A standing stone recalls the legendary Battle of Duncrub. Late 16th-c Keltie Castle lies 1m W, near the memorial to Maggie Wall who was burned as a witch in 1657.

DUNNOTTAR CASTLE, Grampian   35 NO88
An impressive ruined fortress situated 160ft above the sea on a rocky cliff, Dunnottar Castle was a stronghold of the Earls Marischal of Scotland from the 14thc. In 1645 the Royalist Marquis of Montrose failed to dislodge the Earl Marischal, a fierce Presbyterian Covenanter, from the castle. During the civil war it was held by the Royalists and was the last Scottish fortress to hold out against Cromwell's troops; it fell after an eight-month siege in 1652. Scotland's Crown Jewels, which had been kept hidden in the castle until this time, were smuggled out by the wife of the minister at nearby Kinneff and hidden under the pulpit in the church.

In 1685 167 Covenanters were imprisoned in the dungeon. The castle is well preserved, the oldest parts – the tower and chapel – date from c1392; the fine gate-house dates from c1575. Scott met the subject of his Old Mortality cleaning the headstones of graves in the old churchyard 2m inland. Magnificent cliff scenery can be seen along the rocky coast S of the castle.

*DUNOON, Strathclyde   44 NS17
Mary Campbell, Burn's sweetheart and the subject of his *Highland Mary*, was born near Dunoon at Auchnamore Farm. She is commemorated by a statue on Castle Hill, overlooking the Clyde. The town itself boasts two fine bays and is a large Cowal resort on the Firth of Clyde, popular with yachtsmen. Clyde Yachting Fortnight is staged in July and the Cowal Highland Gathering is staged at Dunoon at the end of August.

Dunoon Castle dates from 1822, but traces of another ancient castle can be seen on a rock above the steamer pier. Cruises from this pier take in pleasant views along the neighbouring waters.

The wild country of the Cowal peninsula behind the town includes the wooded slopes and charming waterfalls of Morag's Fairy Glen. A coast road running S from Dunoon for Toward Point affords fine views. Inland and to the W lofty moorland rises to 1,651ft Bishop's Seat, which overlooks Loch Striven to the Kyles of Bute. Across the Firth of Clyde, opposite Dunoon, is the landmark of Cloch Point. Its white-painted lighthouse was constructed in 1797.

DUNROBIN, Highland   37 NC80
Magnificently set in a great park overlooking the sea, Dunrobin Castle has for centuries been the seat of the Earls – and later Dukes – of Sutherland. It was originally a square keep built c1275 by Robert, Earl of Sutherland, from whom it got its name. Extensive alterations were made in 1856, but an old yett is preserved. The house is now a boys' public school, with a museum in the grounds.

DUNS, Borders   31 NT75
Although little more than a village, Duns became the county town of old Berwickshire after Berwick was declared a neutral town in 1551. The border was later revised to make Berwick a part of England. It is a market town at the foot of Duns Law, on which the town stood before being destroyed by English invaders in 1545. The summit of the hill is surmounted by the Covenanter's Stone, commemorating a camp made there in 1639 by General Leslie and his Covenanters before they marched to Newcastle. The Covenanters supported the Scottish Reformed Church in opposition to Charles I's ecclesiastical policy.

Duns church was built in 1880, and a Mercat cross stands in the public park. The Burgh Chambers house the Jim Clark museum, which exhibits trophies won by this world-championship racing driver. Clark lived in Duns and was killed in Germany in 1968. The town hall is of 19th-c date, and modern Duns Castle stands NW. This was designed by Gillespie Graham and retains an ancient tower. Another feature of the house is a fine avenue of lime trees near the tiny loch of Hen Poo.

Manderston House stands in fine gardens 2m E of Duns, and 2m S of the town is 17th- and 18th-c Nisbet House. Its wealth of gun loops are unusual at so late a period. To the NW of Duns rise the foothills of the Lammermuirs, crossed by two narrow roads – the W one heads towards Longformacus, and the E road runs through the valley of Whiteadder Water to Cranshaws.

DUNSCORE, Dumfries and Galloway
25 NX88
Situated in the fertile valley of Cairn Water, Dunscore lies 6m E of Craigenputtock Farm, where Carlyle wrote *Sartor Resartus*. The ruined tower of Lag is associated with Sir Robert Grierson, a notorious persecutor of the Covenanters in the 17thc, and stands 1½m NE of Dunscore. Ellisland Farm, 3½m E, was taken over by Robert Burns in 1788. Burns rebuilt the property and tried to introduce new farming methods. He gave up to become an exciseman the year after, and moved to Dumfries in 1791.

DUNSKEATH, Highland   34 NH76
A passenger ferry crosses the narrows of the Cromarty Firth from here to Cromarty. To the E are the numerous caves of the North Sutor. Major North-Sea oil developments are taking place in the area.

DUNSTAFFNAGE CASTLE, Strathclyde
29 NM83
A castle was originally built here for Alexander II's attack against Norsemen who occupied the Hebrides. The present castle (AM) probably dates back to the 13thc, though most of the parts now standing are of 15th-c origin. It was an ancient Campbell stronghold and stands on a promontory guarding Dunstaffnage Bay, where the waters of Loch Etive and the Firth of Lorne meet. The two round towers, curtain wall, and gatehouse still stand, and some of the walls are as much as 10ft thick.

A brass gun from a Spanish galleon wrecked in Tobermory Bay is preserved on the battlements. The site played an important part in early Scottish history, and the seat of the Scottish government of the original kingdom at Dalriada – before the union with the Picts – was thought to be here. The celebrated Stone of Scone lay here before being moved to Scone, probably in the 9thc. Flora Macdonald was imprisoned here for ten days in 1746 before she was taken to London, and Scott introduced the castle into his *Legend of Montrose* and *Lord of the Isles*. Near the castle is a chapel and burial-place of the Campbells of Dunstaffnage, probably dating from the 13thc.

DUNSYRE, Strathclyde   30 NT04
Newholm Mansion is associated with the Covenanters, and Dunsyre church preserves its old jougs, iron collars used for punishing criminals. Many ancient gravestones can be seen in the churchyard. Black Mount rises to 1,689ft in the S.

DUNTOCHER, Strathclyde   45 NS47
An ancient twin-arched bridge stands here amid woodlands, and to the N are the Kilpatrick Hills, dotted with small lochs. A fragment of the great Roman Antonine Wall (AM) is also of interest.

DUNTULM, Isle of Skye, Highland
32 NG47
Duntulm Castle dates from the 15thc and was once the seat of the Macdonalds of Sleat and Trottenish. It is now a crumbling ruin. The castle was called Duncolmen in the 16thc, and lies near the N tip of Skye overlooking Duntulm Island and bay. The predecessor of the building was Dunscaith Castle, situated near Isle Ornsay at the S end of Skye. On the shore below Duntulm Castle is a groove worn by the keel of the Macdonald galleys. The promontory of Rudha Hunish lies beyond the shore of Score Bay N of Dantulm; NW across the waters of the Minch are the hills of Harris, in the Outer Hebrides.

DUNURE, Strathclyde   24 NS21
A small fishing village with a sand and shingle foreshore, Dunure lies SW of the Heads of Ayr and just W of the Ayr to Girvan road. An ancient dovecot stands beside a ruined castle on the cliff top. The Commendator of Crossraguel Abbey was twice nearly roasted to death in the castle by the 4th Earl of Cassillis in 1570, before surrendering his lands. Brown Carrick Hill rises to 940ft behind the village and affords fine views. On the road to Girvan, 2m S, is the Electric Brae; an optical illusion caused by the configuration of the surrounding countryside makes the road appear to be descending when in fact it is ascending. Croy sands stretch away to the SW at the N tip of Culzean Bay.

DUNVEGAN, Isle of Skye, Highland
32 NG24
Leod, son of a 13th-c king of the Isle of Man, built the curtain wall of Dunvegan Castle in c1270. He also constructed the sea-gate, which was the castle's only entrance until 1748. Slowly added to over the centuries, the building is still the seat of the Macleods of Macleod and houses family portraits by Ramsay and Raeburn. Other features include relics of Prince Charles Edward, the great two-handed sword of the 7th Chief William – who died at the Battle of Bloody Bay off Mull in 1480, and the ancient Irish silver Dunvegan Cup which was given to the 11th Chief Rory Mor c1600. Dunvegan's most treasured possession is a torn, delicate fragment of silk known as the Fairy Flag. This was probably woven on the Island of Rhodes in the 7thc, and is the guardian of Dunvegan Castle and the Clan Macleod.

Tradition says that a fairy gave the flag to William the 4th Chief in the 14thc. The flag is said to have three magical properties – when flown on the battlefield it will ensure a Macleod victory; when spread on his marriage-bed it will endow the Macleod chief with children; when unfurled at Dunvegan it will charm herring into the loch. The gift was made on the condition that it should only be used in emergencies – when the Macleods faced defeat, when the life of the sole heir was in danger, or when the clan was threatened with extinction. Twice the flag was flown in battle, and twice the Macleods won – at the Battle of Glendale in 1490 and at Trumpan in 1597.

A dungeon in the castle has a high slit window which opens on to the kitchen stair – a further torture for the starving wretches. Visitors to Dunvegan have included James V, Rob Roy, and Dr Johnson and Boswell. The castle looks out across island-studded Dunvegan Loch between the Vaternish and Duirinish peninsular, and the hills of Harris can be seen from the ramparts. Fairy Bridge stands 4m NE of Dunvegan, and had an evil reputation in the old days. It was thought that no horse would cross it without shying. The ruined Church of Duirinish lies to the SE of Dunvegan village. Macleod's Tables, twin-flat-topped hills overlooking Loch Bracadale, lie to the SW. Beyond these two hills the peninsula narrows to Idrigill Point, near which are the trio of off-shore stacks of basalt rock known as Macleod's Maidens.

The road round the W shores of Loch Dunvegan leads to Cobost, near which the Isle of Skye Folk Museum exhibits a replica of a whisky still. The road branches W half way along Loch Dunvegan, and leads to Loch Pooltiel, Glen Dale, and eventually Waterstein Head. Some of Skye's finest cliff scenery can be reached on foot from the head. Beyond the head is Neist Point and lighthouse in a magnificent cliff setting overlooking the Little Minch. The road round the W shore of Loch Dunvegan leads to Boreraig, home of the famous MacCrimmon pipers – hereditary pipers to the Macleods. A memorial cairn marks the spot where the famous piping college once stood. Beyond Boreraig the road leads almost to the 100ft-high cliffs of Dunvegan Head. Lonely cliffs soar almost to 1,000ft to the SW of the head.

DURISDEER, Dumfries and Galloway
25 NS80
This tiny village lies to the E of Nithsdale under a lofty ridge of green Lowland hills, just E of the Thornhill to Crawford road. Durisdeer's unusual little 17th-c church preserves fine 18th-c effigies of the 2nd Duke of Queensberry and his wife, sculpted in black and white marble by the Flemish sculptor John Nost. Beneath the effigies is a vault where twelve of the Duke's family were buried.

The churchyard contains the factor's stone, where the children of a Queensberry master of works in 1684, John Lukup, were buried. A martyr's stone to a Covenanter shot in 1685 is also of interest. Well Path may have been part of a Roman road, and leads NE through the hills towards the Dalveen Pass.

DURNESS, Highland   36 NC46
The crofting community of Durness is one of the farthest N villages in Scotland, and offers good trout and salmon fishing. A narrow peninsula extending N terminates at Fair Aird, or Far Out Head, which can be reached on foot. The road to Rhiconich, SW of Durness, runs to the shores of the Kyle of Durness. From the Cape Wrath Hotel a passenger ferry crosses the narrow Kyle. In summer – weather permitting – a minibus takes visitors over 11m of moorland known as The Parph to lonely Cape Wrath lighthouse.

The rugged, reddish cliff scenery here is most striking. A little to the NW of Durness, overlooking the sandy shores of Balnakeil Bay, lie the ruins of 17th-c Durness Old Church at Balnakeil. A quaintly-carved monument to Donald Makmurchou can be seen here, as well as the grave of Robert Donn. Donn died in 1778 and was known as the illiterate 'Burns of the North'. A nearby 18th-c house, now a farm, was once the residence of the Bishops of Caithness. Balnakeil Craft Village is close by.

DUROR, Highland   29 NM95
The famous Appin murder of 1752 was committed in the area. James Stewart, whose home was at the nearby farm of Acharn, was tried at Inveraray and

unjustly hanged at Ballachulish. He lies buried 2m SW in the ruined Kirk of Keil, on the shores of Loch Linnhe.

DURRIS, Grampian *35 NO79*
Magnificent tree specimens grow in the grounds of Durris House.

DYCE, Grampian *35 NJ81*
Dyce lies to the W of the River Don, and is the site of the airport for Aberdeen. Prehistoric remains can be seen to the W on the slopes of Tyrebagger Hill. This is also a good viewpoint, with view indicators at the summit. On the W bank of the river, 1½m NW of the village, the churchyard of a ruined church includes two ancient sculptured stones (AM). Also of interest is a 19th-c watchtower built to keep a look out for body-snatchers, a common problem of the time.

DYKEHEAD, Tayside *35 NO36*
Two roads fork at this Dykehead and traverse the two long and picturesque Angus glens. The right fork follows the South Esk River, dividing into two branches along each bank to reach Clova in Glen Clova. The left fork continues N through beautiful Glen Prosen, passing a fountain erected in memory of the Antarctic explorers Captain Scott and Dr Wilson, who reached the South Pole in 1912. The fountain is overlooked by 1,230ft Tulloch Hill, which carries the prominent Airlie monument. Continuing through Glen Prosen, the road meets Prosen Water and follows it for 7m before ending near Glen Prosen Lodge. Beyond here a path leads into the lonely E Grampians in the Braes of Angus, dominated by 3,043ft Mayar.

DYKENDS, Tayside *31 NO25*
Roads from Alyth and Kirriemuir converge here at the entrance to the delightful Glen Isla. A little to the W flows the River Isla, with 1,630ft Creigh Hill rising to the NE. Loch Lintrathen supplies Dundee with water and lies 2½m SE on the Kirriemuir road.

DYSART, Fife *47 NT39*
A picturesque little Royal Burgh with old houses and a rocky foreshore, Dysart has become united with Kirkcaldy. Cromwell's soldiers damaged the Tolbooth of 1576, and the ruined, 16th-c Church of St Serf carries a fortress-like tower. An old house of 1583 stands near by. An inscription above the doorway reads 'My hoip is in the Lord'. A 16th-c house known as The Towers is also of interest.

EAGLESHAM, Strathclyde *45 NS55*
Rudolf Hess, the deputy German Fuehrer, made his sensational plane landing of 1941 near this village. Eaglesham was created by the 12th Earl of Eglinton in the 18thc, and a number of original houses survive. An eagle weathervane tops the spire of the 18th-c parish church, and the churchyard contains a Covenanter's monument. The road to Kilmarnock, SW of Eaglesham, crosses Eaglesham Moor at a height of over 900ft. Wide views can be enjoyed from these moors. Beyond Lochgoin Reservoir is a monument to the Covenanter John Howe. A farmhouse near by houses an interesting collection of Covenanting relics.

EARLSTON, Borders *26 NT53*
Once named Ercildoune, this town lies in Lauderdale valley near the Leader

Water. A stone inscribed 'Auld Rymer's Tace lies in this place' stands in the churchyard, and just S of the town is the ruined old Rhymer's Tower. The tower is associated with the almost legendary Thomas the Rhymer, a 13th-c poet and prophet. About 1m S of the town near Leader Water is the 16th-c house of Cowdenknowes, which has connections with the Border family of Home.

EASSIE, Tayside *31 NO34*
A fine example of an ancient sculptured stone (AM), inscribed with a cross and Pictish symbols, stands in the churchyard.

EAST CALDER, Lothian *46 NT06*
Illieston House is possibly of 16th-c origin, and lies 2m N of the village. The Scottish Wildlife Trust's Almondell country park lies off the A71 at East Calder. Nature trails are being developed to link up with old drovers' roads over the Pentland Hills.

EASTER ROSS, Highland *37*
In contrast to the wild and beautiful Wester Ross, flatter Easter Ross is pleasant in a more relaxing way. It was once known as Cromarty, and lies between the Dornoch and Cromarty Firths.

EAST KILBRIDE, Strathclyde *45 NS65*
A well-planned new town, East Kilbride is an overspill area for Glasgow. Its industry includes extensive research laboratories, and the area around the town is noted for dairy farming. The Hunter brothers were anatomists in the 18thc and were born near by. A monument has been erected to their memory. East Kilbride saw the first meeting of the Scottish Society of Friends in 1653.

Near the churchyard is an old mounting stone, and above the church's tower entrance is the date 1774. The tower itself is of 19th-c crown design. An 18th-c Stuart mausoleum can also be seen. Among the more modern developments is a covered Olympic-size swimming pool. Jean Cameron, associated with Bonnie Prince Charlie, once lived at Mount Cameron. About 1m N of the town is restored Mains Castle, probably of early 13th-c date.

EAST LINTON, Lothian *31 NT57*
The River Tyne flows through a tiny gorge here and is spanned by a 16th-c bridge. John Rennie, the engineer and builder of London's old Waterloo Bridge, was born E of the village at Phantassie Mansion in 1761, and his memorial can be seen beside the by-pass. On the river bank near East Linton is 17th-c Preston Mill (NTS), still in working condition (see inset opposite). Near by is the Phantassie Dovecot (NTS), a fine, traditionally-Scottish example of this type of building.

To the N is the Church of Prestonkirk, which was built in 1770 and is now used as a mortuary chapel. It retains a 17th-c tower and an interesting 13th-c square chancel from an earlier structure. The extensive ruins of 13th- to 15th-c Hailes Castle (AM) lie 2m SW of the village, and include the original water-gate, dungeons, and a fine 16th-c chapel. Bothwell brought Mary Queen of Scots here on their flight from Borthwick Castle in 1567. The castle was dismantled by Cromwell in 1650.

Traprain Law rises to 724ft S of the castle. A Celtic town once stood here, and a hoard of Roman silver excavated in 1919 was taken to the National Museum of Antiquities in Edinburgh.

EAST MEY, Highland *37 ND37*
The Castle of Mey was built in 1568 by George, 5th Earl of Caithness, and lies NW near Mey Bay. The structure is also known as Barrogill Castle, and remained in the hands of the Caithness family until the late 19thc. In 1952 the Queen Mother saved it from demolition by purchasing it as a summer home. To the N of East Mey is St John's Point and the dangerous reef known as the Merry Men of Mey, overlooking the Pentland Firth. Stroma Island lies off-shore beyond the Inner Sound.

EAST NEUK, Fife *31 NO61*
Several tiny picturesque Royal Burghs and villages lie along the coast in this E corner of old Fifeshire, around Fife Ness.

EAST SALTOUN, Lothian *47 NT46*
Andrew Fletcher of Saltoun, the famous Scottish patriot, was born at Salton Hall in 1653. The 17th-c work of the hall has been added to of late. Saltoun Mill stands near the station and dates from the late 17thc. East Saltoun was the first place in Britain to weave fine hollands, and the first in Scotland to produce pot barley.

EAST WEMYSS, Fife *47 NT39*
This small coal port lies on a rocky stretch of coast riddled with caves or weems, including Glass Cave which lies to the SW near West Wemyss. Macduff Castle's massive ruin lies to the NE, just beyond East Wemyss. An old dovecot is preserved near by.

ECCLEFECHAN, Dumfries and Galloway *26 NY17*
This was the birthplace of historian, critic, and essayist Thomas Carlyle in 1795. Carlyle described the village in his *Sartor Resartus* under the name of 'Entepfuhl'. Arched House (NTS), where he was born, was built over a pond and houses a collection of personal relics. His statue stands in the village, and his grave and those of his parents can be seen in the churchyard. Archibald Arnott, doctor to Napoleon at St Helena, is also buried here.

ECCLES, Borders *31 NT74*
Traces of a Cistercian convent which was burnt in 1545 survive at Eccles. The church dates from 1779, and SW of Crosshall Farm stands a tall ancient cross.

ECHT, Grampian *35 NJ70*
Prehistoric fortifications top Barmekin of Echt, an isolated hill NW of the village. About 1½m W of the village, near Sunhoney Farm, is the Cullerlie stone circle (AM) — probably of late bronze-age origin.

ECKFORD, Borders *26 NT72*
Kale Water joins the River Teviot here. An old watch-house – a look-out to prevent body-snatching – stands in the churchyard, and the church preserves a pair of 18th-c jougs. Jougs are iron collars which were once used to punish wrongdoers.

EDDERTON, Highland *37 NH78*
Edderton Sands, an inlet of the Dornoch Firth, lie to the NE of Edderton. The local church dates from 1793.

Entries marked * are the starting point of drives included in the Day Drive section of the book (pages 95 to 160).

EDDLESTON, Borders   30 NT24

This hamlet lies in the valley of the Eddleston Water, with 2,136ft Blackhope Scar rising from the Moorfoot Hills to the E. The lower Cloich Hills overlook the village to the W. Near the village are the prehistoric Milkieston Rings. The Black Barony Hotel was formerly known as Darnhall and dates from the 17thc. It was once a Murray residence. Portmore Loch lies high in the hills 2½m NNE of Eddleston. To the S on the Peebles road is a memorial to George Meikle Kemp, who served as an apprentice here during the early 19thc. He designed the well-known Scott Memorial in Edinburgh. A narrow road running SW from Eddleston ascends between the twin Meldon Hills before dropping into Tweeddale.

EDDRACHILLIS, Highland   36 NC14

Eddrachillis overlooks Badcall Bay, an inlet of island-studded Eddrachillis Bay. The inland countryside is dotted with lochens, and the sharp gneiss cone of 2,364ft Ben Stack rises to the E. A rough and hilly road leads SE from the village to the ferry at Kylesku, passing close to the shores of little Calva Bay – with its two islands – and then turning inland by Loch Allt nan Airbhe.

EDINBAIN, Isle of Skye, Highland   32 NG35

Aodann Ban is the Gaelic name for this little township, meaning 'the white and grey face'. The town lies near the head of Loch Greshornish, an inlet of Loch Snizort, and is backed by lonely moorland. Loch Snizort Beag lies 4m NE.

*EDINBURGH, Lothian   47 NT27

District plan overleaf
Central plan page 216

Perth was succeeded as capital of Scotland by Edinburgh in 1437. Unlike most of Britain's old cities – which emerged along river valleys – Edinburgh was built on hills. Salisbury Crags rise on the E outskirts of the city, with the celebrated, 823ft extinct volcano known as Arthur's Seat dominant. This fine viewpoint takes in the long range of the Pentland Hills, which almost reach 2,000ft in height and lie to the S of Edinburgh. Traces of iron-age occupation have been found on Castle Rock, Calton Hill, and Arthur's Seat, but medieval Edinburgh grew along the windy ridge between the castle to the Abbey of Holyrood.

In 1450 James II built the King's Wall, which contained the Old Town for a time and separated the city from the castle by the length of a bowshot. By 1513, however, the city had encroached on the area of Greyfriars Church and the present university, stopping near the old Nor' Loch. In the panic which followed Scotland's defeat by the English at Flodden Field the Flodden Wall was built. For 250 years the Old Town remained within these walls, and the buildings grew upwards, sometimes as high as fourteen storeys, to house the growing population. The Royal Mile, which has been admirably restored in recent years ends at the Palace of Holyroodhouse under Salisbury Crags. Repeated attacks – notably the Rough Wooing by Henry VIII in 1544 and 1547, when he attempted to bully the Scots into acceptance of the marriage between young Edward and the infant Mary, Queen of Scots – terrorized the city into keeping behind its walls.

Cromwell occupied the city in 1650. Other major events in the 17thc included the executions of the Marquis of Montrose and the Marquis of Argyll in 1650 and 1661. The Act of Union passed in 1707 heralded winds of change; the Scottish parliament was dissolved and the city was freed from the threat of attack. New trade coming up the Firth of Forth

MONUMENT TO MILLING

A century ago there were 14 water mills powered by the Scottish River Tyne, which flows past Haddington to join the sea near Dunbar. The only one to survive in working order is Preston mill, on the road between East Linton and Tyninghame, which is in the care of the NTS.

Monks from a nearby monastery are thought to have established the first mill on the site, and built the lade which channels water from the Tyne, sometime in the 12thc. The existing buildings are much as they were in 1620, although the splendid 14ft-diameter cast-iron mill wheel was one of the early products of the Carron Ironworks, which were founded in 1759.

Restored, 17th-c Preston Mill is still capable of producing 2¼ cwt of meal per hour.

The grouping of buildings at Preston mill has always attracted artists, partly because of the red pantiled roofs which are so typical of the Lothians. The outbuilding which originally served as a granary and stable has been turned into a display centre, where descriptions and illustrations of relics of the old milling days are on show.

The most picturesque building is the kiln, which has a furnace at ground level and outside stairs leading up to a drying loft. Preston mill dealt almost exclusively with oatmeal. After being taken from the store, the oats were spread over the floor on the upper level of the kiln to a depth of 5 inches, being turned constantly to make sure that the heat of the furnace dried them thoroughly. Moist air was drawn off through a flue in the roof. This has a characteristic cowl which swings in the breeze and ensures that the outlet is always downwind. The kiln roof was the first part of the mill to be restored after the NTS took over in 1950. This work was done while the mill was still working commercially, and the money for it was raised by public subscription.

The milling equipment is housed in the third building. Preston's last miller stopped working in 1955, and little was done to the machinery until 1964 when Joseph Rank Ltd offered to meet the cost of restoration. Most of the repairs and replacements had to be done on the woodwork, because the metalwork was still in very good condition. New wooden paddles were also fitted to the original water-wheel.

The mill was reopened in 1965, back in full working trim. Since then it has never actually ground any meal, although well capable of producing its old quota of 2¼ cwt in an hour; but the machinery is kept turning at a slower rate to demonstrate the intricacies of gear-wheels and spindles, millstones, and sieves, which are not much different from the machinery used in Roman times.

For captions see page 217

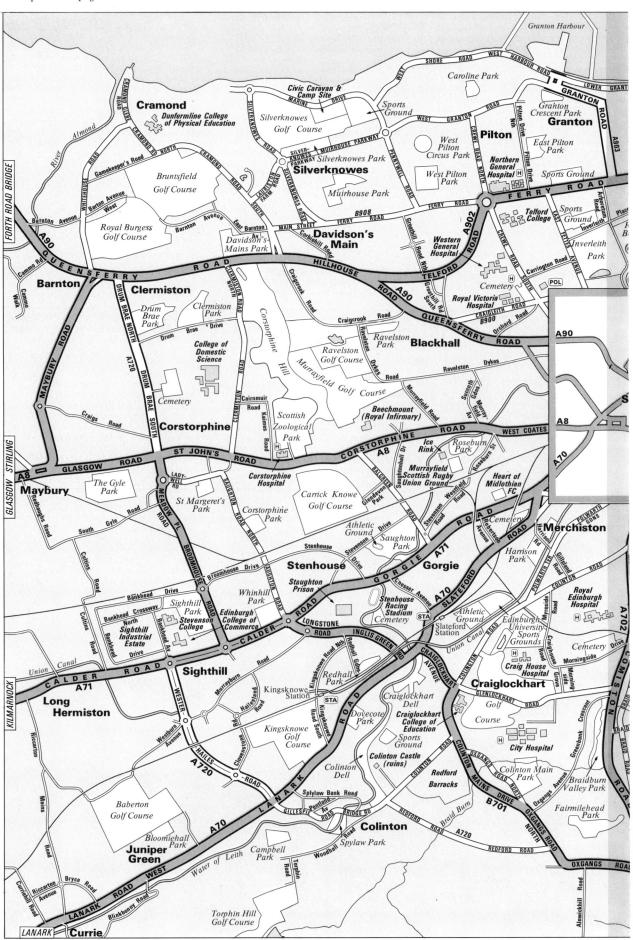

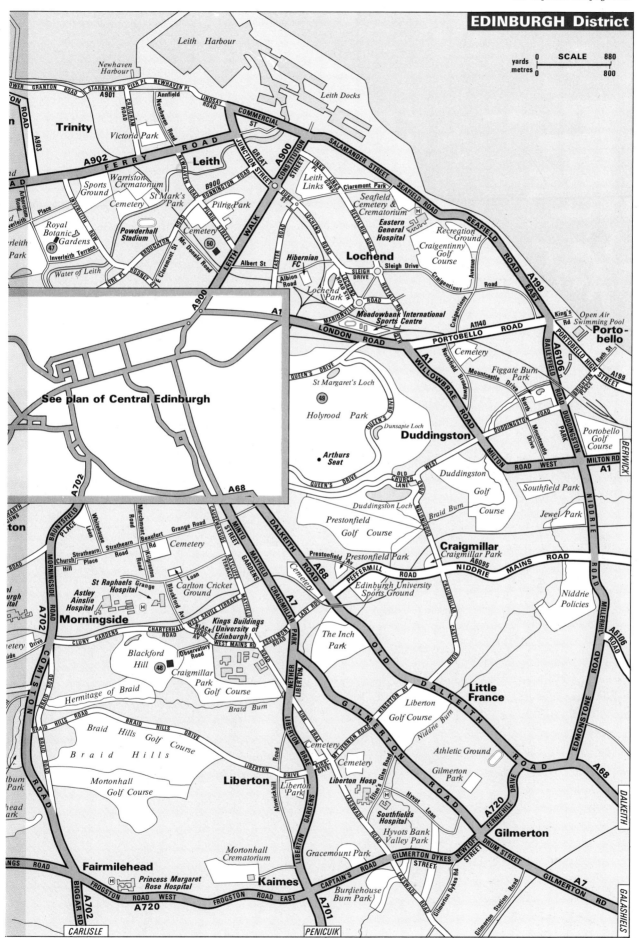

EDINBURGH District

SCALE
yards 0 ——————— 880
metres 0 ——————— 800

Leith Harbour

Newhaven Harbour

Trinity

Leith Docks

Victoria Park

Leith

Warriston Crematorium
St Mark's Park
Pilrig Park
Sports Ground
Cemetery
Powderhall Stadium
Royal Botanic Gardens
Inverleith Terrace
Water of Leith

COMMERCIAL ST

Leith Links
Claremont Park

Seafield Cemetery & Crematorium

Eastern General Hospital

Recreation Ground
Craigentinny Golf Course

Hibernian FC
Albert St
Albion Road

Lochend
Sleigh Drive
Lochend Park

Meadowbank International Sports Centre

LONDON ROAD

King's Rd

Open Air Swimming Pool

Porto-bello

Portobello High Street

Cemetery

Figgate Burn Park

Portobello Golf Course

See plan of Central Edinburgh

St Margaret's Loch

Holyrood Park

Arthurs Seat

Queen's Drive

Dunsapie Loch

Duddingston

Duddingston Golf Course

Duddingston Loch

Prestonfield Golf Course

Craigmillar
Craigmillar Park

NIDDRIE MAINS ROAD

Niddrie Policies

Bruntsfield Place
Whitehouse
Marchmont Road
Grange Road
Cemetery

Strathearn Road
Beaufort Rd

St Raphaels Hospital
Astley Ainslie Hospital
Morningside

Carlton Cricket Ground

Kings Buildings (University of Edinburgh)
WEST MAINS RD

Edinburgh University Sports Ground

Peffermill Road

The Inch Park

Little France

Blackford Hill
Craigmillar Park Golf Course

Hermitage of Braid

Braid Burn

Liberton Golf Course
Niddrie Burn

Braid Hills Golf Course

Braid Hills

Mortonhall Golf Course

Liberton
Liberton Park
Cemetery
Liberton Hosp

Athletic Ground

Gilmerton Park

Gilmerton

Fairmilehead

Princess Margaret Rose Hospital

Mortonhall Crematorium

Kaimes

Southfields Hospital

Hyvots Bank Valley Park

Gracemount Park

Gilmerton Dykes Street

Burdiehouse Burn Park

215

developed the port of Leith, now part of the city. In the late 18thc came the building of the New Town. Nor' Loch was drained in 1760 and the chasm was bridged in 1772 by the North Bridge, which in fact divides the Old and New Towns. The age of Georgian elegance saw fine building by Robert Adam in the shape of the Register House, the university, and the N side of Charlotte Square. Adam was followed by Thomas Hamilton, who built the Royal High School at the foot of Calton Hill in 1829, modelled on the Temple of Theseus in Athens. Adding strength to Edinburgh's nickname of the Athens of the North is Charles Cockerell's unfinished Parthenon, erected on Calton Hill as a monument to Scots killed in the Napoleonic Wars.

The basic plan of squares and broad thoroughfares was James Craig's, who must also take the credit for the buildings on one side only of Queen Street and Princes Street. The opposite sides were

Central Plan

1 Acheson House (Scottish Craft Centre)
2 Assembly Rooms
3 Burns Monument
4 Calton Hill
5 Cannon Ball House
6 Canongate Church
7 Canongate Tolbooth
8 Castle
9 City Chambers
10 Flodden Wall
11 Floral Clock
12 George Heriot's Hospital School
13 Gladstone's Land
14 Greyfriars Church and Greyfriars Bobby Fountain
15 Heart of Midlothian
16 Huntly House (City Museum)
17 John Knox's House
18 Lady Stair's House
19 Magdalen Chapel
20 Mercat Cross
21 Moray House
22 Museum of Childhood
23 National Gallery of Scotland
24 National Library of Scotland
25 National Portrait Gallery of Scotland and National Museum of Antiquities
26 National Trust for Scotland Offices and Bute House

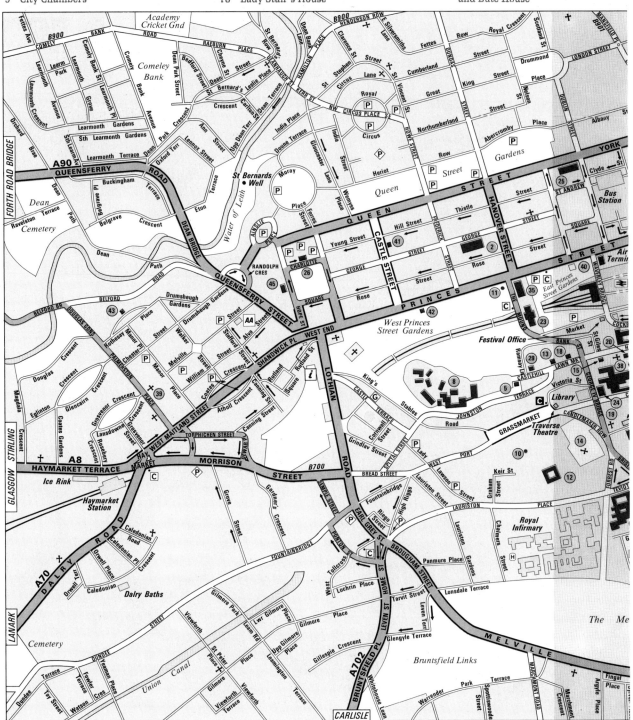

left open as public gardens. During the latter half of the 18thc and the first decade of the 19th, Edinburgh blossomed into one of Europe's cultural centres. The city was the home of literary giants who included James Boswell, Robert Burns, Sir Walter Scott, philosopher David Hume, the political economist Adam Smith, the painter Sir Henry Raeburn, and the engineer Thomas Telford – among very many others.

The Assembly Rooms in George Street date from 1787 and incorporate the Music Hall of 1843, where Paderewski and Pachman gave piano recitals, Dickens and Thackeray lectured, and Gladstone delivered political speeches. Beautiful Princes Street Gardens on the S side of Princes Street contain the prominent Scott Monument, the Scottish-American War Memorial, and the well-known Floral Clock. The guardian bastion of the castle rises impressively in the background.

cont

27	New University	36	Royal Scottish Museum	
28	Old University	37	St Andrew's House	
29	Outlook Tower	38	St Giles's Cathedral	
30	Palace of Holyroodhouse and Holyrood Abbey	39	St Mary's Episcopal Cathedral	
31	Parliament House	40	Scott Monument	
32	Queen Mary's Bath	41	Scott's House	
33	Register House	42	Scottish/American War Memorial	
34	Royal High School	43	Scottish Arts Council Gallery	
35	Royal Scottish Academy	44	Tron Church	
		45	West Register House	

46 White Horse Inn and White Horse Close

District Plan
47 Royal Botanic Gardens and Scottish Gallery of Modern Art (Inverleith House)
48 Royal Observatory
49 St Anthony's Chapel Ruins
50 Transport Museum

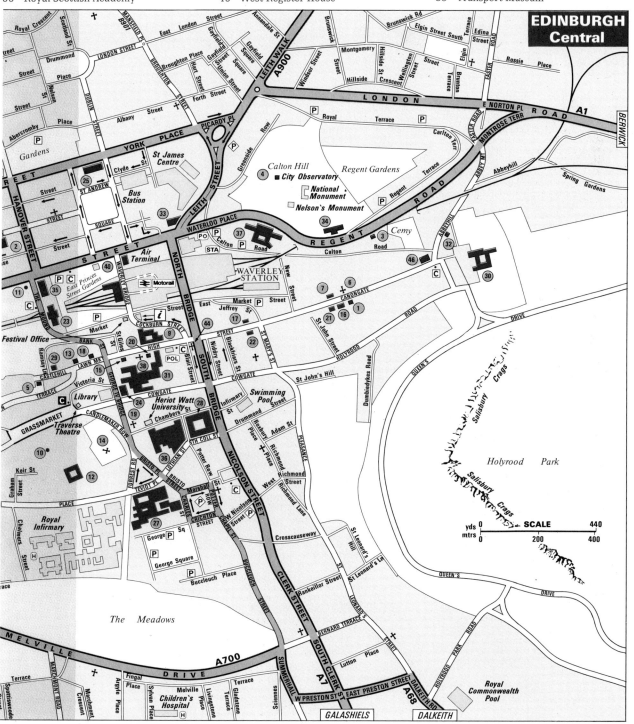

St Giles's beautiful 15th-c crown steeple is the finest of only three examples in Scotland.

Edinburgh is rightly famous for its many parks, gardens, and open spaces; the oldest park is on 300ft-high Blackford Hill, where the Royal Observatory is situated. Scott described the view from the park in *Marmion*. Also here is the Royal Botanic Garden, with perhaps the finest rock garden in the world and a unique group of exotic plant houses. Beyond the famous rugby-football ground at Murrayfield, W of the city, is Corstorphine Hill and the spacious Edinburgh Zoo. In 1947 the Edinburgh International Festival was introduced, a series of concerts, operas, and theatre events now held annually at the end of August or early September. The spectacular floodlit Military Tattoo takes place at the castle every night throughout the festival period. Modern developments in the city include the splendid Meadowbank Sports Centre and the Royal Commonwealth Pool, built for the Commonwealth Games held here in 1970. Extensions have been made to Edinburgh Airport, situated 7m W of the city at Turnhouse.

World-famous for its dramatic beauty and rich history, Edinburgh is also a great centre for education. It is the legal and administrative centre for Scotland, with supreme courts of justice in Parliament Square behind St Giles, in the Royal Mile, and St Andrew's House – headquarters of the Scottish Office – near Calton Hill. A detailed guide-book is essential for a full appreciation of the city, but the following brief descriptions may provide an introduction for the visitor.

On the lower slopes of Arthur's Seat E of the city centre are St Margaret's Well, the remains of St Anthony's Chapel, and tiny St Margaret's and Dunsappie Lochs. Holyrood Park encircles the hill and the beautiful Queen's Drive follows its perimeter, affording wonderful views of Duddingston loch and village and Craigmillar Castle. Edinburgh's river, the little Water of Leith, is spanned by Telford's Dean Bridge of 1831. Farther upstream is picturesque Dean Village, and downstream near Stockbridge is a curious 18th-c Doric temple covering St Bernard's Well.

The following outer districts of the city are dealt with under their individual names elsewhere in the gazetteer:

Barnton; Colinton; Corstorphine; Craigmillar Castle; Duddingston; Fairmilehead; Granton; Hillend; Leith; Liberton; Merchiston; Newhaven; Portobello. Situated some 8m WNW of the city centre are the two famous Forth Bridges, described under Queensferry, South.

CATHEDRALS, CHAPELS, AND CHURCHES

Greyfriars Church

The present church, begun in 1612, was the first church to be opened in Edinburgh after the Reformation. It stands on the site of a monastery established by Dutch friars in the 13thc. In 1638 the first signatures were placed on the National Covenant, a solemn undertaking to resist the 'contrary errours and corruptions' of the Anglican faith imposed on Scotland by Charles I, in this churchyard.

Copies of Covenanting banners hang above the pillars, and among the many ornate tombs is the Martyrs' Memorial to 1,200 Covenanters imprisoned in the open churchyard for five months during an Edinburgh winter in 1679, after being captured at the Battle of Bothwell Brig. Captain Porteus, Allan Ramsay, and the Earl of Morton – executed Regent of Scotland during the minority of James VI – are all buried in the churchyard. In nearby Candlemaker Row is a fountain in memory of Greyfriars Bobby, the famous little Skye terrier who watched over the grave of his master Jock Grey, a Border shepherd, for fourteen years. He was fed by the people of Edinburgh, and when he died in 1872 was buried beside his master.

High Kirk of St Giles

There has been a church here since the 9thc. The present church, also known as St Giles' Cathedral, is the most famous of Edinburgh's churches and dominates the old High Street. The tower carries a beautiful crown steeple dating from *c*1495, which is the finest of only three examples to be found in Scotland – the others are at the Tolbooth in Glasgow, and King's College Chapel in Aberdeen.

The church was subdivided into four churches at one time, and many of its altars and precious relics were destroyed in 1556; considerable and damaging restoration was carried out in the 19thc.

Sir Robert Lorrimer designed the ornate Thistle Chapel, and in the Chepman Aisle are the remains of the great Marquis of Montrose, who was executed in Edinburgh in 1650. Also of interest are the Moray and Albany Aisles. The Colours of the Scottish regiments hang in the nave. Near the Preston Aisle is the Royal pew, and a monument has been erected in a side chapel to Robert Louis Stevenson (1850 to 1894), who is buried in Samoa. A monument to the Covenanter Marquis of Argyll, executed in 1661, stands in St Elio's Chapel.

John Knox was minister at St Giles' until his death in 1572, and preached his own brand of Calvinism from the pulpit. In 1637 an indignant woman threw a stool at the Dean for reading from the Laud's book – an event which foreshadowed the Covenant Wars.

Magdalen Chapel

Found in 1547 under the patronage of the Guild of Hammermen, the chapel still preserves its founder's tomb and is one of Edinburgh's oldest surviving buildings. Pre-Reformation stained glass survives in here, and the chapel was once used as a mortuary. In 1685 the body of the Earl of Argyll was brought here after execution. The building now serves as the chapel of Heriot Watt University.

St Mary's Episcopal Cathedral

In Palmerston Place on the W side of the city is the cathedral designed by Sir Gilbert Scott and built between 1874 and 1917. It carries a 276ft-high central spire and houses an impressive interior. Near by is the charming 17th-c Easter Coates House, probably the oldest house in New Town and now the home of a choir school.

Tron Church

A public 'tron' or weighing beam lies near this church, which was built between 1637 and 1663. After the wooden steeple was burnt a stone one was erected in 1824. Hogmanay celebrations are conducted outside the church, which is no longer used as a place of worship.

FAMOUS BUILDINGS

Calton Hill

Beyond the E end of Princess Street is 350ft-high Calton Hill, with its odd collection of buildings. Charles Cockerell's Parthenon tops the hill and is a monument to the Scots who fell in the Napoleonic campaigns. It was begun in 1822, and in spite of the fact that financial disaster prevented the memorial from being finished, the tall pillars still stand magnificently over the city. Near by is the 102ft-high Nelson Monument, shaped like a telescope and carrying a time-ball. The latter is lowered daily at 13.00hrs for the benefit of mariners. The old City Observatory and the Playfair Monument are two other important structures sited on the hill. The Burns Monument and St Andrew's House – the administrative centre for Scotland – stand on the lower slopes.

Canongate

One of the most fascinating old landmarks of the Royal Mile is the Canongate Tolbooth. This was built in 1591 and variously used as a courthouse and prison. Features include a curious projecting clock, outside stairs, and a turreted tower. The building now houses a collection of Highland dress and tartans. Restored Canongate Church was built in 1688 and displays a pair of stag's antlers supporting a cross on the gable. The celebrated 18th-c political economist Adam Smith was buried in the churchyard, as was Robert Fergusson, the 18th-c poet.

When Burns came to Edinburgh in the 1780's the grave was unmarked but Burns, in debt as he was, paid for a stone to be erected on the grave of a fellow-poet he much admired. Another stone inscribed 'Clarinda' marks the grave of Mrs Agnus Maclehose, an Edinburgh woman with two children, and one of Burns' great loves. She inspired him to write.
Had we never lov'd sae kindly,
Had we never lov'd sae blindly,
Never met – or never parted,
We had ne'er been broken-hearted . . .

Many of Canongate's old houses have been restored. White Horse Close is a group of 17th-c buildings which include White Horse Inn, a staging post for coaches to London now converted into flats. Huntly House was once residence of the Marquis of Huntly and is a fine building of 1570, displaying a timbered front. It contains a museum of Edinburgh's history, including relics of Burns and Scott. The letter 'S' let into the ground at intervals across the road marks the old sanctuary line of Holyrood Abbey. Once a debtor had crossed this line he was safe, and passers-by would watch them being chased down Canongate by bailiffs and bet on the result. The right of sanctuary survived until 1880.

Charlotte Square
'Robert Adam, Architect to the Square, 1791' – this is the signature which appears on original drawings preserved in the City Chambers. The Square is a magnificent example of Georgian architecture. Bute House (NTS), the official residence of the Secretary of State for Scotland, adjoins the offices of the National Trust for Scotland. On the W side stands the one-time St George's Church, which features a green dome and is now West Register House. It contains interesting old documents. Near by are the Scottish Arts Council offices and a gallery where exhibitions are frequently held.

Edinburgh Castle
Overlooking Princes Street and the picturesque streets of the Old Town, Edinburgh Castle (AM) has a history stretching far back into the mists of legend. Its former name Duneadain means 'fort on a slope' and aptly describes its lofty position on Castle Rock. Evidence of habitation in iron-age times has been found on the rock. Edward I occupied the castle in 1296, Edward III refortified it later, and the Scots took it in 1341. Great devastation resulted when Mary Queen of Scots lost the fortress to Regent Morton. In 1650 it was captured by Cromwell, but Bonnie Prince Charlie – though occupying the city in 1745 – failed to take it.

A castle has stood on Castle Hill for at least 1,000 years, and St Margaret's Chapel – the earliest surviving part of the present structure – dates partly from *c*1100. This tiny chapel is dedicated to the saintly Queen Margaret, sister of Edgar Atheling, king-elect of England after Harold died at Hastings. Following the Norman Conquest Edgar and Margaret fled to Scotland, where she married Malcolm III in 1069. Margaret reformed many aspects of the Scottish

church and state, and died in 1093 after hearing of the deaths of her husband and son at the Battle of Alnwick. When Robert the Bruce captured the castle from the English in 1313, he destroyed every building but ordered that the chapel should be left unharmed. After the Reformation the chapel was used to store powder for the 16th-c castle gunners. Mons Meg, a massive cannon which stands at the chapel door, was forged in the 15thc. It burst after firing a royal salute to Charles II in 1680. Behind the chapel lies Palace Yard, on the N side of which is the Scottish National War Memorial erected in 1927 to the memory of 100,000 Scots who died in the first world war.

Opposite the memorial is the Great Hall, built by James IV early in the 16thc and now housing the armoury. One of its features is the fine timbered roof, and the building itself stands over the Casemates – vast vaulted rooms where Napoleonic prisoners were kept. On the E side of Palace Yard is the Old Royal Palace where Mary Queen of Scots gave birth to James VI, later James I of England, in 1566. Housed in the palace are the Scottish Crown Jewels, some dating from the 14thc. When Cromwell occupied the castle the regalia was hidden behind the pulpit of the village church of Kinneff in old Kincardineshire. It was returned to safe keeping in 1682.

Ever since 1861 a gun has been fired each weekday at 13.00hrs as a time check from the Half Moon Battery on the ramparts. Each autumn the three-week floodlit Military Tattoo is held beneath the battlements in the Castle Esplanade, the castle's centuries-old drilling ground. Adjacent to the Old Palace are the barracks, which now house a fascinating Scottish Naval, Military, and Air Force Museum with exhibits of uniforms, Highland weapons, and a collection of tartans. Outside the castle on Castle Hill is the Outlook Tower; its camera obscura throws a bird's eye view over Edinburgh. Near by is a 17th-c Cannon Ball House, with a cannon ball embedded in one of its gables – probably as a water level mark. Opposite this a well marks the spot where over 300 women were burnt to death as witches between 1479 and 1722. Survivals of the ancient Flodden Wall include a tower and can be seen in

the Vennel, which ascends S in the steps beyond Grassmarket towards George Heriot's Hospital School.

Edinburgh University
The university was founded in 1582 and was once known as the College of King James. Buildings designed by Robert Adam in 1789 were completed in 1827 by Playfair, and the dome dates from 1883. The site of the old buildings was once occupied by the house in which Darnley lived, and where he was strangled in 1567. It was blown up with gunpowder the same night.

In recent years many of the old buildings around the McEwan Hall have been demolished, with new university extensions erected in their place. To the S off Meadow Walk is 18th-c George Square, now overwhelmed by high new university towers.

George Heriot's Hospital School
Originally a military hospital, this splendid building was begun in 1628 by William Wallace and founded by George Heriot, a wealthy jeweller and the Jingling Geordie of Scott's *The Fortunes of Nigel*. The building includes a fine quadrangle and is now a well-known school.

Grassmarket
Grassmarket, originally a congregation place for drovers, was an execution site for over a century after 1660. Now it houses antique shops and the famous Traverse Theatre. Burns and Wordsworth were patrons of the White Hart Inn, and the Beehive was once famous for cockfighting.

Heart of Midlothian
Decorative cobbles mark the site of the Old Tolbooth, or prison. The prison was stormed in the Porteus riots of 1736, when Captain Porteus was hanged by a mob from a dyer's pole in the Grassmarket. Captain Porteus had ordered his troops to fire on a crowd that had refused to disperse. He was condemned to death, but a reprieve sent from London incensed the mob. Scott based his *Heart of Midlothian* on these violent events. The well-known Advocate's Close is near by.

John Knox's House
Knox led the Protestant Reformation in Scotland in the 15thc, and is believed to

Protestant Reformer John Knox is said to have lived in this house during the 15thc.

have lived in a 15th-c house in the High Street. The house preserves old timber galleries and is thought to have been built by the goldsmith to Mary Queen of Scots. Near by stood the Netherbow, the city gate farthest away from the castle, which later formed the boundary between the burghs of Edinburgh and Canongate. The Netherbow was removed in 1764. Opposite John Knox's House is the fascinating Museum of Childhood, with its vast collection of children's toys, dress, and books.

Lawnmarket (Gladstone's Land)

A fine old 17th-c six-storeyed house built in Lawnmarket, Gladstone's Land (NTS), was the work of an Edinburgh burgess called Thomas Gladstone. It preserves Edinburgh's last arcaded ground floor, plus several remarkable painted ceilings. The Saltire Society now occupies the house, and across the road are picturesque Riddle's Close and Macmorran's Close. David Hume, the great philosopher who was once refused a chair by Edinburgh University, lived in Riddle's Close.

The old house of Bailie Macmorran, shot dead by a high school boy in 1595 for trying to break a schoolboys' strike, still stands in Macmorran's Close. Deacon William Brodie, town councillor by day and burglar by night, lived in Brodie's Close. He was executed in 1788. Robert Stevenson was also Edinburgh-born, and based his *Dr Jekyll and Mr Hyde* on the character of Brodie. Lady Stair's House dates from 1622 but has been greatly restored. It stands in Lady Stair's Close and now houses a Burns, Scott, and Stevenson museum.

Mercat Cross

Part of an ancient shaft, restored in 1880 by Gladstone, is preserved in the famous cross which faces the City Chambers in the Royal Mile. The old cross was demolished in 1756. Royal Proclamations were read from here, including news of the death of James IV and the Battle of Flodden. Crowds gathered here again in 1745 to hear Prince Charles Edward proclaim his exiled father James III.

Moray House and Acheson House

These two interesting old houses stand in the Royal Mile. Moray House dates from 1628 and preserves fine old ceilings; it is now a college of education. Well-restored Acheson House was built in 1633 and includes a quaint courtyard; it now houses a Scottish Craft Centre display. Facing Moray House are 17th-c Bible Land and Morocco Land, which display interesting carvings. Old-world Bakehouse Close is adjacent. Panmure House, home of Adam Smith, once stood near by.

Palace of Holyroodhouse

At the end of the Royal Mile is the Palace of Holyroodhouse (AM), steeped in tragic memories of the Stuarts. The palace is the official residence of the Queen in Scotland and was commenced by James IV c1550, who enlarged an existing guesthouse of 13th-c Holyrood Abbey (AM) to create the building. Most of the present structure was built for Charles II, who commissioned much of the interior, including the extraordinary Royal Portrait Gallery. James de Witt painted 110 alleged Scottish kings and queens between the years 1684 and 1686 for the modest fee of £120 a year. Leading from the gallery are the

Audience Chamber and the private apartments where Mary Queen of Scots lived from 1561 to 1567. It was here that she had her famous interview with John Knox. David Rizzio, her friend and secretary, was stabbed to death in her presence in March 1566 by a gang of nobles led by the Earl of Morton and her husband Darnley. Darnley himself was found strangled a year later at his house at Kirk o' Field, on the site of the present university. Mary was married to Bothwell at Holyrood in 1567.

A messenger rode 400m, from Elizabeth I's deathbed in Richmond Palace (Surrey) to Edinburgh, in 62 hours to inform James VI of Scotland and I of England of the Queen's death. Prince Charles Edward held a brief court here in 1745, though he never captured the castle, and Scott describes the ball the Prince gave in his *Waverley*. George IV visited Holyroodhouse in 1822, at the time when Britain was spellbound by Scott's novels and all things Scottish. He attended a ball in full Highland dress — wearing pink silk tights. The State Apartments are used by the Queen when in residence and contain rich tapestries and fine period furniture.

Only the nave remains of Holyrood Abbey – the Chapel Royal founded in 1128 by David I as a penance. Legend has it that the King went out hunting on a holy day and was attacked by a stag. About to be gored, he seized the stag's antlers; the beast vanished, leaving in the King's hand a Holy Cross or Rood. The abbey was supposedly built on the spot where the miracle occurred, and for centuries was the burial-place of Scottish kings and queens, including David II, James II, James V, Mary Queen of Scots, and also Darnley and Rizzio. In 1544 the abbey was pillaged by the Earl of Hertford, and again suffered severe damage in 1547. A mob celebrating the accession of William of Orange plundered the abbey in 1688 and desecrated the Royal coffins. Among the objects removed was the head of Lord Darnley. In the grounds of the palace stands Queen Mary's Bath, a small 16th-c tower where a richly carved dagger was found during repairs in 1852. The dagger may well be the murder weapon of Rizzio.

Parliament House

Built in 1640, this was the seat of Scottish government until 1707 and the Act of Union with England. The Courts of Justice are now held behind Parliament Hall, which displays a fine hammerbeam roof. John Knox was buried in Parliament Square in 1572. Sir Walter Scott was born in Edinburgh and spent most of his working life at Parliament House as a lawyer. He lived with his parents at 25 George Square before his marriage, but his favourite home was 39 Castle Street – off George Street – where he lived after his marriage.

Princes Street Gardens

Along the whole S side of this street, which was named after the sons of George III, gardens fall steeply away into the canyon of the Nor' Loch, drained in 1760. Princes Street Gardens contain the Floral Clock of 1903, and the Scottish-American War Memorial. George Kemp erected the fine, 200ft-high Scott memorial between 1840 and 1844. Sixty-four statuettes of Scott characters adorn the monument, with statues of Scott and his dog Maida under the

canopy. To the W stands the Royal Scottish Academy, founded in 1823 and known originally as the Royal Institution.

Register House

This fine Robert Adam building of 1772 serves as the Public Record Office for Scotland. Among many fascinating documents preserved here is the 14th-c Declaration of Arbroath and the 18th-c Treaty of Union. A fine 19th-c statue of the Duke of Wellington stands in front of the building.

ART GALLERIES, LIBRARIES, AND MUSEUMS

National Gallery

The National Gallery stands behind The Mound, a road built on an enormous tip of debris thrown into the Nor' Loch during the 19thc, and is a modern building housing a comprehensive collection. Two other interesting museums are the Transport Museum in Shrubhill, Leith Walk, and the Philatelic Bureau in the Post Office in Waterloo Place, at the E end of Princes Street.

National Library of Scotland

Founded in 1682, the National Library is housed in modern buildings and is Britain's fourth largest library. Many treasures, including the books removed from Parliament House, are preserved here.

National Portrait Gallery and Museum of Antiquities

The exterior of this building is decorated with statues of eminent Scotsmen, and inside are collections of historical portraits and statuary. The National Museum of Antiquities exhibits items illustrating the development of the Scottish way of life. Among many fascinating objects are relics of Mary Queen of Scots, Prince Charles Edward, Scott, and Burns. A remarkable hoard of Roman silver excavated at Traprain Law near East Linton can be seen, as well as a fine oak door from the tower of Amisfield.

Royal Scottish Museum

Opened in 1866, this building houses Britain's most comprehensive museum. Subjects covered are the decorative arts, natural history, geology, mining, shipping, aeronautics, and power. The superb collection of fossil fish is considered the best in the world.

EDNAM, Borders   *26 NT73*

James Thomson, writer of the words to *Rule Britannia*, was born in Ednam in 1700. His obelisk stands to the S at Ferniehill. A plaque on the bridge over Eden Water commemorates Henry Francis Lyte, the hymnologist who wrote *Abide with me*, and who was born near by. Across Eden Water some 2m W is the partly 17th-c mansion of Newton Don.

EDROM, Borders   *31 NT85*

A Norman doorway (AM) leads to a burial vault in Edrom's ruined parish church, which also contains a tomb of 1553 in the Blackadder Aisle.

EDZELL, Tayside   *35 NO56*

This little inland resort lies between Strathmore and the Howe of the Mearns. It is approached through an arch which was erected in 1887 to the memory of the 13th Earl of Dalhousie. A little to the W of Edzell, near the West Water, stand the ruins of early 16th-c Edzell Castle (AM), once home of the Lindsays.

The fine Stirling tower still stands and the castle walls are decorated with bas reliefs indented with large square holes which, when seen from a distance, form the Lindsay arms. A bower once used by Mary Queen of Scots is also preserved, but the most notable feature is the walled garden laid out by Lord Edzell in 1604. This displays unique decorations, and a turreted garden house has also survived. A fine dovecot stands by the adjoining farm.

The North Esk River flows through lovely Glen Esk to the NW. A road penetrates the glen as far as lonely Lochlee in the E Grampians – or Benchinnan Mountains – with 3,077ft Mount Keen rising in the background to the N.

EILDON HILLS, Borders   26 NT53

Scott loved these hills, which form a prominent feature of the landscape. A view indicator has been placed at the highest point of 1,385ft, and two other peaks rise to 1,327ft and 1,216ft. Wonderful views include a long stretch of the River Tweed.

ELDERSLIE, Strathclyde   44 NS46

This town is traditionally the birthplace of William Wallace, and a memorial has been erected near an old house which is thought to be on the site of his home.

*ELGIN, Grampian   34 NJ26

A Royal Burgh and market town, Elgin is perhaps best known for its ruined cathedral (AM) of 1224, one of the finest ecclesiastical buildings in Scotland. The cathedral and part of the town were burnt in 1390 by the notorious Wolf of Badenoch, the outlawed son of Robert II who terrorized the district.

Once known as the Lantern of the North, the cathedral was burned or otherwise damaged several times before after the Wolf's depredations, and in 1711 the central tower collapsed. The structure became a convenient quarry for building stone and remained ruined until 1807. In spite of this a great deal of 13th-c work is still preserved. A notable example is the choir, in which lies the founder's grave and an ancient cross-slab – perhaps of 6th-c date – carved with strange Pictish symbols. Several fine tombs can be seen in the south choir aisle. The nave and chapter house are 15thc, and numerous tombstones with quaint inscriptions abound in the old burial ground S of the cathedral. The Panns Port – or East Gate – is the only surviving gate from the cathedral precincts, and a wing of the Bishop's Palace (AM) dating from 1406 still stands.

Prince Charles Edward, and Dr Johnson and Boswell were visitors to the town in

1746 and 1773 respectively. Prince Charlie stayed at Thunderton House prior to Culloden, which was built in 1650 and is now a hotel. Near St Giles' Church, which was rebuilt in 1826, is the Muckle Cross. This is associated with the raising of the Macleod Highlanders, later to become the Highland Light Infantry, in 1778. Greyfriars Chapel and the 17th-c Little Cross in the High Street have both been restored. Grant Lodge stands in the park and houses a library. Near one of the park entrances is a museum which exhibits collections of fossils and prehistoric weapons. The house of Duff of Braco includes fine arches and dates from 1694. A Gordon monument stands on the site of a former castle on Lady Hill.

The windings of the River Lossie in the fertile Laigh of Moray almost encircle Elgin, and 6m N the well-known resort of Lossiemouth stands where the river enters the sea. The resort's harbour is known as Branderburgh. Innes House, a fine 17th-c mansion situated 5m NE of Elgin, was probably the work of the same person who designed George Heriot's Hospital School in Edinburgh.

ELGOL, Isle of Skye, Highland   32 NG51

This is the village from which Bonnie

1	Bishop's Palace	5	Grant Lodge Library	9	Museum
2	Cathedral Ruins	6	Greyfriars Chapel	10	Panns Port or East Gate
3	Duff of Braco House	7	Innes House	11	St Giles' Church and Muckle Cross
4	Gordon Monument	8	Little Cross	12	Thunderton House (Hotel)

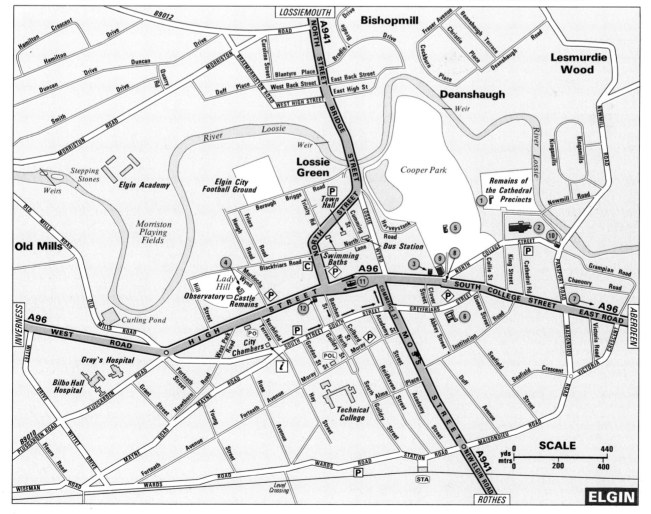

Prince Charlie left for the mainland. It lies at the end of the narrow and hilly road from Broadford, in a beautiful setting on the E shore of Loch Scavaig. The view from 1,128ft Ben Meabost of the Cuillin Mountains grouped above Loch Scavaig has been described as one of the finest in the world.

A long path leading eventually to Loch Coruisk runs N along the side of Loch Scavaig to Camasunary, from which Loch na Creitheach can be reached. The fine 3,042ft peak of Blaven, an outlier of the Black Cuillins, rises above the loch. From Camasunary the path turns W towards the rocky slopes of 1,623ft Sgurr na Stri and fords a stream before reaching the notorious and hazardous Bad Step.

Magnificent Loch Coruisk is described by Scott in *Lord of the Isles* and can be reached from here. This landscape is considered to be the finest loch and mountain scenery in Britain. The best view is from the top of Sgurr na Stri, which faces the great cirque of the Cuillins massed to the W. The views extend beyond the corrie of Coire-uisg to the Inaccessible Pinnacle, perched near the rocky summit of 3,254ft Sgurr Dearg. Loch Coruisk can also be reached by motor boat from Elgol.

The island of Soay lies in Outer Loch Scavaig, with the island of Rum's jagged, mountainous silhouette to the SW. Strathaird Point juts out S of Elgol, and back along the coast NE of the point is Spar Cave. The cave, splendid with stalactites and stalagmites, can be visited by boat. Weird cliffs eroded with deep fissures hang overhead.

ELIE AND EARLSFERRY, Fife   31 NO40
Elie and its twin resort Earlsferry lie on either side of the sandy, crescent-shaped bay between Chapel Ness to the W and Elie Ness to the E. Garnets have been found on the beach near Elie. The parish church carries an octagonal steeple and dates from the 17thc. Gillespie House stands in South Street and has a fine carved doorway dated 1682.

To the E of the town near the sea is Lady's Tower, originally built for Lady Janet Anstruther whom Thomas Carlyle has described. Farther E along the coast are the remains of Ardross Castle. Elie and Earlsferry are noted for their fine golf courses, on one of which a trophy in memory of the great Scots golfer James Braid is played for annually. Braid, who was born in Earlsferry in 1870, won the Open Championship five times between 1900 and 1910. Kincraig House stands in Earlsferry and dates from 1680. To the W of the town is Kincraig Point, with Macduff's Cave close by.

ELLON, Grampian   35 NJ93
Ellon is situated in the agricultural Formartine district and lies on the River Ythan. An ancient mote-hill known as the Earl's Mount stands here, and 5m N is 16th-c Arnage Castle.

ELPHIN, Highland   36 NC21
Situated on the fringe of the wild Assynt country, Elphin lies in a lonely setting of mountains and lochs. To the E is Loch Urigill, and the Cromalt Hills rise to the S. Drumrunie Forest lies W of Elphin and includes 2,786ft Cul Mor, which overlooks Loch Veyatie and the Cam Loch. The spectacular double-topped peak of 2,399ft Suilven rises beyond, and its sharp E cone can be clearly seen from Elphin.

ELVANFOOT, Strathclyde   25 NS91
Elvan Water meets the Clyde at Elvanfoot, which lies in the upper part of Clydesdale amid Lowland hills. A new bridge carrying the A74 across the Clyde has now replaced the old Telford bridge. A plaque in the burial ground near the bridge commemorates 37 men who died of cholera whilst working on the Caledonian Railway. Tiny Clydes Burn joins up with the combined streams of Daer Water and Potrail Water S of the village, making Elvanfoot the first place on the true Clyde river.

Harleburn Head and Clyde Law rise to 1,776ft and 1,789ft E of the village. A road runs S from Elvanfoot towards the Nith Valley, passing through lovely winding Dalveen Pass which climbs to a height of 1,140ft with 1,998ft Comb Head, an outlier of the Lowther Hills, rising to the N. Another road leads E from the village and reaches Nithsdale by way of Leadhills and the Mennock Pass.

EMBO, Highland   37 NH89
A coastal village on the Outer Dornoch Firth, Embo is associated with *Granny's Heilan' Hame.*

ENTERKINFOOT, Dumfries and Galloway   25 NS80
An old track leads through the hills from this Upper Nithsdale hamlet through the narrow and deep Enterkin Pass, overshadowed by 2,403ft Green Lowther. Covenanters once trapped a party of dragoons here – an event described by the author Defoe. To the SE of Enterkinfoot a short link connects with the road through beautiful Dalveen Pass, with 1,998ft Comb Head rising to the W. The pass climbs to a height of 1,140ft before descending to Elvanfoot.

ERIBOLL, Highland   36 NC45
Wild and beautiful Loch Eriboll penetrates deep into mountains, and Eriboll itself lies on the road skirting the E shores of the loch. Grann Stacach and Beinn Spionnaidh rise to 2,630ft and 2,537ft respectively in the W at the head of the loch, and beyond Loch Hope to the SE is 3,040ft Ben Hope. To the SW beyond Strath Beag is Loch Dionard, overshadowed by 2,980ft Fionaven.

ERIKSAY, Western Isles   39 NF70
See Hebrides, Outer.

ERROGIE, Highland   34 NH52
This hamlet lies on the W shores of Loch Mhor, which is now a reservoir uniting the waters of Lochs Garth and Farraline. Loch Mhor flows into the Foyers River, which supplies an aluminium works near Foyers on Loch Ness. Near the E shores of the reservoir is the Easter Aberchalder Estate, noted for its fine rock gardens. To the E moorland stretches as far as 2,618ft Carn Odhar.

ERROL, Tayside   31 NO22
The Earls of Errol take their name from this village, which is situated in the fertile Carse of Gowrie near the Firth of Tay, facing the Fife coast. Megginch Castle lies 2m N and dates partly from 1575. Yew trees in the grounds are thought to be over 1,000 years old. Farther N is Fingask Castle, which was built during the 16thc, and later extended.

ERSKINE, Strathclyde   45 NS47
A fine new bridge which replaces the

former car-ferry here takes traffic away from the centre of Glasgow and across to Old Kilpatrick. Erskine House is a 19th-c building now used as a hospital for disabled ex-servicemen. The house was originally built for Lord Blantyre, whose tall obelisk stands near by. The parish church dates from 1813.

ESKDALEMUIR, Dumfries and Galloway   26 NY29
Roads from Lockerbie and Langholm converge here at the N end of lovely Eskdale. Eskdalemuir Observatory was erected in 1908 and lies 3m N of the road junction at a height of 700ft. Raeburnfoot is the site of a Roman camp and lies to the N of the church. A road running N from the village passes through lonely hill country, with 2,269ft Ettrick Pen to the W, on its way to the valley of Ettrick Water. At one point it reaches an altitude of 1,100ft. Prehistoric remains abound in the vicinity, and Castleoer hill fort stands on a lofty ridge 4m S of the village before the confluence of the White Esk and Black Esk rivers.

ETTRICK, Borders   26 NT21
James Hogg, a poet known as 'The Ettrick Shepherd', lived here. A monument to him stands just E of the church on the site of the cottage where he was born in 1770. He was buried in the churchyard in 1835. Another famous grave is that of well-known Tibbie Sheil, who kept the famous inn of the same name near by St Mary's Loch. She died in 1878 at the age of 96. The village lies on Ettrick Water, which flows from hills in the SW dominated by the remote 2,269ft Ettrick Pen. A road running S from the village towards Eskdalemuir follows the Tima Water, and ascends to more than 1,000ft.

ETTRICK BRIDGE END, Borders   26 NT32
Downstream from Ettrick is Ettrick Bridge End, situated in the one-time Royal hunting ground of Ettrick Forest. An old stone bearing the Harden coat of arms and associated with Sir Walter Scott was saved from a river bridge which was washed away in 1777. It has been built into the present bridge. Scott's grandfather lived in Oakwood Tower, which still stands in a picturesque setting near the river. The tower exhibits characteristic crow-stepped gables and was built by an ancestor of Scott in 1602. Another ancient Scott home, 16th-c Kirkhope Tower, survives 1½m NE of Ettrick Bridge End near the little hill road to Yarrow. Remains of a Roman fort can be seen near Oakwood Tower. William of Deloraine, portrayed in Scott's *Lay of the Last Minstrel*, once lived 5m SW off the road to Tushielaw at Deloraine.

EVANTON, Highlands   34 NH66
Cromarty Firth lies 2m S of this village, which stands on the Allt Grand River. Farther upstream this water is known as the Glass River. Loch Glass, source of the Glass River, lies 5m NW of the village among the foothills of 3,429ft Ben Wyvis. Farther N the smaller Loch Morie is shadowed by 2,419ft Meall Mor. Foulis Castle, 18th-c seat of the Clan Munro, stands 2½m SW of the village and replaces an earlier structure which was burnt down.

EWES CHURCH, Dumfries and Galloway   26 NY39
High up in the fork of a local lime tree

hangs the 300-year-old church bell. Near by on Sorbie Bridge is a tablet in memory of the Rev Henry Scott Riddell, author of *Scotland Yet*.

EYEMOUTH, Borders   31 NT96

Almost the entire male population of Eyemouth – 129 men – lost their lives in a fishing tragedy during a terrible storm in October 1881. The town is chequered by cobbled streets, and narrow pends or archways lead into small courtyards. Wynds or narrow passageways pass between the buildings.

Eyemouth lies between Hare Point and Nestends, and has an old breakwater dating from 1770. Hurkers Rocks protect the fishing harbour, which is overlooked by the gardens of Gunsgreen House, a centre for 18th-c smuggling activities. Cromwell is believed to have erected the nearby tower. Caves honeycomb the picturesque cliffs along the coast N and S, and were used up to 200 years ago by smugglers. Netherbyres was once the home of Sir Samuel Brown, who built the Union Suspension Bridge over the Tweed near Paxton in 1820. Linthill House, dark with its gruesome memories of the murder of wealthy Mrs Patrick Hume in 1751, stands $1\frac{1}{2}$m SW. The culprit was supposedly the butler.

FAILFORD, Strathclyde   25 NS42

A monument at the confluence of the Water of Fail and the River Ayr commemorates the parting of Robert Burns from his Highland Mary – Mary Campbell – on 14 May 1786. Mary was an Argyllshire dairymaid.

FAIRLIE, Strathclyde   44 NS25

This small Firth of Clyde resort has a sandy beach and a pier, and faces the island of Great Cumbrae. Little Cumbrae island lies to the S of Cumbrae, and is separated from the large island of Bute by a narrow channel. The ancient Fairlie Stone lies in St Margaret's church, and N of the town is Kelburne Castle, seat of the Earl of Glasgow. The building comprises a late 16th-c tower attached to a house dating from 1700. Ruined Fairlie Castle is dated 1521 and stands in a glen to the E of Fairlie. The mountains of Arran rise to the SW.

FAIRMILEHEAD (Edinburgh), Lothian   47 NT26

Hunter's Tryst is an inn which was once a cottage associated with Robert Louis Stevenson's *St Ives*. It lies a little to the W of Fairmilehead on the road to Colinton, with prehistoric Caiy Stone (NTS) standing near by.

FAIRNILEE, Borders   26 NT43

Yair House was built in 1788 and lies W of Yair Bridge. The bridge spans the Tweed, and the area is dominated by 1,523ft Three Brethren. Alison Cockburn wrote her version of *Flowers of the Forest* in the now-ruined tower of Fairnilee House during the 11thc. The tower is picturesquely set amid trees high above the River Tweed.

FALKIRK, Central   46 NS87
Plan overleaf

Falkirk is an important industrial centre operating coal mines and the great Carron Ironworks, which began in 1760 with the production of carronades for Nelson's fleet. A carronade is a small naval cannon. The plant now makes light metal castings. In spite of this industrial history, the town was once a collecting place or tryst for cattle brought from all parts of the Highlands along the old drovers' roads.

In 1298 Wallace was defeated in a battle near the town, and Prince Charles Edward was victorious at another in 1746. The bootmaker's shop where the prince spent a night still survives, and can be seen opposite the new Falkirk Steeple. Burns once visited the former Cross Keys Inn in the High Street, and a museum stands in Dollar Park. Falkirk has two old canals – the Forth and Clyde with locks, and the Union. Fascinating 19th-c brewery buildings can also be seen.

An interesting depot of the Scottish Railway Preservation Centre is situated in Wallace Street. Perhaps the best surviving portion of the great Roman Antonine Wall (AM), which ran the width of Scotland, is preserved in the private grounds of Callendar House E of Falkirk. Mary Queen of Scots visited this house many times between 1562 and 1567. The modern buildings of Callendar House College of Education stand near by. A well-preserved fort known as Rough Castle (AM), one of the nineteen forts along the Antonine Wall, lies to the W of Falkirk. Traces of the wall can be seen between Falkirk and Bonnybridge.

FALKLAND, Fife   31 NO20

Picturesque old weavers' cottages and cobbled streets characterize this little Royal Burgh, which is famous for its palace. Falkland Palace (NTS) was a favourite seat of the Scottish Court from the reign of James V. James improved the building considerably before he died there in 1542, and his daughter Mary Queen of Scots used to hunt from the palace. Charles I and Charles II visited the building, Rob Roy occupied it in 1715 after the Battle of Sheriffmuir, and Scott used it as the setting for part of his *The Fair Maid of Perth*. It was in this work that Scott introduced the story of the Duke of Rothesay, who is said to have starved to death in one of the dungeons.

Built in the Renaissance style between 1530 and 1540, the palace boasts a fine façade to the S wing; the E wing was burnt by Cromwell's troops in 1654. The banqueting hall is now a chapel, preserving a good screen and interesting 17th-c tapestries. The Royal Tennis Court dates from 1539.

Falkland's town house and spire date from 1865, and a house with an inscribed panel to Richard Cameron stands in the square. Cameron was a local schoolmaster and Covenanter martyr who was born in 1648. He is associated with the raising of the Cameronian Regiment in 1689. Green Hill bears a monument to O Tyndall-Bruce, an Englishman who restored the palace and built the church in 1849.

The Lomond Hills rise S of the village, with 1,471ft East Lomond in the immediate background and 1,713ft West Lomond lying farther W overlooking Loch Leven. West Lomond is the highest hill of the range.

FALLS OF CRUACHAN, Strathclyde   29 NN02

At the E end of the dark and gloomy Pass of Brander, overlooking the waters of Loch Awe, are the Falls of Cruachan. Robert the Bruce routed the MacDougalls of Lorne in the pass, which is backed by 3,689ft Ben Cruachan. The mountain has twin summits and can be climbed from a point W of the falls. It offers fine views of the lovely Lorne country, including Loch Etive and Loch Linnhe. A river barrage in the Pass of Brander forms part of the Loch Awe hydro-electric scheme.

FALLS OF GLOMACH, Highland   33 NH02

Among the highest waterfalls in Britain, the Falls of Glomach (NTS) are situated above wild Glen Elchaig and cascade from 370ft. They are difficult to reach and special care should be taken in windy or wet weather. The two main starting points are tiny Loch na Leitreach in Glen Elchaig, and Croe Bridge on Loch Duich. The $1\frac{1}{2}$-hour climb from the W end of Loch na Leitreach is arduous; from Croe Bridge the 7m path heads towards the falls by way of Dorusduain climbing over the rough and steep, 2,000ft Bealach na Sroine. Sgurr nan Ceathreamhnan's remote and massive 3,771ft peak rises to the SE of the falls.

FALLS OF ROGIE, Highland   33 NH45

Woodland forms a picturesque backdrop to these lovely falls on the River

The church bell at Ewes hangs in the fork of a lime tree.

Blackwater. They can be reached from the road near Achilty Inn.

FARR, Highland   37 NC76

An ancient sculptured stone stands in the churchyard of Farr's little 18th-c church, which lies SW of the village on lovely Farr Bay. To the N of the village is Farr Point, overlooking the stormy waters of the Pentland Firth.

FASLANE, Strathclyde   44 NS28

Now a Polaris submarine base, Faslane is also involved with breaking up large vessels for scrap. Notable ships that have suffered the fate include the battleships 'Malaya' and 'Renown', and the Cunard liner 'Aquitania'. A local graveyard contains the bodies of men drowned in the submarine K13, which sank in nearby Gare Loch in 1917.

FEARN, Highland   37 NH87

Fearn lies in a fertile stretch of country between the Cromarty and Dornoch Firths. Abbey Church was originally sited at Edderton, but was moved to the town in 1338. The collapse of the chapel roof in 1742 killed several townsfolk. An interesting tomb lies near the Shandwick burial place in the South Chapel. Ruined Lochslin Castle stands 2½m NE, near the shores of Loch Eye. Geanies House stands in fine gardens, which afford views of the Moray Firth, 4½m NE of Fearn.

FEARNAN, Tayside   30 NN74

This small Loch Tay resort lies to the W of wooded Drummond Hill, and is a convenient centre for visiting beautiful Glen Lyon. A short road runs N from Fearnan to Fortingall.

FENWICK, Strathclyde   29 NS44

Fenwick's restored church dates from 1643 and contains a post-Reformation pulpit. Its old jougs – an iron collar once used for chaining wrongdoers to a wall – has been preserved. Numerous Covenanter monuments lie in the churchyard, and one inscription recalls Scott's *Old Mortality*. Fenwick lies on the Fenwick Water, with moorland to the E and Crawfurdland Castle 2m S. This castle was given to the Hewison-Crawfurd family by James V in the 16thc, as a reward for rescuing him from thieves who attacked the king while he was crossing the old bridge at Cramond.

FERNESS, Highland   34 NH94

To the S of Ferness the River Findhorn enters its most beautiful reach, flowing between high rocky banks amid picturesque woodland. Dulsie Bridge lies farther upstream and is a particularly lovely spot. Some 4m NE of Ferness, off the Forres road near Daltulich Bridge, is beautiful Randolph's Leap. This is accessible only on foot, and is named after Randolph, 1st Earl of Moray.

1 Bootmaker's Shop	4 Dollar Park	7 Rough Castle
2 Callendar House	5 Robert Burns' Plaque (Old Cross Keys)	8 Scottish Railway Preservation Society
3 Carron Ironworks	6 Roman Antonine Wall	9 Steeple and Information Centre

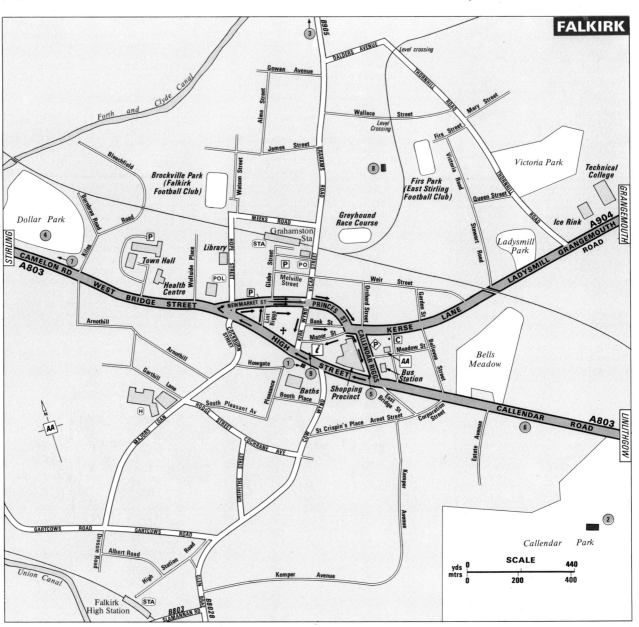

During a combat the earl's opponent jumped the river at this point. The leap lies in Findhorn Glen near the meeting of the waters of the Findhorn and the Divie. This is also close to the fine grounds of Relugas House. A stone near the meeting of the two rivers commemorates the record height of the water during the great floods of 1829.

FERNIEHIRST CASTLE, Borders 26 NT61
Now used as a youth hostel, this fine 16th-c castle stands in woodland just E of Jed Water. It was once a seat of the old Border family of Ker, and replaced an earlier building which was destroyed in 1571. It played its part in many fierce Border skirmishes throughout the ages, was many times besieged, and changed hands frequently. The building is L-shaped and carries the Ker arms on several panels. A huge fireplace dominates the great hall.

FERRYDEN, Tayside 31 NO75
North-Sea oil developments are being carried out at Ferryden, which lies on the estuary of the South Esk River facing Montrose. Scurdy Ness and its lighthouse lie E of the village.

FESHIEBRIDGE, Highland 34 NH80
A bridge over the lovely gorge of the River Feshie, a tributary of the Spey, can be seen E of this little village. The Feshie runs down from the Cairngorms and passes through picturesquely-wooded Glen Feshie. General Wade planned to build a road through the glen to link Speyside with Deeside. It was meant to reach Deeside near the Linn of Dee by Inverie, but was never started. Apart from the long walkers' track through the wild Lairig Ghru Pass, the only road from the Spey to the Dee valleys is via Tomintoul.

FETTERCAIRN, Grampian 35 NO67
Lying on the edge of the fertile Howe of the Mearns, with the E Grampians in the background, Fettercairn was visited by Queen Victoria and Prince Albert in 1861. An arch commemorates this occasion. The shaft of the old 17th-c Kincardine Town Cross stands in the square, and is notched to show the measurements of the Scottish ell — roughly equivalent to a yard.

Interesting papers relating to the Boswell family have been discovered at Fettercairn House. Ruins of Kincardine Castle, once a Royal residence built on the site of the former county town of Kincardine, lie 2m NE off the Stonehaven road. Macbeth's head is thought to have been brought to Malcolm at Kincardine Castle, after Macbeth's defeat at Lumphanan. Balbegno Castle is partly of 16th-c date and stands 1m SW of Fettercairn.

FEUGHSIDE INN, Grampian 35 NO69
Lying on the road from Cairn o' Mounth to Kincardine o'Neil on Deeside, this inn takes its name from the nearby Water of Feugh. Passing near the inn is the road from Aboyne to Banchory, an alternative to the main Deeside road. The great Forest of Birse lies to the W of the inn.

FINCASTLE, Tayside 34 NN86
Old Fincastle, a 17th-c house with a small loch, lies to the NW of this village.

FINDHORN, Grampian 34 NJ06
Once one of the chief exporting towns of

Moray, the fishing village of Findhorn lies on the E side of sandy Findhorn Bay, facing the Moray Firth. Culbin Sands finally engulfed the original village after several near misses, and the second village was devastated by floods in 1701. Distant Forres can be seen across the bay to the S.

FINDOCHTY, Grampian 35 NJ46
A quaint little fishing village with good sands, Findochty lies on a rocky stretch of coast between Craig Head and Long Head. Spey Bay lies to the W.

FINDON, Grampian 35 NO99
Known also as Finnan, Findon has given its name to the famous Finnan haddocks, once cured here in the local peat-reek. The village has a shingle foreshore.

FINHAVEN, Tayside 31 NO45
Ruined Finhaven — or Finavon — Castle lies to the S of the River South Esk. It belonged to the Earls of Crawford and dates from c1500, but was extended in 1593 and collapsed in 1712. Beyond the castle is the Hill of Finhaven, a good viewpoint with a vitrified fort on its E summit.

FINNART, Strathclyde 44 NS29
Situated N of Gare Loch on the E bank of Loch Long, Finnart is an ocean-terminal oil port.

FINTRY, Central 45 NS68
Fintry is set in a hollow on the Endrick Water, between the Fintry Hills to the NE and the Campsie Fells to the S. It occupies a position in the centre of the ancient territory of Lennox. In the Middle Ages, Lennox extended into a large part of the old Stirlingshire, Perthshire, and Renfrewshire counties. These have now been eliminated by recent reorganization. Culcreuch Tower is an ancient structure which was added to in the 17thc, and lies to the N. Some 3m E of Fintry near the Walton reservoir is the Loup of Fintry, a waterfall on the Endrick Water which plummets from a 100ft-high rock ledge.

A narrow, hilly moorland road continues E from here, passing close to the site of former Sir John de Graham's Castle, then keeping to the N of the Kilsyth Hills to reach a flat industrial area at Denny. The Crow Road leads SE from Fintry to Lennoxtown and affords fine views over the Campsies, where dark basalt rocks protrude above the grass.

FIRTH OF CLYDE, Strathclyde 29
This is the name given to a stretch of water separating the coast of the old Ayrshire and Renfrewshire counties from the islands of Arran, Bute, and the Cowal shores of the mainland. Yachting is popular on the Firth; regattas are held here and on the more confined waters of the Kyles of Bute to the NW. Among the well-known resorts on the Firth are Ardrossan, Largs, Wemyss Bay, and Dunoon.

FLODIGARRY, Isle of Skye, Highland 32 NG47
Flora Macdonald spent the early years of her marriage to Allan Macdonald of Kingsburgh at Flodigarry. A hotel adjoins the old house where she lived. In 1746 Flora escorted the fugitive Bonnie Prince Charlie, dressed as her maid Betty Burke, from Benbecula in the Outer Hebrides to Portree in Skye. Dr Johnson and Boswell were entertained at Flodigarry before her

family emigrated to North Carolina. The Macdonalds later returned, and Flora is buried a few miles W of Flodigarry at Kilmuir. Opposite Flodigarry is the off-shore island known as Eilean Flodigarry. A road running S passes below the dark, imposing crags and pinnacles of the Quiraing.

FLOORS CASTLE, Borders 26 NT73
Built by Vanbrugh in 1718, this vast mansion is sited near the Tweed and boasts 365 windows – one for every day of the year. Playfair carried out Tudor-style alterations in c1849. The castle stands in a great park, and the main entrance gates from Roxburgh Street in Kelso were erected in 1929. They display ornate wrought-iron work overlaid with gold leaf. A holly tree in the park is said to mark the spot where James II was killed by a bursting cannon while laying siege to the castle in 1460.

FOCHABERS, Grampian 35 NH35
Situated to the E of the River Spey, Fochabers stands on the edge of Speymouth Forest. Serious soil erosion has taken place here. Only one tower of Gordon Castle remains in the great park to the N, the rest having been demolished in 1955. Fochabers used to lie nearer the castle, but was removed to its present site during the 18thc. The old Market Cross and the jougs – malefactors' iron collar – were left behind during the move. The 19th-c church has a pillared portico, and to the W across the Spey is Mosstodloch river bridge. This replaces an earlier one lost in the disastrous floods of 1829.

FOGO, Borders 31 NT74
Two private laird's lofts of 1671 and 1677 are preserved in the local church. The elder of the two was used by the Trotters of Charterhall, and displays an outside staircase.

FORD, Strathclyde 29 NM80
Ford is a small anglers' resort with a steamer pier, situated between the SW tip of Loch Awe and little Loch Ederline. A road along the S shores of Loch Awe passes ruined Fincharn Castle after about 2m, facing Inverliver Woods across the loch. Another road from Ford traverses Loch Awe's N shores and leads to Dalavich and Kilchrenan.

FORDOUN CHURCH, Grampian 35 NO77
Situated 3m NNW of the Brechin to Stonehaven road on the edge of Drumtochty Forest, Fordoun Church stands on a steep bank over the River Luther. A fragment of the ancient Chapel of St Palladius lies in the churchyard. The dedication is to an Irish bishop. Monboddo House, one-time home of the 18th-c judge Lord Monboddo, lies 1½m NE and was visited by Dr Samuel Johnson in 1773. A road runs NW around Finella Hill and passes Drumtochty Castle – now a school – before reaching Clattering Bridge.

FORDYCE, Grampian 35 NJ56
Delightfully situated just S of the Portsoy to Cullen road, Fordyce has a small 16th-c castle which overlooks the village street. Fine corbelling and good dormer windows are features of the castle. Thomas Nicholson was born at the mansion of Birkenbog, situated in a fine walled garden 1½m NW, in 1665. He

later became the first Vicar-Apostolic of Scotland.

FORFAR, Tayside *31 NO45*
Malcolm III is said to have held the parliament at which he bestowed surnames and titles on Scottish noblemen here in 1057. Forfar is a Royal Burgh and one-time county town in the fertile Howe of Angus between little Lochs Forfar and Fithie. Malcolm's castle was destroyed by Robert the Bruce, but the site is marked by a 17th-c octagonal turret which was once the town cross. William Playfair (1789 to 1857) designed the town hall, which houses the Forfar Bridle – an iron collar with a prong. This was used in medieval times to silence a victim about to be executed.

Fine views are offered by the Hill of Finhaven, which lies to the NE and is crowned by a vitrified fort. Closer to Forfar, near Loch Fithie, is the ruined Restenneth Priory (AM) – a house of Augustinian canons which was possibly founded by David I. Its earliest portions date from the 12thc, though the tall square tower may be older. The broach spire probably dates from the 15thc. Restenneth Priory is the resting place of Robert the Bruce's son.

A track known as King's Codger's Road once ran E from Forfar to the coast at Usan, and was the route by which the Royal Castle was supplied with fresh fish. A battle of great importance to Scotland was fought at Dunnichen, once known as Nectan's Mere, 4m SE of Forfar and E of the Carnoustie road. Ecgfrith, King of the Angles was defeated here, an event which ensured Scotland's independence. The fascinating Angus Folk Collection is housed in Kirkwynd Cottages 5m SW of Forfar, and covers domestic and agricultural life in the county up to the 19thc. Just W of Forfar, near a loch of the same name, is the site of another ancient battle, this time between the Picts and Scots.

FORGUE, Grampian *35 NJ64*
This village stands on the Burn of Forgue, a tributary of the River Deveron. A silver communion cup of 1629 preserved in the church may be the oldest in Scotland.

FORRES, Grampian *34 NJ05*
A Royal Burgh standing near the River Findhorn, Forres is mentioned in Shakespeare's *Macbeth* as the site of King Duncan's Court. The town's museum contains a famous collection of fossils from the local old red sandstone, and the Witches' Stone marks a place where three witches accused of causing the death of King Duffus were burnt in AD965. Nelson Tower was erected on top of densely-wooded Cluny Hill in 1806, and affords a magnificent view of Findhorn Bay, which lies 2m N.

The Sueno's Stone (AM) can be seen 1m NE of Forres, where the roads to Findhorn and Elgin diverge. This remarkable, 23ft-high sculptured stone is elaborately carved and is of unknown origin. One theory is that it commemorates a battle won by the King of Denmark's son, Sweyn or Sueno, over Malcolm II in 1008. Some 6m SW of the town in Darnaway Forest is Darnaway Castle, built in 1810 round the 15th-c hall of an earlier structure. The previous building belonged to the Earls of Moray. Mary Queen of Scots

stayed here in 1562. Farther upstream from Forres the Findhorn flows between Darnaway Forest and the woods of Altyre; the scenery here is of exceptional beauty.

FORSINARD, Highland *37 NC84*
Forsinard lies between Strath Halladale and Achintoul Forest, and is a resort much favoured by anglers. Ben Griam Beg and Ben Griam Mhor rise to respective heights of 1,803ft and 1,936ft in the W. Loch an Ruathair lies 4m S off the Helmsdale road.

FORT AUGUSTUS, Highland *33 NH30*
Historic Fort Augustus was built after the Jacobite rising of 1715, and named after Augustus, Duke of Cumberland. General Wade enlarged the fort in 1730 and built a road linking Fort William and Inverness by way of Glen More in 1725 and 1726. This route is still partly followed by the present main road. Fort Augustus was once known as Kilcummin, or Killichiumen. It was captured by Bonnie Prince Charlie's forces in January 1745, and held until after the Battle of Culloden. A Benedictine abbey of 1876 and a Roman Catholic boys' school now share the site of the old fort. The grave of John Anderson, a carpenter friend of Burns, lies in the churchyard. Although Anderson died in 1832 his name lives on in the verse *John Anderson my jo John.*

Fort Augustus is now a very popular angling centre, situated in wooded hill country at the SW end of Loch Ness near the point where it is entered by the Caledonian Canal, with its six lochs. The old Wade road to Inverness climbs steeply E from Fort Augustus, crossing wooded Glen Doe and passing Loch Tarff before ascending to 1,275ft. The section to Whitebridge affords good views.

Forests have been planted along the W shores of Loch Ness, and the village of Ichnacardoch has been recently established. General Wade's famous road over the Corrieyairack Pass, now no more than a track, runs S from Fort Augustus and climbs to 2,500ft over the pass before descending into the Spey valley in steep zigzags. Neil Munro described the making of this road in his *New Road*, and Bonnie Prince Charlie followed the route with his Highland army in 1745. A disused smithy 2m S of Fort Augustus, on the A82, houses the Great Glen Exhibition. This covers the history of the village, Loch Ness, and the famous monster. Another Wade road ran NW from Fort Augustus to Glen Moriston, and was used by Dr Johnson and Boswell in 1773.

FORTEVIOT, Tayside *30 NO01*
Once a Pictish capital like Dunstaffnage, Forteviot lies just S of the confluence of the River Earn and the Water of May in Strath Earn. The Water of May flows through the village from the heights of the Ochil Hills. Some 2m N the 19th-c Dupplin Castle stands in a fine wooded park E of Dupplin Loch. A battle was fought near here in 1332, and close to Bankhead Farm and the Earn is a hill surmounted by a splendidly carved early-Christian cross. Invermay House lies 1½m SE of Forteviot and has associations with Scott's *Redgauntlet*. Recent excavations SW at Broomhill Farm have revealed the outlines of a large Roman camp.

FORT GEORGE, Highland *34 NH75*
One of the finest late artillery fortifications in Europe, Fort George (AM) lies on a narrow spit of land where the waters of Inner and Outer Loch Moray unite to face Chanonry Point in the Black Isle. The fort and garrison church were built in 1748 as a result of the Jacobite rebellion, and Dr Johnson and Boswell were visitors in 1773. Fort George is still a military garrison, and houses the regimental museum of the Queen's Own Highlanders.

FORTINGALL, Tayside *30 NN74*
This lovely village of thatched cottages lies on the River Lyon just N of Loch Tay. It is separated from the loch by wooded Drummond Hill. Pontius Pilate may have been born here. A huge yew tree in the churchyard may be the oldest alive in Britain; in 1772 its girth was measured at 56ft, and its one remaining live stem is carefully tended. Glen Lyon House was once a Campbell home, and E of Fortingall the River Lyon flows for a further 5m to join the Tay.

To the SW of the village are earthworks which may indicate a one-time Roman outpost. Beautiful Glen Lyon stretches W of Fortingall for 25m through Breadalbane country. It is one of Scotland's longest glens, and is approached via the richly-wooded Pass of Lyon. A feature of the pass is the romantic MacGregor's Leap. Allt do Ghob Falls are situated 2m W along the glen, just S of the road. The road itself continues W between the peaks of 3,419ft Cairn Mairg, to the N, and 3,984ft Ben Lawers to the S.

FORTROSE, Highland *34 NH75*
This quiet Black-Isle resort and Royal Burgh faces the Inner Moray Firth. Its sheltered bay is popular with yachtsmen. Chanonry Point separates Fortrose from the Outer Moray Firth, and overlooks the water to Fort George. The ruins of Fortrose Cathedral (AM) date from the 14th and 15thc, and include a vaulted south aisle which preserves several monuments and an ancient font. The chapter house is now used as a court house. Cromwell is thought to have used stones from the already derelict cathedral to build his fortress at Inverness. Inland to the NW is the elevated, wooded ridge known as Millbuie. Mary Queen of Scots bestowed the lordship of this upon Darnley.

*FORT WILLIAM, Highland *33 NN17*
A touring centre for Lochaber and the W Highlands, Fort William lies near the W end of Glen More by the head of Loch Linnhe. It lies at the foot of the 4,406ft bulk of Ben Nevis, Britain's highest mountain. The Ben is not visible from the town itself, but forms a landmark for many miles around and can be clearly seen from the summit of 942ft Cow Hill, which rises behind the town. The view from Cow Hill includes the lower reaches of beautiful Glen Nevis, backed by the white quartzite peak of 3,601ft Sgurr a' Mhaim.

Ben Nevis can be climbed from the rough but well-defined path at Achintee Farm in Glen Nevis, which can be reached from Fort William by crossing the River Nevis just NE of the town and keeping to the E bank. Fort William's original earth-and-wattle fort was built in 1655 by General Monk, 1st Duke of Albemarle. It was rebuilt in stone in

1690 by order of William III, after whom it was named. The Jacobites failed to capture the fort in 1715, and General Wade strengthened it after this siege. The Jacobites again besieged Fort William unsuccessfully in 1745, and it continued to be garrisoned until 1855. After this it was demolished. A gateway from the fort was re-erected in 1896 at the Craigs, the old cemetery, and W of the gateway is The Rock from which cannons fired on the fort in 1746.

The West Highland Museum in the High Street contains the famous secret portrait of Prince Charles Edward, which can only be seen if the picture is reflected on to the curved surface of a polished cylinder. Also here is a bed in which the Prince slept, plus panelling dating from 1707 and taken from the house of the Fort's governor. A reconstructed croft kitchen is of interest. The Lochaber Gathering takes place in the town every year, usually in the latter half of August.

Fort William received the benefits of electric lighting in 1896, and was one of the first British towns to do so. A large aluminium factory and power house NE of the town is fed by the waters of the Lochaber power scheme, brought by a 15m tunnel through Ben Nevis. Farther NE the ruins of Inverlochy Castle (AM) stand beside the River Lochy. Once the home of the Comyns, this square building is probably of 13th-c date. Comyn's Tower – the largest of its circular towers – had walls 10ft thick and rooms measuring 20ft across. In 1431 the Earls of Mar and Caithness were defeated in a battle here; in 1645 the great Marquis of Montrose, of Clan

Graham, defeated the Covenanters near the castle after remarkable forced marches through the Lochaber Mountains. This later battle is described by Scott in *Legend of Montrose* and Neil Munro in *John Splendid*.

The 19th-c Inverlochy Castle is now part of a cattle farm, and the old castle forms an hotel. The main road continues NE towards Great Glen on the line of General Wade's military road, and reaches Invergarry beyond Loch Lochy. Access to the beautiful district of Ardgour is by a road running SW from Fort William along the shores of Loch Linnhe. The loch is crossed by the Corran Ferry, and the road continues along the shores of Loch Leven to Kinlochleven. The old road from Fort William to Kinlochleven went inland over the lonely hills and past Loch Lundavra.

The waters of Loch Linnhe mingle with those of Loch Eil, NW of Fort William, beyond the narrows near Corpach. A road along the N shores of Loch Eil is the romantic 'Road to the Isles – by Ailort and by Morar to the Sea', leading to Mallaig in countryside poignant with memories of Bonnie Prince Charlie. Thomas Telford built the road as far as Arisaig between 1800 and 1804.

FOULDEN, Borders 31 NT95
An unusual two-storeyed and crow-stepped tithe barn (AM) can be seen here. An inscribed tombstone in the churchyard is dated 1592.

FOWLIS, Tayside 30 NN92
This quaint little village lies a little way N of the Crieff to Perth road, some 25m W

of Fowlis Easter. It has no connection with the latter. A lych-gate to the restored, 13th-c St Bean Church is dated 1644. The church boasts an old jougs and a Celtic cross, and opposite is the Fowlis Wester Sculptured Stone (AM) – a remarkable 10ft-high, 8th-c Pictish cross-slab. Prehistoric standing stones can be seen on moorland to the NW.

FOWLIS EASTER, Tayside 31 NO33
St Marnan's Church dates from 1453 and preserves a series of medieval painted panels, a bell of 1508, and an old carved font. Its elaborately-carved Sacrament House is considered one of the finest in Scotland. Beside the S door are the jougs – an iron collar once used for securing wrongdoers. Fowlis Castle was built during the early 17thc.

FOYERS, Highland 33 NH42
Overlooking Loch Ness, Foyers is best known for its two beautiful waterfalls. The first hydro-electric scheme in Britain was used from 1896 to feed water from the Loch Mhor Reservoir to nearby aluminium works. Although the works are now closed, the waterfalls are still much reduced, and a further extension to the scheme was completed in 1974 (see inset overleaf). Across Loch Ness is 2,284ft Mealfuarvonie the highest point in the extensive Balmacaan Forest. Foyers stands on the line of General Wade's road from Fort Augustus to Inverness. A shelter built here by Wade was known as the General's Hut.

*FRASERBURGH, Grampian 35 NJ96
Situated on Fraserburgh Bay, the town is

1 Fort William
2 Gate of Fort William

3 Inverlochy Castle

4 West Highland Museum

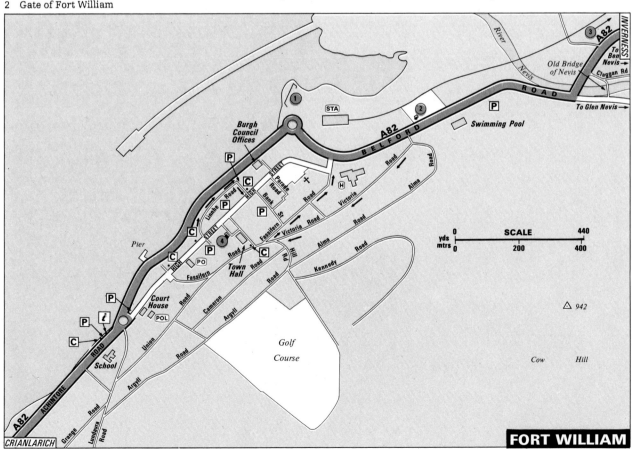

FORT WILLIAM

a herring port and a Buchan holiday resort with fine sands. It dates back to the mid 16thc, when it was founded by Sir Alexander Fraser and known as Farthlie. Its Mercat cross of 1736 is of interest. The town is sheltered to the W by Kinnaird's Head, mentioned by the ancient Greek historian Ptolemy, and the lighthouse stands on the remains of a 16th-c tower and overlooks the North Sea. Near by is the quaintly named Wine Tower, probably of 15th-c date and Fraserburgh's oldest building. It stands above the 100ft-long cave of Scalch's Hole. Restored Cairnbulg Castle lies 3m SE near the Water of Philorth.

FRESWICK, Highland   37 ND36
Freswick Bay lies 1m E of Freswick and is sheltered to the N by Skirsa Head, and to the S by Ness Head. Ruins of 15th-c Bucholly Castle lie near Ness Head. This once belonged to the Mowats. The area is rich in prehistoric sites. The low Warth Hill stands 2m N on the John o' Groats road and affords glimpses of the distant Orkneys.

FRIOCKHEIM, Tayside   31 NO54
This curious placename is probably derived from *Freke*, the name of a one-

BIRTH OF AN INDUSTRY

Set on a steeply sloping hillside on the east side of Loch Ness, Foyers was a lonely place before General Wade blasted a road to it in 1732. In Victorian times tourists came to admire the splendid Falls of Foyers. Few of them could have imagined that the water was about to be harnessed, and that this isolated place would give birth to what was, for Britain, an entirely new industry.

In 1894 the British Aluminium Company was formed, with a capital of £300,000. Its advisers included Lord Kelvin, the greatest physicist of the time, and the company decided to build a pioneer hydro-electric plant at Foyers to provide power for an aluminium factory.

Work began the following year. The company had bought the 8,000-acre Foyers Estate, and negotiated water

time bailie of Forfar, and *heim*, meaning home. It is thought that the suffix may have been added by John Anderson, who had lived in Germany, in 1830.

FURNACE, Strathclyde   29 NN00
Smelting works once stood in this aptly-named Loch-Fyne village, which is still known for its large granite quarry.

FYVIE, Grampian   35 NJ73
Dominating the River Ythan, Fyvie Castle is one of the stateliest castellated mansions in Scotland. It was founded in the 13thc, and its four old turreted towers are named after their builders – Gordon, Meldrum, Preston, and Seton. In 1644 the Royalist Duke of Montrose was pursued here by the Earl of Argyll, a Covenanter he later routed. Fyvie Castle's oldest work dates from the 15thc, and most of the rich south front was built during the 15th and 16thc – with some 17th-c additions. A magnificent stone spiral staircase is preserved inside the castle. Lord Dunfermline, who completed the 17th-c alterations, later worked at Pinkie House in Midlothian.

*GAIRLOCH, Highland   36 NG87
This village resort lies in a superb setting

rights with neighbouring proprietors. Above the falls five sluice-gates were built to divert and regulate some of the water of the River Foyers into an 8ft-diameter tunnel, which fell 350ft to the power house nearer the lochside. Five 700hp turbines were installed by Escher and Wyss of Zurich, and the electricity produced not only powered the aluminium works but also supplied lighting for the Foyers Hotel and the village which the company established for workers.

To increase the storage capacity of the hill lochs which fed the River Foyers, the company devised a scheme to merge Loch Farraline and Loch Garth into the single and much bigger Loch Mhor. This explains why to the east of Loch Ness there is a district called Lochgarthside – but no sign of any stretch of water with the same name.

The aluminium works flourished. Bauxite, the raw material, was mined in Antrim and pounded into a fine powder before being shipped from Ireland

on the Gair Loch, and affords distant views of the Outer Hebrides. Facilities include fine fishing and good bathing from sandy beaches. Gairloch has one of the few golf courses in NW Scotland, and the two islands of Longa and Eilean Horrisdale lie in the loch itself. Salmon are landed at Gairloch in the morning, and the evening fleet brings in whitefish, prawns, lobsters, and crabs.

The fish auctions are an entertainment in themselves. To the S of Gairloch the view ranges over the Flowerdale Forest peaks, dominated by 2,869ft Baeshven. Farther S the 3,232ft Beinn Alligin, one of the magnificent, wild Torridon peaks, overlooks lonely Torridon. The road SE from Gairloch to Loch Maree passes beautifully wooded Kerrysdale and its hydro-electric scheme; a W branch leads back to the coast between Opinan and Red Point. Melvaig is the farthest N point reached by the road running NW from Gairloch, and beyond Melvaig lies lonely Rudha Reidh and its lighthouse.

GAIRLOCHY, Highland   33 NN18
The River Lochy used to flow into Loch Lochy here, but was diverted over the lovely Mucomer Falls into the River

through the Caledonian Canal to the quay at Foyers. In its heyday the plant employed 500 men, and the two villages of Lower and Upper Foyers spread over the hillside.

In time, however, the aluminium company's attentions came to be focused on bigger, more modern enterprises at places like Fort William and Kinlochleven. When Foyers went over to the production of super-purity aluminium, it needed far fewer workers. In January 1967 the company announced an immediate run-down of the old factory; its hydro-electric plant was by then the oldest of its kind still operating anywhere in the world.

Many of the village houses were sold off and it seemed as if Foyers was finished. But it still had advantages to offer, and the North of Scotland Hydro-Electric Board moved in to build a massive pumped storage scheme to generate power for the national grid. Completed in 1974, it incorporates some of the original Victorian ideas, because the water comes from Loch Mhor – although this time via a tunnel through the hills. The aluminium factory, half-forgotten birthplace of a great industry, still stands near the modern power station at Lower Foyers. The road from Fort Augustus passes the sluice-gates above the falls.

Vertical generators of 1895 in the Foyers power house.

Spean, which enters the loch a little to the E. Two locks raise the level of the Caledonian Canal to the height of the loch, and the canal runs along the old course of the River Lochy. Magnificent views of the great 4,406ft Ben Nevis and its neighbours can be enjoyed from the road to Corpach. To the N of this road, 2½m S of Gairlochy, is the entrance to roadless Glen Loy. Prince Charles Edward marched through here in 1745, and traces of the ancient Caledonian Forest survive in the glen.

GAIRNEYBRIDGE, Fife 46 NT19
A monument here commemorates the foundation of the first Secession Presbytery in 1733. Loch Leven lies to the N, with Benarty Hill rising to 1,167ft in the E.

GAIRNSHIEL BRIDGE, Grampian 35 NJ20
Gairnshiel Bridge lies amid lofty hills and moors in Glen Gairn, at the junction of the roads from Braemar and Ballater in the Dee valley. Beyond Glen Finzie 2,862ft Morven rises to the NE. The road continues N from Gairnshiel Bridge and crosses the hills along the steep and narrow Glas Choille section, which is often snowbound in winter. After this it descends the fertile valley of the Don near Cock Bridge.

*GALASHIELS, Borders 26 NT43
The bustling Border town of Galashiels is noted for its tweeds and woollens. Every June there is a pageant, the Braw Lad's Gathering, when the history of the town since its charter was granted in 1599 is re-enacted. Galashiels motto 'Sour Plums' can be seen on the municipal buildings, and refers to a Border foray of 1337 when a party of English soldiers was slain while picking wild plums. The Scottish College of Textiles is situated here, and the town has a 1695 Mercat cross. Sir Robert Lorimer designed the war memorial's clock tower, in front of which is a representation of a Border 'reiver' or moss-trooper.

Old Gala House dates from the 15th and 17thc, with modern alterations, and is

now an art centre. To the N of the town the well-preserved Old Buckholm Tower stands on the slopes of Buckholm Hill. A plaque 1½m SE of the town records Sir Walter Scott's last journey to his home in Abbotsford on his return from Italy in 1832 shortly before his death. It is sited on the Melrose road near Longlee. An old track known as the Catrail, or Pict's Ditch, passes W from Galashiels over high ground and once ran S for more than 50m. Another stretch is visible near Shankend, on the Hawick to Newcastleton road.

GALLOWAY, Dumfries and Galloway
Some of the wildest but least-known scenery in Scotland is to be found in Galloway. The lovely mountain slopes have earned themselves the name of the Galloway Highlands, and are dominated by the 2,764ft Merrick and the fine Rhinns of Kells range. This is the land of the red deer, of the thickly coated black and hornless Galloway cattle, of the golden eagle, and of wild goats with long, curly horns. The breed of horses known as Galloways is thought to have partly originated from animals which swam ashore from Spanish Armada galleons wrecked on local coasts.

The 200sqm Glen Trool forest park spreads around Loch Trool and is about to be renamed Galloway forest park. Galloway was administered in the 14th and 15thc by the Douglas family, and afterwards by hereditary stewards under the crown until 1747. During the 17thc the district was intensely involved with the Covenanters.

An extensive power scheme which harnesses the local water resources and includes the large Clatteringshaws Dam and a number of power houses has been developed here. Galloway's landscape has been a source of inspiration for many famous writers. S R Crockett's *The Raiders* introduces the Merrick of wildest Galloway; Dorothy L Sayers wove the countryside into *Five Red Herrings*; much of the action of John Buchan's *The*

Thirty-Nine Steps takes place around the Cairnsmore of Fleet, a lonely 2,331ft peak to the NE of Creetown.

GALSTON, Strathclyde 25 NS43
Dutch and Huguenot immigrants settled in this lace-making town in the 17thc. Galston lies in wooded country in the valley of the River Irvine. Nearby Barr Castle is an ancient tower, and to the N is mainly 19th-c Loudoun Castle. The latter retains a 15th-c tower, but was badly burnt in 1941. Mostly-modern Cessnock Castle preserves an old tower and stands 1½m SE of Galston near Burn Anne.

GANNOCHY BRIDGE, Grampian 35 NO57
The boundary between the former counties of Angus and Kincardine was formed here by the North Esk, which flows through a lovely rocky and wooded defile. Hills to the NW include 2,220ft Hill of Wirren and 1,986ft Bulg. Upstream from Gannochy Bridge the river flows through a particularly beautiful valley, which is also traversed by the road to Tarfside and Lochlee.

GARDENSTOWN, Grampian 35 NJ86
Nestling beneath striking red cliffs in Gamrie Bay, this picturesque fishing village features a small harbour and interesting tiers of houses. Alexander Garden of Troup founded the village. To the W near More Head is the hill of Gamrie Mhor, with the ruined Old Church of St John near by. This church was founded in 1004 to commemorate a Scottish victory over the Danes. Crovie Head lies E of Gardenstown and shelters the neighbouring fishing village of Crovie.

GARELOCHHEAD, Strathclyde 44 NS29
True to its name, this well-known resort lies at the head of fine Gare Loch and is backed by hills which include a long ridge overlooking Loch Long. This ridge is known as Argyll's Bowling Green. Yachts anchor in Gareloch during the season, and large ships are often laid up in its waters. A ship-breaking yard lies S at Faslane. To the E of Garelochhead a

1 Catrail
2 College of Textiles
3 Mercat Cross
4 Municipal Buildings with Town Crest
5 Old Buckholm Tower
6 Old Gala House
7 War Memorial

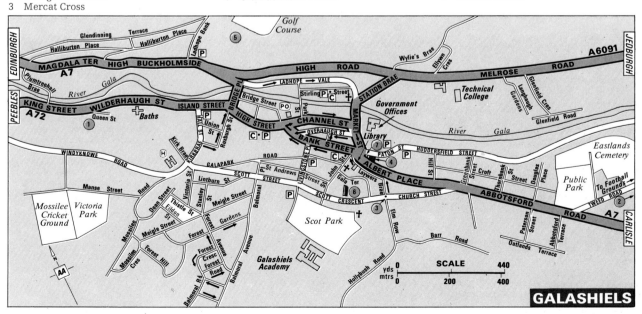

range of lonely hills is dominated by 2,338ft Beinn Chaorach, rising above the head of Glen Fruin. Roads run along both sides of Gare Loch, and the one on the W side skirts the Rosneath peninsula.

GARGUNNOCK, Central   45 NS79
This small village lies in flat country traversed by the serpentine course of the River Forth. To the E lie the Touch Hills, threaded by the Touch Burn; S are the higher Gargunnock Hills and their lofty reservoirs, with the Fintry Hills beyond. Gargunnock House is a 16th- to 18th-c mansion standing to the E of the village, and even farther E is the 15th- to 18th-c Touch House. The latter displays fine old carving. Old Leckie House dates from the 16thc and stands 1½m W of Gargunnock.

GARLIESTON, Dumfries and Galloway   25 NX44
Pleasure craft use the harbour of this Garlieston Bay fishing village, and there are sandy beaches in the area. To the NE there are traces of Eggerness Castle at Eggerness Point, and Galloway House lies 1m S on the coast near Rigg Bay. The Earls of Galloway lived in this 18th-c house, but it now houses a school. The grounds are noted for their wealth of trees and shrubs.

GARMOUTH, Grampian   35 NJ36
Charles II landed near this village – which was then a port – in 1650. He signed the Solemn League and Covenant in a cottage which is now marked with a plaque. Lady Margaret Ker was a 17th-c Royalist who is recalled by the revived Maggie Fair, held on the last Saturday in June.

GARTOCHARN, Strathclyde   44 NS48
Gartocharn is a small resort which lies near the SE shore of island-studded Loch Lomond. Ross Priory is situated by the lochside to the NW. Scott was a visitor to the priory, which stands in lovely grounds graced by a wonderful avenue of yews.

GARVALD, Lothian   31 NT57
Clints Dod, one of the Lammermuir Hills, rises to 1,307ft SE of this tiny hillside village. The summit forms a good viewpoint. Garvald Church displays 12th-c work and preserves a sundial of 1633. Ancient jougs are attached to the W gable. Ruined Stoneypath Tower lies in a wooded glen to the E of the village. Cistercian monks occupying the 19th-c mansion of Nunraw, which lies to the SE, are in the process of building a new abbey. The mansion retains a 16th-c tower. A narrow, hilly road threads its way SE into the hills below Spartleton Edge, and later crosses the Hungry Snout before descending to Cranshaws in the valley of Whiteadder Water.

GARVE, Highland   33 NH36
Lying between Loch Garve and Strath Garve, this little village sits on the main road which runs W along Strath Bran and past Loch Luichart. Distant Fannich peaks can be seen to the NW, from the road beyond Kinlochluichart. A large hydro-electric scheme now operates in the Fannich district. To the S beyond Loch Luichart are the smaller Lochs a'Chuilinn and Achanalt, with Sgurr Vuillin rising to 2,845ft in the background. A lonely road through Strath Garve leads to Ullapool. To the E of the road is 2,497ft Little Wyvis, backed by the larger mass of 3,429ft Ben Wyvis.

GATEHOUSE OF FLEET, Dumfries and Galloway   25 NX65
This former cotton town on the Water of Fleet was the 'Kippletringan' of Scott's *Guy Mannering*. Burns composed *Scots wha ha'e wi' Wallace bled* on the nearby moors and wrote it down in the town's Murray Arms. Cally House, designed by Robert Mylne in 1763 and now a hotel, stands in fine grounds 1m S of the town. About 1m W of the house the Water of Fleet enters Fleet Bay, overlooked by ruined, 15th-c Cardoness Castle.

This castle was built on a rocky outcrop for the McCullochs of Galloway, and comprises four storeys over a vaulted basement. The McCullochs had a sinister murder hole over the entrance passage, through which boiling pitch could be poured over any attackers. Original features of the castle include the stairway, stone benches, and elaborate fireplaces. The A75 passes the castle on its way SW from Gatehouse to Creetown, following the curve of Wigtown Bay and affording views of the Murray Isles beyond Fleet Bay to the S. This is considered one of the most beautiful roads in the S of Scotland; wonderful seascapes can be enjoyed to one side, while fine walking country rises to the other. Dick Hatteraicks Cave, near ruined Barholm Castle where John Knox found refuge, can be seen beyond Ravenshall Point.

Nearer to Creetown the road passes Carsluith Castle (AM), with 1,497ft Cairnharrow to the E. The old road to Creetown went inland to where the lonely Gatehouse of Fleet station once stood, some 6m NW of the town. Some 3m NW of Gatehouse, the ruined but still impressive Ruso Castle of *c*1500 lies in the lovely valley of the Fleet Water. This was the tower of the Gordons of Lochinvar, the family from which sprang the hero of Scott's poem *Young Lochinvar*. Farther to the E Bengray rises to 1,203ft above Loch Whinyeon.

GIFFNOCK, Strathclyde   45 NS55
This town is situated on the SW fringes of Glasgow. Cathkin Braes, an attractively-wooded public park, lies to the E.

GIFFORD, Lothian   31 NT56
Gifford is a delightful 18th-c village which stands on Gifford Water and faces S to the Lammermuir Hills. Sheep graze on these hills, and fine views can be enjoyed from 1,733ft Lammer Law. Gifford's church dates from 1708 and features a late medieval bell and 17th-c pulpit. An older church once stood near 18th-c Yester House, home of the Marquess of Tweeddale. An avenue leads to this Adam House, and the building stands in pleasant grounds SE of the village near Hopes Water.

Beyond the mansion are the ruins of Yester Castle, which contain a vaulted underground chamber known as Goblin Ha'. This was supposedly built in 1267 by a local magician, Hugo the Wizard. Scott has introduced the scene in his *Marmion*. Near the mansion is restored Bothan's Church, a small 15th-c collegiate church which has been the burial place of the Tweeddales since 1710. A narrow and hilly road winds SE from Gifford into the Lammermuirs, climbing to some 1,400ft. It continues over the Hungry Snout to descend to the valley of Whiteadder Water near Cranshaws, on the way to Duns.

GIGHA, ISLE OF, Strathclyde   28 NR64
Separated from the W coast of Kintyre by the Sound of Gigha, this flat little island is 6m long and has a rocky shoreline. Lovely gardens can be seen at Achamore and the ruins of Kilchattan Church are of 13th-c date. Dr Kenneth MacLeod, the Gaelic scholar from Gigha parish, wrote verses for the famous *Songs of the Hebrides*. Steamers sail from West Loch Tarbert to Gigha, and there is a passenger ferry to the island from Tayinloan. The tiny island of Cara lies off the S tip of Gigha.

GILMERTON, Lothian   47 NT26
William Adam, father of the more famous Robert, built a fine mid 18th-c mansion called The Drum which lies a little to the E of Gilmerton.

GILMERTON, Tayside   30 NN82
Exquisite Sma' Glen lies 4m N of Gilmerton, and traces of 13th-c Inchaffray Abbey can be seen 5½m E of the village off the Perth road. Cultoquhey and Inchbrackie mansions lie to the SE of Gilmerton. A by-road NW from the village encircles the fine park of 17th- to 19th-c Monzie Castle, and eventually leads to Crieff.

*GIRVAN, Strathclyde   24 NX19
Girvan is a well-known resort with sandy beaches and good fishing. The town house was once a gaol and was moved to its present site in 1828. Some 3m NE of Girvan, an impressive, 16th-c stronghold of the Cathcarts of Carleton lies in the valley of the Water of Girvan. Restored Ardmillan House lies 2m S of the town and was built between the 16th and 18thc, passing from the Kennedys to the Craufurds in 1658. Mary Queen of Scots once stayed here. Girvan Whisky Distillery, which offers guided tours to visitors, lies E of the stronghold on the B741.

The beautiful coast road running S to Ballantrae negotiates dramatic Kennedy's Pass. Ailsa Craig lies 10m out to sea to the W of Girvan. This 1,114ft-high rock lies halfway between Glasgow and Belfast, and has been dubbed Paddy's Milestone. It is a nesting ground for seabirds, and provides the granite from which the stones used in the Scottish game of curling are made. Other features of the island include a lighthouse and the ruins of an ancient castle.

GLAMIS, Tayside   31 NO34
This picturesque village boasts famous Glamis Castle, which stands in fine grounds bordered by Dean Water. A fortification has been here from very early times and Malcolm II is said to have died here in 1034. The present 14th-c structure is the ancestral home of the Earl of Strathmore, father of the Queen Mother, and was rebuilt between 1675 and 1687 in the style of a French chateau. The building material was locally-quarried stone. Portions of the high square tower's 15ft-thick walls are original, and Duncan's Hall is the oldest complete portion of the castle. The hall is probably the setting of Shakespeare's *Macbeth*, who was Thane of Glamis. A ghost is said to haunt the castle, which preserves the lion-cup of Glamis mentioned in Scott's *Waverley*. A plaster ceiling of 1621 adorns the drawing room and the chapel displays fine panelling.

The Old Pretender – the son of James VII of Scotland and II of England – lodged at the castle in 1715. The Queen Mother spent her childhood at Glamis, and Princess Margaret was born here in 1930. Housed within the building are fine collections of china, tapestry, furniture, paintings, and armour, while the beautiful grounds contain a massive sundial with 84 dials. Lovely views of the Vale of Strathmore can be enjoyed from the battlements.

Old jougs hang near the churchyard gate in the village, and the carved Glamis Stone is preserved at the manse. Restored cottages in the Kirkwynd contain the fascinating Angus Folk Museum, illustrating 200 years of domestic and farm life. The richly-carved, early-Christian St Orland's stone lies 2½m NE near Cossans Farm.

*GLASGOW, Strathclyde   45 NS56
District plan overleaf
Central plan on page 234
Glasgow is the largest city in Scotland, and grew with enormous rapidity after the Industrial Revolution to become one of the major shipbuilding and heavy engineering centres in the world. In recent years there has been a notable run-down of these industries and a switch to lighter engineering. Also in recent years there has been considerable clearing of the infamous slums, and a great deal of new road construction. The 19th-c Clyde tunnel is still open for pedestrians (see inset on page 236).

Traditionally Glasgow was founded by St Kentigern – also called St Mungo – who built his church here in AD543. The first cathedral was erected on the site of the church in 1136, over the remains of the saint's body. The year 1451 saw the birth of Scotland's second university, and in 1454 Glasgow was made a Royal Burgh. Cromwell entered the city in 1650 and 1651, and Prince Charles Edward retreated through Glasgow from England in 1745. During this retreat he levied a toll on the city. The 17th-c Glasgow Cross, where he was proclaimed Regent, was demolished and replaced with a replica of the original cross in 1929. On Glasgow Green, where the prince reviewed his troops after the retreat, is the Nelson obelisk. Glasgow Airport lies 7m W of the city centre.

CATHEDRAL AND MEDIEVAL BUILDINGS
Glasgow Cathedral (AM) is the only complete medieval cathedral on the Scottish mainland. It replaces the original cathedral built over St Mungo's Church between 1123 and 1136, which was burnt down in 1196. Part of the original crypt of 1197 remains, and wonderful 13th-c work survives in the choir and tower. The cathedral's pride is the splendid crypt, or Laigh Kirk, which is now Glasgow's parish church. Its pillars and vaulting around the site of St Mungo's tomb are magnificent. At one time three separate congregations worshipped in the crypt, choir, and the nave – which was not completed until 1480. Below the choir, with its fine 15th-c stone screen, is an interesting vaulted crypt known as Blackader's Aisle. A richly-carved door leads to the 13th-c chapter house, in which lies a gravestone to nine martyred Covenanters. The cathedral's spire dates from the 15thc. Until the Reformation the cathedral was a much-ornamented place of pilgrimage, but 16th-c Presbyterian zeal purged it of all 'monuments of idolatry'

The Necropolis, from where the cathedral is best seen, is full of the graves of Glasgow merchants, including that of William Miller (1810 to 1872), who wrote *Wee Willie Winkie*. Statues to the Reformers and John Knox stand in the Necropolis. A little to the W of the cathedral is Provand's Lordship, which was built in 1471 for the priest in charge of the old St Nicholas Hospital and is probably Glasgow's oldest house. James II, James IV, and Mary Queen of Scots all stayed at the house, which now contains a museum of 17th-c furniture, old stained glass, portraits, and tapestries. Provan Hall (NTS) stands in Auchinlea Road on the E fringe of the city and also dates from the 15thc. This well-restored house was built as the mansion house of the Laird of Provan. Prebendary of Provan's pepperbox tower is pierced for defence; the combination of this and its corbie-stepped gables make it the finest example of a simple pre-Reformation domestic house in Scotland. Crookston Castle (NTS) probably dates from the 13thc and is surrounded by an early defensive ditch. It was visited by Mary Queen of Scots and Darnley in 1565.

CITY CENTRE
Central Glasgow is sooty-grey, years of smoke and grime covering the once creamy stonework. It is essentially Victorian and was designed and built by Glasgow men. The best-known of these is probably Alexander 'Greek' Thompson, whose surprisingly successful mingling of Greek and Egyptian styles is best seen in St Vincent Street Church, the terraces of Great Western Road, and in the Egyptian Halls of Union Street. George Square houses statues to Queen Victoria, Prince Albert, Sir Walter Scott, Robert Burns, Sir John Moore, Lord Clyde, Thomas Campbell, Dr Thomas Graham, James Oswald, James Watt, William Gladstone, and Sir Robert Peel.

The City Chambers in George Square were built in the Italian Renaissance style and opened in 1888 by Queen Victoria. A 240ft-high tower tops the chambers, which have a rich and lavish interior including a unique loggia and a fine banqueting hall with murals depicting Glasgow's progress. Near by in George Street are Stow College and Strathclyde University; the latter occupies

the former Royal Technical College buildings. The Scottish Stock Exchange is housed in a French Venetian building of 1877, in West George Street.

Tolbooth Steeple lies on the E fringe of the city centre and is all that remains of the 17th-c Tolbooth and prison described in Scott's *Rob Roy*. The 113ft-high steeple is topped with a crown, one of only three crown steeples in Scotland; the other two can be seen on St Giles' in Edinburgh, and King's College Chapel in Aberdeen. Near the steeple is the Mercat cross. The Tron Steeple dates from 1637 and forms an arch over the pavement. It is all that remains of St Mary's Church, which was burnt by drunken members of the local Hell Fire Club in 1793. Merchant's Hall Steeple was built by Sir William Bruce in the late 17thc, and is now surrounded by a modern fish market. This tower is noted for the effect of diminishing storeys.

MUSEUMS
The art gallery and museum in Kelvingrove Park were opened in 1901, and the galleries contain the finest municipal collection in Britain. Works including Flemish, Dutch, and French canvases, a wide range of French-Impressionist and post-Impressionist items, and modern Scottish paintings can be seen. The famous Burrell collection is housed here. The main museum halls cover armoury, shipbuilding, and engineering.

The Mitchell Library in North Street preserves many rare books, including an important Burns collection. On Glasgow Green is the People's Palace, containing the Old Glasgow Museum which illustrates Glasgow's domestic history. Exhibits include a purse made by Mary Queen of Scots and relics of the city's grocer-hero Sir Thomas Lipton. Lipton's yachts, all named Shamrock, made five unsuccessful attempts to win the America Cup between 1899 and 1930.

The fascinating Museum of Transport stands in Albert Drive and houses tramcars, motorcars, horse-drawn vehicles, bicycles, and historic Scottish locomotives. In Renfrew Street is the Glasgow School of Art, designed in 1896 by Charles Rennie Mackintosh, a pioneer of the modern style.

cont

Built with stones from the old college, the Old Lodge still forms part of the university.

Apart from these interesting places, Glasgow also offers a number of other museums housing a variety of exhibits. Campshill Museum contains pictures and *objet d'art* from the Burrell Collection, plus several items of natural history interest. Pollock House was designed by William Adam in 1752 and houses the famous Stirling-Maxwell collection of Spanish and other paintings, and fine furniture, silver, and porcelain. The fascinating Tollcross Museum has a collection of dolls, attractive pictures, and an exhibit entitled 'The Story of Cock Robin'. Although basically a children's museum, this is likely to appeal to almost any age group.

GLASGOW UNIVERSITY AND HUNTERIAN MUSEUM

In 1451 Bishop Turnball obtained Papal authority to start a university in Glasgow, and the first lectures were held either in the cathedral or in the Black Friars' monastery in the High Street. The university stood in the High Street for 400 years before it was moved to its present commanding site on Gilmorehill in 1870. Sir George Gilbert Scott's gothic pinnacles overlooking Kelvingrove Park and the Clyde shipyards contrast with the old college façade – that was used to construct the Old Lodge which stands near the entrance. Imposing Bute Hall was added in 1882.

Central Plan

1	Art Gallery and Museum
2	Cathedral
3	City Chambers
4	Egyptian Halls
5	George Square Statues
6	Mercat Cross
7	Merchants' Hall Steeple
8	Mitchell Library
9	Nelson Obelisk
10	People's Palace
11	Provand's Lordship
12	St Vincent Street Church
13	School of Art
14	Scottish Stock Exchange
15	Stow College
16	Strathclyde University
17	Tolbooth Steeple

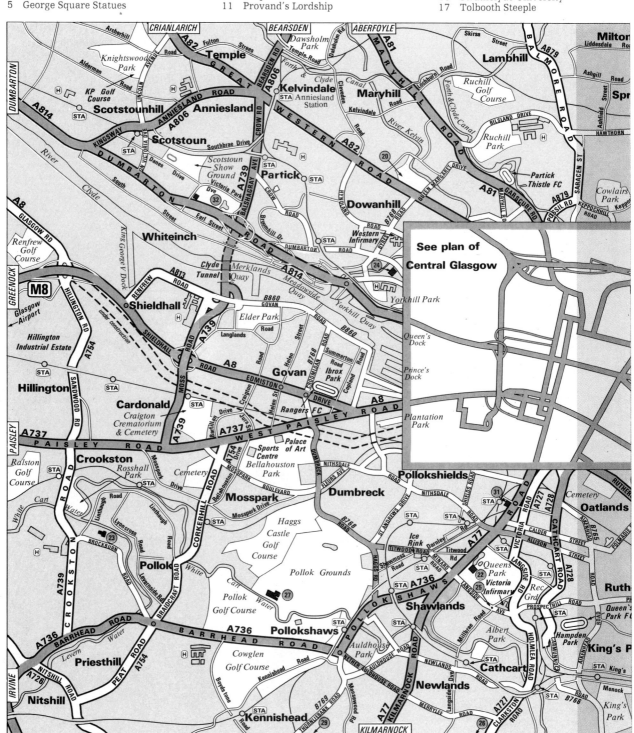

Though enormous by 19th-c standards, the university today is only the nucleus of a large number of institutions scattered over the city. It includes the Hunterian Museum, where collections of early printed books, manuscripts, coins, paintings, and archaeological specimens include those bequeathed by Dr William Hunter, who died in 1783. Kelvin Hall, rebuilt in 1926, is the largest exhibition hall in Britain.

PARKS

For an industrial city Glasgow is fortunate in having so many well-laid out parks and gardens. Linn Park is the loveliest of all, and lies on the banks of White Cart Water. It includes a nature trail and children's zoo. Rouken Glen has more than 200 acres of attractive woods and parkland, including a waterfall and boating lake. Glasgow Green with the People's Palace, Kelvingrove Park with the art gallery and museum, and

Queen's Park to the S are also favourites. Just outside Queen's Park is a memorial marking the site of the Battle of Langside in 1568, which ended the tragic reign of Mary Queen of Scots. To the SE of the park is Hampden Park football ground, which is the biggest football stadium in Britain and is capable of holding 135,000 people. The Hampden Roar in support of Scotland at international matches can be heard a mile away! Even greater passions are

cont page 236

18	Tron Steeple
	District Plan
19	University and Hunterian Museum
20	Botanic Gardens
21	Calderpark Zoological Gardens
22	Campshill Museum
23	Crookston Castle
24	Kelvin Hall
25	Langside Memorial
26	Linn Park
27	Pollock House
28	Provan Hall
29	Rouken Glen
30	Tollcross Museum
31	Transport Museum
32	Victoria Park

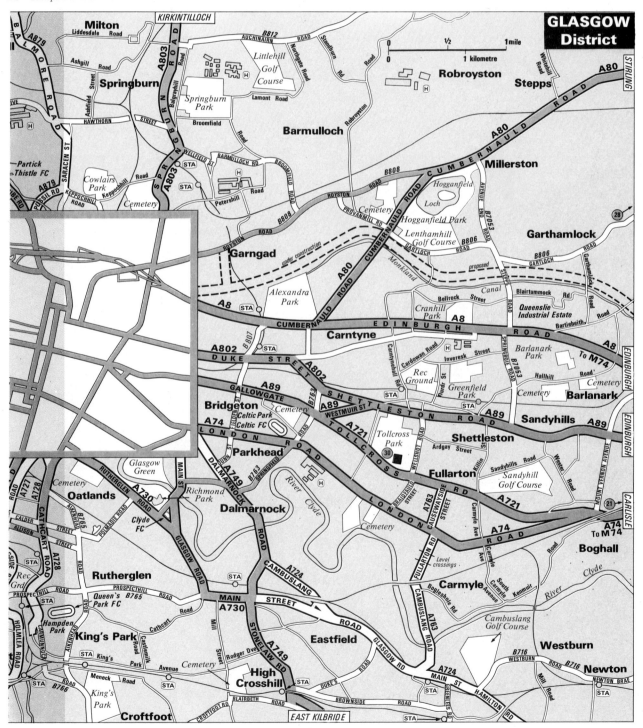

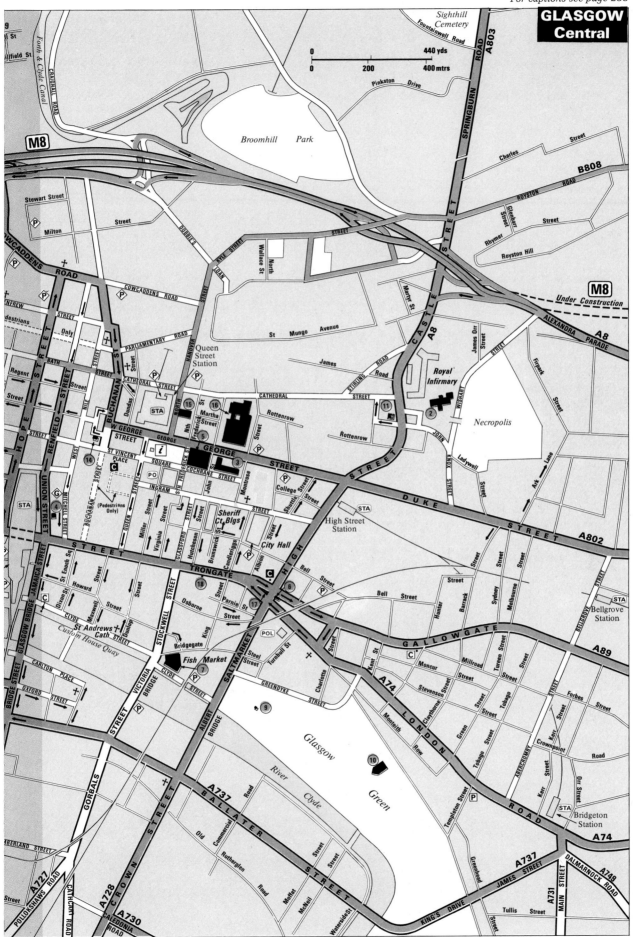

roused when Celtic and Rangers, two Glasgow teams, play one another.

The Zoological Park lies SE of the city near Calderpark, with a fairground near by. The Botanic Gardens cover 42 acres to the NW of the city, and include a pleasant walk along the banks of the River Kelvin. Kibble Palace has a unique collection of trees, ferns, and plants from temperate areas of the world. A

fascinating grove of fossilized tree stumps some 230-million years old can be seen in Victoria Park, Whiteinch.

Glasgow is surrounded by lovely countryside, particularly to the W and the N. Almost on the city's doorstep are the Campsie Fells, the Kilpatrick Hills, and the Kilsyth Hills. Within easy reach are the Kyles of Bute, wonderful Loch Lomond, and the Trossachs.

GLASSERTON, Dumfries and Galloway 24 NX43
A by-road and path lead 2m from Glasserton to St Ninian's Cave (AM) on Port Castle Bay. The cave is said to have been a retreat of the saint, and early-Christian crosses can be seen inside. Burrow Head lies to the SE.

GLENBARR, Strathclyde   24 NR63
Glenbarr lies on the W shores of the

THE FORGOTTEN TUNNEL

In 1895 Glasgow was in the grip of a kind of tunnelling mania. The Central Station low-level line was being dug, the underground railway circuit was nearing completion, and the Glasgow Harbour Tunnel Company's pride and joy was about to be opened after five years of excavating under the Clyde.

Parliamentary approval had been given in 1889 for a pedestrian and vehicle tunnel under the Clyde between Finnieston on the north bank and Mavisbank Quay on the south. Three 16ft diameter tunnels were dug, with shields and compressed air, the centre one being for pedestrians and the others for horse and cart traffic. The entrances on both sides were circular brick towers, which contained not only stairs for pedestrians but also hydraulic lifts for raising and lowering cart traffic to and from the main tunnel level under the river.

In each tower there were six segments of hydraulic hoist, three for up traffic and three for down. The hoists were provided by the Otis Elevator Company of New York, and the chairman of the Harbour Tunnel Company replied to criticisms from the Glasgow engineering establishment about the use of foreign machinery by saying that they were the best available.

It was on July 15, 1895 that the Harbour Tunnel opened for business. This was during the Glasgow Fair holidays, and traffic was light for the first week. On the following Monday, however, when only half the hoists on each side were working, 218 vehicles used the tunnel during its opening period of 05.00 to 19.00hrs.

The next day it was 272, and the secretary of the Otis Company's London subsidiary reported that 'the horses generally have taken most kindly to the lifts, and are carried up and down without trouble.' Carters said that by avoiding the steep inclines at the nearby ferries they could take five extra bags of flour per journey.

Like many similar schemes, the Harbour Tunnel never produced the revenues its promoters expected, and from time to time they threatened closure. In 1915 an arrangement was reached with Glasgow Corporation by which the city authorities came to the financial rescue by making an annual grant, and being given in return an option to buy over the tunnel at a later date.

That later date came in 1926, by which time the corporation paid out almost £30,000 every year to keep the tunnel and the passenger and vehicle ferries near by running. The tunnel passed into the city's control for a payment of £100,000. At the same time the corporation released details of plans for a new cross-river bridge at Finnieston, and it was expected that the tunnel would soon be closed. The bridge was never built. In 1932 a columnist in the *Evening Citizen* could still write about a journey beneath the Clyde:

One of the Glasgow-to-Finnieston Tunnel's brick entrance towers.

'The door of the passenger tunnel has long been disused, and foot-passengers now enter by one of the four elevators for vehicles at the other side of the rotunda. Choosing the company of a horse and lorry as preferable to that of a motor-car, I soon found myself smoothly and quietly descending among a bewildering medley of wheels and cables, through which I could see the mouth of the old disused foot-passenger tunnel as we passed on the way down. At the bottom water oozed through the iron sides of the great tube, which has never been totally watertight. At one place a single stalactite a foot long hung from the roof.'

The tunnel was still of some use to the city, although the ferries were far more popular with those whose business did not take them close to the city-centre bridges. Traffic increased again during the second world war, when dockers and shipyard workers were among the most regular users. In April 1943 there was a request that the tunnel should be restricted to motor traffic, since horse-drawn vehicles were causing delays. Glasgow Corporation, however, had far different ideas, since their Master of Works had recently made a thorough examination of the old tunnel and reported that 'grave responsibilities would be incurred' if it were kept open at all.

In September 1943 it was decided to abandon the vehicle tunnels, and all the hydraulic equipment was removed. The passenger tunnel was to be retained, and £500 was earmarked for pumps to keep it dry.

Despite the derelict appearance of the towers, and the fact that they seem to be no more than a roosting place for half the city's birds, the Harbour Tunnel is still open. The remains of the machinery in the great circular shafts can be glimpsed, and dimly lit stairways plunge eerily down alongside the hydraulic pipeline which took pressure from the south side to the north, to the main level below the Clyde. The Harbour Tunnel remains one of Glasgow's best-kept secrets; most people in the city, if they are even aware of its existence, thought it closed down long ago.

Kintyre peninsula, at the mouth of Barr Glen which leads into lonely hill country. Barr Water flows into the sea beyond the modernized Glenbarr Abbey, with Glencardoch Point to the N.

GLENBERVIE, Grampian   35 NO78

Churchyard tombstones of the Burnes (Burns) family were restored in 1968, and a Burns memorial cairn has been erected on the A94 some 3m S of Stonehaven.

GLENBRITTLE, Isle of Skye, Highland 32 NG42

From the head of Loch Harport a narrow little road runs S through Glenbrittle to a remote village of the same name, set on the shores of the sea Loch Brittle. The road is bordered by Forestry Commission plantations and offers magnificent views of the Cuillins, which rise steeply from the green valley of the River Brittle. The view includes two of the Cuillins' finest corries – Coire Lagan and Coir' a Ghrunnda. The former is dominated by the great precipices of Sron na Ciche. Glenbrittle is a climbers' rendezvous, and 3,309ft Sgurr Aladair is the highest peak of the range. It is famous for its Stone Shoot, and is often scaled from here. A path runs S from the village, along the shores of Loch Brittle to the picturesque headland of Rudh'an Dunain, which affords lovely views.

GLENCAPLE, Dumfries and Galloway 25 NX96

'Portanferry' is the name given to this little village on the Nith estuary, by Scott in *Guy Mannering*. Glencaple is known locally as the Auld Quay, and Burns wrote here during his time as an exciseman.

GLENCARSE, Tayside   30 NO12

Pitfour Castle, a late 18th-c mansion, has now been converted into flats. Inchyra House dates from the same century.

GLENCOE, Highland   29 NN15

Probably the finest and most famous glen in Scotland, Glencoe (NTS) runs through magnificent mountain scenery from Rannoch Moor to Loch Leven in old Inverness. It was the scene of the Massacre of Glencoe, and has been called the Glen of Weeping. In the early hours of a February morning in 1692, a troop of soldiers led by Robert Campbell of Glen Lyon slaughtered some 40 of the Macdonalds of Glencoe after twelve days' hospitality. The Macdonalds had failed to give up the Jacobite cause and swear allegiance to William III by the date set by the government. The order for the savage attack is said to have been written on a playing card – the Nine of Diamonds – since known as The Curse of Scotland.

All the hamlets in the glen were burnt down, and many of those Macdonalds who fled into the mountains died of exposure. MacIan, chief of the Macdonalds, was murdered and is buried on the island of Eilean Munde in Loch Leven, near the entrance to the glen. A monument has been erected to his memory. MacIan's two sons escaped into the hills.

Bidean nam Bian (NTS), at 3,766ft the highest peak in the one-time county of Argyll, overlooks the glen to the S. The mountains of Dalness Forest include the twin Buchaille Etive peaks, separated by the lovely Lairig Gartain Pass, and face

Glen Etive. The main road through Glencoe reaches a 1,000ft summit below a rock platform called the Study or Studdie. This provides magnificent views of the savage mountains which overhang Glencoe. To the E of Bidean nam Bian are the Three Sisters of Glencoe – Beinn Fhada, Gearr Aonach, and Aonach Dubh – all over 2,500ft – plus 3.657ft Stob Coire nan Lochan and Bidean nam Bian. High up on Aonach Dubh is Ossian's Cave, a deep cleft overlooking Loch Triochatan. On the N side of Glencoe the pinnacled 3,000ft ridge of Aonach Eagach faces the Mamore Forest mountains of Lochaber across Loch Leven.

At the W end of this ridge is the well-known Pap of Glencoe, situated at the entrance to the glen and a prominent feature of the view from Ballachulish. Near Loch Triochatan the new road parts company from the old, which passes the little Clachaig Inn on its way to Carnach. Signal Rock, from where the signal was given for the Glencoe massacre, stands near by. Meall a' Bhuiridh rises near the head of Glencoe and offers exciting ski-ing amid splendid scenery.

Glencoe itself offers some of the best opportunities to mountaineers in the whole of Scotland, and includes good routes for the hill walker. Wild life in the glen includes red deer, wildcats, golden eagles and ptarmigan. Robert Louis Stevenson was fascinated by Glencoe and included it in his novel *Kidnapped.*

GLENCORSE, Lothian   47 NT26

Britain's oldest regiment, the Royal Scots, has its barracks here. They now form part of the Lowland Brigade, but were originally formed from Louis XIII's companies and part of the Swedish army in 1633. The regimental march is *Dumbarton's Drums*, and the Earl of Dumbarton was appointed by Charles II as the regiment's Colonel. Robert Louis Stevenson described the old kirk which lies to the N of Milton Bridge in the *Weir of Hermiston*. The building is now ruined. Farther N in the foothills of the Pentlands is Glencorse Reservoir, backed by Black Hill. Nearby Rullion Green is where the Covenanters were defeated by General Tam Dalyell in 1666. A stone erected in 1738 recalls the battle, and every year a service is held in a field to the NE at Flotterstane. A small iron-age fortification can be seen farther N on 1,595ft Castle Law.

GLENDARUEL, Strathclyde   29 NR98

The glen stretches from the head of Loch Riddon – an inlet of the Kyles of Bute – into the hills bordering Loch Fyne. Kilmodan Church houses a memorial to Colin Maclaurin, the mathematician who organized the defence of Edinburgh in the '45 Rising. A narrow, hilly road winds to the S of Glendaruel, reaching a summit of 1,026ft before reaching Otter Ferry on Loch Fyne.

GLENDEVON, Tayside   30 NN90

This little village lies in the heart of lovely, winding Glen Devon. The head of the glen penetrates the Ochil Hills and meets Glen Eagles to the N. Fine views N over Strath Earn towards distant mountains are afforded from the road through Glen Devon. Several large reservoirs lie to the SE near 2,004ft Innerdownie.

GLENEAGLES HOTEL, Tayside 30 NN91

One of Scotland's best-known golf resorts, Gleneagles lies on moorland near Auchterarder between Strath Earn and Strath Allan, a little beyond the N end of Glen Eagles. The Ochil Hills to the S can be seen from Gleneagles Hotel. Some 2m S off the road through the glen stands Gleneagles House, built in 1624. Traces of an ancient castle lie near by. St Mungo's Chapel dates from 1149 and contains memorials to the Haldanes.

GLENELG, Highland   32 NG81

A sleepy hamlet on Glenelg Bay, Glenelg can be reached by only one road. This crosses a high ridge W of Loch Duich via the Mam Rattachen Pass, used by Dr Johnson and Boswell in 1773. The twisting climb through the pass is rewarded by a fine view of the mountain range known as the Five Sisters of Kintail, dominated by 3,505ft Sgurr Fhuaran. In summer a car ferry crosses the Sound of Sleat, noted for its fierce currents, to Kylerhea on the Isle of Skye.

Cattle used to be ferried from Skye to Glenelg (the name of which is a palindrome, *ie* it reads the same backwards as well as forwards), and then driven through the Mam Rattachan Pass and down through the Highlands to the great cattle trysts near Falkirk. On the N side of Glenelg Bay are the ruins of Bernera Barracks, which were erected *c*1722. Soldiers were quartered continuously here for 70 years during the 18thc. A carved stone in the churchyard commemorates one of the garrison officers, and dates from 1730.

Opposite the barracks the narrows of Kyle Rhea face Kylerhea, and are overlooked by the peaks of 2,396ft Beinn na Caillich and 2,401ft Sgurr na Coinnich, rising from Skye. A little road runs S from Glenelg to lovely Glen Beag, where two of the best-preserved iron-age brochs (AM) on the Scottish mainland survive. These brochs – Dun Telve and Dun Troddon – are double-walled stone towers, probably built over 2,000 years ago by the Picts for protection against invaders. Farther E is the Dun Grugaig broch, situated near a waterfall with the wonderful viewpoint of Ben Sgriol rising 3,196ft to the S.

The narrow coast road from Glenelg to the entrance of Glen Beag continues S around Outer Loch Hourn to Arnisdale. This hilly road is one of the loveliest in Scotland, providing wonderful views from high ground towards the islands of Skye and Rum. On the S side of Loch Hourn rises 3,343ft Ladhar Bheinn, one of the highest of the remote Knoydart peaks. A scatter of rocks in the Sound of Sleat comprise Sandaig Islands, which are guarded by a white lighthouse.

GLENFARG, Tayside   30 NO11

Winding through the fringe of the Ochil Hills, Glen Farg wends towards flat countryside near the Earn estuary and eventually flows into the River Tay. Little Glenfarg village lies at the S end of the glen's defile.

GLENFINNAN, Highland   33 NM98

A round tower (NTS) with a statue of a kilted Highlander marks the spot where Bonnie Prince Charlie unfurled his father's standard on 19 August 1745, at the beginning of his attempt to recover that which the nearby inscription calls

Whisky has been produced by the famous Glenlivet distillery since 1824.

'a throne lost by the imprudence of his ancestors'. Erected in 1815 by Macdonald of Glenaladale, a grandson of one of the prince's original supporters, the monument stands at the head of Loch Shiel in a superb mountain setting near the confluence of the little River Finnan and a loch.

Seven men were with the prince when he landed from France at Loch nan Uamh, which runs into open sea 12m W of Glenfinnan. The prince and his men stayed at nearby Kinlochmoidart while the clans rallied at Glenfinnan. St Finnan's Isle rises from Loch Shiel and was for centuries the burial ground of the Macdonalds, who built a chapel here in the 16thc. An old tablet in the RC church which stands in the grounds of Glenfinnan House a little to the W, mentions the prince. The church bell carries the outline of an Irish wolfhound and is situated at ground level.

The romantic Road to the Isles runs through Glenfinnan, and to the W it follows a valley between lofty hills strewn with rocks. Beinn Odhar Mhor rises to 2,853ft to the S, and 2,489ft Fraoch Bheinn can be seen to the N. In about 3m the road begins to descend. A little mound on the right affords wonderful views of Loch Eil, the Sound of Arisaig, and the islands of Eigg and Rum. Lonely Glen Finnan lies N of the village, and beyond it rise the bare and stony peaks of 3,164ft Sgurr Thuilm and the twin Streaps which touch 2,988ft and 2,916ft respectively.

GLENKINDIE, Grampian 35 NJ41
A remarkable weem, or ancient Pict's house, lies near Glenkindie House in the upper Don valley. Across the river and about 1m SSW, an ancient sculptured cross stands in the churchyard near remains of Towie Castle. The 16th-c ruins of Glenbuchat Castle (AM) lie 3m WNW of Glenkindie, beyond the Bridge of Buchat. This ancient seat of the Gordons is a fine example of a Z-plan castle. The last laird was John Gordon, who fought in the 1715 and 1745 risings and escaped after the Battle of Culloden in 1746.

GLENLIVET, Grampian 34 NJ22
The famous Glenlivet distillery was founded in 1824, and whisky has been distilled in the area for many years. For generations the distillers used barley from the fertile fields of Banff and Moray, but now most of this comes from England because of the enormous demand. The grain is converted to malt and then mixed with hot water. A sugary water called wort is extracted from the mixture, and cooled before the yeast is added for fermentation. Yeast attacks the sugar in the wort and converts it to crude alcohol and carbon dioxide. After the gas has escaped the remaining wash is distilled, so that the vaporized alcohol leaves unwanted residues behind. This vapour is condensed into an unpalatable liquid and re-distilled until the spirit has reached the right standard. While in the spirit vat the whisky is diluted until it becomes proof spirit, then run into oak casks to mature. By British Standards 100-degrees proof spirit contains 57.1 per cent alcohol and 42.9 per cent water.

Scotch whisky cannot be sold until it has matured in casks for at least three years. Most whiskies are blended with others, and the blender dilutes the mixture with water. About 70-degrees proof is normal for the home market, and 75-degrees for export.

Ben Rinnes rises to 2,755ft over Glen Rinnes and the Dufftown road. The latter runs through the glen to the NE of Glenlivet village. Glen Livet extends SE from the village towards the Ladder Hills, and was the site of a battle fought by James IV in 1594. Remains of Blairfindy Castle stand near by, and a picturesque ruined bridge can be seen near Livet Water to the N at Bridgend. Glenlivet stands just W of the Tomintoul Tomnavoulin to Delnashaugh Inn road. To the W is another road from Tomintoul to Delnashaugh Inn, which runs through Strath Avon and the Cromdale Hills. Ancient Drumin Tower stands by this road NW of Glenlivet.

GLENLUCE, Dumfries and Galloway 24 NX15
Old Wigtown's largest village, Glenluce lies a little to the W of the Water of Luce near its estuary in Luce Bay. Glenluce Abbey (AM) lies in ruins N of the village on the road to New Luce. This Cistercian house was founded c1192 by the Lord of Galloway, and has an intact 15th-c vaulted chapter house and water pipes which are probably unique. Michael Scott, the Border 'wizard', is said to have lured a plague to the abbey in the 13thc and shut it in a vault.

Some 2m NE of Glenluce off the Newton Stewart road is the ruined, 17th-c Carscreuch Castle, built by the first Lord Stair and associated with Scott's *Bride of Lammermoor*. The tall, imposing castellated Castle of Park (AM) stands 1m SW of Glenluce. Built in 1590 by Thomas Hay of Park, the mansion has been restored and overlooks the village from the brow of a hill.

GLEN MORE, Highland
Also known as the Great Glen of Alban – or the Great Glen for short – Glen More is a remarkable physical feature which divides the mainland of Scotland in two. A chain of lochs, which includes Loch Ness, lies along the glen, and the rift itself stretches from Inverness down to Fort William. Telford's Caledonian Canal completes the link between the North Sea and the Atlantic Ocean, so that small vessels need not navigate the stormy waters round the N coast of Scotland. Lofty hills overlook much of the glen, increasing in height from E to W and culminating in 4,406ft Ben Nevis, the highest mountain in the British Isles.

General Wade's military road from Inverness to Fort William traverses almost the entire length of Glen More, though the present road no longer follows the exact line of the old one. The beautiful Glen More forest park is situated in the foothills of the Cairngorms E of Aviemore.

GLENRINNES, Grampian 35 NJ23
Ben Rinnes rises to 2,755ft NW of Glenrinnes, and 2,563ft Corryhabbie to the S. The village itself lies in the heart of Glen Rinnes.

GLENROTHES, Fife 31 NO20
Glenrothes is a New Town with a wide diversity of industry, particularly in the field of electronics.

GLENSHEE, SPITTAL OF, Tayside 34 NO16
A travellers' hospice once stood here in Glen Shee at the heart of the Grampians, where a fine hill road now links Blairgowrie and the S with Braemar on Royal Deeside. The area is well known for climbing, and the ski runs lie 6m N. Glenshee chairlift ascends the 3,059ft Cairnwell mountain from the summit of the highest mainroad pass in Britain – the 2,199ft Cairnwell Pass – and serves both the difficult Tiger run and an easy traverse to Cairnwell Burn. Another lift at the latter allows access to a ski-run back to the main road. On the E side of the main road beginners can use the draglift, which is also used by experts heading for the Meall Odhar tow.

Near the summit of the pass, 5m NNE of the Spittal beyond Gleann Beag, is the Devil's Elbow. This 1,950ft-altitude road was notorious in the early days of motoring but is now bypassed by a less severe road. Glas Maol rises to 3,502ft and is the highest peak of the range, which ends far to the NE in Lochnagar. This mountain faces the Cairnwell across the pass. A little to the E of the Spittal are a stone circle, and a tumulus known as the Tomb of Diarmid. This has links with the ancestors of the Clan Campbell.

Modern Dalnaglar Castle lies 5m SE of the Spittal beyond Shee Water.

GLEN SHIEL, Highland 33 NG91
One of the two well-known roads to the Isles runs through this lovely glen for 10m from Glen Cluanie to the head of Loch Duich at Shiel Bridge. High mountains overhang the glen. Bonnie Prince Charlie hid in the lower reaches after the '45 Rising. The famous Five Sisters of Kintail (NTS), with 3,505ft Scour Ouran rising up from the roadside, stand to the E overlooking Loch Duich. To the W is a line of hills which end in the serrated outline of the 3,317ft Saddle. Spanish troops landed from frigates in Loch Duich during a Jacobite rising in 1719, and fought a battle in the heart of the glen at Bridge of Shiel, which spans the River Shiel. One of the Five Sisters – Sgurr nan Spainteach – was named after this event.

Glen Shiel's magnificent scenery determined Dr Johnson to write his classic *Journey to the Western Isles* when he and Boswell rode through the glen on horseback in 1773. Clach Johnson is a boulder under which he is supposed to have rested while journeying through the glen. The road follows the line of an old military road, and during rainy weather waterfalls in full spate tumble down the hills on either side.

GLEN TROOL NATIONAL FOREST PARK, Dumfries & Galloway
About to be renamed Galloway forest park, this 200sqm area around Loch Trool is a haven for wildlife and includes spectacular mountain and loch scenery.

GOGAR, Lothian 47 NT17
Picturesque old Gogar House dates from 1625 and displays angle turrets and a balustraded roof. It stands a little to the NW of Gogar, and Edinburgh's airport at Turnhouse lies to the N.

GOLSPIE, Highland 37 NH89
The old county of Sutherland's administrative centre, Golspie is also a busy fishing town and holiday resort which offers good sands. An inscribed Gaelic stone on the old bridge is the rallying point for the Clan Sutherland. Lofty moorland rises behind Golspie, culminating in 1,464ft Beinn Lundie. Nearer the town is 1,256ft Beinn a' Bhragie on which stands a statue of the 1st Duke of Sutherland by Chantrey. Golspie Burn flows through pretty Dunrobin Glen, to the NW of Golspie, and is overlooked by 1,706ft Ben Horn. A bridge spanning the burn has a rare Gaelic (Ogham) inscription.

GORDON, Borders 31 NT64
Associated with the 'Gay Gordons' who moved to old Aberdeenshire in the 14thc, Gordon lies 1m W of the Eden Water. A circular clock tower stands in the main street, and N of the village lie the ruins of a fine turreted tower house known as Greenknowe Tower (AM). This castle was built in 1581 and served as the home of a Covenanter. The iron yett or gate still survives, and above it the date 1581 has been carved between two shields.

GORDON ARMS HOTEL, Borders 26 NT32
This fishing inn and hotel lies on crossroads near the Yarrow Water. It is surrounded by Ettrick Forest, and access to the beautiful St Mary's Loch is easy.

Sir Walter Scott and James Hogg, 'The Ettrick Shepherd', supposedly met here in 1830. A little to the N is Mountbenger Farm, once tenanted by Hogg. The road leading N through the hills towards Traquair is known as the Paddy Slacks. Eldinhope, formerly Altrive Lake Farm, lies to the S of the village and was where Hogg died in 1835. Willie Laidlaw was a friend and amanuensis of Scott who was born in Blackhouse Tower. This now lies in ruins in the valley of the Douglas Burn, 3m W of the hotel. Both Scott and Hogg were visitors to the tower.

GOREBRIDGE, Lothian 47 NT36
Arniston, a fine Palladian mansion and the seat of the Dundas family, lies a little to the SW of Gorebridge. It stands in lovely walled gardens and is guarded by ornate gateposts depicting a lion and an elephant.

GOSFORD HOUSE, Lothian 47 NT47
This magnificent 18th-c house is partly by Robert Adam and is considered one of the best examples of his work. It stands in parkland overlooking Gosford Bay in the Firth of Forth, between Longniddry and Aberlady.

GOURDON, Grampian 35 NO87
Women still bait the handlines in this little fishing port, where the prosperous fish market attracts many visitors. Doolie Ness lies to the N and shelters the village.

*GOUROCK, Strathclyde 44 NS27
Well-known as a yachting centre and holiday resort, Gourock lies in a beautiful position on a bay facing Kilcreggan and the Rosneath peninsula. Loch Long and the Holy Loch lie NW of the resort, and Clyde pleasure steamers sail from the pier for tours of the Firth and the Kyles of Bute. On Tower Hill is Granny Kempock's Stone, which is probably of prehistoric origin. In 1622 Mary Lamont was burned as a witch here for intending to throw the stone into the sea to cause shipwrecks. Some 2½m SW along the coast is ruined Levan Castle, which stands in woodland near the prominent white Cloch lighthouse. The hills of Cowal rise to the NW of Gourock.

GOVAN (Glasgow), Strathclyde 45 NS56
Handloom weavers were the main population of Govan until 1856, but now the village forms part of the industrial Clydeside district of Glasgow. Early-Christian monuments surround the modern church, which was built on the site of an ancient monastery originally founded by St Constantine. The saint undertook missionary work at the request of St Mungo, patron saint of Glasgow. A sarcophagus which exists in the chancel may have once been raised over St Constantine's tomb. Haggs Castle lies to the SE of Govan and is an old home of the Maxwells. Although much altered and restored, the door of the castle displays ornamental panels on which the date 1585 has been carved.

GRAMPIANS, THE
Hector Boece the historian first named the Grampians in 1520, when he found and misread the name *Mons Graupius*. This was the name that the Roman Tacitus had given as the scene of Agricola's victory over the Picts cAD84. This battle is now thought to have taken place some distance N of the Tay. The Grampians are grassy, heather-clad mountains which stretch across the

Highlands from the old county of Argyll in the W, across one-time Perthshire, to old Aberdeenshire in the NE. Originally the range was called the Mounth, a name which has survived in the well-known pass called the Cairn o' Mounth and in the great plateau of the White Mounth which lies S of the Dee valley. The White Mounth includes the famous granite peak of Lochnagar.

The Grampians have the highest and largest mountain mass in Britain, and many of the summits are Munros – *ie* over 3,000ft in height. Sir Hugh Munro was mainly responsible for their classification and has given his name to the 534 Scottish peaks which top this height. To the NE is the even higher mass of the Cairngorms, with lonely lochs and corries and a large area of flat tops which exceed 4,000ft. In the whole of Great Britain this height is beaten only by Ben Nevis.

The passes through the Grampians were used centuries ago by invading Romans and English; the best-known are the Pass of Leny near Callander; the Cairnwell Pass, with the highest main road summit; the bleak Drumochter Pass, with Wade's great highway linking Dunkeld with Inverness; the famous Lecht road linking Cock Bridge in the Don valley with Tomintoul; and the Cairn o' Mounth Pass.

Around the lonely head of Glen Isla in the lovely Braes of Angus district, the E Grampians are sometimes called the Benchinnan Mountains. The by-road from Kirkton of Glenisla ends here and a long track continues up Monega Hill to a height of 3,318ft, the highest right-of-way in Scotland. Grouse are shot in season on some of the high moorland, and deer-stalking takes place in the hills. Much of the area is under snow during winter and ski-ing is possible in some parts – particularly around Glenshee.

GRANDTULLY, Tayside 30 NN95
Canoe slaloms are held here, and a bridge which spans the River Tay links roads which run along each side of the river. Grandtully (pronounced Grantly) Castle lies 2m SW off the Aberfeldy road, and is the ancestral home of the Stewarts of Innermeath. The castle dates from 1560 and was enlarged in 1626 and 1893. It is thought that Scott may have had Grandtully in mind when he described 'Tullyveolan' in *Waverley*. Near the castle is 16th-c St Mary's Church (AM), which has a finely-painted 17th-c wooden ceiling. To the NW 2,559ft Farragon Hill rises above Loch Derculich, the source of Derculich Burn which flows S to join the Tay.

GRANGEMOUTH, Central 46 NS98
This Forth-estuary port boasts Scotland's largest complex of oil installations, refineries, and ancillary works. The River Carron joins Smeaton's Forth and the Clyde Canal here. The canal was built in 1790 and runs 38m across the narrow waist of Scotland to enter the Clyde at Bowling. Grangemouth also includes important docks, and Scotland's first power bridge was opened here in 1880.

GRANTON (Edinburgh), Lothian 47 NT27
The old 19th-c harbour of Granton faces Burntisland over a 5m stretch of the Firth of Forth. George Mackenzie, the first Viscount Tarbat, built the beautiful old mansion of Caroline Park between

Entries marked * are the starting point of drives included in the Day Drive section of the book (pages 95 to 160).

239

1685 and 1696. The picturesque south front includes ogee-shaped tower roofs, and inside the mansion is some fine original ironwork. The building now serves as offices. Farther W is Drylaw, a house of the same period which also contains lovely old ironwork.

GRANTOWN-ON-SPEY, Highland 34 NJ02
This town was founded in 1776 and planned by a local landowner, Sir James Grant, as a centre for the Highland linen industry. It is beautifully situated in Strath Spey and is built mainly of granite. The town's situation makes it a good centre for touring the valley and the fine mountains which grace the district.

The River Spey is famous for its salmon, and Grantown is a popular angling resort. In the winter skiers are attracted by the Cairngorm slopes; this range can be seen to the S. Nearer to the town and to the E are the Cromdale Hills, which rise to over 2,000ft in some places. A bridge by which Craigellachie road crosses the Spey has a concrete arch of 240ft. A little farther E is the older three-span bridge of 1754, which is now closed to traffic. Castle Grant, a fine old mansion and the seat of the Earls of Seafield from the 16th to 18thc, lies 2m N of the town. The oldest portion of the mansion is the keep, which is dated c1530 and often called Barbie's Tower. Castle Grant was extended in the Adam tradition during 1750. A good road with fine views runs SE from the town, and climbs to more than 1,400ft on the way to Bridge of Brown.

GRANTSHOUSE, Borders 31 NT86
Houndwood, an old mansion standing in fine gardens, lies 3m SE of Grantshouse off the Great North Road.

GREENLAW, Borders 31 NT74
Between 1696 and 1853 Greenlaw was the county town of Berwickshire, but lost this status to Duns during the 19thc. It originally stood on a green law, or isolated hill, a little to the SE but was moved to its present site on the Blackadder Water in the foothills of the Lammermuirs.

Greenlaw's church tower dates from 1712, although the style is of late 15th-c appearance, and the church itself was originally built for use as a gaol. Near by is the Mercat cross of 1696, moved from its former site. Rowchester mansion lies in lovely gardens 3m SE of the town. On a hilltop 3m S is ruined Hume Castle, a building which dates back to the 13thc and was once the seat of the Earls of Home. The castle had a turbulent past and changed hands many times before falling to Cromwell in 1651. The Earl of Marchmont restored it as a sham antique in 1794, and in 1804 – when it was thought there was going to be a Napoleonic invasion – a beacon was lit on what was left of the building. The situation of Hume Castle affords fine views.

GREENLOANING, Tayside 30 NN80
Knaik Water joins the Allan Water here after having flowed down from Braco, where there are great Roman earthworks. Greenloaning is also the junction of roads from Crieff and Perth to Dunblane.

GREENOCK, Strathclyde 44 NS27
James Watt, the inventor of the steam engine, was born here in 1736 and his statue can be seen in the Watt Library. Greenock is an important industrial and ship-building town on the Clyde estuary, which suffered severe bomb damage in the second world war. It is now the site of the important Clydeport Container Terminal. A well-known roadstead in the river off Greenock is known as the Tail of the Bank. Watt Cairn can be seen in the cemetery, and near by is the tombstone of Burns' Highland Mary. This was moved here from its former position in the old North Kirk.

A huge cross on Lyle Hill commemorates the Free French sailors who lost their lives in the second world war Battle of the Atlantic. Greenock Waterworks lies surrounded by moorland to the S of the town, in a situation which affords fine views over the Clyde estuary to a mountainous background.

GRETNA, Dumfries and Galloway 26 NY36
Visitors still flock to 18th-c Gretna Hall and the local smithy. Both are famous as the first places over the Scottish border where, for a century, runaway lovers could be immediately married without parental consent. An English law dated 1754 prevented clandestine marriages in England, but in Scotland the couple had only to declare in front of witnesses their wish to become man and wife. In 1856 a law was passed requiring the man or woman to have lived in Scotland for three weeks before the marriage. Marriages were also solemnized at the Sark Toll Bar and in local inns.

The blacksmith's shop still houses the anvil over which couples were married, but since 1940 a change in the law has prevented the smith from performing the ceremony. The little River Sark is the actual border between England and Scotland, but the old bridge is now by-passed by the A74 dual carriageway. A little to the SW the river flows into the Solway Firth, which is notorious for its dangerous tides which sometimes carry a 4ft-high wave known as a bore. A battle fought 3m NE on Solway Moss in 1542 resulted in defeat for the Scots.

A little to the S of Gretna, near the shores of the Solway Firth, is the 7ft-high Lochmaben Stone which has an estimated weight of 10 tons. The stone is thought to have once formed part of a circle which was used as a meeting place for conferences in ancient times. Details of a truce between England and Scotland were discussed here during 1398.

GRIBUN, Isle of Mull, Strathclyde 28 NM43
Beneath the steep cliffs of Loch na Keal, near Gribun, is a road which runs from Salen to Loch Scridain. Dr Johnson and Boswell were entertained on the tiny offshore island of Inch Kenneth during their 'progress' around Scotland, and farther out to sea lie the islands of Ulva, Gometra, Little Colonsay, and Staffa. Ben More, Mull's most magnificent mountain, rises to the E of Gribun and affords wonderful views over the island. The road SE to Loch Scridain follows Glen Seilisdeir, keeping to the E of the almost roadless Ardmeanach peninsula. Such roads as do exist are very poor. Burg Experimental Farm (NTS), lies on the peninsula opposite Loch Scridain. Wonderful cliff scenery makes the coast of the peninsula well-worth visiting.

GROGPORT, Strathclyde 28 NR84
Grogport is situated on a little bay in the Kilbrennan Sound, and faces across the water to 2,345ft Beinn Bharrain. This is one of the lofty Arran peaks.

GRUINARD BAY, Highland 36 NG99
Rocky coves and pink sand characterize Gruinard Bay, one of Scotland's loveliest beaches. It lies in the Wester-Ross area of the NW Highlands, and can be reached from the W via the once-notorious, 1 in 6 Gruinard Hill. Wonderful views across island-studded waters to the Coigach Hills are afforded by the summit of the hill. Second Coast and First Coast are two oddly named clachans lying to the W of the summit. The Gruinard and Little Gruinard Rivers flow into the bay.

In the middle of the bay lies Gruinard Island. Boat landings are prohibited on this island because the ground is still infected with anthrax which was deposited during germ-warfare testing in the second world war. Gruinard House lies on the shores of the bay, in front of a gorge which has been carved out by the Gruinard River. This river flows from Loch na Sheallag in the SE, below the Torridon sandstone peaks of 3,500ft An Teallach. The latter are best visited from Dundonnell. To the S of the bay the lonely Fisherfield Forest is dominated by 2,974ft Beinn Dearg Mhor.

GUARDBRIDGE, Fife 31 NO41
Bishop Wardlaw, an early bishop of St Andrews, built the old bridge which spans the Eden here c1420. His shield of arms and pastoral staff can still be seen on one of the keystones. A new bridge now crosses the river and the old structure no longer carries any traffic. To the N of Guardbridge is a large paper mill. Much of the area is afforested, and the lonely and extensive Tentsmuir plantations lie N of St Andrews Bay.

GULLANE, Lothian 47 NT48
A well-known sandy holiday resort, Gullane boasts three public golf courses and affords magnificent views across the Firth of Forth to the Fife coast, backed by the distant Lomond and Ochil Hills. The championship course of Muirfield lies ½m NE and is the headquarters of the Honourable Company of Edinburgh Golfers, founded in 1744. This is the oldest golfing club in the world. Visitors may only play at the invitation of a member. A little Norman work survives in Gullane's roofless Old Church, which was partly destroyed in 1631. The last vicar was dismissed by James VI for smoking tobacco. Saltcoats Castle dates from the 16thc and lies to the S of the village. A fine old dovecot can be seen here. Robert Louis Stevenson used the character of Gullane as a background for his work *Catriona*.

GUTHRIE CASTLE, Tayside 31 NO55
Originally built by Sir David Guthrie in 1468, Guthrie Castle has been inhabited by the family ever since. The picturesque grounds include a spring garden, best seen in May, and a walled garden. Nearby Gardyne Castle shows 16th-, 18th-, and 19th-c work. To the W off the Forfar road are Balgavies Loch and the larger Rescobie Loch.

HADDINGTON, Lothian 31 NT57
Once a county town, Haddington is a gracious Royal Burgh situated on the River Tyne. The town was laid out in a

long, narrow triangle in the 12thc, and these original boundaries can still be traced by following the line of High Street, Market Street, and Hardgate. The town was burnt by the English several times during the Middle Ages, and its name was once given to the whole one-time county of East Lothian. Alexander II was born here in 1198, and the town is also thought to have been John Knox's birthplace in 1505. William Adam – father of Robert Adam – designed the splendidly proportioned Town House in 1748. The building includes a curfew bell, and the tower was added in 1831 by Gillespie Graham. The Mercat cross is topped by the figure of a goat.

The local library houses the 17th-c book collection of John Gray, who was born in the town in 1646, and St Mary's Church is a cruciform building dating from the 15thc. It has been somewhat restored, and is known as the Lamp of Lothian because of a lantern which once hung in the tower. Although the choir and transepts are ruined, the former still contains the tomb of Jane Welsh, wife of Thomas Carlyle. Services are now held in the nave, which displays an impressive W front and double doorway. St Mary's fine tower was originally surmounted by a crown similar to that of St Giles in Edinburgh. Near by lie the ruins of the 12th-c church of St Martin (AM).

Both Haddington House and Moat House (Eastgate) date from the 17thc, and Kinloch House is the gabled 18th-c town mansion of the Kinlochs of Gilmerton. Two fine old bridges span the Tyne, 16th-c Nungate Bridge was once a place of public hanging, and early 16th-c Abbey Bridge lies 1m E of the town. Remains of 16th-c Barnes Castle lie 2m N near the Garleton Hills, where there is also a monument to the 4th Earl of Hopetown – a hero of the Peninsula Wars.

Farther N off the B1377 is Chester Fort, a good example of an iron-age fortification which displays ramparts and clear remains of many interior buildings. Some 2m NE of the town near the Tyne is restored Stevenson House, which was built in the 16thc and 18thc. Lonely little Church of Morham stands 3m E off a by-road. This was built in 1685 and 1724, and preserves a bell of 1681 which is probably of Dutch origin.

HALKIRK, Highland 37 ND15
This symmetrically-ordered town lies on the River Thurso, with the main Wick to Thurso road running a little to the E. The river is noted for its fishing. Massive 8ft to 10ft-thick walls remain from the possibly 14th-c Brawl Castle, which lies across the river to the N. A modern house now adjoins the old tower. To the E of Halkirk are Loch Scarmelett and the larger Loch Watten, both noted for trout fishing. Prehistoric remains can be found 4m W around Loch Calder.

HAMILTON, Strathclyde 45 NS75
A rare example of an attractive industrial town set in relatively unspoilt surroundings, Hamilton is also a Royal Burgh. Mary Queen of Scots rested here after escaping from Loch Leven Castle, and in 1651 Cromwell made his headquarters in the town. William Adam designed the octagonal parish church in 1732, and opposite stands the Celtic Netherton Cross. In the churchyard is a Covenanters' monument displaying four heads in relief. Hamilton is the hereditary seat of the Dukes of Hamilton, though the palace which once stood in the Low Parks – NE of Hamilton – was demolished in 1927 due to mining subsidence. The extravagant Hamilton Mausoleum, built by the 10th Duke between 1840 and 1855 at a cost of some £150,000, was designed by David Bryce and stands in

the Low Parks near the racecourse. Huge bronze doors lead to the interior, which features a remarkable multi-colour marble construction and six-second echo.

The High Parks are S of Hamilton. Another ducal property, Chatelherault Lodge, stands here and was designed by William Adam in 1732. Near by are the ruins of Cadzow Castle, a 12th-c structure visited by Mary Queen of Scots in 1568. Cadzow has a rare herd of wild cattle, distinguished by their black-and-white markings. The 16th-c house of Barncluith stands in terraced gardens above the Avon.

HANDA, ISLE OF, Highland 36 NC14
This tiny island lies a little to the NW of Scourie Bay, with the Sound of Handa separating it from the mainland. The island was once inhabited by twelve families who appointed their own parliament and queen – the oldest widow in the community. In 1846 the tradition died when the potato famine forced the islanders to leave for the mainland. Handa is now a seabird sanctuary with vast populations of fulmars, shags, gulls, kittiwakes, and auks; Arctic and great skuas frequent the moorland. There are boat trips from Scourie to Handa, and the Torridon-sandstone cliffs which soar to 400ft afford fine views of the mainland.

HARRIS, Western Isles 38
See Hebrides, Outer.

*HAWICK, Borders 26 NT51
Plan overleaf
Hawick is world-famous for knitwear and lies where the Slitrig Water joins the Teviot in the heart of Teviotdale. A large Border town with a sheep market, Hawick has been a woollen-manufacturing centre since the 18thc. Border skirmishes were frequent

1 Barncluith House
2 Cadzow Castle

3 Chatelherault Lodge
4 Hamilton Mausoleum

5 Parish Church and Celtic Netherton Cross

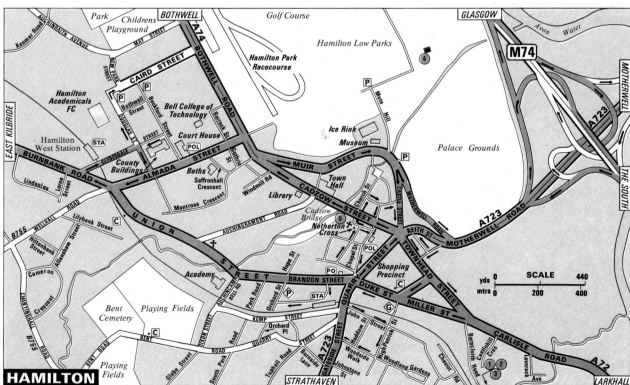

occurrences in the town's history and in 1570 the town was almost completely burned down. An early building which has survived now forms part of the Tower Hotel. Anne, widow of the executed Duke of Monmouth, lived here at one time. Scott addressed the *Lay of the Last Minstrel* to this Duchess, and along with William Wordsworth was a visitor to the house.

St Mary's Church was founded in 1214 but rebuilt in 1763. John Hardie, pioneer of Hawick's woollen industry in 1771, is buried in the churchyard. Hawick Motte measures 30ft high and some 300ft round, and is the mound of a Norman castle which was probably built in the 12thc by one of the Lovels. This family held Hawick at that time. Every year a ceremony called the Common Riding takes place in June, when horsemen ride the town's marches or boundaries to commemorate the local youths who rallied to defeat an English raiding party in 1514. This was a year after Flodden, when practically all the men of Hawick were wiped out. The Horse Monument in the High Street records the event. Hornshole bridge spans the Teviot 2m NE, and another commemorative monument stands near by.

Wilton Lodge Museum contains many fascinating exhibits, one of which illustrates the history of the woollen trade. The building housing the museum was once the home of the Langlands, lords of the domain for 500 years from 1290. In 1859 an extra storey and bow windows were added. Some 2m SW in Teviotdale is the ancient tower of Goldielands. This was once owned by a branch of the Scott family, who also held Branxholm Tower which lies 1m farther on. The original Branxholm Tower was blown up in 1570 and the present building was started in 1571.

Sir Walter Scott's ancestors also owned much-restored 16th- or 17th-c Harden House, which lies 4½m W of Hawick.

HEBRIDES, INNER, Highland 32

Skye is the farthest N of this group of islands which lies off the ragged W coast of Scotland and is separated from the Outer Hebrides by the waters of the Little Minch. Islay lies off the narrow Kintyre peninsula at the farthest S end of the group, and at one point is only 25m from Northern Ireland. The other principal Inner Hebridean islands are Colonsay, Iona, Jura, Mull, Rum (with Eigg), Staffa, and Tiree (with Coll) – all of which are described separately under their own names. Places of interest on Skye, Mull, and Islay have also been indexed individually. Whilst Skye is the largest and most picturesque island, made magnificent by the spectacular Cuillin range, Iona and Staffa are both of unique interest. Iona is famous for its cathedral and associations with St Columba, and Staffa has its strange basaltic rocks and well-known Fingal's Cave.

HEBRIDES, OUTER, Western Isles 38

Also known as Long Island, the Outer Hebrides stretch in a 130m-long line from the Butt of Lewis in the N to Barra Head on the island of Berneray in the S. Long, silvery-white sandy beaches edge the islands, and the W shores are continuously pounded by the full force of the Atlantic. This sea action and the resulting erosion has formed many islands, sea lochs, and pretty coastal inlets. The Minch separates the Outer Hebrides from the mainland, and the Little Minch flows between the islands and Skye – one of the Inner Hebrides.

Lewis is the largest of the islands and Harris is attached to Lewis. The other

principal islands are North and South Uist, Benbecula, and Barra. Flat moorland and numerous lochans characterize the islands, where soil is poor and trees are rare. North Uist, across the Sound of Harris, has so many lochans that the island seems to be more water than land. Harris is the exception in having dramatic mountain peaks, which soar from the sea to over 2,500ft. Peat cut from the moorland by the islanders is stacked to dry for use as winter fuel, and some of the primitive, thatched Black houses can still be seen. Roofing thatch is often held in place by ropes weighted with rocks, as a safeguard against wicked gales which can sweep in from the Atlantic without prior warning.

The manufacture of world-famous Harris Tweed is still a main industry, and a number of fishing vessels operate from island ports. Gaelic is spoken by the islanders and placenames are sometimes bi-lingual. Lewis and Harris have miles of good motoring road, though in S Harris the routes are narrow and winding. The smaller islands have few roads, but a viaduct links Benbecula with South Uist and a causeway connects North Uist with Benbecula.

A wealth of prehistoric evidence litters the islands in the form of chambered cairns, standing stones, brochs, and forts; the ruins of many small churches can also be seen. In the 11thc the Outer Hebrides were over-run by Norsemen who were eventually quashed at Largs in 1263. John of Islay, a supporter of Robert the Bruce, became the first Lord of the Isles in the 14thc. Steamers from various mainland ports connect with several ports on the islands, including Stornoway on Lewis and Castlebay on Barra. Air services operate from Glasgow (Abbotsinch airport) to Barra, Benbecula,

1 Branxholm Tower	4 Hornshole Bridge Monument	7 Tower Hotel
2 Goldielands Tower	5 Horse Monument	8 Wilton Lodge Museum
3 Hawick Motte	6 St Mary's Church	

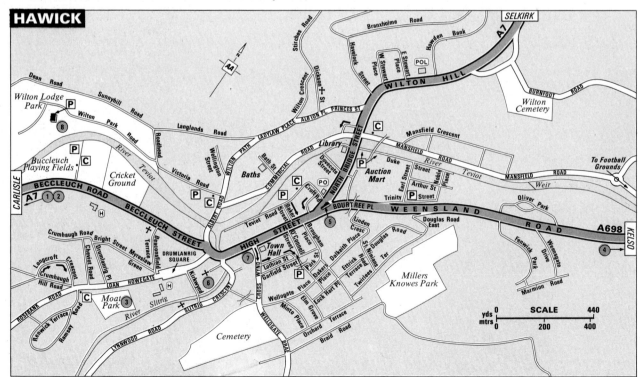

an air link with Inverness. The following entries describe the main islands of the group and are arranged in alphabetical order.

BARRA, Western Isles   *39 NF60*

This infertile little island is separated from South Uist by the Sound of Barra and the island of Eriskay. Castlebay has a pier and is the island's chief link with the mainland. A large herring station is operated here. Picturesque Kishmul Castle stands on a tiny island in Castle Bay, and is the largest stronghold in the Outer Hebrides. The original fortification was built *c*1030 for the pirate-chief of the Macneils of Barra, one of whose ancestors was said to have refused Noah's hospitality as 'the Macneil has a boat of his own'.

At one period a retainer is said to have announced 'Macneil has dined, the kings, princes, and others of the earth may now dine' daily from the castle walls. A large part of the present castle dates from *c*1427, though the main tower is thought to be of 12th-c origin. Restoration was commenced in 1938 by the 45th clan chief, an American architect, and completed in 1960.

Though Gaelic is spoken by many Outer Hebrideans, Barra is noted for its pure Gaelic and also for its folk songs and folklore. Fine views can be enjoyed from the top of 1,260ft Heaval, which rises from the S part of Barra. Some 12m of roads encircle the island, giving access to Traigh Mor – or Great Cockle Shore – in the N, where there is an airstrip. Ben Eoligarry stands at 338ft near by and affords lovely views. Ruined Cille-bharra, with its old carved slabs, was once the church of St Barr. A narrow peninsula extends past the old burial ground of Kilbar and Eoligarry House, once a Macneil seat, to Scurrival Point and the Sound of Fuday.

Vatersay, Sandray, Pabbay, and Mingulay are islands which lie to the S of Barra. The Biulacraig cliffs soar to unbelievable heights on the W coast of Mingulay, and Berneray completes the chain of the Outer Hebrides. A lighthouse tops 580ft Barra Head on Berneray, the farthest S point of the Outer Hebrides.

BENBECULA, Western Isles   *39 NF75*

Lying between North and South Uist, Benbecula is vulnerable to high sea winds and linked to North Uist by a causeway from Gramisdale. Most of the thousand people on Benbecula live at Bailvanish, the principal community near the airfield. Rueval Hill is a prominent high point among the maze of lochs, bays, and islets that make up this island. A road links Gramisdale with Creagorry, where a bridge connects up with South Uist, and ruined Borve Castle lies 2m NW of Creagorry and once served as a stronghold of the Chiefs of Benbecula. Prince Charles Edward escaped from here in a rowing boat in 1746. Dressed as Flora Macdonald's maid, he successfully made the crossing to Port Kilbridge near Uig on Skye.

ERISKAY, Western Isles   *39 NF70*

In 1745 Prince Charles Edward set foot on Scottish soil for the first time when he landed on Eriskay from the French brig Du Teillay. This charming little island has a population of around 300 people, mainly concerned with crofting and fishing. The pale pink sea convolvulus which blooms here is said to have grown from seeds dropped by the prince. Colonies of seals frequently visit the island, and Eriskay's own strain of semi-wild ponies roam the interior. The island is specially noted for its lovely folksongs, particularly the sad Gaelic *Eriskay Love Lilt*. In 1941 the SS 'Politicia' ran aground off the island with a large cargo of whisky. Compton Mackenzie's novel *Whisky Galore* is based on the subsequent events. A film has been based on the novel.

HARRIS, Western Isles   *38*

The landscape changes as the road from Lewis runs alongside the shores of Loch Seaforth, and becomes more hilly with lofty, gneiss peaks to the W dominated by 2,622ft Clisham – the highest mountain in the Outer Hebrides. Its neighbour Mulla fo dheas rises to 2,439ft. The road from Stornoway climbs the mountain's E flanks before descending to Ardhasig Bridge, which affords fine views of West Loch Tarbert and the lonely hills to the NW.

Beyond these hills the rocky mountains of the remote Forest of Harris stretch from Loch Resort to West Loch Tarbert. Some of the highest peaks include 2,392ft Uisgnaval, 2,165ft Oreval, 2,153ft Ullaval, and 2,227ft Tirga More. The great rock face of Strone Ulladale stands at 1,398ft N of Ullaval, and overlooks Glen Ulladale and Loch Resort.

One of the finest passes through the hills runs between Uisgnaval and Oreval, past the craggy Strone Scourst which rises to over 1,600ft above Loch Scourst. This track ends 4m N of West Loch Tarbert at Loch Voshimid. Stulaval rises to 1,887ft from the Lewis border and dominates the S end of narrow Loch Langabhat. To the E of the road from Stornoway is Outer Loch Seaforth, which displays fjord-like scenery. Tarbert, the largest Harris village, stands on a narrow isthmus between East and West Loch Tarbert. Its steamer pier is on the former, and its name means 'a narrow neck of land across which boats may be dragged'. To the W 1,600ft Ben Luskentyre faces the island of Taransay.

A scenic road which runs E from Tarbert ends at Kyles Scalpay, overlooking Scalpay Island. The waters of the area abound in fish. To the N of Tarbert, at Ardhasig Bridge, a lovely but narrow road runs W along the shores of West Loch Tarbert to Amhuinnsuidhe Castle, where James Barrie wrote much of *Mary Rose*. The road ends at lovely Husinish Bay, overlooking the island of Scarp. The 'main' road from Tarbert runs S into the delightful district of S Harris and turns W along Glen Laxdale, where cairns mark ancient prehistoric funeral routes. The road then leads to one of Harris's beauty spots – the silver Luskentyre Sands lining a deep inlet on the Sound of Taransay, sheltered by the protective bulk of Taransay island. Near Luskentyre village is Loch Fincastle, a salmon loch.

The road continues past sandy bays with views of Toe Head, a peninsula stretching out into the Atlantic. Chaipaval Hill affords unforgettable views of the Cuillin range of Skye and the hills of North Uist. Cape Difficulty, on Toe Head, is one of the three real capes in Britain. Continuing through Glen Coishletter, the road passes near the shores of the Sound of Harris and leads to Leverburgh – or Obbe –

where Lord Leverhulme failed in his attempt to create a fishing station. The islanders resisted his efforts to improve trade.

Rodel, a village on Rodel Bay, is notable for cruciform St Clement's Church (AM), which was built in 1500 on a hill overlooking the Little Minch and the Sound of Harris. Curious sculptures decorate the roof of the church, which was built as a chapel by the 8th Macleod Chief of Dunvegan Castle in Skye. A feature of the interior is a fine recessed Macleod tomb dating from 1528, and several interesting Highland grave slabs can be seen in the churchyard. Also in the cemetery is the tomb of a Macleod of Berneray, who fought for Bonnie Prince Charlie. In 1873 the church was restored by the Countess of Dunsmore.

Fine views can be enjoyed from 1,506ft Roneval, which rises to the N of Rodel. Finsbay lies 4m NE of Rodel and is a small port on Finsbay Loch, reached by a treacherous little road with acute corners and blind bends. This road continues to the jagged E coast, past the head of Loch Stockinish. Steamers call at Stockinish, and a little to the N the road meets up with the 'main' road back to Tarbert.

LEWIS, Western Isles   *38*

The Lews is another name for Lewis which, together with Harris, forms a land mass some 60m long and 18 to 28m wide. Stornoway, the largest town in the Outer Hebrides and unofficial capital of Lewis, has a 2m-long natural harbour which has made it the centre of the Hebridean herring industry. There is also a large lobster pond. Tweed weaving is still a cottage industry here, but Stornoway has five mills for spinning and finishing the cloth. Lewis Castle stands in fine wooded grounds facing the harbour and was given to the town by Lord Leverhulme. Leverhulme bought the island in 1918 with the intention of modernizing Lewis' industries. Although he tried to turn the crofters into fish-cannery workers, the project finally failed. The castle was built in 1844 and now serves as a technical college. St Peter's Church has an ancient fort and houses Livingstone's Prayer Book.

Golf and sea-angling are popular pastimes in Stornoway. To the S of the town on Arnish Moor a cairn and a loch commemorate Prince Charles Edward's visit to a local farm after the Battle of Culloden in 1746. Stornoway is linked by a narrow strip of land to the Eye Peninsula, at the NE tip of which is the fine rock scenery and lighthouse of Tiumpan Head. Distant views from here take in the cliffs of Cape Wrath in good weather. In the SW corner of the peninsula is the ruined Eye Church of St Columba, dating from the 14thc or earlier. Its interesting monuments include the Macleod tombs, and one which is thought may be of Roderick Macleod VIII of Lewis. A road runs NE from Stornoway and follows the sandy bays to Gress, where the ruined Church of St Olaf is thought to be the only one in the Outer Hebrides dedicated to a Norse saint. Seal Cave is a remarkable feature accessible by boat.

Farther NE beyond Tolsta is Tolsta Head, with its magnificent cliffs, fine silver sand, and a lighthouse. The bay of Geiraha is one of the most picturesque on Lewis. From Stornoway a road runs

NW over moorland dotted with tiny lochans, passing near the 1,000ft Barvas Hills. A left turn to Shader, 15m along this road, leads to an impressive 18ft-high monolith called Clach an Trushal, or the Thrushel Stone. Near by at the S end of Loch an Duin are the ruined neolithic Steinacleit chambered cairn and stone circle (AM). The main road continues NE to Port of Ness and the Butt of Lewis, with its lighthouse; this is the farthest N point of the Outer Hebrides. Wonderful and primitive rock scenery is offered by the headland, and near by stands the restored 12th-c Church of St Molua.

From Swanibost there is a fine view of the Eye of the Needle, a rugged cape of rock pinnacles and cliffs near the Butt. The islands' programme to reseed and fertilize the barren moorland to make pasture was begun here. The Standing Stones of Callanish (AM), 16m W of Stornoway and beyond Garynahine, are the most remarkable antiquity in the Western Isles – second only in importance to the great Stonehenge in England. An avenue of nineteen stone monoliths leads to a circle of thirteen stones, with more rows of stones fanning out into what were possibly further circles. These stones were probably laid at intervals between 2,000 and 1,500 BC, and may have been used for sun worship. A great cairn measuring 40ft across stands within the circle. Opposite Callanish is the island of Great Bernera, which can be reached by a road bridge. Loch Roag lies to the W and East Loch Roag to the E.

On Loch Carloway, an inlet of East Loch Roag 7m NW of Garynahine, is the famous Dun Carloway Broch (AM) – considered one of the best preserved iron-age brochs in the Western Isles and still standing at about 30ft. A road leads NE along a coastline dotted with small crofting communities. Arnol has a museum in a *tigh dubh* (AM), the traditional black house of the islands. Its thick, drystone walls are pierced by doors and windows made tiny as protection against the harsh weather. Barvas connects up with the Stornoway to Port of Ness road, and is overlooked by 918ft Ben Barvas to the E.

From Garynahine another narrow road runs SW into remote country dotted with numerous lochans, beyond which lies the great expanse of Loch Langabhat. This road leads to some of the farthest W parts of Lewis, round Little Loch Roag and through the lovely Glen Valtos to Uig. Fine cliffs and long stretches of silver sand are to be found here, with the bleak promontory of Gallen Head overlooking island-studded Loch Roag to the N. Views over 20m of sea encompass the Flannan Isles, or Seven Hunters. A lighthouse was built on these islands in 1900; all three lighthouse keepers on duty vanished soon afterwards during a gale. Ardroil Sands lie 4m SW of Uig, backed by a range of remote, rocky hills which include 1,885ft Mealasbhal. Beyond the E flanks of the latter and the hill of Tarain lies the long, narrow Loch Suainaval, which is over 200ft deep in places. This SW corner of Lewis has no roads, and S of the hills the headland of Gearraidh na h-Airde Moire boasts a collection of beehive houses near the mouth of Loch Resort. Tarran Mor is a precipitous, rocky hill in Harris which faces the loch.

The road to Harris from Stornoway passes near the Parish of Lochs, so called because the proportion of water to land is even higher here than elsewhere in the islands. Crofters grow potatoes in lazy beds – rows of banked-up soil with their own drainage system. Ballalan lies at the head of lovely Loch Erisort, and from here the road crosses moorland which was once the hunting ground of the Earl of Seaforth, Chief of the Mackenzies. It was he who raised the Seaforth Highlanders regiment.

Small herds of red deer roam wild in these parts, and a road runs down the W side of beautiful Loch Seaforth to Aline, opposite Seaforth Island. This SE corner of Lewis is known as Park, with its highest point at 1,874ft at Beinn Mhor. The tiny Shiant Islands lie beyond the Sound of Shiant off the SE coast of Lewis.

NORTH UIST, Western Isles   39 NF77
The Sound of Harris separates Harris from North Uist, and is punctuated with many islands which include Berneray and Pabbay. North Uist is covered in lochans, and the views afforded by a road which follows the twisting N shoreline give the impression that the island is more water than land, particularly to the E and S. The road round the island passes a wealth of prehistoric standing stones, cairns, and brochs. Loch Scadavay, with its innumerable inlets, is the largest inland loch. Lochmaddy is North Uist's main village, and has a pier on the trout and salmon-rich Loch Maddy. South Lee rises to 920ft S of Lochmaddy and offers a magnificent panorama of the loch-flecked landscape to the W. Farther S is 1,138ft Eaval, the highest point on the island, overlooking Lochs Obisary and Eport to the N and the tidal island of Grimsay to the S.

The road SW from Lochmaddy leads to the W coast, including the Paible district, and after 5m passes the fine chambered cairn of Langass Barp. Some 3m farther a road branches S to Carinish, where a causeway connects with Grimsay and the larger island of Benbecula. The ruins of the massive Temple of Carinish date from the 14th or 16thc. To the W are Baleshare Island and the Monach Isles. Situated beyond the Sound of Monach, this group now comprises a national nature reserve rich in seabirds and seals. Hoglan Bay lies on the exposed Atlantic coast in the NW corner of North Uist, and the remote Haskeir Isles can be seen far out to sea. Another nature reserve at Balranald – near Hougharry – is the breeding place of the rare red-necked phalarope.

SOUTH UIST, Western Isles   39 NF72
A road running the length of South Uist starts from Carnan – at the end of the viaduct from Benbecula – and runs to Pollachar near Kilbride in the extreme S on the Sound of Eriskay. To the S of Carnan the road crosses Loch Bee by a narrow raised causeway. The contrasting scenery of South Uist can be enjoyed from the road, with lochs lying to the W and mountainous hills dominated by 2,034ft Beinn Mhor and 1,988ft Hecla to the E. Prince Charles Edward sheltered in a forester's hut between these hills for three weeks in 1746.

Loch Druidibeg national nature reserve lies near by. This is the most important surviving breeding ground of the native greylag goose in Britain. Farther S beyond Loch Eynort is 1,227ft Stulaval with Loch Snigisclett stretching below its N slopes. Lochboisdale is South Uist's chief village and has a pier on the loch of the same name. Access to the village is by an E branch off the 'main' road at Daliburgh Church. Near Daliburgh is a primitive, thatched-roof, crofter's black house. Remains of Flora Macdonald's birthplace stand at Milton, 4m N of Daliburgh Church, near the shores of Loch Kildonan. Some 2½m farther N is a by-road which leads to ruined Ormaclett Castle, built c1701 and burnt down in 1715. Several sections of road afford views of St Kilda – the farthest W group of islands in the British Isles, lying 60m out into the Atlantic.

HEILIM, Highland   36 NC45
Fine mountains back Loch Eriboll, a sheltered anchorage safe from storms, on the NE shore of which lies Heilim. By the loch-side to the S of Heilim are the ruins of a broch or Pictish tower. To the NW on the road to Tongue is the head of Loch Hope, at the S end of which rises 3,040ft Ben Hope.

HELENSBURGH, Strathclyde   44 NS28
John Logie Baird, a pioneer of television, was born here in 1888. Helensburgh is a popular resort for anglers, golfers, and yachtsmen and lies at the point where beautiful Gare Loch merges into the Clyde estuary. An obelisk in the town commemorates Henry Bell, who in 1812 designed the 'Comet' – Europe's first steam-driven ship. Henry Bell's anvil and the flywheel from the 'Comet' are preserved in Hermitage Park. Helensburgh is a good centre for exploring the wild hills and glens of Dunbarton. There are few roads but the mountain scenery is magnificent, with the twin peaks of Doune Hill rising to 2,408 and 2,298ft. The shores of Loch Lomond can be reached via a road leading NE from the town. A left fork 1½m from Helensburgh leads into Glen Fruin, also called the Glen of Sorrow, with 2,338ft Beinn Chaorach to the N. A savage clan battle was fought between the Macgregors and the Colquhouns here in 1603.

*HELMSDALE, Highland   37 ND01
Helmsdale River flows to the sea through the green valley of Strath Ullie, and the little fishing port of Helmsdale lies between high moorland ridges. It offers safe anchorage and a sandy beach. The ruined castle was demolished in 1971, and was where the Earl of Sutherland and his wife were poisoned in 1567. To the N of Helmsdale a road to Berriedale winds through the picturesque Nithsdale ravines to enter the one-time county of Caithness near the rocky Ord of Caithness. At this point the road is over 700ft above sea level, and affords fine views of desolate hills to the NW.

HERIOT, Borders   47 NT45
Heriot is sited high up on the main Carlisle to Edinburgh road, and to the W is bordered by the Moorfoot Hills. The church stands 2m SW on a delightful road which follows the Heriot Water and Dewar Burn through the hills. This road reaches a 1,200ft summit at the border of one-time Peebles-shire, and later follows the Leithen Water towards Tweeddale with 2,161ft Windlestraw Law to the E.

Flywheel from Henry Bell's 'Comet', the first steamship in Europe. The anvil was used by Bell during construction of the vessel.

HERMISTON, Lothian   47 NT17

To the S of the road from Hermiston to Mid-Calder are the estates of Riccarton and Dalmahoy, known for their fine trees. A little to the N of the community is the restored Church of Ratho, which was founded in the 12thc. The last Earl of Lauderdale lived at Hatton House and lies in the churchyard. The house itself was demolished after a fire.

HERMITAGE CASTLE, Borders
26 NY49

Outwardly almost perfect, this grim 14th-c castle stands on a hillock amid bleak moorland overlooking Hermitage Water. Its position is a little to the W of the Newcastleton to Hawick road, and the castle was originally a stronghold of the de Soulis family. The structure fell into the hands of the Douglases in 1341 and has a cruel history. It was to here that Mary Queen of Scots came to see her lover the Earl of Bothwell in 1566. Bothwell owned the castle at that time. Mary rode from Jedburgh to see the earl when he was wounded, and rode back the same day – a distance of some 40m. She nearly died from fever as a result. Swinburne has described the castle, which is of immense strength and still has its four towers and connecting walls, in one of his poems. Remains of the original interior tower also survive.

HIGHLANDS, THE

Scotland is traditionally divided into the Lowlands and Highlands – areas on either side of a geological division. Generally speaking the Highlands comprise the district of hills, glens, lochs, and islands lying N and W of and including the grassy heather-clad Grampians. Since the re-organization of counties, one of the new administrative areas that has emerged is known as 'Highland'. The scanty population of Highlanders are largely of Celtic extraction and some still speak Gaelic.

The old county of Argyll, in the S Highlands, once formed the ancient kingdom of Dalriada; the N Highlands were at one time mainly Pictish territory. Seven well-defined peaks exceed 4,000ft, and there are 543 Munros – summits of over 3,000ft. Notable features of the Highlands include the granite Arran peaks; the fine plateau of the Cairngorms, embracing a national nature reserve; the wild hill country around Glencoe, also including the great Ben Nevis and the Mamores peaks; the serrated outline of the magnificent Cuillins on Skye, composed of the black gabbro much favoured by climbers and hill-walkers; the Archaean gneiss rock of the remote Assynt district; the grand Torridon-sandstone and white-quartzite peaks of Wester Ross and one-time Sutherland.

The geological boundary between the Highlands and Lowlands commences in the Firth of Clyde, skirts the Cowal coast of old Argyll, crosses the mouth of the Gare Loch, and later passes over the lower reaches of Loch Lomond. It then follows a rough line linking Aberfoyle with Callander and Comrie. Running NE to SW across one-time Perthshire is the Highland Boundary Fault – a deep fracture in the earth's crust where the 300-million year old rock still gives rise to occasional earth tremors near Comrie. Continuing past the entrance to the Sma' Glen, the line reaches the Tay to the S of Dunkeld and then stretches NE towards the Dee valley at Dinnet. From here it traverses the now defunct counties of Banffshire and Moray in a NW direction, to reach the Moray Firth at Nairn.

To the N of Firth is the old county of Caithness, an area which is not actually part of the Highlands. Glen More, or the Great Glen, is a remarkable rift valley, which extends from Inverness in the NE to Fort William in the SW. This Highland feature divides the mainland into two, and a series of lochs joined together by the Caledonian Canal lie along the trough. Glen More is overlooked at its W end by Ben Nevis – Britain's highest mountain – and its outlying peaks.

Lying to the W of the rift is the area known as the NW Highlands, which contains the wonderful mountain and loch scenery for which Scotland is justly renowned. Offshore is the large and lovely Inner Hebridean island of Skye. Some of the finest inland mainland lochs include Shiel, Morar, Duich, Quoich, and Maree. The mountains of the NW Highlands include the great hills which dominate both sides of picturesque Glen Shiel as far as Loch Duich; the little-known peaks shadowing Glens Affric and Cannich, two of the loveliest glens in Scotland; Suilven and the strange, isolated summits of the lonely Assynt district; the great cirque of An Teallach, near Dundonnell in Wester Ross; and the magnificent Torridon peaks of Liathach and Ben Eighe near Kinlochewe. Ben Eighe national nature reserve, one of the first and wildest of its kind in the British Isles, is the hunting-ground of the rare pine marten.

Much of the mountain area of the Highlands is given over to deer forest; grouse are shot on some of the moors, and many of the lochs and rivers are available to the angler. Pony-trekking has become a popular pursuit in the area. Glencoe and the Grampian and Cairngorm Mountains offer ski-ing, and Aviemore is the chief centre for the pastime in the Cairngorms. It is also a convenient base for visiting the Glen More forest park.

HIGHTAE, Dumfries and Galloway
26 NY07

Hightae lies on the River Annan. The fine 18th-c mansion of Rammerscales stands SW and was built by Dr James Mounsey – at one time chief physician to the Russian Imperial Court.

HILLEND (Edinburgh), Lothian   47 NT26

Situated on the fringe of the Pentlands, Hillend faces W towards the Caerketton Crags and the 1,617ft summit of Allermuir Hill. The longest dry-ski slope in Britain operates on the side of Caerketton and is open all year round. Sir Walter Scott was a frequent visitor to Woodhouselee House, which is sited 2m SSW.

HODDOM BRIDGE,
Dumfries and Galloway   26 NY17

The River Annan flows under this bridge. A little to the W on the S side of the river is the site of Hoddon Castle, demolished in 1953. Trailtrow (or Repentance) Tower stands on a hill above the site of the castle and was built in the 16thc. The tower is linked with John Maxwell, who repented his decision to use force against his compatriots in the 16thc and later defeated the English. Hoddom Church stands on the road to Ecclefechan and was once the see of St Mungo.

HOLY LOCH, Strathclyde   44 NS18

Holy Loch is now a Polaris-submarine base. It is a little inlet of the Clyde estuary near the entrance to Loch Long, and a 166-acre forest garden of eucalyptus and other exotic trees has been planted here by the Forestry Commission.

HOLYTOWN, Strathclyde   45 NS76

Keir Hardie, famous member of the early Labour Party movement, was born near Holytown in 1856. The town itself lies in a mining area to the E of the Clyde valley.

HOPE LODGE, Highland   36 NC46

Hope Lodge lies at the N tip of Loch Hope, to the N of which are the fine cave-riddled cliffs of Whiten Head. There is no road to the head, but the road E from Hope Lodge crosses lonely moorland at A'Mhoine to reach the Kyle of Tongue. At the head of long and narrow Loch Hope rises Ben Hope, the farthest N peak of over 3,000ft in Scotland. A good road runs $3\frac{1}{2}$m E to the shores of Loch Eriboll from Hope Lodge.

HOPEMAN, Grampian   34 NJ16

This small resort and fishing village has a harbour and lighthouse.

HOUNAM, Borders   27 NT71
Heatherhope Loch, now a reservoir for Kelso, lies amid heather-clad moorland to the SE of this little Kale Water village. The main Cheviot range rises beyond the loch, with the 2,676ft Cheviot predominant farther to the E in England. The fine viewpoint of the 2,382ft Auchopecairn – right on the Scottish border – rises from the Cheviot's W slopes.

HOUSTON, Strathclyde   44 NS46
A Mercat cross which was restored in 1713 stands in the town. To the N is St Peter's Well, and Houston House dates mainly from the 19thc. Farther N beyond St Peter's Well is the 11ft-high Barochan Cross (AM), a weathered Celtic structure of possible 12th-c date which has been moved from its original site.

HOWE OF FIFE, Fife   31
This is the fertile area situated to the NE of the Lomond Hills.

HOWGATE, Lothian   47 NT25
Situated on the slopes of the Moorfoot Hills, 4m SE of Howgate, is the large Gladhouse Reservoir. Howgate itself is a hamlet with an attractive old coaching inn.

HOWWOOD, Strathclyde   44 NS36
To the W of Howwood is Castle Semple Loch, with the church of the same name lying near by. To the NW on the road to Lochwinnoch is the ancient Clochodrich Stone. The name of this may have been taken from an early ruler of Strathclyde.

HUMBIE, Lothian   47 NT46
The first German bomber to crash on British soil fell near Humbie during the second world war. The village lies at the foot of the Lammermuir Hills, and is a children's village associated with the Edinburgh Children's Holiday Fund. Johnstounburn House lies in fine gardens to the S of the village.

HUNA, Highland   37 ND37
Farms in the district around Huna use characteristic Caithness flagstones in place of fences. The village lies about halfway between St John's Point and Duncansby Head, on the Inner Sound of the Pentland Firth, facing the island of Stroma.

HUNTER'S QUAY, Strathclyde   44 NS17
This little Firth of Clyde resort lies at the mouth of Holy Loch and is the headquarters of the Royal Clyde Yachting Club. Every July Hunter's Quay becomes the central point for Clyde Yachting Fortnight. To the N across the mouth of the Holy Loch is Strone Point and the small resort of Strone. Hunter's Quay takes its name from the Hunters of Hafton House, which dates from 1828 and lies to the NW.

HUNTERSTON, Strathclyde   44 NS15
Scotland's first commercial nuclear power station was opened here in 1964, and a second one is under construction. There are also plans for the development of a deep-water port, and a steel works with an iron-ore terminal.

HUNTINGTOWER, Tayside   30 NO02
Huntingtower Castle (AM) was the scene of the Raid of Ruthven in 1582. James VI (later James I of England) – then sixteen years old – accepted an invitation from the Earl of Gowrie to his hunting seat. He immediately found himself in the hands of Protestant nobles, who demanded the dismissal of James's favourites. The Master of Glamis barred the King's way when he tried to escape, and James was held for a year while the Ruthven conspirators wielded power. Two years later the Earl of Gowrie was beheaded. The castellated mansion dates from the 15thc and has been restored. It has two towers joined by lower buildings, the space between the towers being known as the Maiden's Leap.

HUNTLY, Grampian   35 NJ53
The attractive market town of Huntly offers excellent fishing. Immediately N the River Bogie joins the better-known Deveron, which flows from higher ground to the W overlooked by 1,229ft Clashmach Hill. Ruined Huntly Castle (AM) is approached through a beautifully wooded park and overlooks a gorge of the Deveron. Formerly known as the Palace of Strathbogie, the castle replaced an earlier medieval fortification which was the seat of the Gay Gordons until 1544. This family were the Marquesses of Huntly, the most powerful family in the North until the mid-16thc.

The castle was destroyed by Moray in 1452, rebuilt twice before 1554, and burned down again in 1594. The present structure dates from 1602, but became derelict in the 18thc when some of its stones were used to build Huntly Lodge, which stands to the N of the town and now serves as a hotel. Its upper storey still displays some of the original, elaborate heraldic ornamentation. Beldorney Castle, dating from the early 17thc, lies 8m W of Huntly.

HURLFORD, Strathclyde   25 NS43
Iron and fireclay works form part of this small town. The house of Carnell is interesting in that it has a 15th-c pele tower.

HUTTON, Borders   31 NT95
Hutton Castle, a modern building with an ancient pele tower, stands on Whiteadder Water. Sir William Burrell was a former owner who donated the famous Burrell Art Collection to Glasgow in 1944.

HYNDFORDBRIDGE, Strathclyde   30 NS94
Overlooked to the E by 1,131ft Cairngryfe Hill, the Hyndford Bridge spans the Clyde and dates from 1773. Lanark racecourse lies on Lanark Moor to the NW.

INCHCOLM ISLAND, Fife   47 NT18
Mentioned in Shakespeare's *Macbeth*, Inchcolm Island lies 1½m out to sea to the S of Aberdour. On the island are the best-preserved of Scotland's early monastic remains. The Abbey of St Columba (AM) was founded in 1123, and the ruins include a fine 13th-c octagonal chapter house and tower, plus examples of 15th-c work. Traces of the original frescoes have been discovered in the choir.

INCHINNAN, Strathclyde   45 NS56
Situated about 1m N of Glasgow Airport, this place is the site of a factory that produced airships during the first world war. The world-famous R34 was built here and later flown across the Atlantic by Major Herbert Scott (see inset opposite).

Inchinnan church was once the property of the Knights Templar, and the modern building that now exists was erected by Lord Blythswood. Celtic Stones, Templars' tombs, and several mortsafes from the old body-snatching days can be seen in the churchyard.

INCHKEITH ISLAND, Fife   47 NT28
Held by the French between 1549 and 1567, the fortified island of Inchkeith lies 3m off the Fife coast and is the site of a powerful lighthouse. Dr Johnson and Boswell were visitors in 1773, and Carlyle came here in 1817. Kinghorn lies NW on the mainland.

INCHNADAMPH, Highland   36 NC22
This fishing village lies in the fascinating though remote Assynt district of the NW Highlands. Many of the surrounding mountains are of Torridon sandstone, sometimes topped with gleaming white quartzite. Much of the area to the NW is formed by the oldest known type of rock in the world – Archaean gneiss – found elsewhere only in the Outer Hebrides and near the St Lawrence River in Canada. Small lochs litter the barren countryside around Inchnadamph, one of which is the habitat of the rare gilaroo trout.

Picturesque Loch Assynt stretches for 7m NW of the village, and ruins of Ardvreck Castle stand on its N shore. This structure dates from the late 16thc and was a Macleod stronghold. After an abortive invasion attempt on behalf of the exiled Charles II, the great Marquis of Montrose took refuge at Ardvreck Castle in 1650. Neil Macleod surrendered Montrose, who was later executed at Edinburgh, for a reward thought to be in the region of £20,000. Near the castle are ruins of 17th-c Calda House, seat of the Mackenzies. A national nature reserve lies in a limestone area near Inchnadamph, and is riddled with underground streams and caves.

The Allt nan Uamh caves on the lower slopes of 3,273ft Ben More Assynt, which lies 4m SE of the village, are the site where 8,000 year-old human bones were found. Ben More Assynt is the highest peak in the one-time county of Sutherland, and is composed mainly of gneiss. Conaveall rises to 3,234ft in the neighbourhood and features a partly subterranean stream. The area which used to be Sutherland is noted for its wierdly shaped mountains formed of ancient rocks. To the SW of Inchnadamph 2,779ft Canisp and 2,399ft Suilven are separated by lonely Loch Gainimh. Suilven, known as the Matterhorn of Scotland because of its dangerous cliff faces, shows part of a sandstone layer formed on top of rock 2,600 million years old.

The road NW from Inchnadamph to Unapool passes E of the seven peaks of Quinag. These are joined together by a long ridge, and form marvellous walking country for the energetic. Glasven rises to 2,541ft E of the road and is the source of the sheer, 658ft Eas Coul Aulin, Britain's highest waterfall. This is said to be several times the height of Niagara. The falls can be reached by a boat which runs from Kylesku Ferry to Loch Glencoul, or on foot from the road below Glasven.

INCHTURE, Tayside   31 NO22
Strawberries are cultivated in the fertile Carse of Gowrie between the Sidlaw Hills

and the Firth of Tay, and Inchture lies in the heart of this district. Rossie Hill rises to the N and Rossie Priory is surrounded by fine grounds.

INNELLAN, Strathclyde   *44 NS17*

A Firth of Clyde and Cowal holiday village, Innellan has a steamer pier and faces Wemyss Bay. The climate is so mild that palm trees grow in some gardens.

THE UBIQUITOUS AIRSHIP

A well-known landmark 1m north of Glasgow airport is a large grey building with 'India Tyres' painted in tall letters round the sides. Now used as a tyre store, it was set up during the first world war with a much more dramatic purpose; for the factory at Inchinnan was one of the centres of Britain's airship industry.

William Beardmore and Company were a giant engineering concern with forges, factories, and yards in Glasgow and the surrounding district. In wartime conditions they poured out not only more than a million tons of steel, but also mines, shells, field guns, naval guns, tanks, marine engines – even cruisers, battleships, and 650 aeroplanes ranging from Baby Sopwiths to Handley-Page bombers. Their total wartime turnover was put at 68-million pounds.

In 1916 the Admiralty decided to explore the possibilities of using airships in fleet reconnaissance. Beardmores were given a contract. They bought 360 acres of Allards Farm at Inchinnan, and the construction of the giant sheds and hangars was started by Sir William Arrol and Company. The main hangar was 720ft long, 150ft wide and 100ft high. While this was going on, the building of the main airship parts was under way at Dalmuir, just across the Clyde.

His Majesty's Airship R24 was laid down in July 1916. She had a capacity of 970,000 cubic feet, with a lifting capability of 6¼ tons. Her flight trial was in September 1917, and she was soon afterwards delivered in two hours to her base at East Fortune, 65m away on the far side of Edinburgh. R27 made her maiden flight in April 1918 and was then based at Howden in Yorkshire.

Toward Point and lighthouse lie 2m SSW near a modern castle. A road runs W past ruined Castle Toward, which boasts a 15th-c square tower and displays battlements on the N wall. The tower rises three storeys. From here the road continues to the S shores of Loch Striven. Views from these shores extend along the Kyles of Bute and across to the bay of Rothesay on the island of Bute. The road

Far more significant was the third Beardmore airship, the world-famous R34. This was a much bigger craft, with a capacity of two million cubic feet and a lifting capacity of more than 30 tons. She was completed after the fighting in Europe was over, in December 1918. Her maiden flight was in January of the following year. On 14 March 1919 there was a grand public showing of the new ship: 'Shortly after 9.30, the large doors of the shed were thrown open, and she floated gracefully at her moorings, steadied by weights and sandbags.' At the controls was Major Herbert Scott, who was soon to make the most famous flight of all.

Her 665ft bulk dominating the factory, R34 was released from her moorings and began a four-hour demonstration flight over Glasgow and the lower Clyde, swinging round above the island of Ailsa Craig as she turned for home. Most of the flight was at 2,000ft, and the highest speed attained was 60mph. Two months later she left Inchinnan on her acceptance trial and settled, like the first of the Beardmore airships, at East Fortune. In June there was a longer flight, 2,000 miles in 56 hours up the Baltic and home again in a stiff gale. R34 was almost ready for her greatest challenge, the pioneer double crossing of the Atlantic.

The historic journey began at 13.42hrs on Wednesday 2 July 1919, when a bugler at East Fortune sounded the signal 'Let Go'. It had been planned that R34 would arrive in America during the Fourth of July celebrations, but severe

The airship factory at Inchinnan was one of the cradles of the infant aeronautics industry in Britain.

comes to an end beyond Inverchaolin Church, which is backed by lonely hills dominated by 1,651ft Bishop's Seat.

INNERLEITHEN, Borders   *26 NT33*

Sir Walter Scott popularized Innerleithen after he published his novel *St Ronan's Well*, in which he associated a local well – known until then as Doo's Well – with the 7th-c St Ronan. Innerleithen is a woollen

weather intervened. There were 50mph head winds and two electric storms. The navigators plotted and replotted new courses to avoid the worst conditions, and when the airship settled triumphantly over Roosevelt Field, Long Island, after a flight of 108 hours 17 minutes, there was only 90 minutes worth of petrol left in the tanks. The return journey to Pulham in Norfolk, with a following wind, took only 75 hours.

Beardmores were seemingly well established at Inchinnan by that time, having built a settlement of 52 houses for airship workers beside the factory. In fact, only one more airship was ever to be built there. Designed for peacetime commercial work, R36 was completed in 1921. She was provided with luxurious accommodation for 50 passengers, and shifts were to be worked by a crew of four officers and 24 men, seven of them riggers and thirteen engineers. Her engines were a curious mixture. Three of them were 350hp Sunbeam Cossacks and the other two were 260hp Maybachs from a surrendered Zeppelin. After leaving the Clyde R36 was based at Pulham.

Although Beardmores never produced another airship, they supplied the engines for the ill-fated R101, built in the Royal Airship Works at Cardington near Bedford. When R101 crashed on a hastily arranged flight to India, the British airship industry was closed down. In 1927 the empty factory at Inchinnan was taken over by the India Tyre and Rubber Company, which a few years later was absorbed in the Dunlop empire. The buildings have changed, but the houses provided by Beardmores are still there, and one of the airship sheds remains to remind travellers through Glasgow airport of a more leisurely way of flying.

town which stands on Leithen Water near its confluence with the Tweed. The town's first tweed mill was opened in 1790. The St Ronan Games, or Cleikum Ceremony, are held every year and symbolize the expulsion of the Devil by St Ronan. To the N of the town are the delightful hill-bound valleys of Leithen Water and Glentress Water.

Windlestraw Law rises to 2,161ft near the meeting of the old Peebles-shire, Selkirkshire, and Midlothian boundaries. Traquair, a picturesque early mansion thought to be the 'Tullyveolan' of Scott's *Waverley*, lies to the S of Innerleithen across the Tweed. The ancient tower of Cardrona stands 2m NW, also on the other side of the Tweed.

INNERMESSAN, Dumfries and Galloway 24 NX06

It is thought that the Roman site of *Rericonium* was a little to the N of Innermessan, overlooking Loch Ryan. Isolated Craigcaffie Castle now stands on the site and is a good example of a late 16th-c square tower house. Its 13th-c foundations are said to have been laid on bags of wool to stop subsidence into the marshy ground.

INNERWICK, Lothian 31 NT77

English invaders destroyed Innerwick Castle in 1547, but ruins of the structure can still be seen. Near by are remains of Thornton Castle, and Innerwick Church dates from 1784. Monynut Edge lies S of the village, with Heart Law rising to 1,283ft near the old Berwick border.

INNERWICK, Tayside 30 NN54

Glen Lyon's green hills make a lovely setting for this lonely community. An ancient bell is preserved in the church.

INSCH, Grampian 35 NJ62

Several sculptured stones can be found in the Insch area, and 2½m away at Myreton is the Pictish Picardy stone (AM), inscribed in an ancient form of Gaelic. To the W of Insch is the conical hill of Dunnideer, crowned by a vitrified fort and the ruins of a 16th-c castle. Christ's Kirk rises to 1,021ft and faces Dunnideer across the Shevock Burn. The Foudland Hills, some of which are over 1,500ft high, lie to the NW of the village.

Insh Church stands on a site which has been used for worship since the 6thc.

INSH, Highland 34 NH80

Insh Church stands on a hillock near a bridge spanning the Spey, on a site which has been used for worship since the 6thc. The present church is of 18th-c origin and preserves an 8th-c bronze Celtic hand-bell, once used to call people to worship.

INVERALLOCHY, Grampian 35 NK06

This village lies at the E end of sandy Fraserburgh Bay. Two castles built by the Comyns stand near Inverallochy – 2m S is ruined Inverallochy Castle, and the restored Cairnbulg Castle stands 2m SW on the Water of Philorth.

INVERAMSAY, Grampian 35 NJ72

The Battle of Harlaw was fought near here in 1411, with great loss of life. The Lord of the Isles was defeated and prevented from marching farther S by the Lowlanders. Beyond the River Urie and to the SE of Inveramsay near Harplaw House, a tall monument commemorates the battle; Scott mentions this in the *Antiquary*.

INVERAN BRIDGE, Highland 37 NH59

Inveran is a three-arched bridge which spans the turbulent River Shin, popular with anglers. About 1m N are the spectacular Falls of Shin which drop through a rocky gorge where leaping salmon can be seen at certain times of the year. The Shin meets the Kyle of Sutherland to the S near Invershin.

INVERARAY, Strathclyde 29 NN00

This beautiful white-walled Royal Burgh lies on Loch Fyne and faces Strone Point, at the E end of little Loch Shira. The town is surrounded by some of the loveliest woodlands in Scotland. Inveraray Castle has been the hereditary seat of the chiefs of the Clan Campbell, Dukes of Argyll, since the early 15thc. In 1644 the original village of Inveraray near the ancient castle was burnt by the Royalist Marquis of Montrose, and the 3rd Duke of Argyll built the new town and castle between 1746 and 1780. The 8th Earl was executed in Edinburgh in 1661, and in 1685 his son fell victim to the same fate.

Scott mentions the 8th Earl in his *Legend of Montrose*, and the 2nd Duke in *Heart of Midlothian*. Roger Morris, William

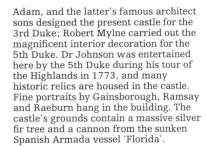

Adam, and the latter's famous architect sons designed the present castle for the 3rd Duke; Robert Mylne carried out the magnificent interior decoration for the 5th Duke. Dr Johnson was entertained here by the 5th Duke during his tour of the Highlands in 1773, and many historic relics are housed in the castle. Fine portraits by Gainsborough, Ramsay and Raeburn hang in the building. The castle's grounds contain a massive silver fir tree and a cannon from the sunken Spanish Armada vessel 'Florida'.

Near the grounds is the 850ft hill of Duniquoich, topped by a tower and described in Scott's *Legend of Montrose*. A tall Celtic burial cross from Iona stands at the junction of Front and Main Street. The parish church was built between 1798 and 1804 by Robert Mylne, and includes a dividing wall which allows services to be held in Gaelic and English at the same time. In 1752 the famous Appin murder trial was heard in the old courthouse. James Stewart (James of the Glen) was accused of shooting Colin Campbell, known as the Red Fox. After an unfair trial he was hanged at Ballachulish.

The end of Robert Louis Stevenson's novel *Catriona* describes the Inveraray area. From the grounds of Inveraray Castle there is a 5m walk along the length of Glen Shira. At the head of Loch Shira, the entrance to the glen, the little River Shira is spanned by a lovely 18th-c ornamental bridge. The road through the glen is bordered by dense woods near the pretty Falls of Aray, and a memorial to Neil Munro, an author who lived in the town, stands in the vicinity. Higher up the glen the road climbs on to open moors and ends at Rob Roy's home, now a ruin. The bandit's dirk handle and sporran have been preserved in Inveraray Castle. To the NE of the glen's head 3,106ft Beinn Bhuidhe towers over local hydro-electric works. On the road to Glen Croe, 4m NE of Inveraray and overlooking Loch Fyne, is the well-restored Dundarave Castle of 1598. Neil Munro describes the structure a Doom Castle in his *John Splendid*.

INVERBERVIE, Grampian 35 NO87

Also known as Bervie, this little textile-milling Royal Burgh is strikingly situated on the S bank of a gorge through which Bervie Water flows to the sea. Beyond the river's mouth is a shingle bar of brilliantly-coloured pebbles. John Coutts, father of the famous London banker Thomas Coutts, was born in Inverbervie in 1699. A memorial set up in 1969 honours Hercules Linten, designer of the 'Cutty Sark' clipper, who was born at 4 Market Square in 1836 and died in the same house 64 years later. Hallgreen Castle stands ½m S of the village near a picturesque stretch of rocky coastline pocked with caves and gullies. Delightful little Allardyce Castle stands on a bend of Bervie Water 1m NW of the town. It dates from c1600, and displays fine corbelling and white-harled walls.

INVERCHAOLIN, Strathclyde 29 NS07

Just beyond Inverchàolin Church a road which follows the E shores of Loch Striven comes to an end, backed by 1,651ft Bishop's Seat. Farther N are high hills overlooking Glen Lean.

INVERESK, Lothian 47 NT37

Almost adjoining Musselburgh, which

also lies on the River Esk, Inveresk was the site of a Roman camp. Excavations at Inveresk House have revealed many Roman artefacts. The parish church was built in 1865 and affords fine views of the surrounding countryside from its high situation. This replaced an earlier church which stood on the same site, and carries a tall spire. The building stands in a very beautiful churchyard which includes a mound said to have served Cromwell as a battery gun. Fine Georgian houses in the town include Halkerston and the Manor House. The 17th-c Inveresk Lodge (NTS) stands in lovely gardens.

INVEREY, Grampian   34 NO08

This Deeside hamlet lies on the road leading W from Braemar to the foothills of the Cairngorms, and is set amid beautiful woodlands. Eye Water joins the Dee here, and a memorial tablet recalls John Lamont who became Johann von Lamont, Astronomer Royal of Bavaria in the 19thc. Inverey makes a good centre for walking, which is particularly enjoyable to the W and N. To the E off the Braemar road is the lovely Linn of Corriemulzie waterfall; to the S, up the rugged valley of the Ey Water, is a deep chasm known as the Colonel's Bed. This was named after Colonel John Farquharson, who fought at Killiecrankie in 1689 and is thought to have hidden in the chasm. The well-known Linn of Dee, where Byron nearly drowned as a boy, is a wild and rocky cleft through which the river cascades by the roadside. This spectacle lies 2m W of Inverey on the edge of the vast Mar Forest.

At the Linn the road crosses Lui Water and passes Mar Lodge, where there are ski-ing developments. The road ends near the Linn of Quoich, a deep wooded ravine where the Quoich Water flows down from Glen Quoich, backed by 3,924ft and 3,860ft Bheinn a' Bhuird. A very rough track has been cut almost to the top of the summit – one of the loftiest peaks in Scotland – but this is too dangerous to be used by the unskilled climber. Beyond the Linn of Dee a path leads alongside the river through wilder country towards the S Cairngorms, and then turns N into Glen Dee. From here it is known as the Lairig Ghru, the famous pass through the Cairngorms for long-distance walkers, dominated to the W by 3,797ft Beinn Bhrotain and later by the 3,303ft Devil's Point. The river is spanned by the White Bridge where the path diverges into Glen Dee, and a little to the E of the bridge is a rock cataract and pool known as the Chest of Dee.

Nearer Inverey another path leads through Glen Lui and Glen Derry into the Cairngorms, under the slopes of 3,788ft Derry Cairngorm. Farther N 3,883ft Beinn Mheadoin overlooks remote Loch Avon. This path is the Lairig an Laoigh Pass, allowing access for hardy walkers travelling to Nethybridge on the edge of the Forest of Abernethy. Another pass leads W from Glen Lui, through Glen Lu Beg to Glen Dee and the Lairig Ghru.

INVERFARIGAIG, Highland   34 NH52

Situated on the E side of Loch Ness, Inverfarigaig has a steamer pier and lies amid beautiful woodland. The picturesque Pass of Inverfarigaig leads E towards Errogie on Loch Mhor. The original 18th-c Wade road includes a section at the foot of the pass near Loch Ness which had to be blasted by miners.

INVERGARRY, Highland   33 NH30

Here, on the W side of Loch Oich, is the start of one of the Roads to the Isles. This runs through magnificent W Highland glens and mountains by way of Cluanie and Glen Shiel, to the Kyle of Lochalsh facing the island of Skye. The River Garry flows into Loch Oich just N of ruined Invergarry Castle. Prince Charles Edward stayed here before and after Culloden, and the castle later suffered the vengeance of the Duke of Cumberland – who had the building burned when in pursuit of the prince. The castle was the seat of the Macdonells of Glengarry, many of whose descendants emigrated to Canada in 1803 to found a new Glengarry. To the W of Invergarry the Road to the Isles climbs through the richly-wooded Glen Garry on the first stage of its journey. After a few miles it follows the lovely tree-lined shores of Loch Garry, with Ben Tee rising to 2,956ft across the loch. A hydro-electric scheme operates in this district.

INVERGORDON, Highland   34 NH76

Invergordon was formerly a naval base and has a fine harbour on the Inner Cromarty Firth, facing Udale Bay and Cromarty Bay on the Black Isle. A large aluminium smelter has been established here, and there are a number of North-Sea oil developments. Views to the E take an expanse from the Bay of Nigg to Cromarty, guarded by the twin Sutors of Cromarty.

INVERGOWRIE, Tayside   31 NO33

St Boniface landed here cAD715, and an interesting ancient sculptured stone is set in the church wall. Invergowrie House dates from the 16th to 19thc.

INVERIE, Highland   32 NG70

Remote little Inverie can only be reached by motor launch from Mallaig. It lies on Inverie Bay in the Knoydart district. The bay is an inlet of Outer Loch Nevis, set amid a wonderful landscape of mountain and loch. A bridle path leads NE from Inverie through Glen Dulochan, overshadowed by 2,612ft Sgurr Coire na Coinnich and the great 3,343ft Ladhar Bheinn. Climbing to nearly 1,000ft at its summit, the path later descends into Glen Barrisdale and continues to Barrisdale Bay on the lovely shores of Loch Hourn. The 3,053ft bulk of Luinne Bheinn lies to the S.

INVERINATE, Highland   33 NG92

Sgurr an Airgid rises to 2,757ft and dominates this village, which is situated on the lovely shores of Loch Duich. The little church and manse of Kintail lie by the lochside 1½m SE, and Carr Brae or Keppoch Hill lies on the road to Dornie 2m NW. The hill affords magnificent views over Loch Duich towards the Mam Rattachan Pass. The view to the SE includes the splendid Five Sisters on Kintail and 3,505ft Scour Ouran.

INVERKEILOR, Tayside   31 NO64

Inverkeilor Church contains the 17th-c Northesk pew, and E of the village is Lunan Bay with its remarkable singing sands. The bay stretches from Boddin Point – with its curious Rock of St Skeagh – to Lang Craig. Red Head lies S of Lang Craig and is mentioned in Scott's *The Antiquary*. On the coast NE of Inverkeilor are the remains of Red Castle, which was burned and sacked in 1579 by Lord Gray's son. He was subsequently declared an outlaw. Ethie

Castle is of 15th-c and later date, and stands 3m SE of the village.

INVERKEITHING, Fife   46 NT18

A 16th-c Mercat cross with carved armorial bearings and topped by a unicorn of 1688 stands in this Royal Burgh. The town is situated on the Firth of Forth and is a centre for shipbreaking. Its interesting old buildings include the Old Town House of 1770, with its outside staircase, and the 15th-c Greyfriars Hospital, which now serves as a museum. The tower is the only remaining 15th-c structure of the church, though an old fort has been preserved. Cromwell defeated a Royalist army led by Maclean of Duart to the N of Inverkeithing in 1651. A private railway on the estate of 16th-c Fordell Castle, 2m N of the town, once carried coal to the coast.

INVERKIP, Strathclyde   44 NS27

Moorland lies to the SE of Inverkip, which is situated a little inland from the sandy coast of the Firth of Clyde. A marina and a power station have recently been developed in the area. Ardgowan House dates from 1798, and stands near 15th-c Inverkip Castle in a park facing Lunderston Bay. Greenock's large reservoirs lie on high ground to the E. The white Cloch lighthouse can be seen 2½m N along the Gourock road at Cloch Point.

INVERKIRKAIG, Highland   36 NC01

The border between the one-time counties of Sutherland and Ross and Cromarty is formed by the River Kirkaig as it flows into Loch Kirkaig near Inverkirkaig. Picturesque waterfalls can be seen near by. The source of this stream is in Fionn Loch, which lies to the SE and is dominated by 2,399ft Suilven. This is one of the strange, isolated Torridon-sandstone peaks of old Sutherland. A picturesque but narrow road known affectionately as the mad little road of Sutherland, leads from Lochinver by way of Inverkirkaig. It follows a tortuous, hilly course along the island-studded shores of Enard Bay, and later turns inland towards Loch Sionascaig past many rocky lochans. The views are magnificent, but the driving is hazardous.

INVERMORISTON, Highland   33 NH41

A small town at the E end of the long Glen Moriston, Invermoriston is bordered to the N by the hills of Invermoriston Forest and faces Loch Ness near the confluence of the loch and River Moriston. Prominent, 2,284ft Mealfuarvonie, rises above Loch Ness 5m NE. The road W from Invermoriston passes through the glen and is the start of the through-road from Loch Ness to the NW coast. To begin with the glen – which has hydro-electric developments – is thickly wooded, but later the road climbs on to bleak moorland and is joined by the remains of the old military road which runs from Fort Augustus and over the mountains through Inchnacardoch Forest. Dr Johnson and Boswell used this route from Invermoriston in 1773 during their tour of the Highlands and Islands.

The River Doe joins the Moriston 13m W of the town, at the head of the glen. A few miles up Doe Glen is Corridoe Cove, where Prince Charles hid in the '45 Rising when he was guarded by the 'eight men of Glenmoriston'. A cairn marks the place where Roderick Mackenzie, one of the Prince's bodyguards, was killed by English troops in 1746. Mackenzie bore a striking resemblance to the prince, and as he lay dying he said, 'You have murdered your prince'. Tempted by the £30,000 ransom on the prince's head, the soldiers believed Mackenzie and their mistake was not discovered until the prince had made good his escape.

*INVERNESS, Highland   34 NH64

Inverness, an attractive and historic town on the River Ness at the NE end of Glen More and the Caledonian Canal, has been dubbed the Capital of the Highlands. The narrows, guarded to the N by Craigton Point, are the meeting place of Beauly Firth and the Inner Moray Firth. Inverness has associations with Shakespeare's *Macbeth*.

Between 1652 and 1657 Cromwell erected The Sconce Fort on the right bank of the Ness, but only the Clock Tower remains. Wade built his Fort George barracks on the site of an old castle, which had surrendered to Mary Queen of Scots in 1562. King David built the first stone castle in Inverness *c*1141. Fort George was blown up by Prince Charles Edward in 1746, and a new Fort George was built to the NE. Inverness was the terminal point of Wade's great military roads from Dunkeld and Fort William. Abertarff House (NTS) dates from the 16thc and contains an ancient spiral staircase; the house is now the headquarters of An Comunn Gaidhealach, the Highland Association which preserves Gaelic language and culture. The High Church is mainly 18thc, with a little surviving late 13th-c work.

Dunbar's Hospital dates from 1668, and the Tolbooth Steeple was built in 1791. The gothic-style Town House, built between 1878 and 1882, was the scene of the first Cabinet meeting ever to be held outside London. This meeting was called in 1921 by Lloyd George, then holidaying in Scotland, to deal with a letter he had received from Eamon de Valera.

In front of the Town House is the Mercat cross, incorporating the Clach-na-Cudainn or stone of tubs, on which women rested their tubs on their way from the river. St Andrew's Cathedral dates from 1866 and 1871 and displays fine carved pillars. Other interesting buildings in Inverness include the modern castle, and the library, museum, and art gallery. A monument to Flora Macdonald

1   Abertarff House
2   Aldourie Castle
3   Castle and Flora Macdonald Memorial
4   Castle Stewart
5   Clock Tower
6   Craig Phadraig
7   Dunbar's Hospital
8   High Church
9   Library, Museum, and Art Gallery
10   St Andrew's Cathedral
11   Tolbooth Steeple
12   Town House and Mercat Cross

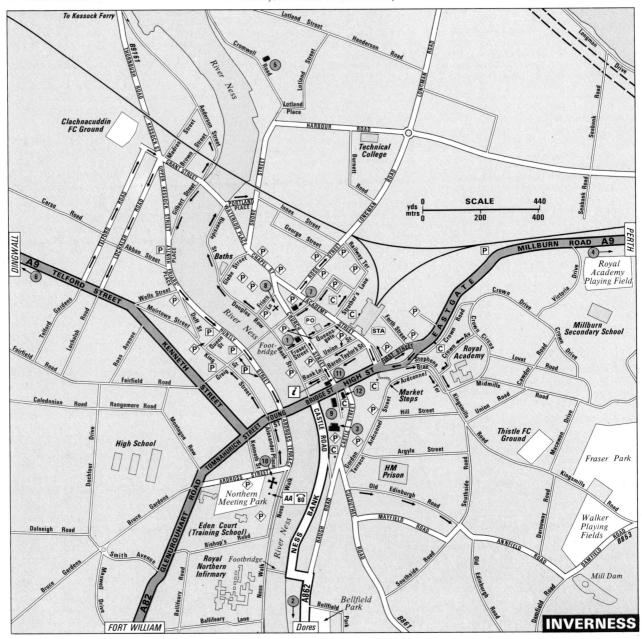

Entries marked * are the starting point of drives included in the Day Drive section of the book (pages 95 to 160).

stands on a terrace to the S of the castle. The Northern Piping Competition takes place every September in Inverness.

Castle Hill affords fine views of highland country, and just N of Inverness the hill of Craig Phadraig is crowned by a vitrified fort. It was here that the Pictish King Brude is believed to have been visited by St Columba in AD565. Restored Castle Stewart, built by the 3rd Earl of Moray in 1625, can be seen on the road to Fort George 6m NE of Inverness. The building, which is near Dalcross airport, is considered a good example of the Scottish baronial style. Aldourie Castle lies 7m SW of Inverness near the N tip of Loch Ness. Built in 1626 by MacIntosh, this has been a seat of the Frasers since 1750. Good views are afforded by Tomnahurich Hill, which rises W of the town. The great bulk of 3,429ft Ben Wyvis dominates the NW.

INVERORAN, Strathclyde *29 NN24*
Duncan Ban MacIntyre – the famous bard – was born near Inveroran in 1724, and his monument stands at Dalmally. Inveroran lies at the W end of Loch Tulla, on the line of the old Glencoe road and at the foot of the Black Mount. The village faces 3,565ft Stob Ghabhar.

INVERSANDA, Highland *29 NM95*
Situated on the picturesque road through the Ardgour country, Inversanda faces Inversanda Bay on Loch Linnhe. Near by is the E end of Glen Tarbert, which contains a road leading round the head and S side of Loch Sunart to Lochaline on the Sound of Mull. Lochaline can also be reached from Inversanda along the shores of Loch Linnhe, by way of Camasnacroise. The wild Coir an Iubhair heads N from Glen Tarbert, 1m W of Inversanda, and leads to the wonderful rock scenery of 2,903ft Garbh Bheinn. The latter is Ardgour's finest peak, and one which is well-known to climbers.

INVERSHIN, Highland *37 NH59*
Invershin is where the River Shin meets the Kyle of Sutherland. A nearby hillock is surmounted by the modern Carbisdale Castle, which now serves as a youth hostel. Montrose fought his last battle near here in 1650, after which he fled to Ardvreck Castle, near Inchnadamph, where he was betrayed.

INVERSNAID, Central *29 NN30*
Splendid mountains, including 3,318ft Ben Ime, 3,004ft Ben Vane, and 3,092ft Ben Vorlich face Inversnaid across Loch Lomond. A fort was built to repress the Macgregors here in 1713, and was at one time under the command of General Wolfe – of Quebec fame. Inversnaid has a steamer pier, and the road from Aberfoyle ends here.

A path N along the lochside leads to Rob Roy's Cave, which has been described by Dorothy Wordsworth. Robert the Bruce is said to have sheltered here in 1306. A little to the E of Inversnaid the Arklet Falls can be seen on the Arklet Water, which flows from a loch of the same name. Arklet Falls are associated with Wordsworth's *Highland Girl*. The 1,762ft Cruachan lies SE and affords good views. The power station at Inveruglas, on the W shore of Loch Lomond, forms part of the Loch Sloy hydro-electric scheme.

INVERUGLAS, Strathclyde *29 NN30*
This is the site of the Loch Sloy hydro-electric scheme power station, situated on the W shores of Loch Lomond. Loch Sloy itself lies away to the NW beyond Glen Sloy, and is overlooked by 3,004ft Ben Vane to the S and 3,092ft Ben Vorlich to the N. This is MacFarlane country, and the clan's ancient rallying cry was 'Loch Sloy'.

INVERURIE, Grampian *35 NJ72*
Inverurie is situated in the Garioch district near the meeting of the waters of the Don and the Urie. It is a Royal Burgh which contains many interesting features. The Bass is a 50ft-high natural mound which was probably once the site of an ancient stronghold. Mary Queen of Scots was a visitor here in 1562.

Several ancient carved stones lie in the vicinity, and the churchyard contains an inscribed Pictish Stone. About ½m NW of the town is the Brandsbutt Stone (AM), which bears Pictish symbols and an Ogham inscription. East Aquhorthies Stone Circle lies 2½m W. The Maiden Stone (AM) is an early Christian monument carved with a Celtic cross and Pictish symbols, lying 4½m NW of Inverurie. Bourtie House stands 2m NE of the town and dates from 1754. Kieth Hall stands near the town on the E bank of the Urie. Close to the Don some 2m S is ruined Kinkell Church (AM), rebuilt in 1528 and preserving a rare sacrament house. To the W of Inverurie is the prominent 1,698ft Mither Tap of Bennachie.

IONA, ISLE OF, Strathclyde *28 NM22*
St Columba came from Ireland to this little Inner Hebridean island in AD563, to found a monastery and to convert Scotland to Christianity. Iona, once known as Icolmkill, is only 3m long and 1½m wide. It is separated from Fionphort, near Bunessan in the SW tip of Mull, by the narrow Sound of Iona. A passenger ferry operates from Fionphort. St Columba died in AD597 and his remains were later taken back to Ireland. Iona became a place of pilgrimage, and many early kings and chiefs were buried here up to 1040.

The monastery suffered great damage from repeated attacks by the Norsemen who overran the Outer Hebrides in the 11thc, but in 1203 the Benedictines founded a new monastery. This was destroyed in 1561, and the remains of a nunnery built in the same year can be seen near the landing place. The chapel adjoining the nave houses the tomb of Iona's last prioress, who died in 1543. Richly-carved McLean's Cross (AM) probably dates from the 15thc, and stands on a road parallel to the ancient Road of the Dead – leading to St Oran's Cemetery, considered the oldest Christian burial ground in Scotland. King Duncan, said to have been murdered by Macbeth in 1040, was the last of the 48 Scottish kings to be buried here.

Among the many carved Celtic slabs are several of old clan chiefs, bearing the designs of their galleys. In 1932 the ashes of Margaret Kennedy-Fraser, the transcriber of Gaelic songs, were buried here. Iona's oldest surviving building is the restored, Romanesque St Oran's Chapel, which is said to have been built by the saintly Queen Margaret in 1080. A carved Norman doorway leads into the restored building.

The cathedral was founded in the 13thc, though the present building is more recent and dates from the 15thc. The original design of the building has been greatly changed over the years. It is cruciform in shape and carries a low tower; the pier capitals inside are carved with birds, animals and flowers. Many interesting tombs have survived, and the so-called St Columba's pillow is preserved below the E window. Fragments of a 13th-c monastery adjoining the cathedral are in the process of restoration, and include the chapter house, refectory, undercroft, and cloister.

Facing the cathedral is the granite Great Cross of Iona, or St Martin's Cross. This 9th- or 10th-c relic is over 16ft high and shows elaborate Runic carving. Near by is 9th-c Celtic St John's Cross. St Columba is thought to have landed at Port na Curaich, on the S end of Iona. A spouting cave lies on the W coast, and fine views over beautiful sands are afforded by Dun I, in the N part of the island. Iona is covered with wild flowers, and a profusion of sea-shells can be found on its shores. Dr Johnson, who came to the island in 1773, described it as 'that luminary of the Caledonian regions'.

IRONGRAY, Dumfries and Galloway *25 NX97*
A stone in Irongray churchyard was erected by Scott in memory of Helen Walker, said to be the original of his Jeannie Deans character portrayed in *Heart of Midlothian*. The community lies in the pleasant valley of the Cluden Water. A knoll ¼m W is surmounted by a Covenanter's inscribed tomb of 1685, and a little N from here across the river is 16th-c Fourmerkland tower. Skeogh Hill lies some 4m W beyond Cairn Water, by way of Routin Bridge. An obelisk on the SE slopes of this hill marks the communion stones where John Welsh, a local minister and great-grandson of John Knox, gave the Sacrament to 3,000 Covenanters in 1678.

IRVINE, Strathclyde *24 NS33*
Robert Burns lived at Irvine between 1781 and 1783, and a plaque on a cottage in Glasgow Vennel records his sojourn as a flax-dresser. The Burns Club was established in 1826 and is now a museum, and a statue of the poet stands on the Town Moor.

Irvine is a Royal Burgh, manufacturing town, and port situated at the confluence of the River Irvine and the Annick Water. The combined waters of the two rivers flow into the sea by the estuary of the Garnock. Another literary figure associated with the town is John Galt, who was born here in 1779. The Academy was founded in 1572 from the revenues of an ancient monastery which once stood here. Ruins are all that is left of 14th-c Seagate Castle, which Mary Queen of Scots visited in 1563. In 1297 the Treaty of Irvine was signed in an earlier structure. The Buchanite Sect was founded in the Relief Church in 1783.

The town's exotic, 120ft-high Tower House faces the old Mercat cross. Marymass Week is held in the town every summer, and includes a Riding of the Marches. The Ardeer explosives factory stands on sandy dunes just NW of Irvine, on a site chosen in 1873 by Alfred Nobel, the Swedish chemist who first produced dynamite and founded the Nobel Prize. Today the factory is one of Britain's main centres for the production of explosives. Irvine and Kilwinning, a smaller town 4m NW, are being combined to form a New Town.

ISLAY, ISLE OF, Strathclyde   28 NR26

The island of Islay is the farthest S of the Inner Hebrides, and lies off the W coast of Kintyre. It is separated from the hillier island of Jura by the narrow Sound of Islay. The island is 25m long and some 20m wide, and offers fine beaches with the added benefit of a warm climate. Steamers call at Port Ellen and Port Askaig from West Loch Tarbert and Kennacraig respectively, and regular flights arrive at Glenegedale airport from Glasgow Airport.

Fishing and agriculture are important to Islay's economy, and the local whisky distilleries are world famous. The island is not actually encircled by a road, but some of the coastal villages are connected by well-surfaced highways. Some of the other roads, which help to make up the islands total of 75 motoring miles, are rough and narrow. Several sculptured stones and Celtic crosses can be seen on Islay; the most finely carved examples of the last-mentioned are at Kildalton and Kilchoman. Lofty cliffs of the Mull of Oa peninsula, SE of Islay beyond Laggan

Bay, can be reached by the road from Port Ellen. Hills to the NE of Port Ellen rise to over 1,500ft. Lochs Indaal and Gruinart lie on the W side of the island and are separated by a narrow neck of land; the lovely coastal district to the SW is known as the Rhinns of Islay.

ISLE OF WHITHORN, Dumfries and Galloway   25 NX43

This small mainland port is a centre for sea angling and dinghy sailing, situated on rocky shores sheltered by Isle Head. St Ninian, the son of a local chieftain, landed here in AD395 on his return from studying in Rome; his mission was to bring Christianity to Scotland. The ruins of a plain 13th-c chapel (AM) can be seen, but there are no signs of an earlier church which is thought to have stood here. Remains of an iron-age fort and the late 17th-c Isle Tower can be seen on the point of the promontory. There is a large caravan site to the SW at Barrow Head. Views from the head extend as far as the coast of Northern Ireland and the Lake District.

St Ninian's Cave (AM) lies 4m W of the Isle of Whithorn on the shores of Port Castle Bay, and can be reached by a

moorland track from the Port William road, near Glasserton. The cave was probably used by the saint as a retreat. Sculptured stones and crosses carved on the walls may have been the work of his followers. The 17th-c house of Tonderghie lies to the E.

ISLE ORNSAY, Isle of Skye, Highland   32 NG61

Once the centre of a thriving fishing industry, Isle Ornsay is situated in the fertile peninsula of Sleat, overlooking a sheltered anchorage which is popular with yachtsmen. Facing the village is an island in the Sound of Sleat, with a lighthouse and the remains of a small nunnery. Some 2m SW off the Armadale road is a rough and hilly by-road which runs NW to Ord on Loch Eishort, where there are fine views over Skye.

Farther along the road is Tokavaig, where the ruins of Skye's most ancient castle, Dunscaith, stand on a rock. Dunscaith Castle was the home of the Macdonalds of Sleat before they moved to Duntulm. It is said that Scathach – female warrior and queen – reigned at Dunscaith, the name of the castle means 'the fortress of Scathach'; she is said to have taught the arts of war to warriors from all parts of Scotland and Ireland.

JEDBURGH, Borders   26 NT62

Jedburgh Abbey (AM) is considered to be the most impressive of the four great Border abbeys. It lies in the lovely valley of the Jed Water, which flows N to join the Teviot beyond Bonjedward, and was founded c1118 by David I. French monks from Beauvais colonized the foundation. The buildings were repeatedly damaged by English invaders during the Middle Ages, and in 1523 the Earl of Surrey ordered it to be burned.

Even roofless and in ruins the abbey is magnificent. Its red sandstone remains include a splendid nave with beautiful detail-work dating from the transitional period, and the west front displays a fine rose window known as St Catherine's Wheel. The richly-carved Norman doorway is of interest, and many fascinating monuments are preserved in the fine 14th-c north transept. The Norman tower has been greatly restored, and the choir has been largely rebuilt.

Jedburgh town is a fine centre for riding, walking, and climbing in the surrounding hills and moorland. Its original name Geddewrd has been corrupted to various forms over the ages, including Jeddart and Jethart. Prince Charles Edward stayed in the town in 1745, and Burns once lodged in a house, now demolished, in Canongate. Other famous visitors included Wordsworth and his sister, who were guests at a house in Abbey Close, off The Bow. Sir David Brewster, founder of the British Association, was a native of Jedburgh and a tablet marks the house in Canongate where he was born.

Many of this attractive town's old houses have typical crow-stepped gables. Queen Mary's House, where Mary Queen of Scots lay ill in 1566 after riding to visit

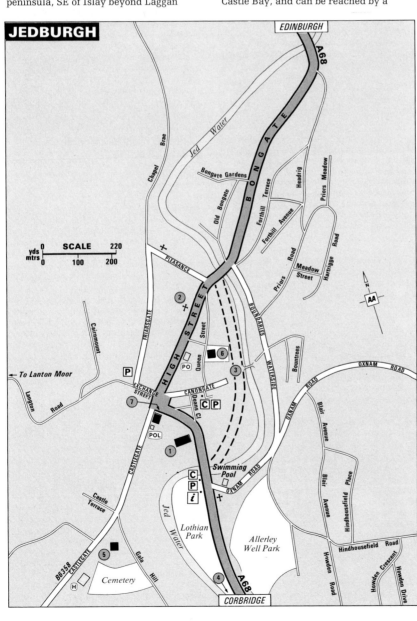

1 Abbey
2 Blackfriars Church
3 Canongate Bridge
4 Capon Tree
5 Castle
6 Queen Mary's House (museum)
7 New Gate

Bothwell at Hermitage Castle, is now a museum containing the queen's death mask, thimble-case, and watch among other relics. Blackfriars Church was built in 1746 and greatly altered in 1818. An ornate iron lantern is set in the portico. A tall steeple tops New Gate, which carries the dates 1720, 1755, and 1761 and gives access to the abbey precincts; near by an interesting 16th-c three-arched bridge can be seen off Canongate.

Jedburgh's ancient castle was once a residence of Scottish kings and dated from the 12thc, but this has now vanished. It had a turbulent history and fell into English hands many times. Finally, the Scottish parliament ordered it to be destroyed in 1409 because it was proving of more use to the English. The site of the fortification, at the top of Castlegate, is now occupied by a modern castle which was built as the county prison in 1823. It now houses the only gaol museum in the country, where display rooms show the 'reformed' system of the early 19thc.

Every Shrove Tuesday the Uppies – those born above the Mercat cross – and the Downies – those born below it, play handball through the streets of Jedburgh – a custom known as Candlemas Ba', dating from medieval times. The Callants' Festival is held here every summer. About 1m S of Jedburgh, to the right of the A68 and near the river, is the 'Capon Tree'. This is said to be the last survivor of the ancient Forest of Jethart, which once covered the whole region. To the SW of the town are 1,095ft Dunian Hill and 1,110ft Black Law, both of which offer wide views of the surrounding countryside. Ancient earthworks and the ruined 17th-c tower of Timpendean lie 1½m NW on Lanton Moor.

JERICHO, Tayside *31 NO44*
This oddly-named hamlet lies just S of the main Glamis to Forfar road. Several handloom weavers' cottages can be seen here.

JOHN O' GROATS, Highland *37 ND37*
John o' Groats lies near the extreme NE tip of the Scottish mainland and overlooks the stormy waters of the Pentland First. Stroma Island lies off-shore beyond the Inner Sound. The village is 873m distant from Land's End in Cornwall by road, and 280m from Kirkmaiden – Scotland's farthest S parish. Kirkmaiden is associated with Burns' *Frae Maidenkirk to Johnny Groats.*

The village is named after a Dutchman, Jan de Groot, who came to Scotland with his two brothers c1500. As time went by the family increased until there were eight families, and a precedency could not be agreed. As a solution Jan built his famous octagonal house, with a door in each side and an octagonal table inside. This gave precedence to nobody and the dispute was settled. The house itself has since vanished, but a mound and flagstaff mark its site. Views N take in S Ronaldsay and the cliffs of Hoy in the Orkneys. Small shells called Groatie Buckies can be found on the beach near by.

Farther E the impressive viewpoint of Duncansby Head, the *Vervedrum* of Ptolemy, features a lighthouse. To the S are the three curious stacks of Duncansby and a fine range of sandstone cliffs which extend towards distant Skirsa

Head. Deep gashes called geos split the cliffs in places. The Pentland Skerries islands lie to the NE of the Head.

JOHNSHAVEN, Grampian *35 NO76*
Situated on a rocky and picturesque stretch of coast, the fishing village of Johnshaven lies just off the Montrose to Stonehaven road.

JOHNSTONE BRIDGE, Dumfries and Galloway *25 NY09*
This picturesque bridge spans the River Annan, which flows S through the delightful Annandale valley, rich in memories of historic Border struggles. The local church dates from 1733.

JURA, ISLE OF, Strathclyde *28 NR57*
Picturesque Jura is one of the Inner Hebridean islands, separated from Knapdale on the mainland by the Sound of Jura and from the island of Islay by the Sound of Islay. This rugged, mountainous little island thrusts from the sea and dominates the skyline with the triple-peaked Paps of Jura. These all attain a height of about 2,500ft, and are notable landmarks from the mainland. A passenger ferry from Feolin Ferry on the Sound of Islay links up with Port Askaig on Islay, and there is a pier at Craighouse.

Measuring some 28m long and 8m across, Jura is not widely visited due mainly to its lack of accommodation. The island's only road runs for 24m, from Feolin Ferry and along the E shoreline to Ardlussa. The sea loch of Tarbert almost divides the island in two, and the strait of Corryvreckan separates the N coast of Jura from Scarba. This contains a treacherous whirlpool which can be heard from afar and is officially classed as unnavigable by the navy.

KAMES, Strathclyde *29 NR97*
Kames is a small Cowal resort on the Kyles of Bute. Millhouse village lies 1½m SW, and from here a road leads NW to Kilfinan. A branch road runs SW to the shores of Loch Fyne, from which the wooded Glenan Bay can be reached on foot. To the W of Kames is a by-road which leads S. It extends almost to Ardlamont Point, which affords views to the island of Bute and to the N tip of Arran across the Sound of Bute.

KEIG, Grampian *35 NJ61*
To the E of Keig, near My Lord's Throat Pass and a winding stretch of the Don, is modern Forbes Castle. Cairn William rises to 1,469ft in the SE.

KEILLS, Strathclyde *28 NR68*
Ruins of a chapel which include a fine Celtic cross can be seen at Keills, which lies between the Sound of Jura and the S reaches of Loch Sween. To the S is Loch na Cille.

KEISS, Highland *37 ND36*
This little fishing village is sited on Sinclair's Bay. Remains of the old Keiss Castle lie near a modern castle on the coast to the N. Beyond here and to the left of the road is a Baptist chapel in memory of Sir William Sinclair, founder of the country's first Baptist church. The main road S towards Wick crosses the Keiss Links, with Loch of Wester lying to the W.

KEITH, Grampian *35 NJ46*
Keith was once famous for its fair and is an agricultural centre in Strath Isla. The Auld Brig o' Keith dates from 1609 and

joins Keith with Fife Keith across the River Isla. This is one of two old bridges, the other dating from 1770. Ruined Milton Tower was once the home of the Oliphant family. Milton Distillery is Scotland's oldest working malt-whisky distillery and was founded in 1785. A fine altarpiece decorates the RC church, and lovely views can be enjoyed from 1,199ft Balloch Hill. The latter rises SE of the town.

*KELSO, Borders *26 NT73*
Plan overleaf
Scott described Kelso as 'the most beautiful, if not the most romantic, village in Scotland'. The town stands on the Tweed, and its abbey (AM) was once the largest and perhaps the finest of the great Border abbeys. Only a small part of this has survived. It was founded by David I in 1128, and when the Earl of Hertford entered Kelso in 1545 the abbey was garrisoned as a fortress, taken only at the point of the sword. The garrison of 100 men, including 12 monks, were slaughtered and the building almost totally destroyed. All that remains are the west façade and transepts, part of the tower, and two of the nave bays showing some fine Norman and early-gothic detail – notably on the north transept.

Kelso's wide, cobbled square includes the Town House of 1816. The town has many historical associations, including visits from Mary Queen of Scots, and Prince Charles Edward. Scott lived here for some months in 1783 and attended the grammar school, which was then held in the aisle of the abbey. The brothers Ballantyne, who later printed and published Scott's works, went to the same school. The first edition of *Minstrelsy of the Scottish Border* was printed in here.

John Rennie built the fine five-arched bridge across the Tweed in 1803 to replace one destroyed by floods in 1797. The bridge is virtually a model for the Old Waterloo Bridge in London, which Rennie built in 1811. Two lamp-posts taken from Old Waterloo Bridge during its demolition in 1934 have been re-erected on the Kelso Bridge. Floors Castle is a vast mansion built by Vanbrugh in 1718 and altered by Playfair c1849; the best views of this are afforded by the bridge. The Turret House (NTS) is of interest, and the Wooden House dates from the early 19thc.

Kelso is an excellent touring centre for the Cheviot Hills, and just outside the town the Tweed is joined by the Teviot. At this point the waters are spanned by the Teviot Bridge, perhaps remodelled on Rennie's bridge in Kelso. William and Robert Adam designed the lovely old Mellerstain House, a mansion which lies 6m NW of the town.

KEMNAY, Grampian *35 NJ71*
Granite from the quarries at Kemnay was used to build the Forth Bridge and London's Thames Embankment. Some 3m SSW off the Monymusk road is the turreted Castle Fraser, dating from 1454 to 1618 and a very fine example of the Scottish baronial style. Fetternear House, once the country seat of the Bishops of Aberdeen, lies W of Kemnay beyond the tree-shrouded curves of the Don.

KENMORE, Tayside *30 NN74*
The little resort of Kenmore lies amid

Entries marked * are the starting point of drives included in the Day Drive section of the book (pages 95 to 160).

hills at the E end of the salmon Loch Tay. Wooded Drummond Hill rises to the N in front of the River Lyon, which flows E from its long and beautiful glen. The town is sited on the River Tay, which flows NE from the loch to join the River Lyon NE of the village. Burns admired the view from the bridge over the Tay and set it to verse – a fact which is recorded in the parlour of the hotel, first licensed over 400 years ago. William and Dorothy Wordsworth were also visitors to Kenmore.

Taymouth Castle is now a school but was once the seat of the Earls of Breadalbane. The present building dates from the early 19thc, and Queen Victoria and Prince Albert visited the castle in 1842. Stone circles at Croftmoraig, 2m E of Kenmore, comprise one of the largest groups of prehistoric stones in the country. A very steep (1 in 4) and narrow road winds S over hill country and reaches a summit of 1,672ft. It passes Loch Freuchie in Glen Quaich on its way to Amulree. Roads run W along the N and S banks of 14m-long Loch Tay.

The best mountain views in the area are from the S road, extending N across the loch to 3,984ft Ben Lawers (NTS). This is the highest peak in the county once known as Perthshire, and is noted for the wide range of Alpine plants which grow on its lower slopes. A small island with ruins of a priory which was built in 1122 rises from the loch near Kenmore, and 1½m S of the town on the S bank of the loch are the falls of Acharn.

KENNACRAIG, Strathclyde   28 NR86
A car ferry leaves here for Port Askaig on the island of Islay.

KENNETHMONT, Grampian   35 NJ52
The full name of this hamlet is Kirkhill of Kennethmont. A little to the N lies Leith Hall (NTS), which for three centuries was home of the Leith and Leith-Hay family. The earliest surviving portion of the building dates from 1650 and is incorporated into the north wing. The hall was extended in the 18th and 19thc. The Exhibition Room contains a writing case which was presented to the family by Prince Charles Edward on the eve of

Culloden in 1746. A rock garden is an attractive feature of the grounds.

KENTALLEN, Highland   29 NN05
Kentallen is backed by the great horseshoe curve of 3,362ft Ben Vair and stands on Kentallen Bay, an inlet of Loch Linnhe. From the summit of Ben Vair the magnificent view encompasses the Glencoe mountains, with 3,766ft Bidean nam Bian dominant. More fine views extend over Loch Linnhe to the Ardgour mountains from the Ballachulish road, NE of Kentallen. The wooded, roadless Glen Duror lies S of the village.

KILBARCHAN, Strathclyde   44 NS46
An 18th-c weaver's cottage (NTS) is preserved here and a fountain has been erected in memory of Robert Allan, a local weaver poet (see inset opposite). A building now used as an old folk's hall bears the statue of Habbie Simpson, a 17th-c local piper.

KILBIRNIE, Strathclyde   44 NS35
Kilbirnie Loch lies to the E of this town, which stands on the River Garnock. An old carved pulpit and the grandiose Garnock gallery of the Crawford family are features of the 17th-c church. Ruins of several fine old buildings can be seen near Kilbirnie, including Kilbirnie Place which lies to the W and was burned in the 18thc. The remains of Ladyland and Glengarnock Castle are also of interest.

KILCHATTAN BAY, Isle of Bute, Strathclyde   44 NS15
Facing the two Cumbrae Islands across the Firth of Clyde, Kilchattan Bay is a quiet resort with a sandy beach and a pier. Some 4m N on the coast is the palatial Mount Stuart mansion, a modern structure and a seat of the Marquis of Bute. Beyond the mansion is the model village of Kerrycroy. Garroch Head lies to the S of Kilchattan Bay and faces towards the island of Arran. A road runs NW from the resort to Kingarth, beyond which are the standing stones of Lubas. From Kingarth itself a narrow road runs S; at a point 3m SW of the resort are the ruined 19th-c Chapel of St Blane and the foundations of a monastery founded by St Blane in the 6thc. Near by on sandy Dunagoil Bay is a vitrified fort. The road from Kilchattan continues NW from Kingarth to the sandy bays of Scalpsie and St Ninian's, the latter facing the island of Inch Marnoch.

KILCHOAN, Highland   32 NM46
This remote village lies on the rocky, picturesque Ardnamurchan coast. Its pier is known as Mingary and is the starting point of a passenger ferry to Tobermory on the island of Mull. The pier lies on a by-road about 1m SE of the village, facing E across the water to the impressive ruins of Mingary Castle, where James IV held his court in 1495. Ancient home of the MacIains, a branch of the Clan Macdonald, Mingary Castle dates from the 13thc and includes inner buildings of 15th-c origin. It was taken for Montrose in 1644, and described by Scott in his *Lord of the Isles*. Beyond the castle rises 1,729ft Ben Hiant which affords fine views E towards Loch Sunart.

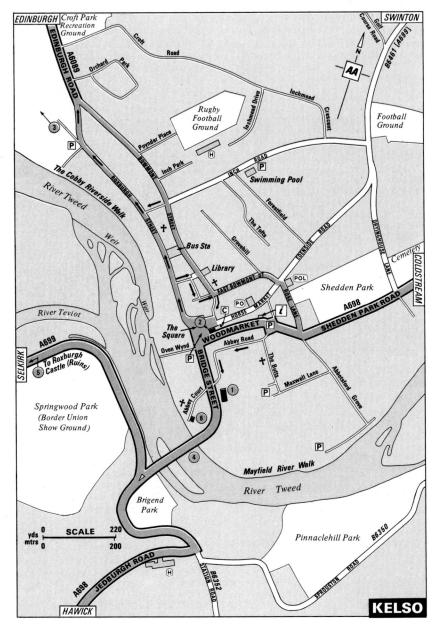

1   Abbey
2   Town House
3   Floors Castle
4   Kelso Bridge
5   Teviot Bridge
6   Turret House

KELSO

Kilmory Bay's silver sands lie 6m NE of Kilchoan and can be reached via a by-road and a short walk. The by-road leaves the road to Salen. Ockle Point lies E of the bay. To the NW of Kilchoan and its bay, a rough road from the B8007 gives access to the farthest W point of the Scottish mainland at Ardnamurchan Point, with its lonely lighthouse. Some 2m from Kilchoan and to the W of this road, the low hill of 1,123ft Beinn na Seilg affords beautiful panoramic views from its rocky summit. A stone circle stands on its E slopes.

KILCHOMAN, Isle of Islay, Strathclyde 28 NR26

A finely-carved Celtic cross stands to the S of the road by the church, and remains of an ancient Macdonald fortress lie to the NE of Kilchoman near Loch Gorm. Good sands can be found at Saligo Bay, which is reached via a narrow road leading N. Machir Bay lies W in the Rhinns of Islay and also offers fine beaches. Several ancient standing stones dot the area, and near Machir Bay are the graves of some of the American sailors lost when the 'Otranto' was wrecked on this rocky coast in 1918.

FABRICS FOR THE WORLD

Kilbarchan is a place apart. In the days of the Scottish cotton boom, its villagers spurned the mills and factories which sprang up in neighbouring towns, and persevered with hand-loom weaving in their own homes. A perfect evocation of two centuries of alternating success and depression is in the weaver's cottage at the Barngreen, now in the care and protection of the NTS.

The Bryden family, for whom the cottage was built in 1723, are commemorated on the carved lintel above the front door. Their house was constructed on the 'cruck' system. An A-shaped framework of timber, and not the walls, supported the original thatched roof, which has now been replaced by slates. One of the ceilings has been cut away to show the well-preserved timber. Good use was made of the sloping site, and windows were easily placed in the basement room where the hand-loom worked.

This weaver's cottage was built on the cruck system and has been restored to house a museum of the industry.

KILCHRENAN, Strathclyde 29 NN02

Kilchrenan faces Portsonachan and is situated a little N of Loch Awe. A block of granite in the churchyard commemorates Mac Cailean Mor, founder of the Argyll fortunes, who was killed in 1294. The road to Taynuilt runs N though wooded Glen Nant. To the SW, near the shores of Loch Awe, are Forestry Commission plantations and the new forestry village of Dalavich.

KILCHURN CASTLE, Strathclyde 29 NN12

Built in a lovely situation beside upper Loch Awe, romantic Kilchurn Castle (AM) stands on land that was once an island. The keep was built in 1440 by Sir Colin Campbell, who founded the Breadalbane family, and the north and south sides of the building were erected in 1693 by Ian, Earl of Breadalbane. Bredalbane's coat of arms and those of his wife hang over the gateway. The castle was occupied by the Breadalbanes until 1740, and in 1746 was used as a garrison for Hanoverian troops. The infamous gale of 1879 – which wrecked the Tay Bridge – also toppled one of the castle's towers.

There had been weavers in Kilbarchan for 40 years when the Brydens came to Barngreen, turning out cambrics and muslins. Candle-makers worked for a family called Barbour. In 1739 the Barbours branched out into linen-bleaching, for which the pure water of the village stream was well suited. Then came silks and lawns, tartans, and fine cotton fabrics, and Kilbarchan was on the way to fortune.

By 1794 there were 383 looms in the village. But the good days had temporarily come to an end, and business was 'in a languid state'. The Brydens' cottage was sold to a family called Brodie, and again to William Christie, whose descendants were to live and work their looms here for nearly 140 years.

The Rivers Orchy and Strae enter Loch Awe here, 3,689ft Ben Cruachan dominates the countryside behind the loch. A hydro-electric power station has been built inside the mountain. A bridge spanning an inner reach of the loch near the castle carries the Dalmally to Taynuilt road.

KILCONQUHAR, Fife 31 NO40

This attractive village lies by a loch of the same name. Kilconquhar House carries a 16th-c tower, and several ancient carved stones are preserved in the local churchyard.

KILCREGGAN, Strathclyde 44 NS28

Kilcreggan lies at the S end of the Rosneath peninsula, overlooking the mouth of Loch Long and the Holy Loch. Both this resort and the neighbouring village of Cove – W beyond Baron's Point – have piers. Knockderry Castle stands over the dungeons of an old tower on the road to Coulport, some 3m NW of Kilcreggan. Scott includes the castle in his *Heart of Midlothian,* where he calls it Knock Dunder.

The busy days returned. In the next 40 years Kilbarchan had more than doubled the number of its looms to 800, and the local minister could write of 'the unprecedentedly flourishing state of the industry', while reporting that a skilled worker could earn as much as ten shillings per day from the merchants who bought up the finished materials.

As the factories inexorably took over, so the number of household looms declined. In 1954 William Christie's great-great-grandchildren presented the old cottage, steeped in memories, to the NTS. It was restored with the help and enthusiasm of many local people, and opened three years later as a museum of the great days of the village weavers. By then Kilbarchan's looms were all but silent.

In the basement weaving room, however, are installed the hand-looms of two of the last of the Kilbarchan weavers. In other rooms are domestic exhibits and displays of the fine shawls and tartans which were Kilbarchan's specialities – as well as an example of the ponchos which were exported from this Lowland village to the gaucho-lands of South America.

KILDALTON, Isle of Islay, Strathclyde
28 NR44
Two finely sculptured Celtic crosses can be seen in the local churchyard, and Kildalton Estate extends towards the shores of island-studded Loch a' Chnoic. Inland and to the NW is 1,136ft Beinn Sholum, the farthest S of a long line of hills which continue towards the Sound of Islay.

KILDONAN, Isle of Arran, Strathclyde
24 NS02
Ruins of Kildonan Castle lie on a rocky stretch of coast, facing the tiny island of Pladda. A lighthouse is sited on the island. To the NE of Kildonan is Dippin Head, which is close to the Dippin Rocks – a vantage point for magnificent seascape views.

KILDONAN, Highland   37 NC92
The small village of Kildonan lies in Strath Ullie, which is threaded by the Helmsdale River – a favourite with anglers. Gold was discovered in the Kildonan Burn in 1868. Prehistoric remains which include parallel rows of stones can be found in the area, particularly NW on Leirable Hill. To the N Suisgill Lodge stands in fine gardens. Lofty moorland rises to the N and S of the valley.

KILDRUMMY, Grampian   35 NJ41
Guarded on two sides by a ravine, Kildrummy Castle (AM) stands at a height of 800ft and overlooks the valley of the upper Don. The imposing ruins of this great castle, built in the 13thc and extensively repaired, have their share of stormy Scottish history. Sir Nigel Bruce mounted a gallant defence here in 1306, and the castle was laid siege to by the son of the Wolf of Badenoch in 1404. After the 1715 Jacobite Rising the castle was dismantled.

One of its two round towers – the Snow Tower – is almost equal in size to the outstanding example at Bothwell. There are also remains of a chapel with a triple lancet window, and the lovely grounds include a Japanese water garden. Near Kildrummy Church, 1m NE of the castle and E of the main road, the remains of an ancient kirk retain a Norman wall plus a vault built in 1605 and restored in 1862. This is known as the Elphinstone aisle and contains some interesting monuments. Farther N and to the left of the Huntly road is Drumnahive Wood, in which lies Lulach's Stone – traditionally associated with the slaying of Lady Macbeth's son.

KILFINAN, Strathclyde   29 NR97
Kilfinan village stands on Loch Fyne to the E of Kilfinan Bay, with the heights of Knapdale rising beyond the farthest shore of the loch. The road S from Kilfinan passes Loch Melldalloch and continues as far as Tighnabruaich on the Kyles of Bute.

KILFINICHEN, Isle of Mull, Strathclyde
28 NM42
Kilfinichen church stands on the N shores of the sea Loch Scridain, near the fossilized McCulloch's Tree – a noted geological specimen. The remarkable Gribun cliffs can be reached by a road which runs N through Glen Seilisdeir. Mull's highest peak, 3,169ft Ben More, rises to the N of Kilfinichen and offers views to the Outer Hebrides on fine days. A by-road leads W along the shores of

Loch Scridain into the lonely and hilly peninsula of Ardmeanach. A 2,000-acre NTS farm known as Burg is situated here, and lofty cliffs rise farther W at the peninsula's tip.

KILKERRAN, Strathclyde   24 NS30
Kilkerran House has been the home of the Fergussons of Kilkerran since the 17thc. Part of the estate is now being developed for outdoor recreation, including riding, and there is a good camp site in the walled garden.

KILLEAN, Strathclyde   29 NR64
Near the modern church are remains of an earlier structure. A good double window has been preserved.

KILLEARN, Central   45 NS58
George Buchanan, the historian and scholar who became tutor to James VI, was born here in 1506 and an obelisk has been set up to his memory. Killearn lies NW of the Campsie Fells, among which 1,896ft Earl's Seat, is the highest point and 1,401ft Dumgoyne has a prominent conical summit. Killearn House dates from 1816 and stands 1½m SW. To the W and N of the village winds Endrick Water, and 2m NW is the Pot of Gartness – where the river cascades through a ravine.

KILLIECRANKIE, Tayside   34 NN96
This hamlet is best known for the bloody battle which took place 1m N at the Pass of Killiecrankie (NTS) in 1689. The battle was won for James VII (James II of England) and the Jacobite cause by Graham of Claverhouse – Viscount Dundee, the *Bonnie Dundee* of Scott's ballad. Dundee defeated General Mackay but was killed in the moment of victory. A stone marks the spot where he fell, and a steep footpath leads to Soldier's Leap, where two rocks almost bridge the gorge.

It is said that a trooper jumped across the River Garry to escape the Royalist Highlanders here. Macaulay, as well as Scott, has vividly described the battle. At the S end of the pass is Bridge of Garry, where the roads to Loch Tummel and Pitlochry diverge. The pass adjoins the Linn of Tummel (NTS). The latter can be reached by road from Pitlochry, or on foot from Bridge of Garry.

KILLIN, Central   30 NN53
Killin is an all-year-round resort which offers fishing on Loch Tay and touring the surrounding mountains in summer, and ski-ing on the Ben Lawers range in winter. The town lies at the E end of the mountain-encircled Glen Dochart and Glen Lochay. Beautiful waterfalls grace both River Dochart and River Lochay as they flow through their glens before joining to flow into Loch Tay. Near the Dochart bridge, built in 1760 and repaired in 1830, are two small islands; one of these is known as Inch Buie and was the burial ground of the Clan MacNab. At the head of the loch, just N of Killin, are the ruins of Finlaig Castle – a one-time seat of the Breadalbanes. An ancient beheading pit lies here, thought to be the sole example surviving in Scotland. Several sculptured stones have also been preserved. Scott describes Finlaig Castle in his *Fair Maid of Perth*.

To the S of the River Dochart is Kinnell House, where one of Europe's largest vines is growing. From Killin fine views

extend across Loch Tay to 3,984ft Ben Lawers (NTS), the highest mountain in the one-time county of Perthshire. Nearer to the town the Tarmachan peaks now form a national nature reserve. The road through Glen Dochart branches S 2½m SW of Killin, at the entrance to gloomy Glen Ogle. It climbs to nearly 1,000ft on the way to Lochearnhead and is bordered by steep slopes.

KILMACOLM, Strathclyde   44 NS36
Good views can be enjoyed from some of the low hills around Kilmacolm, a resort situated in Strath Gryfe. The local church houses tombs of the Earls of Glencairn, and incorporates the aisle of an earlier building. On a by-road leading towards Houston, some 2m SE of Kilmacolm, are the ruined Church of St Fillan and the rock where the saint used to sit when baptising children. Children used to be brought to the nearby Holy Well to be cured of rickets. Scanty remains of Duchall Castle lie 2m SW of the resort, and are supposed to be haunted.

KILMALUAG, Isle of Skye, Highland
32 NG47
St Mo Luag of Lismore practised Christianity here in the 6thc. Kilmaluag River flows N through the village to a bay of the same name. To the NW, Rudha Hunish, the farthest N point on Skye – faces the tiny Eilean Trodday across the water.

KILMANY, Fife   31 NO32
Dr Thomas Chalmers, a preacher famous in the 19thc, is associated with the local 18th-c church. Picturesque Goales Den and the ruins of the 16th-c Mountquhanie Castle can be seen near by. The owner of the castle in the 17thc, Robert Lumsden, refused to give up Dundee to General Monk and was later executed.

KILMARNOCK, Strathclyde   24 NS43
Johnny Walker was a grocer in Kilmarnock's King Street; he started to blend whisky in 1820 and today the whisky bottling concern that he began is the largest in the world. Kilmarnock also manufactures carpets and footwear, and has associations with Burns. The first edition of his poems was printed in the town in 1786, when Burns hoped to raise enough money to emigrate to Jamaica. However, the great success of the poems made him change his mind. A copy of the first edition is exhibited in a museum housed in the red-sandstone Burns Monument in Key Park. The announcement of the poet's death on 21st July 1796, as printed in the *Kilmarnock Standard*, is also preserved here. The Angel Hotel and the former Laigh Kirk are associated with Burns, and the churchyard boasts an epitaph by the poet on *Tom Samson*. Several Covenanters monuments survive here.

A steeple from the Kirk of 1410 outlived a fire of 1668, and the present Laigh Kirk dates from 1802. The Dick Institute contains a fascinating museum of rural life. Two old towers are preserved at Dean Castle, a 15th-c fortification lying 1m N of Kilmarnock near Fenwick Water. To the S of the town is 500ft Craigie Hill, which is surmounted by a view indicator.

KILMARTIN, Strathclyde   28 NR89
Notable prehistoric remains can be seen in and around Kilmartin. Among these are: the Kilmartin Stone, cross fragments

in the churchyard; the Temple Wood circle and cist; Ri Cruin cairn; Ballygowan cup-and-ring marked rocks; Glebe cairn; Dunchraigaig cairn; Baluachraig cup-and-ring marked stones; and Nether Largie cairns – between Kilmartin and Nether Largie. All these items are protected under the Ancient Monuments scheme. Near the village are the ruins of a castle, while 1m N, Carnasserie Castle (AM) overlooks Kilmartin valley from a commanding height. This stronghold is now ruined but was built by John Carswell, first Protestant Bishop of the Isles, who translated Knox's *Liturgy* into Gaelic and published it in 1567 – the first book ever to be printed in that language. The castle was captured and partly blown up during Argyll's

rebellion in 1685. Modernized Duntroon Castle stands about 4m SW of Kilmartin on the shores of Crinan Loch.

KILMAURS, Strathclyde *29 NS44*
Cutlery was once a famous product of this old burgh. The medieval jougs still hangs on the old Tolbooth and parts of Rowallan Castle (AM), 2m NE, date back prior to 1560. This structure includes two impressive circular towers and a Renaissance doorway which leads into the forecourt. Rowallan Castle bears the arms of the Mures of Rowallan, and is the home of Lord Rowallan, the former Chief Scout.

KILMELFORD, Strathclyde *29 NM81*
The small angling resort of Kilmelford

lies at the head of Loch Melfort, sheltered from the open sea by a cluster of islands. These include Luing and Shuna, which are separated by the Sound of Luing from the more mountainous island of Scarba. To the N on the Kilninver road is the lovely, wooded Pass of Melfort, situated above the valley of the River Oude. A very rough and narrow road climbs E from Kilmelford towards Loch Avich, giving a fine distant view of 3,689ft Ben Cruachan. Arduaine House lies 4m SW in lovely gardens by Loch Melfort, just off the road to Ardrishaig.

KILMICHAEL GLASSARY, Strathclyde *29 NR89*
Cattle fairs were once held in this oddly-named River Add village. The community

1   Burns' Monument and Museum
2   Craigie Hill

3   Dean Castle
4   Dick Institute

5   Laigh Kirk

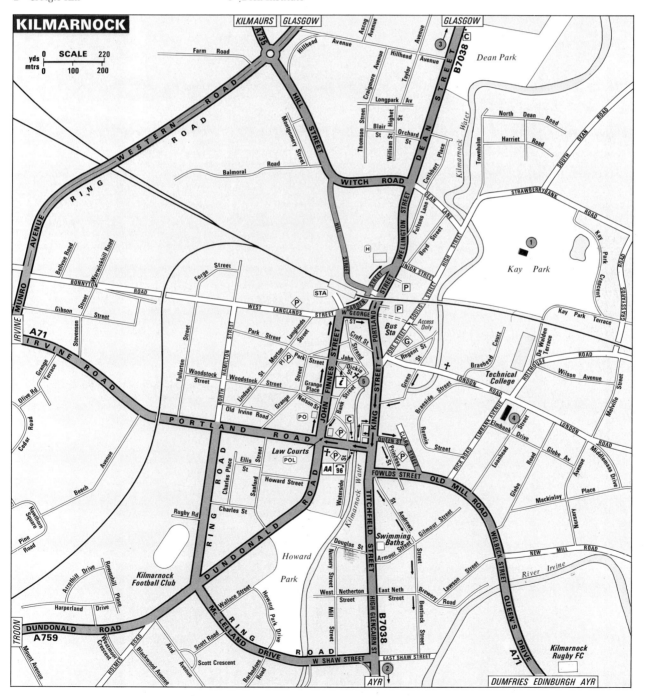

lies on the edge of Moine Mhor – or Great Moss of Crinan – and prehistoric standing stones (AM) can be seen in the vicinity. Dunadd, on an isolated hillock 1½m NW, was the site of the ancient capital of Dalriada cAD500–800 from which the Celtic kingdom of Scotland sprang. Traces of a fort (AM) are still visible, and a fine figure of a boar and the sign of a footprint (AM) are carved on the highest rock. It is likely that this was where the early kings were invested with royal power.

KILMORACK, Highland   33 NH44
Situated on the Beauly River, Kilmorack lies in a district known as the Aird. A waterfall which once cascaded near by has vanished due to the effects of a hydro-electric scheme. Beyond the river and to the SE is the late 19th-c Beaufort Castle, seat of Lord Lovat, Chief of the Clan Fraser. Fire damaged the building in 1937, and the ruins of an older castle can be seen near by.

KILMORY KNAP, Strathclyde   28 NR77
A lobster-fishing centre situated on a narrow neck of land separating the lovely, wooded Loch Sween from Loch Killisport, Kilmory Knap lies in attractive Knapdale. The Chapel of St Maelrubha is a typically small W Highland church, and its famous carved tombstones and the MacMillan Cross (AM) date from medieval times. Sweeping views from the village extend across the Sound of Jura to the conical Paps of Jura. Castle Sween (AM) lies 2½m NNE and is possibly the earliest stone castle in Scotland. Built in the mid 12thc, the main structure is Norman and displays large pilaster and angle buttresses. It incorporates MacMillan's Tower. Now in ruins, the castle was largely destroyed by Sir Alexander Macdonald in 1647. Launches can be hired for a trip to St Cormac's Chapel on Eilean Mor, an island 3m W of the village. This tiny medieval chapel measures 15ft by 8ft, has an upper chamber accessible only by ladder, and contains a fine sculpture of a priest.

KILMUIR, Isle of Skye, Highland   32 NG37
On Score Bay, near the road leading round the N tip of the island and linking Uig with Flodigarry, is an old burial ground where generations of Macdonalds, Martins, MacArthurs, and Nicolsons lie. Flora Macdonald was buried here in 1790, wrapped in a sheet in which Bonnie Prince Charlie slept at Kingsburgh. A large slab of granite covers her grave and a great Iona cross, inscribed with lines by Dr Johnson, stands at her head. The graveyard at Kilmuir commands a magnificent view, with the land to the W sloping down to the cliffs of Score Bay.

To the S is Loch Snizort; N and W are Lewis and the hills of Harris, followed by the long broken line of North Uist and Benbecula. Close by the graveyard is a cottage museum displaying a wall bed, plus farming and domestic implements. Loch Chailuim Cille faces the sea 2m S. It has been drained, and traces of the plan of an ancient Celtic monastery can be made out on what used to be an island in the loch.

KILMUN, Strathclyde   44 NS18
This Cowal peninsula village is situated on the N shore of Holy Loch. Only the tower of the collegiate church of 1442 remains, but the vault is the last resting place of the Marquis of Argyll – executed in Edinburgh in 1661. The churchyard contains many interesting carved tombstones, including that of a shepherd boy found frozen to death on a nearby hillside in 1854. Many of the garden gates in Kilmun have been decorated with pebbles, and fine woods and rhododendrons brighten and soften the area. An obelisk erected in memory of J Duncan, whose chemical research in the 19thc revolutionized the British sugar-refining industry, is also of interest. Strone Point overlooks the Firth of Clyde to the SE. Delightful little Puck's Glen lies 2m NW of Kilmun and offers fine views. Hill-bound Glen Masson stretches to the NW.

KILNINIAN, Isle of Mull, Strathclyde   28 NM44
Stones with carved Celtic inscriptions lie in Kilninian churchyard. The road NW from Kilninian climbs through hairpin bends and over moorland to reach Calgary. Laggan Falls lie 4½m SE, facing Loch Tuath and the island of Ulva.

KILNINVER, Strathclyde   28 NM82
The mountainous island of Mull can be seen to the W of Kilninver, and the village itself lies on Loch Feochan – an inlet of the Firth of Lorne. A road runs SE from the village through wooded Glen Callon on the way to the picturesque Pass of Melfort, where there is a small hydro-electric dam. Loch Scamadale lies amid hills 4m SE of Kilninver beyond Glen Euchar.

KILSYTH, Strathclyde   45 NS77
Montrose defeated the Covenanters here in 1645, and relics from the battle are preserved in rebuilt Colzium House, which adjoins the battle site. Kilsyth itself is a mining town at the foot of the Kilsyth Hills. Meikle Bin is the highest summit and rises to 1,870ft to the NW.

KILWINNING, Strathclyde   29 NS24
Formerly known as Segdoune, Kilwinning is an iron-working town on the River Garnock, claiming to be the earliest home of freemasonry in Scotland. A rare wooden cross tops the shaft of the local Mercat cross, and there are traces of an ancient priory in the town. Archery contests have taken place in Kilwinning for many years. Both Kilwinning and Irvine, which lies to the S, are to be developed as a single new town. Roofless Eglinton Castle dates from 1798 and stands 1½m SE.

KINBRACE, Highland   37 NC83
The 3rd Duke of Sutherland attempted to reclaim land from the sea near this lonely crofting village. Several chambered cairns can be seen in the vicinity, particularly to the S near the Kinbrace Burn.

KINCARDINE, Central   45 NS79
A rare 17th-c Scottish brass is preserved in Kincardine's early 19th-c church, which also houses the Drummond monuments. Blair Drummond House lies 1m NE, near Scotland's first African Safari Park.

KINCARDINE O'NEIL, Grampian   35 NO59
Remains of an Auld Kirk can be seen here, and the village used to have an annual fair. Kincardine O'Neil was once important as the Dee bridgehead of the road over Cairn o' Mounth Pass. The former bridge was replaced by a ferry, but now a modern bridge crosses the river 2m SE at Potarch. The road to the pass proceeds from there by way of Feughside Inn. Near the road leading N from Kincardine O'Neil to the small Loch of Auchlossan and Lumphanan, 1½m W of the village, is the picturesque Slug of Dess waterfall. This is where the Dee is joined by the Dess Burn.

KINCARDINE-ON-FORTH, Fife   46 NS98
Fine Kincardine Bridge is the last bridge across the Forth before the estuary widens. Traffic to Fife and the adjacent counties from Glasgow and the S can avoid Stirling by using the bridge. The port lies on the E bank of the estuary and has a 17th-c Mercat cross, displaying the arms of the Earl of Kincardine. Many of Kincardine's old houses carry date inscriptions. The town was the birthplace of Sir John Dewar, inventor of the vacuum flask, in 1842. Tulliallan Church is a ruined structure dating from 1675. Remains of the late 15th-c Tulliallan Castle lie behind it. This castle displays ground floor vaulting and is of great architectural interest. Modern Tulliallan Castle lies on the outskirts of the town and was the home of Polish General Sikorski during the last war. It now houses a police training college. The Forestry Commission's Tulliallan Forest lies in the background.

KINCRAIG, Highland   34 NH80
The River Spey flows through Loch Insh, and Kincraig is built on the N side of the loch. The Spey is joined by the River Feshie to the NE. The finely-wooded head of Glen Feshie lies beneath the W outliers of the Cairngorm Mountains. Near by is the Highland Wildlife Park, which uses natural surroundings to show creatures that used to live in the Highlands, eg wolves and bears, together with those that still live there, eg deer and the wildcat. In Glen Feshie Forest the Feshie is joined by the Eidart, which flows from the Great Moss on the lofty Cairngorm plateau.

KING EDWARD, Grampian   35 NJ75
The name of this village is a corruption of the Gaelic 'Cean-eador'. Ruined Kinedart Castle lies 1m S on the road to Turriff. Near the River Deveron, 2m NW of King Edward, the modern mansion of Eden stands in fine grounds with the ruins of Eden Castle not far away.

KINGHORN, Fife   47 NT28
King Alexander III died here in 1286 after a fall, and his monument stands on King's Crag on the Pettycur promontory. The promontory itself affords fine views towards Inchkeith Island. Kinghorn is a Royal Burgh on the Firth of Forth, and offers good sands. Pettycur was once a ferry terminal, and various milestones in the area still carry its name.

KINGLASSIE, Fife   47 NT29
Once called Goatmilk, a corruption of Gaytmylkshire, the village lies near 605ft Redwells Hill. This is crowned by an unfinished 52ft-high tower known as Blythe's Folly, erected in 1820.

KINGSBARNS, Fife   31 NO51
Situated a little inland from the stretch of coast between Babbet Ness and Cambo Ness, Kingsbarns has a church with a tall and slender spire. Randerston House, a

Wade's Ruthven Barracks, grim reminders of the 1745 Rising led by Bonnie Prince Charlie.

17th-c building which is now a farm, lies 2m SE off the Crail road.

KINGSHOUSE, Strathclyde   29 NN25

Kingshouse was described in Neil Munro's *John Splendid*, and is a well-known climbing rendezvous standing on a section of the former road through the heart of Glencoe. This ran a little to the E of the present road. Captain Campbell's soldiers are said to have gathered at Kingshouse Inn before the notorious massacre of Glencoe in 1692. Magnificent mountain scenery surrounds Kingshouse. The White Corries ski-ing centre is near by, and the great rock peak of The Shepherd of Etive (Buchaille Etive Mor) towers 3,345ft to the W. The mountain, with its sensational Crowberry Ridge, is a favourite with climbers. Wild Lairig Gartain Pass runs between this peak and 3,129ft Buchaille Etive Bheag, and S of Kingshouse are the Black Mount peaks, notably 2,952ft Sron na Creise; 3,636ft Meall Bhuiridh, with a chair lift and ski tow; 3,602ft Clachlet; and still farther S, 3,565ft Stob Ghabhar.

Glen Etive stretches to the SW, and the mountains which separate it from Glencoe are part of Dalness Forest (NTS). A narrow road from the Glencoe road runs down Glen Etive, coming to an end at the lovely head of Loch Etive and a steamer pier. The 3,541ft bulk of Ben Starav dominates the loch at this point.

Kingshouse was used as a rest-house by General Caulfield's soldiers while they built the old road S from Kingshouse in 1757. Now disused, the road climbed to 1,450ft over the exposed Black Mount. The present road, re-aligned farther E, crosses desolate Rannoch Moor and passes by the shores of Loch Ba. Robert Louis Stevenson describes Rannoch Moor in *Kidnapped*. A cairn on a 1,143ft watershed shows where the waters divide to flow E to the North Sea and W to the Atlantic. To the E beyond Rannoch Moor is lonely Rannoch Station, which is accessible only from the E; there are no roads across the intervening 10m of moorland.

KINGSTON, Grampian   35 NJ36

Two Yorkshiremen who came here to buy timber in 1784 gave the village its name, which was derived from Kingston-upon-Hull. Kingston stands near the Spey Estuary 1m N of Garmouth, where Charles II landed in 1650.

KINGUSSIE, Highland   34 NH70

So-called 'Capital of Badenoch', the pony-trekking centre of Kingussie lies in wooded Strath Spey and offers fine views E to the lofty Cairngorm Mountains. Craig Beg is a good 1,593ft viewpoint which overlooks the resort's attractive golf course. The Highland Folk Museum, known as Am Fasgadh (The Shelter), was originally founded in Iona. It shows a comprehensive collection of domestic items used in the Highlands in bygone days, including Highland dress, tartans, relics of old crafts, farm implements, an old furnished cottage, a mill from Lewis, a black house, and a clack mill. James Macpherson, the 18th-c translator of the Ossianic poems, was born in Kingussie. He built the mansion of Balavil, which still lies 3m NE off the Aviemore road, and his monument stands at the point where Raitts Burn passes under the road on its way to join the nearby Spey.

To the SE of Kingussie is Tromie Bridge, leading to the long valley of Glen Tromie. This glen penetrates into the great Gaick Forest, where Loch an't Seileich lies amid lofty hills. Very hardy walkers can take the wild Minigaig Pass which leaves the glen to the SE, and climbs over the hills before descending into Glen Bruar, N of Struan. Some 1½m S and across the Spey are the ruins of Wade's Ruthven Barracks (AM). These grim reminders of the '45 Rising, stand on a site where the Wolf of Badenoch once had a fortress. The barracks were built to keep the Highlanders in check between 1716 and 1718, and enlarged by Wade in 1734. After the disaster of Culloden in 1746, Prince Charles' Highlanders assembled at Ruthven and waited for him to raise his standard once more. The defeated prince sent them a message of farewell instead, at which the Highlanders blew up the barracks to prevent them falling into government hands.

General Wade's military road from the S reached the barracks over the hills from Glen Truim. To the W of Kingussie lie the little-visited Monadhliath Mountains, where several peaks, including Carn Dearg and Carn Mairg, top 3,000ft. One of Scotland's last wolves was reputedly slain on the N slopes of this range, near the headwaters of the Findhorn, in 1743.

KINLOCHBERVIE, Highland   36 NC25

Beautifully situated on Loch Inchard, on a narrow and winding road leading NW from Rhiconich, Kinlochbervie has important fisheries and a new pier. Its situation affords splendid views towards the lonely mountains of Reay Forest, dominated by 2,980ft Foinavan. The road runs NW for 4m towards the open sea, and also offers wonderful views before it ends at the little fishing village of Sheigra. A coastal track from here leads to remote Sandwood Bay, one of the loveliest in Scotland. Lofty cliffs and red Torridon-sandstone stacks rise above the reddish sands of this completely unspoilt and little-known area. Far away to the N at the tip of this cliff-bound stretch of coastline is lonely Cape Wrath and its isolated lighthouse.

KINLOCHEIL, Highland   33 NM97

Prince Charles Edward stayed here for a few days in 1745, after raising his father's standard at Glenfinnan. Kinlocheil lies on one of the Roads to the Isles near the W end of Loch Eil. The road to Ardgour and Ardnamurchan turns off at the head of the loch and continues along its S shores. Ben Nevis, at 4,406ft the largest mountain in Britain, can be seen rising to the SE. Lofty hills to the W guard Loch Shiel. Fassifern House is encircled by trees 3m E on the Fort William road.

KINLOCHEWE, Highland   33 NH06

Magnificent mountain scenery surrounds Kinlochewe, which has become a centre for hill-walking, climbing and fishing. It lies at the head of beautiful Loch Maree, and on the W bank – a little to the N of the village – are the woodlands of Coille na Glas-Leitire. These, together with lofty slopes of Kinlochewe Forest and 3,188ft Ben Eighe, form the Ben Eighe national nature reserve – the first of its kind to be formed in Britain.

The reserve covers over 10,000 acres and preserves a large remnant of the ancient Caledonian pine forests. Pine martens, deer, wild cats, and golden eagles are protected here, and both Scots pine and birch flourish in the woods. The great Ben Eighe itself is of major geological interest, being composed of 750-million-year-old red sandstone topped by 600-million-year-old white quartzite. A 4m mountain trail climbs 1,800ft through spectacular scenery, and the Glen Torridon road SW from Kinlochewe skirts the base of Ben Eighe and passes Loch Clair. At the loch a beautiful private road branches to Achnashellach by way of Loch Coulin.

Glen Torridon's scenery is wild and rocky with the 3,456ft Liathach overhanging the N side of the road. Considered one of the finest peaks in Scotland, this is built up of parallel red Torridon-sandstone ledges and is treacherous to climb. Behind the peak are wild corries, including the fascinating Coire na Caime. A long and arduous walk through the deep cleft between Liathach and Ben Eighe leads to the breathtaking cliffs of Coire Mhic Fhearchair, rising high above a tiny lochan. From Kinlochewe a road runs NW along the W shores of Loch Maree, dominated here by the 3,217ft Slioch (The Spear) rising from the E shore. To the N and E of the

Slioch is one of the most spectacular and remote mountain districts in Scotland. There are no roads and access to the area is by a few rough paths.

Foot access through Glen Bannisdail to the solitary Lochan Fada can be gained from beneath the E flanks of Slioch. The splendid rock peak of A'Mhaigdhean, rises to 3,060ft above the lonely Dubh and Fionn Lochs, N of Lochan Fada, and farther N the 2,974ft Beinn Dearg Mhor towers above Loch na Sheallag. The great cliffs of Glen Tulacha, part of 2,817ft Ben Lair, rise to the NW of Lochan Fada.

KINLOCH HOURN, Highland 33 NG90
Eucalyptus trees grow near Kinloch Hourn, a hamlet situated in a hollow at the head of Inner Loch Hourn. Access to the village is by a single-track road from the A87, which runs along the often precipitous shore of Loch Quoich and round the shoulder of 3,365ft Sgurr a'Mhoraire. Sgurr nan Eugallt rises 2,933ft to the W. A very steep descent (1 in 6), through a wilderness of glaciated, grey rocks, follows before the road reaches Kinloch Hourn.

One of the loveliest of Highland views – along the whole length of Loch Hourn towards the distant Cuillins of Skye – can be enjoyed from the summit of Sgurr a'Mhoraire. Hourn is Scotland's most fjord-like sea loch, flanked by sheer rock walls and with superb mountain scenery. A path leads for a short distance along the S shore of the Inner Loch, with fine views of the N shores and 2,327ft Druim Fada. Prince Charles Edward wandered in these lonely mountains after his defeat at Culloden in 1746, and narrowly missed the sentries posted on the slopes of Sgurr a'Mhoraire.

KINLOCHLEVEN, Highland 33 NN16
Fine mountains surround this busy little industrial centre, which lies at the head of Loch Leven. The shores of the loch are traversed by a picturesque road affording fine views. To the N of the town rise the grand Mamore Forest Mountains, with 3,700ft Binnein Mor predominant. On the far side of the range, to the S, the ridges of 3,168ft Aonach Eagach overlook Glencoe.

An old military road once ran from Kingshouse, crossing the Devil's Staircase at 1,745ft before entering Kinlochleven from the SE. It then continued NW over the hills, past Loch Lundavra and on towards Loch Leven. To the E of the town is the great Blackwater Reservoir, from which water is drawn to supply Kinlochleven's aluminium works.

KINLOCHMOIDART, Highland 32 NM77
Kinlochmoidart lies at the head of wooded Loch Moidart, where the River Moidart flows into the loch. Prince Charles Edward was given hospitality here by the Macdonalds in 1745, before he raised his father's standard at Glenfinnan. Seven beech trees were planted in a meadow at Kinlochmoidart to commemorate the 'Seven Men of Moidart', who were among the prince's most faithful companions. Six trees still stand in a line; one was blown down in a gale and has been replaced by a young sapling.

To the E of the village the river flows through Glen Moidart, to the N of which a range of lofty hills ends with 2,876ft Fros Bheinn. This height affords fine views across the Sound of Arisaig to Rum and Skye. The road W from the village leads along the N shores of the loch, and passes through Glen Uig to the little village of Glenuig on the Sound. It then continues E towards Loch Ailort, eventually reaching Lochailort on the Road to the Isles. The seaward views are magnificent along the whole length of the road. This highway partly follows the route of an old footpath to Lochailort, and was finished in the late 1960's.

KINLOCH RANNOCH, Perth 30 NN65
This little angling resort lies on the River Tummel at the E end of Loch Rannoch, in Breadalbane country. The river flows E through a reservoir which is part of the vast Tummel-Garry hydro-electric scheme. Power stations stand at the far W end of Loch Rannoch and at Tummel Bridge. Beyond the reservoir a road diverges N to climb to over 1,000ft and later descend through Glen Erochy to Struan in Glen Garry. English invaders are said to have fought Robert the Bruce at Dalchoisnie, SE of Kinloch Rannoch, in 1306. Farther SE is the sharp quartzite cone of 3,547ft Schiehallion, one of the best-known landmarks and viewpoints in the Central Highlands. Away to the E near Loch Tummel is the famous Queen's View, an AA Viewpoint originally made famous by Queen Victoria.

Before reaching the lower slopes of Schiehallion the moorland road running SE from the village passes the ruins of St Blane's Chapel at Lassentulich, on the way to little Loch Kinardochy near White Bridge. Geal Charn, S of Kinloch Rannoch, rises to 2,593ft at the head of Gleann Mor. Farther S are the 3,000ft peaks of the extensive Carn Mairg group. From the S shores of Loch Rannoch, on the edge of the lovely Black Wood of Rannoch where the native Caledonian pine is still to be seen, a path leads over the hills to Glen Lyon. Loch Rannoch has well-wooded roads on both its S and N shores, which converge at the W end of the loch 5m E of remote Rannoch Station. A mansion known as The Barracks was erected for troops near this road junction after the '45 Rising.

The desolate expanse of Rannoch Moor includes Lochs Laidon and Ba, and stretches W from the railhead. Beyond the ridge of the Black Corries are the large Blackwater Reservoir and Lochan a Chlaidheimh, into which a 15th-c Earl of Atholl threw his sword to resolve a land dispute with the Camerons. Views of the lofty Black Mount and the Glencoe and Grampian Mountains can be enjoyed from the moor, which Robert Louis Stevenson describes in *Kidnapped*. A tunnel aquaduct running N links Loch Rannoch with lonely Loch Ericht, overlooked by the fine peak of 3,757ft Ben Alder. This is only accessible from the A9 near Dalwhinnie.

KINLOSS, Grampian 34 NJ06
All that remains of the once-famous 12th-c Kinloss Abbey are the foundations and two fine round-headed arches. An extensive RAF aerodrome is situated at Kinloss. Milton Brodie lies 2½m NE, and has a hexagonal tower and an old abbey garden.

KINNAIRD, Tayside 30 NO22
Lying on the slopes of the Sidlaw Hills, Kinnaird overlooks the fertile Carse of Gowrie and the distant Firth of Tay. Red-sandstone Kinnaird Castle dates from the 12th to 15thc and has been well restored.

KINNEFF, Grampian 35 NO87
After Dunnotar Castle fell to Cromwell at the end of an eight-month siege in 1652, the Crown Jewels of Scotland were smuggled out and hidden under the pulpit of Kinneff's parish church. They stayed in their hiding place for eight years, until the restoration. A monument has been erected to Mrs Grainger, wife of the local minister, who safeguarded the regalia.

KINNESSWOOD, Tayside 30 NO10
Attractively situated at the foot of Bishop Hill and White Craigs to the E of Loch Leven, Kinnesswood was the birthplace of the poet Michael Bruce in 1746. Bruce's cottage has been preserved as a small museum. Alexander Buchan, the meteorologist who first pointed out the recurring cycles of five cold and three warm periods, was also born here.

KINROSS, Tayside 30 NO10
Loch Leven and its famous island castle (AM) lie just E of this small county town, which is popular with anglers who come to fish for the loch's salmon trout. In winter the town is noted for skating and curling. Robert Adam decorated the 17th-c Tolbooth, which was restored by the Crown in 1771. Attached to the carved town cross is the old jougs – an iron collar for wrongdoers. The former town kirk has an 18th-c steeple, and Kinross House was designed by William Bruce – famous for his work at Holyroodhouse. The house at Kinross was built between 1685 and 1692, and stands amid beautiful grounds between the town and the lochside. Three inscribed plaques decorate a bridge on the Ballingry road, which lies S of Kinross off the A90. Benarty Hill rises 1,167ft S of the loch on the Fife border.

KINTAIL, Highland 33
A profusion of mountains, lochs, glens and rivers make this district one of the most scenic areas in Scotland. About 15,000 acres of the area, including the well known Five Sisters of Kintail, belong to the NTS. Red deer and wild goats frequent the mountains, which are dominated by 3,505ft Scour Ouran. The W flanks of this mountain include a long grassy slope which extends from the summit almost down to the roadside in picturesque Glen Shiel. The little church and manse of Kintail lie on the E shore of Loch Duich, near Inverinate. Wonderful views of the loch can be enjoyed from the summit of the Mam Rattachan Pass, on the road to Glenelg. This road diverges W from the highway running along the W shores of the loch. A fine panorama of the Kintail peaks forms a background to Loch Duich.

KINTORE, Grampian 35 NJ71
Kintore is a tiny Royal Burgh which has a Tolbooth of 1740, displaying a dual outside staircase. Balbithan House dates from the 17thc, and the church has a rare Sacrament House – a feature peculiar to churches in E Scotland. The curious Ichthus Stone in the churchyard is carved with a fish on one side and what may be an elephant on the other. Around Kintore are many prehistoric remains such as hill forts and stone circles. Mary Queen of Scots is thought to have visited Hallforest Tower, now in

ruins, in 1562. The tower was built entirely without staircases.

KINTRAW, Strathclyde *28 NM80*

This village lies at the head of Loch Craignish. Just to the N is a by-road which diverges SW for Craignish church, on the shores of the loch. Beyond lies Craignish Castle, a 16th-c keep with a rhododendron garden which was originally laid out by Osgood Mackenzie. Farther S beyond the castle is Craignish Point, facing a turbulent channel known as Dorus Mor or Great Door. The sea loch Craignish is dotted with islands.

KINTYRE, Strathclyde *24*

The long and narrow peninsula of Kintyre stretches S towards the Atlantic and is only 12m from the coast of Northern Ireland at one point. Roads run along the E and W shores of the peninsula, the former affording views across the Kilbrennan Sound to the mountains on the island of Arran. The latter road offers a panorama which includes the islands of Islay, Jura, and the distant coast of Northern Ireland. Gigha, a small island a few miles off the W coast of Kintyre, can be reached by passenger ferry from Tayinloan. West Loch Tarbert forms the N boundary of Kintyre, and almost cuts it off from the district of Knapdale. A ridge of hills which forms a backbone down the middle of the peninsula includes 1,491ft Beinn an Tuirc, near Saddell. The farthest S point of the peninsula is known as the Mull of Kintyre. A lighthouse is sited here.

KIPPEN, Central *45 NS69*

This attractive village faces S towards soaring Standmilan Crag and lies S of the winding River Forth. To the SE and SW are the Gargunnock and Fintry Hills. Although Kippen sees little of the sun, an enormous vine grew in the village for 70 years and is said to have been the world's largest. It produced 2,000 bunches of grapes a year until it was removed in 1964 to make way for new houses. A fine old dovecot (NTS) has been preserved in the village, and the

church of 1825 is considered to be one of the finest of its period in Scotland. Sir David Cameron was involved with the building's 20th-c renovation. To the N of the River Forth is the treacherous Flanders Moss, a wild peat bog where a forest probably once stood. Wrightpark dates from 1750 and stands 1½m SSW of Kippen.

KIPPFORD, Dumfries and Galloway *25 NX85*

Popular with yachtsmen, Kippford lies on Rough Firth – the estuary of the Urr Water – which forms an inlet of the Solway Firth. Solway Firth inlets such as this were used to smuggle wines and tobacco into Scotland during the 18thc, to escape import duties. Robert Burns was a member of the ineffectual customs service for a time. Kippford has a rocky beach. Bathing, even for strong swimmers, is hazardous.

KIRKANDREWS, Dumfries and Galloway *25 NX54*

James Brown, a businessman from Manchester, built the curious castellated buildings of the local church, farm, and laundry. The small Islands of Fleet lie to the W in Wigtown Bay.

KIRKBEAN, Dumfries and Galloway *25 NX95*

Kirkbean is dominated by 1,632ft Boreland Hill and the fine viewpoint of 1,866ft Criffel, and lies inland from the Solway Firth. The ancient Preston Cross stands off the Dalbeattie road. Arbigland was the birthplace of John Paul Jones in 1747 and lies 1½m SE of Kirkbean. Jones was a privateer who became known as the father of the American navy. The local church houses a font which commemorates him and was presented by the American Navy in 1945. Dr Craik, Washington's personal medical assistant, was also born at Arbigland. The nearby House on the Shore is set amid lovely gardens in a situation which affords views across the rocky shores of the Solway Firth, towards the Lake District mountains.

KIRKCALDY, Fife *47 NT29*

Often known as Lang Toun, Kirkcaldy has a 4m-long main street and has been a Royal Burgh since 1450. Nowadays it is a large coal port and industrial town, and one of the country's chief manufacturing areas for floor coverings. Included within its boundaries is Dysart, which lies beyond Pathead. Both Adam Smith, economist and author of *The Wealth of Nations*, and the designer Robert Adam were born in Kirkcaldy and went to the now-demolished Burgh School, where Thomas Carlyle and Edward Irving once taught. Adam Smith was born at a house in the High Street in 1723, opposite which stands 17th-c Old Dunniker House, now used for shops.

Robert Adam was born at Gladney House, which no longer stands, in 1728. The parish church is topped by a 13th-c tower, and several old cottages can be seen in the steep lane of Kirk Wynd. Thomas Carlyle once lived in this road. Several fine 17th-c and earlier houses can be seen in an area near the harbour known as the Sailor's Walk (NTS). These have all been restored. Links Market fair is held every spring and is the largest in Scotland. Gaunt, impressive ruins of Ravenscraig Castle (AM), built by James II in 1460, lie on a rocky promontory between Kirkcaldy and Dysart. The castle later passed into the hands of the Sinclair Earls of Orkney, and is thought to be the first British castle designed for defence by firearms.

Beveridge Park lies to the W of Kirkcaldy and leads into the grounds of Raith House. Farther W lie the sparse ruins of Balwearie Tower, with its 7ft-thick walls. An ancient sculptured cross known as the Dogton Stone lies 5m NW of Kirkcaldy, to the N of the A919.

KIRKCOLM, Dumfries and Galloway *24 NX06*

Situated in the Rhinns of Galloway peninsula on the W side of Loch Ryan, Kirkcolm lies E of attractive little Loch Connel. Sir John Ross the Arctic explorer was born at Balsarroch House

1 Adam Smith's Birthplace
2 Balwearie Tower
3 Old Dunniker House
4 Parish Church
5 Raith House
6 Ravenscraig Castle
7 Sailors' Walk

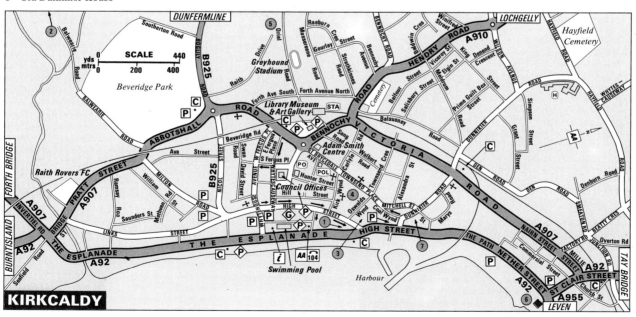

in 1777. This building is sited W of Loch Connel. Robert Stevenson built the lighthouse 4m NW at Corsewall Point in 1815, and the ruins of Corsewall Castle can be seen near by.

KIRKCONNEL, Dumfries and Galloway 25 NS71

The small industrial town of Kirkconnel lies on the River Nith, at the edge of the Ayrshire coalfield. The origins of ancient Devil's Dyke, remains of which can be seen to the S, lie in the depths of history and its purpose is not known.

KIRKCOWAN, Dumfries and Galloway 24 NX36

Remains of an ancient church can be seen in this village, and an external staircase leads to the gallery of the present church. To the SE is the confluence of Tarf Water and the River Bladnoch, and 5m SSW beyond the Tarf Water is the fine, restored Old Place of Mochrum. This is also known as Drumwalt Castle, and most of the structure dates from the 15th and 16thc. Two picturesque early towers are of particular interest. Mochrum Loch lies beyond the house, and Castle Loch is to the W of the loch. Loch Ronald can be seen in the district known as The Moors, 6m NW of Kirkcowan.

*KIRKCUDBRIGHT, Dumfries and Galloway 25 NX65

The town's name means Church of Cuthbert, and Kirkcudbright is an ancient Royal Burgh and market town on the Dee estuary. It is the most important town in the one-time Stewartry or county of Kirkcudbright, and boasts a small harbour at the head of Kirkcudbright Bay. MacLellan's Castle (AM), a handsome castellated mansion overlooking the harbour, was built in 1582 by Sir Thomas MacLellan of Bombie. Sir Thomas was the Provost at that time and his Renaissance tomb lies in the Old Greyfriars Kirk. The mansion has been a ruin for over 200 years, and there is no trace now of two other castles which once stood in the town. The Mercat cross dates from 1610 and stands on the outside stair of the Tolbooth. The town jougs hang on the NW wall of the Tolbooth, which was built between the 16th and 17thc and preserves two old bells. It now forms a memorial to John Paul Jones, dubbed father of the American navy, who was once imprisoned here.

Witches used to be tried here, and the last one to be executed was Elspeth McEwen in 1698. Kirkcudbright is the centre of a lively group of weavers, potters, and painters who work in the town's 18th-c byways. Of the good 17th- and 18th-c houses in the town, Auchengool House (opposite the castle), and Broughton House are particularly fine. The latter belonged to the artist E A Hornel, who bequeathed it to the town, and now houses a collection of his artist's books and paintings. The Stewartry Museum is sited in St Mary's Street, and the Selkirk Arms Hotel in the High Street was where Burns wrote the much-quoted *Selkirk Grace*:

> *Some hae meat and canna eat,*
> *And some wad eat that want it:*
> *But we hae meat and we can eat*
> *And sae the Lord be thankit.*

The churchyard of St Cuthbert's contains the graves of three Covenanters executed in 1684 and 1685, plus the tomb of Billy Marshal, the tinker king who died in 1792 aged 120. According to Scott, Marshal had fathered four children after the age of 100. The entrance to the churchyard is built round part of the old iron yett or gateway to the town. In Kirkcudbright Bay is St Mary's Isle, a peninsula on which a heronry is preserved in private grounds. Burns stayed here as a guest of the Earl of Selkirk. Farther out into the open sea is Little Ross Island, which bears a lighthouse built by Robert Louis Stevenson's father.

KIRKFIELDBANK, Strathclyde 30 NS84

Orchards grow along the Clyde valley near this pretty village, which lies a little to the W of Lanark. Two bridges span the river, the modern one now carrying traffic which used to cross by the 17th-c structure.

KIRKGUNZEON, Dumfries and Galloway 25 NX86

The stream on which this village lies is known as Kirkgunzeon Lane. Situated among farm buildings 1½m NE is Drumcoltran Tower (AM), a good example of a 16th-c Scottish tower-house – simple and severe. Another old tower stands 1m S of Kirkgunzeon and is known as Corra. Criffel rises to 1,866ft SE of the town and can be seen for miles around.

KIRKINNER, Dumfries and Galloway 24 NX45

The churchyard here contains an ancient Celtic cross. Remains of Baldoon Castle, once the home of David Dunbar, lie 1½m N near Bladnoch Water. Dunbar was the bridegroom in Scott's novel *Bride of Lammermoor*.

KIRKINTILLOCH, Strathclyde 45 NS67

Once known as Caerpentulach, this town originated at one of the forts on the Roman Antonine Wall (AM). The wall can still be traced in the neighbourhood. Kirkintilloch and its nearby port of Lenzie both lie on the Forth and Clyde Canal, which flows through flat country to the S of the Campsies and Kilsyth Hills. An old church in the town now houses a museum, and an interesting corbie-stepped house dates from 1644.

KIRKLISTON, Lothian 46 NT17

Parts of Kirkliston's church date from the 12thc, and its saddle-back tower – roofed like an ordinary house – rises above the village. Other features of the church include a carved Romanesque doorway and a 17th-c bell-cote. The tomb of the first Countess of Stair is associated with Scott's *Bride of Lammermoor*. To the E and across the

KIRKCUDBRIGHT

1 Broughton House (museum)
2 MacLellan's Castle
3 Mercat Cross and Tolbooth
4 Old Greyfriars Kirk
5 St Cuthbert's Churchyard
6 Stewartry Museum

Entries marked * are the starting point of drives included in the Day Drive section of the book (pages 95 to 160).

River Almond, on which the village lies, is Turnhouse, where the airport for Edinburgh is situated. Ingliston lies 1½m S of the village and is the scene of the Royal Highland Show, Scotland's national agricultural show held annually during the last two weeks of June.

Newliston House stands 2m SW of Kirkliston and was built by Robert Adam between 1789 and 1792. It is surrounded by trees which are said to have been planted by the 2nd Earl of Stair in the pattern formed by his regiment at the Battle of Dettingen. The ruins of Niddry Castle, or Niddrie-Seton, lie 2m W. This was built between the 15th and 17thc and was the refuge of Mary Queen of Scots, accompanied by Lord Seton, for the first night after her escape from Loch Leven Castle in 1568. Scott includes this dramatic piece of history in his novel *The Abbot*.

KIRKMAIDEN, Dumfries and Galloway
24 NX13
Scotland's farthest S parish, Kirkmaiden is immortalized in Burns *Frae Kirkmaiden to Johnny Groats*. John o' Groats lies 280m from the village. The village has a 17th- to 18th-c windmill, and the churchyard of the ruined church contains ancient sculptured stones.

KIRKMICHAEL, Tayside   34 NO06
Kirkmichael stands amid hills on the River Ardle in Strath Ardle. The road leading N and later W towards Pitlochry climbs steadily to 1,260ft through Glen Brerachan, affording views of 2,757ft Ben Vrackie before descending to the valley of the River Tummel. An old drove road once ran N from Glen Brerachan towards NE Scotland, through Glen Fernalt.

KIRK OF MOCHRUM,
Dumfries and Galloway   24 NX34
A fine carved oak pulpit can be seen in the interesting local church. To the NW, about 7m along the coast road from Port William, is Chapel Finian. This small chapel or oratory probably dates from the 10th or 11thc.

KIRKOSWALD, Strathclyde   24 NS20
Two of Burns' best-known characters, Tam o' Shanter and Souter Johnnie, lie buried in Kirkoswald churchyard. Tam o' Shanter was Douglas Graham of Shanter, who supplied malter grain to a brewhouse in Ayr in Burns' time; Souter Johnnie, his crony, was John Davidson the village cobbler. Souter Johnnie's 18th-c thatched cottage (NTS) is now a Burns museum, and includes life-size stone figures of the Burns characters in the garden. Robert Adam designed Kirkoswald's church in 1777.

KIRKPATRICK DURHAM,
Dumfries and Galloway   25 NX77
John Neilson, the Laird of Corsock, was the Covenanter who was martyred at Edinburgh in 1666. He is commemorated by a stone in the local churchyard.

KIRKPATRICK FLEMING,
Dumfries and Galloway   26 NY27
Beyond Kirtle Water, to the W of Kirkpatrick Fleming on the Cove Estate, is a cave dating back to neolithic times. It is said that this once sheltered Robert the Bruce and was where a spider gave him a lesson in perseverance.

KIRKTON OF GLENISLA, Tayside
34 NO26
This attractive village, with its cumbersome name, lies on the River Isla in a beautiful long glen. Several of these glens thread their way into the E Grampians in the Braes of Angus district. The road up the glen forks 4m N, with the right branch rejoining the River Isla and passing the ruins of Forter Castle. This castle may be the 'Bonnie Hoose o' Airlie', from the lines:
Lady Ogilvie looks o'er her bower window,
And O, but she looks weary,
And there she spied the great Argyle,
Come to plunder the castle o' Airlie.
Forter Castle was burned by Argyle in 1640. A further 5m along this rough road is the lodge of Tulchan, from where a track runs N to picturesque Caenlochan Glen and a national nature reserve.

KIRKTOWN OF ALVAH, Grampian
35 NJ65
Bridge of Alvah lies to the N of Kirktown on a beautifully-wooded reach of the Deveron. Some 2m E across the river are the ruins of Eden Castle, built in 1676 and the seat of the Nicholas family. A reputed reason for its downfall is that the wife of a tenant asked the laird to control her wayward son. The laird drowned him in the river and was subsequently cursed. In 1713 the third Lord Banff was burned to death at Inchdrewer Castle.

KIRKTOWN OF TEALING, Tayside
31 NO43
An iron-age earth house (AM) and a late 16th-c dovecot (AM) can be seen here.

KIRKWALL, Orkney Isles   40 HY41
See Orkney Isles.

KIRN, Strathclyde   44 NS17
This Firth of Clyde resort is adjacent to Dunoon and offers a shingle beach.

*KIRRIEMUIR, Tayside   31 NO35
Sir James Barrie, creator of *Peter Pan*, was born in Kirriemuir in 1860. His birthplace (NTS) at 9 Brechin Road, and the wash-house which he used as a theatre, now form a Barrie Museum containing sections of original manuscripts, personal possessions, and mementoes of actors and producers associated with his plays. Barrie called Kirriemuir 'Thrums' in his novels, and in the weavers' suburb of Southmuir is the cottage which Barrie called 'A Window in Thrums'. The author was buried in the new church cemetery during 1937. The Auld Licht Manse stands opposite his birthplace, and a gable of the Auld Licht Kirk is preserved in the new church – a design by Sir Ninian Comper. A camera obscura can be seen in a pavilion behind the cemetery.

The town lies in the fertile Howe of Angus and is crossed by picturesque narrow streets. It is an important centre for the manufacture of linen and the milling of oatmeal, and a good point from which to explore the beautiful Braes of Angus. The area includes Glen Glova, Glen Prosen, and Glen Isla – all of which penetrate into the E Grampian mountains.

Inverquharity Castle lies 4m NE and is a well-preserved four-storeyed tower dating from c1450. Just over 1m S of Kirriemuir stands Logie, a mainly 17th-c mansion in lovely gardens. Airlie Castle is 6m WSW and has been a seat of the Ogilvies for

centuries. Little remains of the 'Bonnie Hoose o' Airlie', which was plundered in 1640.

KIRTLEBRIDGE, Dumfries and Galloway
26 NY27
Near the Kirtle Water, a little to the SE of Kirtlebridge, are the old towers of Robgill, Woodhouse and Bonshaw. Robgill was built during the 16thc and is now part of a modern mansion. The well-preserved tower of Bonshaw is an ancient and long-inhabited Irving stronghold, retaining its 16th-c clan bell. Sir Robert Irving, captain of the liner Queen Mary, lived at Bonshaw and died in 1954. Some 2½m NE at the ruined Church of Kirkconnell (AM) are the graves of 'Fair Helen of Kirkconnellee' and her lover. A fine 15th-c wayside cross known as the Merkland Cross (AM) stands on a by-road 1½m SE off the road to Gretna. The cross is said to mark the spot where a Master of Maxwell was murdered in 1484.

KISHORN, Highland   32 NG84
Courthill is another name sometimes given to this tiny village near the head of Loch Kishorn, an inlet of the larger Loch Carron. Farther N at the head of Loch Kishorn is Rassall Ashwood, a nature reserve. From Kishorn a road leads E to Lochcarron over the miniature Pass of Kishorn. The view W from the village over the Inner Sound towards Skye is beautiful, with 2,539ft Sgurr a'Charaochain and its rugged outlier The Cioch rising above the loch. Both these peaks form part of the Applecross hills of red Torridon sandstone. The road to Applecross starts 1m N of Kishorn and leads over the spectacular Pass of Cattle – the nearest approach to an Alpine climb in Britain.

KNAPDALE, Strathclyde   28
The area of low hill country that bears this name lies between the Sound of Jura and Loch Fyne, separated from the Kintyre peninsula to the S by West Loch Tarbert. Knapdale is almost encircled by roads, but only one route penetrates the interior – the road from Ardrishaig to the inner reach of Loch Killisport on the W coast. The Crinan Canal links Loch Gilp and Loch Fyne with the Sound of Jura, flowing along the N fringe of Knapdale. On the E shore of Loch Sween stand the remote 12th-c ruins of Castle Sween (AM), possibly the earliest stone castle in Scotland. The main Norman structure of this displays a large pilaster and angle buttresses, and the building was destroyed by Macdonald in 1647.

KNOCKAN, Highland   36 NC21
This is the starting point of a 50m motor trail which runs through the Inverpolly national nature reserve and over the old Sutherland border into the rocky land of Assynt. Knockan Cliff is an AA viewpoint.

KNOCKANDHU, Grampian   34 NJ22
Near here is the Braes of Glenlivet, some 3½m SE beyond Chapeltown, is the old Scalen Seminary. This was founded in the mid-17thc, burned in 1745, and later largely transferred to Blairs.

KNOCKANDO, Grampian   34 NJ14
The originals of Charles Dickens' 'Cheeryble' brothers in *Nicholas Nickleby* were the Grant brothers, who lived in this parish. Knockando's church displays internal gallery, and ancient carved slabs can be seen in the churchyard.

KNOYDART, Highland   32

Some of Scotland's finest mountain and loch scenery exists in Knoydart, though the area has been somewhat affected by the large new hydro-electric scheme in the district around Loch Quoich. Knoydart is sometimes called 'Rough Bounds', because a narrow fringe route from the A87 to Kinloch Hourn is virtually the only road.

KYLEAKIN, Isle of Skye, Highland 32 NG72

This is the arrival point for the car ferry from Kyle of Lochalsh. Kyleakin overlooks the narrow strait of Kyle Akin, through which an early King of Norway sailed on his way to Largs. The village was named after this king. The ruins of Castle Moil are sited on the shore to the E, and afford fine views up Loch Alsh. The castle was once known as Dunakin, and served as a lookout post and fortress against raids by Norsemen. For centuries it was a stronghold of the Mackinnons of Strath. A legend says that it was built by the daughter of a Norwegian king, who installed a chain across the strait to extract a toll from passing ships. She subsequently became known as Saucy Mary. In the background is 2,396ft Beinn na Cailleach, a good viewpoint.

*KYLE OF LOCHALSH, Highland 32 NG72

This is the main ferry-stage for Skye, the shores of which are only a few hundred yards away across the Kyle Akin waters. Kyle of Lochalsh is a busy fishing and shipping village at the W end of Loch Alsh, and is the terminal point for one branch of the romantic Road to the Isles. Also known as the Gateway to Skye, the village is the railhead of the line from Inverness. Steamers sail from Kyle of Lochalsh to Mallaig and Skye, and there is a motor boat service to Loch Toscaig for Applecross.

Many high points around the village offer magnificent views towards the Cuillins of Skye, over Loch Alsh and Loch Carron, and across Inner Sound with the Crowlin Islands. Beyond the Crowlins are the lofty Applecross Hills, with the narrow de-populated island of Raasay to the W. Part of Kyle of Lochalsh lies within the estate of Balmacara (NTS). Coral can be found 2m N on the beach at Erbusaig Bay.

KYLERHEA, Isle of Skye, Highland 32 NG72

A summer car ferry crosses narrow Kyle Rhea from here and connects with Glenelg on the mainland. The road from Kylerhea climbs very steeply (1 in 5) and winds down through Glen Arroch, affording fine views of Broadford Bay and its islands before joining the Kyleakin to Broadford road. To the S of Kylerhea is 1,984ft Ben Aslak, with 2,396ft Beinn na Cailleach, rising to the NW.

KYLESKU, Highland   36 NC23

One of the most beautiful and remote places in the N Highlands, Kylesku lies on an inlet of the lovely Eddrachillis Bay known as Loch Cairnbawn. The island-studded narrows are crossed by a free car ferry which links with Kylestrome at this point. Opposite Kylestrome is the small island of Garbh. Lochs Glendhu and Glencoul lie to the E and have been compared with Norwegian fjords. They penetrate deep into the wild and roadless hills, and the distant peak of 2,597ft Ben Leoid overlooks Loch Glencoul. Beyond

the head of the loch is the remote Eas-coul-Aulin waterfall, which cascades into a valley beyond Loch Beag.

Eas-coul-Aulin is Britain's highest fall, with a sheer drop of 658ft. When in full spate it is three times higher than the mighty Niagara; it can be reached by boat which docks at Loch Glencoul, leaving the rest of the journey to foot power. A walk from the road which runs to the S of Kylesku, below 2,541ft Glasven, also allows access to the fall. This road follows a pass between Glasven, the source of the fall, and 2,653ft Quinag on the way to Inchnadamph. A beautiful though narrow road runs W from Kylesku to pass along the S shores of Loch Cairnbawn, and thence towards Drumbeg and Lochinver. This route affords magnificent views of the mountains and sea along its entire length.

KYLES OF BUTE, Strathclyde   29 NR97

Kyles of Bute is a beautiful curved strait much used by Clyde pleasure steamers. It encircles the N end of the island of Bute, washing the shores of the Cowal peninsula on the mainland. Yachting regattas are held here and farther E on the Firth of Clyde. The Cowal peninsula is penetrated by two long sea lochs – Riddon and Striven. At the mouth of Loch Striven is Strone Point, to the W of which lies South Hall where woods were planted to show the pattern of the opposing armies at Waterloo. Colintrave lies between the two inlets and provides a ferry service to Rhubodach on Bute. Almost blocking the Kyles to the W, facing the N tip of Bute, are the small Burnt Islands where two standing stones known as the Maids of Bute form prominent landmarks.

KYLESTROME, Highland   36 NC23

The wild and lonely road on which Kylestrome lies passes several small lochans on its way to Scourie, to the N of the island-studded Eddrachillis Bay.

LADYKIRK, Borders   31 NT84

James IV is thought to have built the picturesque local cruciform church c1500 as a thank-offering for his escape from drowning in the nearby Tweed. Constructed entirely of stone as a safeguard against fire, the church has a tower which was probably completed by William Adam in 1743. On the English side of the river are the ruins of Norham Castle, which was built in 1121 to defend the ford. In 1160 the original wooden building was replaced by the present stone keep by Hugh de Paiset. Robert the Bruce besieged Norham for a year in 1318, but was successfully repelled. The castle was extended several times up until the 16thc.

LAGG, Isle of Arran, Strathclyde 24 NR92

Lagg stands in an attractive setting of woods and tropical plants on the S shores of Arran, a little SW of the village of Kilmory on the Water of Kilmory. Nearby Torrylin Cairn is a neolithic chambered cairn, and the notable neolithic long cairn known as Cairn Ban lies 3½m N. Bennan Head forms part of the rocky coast beyond Kilmory, and is Arran's farthest S point. The coast road runs NW from Lagg to Torr A'Chaisteil (AM), a barrow with two stone circles, on the way to Blackwaterfoot.

LAGGAN LOCKS, Highland   33 NN29

These locks lie on the Caledonian Canal at the NW end of Loch Lochy, near the point where the main mountain ridge of Scotland cuts across the Great Glen or Glen More. This ridge is known as Drum Allen and forms an important watershed. Rivers to the W flow into the Atlantic and those to the E enter the North Sea. About 1m SW on the N bank of Loch Lochy is Kilfinnan, where the chiefs of Glengarry are buried in a mausoleum.

LAIDE, Highland   36 NG89

Laide has fine sands and offers good views of Gruinard Bay.

LAIGH OF MORAY

This fertile, flat area of countryside is watered by the River Lossie and bordered by the Outer Moray Firth. Elgin stands in the centre of the Laigh of Moray.

LAIR, Tayside   34 NO16

Lair is surrounded by hills, with 2,441ft Mount Blair to the E, and is situated in Glen Shee. A road from Lair runs E across the River Shee and continues to the beautiful valley of Glen Isla, which is threaded by a picturesque road for much of its length.

*LAIRG, Highland   37 NC50

Featureless Loch Shin has been the subject of large-scale hydro-electricity developments. It stretches NW from Lairg, which forms an important junction for roads leading W and N into the wild and beautiful NW Highlands. The highest mountain in the one-time county of Sutherland, 3,273ft Ben More Assynt, rises to the NW. The village is a busy market centre where important lamb sales take place, and is popular with anglers. The area holds a great deal of archaeological evidence, particularly to the N where there are prehistoric hut circles and tumuli. Lairg cemetery contains a quaint old tombstone portraying death. The spectacular Falls of Shin lie 5m S of the village, and at certain times of the year are where springing salmon can be seen leaping through a rocky gorge.

LAIRIG GHRU PASS, Highland 34 NH90

Speyside and Deeside are linked by this famous mountain pass, which cuts right through the heart of the Cairngorm range. Only experienced hikers should attempt the 28m walk which starts at Aviemore and finishes at Braemar. The N end of the pass is overshadowed to the E by the mighty cliffs of 3,983ft Cairn Lochan and 3,448ft Lurcher's Crag. The path descends from here into the woodlands of the great Rothiemurchus Forest.

Farther S the track reaches a height of more than 2,700ft between the shoulders of 4,296ft Ben Macdhui and 4,248ft Braeriach, amid a wilderness of huge boulders. The Pools of Dee lie near this point, though the true source of the Dee lies at over 4,000ft in the remote fastnesses of Braeriach. Devil's Point rises to 3,303ft to the W, on the descent towards Glen Dee and the extensive Mar Forest. Below this is a ruined Corrour bothy – or farm labourer's hut – which has sheltered many walkers in its time. A path diverges SE from the bothy and leads through Glen Lui Beg and Glen Lui to reach Inverey, but the main path stays close to the Dee and follows it to Inverey.

Entries marked * are the starting point of drives included in the Day Drive section of the book (pages 95 to 160).

LAMANCHA, Borders *47 NT25*
Lamancha House dates from 1663 and
stands W of Lamancha.

LAMBERTON, Borders *31 NT95*
Runaway marriages were once performed
by the toll-keeper of the former Lamberton
Toll, although this has not acquired the
fame of Gretna. Lamberton itself lies on
the Great North Road at the Border, a
little to the N of the English Berwick-
upon-Tweed. Lofty cliffs line the North-
Sea coast just to the E of the community.

LAMINGTON, Strathclyde *25 NS93*
This small Clydesdale village faces W
towards 2,335ft Tinto Hill, which offers
fine views. Culter Fell rises to 2,454ft
among a range of lower hills to the E.
Robert Burns was a visitor to the church,
which has a Norman doorway and
preserves ancient jougs. Ruined
Lamington Tower carries the date of
1589 and lies to the N.

LAMLASH, Isle of Arran, Strathclyde
24 NS03
Lamlash Bay is a haven for yachts,
sheltered by Kingcross Point to the S and
Clauchlands Point to the N. Bruce is said
to have embarked for the mainland from
Kingcross Point in 1307. In 1263 King
Haco of Norway rallied his defeated
fleet in the Bay after the Battle of Largs,
when he lost his fight for the Hebrides
and the Isle of Man. Craggy Holy Island
lies in the bay. Below the island's 1,030ft
Mullach Mor is St Molus' Cave, the cell
of a hermit in the days of St Columba.
From Lamlash village the road N to
Brodick stays inland, but a path skirts
the coast and keeps near the low
Clauchland Hills. A by-road SW from
Lamlash climbs 1 in 6 gradients to nearly
1,000ft through the Monamore Glen,
before descending through Glen
Scorrodale to the coast near Lagg.

*LANARK, Strathclyde *30 NS84*
Nothing remains of the 12th-c castle
built here by David I, though there are

still ruins of the 12th-c Church of
St Kentigern. Lanark is an ancient Royal
Burgh situated high above the banks of
the winding River Clyde, which flows
through its loveliest reaches near the
town. Wallace is said to have lived in
here, and his statue stands in the parish
church of 1777.

The Whuppity Scoorie ceremony takes
place every 1 March, and is believed to
be a relic of a pagan festival intended to
chase away winter. On the Thursday
following 6 June, pageants are held to
celebrate Lanimer Day, or Beating the
Bounds. New Lanark lies 1m S and was
founded as a socialist experiment in
1784 by Richard Arkwright and David
Dale. The textile mills and complete
planned community layout became a
European showpiece by the early 19thc,
under the guidance of Dale's son-in-law
Robert Owen. Owen was made a partner
in the mills and developed many welfare
schemes for the workers, including a
reduced 10½ hour working day, a cost-
price shop, and schools for the children.
New Lanark is Scotland's finest example
of industrial and social archaeology.

Braxfield House, on the way to New
Lanark, is mentioned in Robert Louis
Stevenson's *Weir of Hermiston*. The
picturesque falls of the Clyde, S of
Lanark, include Cora Linn and
Bonnington Linn. Due to hydro-electric
schemes these are now almost dry.
Water is allowed to flow over them on
three open days per year. About 1½m W
on the S bank of the Clyde is the pretty
village of Kirkfieldbank, near the
confluence of Mouse Water and the
Clyde. An ancient bridge which is of
possible Roman origin spans Mouse
Water, and nearby Cartland Crags tower
over a deep chasm. Farther down the
Clyde is the Stonebyres Linn Fall, with
Blackhill (NTS) offering fine views.

LANGHOLM, Dumfries and Galloway
26 NY38
Langholm is an angling resort with an

important woollen trade. Wauchope
Water joins the Esk here from the SW,
and the lovely Ewes Water flows into the
main river from the N. Since 1816 a
picturesque Border Riding ceremony has
taken place annually in the town, and
there are traces of Langholm Castle to
be seen on the Castle Holm. The 1,162ft
Whita Hill lies to the E and is surmounted
by a monument to General Sir John
Malcolm (1769–1833), Governor of
Bombay from 1827 to 1830. The General
was born near Langholm and is buried in
Westminster Abbey.

The forbears of Neil Armstrong, first
man on the moon, came from Langholm;
the astronaut has been made a freeman
of the burgh. Johnny Armstrong, the
16th-c sheep rustler who plundered
farms on both sides of the Border, lived
4½m SE at Gilnockie. The restored
defensive pele tower in which he hid
after raids still stands. In 1529 Armstrong
was finally trapped and executed at
Caerlanrig, in the area that used to be
the county of Roxburghshire. The motte
of former Barntalloch Castle lies 2½m
NNW on a bend of the Esk.

LARACHBEG, Highland *28 NM64*
Small-holdings near this tiny Morven
clachan, which lies in a valley between
Lochs Aline and Arienas, were given to
many of the inhabitants of the islands of
St Kilda when evacuated in 1930. During
this year it was realized that it had
become almost impossible to scratch a
living on the island. At the head of Loch
Aline is Kinlochaline Castle, a square,
turreted structure dating from the 15thc.
The road NE from Larachbeg climbs
through Gleann Geal and later divides,
the N branch eventually leading along
the SE shores of Loch Sunart and the
E branch running towards Loch Linnhe.

LARBERT, Central *46 NS88*
Guns used in the Battle of Waterloo were
cast here at the great Carron Ironworks.

1 Blackhill
2 Braxfield House

3 Church of St Kentigern (ruins)
4 New Lanark

5 Parish Church and Wallace Statue

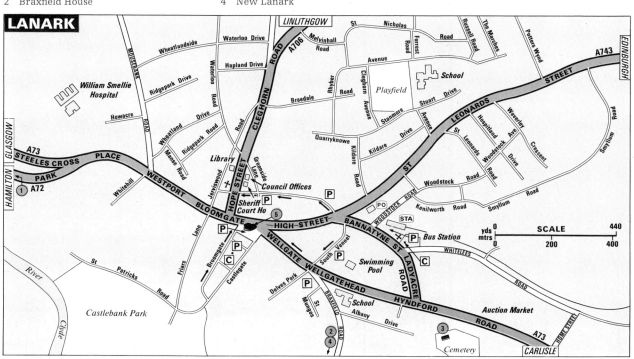

LANARK

LARGO, Fife 31 NO40

Lower Largo lies on Largo Bay, with Upper or Kirkton of Largo lying a little inland under the shadow of 948ft Largo Law. The latter affords good views. In 1676, Alexander Selkirk, Defoe's original for *Robinson Crusoe*, was born in Lower Largo. His statue stands near the harbour. A naval victory over the English was won in the early 16thc by Sir Andrew Wood, who died in 1515 and was buried in the churchyard of the parish church of Upper Largo.

Among his ships was the 'Great Michael', launched at Newhaven in 1507. All that remains of Wood's Castle is a conical capped tower. Upper Largo's church has a 16th-c chancel and tower, and carries a spire which may have been added in 1623. A Celtic cross slab lies near the churchyard gate. The charming glen of Kiels Den lies W of the church, and old Pitcruvie Castle stands 1½m W of Upper Largo.

LARGS, Strathclyde 44 NS25

Lofty hills shelter this popular yachting resort, which lies on the Gogo Water and Largs Bay. The island of Great Cumbrae is situated in the Firth of Clyde opposite the resort, and Largs is the starting point for steamer excursions to the Kyles of Bute and islands in the Firth of Clyde. Sailing courses are available at Inverclyde (AM) and the resort has a pebble beach. Skelmorlie Aisle (AM), a splendid mausoleum of 1636, is all that has survived from the former Church of St Columba. The mausoleum displays elaborately-painted wooden roofs and contains the tomb of the church's founder, Sir Robert Montgomery, and his wife. A fine monument to the Boyles of Kelburne is also of interest.

Every year, usually in early summer, Largs holds the Colm's Day Festival in honour of St Columba. Brisbane House, birthplace of Sir Thomas Brisbane – Governor of New South Wales – once stood NE of the town. Sir Thomas gave his name to the Australian city of Brisbane. A round tower known as The Pencil is situated at Bowen Craig, S of Largs, and marks the naval victory of the Scots over King Haco of Norway in 1263. The Norsemen failed to make a permanent landing here and, as a result of the Battle of Largs, lost the Hebrides and the Isle of Man. Moorland behind the town culminates in the 1,711ft Hill of Stake.

LASSWADE, Lothian 47 NT36

Scott lived in a cottage here between 1798 and 1804, and his 'Gandercleugh' in *Tales of my Landlord* is thought to be a fictional name for Lasswade. Wordsworth was a guest of Scott, and another literary figure associated with the town is Thomas de Quincey, whose house still stands 2m SW of the town near the North Esk River. Mavisbush House, as De Quincey cottage used to be called, was the writer's home between 1840 and 1859.

The churchyard of Lasswade's ruined Norman church contains the graves of William Drummond the poet and Henry Dundas, 1st Viscount Melville. The latter was a famous benevolent despot during the late 18thc, who lived at Melville Castle. The castle now serves as a hotel. William Drummond rebuilt ancient Hawthornden House, which overlooks the river 2½m SW of Lasswade, in a setting of beautiful gardens. The house preserves an old bell tower and artificial caves of great age. Ben Jonson's Tree grows in the grounds and recalls a visit by the poet in 1618 and 1619.

LATHERON, Highland 37 ND13

Church bells used to ring in the unusual detached tower which is sited on a hill above Latheron church. The countryside around Latheron is rich in prehistory and boasts numerous hut circles and Pictish remains. A large ancient standing stone stands near the post office, and NE are several recently-excavated stone structures of very early date – known as the Wag. To the N of Latheron is the moorland road to Thurso, dating from the late 18thc. On the rock-bound coast, 2½m NE of the village stand the ruins of Forse Castle. Latheronwheel, or Janetstown, lies 1m SSW and has a quaint little harbour.

LAUDER, Borders 31 NT54

Lauder is old Berwickshire's only Royal Burgh and is situated in Lauderdale, on the Leader Water. The latter flows S from the Lammermuirs on the old East Lothian border. It is a good angling centre and the Lauder Common Riding, a festival of horse riding held every June, is one of the oldest in the country. Stallholders at the street fairs used to pay their dues at the curious little Tolbooth, which is approached by a flight of steps.

The nearby cruciform church of 1673 may be partly the work of Sir William

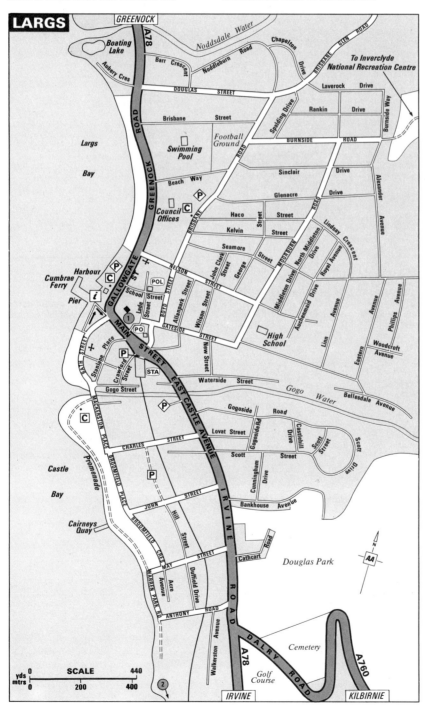

1 Skelmorlie Aisle
2 The Pencil Monument

Bruce. Several of James III's favourites were hanged from the old Lauder Bridge by the Earl of Angus, or Bell-the-Cat as he became known, in 1482. The bridge is no longer standing. James Guthrie, minister at Lauder from 1642 to 1649, was the first Covenanter martyr to be recorded on the Greyfriars churchyard monument in Edinburgh. He was executed in 1661. Imposing Thirlestane Castle stands in parkland just outside Lauder. Its earliest work originates from 1595, and additions date from 1675 and 1841. Sir William Bruce built the fine west front, and the castle has grand entrance gates SE of town on the A697. About 2½m SE off the same road is the ancient tower of Thirlestane, associated with the castle. A lovely moorland road runs W from the town and climbs to over 1,100ft before later descending to the Gala Water at Stow.

LAURENCEKIRK, Grampian   35 NO77
Snuff-boxes were once an important product of this small town, which was founded in 1779 by Lord Gardenstone. Laurencekirk lies in the fertile Howe of the Mearns, with 915ft Garvock Hill rising to the SE and topped by the Johnstone Tower. The latter was erected in the early 19thc with stones left over from the building of his own mansion by James Farquhar. Thornton Castle, dating from the 15thc, lies 3m W of the town.

LAURIESTON, Dumfries and Galloway   25 NX66
Prior to the 18thc this Galloway village was called Clachanpluck. Features include a monument to the author S R Crockett, who died in 1914 at Tarascon in France and whose books contained local colour. Little Woodhall Loch lies to the N, and 3m E near the shores of Loch Ken is the churchyard of Balmaghie. This contains Crockett's grave and Covenanters' gravestones.

LAWERS, Tayside   30 NN63
Lawers is situated on Loch Tay and lies at the foot of 3,984ft Ben Lawers, the highest mountain in the one-time county of Perthshire. The NTS owns about 8,000 acres around the mountain, and the largest number of Alpine plant species in Britain grow on the lower slopes. Ben Lawers can be climbed quite easily from Lawers, and the view from the summit takes in the whole of Breadalbane country and much of the Grampians.

A visitors' centre traces the history of the area and other interesting local features. A lovely descent of the mountain runs W from the summit to the tiny Lochan na Lairige, on the narrow mountain road linking Loch Tay with Bridge of Balgie in Glen Lyon. Ben Lawers and its outliers sometimes provide good ski-ing and Coire Odhar, on 3,657ft Beinn Ghlas, is used by the Scottish Ski Club. To the W of Lochan na Lairige the peaks of the Tarmachan group rise to a height of 3,421ft.

LAXFORD BRIDGE, Highland   36 NC24
A remote place in the N Highlands, Laxford Bridge lies on the salmon river of the same name, which flows into the island-studded Loch Laxford a little to the NW. Apart from the Laxford River, the numerous lochans in the area form a fisherman's paradise; the view from the mountain summits in the vicinity show almost more water than land. The gneiss

cone of 2,364ft Ben Stack rises to the SE and is formed of some of the world's oldest rock – archaean grey gneiss.

Loch Stack lies below the mountain and is drained by the Laxford River. The S shore carries the picturesque road to Lairg, and rough quartzite scree slopes lie at the foot of Arkle, which rises to 2,580ft N of Loch Stack. Farther E is 2,548ft Meall Horn, which together with Arkle lies in the great Reay Forest. A by-road leads N to Tarbert from the Scourie road, 4m W of Laxford Bridge, into the wild and rocky Fanagmore district facing the island of Handa.

LEADBURN, Lothian   47 NT25
Moorland surrounds this village. Some 2m SW over the old Peebles border is the fine 18th-c Adam mansion of Whim, now serving as a hotel.

LEADHILLS, Strathclyde   25 NS81
Lead was mined here in the Lowther Hills between the 13th and 19thc, and some silver has also been dug since Roman times. Gold has been found in local streams, and this metal is believed to have been used in the crowns of Scottish kings. Leadhills lies at a height of 1,350ft – exceeded only by its near neighbour to the SW, Warlockhead – and is a ski resort. A road between the two villages climbs to 1,531ft on the old county border.

Allan Ramsay, the poet who wrote The Gentle Shepherd, was born at Leadhills in 1686. He was the founder of an early Edinburgh theatre and lent his name to Britain's first subscription library (see inset overleaf). The village was also the birthplace of William Symington, a pioneer of steam navigation whose monument stands near the churchyard. John Taylor, a local man who died at the age of 137 years, is also buried here. Hopetown Arms is the highest inn in Scotland, and the nearby golf course is the highest in Britain. The rounded Lowther Hills rise to the SE, including 2,403ft Green Lowther and 2,377ft Lowther Hill. Between them these two hills command panoramic views over the Lowlands and into England.

LEGERWOOD, Borders   31 NT54
A 17th-c monument to the Ker family and a Norman chancel arch are interesting features of Legerwood's church. Corsbie Tower is a ruined 16th-c stronghold.

LEITH (Edinburgh), Lothian   47 NT27
Leith lies at the confluence of the Water of Leith and the Firth of Forth, and is Edinburgh's seaport. The important harbour boasts well-equipped docks and shipyards, and a modern container quay. Sawmills and chemical works make up the major part of Leith's industry, and the town was incorporated within the Edinburgh boundaries in 1920. Once called Port of Leith, the town was sacked by the English many times. The attacks in 1544 and 1547 were devastating. In 1561 Mary Queen of Scots came ashore here from France, where she had spent her childhood, and stayed at the house of the merchant Andrew Lamb. This building, known as Lamb's House (NTS), still stands in Water's Close and has been restored as an old people's day centre.

The Water of Leith divides the town into N and S. Kirkgate features the restored, 15th-c St Mary's Church and Trinity House, which contains an interesting collection of paintings. Scanty remains

of the 19th-c Citadel survive. Near the shore is the so-called Signal Tower, which Robert Mylne originally erected as a windmill in 1686. Charles I played golf on Leith Links, now a park, in 1641. The shore was the old landing place and a stone by the quay wall records George IV's visit in 1822.

LENDALFOOT, Strathclyde   24 NX19
Lendal Water rushes into the sea here, and Bennane Head lies SW of this lovely stretch of coast. A memorial in Lendalfoot records the drowning of several Arran men in 1711. A little inland are the ruins of Carleton Castle, one of a chain of Kennedy watchtowers along the coast. Legend has it that its former baronial owner killed his first seven wives by pushing them over the cliff, but was disposed of himself in the same way by May Cullean, his eighth wife. Beautiful rock scenery can be found on the way to Bennane Head at Gamesloup. Bennane Cove lies beyond the head and has associations with S R Crockett's Grey Man. Kennedy's Pass, NE of Lendalfoot, is dramatic.

LENNOXTOWN, Strathclyde   45 NS67
This small industrial town lies below the Campsie Fells at the foot of a road leading over the hills through the head of Campsie Glen to Fintry. 'Lennox' was once the name given to the one-time county of Dunbartonshire and parts of the bordering counties. Nowadays it is only used when describing the hills of the area which used to comprise NW Stirlingshire. The district is known generally as the Campsies or Lennox Hills.

LERWICK, Shetland Isles   41 HU44
See Shetland Isles.

LESLIE, Grampian   35 NJ52
Leslie lies on the Gady Burn and faces SE towards the long ridge of Bennachie. Leslie Castle was built in 1661, and 2½m E beyond Auchleven is the restored 17th-c mansion of Lickleyhead.

LESLIE, Fife   30 NO20
Leslie's green is claimed to be the scene of the 15th-c poem Christ's Kirk on the Green, and has a bull-stone which was once used for tethering bulls during bull-baiting. Leslie is a small industrial town and has several interesting old houses. To the E of the town stands Leslie House. This was begun in 1670 but two of its wings were destroyed in a fire of 1763.

LESMAHAGOW, Strathclyde   30 NS84
Also known as Abbey Green, Lesmahagow lies on the edge of moorland which stretches to the SW. The River Nethan flows N through the town on its way to join the Clyde at Crossford. Lesmahagow's ancient priory no longer stands but once had fine orchards. It is thought that the monks here may have pioneered the Clydesdale fruit-growing industry. Alexander Muir, associated with Canada's national anthem, was born in Lesmahagow in 1830. The Hunterian Museum at the University of Glasgow preserves the well-known Lesmahagow Flagon of bronze, found here in 1810.

LEUCHARS, Fife   31 NO42
One of Scotland's finest Norman churches stands at this RAF-station community. It was built by the de Quincy family and retains its original chancel and apse. Both the interior and exterior of the

building are richly carved. A 17th-c bell turret has been added above the apse, and also of interest are the two carved Earlshall stones of 1584 and 1635. On the edge of lonely Tentsmuir, with its forestry plantations and nature reserve, lies the picturesque mansion of Earlshall. This was built between 1546 and 1607.

LEVEN, Fife   31 NO30
Largo Bay offers fine sands and is where this Firth of Clyde resort and industrial centre is situated. The River Leven flows into the Firth here. Interesting features of the promenade include a house and car built of shells.

LEWIS, Western Isles   38
See Hebrides, Outer

LEWISTON, Highland   34 NH52
This hamlet lies to the S of Drumnadrochit, at the foot of Glen Urquhart. A 2m walk leads SW to lovely Divach Falls.

LHANBRYDE, Grampian   35 NJ26
Little Loch na Bo lies to the SE of this village, which stands in a wooded setting. The white-harled Coxton Tower lies SW and dates from 1644. Coxton retains its characteristic iron yett, or entrance gate, and is a well-preserved period example of a tower-house.

LIBERTON (Edinburgh), Lothian   47 NT26
Liberton House is an early 17th-c building with a sundial dated 1683. Near by on a ridge stands the 15th-c Liberton Tower of the Dalmahoys, a prominent landmark overlooking Edinburgh. The Inch, 1m NNE of Liberton, is another early 17th-c structure but with modern additions. Just W of Liberton are the Braid Hills, a public park with a good golf course.

LILLIESLEAF, Borders   26 NT52
Lilliesleaf's church was built in 1771, but it has since been extended. Riddell motte lies 2m SW and is crowned by a 19th-c

tower. The old house of Riddell was burned to the ground in 1942.

LIMEKILNS, Fife   46 NT08
The restored, 14th-c King's Cellar here was once a store for the court at Dunfermline. It is now used as a freemason's lodge.

LINCLUDEN ABBEY, Dumfries and Galloway   25 NX97
Founded as a Benedictine convent in the 12thc, Lincluden Abbey (AM) lies near the meeting of the River Nith and Cluden Water – off the Thornhill road a little to the NW of Dumfries. The convent was rebuilt in the 15thc as a collegiate church, and the red-sandstone remains include fine stone carvings and parts of the medieval domestic buildings. Douglas-family arms adorn the ruins of the church, and the richly decorated choir preserves a fine stone rood-screen. Of particular beauty is the tomb of Princess Margaret, daughter of Robert III, who died c1430. Burns loved to visit Lincluden.

A LEAD MINERS' LIBRARY

The first subscription library in Britain was established, not in some comfortable city, but in the lonely village of Leadhills over 1,200ft up in the heart of the Southern Uplands. It was started in 1741 by the lead miners employed by the Scots Mining Company, encouraged by the manager James Stirling, who felt that they should have something to occupy their spare time after he reduced their working shifts to a six-hour day.

At first the rules of the Reading Society restricted membership to workers in the mines. Their tastes were not frivolous and religious, philosophical, and historical books were in great demand. Shakespeare, Johnson, Fielding, Swift, Carlyle, and Congreve appeared early in the catalogue. The Leadhills men did not spend all their off-duty time in reading, because they also made productive farms out of ground offered rent-free by the Earl of Hopetoun, whose estates included the lead mines, and were given one-sixth of the value of all the lead produced.

The library continued to operate even after the mines closed down in 1928. Unavoidably, the village population declined and times became hard. At the beginning of the second world war the library was absorbed in the county service, but by 1965 the building itself had deteriorated badly and the county council felt that the money needed to restore it was not worth spending. A mobile service was arranged instead, and many of the old books were stored elsewhere.

It seemed as if the pioneering library was finished; but the local people refused to give in. After four fruitless years they arranged a grant of £400 from the Pilgrim Trust. More finance became available, and between 1970 and 1972 the original building was refloored, refurnished, damp-proofed and, most important, given electric heating. The stock of books was replaced, and by June 1972 the Leadhills Miners' Reading Society was back in business. It is now called the Allan Ramsay Library, after the Scottish poet who was born in the village, although doubts are expressed about whether he was actually concerned in the founding of the library.

As well as its books, many of which are now rare outside of private collections, the library is a storehouse of information about the great days when the Lowther Hills were so full of minerals – gold and silver as well as lead – that the district was known as 'God's Treasure House in Scotland'. There are detailed records of the mining operations from 1739 to 1854 – original documents, relics, and maps showing the precise locations of the lead seams. Among the photographic collection are many pictures of the Leadhills and Wanlockhead Light Railway, which was opened in 1901 from the main Glasgow-London line at Elvanfoot. With a summit at 1,498ft it was the highest conventional line in Britain. The last run on the railway was in December 1938. Its closure, as well as that of the mines, made Leadhills a lonely place again; but the survival of the library has proved that the independent spirit of the old miners is not lost.

Miner's cottages at Leadhills – the first community to have a subscription library.

LINDORES, Fife *31 NO21*
Lindores lies 2m SE of Lindores Abbey, a great religious centre founded by the Benedictines in 1178, near the reed-encircled Lindores Loch. Abbot Lawrence of Lindores became the Great Inquisitor. He tried many men as heretics and later had them burned at the stake. Little is left of the abbey, and the main survivals include the groined entrance arch and part of the west tower. Near by are ruins of 16th-c Denmylne Castle.

LINLITHGOW, Lothian *46 NS97*
At one time Linlithgowshire was the name given to the old county of West Lothian, but now it just refers to the ancient Royal Burgh which stands on the S shore of Linlithgow Loch. Linlithgow is famous for the fine ruins of its Royal palace (AM) which stands on a knoll above the loch. Successor to an older building which was burned in 1424, the palace was itself destroyed by a fire – probably accidental – started by the General Hawley's troops in 1746. The palace has a rich history. James I started the rebuilding in 1424 and James V and his daughter Mary Queen of Scots were both born here. On the first floor of the Royal Apartments, on the west side of the quadrangle, is the room where the Queen was born in 1542 as her father lay dying at Falkland Palace. Queen Margaret's Bower is a little room in a turret where Queen Margaret kept vigil while James IV fought at Flodden. The last Scottish national parliament met in the palace in 1646, and Prince Charles Edward stayed here in 1745. In 1914 George V held a court in the Lyon Chamber.

The palace's chapel and magnificent Great Hall show late 15th-c work, and the fine quadrangle has a richly-carved 16th-c fountain. A fine gateway in the town leads into the palace precincts, which also contain the famous St Michael's Church. This is considered one of the finest parish churches in Scotland. Also rebuilt after the disastrous fire of 1424, the church carried a crown steeple which was removed in the 1820's. A recent appeal fund provided a modern and controversial, golden spire

in the shape of a crown. The oldest bell dates from 1490 and tolled a knell for the defeat of the Scots by the English at Flodden in 1513. The nave is wonderfully proportioned, and the choir displays two chapels in place of the more usual transepts. Beautiful window tracery includes particularly fine work in Katherine's Aisle. James IV had a vision of his death at Flodden in the south chapel.

Linlithgow town was garrisoned by Cromwell's troops between 1651 and 1659. There are some interesting late 16th-c houses (NTS, not open) in the High Street. Also in the High Street, facing the County Buildings, is a plaque which records the shooting in the street of the Earl of Moray – Regent of Scotland – in 1570. The curious Cross Well has thirteen water jets and was set up in 1807. It is a copy of an ancient well which was destroyed by Cromwell's troops in 1659. St Michael's Well is situated at the E end of the High Street and dates from 1720. A hill 2m N beyond Linlithgow Loch is surmounted by a monument to General Hope, a hero of the Indian Mutiny. Ruins of 15th-c Almond Castle can be seen 2½m W of the town.

LISMORE, ISLE OF, Strathclyde *28 NM84*
This flat, green island is situated in Outer Loch Linnhe where its waters mingle with those of the Firth of Lorne and the Sound of Mull, and is utterly devoid of trees. St Moluag practised here in the 6thc, and Lismore became the seat of the Argyll diocese. Its tiny cathedral is now a parish church. Steamers from Oban call at Achnacroish pier on the east side of the island, which is washed by the Lynn of Lorne. A passenger ferry connects with Port Appin. There are splendid views across to the hills of Morven and the rugged island of Mull from many points on the island. Picturesque ruins of Castle Coeffin can be seen on the W coast of Lismore, near the village of Clachan.

LIVINGSTON, Lothian *46 NT06*
Scotland's fourth New Town, Livingston, was begun in 1962 and operates a wide variety of industries. Howden House

was the 18th-c home of Sir Henry Raeburn, and now serves as a community centre.

LOANHEAD, Lothian *47 NT26*
The Pentland Hills rise to the W of this town, which lies a little N of the North Esk River.

LOCHABER, Highland *33*
One of the loveliest of the Highland districts, Lochaber is closely linked with legends and tales of Bonnie Prince Charlie. Its boundaries have varied through history, and at one time extended from the Atlantic to the country of Strath Spey. Now they stretch roughly E of the Great Glen, from Loch Leven and Loch Linnhe to Loch Lochy and Glen Spean near the beautiful Badenoch country. There was once probably a Loch Lochaber in the district, but this has long since dried up.

Lochaber is divided into Nether and Brae or Upper Lochaber. Nether Lochaber is Cameron country and lies S of the great Ben Nevis, including the Mamores range. The head of the Clan Cameron is Cameron of Locheil, whose ancestral home of Achnacarry House stands near the densely-wooded shores of Loch Arkaig. Brae Lochaber lies beyond the Ben and is the land of the MacDonnells of Keppoch, famous for their Gaelic bards. Every August the Lochaber Gathering is held at Fort William.

LOCHAILORT, Highland *32 NM78*
The 2,876ft height of Fros Bheinn is the most prominent of a range of high hills backing Lochailort, which lies in a lovely position at the head of the sea loch Ailort. Loch Eilt and its tree-crowned islets lies 2m E, and is the source of the little River Ailort which flows into Loch Ailort at the hamlet. The Road to the Isles 'By Ailort and by Morar to the sea' is well known, and runs the length of Loch Eilt backed by steep rock-strewn hills. From the W end of Loch Eilt a path climbs N into the hills, reaching a height of over 1,000ft. Ahead are wonderful views down little-known Loch Beoraid in S Morar, hemmed in by lonely mountains. Some of the latter show rocky, glaciated outcrops. *cont*

1   Almond Castle (ruins)
2   Cross Well
3   General Hope Monument
4   Palace
5   St Michael's Church
6   St Michael's Well

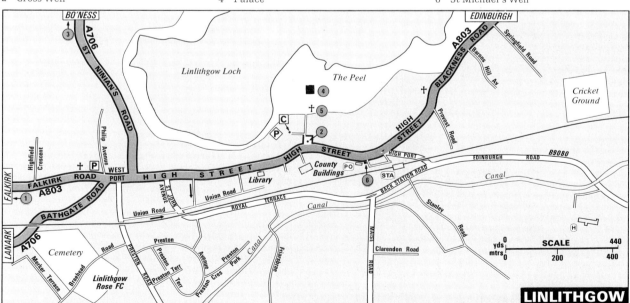

A cave where Prince Charles Edward sheltered during his wanderings is quite close. The path follows the Meoble River down to the lonely clachan of Meoble, and eventually reaches the shores of remote Loch Morar. A picturesque new road runs SW from Lochailort and passes through lovely Moidart to Kinlochmoidart. Wonderful views of the sea and coast are afforded by the road as it heads towards the tiny village of Glenuig on the Sound of Arisaig. Prince Charles Edward landed here from Borrodale House, near the head of Loch nan Uamh, on his way to Kinlochmoidart. To the W of Lochailort, at the seaward end of the Loch, is the tiny island of Eilean nan Gobhar. This is where the French ship bringing the prince anchored in July 1745 at the start of the '45 Rising, which was to end a year later in the same place as it had begun.

LOCHALINE, Highland 28 NM64
Lochaline is a Morven village which lies at the seaward end of Loch Aline and has a steamer pier. It overlooks the Island of Mull across the Sound of Mull, and offers breathtaking views down the Sound to the ruins of Ardtornish Castle. This was a 14th-c stronghold of the Lord of the Isles. The castle is portrayed by Scott in his *Lord of the Isles*, and can be reached by ferry from Lochaline. A 16th-c or earlier slab in Keil churchyard depicts one of the earliest known likenesses of a kilted Scot, and near the church is an old cross which was brought here from Iona.

LOCH ALSH, Highland 32
Loch Alsh extends inland from the narrow strait of Kyle Akin, which separates Skye from the mainland, to the point where it joins Loch Duich and Loch Long at the Dornie bridge. Fine views of Loch Alsh and the 2,396ft hill of Beinn na Cailleach on Skye can be enjoyed from a road running W from Dornie towards Kyle of Lochalsh.

LOCHANS, Dumfries and Galloway 24 NX05
Ruined Garthland Tower lies just SE of this small Rhinns of Galloway village.

LOCH ARKAIG, Highland 33
Beautiful Loch Arkaig is said to contain treasure hidden by the Jacobites, and is separated from Loch Lochy – in the Great Glen – by the little River Arkaig. Achnacarry House is near the point where the river flows into Loch Arkaig. This building lies amid woodlands and is the ancestral home of Cameron of Lochiel, Chief of the Clan Cameron. One of the chief's ancestors – the 'gentle Lochiel' – was a follower of Prince Charles Edward.

The original castle was burned in 1746 because the chief supported the '45 Rising, but the estates were handed back in 1784. Several magnificent tree-lined avenues grace the estate, and of particular beauty is the so-called Dark Mile. This includes the Cia-aig Falls, on the road from Gairlochy near the E end of the loch. The lovely, narrow road leads W along the loch, soon becoming a mere path through progressively wilder country. Rising to the W are the bare peaks of 3,224ft Gulvain and the 2,988ft Streaps. Paths from the W end of the loch continue through Glen Dessary and the rocky Glen Pean, to the remote shores of Loch Nevis and Loch Morar respectively.

Jenny Cameron, who was present when Prince Charles Edward raised his father's

standard at Glenfinnan in 1745, lived in Glen Dessary. The path from here to Loch Nevis crosses the wonderful rugged pass known as the Mam na Cloiche Airde The prince wandered in this wild country around Loch Arkaig after the '45.

LOCH ASSYNT, Highland 36
Set in the heart of the wild and rocky mountains of old Sutherland, Loch Assynt is both beautiful and remote. Around the loch grow rare plants and ferns, and to the E rises the area's highest peak – 3,273ft Ben More Assynt. The long ridge of 2,653ft Quinag rises nearer to the loch on the N side, and 2,779ft Canisp is an odd, isolated Torridon sandstone peak to the S.

Inchnadamph is a fishing resort which lies at the SE end of Loch Assynt. To the NW of the resort lies the shell of 16th-c Ardvreck Castle, where the great Marquis of Montrose was betrayed by the laird in 1650. Montrose was of the Clan Graham. Near by are the remains of Calda House, ancient home of the Mackenzies. Archaean, grey gneiss rocks border the pretty road which skirts the N shores of Loch Assynt towards Lochinver.

LOCH-AWE, Strathclyde 29
Trout and salmon abound in this narrow W Highland loch. Nowadays the loch forms part of Scotland's largest hydro-electric scheme, but 'Lochow' – as the loch was once known – was for years a beautiful, natural moat protecting the Campbells of Inveraray from their enemies to the N. Many reminders of a fortified past survive along the loch's banks and on its islands. Ruins of a castle can be seen at the S end at Fincharn, and there is another on the wooded island of Fraoch Eilean. The latter was built by the McNaughtons and dates from the 14thc. The nearby island of Inishail features an ancient chapel.

This stretch of the loch is drained here by the River Awe and can be considered the most beautiful, with the twin peaks of 3,689ft Ben Cruachan dominating the scene to the N. The world's second largest hydro-electric power station is sited on Ben Cruachan, and pumps water from Loch Awe to a reservoir 1,315ft up on the mountain. Far below are the Falls of Cruachan and the wild Pass of Brander, where Robert the Bruce routed the Clan MacDougall in 1308.

To the SW of Loch Awe station stands the lovely Church of St Conan, built between 1881 and 1930. At the N tip of the loch are the ruins of Kilchurn Castle (AM), built in 1440 by Sir Colin Campbell of Glenorchy, founder of the Breadalbane family. The Innis-Sherrich Chapel, dedicated c1257 to St Findoc, can be seen on an islet near the loch's S end. Lying on the grass near by are two fine carved slabs of the 14th or 15thc.

LOCHBOISDALE, Western Isles 39 NF71
See Hebrides, Outer.

LOCH BROOM, Highland 36
Loch Broom stretches SE from the Coigach district, into the hills which separate the Dundonnell and Inverlael Forests. Ullapool, a small fishing town and resort lies near its mouth and is shadowed by 2,082ft Ben Goleach to the W. Beyond lies Little Loch Broom, skirted by the Ullapool to Dundonnell road, with the great An Teallach range

dominating the countryside to the S. Beinn Dearg stands at 3,547ft and towers above the Strath More valley at the head of the loch.

LOCHBUIE, Isle of Mull, Strathclyde 28 NM62
A village of the same name is situated on the picturesque shores of Loch Buie, overlooked by 2,354ft Ben Buie to the N. Moy Castle, a ruined Maclaine stronghold with a water-filled dungeon, was visited by Dr Johnson. A stone circle stands to the E near little Loch Uisg, and beyond this lies the almost land-locked Loch Spelve. A road along the N shore of Loch Spelve heads towards Craignure. Wonderful cliff scenery can be enjoyed in these parts, with 2,289ft Creach Bheinn rising above the road. Lord Lovat's Cave lies on the E shore of the entrance to Loch Buie, facing the Firth of Lorne. This 300ft-long and 150ft-high cave can be visited by boat only.

LOCHCARRON, Highland 33 NG93
Ties and scarves are woven in this attractive village, which lies on the shores of Inner Loch Carron. Also known as Jeantown, Lochcarron is situated at the start of the road leading to Shieldaig, Torridon, and Kinlochewe. Before reaching Kishorn the road enters the tiny Pass of Kishorn, leading down to the hamlet on a loch of the same name. Slumbay is a little fishing village to the SW of Lochcarron. Farther SW at the entrance of Inner Loch Carron stand the ruins of Strome Castle (NTS), a former MacDonnell fortification which was blown up by the Mackenzies in 1603 during a clan feud. To the NW of Lochcarron is the thickly-wooded Allt-nen-Carman national nature reserve.

LOCH CORUISK, Isle of Skye, Highland 32
Thought by many to be the most spectacular mountain and loch scenery in the whole of Scotland, Loch Coruisk lies in a deep and remote basin below the Cuillins on the Isle of Skye. It is separated from the sea loch Scavaig by a narrow strip of land, and access is usually by motor boat from Elgol to the head of Loch Scavaig. However, there are also two long-distance paths to the loch. The one from Sligachan leads over the Drumhain ridge, and the other runs from Elgol, by way of Camasunary and the notorious Bad Step.

A breathtaking view of Loch Coruisk, with the great Cuillin circle massed to the W, can be enjoyed by climbing the steep and rocky little peak of 1,623ft Sgurr na Stri, situated at the SE end of Loch Coruisk. From this point the view includes the Inaccessible Pinnacle perched near the rocky summit of 3,254ft Sgurr Dearg, beyond the corrie of Coire-uisg. Loch Coruisk's savage beauty has inspired many writers and painters, including Turner, Scott in *Lord of the Isles*, and John Buchan in *Mr Standfast*.

LOCH DOON, Strathclyde 25
Hills surround this long, narrow loch, and the picturesque Ness Glen lies at its N end. A road along the W shores passes Loch Doon Castle (AM), a 14th-c island-castle which was carefully re-erected by the loch-side before the water was raised in connection with the Galloway power scheme. Once known as Castle

Balliol, this stronghold has walls between 7 and 9 ft thick. Beautiful Galloway hills rise to the S of Loch Doon, including 2,520ft Shalloch on Minnoch, 2,562ft Kirriereoch Hill, 2,668ft Corserine, and 2,650ft Carlin's Cairn. To the W of the loch lies Carrick Forest, part of the Glen Trool forest park. This includes the lonely Lochs Recar and Macaterick, and the waters of Eglin Lane and Gala Lane.

LOCH DUICH, Highland 33

This NW Highland sea loch is of great beauty and stretches from Shiel Bridge – at the N end of the magnificent mountain-encircled defile of Glen Shiel – to Dornie, where it is joined by Loch Long. The waters of both lochs join up with Loch Alsh, which extends as far as the shores of Skye. Beyond Shiel Bridge the main road to Dornie and Kyle of Lochalsh crosses the loch by a causeway, and W of Shiel Bridge a road climbs over the steep and narrow Mam Rattachan Pass to Glenelg. One of the finest views of the loch, backed by the fine ridge of the Five Sisters of Kintail, can be enjoyed from the summit of the pass. Scour Ouran stands at 3,505ft and dominates both the Five Sisters' group and Glen Shiel, to the SE of Loch Duich.

LOCHEARNHEAD, Central 30 NN52

Highland Games are held at this small touring centre during July. The community lies at the W end of lovely wooded Loch Earn, which provides good sailing and water ski-ing. Fine walking country is offered by the surrounding hills, which are ablaze with the colour of wild flame nasturtium in the summer. From Lochearnhead a narrow and hilly road runs along the S shores of the loch, passing close to the remains of St Blane's Chapel. Near here is the entrance to Glen Ample, where a waterfall faces the old castellated mansion of Edinample.

Ardvorlich House lies another 2m E and features a tombstone which marks the spot where seven Macdonalds of Glencoe were killed during an attack on the house in 1620. Scott writes about Ardvorlich House and Glen Ample in his *Legend of Montrose*. Inside the building is the famous Clach Dearg, a talisman of rock crystal. To the SE of Lochearnhead are the lofty summits of 3,224ft Ben Vorlich and 3,189ft Stuc a' Chroin, best seen from the road traversing the N shores of Loch Earn on the way to St Fillan's. The hills of Breadalbane country rise to the N of the loch. From Lochearnhead a road runs NW through wooded Glen Ogle towards Glen Dochart and Killin, reaching a maximum height of some 948ft.

LOCH ECK, Strathclyde 44

Lonely Loch Eck is encircled by hills clothed with a forest of variegated spruces, and is situated on the Cowal peninsula. Beinn Mhor rises to the SW, and at 2,433ft is one of the highest points in the area. A lovely road along the E shores of the loch links Strachur with the inner waters of the Holy Loch and the resort of Dunoon.

LOCH ETIVE, Strathclyde 29

A steamer pier lies near the entrance to Glen Etive at the head of this sea loch, from where a narrow road leads NE to Kingshouse, bordered by the Dalness Forest mountains. This end of the loch is dominated by three peaks – 3,541ft Ben Starav, 3,425ft Stob Coir' an Albannaich,

An island in Loch Eilt – the last stronghold of trees against the gales that storm through this valley.

and 2,752ft Ben Trilleachàn. Farther S, between Glen Kinglass and Glen Noe, rises the massive bulk of twin-peaked, 3,689ft Ben Cruachan. The waters at the seaward end of Loch Etive mingle with those of the Firth of Lorne at the Connel narrows, where the Falls of Lora are also situated.

LOCHFOOT, Dumfries and Galloway 25 NX87

This tiny village lies on the N shores of Lochrutton Loch, with restored Hills Castle lying 1½m SE. The castle was built between the 16th and 18thc and is joined to an early 18th-c house. A rare, early 17th-c gatehouse with its original iron yett is preserved.

LOCH FYNE, Strathclyde 29

Famous for its herrings and kippers, Loch Fyne is one of the best-known of the Scottish sea lochs. In common with most sea lochs its finest scenery lies at the head, near Cairndow. Here the peaks of 3,106ft Beinn Bhuidhe, 2,658ft Binnein an Fhidleir, and 3,021ft Beinn an Lochain overlook the loch's waters, and a picturesque road climbs E through Glen Kinglas before descending past Rest and be Thankful to Glen Croe and the head of Loch Long at Arrochar. In the hilly Cowal country beyond Otter Ferry Loch Fyne widens, with the heights of Knapdale forming a background to the W shores. The seaward end of the loch joins the Sound of Bute, facing the island of Bute which lies off the foot of the Cowal peninsula.

LOCHGAIR, Strathclyde 29 NR99

Little Loch Glashan lies to the NW of Lochgair, which stands on a loch of the same name – a tiny inlet of Loch Fyne.

*LOCHGILPHEAD, Strathclyde 29 NR88

Loch Gilp is an inlet of the larger Loch Fyne, and at its head stands the town of Lochgilphead. A little to the N is the chambered cairn of Auchnahoish, from where views to the SW take in the low Knapdale hills. Late 18th-c Crinan Canal flows W to Loch Gilp at Ardrishaig, on its way from Crinan.

LOCHGOILHEAD, Strathclyde 29 NN20

The Victorian township of Lochgoilhead lies in a hollow below the lofty Cowal hills, and has a pier sited on the shingly shores of Loch Goil. A steep and narrow road leading N from the town divides after 2m, with both branches leading into spectacular mountain scenery. The E branch crosses the Rest and be Thankful pass at the N limit of the mountainous Cowal peninsula; rocky and lonely Hell's Glen is traversed by the W branch as it zigzags its way to the E shores of Loch Fyne. A narrow road leads from the town and passes along the head and W shores of Loch Goil as far as the ruins of Carrick Castle. Once a Royal castle, Carrick may have originated in the 14thc and was burned down in 1685. Loch steamers from Lochgoilhead provide good views of the castle ruins.

LOCH HOURN, Highland 32

Many consider magnificent Loch Hourn to be the grandest of all the great sea lochs in the W Highlands. Lying in the remote district of Knoydart, its mountain setting is unequalled. Bare rocky slopes blend into woods of native Scots pine and Forestry Commission plantations. A narrow strait known as Caolas Mor divides Loch Hourn into the Inner and Outer Lochs. The beautiful Inner Loch can only be reached by the road from the A87 in Glen Garry, running W past Loch Quoich. This road becomes very narrow as it descends steeply (1 in 6) through a wilderness of grey, glaciated rocks to Kinloch Hourn.

Perhaps the most breathtaking view of the loch is from the rock-strewn peak of 3,365ft Sgurr a'Mhoraire, which can be approached from the road. Outer Loch Hourn is also only accessible by one road – that from Glenelg. This borders the shores of the Sound of Sleat and affords wonderful views across the Sound to the Isle of Skye. Bending round Outer Loch Hourn the road ends at Arnisdale, to the N of which is 3,196ft Ben Sgriol. Across the loch is the great 3,343ft peak and viewpoint of Ladhar Bheinn, which can be climbed from Inverie on Loch Nevis. A bridle path from Inverie leads NE through Glen Dulochan, climbing to nearly 1,100ft before descending to Barrisdale Bay on Loch Hourn.

LOCHINDORB, Highland 34 NH93

Lochindorb lies on the W side of the wild

Entries marked * are the starting point of drives included in the Day Drive section of the book (pages 95 to 160).

271

and bleak Dava Moor and is best known for the ruins of its sinister island-castle. Edward III occupied Lochindorb Castle in 1303, and during the later part of the 14thc it became a stronghold of the notorious Wolf of Badenoch, who terrorized the Lowlands of Moray. The structure was finally destroyed in the reign of James II. A narrow road SW from the main Grantown-on-Spey to Forres road climbs on to moorland before following the E shores of Lochindorb. It then leads SW towards the lofty road linking Carrbridge with Forres.

LOCHINVER, Highland 36 NC02

A lovely small resort on the wild rocky coastline of the Assynt district, Lochinver has a pier sited at the stony head of Loch Inver. Loch Assynt lies to the NE and is the source of the River Inver, which enters Loch Inver at the resort. Some 300 small lochs surround Lochinver, and it is small wonder that the resort is popular with anglers. The isolated Torridon sandstone peaks of 2,779ft Canisp and 2,399ft Suilven rise SE in Glencanisp Forest.

Suilven is one of the most impressive peaks on the mainland, being formed partly of the oldest rock in Britain, laid down over 2,600 million years ago. Known also as the Matterhorn of Scotland because of its dangerous cliff faces, Suilven has a double peak and affords wonderful views from the sharp E summit. This forms a 1½m ridge which is best seen from the vicinity of Altnacealgach. It is the better-known W peak that is hazardous to climb, and this forms a striking feature in the landscape when viewed from points on the coast around Lochinver – particularly from the rocky shores of Loch Roe, which lies to the NW on the road to Stoer. The 'mad little road of Sutherland' is a name sometimes given to the wild and lovely road leading S from Lochinver towards Inverkirkaig and beautiful Enard Bay. Fine views of Suilven are afforded by this route.

Another picturesque road runs NW from Lochinver, following the coast by way of Stoer and continuing to Kylesku. This road is steep and narrow in places, but offers magnificent views of the old Sutherland peaks and the Isle of Skye across the Minch.

LOCH KATRINE, Central 29

Scott's inspiration for his poem *The Lady of the Lake* came from Loch Katrine, which is considered one of the loveliest in the Highlands. Bare and rocky Ben Venue stands at 2,393ft and is the most prominent of the hills which ring the loch. Water is taken from here by a subterranean aqueduct, and forms part of Glasgow's supply. Ellen's Isle is named after Ellen Douglas, the actual *Lady of the Lake*, and faces the now-submerged Silver Strand which is also associated with Scott's poem.

From the Middle Ages until the early 18thc the MacGregors used Ellen's Isle to hide cattle they had stolen in raids on the Lowlands. No public road traverses Loch Katrine's shore, though pedestrians can use the private road along the N bank to reach Rob Roy's birthplace at Glengyle. A steamer trip on the loch, or short walk from Loch Katrine pier to the Pass of Achraig, gives some idea of the rugged splendour of the Trossachs, which can be seen at the E end of the loch. Part of the Queen Elizabeth forest park extends almost to Stronachlachar, and also to the Pass of Achray.

LOCH LAGGAN, Highland 33

Lochaber power scheme has greatly altered the appearance of wooded Loch Laggan. A large reservoir now lies to the SW, and the great Laggan Dam blocks the far end near the outflow of the River Spean in Glen Spean. A tunnel to the S links up with the waters of Loch Treig. Several ancient dug-out canoes were found in the loch during work in connection with the power scheme. A good road follows Loch Laggan's N shore, with lofty mountains rising in the background.

Beyond the Laggan Dam, on the N side of the road, are parallel 'roads' formed by glacial action, similar to the better-known examples near Roy Bridge. Near Aberarder Farm is the entrance to the wild Coire Ardair and its remote lochan, with 3,700ft Creag Meaghaidh dominant. This mountain is the highest point in a range of hills which stretches for nearly 10m at little below 3,000ft. The River Pattack, on which the Linn of Pattack is situated, flows into the E end of Loch Laggan after accompanying the Kingussie road for 3m in Ardverikie Forest.

LOCHLEE, Tayside 35 NO47

Lochlee lies at the end of the beautiful long valley of Glen Esk, just SW of the local church. The valley is threaded by the North Esk River. Ruined Invermark Castle, ancient home of the Stirlings, stands to the E of the loch where the Water of Mark comes down from Glen Mark. To the NW of Lochlee is 3,077ft Mount Keen, which was climbed by Queen Victoria and Prince Albert in 1861. The Queen's Well on the path to Mount Keen commemorates the Queen's visit. This path is the Mounth Track which leads over the old Aberdeen border towards Aboyne. The White Mounth group is dominated by 3,786ft Lochnagar to the W.

LOCH LEVEN, Tayside 30

Two of Loch Leven's attractions are its fascinating history and its delicious salmon trout. International trout-angling competitions are held on the loch, and curling is a winter sport encouraged here. The loch is also an important wintering ground for thousands of wild geese, mallards, and other wild fowl. Part of it is a nature reserve, and on the SE shore at Vane Farm is a Royal Society for the Protection of Birds study and observation centre. Summer boat trips ply to Castle Island, the site of ruined 14th or 15th-c Loch Leven Castle (AM). Mary Queen of Scots was imprisoned here for eleven months in 1567 and 1568. The queen made a sensational escape with the help of William Douglas, a friend of George Douglas the gaoler's son. As soon as the queen was safely on a boat William Douglas locked the castle and threw the keys into the loch.

The notorious Wolf of Badenoch, son of Robert II, was also imprisoned here after his reign of terror in the late 14thc. Another prisoner was Patrick Grahame, Primate of Scotland. St Serf's Island is also in Loch Leven and includes the remains of an old priory. To the E of Loch Leven are the Lomond Hills, including Bishop Hill and West Lomond. Benarty Hill stands to the S.

LOCH LINNHE, Strathclyde; Highland 29

Like Loch Hourn, Loch Linnhe falls naturally into an Inner and Outer Loch, separated by the Corran narrows. It lies at the extreme W end of the Great Glen, and a car ferry across the narrows links the Lochaber and Ardgour districts. The waters at the head of the Inner Loch mingle with those of Loch Eil near Corpach, and are dominated by the mighty, 4,406ft Ben Nevis and the Mamore Forest mountains. At Corpach the Caledonian Canal flows into Loch Linnhe and provides a navigable link with Loch Lochy. Beyond the Corran Narrows, after being joined by Loch Leven, the loch broadens out. Its waters are overlooked here by the Ben Vair ridges of the Appin country, with the sharp peak of Garbh Bheinn in Ardgour rising behind Inversanda. Loch Linnhe's seaward end extends to Duart Point on the island of Mull, beyond the smaller island of Lismore in the Firth of Lorne. Roads border both shores of the Inner Loch, and fringe the Outer Loch for some distance. Loch Linnhe is best seen from the steamers which sail from Fort William to Oban during the summer.

LOCH LOCHY, Highland 33

One of the chain of lochs along the Great Glen, Loch Lochy is like Loch Linnhe in

Ruined Invermark Castle, a one-time Stirling stronghold near Lochlee.

that it forms part of the Caledonian Canal. At the N end of the loch are the Laggan Locks, and about 10m SW is the entrance to the long, roadless valley of Glen Gloy. This glen leads into lonely hills and displays parallel 'roads' formed by glacial action – somewhat similar to the fine examples near Roy Bridge.

Loch Lochy's shores are hilly and sometimes wooded, the highest mountains rising on the N side in Glengarry Forest. Here Sron a'Choire Ghairbh reaches 3,066ft, and the sharp cone of Ben Tee stands at 2,956ft. The main Fort William to Inverness road follows the E shores of the loch, and about halfway along passes the former Letterfinlay Inn. In the early 18thc General Wade's soldiers used the inn as a road-house while building the original road. Wordsworth and his sister were later visitors.

LOCH LOMOND, Strathclyde; Central 44
Known as the 'Queen of Scottish Lakes', Loch Lomond is the largest lake in Great Britain. Soft green hills slope away from its banks in the S and, farther N, wooded mountains climb dramatically from its W and E shores. Prominent Ben Lomond rises to 3,192ft E of the loch opposite Tarbet, and is best climbed from Rowardennan. The superb panorama from its summit extends from the Arran hills to Ben Cruachan. On the W side of the loch is a narrow neck of land which separates Loch Lomond from the N end of Loch Long at Arrochar. Farther N are 3,318ft Ben Ime, 3,004ft Ben Vane, and 3,092ft Ben Vorlich, crowded into an impressive mountain-scape.

The waters of Loch Sloy, lying in its glen between Ben Vane and Ben Vorlich, are taken by tunnel aqueduct to the power station at Inveruglas. The head of Loch Lomond around Ardlui is particularly beautiful, and from Ardlui a busy road traverses the W shore of the loch. Loch Lomond's islands greatly add to its beauty and attracted Irish missionaries in the 5thc, who wanted to keep their precincts secure from marauders. St Mirren is believed to have founded a monastery in the 6thc on Inchmurrin, the largest island, on which lie the ruins of Lennox Castle.

Loch Lomond national nature reserve covers the SE corner of Loch Lomond and includes five of its islands. On the E side of the loch is a twisting road which follows the shore from Balmaha to Rowardennan, from where a track runs N past the E bulk of Ben Lomond. This path eventually leads to the beautifully situated village of Inversnaid, some 8m N. Loch Lomond's many attractive bays are filled with trout, pike, and powan – a white fish found in Scottish lochs and Welsh lakes. One of Prince Charles Edward's captured followers is said to have composed the song *Loch Lomond* on the eve of his execution in Carlisle Jail. The 'low road' of the song is the path by which the writer says his spirit will return to his native land after death, quicker than his friend travelling to Scotland by the ordinary 'high road'.

LOCH LONG, Strathclyde 44
Norse invaders landed here in the 13thc at the start of a pillaging and plundering raid on villages and islands in the area. Near the head of the loch at Arrochar is the prominent rock peak of 2,891ft Ben

Arthur, popularly known as The Cobbler. Farther S a line of hills known as Argyll's Bowling Green overlooks the meeting point of Lochs Long and Goil. At the mouth of Loch Long is Strone Point, where the waters of Holy Loch meet the Clyde estuary and the Rosneath peninsula divides Loch Long from Gare Loch. The oil-port of Finnart stands on Loch Long's east shore, N of Gare Loch.

LOCH LURGAIN, Highland 36
Little-known Loch Lurgain lies away from any main road and has one of the finest mountain settings in Scotland. It can be reached by a narrow road leading W from the Ullapool to Inchnadamph road. This route follows Loch Lurgain's N shore and passes 2,523ft Cul Beag, and the remarkable 2,009ft An Stack, or Stack Polly. The latter's summit ridge of sharp pinnacles is almost unclimbable, and overlooks Inverpolly Forest. Behind these two peaks is the higher 2,786ft Cul Mor.

Beyond the roadless south shore of Loch Lurgain, Beinn Eun faces the magnificent viewpoint of 2,438ft Ben More Coigach, which overlooks Outer Loch Broom and the Coigach district. Between these two hills lies tiny Lochan Tuath, shadowed by the great crag of 2,285ft Sgurr an Fhidhleir. From Loch Lurgain the road continues past Loch Baddagyle to the picturesque rocky coast around Enard Bay and the village of Achiltibuie.

LOCHMABEN, Dumfries and Galloway 25 NY08
This small Annandale Royal Burgh lies between Castle Loch to the SE, the Kirk and Mill Lochs to the NW, and Brumel Loch to the E. A rare fish called a vendace – about 7ins long and with a heart-shaped mark on its head – frequents Castle and Mill Lochs. Castle Loch and Hightae Lochs are now nature reserves. Lochmaben's Mercat cross has sundials on the faces of its upper portion, and at the south end of Castle Loch is ruined Lochmaben Castle. A predecessor of this may have been the birthplace of Robert the Bruce, although some authorities favour Turnberry Castle.

Lochmaben Castle was built during the early 14thc and changed hands no fewer than twelve times. It withstood six attacks and sieges. Mary Queen of Scots was a visitor here in 1565, and James IV frequently came to the castle. To the N of Lochmaben the Water of Ae is joined by Kinnel Water, both of which flow into the River Annan a little downstream. The River Annan meanders through Annandale to the E of Castle Loch. Skipmyre lies 3m SW of Lochmaben and in 1658 was the birthplace of William Paterson, associated with the founding of the Bank of England. The late 16th-c Elshieshields Tower, partly modernized and joined to an 18th-c house, stands some 2m NNW on the Water of Ae.

LOCHMADDY, Western Isles 39 NF77
See Hebrides, Outer.

LOCH MAREE, Highland 33
Well known to fishermen, beautiful Loch Maree lies amid wild mountain scenery in Wester Ross. The sea loch of Ewe lies farther N but may once have been joined to Loch Maree. The two are separated by a mere 2m strip of land, which is crossed by the River Ewe. Slioch's great mass soars to 3,260ft from Loch Maree's

SE shore. In the vicinity is the finest of Loch Maree's mountain scenery, with the great cliffs of 2,817ft Ben Lair rising to the NW of Slioch. A little more distant is 2,593ft Beinn Airidh Charr.

The road from Kinlochewe, at the head of Loch Maree, runs along the SW shores of the loch; this area lies within the Ben Eighe national nature reserve. The road provides a wonderful view of the loch as it continues along the W shore and passes Grudie Bridge. Here there are magnificent views S towards the grand Torridon peaks – 2,376ft Beinn a Chearcaill, 3,220ft Ben Eighe, and 3,454ft Liathach. Loch Maree Hotel, visited by Queen Victoria in 1877, lies beyond Grundie Bridge opposite a group of the loch's lovely, wooded islands. Druids once worshipped on tiny Isle Maree, where there are traces of a chapel which succeeded an early hermitage of St Maelrubha. Near by are a sacred well and the remains of a wishing tree.

On the opposite roadless shore is Letterewe, where charcoal was used for iron-smelting to make cannons until the mid 17thc. To the S of Loch Maree Hotel rise 2,801ft Beinn an Eoin and 2,896ft Baeshven, overlooking the remote Shieldaig and Flowerdale Forests. The road bears away from the lochside at the clachan of Slattadale, and passes through the narrow and beautiful Kerrysdale on its way to Gairloch. Near Slattadale are the Victoria Falls, named to commemorate a visit by Queen Victoria. One of the most beautiful views of Loch Maree, looking towards Slioch, can be enjoyed just N of the loch from the S fringe of Poolewe.

LOCH MORLICH, Highland 34
Loch Morlich has sandy shores and lies in the heart of the Glen More forest park at a height of 1,046ft. To the N is the 4,084ft Cairngorm, which has given its name to the whole range and to a type of smokey quartz which is found here. Thousands of acres of pine and spruce woods clothe the mountainous slopes around the loch, and the surrounding countryside is probably the finest area in Britain for wild life – eg red deer, reindeer, wildcats, golden eagles, ptarmigan, and capercailize. The Scottish Sports Council runs courses for young people and youth leaders in climbing, sailing, canoeing, fly fishing, and ski-ing at Glenmore Lodge.

There is a camping ground in the neighbourhood, and the district has become Britain's major winter-sports area. Extensive Abernethy Forest lies NE of Loch Morlich and can be reached by a track over the Ryvoan Pass, which affords views of the picturesque little Green Loch. The River Luineag rushes through tall pines from the W end of the loch towards the Spey valley. A track NW of the loch crosses the Sluggan Pass on its way to the Spey valley near Boat of Garten.

LOCHNAGAR, Grampian 34 NO28
This well-known granite peak features prominently in the view from many points on Deeside and even farther afield. It rises at the end of the high-lying White Mounth plateau near the old Angus/Aberdeen border, and has twin summits of 3,786ft and 3,768ft. Overlooking the Royal Forest of Balmoral, Lochnagar is separated from the great Cairngorm range – away to the NW – by the beautifully wooded valley of the Dee.

cont

The Well of Heads near Loch Oich, commemorating the decapitation of seven brothers in the 17thc.

It can be climbed by four routes – Queen Victoria and Prince Albert chose the ascent from Balmoral through Glen Gelder when they climbed the mountain on pony-back in 1848. The other ascents are from Braemar up Glen Callater; from Ballater up Glen Muick and past Loch Muick with 3,552ft Cuidhe Crom, a SE buttress of Lochnagar, rising above the loch; and from Braedownie in Glen Clova. The summit has an indicator and affords magnificent views. Beneath the peak a tiny lochan lies at the bottom of a deep corrie, overhung by tremendous cliffs. Byron was inspired to write one of his finest poems by Lochnagar.

LOCH NAN UAMH, Highland 32

Famous for its associations with Bonnie Prince Charlie, picturesque Loch nan Uamh forms an inlet of the Sound of Arisaig. It was here that the prince landed from a French frigate at Borrodale on 5 August, 1745, at the place where the tiny Borrodale Burn flows into the loch. Borrodale House was burnt after Culloden but still preserves much of its original structure. It was the scene of the fateful interview with Lochiel, when the whole issue of the Jacobite Rising hung in balance. In 1746 the prince returned to the loch as a fugitive with a price of £30,000 on his head, and had to hide in the Glen Beasdale woods before he was able to cross to the Outer Hebrides. Later he returned to the mainland and hid in a cave, now known as Prince Charlie's Cave, near Borrodale. On 20 September 1746 he boarded the French frigate 'L'Heureux', never to return to Scotland again. The '45 Association set up a memorial cairn to the prince in 1956, on the spot where he is thought to have embarked. At the head of Loch nan Uamh, crossed by the road from Lochailort to Arisaig, Gleann Mama leads to Loch Mama in the hills of S Morar. Wonderful seaward views taking in the islands of Eigg and Rum can be enjoyed from here.

LOCHNAW CASTLE, Dumfries and Galloway 24 NW96

Ancient seat of the Agnews, who were once Sheriffs of Galloway, Lochnaw Castle lies in the Rhinns of Galloway peninsula 2m SW of Leswalt. It was built between the 16th and 18thc and stands beside a small loch. The building has been modernized and is now used as a hotel. Pretty Aldouran Glen is traversed by the Stranraer road to the E, and ruined, 16th-c Galdenoch Castle lies to the W.

LOCH NESS, Highland 33

Stories of the monster in Loch Ness date back at least to the 7thc when St Adamnan, Abbot of Iona wrote his biography of St Columba. The biography relates that St Columba prevented a River Ness water monster from eating a Pict in AD565. According to another legend the beast towed St Columba's boat across the loch and was granted perpetual freedom. Gaelic folklore says that the monster is a 'each visge', or fearsome water horse, one of which haunts every dark sheet of water in the Highlands. Loch Ness is not unique in having its monster – Lochs Awe, Rannoch, Lomond, and Morar have all been said to be infested, but there have been hundreds of sightings since the main road along the wooded W shore was opened in 1933. The mystery continues and is probably far more exciting than the final answer.

Loch Ness extends from Inverness to Fort Augustus and is over 700ft deep in places. It has never been known to freeze, and its waters are made very dark by the peaty soil brought down by the numerous streams and rivers which feed the loch. The road along the E shore partly follows the course of an old Wade road from Inverness to Fort Augustus, but then veers away from the loch at Foyers.

There are no high hills around Loch Ness' shores, but 2,284ft Mealfuarvonie is a prominent feature rising above the W shore opposite Foyers. One of the loveliest views from the loch is down Glen Urquhart, which stretches W from its bay and is guarded by the impressive ruins of Urquhart Castle (AM), near Drumnadrochit. Between Drumnadrochit and Invermoriston is a cairn which was set up in memory of John Cobb, who died on the loch while trying to beat the water speed record in 1952. Loch Ness is one of the chain of lochs lying in the Great Glen (Glen More), linked by the Caledonian Canal.

LOCH NEVIS, Highland 32

There is no road access to this magnificent sea loch, which is a close rival to the beauty of Loch Hourn. The narrow strait of Kylesknoydart separates the Inner and Outer Lochs, with the rugged splendour of the Knoydart hills to the N. North Morar's lower hills rise S of the loch and divide it from Loch Morar. Splendid peaks rise at the head of the Inner Loch, dominated by 3,083ft Luinne Bheinn, 2,905ft Ben Aden, and the sharp cone of 3,410ft Sgurr na Ciche.

A path from the loch head crosses the wild pass of the Mam na Cloiche Airde, which long-distance walkers use to reach Loch Arkaig. Apart from several very long tracks, the only way to visit the Loch Nevis is by motor launch from Mallaig to Inverie on its NW shores. Carn a'Ghobhair stands at 1,794ft and can be climbed from Mallaig. This height provides views of Loch Névis which are probably the finest available and include the whole length of Loch Morar.

LOCH OICH, Highland 33

This short but beautiful loch is the highest of the chain of lochs lying in the Great Glen, all linked together by the Caledonian Canal. Along its W shores runs the fine Fort William to Inverness road, passing through Invergarry – gateway to some of the finest scenery in the NW Highlands.

Farther SW is the Well of the Heads, erected by MacDonnell of Glengarry to commemorate the decapitation of seven brothers who had murdered the two sons of a 17th-c chief of Clan Keppoch, a branch of the Clan MacDonnell. The heads were washed in the well before being presented to the chief of the MacDonnells at Glengarry. Four languages on the monument describe the brothers' fate, and seven heads are carved round the top of the pillar, which is surmounted by a hand clasping a dagger.

Aberchalder Lodge stands at the N end of Loch Oich and was where Prince Charles Edward rallied his clansmen before crossing the Corrieyairack Pass on his way to Edinburgh and England in 1745. General Wade built a military road along the E shores of the loch, but this is now only a minor road.

LOCH QUOICH, Highland 33

Penetrating W from Glen Garry into the rugged Knoydart mountains, beautiful Loch Quoich lies in an area which has the highest average annual rainfall in Scotland. The loch has been enlarged as part of a hydro-electric scheme. It was a favourite of Edward VII, who frequently came to Glen Quoich Lodge to shoot. Halfway along the loch's N shore, on the narrow road from Tomdoun to Kinloch Hourn, is Quoich Bridge. This is where the River Quoich flows into the loch from Glen Quoich.

Lofty hills – 3,365ft Sgurr a'Mhoraire to the W, plus 3,395ft Gleouraich and 3,268ft Spidean Mialach to the E – surround this roadless glen, along which General Monk and his troops marched in 1654 towards Glen Shiel. The prominent peak of 3,015ft Gairich rises to the S, and from the SW tip of the loch a track leads past the delightfully rocky Lochan nam Breac into the wild and lonely district of Rough Bounds, dominated by 3,410ft Sgurr na Ciche. This 8m path leads to the shores of Loch Hourn at Barrisdale. Prince Charles Edward had many narrow escapes from capture as he fled through the area from the Duke of Cumberland's men after Culloden in 1746.

LOCH RANNOCH, Tayside 30

Loch Rannoch stretches from Kinloch Rannoch to a point near Bridge of Gaur, on the road to the lonely Rannoch station, and forms part of the Tummel-Garry hydro-electric scheme. The Black Wood of Rannoch borders the loch's S shore, and lofty hills rise beyond it. These include 3,547ft Schiehallion and 3,419ft Carn Mairg to the SE, with 3,054ft Garbh Mheall to the SW.

LOCHRANZA, Isle of Arran, Strathclyde 29 NR95

Arran's farthest N resort, Lochranza lies at the foot of Glen Chalmadale and SW of the Cock of Arran, which faces the Sound and island of Bute which are backed by the hills of the Cowal. This resort has a steamer pier and a summer car ferry service operates to Claonaig on Kintyre. Robert the Bruce is said to have landed here on his return in 1307 from Rathlin in Ireland, at the start of his campaign for Scottish independence.

Lochranza Castle (AM) is a picturesque ruin with two square towers, erected in the 13th to 14thc and enlarged in the 16thc. A fine road runs S from the resort, hugging the coast at the foot of a range of hills all the way to Pirnmill. The delightful bay of Catacol lies 2m S along the road on the Kilbrennan Sound, and from here Glen Catacol penetrates into the hills to the S. Beinn Bhreac and Beinn Bharrain both rise to over 2,300ft and overlook lonely Loch Tanna, which lies at 1,051ft above sea level beyond the head of the glen. Glen Iorsa extends SW to Dougrie on Machrie Bay S of the loch. Glen Diomhan is a small national nature reserve which preserves rare whitebeam trees and lies below 1,870ft Meall nan Damh, SW of Lochranza.

LOCH SCAVAIG, Isle of Skye, Highland 32 NG41

Motor launches from Elgol cross this beautiful sea loch on their way to its head. The grand Cuillin range lies to the N, and a narrow strip of land separates the loch from the magnificent Loch Coruisk, which is overhung at its far end by the jagged Cuillin peaks. The waters of the so-called Mad Burn tumble in spate from a narrow ravine into the water of Loch Scavaig, a little to the W. Above the loch to the NW rises 2,934ft Gars Bheinn, the extreme S Cuillin peak and a fine viewpoint. High points around Elgol afford the finest views of Loch Scavaig and its superb mountainous backdrop. Offshore is the flat island of Soay, with the mountainous Rum and the smaller Eigg farther out to sea.

LOCH SHIEL, Highland 32

This long freshwater loch stretches to Acharacle from the Glenfinnan monument (NTS) raised to Highlanders who followed Prince Charles Edward in the '45 Rising. Romantic Clanranald country forms a beautiful setting, and many consider Loch Shiel to be one of the finest in the W Highlands. The loch forms a natural boundary between the Ardgour district and the Moidart district, and is no more than 1m across at any point. Wonderful mountain scenery frames the loch at its N end, with parallel ranges of rock-strewn hills bordering Glen Finnan to the N of the monument. Bheinn Odhar

Bheag soars to 2,895ft above the W shore, facing across the loch to 2,784ft Meall nan Creag Leac.

Farther down the loch the Moidart mountains recede, but on the E shore Ben Resipol's sharp, rocky peak reaches up to 2,774ft and offers splendid, panoramic views of the whole length of Loch Shiel from its summit – the seaward view including the islands of Eigg and Rum. Below Ben Resipol are the narrows of Loch Shiel and the little island of Eilean Fhionain. The island was used centuries ago as a burial ground, and the Celtic bell preserved here is one of the few surviving examples.

Lonely Glen Hurich cuts through the mountains to the E of Eilean Fhionain and is fringed by woodland. The River Pollock flows into Loch Shiel here from its source in tiny Loch Doilate. Loch Shiel is linked to Outer Loch Moidart by the Shiel River, which flows from its foot amid flat, mossy countryside. There are no public roads along the shores of Loch Shiel, but the Salen to Kinlochmoidart road touches the foot of the loch, and the main road from Corpach to Arisaig passes its head.

LOCH SUNART, Highland 28

The head of this beautiful sea loch lies in an amphitheatre of hills where the districts of Ardgour and Morven meet. Wonderful views are afforded by the summits of 2,903ft Garbh Bheinn, to the NE, and 2,800ft Creach Bheinn, to the SE. Between these two peaks is a road which threads its way through Glen Tarbert from Loch Linnhe. This road is narrow and hilly, but it skirts Loch Sunart's N shore and provides beautiful views of the wooded S shore, backed by gentler hills.

Near the head of the loch is Strontion. This small village gave its name to strontium, a mineral which used to be mined here. Farther W the road passes Salen, behind which Ben Resipol rises to 2,774ft to the NE. The summit of this prominent cone affords one of the finest panoramas in the W Highlands. The whole length of Loch Shiel and the distant islands of Eigg and Rhum can be seen.

LOCH TAY Tayside 30

One of the finest salmon fishing waters in Britain, deep Loch Tay is overlooked at its N end by the great 3,984ft Ben Lawers. Extensive W views of the Breadalbane country and much of the Grampians are provided by the Tarmachans, which face Ben Lawers. Though the main road follows the N shore of Loch Tay, the narrow and hilly S shore road affords the finest views. From Ardeonaig, with its mill and waterfall, a path leads into the hills towards Glen Lednoch, and another at Ardtalnaig runs to Glen Almond. Scott has composed a beautiful word picture of the loch in his *Fair Maid of Perth*. From the E end of the loch the 120m-long River Tay, which carries the largest volume of water of any British river, flows towards Aberfeldy.

LOCH TROOL, Dumfries and Galloway 24 NX47

Situated in Glen Trool in the heart of the remote Galloway Highlands, this beautiful loch is reached from Bargrennan via the Girvan to Newton Stewart road. The area around the loch is included in the Glen Trool forest park.

The park is made up of five separate forests of which Glen Trool Forest is the most beautiful. The Merrick is the highest mountain S of the Highlands and rises to 2,764ft N of Loch Trool within the boundaries of the park. Lochs Enoch and Neldricken, the latter with its 'Murder Hole', lie on the mountain's E and S slopes. To the SE of Loch Enoch are the remote and sinisterly named Round and Long Lochs of the Dungeon.

Much of this wild mountain country is described in S R Crockett's *Raiders*. Robert the Bruce began his fight for independence from the hills in the park, and a granite memorial (NTS) at the E end of the loch recalls how he and his men defeated an English force in 1307 by hurling rocks at them. At the SW end of the loch, near Caldons Farm is an inscribed Martyrs' Stone.

The 4½m circuit of Loch Trool on foot begins at the campsite near here. Away to the NE of the loch are the Rhinns of Kells, prominent among which are 2,668ft Corserine and 2,650ft Carlins Cairn. Farther S are 2,350ft Millfire and 2,446ft Meikle Millyea, with lonely Loch Dungeon lying in between.

LOCHWINNOCH, Strathclyde 44 NS35

This small town lies on Castle Semple Loch, at the S end of which are the ruins of Barr Castle and Peel Castle. Lofty moorland rises to the NW of Lochwinnoch and wonderful views can be enjoyed from 1,663ft Misty Law. Misty Law and the 1,711ft Hill of Stake lie on the one-time Ayrshire border.

*LOCKERBIE, Dumfries and Galloway 26 NY18

A great battle was fought here in 1593, ending one of the last of the infamous Border family feuds. The Johnstones routed the Maxwells, killing Lord Maxwell and 700 of his men. Many of the victims had their ears cut off with a cleaver, and this method of mutilation afterwards became known as the Lockerbie Nick. Lockerbie is an Annandale market town, noted for an August lamb fair which originated in the 17thc. The Old Tower was once the town gaol, and excavations near the flat-topped Birrenswark Hill, SE of Lockerbie, have revealed a 6ft-diameter Roman circular oven. Also here is the site of a well-fortified Roman camp. The mansion of Castle Milk stands in fine gardens by the Water of Milk 3m S of the town. Some 5m NNW of Lockerbie, to the W of the Moffat road and beyond the Annan, is Spedlins Tower. This is dated 1605, though some of its structure is of 15th-c origin.

LOGIE, Grampian 34 NJ05

Altyre Woods and Darnaway Forest lie to the N of the River Findhorn, which flows through a lovely, deep gorge a little to the W of Logie. Randolph's Leap is a beauty spot which lies 2m farther upstream, near the junction of the Findhorn and the Divie. It is named after Randolph, 1st Earl of Moray, whose opponent jumped the river during a combat. There is foot access only. Relugas House lies near by, and farther to the SW the Daltulich Bridge spans the Findhorn off the road to Ferness.

LOGIE EASTER, Highland 37 NH77

Logie Easter lies 3m N of Nigg Bay and is well known for its cattle. Turreted

---

Entries marked * are the starting point of drives included in the Day Drive section of the book (pages 95 to 160).

Balnagown Castle lies 1m SW of the village beyond the Balnagown River, and is surrounded by fine gardens. Once the home of the Earls of Ross, the castle dates from the 13th to 16thc. Several ancient and interesting tombstones are preserved in Marybank churchyard, 2m W of the village near the river.

LOGIERAIT, Tayside 30 NN95
A Royal castle which was the seat of the Regality Courts of Atholl once stood here. Rob Roy made a dramatic escape from its gaol in 1717. Logierait is a Strath Tay village, and a little to the SE the Tay is joined by the Tummel. The interesting local churchyard displays old sculptured stones and several mortsafes – once placed over new graves to foil body-snatchers. On the E bank of the Tay are a number of standing stones and remains of stone circles.

LONGANNET POINT, Fife 46 NS98
This is the site of a coal-fired generating station which has been built on reclaimed land. The 600ft chimney forms a local landmark.

LONGFORGEN, Tayside 31 NO32
Lying in the fertile Carse of Gowrie, Longforgen is situated between the Sidlaw Hills and the Firth of Tay. The 15thc Castle Huntly was once known as Castle Lyon and stands on a rocky site 1m W of the town. It was erected by Lord Gray of Foulis, Master of the Household to James II, and was considerably enlarged from the latter half of the 17thc. It now houses a Borstal institution.

LONGFORMACUS, Borders 31 NT65
This remote little village stands in the foothills of the Lammermuirs on the Dye Water, which is joined by the Whiteadder Water to the NE. Longformacus House is of Georgian date, and the S of the hamlet is dominated by 1,309ft Dirrington Great Law. The road to Duns wends beneath the mountain's slopes. A hilly little road winds NW from Longformacus towards the village of Gifford. The so-called Mutiny Stones, a relic of the stone age, lies W of this road on the Lammermuir heights.

LONGNIDDRY, Lothian 47 NT47
John Knox was a tutor at Longniddry between 1643 and 1647. The community lies just inland from Gosford Bay, a flat section of stony coastline with sand in places and a golf course near by. The ruined 16th- to 17th-c mansion of Redhouse stands 1½m NE.

LONMAY, Grampian 35 NK05
Cairness House dates from 1792 and stands 2½m NE of Lonmay, with the Loch of Strathbeg a little to the E of the village near Strathbeg Bay. Some 3m NW near the village of Rathen is the bronze-age burial cairn of Memsie (AM).

LORNE, Strathclyde 29 NM92
Picturesque Lorne stretches from the Firth of Lorne, at the seaward end of Loch Linnhe, to Loch Awe. The mountains surrounding Loch Etive form Lorne's natural east boundary, beyond which lie the districts of Benderloch and Appin. Strictly speaking these areas are part of Lorne, which extends N as far as Loch Leven and the wild Glencoe mountains. Oban, Lorne's principal town, is a fine centre for exploring this lovely part of the W Highlands. The marvellous countryside is best viewed from the summit of

3,689ft Ben Cruachan, and this peak can be climbed from a point near the Falls of Cruachan – on the NW shores of Loch Awe near the Pass of Brander.

LOSSIEMOUTH, Grampian 34 NJ27
Ramsay MacDonald, the UK's first Labour Prime Minister, was born here at 1 Gregory Place in 1866. Lossiemouth is a bustling and invigorating resort and fishing port on Spey Bay, situated at the mouth of the River Lossie. Good sands offer safe bathing, and extensive sand dunes stretch to the E. Branderburgh lies at the W end of the town and is an important harbour which serves as a port for Elgin. Scanty remains of the Bishops of Moray's castle survive SW of the resort of Kinnedar. The caves near Covesea, which lies 2m W of the harbour, display remarkable rock formations.

LOTH, Highland 37 NC91
It was here that Hunter Polson is said to have killed the last wolf in one-time Sutherland c1700, and a monument a little to the SW of Loth at the foot of Glen Loth recalls this event. Prehistoric remains in the area include standing stones in Glen Loth itself. The glen is backed by 2,060ft Beinn Dobhrain and 2,046ft Ben Uarie. Remains of a long cairn lie at the foot of the glen E of Lothbeg Bridge. The ruined broch of Cinn Trolla, probably of early iron-age origin, stands 2m SW of Loth on the coast.

LOTHIANS
The Lothian region comprises a large expanse of countryside bordered by the Firth of Forth, and roughly extending from Dunbar in the E to Linlithgow in the W. Edinburgh is the capital of the district, and the Lothians once reached as far S as the River Tweed – forming part of the ancient kingdom of Northumbria. Marquis of Lothian is the chosen title of the ancient Kerr family. A magnificent panorama of the district is afforded by the summit of Soutra Hill, on the Edinburgh to Lauder road.

LOUDOUNHILL, Strathclyde 25 NS63
A Roman fort once stood on this isolated 1,043ft cone of rock, and this is also where Robert the Bruce defeated the English in 1307. Adding to Loudounhill's violent history is the Battle of Drumclog, which took place a little to the N in 1679. The battle ended with Claverhouse being defeated by the Covenanters. Loudoun Castle lies 6m W.

LOVAT BRIDGE, Highland 34 NH54
Spanning the River Beauly, Lovat Bridge lies 1m NW of a road which diverges S from the Inverness road to join the Glen Covinth road running through the fertile district of The Aird. Farther S is another little road, which branches SE from the Glen Covinth road and climbs past tiny Loch Laide on its way to Loch Ness.

LOWLANDS, THE
A landscape characterized by rounded green hills, pleasant valleys, and excellent farming country, the Lowlands roughly cover the part of Scotland S of a line linking Glasgow, Stirling, and Edinburgh. More precisely, the Highland line or geological boundary may be said to commence in the Firth of Clyde, to follow the Cowal coast of old Argyll before later crossing the mouth of the Gare Loch to pass later over the lower reaches of Loch Lomond. The boundary then follows a line linking Aberfoyle, Callander, and

Comrie, past the entrance to the Sma' Glen to reach the Tay to the S of Dunkeld. It then runs NE towards the Dee valley at Dinnet, crossing the one-time counties of Banffshire and Moray in a NW line to reach the Moray Firth at Nairn. Even the distant countryside of one-time Caithness, beyond the Moray Firth, is Lowland in character.

Though the name suggests flatness, the Lowlands are more hilly than most parts of England and the climate, particularly in the central area, can be as harsh in mid-winter as at any lonely Highland hamlet. Most of Scotland's industrial area and two-thirds of her population are centred in the Lowlands, particularly between the Clyde and Forth estuaries. A remarkable feature of the region's SW is the district of Galloway, where lonely, rugged hills are dominated by the lofty 2,764ft Merrick and exhibit many of the features of true Highland country. The Lowlands include the delightful Border country, which has a history even more turbulent than that of the Highlands. This area inspired much of the writing of Sir Walter Scott, who lived at Abbotsford until his death in 1832. Burns is considered Scotland's greatest literary figure, and he drew much of his inspiration from the Ayrshire landscape.

LUGAR, Strathclyde 25 NS52
William Murdoch was born here at Bello Mill in 1754, and a nearby cave was the scene of his experiments in coal-gas lighting. Lugar's ironworks were built in 1845.

LUMPHANAN, Grampian 35 NJ50
Macbeth's Cairn lies to the N of Lumphanan and is said to mark the site of Macbeth's last stand in 1057, before he was killed. His head was taken to Malcolm at Kincardine Castle, near Fettercairn. Lumphanan lies beyond the Loch of Auchlossan just N of the winding River Dee.

LUMSDEN, Grampian 35 NJ42
The Correen Hills rise E of Lumsden, and to the W the 2,368ft Buck of Cabrach shadows the valley in which the community lies. Ruins of interesting St Mary's Church (AM) can be seen 2m N off the Dufftown road at Auchindoir, and include a richly-carved 12th- or 13th-c doorway and a rare Sacrament House. A Norman castle once stood on a motte near the church, and W of the church is Craig Castle, which stands on the Burn of Craig. Patrick Gordon, who was slain at Flodden Field in 1513, built the original tower three years before his death.

LUNAN, Tayside 31 NO65
Beside the sandhills in Lunan Bay are the ruins of Red Castle. This red-stone tower probably dates from the 15thc, when it replaced an earlier fort built for William the Lion by Walter de Berkeley. The purpose of the building was to counter raids by Danish pirates. Robert the Bruce gave Red Castle to his son-in-law, Hugh 6th Earl of Ross, in 1328.

LUNCARTY, Tayside 30 NO02
A salmon hatchery is situated on the Tay near Luncarty. Legend has it that the adoption of the thistle as the Scottish national emblem resulted from a battle fought near here in 990. A peasant armed only with a plough yoke successfully rallied the Scots to repel a Danish invasion.

LUNDIE, Tayside *31 NO23*
Lundie is situated in the Sidlaw Hills to the S of Loch Long, and has a church which preserves some of its original Norman structure.

LUNDIN LINKS, Fife *31 NO40*
Popular with golfers, Lundin Links is a sandy resort on Largo Bay. Three prehistoric standing stones are sited near by off the Leven road, and a tall 14th-c tower from a former mansion of the Lundins can be seen in the area.

LUSS, Strathclyde *44 NS39*
This beautiful village lies at the mouth of Glen Luss on the W side of Loch Lomond. It overlooks a group of wooded islands in the loch and faces N towards 3,192ft Ben Lomond. The local church houses a 14th- or 15th-c effigy of 6th-c St Kessog. Wordsworth, his sister, and Coleridge were visitors to the village in 1803. Luss has a steamer service, and 3m at Inverbeg is a passenger ferry which connects with Rowardennan. Lofty hills frame the entrance to Glen Douglas, ½m N of the ferry point, and the glen is threaded by a road leading to the shores of Loch Long. Some 3m S on a promontory facing Loch Lomond is Rossdhu House, a seat of the Colquhouns. Access to the mansion is by a grand gateway on the A82, and the house is now open to the public.

LYBSTER, Highland *37 ND23*
Lybster has a small fishing industry and lies on a wild and rocky stretch of coastline to the SW of Clyth Ness, on Lybster Bay. Its church was built of locally-dressed flagstones, and has a west door and chancel entrance of ancient local design. Two megolithic chambered cairns of *c*3,000–2,000 BC, known as the Grey Cairns of Camster (AM), lie 5m N along the narrow road to Watten. This road leaves the A9 2m E of Lybster and passes the newly-planted Rumster Forest.

LYNE, Borders *30 NT14*
One of Scotland's smallest churches stands at Lyne, and displays a pulpit and two canopial pews of Dutch workmanship. Ruins of a Roman camp built in AD84 lie near the church. The Romans abandoned this, along with several other forts, when they withdrew behind Hadrian's Wall. To the N of Lyne are the twin Meldon Hills, which face each other across a narrow road leading to Eddleston. Farther N and to the W of this road is Crailzie Hill, site of the fascinating Harehope Rings and prehistoric Harehope Fort. Across the Tweed to the S, near its junction with Lyne Water, is the Barns Tower of 1488. This preserves an ancient iron yett or gateway. John Buchan included Barns Tower in one of his early novels, and near by is the white-harled Barns House.

LYNWILG, Highland *34 NH80*
Lynwilg lies on Loch Alvie and is fringed by woodland. A Waterloo cairn and a monument to the last Duke of Gordon stand SE on Tor of Alvie Hill. The view from the top of this hill extends E over the vast Rothiemurchus Forest to the Cairngorms. Alvie Church is the burial place of Sir George Henschel, and lies at the W end of the loch with 2,702ft Geal Charn Mor to the NW. The summit of this height affords one of the finest panoramas of the distant Cairngorms.

MACDUFF, Grampian *35 NJ76*
Macduff is an important herring-fishing town in Banff Bay, and was known as Down until 1783. The town has a large harbour. Across the mouth of the Deveron to the W lies the one-time county town of Banff. Fine views are afforded by the Hill of Down, which is topped by a War Memorial. Tarlair Well lies E near the Howe of Tarlair, and remarkable rocky outcrops can be seen near the bathing pool by the shores.

MACHRIE, Isle of Arran, Strathclyde *24 NR83*
The Machrie Water flows into Machrie Bay, on the Kilbrennan Sound, near this point. The community itself faces the Kintyre peninsula across the sound, and to the N is a coast road to Dougrie Point. The seaward end of long and desolate Glen Iorsa lies near the point, and the head of the loch is hemmed by high hills. One of the few inland roads on Arran runs E just N of Machrie to link up with the String Road, leading to Brodick on the E coast of the island. Remains of ten stone circles – the Standing Stones of Tormore – can be seen 1½m E of Machrie on the S bank of Machrie Water. A path from the coast road runs S from Machrie and leads down to the King's Caves, the largest of which is traditionally said to have sheltered Robert the Bruce and Fingal.

MAGGIEKNOCKATER, Grampian *35 NJ34*
The 1,544ft Ben Aigan and 1,219ft Knockan lie to the NW and NE of this tiny village, which lies in an attractively wooded glen.

MAIDENS, Strathclyde *24 NS20*
This small fishing village and resort lies on Maidenhead Bay and offers a sandy beach dominated by a large caravan site. Shanter Farm, home of Tam o' Shanter, is just inland.

MALLAIG, Highland *32 NM69*
The W end of the songwriter's romantic 'Road to the Isles', Mallaig is a large herring-port on the rocky shores of North Morar, facing towards Skye. Steamers carry cars from Mallaig to the Inner and Outer Hebrides, and one of the most popular tourist routes is to Armadale on Skye. Motor launches carry visitors to remote Inverie on Loch Nevis, which forms the S border of the rugged Knoydart country.

Prince Charles Edward landed at Mallaig as a fugitive in 1746, and wandered among lonely hills before reaching Loch nan Uamh, from where he was taken to safety away from Scottish shores. Carn a' Ghobhair rises to 1,794ft and can be climbed from Mallaig, although this wild and rocky hill has no definite paths. The panorama from the summit is one of the finest in Scotland, taking in the whole lengths of Lochs Morar and Nevis, plus their background of picturesque rocky peaks. The view also extends W over the sea to distant Ardnamurchan Point, and across to the mountainous outlines of Rum and Skye.

MAMORE FOREST, Highland *33*
Also known simply as the Mamores, this fine range of mountains lies in the heart of Lochaber between Glen Nevis and Loch Leven. The highest peak – 3,700ft Binnein Mor – rises above Kinlochleven. A view along Glen Nevis, situated at the foot of Ben Nevis, takes in the white quartzite summit of 3,601ft Sgurr a'Mhaim and its neighbour, 3,274ft Stob Ban. The ridges of the Mamores rarely fall below 3,000ft and run for 8m from E to W, providing some of the finest ridge walking in Scotland. In winter the snow-covered Mamores make an impressive picture from many points around. The best views of this group can be enjoyed from the summit of Ben Nevis and from the lofty peaks around Glencoe.

MAM RATTACHAN (OR RATAGAN) PASS, Highland *33 NG91*
This splendid mountain pass contains the only road leading to the picturesque little village of Glenelg, from where a summer car ferry connects with Kylerhea on Skye. Beginning on the W shore of beautiful Loch Duich, 2m NW of Shiel Bridge, the pass reaches its 1,116ft summit on the old Inverness/Ross and Cromarty border. The steep climb (1 in 6) winds through hairpin bends, and extensive afforestation has obscured the wonderful lower views.

The summit still provides by far the best view of Loch Duich, the jewel of Kintail, which is backed by the famous Five Sisters and dominated by 3,505ft Scour

Trio of prehistoric standing stones near Lundin Links.

Ouran. The whole vista is considered one of the grandest in Scotland. Following the Glenmore River, the pass begins its gradual descent with 3,196ft Ben Sgriol prominent to the SW – one of the rugged guardians of Loch Hourn. Dr Johnson and Boswell crossed the pass on horseback on their way to Glenelg during their Highland tour of 1773, and the Doctor described it as 'a terrible steep to climb'.

MANOR, Borders   26 NT23

Made famous by Sir Walter Scott's *The Black Dwarf*, Manor lies near the foot of the long and beautiful valley of the Manor Water. It was once thickly-populated but is now a graveyard of empty and ruined tower houses, including Castlehill and Posso. The little church stands 1½m SW at the confluence of Manor Water and the Tweed, and preserves the tomb of David Ritchie – the original of Sir Walter Scott's 'Black Dwarf' or 'Bowed Davie'.

Hallyards Manor, where Scott stayed in 1797 when visiting Ritchie, lies to the S of the church. A huge boulder which the Black Dwarf was reputed to have carried 1m from the Tweed lies in Manor, and to the S is the Black Dwarf's Cottage with its special dwarf door. Farther up the valley is isolated Woodhill, on which Macbeth's castle is reputed to have stood. At the valley's head the green, rounded lowland hills become loftier and culminate in 2,680ft Dollar Law.

MARKINCH, Fife   31 NO20

General Leslie the Covenanter was buried in the local St Drostan's Church in 1661. The church is this paper-making town's most prized building, and its 11th- or 12th-c tower includes an upper storey of later date. Ancient Stob Cross stands N of the town and probably marks the limits of an old sanctuary. Bandon Tower stands on high ground 2m NW, and dates from c1580.

Moin House at Melness, built as a shelter for men working on a road during the 1830's.

MARYBANK, Highland   33 NH45

Marybank is situated near the foot of Strath Conon, which is traversed by a narrow road terminating at Scardroy near Loch Beannachan. The head of this wooded glen is backed by lofty hills which include 2,845ft Scuir Vuillin and 2,791ft Bac an Eich. To the S beyond the windings of the River Orrin is the lovely, roadless Glen Orrin, which penetrates W into lonely hills along the one-time Inverness border.

MARYKIRK, Tayside   35 NO66

Situated on the North Esk River, Marykirk lies on the edge of the Vale of Strathmore near the point where it merges into the Mearns country. Inglismaldie Castle lies 3m NW and dates from c1700. It was once a seat of the Earls of Kintore.

MAUCHLINE, Strathclyde   25 NS42

Visitors come to Mauchline for its rich associations with Robert Burns. He began his married life with Jean Armour in a house, now called Burns House, in Castle Street in 1788. The couple were married in a room at Gavin Hamilton's House. Gavin Hamilton, friend and one-time landlord of Burns, is buried in a churchyard which also contains the graves of some of Burns' children. Poosie Nansie's Tavern was Burns' favourite 'howff', as featured in *The Jolly Beggars*, and is still an inn. The former Whiteford Arms also has well-known associations with the poet. A Burns exhibition has been set up at Auld Nanse Tinnock's as part of the Burns Heritage Trail. Adjoining Gavin Hamilton's House is 15th-c Mauchline Castle, or Abbot Hunter's Tower, which retains a fine vaulted hall.

Mauchline was once well-known for its fine snuff boxes, and curling stones are still produced in the town. Five Covenanters were hanged on Loan Green in 1685, and a memorial has been set up

to them. The Burns Memorial Tower houses a museum and lies 1m N of the town. A little farther W lies Mossgiel Farm, rebuilt in 1859, which Burns and his brother rented between 1784 and 1788. Much of his first volume of poems was completed here before he visited Edinburgh in 1786. Burns lived with his family 3m NW at Lochlea Farm from 1777 to 1784. To the SE of the town is the great 19th-c sandstone railway bridge of Ballachmoyle, which spans the Ayr valley. Failford lies 3m WSW of the town on the Ayr road.

MAXTON, Borders   26 NT62

An old cross shaft stands in this little village near a loop of the Tweed, and the much-altered church is of 12th-c foundation. A ruined tower in Maxton was once a seat of the Ker family.

MAYBOLE, Strathclyde   24 NS30

Once capital of the Carrick district, Maybole was also a seat of the Earls of Cassillis – heads of the powerful Lowland Kennedy family. An old rhyme intimates their power:
*Twixt Wigtown and the town of Ayr,
Portpatrick and the Cruives of Cree,
No man may think for to bide there
Unless he court St Kennedie.*
Restored 17th-c Maybole Castle stands in the High Street and was once the earl's town house. It displays picturesque turrets with oriel windows, and now serves as the Kennedy Estate offices. The Tolbooth, part of which dates back to ancient times, was once a Kennedy mansion.

Maybole's collegiate church (AM) was founded in 1371, and on falling into a state of disrepair became a burial chapel for the Earls of Cassillis. No trace now remains of the Provost's house where John Knox and the Abbot of Crossraguel held a three-day theological contest in 1561. Six Covenanters captured after the Battle of Bothwell Brig in 1679 were drowned when the slave ship deporting them sank off the Orkneys, and their monument stands a little to the N near Cargilston Farm. Cassillis House stands near the banks of the Doon 3½m NE of Maybole, and is associated with Burns' *Hallowe'en*. An old pele tower is incorporated in the structure. Kilkenzie Castle was built between the 16th and 17thc and lies 1m S of the town, now serving as a farm. Another fine old building is Kilkerran House, a late 17th-c structure lying some 4m S.

MEARNS, THE, Grampian   35

An alternative name for the one-time county of Kincardine, the Mearns are traditionally supposed to produce efficient men of great strength – 'men o' the Mearns'. The Howe of the Mearns comprises 50sqm of rolling farmland and woodland between the North Esk River and Bervie Water. This area is the NE extension of the fertile valley of Strathmore.

MEIGLE, Tayside   31 NO24

Several interesting old houses still stand in this Strathmore village, which lies to the S of the River Isla. Meigle is reputed to be the burial place of Queen Guinevere. A museum (AM) in the village mounts a magnificent display of ancient sculptured stones from the Celtic Christian period, all found at or near the old churchyard. These exhibits form one of the best collections of dark-age sculpture in

W Europe. The mansion of Drumkilbo lies E and stands in fine gardens.

MEIKLEOUR, Tayside *30 NO13*

The grounds of modern Meikleour House include a 600yd beech hedge which borders the Perth to Blairgowrie road and was planted in 1746. It now stands 85ft high. The jougs stone, or place of punishment, stands opposite the Mercat cross of 1698 in the village.

MELLERSTAIN, Borders *26 NT63*

William and Robert Adam designed this splendid mansion, which is considered one of the most attractive open to the public in Scotland. Mellerstain displays exceptionally beautiful interior decoration and plaster work, and the grounds include fine walled Italian gardens. Views from the grounds extend S across a lake to the distant Cheviots. Lady Grizel Baillie is associated with Mellerstain, and was a heroine of Covenanting times.

MELNESS, Highland *37 NC56*

A sloop carrying French gold for Prince Charles Edward ran aground here in 1745. Melness lies at the mouth of the Kyle of Tongue on Tongue Bay, overlooking the Rabbit Islands. Whiten Head lies near the mouth of Loch Eriboll to the NW, but is without road access. The lonely rocky coastline here is riddled with caves. Beinn Thutaig rises to 1,340ft inland, overlooking the moors of A'Mhoine and a road which crosses this desolate country W to the shores of Loch Eriboll. Moin House, which was built in 1830 as a shelter during the time the road was being laid, lies 6m SW along the highway.

MELROSE, Borders *26 NT53*

Rich in associations with Sir Walter Scott, Melrose lies near the Tweed and is sheltered to the S by the triple-peaked Eildon Hills. Melrose Abbey (AM) was described in Scott's *Lay of the Last Minstrel*, and is perhaps the finest ruined abbey in Scotland. It was battered by the English like all the other Border abbeys. David I first built the abbey for Cistercian monks from Yorkshire's Rievaulx in 1136. Severe damage was inflicted in 1322 and 1385, and final destruction came in the raids of 1543 and 1544. However, enough remains of the nave, transept, and chancel to show how beautiful the building once was. Parts of

the nave and choir date from the rebuilding of 1385 and represent the best and most elaborate work of this period in Scotland. The flying buttresses, pinnacles, and rich window tracery – wrought of red sandstone – are of particular beauty, and the flowing tracery of the five-light window in the south transept is considered the finest of all. A gargoyle on the roof shows a pig playing the bagpipes, and a west buttress of the south side carries carved Royal Arms.

The heart of Robert the Bruce is said to be buried under the east window of the chancel. It was originally to have been buried in the Holy Land, but Sir James Douglas – who was carrying it there – was killed in Spain while fighting the Moors. According to tradition he hurled the casket containing the heart at the enemy shouting 'Go first, brave heart'. Bruce's heart was later returned to Scotland. The chancel of Melrose Abbey contains the supposed tomb of Michael Scott, the wizard associated with Deloraine in Scott's *The Lay of the Last Minstrel*.

Recent excavations at the abbey have revealed the ground plan of the cloisters and other monastic buildings. An abbey museum is contained in the 15th- to 16th-c Commendator's House. Interesting tombs in the old graveyard include those of Scott's wood-forester Tom Purdie, and of his coachman, Peter Matheson. The abbey was presented to the nation by the Duke of Buccleuch in 1918.

Melrose town is the 'Kennaquhair' of Scott's *The Abbot* and *Monastery*, and preserves several fascinating old houses. The Mercat cross carries the arms of Scotland and dates from 1642. On St John's Day (27 December) an old custom called the Mason's Walk is still maintained, involving a torchlight walk from the cross to the abbey and back again. The parish church dates from 1810. A 4m historical walk from Melrose to Newstead includes a Roman camp site by the Eildon Hills, and the return is made via Prior's Walk.

MELVICH, Highland *37 NC86*

Splendid cliffs fringe the coast near Melvich, which lies on Melvich Bay at the end of long Strath Halladale. The best scenery is to be found at Bighouse and Portskerra.

MENNOCK, Dumfries and Galloway *25 NS80*

A fine road which begins at this tiny Nithsdale village runs NE through the Mennock Pass and reaches a summit of over 1,400ft. The 2,377ft Lowther Hill and 2,403ft Green Lowther overlook the pass on the short descent to Wanlockhead – Scotland's highest village. Wordsworth and his sister travelled through the pass in 1803. Eliock House, the birthplace in 1560 of James Crichton, lies N of Mennock across the Nith. J M Barrie based his play *The Admirable Crichton* on the character of James, and Crichton was known as the Marvel of Europe for his physical and intellectual skills. Before he was 20 he could speak twelve languages fluently, and was an expert horseman, fencer, singer, dancer, and musician. Tragically, he was killed in a street brawl in Mantua in Italy at the age of 22.

MENSTRIE, Central *46 NS89*

Menstrie is a small town lying at the foot of 1,375ft Dumyat on the fringe of the Ochil Hills. It now operates a large distillery and bonded warehouses. Restored Menstrie Castle was built during the 16thc and was the birthplace of Sir William Alexander, James VI's Lieutenant for the Plantation of Nova Scotia. The Nova Scotia Exhibition Room displays coats of arms of 107 Nova Scotian baronetcies. In 1734 Sir Ralph Abercromby, victor of the Battle of Alexandria in the Napoleonic Wars, was born in the town.

MERKLAND LODGE, Highland *36 NC42*

This lodge lies at the S tip of Loch Merkland, one of a chain of lochs passed by a road which runs from Lairg to the wild NW coastline near Loch Laxford. To the N 2,864ft Ben Hee rises from the great Reay deer forest, with 2,597ft Ben Leoid farther to the N.

MERSE, THE, Borders *31*

The ancient name 'Merse' means march or boundary, and The Merse comprises an area of old S Berwickshire between the Lammermuir Hills and the Tweed. This is Border country, and the district includes some of Scotland's best agricultural land.

METHIL, Fife *47 NT39*

North-Sea oil platforms are being built at Methil, which is also an important port for the Fife coalfield. The town is linked to Buckhaven to the SW.

METHLICK, Grampian *35 NJ83*

Ruins of an ancient church lie in the burial ground of Methlick's modern church, which is situated near the River Ythan. The fine old House of Schivas stands 3m SE of the town and has been restored. Haddo House, a Georgian mansion built in 1732 by William Adam, stands in the parkland 2m SSE of Methlick. It is built on the site of a house which was the seat of the Gordons of Haddo, Earls of Aberdeen, for over 500 years. Haddo House Theatre stages well-known opera and concert productions. Remains of the ancient Castle of Gight, which was besieged by Montrose in 1639, lie in a lovely wooded setting

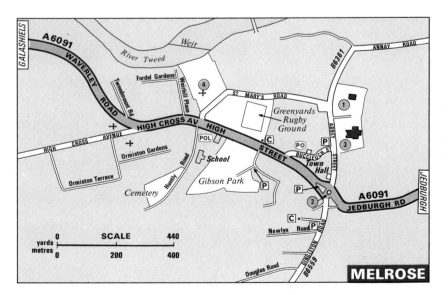

1 Commendator's House and Museum
2 Mercat Cross
3 Melrose Abbey
4 Parish Church

3½m NW near the Ythan. Lord Byron's mother, Catherine Gordon of Gight, was heiress to the estate but had to dispose of it to pay her husband's debts.

METHVEN, Tayside 30 NO02

Two fierce historic battles were fought near this town, which lies at the SW end of the fertile valley of Strathmore. In 1306 Robert the Bruce suffered a defeat at the hands of the English in Methven Wood, and in 1644 Montrose scored a victory over the Covenanters at a site SE near Tibbermuir. Queen Margaret Tudor died at Methven Castle in 1541, a building situated in a splendidly-wooded area, 1½m E of the town. Most of the present structure is of early 17th-c origin. Millhaugh Old Bridge was built in 1619 and carries a narrow road over the River Almond, 3m NW of Methven. About 1½m farther NW from here is Trinity College, Glenalmond – a well-known public school.

MID CALDER, Lothian 46 NT06

Mid Calder was once noted for its oil shales, and is situated on the River Almond. Most of the church is modern, but an apsidal choir rebuilt in 1541 has survived. Also preserved are examples of flamboyant 16th-c window tracery, and corbels carved with heraldic devices. John Knox first administered Communion under the Protestant rite at Calder House in 1556, and Chopin stayed at this partly-ancient mansion in 1848. Another interesting old building in the area is Linhouse, which dates from the 16th and 17thc. An old dovecot survives 2½m SW of the town at Alderston; the house is of 17th-c origin but has been enlarged.

WATER FOR A CITY

From its foundation in 1175 until the middle of the last century, the city of Glasgow depended on wells, rivers, and then private companies for its water supplies. In 1855 the Glasgow Corporation Waterworks Act was passed, permitting the city authorities to take water from Loch Katrine in the Trossachs and pipe it to Glasgow.

John Frederick Bateman was the engineer in charge, and his plan called for a 26-mile aqueduct from Loch Katrine to a new reservoir between Milngavie and the hamlet of Mugdock. Of that distance 13m had to be tunnelled, often through solid rock. The tunnels were 8ft in diameter, pipelines were laid across three wide valleys, and the whole aqueduct was carefully designed to allow a fall of 10in per mile. Mainly because of the difficulties in constructing the aqueduct, the original estimate for the whole scheme of £500,000 was exceeded by nearly £150,000. In October 1859, when Queen Victoria went to Loch Katrine to declare the scheme officially open, it was considered a sound investment. In more than a century nothing has happened to change that opinion.

Bateman considered that, despite the high cost, Glasgow had had a bargain: 'The saving in articles of domestic consumption to which water is applied, such as soap, tea, and coffee, effected by the exquisite purity and softness of the water as compared with the harder water you have been accustomed to use, is nearly equal to your whole water rate, and is equivalent to a free gift to the city of £1,000,000 sterling. In the consumption of soap alone, the saving to the inhabitants on the north of the river will be £30,000 a year.'

As Glasgow expanded, so the original water scheme kept pace. By the 1880's the 500,000,000 gallon capacity of Mugdock reservoir was no longer enough. Between 1883 and 1885 the main road from Glasgow to Strathblane, which ran immediately east of it, was diverted to its present line. In 1886 work started on the 700,000,000 gallon Craigmaddie reservoir; but the excavations were hampered by a stubborn layer of sandstone, and it was only in 1897 that the city's water storage capacity was augmented as planned.

The whole project has been a complete success, and although Glasgow has additional reservoirs south of the city, it is the Loch Katrine scheme which has saved it through the years from the water shortages which so often affect Edinburgh. Control has now passed to the Lower Clyde Water Board, but the reservoir grounds are still laid out as a public park. Rhododendrons, pines, and heather, paths, driveways, and lawns disguise a masterpiece of Victorian municipal engineering.

These 19th-c waterworks at Milngavie still form part of a scheme which supplies Glasgow.

MID CLYTH, Highland 37 ND23

Hill slopes behind Mid Clyth are the site of 22 parallel prehistoric rows – 192 stones in all. The picturesque sandstone inlet of Whaligoe can be seen off the road to Wick 2m NW.

MIDDLETON, Highland 47 NT35

This small village stands on the N slopes of the Moorfoot Hills. A branch from the main Galashiels road runs S from here into the hills, climbing to over 1,200ft before reaching Tweeddale at Innerleithen.

MIDMAR CASTLE, Grampian 35 NJ70

Considered a splendid example of the late 16th- or early 17th-c baronial style, Midmar Castle carries characteristic turrets and lies just off the Aberdeen to Tarland road, to the N of the 1,545ft Hill of Fare. It was once known as Ballogie and was originally built by Sir William Wallace. The building's 17th-c garden is also of interest. The old churchyard of Midmar contains the grave of George Bell, who died in 1575 and was probably the castle's master mason.

MILLERSTON, Strathclyde 45 NS66

On an unclassified road 2m NW of Millerston is a monument which stands on the site of a house in which Sir John Menteith – the 'fause' Menteith – betrayed William Wallace and a companion in 1305.

MILLPORT, Great Cumbrae Island, Strathclyde 44 NS15

Steamers from Largs and Wemyss Bay on the mainland dock at Millport. Millport Bay offers good sands and bathing. The collegiate church was consecrated in 1876 as the episcopal Cathedral of Argyll and the Isles. A good 10m road follows the shores of Great Cumbrae, and a Marine Biological Station with aquaria can be seen on the E coast at Keppel

Pier. The island lighthouse site of Little Cumbrae lies off the S shores of Great Cumbrae. A castle on Castle Island, off the E shore of Little Cumbrae, was destroyed by Cromwell in 1653. Sparse remains can still be seen.

MILNATHORT, Tayside 30 NO10

Loch Leven lies a little to the S of this woollen-manufacturing and market town. Burleigh Castle (AM), to the E of Milnathort, is a fine tower-house of 1582 associated with Scott's *Old Mortality*. James VI visited the castle several times when it was the stronghold of the Balfours of Burleigh. A few miles to the SE are the standing stones of Orwell.

MILNGAVIE, Strathclyde 45 NS57

To the N of this small town lie the Mugdock and Craigmaddie Reservoirs (see inset opposite). Lillie Art Gallery has exhibitions, and Mugdock Castle stands amid woods beyond reservoirs to the N. It preserves an ancient tower. Only the foundations of Craigmaddie Castle, 2m NE of Milngavie, remain to be seen. Curious boulders known as the Auld Wives' Lichts lie E on Blairskaith Muir. Bardowie Castle stands 2m E of the town and faces a tiny loch. Faint traces of the Roman Antonine Wall can be seen S of the town.

MILTON, Tayside 30 NN93

Milton lies at the junction of Strath Bran and Glen Cochill, with the road to Aberfeldy running N through the glen. Meall Dearg rises to 2,258ft in the NW and overlooks lonely little Loch Fender.

MILTON, Highland 37 NH77

This Milton is a picturesque old-world village which is also known as Milntown. Interesting Tarbat House faces the Bay of Nigg.

MILTON OF BALGONIE, Fife 31 NO30

Ruins of 15th-c Balgonie Castle lie 1m W of this village off the Leslie road. Lord Newark, the Covenanting general whom Cromwell defeated in 1650 at Dunbar, died here in 1661. Rob Roy besieged the castle in 1716.

MINARD, Strathclyde 29 NR99

Minard Castle dates from the 19thc and overlooks Minard Bay, an inlet of Loch Fyne.

*MOFFAT, Dumfries and Galloway 25 NT00

Delightfully placed on the River Annan among Lowland hills, Moffat is the centre of a thriving sheep-farming district. This trade is symbolized by the ram which tops the Colvin Fountain in the wide High Street. The town is a good base for walking in Annandale, and there is excellent fishing in the Annan itself. Moffat's popularity as a holiday resort grew from the discovery of a sulphur spring 1½m NE of the town in 1630. Among the distinguished visitors who came to take the waters were Boswell and Burns, who composed the drinking song *O Willie brew'd a peck o' Maut* here. James Macpherson published his *Ossianic Fragments* in 1759 from 18th-c Moffat House, which is now a hotel. John Macadam the road designer lived at Dumcrieff House, to the SE on the Moffat Water, and was buried in the local churchyard in 1836.

St Andrew's Church was built in 1887 on the site of an older church. Roads to the N of Moffat climb into spectacular hill country, with the A701 to Edinburgh leading to the well-known Devil's Beef Tub after about 5m. This sheer-sided hollow is situated by Ericstane Brae, and overshadowed by steep, green slopes. It was once used by Border reivers to hide stolen cattle. Scott mentions the Devil's Beef Tub in *Redgauntlet*. In 1746 a Jacobite captured at Culloden escaped while on his way to Carlisle to be tried by dashing down the steep slopes. He avoided certain death at the hands of the English.

A memorial near the spot commemorates John Hunter, a Covenanter who was shot on a nearby hillside in 1685. Farther to the NW, at a height of over 1,300ft, are the boundaries of the one-time counties Dumfries, Lanark, and Peebles. This is near the watershed where the Annan, Clyde, and Tweed have their sources. The A708 road to Selkirk follows Moffat Water from the town past Burns Cottage, near Craigieburn Wood, which has associations with the poet. Beyond this point, 2,412ft Saddle Yoke, 2,651ft Hart Fell, and 2,695ft White Coomb rise to the W, with the road continuing NE to the Grey Mare's Tail (NTS). This is one of Scotland's highest waterfalls and plunges from a height of some 200ft. The fall is formed by the Tail Burn dropping from lonely Loch Skene to join Moffat Water.

Fine views of the hill country around Moffat can be enjoyed from 2,256ft Lochfell, which rises to the E of the town.

cont

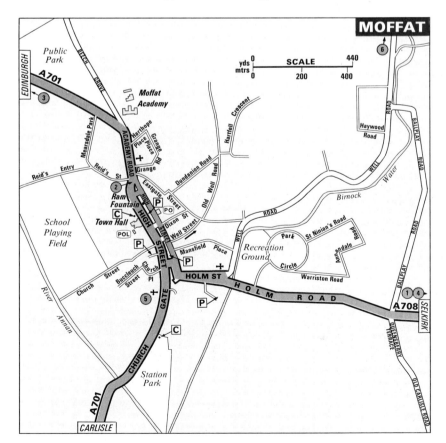

1 Burns' Cottage
2 Colvin Fountain
3 Devil's Beef Tub and Memorial
4 Dumcrieff House
5 St Andrew's Parish Church
6 Sulphur Spring

Two lovely glens within walking distance of Moffat are Bell Craig Glen, 4m SE, and Garpol Glen, 2m SW.

MOIDART, Highland *32*
Closely linked with Prince Charles Edward, Moidart is a district of the wild Clanranald mountains which lie between the W shores of Loch Shiel and the Sound of Arisaig. Loch Moidart divides the district from the remote Ardnamurchan peninsula farther W. Loch nan Uamh, where the prince arrived in Scotland and from where he later fled for his life, is a beautiful inlet of the Sound. Another inlet is picturesque Loch Ailort.

MONALTRIE, Grampian *34 NO29*
The Farquharson Cairn-na-Cuimhne, or Cairn of Remembrance, lies near the river to the SW of ruined Monaltrie House.

MONIAIVE, Dumfries and Galloway *25 NX79*
Three streams meet near Moniaive to form the Cairn Water. The village includes a cross dating from 1638, and a monument to James Renwick – the last of the Covenanting martyrs. Renwick was executed at Edinburgh in 1688, aged 26. Maxwelton House lies 3m ESE and was the seat of the Laurie family. Annie Laurie (1682–1761) was immortalized by William Douglas in the well-known love song of *c*1700. Douglas was a rejected suitor for her hand, and Annie eventually married Alexander Ferguson.

The house was built in the early 17thc and has since been much altered and modernized. To the SW of the house lies Glencairn church and the little village of Kirkland. Annie and her husband are thought to be buried in the churchyard. Craigdarroch, 2½m W of Moniaive off the Carsphairn road, was Annie's married home and the place where she died. William Adam built the house, which stands in lovely gardens, in 1729.

MONIFIETH, Tayside *31 NO43*
A large military training ground is situated on the Barry Links, which lie to the E of this small resort. Buddon Ness reaches out into the sea farther to the SE, and the resort itself offers sandy beaches.

MONIKIE, Tayside *31 NO53*
Monikie is best known for the fine battlemented and turreted 15th-c keep of Affleck Castle (AM), which lies beyond the reservoirs. An exquisite little vaulted chapel includes a very fine upper hall and a solar. The prominent Panmure Monument stands on a hillside S of the town, and commemorates the first Lord Panmure of Brechin, who died in 1852.

MONIMAIL, Fife *31 NO21*
Cardinal Beaton's Tower is the name now given to a surviving fragment of the ecclesiastical Monimail Palace, dating from *c*1578. Monimail's church houses the interesting Melville gallery and displays fine Adam ceiling. Melville House lies to the SW of Monimail and is now used as a school. This splendid, well-proportioned house was built in 1692, and its interior is thought to be the work of Sir William Bruce.

MONKTON, Strathclyde *24 NS32*
Monkton church preserves a Romanesque doorway, and the village itself stands a little inland from Ayr Bay.

MONREITH, Dumfries and Galloway *24 NX34*
Founded in 1770 by Sir William Maxwell, Monreith lies on Monreith Bay in the Machers peninsula between Barsalloch Point and the Point of Lag. Near the Point of Lag stands the ancient, restored church of Kirkmaiden-in-Fernis, on a site associated with an Irish princess called St Medan.

Legend has it that she landed here after floating across Luce Bay on a rock from the Mull of Galloway, where she had plucked out her eyes to discourage an unwanted suitor. She bathed her face on landing, and her sight was miraculously restored. Sir Thomas Maxwell's essays have made the Monreith House of 1799 – situated 2m NE of Barsalloch Point – very famous. Its woodland gardens and rhododendron walks are beautiful, and the carved, wheel-headed Monreith Cross (AM) of possible 5th-c origin stands in the grounds. Part of the White Loch of Myrton, so called as its water is supposed to whiten linen, forms a bird sanctuary. Ruins of Myrton Castle lie in the vicinity.

MONTROSE, Tayside *31 NO75*
Montrose is a well-known sailing, holiday, and fishing port with water on three sides of the town. The South Esk River flows behind through a 2m-wide tidal lagoon known as the Montrose Basin. This curious feature has a curve of sand 5m long and is where pink-footed Arctic geese spend the winter. Also a Royal Burgh, Montrose has a long and interesting history. No trace now remains of the large, important castle which Edward I occupied in 1296 and which Wallace destroyed in the following year.

Gillespie Graham added the spire to the church, and this soars 220ft above the elegant, gable-ended houses of the High Street. Narrow, twisting closes, unchanged in 200 years lead into the

MONTROSE

1 Medicine Well
2 Museum
3 Old Montrose (Government Offices)
4 Parish Church
5 William Lamb Memorial Studio

town's heart from the High Street. Each night at 22.00 hrs the 300-year-old curfew bell is rung from the church steeple. The modern Town Hall stands in Melville gardens and is used for dances and other entertainments.

The Old Pretender sailed from the harbour at the close of the 1715 Rising. A house in Castle Place, Old Montrose, was the birthplace of the great Marquis of Montrose in 1612. The Marquis grew up to become a Royalist leader, and the house is now a government office. Montrose's restored Medicine Well was a popular spa during the 18thc, and the museum shows many relics of Montrose's old seafaring days. The William Lamb Memorial Studio contains an art collection.

MONYMUSK, Grampian   35 NJ61
A priory and later a monastery have both stood at Monymusk, a village lying just off the Alford to Inverurie road. Parts of the ancient priory church, probably of Norman date, have been incorporated into the parish church. The well-known Monymusk Reliquary is a casket of the Celtic period which is now kept by the National Museum of Antiquities in Edinburgh. Modern Cluny Castle stands 1½m S of the village.

Cairn William rises to 1,469ft NW of Monymusk, and its wooded E shoulder is known as Pitfichie Hill. The ruins of Pitfichie Castle lie below the hill, with the River Don flowing through a lovely, wooded gorge beyond. Paradise Wood stands near the gorge and was visited by Queen Victoria in 1866. The Queen came to see larches which were planted in 1741.

MORAR, Highland   32 NM69
Situated on a narrow neck of land between Loch Morar and the outer waters of the Sound of Sleat, Morar looks out across the sea to the islands of Rhum and Eigg. The Falls of Morar on the Morar River are harnessed to a local hydro-electric scheme, and a bay formed by the river's estuary is famed for its white sands. A little to the E stretches the beautiful, 180-fathom Loch Morar, the deepest inland water in Britain. It is said to harbour a monster which appears whenever a death is imminent in the Clan MacDonald. The scenery is finest at the E end of the loch, where the mountain backdrop is highest, but as no roads run near here it is accessible only to long-distance walkers.

Prince Charles Edward wandered among the local hills after his defeat at Culloden in 1746, and one of his followers, Lord Lovat, was captured on an island in the loch and later beheaded. An 18th-c RC college once stood on another loch island, which was also the residence of the Pope's Vicar Apostolic of Scotland. To the N of Loch Morar lies the more impressive Loch Nevis. About halfway along Loch Morar a path leads from the S shore into the hills by way of Meoble, later passing lonely Loch Beoraid on the way to Lochailort. The finest view of Loch Morar is probably afforded by the 1,794ft summit of Carn a'Ghobhair, which can be climbed from Mallaig. The panorama not only includes Loch Morar, but also the whole length of Loch Nevis and the cirque of lofty mountains at its head.

MOREBATTLE, Borders   27 NT72
Persecuted Covenanters once had a refuge in the lonely Kale Water valley,

Ancient Linton Church at Morebattle has been well restored and preserves a Norman font.

to the S of Morebattle. The meandering river flows from the fringe of the Cheviot Hills to join the Teviot, and almost encircles the village. Across the river to the N of the village is ancient Linton church, which has been restored. It preserves a Norman font, a bell of 1697, and the finely-carved Somerville stone set above the porch. Away to the SE the 2,676ft Cheviot rises from England – the highest point in this Border range. Corbet Tower stands 1m S of Morebattle and dates from 1592. Some 2½m SW of the village on the road to Oxnam are the red-stone ruins of Cessford Castle, with walls 14ft thick. The castle surrendered to the Earl of Surrey in 1545.

MORVEN, Highland   28
Also known as Morvern, this Scottish district is bordered to the N by Loch Sunart and to the W and E by the Sound of Mull and Loch Linnhe respectively. Morven is chiefly low hill country, though Creach Bheinn in the NE corner reaches 2,800ft and offers wonderful views. Some of the best views of the district are afforded by steamers which link Fort William and Oban in summer.

MOSCOW, Strathclyde   29 NS44
This small village actually stands on a little river called the Volga. Its moorland setting affords views W towards the Firth of Clyde.

MOSSTODLOCH, Moray   35 NJ35
Fochabers Bridge spans the Spey just E of this village, and replaces an earlier structure which was lost in the floods of 1829. Garmouth, lying 3m N on the left bank of the Spey before it reaches the sea, was once a port.

MOTHERWELL, Strathclyde   45 NS75
Wishaw and Motherwell together form a single Burgh, concerned with iron, steel, and engineering works. Motherwell is the centre of an important coal-mining area, and the great Dalzell works were

founded by David Colville in 1871. The site of the original well in the town's name is marked by a plaque in Ladywell Road. To the N of Motherwell is Jerviston House, a 16th-c tower house of the Baillie family. Carfin Grotto, dedicated in 1922 to Our Lady of Lourdes and visited annually by thousands of pilgrims, lies 2m NE. A 15th-c tower has been preserved SE at Dalzell House, near the Clyde, and the rest of the building dates from the 17th-c and later.

MOULIN, Tayside   30 NN95
Robert Louis Stevenson lived at Kinnaird Cottage to the E of this picturesque little village. It was here that he wrote several of his shorter works, including *Thrawn Janet*. Near the village lie the remains of Castle Dhu, and to the N 2,757ft Ben Vrackie rises as the monarch of the surrounding countryside. A road from Moulin runs NE towards Kirkmichael, climbing to 1,260ft before descending into Glen Brerachan. Craigour stands at 1,300ft in the NW village and offers fine views – particularly W across the Tummel valley to the distant, 3,547ft Schiehallion.

MOUND, THE, Highland   37 NH79
Thomas Telford built this 1,000yd-long railway and road embankment over Loch Fleet in 1815, and had to reclaim some of the land from the water. The Mound Alderwoods national nature reserve covers 689 acres of the surrounding countryside.

MOUNT VERNON (Glasgow), Strathclyde   45 NS66
Mount Vernon lies on the SE outskirts of Glasgow, near the Clyde and adjacent to Calderpark. Glasgow's Zoological Park is situated at the latter.

MOUSWALD, Dumfries and Galloway   25 NY07
A tall, 18th-c tower windmill is preserved at Mouswald.

283

Kilcoy Castle at Muir of Ord is considered a good example of 17th-c baronial style.

MOY, Highland   34 NH73
During the '45 Rising an attack known as the Rout of Moy took place in the Mackintosh country near this village. A force led by Lord Loudoun was successfully dispersed. The village lies at the NW end of Loch Moy, and an island in the loch includes the remains of a castle. Also here is a prominent obelisk to Sir Aeneas Mackintosh, who died in 1820. Modern Moy Hall lies at the N end of the loch and replaces an older house. It is the seat of the chief of the Clan Mackintosh. A main road from Moy runs N towards Inverness, and a wonderful view opens out over Strath Nairn beyond the tiny Lochan a'Chaoruinn. This view extends NW towards the far-distant peak of 3,429ft Ben Wyvis.

MUCHALLS, Grampian   35 NO99
Cliffs and gullies characterize the coastline near Muchalls, which is situated just off the Stonehaven to Aberdeen road. Tiny Muchalls Castle was built by the Burnetts of Leys in 1619. It has ornate plasterwork ceilings, fine fireplaces, and a secret staircase. Skateraw, Porthleven, and Findon are little fishing villages to the N of Muchalls.

MUIRHEAD, Strathclyde   45 NS66
Four small lochs – Johnston, Bishop, Woodend, and Lochend – lie to the SE of Muirhead town.

MUIRKIRK, Strathclyde   25 NS62
Coal-mines are important features of this River Ayr town, and the local church dates from 1650. Prehistoric cairns top Cairn Table, which rises to 1,944ft in the E. Near Cairn Table is 1,843ft Stony Hill, situated on the old Lanark border. Farther S is Three Shire Hill, where a boulder marks the meeting of Ayrshire, Dumfriesshire, and Lanarkshire – three one-time counties of Scotland. A bare expanse of moorland known as Airds Moss lies 5m SW of Muirkirk, and was the site of a battle between the Royalists and the

Covenanters in 1680. A monument recalls this fight, in which Richard Cameron – whose name was adopted by the famous Scottish regiment – was killed.

MUIR OF ORD, Highland   34 NH55
Cattle fairs were once a great attraction of this crofting village. Restored Kilcoy Castle lies 4m ENE, and is a good 17th-c example of the Scottish baronial style. The Stuart arms are carved on the W tower, though the castle later fell into the hands of the Mackenzies. Sir Roderick Murchison was a well-known geologist who was born at Taradale House in the 19thc. The house stands 2m SE of the Muir of Ord on the Beauly Firth.

MULL, ISLE OF, Strathclyde   28
'O Sir! A most dolorous country' was Dr Johnson's description of Mull, which he visited during his Highland tour of 1773. Mull lies in the approaches to Loch Linnhe, separated from Morven and Lorne on the mainland by the Sound of Mull and the Firth of Lorne respectively. It is the largest of the Inner Hebridean islands, and is beautified by moorland, forests, and peaks. Although the actual land mass is only about 30m long, the rocky, indented coastline measures about 300m. Steamers from Oban call at Craignure, Salen, and Tobermory – Mull's main centre and fishing port. A passenger ferry links Fionphort with the little island of Iona, the cradle of Scottish Christianity.

The only good road runs between Salen and Tobermory, and Mull's other 100m of motoring roads are narrow, winding, and difficult for passing. A beautifully-scenic road winds from Tobermory round the NW corner of the island, with hairpin bends and gradients of up to 1 in 6. It passes the shores of Loch Tuath and continues to Loch na Keal, which almost cuts the island into two. Steep Gribun

cliffs overlook Loch na Keal's shoreline road and face the islands of Ulva and Inch Kenneth. The road then proceeds right round the loch's shores, passing the little island of Forsa before heading towards the N shore of Loch Scridain.

Ross of Mull is the name given to the island's SW peninsula, and from here the road continues W beyond Bunessan to the ferry at Fionphort. Picturesque Lochs Buie and Spelve grace Mull's SE corner, and farther N near Craignure is the famous restored Duart Castle, ancient seat of the Macleans. Fine views are afforded by the summit of 3,169ft Ben More, Mull's highest point. Even the outer Hebrides are visible from here at times. The island's wild countryside was the setting for many of David Balfour's adventures in Robert Louis Stevenson's *Kidnapped*.

MULL OF GALLOWAY, Dumfries and Galloway   24 NX13
The Mull of Galloway is the farthest S point of the Scottish mainland, and lies at the tip of the Rhinns of Galloway peninsula. Ancient entrenchments here are thought to have served as the Picts' last defence against the Scots. A 210ft lighthouse commands spectacular views, and traces of St Medan's Chapel overlook Luce Bay near Mull Farm.

MULL OF KINTYRE, Strathclyde   24 NR50
Mull of Kintyre is a wild headland which forms the extremity of the long and narrow Kintyre peninsula – the nearest point in Scotland to the Irish coast. The early lighthouse near South Point was built in 1788 and remodelled by Robert Stevenson. Remarkable views from here extend towards the open Atlantic and the coast of Northern Ireland, with Rathlin Island 12m away. Beinn na Lice rises to 1,405ft behind the lighthouse. Access to the Mull is by a narrow road from Southend. This descends about 1,000ft in 1½m, but the last portion of the road is private.

MULL OF OA, Isle of Islay, Strathclyde   28 NR24
Fine cliff scenery and caves are features of the coastline at the S extremity of the Oa peninsula. A little to the E is a monument to 650 American sailors, lost from two ships wrecked on the rocky coast in 1918. The Port Ellen road ends about 1m short of the Mull, and further travel has to be by foot only.

MUSSELBURGH, Lothian   47 NT37
Mussels are still gathered at Musselburgh, a fishing and manufacturing town on the sandy estuary of the River Esk. The town looks out over the Firth of Forth to the distant coast of Fife, with the Lomond Hills rising dimly in the background. There is a fine golf course, and horse-racing and archery events take place near by on the links. The famous Musselburgh strain of leeks was developed in the extensive market gardens. Upstream from Rennie's 19th-c bridge is an old three-arched footbridge. This probably dates from the mid 16thc and rests on Roman foundations. Musselburgh's Tolbooth dates from c1590 and preserves an ancient clock given by the Dutch in 1496. The Mercat cross stands near by, and a statue in the town commemorates David Moir – the 'Delta' of *Blackwood's Magazine*.

Near the links, on which Cromwell camped after the Battle of Dunbar in 1650, stands the public school of Loretto College. This site was once occupied by the Chapel of Our Lady of Loretto. Stones from the chapel were used to build Musselburgh's Tolbooth, an act which caused the town to be excommunicated for two centuries. Monkton House stands S of the town and dates from the 16thc or later. Every autumn fishermen from the town and the adjoining village of Fisherrow, which lies across the river, take part in the picturesque old custom called the Walks of Thanksgiving. These take the form of thanksgiving for catches of fish.

MUTHILL, Tayside *30 NN81*
Muthill lies in a wooded setting in Strath Earn, on the outskirts of Drummond Castle park. Muthill's ancient church was abandoned many years ago and is mainly of 15th-c date. The fine Romanesque tower dates at least from the 12thc. This, a later gabled roof, and the old chancel arch survive.

NAIRN, Highland *34 NH85*
Fine sands, bathing, golf, and fishing are offered by this well-known resort on the Moray Firth. Once known as Invernairn, this Royal Burgh on the River Nairn enjoys a particularly dry and sunny climate. Lovely wooded countryside and the spectacular reaches of the River Findhorn near Dulsie Bridge and Ferness can be reached from the town.

Near the harbour is Fishertown, built by Telford in 1820 and badly damaged by floods in 1829. Nairn stands on the border between the Highlands and the Lowlands. It is said that at one time Gaelic was spoken in the SW quarter and English in the NE quarter of the town. An ancient cross shaft stands in the High Street. Dr Johnson and Boswell were visitors to Nairn during their Highland tour of 1773. A 17th-c dovecot (NTS) stands on the site of an ancient castle ½m E of the town. This was where Montrose flew the standard of Charles I when he defeated the Covenanters in 1645. Round-towered Rait Castle lies 3m S of Nairn and dates from the 16th to 17thc.

NEILSTON, Strathclyde *45 NS45*
Balgray Reservoir lies to the E of this town, which is situated on the edge of moorland. Near the 18th-c church is a monument to John Robertson, who made the engines for the 'Comet' – the earliest steam-driven craft in Europe. The boat was first launched on the Clyde in 1812. Flat-topped Neilston Pad rises S of the town, and 15th-c Caldwell Tower stands 4m SW above Loch Libo.

NENTHORN, Borders *26 NT63*
Fine 18th-c furnishings and lovely gardens are features of Newton Don, a house 2m E of Nenthorn.

NETHYBRIDGE, Highland *34 NJ02*
A centre for early spring ski-ing, this village lies on the River Nethy which flows to join the Spey a little farther to the N. The ruins of Castle Roy, a curtain wall fortress of the Comyns, Lords of Badenoch, lie near Abernethy church just NE of the village.

Numerous paths cross the great Abernethy Forest, which lies S of Nethybridge, and lead through the Ryvoan Pass near the picturesque little Green Loch on the way to Loch Morlich in the Glen More Forest Park. Other hill tracks lead S towards the Lairig an Laoigh, one of the two well-known passes through the Cairngorms. Only experienced walkers should attempt the trek from Speyside, through the Lairig an Laoigh, to Inverey on Deeside. A road to Aviemore runs SW from Nethybridge and crosses the fringe of Abernethy Forest, keeping E of the Spey. It passes the little church of Kincardine, beyond which lies Loch Pityoulish.

NEW ABBEY, Dumfries and Galloway *25 NX96*
New Abbey is beautifully situated amid woodland on the Pow Burn, backed by 1,300ft Meikle Hard Hill, and the bulky, 1,866ft Criffell. The village is best known for its lovely red-sandstone ruins of the Cistercian New or Sweetheart Abbey (AM). Devorgilla, mother of the vassal king John Balliol, founded the abbey in 1273. When her husband John Balliol the elder died she became one of the richest women in Europe. She owned most of Galloway and had estates and castles in England and land in Normandy.

She built the 13th-c bridge over the Nith at Dumfries, and founded Oxford's Balliol College in her husband's memory. She kept his embalmed heart in a silver and ivory casket by her side for 21 years until she died at the age of 80. Her body and the casket were buried beside her husband in front of the abbey altar, and the foundation was then known as 'Dulce Cor' or Sweetheart. From this time the word became part of the English language.

Much 13th- and 14th-c work survives amongst the abbey ruins, including the 90ft-high central tower, much of the nave and transepts, and a short aisle-less choir. Enormous boulders were used to build the precinct wall. The isolated

Remains of Dundarg Castle perch dramatically on rocks overlooking the bay at New Aberdour.

Abbot's Tower stands a little to the NE, with the Nith estuary a short distance beyond on the Solway Firth. Glen Hill lies to the W and is topped by a circular Waterloo monument. In New Abbey village is 16th- to 18th-c Kirkconnel House; Kirkconnel Tower lies 2m NE and dates from the same period. The finest Scots pines in the country can be seen 1m NW of New Abbey in Shambellie Wood.

NEW ABERDOUR, Grampian *35 NJ86*
Caverns riddle the red-sandstone cliffs of Aberdour Bay, and New Aberdour stands just to the S. Remains of the tower of Dundarg Castle perch on rocks overlooking the bay, with the little River Dour flowing into the bay W of the castle.

NEWBATTLE, Lothian *47 NT36*
Only the crypt and basement chapel remain of Cistercian Newbattle Abbey, which was founded in 1140. The later house was a seat of the Marquess of Lothian, but was destroyed by fire in 1544. Today the buildings are used as a college and house some beautiful old portraits and furnishings. Two fine sundials can be seen in the park. Newbattle church was rebuilt in 1729 and preserves an older pulpit, plus memorials to Archbishop Leighton. Leighton was minister here from 1641 to 1653. The former Sun Inn was well known in the old coaching days and still stands in the town.

NEWBIGGING, Strathclyde *30 NT04*
An old Mercat cross of 1693 date stands here.

NEWBRIDGE, Lothian *46 NT17*
Newbridge has a crow-stepped, gabled inn of 1683. Cliftonhall, to the SW, was the home of Euphame McCalzean who was tried as a witch at Edinburgh and burned alive in 1591. Nearby Ingliston

cont page 287

A GREAT SOCIAL EXPERIMENT

The village of New Lanark is Scotland's most enduring monument to the rise of the cotton trade, and to the great Welsh social experimenter Robert Owen. Lanark itself, on high ground above the River Clyde, was a long-established burgh in 1784 when David Dale, a Glasgow merchant, leased ground in the steep sided valley below the Falls of Clyde from the Braxfield estate. It was described as no more than a marsh, and very difficult to reach; but Dale and his partner Richard Arkwright realised that there was water power in abundance.

A very substantial mill lade was built, and the first mill began working in April 1785. It was destroyed by fire three years later, but by that time the second mill was almost ready and the business survived. Many of Dale's employees were dispossessed crofters from the north and west of Scotland, few of whom in the early days spoke anything but Gaelic. Some arrived at New Lanark almost by accident: 'In 1791 a vessel carrying emigrants from the Isle of Skye to North America was driven by stress of weather into Greenock; about 200 were put ashore in a very destitute situation. Mr Dale, whose humanity is ever awake, offered them immediate employment, which the greater bulk of them accepted. And soon after, with a view to prevent further emigration to America, he notified to the people of Argyllshire and the Isles the encouragement given to families at the cotton mills; and undertook to provide houses for 200 families in the course of 1792.' Many of his workers came from Caithness, Inverness and Argyll, and one of the earliest streets in the village was called Caithness Row.

Richard Arkwright had left the business by that time, but the mill manager William Kelly was a similarly inventive man, and many improvements in cotton machinery were pioneered at New Lanark. Dale himself, as the enterprise grew and the mills and village both expanded, looked after the business side from his offices in Glasgow.

A few years later Robert Owen, then a successful Lancashire cottonmaster and partner in the Chorlton Twist Company, came to New Lanark. He married Dale's daughter Caroline and became managing partner in a new company which bought over New Lanark for £60,000.

Owen soon showed that he meant to do far more than simply run a profitable cotton mill. Working hours were shortened, housing was greatly improved, the entire operation of the mills was overhauled, profiteering shopkeepers were got rid of and the well-stocked company stores became one of the models for the Co-operative movement. Child labour was abolished, which was a change from Dale's time when 500 pauper children, some only five years old, were among the employees. Most notable of all, the village schools promoted Owen's radical educational theories, which stressed that children should enjoy their schooling and offered them a freedom which was a century and a half ahead of its time.

The workers were suspicious at first, although their opinions changed during the ban on cotton imports which caused a four-month shutdown of the mills in 1806. Owen paid full wages throughout. But many of the New Lanark people resented his interference in their private lives, however well-meaning it may have been.

None of this meant that the owners failed to make handsome profits. Owen himself once said that raw cotton bought in at five shillings per pound was worth almost 40 times that when prepared for the muslin weaver. Despite the immense profitability of the cotton business, Owen's partners were always uneasy about his social and educational experiments. In 1809 he had to form another company to buy New Lanark for £84,000. Four years later his new partners forced him to offer the whole enterprise for sale by public auction. Owen raised £114,000 and took over with yet another set of partners. The New Lanark community continued to attract visitors from all over the world, but even Owen's latest partners never fully appreciated what he was doing. He resigned in 1825, and the great social experiment was over.

In 1881 the village and mills were bought over by the Gourock Ropework Company, and rope-making became the staple industry until the 1960's. The company modernized the mills and did its best to keep the houses in good condition. New Lanark, however, had become an unprofitable location, and in 1963, after an unsuccessful attempt to have Lanark town council take over for the nominal price of £250, village and mills passed into the hands of the New Lanark Association, which was dedicated to preserving the buildings and modernizing as many as possible of the 170 houses.

Between 1964 and 1966 sixteen houses in Caithness Row were modernized, and Owen's original counting house renovated. The process has continued slowly, and the village remains externally much as it was in Owen's time. One of the private individuals who founded the Association was Kenneth Dale Owen, great-great-grandson of Robert, who was born in New Harmony, Indiana. This was where Robert Owen moved to set up another of his communities after the final disappointment at New Lanark.

New Lanark, the scene of enlightened social experimentation by Robert Owen in the 18thc.

is the scene of the Royal Highland Show, held annually during the last two weeks of June.

NEW BRIDGE, Dumfries and Galloway
25 NX97
One of the stones making up the stone circle known as the Twelve Apostles at New Bridge has disappeared. The circle straddles two adjacent fields a little to the NW of the bridge, which spans the Cluden Water. Five stones are still in their original upright position.

NEWBURGH, Grampian *35 NJ92*
Floor coverings are made in this small Royal Burgh, which has a harbour on the Firth of Tay. The Mugdrum Cross is more than 1,000 years old and the pedestal of ancient Macduff s Cross stands on a hill to the S of the town. Mugdrum Island lies opposite the harbour and divides the Firth into the North and South Deeps. Overlooking the Firth, 3m NE under the shadow of Norman Law, is ruined Ballinbreich Castle. This was a 14th-c stronghold of the Earls of Rothes. Nearby Flisk church dates from 1790. A little to the E of Newburgh are the remains of Lindores Abbey, which was founded in 1178 and lies NE of Lindores Loch. Mainly 18th-c Pitcairlie House stands 2m S of the town.

NEW BYTH, Grampian *35 NJ85*
Hand-loom weaving was one of the home industries practised on a large scale at New Byth, a small village founded in 1764.

NEWCASTLETON, Borders *26 NY48*
The former weaving village of Newcastleton was founded in 1793 and lies in Liddesdale. Liddel Water forms the boundary between Scotland and England for some miles to the SW, and there are fine views W and E from the village towards the surrounding hills. Liddesdale is associated with Scott's *Guy Mannering*, and some of the hill slopes in the district have been afforested by the Forestry Commission on a large scale. These forests, together with Wauchope Forest, form part of the great Border forest park which extends across the English border. On the border to the NE of Newcastleton the Larriston Fells rise to 1,677ft. A road once linked Liddesdale with the North Tyne valley in Northumberland via the W side of the Fells. The Bloody Bush Stone stands some 2½m E of the Newcastleton to Jedburgh road, and shows the former toll charges. Mangerton Tower is an old Border stronghold 1½m SSW of Newcastleton.

NEW CUMNOCK, Strathclyde
25 NS61
This small industrial town was separated from Cumnock in 1650. It lies near the source of the River Nith, where it is joined by the Afton Water. Lovely Glen Afton is overlooked at its head by 2,298ft Blackcraig Hill, and stretches S from New Cumnock. The glen has associations with Sir William Wallace and Burns, who wrote the lines beginning 'Flow gently, sweet Afton'.

NEW GALLOWAY,
Dumfries and Galloway *25 NX67*
Said to be the smallest Royal Burgh in Scotland, this angling centre lies on the River Ken in the Glenkens District. A

A little to the N of New Galloway is Kells Churchyard, which preserves the curious Adam and Eve stone.

little to the N of the village is Kells churchyard, which features the curious carved Adam and Eve stone and the grave of a Covenanter who was shot in 1685. A close look at the stones here will reveal several fascinating carvings and inscriptions.

Immediately S of New Galloway is Loch Ken, the shores of which are richly wooded farther to the S. The creeper-covered ruin of partly 16th-c Kenmure Castle lies 1m S of the village on the W bank. The Black Water of Dee flows into the loch 5m SE of New Galloway, and Clatteringshaws Dam lies 6m SW near Cairn Edward Forest. The latter forms part of the Glen Trool forest park. Glenlee power station is part of the Galloway power scheme and stands 2m NW. Farther NW are the lofty Rhinns of Kells, with 2,668ft Corserine predominant.

NEWHAVEN (Edinburgh), Lothian
47 NT27
James IV founded this little fishing port *c*1500, and the population was then mainly of Dutch or Danish extraction. Several 16th-c warships were built here, including the 'Great Michael' which was launched in 1507. Sir Andrew Wood of Largo served on this vessel. Newhaven is famed for its fine fish cuisine, and the Peacock Inn has been known for sea food for many years. Newhaven fishwives used to wear a special type of dress, and cries of 'Caller ou' (fresh oysters) and 'Caller herrin' (fresh herrings) were characteristics of Edinburgh in former days.

NEW LANARK, Strathclyde *30 NS84*
Situated on the River Clyde 1m S of Lanark, New Lanark is an old cotton-milling village which was built in the 18thc by David Dale and was later the scene of a social experiment by Dale's son-in-law, Robert Owen. Owen was a man with very advanced ideas on industry and education, and his village

reflects this. The famous inventor of the industrial revolution period, Richard Arkwright, was also connected with the village (see inset opposite).

NEW LUCE, Dumfries and Galloway
24 NX16
The waters of the Main Water of Luce and the Cross Water of Luce meet here to form the Water of Luce, which flows S to Glenluce and Wigtown Bay. New Luce lies in a part of Galloway known as The Moors, and from 1659 to 1662 the minister at the village was Prophet Peden. A narrow road leads N from the village and crosses lovely moorland on the way to Barrhill in the one-time county of Ayrshire.

NEWMAINS, Strathclyde *46 NS85*
Large iron and steel works form the major industrial part of this town, which is situated on the extensive Lanark coalfield. Murdostoun Castle lies N of Newmains and is a partly 15th-c structure which preserves an old dovecot. The Gladsmuir Hills rise to the E of the town.

NEWMILNS, Strathclyde *25 NS53*
Newmilns is noted for its lace and muslin factories and includes a former Tolbooth of 1739. Several Covenanters' tombstones can be seen in the churchyard.

NEW ORLEANS, Strathclyde *24 NR71*
This village stands on the E side of the Kintyre peninsula, overlooking the island of Arran.

NEWPORT-ON-TAY, Fife *31 NO42*
Once linked to Dundee by a car ferry, this small Firth of Tay town now has access via a 42-span road bridge across the river – the second longest bridge in Europe. The town's foreshore is rocky. Beginning SW at Wormit, the famous 2m long Tay Bridge carries the railway line to Dundee and was built between 1883 and 1888. This replaces the original Tay Bridge, which was blown

Granite-built Cree Bridge spans the Cree at Newton Stewart, and was built by John Rennie in 1813.

down soon after it was opened in 1879. A train crossing the Firth at the time of the disaster plunged into the water with a total loss of life. The supports of the old bridge are still visible near by. (See inset on page 208). The strangely named Pickletillem Inn lies on the Leuchars road 2½m S of Newport-on-Tay.

NEWSTEAD, Borders   26 NT53

Newstead is an old-world village situated on the S bank of the Tweed, with the confluence of Leader Water and the Tweed farther to the E. Roman treasures were unearthed from the site of *Trimontium* on Leaderfoot Hill earlier this century, and these relics can now be seen in the National Museum of Antiquities in Edinburgh. Old Melrose, situated in a bend of the Tweed 2m E of Newstead, is the site of a 7th-c monastery of which no trace is left. The famous triple peaks of the Eildon Hills rise to the S of Newstead.

NEWTON BRIDGE, Tayside   30 NN83

Delightful Sma' Glen stretches just S of Newton Bridge, and a little by-road through Glen Almond runs W with views of the River Almond. Ben Chonzie rises to 3,048ft and dominates the glen to the W. The main road N from Newton Bridge leads towards Amulree on the line of a Wade military road.

NEWTON MEARNS, Strathclyde   45 NS55

Mearns lies 1m SE of Newton Mearns, on the edge of a large and lofty expanse of moorland. A feature of the village is the church, which dates from the late 18thc. Nearer to Newton Mearns are 18th-c Blackhouse Castle and restored Pollok Castle. The latter boasts a garden which was originally laid out in the 17thc. A monument to Robert Pollok, the early 19th-c poet, stands SW of Newton Mearns on the Kilmarnock road.

NEWTONMORE, Highland   34 NN79

Visitors can ride Highland ponies into the desolate Monadhliath Mountains from

here, and Newtonmore was the first place in Britain to offer pony-trekking as a sport. The pastime was introduced here in 1952, and this Speyside resort has both a summer and winter-sports season. Fine views extend E to the Cairngorms. Among the many relics in the Clan Macpherson Museum are a fairy gift known as the black charter, and the broken fiddle of freebooting James Macpherson. Sentenced to death in 1701, he is said to have played the *Macpherson's Rant* dirge on his violin as he stood on the gallows. On asking anyone in the crowd who thought well of him to take the instrument, no one accepted, so Macpherson smashed it.

The River Tromie joins the Spey NE of the town, and Long Glen Tromie stretches far into the wilds of the great Gaick Forest – a wilderness of lonely hills. A clan battle was fought 3m SW of Newtonmore, near the meeting point of the Spey and the Truim, in 1386. Overlooking the site to the N is 2,350ft Craig Dhu, the ancient gathering place of the Clan Macpherson. Beautiful wooded areas surround the hill, which gave its name to the Macpherson battle cry. Steep cliffs on Craig Dhu hide the cave where Cluny Macpherson hid for several years after the '45 Rising. A track from Newtonmore climbs through wild and barren scenery, past the Calder River to Loch Dubh and massive 3,087ft Carn Ban. This mountain is a nesting site for the golden eagle.

*NEWTON STEWART, Dumfries and Galloway   24 NX46

Newton Stewart's woollen mills allow visitors to watch mohair rugs and scarves being made. This lovely little Galloway town stands on the banks of the River Cree and operates a livestock market. Pretty riverside houses of almost a continental appearance surprise new-comers. Galloway Monument is an ornate, 57ft-high edifice which was erected in 1875 to commemorate the 9th Earl of Galloway, who died two years previously.

Granite-built Cree Bridge was built by the famous John Rennie in 1813, and replaces an earlier bridge which was washed away by the Cree. It links the town with Minnigaff. Minnigaff's ruined church displays several ancient carved tombstones. Ruins of 16th-c Garlies Castle lie 2½m N, with Cumloden deer park beyond. Farther N near the line of the Devil's Dyke are two stones known as 'The Thieves'. Lovely views from the town take in the distant mountains around Loch Trool, and Newton Stewart itself lies on the edge of Kirroughtree Forest – part of the Glen Trool forest park.

The entrance to the pretty Bargaly Glen lies 4m SE of the town on the Creetown road. Bargaly Glen is traversed by the Palnure Burn, which has its source in the great 2,331ft mass of Cairnsmore of Fleet, a prominent landmark mentioned in John Buchan's *The Thirty-Nine Steps*. Burns has described the Cruives of Cree in verse, and this beautifully wooded stretch of the river lies 4m NW of the town.

NEWTYLE, Tayside   31 NO24

A village in the Sidlow Hills, Newtyle is dominated by 1,399ft Auchterhouse Hill and 1,493ft Craigowl Hill to the E. The Dundee road begins its ascent over the Glack of Newtyle SE of the village, and ruined, 16th-c Hatton Castle lies near this point.

NEW YORK, Strathclyde   29 NM91

New York faces Portinnisherrich across Loch Awe.

NIGG, Highland   37 NH78

The world's largest dock has been constructed here for assembly of oil-production platforms destined for the North Sea. Nigg overlooks the little Bay of Nigg, an inlet of the Cromarty Firth. It is thought that a curious sculptured stone in the church may date from the 17thc. The Hill of Nigg rises 666ft to the E of the village.

NORTH BALLACHULISH, Highland   29 NN05

A road bridge which will replace the busy car ferry to South Ballachulish is to be opened here in the summer of 1975. The main span of this will measure some 600ft.

NORTH BALLOCH, Strathclyde   24 NX39

North Balloch lies at the head of the Stinchar valley, where the Balloch Burn joins the Stinchar. A road to Bargrennan runs SE from here over the lonely Nick o' the Balloch Pass, which touches 1,280ft at its summit.

NORTH BERWICK, Lothian   31 NT58

One of Scotland's most popular E coast resorts, the Royal Burgh and fishing village of North Berwick has a sandy beach and facilities for golf, sailing, and swimming. Behind the town is the 613ft conical peak of North Berwick Law, crowned by a ruined watchtower which dates from Napoleonic times and an arch formed from the jawbones of a whale. Out to sea 3m NE of the town is the famous 350ft-high, 1m-round Bass Rock, with its powerful lighthouse. This rock was used as a Covenanters' prison after 1671 and is mentioned by R L Stevenson in *Catriona*. Traces of old fortifications and a chapel can be seen here, and the rock with its satellite islands forms a nature reserve. The population of the islands now comprises innumerable seabirds and an important gannetry.

Fidra Island has a ternery and lighthouse and lies 3m NW off North Berwick. Nearby Eyebroughty islet, a notable haunt of the eider duck, can be reached from the coast between Dirleton and Gullane at very low tides. Boats from North Berwick take visitors on trips round these Firth of Forth islands. Tantallon Castle (AM) lies 3m E of the town on the coast beyond Canty Bay, and was built in 1375. It remained a Douglas stronghold for centuries. The castle figures in Walter Scott's *Marmion* and perches on a headland, guarded by sheer 100ft cliffs on three sides and a moat on the fourth. According to an old saying, an impossible task was 'like knocking down Tantallon or building a bridge to the Bass'. Despite this, Tantallon was knocked down after withstanding a siege by James V in 1528; General Monk reduced it to ruins after a twelve-day bombardment in 1651. Extensive earthworks survive from the original castle defences, and a 17th-c dovecot stands within the two inner ditches. Fragments of the ancient Auldhame Priory survive SE of the castle in the grounds of Seacliff House. The 16th-c Fenton Tower stands 2m S of North Berwick, off the road to Haddington.

NORTH KESSOCK, Highland   34 NH64
North Kessock faces the narrows between Beauly Firth and the Inner Moray Firth, and has a sailing centre near by. The village is connected by car ferry, which is soon to be replaced by a bridge across the narrows, to South Kessock on the Ness estuary. This allows easy access to Inverness. Ord Hill rises NE above North Kessock, and is topped by a large vitrified fort.

NORTH UIST, Western Isles   39 NF96
See Hebrides, Outer

OAKLEY, Fife   46 NT08
Comrie coal mine, one of the most up-to-date mines in Scotland, lies to the W of Oakley.

*OBAN, Strathclyde   29 NM83
Plan overleaf
Oban is the scene of the Argyll Gathering during the second week in September, and the W Highland Yachting Week during the first week in August. The town is a famous W Highland resort boasting an 18-hole golf course, and makes a fine starting point for drives through the lovely district of Lorne – with its magnificent seascapes and island scenery. Many of the best excursions can be made by steamer to the islands of Mull, Lismore, Iona, and Staffa (all described separately), and also to some of the Outer Hebridean Islands. Pulpit Hill affords wonderful views across the Firth of Lorne and the Sound of Mull, with the occasional unforgettable sunset.

McCaig's Folly, an unfinished replica of the Colosseum in Rome, overlooks the town and was built by a local banker who owned a large amount of property in the area. The idea behind the folly was to curb unemployment during a slump, and local craftsmen were employed on the project from 1897. He intended that

the building should be a museum and art gallery, as well as a memorial to his family. Its walls are 2ft thick and 30ft to 47ft high, and the inside courtyard is landscaped. The folly is floodlit at night. A museum and the County Library are housed in Corran Halls, situated in Corran Parks. Sir Giles Scott built Oban's little granite St Columba's Cathedral.

Offshore from the town is the island of Kerrera, which is linked to Oban by passenger ferry. Alexander II died on Kerrera in 1249, and at the N end of the island is an obelisk to David Hutcheson, who founded the W Highland steamer services. Ruined Gylen Castle lies on the SW shores of Kerrera and dates back to 1587, when it was a MacDougall stronghold. Dr Johnson and Boswell visited Oban in 1773 and found a 'tolerable' inn here. Sir Walter Scott was a visitor in 1814. Between Oban and Ganavan Bay is the Dog Stone – or Clach a' Choin – to which the legendary Fingal is said to have tied his dog Bran. The ruin of the 12th to 13th-c Dunollie Castle, seat of the Lords of Lorne who once owned a third of Scotland, stands near by overlooking the Firth of Lorne. The Brooch of Lorne is supposed to have been worn by Robert Bruce and is preserved in the modern mansion of Dunollie. Ganavan Bay, with its fine, sandy bathing beach, lies beyond the old castle.

Glencruitten House stands E of Oban in Glen Cruitten, surrounded by a park which features the well-known cathedral of trees. The road leading S from Oban to Kilninver passes close to ruined Kilbride church and the restored 16th-c Lerags Cross. A little to the E of the road lies pretty Loch Nell, with the 80yd-long boulder ridge known as Serpent's Mound on its SW shore. At the far end of Loch Nell the tall, granite-built Diarmid's Pillar stands in Glen Lonan and commemorates Diarmid, the ancestor of the Clan Campbell. The clan's ancient burial-place is situated here.

McCaig's Folly in Oban was started to curb local unemployment in the 19thc, but never finished.

OCCUMSTER, Highland   37 ND23
Prehistoric Canister chambered cairns lie 3m N of Occumster and are considered excellent examples of their type.

OCHILTREE, Strathclyde   25 NS52
Former Ochiltree House was where Claverhouse married in 1684, and John Knox was married in an earlier house on the same site in 1564. Ochiltree lies at the junction of Burnoch Water and the Lugar Water, in a dairy-farming district. George Douglas Brown, author of the *House with Green Shutters*, was born in this town in 1869. His book describes much of the local area and renames Ochiltree as 'Barbie'.

OLD DEER, Grampian   35 NJ94
This attractive Buchan village is best known for the scant remains of Deer Abbey (AM), which lie in a charming setting in the grounds of Pitfour House near the South Ugie Water. This Cistercian abbey was founded in 1219, and excavations have revealed its ground plan. An earlier monastery was built here by St Columba in the 6thc, which is mentioned in the famous *Book of Deer*. The latter contains the first-known characters of Gaelic script, and is preserved in Cambridge University Library.

OLDHAMSTOCKS, Lothian   31 NT77
Fairs were once held biennially on Oldhamstocks' village green, but these have disappeared along with the community's old Mercat cross. The local church boasts an elaborate 16th-c sundial.

OLD KILPATRICK, Strathclyde   45 NS47
It is a possibility that this village was the birthplace of St Patrick, and a Holy Well here is inscribed with his name. The village is sited on the N bank of the Clyde near the point where the new Erskine Bridge crosses the river. It is on the line of the Roman Antonine Wall, of which some traces can be made out in the neighbourhood. The Kilpatrick Hills

overlook Old Kilpatrick, and the Forth and Clyde Canal passes through the village to link up with the Clyde at Bowling.

OLDMELDRUM, Grampian *35 NJ82*

Sir Patrick Marson, who researched into tropical medicine in the 19thc, was born here in 1844. Oldmeldrum's church dates from 1684, and Barra Hill rises 1m S to overlook the Formartine and Garioch districts. It is crowned by a prehistoric fort, and Robert the Bruce

probably fought a battle here in 1308. Some 2m SW of the village on the Inverurie road is the fine, partly 17th-c mansion of Barra Castle. Loanhead stone circle (AM), probably of the neolithic-bronze age, can be seen 4m W of Oldmeldrum near Daviot.

OLD RATTRAY, Grampian *35 NK05*

Lonely Rattray Head divides the two bays of Rattray and Strathbeg, and Old Rattray lies a little inland. The shallow Loch of Strathbeg lies W of Old Rattray,

and the remains of Rattray Castle and the 13th-c Chapel of St Mary can be seen at the E end of the loch.

ONICH, Highland *33 NN06*

Attractively positioned on the shores of Loch Linnhe, Onich faces W towards the Ardgour hills which are dominated by 2,903ft Garbh Bheinn. A monument in Onich commemorates the noted Gaelic scholar Dr Alexander Stewart, and near the loch pier is a perforated prehistoric monolith known as the Clach a' Charra.

1 Corran Halls
2 Dog Stone
3 Dunollie Castle Ruins
4 Ganavan Bay

5 Glencruitten House
6 Kilbride Church
7 Loch Nell
8 McCaig's Folly

9 Pulpit Hill
10 St Columba's Cathedral

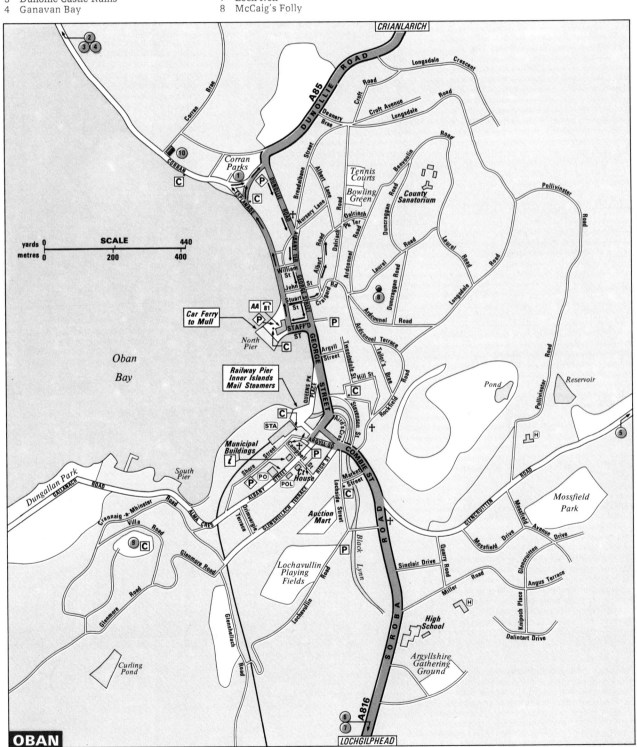

OBAN

Waterfalls cascade along the Amhainn Righ Burn, which tumbles from wooded heights into the loch NW of Onich.

OPINAN, Highland   32 NG77
Views from this clachan extend across the Inner Sound towards the distant Cuillin range on the Isle of Skye. Opinan lies between Gair Loch and the mouth of Loch Torridon.

ORD, Isle of Skye, Highland   35 NJ61
Spectacular sunsets can sometimes be enjoyed from Ord, which lies on the S shore of Loch Eishort. Fine views from here encompass most of the great Cuillin peaks.

ORKNEY ISLANDS
Of the 70 or so islands which make up the Orkneys only 28 are inhabited. The islands lie about 20m to the N of the Scottish mainland over the stormy Pentland Firth, and the largest is itself called Mainland. Most of the 18,000 islanders make their living from farming – the soil is surprisingly fertile and the climate mainly mild. Few trees grow on the islands and trout fishing in the lochs is free. A remarkable feature of both the Orkneys and the Shetlands is that the summer nights are only twilight – or, as Shetlanders call it, simmer dim. The Orkneys display magnificent cliff scenery, notably on Hoy, and the islands abound with prehistoric antiquities and rare bird life. The Romans called the islands the Orcades, but it is thought that the Picts were the first colonizers. Norsemen settled here in the 9thc and stayed for 500 years. In 1468 to 1469 the islands passed to Scotland, given by Christian I of Norway as part of his daughter Margaret's dowry when she married James III of Scotland.

Mainland is linked to several of the smaller islands farther S by the Churchill Barriers, remains of second world war naval defences which now serve a more useful purpose. The Orkneys can be reached by steamer from Scrabster near Thurso (to Stromness), and from Aberdeen (to Kirkwall). Other steamer services connect with the Shetlands. Air services operate from the principal Scottish towns to Grimsetter Airport at Kirkwall. Supply bases for North Sea oil have been planned in some parts of the islands. The following entries list some of the Orkney islands in alphabetical order.

EGILSAY   40 HY43
Egilsay lies E of Rousay and is where St Magnus is thought to have been murdered in 1116. A roofless Norman church (AM) stands on the murder site and has a curious, 48ft-high round tower. This is one of only three examples to be found in Scotland. The little island of Wyre, or Veira, lies to the SW and displays traces of Cubbie Row's Castle (AM). It is possible that this was the earliest stone-built castle in Scotland.

HOY   40 ND29
Hoy is the second largest of the Orkneys, and is also the most spectacular. The island can be reached by steamer from Stromness. Ward Hill rises to 1,565ft and is the highest point in the Orkneys, nurturing many rare plants. Hoy's NW cliffs soar to over 1,000ft and can be reached from Linkness. The latter village is situated in the N of the island, facing

Graemsay Island in Hoy Sound, and has a pier. These fantastic cliffs stretch from St John's Head, where they rise vertically to 1,140ft, to the celebrated Old Man of Hoy, a 450ft pillar of rock rising out of the sea. The Old Man of Hoy was first climbed in 1966 and can be seen from Caithness on the mainland coast. The cliffs are gouged by deep slashes called 'geos'. Beyond the Old Man of Hoy are Rora Head and more cliffs, overlooking the lovely Rackwick Valley. An ancient burial chamber known as the Dwarfie Stone (AM) is situated here. It is inscribed with Hugh Miller's initials and is mentioned by Scott in The Pirate.

Berry Head displays curious coloured cliffs and lies in the S of Hoy. To the E of the head is Melsetter House and its fine gardens, and beyond here are the South Walls peninsula and the village of Longhope. This community of small white houses was the base of the Longhope lifeboat, whose crew of 8 died in 1969 while trying to rescue the crew of the Liberian tanker 'Irene'. The tanker had called for help when short of fuel in mountainous seas. The 'Irene' later came to rest in a rocky bay on the neighbouring island of South Ronaldsay, and her seventeen-man crew was saved. The island of Flotta faces W to the Scapa Flow naval base of Lyness from the mouth of the Loch Hope inlet. Hoy is thought to be the farthest S point of Britain where the rare great skua breeds.

MAINLAND   40 HY41
This is largest of the Orkney islands and has the most roads suitable for motoring – about 200m in all. Several of the minor roads leading to the coast are poor in places. Kirkwall and Stromness, both situated on Mainland, are the two most important ports and towns in the Orkneys. The busy harbour town and Royal Burgh of Kirkwall is the capital of the Orkneys. Narrow, twisting streets and high-gabled greystone houses cluster round the red and yellow sandstone

St Magnus's Cathedral. The cathedral was founded in 1137 by Earl Rognvald, the Norse ruler of Orkney, in memory of his uncle and predecessor Magnus. Magnus was murdered by a rival earl in 1115. The canonized remains of both rulers are sealed in pillars of the cathedral. St Magnus's skull was discovered in 1919 during restoration – split right across by an axe, just as the story tells. After the Battle of Largs in 1263 the body of King Haco rested here on its journey back to Norway. The cathedral was later desecrated by Cromwell's soldiers, and lightning destroyed the spire. This was repaired during restoration work carried out early in the 20thc. St Magnus's Cathedral ranks with Glasgow Cathedral as one of the two finest and most complete gothic cathedral churches in Scotland, and is a most considerable monument to the craftsmanship and staying-power of the Norsemen – it took 300 years to complete. Fine views are afforded by the 133ft-high tower, which was built in 1523.

Characteristic Orcadian 'mort-brods' or memorials can be seen here, and a fine 15th-c tomb lies in the choir. There is also a tablet in memory of 800 men who were lost on board the battleship 'Royal Oak', which was torpedoed in the second world war. To the S of the cathedral is the Bishop's Palace (AM), a partly 13th-c building with a massive mid 16th-c – but much reconstructed – round tower. Nearby Earl Patrick's Palace (AM) has been described as 'the most mature and accomplished piece of Renaissance architecture left in Scotland'. It was built in 1607 for Patrick Stewart, 2nd Earl of Orkney, who was tried in Edinburgh and hanged in 1614 after his reign of tyranny. Earl Patrick's Palace is now roofless and is mentioned by Scott in The Pirate.

A doorway has survived from the 16th-c Church of St Ola, and opposite the cathedral stands the Tankerness House

Remains of the 16th-c Palace of Birsay on Mainland, Orkney Islands.

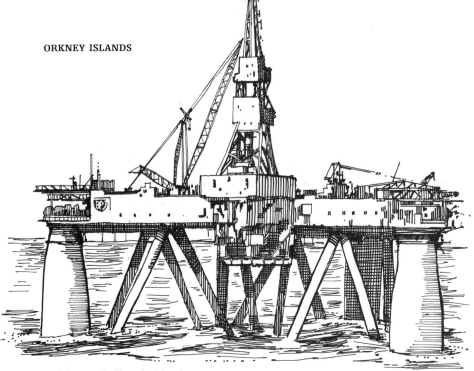

North-Sea oil offers the islands new prosperity and a hitherto unknown scope for development.

of 1574, now housing a museum and art gallery of Orkney life. Kirkwall's public library is the oldest in Scotland and dates from 1683. To the N of the town is the pier on Kirkwall Bay, and beyond the bay lies 19th-c Balfow Castle on the little island of Shapinsay. To the E of Kirkwall are the smaller sandy bays of Meil and Berstone, the latter being an inlet of the larger Ingaress Bay. To the E of the latter is the Tankerness peninsula. Grimsetter Airport lies SE of the town, and S of Kirkwall is the sandy Scapa Bay. Near the W shores of Scapa Bay the road overlooks Scapa Flow, the famous naval anchorage used extensively in both world wars which saw the surrender of the German fleet in 1918. Most of the ships were scuttled by their crews in 1919, but several have since been brought up.

During the last war the Churchill Barriers were built to link Mainland with South Ronaldsay, and thus seal up the E approach to Scapa Flow after the 'Royal Oak' disaster. The road over the barriers begins at St Mary's Holm, a yachtsmen's haven on Holm Sound, and leads to the islands of Lamb Holm, Glims Holm, Burray – with its curious broch – and South Ronaldsay. Italian second world war prisoners created an ornate chapel from a Nissen hut on Lamb Holm. Wideford Hill (AM) affords views which extend S over the Pentland Firth to the mountains of old Sutherland, and also to Fair Isle which is more than 60m N. This hill lies 1m W of Kirkwall. To the W and N are several curious 'weems', or Picts' houses.

Finstown is a sheltered village on the Bay of Firth, and boasts one of the few woods of mature trees in the Orkneys. A ruined broch stands on the tiny island of Damsay in the Bay of Firth. Near the shores of Wide Firth, 7m NE of the village, is the Hall of Rendall. A c1600 dovecot still survives here and includes flagstone landing piers for the birds. Several features of ancient history can be seen near Finstown. The notable gallery grave of Rennibister (AM) lies to the SE of the village, and 3m WSW at Stenness is the famous Maes Howe (AM), an enormous stone-age burial mound dating back to

c2000BC. The chambered tomb is considered one of the finest in Western Europe, and is believed to be 'the tomb of a potentate, a veritable prime-bishop'. The spacious central chamber and three mural cells were furnished with gigantic stones and covered by the 26ft-high by 115ft-diameter mound.

Viking marauders broke into the mound in search of treasure during the 12thc, and Norse crusaders sheltered from a storm in the Howe. While they were there they engraved the richest collection of Runic inscriptions to be found in any one place on the walls. Cuween Hill Cairn (AM) lies 1m S of Finstown and is another chambered tomb of similar age. A narrow causeway between the Loch of Stenness and the Loch of Harray, beyond Stenness church, carries the famous Standing Stones of Stenness (AM). These comprise the Circle of Stenness (AM) and the Ring of Brogar (AM). The former is the remains of a stone circle dated c1800BC, and stands on a mound encircled by a ditch and bank. The Ring of Brogar is a magnificent circle of upright stones surrounded by a ditch.

The Onstan Chambered Cairn (AM), a mound covering a megalithic burial chamber of c2500BC and surrounded by three walls, can be seen by the A965. Several other cairns and earth houses are to be seen in the area between Stromness and Kirkwall. Click Mill (AM), 6m NW of Finstown, is the only watermill designed to a Norse pattern still working today. Its wheel lies horizontally instead of in the more usual vertical position.

Ever since Viking days Stromness has been valued as a safe harbour. The town's narrow paved streets have no footpaths and include quaint closes. An interesting maritime museum faces the hills of Hoy across Hoy Sound, and faces SE to historic Scapa Flow. Steamers from Scrabster on the mainland sail to Stromness, and the port has sea links with Hoy and other islands. The town has a golf course, and the site of Login's Well is associated with explorers Captain Cook and Sir John Franklin. Orphir Church (AM) lies 9m SE of the town, near the shores of Scapa Flow. Near by

are the ruins of a circular church which may have been built by Earl Haakon in the 12thc. To the E of Orphir is sandy Swanbister Bay.

Birsay is a small village in the extreme NW of Mainland, with the Loch of Boardhouse to the E. Ruins of the Palace of Birsay, a residence of the Earls of Orkney which was rebuilt in the late 16thc by Earl Robert Stewart in the style of Falkland Palace, are of interest. Offshore to the NW is the tidal island of Brough of Birsay, with the ruins of a 12th-c church, while to the E is the unruliest spot in Britain – Costa Head. Farther along the coast, by the shores of Eynhallow Sound, is Evie and the nearby broch and secondary buildings of Gurness, at Aikerness. To the SW of Birsay Sound is Marwick Head, which can be reached on foot from Marwick and is the site of a Kitchener Memorial. The cruiser 'Hampshire' was sunk off the coast near here in June 1916, while taking Kitchener to Russia.

Skara Brae (AM) is a remarkable neolithic village settlement of 2500–2000BC which stands on the S shore of the sandy bay of Skaill, beyond Aith and to the W of the Birsay to Stromness road. Narrow covered alleys lead to one-roomed houses containing stone beds, fireplaces, and cupboards. A paved open court was probably the place where communal problems were discussed. The village was occupied for some 250 years and, though uninhabited since c1800BC, is in a remarkably good state of preservation. Modernized Skaill House dates from the 17thc and stands near the freshwater Loch of Skaill.

Deerness also features a ruined broch and stands on Sandside Bay in the SE corner of Mainland – known as East Mainland. A little to the N is a chasm in the cliffs known as the Gloup of Deerness, with the Stack of Deerness beyond. The road running W from the Deerness peninsula to Kirkwall passes the head of Deer Sound at St Peter's Pool. On the narrow isthmus separating this from Taracliff Bay and the North Sea, is the barrow of Dingy's Howe. Copinsay Island lies to the SE. A 2m walk NNW from Deerness leads to a monument overlooking Deer Sound at Scarva Taing commemorating 200 Covenanters who were wrecked here in 1679.

ROUSAY AND EYNHALLOW 40 HY43
Separated from Mainland by the Eynhallow Sound, Rousay offers fine rock scenery on its W coast. Several cairns can be seen here, and of particular interest are: Blackhammer chambered cairn; Knowe of Yarso chambered cairn; Midhowe Broch; Midhowe chambered cairn; and Taversöe Tuick chambered cairn (all AM). A ruined monastic church (AM) stands on the tiny uninhabited Eynhallow Island, now the haunt of seals and birds which include fulmars, eiders, and the rare skua.

SOUTH RONALDSAY 40 ND48
South Ronaldsay is a fertile island linked by the Churchill Barriers to Burray, Glimps Holm, Lamb Holm, and Mainland. On the N coast of the island is St Margaret's Hope, named after Queen Margaret 'Maid of Norway', who died on board ship on her way to Scotland in 1290. A road runs from this pretty village to Burwick in the S of the island, separated from the mainland's Duncansby Head by the 6m-wide storm-torn waters of the Pentland Firth.

STRONSAY 40 HY62

Three large bays – Milk Bay, St Catherine's Bay, and Bay of Holland – bite into the coast of this oddly shaped island. Little Papa Stronsay island lies off its N shores, and farther N across the Sanday Sound is the large, narrow island of Sanday. Features of this include the neolithic chambered cairn of Quoyness. North Ronaldsay, the farthest N of all the Orkney islands, lies beyond Sanday and has an indigenous population of sheep. These have to be kept off cultivated land by 12m of stone wall, and feed largely on seaweed.

WESTRAY 40 HY44

The ruins of 16th-c Noltland Castle (AM), which was destroyed in 1746, preserve a stately hall, vaulted kitchen, and fine, winding staircase. This is considered the finest surviving '2-plan' castle in Britain. The style is named '2-plan' because the central building has wings jutting out from opposite corners. Originally built in 1420 by Thomas de Tulloch, the castle was besieged by Sir William Sinclair of Warsetter and later fell into the hands of Gilbert Balfow of Westray. The present building dates from the time of Balfow, and stands a little inland from Pierowall Bay on the NE coast. Nearby ruins of a church (AM) include several ancient inscribed tombstones.

Across Papa Sound to the NE is the island of Papa Westray, on which stands a ruined chapel. Also on Papa Westray is a large neolithic chambered cairn, displaying beehive cells and rare megalithic engravings. Magnificent cliffs and a lighthouse are features of Noup Head, the extreme NW point of Westray. Just S of the head is the Gentlemen's Cave, where several Jacobites hid after Culloden in 1746. Off the SE shores of Westray is Eday, where numerous ancient weems and tumuli can be seen. Red Head on Eday looks over Calf Sound to Grey Head, on the smaller island of Calf of Eday.

ORMISTON, Lothian 47 NT46

A 15th-c cross (AM) is mounted on modern steps in this Tyne Water village. In 1545 George Wishart took refuge with Alexander Cockburn at Ormiston House, an old building now modernized and enlarged, lying to the S of the village. Near the house is a fragment of the Old Church of Ormiston, in which a fine 16th-c brass to Alexander Cockburn is still preserved.

ORONSAY, ISLE OF, Strathclyde 28 NR38

This small Inner Hebridean island lies to the W of Jura, and is separated from the neighbouring island of Colonsay by a narrow strait which is dry for three hours at low tide. Interesting remains of a 14th-c priory survive on the island, and the churchyard contains a notable sculptured cross and various other ancient stones.

ORTON, Grampian 35 NJ35

Wooded hills rise on either side of the Lower Spey valley, where Orton is situated, with 1,544ft Ben Aigan dominating the landscape to the S.

OSE, Isle of Skye, Highland 32 NG34

Situated on the shores of Loch Bracadale, Ose faces towards the islands of Harlosh, Tarner, and Wiay. Glen Ose extends

Rear view of 17th-c Place of Paisley, showing excellent examples of crow-stepped gables.

inland to the E and bears the ruins of the ancient broch of Dun Arkaig on its S slopes.

OTTER FERRY, Strathclyde 29 NR98

This name derived from 'oitir', meaning 'sand spit'. Otter Ferry lies on the E shores of Loch Fyne and across the loch are the green, rounded hills of Knapdale. These rise above an inlet of Loch Gilp, where Ardrishaig and Lochgilphead are situated. A narrow road from Otter Ferry climbs gradients of up to 1 in 4 to a height of 1,026ft, then winds its way down to the shores of Loch Riddon and Glendaruel.

OVERSCAIG, Highland 36 NC42

Overscaig lies on the N shores of bleak Loch Shin, on the road leading from Lairg to Loch Laxford and Laxford Bridge on the wild NW coast of Scotland. Ben More Assynt rises to 3,273ft in the W, with 2,864ft Ben Hee to the N on the fringe of the great Reay deer forest.

OXNAM, Borders 26 NT61

Oxnam Water flows through the lonely valley which guards Oxnam, cutting through the undulations of the hill country. A Roman station once stood at Cappuck to the N, and the line of the Roman Dere Street can be traced E of Oxnam on its way to the Cheviot ridge. Dere Street crosses the ridge at a height of some 1,500ft to the E of Carter Bar. This is near the famous great camp and earthworks of Chew Green.

OXTON, Borders 47 NT45

The tiny Lauderdale hamlet of Oxton is situated a little W of the Edinburgh to Lauder road through Carfraemill. To the N stands the little parish church of Channelkirk, dedicated to St Cuthbert who is said to have spent his childhood around here. A church has been dedicated to him on this site since before written records. The Romans probably used the pilgrims' track, which once passed through both hamlets on its way from the Lammermuir Hills to Tweeddale.

OYKELL BRIDGE, Highland 36 NC30

The early geographer Ptolemy mentions

Oykell Bridge, which also figures in Icelandic Sagas. The River Oykell flows down the slopes of 3,272ft Ben More Assynt, and through Loch Ailsh, which is noted for fishing. The river's turbulent waters then form the boundary between the one-time counties of Sutherland and Ross and Cromarty for most of its length. A little to the W of Oykell Bridge are picturesque falls, and farther down-stream to the SE of the bridge the Oykell is joined by the Einig. A wilderness of lonely hills in the vast Freevater Forest lie to the S. A low watershed lies 5m NW of Oykell Bridge on the Inchnadamph road, near the small Loch Craggie. This affords fine views towards the distant, isolated peak of 2,779ft Canisp and the sharp E summit of 2,399ft Suilven.

OYNE, Grampian 35 NJ62

Covenanters burned 17th-c Harthill Castle, the ruins of which lie to the SE of Oyne. The village itself lies on Gady Burn in the district of Garioch, overlooked by the forests of Bennachie and 1,733ft Oxen Craig. Westhall is a 16th-c tower house situated in the area, and 3m E is the 17th-c house of Logie-Elphinstone. A remarkable hill fort can be seen on the prominent, 1,698ft Mither Tap, which rises to the S.

PAISLEY, Strathclyde 45 NS46
Plan overleaf

Said to be the largest thread-manufacturing centre in the world, the industrial town of Paisley grew up around the fine cluniac Abbey Church. This was founded in 1163 by Walter Fitz Alan and monks from Wenlock Abbey in Shropshire. Paisley's museum and art gallery houses a priceless collection of famous Paisley shawls, the 'pine' motif of which was introduced from Kashmir in 1770. The English destroyed the Abbey Church in 1307, and most of the present building dates from the mid-15thc. The tower, choir, and north transept have been rebuilt, and the fine nave is still in use as the parish church. Also of note are the west front and doorway. St Mirren's Chapel, standing in place of the south transept, was built in 1499 and contains an effigy believed to be of Marjory Bruce, the daughter of

293

Robert Bruce. Extensive restoration of the abbey was begun by Rowand Anderson and McGregor Chalmers in 1897. This was completed by Sir Robert Lorimer between 1922 and 1928.

Part of the abbey buildings, on the site of the refectory, were incorporated into 17th-c Place of Paisley, now well restored as a War Memorial. Built by the Earl of Dundonald, the Place was the scene of the wedding of John Graham of Claverhouse and Lady Jean Cochrane in 1684. Situated in the very heart of the town is the Town Hall, a fine example of Victorian classical architecture. This 19th-c structure stands beside White Cart Water and carries twin towers with a carillon which rings out a different tune for each day of the month. The Corinthian colonnaded frontage is impressive.

Professor John Wilson, the Christopher North of *Blackwood's Magazine*, was born in the town in 1785. Number 8 Castle Street was the birthplace of Robert Tannahill in 1774, the weaver poet who described the Braes of Gleniffer, a fine viewpoint SW of the town. Thomas Coats Memorial Church was built in 1894. Near the abbey in Incle Street is St Mirin's Cathedral, a large 20th-c building without a tower or spire. The front of the cathedral displays castellations and is very much in the Scottish baronial style.

PALNACKIE, Dumfries and Galloway
25 NX85
Palnackie lies on a creek of Rough Firth, an inlet of the Solway Firth, 3m S of the Craignair granite quarries. These

provided stone for London's Thames embankment. Just N of Palnackie the Urr Water flows into the creek. Orchardton Tower (AM), 1m S of the village, is a circular tower house which is unique in Scotland. Built in the late 15thc by John Cairns, the tower later fell into the hands of the Maxwells. It is probably associated with Scott's *Guy Mannering*. Almorness Point lies S at the tip of a narrow peninsula.

PALNURE, Dumfries and Galloway
25 NX46
Pretty Bargaly Glen carries the Palnure Burn to Palnure, to the S of which it flows into the winding Cree estuary. John Buchan writes about Cairnsmoor of Fleet, which rises to 2,331ft to the NE of Palnure, in *The Thirty-Nine Steps*.

1 Abbey and Place of Paisley	3 St Mirin's Cathedral	5 Thomas Coats Memorial Church
2 Library, Museum, and Art Gallery	4 The Braes of Gleniffer	6 Town Hall

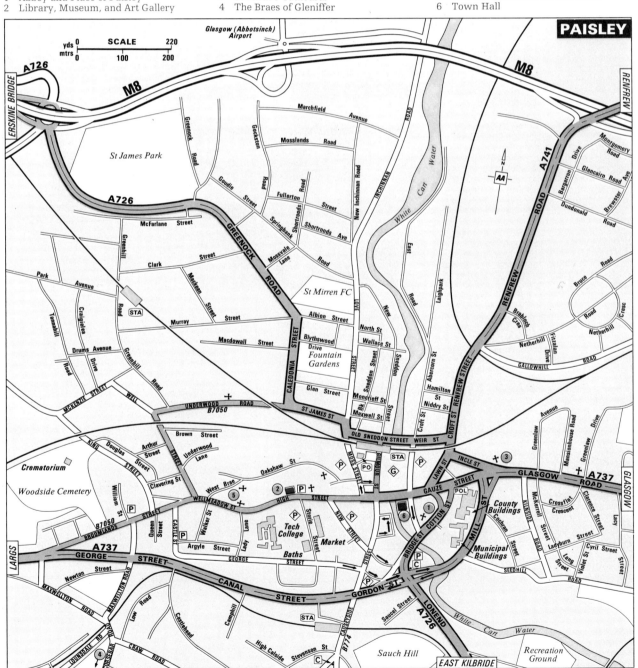

PANNANICH WELLS, Grampian
35 NO49
The wells here became widely known in 1760 and led to the development of the Deeside resort of Ballater, which lies a little to the SW. Fine views N extend over the Dee to 2,862ft Morven, and 2½m E lies Ballaterach Farm, where Byron lived as a child.

PATHHEAD, Fife   47 NT29
Ruined Ravenscraig Castle lies here and was founded by James II in 1460. It later passed into the hands of the Sinclair Earls of Orkney and was perhaps the first British castle to be systematically designed for defence by firearms. Scott renamed the castle, which was dismantled in 1651, as 'Ravensheugh' in his *Rosabelle*.

PATHHEAD, Lothian   47 NT36
Steep banks line the Tyne Water to the N of Pathhead, and beyond the river is Oxenford Castle. This now serves as a school and lies in fine parkland. Preston Hall has fine entrance gates and dates from c1794. Attractive old Ford House dates from 1680. The 17th-c Southside Castle lies 3m W of Pathhead and is now a farm.

PATNA, Strathclyde   24 NS41
Patna is situated on the River Doon and lies on the edge of a coal-mining and steel-producing area.

PAXTON, Borders   31 NT95
Paxton House lies between this village and the River Tweed, and was designed by Robert Adam. Farther S the river is spanned by the fine Union Suspension Bridge originally erected by Sir Samuel Brown in 1820 and the first of its type extant.

*PEEBLES, Borders   31 NT24
Green hills surround this quiet county town and Royal Burgh, which stands on a lovely stretch of the Tweed. Noted for its tweeds and knitwear, Peebles is also a popular centre for anglers who come for the famous Tweed salmon. Many historic and literary figures have made the town their home, including Robert Louis Stevenson; Samuel Crockett; John Buchan and his novelist sister Anna (O Douglas), who lived at Bank House; and Mungo Park, the great African explorer. William Chambers and his brother Robert, who published the first Chambers' encyclopedias and dictionaries, were born in Peebles and donated the Chambers Institute, a library, and a museum to the town. Peebles was occupied both by Cromwell in 1649 and Prince Charles Edward in 1745, but there is no trace left of the old castle. Every June Peebles holds the Border Riding ceremony, when the Beltane Queen is crowned.

Among the town's historical remains are the interesting ruins of the old Cross Kirk (AM), which was built by Alexander II in 1261. The nave and west tower are surviving fragments of this Tristarian friary, and the foundations of the cloistered building have been excavated. The parish church dates from 1784. At the S end of Northgate stands the shaft of the former town cross. Only a tower remains of St Andrew's Church, which stood at the W end of Peebles. Two old inns in the town are the 17th-c Cross Keys Inn – said to be the 'Cleikum Inn' of Scott's *St Ronan's Well*, and the Tontine Inn of 1808. Remains of the 17th-c Queensberry Lodging, birthplace of the spendthrift 4th Duke of Queensberry – the 'Old Q' – were probably incorporated into the Chambers Institute. The Tweed

is spanned here by a bridge which was first built in 1467 and twice widened since. Along the Tweed to the W is 15th-c Neidpath Castle, beautifully positioned above the river.

This was originally a Fraser stronghold but later passed to the Hays of Tweeddale, whose goat's-head family crest surmounts the courtyard gateway. During the Civil War the castle was held by the Earl of Tweeddale for Charles I, until Cromwell's artillery battered its massive 11ft-thick walls and forced its defenders into submission. Neidpath was later restored and sold to the 1st Duke of Queensberry in 1686. His successor, 'Old Q', felled all the fine trees on the estate in the 18thc to raise money. He was denounced in a Wordsworth sonnet beginning 'Degenerate Douglas! Oh, the unworthy lord!' To the E of Peebles the Glentress Forest borders the Innerleithen road, and the beautiful unspoilt valley of Glensax lies to the S. This glen contains attractive burns and is dominated by 2,433ft Dunrig at its head.

PENCAITLAND, Lothian   47 NT46
Tyne Water flows through this delightful village, and Wester Pencaitland boasts an old Mercat cross. Easter Pencaitland includes a church which preserves its original 13th-c north sacristy. The church tower dates from 1631, and other features include a fine 17th-c west doorway, a laird's loft, and three old sundials. Beyond the Tyne Water to the N is Winton House, begun in 1620 but now showing 19th-c additions. Similar in external detail to George Heriot's Hospital in Edinburgh, Winton House is noted for its tall, finely-wrought chimney stacks and ornate plaster ceilings. Penkaet is a beautiful 17th-c house formerly known as Fountainhall, lying 1½m SW. Fine old woodwork is preserved in the building, and the grounds contain two old dovecotes.

PENICUIK, Lothian   47 NT25
For centuries Penicuik was Scotland's paper-making town, and drew power for the mills from the River Esk. The Scottish cotton industry began here in 1778 and the town is one of Scotland's fastest growing communities. The 12th-c tower of the former Church of St Kentigern is now the belfry of the parish church of St Mungo, which also carries a doric portico. Penicuik House was built by Sir John Clark in an elegant Queen-Anne style, but it was largely destroyed by fire in 1899. The stables of the ruins have been rebuilt by the family to form a modern house. An obelisk to Allan Ramsay, a poet born in 1686, stands in the grounds of the house. Ramsay was an Edinburgh wigmaker who later became a bookseller. His most famous poem, *The Gentle Shepherd*, was published in 1725.

Valleyfield Mill was founded in 1709 and used during the Napoleonic wars to confine French prisoners – 300 of whom died here and are commemorated by a monument. To the N of Penicuik rises the Pentland Hills. Scald Law rises to

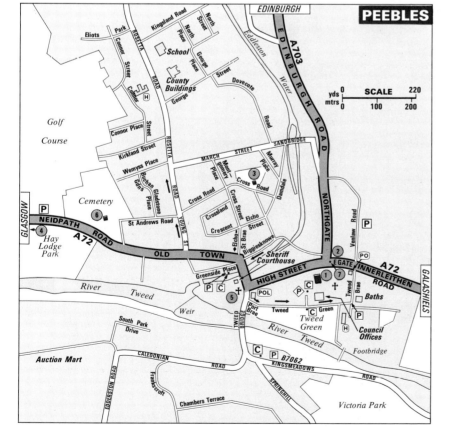

PEEBLES

SCALE
yds 0 ─── 220
mtrs 0 ─── 100 ─── 200

1 Chambers Institute and Queensferry Lodging
2 Cross Keys Inn
3 Cross Kirk Remains
4 Neidpath Castle
5 Parish Church
6 St Andrew's Church Tower
7 Town Cross Remains

Entries marked * are the starting point of drives included in the Day Drive section of the book (pages 95 to 160).

1,898ft and is the highest peak in the range. Beyond the mountain picturesque Loganlee Reservoir lies in a deep trough.

Castlelaw Hill lies 4m N of the town and has a small iron-age fort (AM) comprising two concentric banks and ditches. The fort was last occupied in Roman times, and in the older rock-cut ditch an earth-house has been preserved. Auchendinny House stands 1½m NE of Penicuik, and was built in 1707 by Sir William Bruce. It is considered a good example of this period. Remains of Brunstane Castle lie near the North Esk River 2½m SW of the town.

PENNAN, Grampian 35 NJ86
This small fishing village is sited on a rocky stretch of coast by Pennan Bay, overlooked by Pennan Head. Tore Burn marks the one-time Aberdeen/Banff border, and flows into the sea to the W of Pennan. Farther W is the promontory of Troup Head.

PENNYGHAEL, Isle of Mull, Strathclyde 28 NM52
Pennyghael lies on the S shores of Loch Scridain, with 3,169ft Ben More rising to

the N. The road E to the head of the loch winds through lonely Glen More, overlooked by lofty hills which include 2,354ft Ben Buie to the S. This road later reaches the N shores of almost land-locked Loch Spelve, on the way to Craignure. A narrow road leads S from the village through Glen Leidle to Carsaig Bay.

PENPONT, Dumfries and Galloway 25 NX89
Scar Water, on which Penpont lies, joins the Nith to the E of the village. Penpont stands on the line of an ancient pilgrims' track which James IV followed on his way from Edinburgh to Whithorn in 1507. Auchengibbert Hill rises to 1,221ft N of the village, and the long ridge of the Keir Hills can be seen to the S. Kirkpatrick Macmillan, the inventor of a bicycle in 1839, was born at Courthill Smithy near the hamlet of Keir. His original machine is preserved at the Science Museum in London. Tynron Doon lies W of Penpont and is surmounted by a prehistoric hill fort commanding wide views. Robert the Bruce is said to have sheltered here in 1306.

*PERTH, Tayside 30 NO12
Capital of Scotland for a century until 1437, the 'Fair City of Perth' is an ancient Royal Burgh with a rich history. It is also an important touring centre for Central Scotland. A 70m Scottish Wild Life Trust motoring trail starts from the city. Perth was once known as St Johnstoun, and stands between the meadows of the North and South Inch at the head of the estuary of the River Tay, famous for its salmon. Its livestock market is the most important in Scotland. To the NE rise the Sidlaw Hills, with the Ochil Hills to the SW and the fertile Carse of Gowrie E on the N shores of the Firth of Tay. Perth was over-run by the English on several occasions and Edward I fortified the town in 1298. James I was murdered at the former Blackfriars Monastery in 1437, despite the heroic efforts of Catherine Douglas – a lady of the Queen – to save him. Catherine put her arm in the door in place of a stolen bar to try to keep the murderers out. James' widow and her young son, James II, moved the court to Edinburgh after this.

Perth was also the scene of the Gowrie Conspiracy in 1600, when a band of

1	Balhousie Castle	
2	Branklyn Gardens	
3	County Buildings	
4	Fair Maid's House	
5	Museum and Art Gallery	
6	Old Academy	
7	St John's Church	
8	St Ninian's Episcopal Cathedral	
9	Sir Walter Scott's Statue	

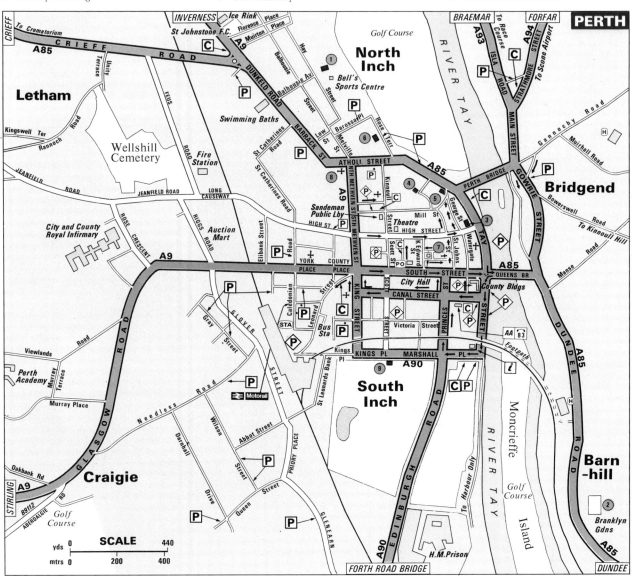

Entries marked * are the starting point of drives included in the Day Drive section of the book (pages 95 to 160).

nobles led by the Earl of Gowrie kidnapped James VI (later James I of England) and held him prisoner for a year. The County Buildings stand on the site of Gowrie House, where the conspiracy was hatched. In 1651 the city surrendered to Cromwell, and in both 1715 and 1745 it was occupied by the Jacobites. St John's Kirk is one of the few buildings which remain from Perth's medieval period. This fine, restored church has a choir of 1450, a central tower with a 15th-c steeple, and a nave built c1490. In 1559 John Knox delivered his rabble-rousing sermon on church idolatry here, which in effect launched the Reformation. Charles I, Charles II, and Prince Charles Edward have all attended services at St John's Kirk, and Scott mentions the church in his *Fair Maid of Perth*. A statue of Scott can be seen in Kings Place. Fine pre-Reformation plate is preserved in the building and the rebuilt north transept houses Sir Robert Lorimer's War Memorial.

In Curfew Row is the Fair Maid of Perth's House, which was restored in 1893. This stands on the site originally occupied by the house where Catherine Glover – the 'fair maid' of Scott's novel – lived in 1396. St Ninian's Episcopal Cathedral is of 19th-c date, and the Old Academy had a façade of 1807. The

academy serves as a school. Perth has an interesting natural history museum and an art gallery, plus the Black Watch Regimental Museum in Balhousie Castle. Late 19th-c stained-glass windows depicting scenes from Scott's *Fair Maid of Perth*, and of Robert the Bruce capturing the town in 1311, decorate the City Chambers. The Salutation Hotel was built in 1699 and has a minstrel gallery near the bedroom occupied by Prince Charles Edward.

The North Inch boasts a fine, spacious park with the huge, domed Bell's Sports Centre. Smeaton built the Perth Bridge across the Tay in 1771, and among Perth's old industrial buildings are some interesting 19th-c dyeworks and glassworks. Waterworks of 1832 have been restored. John Ruskin spent part of his childhood across the Tay at Bridgend, and he was married at the house of Bowerswell in 1848. A view indicator tops Kinnoull Hill, which offers fine views over the city and the River Tay. Branklyn Gardens (NTS) have been described as 'the finest two acres of private garden in the country'. Inchyra House was built c1800 and stands 6m E of Perth.

Beyond Moncreiffe Hill, another fine viewpoint to the SE of Perth, lie the ruins of the 16th-c Elcho Castle (AM). This

ancestral seat of the Earls of Wemyss is a fortified mansion notable for its tower-like jambs or wings, and for its wrought-iron window grills. Another castle which was once on or very near the site of Elcho Castle, was a favourite hide-out of William Wallace.

PETERHEAD, Grampian   35 NK14
Peterhead is a busy Buchan herring port and boat-building town at the mouth of the River Ugie. The town is only 3m from Buchan Ness, Scotland's farthest E point, where extensive North Sea oil developments are taking place. Peterhead Bay is separated from Sandford Bay by Salthouse Head. Near the Head is Peterhead Prison, and prisoners built the harbour breakwater from granite quarried beyond Boddam in the 1880's. Boddam lies S of Buchan Ness.

The town itself was founded in 1593 by the Keiths, who were later exiled for helping the Old Pretender in 1715. The old parish church, or Muckle Kirk, dates from 1806. The links to the S of the town include the remains of 12th-c St Peter's Kirk; the bell tower of 1592 contains a bell which was cast in Holland in 1647. Arbuthnot Museum and Art Gallery has an exhibit on the development of the fishing industry. Peterhead's Town House was built in

1 Arbuthnot Museum, Art Gallery, and Library
2 Bell Tower and Ruins of St Peter's Kirk

3 Inverugie Castle
4 Old Parish Church or Muckle Kirk
5 Ravenscraig Castle (ruins)

6 Town House and Marshall Keith Statue

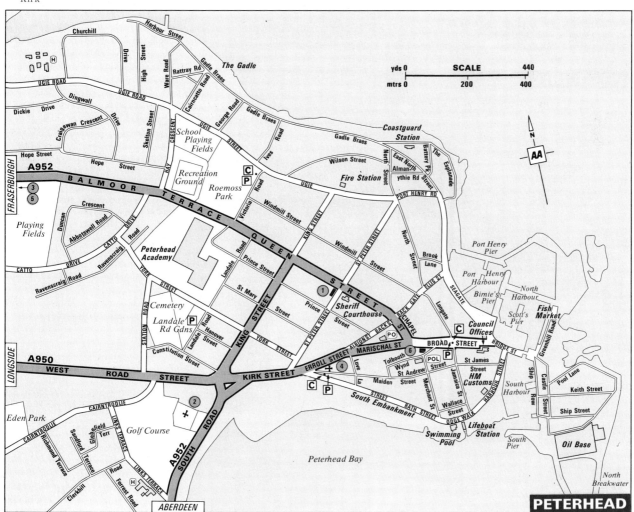

1788 and in front is a statue of Marshal Keith. Keith was born at Inverugie Castle in 1696. This ruined 16th-c stronghold lies 3m NW on the River Ugie. Farther upstream are the remains of the 14th-c Ravenscraig Castle.

PINKIE HOUSE, Lothian *47 NT37*

Dating from 1613, this magnificent Jacobean mansion was enlarged by Lord Dunfermline, who had previously transformed Fyvie Castle in the one-time county of Aberdeenshire. The earliest portion of Pinkie House is the old tower of 1390, but the building is noted particularly for the east front, the long gallery with its splendid painted ceiling, and the wellhead in the courtyard. The Scots were defeated by Lord Hertford at the Battle of Pinkie in 1547. Prince Charles Edward slept at Pinkie House, which now forms part of Loretto College, after the victorious battle of Prestonpans in 1745.

PINWHERRY, Strathclyde *24 NX18*

Ruins of a Kennedy castle are sited here in the delightful valley of the River Stinchar, near its junction with the Duisk Burn.

PIRNMILL, Isle of Arran, Strathclyde *29 NR84*

Situated on the fine road along the W coast of Arran, Pirnmill faces across the Kilbrennan Sound to the Kintyre peninsula. Beinn Bhreac and Beinn Bharrain, both over 2,300ft, rise in the background.

PITCAIRNGREEN, Tayside *30 NO02*

To the NW of this attractive hamlet and near the River Almond are the Lynedoch Woods, where the graves of Bessie Bell and Mary Gray lie. These women came here in 1645 to avoid an outbreak of the plague in Perth.

PITCAPLE CASTLE, Grampian *35 NJ72*

Three sovereigns – James IV, Mary Queen of Scots, and Charles II – have been entertained at Pitcaple Castle. The rebuilt castle is a fine example of the 15th-c 2-plan, and lies near the River Urie. It is still a family home. In 1650 the Marquis of Montrose slept here as a prisoner on his way to execution in Edinburgh.

PITCUR, Tayside *31 NO23*

A remarkable 'weem' or Pict's House, the key of which is kept at Hallyburton House, is preserved here. The village itself lies at the edge of the Sidlaw Hills, on the Coupar Angus to Dundee road.

PITLESSIE, Fife *31 NO30*

Sir David Wilkie the painter was born in the manse of Cults, a little to the NE of Pitlessie, in 1785. One of his pictures entitled *Pitlessie Fair* hangs in the Scottish National Gallery at Edinburgh. A font in Pitlessie church originates from the Crimea. To the NE of the village is 19th-c Crawford Priory.

*PITLOCHRY, Tayside *30 NN95*

Visitors to the Grampians find that Pitlochry makes a fine touring centre and summer resort. The town lies in a wooded setting on the River Tummel, and extensive hydro-electric developments in the area include generating stations at Pitlochry and Clunie. Pitlochry Festival Theatre, known as the 'theatre in the hills', presents plays during the summer. Pitlochry Dam lies on the W side of the town and has a fish pass, where visitors in spring and early summer can watch salmon 'on the run' upstream past the power station. The 54ft-high dam has created the new Loch Faskally. Aldour Bridge gives access to the W bank of the Tummel and the Linn of Tummel (NTS), which can also be reached by footpath from Bridge of Garry.

The road passing Loch Faskally continues by the riverside to reach the E end of Loch Tummel, where there is another dam and salmon ladder. On the other bank of the river, which can be reached by road from Pitlochry via Bridge of Garry, is the famous Queen's View – a magnificent viewpoint along Loch Tummel to the peak of 3,547ft Schiehallion. Queen Victoria came here in 1866. The Loch Tummel Visitor Centre is situated here and illustrates the history, archaelogy, industry, and forestry of the Tummel Valley. To the NE of Pitlochry the A924 climbs on to moorland leading to Glen Brerachan, reaching a summit of 1,260ft and affording views of Ben Vrackie before descending to Kirkmichael in Strath Ardle. An 8th-c Pictish carved slab, known as the Dunfallandy Stone (AM) can be seen 1½m SSE of Pitlochry

PITMEDDEN, Grampian *35 NJ82*

The 600-acre Pitmedden estate contains the 17th-c Great Garden, originally laid out by Sir Alexander Seton. Seen from the lawn above, the four formal motifs have been executed on a grand scale and make a dramatic and colourful spectacle. The thunder houses at either end of the west belvedere are rare in Scotland.

PITSCOTTIE, Fife *31 NO41*

Fossils can be found in the wooded ravine of Dura Den, which contains Ceres Burn and lies N of Pitscottie. A collection of fossils from the area is on display at the University Museum in St Andrews. Magnus Muir lies 3m NE of Pitscottie and features the gravestone of five Covenanters, taken prisoner at the Battle of Bothwell Brig in 1679 and later executed here. In a nearby wood is a cairn which marks the spot where Archbishop Sharp was murdered in the same year by Covenanters. His monument is in the Town Church at St Andrews.

PITSLIGO, Grampian *35 NJ96*

Pitsligo's church dates from 1633 and contains the richly-carved Forbes gallery. Pitsligo Castle stands a little to the N and was built in 1577. It was once the home of Alexander Forbes – Lord Pitsligo – who was outlawed after the Battle of Culloden. Farther E are the 17th-c remains of Pittullie Castle.

PITTENWEEM, Fife *31 NO50*

This picturesque Royal Burgh comprises old houses grouped around a harbour. Incorporated in the parsonage are traces of the Augustinian priory which was founded here in 1141. The church's lovely tower of 1592 is more like a castle than a tower. Historically

1 Dunfallandy Stone
2 Festival Theatre
3 Linn of Tummel
4 Power Station (dam and salmon ladder)
5 Queen's View Viewpoint

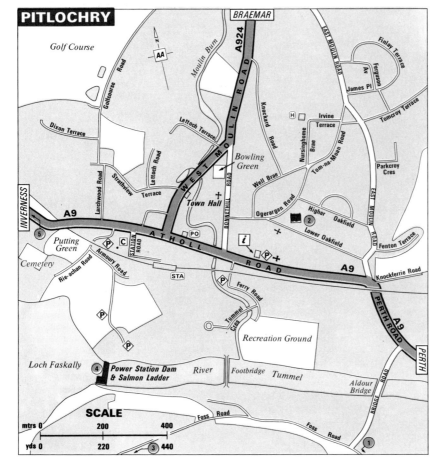

Entries marked * are the starting point of drives included in the Day Drive section of the book (pages 95 to 160).

Pittenweem is noted for the robbery from James Stark, a customs collector, in 1736. This event led to the famous Porteous Riots in Edinburgh. Near the harbour is the cave-shrine of St Fillan, and 3m NE of the town at West Pitkierie is a fluted octagonal dovecot dating from 1782. Balcaskie House lies 2m NW of Pittenweem and was designed by Sir William Bruce c1675. It stands in beautiful terraced gardens.

Sir Robert Lorimer the eminent architect spent his childhood 3m NNW of the town at Kellie Castle (NTS). The castle carries towers and turrets and is considered a fine example of 16th- to 17th-c domestic architecture. Some portions date from the 14thc. First owned by the Oliphants for 200 years and then by the Earls of Mar and Kellie, the castle was restored nearly a century ago by Professor James Lorimer. The interior displays notable plaster work and painted panelling, as well as fine Italian paintings.

PLOCKTON, Highland   32 NG83
The white houses of Plockton line a beautiful sheltered inlet of Loch Carron and face the wild Applecross and Torridon mountains to the N. The village is a fishing and craft community which forms part of the Balmacara estate (NTS). To the E a line of crags facing the shores of the loch rise above modern Duncraig Castle, now a school. This lies in a wooded setting.

PLUSCARDEN PRIORY, Grampian   34 NJ15
Originally a Valliscaulian house, Pluscarden Priory lies in a fertile valley overlooked by a wooded ridge, with Heldon Hill rising to the W. The monastery was founded in 1230, and surviving 13th-c work includes the choir and transepts, the tower, and part of the charter-house. The dreaded Wolf of Badenoch burned the church in 1390 – round about the same period in which he sacked Elgin. After the burning the church was restored. Large circular windows are an interesting feature of the transepts. The abbey was taken over by the Benedictines in 1454, and in 1948 a group of monks from Prinknash Abbey in Gloucestershire returned to rebuild it. The calefactory, now used as a church, contains a pulpit of 1680 which was originally in the old High Kirk of Elgin. Preserved in the Abbey is the jet Burgie Necklace, an ornament of bronze-age origin.

POLLOKSHAWS (Glasgow), Strathclyde   45 NS56
The fine mansion of Pollok House stands here N of the White Cart River. It was built by William Adam in 1752, and displays additions by Rowland Anderson. The house was a Maxwell home and contains rare art treasures. The fine grounds include formal rose gardens and woodland. Part of the estate is now used as a recreation ground.

POLMONT, Central   46 NS97
Just to the N of Polmont is the line of the great Roman Antonine Wall (AM). The River Avon once formed the old Stirling/West Lothian boundary as it flowed into the Forth estuary NE of the town. Off the road to Falkirk, 1m W of Polmont, is the Westquarter dovecot (AM) of 1647. Arms of William Livingstone of Westquarter are displayed over the doorway.

POLWARTH, Borders   31 NT75
A thorn tree associated with a poem by Allan Ramsay once grew on Polwarth's village green. Sir Patrick Hume, a follower of Argyll in 1685, hid for a month in the vaults of a church in the grounds of Marchmount House, which lies to the S. The mansion was the work of William Adam, and the park includes a huge oak tree – 128ft tall and nearly 15ft in girth.

POOLEWE, Highland   36 NG88
Salmon-rich River Ewe flows into the head of Loch Ewe at Poolewe after its short course from Loch Maree. Poolewe lies near the 58th parallel, a latitude farther N than Moscow, and features a remarkable collection of sub-tropical plants which thrive 1m N in the gardens (NTS) of Inverewe House. The gardens were created from barren land by Osgood Mackenzie over 100 years ago.

Across the river and to the E of Poolewe lies Loch Kernsary. Beyond this the larger Fionn Loch borders the lonely Fisherfield Forest and is dominated by the rock peaks of 3,060ft A'Mhaighdean and 2,974ft Beinn Dearg Mhor. Experimental work on croft rehabilitation has recently been carried out 4½m NW of the village at Inverasdale on the shores of Loch Ewe. This loch was of great naval importance in both world wars.

PORT APPIN, Strathclyde   29 NM94
This quiet little village lies between Loch Laich – an inlet of Loch Linnhe – and Airds Bay on the Lynn of Lorne. Steamers call here and a passenger ferry operates to the NE tip of the island of Lismore. Airds House, built in the mid 18thc, stands a little to the SE of Port Appin. Appin Church lies in the Strath of Appin 2m ENE of the village along the Ballachulish to Oban road. This road continues round the head of lovely mountain-backed Loch Creran and affords views along lonely Loch Creran.

Clunie Memorial Arch at Pitlochry was built in the same shape as the water conduits used in the Tummel/Garry hydro-electric scheme.

PORT ASKAIG, Isle of Islay, Strathclyde   28 NR46
A passenger ferry from here connects to Feolin Ferry on the island of Jura. Port Askaig also has a pier for steamers. Bonahavan Bay lies 4m N, and is reached via a narrow, hilly road which passes the Caol Isla distillery. Fine views extend from the bay and across the sound towards the prominent Pap of Jura and the more distant Mull coast. Some 3m SW of Port Appin off the Bridgend road is Loch Finlaggan, where a ruined island castle proclaims the one-time strength of the Lords of the Isles.

PORT BANNATYNE, Strathclyde   20 NS06
The small resort of Port Bannatyne stands on Kames Bay and faces across the Firth of Clyde to Toward Point on the mainland. Kames Castle overlooks the Bay and carries a 14th-c tower. The building now serves as a children's home. A road W across the narrow waist of Bute runs to sandy Etterick Bay, affording views over the Kyles of Bute to Ardlamont Point on the way. This road then continues N as far as Kilmichael, where there is an ancient, ruined chapel dedicated to St Michael. Inland from Port Bannatyne is the highest ground on Bute, where aptly-named Windy Hill rises to a height of 911ft. The coast road N from the resort ends at Rhubodach, where a car ferry links with Colintraive on the mainland.

PORT CHARLOTTE, Isle of Islay, Strathclyde   28 NR25
Near Port Charlotte, which lies on the W shores of Loch Indaal, are the graves of American soldiers drowned when the 'Tuscania' sank in 1918. A road runs W from the village across the Rhinns of Islay peninsula to Kilchiaran Bay, from

cont page 301

THE HARBOUR-BUILDING EARL

In 1793 the Reverend Alexander Cock contributed a chapter about his parish of Cruden on the Buchan coast to the first Statistical Account of Scotland. It was an ideal opportunity to publicise what he thought should be done to regenerate the tiny fishing hamlet of Ward of Cruden, set among rocks at the northern edge of the sweeping Ardendraught Bay. The village was not far from the splendid Slains Castle, home of the Earl of Erroll, who owned most of the district.

Mr Cock wrote that 'if a small brook, which passes along the south end of the Earl of Erroll's gardens, were introduced into the sea, at the end of the beach near the Ward, there is every reason to believe, that a very safe landing place could be made for boats or larger vessels. . . . A flourishing village would be the certain consequence.'

In 1798 the Water of Cruden was indeed diverted, from the north to the south side of Ward Hill. But there was still no attempt to build a proper harbour. In the Statistical Account of 1840 Mr Cock returned to the attack, although he was by then an old man and, indeed, died before the book was published.

It took until 1875 before a later Earl of Erroll realised the old minister's dream and devoted £8,000 over five years to building the sturdy harbour which still stands today. The inner basin was 300ft long and half that wide. To celebrate the work the name of the place was officially changed from Ward of Cruden to Port Erroll.

Within five years it was 'a promising station of the herring fishing'. No fewer than 68 boats were based there; a lifeboat and a rocket apparatus were useful additions on this cliff-bound coast. The Aberdeen Lime Company was busily engaged in shipping corn, coal, and other materials.

In 1899 the fishing village found itself overshadowed by a palatial hotel built above the sands of what was by that time referred to as Cruden Bay, by the Great North of Scotland Railway Company. It became a resort of the rich and the famous, and a more modern village grew up near by. So important did the new settlement of Cruden Bay become that in 1924 it became the name of the joint village.

Despite the steady decline of the fishing trade, it was Port Erroll which had the last laugh. The Cruden Bay Hotel was dismantled soon after the second world war. Today, fishing nets are still spread out to dry on timber frames and along the harbour wall, and the old cottages are mostly renovated. Weekenders use the harbour for motor boats and small yachts. Beside the congregational church, founded in 1882 by the harbour-building earl, is a car park. It stands on top of the original course of the Water of Cruden, and the wooded valley beyond now takes a much smaller burn to the old outlet by the sea, close to the earl's castle of Slains – for half a century now a roofless ruin.

A short diversion of a small local stream allowed the construction of a safe, prosperous harbour at Port Erroll.

where a rough and narrow road follows the peninsula S towards Portnahaven at its SW tip.

PORT ELLEN, Isle of Islay, Strathclyde 28 NR34

Islay's main port, Port Ellen lies on a little rocky bay facing the prominent lighthouse on the Mull of Oa peninsula. There are distilleries in the area, and to the E is a coast road which passes Lagavulin. A ruined round tower here is thought to have been a Macdonald stronghold. After 7m the road reaches the churchyard of Kildalton. Facing the sandy Kilnaughton Bay, 1½m W of Port Ellen, is the memorial to American troops drowned in the sinking of the 'Tuscania' in 1918.

From the memorial the road continues NW to Machrie, on Laggan Bay. This can also be reached via the low road from Port Ellen, which eventually leads to Bowmore. Farther N along the low road is Glenegedale Airport, from where there are regular services to Glasgow (Abbotsinch) Airport. The high road to Bowmore from Port Ellen keeps well inland all the way, and a branch leading NE to Port Askaig is known as the glen road.

PORT ERROLL, Grampian 35 NK03

Once known as Ward of Cruden, this Buchan-district village was once the scene of enlightened industrial development. In the late 18thc this was a tiny fishing village which was rapidly going downhill. However, due to the efforts of a local minister and the Earl of Erroll, the village became a thriving harbour by 1875. Slains Castle, a seat of the Earl of Erroll, lies in a ruined state near by. The harbour itself lies on the N edge of the wide Ardebdraught Bay and nowadays is used mostly by small pleasure craft (see inset opposite).

PORTESSIE, Grampian 35 NJ46

Old cottages grace this picturesque fishing village, which is situated on a sandy crescent-shaped bay. Craig Head shelters Portessie Bay to the E.

PORT GLASGOW, Strathclyde 44 NS37

Founded in 1668, this Clyde ship-building town was the chief custom-house port of the river before the waterway was deepened and widened. Newark Castle (AM) is a large, finely-turreted mansion house of the Maxwells. It overlooks the Clyde and dates mostly from the 16th and 17thc. The mansion is well-preserved and has a 15th-c tower, a fine courtyard, and a hall dated 1597.

PORTGORDON, Grampian 35 NJ36

The Duke of Richmond and Gordon built the harbour at Portgordon, which lies near the old Moray border, in 1874.

PORTGOWER, Highland 37 ND01

Moorland rising behind the rocky stretch of coast on which this small fishing village is situated culminates in 1,940ft Beinn na Meilich.

PORTINCAPLE, Strathclyde 44 NS29

Situated on Loch Long, Portincaple faces Loch Goil and a range of hills known as Argyll's Bowling Green.

Sea fish come into this tidal pond at Port Logan to be fed by hand.

PORTINNISHERRICH, Strathclyde 29 NM91

This village stands on the E shore of Loch Awe, and faces the island of Innis Shearaich. The smaller islands of Innis Connel lie N and bear the remains of Ardconnel Castle, an ancient Campbell stronghold. Waterfalls can be seen near the outflow of the Allt Blarghour Burn, 2m N along the lochside road.

PORT LOGAN, Dumfries and Galloway 24 NX04

Port Logan is a small Rhinns of Galloway fishing village situated on Logan Bay. The opposite side of the bay features a tidal fish-pond which was built in the 18thc. Sea fish here are extraordinarily tame, and cod can be fed by hand when summoned by a bell. Logan House lies 2m N of Port Logan and was the Georgian home of the McDoualls – a family of Pictish origin who had lived in houses on the same site for many centuries. The house is famous for its sub-tropical gardens, which belong to the Logan Gardens Trust.

PORTMAHOMACK, Highland 37 NH98

This Dornoch Firth fishing village lies on a narrow peninsula jutting out into the Moray Firth. The tip of the peninsula is called Tarbat Ness and lies 4m NE. This area enjoys the lowest rainfall in Scotland. Wide views are afforded by the ness, and there is a lighthouse sited here. Ballone Castle stands SE of Portmahomack and probably dates from the 16thc. To the SW of the village near the church are the sandhills of Gaza.

PORTMOAK, Tayside 30 NO10

Now a popular gliding centre, Portmoak lies to the E of Loch Leven between the Lomonds and Benarty Hill. The parish boundary includes both Kinnesswood

and Scotlandwell. Three earlier churches have stood on the site occupied by Portmoak church, and the early 18th-c minister here was Ebenezer Erskine – founder of the Scottish Secession Church. His wife and children lie buried in the churchyard. The cottage of a local 18th-c poet, Michael Bruce, now houses a small museum.

PORTNACROISH, Strathclyde 29 NM94

Portnacroish stands on Loch Laich, an inlet of Loch Linnhe in the Appin district, and faces towards the island of Shuna. To the N is 17th-c Appin House, and beautiful Castle Stalker lies on a tiny offshore island which is clearly visible from both the road and the steamer route along Loch Linnhe. This was once the ancient home of the Stewarts of Appin, and was built c1500 as a hunting lodge in order to entertain James IV. Royal Arms are displayed over the entrance.

PORTNAHAVEN, Isle of Islay, Strathclyde 28 NR15

Situated at the SW end of the Rhinns of Islay, Portnahaven stands NW of Rhinns Point and faces the lighthouse on Orsay island. NE along the rocky W side of the Rhinns peninsula leads to Kilchiaran Bay.

PORTOBELLO (Edinburgh), Lothian 47 NT37

The town's name was given by a sailor who had served under Admiral Vernon at Portobello, Panama, in 1739. Portobello offers good sands and is a resort for people from nearby Edinburgh. Sir Harry Lauder was born here in 1870. The E end of the town is linked to Joppa, and a little to the W lies ancient Restalrig Castle. This was destroyed in 1560 but has been restored. Adjacent is the 15th-c, six-sided Chapel of St Triduana (AM),

Portree, the capital of Skye and centre of the island's road system.

dedicated to a saint who was supposed to have cured eye ailments with water from a nearby spring.

Also near by is late 16th-c Craigentinny House. The building was enlarged in the 19thc, and its eccentric owner – W H Miller – died in 1849. He was known as Measure Miller, after his habit of measuring all the books he bought with a ruler which he carried for this purpose. His strange mausoleum lies off the Portobello Road and displays fine decorative panels.

PORT OF MENTEITH, Central   30 NN50
This resort lies on the shores of the Lake of Menteith. Menteith is Scotland's only lake, apart from the little artificial Pressmennan Lake near Whittinghame in Lothian. Ferries operate to the largest of the lake's three islands, which is the site of the lovely remains of Inchmahome Priory (AM). This Augustinian priory was founded in 1238 by Walter Goreyn, 4th Earl of Menteith, but it is thought that the site was first occupied by a Celtic monastery. Robert the Bruce visited the island in 1306, 1308, and 1310. At the age of four Mary Queen of Scots was taken by her mother to the priory after the disastrous Battle of Pinkie in 1547. The battle meant that the Stirling Castle was no longer secure. The garden where Mary played, now known as Queen Mary's Bower, still survives. Three weeks later the Queen was taken to Dumbarton before sailing to France. R B Cunninghame Graham, a writer who died at Buenos Aires in 1936, is buried on the island.

Parts of the choir and presbytery remain from the priory's 13th-c origins, and later remains include the nave, its fine west porch, and the tower arch. The choir houses the richly-carved grave slab of Sir John Drummond, together with a 13th-c slab depicting a knight. Another island in the lake, Inch Tulla, bears the ruins of a castle where the Earls of Menteith once lived. Near the lake stands Cardross House, dating from the 16th to 18thc. Along the road to Callander, NE of Port of Menteith, is Loch Rusky. This is sometimes frozen over in winter.

To the S of the lake lies an area of flat land known as Flanders Moss. Tiny Loch Macanrie lies near the SW shores of Lake of Menteith, and a legend tells how a king's son was saved from drowning here by a girl. Overlooking Lake of Menteith to the W are the Menteith Hills, with Loch Ard Forest in the vicinity. Tiny Loch an Balloch lies between 1,401ft Beinn Dearg and 1,344ft Ben Gullipen, which rise E of the Menteith hills. The name Menteith, or Monteith, is applied generally to that part of the county lying S of the resort towards the River Forth.

PORTPATRICK, Dumfries and Galloway 24 NX05
Until 1849 steamers sailed the 21m from Donaghadee in N Ireland to Portpatrick, which became a 'Gretna Green' for Irish couples. The steamer crossing was always hazardous due to prevailing SW gales, and when the railway was extended to Stranraer the steamer service was also transferred there.

In 1947 Thomas Blower swam across the North Channel from Donaghadee in just over 16 hours. Portpatrick itself is a small resort with rocky shores, though there are several sandy bays for bathing. The seaward views extend to the N Ireland coast and the Isle of Man. To the S of Portpatrick the Craigoch Burn flows into the sea. Here on the cliffs are the ruins of Dunskey Castle, built c1510.

*PORTREE, Isle of Skye, Highland 32 NG44
Portree is the capital of Skye and the centre of the island's road system. It makes a fine centre for touring the island. Portree Bay is sheltered by high cliffs on three sides, and looks S towards 1,352ft Ben Tianavaig and over the Sound of Raasay to the lovely wooded island of Raasay. James V visited Portree in 1540 and the village has associations with Bonnie Prince Charlie. The prince hid for four days on Skye before he found a boat at Loch Fada to take him to Raasay. One of his hiding places was Prince Charlie's Cave, which lies 4m N and can be reached by boat from Portree harbour. Skye Week – usually the last week in May – opens at Portree, and the provincial Gaelic Mod, or festival of song, is held here in June. The end of July marks the Skye Agricultural Show in Portree, and the third Thursday in August sees the annual Highland Games. To the N of Portree lies the high plateau of the Storr, below which rises a 150ft-high pillar of rock known as The Old Man of Storr. Loch Fada is linked to a hydro-electric scheme and lies near Loch Leathann to the S of the Storr. Both are rich in trout. A hill road leads W from Portree to Bracadale on Loch Beag, an inlet of Loch Harport.

The hilly island of Raasay is some 15m long and a mecca for geologists and botanists. It offers accommodation, and the many ruined groups of cottages show a history of depopulation. Dr Johnson and Boswell were entertained at Raasay House in 1773, and Boswell performed a solo dance on the flat-topped, 1,456ft Dun Caan. Ruins of the Macleod Castle of Brochel can be seen on the island's NE coast, with the little uninhabited island of Rona beyond. Rona is the site of a lighthouse.

PORTSOY, Grampian   35 NJ56
Portsoy marble, or serpentine, is found on the rocky coast near this small fishing port. It was used for two of the chimney-pieces in the Palace of Versailles. Ruined Boyne Castle stands amid woodland and overlooks the Burn of Boyne 2m E. This castle dates from 1485 and is an early Ogilvie fortress. Redhythe Point and Garron Point shelter Sandend Bay 2½m W of Portsoy.

PORT VASCO, Highland   37 NC56
This tiny coastal hamlet is situated at the mouth of the Kyle of Tongue and faces W towards Eilean Iosal and Roan Island. Beinn Thutaig rises 1,340ft to the W beyond Strath Melness.

PORT WILLIAM, Dumfries and Galloway 24 NX34
Sir William Maxwell founded this little port and resort on sandy Luce Bay in 1770. A road climbs inland past the well-known house and park of Monreith. Druchtag Motehill (AM), the earthwork mound of an early medieval castle, can be seen off the A714 at Mochrum village. The mound includes traces of early stone buildings. Drumtrodden stones (AM) are a group of bronze-age cup-and-ring marked rocks 2m NE.

POWFOOT, Dumfries and Galloway 26 NY16
Powfoot was once only a fishing village, but nowadays is a pleasant little resort

offering sandy shores. It lies on the Pow Water at its confluence with the Solway Firth.

PRESTON, Borders *31 NT75*

A little to the S of this village is Whiteadder Water, which flows from its source in the Lammermuir Hills. The shaft of the old cross still survives in Preston, and the rebuilt church of Bunkle lies 2½m E below the foothills of the Lammermuirs. This church preserves one of the earliest Norman arches in Scotland. The original Norman church was demolished in 1820.

PRESTONPANS, Lothian *47 NT37*

Salt panning has been conducted here from the 12thc, when the monks from Newbattle Abbey extracted their salt in this way. Some time later Prestonpans became the exclusive supplier of salt to E Scotland, but this monopoly was broken in 1707 when the Act of Union permitted the import of salt from England. This seaside town was also once noted for its oysters. The famous Battle of Prestonpans took place 1m E of the town in 1745, when Prince Charles Edward defeated Sir John Cope's army in an astonishing 10 minutes.
A fine 17th-c Mercat cross ½m from Prestonpans is thought to be the oldest in Scotland. It survives in an unaltered state and stands on its original site.

Several outstanding 17th-c houses include the well-restored Hamilton House (NTS) of 1628; 17th-c Northfield House with its contemporary dovecot and sundial; Bankton House, which is now a farm. A monument to Colonel Gardiner, who died at Tranent from wounds received in the Battle of Prestonpans, stands in the grounds of Bankton. Scott visited the town as a child and relates the story of the battle in his novel *Waverley*. The novel contains a great deal of other local history. Ruined Preston Tower dates from the 15thc and includes a 17th-c dovecot.

Prestongrange Colliery Beam Engine of 1874 was in operation until 1954. This has been scheduled as an industrial monument. The engine and engine house have been restored and may be visited. Morrisonhaven lies to the W of Prestonpans and was once the town's port.

PRESTWICK, Strathclyde *24 NS32*

Scotland's international airport is situated at Prestwick, a golfing resort which almost joins with Ayr to the S. The town boasts an ancient Mercat cross, and the ruined Church of St Nicholas is a well-known landmark for mariners. The building is said to date from 1163. Ayr Bay offers a sandy bathing beach and pool. Views across the Firth of Clyde take in the mountains of Arran. Adamton House is a Georgian-style mansion with 15th-c associations. Burns-style banquets are held here throughout the year.

QUARTER, Strathclyde *45 NS75*

Gordon of Earlston was killed in a field near Quarter after the Battle of Bothwell Brig in 1679.

QUEENSFERRY, NORTH, Fife *46 NT18*

Queen Margaret of Scotland gave her name to Queensferry. She was a regular

The 17th-c Mercat cross in Prestonpans is remarkably well preserved and may be the oldest in Scotland.

traveller on the ferry, which plied across the Firth of Forth for over 800 years. The queen used the ferry on her way from Edinburgh to her favourite home at Dunfermline in Fife. Queensferry North is situated on the Ferry Hill peninsula, at the N end of the two splendid bridges now spanning the Firth. The older bridge carries the railway and the bridge of 1964 carries the road. Both bridges are described under Queensferry South. St Margaret's Bay lies NW of Queensferry North, and forms part of the naval base of Rosyth.

QUEENSFERRY, SOUTH, Lothian *46 NT17*

Situated at the S end of the two great Forth bridges, Queensferry South is an ancient ferry point on the Firth of Forth. The old ferry used to leave from Hawes Pier, opposite which stands partly 17th-c Hawes Inn. This was described by Scott in *The Antiquary* and by Robert Louis Stevenson in *Kidnapped*. A Carmelite chapel was founded here in 1330 by the Laird of Dundas, and the existing 15th-c structure displays a central tower and barrel vaults. It is now used as an episcopal church, and is the only medieval church of this order still functioning in Britain. The Burgh Museum preserves two ancient charters, and an old Tolbooth in the town was rebuilt in 1720. Plewlands House (NTS) dates from 1643 but has been restored and converted into flats. Blackness Castle of 1626 shows characteristic crow-stepped gables.

Queensferry's picturesque Ferry Fair is held every summer; the quaint Burry Man's procession is another interesting annual custom. Sir John Fowler and Sir Benjamin Baker built the cantilevered railway bridge between 1883 and 1890.

This great bridge is considered one of the finest examples of engineering in the world and measures some 2,765yds long. It gives a headway of 150ft above the water, and the two main spans each have a dimension of 1,710ft. The ferry stopped in 1964 when the queen opened the impressive, 2,000yd-long Forth Road Bridge, one of Europe's longest suspension bridges. This structure has a centre span of 3,300ft and side spans of 1,337ft each.

Inchgarvie Island lies in the firth and supports the railway bridge. It was once the site of a 15th-c fort which opposed Cromwell in 1650. Dundas Castle, for many years the seat of the Dundases, stands 1½m S of Queensferry South. This is one of Scotland's oldest families, and the building dates between 1416 and 1424. The modern castle was erected in 1818.

QUEEN'S VIEW, Tayside *30 NN85*

Queen Victoria gave her name to this famous outlook when she visited it in 1866. It lies on the N bank of the River Tummel, just E of Loch Tummel, and can be reached via a gate leading to a rocky spur. The magnificent, panoramic view encompasses rivers, lochs, and a grand array of mountains to the N and W in Breadalbane country. The sharp quartzite cone of 3,547ft Schiehallion dominates the landscape. A Forestry Commission visitors' centre opened here in 1972 tells the story of the Tummel Valley. Maskelyne, a one-time Astronomer Royal, made use of Schiehallion while conducting experiments on the earth's centre of gravity in 1777.

A dam built at the E end of Loch Tummel has lengthened the loch, which now forms part of the Tummel-Garry hydro-electric scheme. This has marred the view somewhat. The dam includes a salmon-ladder by which the migrating fish can climb into the loch. Of several roads which run along both shores of Loch Tummel, the best leads along the N shores towards Tummel Bridge.

QUIRAING, Isle of Skye, Highland
32 NG46
The remarkable rock pinnacles of the Quiraing form one of Skye's most notable sights, and lie a little inland from the road which runs along the shores of Staffin Bay in the Trotternish peninsula. Needle Rock is 120ft high, and behind it an amphitheatre surrounds a grass-covered rock known as The Table. Near by is The Prison, and a little to the N are the rocks and pinnacles known as Leac na Fionn. The Quiraing can only be reached on foot, but offers splendid views over the hills of Trotternish and E to the Torridon mountains on the mainland. 1,799ft Meal na Suiramach rises to the N of the road and overlooks this rocky wilderness. The view from here extends over N Skye and across the sea towards the distant Outer Hebrides. An inland road links Staffin and Quiraing with Uig.

QUOICH BRIDGE, Highland   *33 NH00*
Hydro-electric developments here have raised the level of Loch Quoich, which

is dominated by 3,015ft Gairich. General Monk and his soldiers marched along the roadless Glen Quoich, which lies to the N, in 1654.

RANNOCH STATION, Tayside   *29 NN45*
A road from the W end of Loch Rannoch leads 6m to this remote W Highland station, situated almost on the border of the one-time county of Argyll. Lonely Rannoch Moor was described by Robert Louis Stevenson as being 'as waste as the sea', and stretches for some 10m towards the main road from Tyndrum to Glencoe. The moor itself is roadless, and some 3,500 acres of its area now form a nature reserve. Loch Laidon, with the Black Corries rising to the N, lies SW of the station. Beyond the Black Corries is the Blackwater Reservoir. To the NE of Rannoch is lonely Loch Ericht, situated in the Grampian mountains to the N of the Kinloch Rannoch road.

RATHO, Lothian   *46 NT17*
Ratho lies near the River Almond and is the site of a spectacular railway viaduct which carries the Edinburgh to Glasgow railway line. The viaduct was built in the 19thc and has been reinforced at various times since. It is still capable of carrying the modern, high-speed trains operated by British Rail, and remains the greatest spectacle on the line (see inset opposite).

REAY, Highland   *37 NC96*
Lord Reay, Chief of Clan Mackay, took his name from this Sandside Bay village. Reay church dates from 1739 and is typical of the area. It features an unusual external staircase to the belfry. Remains of an older church and a carved Celtic cross-slab survive in the churchyard. Dounreay Castle lies 2m NE and preserves a 16th-c tower. The castle was once a seat of the Mackays and now serves as a farm. Near the wild NW seaboard lie the lonely mountains and deer forest of Reay, in the new county of Highland.

REDCASTLE, Highland   *34 NH54*
An old home of the Mackenzie family, the estate of Redcastle lies on the N shore of the Beauly Firth. Some 16th-c work has been incorporated in the modern mansion.

REISS, Highland   *37 ND35*
Once a seat of the Earls Marischal, modernized Ackergill Tower stands on the shore of Sinclair's Bay. It retains a 25ft-deep well and two 18th-c dovecots. Reiss itself lies a little inland from the Bay, at the junction of roads leading to Thurso and John o'Groats.

RENFREW, Strathclyde   *45 NS56*
Generally considered to be the cradle of the Royal House of Stuart, Renfrew is an ancient Royal Burgh with a charter
cont page 306

19TH-C INTER-CITY

Although the Edinburgh-Glasgow railway line provided its builders with few of the spectacular bridging problems so common in hillier areas, it includes – in the comparatively flat country around Ratho – one of Scotland's finest railway viaducts. A striking design of 36 graceful arches takes the main line in a curve that sweeps high above the valley of the River Almond.

Attempts were made to link the two cities by rail as early as 1831. Opposition from landowners and from the proprietors of the Forth and Clyde Canal, which had been operating since 1790, delayed the passing of a suitable Act of Parliament until 1838. Work started immediately, and the Edinburgh and Glasgow Railway, its original eastern terminus at Haymarket instead of at Waverley as today, opened for traffic in 1842.

The Almond viaduct combined solid engineering with attractive design. It is 720yds long, with 50ft between each arch. To take the line on the required route from Winchburgh, clear of the rising ground at Ratho village, it was built on a 73-chain radius curve. East of the bridge a new settlement called Ratho Station grew up to augment the existing village.

Very soon after its opening the small Edinburgh and Glasgow Company, which never during its years as an independent concern made any extensions to its original 47m inter-city route, ran head-first into a bigger rival. Its monopoly was challenged by the Caledonian Railway, which in 1849 began to run services on a longer and at first sight inefficient route between the two cities. The Caley route was by way of Carstairs, Motherwell, and Coatbridge; but its trains were faster and its coaches more comfortable.

A price-cutting war developed, during which the Edinburgh and Glasgow also had to contend with competition from the Forth and Clyde Canal. At the end of it, the two railway companies had slashed their single fares between the cities to only sixpence, and both were brought close to ruin.

In 1856 they decided to bury their differences, and formulated an agreement on joint working. The E & G took 30 per cent of the profits on the Glasgow-Edinburgh traffic, and the Caledonian 70 per cent. But the inter-company rows were not yet over, and in 1864 the E & G decided to join forces with Caledonian's bitter enemy, the North British. Within another year the NB had absorbed the Edinburgh and Glasgow, which ceased to exist as a separate company.

The Almond viaduct has remained the greatest spectacle on the line. Strengthened, reinforced, and rebuilt through the years, it still copes with heavy traffic from British Rail. There are 130 train movements on an average day. More than 70 are by the high-speed inter-city trains between Glasgow and Edinburgh. There are also Edinburgh to Stirling, Edinburgh to Perth, and Edinburgh to Inverness passenger trains, as well as a variety of freight traffic. The bridge copes well, with a speed limit of 80mph applied: faster than motorists are allowed to drive on the M8 motorway which runs near by.

The superb, 36-arch viaduct at Ratho carries the railway line in a graceful curve that sweeps high above the River Almond valley.

dating from 1396. It gives its name to the title of Baron granted to the Prince of Wales. Renfrew's industries include boiler making, engineering, and the manufacture of electric cables. A fine sculptured tomb lies in the parish church, which also features a 15th-c effigy on the tower. To the N of the town is a car ferry which plies across the Clyde to Yoker. Abbotsinch Airport lies 2m SW of Renfrew, and 1m W of the town across the Black Cart Water stands Inchinnan Church, once the property of the Knights Templar. The present building was erected by Lord Blythswood early in this century. The fascinating churchyard includes ancient Celtic stones, tombs of the Templars, and several mortsafes. The latter were once placed over new graves to foil body-snatchers.

Close by is a swing-bridge near the confluence of the Black and White Cart Waters. Argyll Stone, which was at one time thought to be stained with the Earl of Argyll's blood, can be seen near the bridge. In 1685 the earl was captured at Blythswood House, to the W of Renfrew Ferry, and later executed at Edinburgh for his part in the Monmouth rebellion.

REST AND BE THANKFUL, Strathclyde 29 NN20

This curiously-named spot is so called because the 900ft summit of the steep old road through Glen Croe was once marked by a rough stone seat inscribed 'Rest and Be Thankful'. The seat, which Wordsworth described in verse, has long gone but the inscribed stone still remains. The old road is still used for motor trials, but the reconstructed road has been more easily graded for normal traffic. Wonderful views are afforded by the top of 3,318ft Ben Ime, which rises to the

A field near the church at Rhynce contains the Pictish Crow Stone, an important historical relic.

NE and can be climbed from the pass. Ben Arthur, more familiarly known as The Cobbler, stands at 2,891ft to the E of the glen. The S side of the valley is dominated by the rough, rocky slopes of the 2,580ft Brack. Ben Donich rises to 2,774ft in the W. These Cowal peaks all lie within the Ardgoil Estate of the Argyll forest park, while the N summits of Glen Croe form part of the Ardgartan Estate.

From Rest and Be Thankful a descent passes lonely Loch Restil, which lies under the slopes of 3,021ft Beinn an Lochain to the W. The road then runs down Glen Kinglas towards the shores of Loch Fyne. Another road, also steep and narrow, leads from Rest and Be Thankful into the rocky Hell's Glen and down alongside the River Goil to Lochgoilhead, at the head of Loch Goil.

RHICONICH, Highland 36 NC25

An old coaching inn once stood in this little clachan at the head of Loch Inchard. Fine SE views from this hamlet take in the great quartzite peaks of the deer forest of Reay – once the hunting grounds of the chiefs of the Clan MacKay. Foinaven dominates the range at 2,980ft, and the rocky Creag Dionard overlooks the bleak head of Strath Dionard and its lonely loch farther to the SE. The Amhainn Dionard flows N from the loch into the Kyle of Durness. To the S of Rhiconich rise the rough scree slopes of 2,580ft Arkle, backed by 2,548ft Meall Horn.

Innumerable lochans lie amid outcrops of Archaean grey gneiss, some of the world's oldest rocks, around the clachan and in the mountainous region to the SE. A picturesque little ravine threaded by the Achriesgill Water lies just N of

Rhiconich. Lovely Strath Dionard, backed by 2,630ft Grann Stacach and 2,537ft Beinn Spionnaidh, extends to the NE. An adventure school is sited some 4m SW of Rhiconich, near Skerricha.

RHU, Strathclyde 44 NS28

Henry Bell, who launched the pioneer Clyde steamboat 'Comet' in 1812, lies buried in the churchyard of this village. Rhu faces the Gare Loch and Rosneath Bay and has a pier. It is very popular with yachtsmen. A deep glen to the N is known as Whistler's Glen and was mentioned in Scott's *Heart of Midlothian*.

RHUBODACH, Strathclyde 29 NS07

Also known as Rudhabodach, this village is situated on the shores of the Kyles of Bute and linked to Colintraive on the mainland by car ferry. In past days cattle bound for Bute were made to swim this strait.

RHYNIE, Grampian 35 NJ42

The Tap o' the Noth rises 1,851ft from Clashindarroch Forest and dominates Rhynie. It can be seen from as far away as the North Sea. A vitrified fort can be seen in the area, and a field near the church contains the ancient Pictish Crow Stone. This important relic displays various Pictish symbols. Druminnor Castle lies 1m SE and is the restored 15th-c house of the Forbes family. Ruins of Lesmore Castle, once a Gordon stronghold, can be seen 2½m W of Rhynie off the Dufftown road. This road climbs to a height of nearly 1,400ft near the one-time Banffshire boundary. A hill known as the Buck of Cabrach rises 2,368ft to the S.

RICCARTON, Borders 26 NY59

Situated in a remote part of Liddesdale, Riccarton lies amid hill country with the Larriston Fells rising to 1,677ft in the S. Beyond the Liddel Water, some 2m NE, is Thorlieshope – well known as the home of Dandie Dinmont in Scott's *Guy Mannering*. A road leading NE towards Jedburgh climbs to 1,250ft at Note o' the Gate, in the Lowland hills. To the E of Riccarton is a lonely road which runs through the Cheviots and leads to the North Tyne valley in England. Peel Fell rises to 1,975ft E of Riccarton and is one of the Cheviot range. A remarkable boulder known as the Kielder Stone stands on the hill's NE slopes, near the English/Scottish border.

RINGFORD, Dumfries and Galloway 25 NX65

This Galloway hamlet stands on Tarff Water. Grierson of Lag killed five Covenanters near here in 1685, and their memorial lies 2m N of Ringford to the left of the New Galloway road. The tower of Lag, seat of Grierson of Lag, is described under Dunscore.

RISPOND, Highland 36 NC46

A remote little place situated on Rispond Bay, Rispond itself lies just off the Durness to Eriboll road. The lovely sea loch Eriboll stretches SW and offers fine cliff scenery. There are several sandy bays at its mouth near Rispond. To the N of the village is the island of Eileen Hoan, and across the mouth of the loch to the NE rises Kennageall or Whiten Head – a prominent feature in a stretch of cave-riddled cliffs which stand at nearly 850ft high.

ROBERTON, Borders 26 NT41

Borthwick Water flows near the hamlet of Roberton, and the local church dates from 1650. Also near the village are two fine 18th-c houses – Chisholme and Borthwickbrae. Early 19th-c Greenbank toll-house is now part of a farm, and beyond this is the fine viewpoint of Firestane Edge. Little Alemoor Loch, drained by the Alemoor Water, lies farther W. To the S of Firestane Edge stretches the lonely valley of the Borthwick Water.

ROCKCLIFFE, Dumfries and Galloway 25 NX85

Smugglers of wine and tobacco used the little inlets and bays of the Solway Firth near Rockcliffe in the 18thc. The resort lies on Rough Firth, the estuary of the Urr Water on the Solway Firth. A hill-walk to the neighbouring village of Kippford passes the Mote of Mark (NTS), an ancient vitrified hill fort overlooking the Rough Island bird sanctuary (NTS).

RODEL, Western Isles 39 NF77

See Hebrides, Outer

ROMANNO BRIDGE, Borders 30 NT14

Ruins of an old church and churchyard lie to the S of this hamlet on the Lyne Water. A hillside near Newlands church is cut into the old Romanno Terraces, which were probably medieval cultivation platforms. Halmyre House lies 1m NE of Romanno Bridge and is an ancient Gordon seat dating from the 16thc. The river valley 3m S of Romanno Bridge contains the unfinished Drochil Castle, near the confluence of the Lyne and Tarth Waters. It was owned by the Regent Morton, who was executed in 1578 for his part in Darnley's death.

ROSEHALL, Highland 36 NC40

Traces of several brochs can be seen in the district around Rosehall, and the village lies in Strath Oykell on the River Oykell. Near here the Oykell joins with the River Cassley. The turbulent Cassley flows from the N down the long and little-known Glen Cassley. Remains of Auchness Castle can be seen near the point where the Lairg road crosses the Cassley. To the E of the village the road divides, the left fork leading to Lairg and the right fork to Bonar Bridge. In 1408 a fierce clan battle was fought at Tutim on the Oykell, which lies to the W of the village.

ROSEHEARTY, Highland 35 NJ96

Sands and shelving rocks lie to the E of this pretty Buchan fishing village. Beyond Braco Park to the W is the cave of Cowshaven, which was the hiding place of the last Lord Pitsligo when he was outlawed after the '45 Rising.

ROSEMARKIE, Highland 34 NH75

Opposite this lovely little Black-Isle resort, across the Moray Firth, is Fort George. Rosemarkie's fine beach on Rosemarkie Bay is surrounded by attractive rocky scenery. The village was the seat of a bishopric before this was transferred to Fortrose. An ancient grave slab in the churchyard displays a cross

on one side and Pictish symbols on the other. Hugh Miller, who was born at Cromarty, made the cliffs to the NE of Rosemarkie famous when he wrote of their geological interest.

ROSSLYN, Lothian 47 NT26

Famous for its chapel and castle, this mining village lies on the North Esk River and is also spelt Rosslin. The Scots defeated English invaders in a battle near the village in 1303. Rosslyn Chapel, mentioned by Scott in *Lay of the Last Minstrel*, was founded in 1446 by William Sinclair – later Earl of Caithness. It has an abundance of beautiful stone carving which shows Continental influence. Originally the chapel was intended to be part of a collegiate church, but only the choir was finished. This later became the burial place of the Sinclairs. The richly-carved Prentice Pillar is perhaps the chapel's finest feature. A story relates that the pillar was carved by an apprentice during his master's absence to examine the original of his proposed design in Italy. On his return the master is said to have killed his apprentice in a fit of jealousy. Finely-carved pinnacles and flying buttresses enhance the exterior.

In 1688 the chapel was damaged by rioters and restoration was not completed until 1842. There is a little 15ft-high vaulted Lady Chapel and a crypt which may also once have been used as a chapel. On Castle Hill stands the former Old Rosslyn Inn, visited by William and Dorothy Wordsworth, Burns, Dr Johnson and Boswell, Queen Victoria in 1856, and Edward VII when Prince of Wales. Rosslyn Castle overlooks the North Esk and the picturesque Rosslyn Glen from the edge of a cliff. It was the 14th-c stronghold of Sir Henry Sinclair, 3rd

Earl of Orkney. Some of the early 14th-c structure survives, and although nearly destroyed in 1544 the buildings were later restored. The dungeons and 16th- and 17th-c rooms may be visited. Bilston Burn flows to the N of Rosslyn and is of geological interest.

ROSNEATH, Strathclyde 44 NS28

Overlooking Rosneath Bay, this small Gare Loch resort and sailing centre lies in the SE corner of the narrow Rosneath peninsula. St Modan's Well is named after a 7th-c missionary who is said to have had his cell at Rosneath. Pilgrims came here for centuries to take the waters, said to have healing properties.

ROSYTH, Fife 46 NT18

During both world wars the naval base at Rosyth – on the Forth estuary – was of great importance. The dockyard church contains a memorial of the second world war. In 1935 the Cunard liner 'Mauretania' was broken up here. Scott mentions the 16th-c Rosyth Tower (AM) which stands in the dockyard in his novel *The Abbot*.

ROTHES, Grampian 35 NJ24

In 1829 this town was wrecked by the flooding of the Spey. Opposite Rothes on the other side of the valley is the wooded viewpoint of Conerock Hill. Edward I of England traversed the Glen of Rothes, which lies to the N and carries the road to Elgin. To the NE are ruins of a castle which was built in a loop of the Spey. Near the town are the newly-planted Rosarie Forest and Teindland Forest, both well known to forest scientists.

ROTHESAY, Isle of Bute, Strathclyde 29 NS06

The popular resort and Royal Burgh of Rothesay is sited on sandy Rothesay Bay

One of the finest examples of the rich carving displayed by Rosslyn Chapel is the elaborate Prentice Pillar.

An island in Loch an Eilean near Rothiemurchus carries the remains of a castle which once housed the notorious Wolf of Badenoch.

and is the principal town of Bute. Toward Point is across the Firth of Clyde on the mainland. Rothesay's harbour is full of small craft in July, when the Clyde Yachting Fortnight is in full swing. Clyde steamers call at the pier, near which lie the remains of Rothesay Castle (AM), one of the most important of the surviving Scottish medieval castles. The Normans stormed the castle in 1240, and their breach can still be detected. Some 23 years later King Haco of Norway captured the building. Most of the original structure was probably destroyed later by Robert the Bruce, and the castle suffered further damage at the hands of Cromwell in the 17thc. Today the building's strong walls, heightened and provided with four round towers in the late 13thc, still enclose a circular courtyard. A deep moat surrounds the castle, and near by is the Chapel of St Michael which probably dates from the 14thc.

Rothesay has given its name to the Prince of Wales' dukedom, and Scott introduced the fascinating tale of the Duke of Rothesay and the castle. Near the parish church is the ruined chancel of the old Church of St Mary (AM), with its ancient tombs. Mansion House dates from the 17thc and behind the town, on the W shore of narrow Loch Fad, stands Kean's Cottage. This was built by the great 19th-c actor Edmund Kean.

The road along the E shore of the loch provides an alternative route to Kilchattan Bay, the main route being via the coast road past Bogany Point. This road leads to the model village of Kerrycroy, 3m SE of Rothesay. Woods beyond the village contain Mount Stuart, the palatial modern seat of the Marquis of Bute. A road leading SE from Rothesay passes little Greenan Loch as it heads

towards the sandy bay of St Ninian's and Scalpsie. Views to the island of Inch Marnock are afforded along the route. A branch from this road runs N to sandy Etterick Bay, facing across the Kyles of Bute to Ardlamont Point.

ROTHIEMAY, Grampian   35 NJ54

An old bridge straddles the Deveron here. The River is joined by the Isla a little farther to the SE. James Ferguson, an early 18th-c astronomer, is commemorated by a monument at Milltown of Rothiemay. Rothiemay Castle stands in parkland beyond the Deveron. Some of the old building work survives, and the gardens are lovely. Vast Bin Forest extends to the S of the village, and 16th- to 18th-c Auchanechy Castle can be seen 4m WSW of Rothiemay.

ROTHIEMURCHUS, Highland 34 NH80

Many lovely paths and tracks lead through the Forest of Rothiemurchus, which once formed part of the great Caledonian Forest. A large part of this now forms a nature reserve. The community of Rothiemurchus lies on the Spey at the fringe of the forest. Reindeer, once indigenous to Scotland, have been reintroduced into the forest area. Roofless Rothiemurchus church stands in a bend of the Spey near The Doune, a 16th-c and later mansion with an interesting interior. To the E is the Glen More forest park, centred around beautiful Loch Morlich. Cairn Gorm rises to 4,084ft SE of Loch Morlich. A road climbs from the loch to a large car park at about 2,500ft, giving access to the chair lifts and ski tows of the Cairngorms. This is the major winter-

sports area in Britain. At the top of the upper chair lift is The Ptarmigan, the highest restaurant in Britain.

The walkers' track leading to well-known Lairig Ghru Pass runs through the forest to the SE of Rothiemurchus. Nearer to the village is the beautiful Loch an Eilean, reached via a by-road on which stands the carved Martineau monument. The loch is surrounded by forest and is known for its triple echo. Sinister ruins of the castle of the Comyns survive on an island in the loch. The notorious Wolf of Badenoch, son of Robert II, maintained a reign of terror along the Spey valley from this medieval castle during the later 14thc.

A cottage by the lochside houses a visitor centre and small exhibition. A 2½m nature trail encircles the loch. To the S of Rothiemurchus Forest, at the head of Glen Einich, is lonely Loch Einich – one of the wildest of the Highland lochs. It lies at a height of 1,650ft and is framed by Cairngorm peaks, with 4,248ft Braeriach to the E, and the great cliffs of 3,658ft Sgoran Dubh to the SW. Beyond Sgoran Dubh is a long ridge of 3,000ft hills which overlooks Glen Feshie and its remote forest.

ROWANTREE HILL, Strathclyde 24 NX39

Two narrow winding roads fork to the S of Rowantree Hill, the left branch crossing the lonely Nick o' the Balloch Pass at 1,280ft and descending towards Maybole. The right branch climbs even higher to 1,421ft, with 2,520ft Shalloch on Minnoch rising to the E. It later reaches Straiton in the valley of the Water of Girvan.

ROWARDENNAN, Central   44 NS39

A road along the E shore of Loch Lomond ends at Rowardennan. A steamer pier is situated here and there are fine views across the loch to Glen Douglas, which can be reached by a passenger ferry. Wonderful 3,192ft Ben Lomond can be climbed from the village and affords magnificent views from its summit. The panorama E towards the wooded Trossachs is particularly fine. A little to the W of the Ben rises 2,398ft Ptarmigan, with Rowardennan Forest to the SE. The whole area lies within the Queen Elizabeth forest park.

ROXBURGH, Borders   26 NT63

In the 13thc the town of Roxburgh was one of the four Royal Burghs of Scotland, but the town has since disappeared completely and the name only applies to a small village on the W bank of the Teviot. Andrew Gemmels, the 'Edie Ochiltree' of Scott's *The Antiquary*, died at the age of 106 and was buried in the local churchyard. Traces of Roxburgh Castle can be seen 3m NE, between the Tweed and the Teviot. James II besieged the castle, once a Royal residence, in 1460. During the siege the king is said to have been accidentally killed when a cannon burst in the park of Floors Castle, just NW of Kelso. Late 17th-c Fairnington House stands 3½m SW of Roxburgh.

ROY BRIDGE, Highland   33 NN28

In 1688 the last of the great clan battles was fought here between the MacDonells of Keppoch and the MacIntoshes. It is thought that this was the last time the Highlanders used the bow and arrow as a weapon. The MacDonells were the victors, but failed to deal with the MacIntoshes' standard bearer who jumped the River Roy and escaped. A very rough and narrow road runs N alongside the river and through Glen Roy from here, leading to the famous Parallel Roads – hillside terraces marking the levels of lakes dammed by glaciers during the ice age. The 'roads' are the most striking example of glacial action in Scotland, and are distinct on the hillside some 4m from Roy Bridge. The uppermost roads are about 80ft apart, and the lowest situated some 200ft below them. Montrose made a forced march through Glen Roy before the Battle of Inverlochy in 1645.

The 18th-c Keppoch House succeeds an older mansion of the MacDonells of Keppoch, where a young Chief of Keppoch and his brother were murdered in the 17thc. Revenge came seven years later when the assassins, seven brothers, were themselves killed by Iain Lom, the family bard. The seven were beheaded and the heads were washed in the Well of Heads on the shores of Loch Oich before being presented to the Chief of the Clan MacDonell at Glengarry. To the E of Roy Bridge the road and railway cross the Achluachrach Gorge on the River Spean. The fine rocky Monessie Falls can be seen well from the railway, but the cascade has been reduced somewhat since the Lochaber Power Scheme took effect. Just S of Roy Bridge the River Roy flows into the Spean in Lochaber country. Farther S rise the remote peaks of the 3,858ft Grey Cormes, the farthest E in the series of lofty ridges ending in mighty 4,406ft Ben Nevis – the highest mountain in the British Isles.

RUM, ISLE OF, Highland *32 NM39*
Sometimes spelt Rhum, this mountainous Inner Hebridean island is owned by the Nature Conservancy and is a centre for botanical and geological research and the study of red deer. A weekday steamer service from Mallaig is the only way of reaching the island, which has no visitor accommodation. Camping may be allowed with prior permission. A splendid group of peaks – Askival, Sgurr nan Gillean, and Ashval – rise from the S half of the island and all exceed 2,500ft. They provide wonderful viewpoints and offer fine opportunities to the climber.

The little township and castle of Kinloch lie at the head of Loch Scresort on the E side of Rum. A mausoleum is situated in Glen Harris on the W side of the island. To the N of Rum is the Cuillin Sound, beyond which lies the island of Skye – the largest of the Inner Hebrides. Off the SE coast of Rum the Sound of Rum separates the island from Eigg. The remarkable and prominent 1,289ft Sgurr of Eigg rises from the S side of this island. The Sgurr is best seen from Galmisdale, a village with a pier on the S coast of Eigg, but is also prominent in views from the mainland. Scott's *Lord of the Isles* describes a tragedy in a cave on this island, when several hundred Macdonalds were deliberately suffocated by the MacLeods of Skye in the 16thc. On the NW coast of Eigg is the Bay of Laig and the clachan of Cleadale, with singing sands in the vicinity.

Across the Sound of Eigg and to the SW lies the little island of Muck, with a laird's residence at Gallanach and a small harbour at Port Mor. To the NW

Two bridges span the tumbling River Deveron at Rumbling Bridge.

of Rum is the island of Canna, separated from its neighbour by the Sound of Canna. Iron deposits in the low Compass Hill sometimes affect ships' compasses. Eigg and Canna, like Rum, can be reached by steamer from Mallaig. Rum is a prominent feature in views from the mainland, particularly from the Ardnamurchan peninsula, Arisaig, Morar, and Mallaig. Collectively Rum, Eigg, Canna, and Muck are known as the Small Isles.

RUMBLING BRIDGE, Tayside *46 NT09*
When in spate the River Devon rumbles as it rushes under the two bridges at this beauty spot – thus the name. Spectacular gorges and picturesque falls can be seen in the area. The best-known falls are the Devil's Mill and Caldron Linn, which lie to the NE and SW respectively. The narrow arched bridge dates from 1713, and the other from 1816. Restored Aldie Castle stands 3m SE and overlooks the Cleish Hills across the Pow Burn.

RUTHERGLEN, Strathclyde *45 NS66*
Rutherglen was given its charter by David I early in the 12thc, and claims to be Scotland's oldest Royal Burgh. Although now on the fringe of Glasgow the town has retained its independence. Rutherglen Castle was burnt by the Regent Murray after the Battle of Langside in 1568, after which Mary Queen of Scots began her flight from Scotland. All traces of the castle have since vanished. In 1679 the Covenanters affixed a declaration to the Town Cross. This led to the Battles of Drumclog, near Loudounhill, and Bothwell Brig.

The present Mercat cross is modern but the Kirk Port dates from 1663 and

preserves a pair of 18th-c sentry boxes. A gable from the Norman church which once stood in the town rests against an early 16th-c steeple containing a Dutch bell of 1635. Clydesdale horses were at one time tethered in the wide main street during important sales. Rutherglen is a manufacturing town noted for chemicals and paper mills. Castle Milk lies 1½m S and incorporates a 15th- or 16th-c tower. The house may have sheltered Mary Queen of Scots before the Battle of Langside.

RUTHWELL, Dumfries and Galloway *26 NY16*
Famous for the remarkable Ruthwell Cross (AM), the town of Ruthwell lies just S of the Dumfries to Annan road. The 8th-c cross is one of the best dark-age monuments surviving in Europe, and is of the greatest interest to archaeologists. It is preserved inside a special apse in the parish church, just N of the Dumfries to Annan road. The cross is 18ft high and is inscribed with Runic characters. Earlier written phrases are in the Northumbrian dialect of English. These make up the *Rood Lay* or *Dream of the Cross*, a poem possibly written by the Anglo-Saxon poet Caedmon. This verse is in the first person, as if the cross itself is speaking. The monument lay under the church floor during the 17th and 18thc, but was recovered and restored again in 1823. The Reverend Henry Duncan set up Scotland's first savings bank at Ruthwell in 1810.

SADDELL, Strathclyde *24 NR73*
Picturesquely set on Saddell Bay at the foot of Saddell Glen, this village includes

interesting remains of an abbey and castle. Only the walls have survived of the original 12th-c Cistercian abbey, which was probably founded by Somerled, 1st Lord of the Isles. The Clan Donald sprang from Somerled. The abbey is noted for sculptured Celtic tombstones which lie in its churchyard, and it is thought that one of the recumbent effigies may be Somerled himself. Battlemented Saddell Castle is situated on the S side of the bay and dated 1508. It was once the residence of the Bishops of Argyll. Robert the Bruce was concealed in an earlier structure after his defeat at Methven in 1306. Above the date panel over the door is carved a representation of the 'Galley of Lorne'. To the W of Saddell rise the highest of the Kintyre hills, with Beinn an Tuirc standing at 1,491ft and Beinn Bhreac at 1,398ft.

ST ABB'S, Borders *31 NT96*

This small resort and fishing village is situated on a cliff-fringed stretch of coast and offers a sandy beach. Fishermen's gear is stored in a picturesque row of tiny buildings. Red cliffs rise to over 300ft in the N, towards the impressive headland of St Abb's Head. A lighthouse is sited here. In years gone by the caves in these cliffs were used by smugglers. The rugged cliff scenery near St Abb's is perhaps best seen from the small inlet of Pettycarwick Bay.

*ST ANDREWS, Fife *31 NO51*

Historically St Andrews is one of the most fascinating places in Scotland, and a wealth of ancient buildings has survived the rigors of Scottish history. The town was once the ecclesiastical centre for Scotland and has many associations with John Knox, who led the

Scottish Protestant Reformation. The town makes a good centre for exploring the old-world Royal Burghs along the Fife coast, from Crail in the E to Culross beyond Dunfermline in the W. St Andrews is also popular as a summer resort, standing on a promontory with steep cliffs guarding the narrow harbour. Sands fringe shallow St Andrews Bay to the NW of the town, where the four famous golf courses lie. The Royal and Ancient Golf Club is the ruling authority on the game throughout the world, and was founded in 1754. Written records of the Old Course, the oldest in the world, date back to the 15thc. Anyone can play on this course for a small fee. During the annual autumn meeting the captain for the following year plays himself into office. Near the Club House of the Royal and Ancient is the Martyrs' Monument,

1 Blackfriars Chapel
2 Cathedral
3 Holy Trinity Church
4 Martyrs' Monument

5 The Pends
6 St Andrews Castle
7 St Mary's College
8 St Rule's Church

9 Town Hall
10 University and Church of St Salvator
11 West Port

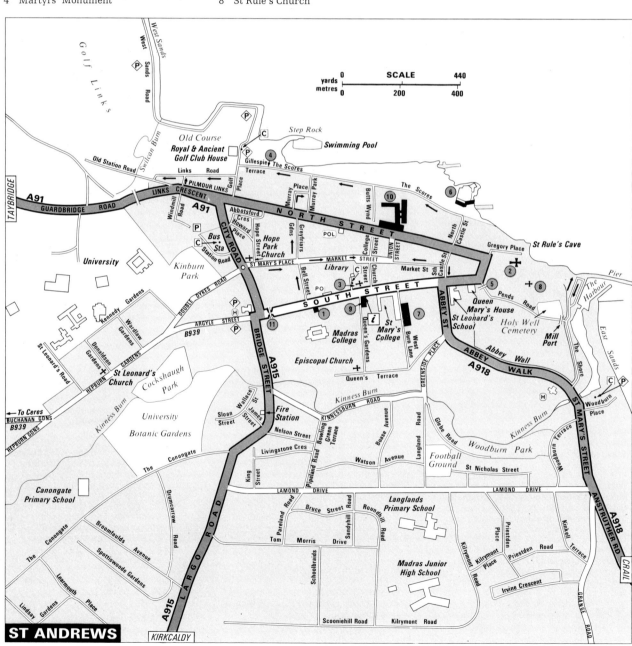

ST ANDREWS

Entries marked * are the starting point of drives included in the Day Drive section of the book (pages 95 to 160).

commemorating reformers burnt in the town in the 15th and 16thc.

St Andrews was made a Royal Burgh in 1140. In 1160 the cathedral (AM) was founded and was destined to become the largest church in Scotland by the time it was completed in 1318. Robert the Bruce attended its consecration in the year of completion. James V and Mary of Guise were married here, and in 1559 some of the cathedral's ornamentation was destroyed after sermons by John Knox. By 1649 the building was reduced to a state of ruin, mainly through neglect, and today only parts of the west and east gables and a portion of the south nave wall still stand. The ground plan can still be traced, however. Beside the cathedral stands the even older little St Regulus' or St Rule's Church (AM), built c1130. A spiral staircase leads to the top of the 108ft-high tower, which affords a splendid view of the city beneath. The nave has vanished but the narrow, roofless choir, with its round-headed windows, has survived.

The town's university is the oldest in Scotland and was founded in 1412. For 70 years up to 1967 it also included University College Dundee. The United Colleges of St Salvator and St Leonard, founded in 1455 and 1512, were combined in 1747 and are famed for the Church of St Salvator – now the college chapel. This 15th-c church has a tall tower with an octagonal broach spire, and contains the tomb of its founder Bishop Kennedy. Other features include the oldest Sacrament House in a Scottish church, and John Knox's pulpit. The latter was originally in the town church.

Cardinal Beaton founded St Mary's College in 1537, and the quadrangle between the older buildings has survived. A thorn tree planted by Mary Queen of Scots can still be seen. Traces of the original St Leonard's College – in which John Knox resided – also survives. Near by stands the little St Leonard's Chapel, with its interesting monuments. In the grounds of the modern Madras College stands the Blackfriars Chapel (AM), which dates from 1525 and is a fragment of an ancient monastery founded in 1274. The University Museum exhibits a fascinating collection of fossils found near Pitscottie in Dura Den.

Holy Trinity is the town church and was founded in 1412. It has been greatly altered over the years, though its 16th-c 'Fife-type' tower remains. John Knox preached his first public sermon in Holy Trinity in 1547. Inside the church is the elaborately-carved 17th-c marble monument to Archbishop Sharp, who was murdered in 1779 near Pitscottie at Magnus Muir. The Playfair Aisle contains family memorials, and other interesting features include two choir stalls of c1505, some fine modern windows by Douglas Strachan, and a wall tablet to Tom Morris the golfer. In the Session House are interesting relics which include two 'cutty' or repentance stools and a scold's bridle. Other old town relics are housed in the Town Hall – the headman's axe, a stone dated 1565 which came from the old Tolbooth demolished in 1862, and some portraits. Mary Queen of Scots may once have stayed in a house in South Street. This was built by Hugh Scrymgeour in 1523, and is now St Leonard's School's library. Near by are The Pends (AM), two gothic arches,

which may date from the 14thc and once formed part of a vaulted gatehouse to the priory precincts. These precincts were originally completely encircled by a wall. Prior Hepburn built the wall (AM) in the 16thc, and much of it still stands. Several fine old houses are to be seen in South Street, the W end of which is spanned by the 16th-c West Port (AM). This was enlarged and restored in 1843. Another old gate stands in Abbey Walk and is known as Teinds Yett. A picturesque custom held each spring is the Kate Kennedy procession.

On a rock overlooking the North Sea is St Andrews Castle (AM), isolated and guarded by a deep, wide ditch. The castle was founded in 1200 and rebuilt late in the 14thc. Cardinal Beaton was murdered here in 1546, and the first round of the Reformation struggle that resulted was fought out in a siege that followed. The 24ft-deep Bottle Dungeon is in the Sea Tower, and to the SE of the courtyard is an underground passage which was dug by the besieged garrison in 1546 – a vain attempt to escape. In 1547 the castle was taken by the French fleet, and John Knox was amongst the prisoners transported to France. The oldest parts of the castle date from the 13thc, but much of the work is later than the partial destruction of 1547. Kinkell Ness lies 2m SE of St Andrews and features strange, basalt-rock pillars known as the Rock and Spindle. G J Whyte-Melville the 19th-c novelist lived 2m SW of St Andrews at Mount Melville. The grounds of the house now form the Craigtown public park.

ST ANN'S, Dumfries and Galloway
25 NY09
Kinnel Water flows through the village of St Ann's, and the lovely Raehills Glen lies

The Pends are two possibly 14th-c arches in St Andrews which may once have formed a gatehouse to the priory precincts.

a little to the NW. St Ann's Bridge dates from c1800. Ruined Lochwood Tower was a stronghold of the Johnstones and was burnt in 1592. Its remains lie in a nearby wood.

ST BOSWELL'S GREEN, Borders
26 NT53
A spacious common separates the village of St Boswell's Green from St Boswell's, which lies NE nearer the Tweed and was once noted for livestock sales. Lessudden House, a fine, modernized 16th- and 17th-c house, stands here. Across the Tweed to the NE is Mertoun House, designed by Sir William Bruce in 1703. A dovecot dated 1576 stands near by. Old Mertoun House has a history dating back to 1677. To the NW of St Boswell's Green is Newtown St Boswell's, with the triple-peaked Eildon Hills rising in the background.

ST CATHERINE'S, Strathclyde
29 NN10
Situated on the E shore of Loch Fyne, St Catherine's faces across the loch to Inveraray. Two roads NE of the village lead E from the loch side road, leading towards Hell's Glen and Glen Kinglas respectively. These highways meet again at the mountain-encircled summit of Glen Croe, known as Rest and Be Thankful.

ST COMBS, Grampian   35 NK06
The fishing village of St Combs lies under Inzie Head, with Strathbeg Bay lying farther to the SE.

ST CYRUS, Grampian   35 NO76
St Cyrus national nature reserve covers 227 acres round the village, and breeding

This ancient circular dovecot stands on cliffs to the SW of St Monans.

seals and eider ducks visit the bay. Fulmars can be seen around the cliffs. Fine rock scenery can be enjoyed NE of the village and its sandy beach, and the Keim of Mathers lies near the promontory of Milton Ness. The Keim is a refuge built by David Barclay of Mather in 1421 after he had killed a sheriff of the Mearns. The village of Mather was once situated near here but was washed away by the sea in 1795. Wooded Den Finella features a waterfall and can be seen 2m NE of St Cyrus – W of the Inverbervie road.

ST FILLAN'S, Tayside 30 NN62
St Fillan's is delightfully set at the E tip of Loch Earn, on the River Earn. Dundurn's wooded slopes rise to 2,011ft to the S of the village, and the hill was once fortified by the Picts. Below rises Dunfillan Hill, topped by the rock known as St Fillan's Chair. In the cemetery on the edge of the village are ruins of a chapel which for generations was the burial-place of the Stewarts of Ardvorlich House, near Lochearnhead. The chapel's font is now preserved in the parish church. Roads to the W of St Fillan's run along both sides of Loch Earn. The main road on the N bank affords fine mountain views which take in 3,224ft Ben Vorlich and 3,169ft Stuc a' Chroin to the S. Wooded Neish Island lies in the loch, and there is a large power station for the Breadalbane scheme near by.

ST KILDA, ISLES OF, Western Isles 38
The farthest W group of islands in Britain, the spectacular isles of St Kilda lie 45m W of the Outer Hebrides. They were owned by the Macleod of Macleod for many generations, but were given to the NTS in 1957 and later leased to the

Nature Conservancy. In 1734 Lady Grange was exiled to St Kilda for harbouring Jacobite secrets, and was buried at Trumpan on Skye. By 1930 the St Kildans had found it impossible to eke a living from the islands, and were evacuated to the mainland. Their primitive dwellings are maintained by working parties which visit St Kilda every summer.

The cliffs on the largest island soar to 1,397ft at Conachair, and are the highest in Britain. St Kilda fosters unique wild life – the wild Soay sheep, the St Kilda mouse, and the St Kilda wren – plus numerous fulmars and puffins. Boreray and the Stacs make up the world's largest gannetry, and the rare Leach's fork-tailed petrel can also be found here. A radar tracking-station has been established on Hirta. Some 180m farther out into the Atlantic lies the minute island of Rockall, only 85ft in diameter and 70ft high. This was first discovered in 1810, when it was actually mistaken for a French privateer!

ST MARY'S LOCH, Borders 26 NT22
Rounded green hills surround this beautiful 3m-long loch, which has been praised by both Wordsworth in *Yarrow Visited* and Scott in *Marmion*. The Megget Water flows into the NW end of the loch at Coppercleuch, and a rough track leads along its valley to the lonely Talla Reservoir, near Tweedsmuir. This is overlooked by 2,754ft Broad Law, one of the highest of the Lowland hills. A hillside N of the loch bears the old churchyard of St Mary's Kirk, and near the NE tip of the loch lie the ruins of Dryhope Tower. The latter was rebuilt *c*1600 and is said to have been the birthplace of Mary Scott – the Flower of Yarrow. Mary married the freebooter Auld Wat of Harden – ancestors Sir

Walter Scott was proud to claim. Farther NE the beautiful Vale of Yarrow is surrounded by the vast Ettrick Forest. This is considered one of the loveliest of all the Border valleys.

A narrow spit of land which separates St Mary's Loch from the little Loch of the Lowes, to the S, is the site of the famous Tibbie Shiel's Inn. This was frequented by James Hogg, the 19th-c poet also known as the Ettrick Shepherd. He once herded sheep on the hills near the loch, and his statue stands just W of the inn. Rodono Hotel stands 1½m N of the Hogg Monument and takes its name from the old barony of Rodonna, of which the Megget family formed a part.

ST MONANS, Fife 31 NO50
Until recently known as St Monance, this lovely little fishing port has old houses clustered near the water's edge. The beautiful 14th-c Old Kirk of St Monance was restored in 1828 and stands almost on the foreshore. In stormy weather spray is flung right to the church door. The unfinished cruciform structure of the church is topped by a curious stone steeple, and a model of a three-masted ship hangs down from one of the transept roofs. St Monans' shipyard now produces pleasure yachts, but once made the original 'Fifie' fishing boats. On the cliffs to the SW are remains of 17th-c Newark Castle, once the home of General Leslie. Leslie was the Covenanter who won the Battle of Philiphaugh, but was later defeated by Cromwell at the Battle of Dunbar. An ancient circular dovecot stands near by.

ST NINIAN'S, Central 45 NS79
St Ringan's is another name for this old village, which is situated S of Stirling at the junction of the Airdrie and Falkirk roads. A little to the SW is the site of the Battle of Bannockburn, which established Robert the Bruce on the throne of Scotland in 1314. Some 2½m S of the village off the road to Denny is the 16th-c mansion of Auchenbowie. The Battle of Sauchieburn, after which James III was defeated, wounded, and later murdered, is thought to have been fought in an area to the W of St Ninian's. Old Sauchie, also W of the village, dates from the 16thc.

ST VIGEANS, Tayside 31 NO64
Noted for its 11th-c church, St Vigeans lies on the Brothock Water a little to the N of Arbroath. There is a remarkable collection of Pictish gravestones here, forming one of the most important groups of early-Christian sculpture in Scotland. Outstanding is the richly-carved Drosten Stone. St Vigeans Museum is of interest (AM). Colliston House is sited 3m N of St Vigeans near Brothock Water and dates from 1583.

SALEN, Highland 32 NM66
Situated on the lovely wooded N shores of Loch Sunart, the small fishing resort of Salen stands on a road which leads N to Acharacle at the W end of Loch Shiel. Acharacle has memories of Prince Charles Edward and the '45 Rising. Loch Sunart is a long and narrow sea loch which divides Ardnamurchan from Morven. Its waters mingle with those of the Sound of

Mull to the W. To the E of Salen rises the splendid viewpoint of 2,774ft Ben Resipol.

SALEN, Isle of Mull, Strathclyde
28 NM54
Only 3m of land separates Salen, on the Sound of Mull, from the beautiful sea loch of Loch na Keal. This loch may be the 'Loch Gyle' of Campbell's famous poem *Lord Ullin's Daughter*, though some authorities think that Loch Goil in the Cowal district is more likely. To the E of Salen a road leads along the shores of the sound and is overlooked by 2,500ft-high hills. In 2m it passes the ruins of Pennygowan Chapel, which displays ancient carved cross-slabs. Loch na Keal is bordered by roads along both its N and S shores. The S shore road passes near the NW tip of the attractive freshwater Loch Ba, and later affords views of the cave-riddled island of Ulva. The smaller isle of Gometra can also be seen.

The road then runs beneath the magnificent Gribun cliffs on its way to Loch Scridain, with Mull's highest peak 3,169ft Ben More rising to the E. A road along Loch na Keal's N shore leads to Loch Tuath, in which lies the island of Ulva, and eventually reaches Calgary. On the inland road to Dervaig, near the entrance to Glen Aros and 2m NW of Salen, lie the ruins of Aros Castle. This was once a stronghold of the Lords of the Isles, and faces the Sound of Mull.

SALINE, Fife   46 NT09
Walter Scott visited Saline several times. The village lies at the foot of 1,178ft Saline Hill, an outlier of the Cleish Hills which stretch away to the NE. Dumglow rises to 1,241ft and is the highest point in the range.

SALTBURN, Highland   34 NH76
Salt was taxed many years ago, and it used to be smuggled ashore here and hidden near by, giving this Cromarty Firth village its name. A new pier and aluminium-smelting works has greatly altered the appearance of the village.

SALTCOATS, Strathclyde   29 NS24
In the 16thc James V established salt-works at this well-known resort, which has a harbour, sands, and good bathing. The North Ayrshire and Maritime museums are interesting. To the NE is Irvine Bay, and across another bay to the NW lies the resort and steamer pier of Ardrossan. See Ardrossan town plan.

SANAIGMORE, Isle of Islay, Strathclyde
28 NR27
The emigrant ship 'Exmouth' went down near Sanaigmore in 1847, with many lives lost. Ardnave Point lies NE on a rocky stretch of coast near the mouth of Loch Gruinart, and large caves have been eroded in the rocks to the S of Sanaigmore. The road S keeps inland and passes near the shores of Loch Gorm, where there are remains of an ancient castle of the Macdonalds. The route eventually leads to sandy Saligo Bay in the Rhinns of Islay.

SANDBANK, Strathclyde   44 NS18
'Sceptre' and 'Sovereign' were two yachts launched from Sandbank, both of which were unsuccessful challengers for the America's Cup. Sandbank lies on the S shores of the Holy Loch, on the road which runs from Dunoon to Ardentinny. This road affords wonderful seaward views the whole way. A little to the NW of Sandbank lies the entrance to Glen Lean, threaded by a narrow, hilly road which leads to the heads of Lochs Striven and Riddon. From here it continues to Glendaruel and Loch Fyne.

SANDHAVEN, Grampian   35 NJ96
A little inland to the SW of this coastal village is ruined 17th-c Pittullie Castle.

SANDHEAD, Dumfries and Galloway
24 NX04
Picts and Scots once fought a battle on the sand dunes of Torrs Warren, to the NE of Sandhead. The community itself lies on Luce Bay, with the vast sands of Luce to the NE. Three of the earliest Christian monuments (AM) in Britain can be seen 2m SW outside Kirkmadrine Church. These show the Chi-Rho symbol and inscriptions which date from the 5th or early 6thc. They show that a very early Christian settlement must have existed here.

SANDYKNOWE, Borders   26 NT63
Sir Walter Scott spent some of his childhood years living with his grandfather at this farmhouse, which is situated near the picturesque Smailholm Tower.

SANNOX, Isle of Arran, Strathclyde
29 NS04
Lonely, picturesque Glen Sannox reaches the sea at Sannox, and from Sannox Bay there are views of the Cumbrae Islands and the Isle of Bute. Roadless Glen Sannox penetrates deep in the heart of the granite hills of Arran, overlooked at the seaward end by 1,756ft Suidhe Fhearghais to the N and 2,168ft Cioch na'h Oighe to the S. Dominating the head of the valley are 2,817ft Caisteal Abhail and 2,168ft Cir Mhor. Climbers can cross the ridge S of Cir Mhor to reach Glen Rosa and Brodick. The road NW from Sannox to Lochranza runs through the lovely North Glen Sannox.

SANQUHAR, Dumfries and Galloway
25 NS70
A granite monument here marks the site of the old Town Cross to which the Covenanters affixed the two famous Declarations of Sanquhar in 1680 and 1685 in their fight to defend Presbyterianism against the Stuarts. Sanquhar itself is a small Royal Burgh on the River Nith. A Tolbooth of 1735 is preserved, and above the river is the ruined castle. This was once owned by the Crichtons and later by the Douglases. Every August the town holds its Riding of the Marches festival. Persecuted Covenanters, or Men of the Moss Hays, hid in the Lowther Hills to the E of the town during the late 17thc. To the W of Sanquhar are the remains of an ancient earthwork called the Devil's Dyke, the origin of which is obscure. The River Nith is joined by Crawick Water 1m NW of Sanquhar. The Crawick flows down from lonely hills on the one-time Lanark Border. Alongside Crawick Water is a narrow road which winds over the hills and eventually leads to Clydesdale by way of Crawfordjohn.

SARCLET, Highland   37 ND34
Sarclet lies to the N of the Stack of Ulbster, near Loch Sarclet, and is situated on a rocky coast line.

Sir Walter Scott spent part of his childhood at this farmhouse near Sandy Knowe.

SARK BRIDGE, Dumfries and Galloway
26 NY36

Part of the River Sark S of Gretna forms the border between England and Scotland here. Just before the river enters the Solway Firth it is spanned by Sark Bridge, now by-passed by the main road from Carlisle to Glasgow and Stranraer. Runaway marriages were once performed at the Sark Toll Bar house, the 'First House in Scotland'. The marriage room tablet is set above the entrance door. The old main road to Scotland followed the A6071 by way of Longtown and Springfield before 1830, and elopement marriages were first held at Springfield.

SCALLOWAY, Shetland Isles *41 HU33*
See Shetland Isles

SCONE, (NEW & OLD), Tayside
30 NO12

Alexander I founded the famous abbey at Scone c1114 on a site 2m W of New Scone between Old Scone and the River Tay. All the early kings of Scotland up to James I were crowned here, but a mob from Perth destroyed the abbey and palace in 1559 after having been incensed by the oratory of John Knox. The ancient mote-hill of Scone was already known in the 8thc, and it was to here that Kenneth MacAlpine – the man who visited Scotland after defeating the Picts at Scone – is thought to have brought the legendary Stone of Scone in the 9thc. Traditionally identified with Jacob's pillow at Bethel, and later the Stone of Destiny at Tara in Ireland, the Stone of Scone was taken to England by Edward I in 1297. It was later placed under the seat of the Coronation Chair in Westminster Abbey, to be sensationally stolen in 1950 and found in Arbroath. Scone Palace was rebuilt in the 16thc,

and Charles II was the last king to be crowned here in 1651. The Old Pretender kept court here in 1716, and some 29 years later Prince Charles Edward slept here. Between 1803 and 1808 the present castellated Scone Palace, home of the Earl of Mansfield, was built. The building houses fine collections of furniture, china, and ivories. The notable gardens include a pinetum, and the old Cross of Scone is preserved in the park. Bonhard House lies SE of New Scone and features a restored 17th-c dovecot.

SCONSER, Isle of Skye, Highland
32 NG53

Sconser Lodge Hotel was built in 1885, on the site of an old inn which was visited by Dr Johnson and James Boswell in 1773. Three Highland chiefs met here in 1745 – Clanranald, Chief of the Macdonalds of Uist; Sir Alexander Macdonald of Sleat; and Macleod of Macleod – to decide against 'rising' with Bonnie Prince Charlie.

SCOTLANDWELL, Tayside *30 NO10*

A spring to the W of Scotlandwell's main street gave the village its name and still bubbles up in a parapeted stone cistern. White Craigs, an outlier of the Lomonds, rises to 1,492ft N of the village. Benarty Hill stands at 1,167ft to the SW.

SCOTT COUNTRY, THE

Scott Country is centred on Melrose and comprises the central Borders. Many places in the area have links either with Scott or his novels, and Abbotsford House, his last and best-loved home, is the most famous. He was buried 5m SE of Melrose at Dryburgh Abbey, near the Tweed. Although not part of the true Scott Country, the beautiful Trossachs

country was made famous by Scott's *Lady of the Lake* and *Rob Roy*. Riccarton and Gatehouse of Fleet are particularly associated with *Guy Mannering*. Scott's *Old Mortality* was based on Robert Paterson, who lies buried at Caerlaverock.

SCOTT'S VIEW, Borders *26 NT53*

This panorama across the Tweed towards the Eildon Hills was much loved by Scott. It is said that the horses drawing his hearse to Dryburgh Abbey stopped here of their own accord, as they had done many times before in their master's lifetime. An AA viewpoint is situated here.

SCOURIE, Highland *36 NC14*

Popular as a fishing resort, the crofting village of Scourie lies on Scourie Bay and affords views E to the sharp gneiss cone of 2,364ft Ben Stack. Palm trees growing near Scourie are thought to be the farthest N in the world. Inland from the resort the countryside is dotted with hundreds of tiny lochans. To the S lies Badcall Bay, which is part of the larger island-studded Eddrachillis. The Sound of Handa separates the island of Handa, a sea-bird sanctuary, from the mainland NW of Scourie Bay.

SCRABSTER, Highland *37 ND07*

A mail steamer crosses the turbulent Pentland Firth from Stromness in the Orkneys to the Scrabster pier on sandy Thurso Bay. Scrabster is sheltered to the NE by remarkable Holborn Head. This headland appears to be split from top to bottom in many places. The largest of these chasms is open to the sea on one side and is spanned by two natural arches. Clett, a 150ft-high sea-girt rock near by, is covered with seabirds during nesting time.

SELKIRK, Borders *26 NT42*

A fine centre for exploring the lovely Yarrow and Ettrick valleys, Selkirk lies on Ettrick Water at the edge of Ettrick Forest. Also a Royal Burgh, the town is noted for the manufacture of tweed. The picturesque old Border Riding ceremony is held here every year, and a nightly curfew is sounded from the Town Hall. The latter is surmounted by a 110ft-high spire, and statues in the High Street commemorate Sir Walter Scott, Sheriff of Selkirk from 1799 to 1832; and Mungo Park, the famous explorer, who was born near the town.

The town museum contains relics of the explorer's expeditions to Sumatra and the Niger. Other exhibits include a flag which is said to have been captured at Flodden, plus relics of James Hogg the Ettrick Shepherd, and Andrew Lang the writer. Burns lodged at the former Forest Inn, which stands in the West Port and is marked by a tablet. Another monument recalls the tragic news of Flodden Field. Selkirk's Mercat cross is modern. The men of Selkirk were once called 'routers', recalling the days when the town was an important shoe-making centre.

To the S of Selkirk stands The Haining, a Palladian house built between 1794 and 1819, and near by is the shell of an earlier mansion which was burnt down in 1944. The mansion of Philiphaugh recalls a battle of 1645, when Leslie and the Covenanters defeated Montrose. This

One of several Henry Moore bronzes set up on a hillside near Shawhead.

house stands in fine gardens to the SW of the town, where the Yarrow Water flows into the Ettrick Water. Carterhaugh, scene of the ballad of *Tamlane*, stands between the two rivers. Bowhill is a fine house which was enlarged by Sir Charles Barry in the 19thc and stands in a large park. Notable portraits are preserved here.

SETON, Lothian 47 NT47
Robert Adam began Seton Castle in 1790, and the building replaces the magnificent old Seton Palace. Charles I was entertained here in 1633. Mary Queen of Scots came to the palace with Darnley after the murder of Rizzio in 1566. She again visited the old building in 1567, this time with Bothwell after Darnley had been murdered. In the grounds of the castle is the unfinished Seton collegiate church (AM), an important ecclesiastical monument of the late 14thc displaying a fine vaulted chancel and apse with lovely window tracery. Also to be seen is a good example of a piscina, and several splendid tombs. A little to the N of Seton lie the twin fishing villages of Port Seton and Cockenzie.

SHANKEND, Borders 26 NT50
Shankend is set on the Slitrig Water and is encircled by Lowland Hills. The ancient Catrail, or Pict's Ditch, can be seen to the S of Shankend on both sides of the road which leads to Liddesdale and the English border. This road climbs to 1,200ft over Limekiln Edge, 3m S of Shankend, overlooked to the W by the strangely shaped 1,677ft Maiden Paps. Another stretch of the Catrail keeps to the N of the Paps and can be seen near Galashiels.

SHAWHEAD, Dumfries and Galloway 25 NX87
A group of Henry Moore bronzes, a head

by Rodin, and other sculptures stand on the slopes of a hill NW of Shawhead, at Glenkiln.

SHETLAND ISLANDS 41
More than 100 islands make up Shetland, though less than 20 of these are inhabited. Muckle Flugga is the farthest N point in Britain – more than 170m from John O'Groats. Although farther N than parts of Alaska, the climate is considerably softened by the benevolent Gulf Stream. Mainland is the largest island, and its capital Lerwick is the only town of importance in Shetland. The islands lie at the centre of rich fishing grounds which support the islands' 18,000 population. Shetland has more known prehistoric sites than any area of its size in Britain, and visitors are enthralled by the splendid cliff and sea loch scenery. The local name for the latter is 'voes'. Apart from fishing, knitting and crofting are the principal industries. Shetland hosiery is famous the world over. Shetland wool and Shetland ponies have a worldwide reputation too. No trees grow on the islands and the summer is short. During June and part of July the nights have little or no darkness – the beautiful 'simmer dim' which has to be seen to be fully appreciated. Sea trout abound in the islands' lochs, and in many places fishing is free. Mainland has many excellent roads, but the smaller islands are less well-equipped and motoring is often hazardous.

The Picts are thought to have been the first colonizers of the Shetland Islands, followed by the Norsemen in the 9thc. Christian I of Norway, Sweden, and Denmark, pledged the Shetlands to James III of Scotland as part of his daughter Margaret's dowry. James married Margaret in 1468. The value of the islands was then ascertained at

8,000 florins. Mainland can be reached by an air service which leaves from the principal Scottish towns and ends at Sumburgh airport. Steamer services link Lerwick with Aberdeen and Orkney. The following entries list the main islands in alphabetical order.

FAIR ISLE 40
The most remote inhabited island in Britain, Fair Isle (NTS) lies 23m from the nearest land and midway between the Orkneys and the Shetlands. Ornithologists have a migration observatory on the island and have recorded more than 300 species, including the Alpine swift and the osprey. A hostel for 24 added to the observatory in 1969 will accommodate tourists when not occupied by ornithologists. A Spanish Armada vessel was wrecked on Fair Isle in 1588, and the island now operates two lighthouses.

The 50 or so islanders fish, farm, and organize a coastguard system. A twice-weekly boat service plies to Grutness in the S of Mainland. Fair Isle women still knit the colourful intricate Fair Isle patterns – which are probably of Norse origin – and produce world-famous woollens.

MAINLAND 41
The farthest S of the Shetlands Islands, Mainland includes the islands' capital Lerwick. This lies on the E shore of Mainland on Bressay Sound. Lerwick's picturesque harbour bustles with fishing boats from many countries, and some of the old merchants' houses at the S end of the town have lodberries – loading piers built out over the harbour. Ships used to sail up to the lodberries' doors and unload straight into the merchants' premises. King Haco of Norway visited the harbour on his way to the Battle of Largs in 1263. On the last Tuesday in January Lerwick celebrates the old Norse festival of Up-Helly-Aa – the fire

1 Bowhill
2 The Haining

3 Market Place and Mercat Cross
4 Philiphaugh

5 Town Hall

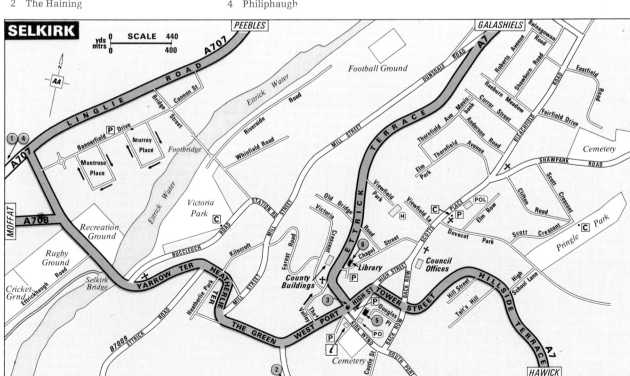

Sturdy little Shetland ponies were once in great demand for mine work and are now popular as pets.

festival – to mark the beginning of the end of long winter nights and the return of the sun. At the climax of Up-Helly-Aa a 30ft-long replica of a Viking longship is burned. Fort Charlotte (AM) overlooks Lerwick and was built in 1665 to guard the harbour. Its high walls contain gun ports pointing seawards. In 1673 it and the town were burned by the Dutch. The castle was repaired in 1781, and subsequently became known as Fort Charlotte after the Queen of George III. Until recently it was used as a headquarters by the Royal Naval Reserve, who drilled there in winter.

A narrow, paved street runs the length of the old town, and narrow closes lead to the top of the hill. Fine stained glass windows grace Lerwick's Town Hall. About ½m offshore lies the island of Bressay, which shelters Lerwick harbour and includes Lerwick golf course.

Bressay is guarded by spectacular cliffs, one of which includes the curious Giant's Leg. This pillar of stone stands in the sea but is attached to the cliff at its top. Near Bard Head, at the S end of Bressay, the stalactite Cave of the Bard is famous for its echo. A few hundred yards E of Bressay lies the smaller Isle of Noss, which is now a nature reserve with thousands of birds wheeling around its great cliffs.

From Lerwick a road runs S towards the parish of Dunrossness, passing Clickhimin Loch and the Pictish broch of Clickhimin (AM), with its secondary buildings. The road then follows the E coast and passes Sandwick, on the Mousa Sound. A boat from Leebotten takes visitors to the uninhabited island of Mousa, where the most complete iron age broch (AM) in existence can be seen. Mousa Broch stands 45ft high and is the only fortress

tower of its kind to survive at approximately its original height. Its 20ft-thick double walls of drystone masonry surround a courtyard 22ft in diameter, and stairs in the walls lead to galleries. Some 8m further S along the road from Lerwick is the parish of Dunrossness, frequently mentioned by Scott in *The Pirate* as the abode of Norna of Fitful Head. The main road ends near Jarlshof, where the 16th-c laird's house also has associations with Scott's *The Pirate.*

Jarlshof (AM) is most famous for the remains of three extensive village settlements, dating from the bronze, iron-age, and the Viking periods. This three-acre site is one of the most remarkable archaeological discoveries in Europe, and was first inhabited by stone-age men *c*2000 BC. Sumburgh Airport lies between the West Voe of Sumburgh and the Pool of Virkie, N of Jarlshof. A tiny road from Jarlshof leads to Sumburgh Head lighthouse, which was erected by Robert Stevenson in 1820 to beam out over the Roost – a dangerous current. On the returning to Dunrossness a detour can be made from the parish church SW of Quendale school. This route then continuing round the W side of Loch Spiggie to Scousburgh, where there are two hotels. To the NW of Quendale Bay is 928ft-high Fitful Head. Those energetic enough to climb to the top are rewarded by magnificent views. St Ninian's Isle, a peninsula where St Ninian founded a chapel in the 5thc, lies farther N. Students excavating the chapel site in 1958 discovered a hoard of beautifully-worked silver bowls and ornaments, which are now on display in the National Museum of Antiquities in Edinburgh. The road rejoins the main road at Channerwick.

Scalloway lies 6½m W of Lerwick and was once the capital of the Shetland Islands. It is still the seat of the islands' judiciary. The village lies at the head of Clift Sound, which is sheltered by the islands of Trondra, Papa, and Oxna, with East and West Burra farther down the Sound. Early-Christian stones have been found in West Burra, on the site of an ancient church. Scalloway's houses cluster around the well-preserved ruins of the castle (AM), which was originally built by the notoriously cruel 2nd Earl of Orkney in 1600. The building was constructed in the medieval style, and legend says that blood was mixed with the mortar. The earl was executed in 1615, after which the castle fell into disuse. To the N of Scalloway the fertile valley of Tingwall contains the lochs of Asta and Tingwall, both of which offer good trout fishing.

At one time the Shetland parliament met on an islet in Tingwall Loch, which could then be reached by stepping stones. The level of the loch has been lowered since, and the stones are no longer required. Just W of Scalloway is Gallows Hill, where witches were burned centuries ago. To the NE of Scalloway a main road encircles Weisdale Voe and heads into the W part of Mainland. This road climbs S with fine views from the higher points, and at Twatt turns S to Reawick and a fine sandy bay. Farther W from Twatt, just beyond the Bridge of Walls, is the Vaila Sound and Walls village. Walls is the port for the Foula mail boat. Foula has a cliff which soars to 1,220ft, and is the home of the great skua and a fitting setting for the film *The Edge of the World.* This was shot here in 1938. The district of Sandness forms part of Walls parish and lies to the NW. Across the Sound of Papa is the island of Papa Stour, which has caves described as the finest in Britain. Out to sea lie the dangerous Vee Skerries. The islands are the haunt of the common seal, particularly in June and July. In N Scotland the common seal is called the tangfish – 'tang' being Shetlandese for 'seaweed' – because of its liking for low water and weed-covered rocks.

The main road from Lerwick towards North Mainland skirts Girlsta Loch. To the NE of the loch the Nesting peninsula faces Whalsay Island, and at South Nesting Bay a road turns inland to Dury and Laxo. From Laxo there is a gated little road which switchbacks N, passing close to Vidlin and eventually leading to Lunna, with its fascinating ancient church. During the second world war the nearby mansion was used as part of the Norwegian escape route. The main road continues W from Laxo, past the shores of Voe Loch to the little township of Voe at the head of Olnafirth Voe. Here the road is joined by the direct road from Lerwick. Farther N the road overlooks Dales Voe (Delting) and later reaches Mossbank. Here at Toft's Voe it connects with the passenger ferry to Ulsta, on the island of Yell. The 50yd-wide isthmus of Mavis Grind lies 6m NW of Voe, separating the parish of Northmavine from the rest of Mainland. A stone thrown over Mavis Grind passes from the waters of the Atlantic Ocean to those of the North Sea. To the N of Mavis Grind lies Hillswick, situated on the Ura Firth which is an inlet of St Magnus Bay. Hillswick is popular with trout anglers and offers good accommodation. Remarkable rock scenery lies to the W at Eshaness.

The natural rock bridge between the two Holes of Scraada fell in some 50 years ago, leaving a single hole. The Grind of Navir is a breach smashed into the cliff face by the sea. Shetland's highest point is 1,475ft Ronas Hill which rises on the N side of Ronas Voe and provides a wonderful panorama of most of the Shetland Islands on a clear day. To the E and NE lie the townships of Collafirth and Burravoe. The road ends at Isbister in North Roe. Still farther N is Fethaland, the farthest N point on Mainland.

UNST 41
Scenically and geologically perhaps the most interesting of all the Shetland islands, Unst lies farther N than any other part of the group. A passenger ferry which operates from Gutcher, on Yell, crosses the Blue Mull Sound to Belmont. The mail steamer 'Earl of Zetland' calls at Uyeasound on the S side, and Baltasound on the E side of the island. Unst was one of the haunts of the rare great skua, which was preserved from extinction by the efforts of the Edmonston family. At the SE end of the island lies the ruined 1598 Muness Castle (AM), which was built of rubble but shows fine architectural detail. Out to sea from Uyeasound is the small island of Haaf Gruney, now a national nature reserve. Baltasound lies farther N and is Unst's principal port.

Still farther N is Haroldswick, with the farthest N post office in Britain. Fine caves riddle the shores of Burrafirth, a large sea loch opening to the N, and the Hermaness district on its W shores is now a national nature reserve. The great skua breeds here, and many other species of sea bird frequent the cliff-girt coast. Mukkle Flugga lighthouse, the farthest N habitation in Britain, stands out to sea on a lonely rock and is only 300m away from the Arctic Circle. A new airport is planned for Unst.

YELL 41
Separated from Mainland by the Yell Sound, this island is almost cut in two by Whalefirth on the W side and Raefirth or Mid Yell Voe on the E side. Gloup Voe, in the N of the island, has the appearance of a miniature Norwegian fiord. Ulsta is situated in the S of Yell and linked by passenger ferry to Toft's Voe (Mossbank) on Mainland. Gutcher, on Yell's NE coast, connects by passenger ferry with Belmont on the island of Unst. The mail and passenger steamer 'Earl of Zetland' operates from Lerwick and calls at the E coast ports of Mid Yell and Cullivoe.

Off the E coast is the island of Fetlar, where generations of breeding have produced the sturdy little Shetland pony – only 42in high at the shoulder when fully grown. Formerly in great demand as work ponies for pits and farms, they have now become popular pets all over the world. Also on Fetlar is a Royal Society for the Protection of Birds sanctuary which includes the red-throated diver, Manx shearwater, red-necked phalarope, Arctic skua, and black guillemot. The snowy owl returned to Scotland to breed here in 1967.

The Osprey, just one of 300 species of birds recorded by ornithologists on Fair Isle.

SHIEL BRIDGE, Highland 33 NG91
Beautifully situated at the head of the lovely sea loch Duich, near the clachan of Invershiel, Shiel Bridge lies in the heart of the 15,000-acre Kintail Estate (NTS). Ben Attow rises to 3,383ft in the area, and the famous Five Sisters of Kintail are dominated by Scour Ouran. These peaks lie within the estate. At Shiel Bridge the road descending from the grand defile of Glen Shiel between the Five Sisters to the E and the 3,317ft Saddle to the W, divides. The E fork crosses lovely Loch Duich via a causeway beyond the village, and leads towards Dornie.
The W fork climbs over the well known pass of Mam Rattachan on its way to Glenelg. A road from the Mam Rattachan road skirts the W shore of Loch Duich and passes Glen Shiel Church on its way to Totaig. A passenger ferry from here links with Ardelve.

SHIELDAIG, Highland 32 NG85
This little crofting and fishing village is picturesquely situated on Loch Shieldaig, an inlet of Loch Torridon, with Shieldaig Island (NTS) to the N. A new road links with Torridon at the head of the loch, providing magnificent views of the great Torridon sandstone peaks of 3,456ft Liathach, 3,232ft Ben Alligin, and 2,995ft Beinn Dearg. This route passes near the Falls of Balgy and the head of Loch Damh, with the fine peak of 2,958ft Ben Damh and the cone of 3,060ft Meall a' Chinn Deirg rising to the S. To the SE of Shieldaig is the road to Tornapress, which climbs to over 400ft and then continues to Loch Coultrie. At this point there are wonderful views of Coir Each and Coire na Poite, two wild corries of 2,936ft Beinn Bhan – the highest of the Applecross hills. The rocks of this hill show characteristic horizontal bands of red Torridon sandstone.

A new road which is being built W from this village to Applecross should be completed by the mid 1970's. When finished it will offer fine views over the Inner Sound to the islands of Raasay and Skye.

SILVERBURN, Lothian 47 NT26
Scald Law, the highest of the Pentland Hills at 1,898ft, can be climbed from Silverburn. The hamlet lies at the foot of the hill above the picturesque Loganlee Reservoir.

SKEABOST BRIDGE, Isle of Skye, Highland 32 NG44
A lovely old churchyard can be seen near Skeabost Bridge. The bridge itself spans the River Snizort where it flows into an inlet of Loch Snizort Beag.

SKELMORLIE, Strathclyde 44 NS16
Skelmorlie is a Firth of Clyde resort which affords fine views across to Toward Point and W to the island of Bute. Opposite Skelmorlie in the waters of the firth is a measured mile, where small vessels are tested for speed. Kelly Burn separates Skelmorlie from the neighbouring resort of Wemyss Bay. Parts of Skelmorlie Castle, 1½m S of the resort on the coast road to Largs, date back to 1502.

SKERRAY, Highland 37 NC66
Views towards the islands of Roan and Eilean Co'omb are afforded by this crofting township. The resort offers a sandy beach and has a steamer pier.

SKIPNESS, Strathclyde 29 NR85
Remains of an ancient chapel and a large 13th-c castle can be seen at Skipness, which lies on the E side of the Kintyre

317

peninsula. The settlement faces Kilbrennan Sound and the Sound of Bute, affording fine views of the N half of the island of Arran.

SKIRLING, Borders   25 NT03

An attractive village with a green, Skirling is noted for its wrought-iron work and numerous painted animals and birds that can be seen dotted around the village. This decoration was the idea of Lord Carmichael, who designed the local house in which he lived. Carmichael died in 1926. Skirling once had an ancient castle but this was destroyed in 1568.

SKYE, ISLE OF, Highland   32

The Gaelic description of Skye is *Eilean A' Cheo fo sgail nam beannmor* – 'The Isle of Mist under the shadow of great mountains'. Considered by many to be the loveliest of all Scottish islands, Skye measures some 50m in length and is the largest of the Inner Hebrides group. It is deeply indented by sea-lochs and rocky headlands which form a series of peninsulas. No part of the island is more than 5m from the sea. Mists often envelope the land, adding to its romantic beauty and enshrouding the tops of the famous Cuillin peaks. The Cuillins provide perhaps the best rock scenery in Britain, and nowhere in the country are there finer peaks to climb. The range is partly composed of black gabbro rock, one of the safest climbing rocks in the world owing to its rough surface.

Roads between the chief places of interest have been greatly improved in recent years. Most of the islanders still make their living from crofting and fishing and traditions are very strong. Myth and magic are part of Skye's

heritage. Almost every place on the island has its tales of fairy bridges, fairy cattle, boys kidnapped by fairies, water kelpies etc, but the island's richest store of legend is bound up with its brief encounter with Bonnie Prince Charlie. The prince was loyally assisted by the brave Flora Macdonald, whose grave can be seen at Kilmuir. In 1773 Dr Johnson and Boswell paid a visit to Skye.

The coastline of the island is mainly rocky with a little sand. Some of the finest cliff scenery can be found in the Duirinish district, which is only accessible on foot. Among the most notable sights of Skye are the wild and beautiful Lochs Coruisk and Scavaig, which lie near Elgol; the fantastic rock formations of the Quiraing near Staffin; ancient Dunvegan Castle, seat of the chief of the Clan MacLeod; and the magnificent panoramic view of the Cuillins rising beyond Loch Scavaig, best seen from above Elgol. The easiest route to Skye is from Mallaig via the car-carrying steamer service. The alternative is the Kyle Akin car ferry from Kyle of Lochalsh. Places of interest in Skye have been indexed separately.

SLIGACHAN, Isle of Skye, Highland   32 NG42

This excellent centre for mountaineers, anglers, and geologists is situated near the head of Loch Sligachan. Overlooking the village to the S is the jagged, pinnacled 3,167ft Sgurr nan Gillean – the Hill of Gullies. Boggy Glen Sligachan extends S into the Black Cuillins, and is considered an excellent example of a U-shaped glacial valley. The course of The River Sligachan, on which the village lies, forms the boundary between the black gabbro of the Black Cuillins and

Skirling House is noted for its abundance of curious wrought-iron work.

the pink granite of the Red Cuillins. The latter lie in Lord Macdonald's Forest and include 2,537ft Glamaig and the lovely 2,414ft Marsco. This range forms a striking contrast to the severe, precipitous Black Cuillins.

A path from Sligachan leads down the glen and allows access to several of the well-known Cuillin rock peaks. Farther down the glen a rough, poorly-defined path leads over the Drumhain ridge to spectacular Loch Coruisk in its deep basin below the peaks – a long walk but very worthwhile. From Sligachan a road to the E follows the coast before cutting across the peninsula to Dunan and Broadford. To the N of Sligachan is a good road which runs through Glen Varragill to Portree. Numerous little hillocks of sand and clay along the glen are evidence of ancient glacial action in the region. The path over Bealach a' Mhaim, SW of Sligachan, is the best way of approaching 3,143ft Bruach na Fritle. This wonderful viewpoint is easy to climb. Below the peak lies gloomy Harta Corrie, in which the Bloody Stone commemorates the final clan battle between the Macdonalds and the MacLeods in 1610.

Another good road leads NW from Sligachan and passes through Glen Drynoch to Loch Harport, later reaching the Duirinish and Vaternish peninsulas. The area between these two features is occupied by the famous castle of Dunvegan. Near Loch Harport is a narrow road which branches S from the main road to Glenbrittle, another well-known climbing centre.

SLOCHD SUMMIT, Highland   34 NH82

A road and railway run through lonely Slochd Mor gorge at this point, reaching a summit of some 1,332ft. Slochd Summit is the highest point on the main road between Strath Spey and Inverness.

SMA' GLEN, Tayside   30 NN83

Heatherclad Sma' Glen carries a road linking Crieff with Dunkeld. This highway was originally built by General Wade in 1730, and runs close to the River Almond. Overlooking Sma' Glen on the E side is 1,520ft Dun Mor, topped by a partly vitrified hill fort. Between the road and the river below Dun Mor is Ossian's Stone, which may have once marked the grave of the legendary 3rd-c Gaelic bard and warrior Ossian, son of Fingal. Wordsworth described the stone in verse after it had been moved from its original site by Wade's soldiers.

SMAILHOLM, Borders   26 NT63

Smailholm House dates from 1707 and stands near the church. The most notable feature of the village is the well-preserved 16th-c Smailholm Tower (AM), which lies SW in a wild, romantic situation on a rocky outcrop. This fine, 57ft-high Border pele tower overlooks a wide expanse of countryside, affording particularly lovely views of the triple-peaked Eildon Hills. The land here was acquired by the Scotts of Harden in the 17thc, and Sir Walter Scott himself spent some of his formative years at the nearby farm of Sandyknowe. Obviously much inspired by Smailholm, Scott included it in both the introduction of the third canto of *Marmion* and his ballad *Eve of St John*. Scott last visited

Smailholm a year before he died, when he came here with Turner who sketched Smailholm Tower. Brotherstone Hill carries the ancient Brothers' Stones and the Cow Stone.

SMOO CAVE, Highland   36 NC46
Sir Walter Scott was much impressed with famous Smoo Cave when he came here in 1814. The name Smoo probably comes from *smjuga* meaning a rock. It lies in limestone cliffs on the wild N coast of old Sutherland, and has three vast chambers. The first chamber is 203ft long and can be reached by boat. Only experienced potholers are able to reach the other chambers.

SNIZORT, Isle of Skye, Highland   32 NG45
Snizort is situated on the shores of Loch Snizort Beag. A little SW of the church, on the right bank of the River Haultin, is the noted chambered cairn of Cairn Liath.

SOCIETY, Lothian   46 NT07
It is quite possible that this odd name is a corruption of sea city, because Society lies near Abercorn on the shores of the Firth of Forth.

SOLWAY FIRTH, Dumfries and Galloway   25
Smugglers and pirates once used the waters of the Solway Firth to move contraband. The firth divides the W coast of Scotland from England, and the fast tide makes the sandy beaches dangerous. Criffell rises to 1,868ft and dominates the firth from its position overlooking the Nith estuary. This hill affords views of the firth that also take in the distant Lake District mountains to the S.

SORBIE, Dumfries and Galloway   24 NX44
To the E of this village is the ruined Old Place of Sorbie. The small port of Garlieston lies farther E on Garlieston Bay.

SORN, Strathclyde   25 NS52
Ancient jougs, an iron collar used to punish wrongdoers, still hang in the 17th-c church of this attractive village. External stairs lead to the church's lofts. A little to the NW is Sorn Castle, which dates from 1409. Other parts of the castle were built between 1795 and 1805. A lonely moorland farm to the N of Sorn is where Alexander Peden the preacher was born in the early 17thc. He ended his days as a fugitive in a nearby cave.

SOUTHDEAN, Borders   26 NT60
In 1575 the Redeswire Raid – last of the great Border battles – was fought in Southdean parish. The parish church includes a window in memory of James Thomson, the author of *Rule Britannia*. To the S of Southdean is the Jed Water, and the ruins of Souden Kirk can be seen near the river. James the Earl of Douglas and various other leaders met at the kirk before the Battle of Otterburn in 1388. Relics excavated from the 13th-c church include a super-altar measuring only 9¼in long and with five carved crosses. Numerous prehistoric remains have survived in the vicinity

and Souden Law, rising above the river, is topped by a hill fort. Peel Fell rises to 1,975ft, and with 1,815ft Carter Fell dominates the long line of the Cheviots to the S.

SOUTHEND, Strathclyde   24 NR60
Situated near the S tip of Kintyre, the small resort of Southend offers two sandy beaches. Offshore beyond the Sanda Sound is the little island of Sanda. The ruined chapel of Keil is traditionally the landing place of St Columba (AD 521–97), who came from Ireland with his disciples to convert the Picts to Christianity. A flat stone is imprinted with two right feet known as 'St Columba's foot prints', but they may have been carved to mark the place where pre-Christian chiefs took their tribal vows. Only 100yds away are traces of a Druid altar. Remains of Dunaverty Castle, where some 300 were executed by the Covenanters, are sparse.

SOUTHERNESS, Dumfries and Galloway   25 NX95
Also known as Satterness, this popular little resort offers accommodation in the form of caravans and chalets and has extensive sands. There are golf links in the area. A disused lighthouse stands on Southerness Point overlooking an inlet of the Solway Firth called Gillfoot Bay. Criffell stands at 1,866ft to the N, beyond the village of Kirkbean. Across the Firth are views of the English coast, with the Lake District visible on a clear day.

SOUTH KESSOCK, Highland   34 NH64
Situated on the estuary of the Ness, South Kessock lies 1½m N of Inverness and faces the narrows which divide the waters of the Beauly Firth from the Inner Moray Firth. A car ferry is to be replaced

by a bridge connecting with North Kessock on the opposite shore.

SOUTH UIST, Western Isles   39
See Hebrides, Outer.

SOUTHWICK, Dumfries and Galloway   25 NX95
Lying just off the Kirkbean to Dalbeattie road, Southwick is built on the Southwick Water which meanders SW into the Solway Firth. Offshore are the Mersehead and Barnhourie Sands. To the NE of Southwick rise the the fine viewpoint of 1,866ft Criffell and its 1,632ft spur.

SOUTRA HILL, Borders   47 NT45
Three one-time counties – Berwick, East Lothian, and Midlothian – used to meet near Soutra Hill, a 1,331ft-high viewpoint on the Edinburgh to Lauder road. This road was known to the Romans and stands on the same line as an ancient pilgrims' way. Edward I, Edward II, and James IV all used the route at some time. Evidence of prehistory has been found on the hill. A little to the SW, on a lonely moorland road leading to the valley of the Gala Water, stands Soutra Aisle. These ruins were once a hospice or chapel, probably of 15th-c date and once used by pilgrims. To the SW of Soutra Hill rise the Moorfoot Hills, with the main ridge of the sheep-cropped Lammermuirs extending NE towards the coast near Cockburnspath. The wonderful view from the hill stretches as far S as the Eildon Hills, and away to the NE across the Firth of Forth to the Ochil Hills.

SPEAN BRIDGE, Highland   33 NN28
Thomas Telford built this bridge over the turbulent River Spean in 1819. The

Scott Sutherland's Commando Memorial near the second world war training grounds at Spean Bridge.

river flows W through Glen Spean from the sandy and wooded shores of Loch Laggan, and negotiates this picturesque reach before entering Loch Lochy near Gairlochy. Farther E along Glen Spean lies Roy Bridge. A rough, narrow road leads N from here to the famous parallel roads in Glen Roy. These 'roads' are terraced ledges left over from the Ice Age. From the hamlet of Spean Bridge a road runs SW towards Fort William over a lofty moorland ridge affording magnificent views of the 3,858ft Grey Corries, 3,999ft Aonach Mor, and the great N corries of distant 4,406ft Ben Nevis. The latter are sometimes streaked with snow all year long.

General Wade's military road to Fort Augustus from Fort William crossed a gorge 2m W of Spean Bridge, with the Spean flowing 100ft below. Across the gorge are the remains of a Wade bridge built in 1736 for £1,087 6s 8d. Eleven years later and three days before Prince Charles Edward raised his father's standard at Glenfinnan, a skirmish – probably the first of the '45 Rising – took place by this old bridge.

Repairs carried out on the bridge were not enough to stop part of it collapsing in 1913, and it has remained in the same state ever since. The angle between the A82 and the B8004, 1½m NW of Spean Bridge, contains an impressive memorial by Scott Sutherland to the commandos of the second world war. Some of these were trained in the area. Fine views of Ben Nevis and Lochaber are available from the memorial.

SPEY BAY, Grampian   35 NJ36
This small resort lies at the mouth of the Spey. The river is the second longest in Scotland and is famous for its salmon. Its best-known reaches lie to the SW in the foothills of the Cairngorms, around Grantown-on-Spey and Aviemore.

SPINNINGDALE, Highland   37 NH68
Remains of an 18th-c mill, erected here to relieve poverty following the 1745 Rising, overlook the Dornoch Firth.

SPOTT, Lothian   31 NT67
An old watch house stands near the church gate here, recalling the days when a lookout had to be posted against body snatchers. The old jougs still hang near the door of Spott's modern church, which preserves a beautifully-carved 18th-c pulpit complete with sounding board. At Spott Loan is a Witch's Stone recalling the last witch to be burnt S of the Forth. Traces of prehistoric hut circles, cairns and other remains are to be seen in the vicinity near Spott.

SPRINGFIELD, Dumfries and Galloway   26 NY36
Weavers founded the village of Springfield in 1791, and runaway marriages were performed here during the 19thc. The village stands on the former main road which passed from Carlisle to Glasgow through Longtown. The marriage trade was lost when the A74 road was built in 1830.

SPYNIE PALACE, Grampian   34 NJ26
Slightly to the E of the Elgin to Lossiemouth road, near the shores of little Loch Spynie, are the ruins of this ancient castle of the Bishops of Moray. The prominent square tower of c1470 is known as Davie's Tower, and over the

main entrance to the courtyard are the arms of the early 15th-c Bishop John Innes. The courtyard contains three small towers. Only the churchyard remains of the Church of Spynie, which was once the Cathedral of Moray and stood until 1736.

STAFFA, ISLE OF, Strathclyde   28 NM33
Steamers from Oban can land on this tiny, uninhabited Inner Hebridean island in calm weather. Staffa is famous for its extraordinary caves and basaltic formations, the best known of which is Fingal's Cave – named after the legendary Ossianic giant Finn McCoul. This giant was supposed to have made Staffa and the Giant's Causeway in Northern Ireland. Fingal's Cave measures 227ft long and 66ft high at mean tide, and inspired Mendelssohn's *Hebrides Overture*. Queen Victoria and Prince Albert were brought here by barge in 1847. Smooth black columns of basalt rise out of the sea like great organ pipes at its entrance. The cave's original Gaelic name is An Uamh Ehirn – the musical cave – from the sounds of the sea echoing through its depths.

Staffa has other fascinating caves including the Boat Cave, Mackinnon's Cave, and the remarkable Clam Shell Cave where the columns suggest the ribs of an old wooden ship. Boats usually land on Staffa at Clam Shell Cave, and the nearby Great Causeway is similar to the Giant's Causeway in Northern Ireland. Sir Joseph Banks first publicized Staffa when he visited it on his way to Iceland in 1772, and the first description of the island appeared in Pennant's *Tour in Scotland* in 1774. To the W of Staffa lie the tiny Treshnish islands, the farthest S of which is known as the Dutchman's Cap, because of its shape.

STAFFIN, Isle of Skye, Highland   32 NG46
Staffin Island faces beautifully sandy Staffin Bay, which faces the village of this name. The road S to Portree approaches the very edge of the cliffs and affords good views of the Kilt Rock. The columnar and horizontal beds of basalt in this rock suggest pleats in a kilt – hence the name. Farther along the road, some 2m SE of Staffin, the waters of Loch Mealt tumble over cliffs into the sea. A hydro-electric scheme operates near the road to Portree. To the NW of Staffin the coast road continues round the Trotternish peninsula by way of Flodigarry, and a branch turns inland to climb nearly 900ft on the way to Uig. This road, with its hairpin bend, is one of the most picturesque on Skye and offers the best view of the Quiraing – a splendid group of rocky crags and pinnacles.

STAIR, Strathclyde   24 NS42
Picturesque Stair House is of early 17th-c date and lies in a bend of the River Ayr. The building has been modernized.

STANLEY, Tayside   30 NO13
Campsie Linn rapids lie a little to the NE of this Strathmore village on the River Tay. Kinclaven Castle stands 4½m NE of Stanley off a byroad near the Tay, and is said to have been destroyed in 1336. The rectangular enclosure can still be seen today.

STAXIGOE, Highland   37 ND35
This fishing village includes a small harbour and lies on a rocky stretch of

coast between the Tails of Elzie and Silkey Head. Further N prominent Noss Head reaches out into the sea, overlooking Sinclair's Bay. A little to the SW of Staxigoe is the airport for Wick.

STENTON, Lothian   31 NT67
A 14th-c Rood Well surmounted by a cardinal's hat here has associations with Melrose Abbey. The medieval Wool Stone stands on the village green and was once used for weighing wool at Stenton Fair. Behind the stone is an old dovecot, formerly the tower of an ancient church. To the NE of Stenton the fine old mansion of Biel stands in 16th-c terraced gardens. The house has been modernized.

STEVENSTON, Strathclyde   29 NS24
The ancient industrial town of Stevenston overlooks Irvine Bay in the Firth of Clyde. An old explosives factory at nearby Ardeer now produces chemicals and fertilizers, and accounts for most of the town's industry. Silicone and nylon are also produced in the area.

STEWARTON, Strathclyde   29 NS44
Knitwear is produced at this Annick-Water town.

STEWARTRY, THE, Dumfries and Galloway
Another name for the one-time county of Kirkcudbrightshire, the Stewartry recalls its former jurisdiction by a Royal Steward. The lordship of the Balliols was taken away from the family and held by the Maxwells – as hereditary Royal Stewards – between 1526 and 1747. Old Kirkcudbrightshire and the adjacent obsolete county of Wigtown make up the district of Galloway.

*STIRLING, Central   45 NS79
Known as the Gateway to the Highlands, this historic Royal Burgh stands on a bend of the Forth and was for years of great strategic importance as the sole route to the N of Scotland. Until the opening of the Kincardine-on-Forth bridge in 1936, Stirling was the last place where the river could be crossed before the estuary widens. An arch of the Old Bridge (AM) of c1400, now used for pedestrians only, was blown up in 1745 to prevent the Highlanders reaching the S. Near the Old Bridge at the N end of Stirling is the Stirling Road Bridge. Wallace defeated the Earl of Surrey in 1297 at the Battle of Stirling Bridge, thought to have been a long-vanished wooden structure about 1m upstream.

Stirling is dominated by its imposing Castle (AM), perched on a 250ft rock and overlooking the battlefield of Bannockburn. The building's early years saw savage tussles between the Scots and the English for possession, and Wallace recaptured it from the English in 1297. Edward I took it in 1304 and in 1314 Robert the Bruce fought for it near by at the Battle of Bannockburn. This fight established him on the Scottish throne. Later the castle became a Royal residence. James II and James V were born here in 1430 and 1512, and both Mary Queen of Scots and James VI spent several years in the castle. General Monk took Stirling in 1651 and Prince Charles Edward was unsuccessful in capturing it in 1746. For years the castle has been used as a barracks, and at present is undergoing restoration.

Entries marked * are the starting point of drives included in the Day Drive section of the book (pages 95 to 160).

The structure has frequently been rebuilt, and the oldest parts surviving today date back to the reign of James III in the 15thc. These include the old tower and 125ft-long Parliament Hall. James IV added the fine gatehouse and James V created a splendid Renaissance Palace in the 16thc, turning Stirling Castle into one of the most sumptuous buildings of its type in the land. James VI rebuilt the Chapel Royal for the christening of Prince Henry in 1594, and several early 17th-c wall paintings have survived here. Various relics of interest are housed in the historic Douglas Room, which has been restored. The hereditary keeper of Stirling Castle

is the Earl of Mar and Kellie. A magnificent view extending well into the Highlands can be enjoyed from 420ft-high Queen Victoria's lookout. Another good viewpoint is Ladies' Rock, overlooking the King's Knot (AM) and King's Garden. The Esplanade features a statue of Bruce, and Queen Mary's lookout bears the inscription M R 1561. Stirling Landmark Centre can be visited on the approach to the castle, and depicts life in the town as it was over the past centuries.

Near the Castle gates is the fine Church of the Holy Rude, where Mary Queen of Scots and James VI were crowned as babies. The nave was built c1414 and its

original oak roof has survived. A remarkable five-sided apse is a notable feature of the choir, which was built between 1507 and 1520. The 90ft-high, square battlemented tower bears the scars of a siege held in 1651. This was when General Monk took the castle. Between 1656 and 1936 the nave and and choir were used as two separate churches. An ancient tilting ground between the church and the castle is now a cemetery. A marble representation of the Covenanting Wigtown Martyrs – a woman and a young girl – can be seen here in a glass case. The martyrs were tied to stakes and drowned by the incoming tide of the Solway Firth in 1685.

cont

1	Argyll's Lodging	6	Darnley's House	11	Old Bridge
2	Bruce's Statue	7	Guildhall	12	Smith Institute
3	Cambuskenneth Abbey	8	King's Knot	13	Tollbooth and Mercat Cross
4	Castle	9	Landmark Centre	14	Wallace Monument
5	Church of the Holy Rude	10	Mar's Wark		

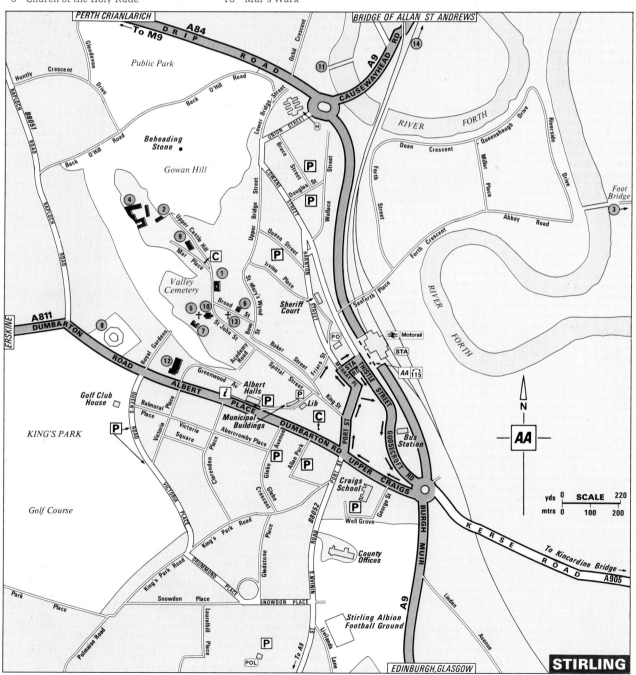

Stirling has a fine Tolbooth dated 1701, and its old Mercat cross has a modern shaft. Several 17th-c houses exist in the town, including Darnley's House which was greatly restored in 1957. Darnley's House may have been the nursery of James VI and his son Prince Henry, but there are stronger associations with the Erskines of Gogar. Argyll's Lodging (AM) was built by the Earl of Stirling in 1630 and was the home of the Marquis of Argyll, the nobleman who crowned Charles II King of Scotland at Scone in 1651. From 1799 to 1963 this mansion was used as a military hospital. Today it is a youth hostel. The 17th-c Guildhall, or Cowane's Hospital, houses old relics and includes a statue of the founder John Cowane. Cowane died in 1634. Pictures and fascinating relics are preserved in the Smith Institute, including several Stirling heads – oaken roundels taken from the ceiling of the King's Presence Chamber in Stirling Castle. In Broad Street is the unfinished Mar's Wark (AM), which was started in 1570. This was to have been the town house of the Regent Mar, and carries Royal Arms and several curious inscriptions above the entrance.

A little beyond Stirling Bridge is Causewayhead, overlooked by the 362ft-high Abbey Craig which is topped by the famous pinnacled Wallace Monument. This commemorates Sir William Wallace, who defeated the English army at the Battle of Stirling Bridge in 1297 and became ruler of Scotland. Built in 1869 at a cost of £16,000, the tower includes a statue of Wallace and preserves a two-handed sword said to have belonged to the Scottish patriot. However, historians say this type of sword is not known to have been used by knights until the late 15thc. Wallace cleared the English out of Perth, Stirling, and Lanark, but was defeated at Falkirk in 1298 and executed in London in 1305.

Bruce held a Scottish parliament at Cambuskenneth, 1m NE of Stirling near one of the bends of the River Forth, in 1326. Fragments of Cambuskenneth Abbey (AM), which was founded in 1147 by the Augustinians, can still be seen. The best-preserved portion is a fine late 13th-c detached tower which can still be climbed and affords an excellent view. James III and his Queen were buried in front of the abbey's high altar, and Queen Victoria unveiled a monument to their memory 1864.

STOBHALL, Tayside   30 NO13
Ancient home of the Drummonds, a picturesque group of buildings around a courtyard stands on a ridge above the E bank of the Tay at Stobhall. The house consists of a chapel and tower of 1578. The chapel preserves the old Holy Water stoup and the aumbry – a small cupboard for altar vessels – with its original door. Above the painted ceiling is a loft. Millais the painter lived at Stobhall for a time. Near by is an 18th-c dower-house, and attached to it is a gateway with a heraldic panel. This leads to the enclosure. Campsie Linn rapids lie SW of Stobhall.

STOBO, Borders   26 NT13
A restored Norman church with 16th- and 17th-c additions overlooks the Tweed in this little hamlet. Over the 13th-c doorway is a barrel-vaulted porch where the jougs, an iron collar for wrongdoers, still hang. Stobo Castle lies a little to

the SW and was restored in the 19thc. Across the river is Dawyck House, situated near the remarkable Dawyck Woods. This is some of the best-known woodland in Scotland. Carl von Linne, the 18th-c Swedish naturalist, came to the house to visit his pupil Sir James Naesmyth. After the visit Naesmyth introduced many species of tree – including the larch – into Scotland. Dawyck Woods contain huge old Douglas firs, a pinetum, plus a wealth of Chinese rhododendrons and other shrubs and trees.

STOCKIE MUIR, Central   45 NS48
Glimpses of Loch Lomond can sometimes be seen to the NW from this lofty moorland, which affords panoramic views. A little to the W are the slopes of 1,171ft Auchineden Hill, which include a curious chasm known as the Whangie.

STOER, Highland   36 NC02
Remotely situated on the lovely but narrow and hilly road linking Lochinver with Kylesku, Stoer is surrounded by dozens of tiny lochans. Many of these abound with fish. Bathing is offered by the sandy shores of the Bay of Stoer, and SE off the Lochinver road is sandy Achmelvich Bay. The rocky inlet of Loch Roe is situated near by. Views inland include the strange, isolated, red Torridon sandstone of one-time Sutherland's mountains, which are best seen from Cnoc Poll. This low hill lies to the NW of Stoer. The Torridon peaks include 2,653ft Quinag, 2,779 Canisp, and the double-peaked 2,399ft Suilven. Beyond Cnoc Poll lies the Stoer peninsula, at the end of which the Rhu Stoer and the Point of Stoer lie each side of a rock pillar known as the Old Man of Stoer.

STONEHAVEN, Grampian   35 NO88
Lovely cliff scenery lies to the N and S of this fishing port and holiday resort, which has a stone and shingle beach. Stonehaven offers good fishing both in the sea and along the Carron Water. The river divides the old and new parts of the town, and just before entering the sea is joined by the Cowie Water which flows through a lovely glen from lonely hills to the W. The 16th-c Tolbooth stands on the quay and is a former storehouse of the Earls Marischal. It was later a court and prison. From 1748 to 1749 it held episcopal ministers, who baptized children through the windows. The Tolbooth has since been modernized and now houses a museum. In summer it becomes a restaurant. A plaque on a house at the S end of Market Square marks the birthplace of Robert William Thomson (1822–1873), inventor of the pneumatic tyre, the fountain pen, and the dry dock. Every June a veteran car rally is held in his memory. Near the harbour stands the Mercat cross and an 18th-c steeple where the Old Pretender was proclaimed king in 1715. Fireballs made from tallowed rope are carried through the town at Hogmanay.

From Stonehaven the Slug Road runs NW past Fetteresso Forest and over the hills to Banchory, reaching 800ft near Durris Forest. To the N of this road, some 4m from the town is the Roman Camp of Raedykes. The Romans used the Elsick Mounth road, which lies E of the camp and runs from Stonehaven to the Dee Valley.

STORNOWAY, Western Isles   38 NB43
See Hebrides, Outer.

STORR, THE, Isle of Skye, Highland 32 NG45
This 10m-long ridge along the Trotternish peninsula rises to 2,000ft in height and is precipitous in many places to the E. The lofty 2,360ft Storr plateau includes wild crags and dominates the ridge, offering magnificent views S to the splendid Cuillin range. The views also extend farther W over the Minch to the Outer Hebrides, and E towards the Applecross mountains on the mainland. The well-known Old Man of Storr, a detached 160ft pinnacle of rock beneath the Storr, was not climbed until 1955. Good views of The Storr are offered by a road running N from Portree. This actually passes beneath the cliffs of the ridge. Also on this road are the Storr Lochs, now harnessed to a hydro-electric scheme.

STOW, Borders   31 NT44
Stow lies on the Gala Water and includes a fine pack-horse bridge dating from 1655. The old church is ruined, and the modern church carries a 140ft-high spire. It is said that King Arthur once routed the Saxons in this area, which at one time was called the Stow of Wedale. He later founded a church as a thanksgiving. A delightful road from Stow climbs to over 1,100ft across moorland before descending to Lauder. To the W of Stow rises 2,161ft Windlestraw Law, where the one-time counties of Midlothian, Selkirk, and Peebles met.

STRACHAN, Grampian   35 NO69
Strachan is situated near the meeting of the Water of Feugh and the Water of Dye. The Dye flows along the long valley of Glen Dye, which can be followed via the famous road which climbs over the Cairn o' Mounth. Kerloch rises to 1,747ft SE of Strachan, and the vast Forest of Birse stretches W of the village towards the lonely hills on the old Angus/Aberdeen border. Some 12m W of Strachan is the partly 16th-c Castle of Birse, which was once the home of the Gordons of Clunie.

STRACHUR, Strathclyde   29 NN00
Chopin once visited Strachur, a small resort in the Cowal peninsula lying near Loch Fyne. A pier lies about 1m NW, and the loch hereabouts measures almost 600ft in depth. The former seat of the McArthur Campbells dates from c1783. A road from Strachur leads inland to Loch Eck, a long and narrow sheet of water surrounded by hills. The highest of these are 2,557ft Beinn Bheula to the NE and 2,433ft Beinn Mhor.

STRAITON, Strathclyde   24 NS30
This attractive Carrick village lies on the Water of Girvan. Straiton's restored church preserves a pre-Reformation aisle. To the E off the Dalmellington road is the lovely glen of the Lambdoughty Burn, made splendid by its attractive waterfalls. One of these is known as the Rossetti Linn, and was much admired by Dante Gabriel Rossetti while he was staying at Penkill Castle, near Dailly. A narrow, hilly road climbs S over moorland from Straiton and leads towards Rowantree, reaching a height of 1,421ft. Views from the road encompass 2,520ft Shalloch on Minnoch to the SE, with

remote Loch Macaterick beyond. Just W of the village near the Water of Girvan stands the old mansion of Blairquhan.

*STRANRAER, Dumfries and Galloway 24 NX06

Old Wigtownshire's largest town, Stranraer is the terminal of the 35m crossing from Larne in Northern Ireland. The town lies in the Rhinns of Galloway at the head of Loch Ryan and was known as *Rerigonius Sinus* by the Romans. Facilities include a marine lake, paddling pools, a rock garden, and parks. Stranraer Castle lies in the centre of the town and is probably of early 16th-c date. Some 17th-c work is evident, and the structure was long used as a jail. Graham of Claverhouse is said to have lived here in 1682 while conducting his campaigns of religious persecution against the Covenanters. Near the pier is a hotel called the North West Castle, once the home of the Arctic explorer

Sir John Ross in (1777–1856). Stranraer was the home port of the cross-channel steamer 'Princess Victoria', which went down in a great storm in January 1953.

STRATHAVEN, Strathclyde 30 NS74

Prosperity first came to Strathaven during the Middle Ages, when its silk industry was founded. It now produces rayon and knitwear goods. Extensive lofty moorland stretches away to the W, and an ancient bridge spans Powmillon Burn. This river threads its way through the town to join the Avon Water to the SE. Strathaven Castle is a 15th-c ruin overlooking the burn and is also known as Avondale Castle. It was last occupied by the Duchess of Hamilton in the 17thc. Dungavel House, once the shooting lodge of the Dukes of Hamilton, is now a training centre for miners. To the W of the town on the Kilmarnock road is Lauder Ha', Sir Harry Lauder's home until his death in 1950.

STRATHBLANE, Central 45 NS57

Situated on the Blane Water, this small resort lies at the foot of the Strathblane Hills and the higher Campsie Fells. Earl's Seat rises to 1,896ft and is the highest point of the range. About 1m E on the Ballagan Burn are falls known as the Spout of Ballagan. Partly 15th-c Duntreath Castle preserves its medieval stocks and dungeons and lies some 2m NW of Strathblane off the Killearn road.

STRATHCARRON STATION, Highland 33 NG94

Attadale Forest's lonely hills include 2,612ft Beinn Dronnaig and overlook Strathcarron Station, which lies just S of the Inverness to Kyle of Lochalsh road. The NE end of Loch Carron lies about 1m SE of the station.

STRATHDON, Grampian 35 NJ31

At Strathdon the angling River Don is joined by the Water of Nochty, which

1 Castle   2 North West Castle Hotel

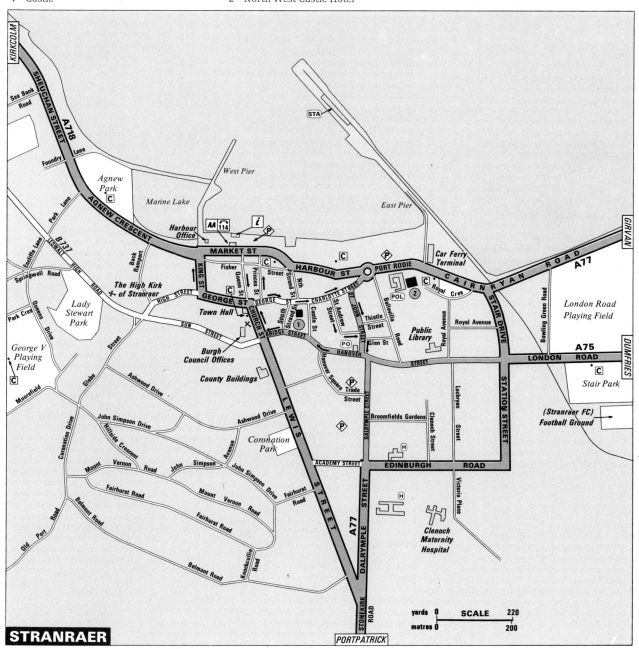

STRANRAER

flows down from the Ladder Hills. The spire of the local church can be seen for miles around, and just SW of the village the Don is spanned by the Poldullie Bridge of 1715. The river and hill country around Strathdon is particularly lovely. The Lonach Highland Gathering is usually held here in mid August. Colquhonnie Castle dates from the 16thc and was never completed. Its ruins can be seen 1½m ESE near the Don. Fine views are afforded by the summit of 1,213ft Tillypronie Hill, which lies 7m SE of Strathdon on the road to Cambus O'May.

STRATHKANAIRD, Highland   36 NC10
This village lies in the valley of Strathkanaird between the remote Rhidorroch Forest and the Coigach Hills. The picturesque Ullapool to Inchnadamph road crosses the valley, and SW of the village it skirts the shores of Loch Kanaird. Isle Martin lies just offshore of this loch. The N side of the Kanaird River estuary, W of Strathkanaird, carries a ruined broch known as Dun Canna. The distant Coigach district is dominated by 2,438ft Ben More Coigach.

STRATHLACHLAN, Strathclyde   29 NS09
Near here Castle Lachlan stands in woodland on Lachlan Bay, a little inlet of Loch Fyne. The road 2m NE of Strathlachlan climbs over the hills of Cowal and descends towards the long and pleasant valley of Glendarnel.

STRATHMIGLO, Fife   30 NO21
Stones from an ancient castle owned by Sir William Scott of Balwearie were used to build the spired Tolbooth of 1734. The parish of Strathmiglo includes some late 18th-c weavers' cottages, and to the S of Strathmiglo are the Lomond Hills. Some 3m NW of the village is 15th-c Balvaird Castle.

STRATHMORE, Tayside and Central
Sited between the foothills of the Grampians to the N and the gentle Sidlaw Hills to the S, the long Vale of Strathmore includes many fine farms and is the home of the championship black Aberdeen Angus breed of beef cattle. These animals do not have horns. To the SE of Strathmore a road runs parallel with the Tay, then later continues alongside a tributary of the Tay called the Isla. Farther NW Strathmore is known as the Howe of Angus. The vale can be seen at its best from the battlements of Glamis Castle, the ancestral home of the Queen Mother's family and birthplace of Princess Margaret.

STRATH NAVER, Highland
In the early 19thc the lonely valley of Strath Naver, which stretches from Altnaharra on Loch Naver to the coast at Bettyhill, became depopulated by the Highland Clearances. The valley is rich in prehistoric remains, and the salmon River Naver was known to Ptolemy – a historian from ancient Greece.

STRATHPEFFER, Highland   33 NH45
European royalty first popularized Strathpeffer in the 19thc, when they came here for the chalybeate springs (see inset opposite). The town shelters in a wooded setting to the N of Strath Conon and is now a well-known Highland resort. It forms a good centre for touring Easter Ross and the Black Isle, and for exploring the beautiful mountains and lochs of Wester Ross. A fierce clan battle was fought at Strathpeffer in 1478, and the Eagle Stone marks the battlefield. Turreted Castle Leod stands 1m N, and dates from 1616 but shows later alterations. Farther N rises the great 3,429ft Ben Wyvis, the highest mountain in Easter Ross and a prominent landmark for miles around. Views from its summit encompass both the North Sea and the Atlantic. Knockfarril is a vitrified fort on the ridge of Druim Chat, to the E of Strathpeffer.

STRATH SPEY, Highland
Speyside, or Strath Spey, is the name given to the wide lower valley of the Spey, which flows partly along the old Banff/Moray border to reach the sea at Spey Bay. The Spey is an important salmon river which also yields sea trout and brown trout. Its pools are well defined and easily accessible. In summer the river is the centre of a pearl-fishing industry – one out of every 100 mussels scooped up from the river bed contains a pearl. The swift-flowing waters of the Spey serve several distilleries and contribute to the quality of Scotch whisky. The upper Spey rises near the Monadhliath mountains, entering Strath Spey as it flows NE down the valley between these mountains and the lofty Cairngorms.

STRATHY, Highland   37 NC86
Strathy lies inland from Strathy Bay and was once known for its flagstone quarries. Prehistoric remains can be seen on the W bank of the Strathy Water, and W of the bay is a peninsula which ends at cave-pocked Strathy Point. A lighthouse was erected here in 1958. Strathy Bog national nature reserve covers 120 acres and lies 8m SSW of the village.

STRATHYRE, Central   30 NN51
Lying in the heart of hills that were graphically described by Scott in *Lady of the Lake* and *Legend of Montrose*, Strathyre is a little summer resort popular with people who like to walk in the surrounding countryside. A large forest has been planted near the village, and the small forest centre and museum are of interest. In 1968 a hurricane blew down 80,000 young trees. An old bridge spans the Balvaig Burn, which flows through Strathyre, and narrow Loch Lubnaig is noted for its fishing. This water stretches S from the village, and its wooded E shore is bordered by a road which leads towards the Pass of Leny, where the River Leny rushes through a narrow gorge. At the S end of the loch a tiny churchyard lies on the site of St Bride's Chapel, with Ben Ledi rising to 2,875ft across the water. Some of the highest peaks near Strathyre include 3,189ft Stuc a' Chroin to the E and 2,685ft Ben Vane to the SW.

STRICHEN, Grampian   35 NJ95
Mormond Hill rises to 749ft 2m NE of Strichen, and is the only high point in the flat Buchan country. A White Horse carving which dates from 1700 can be seen on the hill's S slopes, and a later carving of a stag was produced on the hill's E slopes in 1870. The latter has been partly obliterated by undergrowth.

STROMA, Highland   37 ND37
Few people now live on this small island in the turbulent Pentland Firth. It lies between the mainland and the Orkneys, and E are the smaller Pentland Skerries.

STROME FERRY, Highland   33 NG83
In 1970 a road built along the S side of Loch Carron replaced the car ferry by joining with the N shore road beyond the head of the loch. Telford built the road leading to the N shore, and in 1819 he and the poet Southey were the first to travel the highway in a wheeled carriage. Remains of Strome Castle (NTS) overlook the N shores of the loch. This ancient stronghold was destroyed in 1609 after a long siege. Fine views of the distant Cuillin range on the island of Skye can be enjoyed from here. The road which runs S from Strome climbs steeply before descending to Strath Ascaig.

STROMNESS, Orkney Isles   40 HY20
See Orkney Isles.

STRONACHLACHAR, Stirling   29 NN41
A road S from this village leads past Loch Chon to Aberfoyle, and a little road W skirts the shores of Loch Arklet before reaching Loch Lomond at Inversnaid within 4m. Stronachlachar itself boasts a steamer pier. A path from the village leads NW to the lonely house of Glengyle, situated in a glen of the same name. This was the birthplace of Rob Roy, the famous freebooter immortalized by Scott in 1671.

STRONE, Strathclyde   44 NS18
Strone is a small holiday resort situated where the waters of Loch Long and the Holy Loch meet. Strone Point is the site of a steamer pier and faces across the mouth of Holy Loch to Hunter's Quay. To the N, almost adjoining Strone, is the little resort of Blairmore.

STRONTIAN, Argyll   32 NM86
Rare minerals found in the vicinity of this village during the 18thc included Strontium – the radioactive form of which is present in nuclear fallout. Strontian lies in a lovely position at the E end of long Loch Sunart, which divides the districts of Sunart and Ardnamurchan from Morven to the S. The River Strontian flows between the mountains of Sunart and Ardgour and joins Loch Sunart from a glen to the N.

Deserted lead mines and the Arriendle Forest nature reserve can be seen here. Scotstown, 2m N of Strontian, is one of the glen's hamlets and recalls lead miners who came here in the 18thc from the Lowlands. The 2,774ft Ben Resipol can be scaled from the glen and affords magnificent views of Loch Shiel to the N and Morven to the S. A fine road which runs W of Strontian passes along the N shore of Loch Sunart and continues through beautiful wooded scenery on the way to Salen.

STRUAN, Tayside   34 NN86
Situated at the junction of Glens Garry and Erochy, Struan is divided from Calvine in the N by the River Garry, which features well-known falls and a salmon leap. Calvine stands on the main Perth to Inverness road. A little to the E of this village are the fine Falls of Bruar. These falls lie in Glen Bruar, with the upper fall a short way up the glen. Hikers can take a path through Glen Bruar, which is dominated to the E by 3,304ft Beinn Dearg rising from the Forest of Atholl hills. This path crosses

the lonely hills of wild Gaick Forest and runs through the remote Minigaig Pass as far as Kingussie in the Spey valley. The Clan Donnachie has associations with Struan, and a clan museum at Calvine exhibits relics from the 1715 and 1745 Risings. Clans Reid, Robertson, MacConnachie, Duncan, and MacInroy make up Clan Donnachie. The road W from Struan passes through Glen Erochy

TAKING THE WATERS
But for the Jacobite rebellion of 1745, the healing waters of Strathpeffer might never have been widely known, and Britain's most northerly spa might never have been built. After the Jacobites' defeat, the estates of the Earl of Cromartie were among those forfeited to the government. A report about a healing well resorted to by local people had been forwarded in 1772 to the Royal Society in London, but its most enthusiastic advocate was Colin Mackenzie, the government factor on the Cromartie estates.

In 1777 Mackenzie urged that a village should be built near the well. He knew of two people 'both so lame and feeble that they were obliged to be carried to the well on feather beds on carts; but by the use of the water for some weeks they so far recovered as to be able to walk upon their own legs for miles'. Nothing official was done, although Highland people continued to favour the well. In a short time the Earl of Cromartie was restored to his estates, and there was no longer a government interest.

By 1810 the well was beginning to be neglected. Then a Dr Thomas Morrison found that the water cured his own ailments, decided to settle in the place, and in 1819 built a pump room over what was known as the Strong Well. There was still little in the way of accommodation for visitors, but with professional attention now available modern Strathpeffer began slowly to grow up.

The once-prosperous spa buildings at Strathpeffer have been considerably reduced in recent years, but still entertain the occasional customer.

and climbs to over 1,000ft before heading to the Tummel valley and Kinloch Rannoch.

STRUIE HILL, Highland   37 NH68
This lofty hill overlooks the waters of Dornoch Firth and is an AA viewpoint. The panorama from its summit takes in glimpses of the distant Ben More Assynt to the NW.

In 1861 a stone pump room replaced Dr Morrison's original wooden building. Ten years later a second storey was added. In 1881 a range of ladies' baths was built to cater for the increasing trade. By that time the Countess of Cromartie, owner of the estate, had married the Duke of Sutherland. Both interested themselves in Strathpeffer's development into a health resort and a place of some fashion. Also in 1881 the Duchess opened a spa pavilion, where dances and concerts were held, there was a reading-room and a billiards-room, and visitors could promenade in wet weather.

In June 1862 Strathpeffer's out-of-the-way situation for a spa had been greatly improved by the opening of the Dingwall and Skye Railway, which had a station not far from the village. The line might have come right through Strathpeffer but for fierce opposition from landowners, which prevented the railway from taking the obvious easy line through the village, and forced it through the hills to the north. In June 1885 a branch line was opened, with a terminus on the edge of Strathpeffer itself.

The spa entered into its greatest period. More houses and hotels were built, all keeping the same pleasant atmosphere. The baths and pavilion gardens occupied two sides of the village square, and the imposing Highland Hotel towered over it from a hill. Visitors could take their choice from a variety of sulphur springs or sample a chalybeate well. Medical directories were published, giving full details of the available cures and treatments. Peat baths were introduced to Britain here in 1887. In addition there were immersion baths, sulphur baths, and a Strathpeffer invention with the forbidding title of 'low-pressure subthermal reclining manipulation douche'.

STRUY BRIDGE, Highland   33 NH44
The River Farrar joins the River Glass to form the Beauly River near Struy Bridge. Immediately to the NE of the bridge is modernized Erchless Castle, once the seat of the head of Clan Chisholm. Large numbers of the clan emigrated to America or Canada in the 18th and 19thc. Delightful Strath Glass extends to the SW and is threaded by a river. The

A fine golf course was built, for Strathpeffer was never intended simply for invalids. There were strenuous walks in the hills and woods, and the social whirl continued. Carriages would gather in the village square so that visitors from all over Britain could hear the resident orchestra play in the bandstand, although it retreated to the pavilion in wet weather.

An English syndicate took over the spa and continued to increase its facilities, even though the appeal of taking the waters dwindled as the 20thc advanced. During the second world war the main baths building suffered the indignity of being turned into a weapons store, while the biggest hotels housed army trainees. After the war the spa buildings were restored, and for a time hopes were high for a return to the old splendour. But times had changed. The grand pump room was dismantled, and became what looks like an ordinary part of the village square. That it is by no means ordinary can be seen by watchful visitors who notice that parts of the car park are surfaced with tiles – the original flooring of the pump room. A small tourist information centre is actually built on top of one of the old baths, as can be seen by the circular stonework which supports it.

The pavilion remains, among its gardens, and has a new reputation for Highland cabarets. In the grounds is a smaller pump room opened in 1909. It was closed at the start of the second world war and restored in 1960. Sulphur water is still sold there, and the interior is complete with its original white and green tiling and cane furniture.

Strathpeffer is still a restful holiday resort, and there are regular customers for the spa water. In fine surroundings, and as closely grouped as ever about the village square, it remains 'a Victorian period-piece with the charm of an Indian hill station'.

Now a museum, this thatched house was once the venue for the Bachelor's Club formed by Robert Burns.

roads on both sides of the valley meet near Cannich. A private road runs down the long and beautiful Glen Strathfarrar, which lies W of Struy Bridge and has been subject to hydro-electric developments.

The valley penetrates deep into 3,000ft-plus mountains, extending as far as lonely Loch Monar. Beyond the loch stretches West Monar Forest, where 3,452ft Sgurr a' Chaorachain faces towards the remote Glencarron Forest. Ptolemy of Alexandria, the early historian, mentions the River Farrar in his writings.

SWANSTON, Lothian   47 NT26
Robert Louis Stevenson spent many holidays here between 1867 and 1881. Swanston Cottage was the Stevensons' summer home. Relics belonging to the writer, who mentions the hamlet in *St Ives* among other novels, are preserved here. The Caerketton and Allermuir Hills form part of the Pentland range and overlook Swanston from the S.

SWINTON, Borders   31 NT84
Swinton's Church houses a tomb which is thought to originate from *c*1200. The Mercat cross of 1769 displays several sundials.

SYMINGTON, Strathclyde   24 NS33
Interesting historical features in Symington town include the church's three round-headed, 12th-c windows and ancient open-work timber roof. The main building has been greatly reconstructed. Nearby Bogend features an old toll-house and ruined Craigie Castle. The latter lies to the NE and was a Wallace stronghold.

SYMINGTON, Strathclyde   25 NS93
Quothquan Law rises to 1,097ft N of this village, beyond the River Clyde. The 2,335ft Tinto Hill is a prominent landmark to the W of Symington, and views from its summit encompass the mountains of the Lake District and the coast of Northern Ireland. On the E slopes of Tinto Hill is ruined Fatlips Castle, former seat of the Lockharts.

SYRE, Highland   37 NC64
Ruined prehistoric brochs and hut circles can be seen in the Strath Naver Valley to the N and S of Syre Church. To the N at Skail a stone commemorates the founding of the 93rd Sutherland Highlanders, who fought at Balaclava. Lonely little Loch Syre lies to the W of Syre Church, and farther W beyond Loch Loyal is the fine multi-peaked Ben Loyal. This 2,504ft peak is best seen from around Tongue.

TAIN, Highland   37 NH78
Tain is an ancient Royal Burgh which stands on the Dornoch Firth. Its 17th-c Tolbooth has a peal of bells, and the restored market cross stands near by. The town also features two ruined chapels dedicated to St Duthac, who died in 1065 and was buried in Ireland. His remains were later transferred to the chapel which lies in the churchyard and was destroyed by fire in 1427. The nearby collegiate Church of St Duthac was built in 1371 by William, Earl and Bishop of Ross. It is of decorated style and displays fine fenestration.

The wife and daughter of Robert the Bruce sought sanctuary in the second chapel during 1306, but were later given up to Edward I. Remains of this chapel can be seen near the golf links. James IV made regular pilgrimages to Tain and travelled along a route now followed by the road which runs S from the town and crosses Glen Aldie in the direction of Logie Easter. This road is still called King's Causeway. It is also known that James V travelled this way on foot in 1527. Loch Eye and the ruins of Lochslin Castle lie to the E of Tain. A large expanse of sandy links lying to the N of Loch Eye and bordering the Dornoch Firth is known as Morrich More.

TALISKER, Isle of Skye, Highland   32 NG33
The well-known Talisker malt whisky distillery is situated just outside the village of Carbost on the W shores of Loch Harport. It can be reached via the B8009 off the Sligachan to Bracadale

road. At Carbost a rough and narrow road leads over hills to Talisker Bay, with impressive Preshal More rising to the S of the road. To the S of the bay is a magnificent range of cliffs which can only be reached on foot. The road round the W shores of Loch Harport branches 3m NW of Talisker. The W fork leads towards Fiskavaig Bay, and the NW fork continues almost to Ardtreck Point.

TANNADICE, Tayside   31 NO45
A small village situated in the fertile Vale of Strathmore, Tannadice lies on the South Esk River and affords views of the nearby Hill of Finhaven. This height is surmounted by a vitrified iron-age fort.

TARBERT, Western Isles   38 NB43
See Hebrides, Outer

*TARBERT, Strathclyde   29 NR86
Tarbert is the centre of the Loch Fyne herring fishing industry and lies on the tiny ithsmus on the shores of East Loch Tarbert. This little neck of land links Knapdale and Kintyre, and divides the loch from West Loch Tarbert. Magnus Barefoot of Norway is said to have been dragged in a galley across the 2m isthmus in 1093. Hills almost encircle Tarbert and its harbour, with Sliabh Gaoil rising to 1,840ft in the hills of South Knapdale to the NW. Tarbert offers good sands and bathing, and the ruins of a 14th-c castle overlook the harbour. This was once the stronghold of Robert the Bruce, and later of James II.

Car ferries to Islay sail from Kennacraig, 4m SW on beautiful West Loch Tarbert. Roads encircle the 10m loch, and the sometimes hilly N shore road leads towards the waters of the Sound of Jura and Loch Killisport, passing Kilberry Castle on the way. This was the seat of the Campbells of Kilberry for 500 years, and several late-medieval sculptured stones can be seen here. The road along the S shore follows the W coast of the Kintyre peninsula, and affords views of the island of Gigha before it eventually reaches Campbeltown.

TARBET, Strathclyde   29 NN30
King Haakon of Norway dragged his ships from Tarbet on Loch Lomond across the narrow strip of land to Arrochar on Loch Long when laying waste the countryside in 1263. Views E from the resort of Tarbet extend across Loch Lomond and take in the fine peak of 3,192ft Ben Lomond. To the W beyond Loch Long is 2,891ft Ben Arthur, popularly known as The Cobbler. The road leading N along Loch Lomond's W shores passes Inveruglas power station of the Loch Sloy hydro-electric scheme.

TARBOLTON, Strathclyde   24 NS42
From 1777 to 1784 the Burns family lived near Tarbolton at Lochlea Farm, and it was here that the poet's father died. The town was enlivened at this time by the Bachelors' Club, a debating society founded in 1780 by Burns and his friends at a house (NTS) which still stands. A year earlier Burns attended dancing classes at the same house, and was initiated as a freemason here in 1781. The thatched house now contains a Burns museum exhibiting relics mostly from the Lochlea period.

Tarbolton's church includes stone stairs leading to a loft, and carries a 90ft spire. The tall 19th-c Barnweil Monument stands

2m N of the town and commemorates the burning of the Barns of Ayr by William Wallace. John Knox preached in Barnweil Church, which now lies in ruins. Willie's Mill stands on the Water of Foil to the NE of Tarbolton and has associations with Burns. Montgomerie and the village of Failford, further downstream, are also connected with the poet. Burns' *Highland Mary* – ie Mary Campbell – was in service at 19th-c Montgomerie House. The house was originally known as Coilsfield, from the tradition that 'Auld King Coil' was killed here by Fergus King of the Scots.

TARFSIDE, Tayside   35 NO47
The Water of Tarf joins the North Esk River here, amid the foothills of the Eastern Grampians and in the lovely valley of Glen Esk. Near by at Glenesk is a tiny museum called The Retreat. A lofty walkers' track known as the Fir Mounth Road leads N through hills and crosses a flank of 2,435ft Hill of Cat. It then heads towards Glen Tanner and Aboyne. To the NE of Tarfside is 2,555ft Mount Battock, near the old boundaries of one-time Angus, Kincardine, and Aberdeen. Mount Keen rises to 3,077ft and forms a prominent feature NW of the village.

TARLAND, Grampian   35 NJ40
Alastrean House was originally called the House of Cromar and is situated on the NE fringe of the village. This was given to the Royal Air Force by the late Lady MacRobert in memory of her three sons killed during the second world war. Near the village is Culsh earthwork, a large iron-age chamber and entrance which has its roofing slabs intact. On the Aberdeen road 4m NE of Tarland rises the Slack of Tillylodge, providing lovely views W towards 2,862ft Morven and the distant Cairngorms. About 1m farther lies ruined Corse Castle, which was built in 1581. Patrick Forbes, who owned an earlier structure in the early 16thc, was said to have been visited by the Devil who carried off the front of the castle after an argument. Remains of Coull Castle lie on a rocky knoll near a church off the Aboyne road, 3m SE of Tarland. Also in the vicinity is the stone circle of Tomnaverie (AM), probably of bronze-age origin.

TARVES, Grampian   35 NJ83
In the 19thc the Duthie family perfected the famous Collynie breed of shorthorn cattle here. Tolquhon Castle (AM) lies 2m S off the B9004, and was once a seat of the Forbes family. This interesting ruin comprises an early 15th-c rectangular tower and a large quadrangular mansion, built between 1584 and 1589. Other features include two round towers with grated windows, a fine carved panel over the door, and a courtyard.

TAYINLOAN, Strathclyde   28 NR64
A passenger ferry links Tayinloan, on the W side of the Kintyre peninsula, with the island of Gigha across the Sound of Gigha.

TAYNUILT, Strathclyde   29 NN03
Splendid views of 3,689ft Ben Cruachan and the mountains overlooking Upper Loch Etive are afforded by the area around Taynuilt. This small resort lies beside the village of Bonawe on the narrows of lovely Loch Etive. Near Muckairn Church is a monument erected

to Lord Nelson before his remains were returned to England. To the SE of Taynuilt a road crosses the River Awe to enter the gloomy Pass of Brander and reach the Falls of Cruachan. Wooded Glen Nant stretches S from Taynuilt and is traversed by the road to Kilchrenan. A hazardous road with gates and sharp bends runs SW from the resort by way of Glen Lonan, passing near Loch Nell before reaching Oban.

TAYPORT, Fife   31 NO42
Tayport was originally called Ferry-Port-on-Craig and overlooks the Firth of Tay. The ferry to Broughty is no longer operated. Tayport's church was rebuilt in 1794 and carries a 17th-c tower. Scotscraig, a mansion to the SW below Hare Law, preserves an archway dated 1667. This bears the crest of Archbishop Sharp, who once lived here and was murdered at Magus Muir by Covenanters in 1679. Tents Moor lies to the SE of Tayport, with the Morton Lochs on its W extremity. A national nature reserve of 47 acres surrounds the lochs, an important breeding ground and resting place for migratory birds. Corsican pinewoods, part of which make up the 92-acre Tentsmuir Point national nature reserve, enclose the Morton Lochs area.

TAYVALLICH, Strathclyde   28 NR78
This village lies on a small inlet of tree-shrouded Loch Sween in the Knapdale district. The road SW from Tayvallich ends at Keills, and beyond a small neck of land to the W of the village is Carsaig Bay on the Sound of Jura.

TEANGUE, Isle of Skye, Highland   32 NG60
The hamlet of Teangue faces Knock Bay, an inlet of the Sound of Sleat, in the fertile Sleat peninsula. A rocky headland above the bay carries the ruins of Knock Castle or Castle Camus, an ancient stronghold of the Macdonalds. A story tells how John Ban MacPherson defended the castle single handed against a band of the MacLeods of Dunvegan c 1620. Fine views from

the castle extend towards the mainland mountains. About 1m NW of Teangue a hilly road crosses the Sleat peninsula to Ord, on Loch Eishort.

TEMPLE, Lothian   47 NT35
In the early Middle Ages Temple was the chief Scottish seat of the Knights Templar. When the order was suppressed in 1312 the property passed to the knights of St John of Jerusalem. The main feature of the village, which lies on the steep banks of the South Esk River, is the roofless 13th- to 14th-c church. Features of this include a 17th-c east gable belfry. The churchyard of the modern church contains an unusual gravestone to the Rev James Goldie, giving details of his will. Deuchar's Arch lies E of the village and is the sole remaining fragment of a large mansion. Large Gladhouse Reservoir lies 3m SW on the lower slopes of the Moorfoot Hills at a height of 900ft. Beyond rises the lonely hill of 2,136ft Blackhope Scar.

TEVIOTHEAD, Borders   26 NT40
James V ordered the hanging of the famous early 16th-c Border outlaw Johnny Armstrong near Teviothead. A memorial to Armstrong lies in the churchyard of the lonely local church. The outlaw plagued the district around Canonbie and Langholm when he was alive. The village lies amid the rounded hills of Teviotdale, and a little to the N is a monument to the song writer Henry Scott Riddell, who was buried in the churchyard in 1870. He was a writer of patriotic songs, including *Scotland Yet* and *Oor ain Folk*, and also a minister of the parish.

*THORNHILL, Dumfries and Galloway   25 NX89
Known also as the Ducal Village because of its long association with the Dukes of Queensberry and Buccleuch, Thornhill lies in the Nith valley and is backed by Lowland Hills. Queensberry rises to 2,285ft in the E, and North Drumlanrig Street is lined with lime trees planted by the 6th Duke of Buccleuch during the last century. A museum in the town house

Deuchar's Arch lies E of Temple and is the sole surviving fragment of an old mansion.

327

exhibits relics of Burns and the Covenanters, and a tall column set up in 1714 at the town centre supports a winged horse – the emblem of the Queensberrys. This was restored after gale damage in 1955. To the W near a bridge over the Nith the 15th-c Boatford Cross marks the position of an old ford and ferry. Dalgarnock churchyard lies 2m S off the Dumfries road near the river, and contains a cross commemorating 57 Covenanting martyrs of Nithsdale.

THORNTON, Fife 47 NT29
Thornton is an important mining centre on the East Fife coalfield.

THRUMSTER, Highland 37 ND34
Three small lochs lie near this tiny village. Bare Loch Hempriggs is situated to the NE, and Loch Sarclet lies S near the village of Sarclet and the rocky coast between Sarclet Head and the Stack of Ulbster. The Loch of Yarehouse is situated SW of Thrumster.

THURSO, Highland 37 ND16
The Thurso River wends its way into Thurso Bay between craggy Holborn Head and Clairdon Head via this town. Thurso itself was once an important port, but today is a pleasant fishing town and resort. Locally-quarried flagstones line many fields and roads in the area instead of fences or hedges. Views NE from Thurso take in Dunnet Head, the farthest N point on the Scottish mainland, and extend across the stormy Pentland Firth to the distant cliffs of Hoy in the Orkneys. In the old part of Thurso are ruins of the Church of St Peter, which was used since the days of the Vikings. The present remains are of 17th-c date. The last sermon to

have been preached here was delivered in 1862. The town also includes interesting 17th-c houses, and the museum displays a collection of plants and fossils plus a small Runic cross. In Manson's Lane is the ancient Meadow Well.

Thurso Castle lies on the shore 1m NE of the town, and was where Sir John Sinclair the 18th-c statistician and agriculturalist was born. His statue stands by the church. The castle has been partly demolished, and beyond it stands Harold's Tower – the Sinclair burial place. This was erected over the grave of Harold, an Earl of Caithness, who was killed in 1196. To the W of the town on the shores of Thurso Bay are remains of the medieval Bishop's Palace, with Pennyland House in the vicinity. Sir William Alexander Smith, founder of the Boys' Brigade, was born in this house in 1854. Farther along the coast lies Scrabster, the port for the Orkney steamer. Some 2½m W near the foot of Scrabster Hill is a Pictish broch known as 'Things Va'.

TIBBIE SHIEL'S INN, Borders 26 NT22
Famous Tibbie Shiel's Inn is situated between the beautiful St Mary's Loch and the Loch of the Lowes. Tibbie Shiel was a well-known 19th-c character who died in 1878 at the age of 96. Among the inn's past visitors have been de Quincey, Brewster, and Lockhart. One of Christopher North's (Professor Wilson) and James Hogg's (the Ettrick Shepherd) Noctes Ambrosianae took place here. Today the inn is popular with anglers.

TIGHNABRUAICH, Strathclyde 29 NR97
Tighnabruaich is a Gaelic name meaning House on the brae, and refers to the

solitary house which once stood here. The settlement is now a popular Kyles of Bute and Cowal resort, and has a steamer pier facing the island of Bute. Next to the town lies the smaller resort of Auchenlochan, also with a pier. The road N from Tighnabruaich follows Loch Riddon to Glendaruel. Off this road some 2m N of the town is the 9-acre Tighnabruaich wildlife centre and forest trail. Photo-safari hides overlook a small lochan in an area frequented by wild ducks, roe deer, Soay sheep, and blue hares.

TILLICOULTRY, Central 46 NS99
Tartans and woollens are manufactured at this River Devon town, which lies at the foot of the main ridge of the Ochil Hills. Ben Cleuch, the highest point in the range at 2,363ft, rises to the N of Tillicoultry and the lovely glen behind the town is the meeting point for many burns. Harviestoun dates from 1804 and is situated in the hills to the NE; it was once the home of Archibald Campbell Tait, headmaster of Rugby School and later Archbishop of Canterbury.

TILLYFOURIE, Grampian 35 NJ61
Below wooded Tillyfourie Hill lies Tillyfourie, with the ivy-covered ruins of L-shaped Tillycairn Castle 2m SE. The tree-clad hills of Corrennie Forest and Pitfichie Forest lie to the SW.

TINWALD, Dumfries and Galloway 25 NY08
The churchyard of Tinwald's church, which was rebuilt in 1763, preserves a martyr's monument.

TIREE, ISLE OF, Strathclyde 28
The Inner Hebridean islands of Tiree

1	Bishop's Palace (ruins)	4	Meadow Well	7	'Things Va' Broch
2	Castle and Harold's Tower	5	Museum		
3	Church of St Peter (ruins)	6	Pennyland House		

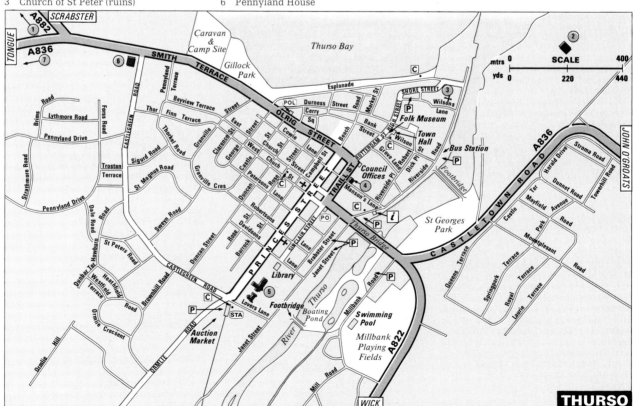

THURSO

and Coll are flat and mainly devoted to crofting. They can be reached by steamer from Oban, and flights from Glasgow land at an airport in Tiree. Fertile Tiree is sometimes called the Granary of the Hebrides and is noted for the breeding of horses. Its variegated coloured marble is also well-known. On the E side of the island, between Goth and Hynish Bays, are the pier and lighthouse of Scarinish. Dr Johnson visited Coll in 1773 to see ruined Breachacha Castle and the remains of several ancient forts. Famous 135ft-high Skerryvore Lighthouse tops an isolated rock in the Atlantic some 10m W of the island. Erected in 1843, this structure was the magnificent achievement of Alan Stevenson.

TIUMPAN HEAD, Isle of Lewis, Western Isles 38 NB53

Fine rock scenery and a lighthouse are features of Tiumpan Head, farthest N point of the Eye peninsula. Across the Minch are distant views of Cape Wrath.

TOBERMORY, Isle of Mull, Strathclyde 28 NM55

In 1588 a Spanish Armada galleon, probably called the 'Florida', was sunk in Tobermory Bay after being blown up by a Scottish hostage. Many unsuccessful attempts have been made to find the galleon's supposed treasure, but relics that have been recovered include a cannon which is now at Inveraray Castle. Tobermory's name means St Mary's Well, and the town is the largest resort on Mull. It is also a fishing port, sheltered by Calve Island in the Sound of Mull. Woods surround the town, and it faces towards the Ardnamurchan and Morven coast on the mainland to the N and E.

Tobermory was visited in 1773 by Dr Johnson and Boswell, who counted twelve to fourteen ships in the harbour. Steamers from the pier link up with Mingary, near Kilchoan on the Ardnamurchan coast. Modern Glengorm Castle lies in fine grounds to the N of Tobermory, and to the SE of the resort is the lovely parkland of Aros House. The Calgary road leads W from the resort and passes near the Mishnish Lochs to the N of Loch Frisa. After this it continues through hairpin bends to Dervaig on narrow Loch Cuan.

TOMATIN, Highland 34 NH82

To the SW of this Strath Dearn village is a wilderness of lonely mountains which are dominated by the Monadhliath range – the source of the River Findhorn. The Findhorn flows through the Tomatin, and farther downstream the river is overlooked by hills over 2,000ft high in a roadless part of Strath Dearn known as the Streens. The loveliest stretch of the river is at Dulsie Bridge. Telford built a bridge at Tomatin in 1833, but this has now been replaced.

TOMDOUN HOTEL, Highland 33 NH10

Hydro-electric developments have greatly altered the still lovely scenery around this anglers retreat. Enlarged Loch Garry merges with Loch Poulary at Tomdoun Hotel, but the road which used to climb N over a 1,424ft-high shoulder of Creag a' Mhaim to Cluanie can no longer be used because of the construction of the Loch Loyne Reservoir.

Cluanie is now reached by a road from the N shore of Loch Garry, which leads across low hills to follow the N shores of Loch Cluanie to Cluanie. These lochs are also used as reservoirs.

The road leading W from Tomdoun Hotel is the only route penetrating the fringe of the picturesque mountainous district of Knoydart, sometimes referred to as Rough Bounds. This road leaves Glen Garry to border the N shores of the very lovely Loch Quoich, before ending at Kinloch Hourn at the head of Loch Hourn. Hourn is considered by many to be the most beautiful of the great W Highland sea lochs. Gairich rises to 3,015ft and dominates Loch Quoich from the S. It is also prominent in the W view from Tomdoun. Many people from these parts emigrated to Canada in the 18th and 19thc to found a new Glengarry.

TOMINTOUL, Grampian 34 NJ11

Although situated at 1,160ft and thus considered the highest village in the Highlands, Tomintoul is not the highest in Scotland. This distinction curiously falls to 1,380ft-high Wanlockhead, a Lowland village. In summer Tomintoul is an anglers' resort. The Avon and its many feeder streams flow near by. A road which leads NW from Tomintoul to Grantown-on-Spey affords views of the Cairngorm foothills and the distant peak of 3,843ft Ben Avon. Just E of Tomintoul the Conglass Water is crossed by a lofty road leading NE from the village and climbing to 1,200ft near the Braes of Glenlivet. After this it descends to Tomnavoulin and Glenlivet.

From Tomintoul the famous Lecht road, built as a military route in 1754, leads SE alongside the Conglass Water. This road reaches 2,090ft near the old Aberdeen/Banff border on its way to the valley of the Don, and is very often snow-bound in winter. Away to the SW of the village the source of the Avon lies in the heart of the Cairngorms. Just outside the village the Avon is joined by the Water of Ailnack, near Delnabo. Together with the Water of Caiplach this stream flows through a series of inaccessible spectacular gorges, with 2,692ft Geal Charn rising in the background. Farther downstream and to the NW of Tomintoul the Avon is joined by Conglass Water. A road alongside the river runs through Strath Avon and the Cromdale Hills towards Delnashaugh Inn, in the Spey Valley.

TOMNAVOULIN, Grampian 34 NJ22

Tomnavoulin lies in Glen Livet, with lonely hills and moorland to the E dominated by 2,563ft Corryhabbie. This height overlooks Glens Suidhe and Fiddich. The lofty road S from the village to Tomintoul rises to over 1,200ft beyond the Braes of Glenlivet. On a by-road to the NW of Tomnavoulin lies the famous Glenlivet whisky distillery.

TONGLAND, Dumfries and Galloway 25 NX65

This village is closely involved with the important Galloway hydro-electric scheme, which utilizes the fall in the level of the River Ken before it joins the Dee at the foot of Loch Ken. Tongland has a generating station, and the dam has a fish pass which is thought to be one of the highest in Scotland. Telford designed the bridge which spans the Dee here.

Traces of 12th-c Tongland Abbey remain in the burial ground near the parish church. A story says that one of the abbots once tried to fly from the battlements of Stirling Castle, wearing wings made of birds' feathers, in the presence of James IV – only to land in a manure heap.

TONGUE, Highland 37 NC55

Also known as Kirkiboll, Tongue lies on the Kyle of Tongue, the outer waters of which form Tongue Bay. The Kyle is now bridged to the N of Tongue, saving a detour round the head of the sea loch. Anglers frequent this little resort, with its sandy, wind-blown shores, and ruined Castle Varrich stands on the Allt an Rhian where it flows into the Kyle. This was once the home of an 11th-c Norse king and later formed a Mackay stronghold. To the N of the village stands 17th- and 18th-c Tongue House, on the site of the ancient seat of the Lords of Reay. Beyond it rises the rocky 1,009ft height of Cnoc an Freiceadain, which can be seen from the road to Bettyhill.

The road S from Tongue skirts Loch Loyal on the way to Altnaharra. To the W rises the many-peaked, 2,504ft Ben Loyal, one of the finest granite mountains in the area but not of great interest to the climbers who make Tongue their rendezvous. The peak is prominent in the view afforded by the little road SW from Tongue, which rounds the Kyle of Tongue and passes near little Loch Hacoin before turning N for the desolate moorlands of A' Mhoine.

TORGYLE BRIDGE, Highland 33 NH31

The road through Glen Moriston uses this bridge to cross the Moriston River, which is known for its fine rapids. Woodland covers the glen to the E but to the W the landscape is bare. Mountains rising to the W of the glen are dominated by 3,634ft Sgurr nan Conbhairean.

TORNAPRESS, Highland 32 NG84

This is the beginning of the famous mountain road over the Pass of Cattle, or Bealach nam Bo, to Applecross. In winter this spectacular road, which climbs from sea level to 2,054ft within 6m, often becomes blocked by snow. It is almost the highest road in Scotland. Maximum gradients approach 1 in 4, and several hazardous hairpin bends have to be negotiated near the summit. The view from the top ranges W towards the dark Cuillins of Skye and the distant Outer Hebrides, and E over Lochs Kishorn and Carron to the serried peaks in the one-time counties of Ross & Cromarty and Inverness. The descent from the Pass of Cattle to Applecross is less hair raising. Peaks of red Torridon sandstone rise near the pass – 2,325ft Meall Gorm to the S, and 2,539ft Sgurr a' Chaorachain to the N. Nearer Tornapress is 2,936ft Beinn Bhan, with its remarkable E corries – notably Coire na Poite.

TORNESS, Highland 34 NH52

To the NE of this River Farigaig village lie the three lochs of Ruthven, Duntelchaig, and Ashie.

TORPHICHEN, Lothian 46 NS97

Although far from any main roads, this village attracts many visitors who come to see the fine 12th- to 15th-c Torphichen Preceptory (AM). Outwardly resembling a castle, this church was once the property of the Knights Hospitallers of St John of Jerusalem, who held their first meeting for 400 years here in 1947. Of the original Norman church which was built for the Knights Templar, only the chancel arch has survived. The foundations are all that remains of the choir. The transepts date from the 13thc, and the 16th-c parish church was built over the ancient nave. The crossing and the saddle-back roofed tower are of 15th-c date. The upper storeys of the tower formed part of the original hospital, or domestic buildings.

In the churchyard lies a cup-marked sanctuary store. Torphichen Mill was the birthplace of Henry Bell, designer of the early 'Comet' steamboat, in 1767. The bridge which spans the Avon near the mill is of c1800 date, and had to be repaired in 1930. To the NE of Torphichen rises Cocklerue, a hill originally known as Cuckold le Roi and mentioned in one of Robert Louis Stevenson's poems. Good views are to be had from the top of The Knock, one of the Bathgate hills which rises to 1,017ft in the SE. Near by is Cairnpapple Hill (AM), one of Scotland's most important prehistoric sites.

Originally a neolithic sanctuary, the site was altered in the early bronze age (c1800BC) and a monumental, circular open-air temple was erected within a ditch. During c1500BC a bronze-age cairn was built and was considerably enlarged several centuries later. Recently the site was excavated and laid out for public view. Bridge Castle crowns a rocky height 2m SW of Torphichen, and is mainly of 16th- and 17th-c date. This was once a seat of the Earls of Linlithgow.

TORPHINS, Grampian 35 NJ60
It is likely that the origin of this village name was Thorfinn, who was a Scandinavian ally of Macbeth killed in the vicinity of nearby Lumphanan. The ruins of Castle Maud lie 2m S and may date back to the time of Robert the Bruce.

TORRIDON, Highland 33
Over 14,000 acres of this wonderful mountainous district are preserved by the NTS. Glen Torridon is considered by many to be the finest and wildest of the Wester Ross glens, and on both sides rise the famous mountains of red Torridon sandstone. Some of these peaks, of great interest to geologists, are capped with quartzite and make a striking scene when lit by the evening sun. Liathach is one of Scotland's finest mountains and at 3,456ft the highest Torridon peak. Its 3m of steep terraces present a challenge to the most experienced climber and tower over the spectacular corrie of Coire na Caime to the N. In Glen Torridon is the curious glacial moraine deposit known as the Corrie of a Hundred Hills. Farther NE rise the magnificent quartzite peaks of Ben Eighe, all over 3,000ft high, forming part of the Ben Eighe national nature reserve. This extends to the shores of Loch Maree.

At the W end of Glen Torridon lies the hamlet of Torridon, where there is a visitor centre. The road branches here, with the narrow N fork following the N shore of Inner Loch Torridon, with

hairpin bends and gradients of 1 in 5 before ending at Diabaig on the Outer Loch. Above the Inner Loch and beyond Care Mhic Nobuil, 3,232ft Ben Alligin shows the curious Horns of Alligin. Farther NE is 2,995ft Ben Dearg, which affords fine views over all the Torridon peaks. The S fork from Torridon is a new road which climbs above the S shore of Inner Loch Torridon on the way to Shieldaig, affording superb views of the terraced Torridon peaks to the N – particularly of Liathach.

TORRIN, Isle of Skye, Highland 32 NG52
The crofting township of Torrin faces Loch Slapin. Beyond the loch on the Strathaird peninsula rises the great Black Cuillin peak of 3,042ft Blaven, where a fine rocky ridge known as Clach Glas is well known to climbers. To the NE of Torrin rise the gentler Red Cuillins. The road to Broadford runs E of Torrin and passes little Loch cill Chriosd in Strath Suardal. Beside the loch the creeper-covered ruins of the 16th- or 17th-c Church of Kilchrist stand in an ancient cemetery. St Maolrubha set up his church here in the 7thc. Between the ruined church and the loch is Cnoc-na-Aifhreann – the Hill of the Mass – where the saint and his successors administered to the people of the valley before the church was built.

TORRYBURN, Fife 46 NT08
This small coal port lies on Torry Bay, which is an inlet of the Forth estuary. Robert Louis Stevenson's nanny Alison Cunningham was born in the village in 1822. The poet dedicated his *Child's Garden of Verse* to her. A nearby field contains a bronze-age 8ft-high standing stone. The famous little Royal Burgh of Culross lies 2½m W on the coast.

TORTHORWALD, Dumfries and Galloway 25 NY07
A late 14th-c ruined keep of the Carlyles looks W from here to the fertile Nithsdale valley. These remains stand on a 250ft-high hill. One of the castle's earlier owners was given the title of Earl Torthorwald by James VI.

TRANENT, Lothian 47 NT47
This mining town lies a few miles inland from the Firth of Forth. In 1745 Colonel Gardiner died here from wounds received at the Battle of Prestonpans, but lives on in Scott's novel *Waverley*. Although the parish church is only of 19th-c date it sits on ancient foundations and has many fascinating stones in its churchyard. Near by is a dovecot of 1587. High ground 2m SW of Tranent is occupied by the ruins of 15th- and 16th-c Falside Castle.

TRAQUAIR, Borders 26 NT33
Lying on a tributary of the Tweed known as Quair Water, this lovely hamlet is usually visited for Traquair House – probably the oldest inhabited house in Scotland. A thousand years of history lie behind the grey walls of this picturesque, turreted mansion, and it may be the original of Scott's Tully-Veolan in the novel *Waverley*. William the Lion held court here in 1209, and since that time the mansion has been visited by 26 other English and Scottish monarchs. Mary Queen of Scots and Darnley were guests here in 1566, and some of the Queen Mary's relics are preserved in the house. Prince Charles Edward stopped here

during the '45 Rising and in 1746 the Earl of Traquair decreed that the well-known Bear Gates to the main avenue should not be opened again until a Stuart was once more on the throne.

Most of the mansion was rebuilt in 1642, but the tower is earlier and the wings were added on at a later date. Ale is still brewed at the 18th-c brewhouse (see inset opposite), and the house contains silver, glass, tapestries, and embroideries of the 13thc, as well as Mary's relics. Montrose is said to have sheltered at the house during his flight after the Battle of Philliphaugh in 1645. He used an old drovers' track over 1,856ft Minchmuir as his escape route from Selkirk to Peebles.

To the SW of Traquair church, which has an exterior galleried stairway, the house of Glen stands in fine gardens. This was an early home of the 1st Countess of Oxford and Asquith. A road from Traquair known as Paddy Slacks runs S towards the lovely Vale of Yarrow, reaching 1,100ft near the one-time Peebles/Selkirk border on the N fringe of the Ettrick Forest.

TRINAFOUR, Tayside 34 NN76
Trinafour lies in the lonely moorland of Glen Erochy and stands on the road which links the Tummel valley with the main Perth to Inverness road. These roads join in Glen Garry at Calvine, near Struan. Hydro-electric developments near Trinafour harness the River Errochty and include Errochty Reservoir and a power station. The scheme is connected to the vast Tummel-Garry developments. A rough track leading N from Trinafour to Dalnacardoch is part of an original Wade military road built in 1730. It climbs to 1,542ft before descending into Glen Garry, and affords a magnificent view of the Forest of Atholl mountains to the N from the hairpin bend above Trinafour.

TROMIE BRIDGE, Highland 34 NN79
Although there are no roads in the lonely Grampian Gaick Forest, it can be reached from Tromie Bridge along paths leading S down long Glen Tromie. Loch an't Seilich is set amid the steep hills of Gaick Forest and linked to Loch na Cuaich. Their combined waters are taken by aqueduct to Loch Ericht as part of the important Rannoch hydro-electric scheme. Vrotten Loch is passed by a footpath running S to the old Inverness/Perth border, where Loch-an-Duin lies at 1,700ft amid fine mountain scenery. Paths from the loch continue S through the vast Forest of Atholl, reaching Glen Garry near Dalnacardoch.

TROON, Strathclyde 24 NS33
This well-known golf resort lies on a narrow piece of rocky coast dividing Ayr Bay from Irvine Bay, facing the Firth of Clyde. In the 18thc the 4th Duke of Portland began the building of Troon harbour. The S sands provide good bathing, and beyond the N sands lie Barassie and Gailes – both well known to golfers. Marr College was built in 1919 from money donated to the town by Charles Kerr Marr, who was born here. Distant views from Troon extend across the Firth to the mountains of Arran, and the bird sanctuary of Lady Isle lies off-shore. Louis Philippe of France stayed 2m E of Troon at Fullarton House in 1801.

TROSSACHS, THE, Central *29*

Unparalleled landscapes of mountains, lochs, rivers, and woodland make up the Trossachs, the name of which means 'bristly country'. The richly-wooded gorge of the Trossachs stretches from Loch Achray to Loch Katrine, with the road through the pass now following a slightly different course from the time of Sir Walter Scott. The poet's *Lady of the Lake* and *Rob Roy* started a rush of visitors to the area early in the 19thc. No public roads encircle the shores of beautiful Loch Katrine, but the summer steamer from Loch Katrine pier gives some idea of the rugged splendour of the Trossachs. The steamer puts down at Stronachlachar, where Rob Roy's birthplace at Glengyle can be visited. Walkers can use the private road along Loch Katrine's N shore from Loch Katrine pier to Glengyle. Ellen Douglas was the 'Lady' in Scott's *Lady of the Lake*, and her lake was Loch Katrine.

The places in the poem can still be identified but the 'Silver Strand' opposite Ellen's Isle has submerged since the level of the loch was raised to improve Glasgow's water supply. Rugged Ben Venue rises to 2,393ft and dominates the scene, overlooking the E end of Loch Katrine and the Pass of Achray. Part of

ALE AS IT WAS

The fine mansion of Traquair near Innerleithen is believed to be the oldest inhabited house in Scotland. Part of the existing building was in use as early as 1107. Traquair is open to the public, and the house itself contains many architectural and historical mementoes of the Stuart lairds who have lived here since 1491, and of the Scottish kings and queens to whom the house offered hospitality.

The west wing was completed in 1664. In it, underneath the chapel, is a restored brew house where one of the rarest drinks in Scotland is produced. Almost all the equipment is original, having been installed in 1739 during the time of Charles Stuart, the 4th Earl of Traquair. Ale was brewed for the family, estate workers, and tenants until 1770. The brew house became almost derelict until it was rescued by Peter Maxwell Stuart, the present and 20th laird. Now Traquair House Ale is produced in limited quantities for sale to the public.

the district lies within the 45,000-acre Queen Elizabeth forest park. Paths lead E from Loch Katrine pier to the picturesque Pass of Achray. The road leads E along the N shore of wooded Loch Achray, where there is water ski-ing. It then passes the Trossachs Hotel, behind which rise the fine viewpoints of 1,149ft Sron Armailte and 1,750ft Ben A'an. Farther E is famous Brig o' Turk, a village of white-walled cottages amid steep, wooded hills familiar to lovers of *Lady of the Lake*.

An early 19th-c bridge carries the main road over the Finglas or Turk Water, which descends from Glen Finglas. Beyond the bridge stretches picturesque Loch Vennachar, with 2,875ft Ben Ledi rising to the N. From the shores of Loch Achray the picturesque Duke's Pass runs S over the hills to Aberfoyle, with views to the E of Loch Drunkie.

TRUMPAN, Isle of Skye, Highland *32 NG26*

The Macdonalds of Uist set fire to the church here in 1597, killing all but one of the congregation of Macleods. The Macleods of Dunvegan rushed to the spot and waved the Fairy Flag, the most treasured possession of the Clan Macleod and a relic preserved at Dunvegan

Peter Maxwell Stuart himself looks after the brewing. Traquair House Ale is brewed five or six times every year, with 150 gallons produced on each occasion. Five bags of barley are boiled in the mash tun, which is entirely original, and then allowed to stand for an hour. The mash is then pumped electrically into the hot liquor tank and copper, which is now heated by gas, and yeast is added. Apart from pumping and heating, there are no modern refinements. The copper itself holds 200 gallons, and estate accounts show that in 1739 it cost £8. After the mixture is ready it is run off into coolers. The original hand stirrers are kept on display above them, still in fine condition after more than two centuries.

Next door are the fermenting vessels, which needed virtually no repairs when the brew house was reopened, and are a fine tribute to the original cooper's craft. In the same room is a display explaining the process and showing some of the old estate papers. A more prosaic modern

Castle to this day. Because of the ebb tide the Macdonalds could not flee in their boats and only two of them escaped death at the hands of the Macleods. The ruins of the church lie in a lonely setting on the narrow Vaternish peninsula, and the ancient churchyard contains the tomb of Lady Grange, who was exiled to the remote islands of St Kilda in 1734 for harbouring Jacobite secrets. To the N of Trumpan is Vaternish Point and E lie the Ascrib Islands in Loch Snizort.

TULLIBARDINE, Tayside *30 NN91*

Tullibardine Chapel (AM) was founded in 1446 and is one of the few collegiate churches in Scotland to be entirely finished and still preserved unaltered. It lies in delightful Strath Earn and displays a remarkable open-timber roof. There is a small tower at the fortified west end of the building. At one time this was the Atholl mausoleum, but it is now the burial-place of the Strathallan family. The Strathallan's castle lies a little to the N near the confluence of Machany Water and the Earn.

TULLIBODY, Central *46 NS89*

Old Bridgend Bridge spans a stream here, and to the SW the River Devon flows into the Forth. Robert Dick the geologist was

document is a current Customs and Excise licence, for Traquair House Ale is subject to all the usual legal requirements. Once brewing is completed, the ale is taken in bulk to the Belhaven Brewery in Dunbar, where it is bottled and returned to Traquair.

The pond outside the brew house is itself of interest. In the beginning Traquair House was built in a bend of the River Tweed. Over the years the river began to threaten the foundations, and in the 1640's the 1st Earl had a new channel dug some way to the north of the house. The Tweed was diverted into it, and only the Well Pool survives to show the original course.

Interior of the brewhouse at Traquair – one of the few places where traditional ale is still made.

born in Tullibody in 1811. An early 18th-c house called Brucefield is an interesting feature of the village.

TULLOCH, Highland   33 NN38

Tulloch stands on the River Spean in Glen Laggan. A hillside to the N shows a curious parallel road, which was formed by glacial action. From Tulloch the road NE passes a reservoir which is dominated to the N by the great mass of 3,700ft Creag Meaghaidh. This route later reaches the shores of Loch Laggan. Only a railway borders the shores of Loch Treig, which lies to the SE of Tulloch under lofty, 3,000ft hills. Loch Treig's waters are now harnessed as part of the great Lochaber power scheme, and are carried along a 15m tunnel beneath Ben Nevis. Lonely Loch Ossian lies in Corrour Forest to the SE of Loch Treig, and beyond its shores rise 3,611ft Beinn Eibhinn and 3,757ft Ben Alder.

TULLOCHGORUM, Highland   34 NH92

Tullochgorum is sited on the N bank of the Spey, and gave its name to a well-known, 18th-c Strathspey tune. In the W the wooded Creag an Fhithich rises to 1,325ft.

TULLYNESSLE, Grampian   35 NJ51

Suie Burn, a tributary of the Don, flows through Tullynessle. Ruins of three-storeyed Terpersie Castle stand in a farmyard to the NW. The castle was built in 1561 and one of its window sills displays the Gordon crest.

TUMMEL BRIDGE, Tayside   30 NN71

General Wade built this bridge over the River Tummel in 1730 on the line of his military road from Crieff to Dalnacardoch. Near by on the S bank of the river is a power station which forms part of the great Tummel-Garry hydro-electric scheme. Mendelssohn spent some time at an inn near Tummel Bridge in 1829. Roads to the E border the shores of Loch Tummel. The N shore road is considered the best and leads to the famous Queen's View, a magnificent viewpoint which provides a panorama of Loch Tummel and the peak of 3,547ft Schiehallion. To the S of Tummel Bridge the Wade road climbs to nearly 1,300ft before descending into Strath Appin.

TURNBERRY, Strathclyde   24 NS20

Well known for its golf course, Turnberry lies on sandy Turnberry Bay and faces across to the mountains of Arran. Robert the Bruce was possibly born at Turnberry Castle in 1247. Traces of the castle lie N at Turnberry Point. Some authorities, however, consider that the king was born at Lochmaben Castle in the one-time county of Dumfries-shire. The Scottish Barons met at Turnberry Castle in 1286, and Bruce landed here in 1307 to win his first battle against the English. Seven years later at Bannockburn he won his fight for Scotland's independence.

TURRIFF, Grampian   35 NJ74

Covenanters and Royalists battled here in 1639 – a skirmish known as the Trot of Turriff. The town stands on the Idoch Water and once had a church belonging to the Knights Templar. The present church has an unusual double belfry of 1635, a 16th-c choir, and several interesting monuments. Turriff's Market Cross was re-erected in 1865. Craigston Castle, built between 1604 and 1607, lies 4½m NE and has been the seat of the Urquhart family since its first building.

To the E is Turriff Delgatie Castle amid pleasant woodland. Seat of the Clan Hay, this tower house has been in the family's possession for nearly 700 years and was built by the Hays of Delgatie in the 13thc. The castle shows alterations dating up to the 16thc and its contents include pictures, arms, and fine painted ceilings of c1590. Mary Queen of Scots stayed here for three days in 1562, and her portrait hangs in the room she used. Hatton Castle lies 3m SE of Turriff off the Fyvie road, and incorporates part of the ancient Balquholly Tower. A little to the NW of the town is the confluence of Idoch Water and the Deveron.

TUSHIELAW INN, Borders   26 NT31

Picturesquely situated on the Ettrick Water, Tushielaw Inn is surrounded by green, rounded Lowland hills. A fine moorland road climbs E from the inn and heads towards Hawick.

TWEEDDALE, Borders

One of Scotland's great salmon rivers, the Tweed flows through the centre of the area which was once the county of Peebles-shire but was more generally known as Tweeddale. Sheep graze on the hills above the river, providing wool for the tweed cloth that has been woven in the small towns for two centuries.

Numerous streams join the main river, the loveliest reaches of which extend from Melrose, through the town of Peebles, to the lonely head of the river at Tweedsmuir – associated with the novels of John Buchan. The source of the Tweed is known as Tweed's Well, and the nearby ranges of lofty hills close in near the borders of the one-time Dumfries-shire, Lanarkshire, and Peebles-shire counties; 2,695ft White Coomb and 2,651ft Hart Fell are the highest of these hills.

TWEEDSMUIR, Borders   26 NT12

John Buchan spent some of his boyhood in this parish, and his novels include much of the local colour. Tweedsmuir's church carries a lofty spire which is a landmark for many miles around, and the churchyard contains an inscribed Covenanter's stone of 1685. An ancient 5ft standing stone is situated near the church. The village itself is surrounded by lofty lowland hills, with flat-topped, 2,754ft Broad Law and 2,680ft Dollar Law to the E. A track leads SE from Tweedsmuir through the hills beside Talla Reservoir, which holds water for Edinburgh. Near by is Fruid Reservoir, which was opened in 1969 as an additional water supply for the city.

To the SE of Tweedsmuir is the Megget Stane and the source of Megget Water, which flows NE towards St Mary's Loch. At the SE end of Talla Reservoir the Gameslope Burn flows down 2,571ft Molls Cleuch Dod via the cascades of Talla Linnfoot. It was here in 1682 that Covenanters held the secret meeting described by Scott in *Heart of Midlothian*. Three great rivers – the Annan, Tweed, and Clyde – all rise some 8m SW of Tweedsmuir. Tweed's Well is the source of the Tweed and lies at a height of 1,500ft a little to the E of the Moffat road at Tweedshaws. A cairn on the road here tells the story of a great snowstorm which occurred in 1831, taking the lives of the guard and driver of the Edinburgh mailcoach. The road reaches 1,348ft a little farther S.

TWYNHOLM, Dumfries and Galloway   25 NX65

Barwhinnock lies to the NW of Twynholm and is a notable example of a small Regency mansion. One of its features is a walled garden.

TYNDRUM, Central   29 NN33

Anglers and climbers come to Tyndrum, which lies in Strath Fillan near its junction with Glen Lochy. Beinn Chaluim and Creag Mhor are the principal peaks to the NE of Tyndrum, and rise to 3,354ft and 3,305ft respectively among the Forest of Mamlorn mountains. These two peaks face the head of Glen Lochay in the Breadalbane country. At Dalry, 2m SE of Tyndrum and near the Fillan Water, Robert the Bruce was wounded in a skirmish in 1306 and lost the famous brooch which is now preserved in the Macdougall mansion of Dunollie, near Oban.

To the SE of the village is a fine group of mountains which rises at the meeting point

The unusual double belfry carried by Turriff Church, which once belonged to the Knights Templar.

of Glens Falloch and Dochart, near Crainlarich. Glen Lochy is dominated by the grand peak of 3,708ft Ben Lui, which rises to the SW of Tyndrum. Ben Lui is well known for its great N corrie and is also the source of Fillan Water. Later known as the Dochart, this river emerges from Loch Tay and becomes the Tay – the river with the greatest volume of water in Scotland. Above Glen Coninish to the E of Ben Lui is 3,374ft Beinn Oss.

TYNET BRIDGE, Grampian   35 NJ46
Tynet Church is one of Scotland's oldest post-Reformation structures. It stands in the vicinity of Tynet Bridge and is still in use.

TYNNINGHAME, Lothian   31 NT67
Remains of a 12th-c church which is now the burial chapel of the Earls of Haddington lie in the well-wooded grounds of 18th- and 19th-c Tynninghame House. This building lies to the NE on the coast by the Tyne estuary, near Tynninghame sands. The chapel was once one of the finest examples of parochial-Romanesque architecture in Scotland, and some beautiful carving can still be seen on the surviving arch of the apse. Beyond the park are the links, which end as a narrow promontory. A rock here is known as St Baldred's Castle, and near by is a bronze-age cairn. Peffer Sands lie farther N.

TYNRON, Dumfries and Galloway   25 NX89
A small national nature reserve covers some of the countryside by this Shinnel Water village. Tynron's churchyard contains an inscribed martyr's stone.

UDNY, Grampian   35 NJ82
This village is situated in the district of Formartine, which covers much of the country between the Rivers Don and Ythan and offers a sandy coast farther E. Udny's Castle retains an ancient four-storeyed tower.

UIG, Isle of Skye, Highland   32 NG36
Picturesque Uig is situated in a fine bay and has a steamer pier which is used by car ferries to the Outer Hebrides. The village faces across Loch Snizort and its islands to the Vaternish peninsula. This part of Skye is rich in associations with Bonnie Prince Charlie. The road leading N round the tip of the Trotternish peninsula climbs steeply up Idrigil Hill through a double hairpin bend. Near Port Kilbride is the old grey Monkstadt House. Flora Macdonald landed with the prince at Kilbride Bay after their journey from the remote island of Benbecula in the Outer Hebrides on 29 June 1746.

He had been disguised as Flora's Irish maid, Betty Burke. They travelled S past Uig towards Loch Snizort Beag and Kingsburgh House, where a successor to the original house stands today. The prince sheltered here for a while, and four years later Flora married Kingsburgh's son Alan. When Dr Johnson and Boswell visited Skye in 1773 they were entertained here by Flora. A little to the N lies Prince Charles' Well, where the prince quenched his thirst. To the NE of Uig is a reconstructed road which runs across the Quiraing to Staffin. Stack Skudiburgh lies in a setting of rocks on the coast a little NE of Uig.

ULBSTER, Highland   37 ND34
On the coast near Ulbster in the little hamlet of Whaligoe, which perches on the cliff top and has 365 precarious steps leading to the fishing boats in the tiny harbour below.

*ULLAPOOL, Highland   36 NH19
Founded in 1788 by the Fisheries Association to expand the herring industry, Ullapool today is a resort as well as a fishing town. It is a leading centre for sea angling, including big-game fishing for sharks, and lies in a lovely position near the mouth of Loch Broom. A passenger ferry plies this sea loch to Aultnaharrie, which is dominated by 2,052ft Ben Goleach. Ullapool's wide streets are named in both Gaelic and English, and the town boasts what is probably the only public convenience in Britain with a turf-thatched roof! A fine memorial clock stands in memory of Sir Arthur Fowler of Braemore, who died in 1899. Several ruined brochs can be seen in the vicinity of Ullapool, particularly Dun Canna 4m N on the N side of the Kanaird estuary. Two other examples lie on the W shore of Loch Broom SE of Aultnaharrie. The Ullapool River flows into Loch Broom after emerging from Loch Achall 4m E. Farther E Glen Achall penetrates lonely hills, with Rhidorroch Forest to the N.

Ullapool makes a convenient centre for exploring some of the finest mountain scenery in the NW Highlands. Away to the SE beyond the head of Loch Broom stretches the fertile wooded valley of Strath More, with the lofty peaks of the Ben Dearg group soaring above. A rugged, picturesque coast road NW of Ullapool skirts the shores of Loch Kanaird on the edge of the wild Coigach district. It affords views of the off-shore Isle Martin, then turns inland through Strath Kanaird with 2,438ft Ben More Coigach dominating the scene to the NW. Some 12m NW of Ullapool in Outer Loch Broom the lovely Summer Isles face towards Achiltibuie on the mainland coast. Motor launches from Ullapool visit the islands, the largest of which is Tanera More. The community of inshore fishermen who once lived here left before 1946, when the herring shoals diminished.

ULVA, ISLE OF, Strathclyde   28 NM43
The tiny Sound of Ulva separates this island from Mull, and a passenger ferry links the two. Dr Johnson and Boswell visited Ulva to see its caves and basalt cliffs in 1773. Sir Walter Scott and David Livingstone were later visitors. Campbell's famous poem *Lord Ullin's Daughter* is associated with Ulva, but many think that the 'Loch Gyle' in the poem is Loch Goil in the Cowal district. To the SW of Ulva lie Little Colonsay and the well-known island of Staffa. The island of Gometra, with its basaltic columns, lies to the W and faces towards Lunga and Fladda in the Treshrish group.

UNAPOOL, Highland   36 NC23
The waters of Loch Glendhu and Loch Glencoul meet here. A ferry operates just N of Unapool at Kylesku, which is situated on the narrows separating the two lochs from Loch Cairnbawn to the W. To the SE prominent Ben Leoid rises to 2,597ft at the head of Glencoul. The road S from Unapool passes the seven peaks of Quinag. These are joined by a long ridge and provide excellent hill-walking country for the energetic. To the E of the road is 2,541ft Glasven, the source of Britain's highest waterfall –

Eas Coul Aulin. This has a sheer drop of some 600ft and is higher than Niagara Falls. The waterfall can be reached on foot from the road, or by boat from Kylesku ferry.

UPHALL, Lothian   46 NT07
The partly-Norman church at Uphall includes a 17th-c burial-vault and several fascinating tombs. The manse was the dower-house of Dowager Lady Cardross in the 17thc. Principal Shairp the writer lies buried in the church and was born at Houston, a 16th-c mansion to the S of the village. This is now a hotel.

UPLAWMOOR, Strathclyde   44 NS45
Ouplaymuir was the original name of this village. The Adam mansion of Caldwell dates from 1772 and lies to the SW.

USAN, Tayside   31 NO75
Once known as Fishtown of Usan, this was an important fishing port some centuries ago and had a port and mill which were mentioned in records dating from 1608. Fresh fish were taken along a track known as 'King's Codger's Road', which once led W to a Royal Palace at Forfar. Nowadays Usan is a quiet little place with a coastguard station and rocky foreshore. The village lies between Scurdy Ness and Boddin Point. Near the latter is the curious rock of St Skeagh, with wide Lunan Bay sheltered beyond by Lone Craig and Red Head to the S.

VALLEYFIELD, Fife   46 NT08
A village on Torry Bay, Valleyfield lies a little NW of the small coal-port of Torryburn. The colliery is linked to the village by a tunnel under the Forth to Kinneil.

WADE ROADS
Many of the great military roads through the Highlands were begun by General George Wade between 1726 and 1740. Until this time many parts of the area were inaccessible except on foot, and though some of Wade's roads have degenerated many others have been incorporated in the present main highways. It is known that Wade built 234¾m of road, and that between c1728 and 1737 he spent £23,316 0s 6d on these projects. Wade's best achievement was probably the road linking Dunkeld with Inverness, which crosses the Grampians and is very largely followed by the present main road.

Crieff is the start of a link road which ran N through the Sma' Glen to Aberfeldy, where Wade's finest bridge still spans the Tay. Part of the link over the hills in old Perthshire, by way of Tummel Bridge to the main road at Dalnacardoch, is followed by modern roads; other portions remain as rough tracks. In a lonely setting of hills 2m NW of Dalnacardoch stands the Wade Stone of 1729, marking the completion of that portion of the road. The present main road through Glen Garry to Inverness runs partly on the Wade course.

Another famous Wade road diverged to the left at Dalwhinnie for the Upper Spey valley. From here a short spur was constructed to rejoin the more important road nearing Kingussie, which was where Wade enlarged the Ruthven Barracks in 1736. Prince Charles Edward's Highlanders destroyed the barracks in 1746, and their ruins can be seen today. Wade's great road from Kingussie continued to Fort George, now called Inverness. A new Fort George was constructed to the NE of the town at a later date.

Wade's road through the Upper Spey valley ran NW, zig-zagging up the famous Corrieyairack Pass and reaching a 2,000ft summit in a setting of lonely hills before descending through Glen Tarff. This great road, along which Prince Charles Edward marched in 1745, has deteriorated to little more than a track which can hardly be made out in places. The long route can be followed on foot but makes an arduous journey. From Glen Tarff the road ran to Fort Augustus in the Great Glen. Here Wade rebuilt and enlarged barracks, on the remains of which a Benedictine monastery was built in 1876. At Fort Augustus the road linked up with Wade's road from Fort William to Inverness, following Glen More. Parts of the military road are still followed by the present main road, but N from Fort Augustus the Wade road kept to the E and the present main road runs to the W of Loch Ness. Thus Inverness was the junction of Wade's two best-known roads, which in places are incorporated in today's highways.

After 1740 Wade built no more roads in Scotland, for he was relieved of his command. He fought a campaign in Flanders in 1744 and returned to Scotland the following year to help deal with the Rising. When the Duke of Cumberland took over as supreme commander of the English army, Wade retired to live at Highgate in London. In 1784 he died aged 78 at Bath, and his body lies in Westminster Abbey near his monument by Roubiliac. General Caulfield carried on much of the Scottish military road building after Wade and is reputed to have written the lines:
"If you'd seen these
roads before they were
made,
You'd lift up your
hands, and bless
General Wade"

Among the roads Caulfield built for £167,000 were from Dumbarton to Inveraray (1746–1750); Coupar Angus to Braemar and over the Lecht Road to Tomintoul, Grantown-on-Spey, and the present Fort George (1748 onwards); Stirling to Tyndrum, Kinlochleven, and Fort William by way of the now disused Devil's Staircase near Kingshouse (1748–1751); and from Fort Augustus to Bernera Barracks at Glenelg (1750–1784). The first 7m of the latter were later abandoned. The first military road map was published in 1755, and a list of these roads towards the end of the 18thc mentions the total mileage as 1,103m. Only 600m had been kept up by 1800. The Commissioners of the Road and Bridge Act of 1812 took over the roads in 1814.

WALKERBURN, Borders 26 NT33
Founded in 1854, Walkerburn is a textile village on the River Tweed. Remarkable earthwork terraces can be seen N of the village on Purvis Hill, and the ruins of Elibank Tower lie 2½m E and may date from 1595. This structure was either built or enlarged by one of the Murrays of Darnhall, near Eddleston. The daughter of this Murray was 'Muckle Mouthed Meg', who married a Scott of Harden and is portrayed in ballads by both Hogg and Browning.

WANLOCKHEAD, Dumfries & Galloway 25 NS81
Wanlockhead lies at 1,380ft above sea level and is Scotlands highest village. Tomintoul, the highest village in the Highlands, stands at 1,160ft. The rounded Lowther Hills surround this village, and the highest points are 2,403ft Green Lowther and 2,377ft Lowther Hill. Both are good viewpoints.

Persecuted Covenanters found refuge in these hills during the late 17thc. Gold, silver, and lead have been mined here at least since Roman times, and at the appropriately named village of Leadhills – which is almost as high as Wanlockhead (see inset on page 268). Remains of the 18th- and 19th-c workings can still be seen. Between the two villages the road climbs to 1,531ft, and from Wanlockhead this same road continues SW towards the Nith Valley through the fine Mennock Pass, reaching a 1,400ft summit.

WATTEN, Caithness, Highlands 37 ND25
Trout are fished in Loch Watten, which lies a little to the N of this hamlet. The old Mill of Watten stands at the SE end of the loch.

WEEM, Tayside 30 NN84
Overlooking this village, which lies on the N bank of the Tay at the E end of Strath Appin, is the 800ft-high Rock of Weem – a fine viewpoint. An inn here has a sign commemorating a visit by soldier and engineer General Wade in 1733. Monuments to the Menzies lie in the Renaissance church. Menzies Castle stands in lovely wooded grounds to the W of the village, and is the chief seat of the clan. It is considered a fine example of an old Scottish mansion, with its small door and immensely thick walls, and dates from between 1571 and 1577. It was restored in 1957 and houses a clan museum.

WEMYSS BAY, Strathclyde 44 NS16
The main car ferry link with Rothesay on the Isle of Bute operates from here, and Wemyss Bay is a small Clyde holiday resort with a rock and pebble beach. The view from the resort takes in the hills of Bute and the Cowal peninsula. Kelly Burn separates Wemyss Bay from the neighbouring resort of Skelmorlie, which lies farther S.

WESTERKIRK, Dumfries & Galloway 26 NY39
Thomas Telford the great engineer was born near this village in 1757. He was buried at Westminster Abbey, but his memorial stands in the village. One of Telford's many achievements in Scotland was the building of the Caledonian Canal, which enabled sailing ships to avoid the stormy journey around Cape Wrath. Westerkirk, also known as Bentpath, is surrounded by green lowland hills.

WESTERN ISLES
For many years this name has encompassed the Inner and Outer Hebrides, together with the islands of Arran, Bute, and the Cumbraes which lie farther S in the Firth of Clyde. It is now the official title of a new administrative region.

WESTER ROSS 33
Picturesque and hilly Wester Ross is an area which comprises the W half of the one-time county of Ross and Cromarty –

as distinct from the flatter Easter Ross, which faces the North Sea. Wester Ross portrays some of the finest of the NW Highland scenery, and its coast is indented by many beautiful sea lochs including Loch Alsh, Loch Carron, Loch Torridon, and Loch Broom. Kyle of Lochalsh faces Skye and is the Wester Ross railhead of a line from Inverness. This makes a convenient centre for touring the district, as do the beautiful little resorts of Gairloch, near delightful Loch Maree, and Ullapool, which lies between the Teallach range and the Coigach mountains. Other outstanding features in the district are the very ancient, red-sandstone Torridon mountains and the Ben Eighe national nature reserve – both near Kinlochewe.

WEST KILBRIDE, Strathclyde 29 NS24
Situated just inland from Seamill, with its good sands bordering the Firth of Clyde, the old village of West Kilbride lies off the main road. A little to the E of the village is Kilbride Tower. This stands on high ground and is also known as Law Castle.

WEST LINTON, Borders 47 NT15
Once noted for its stonemasons, West Linton lies at the foot of the Pentland Hills. Fine examples of 17th-c stone carving are to be seen in the village, notably a figure of 1666 which was re-erected in 1861 at Lady Gifford's Well. Opposite the well is a house with carvings dated 1660 and 1678, probably made by the same hand. An older name for the village was Linton Roderick, and 9m SW of West Linton above the hamlet of Dunsyre rises 1,460ft Black Law. The grave of an unknown Covenanter, killed at Rullion Green in 1666, lies on the slopes of this hill.

A narrow road NW from West Linton leads alongside the Lyne Water and later deteriorates into a track. This is the Cauld Stane Slap, one of the best-known of the ancient drove roads. For centuries cattle were driven along the track to cross the Pentlands, and the path reaches a summit of 1,430ft below the slopes of 1,839ft East Cairn Hill. West Cairn Hill rises 1,844ft to the SW. The track led as far as Stenhousemuir near Falkirk.

WESTRUTHER, Borders 31 NT64
Dirrington Great Law rises to 1,309ft NE of this village, which is situated on the S slopes of the Lammermuir Hills. Remains of an old church lie near the modern replacement. Partly 17th-c Wedderlie House lies 1½m NE, and a pair of gatehouses 3m SW on the Lauder road once led to former Spottiswoode House. These gatehouses have interesting milestones and carry coaching clocks over their gables.

WEST WEMYSS, Fife 47 NT39
This small Firth of Forth town lies a little to the SE of the Leven to Kirkcaldy road. The old, curiously inscribed Tolbooth has an outside staircase, and Wemyss Castle dates from 1421 with 17th- and 19th-c additions. In 1565 Mary Queen of Scots met Darnley here for the first time. Historians believe it was a love match, and the pair were married five months later. Rocky coastline to the NE of West Wemyss is riddled with caves or weems, notable for their bronze-age, iron-age, and early-Christian carvings. Some of these caves have now collapsed.

WHISTLEFIELD, Strathclyde *44 NZ29*
Situated on the watershed between the
Gare Loch and Loch Long, Whistlefield
faces towards hills known as Argyll's
Bowling Green.

WHITEBRIDGE, Highland *33 NH41*
General Wade's military road from Fort
Augustus to Inverness passed through
Whitebridge, and a military rest-house
that once stood here later became an inn.
At Whitebridge the River Foyers is
joined by the Fechlin, which flows
from Loch Killin in the hills to the SE.
Following the River Foyers the hilly
Wade road continues N from the village
to Foyers, then runs along the edge
of Loch Ness to Dores and Inverness.
Another road runs NE from Whitebridge
by way of Errogie to Dores. Remote
Loch Killin is surrounded by hills and
can be reached via a rough little road
SE from the village.

The Fort Augustus road runs SW, at first
following the River Foyers and then
climbing on to moorland at a height of
1,275ft. Before reaching Loch Tarf the
road affords fine views, then later
descends steeply into wooded Glen Doe.

WHITE BRIDGE, Tayside *30 NN75*
Also on the line of a Wade road, White
Bridge lies at a height of over 1,000ft
in the old Perthshire hills. Near by the
road forks, with both branches leading
N to the Tummel valley. Between the two
roads lies little Loch Kinardochy,
bordered by the W fork. The latter climbs
over moorlands below 3,547ft
Schiehallion and provides wonderful
views before descending to Kinloch
Rannoch. Shortly after leaving White
Bridge the E fork reaches a height of
1,263ft.

WHITEHILLS, Grampian *35 NJ66*
Sheltered by Stake Ness and Knock Head,
Whitehills is a fishing village situated on
a sandy and rocky bay. To the W the
coastline is also rocky, and there are
several lonely headlands near Portsoy.
Inland from Whitehills stand the ruins of
St Branden's Church, preserving Jacobean
churchyard tombstones.

WHITEKIRK, Lothian *31 NT58*
Suffragettes damaged Whitekirk's
fascinating 15th-c cruciform church
in 1914, but it has since been repaired.
The church carries a massive tower
with a wooden spire and features a
barrel-vaulted chancel and porch, plus
a 17th-c carved wooden front to the
north gallery. Long before the church
was built a holy well stood near by.
This was visited by Aeneas Silvius, later
Pope Pius II. Another of Whitekirk's
historical features is a two-storeyed
tithe barn which incorporates part of a
16th-c castle and stands beyond the
churchyard. Monks from Holyrood used
to store grain here. Fine walled gardens
grace the mansion of Newbyth, 2m SW
of Whitekirk, and 2m NW of the village
stands the late 18th-c Leuchie House.

WHITE MOUNTH, Grampian *35 NO28*
Lochnagar, with its twin summits of
3,786ft and 3,678ft, is the monarch of
the great mountain plateau known as the
White Mounth. Other principal peaks are
3,268ft Broad Cairn, 3,314ft Cairn
Bannoch, 3,274ft Fafernie, and 3,430ft
Cairn Taggart. The White Mounth is
bordered to the W and E by Glen
Callater and Glen Muick, both of which

Royal Arms of Scotland mounted over
the 17th-c Pend archway in Whithorn.

contain lochs. To the N lies Deeside and
Balmoral Forest, which separate these
mountains from those of the Cairngorm
range away to the NW. By-roads run
down both Glen Callater and Glen
Muick from Braemar and Ballater.
Mountain paths lead N from Braedownie,
at the head of Glen Clova, and then to the
White Mounth.

WHITHORN, Dumfries & Galloway
24 NX44
St Ninian, the son of a local chieftain,
founded a monastery at Whithorn in
AD 397 and may have built his *Candida
Casa* or White House here – probably
the first Christian church in Scotland.
Other authorities hold that the church
was built 4m SE at Isle of Whithorn,
where St Ninian landed cAD395 on his
return from studying in Rome. Fergus
Lord of Galloway built the priory (AM) in
the 12thc, and a good late 12th-c carved
doorway has survived.

Excavations of the priory ruins have
revealed fragments of a wall covered in
pale plaster – maybe the *Candida Casa.*
The ruins show some 15th-c work and
are entered through the Pend, a 17th-c
arch on which the Royal Arms of
Scotland before the Union are displayed.
Attached to the priory is a museum (AM),
which preserves some ancient carved
stones including the 7th-c St Peter's
Stone and the 5th-c Latinus Stone –
possibly the oldest in Scotland. St
Ninian's Shrine became an important
place of pilgrimage and was visited
regularly by James IV.

Whithorn itself is an ancient Royal Burgh
and preserves a number of small 18th-c
houses in George Street. A 4m moorland
walk to the W coast of the Machars
peninsula leads to St Ninian's Cave,
the seashore retreat of the saint. Crosses
in the cave walls were probably carved
by St Ninian's followers. Some 2m W of
the village off the Port William road is
Rispain Camp, a rectangular enclosure
defined by double banks and ditches
which was probably a medieval
homestead site. Some 5m further W lies
Barfalloch Fort, remains of an iron-age
fort overlooking the sea and enclosed
by a large ditch.

WHITING BAY, Isle of Arran, Strathclyde
24 NS02
Facing the Firth of Clyde, Whiting Bay
is an attractive resort offering safe

bathing. Pretty Glen Ashdale includes
waterfalls and extends inland from
Whiting Bay. Holy Island lies NE beyond
Kingscross Point.

WHITTINGHAME, Lothian *31 NT67*
The Earl of Balfour was born at 19th-c
Whittinghame House in 1848, and his
tomb lies in the grounds. Also in the
grounds is an ancient yew tree which is
supposed to mark the spot where
Darnley's murder was plotted. Near the
house stands 15th-c Whittinghame
Tower. Ruchlaw House lies 1½m E of the
village and is a modernized 17th-c
building with two old sundials and a
dovecot. Apart from the well-known
Lake of Menteith, Pressmennan Lake
is the only other 'lake' in Scotland. This
lies 2m SE of Whittinghame and was
artificially formed in 1819.

WICK, Highland *37 ND35*
Plan overleaf
Telford designed Wick harbour, which
was later improved by Thomas
Stevenson. In spite of these great names,
large steamers are only able to dock
at high tide. The town is an ancient
Royal Burgh and a busy herring port,
situated where the Wick Water flows into
Wick Bay. The suburb of Pulteneytown
was founded by the British Fishery
Society early in the 19thc. The quaint
Town Hall is surmounted by a cupola,
and the old Sinclair Aisle in the parish
church is the burial-place of the Earls
of Caithness. About 2m NE of Wick is the
airport, and about 1m farther Noss Head
overlooks sandy Sinclair's Bay. The cliff
edge here is occupied by the adjacent
castles of Girnigoe and Sinclair, one-
time strongholds of the Sinclairs. Girnigoe
dates from the end of the 15thc and
had a complicated system of moats,
portcullis, and guardrooms. Sinclair
was built between 1606 and 1607. Both
castles were demolished in the clan
battles during the 17thc.

A headland above the sea and over a
deep cleft in the rocks 1½m SE of Wick
is occupied by the 14th-c Castle of Old
Wick, once known as Castle Oliphant.
This windowless square tower is known
to seamen as the Old Man of Wick. The
castle was taken in 1569 by the Master
of Caithness, son of the 4th Earl of
Caithness. In the following year he was
imprisoned for six years in castle
Girnigoe before being put to death. Near

the Castle of Old Wick are curious rock stacks known as Brig o' Tram and the Brough.

WIGTOWN, Dumfries & Galloway 24 NX45

Although Wigtown's harbour is now silted up the town is still one of the main centres of the bleak Machars peninsula. Fishing and wild-fowling are popular pursuits here. Wigtown became a Royal Burgh in 1457, and the old cross of 1748 carries a sundial. Near by is a cross which was erected in 1816. An enclosure in the broad main street was once used to pen cattle.

The town has cruel associations with the Covenanters, and a post in the Bladnoch estuary marks the site of the drowning of the Wigtown Martyrs. Margaret Mchauchlan aged 63 and Margaret Wilson aged 18 were accused of attending meetings of their sect in 1685. They were tied to stakes in the estuary and drowned by the rising tide. A Covenanters' memorial was erected in 1858 on Windyhill, a fine viewpoint rising behind the town. Some 3m NW off the road to Kirkcowan are the standing stones of Torhouskie (AM), probably of bronze-age origin. The nineteen stones form a circle 60ft in diameter.

WILSONTOWN, Strathclyde 46 NS95

Lonely moorland and fells surround this mining village, which is situated at a height of over 900ft. Wilsontown was the site of the first iron works in the one-time county of Lanarkshire, built between 1779 and 1781.

WINCHBURGH, Lothian 46 NT07

Much of the countryside around Winchburgh has been spoiled by the workings of the one-time oil-shale industry. Ruins of late 16th-c Duntarvie Castle lie 1m N.

WISHAW, Strathclyde 45 NS75

Gillespie Graham designed the Victorian mansions of Wishaw House to the N, and Cambusnethan Priory. Scott's biographer J G Lockhart was born at Cambusnethan House in 1794.

WISTON, Strathclyde 25 NS93

Wiston's old church was replaced in the 19thc. Tinto Hill rises to 2,335ft in the N and provides fine views.

WORMIT, Fife 31 NO32

The 2m-long Tay Bridge which spans the Firth of Tay here was built between 1883 and 1888 to carry the railway line into Fife. Visible near by are the supports of the ill-fated bridge of 1871, which was blown down in 1879 while a train was roaring across it. Many lives were lost when the train plunged into the raging firth. Wormit is said to have been the first Scottish village to have had electricity. The 42-span Tay Bridge crosses the Forth 2m E and is the second largest structure of its type in Europe.

YARROW, Borders 26 NT32

Beautiful Vale of Yarrow lies amid the green, rounded hills of the Ettrick Forest and is threaded by Yarrow Water. This lovely countryside is rich in remains of ancient Border keeps and has inspired many great writers and composers, including Wordsworth, Scott, and James Hogg – the Ettrick Shepherd. Scott's great-grandfather was once minister of Yarrow Kirk, which has twice been burnt down and now contains relics of Wordsworth and Hogg. Both poets lived in the area. Nearby Deuchar Bridge is now derelict and dates from 1653.

To the S of the Kirk is a by-road which leads to Ettrick Bridge End. In the 19thc a plough excavated the Yarrow or Liberalis Stone, which lies ½m W of the Kirk at Whitefield. The stone is a memorial to Nudus and Dumnogenus, the two sons of Liberalis who were killed at the Battle of Yarrow in AD 592. Some of the most beautiful of the vale's scenery can be found near Broadmeadows, which lies in a richly wooded setting to the NE.

YETHOLM, Borders 27 NT82

The two villages of Town Yetholm and Kirk Yetholm are less than ½m apart and divided by the Bowmont Water. Both lie at the foot of the Cheviots. Away to the SE across the English border, rises the 2,676ft Cheviot itself. Nearer the villages the Border line crosses 1,849ft Curr and 1,985ft Schel, which rise above the lonely valley of the College Burn. Kirk Yetholm is the end of the 250m-long Pennine Way from Edale in the English Peak District.

A cottage in the village was the palace of the Scottish gipsies until the royal line died out in 1902. The last gipsy queen, Esther Faa Blythe, was buried here in 1883 and described the scattered village as 'sae mingle – mingle that ane micht think it was either built on a dark nicht, or sawn on a windy ane'. Scott's 'Meg Merrilees' in Guy Mannering may have been modelled on an earlier gipsy queen. Esther Faa Blyth's son became king in 1898, and died four years later with no heir. Overlooking the villages are the Cheviot foothills of 1,086ft Staerough.

YETTS OF MUCKHART, Central 30 NO00

Many hill roads meet here in Glen Devon and the River Devon flows SE under 1,496ft Lendrick Hill.

YOKER (Glasgow) Strathclyde 45 NS56

A car ferry operates on the Clyde for Renfrew here. Nearer to Glasgow is a road tunnel beneath the Clyde which links Whiteinch and Linthouse.

YTHAN WELLS, Grampian 32 NJ63

Near here is the source of the River Ythan, which follows an E course to enter the North Sea near Newburgh. Ythan Wells lies in the Strathbogie district of old Aberdeenshire, and 3m N stands the ancient house of Frendraught. In 1630 the tower was set alight, killing Lord Aboyne and Gordon of Rothiemay. Traces of Roman occupation, probably the farthest N penetration of the Romans into Scotland, survive 1½m W of Ythan Wells at Glenmailen.

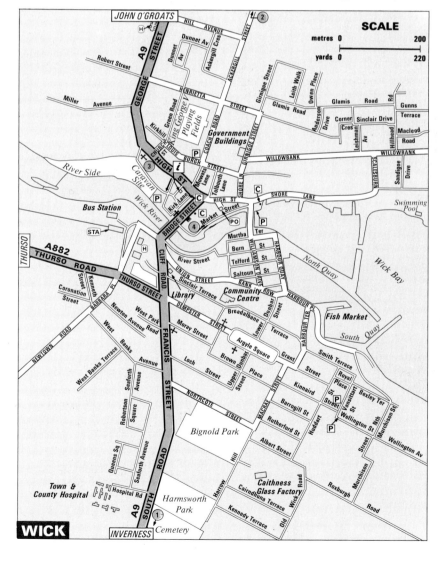

1 Castle of Old Wick
2 Castles of Girnigoe and Sinclair (ruins)
3 Parish Church
4 Town Hall

Scotland at Leisure

Scotland is a sportsman's paradise. The mecca of St Andrews draws golfing pilgrims from all over the world, enthusiasts who do not consider themselves complete until they have trodden in the footsteps of past monarchs over the ancient greens. Scottish waters teem with fish to gladden the heart of any angler – huge trout and pike in the lochs, furious Tweed salmon, and salt-water catches that are measured in stones rather than pounds. Wild coasts and headlands shelter bays and sea lochs where yachtsmen fly before the wind and skin-divers discover other-world fantasies on the ocean's bed. Water skiers defy gravity, surfers race towards the golden arcs of exposed beaches, and inland lochs – small, mountain-encircled seas in themselves – offer havens of magnificence for small-boat sailors and the casual walker. And the Scottish landscape has even more to offer – winter sports for the skier; mountains and glens for climbers and hill walkers; wide moorlands and open rides where the lone pony-trekker can be the only person in the world; plus numerous nature reserves, sanctuaries, trails, forest walks, wildlife parks, etc.

The following gazetteer of towns able to offer comprehensive leisure facilities is not exhaustive, but should be used to select bases from which to tour areas offering particular activities. All places listed here are described in the main gazetteer and appear on the touring atlas in red type. Each is also referenced to the five special maps at the end of this article. Keys to symbols used in the text appear on the relevant maps.

Visitors to Scotland should remember a few basic rules and courtesies. Most land and water is owned by somebody and permission should be sought before crossing a field, launching a boat, or casting a fishing line. Freshwater anglers should take particular care to ensure that they have all the requisite permits and rod licences, plus details of number and weight restrictions over fish that may be taken. Information of this nature can usually be supplied by tourist offices, post offices, inns, and hotels. Hill walkers and climbers should use the same sources to determine restricted areas during the shooting seasons, and should never set out without telling somebody where they are going. Even in summer sudden and extreme changes in weather can make the Scottish countryside dangerous, and rescue parties can work more efficiently if they know where to start looking. Warm, waterproof clothing and strong footwear are essential, and it is best to venture forth in parties rather than alone – particularly if inexperienced. Sea anglers should seek local information regarding boat hire, beach-fishing restrictions, pier tarrifs, etc.

Nature reserves, walks, and trails are set aside and preserved to protect wildlife, so visitors should stay on the paths unless they have obtained a permit to do otherwise. In many cases it may be against local by-laws to pick or uproot plants and flowers, and dogs and children must be kept under control. Observe the country code and help preserve a valuable natural legacy for future generations. See feature starting page 39 for information concerning the Scottish Islands.

*ABERDEEN, Grampian *B2*
A long stretch of sandy beach lies N of the city and there is fine coastal scenery to the S. The scenic beauty of the rivers Dee and Don is famous. All but one of Aberdeen's seven golf courses have eighteen holes and the facilities are generally good. Brown trout can be fished in Gormack Burn, which lies within the Drum Estate, and other opportunities for game fishing are offered by some stretches of the River Don. The sea angler has excellent prospects, particularly off Girdle Ness. Catches off this coast might include codling, dabs, flounders, mackerel, and saithe from the beach; cod, haddock, and saithe from boats. The area is popular with small boat sailors, and W off the A944 is the yachting venue of Loch Skene. Aberdeen also has skin-diving facilities and a water ski-ing club. An artificial ski slope at Kaimhill Playing Field is open to the general public on Saturday afternoons. There are pony trekking centres in the area, and a nature trail has been laid out at Hazlehead Public Park. Some 5m W are the Kirkhill Forest Walks. The tourist-information office at Aberdeen is in St Nicholas House, Broad Street.

ABERFELDY, Tayside *B2*
Aberfeldy is a small touring centre in the Highlands of old Perthshire, near the well-known beauty spot of the Falls of Moness. Golfing facilities are provided by a nine-hole course and the Tay River can be fished for salmon, brown trout, and grayling. Canoeing can be enjoyed on the Tay at Grandtully, and pony trekking is amply catered for. Strath Tay history trails comprise four walks of archaeological and historical interest which radiate from Aberfeldy. The Birks of Aberfeldy nature trail passes the Falls of Moness, and woodland walks on the N shore of Loch Tay penetrate Drummond Hill Forest. A tourist information office is sited in the Square at Aberfeldy.

ABERFOYLE, Central *A2*
Set in a landscape of hills, lochs and forests, Aberfoyle has a great deal to offer those in search of beauty and active leisure pursuits. The area offers many possibilities for the angler, including the brown-trout lochs Ard, Chon, Drunkie, and the Lake of Menteith. Pike can be caught in Lochs Ard, Chon, and Dhu. Loch Katrine lies N and provides facilities for sailing. Several places around Aberfoyle cater for pony trekking. The beautiful and justly-famous Trossachs offer limitless prospects for the hill walker, and the Queen Elizabeth forest park comprises 46,000 acres of Highland scenery. The park offers over 60m of well-signposted walks and has a picnic site. Aberfoyle has an information office in Main Street.

AIRDRIE, Strathclyde *B3*
Hillend Reservoir lies E of Airdrie and can be fished for trout, pike, and perch in season. Lily Loch, Black Loch, and Roughrigg Reservoir are also water-sports venues. To the E of the town on the A17 is Caldercuix, which offers pony trekking

facilities, and Airdrie itself includes two eighteen-hole golf courses. The town's tourist information office is in the Municipal Buildings.

ALLOA, Central   *B2*
This Forth-side town has two eighteen-hole golf courses, and Gartmorn Dam can be fished for pike and perch. The area around this water comprises a nature reserve. Sailing can be enjoyed on the Firth of Forth.

ANNAN, Dumfries and Galloway   *B3*
Annan is a small town surrounded by agricultural countryside and lies close to the Solway Firth. An eighteen-hole golf course exists at nearby Powfoot, and the Annan is noted as a game fishing river. Coarse fishing is also offered by the Annan, and catches here might include pike, perch, roach, and chub. Solway Firth is excellent for small-boat sailing and sea angling.

ARBROATH, Tayside   *B2*
Arbroath is a popular seaside resort with a good harbour and a safe sandy beach. The cliffs and caves to the N of the town are a great attraction, and golfing facilities are provided by an eighteen-hole course. The sea angler can expect a wide variety of fish, including cod, codling, conger, flounder, haddock, mackerel, plaice, pollack, saithe, and sole. Small boats put out from the harbour, and the gliding centre at Condor offers facilities which include instruction for the inexperienced. East Seaton lies 1½m from Arbroath and includes pony trekking stables. The Scottish Wildlife Trust has a 3m-long nature trail N of the town. A guide to the cliff geology, shore, and wildlife likely to be seen on the trail is available. Arbroath's tourist information office is situated at 105 High Street.

ARDROSSAN, Strathclyde   *A3*
This W coast holiday resort is near Saltcoats and offers safe bathing, especially from the sandy sweep of Irvine Bay. Busbie, Mill, and Whitlees Reservoirs can be fished for brown trout. Opportunities for sea angling are large and yield cod, conger, dabs, flounders, haddock, pollack, and whiting. Small boats can be launched on Irvine Bay. Troon lies at the S end of Irvine Bay and is a skin-diving centre. Horse Island, a nature reserve lying off the coast NW of Ardrossan, belongs to the RSPB and has a large population of birds including various gulls, terns, eider ducks, oyster-catchers and rock pipits. Lady Island is a bird sanctuary which lies offshore from Troon.

A tourist information office is housed in the Council Chambers at Saltcoats.

*AVIEMORE, Highland   *B2*
This major sporting resort is used as much in the winter as it is in the summer. It lies in Strath Spey and is surrounded by mountains and forests. Loch-an-Eilean lies in Inshriach Forest S of Aviemore and includes a visitor centre. The Scottish Centre for Outdoor Training is situated at Glenmore Lodge. Several pony-trekking centres operate in the area. Aviemore is probably best known for the winter sports which take place on the Cairngorm Mountains. Facilities include ski schools, ski shops, and the Aviemore Centre. The latter has an ice rink, indoor heated swimming pool, and the Drambuie plastic ski slope – open to the public all day and by arrangement in the evening. This region is particularly good for the hill walker and the climber, with the Monadhliath Mountains to the W and the Cairngorms with 4,300ft Ben Macdhui to the S.

Opportunities for the angler are offered by the River Spey, and many of the local lochs can be fished for trout. Sailing can be enjoyed on lochs Morlich and Insh, while the canoeist will find the Spey an exciting prospect. There is a gliding club between Aviemore and Kingussie. The 12,000 acre Glen More forest park has something to engage everybody's interest – Loch Morlich has fishing and bathing, and the pine forests and mountains abound with wildlife. Within the park there are three nature trails and five longer treks. N of Aviemore at Boat of Garten is Loch Garten, which is famous as being a nesting site of the rare osprey. Part of the shore around Loch Alvie forms the Craigellachie nature reserve, an area of birchwood which is of particular interest for its insects and moths. There is also a nature trail here. Aviemore has a tourist information centre.

*AYR, Strathclyde   *A3*
A popular and attractive resort offering a whole host of leisure activities, Ayr includes some fine parks – notably Belleisle and Craigie. The local beaches are excellent and have many amenities – *eg* ponies on the sands, paddling pools etc. Putting greens, miniature golf, a fairground, tennis courts, a famous horse-racing course, and three eighteen-hole golf courses ensure that the holidaymaker need never be bored. The River Ayr can be fished for salmon, sea trout, and brown trout in season, and grayling can be caught in the upper reaches. Sea anglers can expect cod, dogfish, flounders, haddock,

pollack, skate, tope, and whiting. The Firth of Clyde is a popular venue for sailing, and small boats can be launched at Ayr. There are yachting facilities just along the coast at Prestwick. Pony trekking stables exist in the area, and the Rozelle nature trail lies S of the town. This fascinating walk illustrates plant and animal life in pond and woodland environments. Ayr's tourist information centre is at 30 Miller Road.

*BALLATER, Grampian   *B2*
Set in the wooded valley of the Dee, Ballater is a popular resort surrounded by splendid scenery. Of particular note are the Linn of Muick Falls, which lie S on a minor road. Highland games are held in the town every August. Golfers will enjoy the challenge of the local eighteen-hole course, and the game fisherman can pit his skill against furious Dee salmon. This is an excellent area for hillwalking and climbing, particularly N of Ballater around 2,862ft Morven and 2,456ft Cairn Mona Gowan. The Deeside Gliding Club is situated 2m W of Aboyne and operates from Aboyne Airfield at Dinnet. Its facilities are open to the public and instruction is available. A tourist information office is sited in Station Square, Ballater.

*BANCHORY, Grampian   *B2*
Some 4m W of Banchory in Blackhall Forest are the interesting Midmar forest walks. Banchory itself boasts an eighteen-hole golf course and has a tourist centre.

*BANFF, Grampian   *B1*
Safe bathing and a sandy beach can be enjoyed at Banff, and the eighteen-hole golf course is excellent. Salmon, sea trout, and brown trout can be fished in the River Deveron. Facilities for small boat launchings are provided. Tourist information is available.

*BLAIRGOWRIE, Tayside   *B2*
Dean Water and the River Isla can be fished here for brown trout and grayling. Drumore Loch has a water ski-ing centre, and the town has a golf course. Tourist information is available.

*BRAEMAR, Grampian   *B2*
Set amid splendid scenery, this famous holiday resort offers an eighteen-hole golf course and a 9m stretch of the River Dee which can be fished on application to the Invercauld Arms Hotel. Even by Scottish standards this is expensive water, but the fishing is renowned. Braemar makes a good centre for the winter-sports enthusiast, and 3,924ft Beinna Bhairijh is one of the

best and most popular ski slopes in the area. There are no facilities on this mountain and it can only be approached via a rough track. Ski facilities are provided at nearby Glenshee however, and on Cairn Gorm. The latter is best approached from Aviemore. This is superb country for the hill walker and climber. To the SW the magnificent Cairngorms culminate with 4,300ft Ben Macdhui, and W of Braemar is the picturesque Linn of Dee. Access to the latter is via a beautiful route along the heavily-wooded banks of the Dee. From Linn of Dee the mountains can be approached via glens Dee, Lui, or Quoich. Glen Lui wanders among stands of magnificent pine woods and along dancing waters right up into the heart of the Cairngorms, and is perhaps the most rewarding of the three routes. To the E of Braemar is Balmoral Forest. Lochnagar, at 3,786ft the highest point in the forest, is popular for rock, snow, and ice climbing, ski-ing, and walking. Much of beautiful Deeside was preserved when Queen Victoria purchased the Lochnagar Estate. The area is especially famous for its profusion of heather, which is purple with blooms at the end of August. The local pinewoods are used as nesting sites by the golden eagle, a bird which elsewhere builds on cliffs. Braemar has an information caravan at Fife Arms Mews.

BRECHIN, Tayside *B2*
Brechin has an eighteen-hole golf course, pony trekking facilities, and trout fishing in Saugh Loch.

CAIRNGORMS *B2*

In recent years the Cairngorms have become the centre of Scotland's winter sports industry. The very wide range of facilities include three chair lifts – one of which ascends to 3,600ft – and seven ski tows. Car parks, toilets, restaurants, and snack bars are also provided. Surrounding towns and villages feature ski-schools, ski-shops, apres-ski amenities, etc, and the whole of this mountainous region is popular with hill walkers and climbers. Many of the peaks should only be tackled by the experienced, but there are several excellent scrambles for those possessing only good sense and stamina. The 4,084ft Cairn Gorm is the most easily accessible high mountain in Scotland, for instance. Ben Macdhui stands at 4,296ft and is Scotland's second highest mountain. The challenge which it presents should only be accepted by the experienced. An extensive part of the Cairngorms – which comprise Scotland's largest area of high mountains – has been set aside as a nature reserve. The Glen More forest park covers 12,500 acres.

*CALLANDER, Central *A2*
Known as the gateway to the Highlands, this popular touring centre has an eighteen-hole golf course. Pony trekking facilities are offered 9m N at Strathyre and in the Trossachs. Many opportunities exist for both game and coarse fishing. River Teith holds salmon, sea trout, and brown trout, plus pike and perch. Loch Venacher can be fished for salmon, brown trout, pike, and perch. The Trossachs include a water ski-ing and sailing school, and comprise some of Scotland's most beautiful scenery. This area offers ample scope for the climber and hill walker. Strathyre has a forest centre and walk, and the huge Queen Elizabeth forest park stretches to the W. Callander's information office is situated at 2 Ancaster Square.

CAMPBELTOWN, Strathclyde *A3*
Campbeltown is a Kintyre-peninsula resort with a pebble beach and two eighteen-hole golf courses within easy reach – 4m W at Machrihanish and 7m S at Southend. Lussa Loch contains brown and rainbow trout, and the coastal waters yield cod, dabs, haddock, mackerel, pollack, and skate – all of which can be caught from the shore. Boat fishing might produce cod, coalfish, conger, dogfish, haddock, ling, mackerel, pollack, and wrasse. Campbeltown Loch is suitable for sailing and skin diving. A tourist information office exists in the town.

CRIEFF, Tayside *B2*
Another 'gateway to the Highlands', Crieff is a popular resort with an eighteen-hole golf course and a riding stable. Loch Earn can be fished for salmon and brown trout, and the River Earn holds excellent brown trout and grayling. A sailing school is situated on Loch Earn. A nature trail runs along the wooded banks of the River Turret, while farther upstream are the very attractive falls of Turret. There is a tourist information office in James Square.

CUPAR, Fife *B2*
Horses and ponies may be hired for riding and trekking from the local riding school. Golfers may find the little nine-hole course interesting.

DOLLAR, Central *B2*
Dollar boasts an eighteen-hole golf course, and pony trekking facilities are available at nearby Muckhart Mill. Glenquay Reservoir can be fished for brown trout.

DORNOCH, Highland *B1*
The Royal Dornoch eighteen-hole golf course is renowned, and the resort also includes a nine-hole relief course. Buidhe Loch can be fished for brown trout, and the sea angler can expect cod, haddock, and all types of flatfish from boats. Sea trout are caught from the beach. The Masonic Buildings house the tourist information centre.

DRYMEN, Central *A2*
Situated in a region of magnificent mountain scenery, Drymen has a great deal to enchant and exhaust the active sportsman. Two golf courses near by are the Buchanan Castle eighteen-hole and Strathendrick nine-hole. Fishing rights in both Endrinct Water and Loch Lomond belong to the Loch Lomond Angling Improvement Association. There is a considerable waiting list for membership, but a permit for coarse fishing may be obtainable. Boating and canoeing are popular pastimes on Loch Lomond. The walker will find it difficult to choose from the many beautiful routes available. Loch Lomond is renowned for its beauty, and the 3,182ft peak of Ben Lomond rises from within the boundaries of the Queen Elizabeth forest park on the NE shore of the loch. A well-used footpath leads to the summit, and the journey to the top and back will take about six hours.

*DUMFRIES, Dumfries and Galloway *B3*
Dubbed 'The Queen of the South', Dumfries has two eighteen-hole golf courses and there is a pony-trekking stable 5m W at Lochanhead. River Nith can be fished for salmon, sea trout, brown trout, grilse, grayling, perch, and roach, and its estuary is ideal for sailing and boating. Some 7m SW is the Dumfries and District Gliding Club, which caters for visitors and provides instruction for beginners. The club is situated on Glaisters Farm at Kirkgunzeon. Of the several nature reserves close to Dumfries, some restrict admission and require the would-be visitor to obtain a permit. To the NE of Dumfries is the Forest of Ae, where attractive forest walks provide an opportunity to spot a variety of animals and birds. Access to these walks is not restricted. Mabie Forest lies about 5m SW of Dumfries and includes several walks and trails which afford exceptional views. Again access to this is not restricted. Caerlaverock Nature Reserve lies 8m SE of Dumfries and encompasses areas of saltmarsh plus a sandy foreshore. A complex ecosystem of sea and land flora and fauna may be observed here, and access to this part of the reserve is not

restricted. Also at Caerlaverock is a wildfowl refuge, to which admission is very restricted and a fee is charged. Dumfries has a tourist information office at Whitesands.

*DUNBAR, Lothian *B2*

Proud possessor of a record which shows more hours of sunshine than any other Scottish resort, this E Lothian town offers a sand and pebble beach and an open-air swimming pool. Leisure facilities here include two eighteen-hole golf courses and pony-trekking amenities. The coastal waters between Dunbar and Eyemouth are very popular with the beach angler and can be expected to yield codling, haddock, flounders, mackerel, and whiting. Sailing facilities are available at Tynemouth. A cliff-top nature trail at Dunbar illustrates various aspects of geology and animal life. Farther along the coast, about 2m E of Dunbar, is the Barnsness Coastal Park. This comprises 142 acres of coastline considered to be of special interest. Some 6m SW of Dunbar at Stanton is the Pressmennan Wood forest trail, a 2m walk through mixed woodland. Innerwick lies 5m SE of the resort and includes the East Lammermuir Deans nature reserve – four deep valleys in the Lammermuir Hills which provide a habitat for a rich variety of flora. This reserve cannot be visited without a permit. Dunbar has a tourist information centre at the Town House, High Street.

*DUNDEE, Tayside *B2*

Dundee has three eighteen-hole golf courses and there is a pony-trekking stable at Camperdown Park. A riding stable is situated 11m SW at Errol. Beach fishing on the Firth of Tay can produce cod, and the boat-based angler can expect cod, haddock, ling, plaice, pouting, and saithe. The Firth is also a good area for sailing and small craft. An artificial ski-slope at 10 Ancrum Road is only available to members, but the general public are at liberty to join the club. Camperdown Park covers 600 acres and lies on the outskirts of the town. It includes nature trails, several ponds, and a fascinating children's zoo. On the other side of the Firth at Tayport is the Tentsmuir Point nature reserve, where two nature trails give an insight into the flora and fauna of the area. Also at Tayport is the Morton Lochs nature reserve, based around an artificial loch which is on the

migratory route of several species of wildfowl and waders. Permits must be obtained by any person wishing to move away from the road. Dundee's tourist information office is in City Square.

*DUNFERMLINE, Fife *B2*

There are three eighteen-hole golf courses here, and Loch Fitty holds brown trout and rainbow trout. There is a tourist information office in the City Chambers.

DUNKELD, Tayside *B2*

The beautiful woodland scenery which surrounds this Tay-valley town can be explored on horseback from the several pony trekking centres in the area. The $\frac{1}{2}$m-long Hermitage nature trail is an interesting woodland walk which shows a wide variety of trees and birds, and the Craigvinean forest walks through coniferous plantations provide a car park, picnic area, and viewpoint. Loch of Lowes nature reserve lies 2m E of Dunkeld and displays a wide variety of flora and fauna. A pair of ospreys have been nesting in the area since 1969 and can be watched from an observation hide, and a visitor centre here supplies information. The Tay offers fishing, and there is a golf course in the area.

*DUNOON, Strathclyde *A2*

A resort on the W bank of the Firth of Clyde, Dunoon has an eighteen-hole golf course and a reservoir which may be fished for brown and rainbow trout. Eck Loch holds salmon, sea trout, and brown trout, and sea fishing in the Firth of Clyde and Loch Long is productive. Many opportunities for sailing and boating exist on Holy Loch, Loch Long, and the firth. Forest trees from all over the world are grown at the Forestry Commission's Kilmun Arboretum, and there are various interesting woodland walks. Dunoon has a tourist information centre at Pier Esplanade.

DURNESS, Highland *A1*

Superb cliff scenery on this N coast includes 800ft Cló Mor, the highest mainland cliff in Britain. The cliff face provides a precarious footing for numerous sea-bird colonies. Limestone cliffs around Smoo Cave – in itself of great interest – hold much to interest the botanist. Balnakeil Bay has a sandy beach, and Loch Eriboll is popular with small-boat sailors. Lochs Inchard, Laxford, and a'Chairn Bhairn are situated on the NW coasts and are also suitable for small craft. Many of the local lochs hold trout. Durness has a tourist informaton caravan.

EARLSFERRY, Fife *B2*

Twin resort of Elie, Earlsferry offers good beaches and safe bathing. Golfers will find the eighteen- and nine-hole courses rewarding, and there is a pony trekking stable at Elie. Sea anglers can expect to catch cod, flounders, haddock, and saithe here, and the coastal waters are suitable for small boats. Largo Bay lies round the headland and has facilities for larger launchings.

*EDINBURGH, Lothian *B3*

Edinburgh's administrative and cultural capital offers – as is to be expected – a full spectrum of leisure possibilities. An indication of the esteem in which golf is held throughout Scotland is the number of courses in the country's premier city – 24, all but one of which have eighteen holes. Rugby enthusiasts the world over are familiar with the famous Murrayfield ground. Edinburgh's Botanic Garden is one of the most renowned in the world, and the zoo and museums are places where many happy hours – if not days – can be spent. There are three pony-trekking and riding stables within 3m of the city centre. The ones at Silverknowes and Liberton Drive provide both horses and ponies, and the one at Juniper Green specializes in horses.

Although Edinburgh does not have any of the great fishing waters, excellent sport is provided by local, lesser-known lochs and reservoirs. Brown trout can be taken from Clubbiedean, Gladhouse, Glencorse, and Roseberry reservoirs, and from the Water of Leith. For the coarse fisherman Duddington Loch holds wild carp, roach, and tench. Beach fishing on the Firth of Forth yields coalfish, flatfish, and whiting, while the boat angler can expect to take coalfish, codling, conger, flatfish, gurnard, haddock, mackerel, and whiting. The firth is also suitable for sailing and boating. Excellent walks penetrate the attractive countryside around Edinburgh. To the SW are the beautiful Pentland Hills with 1,898ft Scald Law, 1,570ft Cock Rig, and 1,752ft Byrehope Mount, while to the S and SE is the beautiful scenery of the Moorfoot and Lammermuir Hills. Hermitage of Braid Public Park includes a two-hour nature trail which is described in a leaflet written by children. Some 12m W of Edinburgh is the Almondell country park, is a 90-acre estate with a river, canal, woodlands, and a nature trail. An artificial ski-slope at the Hillend Ski centre in Biggar Road is open to the public throughout the year from 09.00 to 21.00 hrs. A tourist information office is situated at 1 Cockburn Street, and the Scottish Tourist Board has its headquarters at 23 Ravelston Terrace.

*ELGIN, Grampian *B1*

Although not actually on the coast, Elgin is very near the sea and close to large areas of sandy beach at Burghead Bay and Buckie. Buckie and Lossiemouth are popular seaside resorts with fine sporting facilities. Elgin itself has an eighteen-hole golf course, and there are two more on the coast at Newtown and Lossiemouth. The former is a nine-hole course and the one at Lossiemouth has eighteen holes. The River Lossie can be fished for salmon, sea trout, and brown trout, and sea angling is particularly good at Lossiemouth, Branderburgh, and Burghead. The area is popular with small-boat sailors and yachtsmen, and coastal centres for these pursuits include

Findhorn, Findhorn Bay, Burghead, Lossiemouth, and Spey Bay. Pony trekking facilities are offered at Lossiemouth and 7m W at Kinloss. Some 4m SW of Elgin is Monaughty Forest, where there are four interesting walks and various visitor amenities. A tourist information office is situated in Elgin's High Street.

EYEMOUTH, Borders B3

A good bathing beach which is sandy in parts can be enjoyed at this Border-country resort, and there is a nine-hole golf course. Pony trekking facilities are available in the area. Eye Water may be fished for brown and rainbow trout, while the sea angler can take cod, codling, haddock, flounders, mackerel, plaice, saithe, and sole. Skin diving is a popular pastime here, and the underwater visibility around the local coast is very good. Divers will find plenty to occupy their interest, including wrecks and unusual rock formations. The Lammermuir Hills offer great scope to the hill walker.

FALKIRK, Central B2

Four golf courses exist within 5m of Falkirk – three eighteen-hole and one nine-hole. A pony trekking stable operates in the area, and brown trout can be taken from the River Avon. Trout fishing is also offered by the Carron Valley Reservoir.

FORFAR, Tayside B2

Opportunities for fresh-water fishing here are extensive. Brown trout can be taken in Dean Water, Forfar Loch, Glenogil Reservoir, Kerbert Water and Noran Water, and there are grayling in Dean Water and Kerbert Water. Forfar Loch holds pike. The Sidlaw Hills lie to the SW and provide good hill-walking country. Forfar has an eighteen-hole golf course.

FORT AUGUSTUS, Highland A2

Situated at the S end of Loch Ness amidst a setting of wooded heights, Fort Augustus is a good centre from which to explore the central and W Highlands. Pony trekking centres provide an enjoyable means of exploring the area, and golfers can match their skill against the local nine-hole course.

This region is well known to anglers – Loch Ness can be fished for salmon, brown trout, sea trout, eels, and pike; Moriston River has salmon, sea trout, and brown trout; and lochs Garry and Cluanie contain brown trout. Loch Ness and Loch Lochy are ideal for small-boat sailing, and Lochy is also a canoeing centre. To the W of Fort Augustus is superb hill-walking country, but some of the terrain is rough and difficult and should only be attempted by those who are well-equipped and the physically fit. Some of the more well-known summits are 3,634ft Sgurr Nan Conbhairear and 3,673ft A'Chralaig. Both of these are approached from a road running along the N side of Loch Cluanie, and are strenuous but not difficult climbs. Farther W along Glen Shiel are the five Sisters of Kintail, a well-known range which culminates in 3,505ft Sgurr Fhuaran and can be approached from a point 1½m E of Glen Shiel Bridge. The climb up Sgurr Fhuaran is steep and gruelling. Carn Eige, at 3,877ft the highest mountain in the W Highlands, lies S of Loch Mullardoch and is best approached from Loch Beneveian. The long, arduous climb to its summit is only

suitable for the really fit. Those who are not quite so adventurous can enjoy the many fine walks to be had around Glen Moriston, Glen Affric, Dog Falls etc. Inchnacradoch Forest contains two interesting forest trails. Fort Augustus has a tourist information office in the car park.

FORTROSE, Highland B1

Extensive sandy beaches and an eighteen-hole golf course are offered by this small, inner Moray-Firth resort. The firth is famous for its fishing and teems with cod, flatfish of all kinds, haddock, mackerel, pollack, saithe, and sea trout. Avoch Bay and the inner firth are excellent for boats of all sizes. To the N of Fortrose is the good sailing area of Cromarty Firth, which is also good for sea fishing. Nigg Bay lies on the N shore of Cromarty Firth and has a sandy beach.

*FORT WILLIAM, Highland A2

Fort William is overshadowed by the highest mountain in Great Britain – 4,406ft Ben Nevis. Loch Arkaig lies N and can be fished for brown trout, sea trout, and salmon. Loch Linnhe holds salt-water fish, and the fishing is particularly good at Corran. Most of piers provide good vantage points from which fish may be taken. Lochs Eil and Linnhe are suitable for sailing.

The town forms an excellent centre for the hill walker and climber. Ben Nevis is an obvious goal and is accessible by three main routes, each of varying difficulty. Beneath the Ben is beautiful Glen Nevis, which can be followed by a road which is contained by the Glen for 7m and terminates at a car park. Beyond this is the Gorge of Nevis, one of Scotland's most dramatically beautiful places – a combination of rock, water, and trees. On the S side of Glen Nevis the Mamore Mountain chain provides a taxing ground for experienced climbers, and Loch Arkaig is a place of quiet and secluded beauty. To the W of Fort William, bounded by Loch Shiel and the Sound of Arsaig, is the Moidart region. This is another area which defies any description – it has to be seen to be appreciated. Some 10m NE of the town is the Glen Roy nature reserve, which includes a post-glacial terrace system. Fort William has a tourist office. Pony trekking stables exist in the area.

*FRASERBURGH, Grampian B1

Fraserburgh Bay offers a sandy beach and is suitable for small boat sailing. The town itself boasts an eighteen-hole golf course. Opportunities for the fisherman include brown trout in Fedderate Reservoir, rainbow and brown trout in Red Loch, and Loch-Leven trout and sea trout in Loch of Strathbeg. Loch of Strathbeg is also of interest for its wildfowl and flora. Good salt-water catches which can be expected from the pier at Fraserburgh and from Kinnairds Head might include codling, mackerel, and saithe. Boat fishing can yield codling, haddock, mackerel, plaice, and saithe. There is a tourist information office in Saltoun Square.

*GAIRLOCH, Highland A1

Beautifully-situated Gairloch is a small resort with a good stretch of sandy beach. Similarly fine beaches can be enjoyed N at Seana Chamas and on the N shore of Loch Torridon. The resort has a nine-hole golf course and is a very popular sea-angling centre. Pollack and saithe may be caught from the shore, and conger, haddock, ling, skate, and whiting from boats. This region is one of the most wildly beautiful in Scotland and a paradise for the climber and the hill walker.

An excellent walking path runs N from Applecross village to Shieldaig, and thence E to scenic Glen Torridon. Coulin Forest and Ben-damph Forest are bounded by Glens Coulin and Torridon, and criss-crossed by deer-stalkers trails. One of the best walks in this region is from Achashellach in Glen Carron, past Lochs Coulin and Clair, thence to Glen Torridon. This is a private road which is open to walkers only and affords magnificent views. Torridon Forest contains some of the most dramatic and compelling mountain scenery in Scotland. Details of routes for walkers and climbers in this region can be obtained from the trust warden at Torridon or the conservancy warden at Kinlochewe.

Beautiful Loch Maree has only one rival – Loch Lomond – and is overlooked by 3,217ft Slioch. This height offers good climbing but should not be attempted during the deer-stalking season. To the N of Loch Maree and bounded in the N by Little Loch Broom is a mountainous region which includes Loch Fionn and 3,774ft An Teallach. This remote and rugged region has a thread of paths which open it up to walkers and climbers. The W shores of Loch Maree include the two Slattadale forest trails, walks of 5m and 1½m length respectively. Beinn Eighe nature reserve was the first of its kind to be established in Britain and is situated on the E slope of Beinn Eighe. The magnificent golden eagle is not an uncommon sight here. To the N of Glen Torridon is Torridon Forest, a vast 14,000-acre estate belonging to the NTS. Fine scenery and large numbers of rare animals, birds, and plants are featured here. Tourist information can be obtained from Achtercairn in Gairloch and from the centres at Kinlochewe and Torridon.

*GALASHIELS, Borders *B3*

An eighteen- and nine-hole golf course exist at Galashiels, and there are opportunities for pony trekking in the vicinity. River Tweed can be fished for brown trout and grayling.

GATEHOUSE OF FLEET, Dumfries and Galloway *B3*

Situated near Wigtown Bay, this attractive town is set amid fine scenery and includes a nine-hole golf course. Pony trekking facilities are offered 5m SW. This is good fishing country, and the numerous little lochs are well stocked. Sea trout and sometimes salmon and grilse may be caught in the Water of Fleet. Lochs Whinyeon and Grannoch can be fished for brown trout, while Loch Skerrow offers brown and rainbow trout. Bush Moss Loch contains rainbow trout. Fleet Bay is a good venue for small-boat sailing. Fleet Forest lies S of the town and includes the Murray Forest Centre. Three walks and an information centre are provided for the benefit of visitors. There is an information office in Horatio Square.

*GIRVAN, Strathclyde *A3*

Features of this popular resort include a sandy beach and an eighteen-hole golf course. Pony-trekking facilities are available down the coast at Lendalfoot. Water of Girvan is said to provide some of the finest fishing in W Scotland, and although a lot of the river is privately fished some stretches are still open. The angler can expect salmon, sea trout, and brown trout here. Sea anglers have good prospects too, especially off the pier and from Horse Rock. Codling, flounders, gurnard, haddock, monkfish, plaice and skate are all to be found in these waters. Facilities for launching both large and small sailing vessels exist at Girvan. About 15m E of Girvan is the huge Glen Trool forest park – some 200sqm of magnificent upland scenery. Several excellent walks cross this region, and the 2,764ft Merrick is the highest point. This and Loch Trool itself are the main features. Glen Trool forest park is about to be renamed Galloway forest park. Girvan has a tourist information office at the Town House.

*GLASGOW, Strathclyde *A3*

As befits its size Glasgow has a total of 23 golf courses, four of which have nine holes and the rest eighteen. Somewhat surprisingly Glasgow also has a pony trekking and riding stable, and offers sea angling.

Much of the fishing in the Glasgow area belongs to Loch Lomond Angling Improvement Association. Membership to this club is restricted and there is a long waiting list, but there are several 'open' waters that may be fished. These include the Luggie River for brown trout, and rainbow trout; Sloy Loch for brown trout; Lochen Loch for brown trout; Springfield Reservoir for brown trout; the Clyde for brown trout, grayling, and roach. A water in Clyde Park holds roach, perch, and pike and is completely free. An artificial ski-slope which is open to the public seven days a week from 10.00hrs until one hour before the park closes is situated in Bellahouston Park, but prior bookings are required. Excellent walking may be had N of Glasgow in the Loch Lomond region, and Glasgow's parks contain numerous nature trails. These have primarily been laid out for children, but all age-groups will enjoy them, and are situated in Dawsholm Park, Kelvingrove Park, Rosshall Park, and Springburn Park. Some 9m SE at Bellshill is the Orbiston Glen nature trail, a 1¾m walk again designed mainly for children, and about 13m NE at Cumbernauld is the Palacerigg country park. Glasgow has an excellent Botanical Garden. The tourist information office is in George Square.

GLENCOE, Highland *A2*

Coe River may be fished for salmon, sea trout, and brown trout, but Glencoe's greatest attraction is its mountains. These are ideal for walking, climbing, and winter sports of all types. Ski-ing facilities are centred on Meall a Bhuiridh, which is situated off the approach road a few miles SE of the descent into the glen. Among the many amenities provided are chairlifts, T-bar tows, car parks, a cafe, and several good hotels. Facilities are only fully operational at weekends, Easter, and New Year, but the services can be hired for a club or party at very reasonable rates. The most popular climbing mountain in Scotland is 3,245ft Buchaille Etive Mor, which is situated at the E entrance of Glen Coe. To the S of Glen Coe is the mountain complexity of 3,766ft Bidean nam Bian, which should only be attempted by experienced rock-climbers. The N side of the glen is enclosed by Aonach Eagach, 2m of jagged ridge which culminates at 3,168ft and is again only suitable for experienced climbers. A less daunting mountain is 3,362ft Bein a Bheithir, which has twin peaks overlooking the mouth of Loch Leven. A forest road may be taken to the tree line, from whence a glen may be followed to the main ridge. To the E of Glen Coe the vast, open expanse of Rannoch Moor is interlaced by lochs and rivers. The centre of the moor affords the best views of the mountains of Glen Coe, and the entire region offers excellent, if rough, walking. Some 12,800 acres of Glen Coe belong to the NTS and include two forest walks – one historical and one botanical. An information centre is sited here.

GLENROTHES, Fife *B2*

Glenrothes is a new-town development in the Kingdom of Fife. The town has an eighteen-hole golf course and the area offers good opportunities for pony-trekking. Loch Leven lies 7m W and offers fishing, gliding, a nature reserve, etc. Near by to the S and E is the sea. There is an information kiosk in the town.

GLENSHEE, Tayside *B2*

In recent years Glenshee has become very popular as a ski-ing centre. Activities are centred round the 3,059ft Cairnwell Mountain, which has T-bar tows, a chairlift, car park, toilets, and a café. A ski school and a sports shop are situated in Spittal of Glenshee. The region also holds much to please the climber and hillwalker, particularly among the notable peaks of Cairnwell, 3,502ft Glas Maol, and 3,786ft Lochnagar.

GRANTOWN-ON-SPEY, Highland *B2*

Popular for both summer and winter holidays, Grantown-on-Spey is conveniently close to the Cairngorm ski-ing centre and includes a ski shop among other winter-sports facilities. There are two ski schools, an eighteen-hole golf course, and pony-trekking facilities. River Spey is famous for its salmon and holds sea and brown trout. Trout can also be taken from Lochindorb, and Mallochie Loch is well known for its pike. The Spey is a popular canoeing venue. Fine hill walks in the area penetrate beautiful Strath Spey and the Hills of Cromdale, which rise to the E. There is a tourist information office in the Square.

GREENOCK, Strathclyde *A2*

As well as the eighteen-hole golf course in the town, there are three other courses within 5m of Greenock. Brown trout can be taken from many of the local lochs and reservoirs, and S of Greenock is the Renfrewshire regional park. This comprises 30,000 acres of high moorland, wooded valleys, stretches of water, and affords marvellous views over the Clyde. Cornalees Bridge Trail runs near Loch Thom and visitors are guided by a ranger. Features of interest along this walk include several industrial and archaeological items.

HADDINGTON, Lothian *B3*

This attractive town has an eighteen-hole golf course and facilities for pony trekking. The area is well known for its brown trout fishing in the local burns, streams, and reservoirs – including Birns Water, Donolly Reservoir, Gifford Water, Hopes Reservoir, Keith Water, and the River Tyne. Roach can be caught in the Tyne and carp in Danskine Loch. Good hill-walking country includes the Lammermuir Hills, with 1,307ft Clints Dod, 1,750ft Meikle Says Law, 1,625ft Hunt Law, and 1,245ft Cranshaws Hill.

HAMILTON, Strathclyde A3

Set amid very pleasant countryside with the attractively-wooded valleys of the Clyde and Avon to the S and E, Hamilton has an eighteen- and a nine-hole golf course. The Neilsland Park nature trail introduces the visitor to a variety of plants and trees.

*HAWICK, Borders B3

Pony trekking facilities exist in the area around Hawick, and angling prospects include brown trout fishing in many of the local lochs. River Teviot holds salmon, brown trout, and grayling. Excellent hill-walking country around Hawick includes Teviotdale, Eskdale to the S, and the Cheviot Hills to the SE. Also SE and right on the Border is the 125,000-acre Border forest park. The town of Hawick has two golf courses – one eighteen and one nine hole. Hendersons Travel Agency in the High Street will supply tourist information.

HELENSBURGH, Strathclyde A2

Much of the fishing in the lochs around Helensburgh is owned by angling clubs and is not open to the public, but local inquiries may reveal less restricted waters. Sea angling from shore or boat is good and can yield cod, conger, dabs, dogfish, flounders, haddock, rays, saithe, and whiting. Sailing is popular on Gare Loch, Loch Long, and the River Clyde. A great deal of this beautiful area is popular with hill walkers, and the Argyll forest park and Loch Long lie to the W. Loch Lomond and The Queen Elizabeth forest park lie to the E. Renowned as one of the loveliest places in the world, Loch Lomond is surrounded by thick deciduous woodland and the area around the village of Luss is famous for its flowers. The Ardmore nature reserve covers both fresh and saltwater marsh as well as foreshore areas, and is of great biological and geological interest. Access to the foreshore is not restricted, but a permit is required to visit the rest of the reserve. To the E on the shores of the loch is the Loch Lomond Bear Park. Helensburgh itself includes an eighteen-hole golf course.

*HELMSDALE, Highland B1

Leisure facilities at Helmsdale include a nine-hole golf course and a sandy beach which allows access for safe bathing. The waters in the area are reputed to offer some of the finest fishing in Scotland, and the coast is suitable for small-boat sailing. A tourist information office is situated in Dunrobin Street.

HUNTLY, Grampian B1

Rivers Deveron and Isla flow through a pleasant landscape of hills and woods before uniting N of Huntly. There is a lido on the Deveron and the local eighteen-hole golf course is noted as being excellent. Pony trekking facilities exist in the area. Huntly is a fine centre for angling and rivers Bogie, Deveron, and Isla can all be fished for salmon and trout. A tourist information caravan is in the Square.

*INVERNESS, Highland B1

Superbly situated at the mouth of the River Ness, this excellent tourist centre is called the 'Capital of the Highlands' and includes an eighteen-hole golf course. Opportunities for fishing are good – Choire Loch has brown and rainbow trout, the N sides of Dochfour Loch and the Caledonian Canal can be fished for brown trout, and Loch Ness and Ness River offer salmon, sea trout, and brown trout. Beauly Firth and Moray Firth are known to sea anglers and provide sailing facilities. Inverness has a sub-aqua club. Some 3m E is the 2m-long Culloden forest trail, and to the W at Leachkin is the Craig Phadraig forest walk. The tourist office is at 23 Church Street.

INVERURIE, Grampian B2

Confluence of rivers Urie and Don is just S of Inverurie, and stretches of both these rivers can be fished for salmon and brown trout. About 1½m W are the Bennachie forest walks, which pass through varied scenery including forests. Golf and tourist information are also offered.

IRVINE, Strathclyde A3

A large expanse of sandy beach on the coast here stretches from Saltcoats in the N to Ayr in the S. Irvine has two eighteen-hole golf courses and there is a riding stable 4m N at Kilwinning. Rivers Irvine, Garnock, and Lugton, and Annick Water offer salmon, sea trout, and brown trout, and sea angling in Irvine Bay produces cod and flounders from the shore and coalfish, cod, conger, dogfish, flounders, haddock, skate, and whiting from boats. Sailing is good all along this coast, and a sub-aqua centre operates from Troon.

JEDBURGH, Borders B3

This border town is well known for its rugby football and has a nine-hole golf course plus pony-trekking facilities. Jed Water, Teviot River, and Kale River can all be fished for brown trout, and the Teviot also holds salmon and sea trout. Grayling and roach can be caught in both the Teviot and Jed Water. Good hill walking country includes the beautiful valley of the Jed and Teviotdale to the NW. To the S are the splendid Cheviots and the 125,000-acre Border forest park. The latter is the largest planted forest system in the Kingdom. Jedburgh has a tourist information office at The Toll House, Lothian Park.

KEITH, Grampian B1

Keith is situated in Strath Isla and has an eighteen-hole golf course. The River Isla offers salmon, sea trout, and brown trout, and can be fished by permit obtainable from Huntly's Town Clerk. There is a tourist information office in Church Road.

*KELSO, Borders B3

Pony-trekking stables exist 4m NW of Kelso at Nethorn and 12½m SE at Yetholm. Golfers are catered for with a nine-hole course. The River Tweed is renowned as one of the finest of all salmon rivers, but also holds trout and various coarse fish. Brown trout can be caught in Jed Water, Teviot River, and Kale River, and the Teviot also has salmon and sea trout. There is a tourist information office at 66 Woodmarket.

KILLIN, Central A2

Resort for both winter and summer sports, Killin is situated in the midst of fine Highland scenery and includes a nine-hole golf course. Anglers will find plenty of sport in the area; Dochart River and Loch na Lairige have brown trout, and Loch Tay and the River Lochay have both salmon and trout. Dochart River is also known for its pike and perch. Sailing facilities are available S at Loch Earn.

Ben Lawers is particularly well known as a ski slope, and the entire region is a popular winter-sports venue. Magnificent areas for hill walking and climbing include 3,984ft Ben Lawers – the highest mountain in the S Highlands – which can be approached via a track from the car park on the road from Loch Tay to Glen Lyon. A short nature trail also starts from the car park, and much of Ben Lawers forms a nature reserve. The mountain is the habitat of some of the finest and rarest alpine flora in the Kingdom. Much farther N is 3,547ft Schichallion, a well known climber's mountain with a peak covered in boulders which make the going difficult. The scramble to the top is amply rewarded by extensive views in all directions. Glen Lyon is superb and an excellent walk can be taken along its entire length from Loch Lyon down to Fortingall. Nearer to Killin is Glen Lochay, which is noted for its waterfalls and affords good views of Loch Tay from the wooded S bank. To the SW of Killin are the peaks of 3,843ft Ben More and 3,821ft Stob Binnein. There is an information centre at Myrtle Grove.

KILMARNOCK, Strathclyde A3

There are two eighteen-hole golf courses here. Brown trout can be taken from Annick Water, and both salmon and trout from the River Irvine.

KINGUSSIE, Highland B2

Closely associated with the Cairngorms winter-sports centre, this Highland resort offers a very wide range of leisure activities which include a famous eighteen-hole golf course. Pony trekking facilities

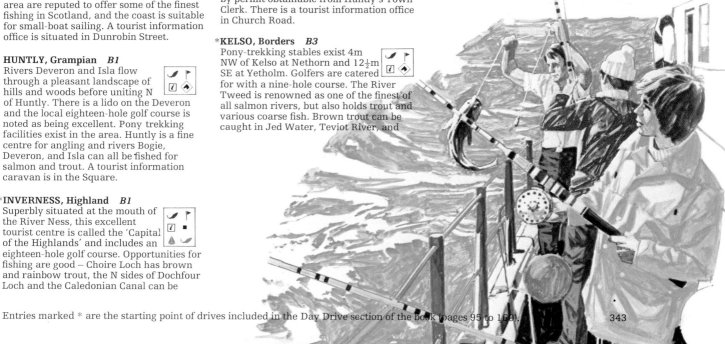

exist in the area, and the River Spey's salmon and trout attract anglers. The Spey is also popular with canoeists and Loch Insh is a favourite venue for yachtsmen. Facilities for the winter-sports enthusiast include a ski school, and the Cairngorm Gliding Club is situated at Feshiebridge. Visitors are welcome to the latter and training is available.

To the NE of Kingussie on the A9 is the Highland wildlife park, a 260-acre area abounding with animals which were and are indigenous to Scotland. Vast opportunities exist for the hill walker and climber. To N and W are the Monadhliaths, and the magnificent Cairngorms rise to the E. Glen Feshie lies E of Kingussie and is particularly wild and remote. A track from Feshiebridge to the Dee leads through magnificent stands of Caledonian Pine and on through high and desolate ravines. Kingussie has a tourist information office at 26 High Street.

KINROSS, Tayside *B2*
Above all else Kinross is famous for Loch Leven, and is situated on this famous water's W shore. To the angler the name spells trout – in fact Loch Leven Trout, a name famous the world over. Brown trout can be taken from a section stretching from Leven sluices to Auchmuir Bridge. To the ornithologist the name spells wildfowl, for this is the most important freshwater breeding and migratory area for ducks and geese in the Kingdom. On the S shore of the loch is the Vane Farm nature reserve, which comprises 300 acres of mixed habitats and includes a nature trail through birch woods to moorland. Facilities include an ecological display room and an observation post. A small charge is levied for use of the car park but otherwise access is free – although not unlimited. At Scotlandwell, E of Loch Leven, is a gliding club run by the Scottish Gliding Union. Kinross itself has golfing facilities. Tourist information can be obtained from the Green Hotel at Kinross.

KIRKCALDY, Fife *B2*
Among the leisure facilities in this town are two eighteen-hole golf courses, and there are pony-trekking facilities in the area. Opportunities for the freshwater angler are not large but Raith Lake does hold brown and rainbow trout. The sea angler has the chance of good catches at West Wemyss, East Wemyss, Buckhaven, and Methil and can expect to beach cod, eels, flounders, haddock, mackerel, saithe, and whiting. Yachtsmen and small-boat sailors favour the Firth of Forth and there are launching facilities at Kirkcaldy.

Ravenscraig Park nature trail introduces the visitor to many exotic trees, and the 1m Dunrikier Park nature trail illustrates various aspects of plant and bird life.

*KIRKCUDBRIGHT, Dumfries and Galloway *B3*
Home of many artists, Kirkcudbright is an attractive town which provides holiday courses for aspiring painters – no matter how meagre their skill. Golfing enthusiasts may like to meet the challenge of the local nine-hole course, and the sea angler can expect to catch bass, coalfish, cod, conger, dogfish, flounders, plaice and pollack from the beach. Boat fishing will yield coalfish, codfish, conger, dogfish, flatfish, haddock, mackerel, pollack, and tope. Kirkcudbright Bay is a good boating area and offers sailing facilities. The tourist information office is in the Town Hall.

*LAIRG, Tayside *A1*
Holiday resort and Highland touring centre, Lairg is a handy base for anglers intent on the salmon, brown trout, and sea trout in Loch Shin. Mallart River and Mudale River can be fished for salmon, and Loch Beannach has brown trout. Full information concerning the numerous other waters in the area is usually obtainable from local hotels. Moorland lies to the N and a particular attraction to the S are the Falls of Shin. Also S off the Bonar Bridge road are the Kyle of Sutherland forest walks. Tourist information can be obtained at Lairg Library.

*LANARK, Strathclyde *B3*
Lanark has an eighteen-hole golf course and a pony-trekking and riding stable. The River Clyde may be fished for brown trout, grayling, roach, and other coarse fish. Corehouse nature reserve lies on the outskirts of Lanark and features a wide variety of birds, animals, and plants in woodland. It includes two trails, but except for certain open days which are announced in the local press, a permit is required by would-be visitors. Permits can be obtained from the reserve secretary, 18 Ladyacre Road. There is a tourist information office at 26 Hope Street.

LARGS, Strathclyde *A3*
This popular holiday resort has a sandy, protected bay. There are two eighteen-hole golf courses on the mainland and another at

Millport on Great Cumbrae Island, which is connected to Largs by ferry. Pony-trekking facilities are available in the area and the sea angling is good. Sea anglers can expect to meet cod, conger, dabs, dogfish, haddock, mackerel, plaice, saithe, and sea trout. A very popular boating and yachting centre, Largs is conveniently close to sheltered waters and offers various sailing facilities. There is a tourist information office at Cumbraen Pavilion.

LINLITHGOW, Lothian *B2*
Linlithgow Loch is stocked with brown trout, but advance booking for a permit is essential. Tickets are available from 2 Carmuirs Street, Camelon, Falkirk, and there is a weight restriction – only fish over 8lb may be taken. The loch is suitable for dinghy sailing, also by permit. There is an eighteen-hole golf course in the area.

*LOCHGILPHEAD, Strathclyde *A2*
Leisure facilities here include a nine-hole golf course, and there are pony trekking stables in the area. River Add can be fished for salmon, and Add Loch holds brown trout. Most of the usual saltwater fish can be caught at Ardrishaig, which is situated at the mouth of Loch Gilp. Loch Gilp and Loch Fyne are suitable for sailing, but the waters are extremely deep and can be dangerous. To the W on the opposite side of the Knapdale peninsula are lochs Sween and Crinan, which are also suitable for sailing. Knapdale forest lies at the W entry of the Crinan Canal and offers several walks through mixed terrain. A forest information centre is located here, and Lochgilphead has an information centre.

*LOCKERBIE, Dumfries and Galloway *B3*
Set in a farming landscape, this market town has a nine-hole golf course and is close to several excellent game- and coarse-fishing waters. River Annan holds salmon, sea trout, brown trout, grayling, chub, roach, perch, and pike. Dryfe and Kinnell waters have salmon, sea trout, and brown trout. Eels, pike, perch, roach, bream, and vendace can be taken from Castle Loch at Lochmaben, which is also suitable for sailing. Lockerbie's tourist information office is at 55 High Street.

MELROSE, Borders *B3*
Riding and pony trekking stables are based in and near Melrose respectively, and the town has a nine-hole golf course. The world-famous

fishing offered by the Tweed is available here, and the river holds salmon and trout. Eildon Walk is a 4m history trail situated SE in the Eildon Hills.

*MOFFAT, Dumfries and Galloway   B3

Beautifully set among lowland mountains, Moffat is an ideal holiday centre with facilities for pony trekking and eighteen-hole golf. The region is well known to anglers and includes the River Annan, Evan Water, and Moffat Water; these all hold salmon, sea trout, and brown trout. Hill walkers will find the surrounding countryside interesting and challenging. To the NW the Lowther Hills culminate with 2,404ft Green Lowther, and N is the Devils Beef Tub – a giant depression gouged out of the hills. Beyond the Beef Tub is the source of the Tweed, and E are the heights of 2,652ft Hart Fell, 2,413ft Saddle Yoke, and 2,696ft White Coomb. Some 2,000 acres of NTS land lie E of Saddle Yoke and W of the A708 road, and include the spectacular, 200ft Grey Mares Tail waterfall. Hills and moors to the E of Moffat lie round 2,270ft Ettrick Pen, the highest point in the area.

MONTROSE, Tayside   B2

Sands and bathing at this popular seaside town and touring centre are excellent, and the leisure amenities include two eighteen-hole golf courses. There is a pony trekking and riding stable 2½m from Montrose at Langley Park. South Esk River may be fished for salmon, sea trout, grilse, and finnock, and the North Esk holds sea and brown trout. Prospects for beach anglers are good, and codling, mackerel, plaice, saithe, and wrasse can all be caught from the shore. Boat fishing might yield catfish, cod, haddock, etc. Sailing is popular both in the local coastal waters and in Montrose Basin – a large stretch of water some 9m round fed by the South Esk. The basin also holds a great deal to interest the ornithologist, including wild fowl and waders all year round plus thousands of geese in the winter. Some 5m N of Montrose is the St Cyrus nature reserve, 227 acres of salt marsh, sand dunes, and cliffs noted for its abundance of very rare plants and plant communities. A 1½m nature trail here is open to the public at all times. There is a tourist information office in the Town Buildings at Montrose.

MOTHERWELL, Strathclyde   B3

A 2-acre pond in Clyde Park can be fished for roach, perch, and pike, and this industrial town has an eighteen-hole golf course. The surrounding countryside can be explored on horseback from Motherwell's pony trekking and riding stables.

MUIR OF ORD, Highland   A1

Situated in the centre of a large crofting district, the 'muir' is now an eighteen-hole golf course. Pony trekking parties explore the area and the River Conon can be fished for salmon and brown trout. Canoeists use the River Orrin, and there are sailing and sea-angling facilities at Beauly Firth. Muir of Ord has a tourist information office.

NAIRN, Highland   B1

Renowned for its sunny climate, its beach, and its safe bathing, Nairn is sometimes called 'The Brighton of the North'. There are two eighteen- and one nine-hole golf

courses here, and the River Nairn can be fished for salmon and trout. Lochindorb lies to the S off the A939 and holds trout. Two small piers provide good points from which the sea angler may try for dabs, lythe, mackerel, and small saithe. Sailing is also possible here. The tourist information office is situated at the Bus Station in King Street.

NEW GALLOWAY, Dumfries and Galloway   A3

Smallest of all Scottish royal burghs, New Galloway is renowned as an angling centre. Permits for many of the waters in the area can be obtained from places in the town, but several of the waters are controlled from Newton Stewart, Gatehouse of Fleet, and Castle Douglas. The River Ken holds salmon, trout, pike, and perch. Carsfad River and Clatteringshaws Reservoir both have brown trout. Lochinvar has Loch-Leven trout and Stroan Loch offers brown trout, salmon, pike, and perch. Earlston Loch contains brown trout, and salmon. The town has a nine-hole golf course, and there are good opportunities for the hill walker in the area. Immediately SW is Cairn Edward Forest, and W is the vast and exciting Glen Trool forest park. The latter is to be renamed Galloway forest park.

*NEWTON STEWART, Dumfries and Galloway   A3

Fishing resort and holiday centre set in fine scenery, Newton Stewart offers pony trekking from Creetown and Kirkcowan, plus excellent fishing on the Cree River, Bladnoch River, Minnoch River, Palnure Burn, and Penkill Burn. All these waters hold salmon, sea trout, grilse, pike, and perch. Lochs Clatteringshaws, Dee, Kirriereoch, and Ochiltree may be fished for trout, and pike, and Tarf Water contains brown trout, and sea trout. Newton Stewart lies just S of the Glen Trool forest park and is a good base for excellent hill walks and trails. The park, about to be renamed Galloway forest park, covers some 200sqm and contains some of the highest and most beautiful country in S Scotland. Loch Trool forest begins at the W end of Loch Trool and leads round the shores through mixed woodland; Stroan Bridge forest walk starts and ends at Stroan Bridge 1m E of Gentrool Village; Larg Hill and Bruntis

forest trail starts at the Daltamie Nursery in Kirroughtree Forest and leads to a viewpoint overlooking Loch Bruntis, some 3m SE of Newton Stewart; Talnotry forest trail is situated on the Newton Stewart to New Galloway road opposite Talnotry campsite. Newton Stewart has a tourist information office in Dashwood Square.

NORTH BERWICK, Lothian   B2

Two sandy bays, a heated outdoor swimming pool, and two fine eighteen-hole golf courses are features of this popular holiday town. Pony trekking facilities are available 6m SW at Drem, and the Whisky Bottle Reservoir can be fished for brown trout. Sea angling yields good catches of cod, conger, haddock, mackerel, plaice, saithe, and skate, and the fishing is good from boat or beach. Sailing is popular, and there are facilities for both small and large vessels. The 350ft-high Bass Rock measures 1m round and lies 3m offshore NE of Berwick. It is a haven for countless thousand sea birds, and permission is required to land here. Boat trips around the rock can be made from the harbour at North Berwick. Yellowcraig Coastal Park lies W of the town and comprises 94 acres of woodland and foreshore. It includes a nature trail which can be followed with the aid of a descriptive leaflet, and access to the park is unlimited. Just offshore of the park are the islands of Fidra, Eyebroughty, and Lamb – all very rich in bird life. Permission to visit these must be obtained from the RSPB in Edinburgh.

Farther W at Aberlady Bay is Aberlady Bay nature reserve, which covers an intertidal estuary and includes mud, rock, sand, dunes, and marsh. The reserve is the habitat of a rich variety of bird life – especially terns – and access is unlimited. Dogs should be kept on a lead, especially during the breeding season. This is common sense on all reserves. North Berwick has a tourist information office at 18 Quality Street.

*OBAN, Strathclyde   A2

Highland games are held at this very popular resort during September, and the town is known as a gateway to the Western Isles.

Visitors not intending to take the journey into island magic will find enchantment enough at their feet. The viewpoint of Pulpit Hill above the town affords fine views over beautiful land and seascape. Leisure facilities include an eighteen-hole golf course, and pony trekking stables exist 5m NE at Connel. Local fishing waters include Dubh Loch for Loch Leven trout and brown trout; Loch Scamadale for salmon, sea trout, and brown trout; River Euchar for salmon, sea trout, and brown trout. Sea angling in the Firth of Lorne is excellent and beach fishing might produce dogfish, mackerel, pollack, saithe, and sea trout. Boat anglers can expect codling, conger, dabs, and whiting. Oban harbour is protected by the Island of Kerrera, and the sheltered waters are ideal for sailing and boating. Facilities for these sports are very good, and skin diving is a popular pastime off these shores.

Landscapes here are particularly noteworthy and will amply reward the hill walker. Oban has a tourist information office in Albany Street.

PAISLEY, Strathclyde A3
Lochwinnoch lies 10m SW of Paisley and is a major leisure amenity which offers coarse fishing, dinghy sailing, rowing, and canoeing. Close to Lochwinnoch is Muirshiel country park, comprising 70 acres of woods and moorland. In Paisley itself is the Paisley Glen nature trail, mainly designed for children, and two eighteen-hole golf courses. Pony trekking facilities exist W of Paisley at Johnstone, and Barcraigs Reservoir holds trout.

*PEEBLES, Borders B3
Attractively set by the River Tweed in the Tweeddale Hills, Peebles boasts an eighteen-hole golf course and there are two pony-trekking stables in the area. Although the River Tweed is justifiably famous for its salmon and trout fishing, it also holds some fine coarse fish. Talla and Portmore Reservoirs contain brown trout. Fine hill-walking country surrounds the town: the Moorfoot Hills with 2,162ft Windlestraw Law and 2,137ft Blackhope Scar lie to the N; 241ft Pkyestone Hill, 2,681ft Dollar Law, and 2,727ft Broad Law lie to the S. The 2,360-acre Glentress Forest lies close to the town, is well established, and contains a large number of forest walks varying from 2 to 5m in length. There is a tourist information office in Peebles High Street.

*PERTH, Tayside B2
Once capital of Scotland and now called 'The Fair City', Perth owes its title and much of its attraction to the very handsome countryside that surrounds it. Golfing enthusiasts have three reputable eighteen-hole courses to choose from, and the countryside can be explored on horseback from the town's pony trekking stable. Salmon, sea trout, and brown trout may be taken from the rivers Tay and Earn, and the Tay also holds roach, perch, and grayling. Glenfarg Reservoir may be fished for brown trout. The Firth of Tay is popular with yachtsmen. The Ochil Hills lie SW and the Sidlaw Hills NE of the town. Kinnoull Hill lies on the outskirts of Perth and affords spectacular views. A nature trail has been laid out on the hill. Interesting features of old Perthshire are described in a leaflet entitled *Countryside by Car*, which is available at information centres. Perth's tourist office is in Marshall Place.

PETERHEAD, Grampian B1
Functional above all else, this important fishing town has sandy beaches S at Cruden Bay and N at Rattray. Golfers are catered for with an eighteen- and a nine-hole course, and the River Ugie offers good catches of salmon, sea trout, brown trout, and finnock. Anglers can use two long breakwaters to reach codling, dabs, mackerel, and saithe. Boat-based anglers can expect codling, dabs, haddock, ling, mackerel, and saithe. The area is popular with small-craft sailors and Peterhead provides launching facilities. The Forest of Deer has several interesting walks and lies NW of Peterhead at Strichen. On the coast between the town and Fraserburgh is the Loch of Strathbeg, a wildfowl habitat where the extensive sand dunes also support complex plant communities.

*PITLOCHRY, Tayside B2
Pitlochry is a famous and very popular resort situated in the beautiful valley of the Tummel. Its two golf courses are eighteen- and nine-hole respectively, and the fishing opportunities are both extensive and varied. BHAC Loch holds brown and rainbow trout; Loch Faskally has salmon, brown trout, sea trout, and perch; Loch Tulochcunnan has trout; River Tummel has salmon and brown trout; River Tay has salmon, trout, pike, perch, and grayling. Loch Tummel is a popular sailing venue and Pitlochry, Blair Atholl, and Grandtully all have pony trekking facilities. Ben Vrackie rises to 2,757ft and is one of the best-known climbing peaks in the area. Some 6m N of Ben Vrackie is 3,671ft Beinn a Ghlo, a mountain made up of three peaks. The lowest and most easily accessible summit can be readily approached from Blair Atholl. Tummel Valley contains the lochs Rannoch, Tummel, and Faskally and displays remarkable scenery which exudes an altogether more pastoral atmosphere than many other Highland glens.

One of the most exciting features of the river is the waterfall known as Falls of Tummel. Situated above Loch Faskally, the fall is not high but the waters cascade spectacularly over and between rocks into the loch. Linn of Tummel has a 2m woodland nature trail, and Tummel Forest features a number of walks laid out and organized by the Forestry Commission. An additional feature of the forest is its information centre. The Pass of Killiecrankie is a well-known beauty spot and parking is available here for a small fee. Above the golf course is 1,300ft Craigower, the summit of which affords a panoramic view of the whole Tummel Valley. Pitlochry has a tourist information office at 28 Atholl Road.

POLMONT, Central B2
Polmont Ski Centre has an artificial ski slope and is open to the public from 09.00 hrs to 21.00 hrs – subject to prior booking. The town also has a nine-hole golf course.

PRESTWICK, Strathclyde A3
This is one of several towns situated on the sandy coast which stretches from Ayr to Ardrossan. Prestwick's golfing history stretches back some 400 years, and the three eighteen-hole courses here are of a very high standard. The local reservoir can be fished for brown trout, and the entire coast offers excellent prospects for the sea

angler. The waters are also popular with yachtsmen, and Troon is a skin-diving centre. Pony trekking stables exist at Monkton. The town's information office is in Station Road.

*ST ANDREWS, Fife B2
It would be too easy to say that St Andrews has four superb golf courses. If Scotland is the home of golf, then St Andrews is the throne of that sport. Golf of one type or another has been played on the world famous Old Course since the 15thc, and it can still break golfer's hearts. Although the New, Eden, and Jubilee courses are magnificent, the golfer's thoughts always return to the challenge of the Old. The town itself is a delightful holiday resort with good beaches, safe bathing, swimming pools, and skin-diving facilities. Eden Mouth has yachting amenities and is a popular sailing centre. Cameron Reservoir and Kinness Burn hold brown trout, and the sea angling on this stretch of coast is good. Tentsmuir nature reserve is an area of sand and marsh situated N above Leuchars and noted for its plants and wintering wildfowl. Access to the reserve is by permission from the Warden, Kinshaldy Cottage, Tentsmuir Forest. St Andrews has a tourist information office in South Street.

SELKIRK, Borders B3
Picturesquely set amid hills which overlook Ettrick Water, Selkirk has a nine-hole golf course and there are pony-trekking facilities in the area. Brown trout may be caught in Ettrick and Yarrow Waters, and St Marys Loch – situated SW on A708 – holds pike, perch, and eels. The loch is also suitable for small-boat sailing. Superb hill-walking country exists around Selkirk, especially above the valley of the Ettrick and Yarrow rivers. A tourist information office is situated at Halliwells House in the Market Place.

*STIRLING, Central B2
Stirling occupies a position of historical and topographical importance and is popularly called the 'Gateway to the Highlands.' Every year thousands of tourists pass through here on their way to the Trossachs, Loch Lomond, the Perthshire Highlands, etc. The town has an eighteen-hole golf course and there are pony trekking facilities in the area. River Forth holds salmon, sea trout, and brown trout, while Loch-Leven, brown and rainbow trout can be taken from Loch Coulter. Hillwalking country lies to the W in the Gargunnock Hills and SW in Campsie Fells. Stirling's tourist information office is situated in Dumbarton Road.

*STRANRAER, Dumfries and Galloway A3
Situated on the Rhinns of Galloway, Stranraer is an important contact point with Ireland and offers excellent holiday facilities which include a very good bathing beach. Fine sands and safe bathing may also be enjoyed on the other side of the peninsula at Luce Sands. Golfers can choose between two eighteen-hole courses, one in the town itself and the other 6m SW at Portpatrick. Pony trekking facilities are available 6m N at Kirkcolm and 3m E at Aird. Cross Water of Luce can be fished for salmon and sea trout, while several local lochs and reservoirs hold brown trout. Loch Ryan offers good prospects for sea angling and yields coalfish, codling, conger,

haddock, mackerel, plaice, pollack, skate, and whiting. Excellent salt-water fishing is also available at numerous places on the Rhinns including, Drummore, Port Logan, Portpatrick, and Kirkcolm. Loch Ryan provides excellent sailing and water ski-ing water. There is a tourist information office at the Breastwork Car Park.

STRATHPEFFER, Highland A1

Anglers can try their luck for salmon and brown trout in Loch Achonachie and Rivers Conon and Blackwater. Loch Luichart holds brown trout, pike, and perch. To the N of Strathpeffer is 3,433ft Ben Wyvis, a climbing and ski slope. Close to the resort are several noted beauty spots, including the Falls of Conon and the Falls of Rogie, and 2m S is the 3¼m long Torrachilty forest trail. A tourist information office is situated in The Square at Strathpeffer.

TAYNUILT, Strathclyde A2

Pony trekking stables exist near this little resort. Both the Awe River and Loch Avich can be fished for salmon, sea trout, and trout. Loch Awe holds pike and perch in addition to game species. Good hill-walking and climbing country lies E at 3,689ft Ben Cruachan – a mountain which is split into several peaks and can be approached from the Allt Cruachan Reservoir. Glen Nant lies 1m S of Taynuilt and contains interesting natural woodland, comprising mixed deciduous species. Would be visitors must obtain prior permission from the Forestry Commission. About 15m S of Taynuilt by the shores of Loch Awe are the Inverliever forest walks and trail. The walks vary from 1 to 5m in length and the 2¼m trail identifies a varied selection of forest wildlife.

THURSO, Highland B1

Dunnet Bay lies E of Thurso and provides a wide sweep of sandy beach. The town itself has an eighteen-hole golf course, and the River Thurso is a famous salmon and sea trout water. Loch Calder may be fished for brown trout. Excellent sea angling prospects are offered by Thurso Bay and Dunnet Bay, and boats can be taken to the fishing grounds of the Pentland Firth from Scrabster. Fish from these waters include

coalfish, cod, conger, dabs, dogfish, haddock, halibut, ling, mackerel, plaice, pollack, skate, turbot, whiting, and wrasse. Thurso Bay is a suitable sailing and skin-diving area. There is a tourist information office at the Car Park, Riverside.

TONGUE, Highland A1

Good but rather exposed sands allow access for bathing here, and Lochs Loyal, Craggie, and Coulside can all be fished for brown trout. Loch Hope holds salmon and sea trout and the Kyle of Tongue is suitable for sailing. The two most prominent mountains in this far-N region are 3,042ft Ben Hope and 2,504ft Ben Loyal. The former is most easily climbed from a point 1m N of the broch at Dun Dornadilla in Strathmore, and Ben Loyal can be approached from a point 2m S of Tongue at Ribigill Farm. Some 6m E of Tongue is the Forestry Commission's Borgie forest walk through well-established woodland. Invernaver nature reserve lies NE at Bettyhill and protects the rarest collection of plants existing in N Scotland. Permission to enter the reserve must be obtained from the warden in Bettyhill.

*ULLAPOOL, Highland A1

Pony trekking facilities exist here, and the Ullapool River can be fished for salmon, sea trout, and brown trout. Other waters in the area include Loch Achall for salmon, sea trout, and brown trout; the Polly Lochs and Polly River for salmon and sea trout. Salt-water species likely to be caught in Loch Broom by shore anglers include haddock, pollack, and skate from the shore. Boat fishing in the loch will produce coalfish, cod, conger, haddock, mackerel, plaice, pollack, and whiting. Loch Broom is also suitable for sailing and provides launching facilities.

Between Ullapool and Lochinver to the N is a singularly beautiful landscape which is ideal for the hill walker and climber. Overlooking Loch Lurgain is 2,009ft Stac Polly – or Stac Pollaidh – a conical sandstone mountain which is easily climbed for most of its height, although care is required near the summit. Some

4m N of Cul Mhor is 2,399ft Suilven, a spectacular mountain and the best known in the one-time county of Sutherland. It has a long summit ridge and is best approached from Lochinver. An extraordinary panorama of the area's intricate pattern of lochs and lochans can be enjoyed from the peaks. An Teallach is a complex and magnificent mountain which rises to 3,483ft S of Ullapool and offers several challenging scrambles. The mountain is known for its particularly beautiful scenery.

Inverpolly Forest contains Inverpolly nature reserve and lies N of the town. The reserve covers a large, remote area which contains different environments and has much to interest the naturalist and geologist. Parties of six or more must obtain prior permission before visiting the reserve, and permits are required by any person wishing to visit in late summer or autumn. Facilities include a car park, information centre, and nature trail at Knockan Cliff. Ullapool has an information centre.

WICK, Highland B1

Apart from anything else the superb coastal scenery around Wick makes the town an exciting place to visit. Leisure amenities here include a fine harbour, an outdoor swimming pool, numerous sports facilities, and an eighteen-hole golf course. The River Wick can be fished for salmon and sea trout, and lochs Watten and Scarmclate hold brown trout. Local sea angling is very good – especially off Noss Head – and is likely to produce coalfish, cod, conger, dogfish, eels, mackerel, and pollack from the shore and coalfish, cod, ling, mackerel, and pouting from boats. Yachtsmen and small-boat sailors favour Wick and use the launching facilities at Sinclairs Bay. Wick's tourist information office is sited in Whitechapel Road.

WIGTOWN, Dumfries and Galloway A3

Pony trekking stables exist at nearby Creetown and Whithorn, and Wigtown itself boasts a good nine-hole golf course. River Bladnoch holds salmon, grilse, pike, and perch, but permits must be obtained from Newton Stewart before fishing. Garlieston lies 8m S of Wigtown and offers excellent sea-angling prospects for blockans, cod, lythe, and mackerel from the shore and blockans, cod, dabs, flounders, lythe, mackerel, plaice, and rays from boats. Isle of Whithorn lies farther S and is also a good sea-fishing area. Sailing in Wigtown Bay can be enjoyed from Garlieston and the Isle of Whithorn. About 5m S of Wigtown is the 1m Kilsture forest walk through Forestry Commission afforestation. Lochs Mochrum and Castle lie W of Wigtown and are unofficial wildfowl refuges. Loch Mochrum has Scotland's only inland cormorant colony.

The Scottish Countryside

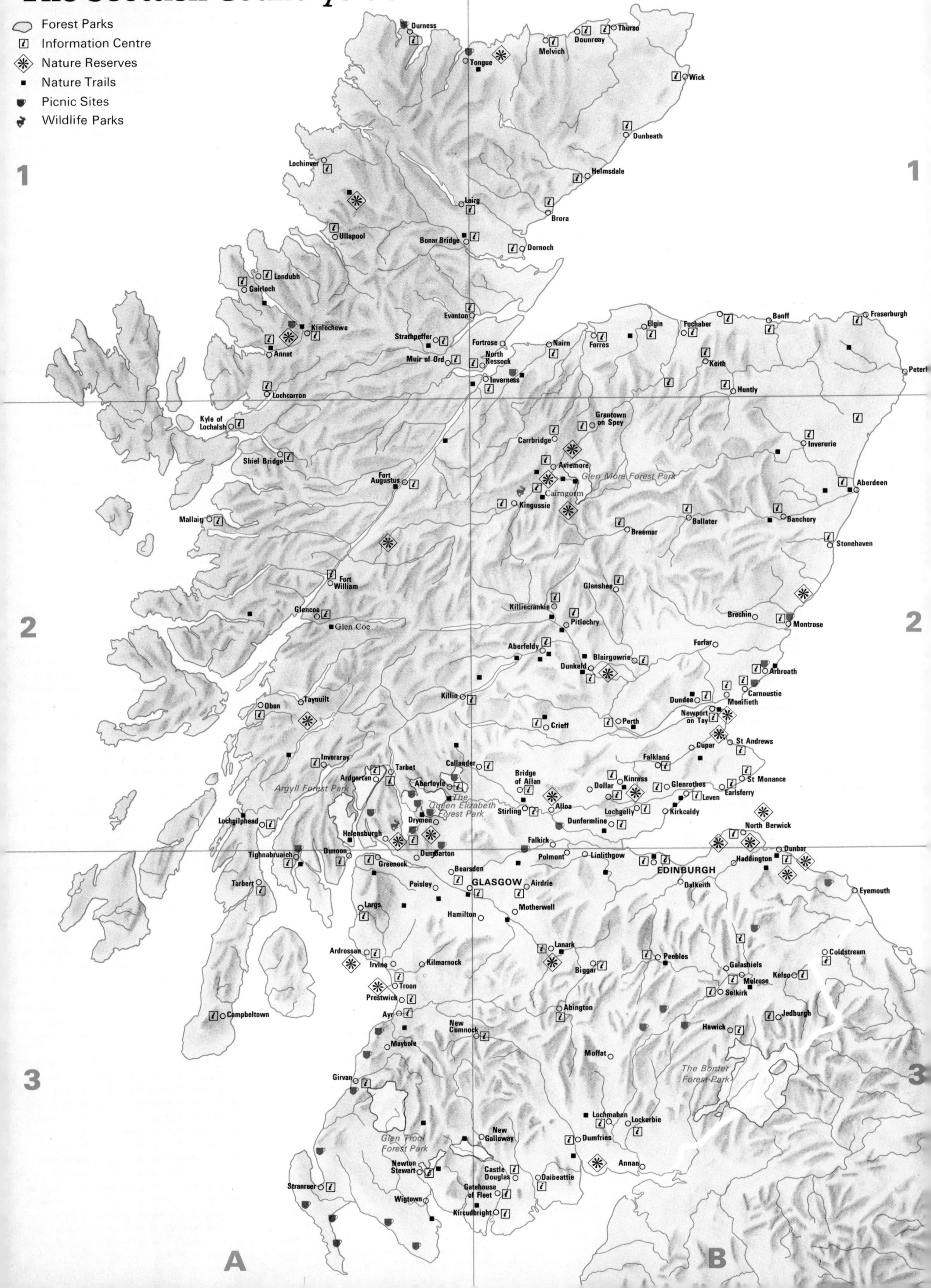

- Forest Parks
- Information Centre
- Nature Reserves
- Nature Trails
- Picnic Sites
- Wildlife Parks

1

2

3

Durness
Thurso
Dounreay
Melvich
Tongue
Wick
Dunbeath
Helmsdale
Lochinver
Lairg
Brora
Ullapool
Bonar Bridge
Dornoch
Londubh
Gairloch
Kinlochewe
Evanton
Elgin
Fochaber
Banff
Fraserburgh
Annat
Strathpeffer
Fortrose
Nairn
Forres
Keith
Peterl
Muir of Ord
North Kessock
Huntly
Lochcarron
Inverness
Kyle of Lochalsh
Grantown on Spey
Shiel Bridge
Carrbridge
Inverurie
Aviemore
Glen More Forest Park
Aberdeen
Fort Augustus
Cairngorm
Ballater
Banchory
Kingussie
Mallaig
Braemar
Stonehaven
Fort William
Glenshee
Glencoe
Killiecrankie
Brechin
Montrose
Glen Coe
Pitlochry
Aberfeldy
Forfar
Blairgowrie
Arbroath
Dunkeld
Carnoustie
Killin
Dundee
Monifieth
Taynuilt
Crieff
Perth
Newport on Tay
Oban
St Andrews
Inveraray
Callander
Cupar
Tarbet
Falkland
St Monance
Ardgartan
Bridge of Allan
Kinross
Glenrothes
Aberfoyle
Dollar
Earlsferry
Argyll Forest Park
The Queen Elizabeth Forest Park
Stirling
Alloa
Lochgelly
Leven
Lochgilphead
Drymen
Dunfermline
Kirkcaldy
Helensburgh
North Berwick
Tighnabruaich
Dunoon
Dumbarton
Falkirk
Polmont
Linlithgow
Haddington
Dunbar
Greenock
Bearsden
EDINBURGH
Tarbert
Paisley
GLASGOW
Airdrie
Dalkeith
Eyemouth
Largs
Motherwell
Hamilton
Ardrossan
Lanark
Coldstream
Irvine
Kilmarnock
Peebles
Galashiels
Troon
Biggar
Melrose
Kelso
Prestwick
Selkirk
Campbeltown
Abington
Jedburgh
Ayr
New Cumnock
Hawick
Maybole
Moffat
The Border Forest Park
Girvan
Lochmaben
Lockerbie
Glen Trool Forest Park
New Galloway
Dumfries
Newton Stewart
Castle Douglas
Daibeattie
Annan
Stranraer
Gatehouse of Fleet
Wigtown
Kircudbright

A

B

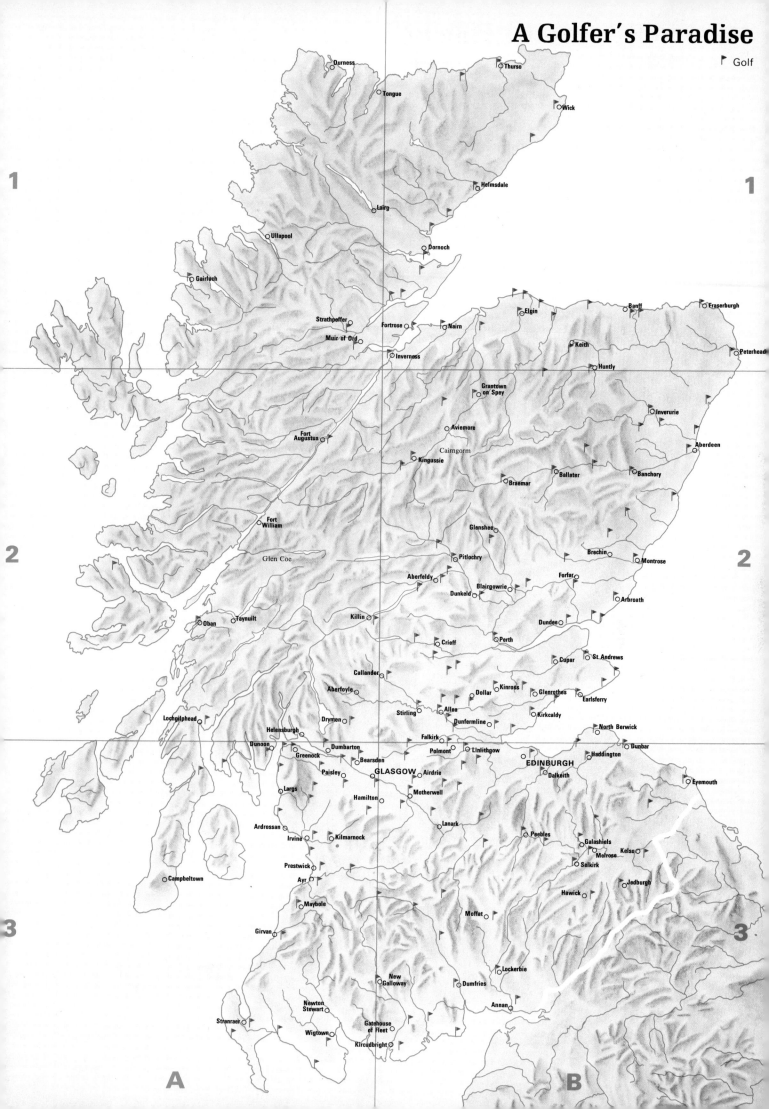

A Golfer's Paradise

⚑ Golf

Salt and Freshwater Fishing

- Freshwater Fishing
- Sea Fishing

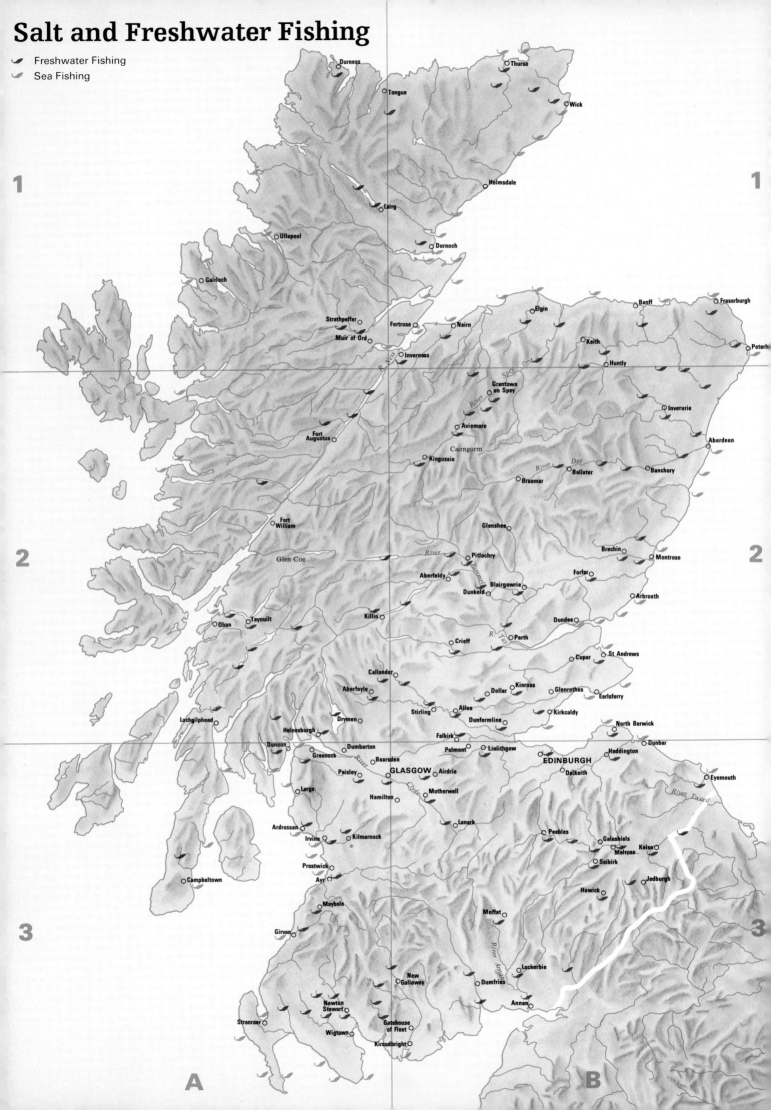

1

1

2

2

3

3

Durness

Thurso

Tongue

Wick

Helmsdale

Lairg

Ullapool

Dornoch

Gairloch

Banff   Fraserburgh

Elgin

Strathpeffer   Fortrose   Nairn   Keith   Peterh

Muir of Ord   Huntly

Inverness

Spey

River

Grantown
on Spey   Inverurie

Aviemore

Cairngorm   Aberdeen

Fort
Augustus   River   Dee

Kingussie   Ballater   Banchory

Braemar

Glenshee

Fort
William   Brechin

Glen Coe   River   Pitlochry   Montrose

Aberfeldy   Forfar

Blairgowrie   Arbroath

Dunkeld

Oban   Taynuilt   Killin   Dundee

R. Tay

Crieff   Perth

Cupar   St Andrews

Callander

Aberfoyle   Dollar   Kinross   Glenrothes

Earlsferry

Lochgilphead   Stirling   Alloa   Kirkcaldy

Drymen   Dunfermline

Helensburgh   Falkirk   North Berwick

Dunoon   Dumbarton   Polmont   Linlithgow   Dunbar

Greenock   Bearsden   EDINBURGH   Haddington

Paisley   GLASGOW   Airdrie   Dalkeith   Eyemouth

Largs   Motherwell

Hamilton   River Tweed

Ardrossan   Lanark

Irvine   Kilmarnock   Peebles   Galashiels   Kelso

Melrose

Prestwick   Selkirk   Jedburgh

Ayr   Hawick

Maybole

Moffat

Girvan

River

Annan

Lockerbie

New
Galloway   Dumfries

Newton   Annan
Stewart

Stranraer   Gatehouse
of Fleet

Wigtown

Kircudbright

Campbeltown

A

B

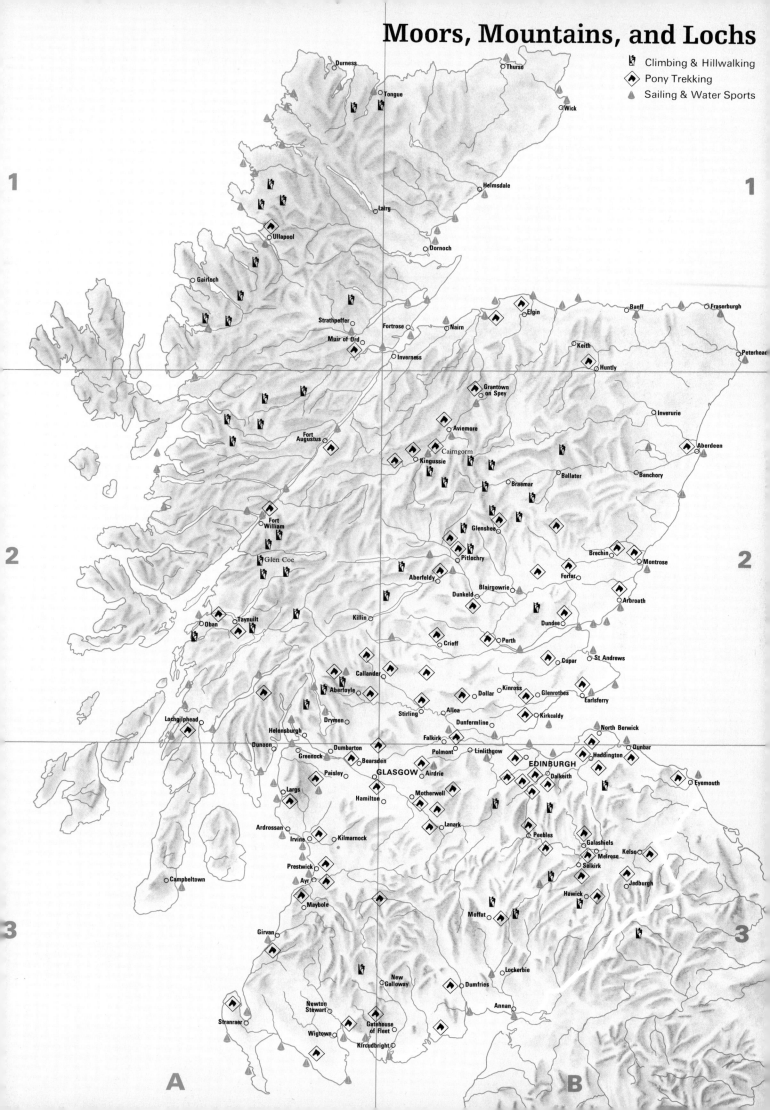

Moors, Mountains, and Lochs

Climbing & Hillwalking
Pony Trekking
Sailing & Water Sports

1

Durness
Thurso
Tongue
Wick
Helmsdale
Lairg
Ullapool
Dornoch
Gairloch
Strathpeffer
Fortrose
Nairn
Banff
Fraserburgh
Muir of Ord
Keith
Peterhead
Inverness
Huntly
Inverurie
Grantown on Spey
Fort Augustus
Aviemore
Aberdeen
Cairngorm
Kingussie
Banchory
Ballater
Braemar
Fort William
Glenshee
Brechin
Glen Coe
Pitlochry
Montrose
Aberfeldy
Forfar
Dunkeld
Blairgowrie
Arbroath
Taynuilt
Killin
Dundee
Oban
Crieff
Perth
St. Andrews
Callander
Cupar
Aberfoyle
Dollar
Kinross
Glenrothes
Earlsferry
Stirling
Alloa
Lochgilphead
Drymen
Dunfermline
Kirkcaldy
Helensburgh
Falkirk
North Berwick
Dunoon
Dumbarton
Polmont
Linlithgow
Dunbar
Greenock
Bearsden
Haddington
Paisley
GLASGOW
Airdrie
EDINBURGH
Dalkeith
Eyemouth
Largs
Motherwell
Hamilton
Ardrossan
Lanark
Irvine
Kilmarnock
Peebles
Galashiels
Kelso
Prestwick
Melrose
Ayr
Selkirk
Campbeltown
Jedburgh
Maybole
Hawick
Girvan
Moffat
Lockerbie
New Galloway
Dumfries
Newton Stewart
Annan
Stranraer
Gatehouse of Fleet
Wigtown
Kircudbright

A

B

1

2

2

3

3

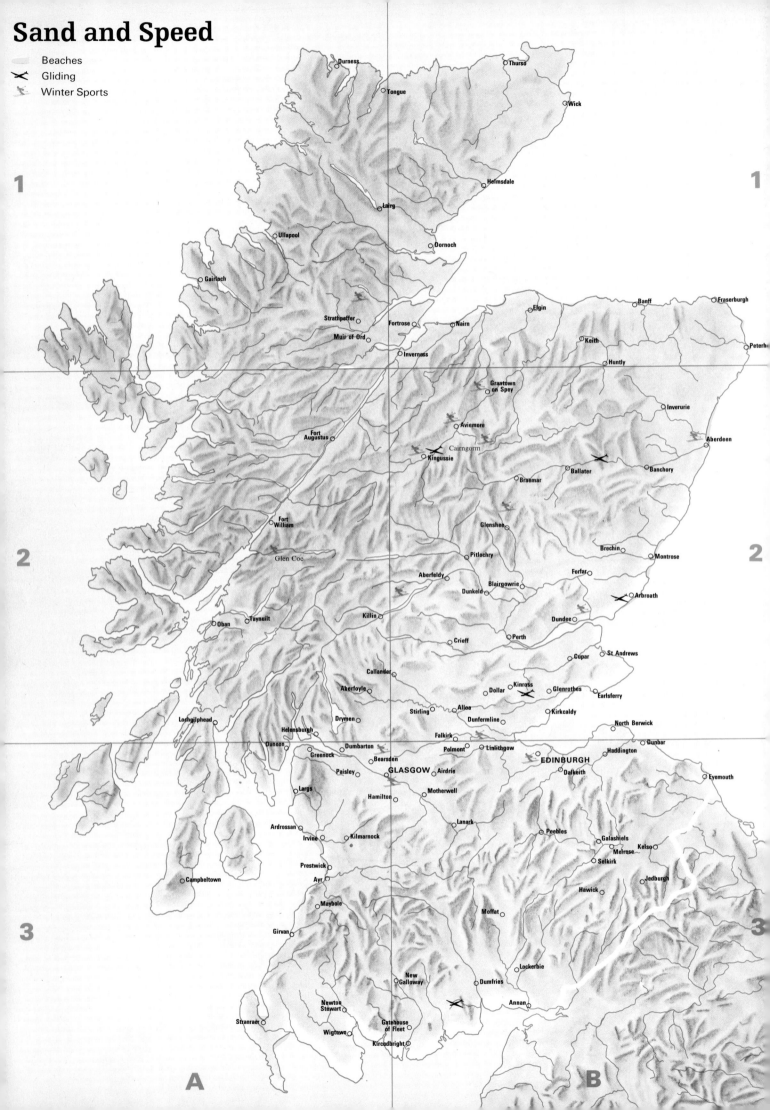

Sand and Speed

- Beaches
- Gliding
- Winter Sports

1

2

3

Durness
Thurso
Tongue
Wick
Helmsdale
Lairg
Ullapool
Dornoch
Gairloch
Elgin
Banff
Fraserburgh
Strathpeffer
Fortrose
Nairn
Keith
Peterh
Muir of Ord
Huntly
Inverness
Inverurie
Grantown on Spey
Aviemore
Fort Augustus
Aberdeen
Cairngorm
Kingussie
Ballater
Banchory
Braemar
Fort William
Glenshee
Glen Coe
Brechin
Pitlochry
Montrose
Aberfeldy
Forfar
Dunkeld
Blairgowrie
Arbroath
Killin
Dundee
Oban
Taynuilt
Crieff
Perth
Callander
Cupar
St Andrews
Aberfoyle
Dollar
Kinross
Glenrothes
Earlsferry
Drymen
Stirling
Alloa
Kirkcaldy
Helensburgh
Dunfermline
North Berwick
Lochgilphead
Falkirk
Dunoon
Dumbarton
Polmont
Linlithgow
Dunbar
Greenock
Bearsden
Haddington
Paisley
GLASGOW
Airdrie
EDINBURGH
Largs
Dalkeith
Eyemouth
Hamilton
Motherwell
Ardrossan
Lanark
Irvine
Kilmarnock
Peebles
Galashiels
Kelso
Prestwick
Melrose
Selkirk
Campbeltown
Ayr
Jedburgh
Maybole
Hawick
Girvan
Moffat
Lockerbie
New Galloway
Dumfries
Annan
Newton Stewart
Stranraer
Gatehouse of Fleet
Wigtown
Kircudbright

A

B

The National Grid

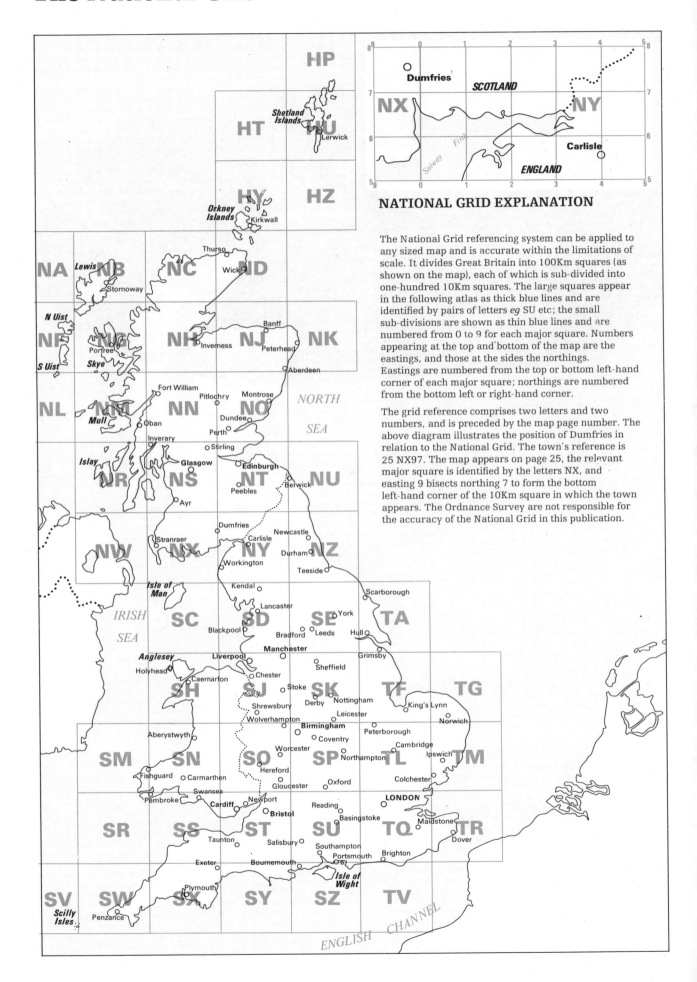

NATIONAL GRID EXPLANATION

The National Grid referencing system can be applied to any sized map and is accurate within the limitations of scale. It divides Great Britain into 100Km squares (as shown on the map), each of which is sub-divided into one-hundred 10Km squares. The large squares appear in the following atlas as thick blue lines and are identified by pairs of letters eg SU etc; the small sub-divisions are shown as thin blue lines and are numbered from 0 to 9 for each major square. Numbers appearing at the top and bottom of the map are the eastings, and those at the sides the northings. Eastings are numbered from the top or bottom left-hand corner of each major square; northings are numbered from the bottom left or right-hand corner.

The grid reference comprises two letters and two numbers, and is preceded by the map page number. The above diagram illustrates the position of Dumfries in relation to the National Grid. The town's reference is 25 NX97. The map appears on page 25, the relevant major square is identified by the letters NX, and easting 9 bisects northing 7 to form the bottom left-hand corner of the 10Km square in which the town appears. The Ordnance Survey are not responsible for the accuracy of the National Grid in this publication.

Key to Atlas

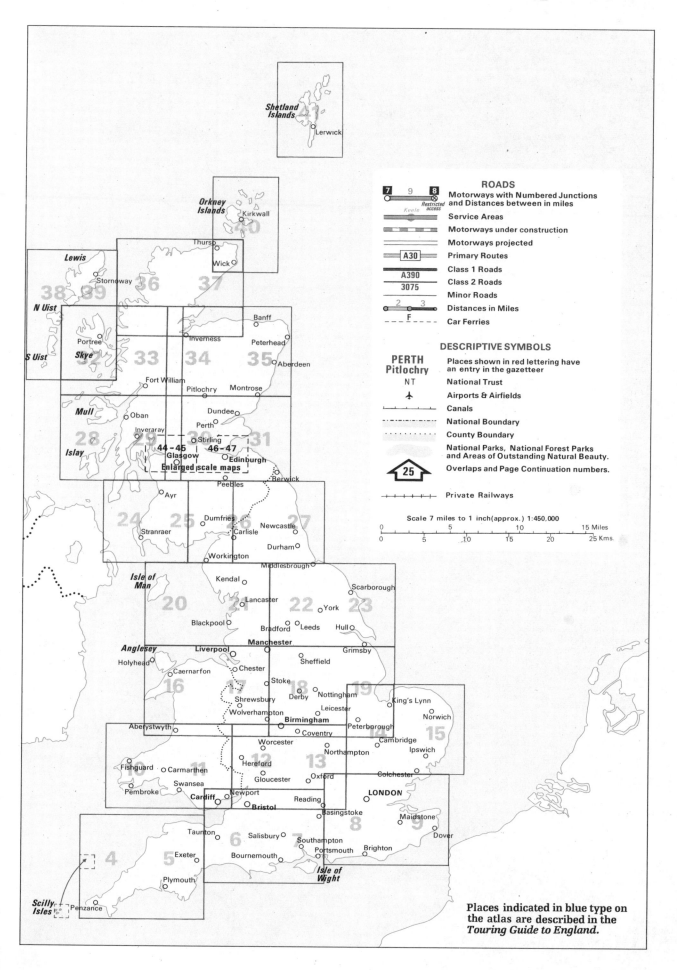

ROADS

Motorways with Numbered Junctions and Distances between in miles

Service Areas

Motorways under construction

Motorways projected

A30 — Primary Routes

A390 — Class 1 Roads

3075 — Class 2 Roads

Minor Roads

Distances in Miles

F — Car Ferries

DESCRIPTIVE SYMBOLS

PERTH
Pitlochry — Places shown in red lettering have an entry in the gazetteer

NT — National Trust

Airports & Airfields

Canals

National Boundary

County Boundary

National Parks, National Forest Parks and Areas of Outstanding Natural Beauty.

25 — Overlaps and Page Continuation numbers.

Private Railways

Scale 7 miles to 1 inch (approx.) 1:450,000

0   5   10   15 Miles

0   5   10   15   20   25 Kms.

Places indicated in blue type on the atlas are described in the *Touring Guide to England*.

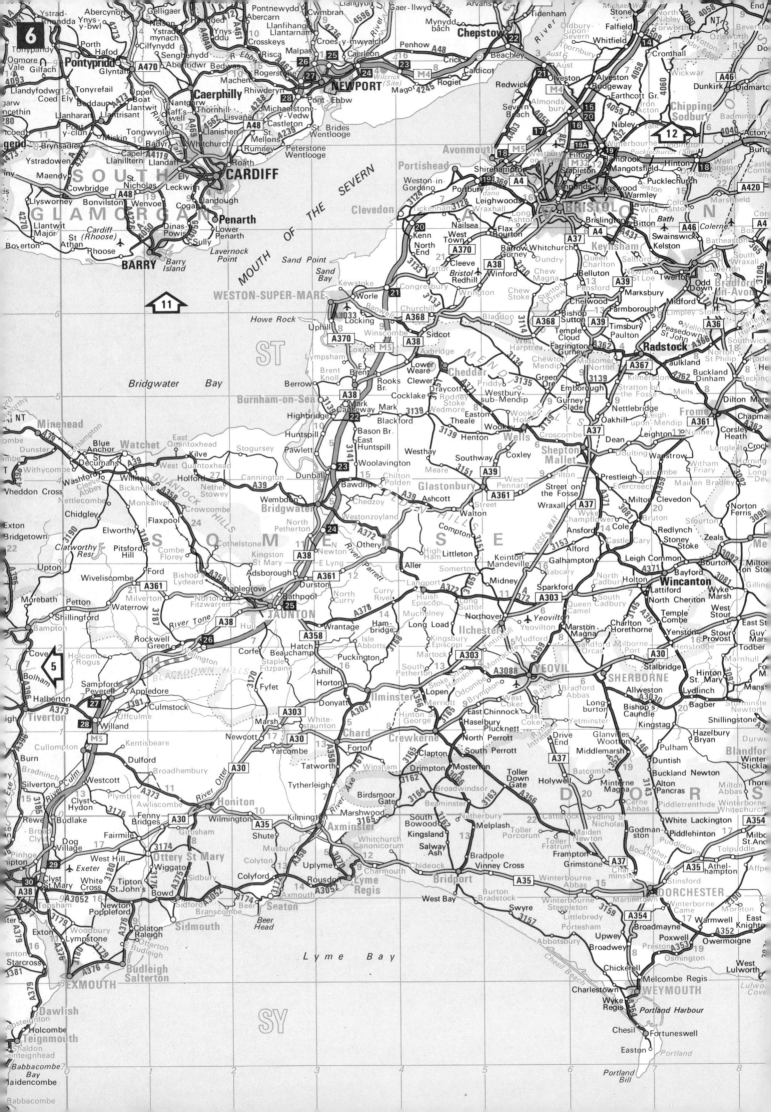

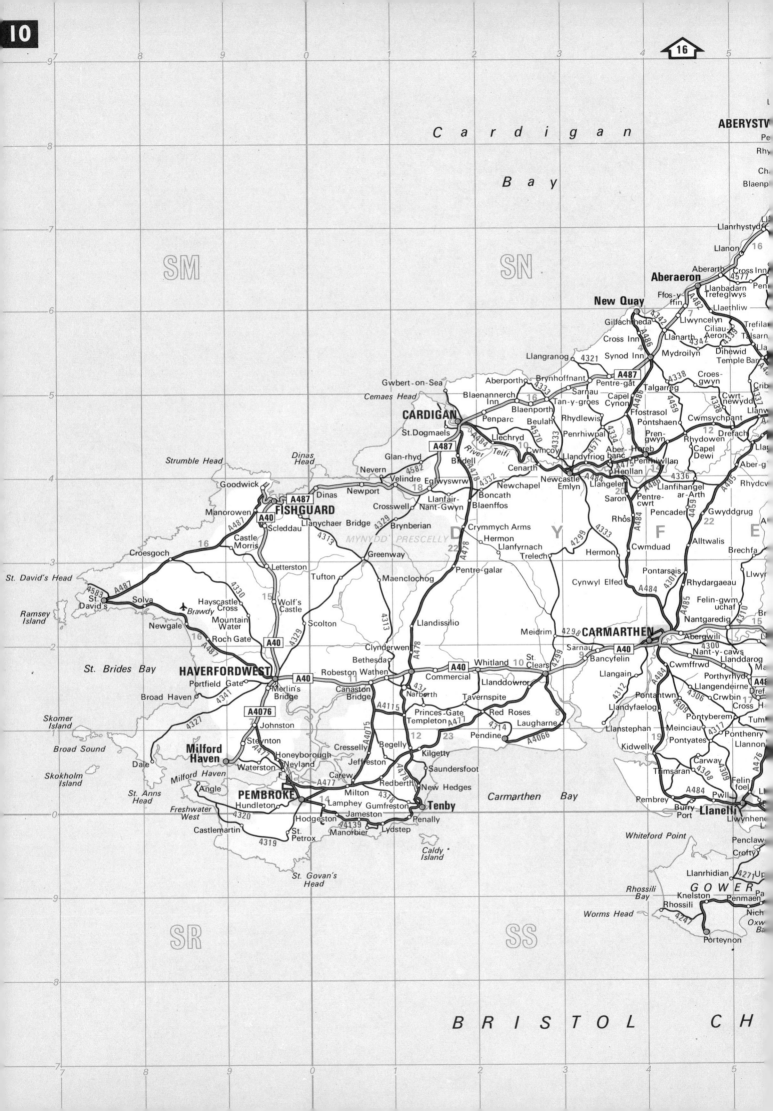

Cardigan Bay

ABERYSTW

SM

SN

Llanrhystyd

Llanon

16

Aberarth   Cross Inn
Aberaeron   4577
Ffos-y-   Llanbadarn
New Quay   ffin   Trefeglwys
Llaethliw
Gilfach-reda   Llwyncelyn
Cross Inn   Ciliau   Trefila
Llangranog   4321   Llanarth   Aeron   4334   Talsarn
Aberporth   Pentre-gât   Synod Inn   Mydroilyn   Dihewid   Temple Bar
Blaenannerch   Talgarreg   Croesgwyn
Inn   16   Tan-y-groes   Capel   Cwmsychpant
CARDIGAN   Penparc   Blaenporth   Cynon   Ffostrasol   12   Drefach
Beulah   Rhydlewis   Pren-   Rhydowen
St.Dogmaels   Llechryd   Penrhiwpal   gwyn   Capel
A487   River   Pontshaen   Aber-   Horeb   Dewi
Glan-rhyd   Teifi   Cwmcoy   Llandyfriog banc   Henllan   4336
Nevern   Bridell   Cenarth   Newcastle   Llangeler   Llanfihangel
Velindre   4582   Emlyn   Saron   Pentre-   ar-Arth
Dinas   Eglwyswrw   4332   Newchapel   cwrt   Pencader   Gwyddgrug
Head   18   Llanfair-   Boncath   Rhôs   22
Goodwick   Newport   Nant-Gwyn   Blaenffos   Cwmduad   Alltwalis   Brechfa
A487   Dinas   Crosswell   Crymych Arms   Hermon
FISHGUARD   Brynberian   Hermon   Llanfyrnach   Pontarsais
Manorowen   Llanychaer Bridge   4329   Trelech   Rhydargaeau
A40   Scleddau   4313   MYNYDD PRESCELLY   Pentre-galar   Cynwyl Elfed   A484   Rhydcv
Castle   Greenway   4478   4299   4333
Croesgoch   Morris   Letterston   Tufton   Maenclochog   Felin-gwm
Solva   4330   Wolf's   Llandissilio   Meidrim   4298   CARMARTHEN   uchaf
St.   A487   Hayscastle   15   Castle   4313   Sarnau   Abergwili   15
David's   Cross   Scolton   4478   Whitland   St.   Bancyfelin   A40   Nant-y-caws   Llanddarog
Newgale   Mountain   Clynderwen   Clears   4299   9   Cwmffrwd
Roch Gate   Water   Bethesda   Commercial   Llanddowror   Llangain   Porthyrhyd   Llangendeirne
HAVERFORDWEST   A40   Robeston Wathen   A40   10   Pontantwn   4306   Crwbin
Portfield Gate   Merlin's   Canaston   A4115   Narberth   Tavernspite   Red Roses   Laugharne   Llandyfaelog   Pontyberem
Broad Haven   4341   Bridge   Bridge   Princes-Gate   4477   8   Llanstephan   Meinciau   Ponthenry
A4076   Templeton   Laugharne   Kidwelly   Pontyates   Llannon
Johnston   12   23   Pendine   Carway
Steynton   Begelly   A4066   Trimsaran   4308
MILFORD   Honeyborough   Cresselly   Kilgetty   Pembrey   4309   Felin
HAVEN   Neyland   Jeffreston   Saundersfoot   A484   Pwll   foel
Dale   Waterston   Carew   Redberth   New Hedges   Burry   Llanelli
Angle   Milford Haven   A477   Milton   4370   Tenby   Port   Llwynhen
PEMBROKE   14   Lamphey   Gumfreston   Penally   *Carmarthen Bay*   *Whiteford Point*
Hundleton   Jameston   Lydstep   Penclaw
4320   Hodgeston   4139   Crofty
Castlemartin   St.   Manorbier   *Caldy*   Llanrhidian   4271
4319   Petrox   *Island*   GOWER
St. Govan's   Knelston   Penmaen
Head   *Rhossili*   Rhossili   Nich
Bay   4247   Oxw
Worms Head   Porteynon

St. David's Head
Ramsey Island
St. Brides Bay
Skomer Island
Skokholm Island
Broad Sound
St. Anns Head
Freshwater West

SR

SS

BRISTOL CH

Wells-next-the-Sea · Point · Overy Staithe · Holkham · Stiffkey · Morston · Blakeney · Cley · Salthouse · Weybourne · Sheringham · West Runton · East Runton · Cromer
Burnham Deepdale · Burnham Overy · Langham · Wiveton · Upper Sheringham · Aylmerton · Overstrand · Sidestrand
Brancaster · Burnham Market · Burnham Thorpe · Wighton · Binham · Glandford · Bodham Street · Felbrigg · Crossdale Street · Trimingham
North Creake · Little Walsingham · Great Walsingham · Letheringsett · Holt · Gresham · Roughton · Thorpe Market · Mundesley · Paston · Bacton · Walcott
Stanhoe · South Creake · East Barsham · Thornage · Edgefield Green · Erpingham · Gunton · Knapton · Happisburgh · Whimpwell Green
Great Bircham · Sculthorpe · Briston · Melton Constable · Saxthorpe · Antingham · Swafield · North Walsham · Lessingham · Ingham · Sea Palling
Tattersett · Hempton · The Heath · Fakenham · Corpusty · Heydon · Blickling · Aylsham · Felmingham · Worstead · Smallburgh · Low Street · Stalham · Horsey
East Rudham · Harpley · South Raynham · East Raynham · Broom Green · Twyford · Guist · Sall · Reepham · Marsham · Fairstead · Buxton · Tunstead · Hickling · Waxham · Horsey

NORFOLK · BRECKLAND · SUFFOLK · ESSEX

NORWICH · GREAT YARMOUTH · LOWESTOFT · BECCLES · Bungay · Halesworth · Southwold · Walberswick
Wymondham · Attleborough · Thetford · Brandon · Diss · Harleston · Bressingham
IPSWICH · Woodbridge · Felixstowe · Aldeburgh · Leiston · Saxmundham · Framlingham · Stowmarket
Sudbury · Lavenham · Long Melford · Hadleigh · Manningtree · HARWICH · Dovercourt
COLCHESTER · Wivenhoe · Brightlingsea · Mersea Is. · Walton-on-the-Naze · Frinton-on-Sea · CLACTON ON SEA
ST EDMUNDS

TG · TM

20

Carmel Head
Cemaes Bay
Bull Bay
Tregele
Burwen
Amlwch
Penysarn
Llanrhyddlad
Holyhead Bay
Rhosybol
City Dulas
Moelfre
Llanfaethlu
Llanallgo
Marianglås
Red Wharf Bay
Carmel
Coedana
Llanerchymedd
Benllech
Puffin Island
Trefor
Llangoed
Alaw Resr.
HOLYHEAD
Holy Island
Bodedern
Valley
Trearddur Bay
Caergeilliog
Bryngwran
Pentraeth
Four Mile Bridge
Valley
Anglesey
Rhosneigr
Llanfaelog
Cerrigceinwen
Gwalchmai
Menai Br
Llanfaes
Llangefni
Beaumaris
Bethel
Pentre Berw
Aberffraw
Hermon
Llangaffo
Port Dinorwic
BANGOR
Newborough
Bryn-Siencyn
Llandegai
Llanfairisgaer
Saron
Tregarth
Bethesda
Caernarfon
Llanrug
Cym-y-glo
Llanddeiniolen
Caeathraw
Llyn Padarn
Pont Dolgarrog
Bont-newydd
Waunfawr
Llyn Peris
Glyder Fawr 3279
Nant Peris
Betws-Garmon
Llanberis
Caernarvon Bay
Groeslon
Salem
Snowdon 3560
Pen-y-pass
Llyn Gwynant
Penygroes
Nantlle
Rhyd-Ddu
Pont-y-pant
Dolwyddelan
Talysarn
Llanllyfni
Beddgelert
Glanaber
Penmachno
A470
Pontllyfni
Gyrn-gôch
Pant-glas
Aber Glaslyn
Ysbyty-Ifan
Llanaelhaearn
Bryncir
Prenteg
Rhyd-y-sarn
Blaenau Ffestiniog
Congl-y-wal
Llithfaen
Glan Dwyfach
Dolbenmaen
Penmorfa
Festiniog
Morfa-Nefyn
Nefyn
Fron
Four Crosses
Llanystumdwy
Tremadog
Maentwrog
Pistyll
Rhoslan
Pentrefelin
Porthmadog
Minffordd
Edern
Allt-gam
Rhos-fawr
Chwilog
Criccieth
Talsarnau
Pont Islyn
Tudweiliog
Efailnewydd
Pwllheli
Llanfihangel-y-traethau
Glyn Cywarch
Llyn Trawsfynydd
Trawsfynydd
Meillteyrn
Rhyd-y-clafdy
Penrhôs
Tremadoc Bay
Harlech
Bronaber
Pen-y-groeslon
Sarn
Nanhoron
Llanbedrog
Llanfair
Llanuwchllyn
Llidiardau
Mynytho
Abersoch
Llanbedr
Y Llethr 2475
A470
Aberdaron
Trwyn Cilan
Ystrumgwern
Ganllwyd
Wenallt
Aran Fawddwy 2970
Dyffryn Ardudwy
Bont Newydd
Henfaes
Tal-y-bont
Llanelltyd
Brithdir
Bardsey Island
Llanaber
Bontddu
Penmaenpool
Caerdeon
Cae'r-tyddyn
Barmouth
Cutiau
Aber-gwynant
Dolgellau
Cross Foxes Inn
Barmouth Bay
Arthog
Cader Idris 2927
Dinas Mawddwy
Cwm-Cewydd
A458
Friog
Mallwyd
Foel
Llwyngwril
Tal-y-llyn
Upper Corris
A487
Cwm-Llinan
Llangelynin
Esgairgeiliog
Cemmaes
Abergynolwyn
Mathafarn
Cemmaes Rd.
Rhoslefain
Dolgoch
Pantperthog
Llanwrin
Llanbrynmair
Tywyn (Towyn)
Bryncrug
Pennal
Penegoes
Machynlleth
A489
Commins Coch
Talerddig
Cardigan Bay
Trefri
Cwrt
Derwen-las
Pennant
Carno
Glandyfi
Pont Crugnant
Frankwell
Aberdovey
River Dovey
Ysgubor-y-coed
Dylife
Clatter
A487
Tre'r-ddôl
Staylittle
Trefeglwys
Caersws
Llancynfelyn
Taliesin
Eisteddfa-Gurig
Pant Mawr
Borth
Talybont
Nant-y-moch Resr.
Upper Borth
11
Llanidloes
Llandre
Rhyd-y-pennau
Llangorwen
Rhyd-y-felin
Bow Street
Capel Dewi
Pont-erwyd
Duffryn Castell
Cwmbelan
ABERYSTWYTH
Llanbadarn Fawr
Penparcau
Moriah
Llangurig
Capel Bangor
Goginan
Llanfihangel
A44
Ysbyty Cynfyn
A470
Rhyd-y-felin
New Cross
Devil's Bridge
Chancery
Afon Ystwyth
Blaenplwyf

LLANDUDNO
Great Ormes Head
Penrhyn Bay
Rhos-on-Sea
RHYL
Conway Bay
Llanrhos
Deganwy
COLWYN BAY
Kinmel Bay
Towyn
Penmaenmawr
Conway (Conway)
Llandudno Junc.
Dolwyd
Old Colwyn
Abergele
Pensarn
Llanfairfechan
Bryn-y-maen
Llanddulas
Aber
Gyffin
Ty'n-y-groes
Dolwen
Glascoed
Tal-y-cafn
Betws-yn-Rhôs
A548
Llanfair Talhaiarn
Tal-y-bont
A470
Pentre Isaf
Llangernyw
Plas Isaf
Denbigh
Carnedd Llywelyn 3485
Trefriw
Llansannan
Groes
Llanrwst
Pentre-tafarn-y-fedw
Gwytherin
Bylchau
Peniel
Capel Curig
Glyn
Nantglyn
Betws-y-coed
Nebo
Hafod Dinbych
Alwen Resr.
Sportsman's Arms Inn
Pont Cyfyng
Rhyd-lanfair
Clocaenog Forest
R. Conway
Padog
Cerrigydrudion
Glasfryn
Llanfihangel Glyn Myfyr
Pentrefoelas
Rhyd-lydan
Gellioedd
Glan-yr-afon
Bethel
Chitalgarthrn
Glan-yr-afon
A494
Llyn Celyn
Llandderfel
Cefn-ddwysarn
Llanfor
Bala
Pale
Croge
Bala Lake
Llangower
Pentre-piod
Pencraig
Ty-nant
Talardd
Llangynog
A494
Alltforgan
Peny Hirn
Lake Vyrnwy
Llanymawddwy
Llanwddyn
Pont-Llogel
A470
Llanerfyl
Llan
Plas Llysyn
A470
Dolfach
Sychnant
Nantgwyn
Van
Upper Penrhuddl

SH
SN
P O W
D Y F E D
C A D E R I D R I S
G W Y N E D D
S N O W D O N I A
A5   **A55**   **A487**   **A499**   **A497**   **A498**   **A496**   **A493**   **A489**   **A44**

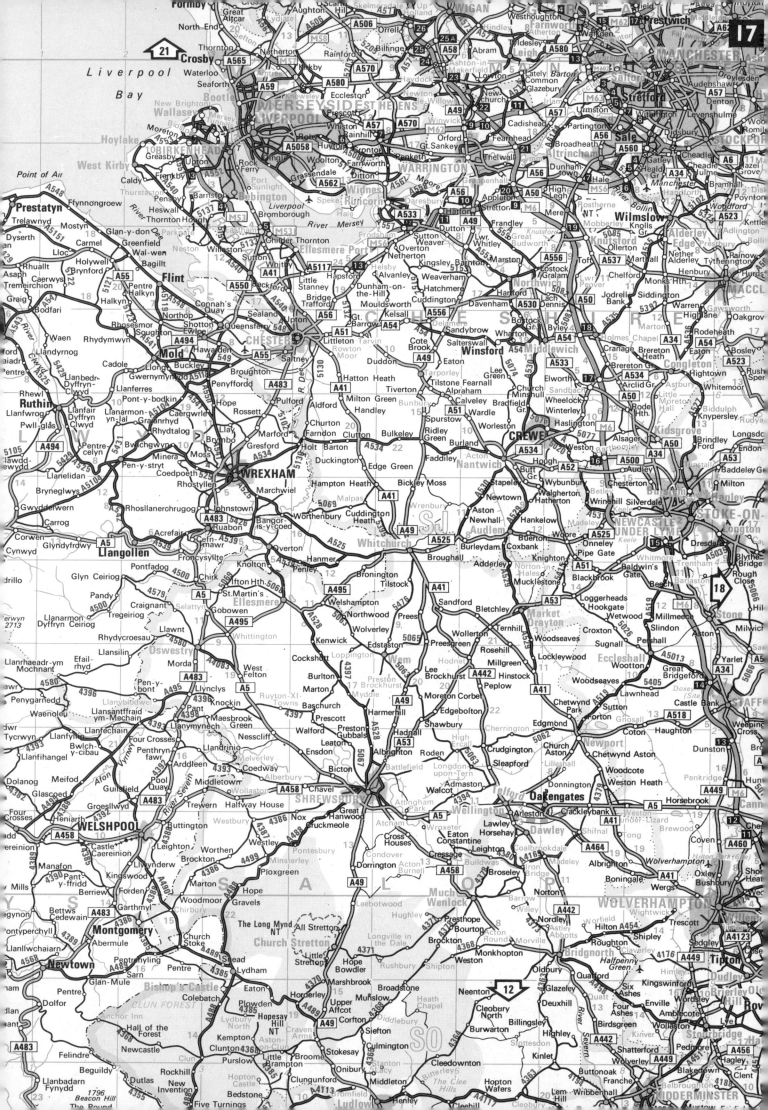

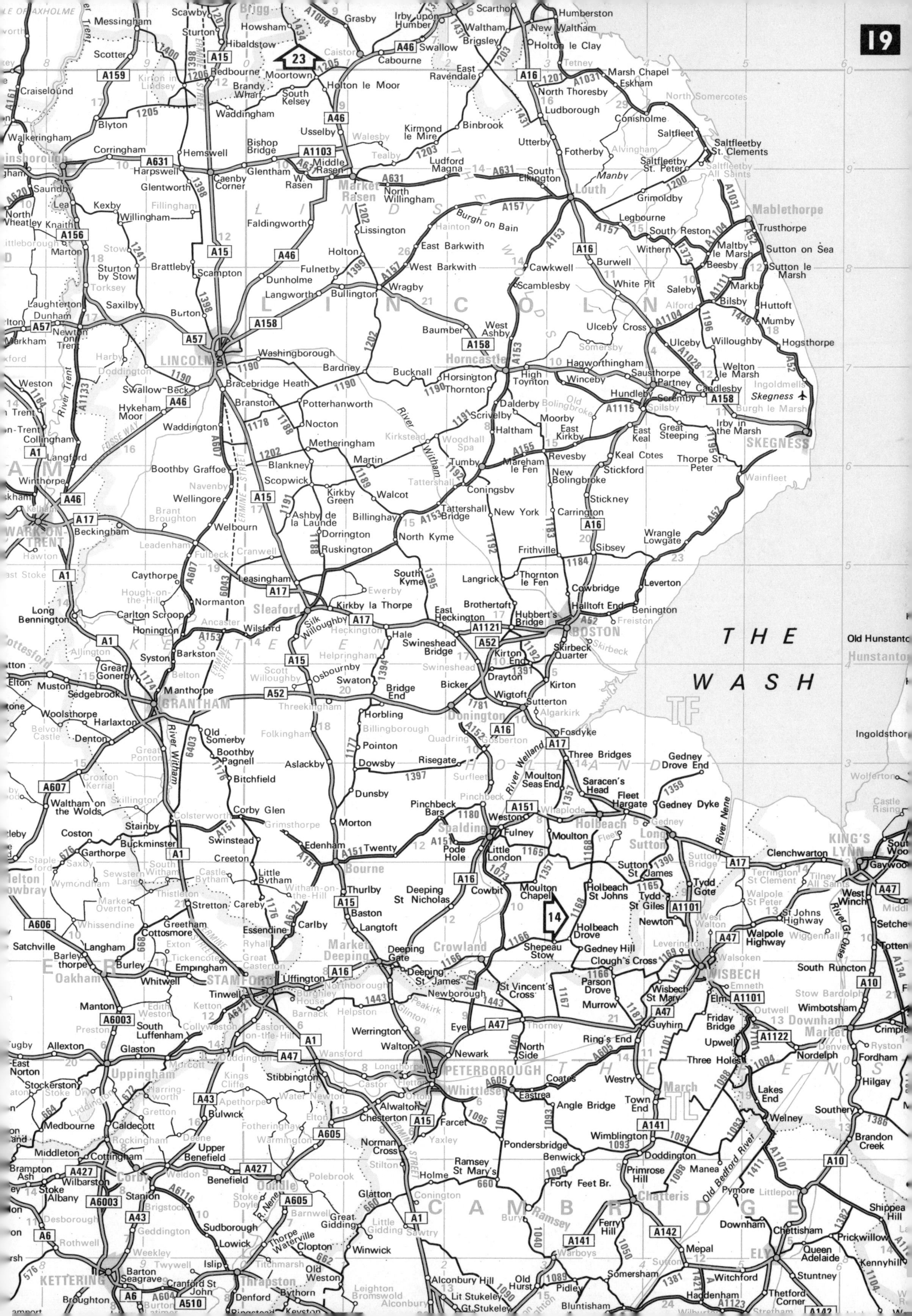
Messingham
Scawby
Brigg
Howsham
Grasby
Irby upon Humber
Scartho
Humberston
Waltham
New Waltham
Brigsley
Holton le Clay
Tetney
Sturton
Hibaldstow
Caistor
Swallow
Cabourne
Scotter
Redbourne
Moortown
Kirton in Lindsey
Holton le Moor
East Ravendale
Marsh Chapel
Eskham
Craiselound
Brandy Wharf
South Kelsey
North Thoresby
Ludborough
North Somercotes
Waddingham
Blyton
Conisholme
Usselby
Binbrook
Walesby
Kirmond le Mire
Utterby
Saltfleet
Walkeringham
Bishop Bridge
Tealby
Fotherby
Alvingham
Saltfleetby St. Clements
Corringham
Hemswell
Middle Rasen
Ludford Magna
Saltfleetby St. Peter
Saltfleetby All Saints
Harpswell
Caenby Corner
Glentham
W. Rasen
Market Rasen
South Elkington
Manby
Glentworth
North Willingham
Louth
Grimoldby
Saundby
Lea
Kexby
Fillingham
Mablethorpe
North Wheatley
Knaith
Willingham
Faldingworth
Lissington
Burgh on Bain
Legbourne
Trusthorpe
Marton
Stow
Hainton
South Reston
Maltby le Marsh
Sutton on Sea
Sturton by Stow
Brattleby
Holton
East Barkwith
Withern
Beesby
Scampton
Torksey
Fulnetby
West Barkwith
Cawkwell
Burwell
Sutton le Marsh
Dunholme
Wragby
Scamblesby
White Pit
Saleby
Markby
Laughterton
Saxilby
Langworth
Bullington
Alford
Bilsby
Huttoft
Dunham
Burton
Mumby
Newton on Trent
Ulceby Cross
Markham
Baumber
West Ashby
Somersby
Ulceby
Willoughby
Hogsthorpe
LINCOLN
Washingborough
Horncastle
Hagworthingham
Harby
Doddington
Bardney
Bucknall
Horsington
High Toynton
Sausthorpe
Welton le Marsh
Weston
Swallow Beck
Bracebridge Heath
Thornton
Winceby
Partney
Ingoldmells
Skegness
Hykeham Moor
Branston
Potterhanworth
Dalderby
Hundleby
Scremby
Candlesby
Waddington
Nocton
Scrivelby
Moorby
Spilsby
Burgh le Marsh
Collingham
Haltham
East Kirkby
East Keal
Great Steeping
Irby in the Marsh
Langford
Metheringham
Kirkstead
Woodhall Spa
SKEGNESS
River Witham
Revesby
Keal Cotes
Boothby Graffoe
Blankney
Martin
Tumby
Mareham le Fen
Thorpe St Peter
Stickford
Winthorpe
Scopwick
Tattershall
New Bolingbroke
Wainfleet
Navenby
Kirkby Green
Coningsby
Wellingore
Walcot
Stickney
Kelham
Brant Broughton
Tattershall Bridge
New York
Carrington
Beckingham
Ashby de la Launde
Billinghay
Welbourn
NEWARK-ON-TRENT
North Kyme
Wrangle Lowgate
Dorrington
Hawton
Leadenham
Cranwell
Fulbeck
Ruskington
Frithville
Sibsey
Caythorpe
Leasingham
South Kyme
Ewerby
Langrick
Thornton le Fen
Leverton
Hough-on-the-Hill
Normanton
Cowbridge
Long Bennington
Sleaford
Kirkby la Thorpe
Brothertoft
Halltoft End
Benington
Carlton Scroop
Ancaster
Silk Willoughby
East Heckington
Hubbert's Bridge
Freiston
Honington
Wilsford
Heckington
Hale
BOSTON
Allington
Swineshead Bridge
Kirton End
Skirbeck
Skirbeck Quarter
Old Hunstanton
Hunstanton
Syston
Barkston
Helpringham
Great Gonerby
Belton
Scott Willoughby
Osbournby
Swineshead
Muston
Swaton
Drayton
Kirton
Elton
Sedgebrook
Manthorpe
Bicker
THE WASH
GRANTHAM
Bridge End
Wigtoft
Sutterton
Woolsthorpe
Threekingham
Algarkirk
Harlaxton
Horbling
Donington
Belvoir Castle
Old Somerby
Folkingham
Billingborough
Fosdyke
Denton
Quadring
Gosberton
Ingoldsthorpe
Boothby Pagnell
Pointon
Three Bridges
Great Ponton
Gedney Drove End
Dowsby
Risegate
River Welland
Aslackby
Surfleet
Croxton Kerrial
Bitchfield
Moulton Seas End
Saracen's Head
Wolferton
Dunsby
Skillington
Pinchbeck
Fleet Hargate
Gedney Dyke
Castle Rising
Waltham on the Wolds
Colsterworth
Corby Glen
Pinchbeck Bars
Whaplode
Holbeach
Gedney
River Nene
Coston
Stainby
Grimsthorpe
Morton
Spalding
Weston
Fulney
Long Sutton
KING'S LYNN
Buckminster
Swinstead
Edenham
Moulton
Fleet
Garthorpe
Twenty
Pode Hole
Little London
Sutton Bridge
Clenchwarton
Gaywood
Saxby
Staple ford
South Witham
Creeton
Bourne
Sutton St James
Terrington St Clement
Tilney All Saints
Melton Mowbray
Wymondham
Sewstern
Castle Bytham
Little Bytham
Witham-on-the-Hill
Cowbit
Moulton Chapel
Holbeach St Johns
Tydd Gote
West Winch
Market Overton
Thistleton
Thurlby
Deeping St Nicholas
Tydd St Giles
Walpole St Peter
Stretton
Careby
Baston
St Johns Highway
Whissendine
Greetham
Carlby
Langtoft
Newton
West Walton
Cottesmore
Essendine
Holbeach Drove
Walpole Highway
Satchville
Langham
Exton
Ryhall
Market Deeping
Crowland
Shepeau Stow
Gedney Hill
Leverington
Wiggenhall
Barleythorpe
Burley
Tickencote
Great Casterton
Deeping Gate
Clough's Cross
Walsoken
Oakham
Empingham
Uffington
Deeping St James
Parson Drove
WISBECH
South Runcton
Whitwell
STAMFORD
Northborough
Tinwell
Burghley House
Newborough
St Vincent's Cross
Wisbech St Mary
Emneth
Stow Bardolph
Manton
Edith Weston
Ketton
Barnack
Helpston
Peakirk
Murrow
Elm
Wimbotsham
Preston
Collyweston
Easton-on-the-Hill
Glinton
Thorney
Guyhirn
Friday Bridge
Outwell
Downham Market
South Luffenham
Werrington
Eye
Ring's End
Upwell
Crimplesham
Tugby
Allexton
Glaston
Duddington
Wansford
Walton
Newark
North Side
Denver
Ryston
East Norton
Morcott
Longthorpe
PETERBOROUGH
Three Holes
Nordelph
Fordham
Uppingham
Kings Cliffe
Stibbington
Castor
Fletton
Coates
Westry
Hilgay
Stockerston
Stoke Dry
Harringworth
Water Newton
Orton
Whittlesey
Eastrea
March
Lakes End
Lyddington
Gretton
Apethorpe
Alwalton
Angle Bridge
Town End
Southery
Bulwick
Elton
Chesterton
Farcet
Welney
Medbourne
Caldecott
Fotheringhay
Warmington
Yaxley
Pondersbridge
Wimblington
Brandon Creek
Rockingham
Deene
Norman Cross
Benwick
Doddington
Middleton
Cottingham
Upper Benefield
Stilton
Ramsey St Mary's
Primrose Hill
Manea
Brampton Ash
Wilbarston
Corby
Weldon
Benefield
Oundle
Polebrook
Holme
Forty Feet Br.
Old Bedford River
Stoke Albany
Stanion
Brigstock
Stoke Doyle
R. Nene
Barnwell
Glatton
Conington
Chatteris
Pymore
Littleport
Shippea Hill
Desborough
Geddington
Sudborough
Great Gidding
Little Gidding
Sawtry
CAMBRIDGE
Ramsey
Downham
Chettisham
Prickwillow
Rothwell
Lowick
Thorpe Waterville
Clopton
Winwick
Bury
Ferry Hill
Mepal
Queen Adelaide
Weekley
Twywell
Islip
Titchmarsh
Warboys
Sutton
ELY
Kennyhill
KETTERING
Barton Seagrave
Cranford St John
Thrapston
Old Weston
Alconbury Hill
Old Hurst
Somersham
Witchford
Stuntney
Broughton
Burton
Denford
Bythorn
Leighton Bromswold
Lit Stukeley
Gt Stukeley
Pidley
Haddenham
Thetford Corner
Alconbury
Bluntisham
Keyston
Ringstead
Stretham
Wilburton
THE FENS
HOLLAND
KESTEVEN
LINCOLNSHIRE WOLDS
TF
TL
A15
A16
A17
A46
A52
A57
A1
A159
A631
A1103
A156
A158
A153
A157
A155
A1104
A1121
A151
A6003
A43
A427
A47
A606
A607
A605
A141
A142
A1101
A1122
A10
A6
A510
A604
23
14

NX

High Harrington
Distingto
A595
Moresby
Parton   Row
WHITEHAVEN   Hensingham
Cleator Moor   Wath
Woodend   Cleator
St Bees   Egremor
Thornhill
New
Mill
Sellafield   Seascale
Ra

Point of Ayre
The Lhen   Smeale   Cranstal
A10   A16
Jurby East   A17   Bride
Jurby West   Andreas
Ballasalla   Sandygate   Regaby
Jurby   St. Judes   Dhoor
The Cronk   Sulby   Ramsey
Ballaugh   Ramsey Bay
A14   A18   Port e Vullen
Kirk Michael   14   15   Corrany   Maughold
Isle   A3   Ballajora
Shaughlaige-   Barregarrow   Glen Mona
e-Quiggin   Snaefell   A2
Knocksharry   Cronk-y-Voddy   2034   Dhoon
Lambfell   *Man*   A18
Moar   Laxey
Peel   St John   Ballacraine   Old Laxey
Patrick   Greeba   Baldwin   Baldrine
Glenmaye   A1   Crosby Union   Hillbury   Clay Head
Dalby   Foxdale   Glen Vine Mills   Onchan
NT   Eairy   Garth   Kirk
Ballamodha   St.   Braaid   Bradden   **DOUGLAS**
Lingague   Silverburn   Newtown   Oune's Hill
Bradda   Ballabeg
West   Colb
Port Erin   Ballasalla
regneish   A7   Ronaldsway
A31   Port St   Derbyhaven
NT   Spanish   Mary   **Castletown**
Head
Calf of
Man

SC

I R I S H   *S E A*

NORTH SEA

NZ

TA

A171
Staithes
Hinderwell
Runswick Bay
Ellerby
Lythe
Sandsend
Whitby
A174
Briggswath
Ruswarp
Sleights
Sneaton
High Hawsker
B1416
Egton
Grosmont
A169
A171
Robin Hoods Bay
Goathland
Ravenscar
MOORS
PARK
FYLINGDALES MOOR
Saltergate
Staintondale
Cloughton Newlands
Bridestones Moor NT
Cloughton
Langdale End
Burniston
Scalby
A169
Hackness
Newby
Everley
Falsgrave
SCARBOROUGH
Wrelton
Middleton
East Ayton
Osgodby
A64
Wilton
Ebberston
A170
West Ayton
Irton
Cayton
Pickering
Thornton Dale
Allerston
Brompton
Wykeham
Seamer
A165
Yedingham
Willerby
Flixton
A1039
Filey
East Heslerton
Staxton
Muston
Filey Bay
Sherburn
Ganton
A64
West Heslerton
Foxholes
Reighton
Buckton
Rillington
Scagglethorpe
Weaverthorpe
Bempton
Dalton
Norton
Burton Fleming
A165
Flamborough Head
Octon Cross Roads
1253
A165
1255
Flamborough
North Grimston
Langtoft
Rudston
Boynton
BRIDLINGTON
Duggleby
Carnaby
Bridlington Bay
Wharram le Street
1253
Sledmere
Haisthorpe
Hilderthorpe
Thornholme
Fimber
Garton-on-the-Wolds
Great Kendale
A166
Burton Agnes
Fraisthorpe
1251
1252
1249
Fridaythorpe
Wetwang
Great Driffield
Lissett
A165
A166
Little Driffield
Wansford
Ulrome
Bishop Wilton
Kirkburn
Eastburn
1249
Beeford
Skipsea
North Dalton
A163
Bainton
Hutton Cranswick
North Frodingham
Skipsea Brough
1242
Warter
Watton
Atwick
Barmby Moor
Pocklington
Beswick
Middleton-on-the-Wolds
Hayton
Thorpe le Street
Kipling Cotes
Scorborough
Brandesburton
Hornsea
Leconfield
A165
1244
Seaton
Rolston
Shiptonthorpe
A163
Market Weighton
Leven
Catwick
A1079
Molescroft
Routh
Long Riston
Mappleton
Holme upon Spalding Moor
Sancton
Bishop Burton
Beverley
Tickton
South Skirlaugh
North Skirlaugh
Aldbrough
Foggathorpe
A614
North Newbald
Walkington
Woodmansey
Coniston
Flinton
Garton
HUMBERSIDE
High Hunsley
Dunswell
Skidby
Ganstead
Wyton
Sproatley
North End
North Cave
South Cave
1233
Sutton-on-Hull
Bilton
HOLDERNESS
Cavil
Scalby
Newport
A63
Willerby
A165
Preston
Roos
Gilberdyke
Swanland
Anlaby
A1079
Marfleet
Hedon
Burstwick
Withernsea
Elloughton
Welton
A1105
KINGSTON UPON HULL
A1033
Thorngumbald
1362
Brough
North Ferriby
Hessle
Paull
Keyingham
Ottringham
Hollym
Swinefleet
A161
Barton-upon-Humber
New Holland
River Humber
Welwick
1445
Alkborough
Barrow upon Humber
Patrington
Easington
Burton upon Stather
South Ferriby
Horkstow
A1077
Thornton Curtis
Thornton Abbey
Eastoft
Luddington
Normanby
Roxby
Saxby All Saints
Bonby
Wootton
A160
Spurn Head
Amcotts
Appleby
Worlaby
A160
Ulceby
Immingham
Habrough
Keadby
Crosby
A1136
Stallingborough
GRIMSBY
A18
Ealand
Brumby
SCUNTHORPE
Melton Ross
Croxton
A18
Brocklesby
Healing
Gt Coates
Cleethorpes
Althorpe
Ashby
Broughton
Wrawby
Keelby
A18
Laceby
Scartho
Humberston
Messingham
Brigg
Bigby
Riby
Irby upon Humber
Waltham
New Waltham
Sturton
Howsham
Grasby
Brigsley
Holton le Clay
Scotter
Hibaldstow
A1084
Swallow
A46
A16
Marsh Chapel
Redbourne
Moortown
Caistor
Cabourne
East Ravendale
North Thoresby
Eskham
A15
Holton le Moor
A46
Kirmond
Binbrook
Ludborough
North Somercotes
Conisholme

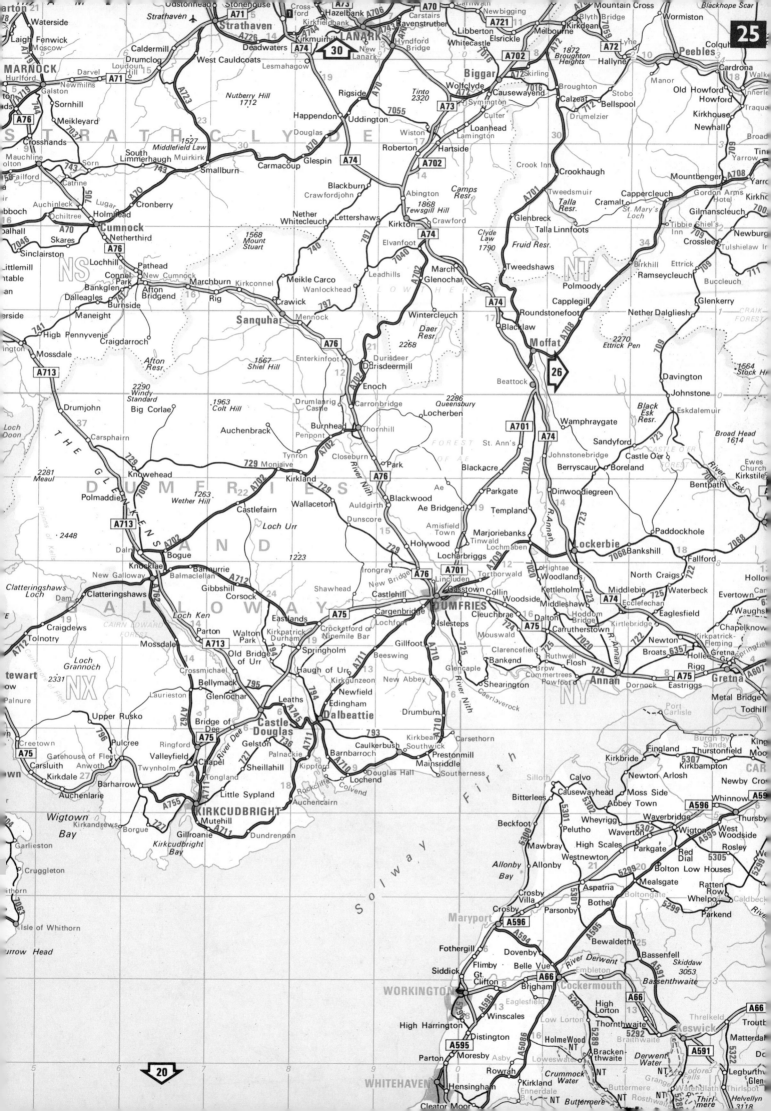

NORTH SEA

NU

NZ

NORTHUMBERLAND

DURHAM

NATIONAL PARK

NEWCASTLE UPON TYNE

GATESHEAD

SUNDERLAND

SOUTH SHIELDS

HARTLEPOOL

STOCKTON-ON-TEES

MIDDLESBROUGH

BARNARD CASTLE

BISHOP AUCKLAND

DURHAM

Swintonmill, Leitholm, Simprim, Orange Lane, Lennel, Coldstream, Birgham, Carham, Sprouston, Mindrummill, Mindrum, Blakelaw, Frogden, Linton, Morebattle, Gateshaw, Hownam, Chatto, Town Yetholm, Kirknewton, Yeavering, Akeld, Wooler, Kirknewton

Norham, Allerdean, Ancroft, West Mains, Beal, Holy Island, Lindisfarne, Duddo, West Kyloe, Fenwick, Buckton, Lowick, Twizel Bridge, Cornhill-on-Tweed, Crookham, Etal, Ford, Middleton, Waren Mill, Budle, Bamburgh, Belford, Outchester, Glororum, Seahouses

The Cheviot 2676, Wark, Flodden, Howtel, Milfield, Doddington, Bellshill, Adderstone, Warenford, Chatton, Greendikes, Brownyside, North Charlton, Christon Bank, Newton Links NT, Embleton, Beadnell, Beadnell Bay, Dunstanburgh Castle, Craster, Howick, Chillingham, New Bewick, South Charlton, Charlton Mires, Rennington, Longhoughton

Windy Gyle 2036, Barrowburn, Shillmoor, Ravens Knowe 1729, Catcleugh, Byrness, Rochester, Horsley, Elishaw, Harbottle, Holystone, Hepple, Flotterton, Thropton, Rothbury, Lorbottle, Cartington, Callaly, Whittingham, Ingram, Powburn, Glanton, Alnwick, Hawkhill, Denwick, Lesbury, Alnmouth, Alnmouth Bay, Birling, Warkworth, Amble, Nth. Togston, Togston, Broomhill, Sth. Broomhill, Red Row, Druridge Bay

A68, A696, A697, A1, A1068, Tosson Hill 1447, Pauperhaugh, Weldon Bridge, Longframlington, Forestburn Gate, Longhorsley, Swarland, West Thirston, Acklington, Felton, Acklington, Widdrington, Widdrington Sta., Ellington, Ulgham, Longhirst, Lynemouth, Longhirst, Ashington, Pegswood, Newbiggin-by-the-Sea

West Woodburn, Knowesgate, Ridsdale, Cambo, Hartburn, Throphill, Mitford, Bothal, Guide Post, Stakeford, Morpeth, Sleekburn, Blyth, Bolam, Whalton, West Edington, Clifton, Bedlington, Bebside, A192, A193, A189

Rayless, Scots Gap, 6343, 6342, Steng Cross, Colt Crag Resr, Little Bavington, West Belsay, Belsay, Higham Dykes, Stannington, Cramlington, East Cramlington, New Delaval, Seaton, Seaton Sluice, A189

Park End, Hallington Resr, Black Heddon, Heugh, Seaton Burn, Dudley, Seaton Delaval, Seghill, Earsdon, Whitley Bay, Cullercoats, Tepper Moor, Carrawbrough, Chollerton, Matfen, Ponteland, Killingworth, Wide Open, Burradon, Backworth, New York, Lynemouth, North Shields

Housesteads, Fourstones, Allerwash, Wall, Hill Head, Stagshaw Bank, Corbridge, Aydon, Heddon on the Wall, Horsley, Wylam, R. Tyne, Newburn, Gosforth, Wallsend, Jarrow, South Shields, Marsden, Whitburn, Roker

Haydon Bridge, Low Gate, A69, Hexham, Dilston, W. Nubbock, Broomhaugh, Stocksfield, High Spen, Greenside, Prudhoe, Blaydon, Ryton, Whickham, Gateshaw, Walker, Monkton, Boldon, A19, A184

Langley, Catton, Allendale Town, Studdon, Sinderhope, Apperley Dene, Whittonstall, Newlands, Shotley Bridge, Medomsley, South Moor, Stanley, West Pelton, Birtley, Washington, Usworth, Springwell, Castletown, Sunderland, Hendon, Ryhope, New Silksworth, Herrington

Spartylea, Dirt Pot, Allenheads, Bolt's Law 1773, Blanchland, Edmondbyers, Castleside, Rowley, Lanchester, Consett, Annfield Plain, Maiden Law, Chester Moor, Chester-le-Street, Houghton-le-Spring, Seaton, Dalton-le-Dale, New Hesledon, Seaham

Lanehead, Cowshill, Wearhead, Ireshopeburn, Ashgill Head, St. John's Chapel, Daddry Shield, Eastgate, Stanhope, Frosterley, Wolsingham, Tow Law, Sunniside, Crook, Willington, Hunwick, Brandon, Croxdale, Sunderland Br, Bowburn, Wingate, Quarrington Hill, Wheatley Hill, Castle Eden, Blackhall Colliery

Witton Gilbert, Ushaw Moor, Esh Winning, Broom, Durham, West Rainton, Sherburn, Sherburn Hill, Shotton Colliery, Trimdon Grange, Trimdon, S. Wingate, Hart, A690, A691, A177, A179

Langdon Beck, Newbiggin, Middleton-in-Teesdale, High Force 2512, Ettersgill, Forest, Fir Tree, Howden le Wear, Witton le Wear, Escomb, Spennymoor, Tudhoe, Ferryhill, Kirk Merrington, Middlestone, Coundon, Rushyford, Woodham, Sedgefield, Fishburn, Station Town, Trimdon Colliery, Peterlee, Easington, Easington La., South Hetton, Hetton-le-Hole, A19, A689

Grains o'th' Beck Bridge, Bowbank, Romaldkirk, Cotherstone, Eggleston, Woodland, Copley, Butterknowle, Evenwood Gate, Ingleton, High Etherley, St. Helen Auckland, West Auckland, Toft Hill, Bishop Auckland, Woodham, Newton Aycliffe, Aycliffe, Great Burdon, Sadberge, Wolviston, Newton Bewley, Haverton Hill, Port Clarence, Seal Sands, Tees Mouth, Greatham, Seaton Carew, Redcar, Dormanstown

North Stainmore, Balderhead Resr, Hury Resr, Selset Resr, Grassholme Resr, Lartington, Startforth, Stainton, Winston, Gainford, Piercebridge, Summerhouse, High Coniscliffe, Coatham Mundeville, Heighington, Darlington, Middleton St. George, Dinsdale, Hurworth, Neasham, Croft, Great Stainton, Bishopton, Thorpe Thewles, Stillington, Whitton, Stockton-on-Tees, Thornaby-on-Tees, Ingleby Barwick, Yarm, Eaglescliffe, Elton, Maltby, Marton, Ormesby, Eston, Guisborough, A66, A67, A19, A171, A174, A1027, A1085

A1, A68, A688, A689, A690, A691, A177, A179, A167, A174

A697, A696, A695, A69, A686, A689

NORTH TYNE, River North Tyne, River Wear, River Tees, Lune Forest, Hamsterley Forest, Slaley Forest, Rothbury Forest, Harwood Forest, Cheviot Hills

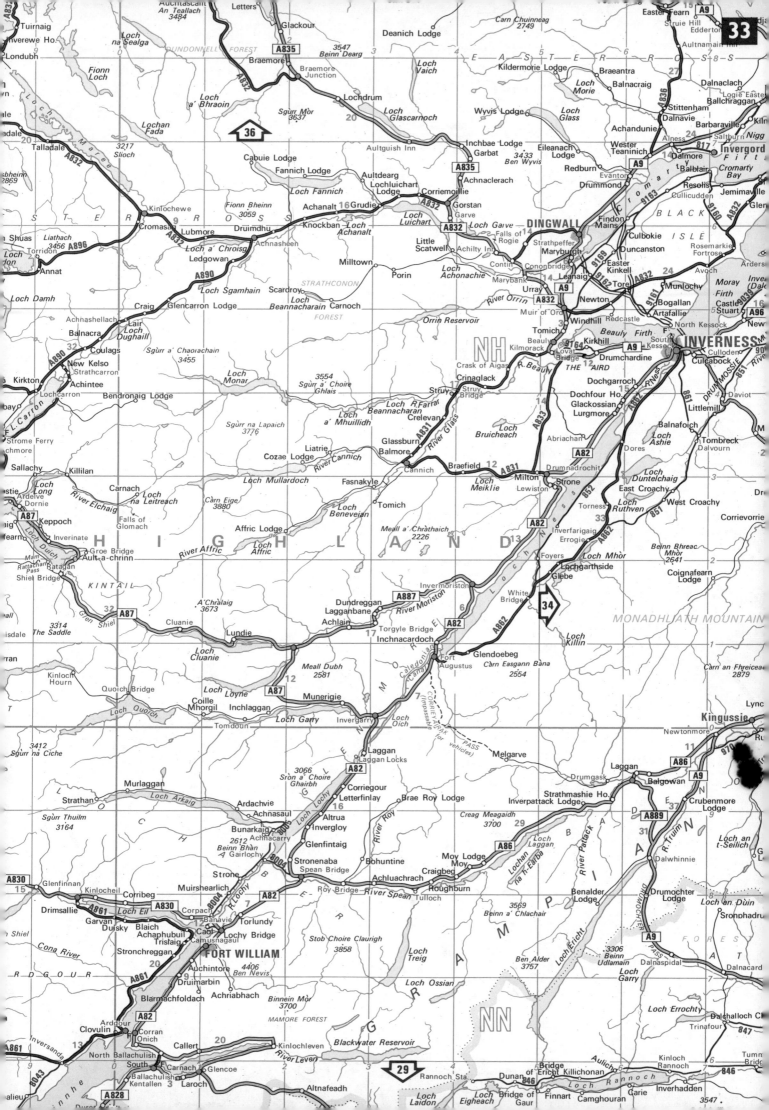

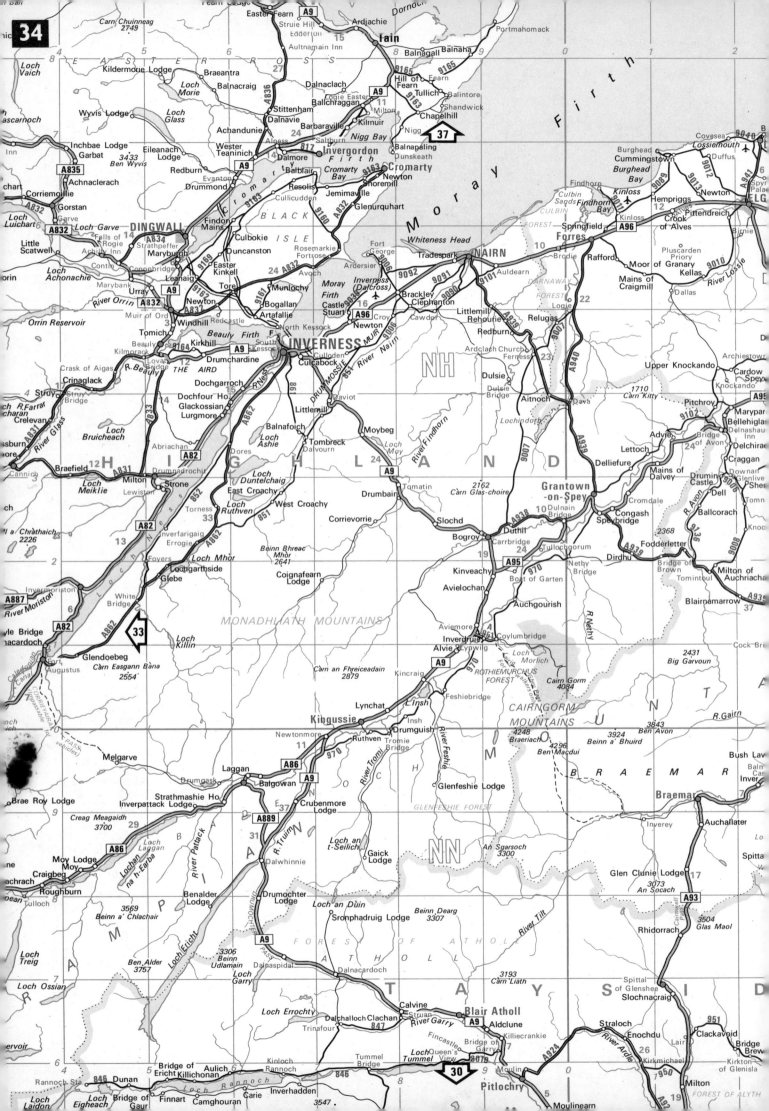

Spey Bay Portknockie Cullen Bay Sandhaven Rosehearty Fraserburgh
Kingston Findochty Cullen Portsoy Whitehills Crovie Pennan Coburty Fraserburgh Bay
siemouth Spey Bay Portessie Buckie Lintmill 9139 Macduff Silverford Gardenstown 9031 Percyhorner Pitsligo 9037 Inverallochy
Calcots Garmouth Bogmuir A98 Portgordon Slackhead Fordyce Deskford Ordens Longmanhill Banff Dubford Protstonhill New Aberdour Mid Ardlaw Memsie 9033 St.Combs
Lhanbryde 9015 Berryhillock Kirktown of Alvah Keilhill King Edward Cauldwells Craigmaud New Pitsligo A981 Strichen Lonmay Old Rattray
A96 9104 Tynet Bridge 9022 A95 9025 A97 Greenlaw Brigend of Mountblairy A98 9105 New Byth A950 9093 New Leeds Crimond Blackhill A952
Mosstodloch Fochabers 17 9016 Gordonstown Peatknowe Cornhill Finnygaud Plaidy Fintry Denhead 17 St.Fergus
Inchberry A96 9018 9023 9121 9027 Cuminestown A950 Dunshillock Mintlaw Longside
Orton Forgie Aultmore Newmill Lootcherbrae Drumnagorrach Aberchirder 9025 Turriff 922 Mains of Idoch New Deer Maud Old Deer Flushing Peterhead
Newlands 9103 Mulben Auchinhove Farmtown Marnoch River Deveron 9024 Darra Birkenhills Drymuir Stuartfield Millbreck 9 A950
Crofts Blackhillock Keith Davoch of Grange Rothiemay 22 Milltown Parkdargue Fortrie Mains of Towie Cairnorrie Brownhill 9030 Auchnagatt Clola Burnhaver Boddam
Towiemore Newtack Bogniebrae Forgue Auchterless 9947 Cot-town 9005 Methlick Backhill Auchiries Hatton Stirling
Maggieknockater 9115 Newton 11 Westerton Fyvie 17 Woodhead St.Katherines Michael Muir Hilton Toll of Birness Coldwells Cruden Bay Port Erroll
Craigellachie 9074 A96 9022 A97 Badenscoth Rothienorman Fisherford Wedderlairs 9005 A92 Bogbrae Chapel Hill
Aberlour 23 Milltown of Auchindown A920 Huntly Ythan Wells Culsalmond Tarves Ellon A92 Collieston
Dufftown Haugh of Glass STRATHBOGIE Dumeath Newtongarry Croft Bainshole Skares Colpy Cairnhill Pitmachie A920 Pitmedden 9000 Bridgend A975
Rinnes 2755 Glenrinnes Auchindown Castle Laggan CLASHINDARROCH FOREST Culdrain 22 Insch Pitcaple Oldmeldrum Udny Kingoodie Housieside Newburgh
Aultbeg 9009 Bridgend Eastertown Millton of Noth Kennethmont 9002 Pitachie Oyne Kirkton of Oyne Inveramsay Whiterashes Pettymuck Foveran
Shabbie Hill 2563 Cabrach A941 Belhinnie Rhynie Clatt Hardgate Leslie Auchleven Chapel of Garioch 993 Rashiereive 17
Craig Castle 9002 Newton The Buck 2368 1588 Correen Hills Burgh Muir Inverurie Reisque 979 Whitecairns Balmedie
Badenyon Lumsden 5 Mossat Invermossat Tullynessle Keig Port Elphinstone Newmachar 979 North Kinmundy A92
GRAMPIAN Belnacraig Kildrummy A944 Milltown of Alford Alford Kenmay Kintore Hatton of Fintray 977 Little Fintray 999
Mains of Glenbuchat A97 Bridge of Alford PITFICHIE FOREST Whitehouse 993 A941 R.Don Aberdeen (Dyce) Dyce Stoneywood
Bellabeg 973 Strathdon Boultenstone Milton of Cushnie Muir of Fowlis 33 Tillyfourie Monymusk Leylodge 16 Blackburn Buxburn Bridge of Don
Garchory Colnabaichin 26 2032 Pressendye Ordhead 994 A96 Kirkton of Skene Kirkton of Skene Elrick Kingsford ABERDEEN Girdle Ness
Cairn 'Mona Gowan 2456 Craigievar Castle Kintocher Craskins Dunecht 9125 Garlogie Cairnie Bieldside Craighton Cults Nigg
Gairnshiel Lodge Newkirk Tarland 9119 Lumphanan 25 Midmar Castle Echt South Kirkton 9119 Cullerlie 18 Banchory Milltimber Cove
Gairnshiel Bridge Torbeg Lochhead Ordie 9094 Tornaveen Hill of Fare 1545 Loch of Skene 977 Culter Blairs 9011 Charlestown
Geallaig Hill 2439 Cambus o'May A93 Aboyne Dinnet Kincardine O'Neil 13 Torphins Mid Beltie Milltown of Campfield Mains of Drum Park Drumoak 14 Hillside Findon
Bridge of Gairn 976 Birsemore Bridge of Ess Marywell 993 Bridge of Canny R.Dee Crathes Castle A93 Craiglug A92 Cammachmore
Ballater Deecastle Pannanich Wells Ballogie 998 976 Banchory Durris Netherley 979 Newtonhill
Littlemill Ballochan Feughside Inn Bridge of Feugh Blairydryne Craiggiecat Muchalls
Aucholzie Whitestone Strachan A957 Rickarton Mowtie
Mount Keen 3077 Kerloch 1747 1051 Hill of Trusta New Mains of Ury STONEHAVEN
Loch Muick Mount Battock 2555 Spitalburn 974 NO Cowie Dunnottar Castle
Invermark Lodge Cairn O'Mount Auchenblae Glenbervie Fiddes Mill of Uras
Tarfside Millden Lodge Fordoun Church Drumlithie 10 A94
Braedownie Ben Tirran 2939 Loch Lee Mid Cairncross Clattering Bridge HOWE OF THE MEARNS Parkneuk Roadside of Kinneff A92
River Sth.Esk Clova 955 Wheen Haughend Woodhead Redmyre Scotston Arbuthnott 96 Kinneff A92
Newbigging Hunthill Lodge 9120 Fettercairn Inverbervie
Rottal Gannochy Bridge Laurencekirk Gourdon
Clachnabrain Bridgend Dunlappie Edzell Sauchieburn 25 A937 Marykirk St.Cyrus Johnshaven
Kirkton of Menmuir Inchbare 966 13
Shandford Tigerton N.Craigo Pathhead
Cat Law 2196 Fern West Muir Trinity Brechin A935 MONTROSE
Pearsie Tannadice 513 A94 Mains of Dun Montrose Basin 31
Cortachy Finhaven Netherton Ferryden
Northmuir A957 Aberlemno Maryton

THE MINCH

NB

NC

NG

NH

Cape Wrath
Faraid Head
Balnakeil Bay
Balnakeil
Whiten Head
Durness
Achiemore
Leirinmore
Smoo Cave
Ben Hu 1338
Sandwood Loch
Keoldale
Kyle of Durness
Sangobeg
Rispond
1592 Creag Riabhach
50
Portnancon
Hope Lodge
Achuvoldr
Heilam
Loch Eriboll
Kempie
Loch Hope
Eriboll
Kinloch Lodge
Blairmore
Sheigra
Oldshore
A807
Kinlochbervie
Badcall
Gualin Ho
R. Dionard
2980 Foinaven
3040 Ben Hope
Loch Dhe
Loch Inchard
Achriesgill
Alltnacaillich
Fanagmore
Foindle
Rhiconich
R. Strathmore
Handa Island
Laxford Bridge
Gobernuisgach Lodge
Loch Me
Scourie
A894
Loch Stack
A838
Achfary
Eddrachillis
Point of Stoer
Oldany Island
Eddrachillis Bay
Kylestrome
Loch Glendhu
Kinloch
Ben Hee 2864
Mudale
Altna
Culkein
Oldany
Drumbeg
Kylesku Ferry
Kylesku
Unapool
Loch Glencoul
Merkland Lodge
Fiag Lodge
Achnacarnin
869
Nedd
Glenleraig
Quinag 2653
Loch Glencoul
HIG
Balchladich
Clashnessie
Stoer
Lochassynt Lodge
19
A894
34
Gorm Loch Mòr
Fiag Bridge
Clachtoll
869
Little Assynt
A837
Loch Assynt
Inchnadamph
Overscaig
A836
Rhicarn
3273 Ben More Assynt
Loch Shin
River Ti
A838
L.Inve
Lochinver
Inverkirkaig
ASSYNT
Canisp 2779
Suilven 2399
Duchally
Rubha Coigeach
Enard Bay
Cam Loch
Ledmore
Beinn Sgeireach 1562
Cra
Reiff
Loch Veyatie
Loch Ailsh
Badintagairt
Alltan Dubh
Baddagyle
Loch Sionascaig
Knockan
Elphin
Altnacealgach
1785 Beinn an Eòin
Glencassley Castle
Colo
L. Osgaig
Loch Urigill
River Oykel
R. Cassley
Salla
Polbain
Loch Bad a' Ghaill
Achiltibuie
Loch Lurgainn
CROMALT HILLS
A837
Rosehall
A839
Summer Isles
COIGACH
1895 Meall an Fhuarain
Lubcroy
Achuirgill
Priest Island
Culnacraig
Strathkanaird
A835
18
Oykel Bridge
Linsic
Isle Martin
Meall Dheirgidh 1659
Greenstone Point
Ardmair Bay
Ardmair
RHIDORROCH FOREST
Opinan
Annat Bay
Morefield
Ullapool
Loch Achall
Mellon Udrigle
Gruinard Island
Little Loch Broom
Braes of Ullapool
Loch an Daimh
River Carron
Rubha Rèidh
Cove
Mellon Charles
Laide
Gruinard Bay
Mungasdale
Badcaul
Aultnaharrie
Badrallach
Leckmelm
2762 Carn Bàn
Alladale Lodge
The Craigs
Ormiscaig
Gruinard House
57
A832
Blarnaleyoch
Ardcharnich
Up
Loch Squod
Aultbea
Coast
Little Gruinard
Ardessie
Camusnagaul
Rhiroy
12
Melvaig
Inverasdale
Loch Ewe
Dundonnell
Ardindrean
Carn Chuinneag 2749
Aultgrishan
Midtown Brae
Auchtascailt
Letters
Deanich Lodge
Peterburn
Tuirnaig
An Teallach 3484
Glackour
Kildermorie Lodge
Naust
Inverewe Ho
Loch na Sealga
Loch Vaich
North Erradale
B021
Poolewe
Londubh
DUNDONNELL FOREST
Braemore
E A S T
Longa Island
L.Tollaidh
Fionn Loch
3547 Beinn Dearg
Braemore Junction
Smithstown
Gairloch
Charlestown
Lochdrum
Loch Glascarnoch
Wyvis Lodge
Loc Gla
Loch Gairloch
Kerrysdale
Loch a' Bhraoin
A835
Port Henderson
Badachro
20
Lochluichart Lodge
Opinam
B8056
Shieldaig Lodge
Slattadale
Sgurr Mòr 3637
Aultguish Inn
Inchbae Lodge
Garbat
Eileanac Lod
Redpoint
20
Talladale
A832
3217 Slioch
33
A835
Baosbheinn 2869
Cabuie Lodge
Aultdearg
3433 Ben Wyvis
Achnaclerach
Fannich Lodge
Lochluichart Lodge
A832
Gorstan
Lower Diabaig
Kinlochewe
Fionn Bheinn 3059
Corriemoillie
WESTER
Grudie
A832
Loch Garve
DINGWA
Alligin Shuas
Liathach 3456
Cromasag
Lubmore
Druimdhu
Knockban
Loch Fannich
Grudie
Loch Luichart
A835
14
A834
Torridon
ROSS
Loch Achanalt
Achilty Inn
Falls of Rogie
Maryb
Upper Loch Torridon
A896
Loch a' Cnroisg
Ledgowan
Achnasheen
Little Scatwell
Contin
Annat
Milltown
Loch Achonachie
Cononbridge
Shieldaig
Balgy
Porin
Marybank
Lê
A896
Loch Damh
A890
Loch Sgamhain
Scardroy
STRATHCONON
Urray
AS
Loch Lundie
Craig
Glencarron Lodge
Loch Beannacharain
Carnoch
Orrin Reservoir
River Orrin
Muir of Ord
14
Beinn Bhàn 2938
Achnashellach
Lair
Loch Dughaill
Sgurr a' Chaorachain
Beauly
Kilmorack
Coulags
Balnacra

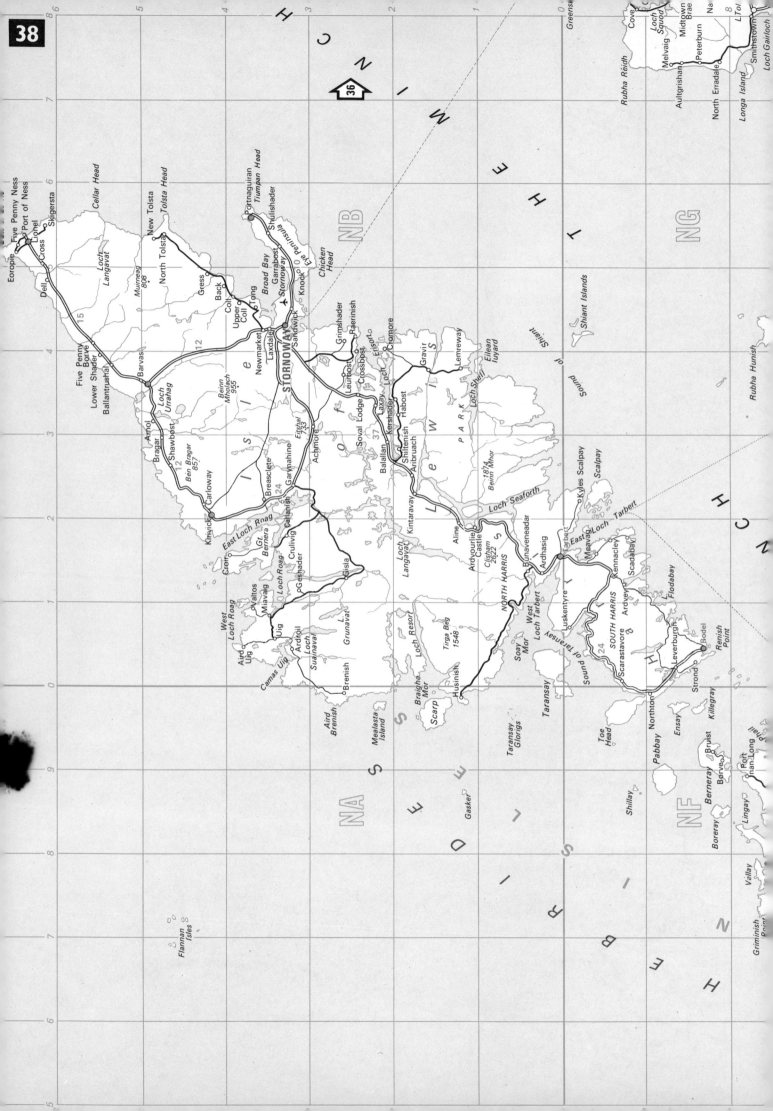

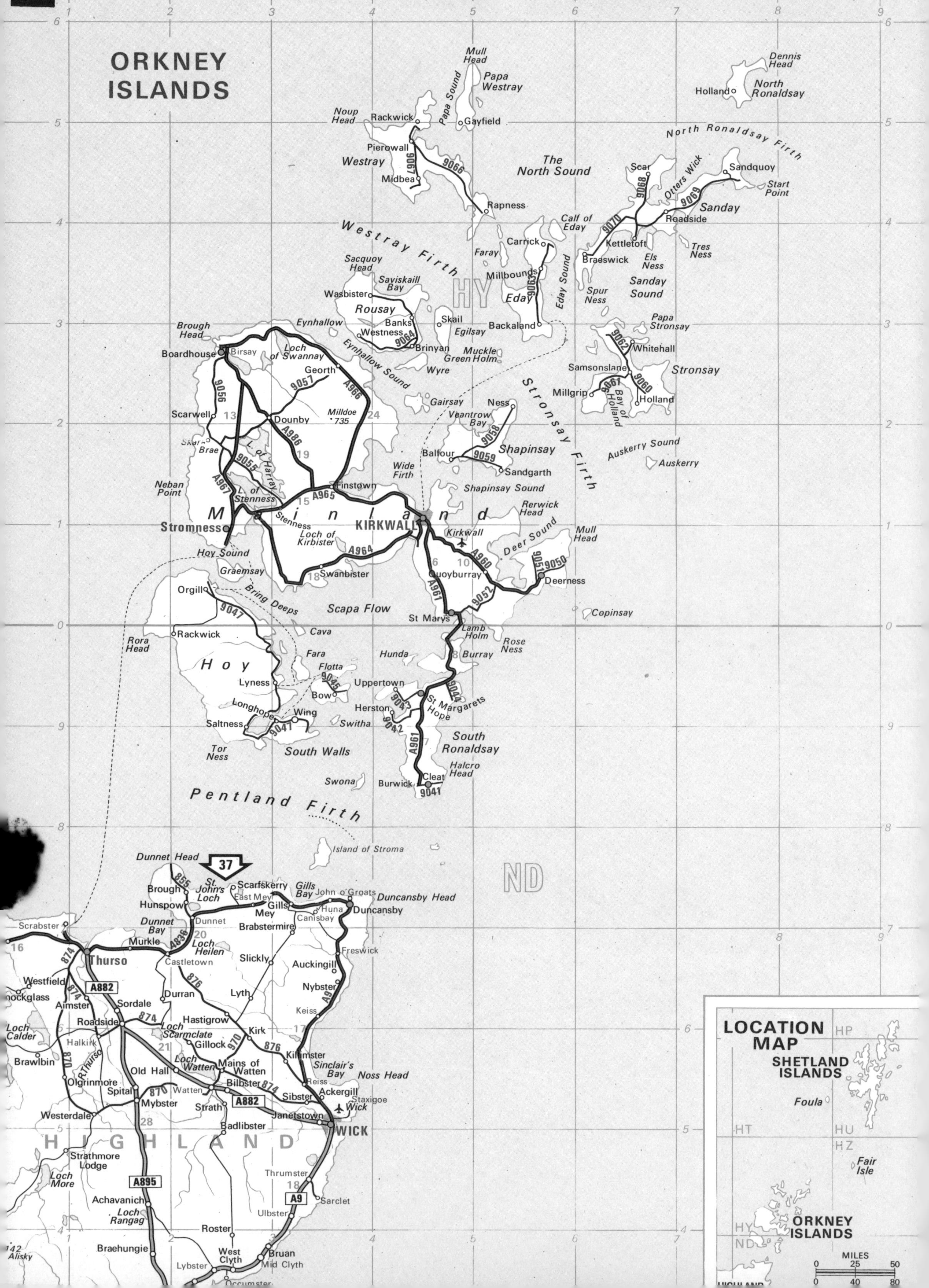

ORKNEY ISLANDS
Mull Head
Papa Westray
Papa Sound
Gayfield
Dennis Head
North Ronaldsay
Holland
Noup Head
Rackwick
Pierowall
Westray
Midbea
9067
9066
The North Sound
North Ronaldsay Firth
Scar
Otters Wick
Sandquoy
Start Point
9068
9069
Sanday
Roadside
9070
Kettletoft
Rapness
Westray Firth
Calf of Eday
Carrick
Faray
Braeswick
Els Ness
Tres Ness
Sacquoy Head
Saviskaill Bay
Millbounds
Wasbister
Rousay
HY
Eday
9063
Eday Sound
Spur Ness
Sanday Sound
Brough Head
Eynhallow
Banks
Westness
9064
Brinyan
Skail
Egilsay
Backaland
Papa Stronsay
Boardhouse
Birsay
Loch of Swannay
Eynhallow Sound
Muckle Green Holm
Whitehall
9062
Samsonslane
Stronsay
Georth
9057
A966
Wyre
9056
Gairsay
Stronsay Firth
Millgrip
9061
9060
Bay of Holland
Holland
Scarwell
13
Dounby
Milldoe 735
24
Ness
Veantrow Bay
Skara Brae
A986
19
9058
Shapinsay
Auskerry Sound
Auskerry
L. of Harray
9055
Balfour
9059
Sandgarth
Wide Firth
Neban Point
A967
L. of Stenness
15
A965
Finstown
Shapinsay Sound
Rerwick Head
Mainland
Stromness
Stenness
Loch of Kirbister
KIRKWALL
Kirkwall
Mull Head
Deer Sound
Hoy Sound
A964
A960
9051
9050
Graemsay
6
10
18
Swanbister
Quoyburray
Deerness
Orgill
Bring Deeps
A961
9052
9047
Scapa Flow
St Marys
Copinsay
Rora Head
Rackwick
Cava
Lamb Holm
Rose Ness
Hoy
Fara
Hunda
Burray
Flotta
9045
Lyness
Uppertown
Bow
9044
9043
St Margarets Hope
Longhope
Wing
Herston
Saltness
9047
Switha
9042
South Ronaldsay
Tor Ness
South Walls
A961
Halcro Head
Swona
Burwick
Cleat
9041
Pentland Firth
Island of Stroma
Dunnet Head
37
ND
855
Brough
St. John's Loch
Scarfskerry
East Mey
Gills Bay
John o'Groats
Duncansby Head
Hunspow
Gills
Huna
Duncansby
Mey
Canisbay
Dunnet
Scrabster
Dunnet Bay
Brabstermire
16
Murkle
B876
20
Loch Heilen
874
Thurso
Castletown
Slickly
Freswick
Westfield
A882
Auckingill
Knockglass
874
Aimster
876
Durran
Lyth
Nybster
Sordale
Roadside
874
Loch Scarmclate
Hastigrow
Keiss
A99
Loch Calder
Halkirk
Gillock
Kirk
17
21
970
876
Brawlbin
870
R. Thurso
Loch Watten
Mains of Watten
Killimster
Sinclair's Bay
Noss Head
Old Hall
Olgrinmore
Spital
870
Watten
Bilbster
874
Reiss
Ackergill
Mybster
A882
Sibster
Staxigoe
Wick
Westerdale
Strath
Janetstown
28
Badlibster
WICK
HIGHLAND
Strathmore Lodge
Loch More
Thrumster
18
A895
A9
Sarclet
Achavanich
Loch Rangag
Ulbster
Roster
Braehungie
West Clyth
Bruan
Mid Clyth
Lybster
Occumster
Alisky
LOCATION MAP
HP
SHETLAND ISLANDS
Foula
HT
HU
HZ
Fair Isle
HY
ORKNEY ISLANDS
ND
MILES
0
25
50
0
40
80

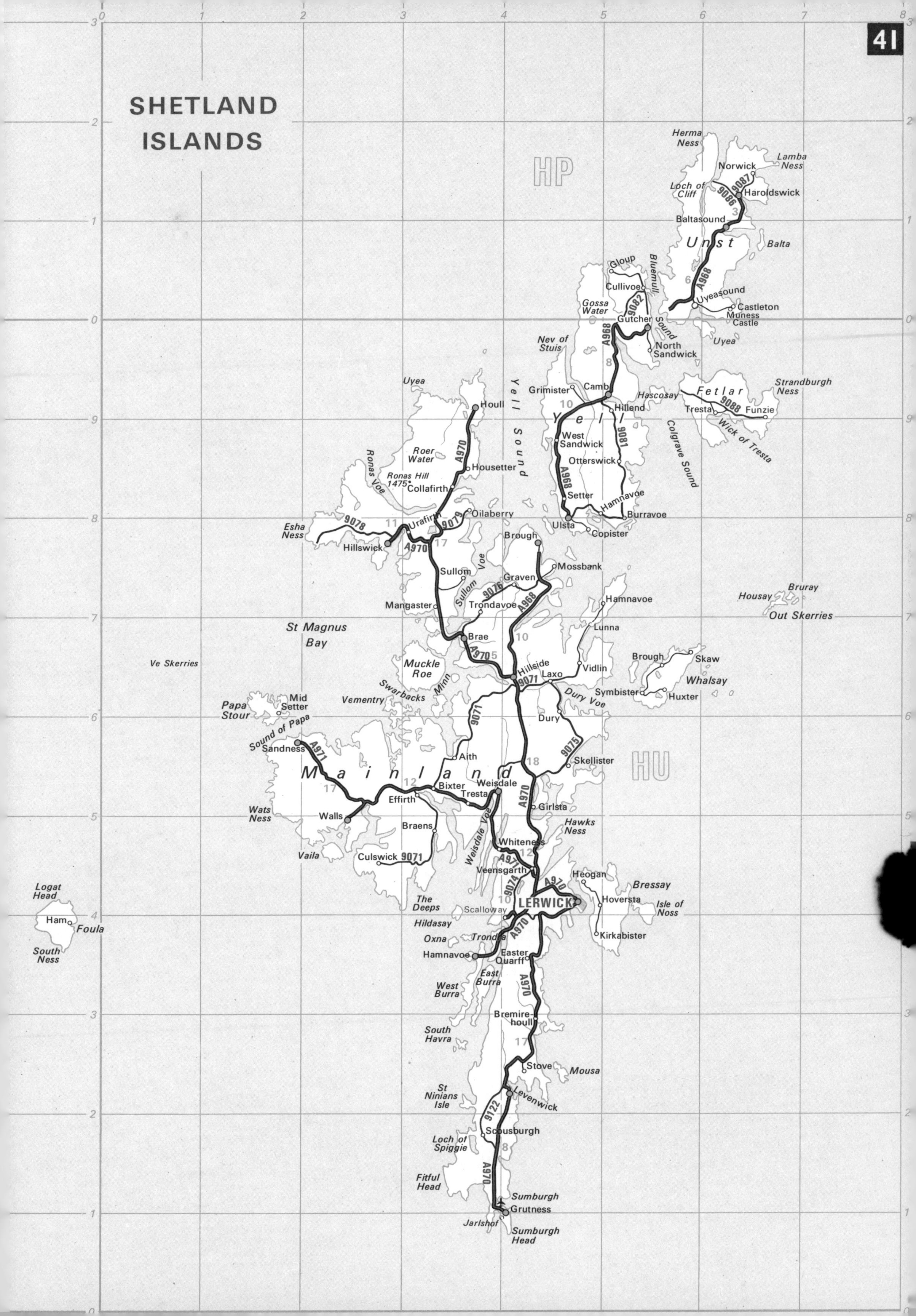

SHETLAND ISLANDS

HP

HU

Herma Ness
Norwick
Lamba Ness
Loch of Cliff
9086 9087
Haroldswick
Baltasound
3
Unst
Balta
Gloup
Cullivoe
9082
Gossa Water
Gutcher
North Sandwick
Castleton
Muness Castle
Uyea
Nev of Stuis
Grimister
Camb
8
Hillend
Hascosay
Fetlar
9088 Funzie
Tresta
Strandburgh Ness
Uyea
Houll
10
Yell
West Sandwick
Otterswick
Yell Sound
Colgrave Sound
Wick of Tresta
9081
A968
Roer Water
A970
Housetter
Ronas Hill 1475
Collafirth
9079
Oilaberry
Setter
A968
Hamnavoe
Burravoe
9078
11
Urafirth
17
A970
Ulsta
Copister
Esha Ness
Hillswick
Brough
Mossbank
Housay
Bruray
Out Skerries
Sullom
9076
Graven
A968
Hamnavoe
Mangaster
Trondavoe
St Magnus Bay
Sullom Voe
Brae
10
Lunna
Ve Skerries
A970 5
Hillside
Laxo
Brough
Skaw
Muckle Roe
9071
Vidlin
Whalsay
Swarbacks Minn
Symbister
Huxter
Mid Setter
Vementry
Dury Voe
Papa Stour
Sound of Papa
9071
Aith
Dury
9075
Skellister
Sandness
A971
Weisdale
18
A970
Mainland
12
Bixter
Tresta
Wats Ness
17
Effirth
Girlsta
Hawks Ness
Walls
Braens
Heogan
Vaila
Culswick 9071
Weisdale Voe
Whiteness
12
A97
Veensgarth
A970
Bressay
Logat Head
9074
Hoversta
Isle of Noss
10
The Deeps
Scalloway
LERWICK
Ham *Foula*
Hildasay
Trondra
A970
Kirkabister
Oxna
Easter Quarff
South Ness
Hamnavoe
West Burra
A970
East Burra
Bremirehoull
South Havra
17
Stove
Mousa
St Ninians Isle
9122
Levenwick
Scousburgh
Loch of Spiggie
8
Fitful Head
A970
Sumburgh
Grutness
Jarlshof
Sumburgh Head

Scottish Battlefields

The Little Minch

NORTH WEST HIGHLANDS

Carbisdale 1650 ✕ ○ Invershin

Moray Firth

Nairn ○
✕ *Auldearn 1645*

Inverness ○ ✕ *Culloden Moor 1746*

Cromdale Braes 1690 ✕

Grantown-on-Spey ○

✕ *Glenlivet 1594*

Old Meldrum ○

Harlaw 1411 ✕ ○ *Barra Hill 1308*

Alford 1645 ✕

○ Inverurie

Tomintoul ○ ○ Alford

Shiel Bridge ○
✕ *Glenshiel 1719*

○ Aberdeen

Battle of the Shirts 1544 ✕ ○ Invergarry

Lumphanan 1057 ✕
○ Lumphanan

✕ *Hill of Fare 1562*

○ Banchory

GRAMPIAN MOUNTAINS

Inverlochy 1645 ✕

Roy Bridge 1688 ✕
○ Spean Bridge

○ Fort William

Bloody Bay 1439 ✕

○ Tobermory

✕ *Killiecrankie Pass 1689*

○ Pitlochry

✕ *Glasclune Castle 1392*
○ Blairgowrie

○ Montrose

Nethven Wood 1306 ✕

✕ *North Inch 1396*

✕ Perth

○ DUNDEE

○ Oban

Firth of Lorn

✕ *Tippermuir 1644*

○ St Andrews

Sheriffmuir 1715 ✕

Dunblane ○
✕ *Stirling Bridge 1297*

Stirling ○ ✕

○ Kirkcaldy

Sauchieburn 1488 ✕ ✕ *Bannockburn 1314*

Glen Fruin 1603 ✕

Helensburgh ○

Firth of Forth

Kilsyth 1646 ✕ ✕ Falkirk

Kilsyth ○

Falkirk 1746 & 1298 ✕

○ EDINBURGH

Pinkie 1547 ✕

Prestonpans 1745 ✕

○ Prestonpans

○ Dunbar

✕ *Dunbar 1650*

✕ *Dunbar 1296*

Largs ○

✕ *Langside 1568* ○ GLASGOW

Rullion Green 1666 ✕ ✕ *Roslin 1303*

○ Penicuik

✕ *Largs 1263*

Firth of Clyde

○ Hamilton

✕ *Bothwell Bridge 1679*

○ Kilmarnock

✕ *Drumeclog 1679*

✕ *Loudoun Hill 1307*

SOUTHERN UPLANDS

Philiphaugh 1645 ✕ ○ Selkirk

✕ *Ancrum Moor 1545*

○ Jedburgh

○ Ayr
○ Cumnock

✕ *Airds Moss 1680*

✕ *Carter Bar 1575*
○ Carter Bar

SOUTHERN

Dryfe Sands 1593 ✕

✕ *Glentrool 1307*

○ Dumfries

○ Lockerbie

○ Newton Stewart

○ Stranraer

Solway Firth

A selection of sites where some of the major battles in Scotland's turbulent history were fought. These battles ranged from border raids and inter-clan feuds to religious crusades, political conflicts, and all-out war between Scotland and England.

The Glasgow-Edinburgh Corridor

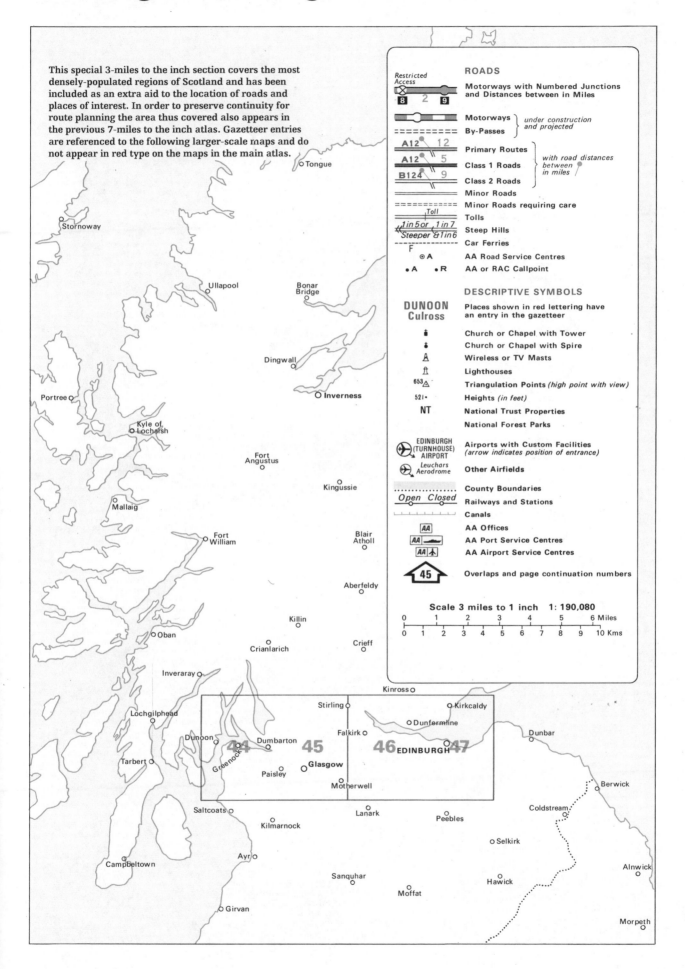

This special 3-miles to the inch section covers the most densely-populated regions of Scotland and has been included as an extra aid to the location of roads and places of interest. In order to preserve continuity for route planning the area thus covered also appears in the previous 7-miles to the inch atlas. Gazetteer entries are referenced to the following larger-scale maps and do not appear in red type on the maps in the main atlas.

ROADS

Restricted Access

Motorways with Numbered Junctions and Distances between in Miles

Motorways *under construction and projected*

By-Passes

A12 Primary Routes

A12 Class 1 Roads *with road distances between in miles*

B124 Class 2 Roads

Minor Roads

Minor Roads requiring care

Tolls

1 in 5 or 1 in 7 Steeper & 1 in 6 Steep Hills

Car Ferries

AA Road Service Centres

AA or RAC Callpoint

DESCRIPTIVE SYMBOLS

DUNOON Culross — Places shown in red lettering have an entry in the gazetteer

Church or Chapel with Tower

Church or Chapel with Spire

Wireless or TV Masts

Lighthouses

653 Triangulation Points *(high point with view)*

521 Heights *(in feet)*

NT National Trust Properties

National Forest Parks

EDINBURGH (TURNHOUSE) AIRPORT — Airports with Custom Facilities *(arrow indicates position of entrance)*

Leuchars Aerodrome — Other Airfields

County Boundaries

Open Closed — Railways and Stations

Canals

AA Offices

AA Port Service Centres

AA Airport Service Centres

45 Overlaps and page continuation numbers

Scale 3 miles to 1 inch   1: 190,080

0 1 2 3 4 5 6 Miles
0 1 2 3 4 5 6 7 8 9 10 Kms

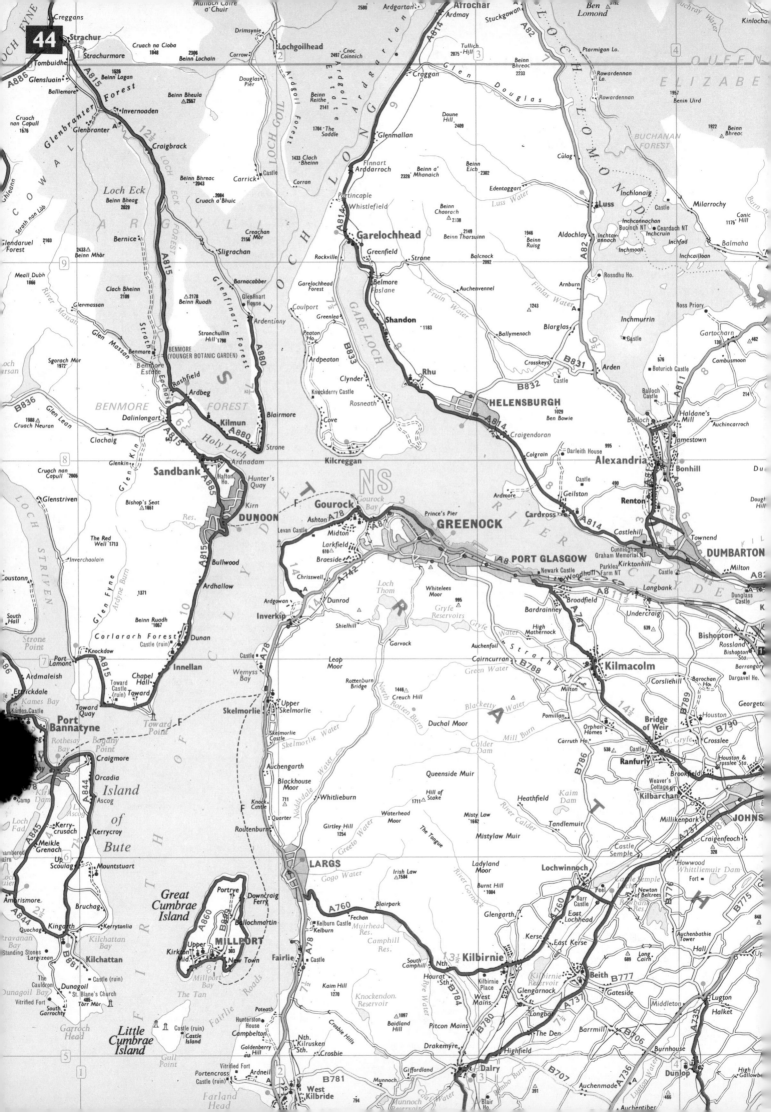

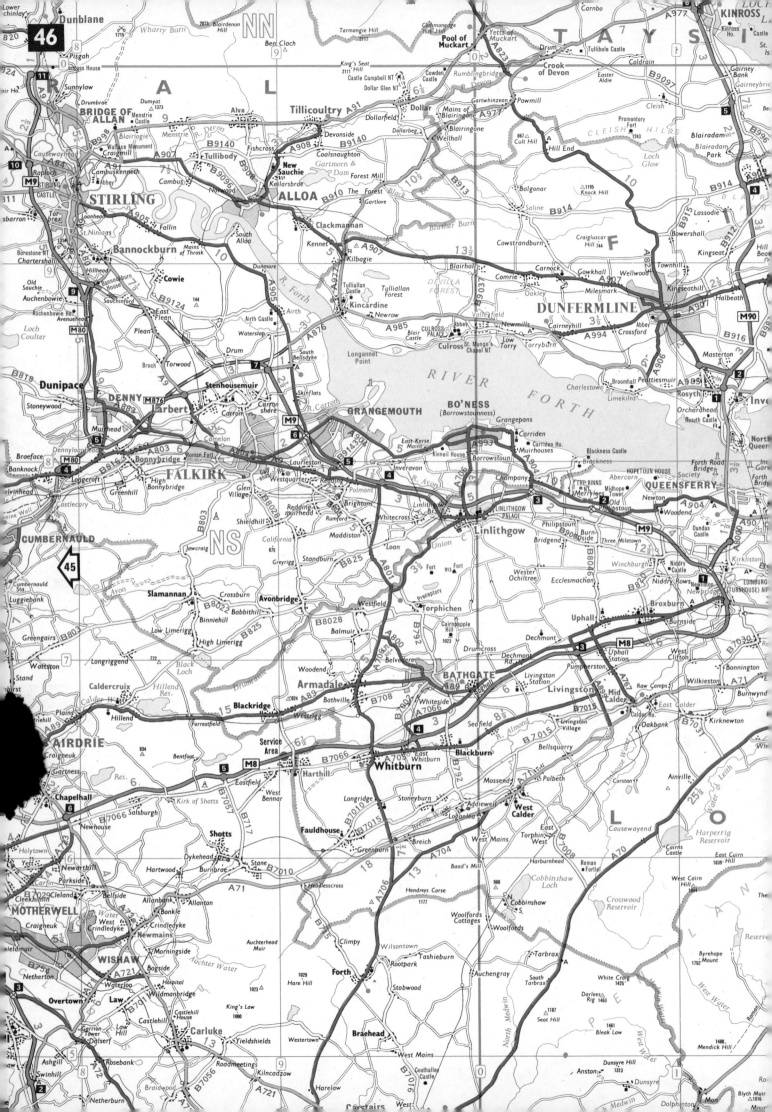

Geological Map of Scotland

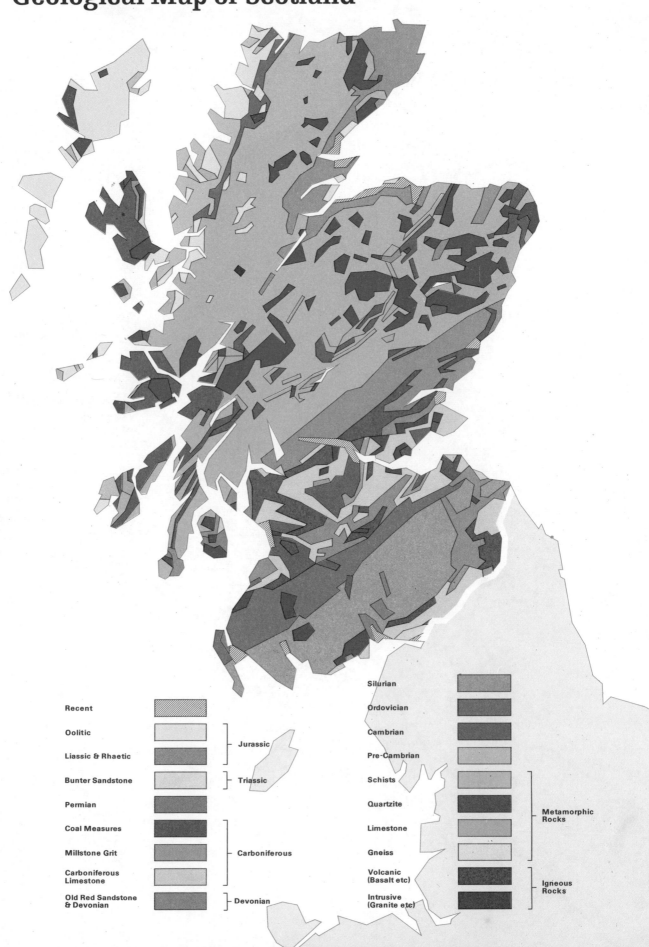

Recent

Oolitic ⎫
         ⎬ Jurassic
Liassic & Rhaetic ⎭

Bunter Sandstone ⎤ Triassic

Permian

Coal Measures ⎫
              ⎬ Carboniferous
Millstone Grit ⎬

Carboniferous
Limestone ⎭

Old Red Sandstone
& Devonian ⎤ Devonian

Silurian

Ordovician

Cambrian

Pre-Cambrian

Schists ⎫
        ⎬ Metamorphic
Quartzite ⎬ Rocks

Limestone ⎬

Gneiss ⎭

Volcanic
(Basalt etc) ⎫ Igneous
             ⎬ Rocks
Intrusive
(Granite etc) ⎭